Time-Saver Standards for Architectural Design

TIME-SAVER STANDARDS FOR ARCHITECTURAL DESIGN

Technical Data for Professional Practice

Donald Watson, FAIA, Editor
Michael J. Crosbie, Ph.D., Editor

Eighth Edition

McGRAW-HILL
New York   Chicago   San Francisco   Lisbon   London   Madrid
Mexico City   Milan   New Delhi   San Juan   Seoul
Singapore   Sydney   Toronto

The McGraw·Hill Companies

Library of Congress Cataloging-in-Publication Data

Time-saver standards for architectural design / Donald Watson, editor ;
    Michael J. Crosbie, editor.—8th ed.
        p.   cm.
Includes bibliographical references and index.
ISBN 0-07-143205-1
1. Building—Handbooks, manuals, etc.   2. Standards, Engineering—Handbooks,
manuals, etc.   3. Architectural design—Handbooks, manuals, etc.
I. Watson, Donald, date.   II. Crosbie, Michael J.

TH151.T55   2004
721—dc22

                                                                2004053873

3 4 5 6 7 8 9 0   QWC/QWC   0 1 0 9 8 7

P/N 143206-X
PART OF
ISBN 0-07-143205-1

*The sponsoring editor for this book was Cary Sullivan and the production supervisor
was Sherri Souffrance. It was set in Sabon by North Market Street Graphics. The art
director for the cover was Anthony Landi.*

Printed and bound by Quebecor/Bogota.

This book was printed on acid-free paper.

CONTENTS

Preface ix

About the Editors xi

Introduction xiii

A SUBSTRUCTURE

Foundations and basement construction

A1.1   Philip P. Page, Jr. and Martin D. Gehner   **Soils and foundation types**

A1.2   Martin D. Gehner   **Retaining walls**

A1.3   Donald Baerman   **Subsurface moisture protection**

B SHELL

Superstructure

B1.1   Donald Watson   **Overview of structures**

B1.2   Martin D. Gehner   **Design loads**

B1.3   Martin D. Gehner   **Structural design—wood**

B1.4   Jonathan Ochshorn   **Structural design—steel**

B1.5   Robert M. Darvas   **Structural design—concrete**

B1.6   Martin D. Gehner   **Structural design—masonry**

Exterior closure

B2.1	Donald Watson	**Overview of exterior wall systems**
B2.2	Donald Baerman	**Thermal insulation**
B2.3	Donald Baerman	**Building movement**
B2.4	Donald Baerman	**Corrosion of metals**
B2.5	Joseph Lstiburek	**Moisture control and the building envelope**
B2.6	Stephen S. Ruggiero and James C. Myers	**Watertight exterior walls**
B2.7	Timothy T. Taylor	**Exterior doors and hardware**
B2.8	John Carmody and Stephen Selkowitz	**Windows**
B2.9	Donald Watson	**Solar control**

Roofing

B3.1	Donald Baerman	**Roofing systems**
B3.2	Donald Baerman	**Gutters and downspouts**
B3.3	Donald Baerman	**Roof openings and accessories**

C INTERIORS

Interior constructions

| C1.1 | William Hall | **Suspended ceiling systems** |
| C1.2 | William Hall | **Interior partitions and panels** |

Staircases

| C2.1 | John Templer | **Stair design** |
| C2.2 | Donald Watson | **Stair dimensioning** |

Dimensions

C3.1	Donald Watson	**Dimensions of the human figure**
C3.2	Elaine Ostroff and John P. S. Salmen	**Universal design and accessible design**
C3.3	John J. Fruin	**Design standards for pedestrian circulation**
C3.4	Mark C. Childs	**Parking and vehicular circulation**

D SERVICES

Conveying systems

| D1.1 | Peter R. Smith | **Elevators and escalators** |

Plumbing

D2.1   Arturo De La Vega   **Plumbing systems**

D2.2   Arturo De La Vega   **Sanitary waste systems**

D2.3   Arturo De La Vega   **Special plumbing systems**

HVAC systems

D3.1   Richard Rittelmann and Paul Scanlon   **HVAC systems for commercial buildings**

D3.2   Catherine Bobenhausen   **Special HVAC equipment**

Fire protection

D4.1   Bruce W. Hisley   **Fire protection sprinkler systems**

D4.2   Bruce W. Hisley   **Special fire protection systems**

D4.3   Walter Cooper   **Fire alarm systems**

Electrical systems

D5.1   Walter Cooper and Robert DeGrazio   **Communication and security systems**

D5.2   Andrew Prager   **Electronic system specialties**

D5.3   John D. Bullough   **Lighting**

APPENDICES

Appendix 1   **Mathematics and drawing**

Appendix 2   **Units of measurement**

Appendix 3   R. E. Shaeffer   **The SI metric system**

CD-ROM table of contents

Index

Preface

Time-Saver Standards for Architectural Design, 8th edition, is a reference for architects, design and construction professionals, and educators.

It represents the result of more than a half-century of documenting the knowledge and technical database for architectural practice. Over 80 authors and experts have contributed to the present volume, either with entirely new articles or, in other cases, updating topics and recommendations developed over many decades.

How to Use This Book

Scan the first-page summaries. The volume can be quickly scanned to provide an overview of the entire scope of architectural practice data. On the first page of each article, there is an introductory summary as well as key words, also found in the Index.

Use the Index for topic search. All topics covered in text, figures, and tables are listed in the Index, providing a cross-reference to locate specific content items.

Read introductory articles and each specific topic article. Each topic area and separate article presents a series of layers of increasing detail, beginning with introductory articles. Highlights of each article are presented through illustrations and text, including checklists of key design criteria. References at the end of each article list sources and citations.

Use the CD-ROM for easy access to selected articles with more data and detail. The CD-ROM Table of Contents is at the end of this volume, just before the Index.

Build your knowledge like a building. Topics in this volume are organized like the process of building a building, "from the ground up." This conforms to the *Uniformat II* classification system, beginning with foundations and proceeding through superstructure, enclosure, interiors, and services. It parallels the sequence and elements by which the architecture and construction process is logically conceived.

Companion Volumes in the Time-Saver Standards Series

The focus of this volume of *Time-Saver Standards for Architectural Design,* 8th edition, is the architectural design and building project, as defined in architectural practice, including all technical aspects of its design and construction.

Two additional recent titles of the *Time-Saver Standards* series follow a similar format and serve as companion volumes and additional references:

Time-Saver Standards for Building Materials and Systems, 1st edition (2000), is a compilation of technical details and checklists for specification and selection data. It is an ideal companion volume for the building designer and construction specifier.

Time-Saver Standards for Urban Design, 1st edition (2003), is an archival compilation of articles and references from the past 100 years, documenting the values and knowledge base of urban design. It covers topics beyond the scale of building to include urban design and planning.

About the Editors

DONALD WATSON, FAIA, NCARB is an architect in private practice. He is former Dean and Professor of Architecture at Rensselaer Polytechnic Institute, Troy, New York (1990–2000) and former Visiting Professor at Yale School of Architecture and Chair of Yale's Master of Environmental Design Program (1970–1990). He has received the 2002 ASCA Distinguished Professor Award and a AIA Educational Honors Award (1997). His architectural work has received national and international design awards. His books include *Designing and Building a Solar House* (Garden Way) 1977, and *Climatic Building Design,* co-authored with Kenneth Labs (McGraw-Hill) 1983, recipient of the 1984 Best Book in Architecture and Planning Award from the American Publishers Association. He is editor-in-chief of *Time-Saver Standards for Building Materials and Systems* (2000) and *Time-Saver Standards for Urban Design* (2003).

MICHAEL J. CROSBIE, PH.D., is active in architectural journalism, research, teaching, and practice. He received his Doctor of Philosophy in Architecture from Catholic University. He has previously served as technical editor for *Architecture* and *Progressive Architecture* magazines and is a former contributing editor to *Construction Specifier.* He is a licensed architect and a senior associate at Steven Winter Associates, a building systems research and consulting firm in Norwalk, Connecticut, and the editor-in-chief of *Faith & Form* magazine. Dr. Crosbie has won several journalism awards. He is the author of more than a dozen books on architectural subjects and several hundred articles that have appeared in publications such as *Architectural Record, Architecture, Collier's Encyclopedia Yearbook, Construction Specifier, Fine Homebuilding, Historic Preservation, Landscape Architecture, Progressive Architecture,* and *Wiley's Encyclopedia of Architecture, Design, Engineering & Construction.* He has been a visiting lecturer/critic at University of Pennsylvania; Columbia University; University of California, Berkeley; University of Wisconsin/Milwaukee; Yale School of Architecture; and the Moscow Architectural Institute and is adjunct professor of architecture at the Roger Williams University School of Architecture.

(Photo: SAFA)

Tuberculosis Sanatorium, Paimio, Finland. Alvar Aalto, Architect. 1928–1933.

INTRODUCTION Donald Watson, FAIA

1 KNOWLEDGE OF BUILDING

The technological knowledge base of architecture

Information" is defined in communications theory as "that which resolves doubt." Information, in this view, is dependent upon the act of questioning and curiosity in the mind of the seeker. Informational data, in and of itself, does not "make sense." Interpreting information depends upon a larger framework of knowledge, insight, and reflection. In the practice of architecture, knowledge of building technique is an essential and motivating requirement of design.

Technique, derived from the Greek *techne,* is a shared root of both "Architecture" and "Technology." Architecture in its root meaning is the "mastery of building." Technology, from *techne logos,* means "knowledge of technique." The term *techne* can be variously defined. It combines the sense of craft and knowledge learned through the act of making, that is to say, through empirical experience. Craftspeople gain such knowledge in the skill of their hands and communicate it through the formal accomplishment of their art and craft.

Technological knowledge in architecture can thus be defined as "knowledge gained in the making" of buildings. The aspiration of the architect or master builder, by definition, is to gain mastery of the knowledge of construction technology. This is a daunting aspiration, made challenging by changes in construction technologies and in the values—economical, aesthetic, and cultural—given to the task by architect and society.

Vitruvius gave the classic definition of architecture in pronouncing three "conditions of building well, *utilitas, firmitas* and *venustas,*" translated by Henry Wolton as "commodity, firmness and delight." Vitruvius's *de Architectura* is the first compendium of architectural knowledge, at least the oldest of known and extent texts. It includes in its scope all aspects of design and construction, from details of construction and building to city planning and climatic responses.

Geoffrey Scott, in *The Architecture of Humanism* (1914), was not above offering pithy definitions of architecture, such as, "architecture is the art of organizing a mob of craftsmen." Scott's widely read treatise offers a view that emphasizes the importance of architectural style as a reflection of culture. Scott defines architecture as "a humanized pattern of the world, a scheme of forms on which our life reflects its clarified image: this is its true aesthetic, and here should be sought the laws of that third 'condition of well-building, its delight.' "

Kenneth Frampton, in *Studies in Tectonic Culture,* defines architecture as inseparable from construction technique and material culture. He cites the 1851 view of architecture defined by Gottfried Semper in terms of construction components: (1) hearth, (2) earthwork, (3) framework/roof, and (4) enclosing membrane. This definition anticipates the classification of architectural elements used in this volume, in terms of elements in their place or sequence in the process of construction and assembly.

Describing architecture in terms of its physical and technological elements does not convey the reasoning and the evaluation needed to guide the designer, the why and how by which particular materials and systems are selected. If the elements of construction are the "nouns," principles of design are still needed, "verbs" that give the connective logic.

Implicit in selecting one thing over another are qualifying "adjectives and adverbs," that is, the value and qualitative evaluations represented by commonly accepted practices. Technical standards represent the assumed values that buildings should stand up, that they should keep the rain out, that they should accommodate human habitation, comfort and productivity, that they should be equally accessible and enabling to all people of all ages, that they should not create negative environmental impact, and so forth. Some of these "design values" are required by law; others are not, but are dependent upon the values and ethical decisions of the designer, as described by Francis Ventre in "Architecture and Regulation: A Realization of Social Ethics" (Ventre 1997). Ventre describes how, early in his career, Alvar Aalto defined as a guiding principle "to do no harm," adopting the adage from the Hippocratic oath. Aalto did not propagandize or preach, but expressed this essentially humanistic and environmental value through his built work.

How architects use information

D. W. MacKinnon (1962) provides a frequently referenced study of the ways that architects work, including how they process information, biased either by habit of mind or talent or by education and training. The study analyzed the personality and work habits of approximately 100 architects, selected to represent both "most creative" and a "representative cross section" of architectural practitioners. The findings of the study determined that architects, particularly those considered "most creative," represent a set of personality traits and work habits that does distinguish the profession's ways of creative learning and practicing, which MacKinnon described as, "openness to new experience, aesthetic sensibility, cognitive flexibility, impatience with petty restraint and impoverishing inhibitions, independence of thought and action, unquestioning commitment to creative endeavor." MacKinnon's work was referred to by Charles Burnette and Associates (1979) in an investigation of how architects use information, sponsored by AIA Research Corporation and National Engineering Laboratory, published as, "Architect's Access to Information" and "Making Information Useful to Architects." The reports cite the recommendations of Richard Kraus (1970) in formatting information for architects (Kraus's interest was computer-based information systems, but his recommendations apply broadly). Kraus suggests that to respond to ways of thinking that are uniquely "architectural," an information system should:

(1) focus on geometric form, permitting visual assimilation;

(2) permit the designer to select the scale at which to operate, that is, in parts or wholes, or the broader context of the building;

(3) enable simultaneous consideration of a number of variables;

(4) help the designer to improve the creative insights during the design process.

These reports provide guidelines for an information system for architectural practice that are noteworthy. Burnette recommends that an information system for architects should be:

(a) up-to-date,

(b) presented in a form to be readily used,

(c) consistent in format appearance,

(d) stated in performance terms, that is, be operationally useful,

(e) accurate and complete, with drawings precise and to scale,

(f) equipped with an evaluation and feedback system.

Organization of *Time-Saver Standards* for *Architectural Design*

The organization of *Time-Saver Standards* is based upon a classification of topics placed in the sequence of the process of construction, as defined by the Uniformat II classification system.

The Uniformat system (its most recent version is Uniformat II) is described in an article in the accompanying CD ROM by its originators,

Robert Charette and Brian Bowen. It is widely adopted for building-related design data, and was first developed as an industry-wide standard for economic analysis of building components. It defines categories of the elements of building in terms of their place in the sequence of construction.

This classification has several advantages. First, it follows the sequence of construction, from site preparation, foundation, and so forth through to enclosure and interior constructions and services. Second, it defines design and construction data by system assemblies, creating an easily understood locus of information by its place as a building element, easily visualized and understandable to architects while designing.

Uniformat II is reasonably compatible with MasterFormat, the long-established classification system used since the 1920s in construction specifications, described in Donald Baerman's article, "Specifications," found in the accompanying CD ROM. Historically, MasterFormat developed a listing of construction materials out of convenience to the builder in organizing construction, including quantity take-offs and purchase orders for materials from different suppliers. In other words, MasterFormat classifies construction material categories as (they might be) ordered from suppliers, a format most convenient for contractors. Uniformat II classifies design, construction and materials data as components and assemblies in the order they are placed in the sequence of construction, a format following the way an architect conceives of the building construction process. The relationship between topics listed according to the Uniformat II classification is correlated to MasterFormat divisions in Table 1. ■

REFERENCES

Bowen, Brian, Robert P. Charette, and Harold E. Marshall, "UNIFORMAT II—A Recommended Classification for Building Elements and Related Sitework." Publication No. 841. Washington, DC: U.S. Department of Commerce National Institute of Standards and Technology, Washington, 1992.

Burnette, Charles and Associates, "The Architect's Access to Information," NTIS # PB 294855; and "Making Information Useful to Architects—An Analysis and Compendium of Practical Forms for the Delivery of Information," NTIS # PB 292782. U.S. Department of Commerce National Technical Information Service, Washington, 1979.

Frampton, Kenneth, *Studies in Tectonic Culture: The Poetics of Construction in Nineteenth and Twentieth Century Architecture.* MIT Press, Cambridge, 1995, p. 85.

Kraus, R. and J. Myer, "Design: A Case History and Specification for a Computer System," in G. Moore (ed.), *Emerging Methods in Environmental Design and Planning,* MIT Press, Cambridge, 1970.

MacKinnon, D.W., "The Personality Correlates of Creativity: A Study of American Architects," *Proceedings of the 14th Congress on Applied Psychology,* Vol. 2. Munksgaard, 1962, pp. 11–39.

Scott, Geoffrey, *The Architecture of Humanism: A Study of the History of Taste,* 2nd ed., Constable and Company, London, 1924, pp. 41, 240.

Ventre, Francis T., "Architecture and Regulation: A Realization of Social Ethics," originally published in *Via 10,* Graduate School of Fine Arts, University of Pennsylvania and reprinted in *Time-Saver Standards for Architectural Design Data,* 7th ed., McGraw-Hill, New York, 1997 (included in the CD accompanying this volume).

Table 1. Matrix of Uniformat II Categories (horizontal) and MasterFormat Divisions (vertical)

MasterFormat Divisions	A1	B1	B2	B3	C1	C2	C3	D1	D2	D3	D4	D5
1 GENERAL CONDITIONS	√											
2 SITE CONSTRUCTION	√								√		√	
3 CONCRETE	√	√	√									
4 MASONRY	√	√	√		√							
5 METAL	√	√	√		√							
6 WOOD & PLASTICS	√	√	√	√	√							
7 THERMAL/MOISTURE	√	√	√	√					√	√	√	
8 DOORS & WINDOWS			√	√	√	√						
9 FINISHES					√		√					
10 SPECIALTIES	√				√		√		√	√	√	
11 EQUIPMENT					√				√			√
12 FURNISHINGS					√		√				√	
13 SPECIAL CONSTRUCTION		√	√							√	√	√
14 CONVEYING SYSTEMS	√	√				√		√				√
15 MECHANICAL				√					√	√	√	√
16 ELECTRICAL						√	√			√	√	√

Design data (after Uniformat II classification)

LEGEND

A	SUBSTRUCTURE
A1	Foundations and basement construction
B	SHELL
B1	Superstructure
B2	Exterior closure
B3	Roofing
C	INTERIORS
C1	Interior constructions
C2	Staircases
C3	Interior finishes
D	SERVICES
D1	Conveying Systems
D2	Plumbing
D3	HVAC
D4	Fire Protection
D5	Electrical

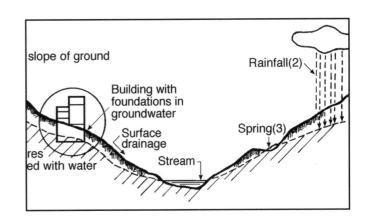

A • SUBSTRUCTURE

A1 Foundations and basement construction

A1.1   Soils and foundation types   *Philip P. Page, Jr.*

A1.2   Retaining walls   *Martin D. Gehner, P.E.*

A1.3   Subsurface moisture protection   *Donald Baerman*

Philip P. Page, Jr., edited by Martin D. Gehner, P.E.

Summary

This article provides an overview of soils and foundation types. Soil bearing capacity and soil tests are reviewed along with substructure foundations, including piers, piles, caissons, and footing design.

Key words

borings, caissons, piers, piles, soil bearing capacity, spread footings, wall footings

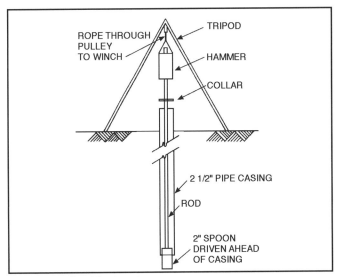

Fig. 1. Typical soil-boring rig.

Soils and foundation types

1 EVALUATING THE BEARING CAPACITY OF THE SOIL

The first step in evaluating the bearing capacity of the soil is site reconnaissance, noting existing buildings, rock outcroppings, streams, and bodies of water. A topographical survey locating these items plus important trees should follow. In areas of substantial previous construction, reference to old maps may indicate features long removed from the landscape.

Subsurface investigation is most often done by borings, but test pits are also used. A typical boring rig (**Fig. 1**) consists of a tripod or frame with a pulley and a small winch.

A hammer is raised by the winch and allowed to fall free, driving a pipe casing into the ground. The casing is cleaned out by a water jet. At stated intervals, normally every 5 ft (1.5 m), a piece of split pipe (called a spoon) is guided through the casing and driven ahead of the lead end to obtain a sample. The spoon is then withdrawn and opened so that the samples may be identified and placed in a sample jar.

The number of blows necessary to drive the spoon 1 ft gives important information as to the compactness of the soil. Generally a 300-lb hammer falling 18 in is used for advancing the casing, and a 140-lb hammer falling 30 in is used to drive the spoon. When rock is reached, a rotary power takeoff on the hoist drives a core bit uncased into the rock. Rock core samples are recovered, identified, and placed in sample boxes. The soil-boring contractor then furnishes a drawing giving the location and ground elevation of the holes, a scale section of each hole showing materials encountered, and a log of the casing and spoon blows.

Many codes as well as good engineering practice dictate boring locations about 50 ft (15 m) on center within the building outline. Soils or geotechnical engineers may typically designate critical points with respect to either site configuration and/or the proposed building footprint. Abnormal ground conditions may require closer spacing. Depth of borings are typically 15 to 20 ft (4.5 to 6 m) below foundation level, with one or more borings deeper to look for weak lower levels.

Test pits give a more immediate idea of the soil conditions but are limited to a depth of approximately 10 ft (3 m). Dug with a backhoe, they provide a method for economical and visually evident evaluation. Where rock is near the surface, a possible picture of the rock profile can be obtained.

Once the type and degree of compactness of soil has been established, its supporting ability must be evaluated. **Table 1** shows representative values for presumptive bearing capacities as listed in two national codes. Local codes may have different values.

When a soil load test is required, a 2-ft (60 cm) square plate is loaded to the proposed design load and held until no settlement is observed in 24 hr. The load is then increased 50 percent and held until no settlement is observed in 24 hr. The test is satisfactory:

- if the settlement does not exceed ¾ in (20 mm) under the design load and,

- if under the overload, it does not exceed 60 percent of that observed under the design load.

Table 1. Presumptive soil bearing values.

Sources: Building Officials and Code Administrators International (BOCA) and American Insurance Association National Building Code (NBC).

Class of Material	Allowable values: pounds per sq. ft.	
	BOCA[1]	UBC[2]
1. Crystalline Bedrock	12,000	12,000
2. Sedimentary Rock	6,000	6,000
3. Sandy Gravel and Gravel	5,000	6,000
4. Sand, Silty Sand, Clayey Sand, Silty Gravel and Clayey Gravel	3,000	4,500
5. Clay, Sandy Clay, Silty Clay and Clayey Silt	2,000	3,000

[1] The BOCA National Building Code/1993. Building Officials and Code Administrators International. Inc.
[2] The Uniform Building Code, 1997. International Conference of Building Officials, 1997
These values are taken for a footing 3' - 0" below grade. Refer to the Code for other widths and shallower depths of footings.

Table 2. Square column footings—soil bearing value: 3000 psf.

Note: Table 2 has been prepared according to ACI 318-89 strength design: $f_c' = 3,000$; $f_y = 60,000$. Tabulated column loads are actual not unfactored.

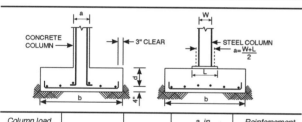

Column load, kips	b, ft	d, in.	a, in. (minimum)	Reinforcement each way
45	4'-0"	12	12	6- #4
57	4'-6"	12	12	6- #4
70	5'-0"	12	12	7- #4
85	5'-6"	12	12	5- #5
101	6'-0"	12	12	6- #5
118	6'-6"	12	12	7- #5
136	7'-0"	14	12	8- #5
156	7'-6"	14	12	7- #6
176	8'-0"	16	12	7- #6
199	8'-6"	16	12	9- #6
221	9'-0"	18	13	9- #6
246	9'-6"	18	13	8- #7
270	10'-0"	20	14	8- #7
298	10'-6"	20	14	10- #7
324	11'-0"	22	14	10- #7
354	11'-6"	22	14	9- #8
382	12'-0"	24	15	9- #8
443	13'-0"	26	15	11- #8
509	14'-0"	28	16	10- #9
580	15'-0"	30	17	11- #9
653	16'-0"	32	18	13- #9

2 SELECTING A FOUNDATION TYPE

One of the most important decisions in designing and constructing any building is determination of the connection to the earth supporting the structure. The earth's substrata is investigated and tested to help define the soil conditions beneath a site of a proposed foundation. Yet even the most thorough investigation encounters only a small portion of the soils, and a foundation design relies heavily on interpretation of the data from soil tests.

The most common types of footings are the spread footings and wall footings. These are used where the soil bearing capacity is adequate for the applied loads. The applied loads accumulate from either column loads or bearing wall loads. Variations of spread footings include eccentric footings, where the center of the superimposed load does not line up with the resultant center of the soil bearing pressure; combined footings, where two or more columns must share one footing; and mat footings, where the required superimposed loads require most of the building's footprint to transfer the accumulated loads to relatively weak soil bearing capacity.

Pile foundations are required where poor surface and near surface soils are weak, and column-like shafts must be used to penetrate the weak soil to reach acceptable supporting stratum and greater depths below grade. Piles are tied together with pile caps upon which the building's columns or walls are supported. When large column loads exist, caissons are used as extensions to columns. Caissons typically are larger in diameter and longer. They rely on end bearing directly on earth with very high bearing capacity.

Retaining walls are used where a grade change occurs and the upper levels must be stabilized behind a wall. The wall portion of the foundation extends vertically cantilevered from a substantial and carefully designed footing.

When good bearing material occurs directly under the building excavation, spread footings are designed for uniform bearing on the soil. The most common footings for square and round columns are square footings. **Table 2** illustrates sizes of square column footings reinforced with steel bars of grade $F_y = 60$ ksi [kips per square inch. A kip is equal to 1000 lb].

The concentrated load of the steel column requires a steel bearing plate to distribute and transfer the load to an acceptable stress on the concrete footing, which in turn distributes the load to the soil at the allowable soil pressures. **Fig. 2** indicates this condition as generally detailed.

Sometimes the load must be distributed over a large area to lower-strength material by an I-beam grillage as schematically shown in **Fig. 3**. A reinforced concrete column often bears directly on the footing and the stress in the column reinforcing is transferred to the footing by steel dowels as indicated in **Fig. 4**.

Bearing walls have continuous footings under them as shown in **Fig. 5**. When the footing projection beyond the face of the wall equals D/2 or less, the footing requires no tensile reinforcement. When the projection is greater than D/2, reinforcement across the footing is required to carry the tensile stresses. As a rule, a footing that is twice as deep as its projection will require no reinforcing. Longitudinal reinforcement is desirable to help distribute more uniform pressures on the soil.

Where a lot line or interference from another footing precludes the use of square footings, a combined footing may serve two or more columns. **Fig. 6** shows examples of popular types of combined footings. Note that the centers of gravity of the plan area of the footing and the load from the column must coincide.

Wall footings often intersect column footings or column piers. **Fig. 7** illustrates such a condition. Footing and wall reinforcement is required to develop continuity through the intersection unless specific expansion joints are properly installed.

Piers supporting grade beams extend to footings placed on bearing strata substantially below the general excavation. The grade beams, designed as flexural members, carry wall and floor loads to the piers as diagrammed in **Fig. 8**.

If the grade beam is shallower than the frost penetration depth, frost bevels may be placed on the beam soffits to prevent frost heave. Unreinforced concrete piers are limited to a height-to-thickness ratio of 1 to 6. A more slender pier must be designed as a reinforced column.

Dowels develop the strength of the column reinforcing into the pier. Small dowels between the pier and the footing prevent pier displacement during backfilling. In areas of varying and unpredictable bearing elevations, field adjustments may easily be made to the height of the pier.

For even deeper bearing strata, piles are used. Concrete pile caps then support the columns and grade beams. The choice between walls and footings, piers and grade beams, or piles and grade beams is determined by soil conditions, by the requirements of the building's structural system, and cost. The requirement of many codes—that a pile be at least 10 ft (3 m) long in order to provide adequate lateral stability—often determines the changeover depth between piers and short piles.

Mats can distribute loads to large areas, permitting light soil bearing loads on weak material. Hydraulic mats resist upward water pressure. Because of the various possible arrangements and loads, each mat becomes a specialized custom design.

Eccentric footings

When the center of a footing's upward pressure cannot be placed directly under the column or wall, methods must be employed to distribute the resulting eccentric footing loading without the uneven pressure exceeding the allowable bearing pressure. Building codes generally limit the projection into the street to 1 ft (≈30 cm) beyond the property line. Thus footings under columns located on the property lines are eccentric to the columns as illustrated in **Fig. 9**.

Straps, reinforced concrete beams, are carried back to an adjacent column for a hold-down load to counterbalance the eccentric moment. The footings are proportioned so that the pressures are uniform and similar under both footings. The strap is reinforced to resist the bending caused by the eccentricity and is not considered as furnishing bearing support. The bending caused by the eccentric loading may be resisted vertically rather than horizontally by a couple composed of tension in the first floor and compression in the basement as seen in **Fig. 10**.

The wall reinforcing required may be substantial. At corners, walls or grade beams permit the employment of special footing as seen in the example of **Fig. 11**.

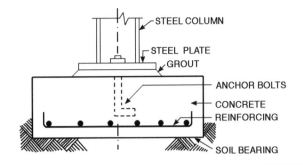

Fig. 2. Steel column on spread footing.

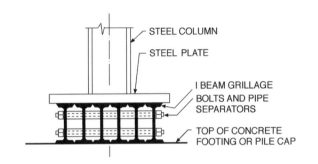

Fig. 3. Steel grillage.

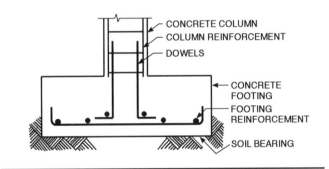

Fig. 4. Concrete column on spread footing.

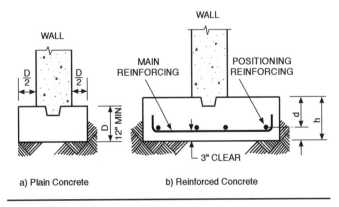

Fig. 5. Typical wall footings: (a) plain concrete; (b) reinforced concrete.

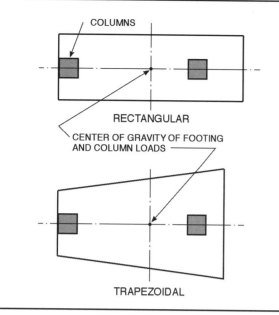

Fig. 6. Plan views of trapezoidal footings.

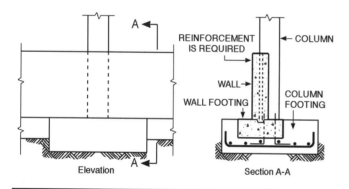

Fig. 7. Typical foundation wall and column footings.

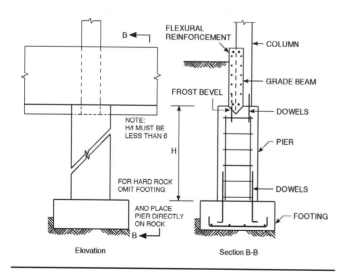

Fig. 8. Typical grade beam and pier.

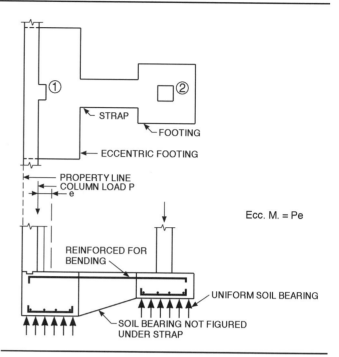

Ecc. M. = Pe

Fig. 9. Pump-handle footing. Note: footing cannot be concentric with column 1 because it would cross the property line. Therefore, the eccentricity is balanced by the use of the strap and hold-down load of column 2.

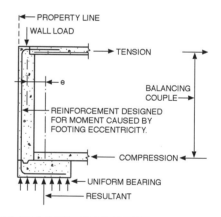

Fig. 10. Eccentric wall footing section.

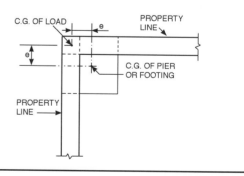

Fig. 11. Eccentric corner footing plan. Note: eccentricities are removed by walls acting as pump handles. Each wall removes the eccentricity normal to it.

Foundations to rock

Rock, having the highest bearing capacity, is often the only acceptable foundation available for heavy loads. Piers carry the loads directly to rock. On hard rock, piers require no footing, as the capacity of the rock is almost that of concrete. Typical column and grade beam construction is employed.

Where rock occurs more than 10 to 15 ft (3 to 4.5 m) below the grade beam soffits, piers become too costly. Clusters of piles driven to rock and encased in a pile cap can support substantial loads. For heavier loads, caissons are used. Caissons are big holes drilled through the weak soil strata down to rock. The drilled voids are then filled with concrete. Piles or caissons may vary in length from 15 to over 100 ft (4.5 to over 30 m).

Piles

Piles carry loads to strata below the ground surface either by end bearing, which are called bearing piles, or by surface friction along their sides, which are called friction piles. The soft material through which the pile is driven provides lateral stability. For structures over water, the piles must be designed as columns.

Pile capacity is established by test load or driving resistance. Load tests are used to establish capacity. Driving resistance measurements are used to ensure that all piles are driven as hard as the test piles. Piles are generally grouped in clusters connected by pile caps.

Borings are essential for proper pile evaluation. Individual piles may test to a capacity greater than their contribution to the capacity of a cluster. A soft stratum underlying a hard one may not be able to support the total load delivered from the hard stratum even though the resistance of the hard stratum may indicate satisfactory pile support (**Fig. 12**).

Different piles shown in **Fig. 13** have evolved with certain characteristics as follows:

- Types I and II are cast-in-place concrete piles. A light-gauge steel shell, driven on a mandrel, which is then withdrawn, is inspected and filled with concrete. Care must be taken to avoid collapsing the shell when an adjacent pile is driven.

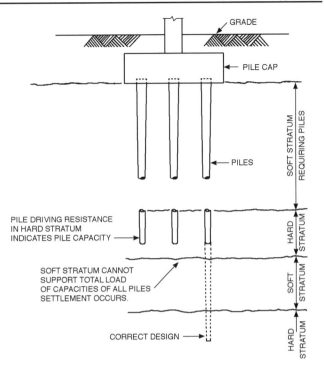

Fig. 12. Piles incorrectly seated in hard stratum above soft stratum.

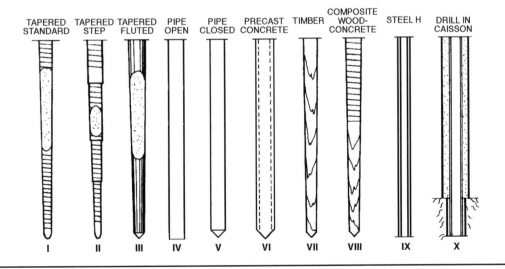

Fig. 13. Types of piles.

- Type III is similar to Types I and II except that the shell gauge is heavier and no mandrel is required.

- Type IV is an open-end steel pipe. It is excavated, often by air jet as it is advanced, and then filled with concrete after refusal has been reached. In lieu of reaching refusal, driving may stop while a concrete plug is placed and then redriving to seat it. The advantage is less disturbance to adjacent structures.

- Type V is a closed-end pile. After driving, it is filled with concrete. Often it is used inside buildings with low headroom. Shorter lengths are simply spliced with steel collars.

- Type VI is a precast concrete pile. It is good in marine structures but requires heavy handling equipment and accurate estimation of tip elevation as it is difficult to cut off in the field.

- Type VII is a wood pile—the least expensive. Where the pile is partially exposed permanently above water level, it must be treated with a wood preservative.

- Type VIII, a composite wood and concrete pile, is seldom used. The timber is kept below groundwater and a greater overall length is achieved. A closed-end pipe pile may be used in place of the timber section.

- Type IX is a rolled steel H section. It is the cheapest of the higher-capacity piles. Protection must be provided when driving through cinder fill or other rust-producing material.

- Type X is a drilled-in caisson. A 24-in (60 cm) round pipe is driven to rock and cleaned out. A rock socket is drilled and cleaned, a steel H-section core is set, and the shell is filled with concrete. This is appropriate for very heavy loads.

Piles are located with a low degree of precision. They can easily be 6 in (15 cm) or more from their desired location. If building columns, which are located with much greater precision, were to be located on single piles, the centerlines would rarely coincide. The resulting eccentric loads in both the column and the pile would generate unwanted moments in both members. A similar condition could exist around one axis for a column supported by a two-pile foundation. Piles almost always are installed in groups of three or more. Groupings of three or more piles provide a degree of safety and redundancy should one pile be driven slightly out of alignment. Lateral stability of the group increases with three piles as compared to fewer piles.

Table 3 illustrates a few simple examples of pile cap sizes and shapes along with representative capacities of the cap and the column being supported. For heavier column loads, the designer is referred to a structural engineer for analysis of specific foundation requirements of the building(s) under consideration. ■

Table 3. Standard pile caps

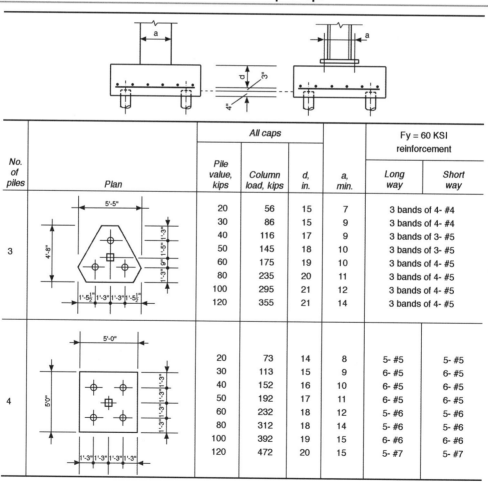

No. of piles	Plan	All caps				Fy = 60 KSI reinforcement	
		Pile value, kips	Column load, kips	d, in.	a, min.	Long way	Short way
3	5'-5" / 4'-8"	20	56	15	7	3 bands of 4- #4	
		30	86	15	9	3 bands of 4- #4	
		40	116	17	9	3 bands of 3- #5	
		50	145	18	10	3 bands of 3- #5	
		60	175	19	10	3 bands of 4- #5	
		80	235	20	11	3 bands of 4- #5	
		100	295	21	12	3 bands of 4- #5	
		120	355	21	14	3 bands of 4- #5	
4	5'-0" / 5'0"	20	73	14	8	5- #5	5- #5
		30	113	15	9	6- #5	6- #5
		40	152	16	10	6- #5	6- #5
		50	192	17	11	6- #5	6- #5
		60	232	18	12	5- #6	5- #6
		80	312	18	14	5- #6	5- #6
		100	392	19	15	6- #6	6- #6
		120	472	20	15	5- #7	5- #7

Martin D. Gehner, P.E.

Summary

This article provides an overview of the structural requirements of retaining walls with illustrative examples, including freestanding cantilevered designs.

Key words

retaining walls, basement walls, lateral pressure, Rankine theory, weep holes

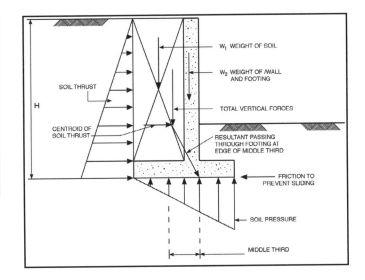

Retaining walls

Retaining walls hold back or retain earth between disparate grade levels. Typically, the wall is cantilevered from a footing extending up beyond the grade on one side and retaining a higher level grade on the opposite side. Basement walls may also be considered retaining walls. However, they are supported at the lowest end by the basement floor slab and at the top by the floor framing system. Both types of walls must resist the lateral pressures generated by loose soils or, in some cases, by water pressures. The soil being retained should be well drained in order to minimize the forces of water and ice.

A basement wall must be designed to resist lateral pressures from adjacent earth. Typically the wall spans from the basement floor to the first floor, depicted in **Fig. 1a,** and acts as the structural element between those two points. **Fig. 1b** illustrates typical forces on a basement wall. The first-floor structural plane must act as a diaphragm able to transfer the reaction from the top of wall to the end walls, or to intermediate cross walls. The diaphragm plane must be secured to the top of the end walls that in turn act as shear walls transmitting the forces down to the footings. To indicate typical wall thickness and the reinforcement required relative to wall height, **Table 1** lists several cases analyzed for lateral loads.

Freestanding-cantilevered retaining walls rely on the weight of the wall plus the weight of earth over the footing for stability. In addition, the friction between the earth and the footing is essential to resist sliding of the footing. The characteristic elements of a retaining wall design are shown in **Fig. 2a.** The Rankine theory of earth thrust, represented in **Fig. 2b,** assumes that the thrust is zero at the top and a maximum at the base, giving a triangular loading. The thrust is produced by the sliding of the wedge of soil between the earth below the angle of repose and the ground surface. The thrust for earth backfilled against the wall is commonly computed as 28.6 psf per foot of height of grade above the footing. If groundwater saturates the soil throughout this height, the design lateral force against the wall increases to 62.5 psf per foot of height of grade above the footing.

The importance of effective water drainage and release of any hydrostatic pressure behind the wall cannot be overemphasized. Weep holes through the vertical wall along with footing drains used in conjunction with gravel or crushed stone backfill allow water to drain away from the wall.

A wide variety of site conditions and retaining wall requirements influence the design of retaining walls. The determination of the specific site's variant conditions along with the applicable wall design criteria require consideration by an engineer experienced with soil mechanics.

To illustrate the design of one simple type of cantilevered retaining wall, the example of **Table 2** takes one set of assumptions and varies the wall height. This freestanding retaining wall is designed so that the resultant of the force of the soil pressure and the gravity loads passes through the middle third of the footing, preventing uplift. The advantage of this approach is to easily proportion the footing and wall based on the limit of the peak allowable soil bearing pressure. Where the soil is particularly compressible, the resultant should pass near the center of the footing to give uniform soil loading. With the resultant at the edge of the middle third, compressible soils may give differential settlement, causing the wall to tilt. Such rotation is very detrimental to a retaining wall.

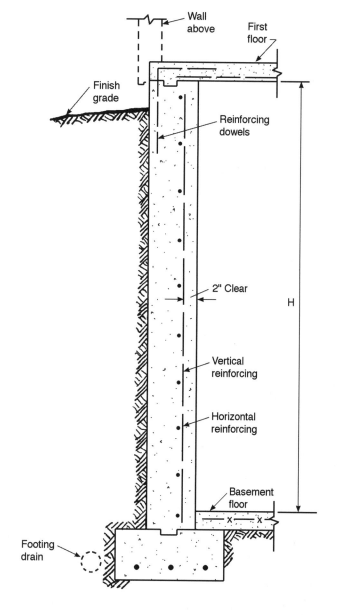

(a) Typical basement wall reinforced concrete

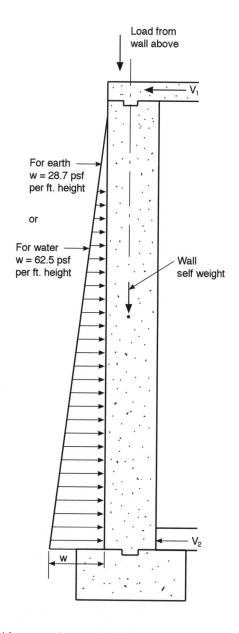

(b) Typical forces on a basement wall

Fig. 1. Basement foundation wall.

Table 1. Basement wall resisting lateral pressure
(ASI 318-89). Strength design: f′$_c$ = 3,000 psi; F$_y$ = 40,000 psi.

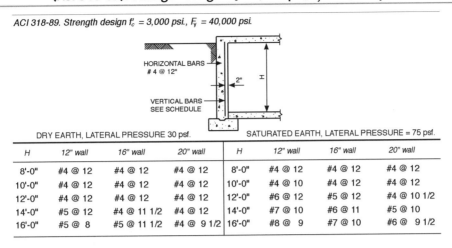

ACI 318-89. Strength design f′$_c$ = 3,000 psi., F$_y$ = 40,000 psi.

DRY EARTH, LATERAL PRESSURE 30 psf.				SATURATED EARTH, LATERAL PRESSURE = 75 psf.			
H	12" wall	16" wall	20" wall	H	12" wall	16" wall	20" wall
8'-0"	#4 @ 12	#4 @ 12	#4 @ 12	8'-0"	#4 @ 12	#4 @ 12	#4 @ 12
10'-0"	#4 @ 12	#4 @ 12	#4 @ 12	10'-0"	#4 @ 10	#4 @ 12	#4 @ 12
12'-0"	#4 @ 12	#4 @ 12	#4 @ 12	12'-0"	#6 @ 12	#5 @ 12	#4 @ 10 1/2
14'-0"	#5 @ 12	#4 @ 11 1/2	#4 @ 12	14'-0"	#7 @ 10	#6 @ 11	#5 @ 10
16'-0"	#5 @ 8	#5 @ 11 1/2	#4 @ 9 1/2	16'-0"	#8 @ 9	#7 @ 10	#6 @ 9 1/2

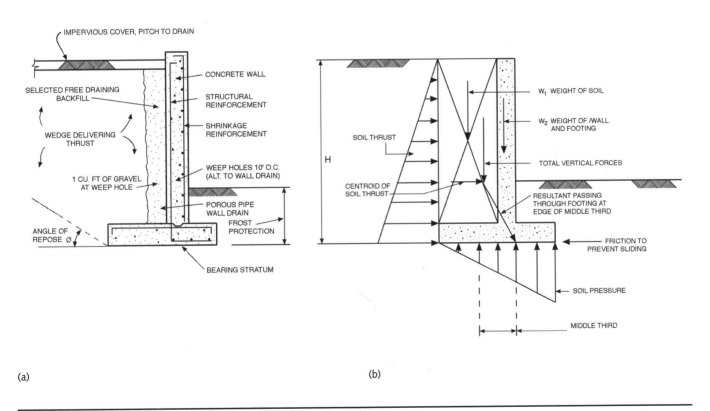

(a)   (b)

Fig. 2. Retaining wall: (a) essential elements of a retaining wall; (b) essential forces for a retaining wall.

Table 2. Cantilever retaining walls
(ACI 318-89). Strength design: $f'_c = 3,000$ psi; $F_Y = 60,000$ psi.

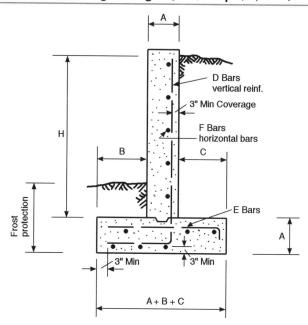

Height H	A	B	C	Toe pressure psf	D Bars	E Bars	F Bars
4'-0"	1'-0"	6"	1'-2"	872	#4 @ 12"c/c	—	#4 @ 8" c/c
5'-0"	1'-0"	8"	1'-5"	924	#4 @ 12"	—	#4 @ 8"
6'-0"	1'-0"	10"	1'-8"	1000	#4 @ 12"	—	#4 @ 8"
7'-0"	1'-0"	11"	1'-11"	1079	#4 @ 12"	—	#4 @ 8"
8'-0"	1'-0"	1'-0"	2'-2"	1207	#4 @ 12"	#4 @ 12" c/c	#4 @ 8"
9'-0"	1'-0"	1'-2"	2'-5"	1352	#4 @ 10"	#4 @ 12"	#5 @ 12"
10'-0"	1'-0"	1'-5"	2'-8"	1452	#5 @ 12"	#4 @ 12"	#5 @ 12"
12'-0"	1'-0"	1'-11"	3'-2"	1649	#5 @ 11"	#4 @ 12"	#5 @ 12"
14'-0"	1'-2"	2'-3"	3'-8"	1873	#6 @ 12"	#4 @ 12"	#5 @ 11"
16'-0"	1'-4"	2'-6"	4'-2"	2128	#6 @ 10"	#4 @ 10"	#5 @ 10"

Retaining walls may also be built with masonry. Stone masonry, concrete masonry, or brick masonry may be used. These materials may also be reinforced. Using a built-up modular unit for a retaining wall always means that the wall must be thicker and more massive. For walls of shorter height, these materials can be interesting and successful. Because they are more vulnerable to cracking and breaking, these materials are often used with undulating or zigzag plan forms. The masonry TEK (NCMA 1996) notes should be referenced for further structural design and detailing. ■

REFERENCES

ACI, *Building Code Requirements for Reinforced Concrete,* ACI 318-89, American Concrete Institute, Detroit, 1989.

CRSI, *CRSI Handbook,* Concrete Reinforcing Steel Institute, Schaumburg, 1996.

NCMA, *TEK Manual for Concrete Masonry Design and Construction,* National Concrete Masonry Association, Herndon, 1996.

Donald Baerman

Summary

Controlling water entry into the subsurface parts of a building is critical, in that the uses and contents of such spaces may be harmed by water and dampness. Moisture protection strategies discussed in this article include dampproofing, waterproofing, and subsurface drainage systems.

Key words

crawl space, dampproofing, footing drain, groundwater, perimeter drainage, subsurface drainage, vapor retarder

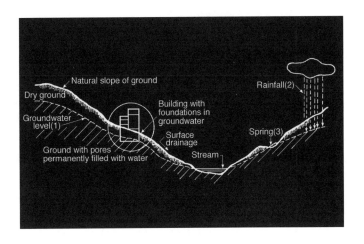

Subsurface moisture protection

Since waterproofing of the subsurface portions of a building is difficult to remedy, the reliability of the waterproofing and moisture control strategies is critical. Methods of moisture control of substructures include:

1. *Dampproofing*, which retards the passage of water in the absence of hydrostatic pressure.

2. *Waterproofing*, which prevents the passage of water, under hydrostatic pressure, through subsurface foundation walls, slabs, or both.

3. *Subsurface drainage*, which removes water from proximity to the foundations and subsurface slabs.

Groundwater

In most regions, there is some dampness in the soil under and around buildings from both surface and underground water conditions (**Fig. 1**). The dampness usually comes from rainwater or local groundwater near the surface, but in some desert regions the moisture movement is up from deep earth. Under the most severe conditions, there is standing water under hydrostatic pressure above or near the bottom of the foundations, either all the time or some of the time. More commonly, there is water in the ground during and after rain, and there is dampness that can penetrate the walls and slabs-on-grade by capillary action and through small cracks and voids.

1. Groundwater level tends to follow ground contour—deeper on hills, shallower in valleys.

2. Rainfall percolates through ground to recharge groundwater. Groundwater level varies with amount of rainfall.

3. Springs occur where local ground depressions place ground level below groundwater level.

Sources of information on the soil and water conditions that prevail in the locality and at specific building sites include all-season measuring of groundwater in a test boring, consultation with a geotechnical engineer, and consultation with local building officials. Long-term flooding records, as well as recent storm patterns (which in many localities are exceeding long-term records), provide equally critical reference data.

Conditions requiring subsurface moisture protection

In some cases, the subsurface spaces of a building are not critical; valuable goods are not stored there, and the spaces are not used for critical operations. In these instances, occasional leaking may be tolerated, and neither dampproofing nor waterproofing may be needed.

Dampproofing is generally adequate to retard passage of water into a basement, and subsurface drainage is provided by natural ground absorption and/or evaporation, under the following combination of conditions:

– If a building is built on very porous soil,

– If the standing groundwater level is always well below the basement, and

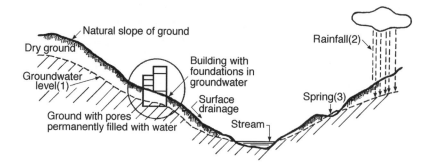

Fig. 1. Factors influencing groundwater flows: (1) groundwater level tends to follow ground contour; (2) rainfall percolates through ground to recharge groundwater; (3) springs occur where ground depressions are below groundwater level.

– If moisture from ground runoff, roof drainage, and similar sources is directed away from the building (by swales, underground drainage pipes, and similar means).

Waterproofing, which is intended to exclude all water from a building under all foreseeable conditions, is the safe choice if any combination of these factors exists:

– If the standing groundwater is near or above the basement floor level,

– If water from other sources is not directed away from the building,

– If building contents and activities in the belowground spaces are valuable and critical,

– If discharge of water from a subsurface drainage system is not practical.

Subsurface drainage is an excellent method of avoiding water entry into the basement:

– If a building site has standing groundwater that is sometimes above the basement floor, or

– If the soil is not sufficiently porous to act as a natural drainage bed.

A redundant combination of surface drainage, subsurface drainage, and dampproofing or waterproofing is a prudent design choice.

If the cost of achieving total protection from substructural leaking under all conditions is very high, the building owner/manager may choose to tolerate the cost of replacing equipment periodically. An example is the decision to save the cost of fully waterproofing a basement balanced against the cost of replacing the heating system if a 100-year storm should occur. This decision should be made explicitly and accurately recorded as part of the design record.

Caution: If a basement is exposed to high standing groundwater, its substructure must be able to sustain the maximum possible pressure (62.4 pounds per foot of depth per square foot). One way to achieve such protection is to design the basement floor slab to be heavier than the water displaced and the walls to resist the water load, and another way is to design the entire substructure to resist the load of the displaced water, in the manner of a boat. The author has seen a floor slab that was broken and forced by underground water pressure up into the first floor. If basement flooding under extreme conditions is tolerable, the substructure can be designed with "burst-in" panels to relieve the stress by allowing the basement to fill with water. In any case, design of a basement to resist a significant hydrostatic head of water should be performed by a structural engineer.

In critical or questionable situations, a good design decision might be to eliminate subsurface spaces or to make them noncritical:

– If there is no reliable outfall for subsurface drainage,

– If analysis shows that there may be troublesome groundwater, and

– If the construction and maintenance budget will not permit waterproofing.

With any system of subsurface moisture protection, it is highly desirable to keep surface water away from the building. Slope the grade down away from the building, incorporating swales and area drains as needed. Do not discharge rainwater, parking lot drainage, and other surface water to areas near the foundations. Keep basement windows and hatches well above grade or in drained areaways.

If subsurface drainage is used to remove significant volumes of water, a civil engineer should be consulted to determine the size and slope of the pipe and the outfall. Many urban and suburban localities require that on-site storm water retainage tanks and/or on-site swales for percolation of surface runoff be provided. In most localities, surface runoff to adjacent properties is not allowed. Some surface runoff may contain harmful chemicals or pollutants. Discharging large volumes of water may also require approval by the Environmental Protection Agency, city engineer, and other officials.

Permeability of concrete and masonry foundations

If concrete is designed, formulated, and placed with sufficient care, it can be made waterproof. Requirements for waterproof concrete are stated in American Concrete Institute publications. Full-time observation of the placement by a structural engineer is recommended.

Unless very special controls are applied to concrete foundation construction, and at masonry foundations, it is prudent to assume that there will be voids and cracks in the foundation materials that will admit water. Water may wick through the foundation walls, and the ground may be temporarily saturated outside the walls during heavy rainfall.

In addition to water entry through basement slabs and foundation walls, water may "wick" slowly by capillary action upward in foundation walls that are in contact with damp ground. This process is known as "rising damp." In new buildings the inclusion of a waterproof flashing course at the base of foundation walls is a good method of avoiding rising damp. For recommendations regarding remedial work on existing buildings, see Massari, Giovanni and Ippolito (1985).

1 DAMPPROOFING

Under those conditions listed above, when dampproofing is judged to be adequate, a brush or trowel coat of waterproofing material applied to the outside of the foundations is an inexpensive way to bridge over minute imperfections and cracks and to retard capillary infiltration. The surface should be cleaned and repaired first. A thick ⅛-in (3.6-mm) coating with a non-asbestos fibrated trowel mastic will be more effective at filling voids and bridging small cracks than a thinner coating.

Waterproofing materials, as described below, may be used as dampproofing. They are generally more effective, and more expensive, than dampproof brush and trowel coatings.

Subslab vapor retarders

Subsurface and subslab vapor retarders serve to retard the passage of water vapor from the earth up through a crawl space or basement slab on grade and to retard the wicking of moisture from the earth into the slab. Subslab vapor retarders are not waterproofing; they are not intended to stop water under hydrostatic pressure. Granular fill under slabs on grade is more reliable than a vapor retarder in resisting capillary action.

Labs (1988) recommends that for selected climatic zones (**Fig. 2**) a vapor-retarding ground cover for a crawl space is the single most important way to prevent condensation and wood decay problems in crawl spaces. A ground cover material should have a perm rating of no more than 1.0 and must be rugged enough to withstand construction-related foot and knee traffic. Recommended materials include 6-mil polyethylene, or 45-mil EPDM membranes.

Factors determining whether to use a subslab vapor retarder include:

- Based on an analysis of vapor flow, is the net vapor flow up from the earth or down to the earth? Under many conditions, a subslab vapor retarder will make the basement slab damper.

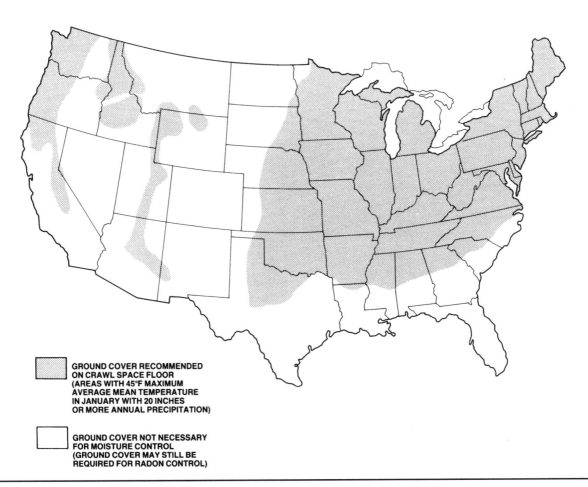

GROUND COVER RECOMMENDED ON CRAWL SPACE FLOOR (AREAS WITH 45°F MAXIMUM AVERAGE MEAN TEMPERATURE IN JANUARY WITH 20 INCHES OR MORE ANNUAL PRECIPITATION)

GROUND COVER NOT NECESSARY FOR MOISTURE CONTROL (GROUND COVER MAY STILL BE REQUIRED FOR RADON CONTROL)

Fig. 2. Approximate areas where a vapor-retarding ground cover is recommended for crawl space. (Labs et al. 1988)

- Will a subslab vapor retarder slow the initial drying of the concrete? The answer is often yes.

- Do the requirements of manufacturers' associations and manufacturers require a vapor retarder? Example: The Resilient Floor Covering Institute.

See ACI 360R-92, *Design of Slabs on Grade*, para. 9.8, which recommends not using vapor retarders in direct contact with slabs on grade. The recommendation is to place the vapor retarder, if there is one, under the porous fill and to "choke off" the top of the porous fill with sand. Excess bleed water can then pass out the bottom of the slab, allowing faster finishing.

A major cause of basement dampness is condensation of humid air on cool surfaces. A vapor retarder, waterproofing, and dampproofing will have little effect on this process. In general, condensation can be reduced by keeping the partial vapor pressure in the basement low (dry air) and keeping the surfaces in the basement warm. Expanded, extruded polystyrene insulation or foamed glass insulation under the slab and outside the walls helps keep the basement surfaces warm. Designing the mechanical system to keep the basement warm in winter and dry in summer, or providing dehumidifiers, helps keep the partial vapor pressure low.

2 WATERPROOFING

First, and most important, determine the nature of the surface and subsurface water. This may require consultation with a geotechnical engineer and people familiar with the site. The author has seen a shallow river completely surround a house and fill the basement during spring melting, while the site was dry in other seasons. Determine whether there will be water under hydrostatic pressure under the basement slabs on grade.

Make sure that the structure is designed to resist the full displacement force of the water under all conditions.

Methods, materials, and details for waterproofing are included in NRCA (2001). The following is a summary. In all cases the substrate should be clean, repaired, dry, and at the temperature recommended by the manufacturer.

- Hot asphalt or coal tar bitumen built-up membranes (applied to earth side). These are similar to built-up roofing. The number of plies is recommended in NRCA (2001).

- Modified bitumen membranes, either hot-applied or self-adhesive (applied to earth side). Hot-applied modified bitumen membranes are similar to modified bitumen roofing. Self-adhesive rubberized asphalt membranes are placed over patched, primed surfaces.

- Butyl and EPDM rubber membranes (applied to earth side).

- PVC membranes (applied to earth side).

- Rubber and PVC membranes should be installed with water cutoffs dividing the waterproofed area into sections, since water that penetrates may travel between the foundation and the membrane.

- Fluid-applied elastomeric membranes (applied to earth side). These materials achieve intimate bond to surfaces, and thus water travel between the membrane and the wall is resisted.

- Hot rubberized asphalt materials (applied to earth side). These are similar to fluid-applied elastomeric membranes.

- Bentonite clay waterproofing (applied to earth side). This material swells greatly upon contact with water, and the gel thus produced waterproofs the surface. These materials can migrate and "heal" small voids and cracks, and they achieve intimate contact with the surface. They must be applied directly to the slab or wall. They are not suitable for aboveground use.

- Metallic waterproofing (applied to earth side or interior side).

- Cementitious waterproofing (applied to earth side or interior side).

- Crystalline waterproofing (applied to earth side or interior side).

- Metallic, cementitious, and crystalline waterproofing are rigid. Movement in the substrate may crack them. However, the substructure of a building is usually stable.

- Other miscellaneous materials are listed in NRCA (2001).

Waterproofing systems applied to the earth side have the advantage of being compressed between the foundations and the water. Systems applied to the interior side have the advantage of being applied after some or all of the foundation shrinkage and settlement has occurred, and they may be inspected, maintained, and repaired while the building is in use, without disruptive, expensive excavation. It is good design to allow access to the basement surfaces that are waterproofed by this method.

Application of a membrane waterproofing system under slabs on grade may require the placement of a subslab over which the waterproof membrane is installed. Protection board is then applied over the waterproofing, and the wearing slab is installed over that.

In all cases, the waterproofing must be protected against construction damage. If insulation is installed over the waterproofing, it may serve as protection. Otherwise, a special protection board is recommended. Full-time observation during backfilling is prudent.

Quality control of subsurface waterproofing

Subsurface waterproofing is not a forgiving system, since even a small imperfection in the system may allow an intolerable amount of water to enter. Whereas a roof can be inspected and repaired, many subsurface waterproofing systems cannot be inspected and repaired, and they must perform without fail for the life of the building. Some methods of special quality control include:

- Special observation of the work, especially the joints such as that between the slab waterproofing and the wall waterproofing. Special observation may be performed by the manufacturer's representative as well as the architect or engineer.

- Redundancy, such as membrane plus bentonite, membrane plus subsurface drainage, and bentonite on the outside and cementitious, metallic, or crystalline waterproofing on the inside.

- Automatic sump pumps with a perimeter drainage trench and with an emergency generator. Sump pumps have the added advantage of taking care of water from burst pipes, severe roof leaks, and similar water that finds its way to the basement.

- Sumps with power and through-wall sleeves for emergency use of a sump pump.

- Special attention to penetrations through the slabs and walls.

3 SUBSURFACE DRAINAGE

Requirements of subsurface drainage

Subsurface drainage should, at best, drain to a fully reliable outfall such as a lower part of the site, a storm drain, or a drywell of adequate capacity. Although subsurface drainage can be directed to a sump pump, the same heavy rainstorm may cause a power failure. If subsurface drainage is critical, and if it depends on a sump pump, the pump and its power source should be highly reliable, for example, more than one pump and an emergency generator backup. If the outfall is a storm or combination sewer, there must be provisions against backflow during deluge conditions.

If the outfall is to grade or a natural waterway, there should be durable screening to keep animals out, and there should be riprap (fist-sized broken face rock) to prevent soil erosion. The proper functioning of subsurface drainage system may be critical, so there should be intense observation of its installation and backfill. There are documented cases in which such systems were crushed and made inoperable by boulders in the backfill.

To check and maintain subsurface drain lines, there should be one or more cleanouts extended to grade. Upon completion of the system, the system must be tested by discharging water into the cleanouts to verify free and positive drainage.

If grade discharge, a storm sewer, or a reliable drywell system is not available, the storm water may drain to a sump pump. However, the sump pump and its power should be highly reliable and redundant.

Footing drainage systems

Elements of a subsurface drainage system (**Fig. 3**):

- There must be a reliable outfall. The pipe from the collection pipe to the outfall should not be perforated.

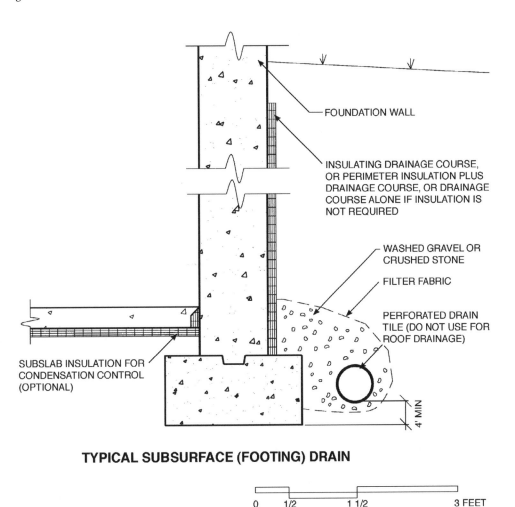

TYPICAL SUBSURFACE (FOOTING) DRAIN

FOUNDATION WALL

INSULATING DRAINAGE COURSE, OR PERIMETER INSULATION PLUS DRAINAGE COURSE, OR DRAINAGE COURSE ALONE IF INSULATION IS NOT REQUIRED

WASHED GRAVEL OR CRUSHED STONE

FILTER FABRIC

PERFORATED DRAIN TILE (DO NOT USE FOR ROOF DRAINAGE)

SUBSLAB INSULATION FOR CONDENSATION CONTROL (OPTIONAL)

4' MIN

0   1/2   1 1/2   3 FEET

Fig. 3. Typical subsurface (footing) drain.

- The foundation wall should, under most conditions, be damp-proofed or waterproofed.

- The collection pipe should always be separate from other storm drainage such as rainwater leader discharge, out to a point well below the footing elevation.

- The collection pipe is normally about 4 in (10 cm) above the level of the adjacent footing bottom.

- The collection pipe can be perforated plastic or porous concrete. A reasonable minimum size is 6-in (≈15-cm) diameter. The perforated collection pipe should be sloped a minimum of 1 percent (about ⅛ in/ft) toward the outfall.

- Around the collection pipe, there should be a porous bed of washed gravel or crushed stone without fines, large enough not to pass through the perforations in the pipe. Around the crushed stone there should be a wrapper of filter fabric.

- There should be a porous drainage course or bed immediately outside the foundations, from grade down to the footings, embedded in the gravel or crushed stone that surrounds the collection pipe.

- Gravel and crushed stone have been used as a drainage course. They should be separated from the soil with filter fabric, and they should be continuous full height. The filter fabric, gravel or crushed stone, and backfill must be placed together. The difficulty in achieving a functioning gravel or crushed stone drainage course explains the wide use of proprietary products instead.

- A number of commercial products function as drainage courses. They include deformed plastic sheet with filter fabric overlay, and deformed plastic filament with filter fabric overlay. There are also several commercial products that combine a drainage course with perimeter insulation, including scored expanded, extruded poly-styrene foam with filter fabric overlay. In addition to serving as perimeter insulation, such products keep the foundations warm, thus reducing condensation of humid air on the basement surfaces.

- A proper drainage course outside the foundations has another function besides drainage: it reduces the capillary movement of soil moisture into the foundations.

It is good practice to keep surface water away from the foundations, even if there is a subsurface drainage system. Grades should slope down away from the building. Rainwater leaders and area drains should discharge into drainpipes separate from the subsurface drainage. If rainwater drips directly from the roof eaves, provide a wide porous drip bed with its own perforated drainage system.

Other types of subsurface drainage

If there is persistent or occasional water under hydrostatic pressure under the basement floor slab, especially if there is no effective waterproofing under the slab, an overall system of underfloor drainage may be used. Over filter fabric a bed of washed gravel or crushed stone is placed, at least 8 in (≈20 cm) deep, with perforated drainpipe distributed throughout. The perforated drainpipe should be sloped at least 1 percent (about ⅛ in/ft) toward the outfall. There should be openings in the footings through which the drainpipes pass. On top of the gravel or crushed stone, place an additional sheet of filter fabric, and then a bed of sand to permit the slab to shrink as it cures and dries.

If there is persistent or occasional water under hydrostatic pressure outside the foundations or under the slab, waterproofing may be more appropriate than subsurface drainage, or it may be used in addition to subsurface drainage. For moisture-prone sites and/or critical subsurface construction on sites sloping toward the building, the additional provision of swales, intercepting drains or curtain drains placed on the uphill sides offers a further prudent "first line" defense of water diversion and moisture control (**Figs. 4** to **6**).

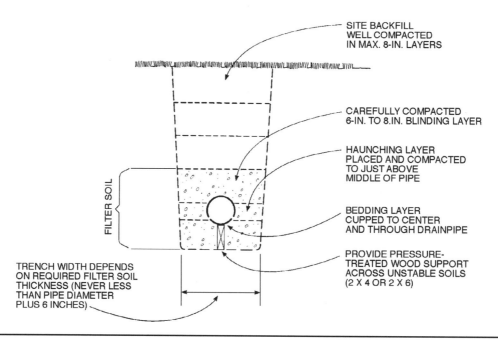

Fig. 4. Drain line using soil filter. (Labs et al. 1988)

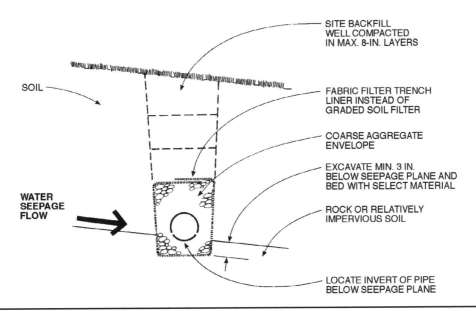

Fig. 5. Intercepting drain using fabric filter. (Labs et al. 1988)

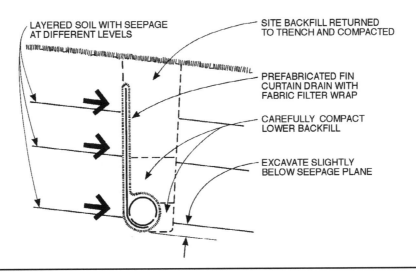

Fig. 6. Curtain drain. (Labs et al. 1988)

If the volume of water is great, its disposal may be a problem, and it may affect other parts of the project and neighboring sites. Also, sub-surface drainage, like a well, tends to run more freely with time, as the silt clears from the soil.

Areaways sometimes become clogged with leaves and other debris and with silt, and they may cease functioning. Since areaways are seldom seen, they may not be maintained. During heavy rain, the areaways may overflow through doors or windows into the building. Some ways to avoid problems include:

- The areaway gratings should be as large as practicable. Small, flat gratings can be clogged easily.

- For small areaways, a bed of washed gravel or crushed stone makes a good bottom.

- If the areaway does not need to be open, a cover will keep rain and debris out.

- If the areaway does need to be open for ventilation, a mesh cover with screening small enough to keep leaves out is desirable. The cover should be removable for cleaning. ■

REFERENCES

American Concrete Institute, *Design of Slabs on Grade,* ACI 360R-92, American Concrete Institute, Detroit, 1992.

Henshell, Justin, *The Manual of Below-Grade Waterproofing Systems,* John Wiley & Sons, New York, 2000.

Labs, Kenneth et al, *Building Construction Design Handbook,* University of Minnesota Underground Space Center, Minneapolis, 1988.

Massari, Giovanni and Ippolito, "Damp Buildings Old and New," *Association for Preservation Technology Bulletin* XVII-1-85, Association for Preservation Technology, Williamsburg, 1985, (540) 373-1621.

National Roofing Contractors Association, *The NRCA Roofing and Waterproofing Manual,* 5th ed., National Roofing Contractors Association, Rosemont, 2001.

B • SHELL

B1 Superstructure

B1.1 Overview of structures

B1.2 Design loads — *Martin D. Gehner, P.E.*

B1.3 Structural design—wood — *Martin D. Gehner, P.E.*

B1.4 Structural design—steel — *Jonathan Ochshorn*

B1.5 Structural design—concrete — *Robert M. Darvas*

B1.6 Structural design—masonry — *Martin D. Gehner, P.E.*

B2 Exterior Closure

B2.1 Overview of exterior wall systems

B2.2 Thermal insulation — *Donald Baerman*

B2.3 Building movement — *Donald Baerman*

B2.4 Corrosion of metals — *Donald Baerman*

B2.5 Moisture control and the building envelope — *Joseph Lstiburek, P.Eng.*

B2.6 Watertight exterior walls — *Stephen S. Ruggiero, P.E. and James C. Myers*

B2.7 Exterior doors and hardware — *Timothy T. Taylor*

B2.8 Windows — *John C. Carmody and Stephen Selkowitz*

B2.9 Solar control — *Donald Watson*

B3 Roofing

B3.1 Roofing systems — *Donald Baerman*

B3.2 Gutters and downspouts — *Donald Baerman*

B3.3 Roof openings and accessories — *Donald Baerman*

Summary

This article is an outline of basic structural approaches with emphasis upon system types and constructability. It provides an introduction to subsequent articles in this section and a guide for preliminary architectural design.

Key words

column, concrete, decks, deformation, floor, frame, roof, slabs, steel, trusses, wood

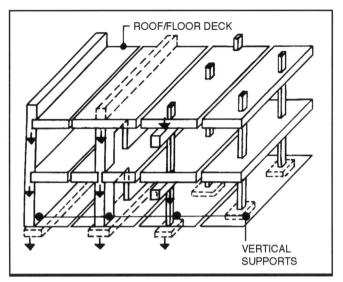

Fig. 1. Structural frame.

Overview of structures

1 FRAMING SYSTEMS

Frame

The structural frame of a building (**Fig. 1**) should be selected to provide the most economical means of support for all loads and resistance to all forces that may be imposed upon the enclosure during its intended in-service life:

– without creating any hazard to its occupants or users.

– without excessive deformations.

– with proper provisions for possible abnormal in-service conditions, such as fire, explosions, and inadvertent overloading.

The structural frame generally consists of:

• Roof deck: either horizontal, pitched, or curved assemblies.

• Floor decks: commonly flat horizontal assemblies:

– suspended above grade.

– supported above grade by piles driven into the ground.

– supported on the ground and independent of the structural frame.

• Vertical supports or primary framing: to hold roof/floor decks in place and to carry all loads to the foundations.

• Foundations: to transfer all loads to the ground.

Vertical support: types

Roof and floor decks (**Fig. 2**) may be supported by various means:

• Bearing walls: which provide continuous support for the decks:

– bearing walls may be wood framed, of masonry, or of cast-in-place or precast concrete.

• Pilasters: load-bearing segments of nonbearing walls supporting girders, the horizontal component of a vertical support assembly, which in turn carry the roof/floor decks:

– pilasters are commonly tied into the nonbearing wall of which they are a part; when incorporated into a framed nonbearing wall, they are also referred to as "posts."

• Column and girder assemblies: of wood, steel, or of reinforced concrete, either cast-in-place or precast:

– reinforced masonry columns are also used.

• Columns only: which provide point support for decks, usually of monolithic reinforced concrete.

– columns are either of structural steel or of reinforced concrete.

Roof/floor deck: types

Roof/floor decks (**Fig. 3**) carry all loads and resist all forces they are subjected to and transmit them to the vertical support assemblies between which they span.

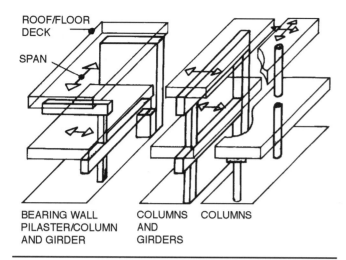

Fig. 2. Vertical support types.

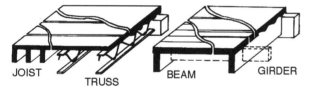

Fig. 3. Roof/floor deck types.

The principal components of roof/floor deck assemblies are:

- Decking: the structural top surface component of the deck.

- Framing: structural components that support the decking. Framing and decking may be separate and distinct components or they may form a single element without any differentiation between them.

The assembly of framing and decking—the deck—may consist of:

- Monolithic framing/decking: such as in cast-in-place reinforced concrete decks.

- Fabricated components: which combine framing and decking into a single unit, such as precast concrete shapes, long-span metal decks, and stressed skin panels.

- Framing and decking assembled at the site to function as roof/floor decks:

- framing may be prefabricated off-site to simplify site assembly, such as in pre-engineered space frames.

Framing/decking: cast-in-place

Decks: cast-in-place reinforced concrete combining framing and decking into a single element (**Fig. 4**):

- Two-way slabs: generally of uniform thickness, may be thickened at columns to increase resistance to shear thus increasing load-carrying capacity:

- minimum of three continuous spans in each direction required for direct design of flat decks.

- generally limited to square or rectangular bays with ratios of width to length of less than two.

- relatively shallow depth of construction but extensive formwork generally required.

- when of uniform thickness throughout, slabs may be cast on the ground stacked, thus requiring minimal formwork, and then lifted into their final position.

- two-way slabs are generally not recommended when numerous larger openings through decks are required: larger openings require special framing.

- conduits for electrical and communications wiring may be embedded in decks, but the size of conduits is generally limited.

- effects of deflection in decks and of cold flow, or creep, in concrete columns of multistory structures must be considered during selection and detailing of exterior walls, partitions, and nonresilient flooring.

- One-way slabs: thin sections functioning as decking cast-in-place monolithically with framing of uniformly spaced ribs of various depths:

- when closely spaced, the ribs are generally referred to as "joists," when spaced further apart, as "beams."

- the ribs are supported by girders spanning in one direction between columns.

- uniform depth construction may be attained by casting joists integrally with wide concrete girders of the same depth.

Supports are generally concrete columns except for lift slabs where structural steel pipe columns are used:

- point support of columns only for two-way flat and waffle slabs.

- columns and girders for two-way framed and one-way slabs.

• Assemblies with concrete girders and/or columns may have fire resistance rating without the need for additional fireproofing.

Framing/decking: separately fabricated units

Decks of precast reinforced concrete components of essentially uniform overall depth, which combine decking and framing into a single unit and are capable of spanning between vertical supports (**Fig. 5**):

- generally are used for light to moderate loading conditions only.

- larger openings through decks require supplementary means of support.

- acceptable extent of deflection rather than strength of components may be the governing consideration during selection.

- when used for floor decks, addition of concrete topping is required to level the surface; topping may be required, and is often recommended, for roof decks.

- joints between units require grouting during installation.

- wiring may be run through cores of hollow-core plank.

- decks may have fire resistance rating without need for additional fireproofing.

Supports may be any combination of: bearing walls, masonry or concrete, columns and girders of structural steel, or concrete.

- spacing of supports: from about 12 ft up to 40 ft for hollow-core plank; 12 to 24 ft for solid slabs.

Framing/decking: monolithically fabricated units

Monolithic decks: assemblies of precast reinforced concrete components in which framing and decking are cast monolithically (**Fig. 6**):

- essentially precast sections of one-way slabs.

- generally used with widely spaced supports.

- smaller openings in decks may be made by cutting out decking between framing ribs; large openings require supplementary supports.

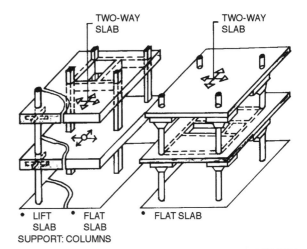

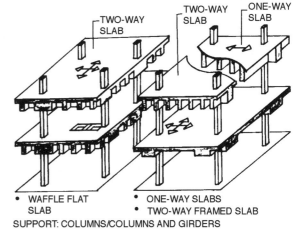

Fig. 4. Framing/decking: cast-in-place.

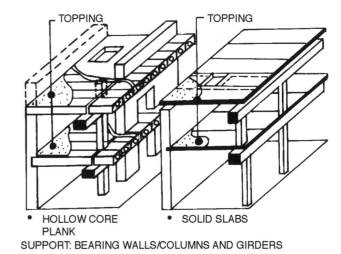

Fig. 5. Framing/decking: fabricated units.

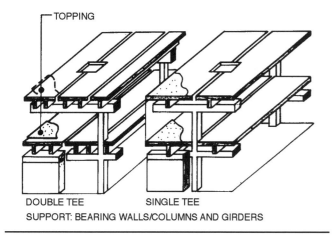

Fig. 6. Framing/decking: fabricated monolithic units.

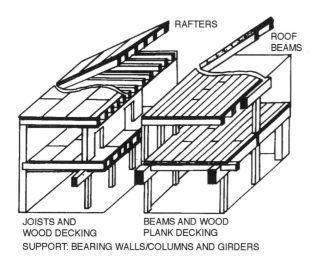

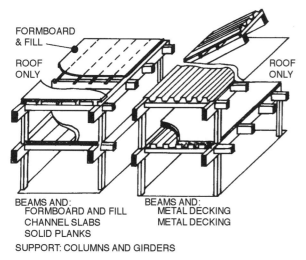

Fig. 7. Solid frame and decking: site assembled.

– acceptable extent of deflection rather than strength may govern selection, especially for upper ranges of allowable spans, camber usually provided.

– concrete topping required for floor decks, may be required for roof decks to provide level substrate for roofing.

– conduits for electrical/communications wiring may be embedded in topping, but size of conduit is quite limited, and may otherwise cause cracking in topping.

– decks may have fire resistance rating without need for additional fireproofing.

Supports may be any combination of: bearing walls of reinforced masonry or concrete, columns and girders of reinforced concrete or structural steel.

– spacing of supports from 40 to approximately 120 ft.

Solid framing and decking: site assembled

Decks: framing and decking as separate components assembled on-site in their final location (**Fig. 7**).

• Solid framing is commonly referred to as:

– joists: when horizontal and spaced 12 to 24 in on centers; rafters or roof joists: when pitched and part of a roof deck.

– beams: when spaced 4 to approximately 8 ft on centers and spanning between girders or bearing walls; also referred to as "purlins" when horizontal and spanning between pitched roof framing girders.

• Spacing of framing is principally determined by properties of decking used:

– load-carrying capacity of decking.

– extent of deflection allowable or acceptable.

– size of decking when joints between individual pieces have to extend over framing members for proper support.

– spacing may be reduced below the maximum allowable for specific type of decking in order to provide increased load-carrying capacity or to span between supports of a section of a roof/floor deck while maintaining the same overall depth of construction throughout.

• Size of framing is generally controlled by allowable stresses in bending and/or shear for short spans, allowable deflection for long spans: especially when inelastic components of an enclosure are also supported by such framing, such as ceiling membranes of plaster or gypsum board, or inelastic flooring.

• Framing may be of solid wood, laminated wood, light-gauge steel, and structural steel:

– precast reinforced concrete beams may also be used with some types of decking, but such usage is not common.

- Decking generally spans one-way between framing members and may be: solid wood; laminated wood; wood composites; precast gypsum, or precast concrete of various densities; formed light-gauge steel with or without cementitious fill; composite of form boards, steel subpurlins, and cementitious fill.

Supports may be any combination of: framed, masonry or concrete bearing walls; columns and girders of solid wood, laminated wood, and structural steel:

- reinforced concrete girders may also be used with some decks but such usage is not common.

Open framing and decking: site assembled

Decks: framing and decking as separate components assembled on-site in their final location (**Fig. 8**). Open framing may be:

- Light trusses of solid wood or wood and steel bar composites: generally spaced 24 in on centers and supporting solid or composite wood decking.

- Short-span and long-span steel bar joists: commonly 24 in or more on centers for floor decks, 4 to 6 ft or more on centers for roof decks, depending on properties of deck used:

- decking commonly used: formed light-gauge steel with or without cementitious fill; form board, steel subpurlins, and cementitious fill; precast cementitious slabs or planks; cementitious fill on metal lath; wood composites when nailing strips are attached to top flanges of steel bar joists.

- proprietary system of steel bar joists and cast-in-place concrete decking providing composite action under load in the deck assembly is available.

- steel bar joists may be used as rafters in pitched roof decks but such usage is not common.

- objectionable vibrations may occur in floor decks framed with short-span steel bar joist when their spans are in the upper range of those allowable.

- deflections in steel bar joists used in dead level roof-decks may result in ponding of rainwater unless drains are provided in all such low spots.

- Purlins/beams in pitched roof-decks should be braced against rotation under eccentric load and lateral sag due to their own weight.

Open framing allows running electrical/communications wiring, small diameter piping, and small size ductwork within the depth of the deck assembly:

- more easily accomplished when deck assembly is supported on girders of open cross section.

Supports may be:

- For light wood trusses: bearing walls of wood frame, masonry, concrete; columns and girders of wood, structural steel, and less often of concrete.

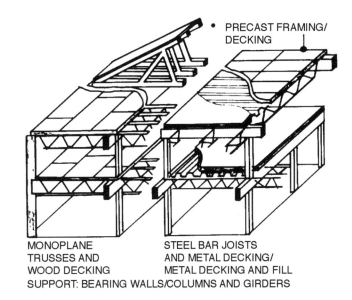

MONOPLANE TRUSSES AND WOOD DECKING

STEEL BAR JOISTS AND METAL DECKING/ METAL DECKING AND FILL

SUPPORT: BEARING WALLS/COLUMNS AND GIRDERS

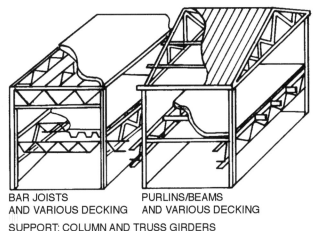

BAR JOISTS AND VARIOUS DECKING

PURLINS/BEAMS AND VARIOUS DECKING

SUPPORT: COLUMN AND TRUSS GIRDERS

Fig. 8. Open framing and decking: site assembled.

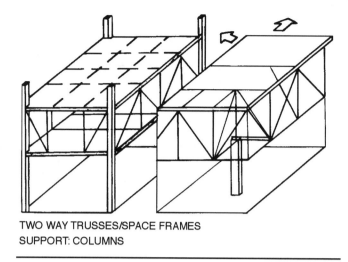

TWO WAY TRUSSES/SPACE FRAMES
SUPPORT: COLUMNS

Fig. 9. Open framing and decking: pre-engineered.

- For steel bar joists: bearing walls of light-gauge steel frame, masonry, concrete; columns and girders of structural steel, and less often of concrete.

Open framing and decking: pre-engineered

Decks: framing and decking as separate components, site assembled (**Fig. 9**).

- Framing:

- two-way interlocking braced truss system, in triangular, diagonal, hexagonal, or rectangular grid of structural steel or aluminum.

- horizontal or curved, used to roof over large open spaces.

- supported by columns, which may be randomly located, may be supported on bearing walls. System permits two-way overhangs.

- to simplify construction, the size of members is either the same throughout, or a limited number of sizes is used: the majority of members must be oversized so that the most heavily loaded would not be overstressed.

- may be assembled on the ground and lifted into place.

- ductwork, piping, and conduits for electrical and telephone wiring may be run within space frame.

- Decking may be: transparent or translucent, such as plastics, glass; formed light-gauge metal; cementitious; wood or wood composites where permitted by building codes.

- Most commonly used for roofs, but can be designed for floor loading also; full-story–height space frames have been built to serve as mechanical equipment floors.

2 DEFORMATION IN STRUCTURAL FRAMES

All structural frames are subject to deformations (**Fig. 10**):

- *Deflection:* the differential change in length between two opposite faces of a horizontal or vertical assembly or component of a structural frame. Deflection may result from:

- bending loads: when one face shortens under compression while the other elongates under tension.

- temperature differential: when one face remains stable or contracts while the other expands.

- moisture differential: when one face remains stable or shrinks while the other swells.

- *Plastic flow:* shortening of vertical components, such as columns, or deflection in horizontal assemblies and/or components, such as monolithic concrete decks, under long-term sustained loading; also commonly referred to as "creep":

- concrete in particular and wood are subject to creep, while its effect on structural steel is insignificant.

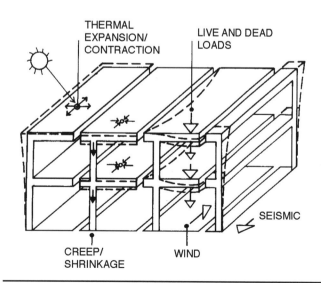

THERMAL EXPANSION/ CONTRACTION

LIVE AND DEAD LOADS

SEISMIC

CREEP/ SHRINKAGE

WIND

Fig. 10. Deformations defined.

- *Shrinkage:* the overall volumetric change due to changes in moisture content.

- *Lateral displacement:* also often referred to as "sway" or "drift," displacement of frames due to wind or seismic forces.

Deformation in decks and girders

Components of horizontal frames such as framing, decking, and girders are always subject to deflection due to bending and to a varying extent the effects of lateral displacement (**Fig. 11**):

– they may also be subject to: deflection due to temperature differential, especially in roof decks, and moisture differential when of materials thus affected.

– plastic flow and shrinkage may further aggravate the effects of deflection.

Deformations to be expected in specific materials and their effects should be considered during preliminary selection of a structural frame:

- *Steel* is essentially elastic within allowable stresses, is not affected by moisture, and does not creep to any significant amount:

– deflection due to live load is the principal consideration, differential thermal expansion/contraction generally being a less significant factor.

– camber may be provided in girders to compensate for deflection due to dead load only, which will also add to the cost of fabrication.

- *Concrete* is subject to deflection under load, creep, shrinkage, and thermal expansion/contraction:

– deflection under permanent load continues to increase for several years due to shrinkage and creep: the total deflection to be provided for in design is the sum of creep deflection from permanent or sustained long-term loads (largely irreversible deflection due to live loads), plus the deflection effects of temperature and moisture differentials.

– creep, which may amount to as much as 2.5 to 3 times the load-induced deflection, will result in loss of prestress, but will also relieve stress concentrations that otherwise might develop.

- *Wood* is affected by changes in overall moisture content, moisture and temperature gradients across a given section, deflection due to loads, and creep:

– wood is subject to continuous volumetric changes of about 3 percent across the grain due to changes in its moisture content under normal in-service conditions.

– creep will occur in wood when under sustained load, with the amount to be expected varying with different species.

Deformation in columns and walls

Vertical elements of a structural frame such as columns and bearing walls are always subject to deflection due to lateral loads, lateral dis-

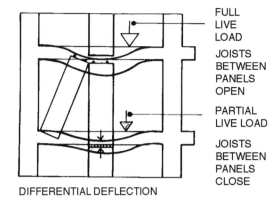

FULL LIVE LOAD

JOISTS BETWEEN PANELS OPEN

PARTIAL LIVE LOAD

JOISTS BETWEEN PANELS CLOSE

DIFFERENTIAL DEFLECTION

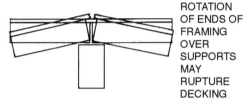

ROTATION OF ENDS OF FRAMING OVER SUPPORTS MAY RUPTURE DECKING

SIMPLY SUPPORTED DECK AT SUPPORTS

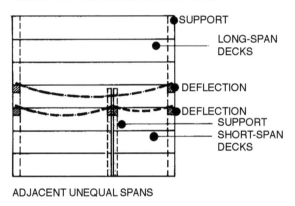

SUPPORT

LONG-SPAN DECKS

DEFLECTION

DEFLECTION SUPPORT SHORT-SPAN DECKS

ADJACENT UNEQUAL SPANS

Fig. 11. Structural deformation in decks and girders.

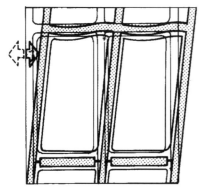

FRAME WILL DEFORM UNDER WIND OR SEISMIC FORCE AND MAY AFFECT EXTERIOR WALLS AND/OR FACINGS IN ADDITION TO POSITIVE OR NEGATIVE WIND PRESSURES ACTING ON SUCH WALLS

LATERAL DISPLACEMENT

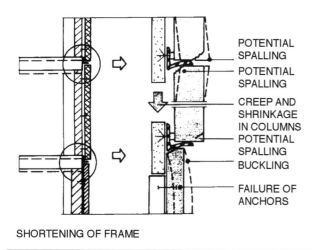

POTENTIAL SPALLING

POTENTIAL SPALLING

CREEP AND SHRINKAGE IN COLUMNS

POTENTIAL SPALLING

BUCKLING

FAILURE OF ANCHORS

SHORTENING OF FRAME

Fig. 12. Structural deformation in columns and walls.

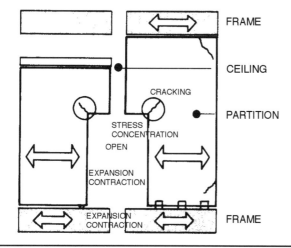

FRAME

CEILING

CRACKING

PARTITION

STRESS CONCENTRATION

OPEN

EXPANSION CONTRACTION

EXPANSION CONTRACTION

FRAME

Fig. 13. Deformation effects on partitions.

placement, and to a varying extent effects of bending due to vertical loads (**Fig. 12**):

– axial loads are seldom truly that, and any eccentricity will cause bending stresses to develop.

– lateral displacement or sway in tall structures may be well within safe limits structurally, but may be far in excess of maximum allowable values for a particular curtain wall system to function properly.

– columns and bearing walls may also be subject to deflection due to temperature or moisture differential through their section and to plastic flow, depending on the properties of their constituent materials.

• *Steel:* is generally affected by lateral forces, bending due to eccentric loading, and differential thermal expansion/contraction.

• *Concrete:* is subject to creep and shrinkage in addition to bending, and thermal and moisture differentials.

– shrinkage and creep in concrete during and after construction will result in shortening of the structural frame, which may amount to as little as 0.10 in or more than 0.60 in for a 60-ft-high structure, depending on: at which stage of construction the frame is fully loaded, size of columns, reinforcing provided, and differences in ambient relative humidity.

– reinforcing of concrete will tend to minimize creep but will not prevent it.

– when connections between a structural frame of concrete and a rigid wall assembly supported by it do not allow for creep-related shortening of the frame, shearing action between the frame and the wall may develop, which may lead to damage or failure of the wall.

• *Wood* columns will be affected by moisture and temperature differential across their section and bending:

– shrinkage along the grain is considerably less than across the grain and generally is not a significant factor.

– when vertical components of a multistory wood-framed structure bear on horizontal framing at intermediate levels, the shrinkage and creep across the grain in such framing will result in shortening of the frame, with the extent varying constantly with changes in ambient relative humidity.

Deformation effects on partitions

Deformations in the structural frame will also affect interior elements of enclosures (**Fig. 13**). Movement and subsequent cracking of partitions may be caused by:

– deflection in floor deck and/or girders that support the partition and/or foundation settlement, with either resulting in vertical cracking, commonly the full height of the partition.

– lateral displacement or distortion of the frame, often leading to corner cracking in partitions.

– thermal expansion/contraction in the frame, when at a different rate than the corresponding movement in the partition.

– shrinkage or moisture-induced volumetric changes in the frame and/or partition.

Cracking in partitions may also be caused by factors not directly related to deformations in the structural frame:

– expansion/contraction in the partition itself.

– stress concentrations in abrupt changes in cross-sectional area, such as at openings.

3 ROOF AND FLOOR DECKS

Roof and floors: typical assemblies

Decking component of site-assembled roof/floor decks may be:

• Composition or wood particleboard: generally used in framed structures as roof sheathing only:

– usually 4 ft wide, 8 to 12 ft long.

– strength in bending and dimensional stability under varying moisture conditions are primary considerations.

• Plywood: for roof sheathing and floor decking in wood or metal framed structures:

– thickness varies from ⅜ in for roof sheathing up to 1¼ in with tongue and groove edges for floor decking.

– 4 ft wide, 8 to 12 ft long, with 8 ft being the most readily available length.

• Wood plank: either solid or laminated:

– solid wood boards of 1 or 1¼ in nominal thickness may be used as roof sheathing or subfloor decking, but such usage is no longer common.

– solid wood decking of 2 to 4 in nominal thickness is available, but has largely been replaced by laminated decking. Laminated decking is available either 3-ply or 5-ply with thickness ranging from 3 to 5 in, in lengths of 6 ft or longer, and in increments of 1 ft.

– spans for planks range from 5 to approximately 16 ft; lay-up generally random over two or more supports.

• Planks of precast concrete or cement-bound wood fiber; also precast concrete channel slabs:

– generally 2 to 4 in thick, 16 to 48 in wide, spanning 8 to 10 ft, plank generally tongue and groove, metal-edged tongue and groove available.

– commonly secured to steel framing by metal clips; some may also be nailed.

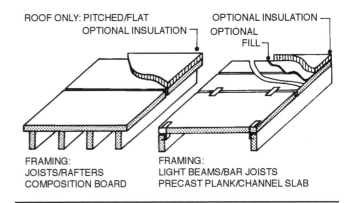

Fig. 14. Framing and decking: site assembled.

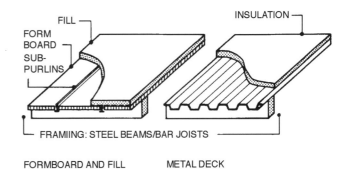

Fig. 15. Roof only: flat.

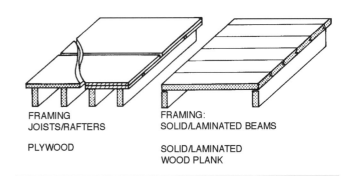

Fig. 16. Roof: flat or pitched/floor.

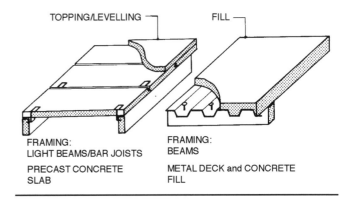

Fig. 17. Roof/floor: flat.

- common usage is as roof decking only; has been used for lightly loaded floors.

• Precast concrete slabs are similar to precast plank except that they are thicker, generally 4 to 8 in, and used principally for floor decking:

- concrete topping of approximately 2 in thickness required for floors.

- spans range from 12 to 24 ft, may function as framing/decking combined.

• Form boards of cement-bound organic or mineral fibers, supported by steel subpurlins between framing, with site-placed usually lightweight concrete fill:

- subpurlin spacing 24 to 33 in: spans 6 to 10 ft.

• Metal deck: usually of formed light-gauge steel either coated or galvanized; generally 28 to 20 gauge for depths of ½ to 1½ in, 22 to 16 gauge for depths of 1½ to 3 in commonly, but available up to 6 in of various configurations.

- ½ to 1½ in deep often used as centering or permanent formwork for cast-in-place concrete floor decks over steel bar joist or light steel beam framing, spaced 2 to 8 ft on centers.

- metal decking for roofs may be used with site-placed lightweight concrete or gypsum fill or more commonly with insulation only; types incorporating sound-absorbing materials in ribs are available; spans for 1½ in depth 4 to 8 ft, for 3 in depth 8 to 12 ft.

Framing and decking: site assembled

• Metal decking for floors: generally 22 to 16 gauge, 1½ to 3 in deep (**Fig. 18**):

- spans range from 6 to 14 ft depending on gauge and depth of deck, and thickness of concrete fill.

- available with closed cells, also referred to as cellular deck, to provide space for electrical/communications wiring.

- always filled with site-placed normal weight or lightweight concrete, usually reinforced.

- decking may be formed to interlock with concrete fill for composite action; in addition metal studs may be welded through decking to top flanges of framing for their composite action with fill, thus reducing their size.

• Grating: of metal or glass fiber reinforced plastic.

Framing/decking combined: fabricated

• Single or double tee's: precast of reinforced commonly prestressed concrete, combining framing and decking into a single unit (**Fig. 19**).

- double tee: generally 12 to 32 in deep and 8 to 10 ft wide; normally spanning 20 to 80 ft, potentially up to 95 ft.

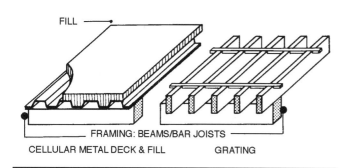

FILL

FRAMING: BEAMS/BAR JOISTS

CELLULAR METAL DECK & FILL   GRATING

Fig. 18. Metal framing and decking: site assembled.

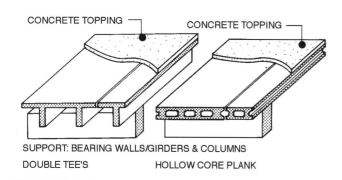

CONCRETE TOPPING   CONCRETE TOPPING

SUPPORT: BEARING WALLS/GIRDERS & COLUMNS

DOUBLE TEE'S   HOLLOW CORE PLANK

Fig. 19. Precast framing/decking: fabricated.

- single tee: Usually 24 to 48 in deep and 8 to 10 ft wide; normally spanning 50 to 110 ft, potentially up to 120 ft.

- camber generally provided to minimize apparent deflection under load.

• Hollow-core plank: precast of reinforced commonly prestressed concrete, combining framing and decking into a single unit:

- depth varies from 4 to 12 in; width, from 16 in. to 8 ft.

- spans generally from 12 to approximately 50 ft; potentially up to 55 ft.

Framing/decking combined: cast-in-place

Reinforced in directions monolithically placed concrete decks combining framing and decking (**Fig. 20**):

- spans for light loading to approximately 30 ft; 20 to 25 ft for heavy loads.

• Flat plate: a two-way slab of uniform thickness throughout.

• Flat slab: generally thickened over columns by drop panels to increase resistance to shear; tops of column may also be flared out for the same purpose.

• Waffle flat slab: thin decking and a grid of joists cast-in-place monolithically:

- joists are omitted over columns to form solid panels, which may also be deeper than the joists to increase resistance to shear.

• Two-way slab: solid relatively thin decking supported by girders along column centerlines.

Decking/roofing combined

Formed metal panels that function as combined roof decking and roofing (**Fig. 21**):

- available in: galvanized steel, either plain or prefinished, aluminum-coated steel, aluminum, either plain or prefinished.

- may be single thickness or a built-up sandwich consisting of: exterior face panel, insulation, and interior face panel.

- composite: with a rigid insulating core sandwiched between two face panels.

- spans generally 6 to 12 ft.

- supported by purlins which span between roof girders spaced about 20 to 30 ft on centers.

Roof/floor decks: typical framing

Joists/rafters

• Cold-rolled light-gauge shapes used as roof/floor framing:

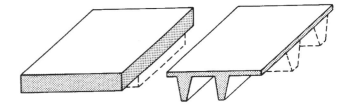

SUPPORT: COLUMNS/COLUMNS AND GIRDERS

FLAT PLATE/SLAB   ONE-WAY JOISTS
ONE- TWO-WAY SLAB   TWO-WAY JOISTS

Fig. 20. Framing/decking: monolithic concrete.

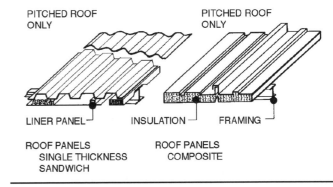

PITCHED ROOF ONLY   PITCHED ROOF ONLY

LINER PANEL   INSULATION   FRAMING

ROOF PANELS   ROOF PANELS
SINGLE THICKNESS COMPOSITE
SANDWICH

Fig. 21. Framing/decking: metal panels.

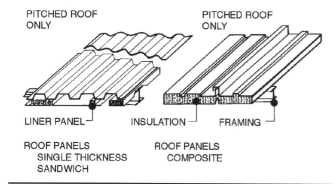

Fig. 22. Joists/rafters.

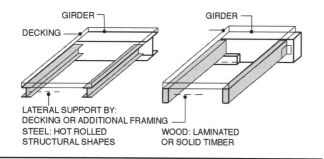

Fig. 23. Beams.

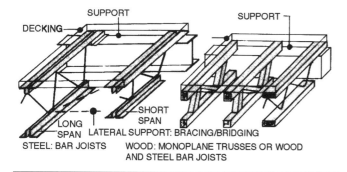

Fig. 24. Trusses: flat top chord.

– gauge varies from 20 to 12; depth, from 6 to 12 in.

– connections are made by welding and/or by self-drilling, self-tapping screws.

– allowable stresses and design in accordance with Specification for the Design of Cold-Formed Steel Structural Members, American Iron and Steel Institute (AISI).

• Dimensional lumber, 2 to 4 in thick, and 6 in or more in width, used as roof/floor framing:

– moisture content should not exceed 19 percent.

– allowable stresses and design generally in accordance with National Design Specification for Wood Construction, National Forest and Paper Association (NFPA).

Beams

• Hot-rolled structural shapes:

– spacing usually 6 to 14 ft when used as framing supported on girders.

– connections welded and/or bolted.

– rolling mill tolerances have been established under ASTM Standard Specification for Rolled Steel Plates, Shapes, Sheet Piling, and Bars for Structural Use.

– decking usually used include: formed metal; precast concrete slabs, plank, channel slabs; cement-bound organic fiber plank and boards.

• Laminated dimensional lumber or solid timber:

– spacing depends on decking selected: up to 4 ft for plywood, 6 to 8 ft for 2 in nominal plank, 9 to 16 ft for 3 in plank, up to 20 ft for 5 in plank.

– available treated for resistance to decay.

Trusses: flat top chord

• Steel bar joists available as short-span and long-span framing:

– short-span bar joists usually 8 to 30 in deep with spans from about 10 to 60 ft.

– long-span: 18 to 72 in deep with spans from about 30 to 140 ft.

– connections to supports generally used: welding to steel girders or to steel-bearing plates anchored in concrete or masonry; anchors to masonry.

– may be doubled, or tripled, to carry localized concentrated loads.

Trusses/beams: pitched/curved

• Monoplane trusses of dimensional lumber, or of top and bottom chords of wood with steel bar webs:

- spacing generally between 12 to 24 in on centers.

- depth varies from 12 to 48 in; spans for light loading, from 20 to 60 ft.

- Monoplane trusses of dimensional lumber:

- spacing generally 2 ft on centers using ⅜ in thick plywood decking.

- spans up to 60 ft based on allowable tension value in bottom chord.

- slope usually from 2 in per ft to 6 in per ft, allowable spans increase with increase in slope.

- monoplane trusses, either with pitched or flat top chord, available of fire-retardant treated wood.

- Curved beams and arches of laminated surfaced dimensional lumber in various shapes:

- nominal width commonly from 3 to 10 in for beams, up to 16 in for arches.

- available treated for resistance to decay, but not fire-retardant treated.

- commonly used with solid or laminated wood plank decking.

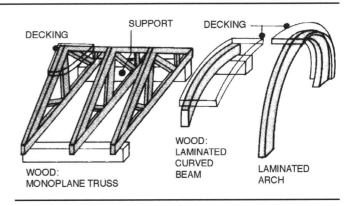

Fig. 25. Trusses/beams: pitched/curved.

4 SUMMARY OF PRELIMINARY CONSIDERATIONS

Structural frame

The structural frame is an integral part of any site-assembled enclosure. Often a clear distinction cannot be made between what might be termed a purely structural or a purely architectural component of such enclosure:

- Decking and framing of roof/floor decks may function:

- structurally: by carrying all superimposed gravity loads between vertical supports, and commonly by transferring lateral loads to vertical supports or other elements of the structural frame.

- architecturally: by serving as the substrate for roofing or flooring, or as substrate and flooring combined.

- Bearing walls are both a structural support for roof/floor decks and the vertical component of the envelope of such enclosure.

- Movement and/or deformations in the structural frame will affect most or all architectural components; conversely, movement or deformation in such components may affect the structural frame.

Preliminary considerations of a structural frame should primarily include roof/floor-decks that shelter and support the activities for which an enclosure is being provided.

Framing/decking combined:

Three basic types within the group are:

- Flat plate: has a completely flat underside.

- Flat slab: with dropped panels at columns, columns generally round, with flared tops.

- Waffle slab: with solid panels of the same depth as slab at columns, and the rest of slab waffled to reduce the dead load of construction.

- Flat plates and flat slabs present few or no obstructions to horizontal distribution of mechanical/electrical systems, but the vertical distribution must be carefully considered as openings in these assemblies are limited in location and size.

Standard reusable forms available to be used in forming flat and waffle slabs include:

- forms for waffle slabs.

- steel forms for round columns with flared capitals, generally used for flat slab construction; and fiber tubes for forming round columns, often used with waffle slabs.

Two-way slabs are:

- generally economical for moderate spans and heavy loads.

- when minimum depth of construction is needed, edge beams may be made shallow and wide, in which case the columns need not line up as long as they fall within the width of the shallow beam.

- Two-way slabs with shallow beams may be used in multistory apartment construction when the underside of the slab can remain exposed.

- Ceilings are generally not used with two-way slab assemblies, nor are they required for a fire-rated assembly.

Fabricated framing/decking:

- Precast concrete units used for flooring usually require a concrete topping:

- to even out all irregularities between individual units.

- to improve the load-carrying ability of the units.

- to improve fire resistance of the assembly.

- Concrete toppings may also be required for roofs:

- to provide a smooth surface for the roofing.

- to improve the thermal resistance of the assembly when insulating concrete fill is used.

Framing and decking—site assembled:

- Joist framing utilizes light, closely spaced members. A variety of materials, sizes, and shapes is available. Joist framing is:

- versatile, economical system for residential, commercial, and light industrial construction where: spans are short to moderate, loads are light.

- prefabricated stressed skin panels consisting of plywood faces and wood joist ribs, widely used in prefabricated housing.

- Beam framing is the most versatile type with a wide choice of materials, sizes, and shapes. Beam framing is:

- most economical for moderate spans and moderate loads,

- can also be adapted to carry heavy loads, with a corresponding increase in unit cost.

- not suitable for long spans.

- when beams frame into girders, the depth of girder usually determines the overall depth of construction.

- Framed assemblies, with the exception of steel bar joists, will not permit ductwork, piping, and conduits to be run within the depth of the framing members, thus requiring additional depth between floors to accommodate such services.

Decking component selection will be influenced by the framing components:

- Wood planking or plywood may be used over metal framing:

- should be secured using self-tapping metal screws, or

- a wood nailer should be attached to the top flange of the member first.

- Roll-formed metal decking, when in light gauges, is difficult to weld to supporting steel framing; the use of welding washers is recommended:

- decking spanning between widely spaced framing may require temporary shoring during placement of concrete fill.

- Precast planks, whether of concrete or fiberboard:

- are generally secured to metal framing using special clips supplied by plank manufacturer.

- diaphragm action is not provided in a roof assembly by precast planks attached in this manner.

- Wood planking, either solid or laminated, is best suited for:

- post-and-beam or heavy timber framing.

- to span between laminated arches or rigid frames where it generally also serves as the finished interior surface.

Spans

Combined dead and live loads and the relative capacities of the various materials and systems determine allowable spans of any structural system. Structural and construction considerations include:

- Stress capacity of components of a given structural system.

- Allowable or acceptable deflection limits, which may vary:

– allowable deflection is often given as a ratio of 1/360 of clear span, without regard to properties of the frame and/or components affected by it, and may not be sufficient to prevent deformations developing: inelastic materials may crack considerably before the limit of 1/360 of span is reached.

• Camber is normally provided in steel, glue-lam, and precast concrete members to compensate for live and dead load deflections. In roof framing such camber may be increased to facilitate storm drainage.

• Bracing between framing members is required in many structural systems as the forces on the beams, trusses, or joists may cause lateral buckling.

• Diaphragm action to resist lateral wind and seismic forces can be achieved in a number of ways to reduce isolated stresses and transmit them through the entire system:

– in wood framing assemblies, usually by diagonal planking or plywood used for decking.

– in steel-framed assemblies, by diagonal bracing, or by roll-formed metal decking.

– in concrete assemblies by combined stress capacities of steel reinforcement and concrete coverage.

• To qualify as a diaphragm, a floor and/or roof assembly must be capable of transmitting lateral forces to vertical components of the structural frame, such as shear walls, without deflecting to a degree in which such deflection could cause damage to a vertical component.

– the effects of lateral loads on the exposed components of roof and floor assemblies

– the roofing membrane and flooring

– should be investigated: structural frames adequate to resist all vertical and lateral loads may still deform too excessively for some types of flooring and/or roofing.

Other considerations may include:

• A column, once installed, can, in most instances, no longer be removed.

• Each type of floor and roof assembly has a certain range over which it is most economical.

• The longer the span, the greater the overall depth of the assembly and the greater the cost per unit of area covered.

Trusses as primary supports

Heavy trusses are used as girders, the primary supports, to carry roof/floor-decks:

• Typical configurations for trusses are: crescent, also known as bowstring, with straight or curved bottom chord; double-pitched with straight bottom chord; double-pitched with pitched bottom chord, also known as scissors truss; single-pitch with straight bottom chord, referred to as sawtooth:

– lateral bracing for top chords must be provided; secondary framing selected will influence spacing of trusses.

– thermal expansion of long-span trusses must be considered in the details of supports.

– concentrated loads to be supported at panel points only.

– long-span, flat top chord trusses are not economical in wood.

– pitched top chord trusses in wood are not economical for spans over 60 ft; in long-span trusses, wood is best suited for bowstring types.

– ceilings, light fixtures, or equipment may be suspended from the bottom chords of trusses.

– long-span trusses generally fabricated off-site. Shape and size of individual panels will be influenced by available transportation facilities, clearances at underpasses, and limitations imposed by applicable state laws.

• Floor to floor height trusses, incorporated in partitions, have been used:

– in residential construction.

– in industrial buildings where mechanical equipment and services to the floor above could be located within the trusses.

– such trusses have also been used in multistory construction to carry suspended lower floors.

Arches

Arches are curved frames combining girders and columns into a single unit. The configurations may be:

– radial, parabolic, tudor, gothic, A-frame, rigid frames.

– rigid frames are arches with straight rather than curved or sloping vertical components.

– arches may be two-hinged at supports, or three-hinged at supports and crown.

• waterproofing of hinged joint at crown may present a problem.

– outward thrust at supports must be resisted by foundations, buttresses, or horizontal ties.

• Site-assembled arches functioning as girders may be:

– structural steel shapes, approximately 20 ft on centers.

– reinforced concrete, approximately 20 ft on centers.

• Arches, domes, and vaults, consisting of curved monolithic decks, which combine means of support and envelope into one:

– of cast-in-place reinforced concrete.

– of essentially constant cross section throughout, or of heavier sections such as ribs, curved girders connected with thin diaphragms.

– small domes may be cast over flexible membranes inflated to resist the weight of fresh concrete.

• Barrel vaults generally used in multiples, with adjacent shells bracing each other.

A comparison of wood, steel, and concrete systems is provided in **Figs. 26** to **28** from Schodek (1992), which provides a thorough discussion of the various system options. In Fig. 26, note that in order for typical sizes of different timber members to be relatively compared, the diagrams are scaled to represent typical span lengths for each of the respective elements. The span lengths that are actually possible for each element are noted by the "minimum" and "maximum" span marks. ■

REFERENCES

Schodek, Daniel L., *Structures,* 2nd ed., Prentice Hall, Englewood Cliffs, 1992.

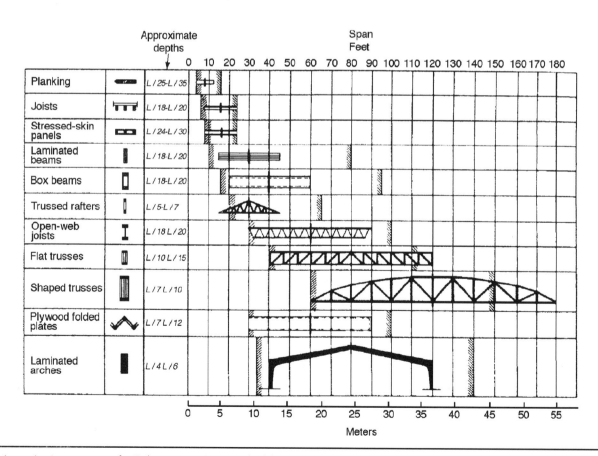

Fig. 26. Approximate span ranges for timber systems. Source: Schodek (1992). Reproduced by permission of Prentice Hall.

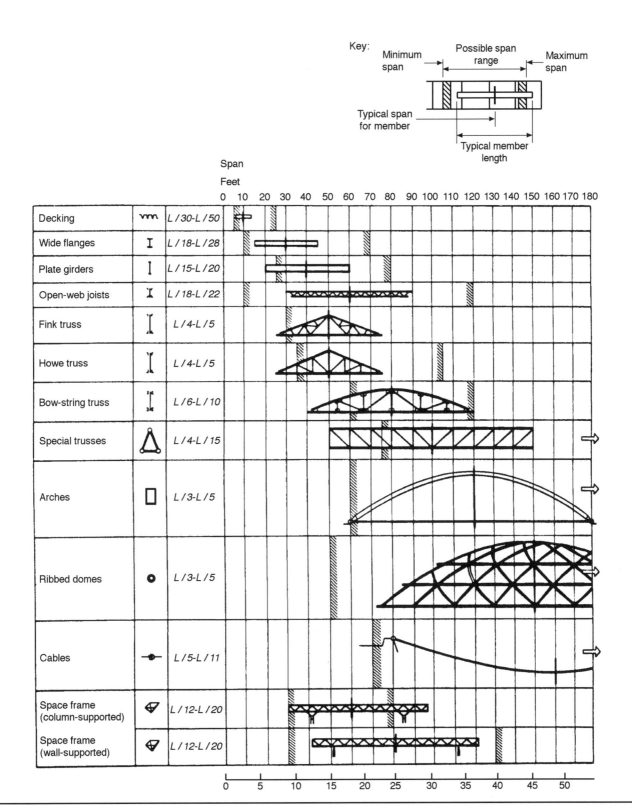

Fig. 27. Approximate span ranges for steel systems. Source: Schodek (1992). Reproduced by permission of Prentice Hall.

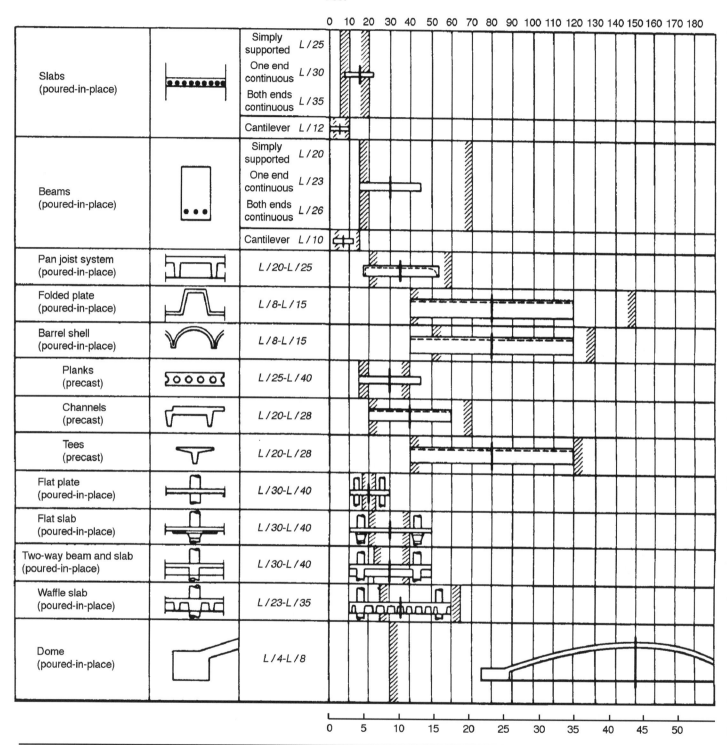

Fig. 28. Approximate span ranges for reinforced concrete systems. Source: Schodek (1992). Reproduced by permission of Prentice Hall.

Martin D. Gehner, P.E.

Summary

The various loads imposed on a building's structure are defined as "design loads," made up of *dead loads,* defined as the permanent forces in and on a building, and *live loads* defined as those generated by variable conditions internally and externally. Internal live loads are created by occupants, movable equipment, and thermal or vibratory conditions caused from internal operations. External live loads are imposed by wind, water, snow, earthquakes, thermal changes, and soil pressures.

Key words

earthquake, engineering calculation, live loads, dead loads, occupancy loads, snow, wind

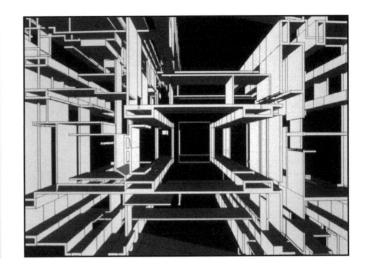

Design loads

1 OVERVIEW OF DESIGN LOADS

Assessing the varied forces imposed on a building during its lifetime requires a thorough understanding of the building, including:

– how it will be used,

– where it is located,

– the geologic soil conditions of the site,

– applicable code requirements,

– the characteristics and interactions of materials used, and

– the methods employed to construct it.

Classification of all such forces are commonly translated into the type of design loads, as follows:

• Dead loads: consist of all forces that are permanent forces in and on a building. These include:

– Gravitational forces accumulated from the materials used to construct the frame, the enclosures, the finishes, and the fixed operating systems.

– Loads from equipment installed permanently in identified locations within the building.

• Live loads: consist of all forces generated by variable conditions internally and externally.

– Internal live loads are created by occupants, movable furniture, temporary storage items, movable equipment, and thermal or vibratory conditions caused from internal operations.

– External live loads are imposed by wind, water, snow, earthquakes, thermal changes, and soil pressures.

– Impact loads from any source may add to live load considerations.

Dead loads

The source of dead loads is primarily generated by the accumulation of weights from all permanently fixed parts of the constructed building. Typical examples of common dead loads are:

– All the structural elements, enclosing walls, floors, roofs, ceilings, interior walls, built-in furniture, and

– Fixed-in-place equipment like heating/cooling equipment, plumbing, light fixtures, fans, and ducts.

For these types of loads, the recommended minimum loads have been established in order to maintain some consistency in basic values for materials and construction systems. **Table 1** lists the weights of common building materials and constructions. **Table 2** contains volumetric weights of materials. Actual dead loads must always be figured on the basis of the actual amount of material used at the location being analyzed. Both tables are useful resources for known quantities of materials contributing to the dead load portion of total load on a structure.

Dead loads are often approximated as uniformly distributed loads for known structural systems such as floor framing systems including all finishes. The following is an example of the dead load summary of a common structural floor system:

Item	Uniform dead load (pounds per sq ft)
Vinyl tile finish flooring	1.4
3 in concrete deck over	37.5
Steel deck form	1.2
Steel floor joists (estimated)	5.1
Suspended ceiling w/ metal lath and plaster	10.0
Light fixture allowance	.8
Total uniform dead load =	56.0 psf

Concentrated loads are large loads applied at a point or over a very small area. The typical illustration of a concentrated dead load is where one end of a secondary beam is supported at a designated location by a primary beam. For instance, a structural floor slab is supported by secondary beams spaced at 8 ft (2.43 m) center-to-center (c/c). These secondary beams are in turn supported by another more primary beam. The first causes a concentrated load on the primary beam at the points of connection, occurring at 8'-0" c/c.

Another example: consider a piece of equipment that has a fixed location and weighs 2800 lbs. It has four legs, each attached to the supporting floor structural system. Each leg transmits 700 lbs on the floor at an identifiable point of application. That unique point of application will determine the requirements of the supporting structural element. The size of the concentrated load and its location will significantly influence the required size, shape, and bracing of the supporting structural element, along with the detailed connection securing the leg to the structure.

Live loads

All variable loads imposed on a building are live loads by definition. Live loads are always additive to dead loads to determine the structural requirements of the building. For reasons of analytical clarity and to understand the structural requirements under different combinations of live and dead loads, gravitational live loads are investigated separately from lateral or angular-applied live loads imposed from winds and earthquakes.

Occupancy loads

Occupancy loads are the typical gravitational loads that a structure must safely support. Occupancy loads include forces not only from people's movements but also from reasonable allowances for movable furniture within a space. **Table 3** lists the minimum uniformly distributed live loads established by U.S. Codes for the design of building structures. A prudent designer will always assess the adequacy of these minimum values in order to match the design requirement with the real conditions associated with the building's functions.

Concentrated live loads

In addition to the uniform occupancy loads, in cases where live loads generate concentrations, the concentrated loads shown in **Table 4** must be included. Unless otherwise specified, the indicated concentration of load is assumed to occupy an area of 2'-5" (76 cm) square, located to represent a "test" maximum stress condition in the supporting structural member.

Machinery and elevators

For structural safety, the weight of machinery and moving loads shall be increased as follows to allow for impact conditions:

– For elevator machinery, the loads are to be increased 100 percent;

– For lightweight machinery driven by motor or shaft, the loads are to be increased by 20 percent;

– For power-driven reciprocating machinery, the load is to be increased by 50 percent;

– For hangers of floors and balconies, the loads are to be increased by 33 percent. The increases for all machinery should be verified by the manufacturer's recommendations.

Cranes moving on fixed tracks

All craneways shall have their design loads increased for impact as follows:

– A vertical force equal to 25 percent of the maximum wheel load;

– A lateral force equal to 20 percent of the trolley weight plus the lifted load applied one-half at the top of each rail;

– A longitudinal force equal to 10 percent of the maximum wheel loads of the crane applied at the top rail.

2 DESIGN LOAD CALCULATIONS

Reduction in live loads

Design live loads on a structure may be reduced under certain limitations as specified by the governing code. Generally, as stated in ANSI (1996), it is permissible to reduce the minimum design live load for members having an influence area of 400 sq ft or more in accordance with the following equation:

$$L = L_o \left(0.25 + \frac{15}{A_i} \right)$$

where:

L = the reduced live load in pounds per square foot (psf)

L_o = the unreduced live load in pounds per square foot

A_i = influence area in square feet, taken as four times the tributary area for a column, two times the tributary area for a beam, and the panel area for a two-way slab.

The limitations of this reduction shall not be less than:

– 50 percent of the unreduced live load for members supporting one floor, and

– not less than 40 percent of the unreduced live load for members supporting more than one floor.

For live loads of 100 psf or less, no reduction may be made for occupied areas of public assembly, for garages, for one-way slabs or for roofs. For live loads greater than 100 psf, the design live loads have some limitations, which must be determined by the code authority having jurisdiction for the building. For live loads greater than 100 psf, no reduction shall be made for design live loads except for the design live loads on columns that may be reduced 20 percent.

Minimum roof loads and snow loads

Ordinary roofs shall be designed for minimum design live loads as stated in **Table 5** or as snow loads as specified for the specific building location, whichever is greater. Each roof must be carefully considered for proper water drainage. If deflections of members or roof slope configurations might cause ponding of water or snow, then additional associated loads should be added to the design live load.

When roofs are used for incidental promenade purposes, they shall be designed for a minimum live load of 60 psf. If the roof is used for assembly purposes or for roof-gardens, then the minimum design live load shall be 100 psf. Design live loads for other special roof uses should be directed and approved by the building official of the code authority having jurisdiction.

Snow live loads to be used for the design of buildings or other structures are given on a snow load map, as in **Fig. 1**. Basic ground snow loads are given in pounds per square foot for a 50-year recurrence interval.

For buildings that present a high degree of hazard to life and property, a design snow load for a 100-year recurrence interval or equivalent value shall be used. For regions where unusually high snowfall accumulation occurs, such as in mountain regions, the design snow load should be determined by the local requirements. For buildings with no human occupants, the snow load may be taken for a 25-year recurrence interval.

Snow loads on roofs vary according to the multiple complications of roof forms, wind patterns, and exposure. All codes have provisions that must be met according to the specific roof conditions. These must be assessed carefully in order to determine the possible increased loads due to drifting or accumulations. Some highly pitched roofs over heated areas may create slides to accumulate on adjacent roofs or roof segments over unheated portions. The variables are numerous, and worst cases must be understood to determine the governing condition for maximum stress on supporting members.

Soil and hydrostatic pressures

For vertical structures below grade, provision must be made to determine the superimposed pressures from soils, from high water tables, or from surcharges on the soils from fixed or moving loads. Lateral pressures from adjacent soils place an increasing uniform load on the wall from grade down to the height of the wall. If the wall restrains water, the full hydrostatic pressure on the wall must be included as a design load.

In the design of basement floors and similar horizontal construction below grade, the upward pressure of water, if any, shall be taken as the full hydrostatic pressure over the entire floor area.

Wind loads

Assessing the magnitude of wind loads on buildings requires extensive investigation of basic velocity wind pressures prevailing at the building site, the building's form(s), its structural system(s), its foundations and soil conditions, and its surrounding urban or open terrain. Sustained pressures on the whole structure must be considered from each potential face of incidence. Further consideration must be given to forces from wind gusts and to limits of lateral movement. Building elements, such as individual windows, doors, wall panels, roof eaves, and similar building parts, must be investigated for the higher pressures from larger local wind forces dislodging these elements from their secured locations.

Representative values for wind in U.S. locations are indicated in **Fig. 2**. For guidance in assessment of wind loads on buildings and other structures, see the applicable code having jurisdiction or ASCA Standard, Section 6 (ASCE 1996).

Earthquake loads

Every building and portions thereof are designed and constructed to resist the stresses produced by lateral forces. Such forces are assumed to come from any horizontal direction. The source of lateral forces may be either from winds or from earthquakes and the engineer may assume that the loads therefrom will not occur simultaneously. Recent research and study of the effects of earthquakes on buildings and structures has permitted extensive development of the analysis and design of earthquake-resistant buildings.

For guidance in the assessment of earthquake loads on buildings and other structures, refer to the applicable code having jurisdiction or to the standard described in detail in Section 9, Earthquake Loads (ANSI 1996).

Combining loads

Except when applicable codes make other provisions, all the loads listed herein shall be considered to act in the following combinations, whichever produce the greatest resistant requirements in the building, foundation, or structural member concerned. The most demanding strength requirement may occur in one or more of the following general combinations of loading:

1. D	where: D = dead load
2. D + L	L = live load
3. D + (W or E)	W = wind load
4. D + T	E = earthquake load
5. D + L + (W or E)	T = load due to contraction
6. D + L + T	or expansion resulting
7. D + (W or E) + T	from temperature changes
8. D + L + (W or E) + T	or other causes

When using the analysis method Allowable Stress Design, the total of the combined load effects may be multiplied by the following applicable probability factors:

– 1.0 for combinations 1 through 4

– 0.75 for combinations 5 through 7

– 0.66 for combination 8

When using the Strength Design analysis method, the service loads are multiplied by safety factors identified as load factors. Common load factors are 1.4 for dead loads and 1.7 for live loads. When combined, the total design loads are then referred to as ultimate loads. Load factors for wind and earthquake loads are described in ANSI (1996). ■

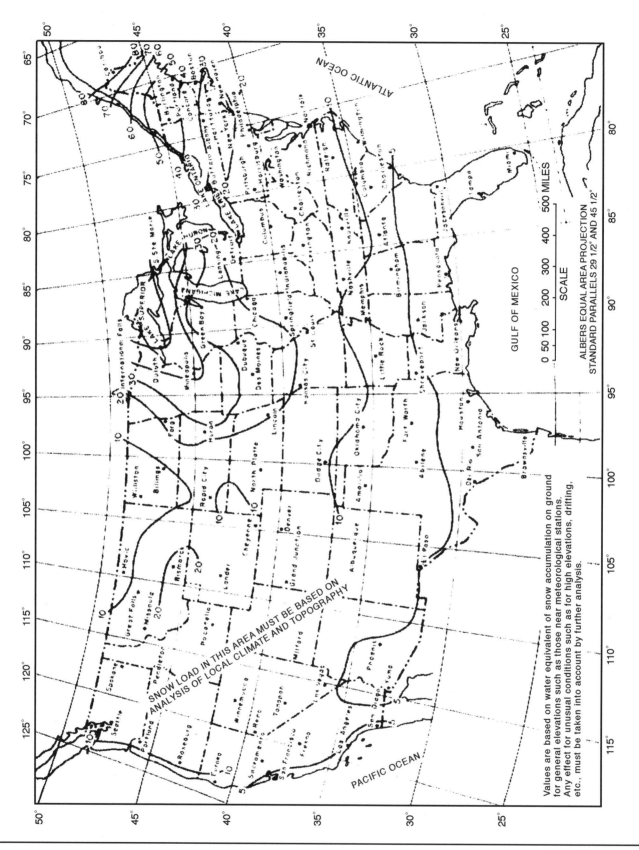

Fig. 1. Basic ground snow loads.

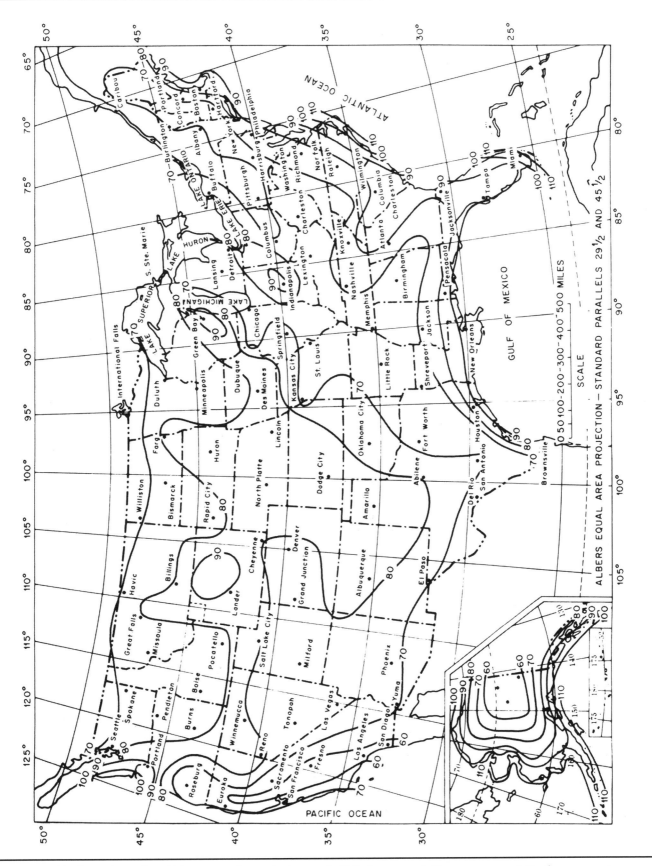

Fig. 2. Basic wind loads in miles per hour. Values represent annual extreme-mile 30 ft above ground, 50-year occurrence interval.

Table 1. Dead Loads—weights of building materials and construction[1]

Weights of masonry include mortar but not plaster coatings. For coatings add the weight appropriate for the type of coating material. Average values of weights are given. In some cases there is considerable range of weight for the same construction due to different manufacturers of similar products.

	Load, psf			Load, psf			Load, psf
Walls:			**Walls** (continued)			**Floors:** (continued)	
Clay brick:			Wood: (continued):			Wood joists:	
4 in. high absorption	34		2x4 studs plastered one side	12		2x8 @ 16 in. o.c.	2.3
4 in. medium absorption	39		2x4 studs plastered two sides	22		2x10 @ 16 in. o.c.	2.9
4 in., low absorption	46		2x6 studs plastered one side	13		2x12 @ 16 in. o.c.	3.5
8 in., high absorption	69		2x6 studs plastered two sides	23		1 3/4x12 Trus Joist @ 16 in.	2.1
8 in., medium absorption	79					1 3/4x14 Trus Joist @ 16 in.	2.3
8 in., low absorption	89		**Floors:**			1 3/4x16 Trus Joist @ 16 in.	2.6
Sand-lime brick:			Cement finish, per inch thick	12		Waterproofing, 5 ply membrane	3
4 in.	38		Concrete slab: per inch thick				
8 in.	74		Plain, stone aggregate	12		**Ceilings:**	
Concrete brick:			Plain, lightweight aggregate	8.5		Acoustic fiber tile	1
4 in., heavy aggregate	46		Reinforced, stone aggregate	12.5		Plaster on tile or concrete	5
4 in., lightweight aggregate	33		Reinforced, lightweight	9.5		Plaster on metal lath	10
8 in., heavy aggregate	89		One way ribbed 20 in. forms			Suspended metal lath and plaster	15
8 in., lightweight aggregate	68		with 5 in. wide by 10 in.			Solid i in. T.&G. wood	2.5
Concrete block:			high rib and 2.5 in. topping	60			
4 in., heavy aggregate	30		One-way ribbed 30 in. forms			**Roofs:**	
4 in., lightweight aggregate	20		with 5 in. wide by 10 in.			Asphalt shingles	2
6 in., heavy aggregate	42		high rib and 2.5 in. topping	52		Cement tile:	
6 in., lightweight aggregate	28		Two-way ribbed slab19 in.			2 in. book tile	12
8 in., heavy aggregate	55		forms with 5 in. wide by			3 in. book tile	20
8 in., lightweight aggregate	37		10 in. high ribs and 3 in.			Roman tile	12
12 in., heavy aggregate	85		topping	71.3		Spanish tile	19
12 in., lightwt. aggregate	55		Two-way ribbed slab 30 in.			Composition built-up:	
Clay tile, 4 in.	23		forms with 6 in. wide by			Three-ply ready roofing	1.5
Facing tile, 4 in.	25		10 in. high ribs and 3 in.			Three-ply felt and gravel	5.5
Glass block, 4 in.	18		topping	79.8		Five-ply felt and gravel	6.5
Gypsum block, 4 in.	12.5		Precast hollow core slab			Copper or tin	1.4
Plaster:			6 in. with 2 in. topping	70		Corrugated metal:	
Solid plaster, 1 in.	10		Precast hollow core slab			20 gauge steel	1.7
Solid plaster, 2 in.	20		8 in. with 2 in. topping	82		24 gauge steel	1.2
Hollow plaster, 4 in	22		Cork tile	0.5		28 gauge steel	0.8
Gypsum, 1 in. on metal lath	8		Gypsum slab, per in. thick	5		Decking: per in. of thickness	
Cement, 1 in. on metal lath	10		Hardwood, per in. thick	4		Concrete plank	12.5
Stucco, 7/8 in.	10		Linoleum or vinyl tile	1.4		Poured gypsum	6.5
Terra-cotta tile	25		Plywood, per in. thick	3		Vermiculite concrete	2.6
Windows, glass, frame and sash	8		Terrazzo, 1 in. on 2 in. concrete			Wood plank or plywood	3.4
Wood:			base	32		Insulation: per in. of thickness	
2x4 studs @ 12 in. o.c.	1.8		Timber decking:			Fiberglass, bat	0.5
2x4 studs @ 16 in. o.c.	1.4		2 in. nominal thickness	4.1		Fiberglass, rigid	1.5
2x6 studs @ 12 in. o.c.	2.9		3 in. nominal thickness	6.8		Loose fill	0.5
2x6 studs @ 16 in. o.c.	2.2		4 in. nominal thickness	9.6		Polystyrene board	0.2
						Skylight, frame and lexan	8
						Slate, 1/4 in. thick	10
						Wood Shingles	3

[1]Data is adapted from American National Standard Building Code Requirements For Minimum Design Loads in Buildings and Other Structures (ANSI A58.1)

Table 2. Volumetric weights of materials for design loads

Values are representative of materials only and may vary slightly.

	lb/ft³		lb/ft³		lb/ft³
Concrete and Masonry:		**Liquids:**		**Minerals:**	
Concrete, Plain:		Alcohol	49	Asbestos	143
Lightweight aggregate	108	Acids:		Bauxite	159
Stone aggregate	144	Muriatic	75	Borax	109
Concrete, reinforced:		Nitric	94	Chalk	137
Lightweight aggregate	111	Sulfuric	112	Dolomite	181
Stone aggregate	150	Gasoline	42	Feldspar	159
Masonry:		Petroleum, crude	55	Gypsum, alabaster	159
Brick, Soft	100	Oils:		Lime, hydrated	45
Brick, Medium	115	Vegetable	75	Magnesite	187
Brick, Hard	130	Mineral and lubricants	57	Pumice	40
Granite	153	Water:		Quartz, flint	165
Limestone	147	Fresh	62.4	Sandstone, bluestone	147
Marble	156	Ice	57	Shale, slate	172
Sandstone	137	Sea water	64		
Terra cotta	120	Snow, fresh fallen	8	**Plastics:**	
				Acrylics	74
Earth excavated:		**Metals and Alloys:**		Cellulosics	80
Clay:		Aluminum, cast or rolled	165	Fluorocarbons	137
Dry	63	Antimony	416	Melamine	94
Damp and plastic	110	Brass, cast or rolled	526	Phenolics	119
Mixed with gravel, dry	100	Bronze	552	Polyethylene	56
Coal:		Chromium	443	Polystyrene	66
Anthracite	58	Copper, cast or rolled	556	Polyurethane	81
Coke	32	Gold, cast or hammered	1205	Reinforced polyesters	131
Earth:		Iron, cast	450	Silicones	117
Dry	95	Wrought	480	Vinyls	104
Moist	96	Steel	490		
Mud	115	Stainless	500	**Other Solids:**	
Peat, turf	32	Lead	710	Asphaltum	81
Riprap:		Magnesium	109	Glass:	
Sandstone	90	Manganese	456	Common	156
Shale	105	Nickel	545	Plate or crown	161
Sand and gravel:		Monel metal	556	Grains:	
Dry and loose	105	Platinum	1330	Barley	39
Packed	115	Silver, cast or hammered	590	Corn, rye, wheat	48
Wet	120	Tin, cast or hammered	459	Oats	32
		Tungsten	1180	Pitch	69
		Vanadium	372	Tar, bituminous	75
		Zinc, cast or rolled	449		

Table 3. Minimum uniformly distributed live loads

Occupancy or use	Live load, psf[1]	Occupancy or use	Live load, psf[1]
Office buildings:		Offices	50
Apartments (see Residential)		Lobbies	100
Armories and drill rooms	150	Corridors above first floor	80
Assemby halls and other places of		File and computer rooms require	
assembly		heavier loads based upon	
Fixed seats	60	anticipated occupancy	
Movable seats	100	Penal institutions:	
Platforms (assembly)	100	Cell blocks	40
Balcony (exterior)	100	Corridors	100
On one- and two- family residences only		Residential:	
and not exceeding 100 sq.ft.	60	Multifamily houses:	
Bowling alleys, poolrooms, and		Private apartments	40
similar recreational areas	75	Public rooms	100
Corridors:		Corridors	80
First floor	100	Dwellings:	
Other floors same as occupancy		First floor	40
served except as indicated		Second floor and habitable attics	30
Dance halls and ballrooms	100	Uninhabitable attics	20
Dining rooms and restraurants	100	Hotels:	
Dwellings (see Residential)		Guest rooms	40
Fire escapes	100	Public rooms	100
On multi- or single-family residential		Corridors serving public rooms	100
buildings only	40	Corridors	80
Garages (passenger cars only)	50	Reviewing stands and bleachers	100
For trucks and buses use AASHTO HB-15*		Schools:	
lane loads		Classrooms	40
		Corridors	80
Grandstands (see Reviewing stands)		Sidewalks, vehicular driveways, and yards	
Gymnasiums, main floors and balconies	100	subject to trucking	250
Hospitals:		Skating rinks	100
Operating rooms, laboratories	60	Stairs and exitways	100
Private rooms	40	Storage warehouse, light	125
Wards	40	Storage warehouse, heavy	250
Corridors above the first floor	80	Stores:	
Hotels (see Residential)		Retail:	
Libraries:		First-floor, rooms	100
Reading rooms	60	Upper floors	75
Stack rooms (books and shelving at		Wholesale	125
65 pcf) but not less than	150	Theaters:	
Corridors above first floor	80	Aisles, corridors, and lobbies	100
Manufacturing:		Orchestra floors	60
Light	125	Balconies	60
Heavy	250	Stage floors	150
Marquees	75	Yards and terraces, pedestrians	100

American Association of State Highway and Transportation Officials

[1] *1 psf = 4.88 kg/m^2*

Table 4. Concentrated loads

Location	Load lb
Elevator machine room grating (an area of 4 sq in.)	300
Finish light floor plate construction (an area of 1 sq in)	200
Garages	*
Office floors	2,000
Scuttles, skylight ribs, and accessible ceilings	200
Sidewalks	8,000
Stair treads (on center of tread)	300

Floors in garages or portions of buildings used for storage of motor vehicles shall be designed for the uniformly distributed live loads of Table 3 or the following concentrated loads:

For passenger care accommodating not more than nine passengers. 2,000 lb. acting on an area of 20 sq. in.

Mechanical parking structure without slab or deck, passenger cars only. 1500 lb per wheel.

For trucks or buses, maximum axle load on an area of 20 sq in.

Table 5. Minimum roof live loads

in pounds per square foot of horizontal projection

Roof slope	Tributary loaded area in square feet for any structural member		
	0 to 200	201 to 600	Over 600
Flat or rise less than 4 in. per ft Arch or dome with rise less than 1/8 of span	20	16	12
Rise 4 in. per ft to less than 12 in. per ft Arch or dome with rise 1/8 of span to less than 3/8 of span	16	14	12
Rise 12 in. per ft and greater Arch or dome with rise 3/8 of span or greater	12	12	12

REFERENCES

AASHTO, *Standard Specification for Highway Bridges,* HB-15-92, American Association of State Highway and Transportation Officials, Washington, 1992.

ASCE, *Minimum Design Loads for Buildings and Other Structures,* ANSI/ASCE 7-95, American Society of Civil Engineers, New York, 1996.

BOCA, *National Building Code,* 12th ed., Building Officials & Code Administrators International, Country Club Hills, 1993.

Martin D. Gehner, P.E.

Summary

This article provides an overview of common applications of wood as a structural material. Topics covered include light wood framing and trusses, timber and stressed-skin panels, and engineered wood construction.

Key words

engineered wood, joist, laminated wood, plywood, purlin, rafter, stressed-skin panel, timber, trusses, wood

Humpback Bridge near Covington, Virginia. 1857. Reportedly saved during the Civil War by agreement of Union and Confederate Troops.

(Courtesy: Eric DeLony)

Structural design—wood

One of the oldest construction materials throughout history, every building tradition has discovered ways to design and craft wood materials at hand into unique applications, including substantial bridge and architectural structures. The wide variety of wood species offers distinct properties for unique and beautiful interpretations for design and construction. The following information provides guidance for common structural applications. As a renewable resource, many species of wood are excellent sustainable yield materials of importance to the designer and builder. Due to increasing demand, engineered wood products are being produced that decrease the waste of wood fragments while increasing the predictability of performance of structural wood members.

Classifications and grading processes of wood material respond directly to the identification of specific properties and applications. The variables of grain, density, knots, shakes, and moisture content present a material, which in its natural state must be used with sensitive insight to properly design for its unique characteristics and properties. The material is very strong by nature. Natural variations can be controlled by selective cutting and bonding. The newer structural wood products are produced by cutting out the weak and variable portions of the natural material and then reforming it into products that enhance the natural material's properties. Such processes reduce the negative influence of knots, splits, and shakes in the manufactured product.

This section presents wood products important to structural applications in buildings. The products included are lumber, timber, wood decking, plywood, laminated members, truss-joist, and proprietary engineered wood combinations. **Fig. 1** shows typical wood sections.

1 WOOD USED IN BUILDING CONSTRUCTION

Lumber

Structural lumber is rough-sawn from logs and then planed and surfaced to a standard net size. A full-cut piece is referred to as the nominal size; however, the rough-cut piece is cut smaller and then finished to the actual size, sometimes referred to as the dressed size, of the piece. A complete listing of all sizes, with associated section properties, can be found in the National Design Specification (AFPA 1992) and in most wood reference manuals. Representative examples are shown in **Table 1**.

Sawn lumber is cut into lengths with rectangular and square cross sections. The narrow dimension is always referred to as the thickness and the larger dimension referred to as the width. Normal identifying reference is by nominal size, such as a 2 × 8 or 2 × 12, whereas actual detailing and construction must use the actual piece size. Lumber of rectangular cross sections, 2 to 4 in in thickness and 4 in or more in width are typically used for structural framing purposes like floor joists, roof rafters, and similar structural elements. These types of members are loaded on the narrow face. Wood studs, commonly 2 × 4s or 2 × 6s spaced 12 to 16 in on center, are installed as wall framing to carry gravitational loads primarily with additional capacity for lateral wind loads.

Timber

Timber beams have cross sections 3 in or more in thickness and 8 in or more in width, and are graded according to strength in bending when loaded on the narrow face. Lumber of square, or nearly square,

---

Credits: Illustrations are developed from publications of National Forest Products Association (now American Forest and Paper Association). The section on stressed-skin panels, updated from *Time-Saver Standards, 6th edition,* was originally authored by William J. LeMessurier and Albert G. H. Dietz.

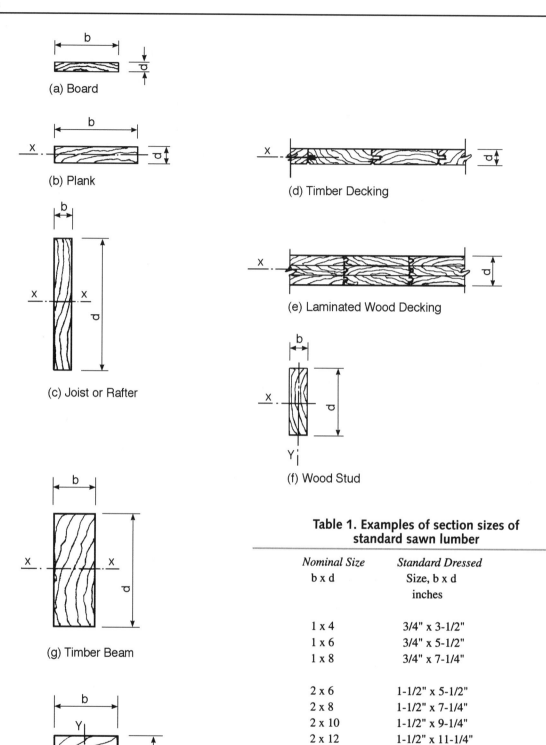

Table 1. Examples of section sizes of standard sawn lumber

Nominal Size b x d	Standard Dressed Size, b x d inches
1 x 4	3/4" x 3-1/2"
1 x 6	3/4" x 5-1/2"
1 x 8	3/4" x 7-1/4"
2 x 6	1-1/2" x 5-1/2"
2 x 8	1-1/2" x 7-1/4"
2 x 10	1-1/2" x 9-1/4"
2 x 12	1-1/2" x 11-1/4"
3 x 12	2-1/2" x 11-1/4"
4 x 4	3-1/2" x 3-1/2"
4 x 6	3-1/2" x 5-1/2"
4 x 8	3-1/2" x 7-1/4"
4 x 10	3-1/2" x 9-1/4"

Fig. 1. Typical wood sections. Note: TJI™, Microlam™, and Parallam™ are registered trademarks of TrusJoist MacMillan, Boise, Idaho.

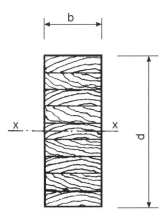

(i) Laminated Beam

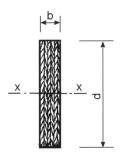

(j) Microlam Beam

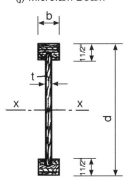

(k) Trus Joint

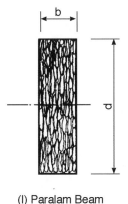

(l) Paralam Beam

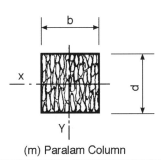

(m) Paralam Column

Fig. 1. Typical wood sections (continued).

sections, 5″ × 5″ or larger are graded for the primary use as columns and posts carrying longitudinal loads. They are suitable for uses in which strength in bending is possible but not the primary stress.

Wood decking

When a piece of lumber is placed in a position where it is loaded on the wide face of the member, it is referred to as a plank. Plank boards are frequently milled so that edges are shaped with tongues and grooves so that when installed against another they form a deck. Decking may be used in residential or industrial buildings for floors or roofs. In residential construction where loads are light, deflection and bending usually govern the structural design while appearance will govern the quality of grade specified. The most common nominal depths of timber deck are 2, 3, and 4 in. Typical spans for tongue and grooved deck systems range from 3′-0″ to 12′-0″. In light frame floor and roof framing systems where joists and rafters are spaced 16 in on center, the deck is called a subfloor. The most popular subflooring material is plywood with thickness of ⅝ to 1 in depending on the joist spacing.

Although 6 to 10 in depths of timber deck are possible for spans up to 20′-0″, these depths of deck will likely be laminated from smaller boards. When decking is used for longer spans, or for heavy industrial loads, deeper sections are required. For those types of applications boards or planks are glue laminated to standard depths and then milled with tongues and grooves. Wood lamination may also be accomplished using mechanical fasteners like nails. Obviously, nailed lamination requires the piece to be used with the narrow face positioned upright in the same position as a joist or rafter. A large amount of material is required for this type of wood deck construction. Therefore such a structural system needs careful assessment as to its proper use compared to more efficient structural systems.

Laminated wood

Laminated wood members are sections larger and longer than most natural timbers. They are made from smaller select wood boards that are glued and pressure clamped. Knots and other natural defects are removed from the wood pieces and then rejoined with fingered type lap joints. When the glue has dried, the sections are planed and sanded to a finished size. The individual pieces to be laminated are either ¾ or 1-½ in thick boards. For straight rectangular beams or columns 1-½ in thick, plank are stacked and glued together. For curved members, such as arches, ¾ in thick boards are stacked, bent, and glued together. All bent wood has a limited radius of curvature permitted based on the thickness of the individual ply. Laminated wood members range in size from 2-½ to 8-¾ in thick by 6 to 48 in deep. Spans for laminated beams range from 10′-0″ up to 50′-0″.

Some unpredictable wood variables are removed in laminated members, thereby allowing higher strengths to be achieved. For instance, knots are removed from all fibers that will be subjected to tension stress. Allowable stresses in bending and shear increase significantly. Both add valued predictability to the strength of the material in the composite section. With relatively modest increases in modulus of elasticity, the deflection of a bending member may govern the size and proportion of the member.

A second form of glue-laminated wood members are sections built up from wood veneers. In the most common form, plywood is manufactured with veneers, approximately 0.1 in thick, layered with grain alternated at 90 degrees glued together. The typical 4 × 8 sheet comes in ¼ to 1-⅛ in thickness. Plywood is designated by two basic types according to exposure and durability. Exterior type is manufactured with waterproof glue and the higher grade of veneers. Interior plywood sheets are manufactured with the inclusion of lower grade veneers and may use glue less resistant to moisture.

Plywood can be manufactured from over 70 species of wood. The numerous variations can accommodate rough framing construction or the best of furniture and finished cabinetry. When selecting and specifying plywood for specific applications, refer to plywood performance standards in publications from the American Plywood Association.

Thin wood veneers can be glued with the natural grain running in one direction. Products manufactured from it have strength properties significantly more predictable due to the control over conservative safety allowances for stress reductions due to moisture, knots, splits, shakes, and other features of natural wood. These laminated members are referred to as "Microlam" sections produced as Microlam™. Available sections are 1-¾ and 3-½ in thick by depths of 5-½ to 18 in. Lengths may be cut to meet the specific applications. These sections provide higher strength for wood beams and framing headers.

A product that combines the strength advantages of Microlam with the strength of plywood in shear through the thickness is the Trus Joist manufactured as TJI™, a registered trademark of Trus Joist MacMillan, and is for joists and rafters. The top and bottom chords are made from laminated wood veneers with parallel grain and the member's web is plywood. The members are available with several choices of chord width along with several choices of overall depth from 9-½ to 16 in. This I-shaped section is a very efficient use of material. The higher flexural and shear strengths can achieve longer spans in typical residential floor and roof construction. Accordingly the de-

signer must assess the deflection criteria. Equally important are the ways this product is detailed for anchorage, lateral bracing, blocking, and bridging of each member.

Bonded parallel strands of wood are bonded together to form a rectangular section called Parallam™. This product has strength properties similar to Microlam. Its dimensional stability is very useful for applications such as wood columns. Rectangular sections are manufactured with selected thickness ranging from 1-¾ to 7 in and depths ranging from 9-½ to 18 in. Column sections may be selected from 3-½ to 7 sq in. Connection details must be carefully considered. Bolts, metal plates, and pins are mechanical fasteners used for securing and creating continuity of load to these members.

2 FRAMING METHODS AND TYPES

Light wood framing

For many small-scale buildings, including residential types, light wood framing systems are used for economy of structure. As worldwide demand increases for building materials, the use of wood as a renewable resource gains importance for building. The craft of working with wood continues to attract individuals not only for general framing construction but also for the highly skilled levels of crafting furniture and cabinetry.

After trees are cut into boards, veneers, lumber, and timbers, the pieces are processed to meet the standards of moisture, strength, and grading appropriate for designated applications. In light framing construction a variety of lumber sizes are nailed together to form a whole building. Walls are typically 2 × 4 or 2 × 6 studs spaced at 16 in on center. Floors and roofs are made with 2 × 8s, 2 × 10s, or 2 × 12s spaced 12 or 16 in on center. In residential construction one common framing system is the platform frame construction as shown in **Figs. 2a** and **2b**. These figures identify the terminology and location for each wood piece. **Table 2** lists recommended nail fasteners for connecting the parts together.

The advantage of platform frame construction is that when each floor system is completed it becomes an excellent working platform for constructing the next story or the roof of the building. Fig. 2b shows a detail of the position of each piece of lumber relative to the supporting foundation wall, to the first floor framing, and to the exterior wall of the next story. (The sill must be anchored to the foundation wall by anchor bolts shown in **Fig. 9**). Remembering that wood shrinks more across the grain than in the direction parallel to the grain, this sill detail will have measurable shrinkage across the combination of sole plate, joists, and sill plate. The designer is challenged with the need to maintain the same amount of shrinkage throughout any single horizontal floor plane.

Balloon frame construction is an historic system of light frame construction (**Figs. 3a to 3c**). As shown in Fig. 3a, the primary advantage of this system is the continuity of the vertical exterior wall studs. Longer studs are harder to install and align. Less vertical shrinkage occurs in two stories of height because the vertical studs pass through the second floor. A comparison of the sill detail, Fig. 3b, with the sill detail of platform frame construction, Fig. 2b, reveals fewer pieces of lumber shrinking under the bearing wall structural studs.

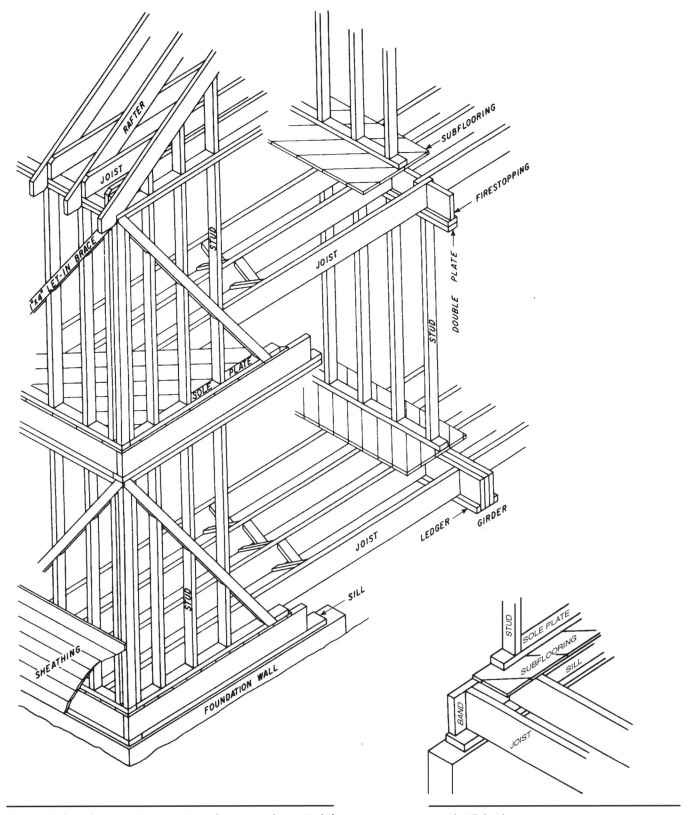

Fig. 2a. Platform-frame construction. Corner braces may be omitted if sheathing is applied diagonally or if plywood sheathing is used. Use double joints under partitions. (Manual for House Framing, National Forest Products Association.)

Fig. 2b. Sill detail.

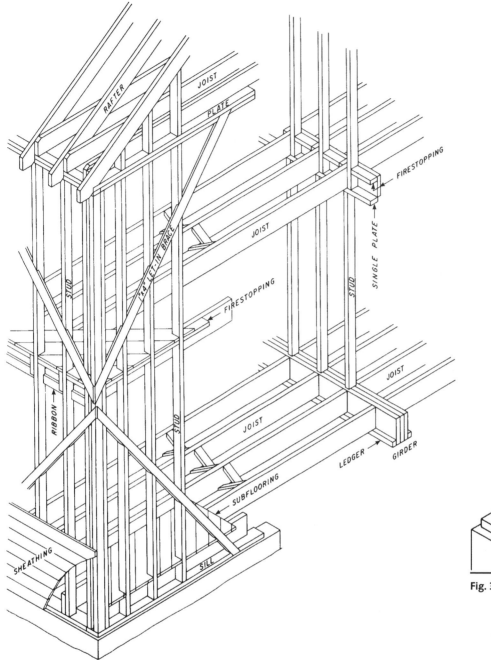

Fig. 3a. Balloon-frame construction (included for historical reference). Corner bracing omitted if sheathing applied diagonally or if plywood sheathing is used.

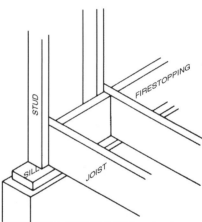

Fig. 3b. Sill detail—balloon-frame construction.

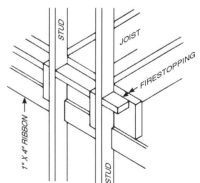

Fig. 3c. Second-floor framing of exterior wall—balloon-frame construction.

Table 2. Common nails and schedule for light framing

RECOMMENDED NAILING SCHEDULE USING COMMON NAILS

Joist to sill or girder, toe nail	3-8d
Bridging to joist, toe nail each end	2-8d
Ledger strip	3-16d
	at each joist
1" x 6" subfloor or less to each joist, face nail	2-8d
Over 1" x 6" subfloor to each joist, face nail	3-8d
2" subfloor to joist or girder, blind and face nail	2-16d
Sole plate to joist or blocking, face nail	16d @ 16" oc
Top plate to stud, end nail	2-16d
Stud to sole plate, toe nail	4-8d
Doubled studs, face nail	16d @ 24" oc
Doubled top plates, face nail	16d @ 16" oc
Top plates, laps and intersections, face nail	2-16d
Continuous header, two pieces	16d @ 16" oc
	along each edge
Ceiling joists to plate, toe nail	3-8d
Continuous header to stud, toe nail	4-8d
Ceiling joists, laps over partitions, face nail	3-16d
Ceiling joists to parallel rafters, face nail	3-16d
Rafter to plate, toe nail	3-8d
1-inch brace to each stud and plate, face nail	2-8d
1" x 8" sheathing or less to each bearing, face nail	2-8d
Over 1" x 8" sheathing to each bearing, face nail	3-8d
Built-up corner studs	16d @ 24" oc
Built-up girders and beams	20d @ 32" oc
	along each edge

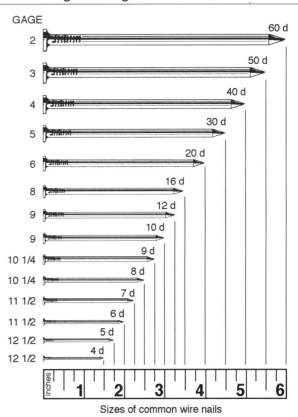

Sizes of common wire nails

The second floor detail of Fig. 3c illustrates the use of a ledger support under the floor joists. In this system of construction each floor joist is secured directly to a stud and to the ledger.

Figs. 4 to **19** illustrate a variety of ordinary details inherent with light frame construction. In Fig. 4, the important issue is to keep the wood framing at least 8 in above the finish grade and to slope the grade away from the building so the water drains away from the building. One example of a foundation wall with footing is illustrated in **Fig. 5.** On the interior of a building, wood columns are often supported by footings just below a concrete floor slab. For this type of column, **Fig. 6** shows two important requirements. First, the column should be raised above the finished floor in order to minimize the moisture contacting the end grain of the wood. A fastener is required to secure the column end in position.

All corners and wall intersections of light frame construction must meet a structural requirement to carry axial load and also accommodate the attachment of wall finishes. The corner column shown in **Fig. 8** is a typical example of how multiple studs are positioned and joined to serve both of these requirements.

Wood joists and rafters are installed at a spacing of 12, 16, or 24 in on center. The module of 16 in on center is the most frequently used. This repetitive use of the same sized member results in a distribution of live load over more than one member. In cases of floor joists, either diagonal cross-bridging or solid block bridging is recommended at intervals of 5 to 8 ft. Bridging helps to distribute concentrated loads

onto multiple adjacent joists. Bridging also has the added advantage of laterally bracing the top and bottom edges of the joists thereby restraining them from buckling. A floor or roof deck that is well secured to the repetitive members will continually brace it.

Many tables exist in the referenced publications to aid in the selection of members for specific loads, spans, and specified grades of material. When designing a member for strength, the critical basic requirements are shear, bending, and deflection. Each requirement has a direct relation to the size and proportion of a section. The design of a joist for shear requires adequate area for the cross section. To meet the maximum bending moment requirement a section modulus relative to a designated axis of bending must be provided. Restraint of the bent member from vertical movement is achieved by providing sufficient moment of inertia in a section relative to the bent axis. For shorter spans with heavy loads shear stress tends to be the condition determining the member size. With light loads and long spans either the flexural condition or the deflection of the member will generally govern the size and proportion requirements of the member.

Most wood data source references are filled with specific information to design wood members. These references are valuable resources in the design and comparison of wood structural systems. The National Design Specification (AFPA 1992) establishes many adjustment factors to modify the allowable stress design values for structural members. There are 14 such factors listed in AFPA (1992). Ten of these influence the allowable bending stress, F_b. Three adjustment factors apply to the allowable shear stress, F_v, and two adjustment factors apply to the modulus

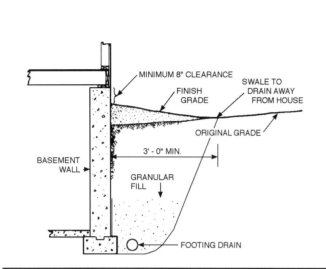

Fig. 4. Foundation plate.

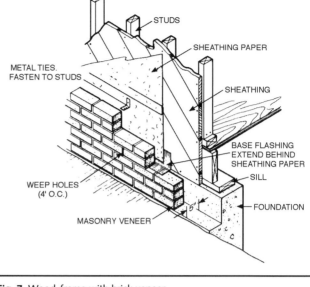

Fig. 7. Wood-frame with brick veneer.

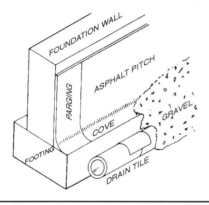

Fig. 5. Foundation and footing.

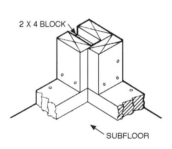

Fig. 8. Standard corner detail.

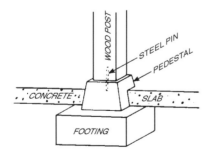

Fig. 6. Footing for basement column.

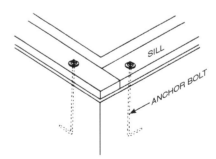

Fig. 9. Anchorage of sill to foundation wall. Anchor bolts, ½ in diameter, should be spaced not more than 4 ft apart and embedded at least 8 in for concrete or 15 in for masonry.

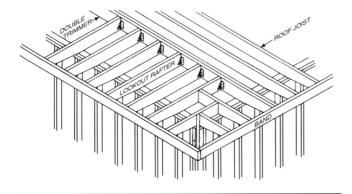

Fig. 10. Corner detail of flat roof, with overhang of less than 3 ft.

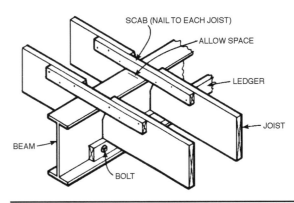

Fig. 13. Steel girder with ledger and wood scab ties.

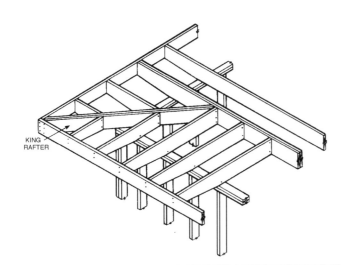

Fig. 11. Corner detail of flat roof with overhang of more than 3 ft.

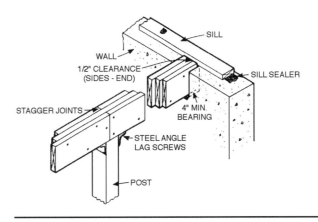

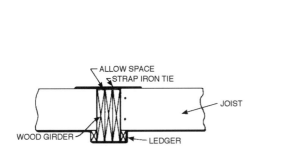

Fig. 12. Wood girder with ledger and metal ties.

Fig. 14. Built-up wood girder on wood column and foundation pocket.

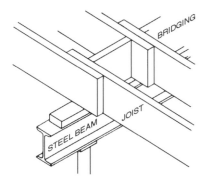

Fig. 15. Joists on steel girder.

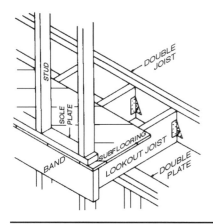

Fig. 16. Overhanging second floor with joists parallel to wall below.

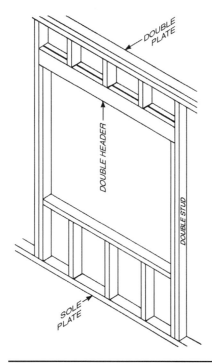

Fig. 17. Framing around exterior wall opening. For openings over 6 ft wide, use triple studs, with the header bearing on two studs at each side.

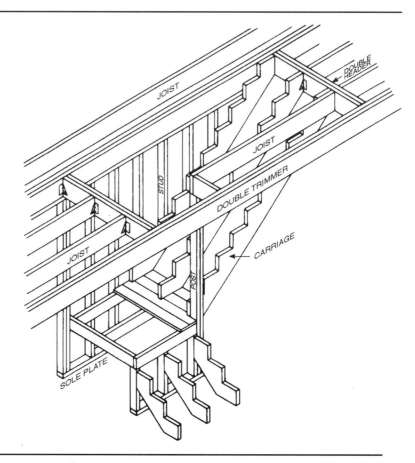

Fig. 18. Framing for stairway with landing.

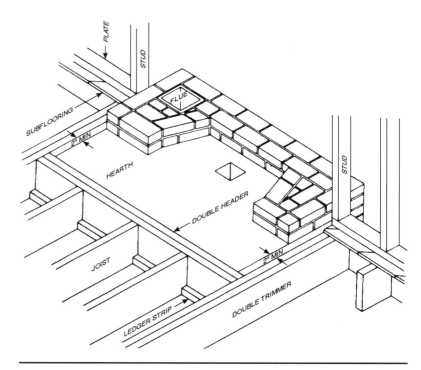

Fig. 19. Floor framing around fireplace. Wood framing must be kept 2 in clear of all fireplace and chimney masonry.

of elasticity, E. When designing wood members, the engineer must assess which factors apply to a specific building and the importance of each applicable factor. A process of preliminary design of members may be appropriate to establish workable architectural dimensions followed by an analysis to assure that each applicable factor has been considered.

In order to gain insight into common and efficient uses of specific wood members, the following illustrations are presented to compare applications.

Example 1 provides some insight into strength requirements. With a constant load imposed on a simply supported floor framing system as shown, the shorter spans between 6 to 14 ft have bending stresses determining the minimum size joist that must be used. The longer spans above 16 ft will have both the flexural and the deflection requirement governing the minimum size of member to be selected. Variables such as joist spacing and grade of material are viable considerations in the selection of an appropriate section. Once a basic section size is determined, then the wood adjustment factors must be considered in order to meet the additional requirements of the Na-

tional Design Specification. These adjustment factors include adjustments for duration of load, moisture exposure, size, and others noted in the specification.

Spans up to 20 ft are shown in this example only because they fall in the range of stock lumber. For spans greater than 20 ft, wood products such as the Trus Joist or a truss type member are efficient alternatives. The longer the span, the more careful one must be to the vertical deflection and the lateral stability criteria. Long thin members may require precautions for handling and installation.

Timber beams are used less today than historically. Not only are large timber members scarce they require lower allowable stresses associated with natural wood. The result is that bigger sections are required compared to laminated members. *Example 2* illustrates such a comparison. As spans increase, the deflection requirements control the selection criteria. When deflection controls the design, the laminated wood member has the advantage over other beam types because it can be built with a camber. The camber frequently used is 1.5 times the dead load deflection.

Example 1. Comparative floor joists

A wood joist floor framing system having a constant load is investigated to show the limits of the spans which may be used based on a specified species of wood and on using the wortking stress method of analysis.

Live load = 40 psf	Dead loads: 3/4" hardwood flooring	= 4.0 psf	Material:
Dead load = 21 psf	3/8" plywood underlayment	= 1.2	Douglas Fir-Larch , No.1 & Btr.
w = plf	5/8" plywood subfloor	= 1.8	F_b = 1150 psi
	estimated joist self-weight	= 3.0	F_v = 95 psi
span, ft.	plaster ceiling	= 10.0	E = 1,800,000 psi
	misc. equipment allowance	= 1.0	
		21.0 psf	

joists spaced @ 16" o.c.;   w = 61 psf x 1.33 ft. = 81.1 plf; $V_{maximum} = \dfrac{wL}{2}$; $M_{maximum} = \dfrac{wL^2}{8}$; $\Delta_{maximum} = \dfrac{L}{360}$

allowable stresses: F_b = 1150 x C_r (1.15) = 1322 psi C_r is the repetitive member factor
F_v = 95 x C_h (1.33) = 126 psi C_h is the shear stress factor for limiting splits on the wide face

Span ft.	V_{max} lbs.	$A_{required}$ "2	M_{max} ft. lbs.	$S_{required}$ "3	Δ max "	$I_{required}$ "4	Joist size
6'-0"	243	2.9	365	3.3*	0.20	6.5	2 x 6
8"-0"	324	3.9	649	5.9*	0.27	15.4	2 x 6
10'-0"	406	4.8	1014	9.2*	0.33	30.8	2 x 8
12'-0"	487	5.8	1460	13.3*	0.40	52.5	2 x 10
14'-0"	568	6.8	1987	18.0*	0.47	82.8	2 x 10
16'-0"	649	7.7	2595	23.6	0.53	141.0*	2 x 12
18'-0"	730	8.7	3285	29.8	0.60	178.0*	2 x 12
20'-0"	811	9.7	4055	36.8	0.67	242.0*	2 x 14

* indicates the governing condition

Example 2. Comparative floor beams

A wood floor framing system with a uniformly distributed load has joists supported by wood beams.
The beams carry a tributary width of 8 feet. Three different wood beam products are compared for
the sampling of spans shown. The comparative choices of beam types have different allowable stresses.

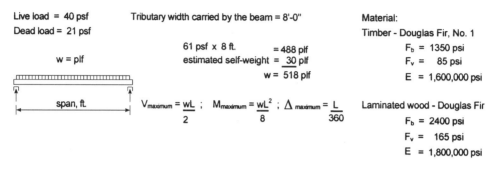

Live load = 40 psf
Dead load = 21 psf

Tributary width carried by the beam = 8'-0"

61 psf x 8 ft. = 488 plf
estimated self-weight = 30 plf
w = 518 plf

w = plf

span, ft.

$V_{maximum} = \dfrac{wL}{2}$; $M_{maximum} = \dfrac{wL^2}{8}$; $\Delta_{maximum} = \dfrac{L}{360}$

Material:
Timber - Douglas Fir, No. 1
F_b = 1350 psi
F_v = 85 psi
E = 1,600,000 psi

Laminated wood - Douglas Fir
F_b = 2400 psi
F_v = 165 psi
E = 1,800,000 psi

Laminated Microlam
F_b = 2925 psi
F_v = 285 psi
E = 2,000,000 psi

Comparative required wood sections

Span, ft.	V_{max} lbs.	M_{max} ft.lbs.	Δ_{max} in.	Timber Nominal size, in.	Laminated size, in.	Microlam size, in.
12'-0"	3,108	9,324	0.40	6 x 10	3-1/8 x 12	1-3/4 x 14
16'-0"	4,144	16,576	0.53	6 x 14	3-1/8 x 15	3-1/2 x 14
20'-0"	5,180	25,900	0.67	6 x 18	5-1/8 x 16-1/2	3-1/2 x 18
24'-0"	6,216	37,296	0.80	6 x 20	5-1/8 x 19-1/2	5-1/4 x 18
28'-0"	7,252	50,764	0.93	6 x 24	5-1/8 x 25-1/2	n.r.[1]

[1]. Not recommended, design requirement exceeds standard product sizes.

Light-frame trusses

Wood trusses are often used in the roof framing system of residential and light commercial buildings. They are very efficient structural members easily manufactured from stock lumber of 2 × 4s, 2 × 6s, 2 × 8s, and 2 × 10s. Typical spans range from 20 to 50 ft at a common spacing of 16 or 24 in on center. A ¾ inch thick plywood deck is secured to the top chord, and internal bracing must be used to maintain alignment and hold the entire array vertical. Repetitive units are produced in quantities at fabricating plants and then the units are bundled and shipped via truck to the building site.

The chords and web members are connected with 18 or 20 gauge galvanized steel gusset plates. These plates have ½-in prongs punched and twisted. They are pressed and nailed into each member at a joint on both faces of the truss. Gusset plates are offset ¼ in with respect to each other on each face of the joint. Camber of 1.5 times the dead load deflection is recommended for the bottom chord and is to be introduced during fabrication. Data on different truss types, member sizes, plate sizes, and designs for other roof pitches are available from local wood truss manufacturers and from companies marketing the metal connectors. *Example 3* illustrates one light-frame truss type with a typical roof and ceiling load. The four spans in the example begin to show the incremental increases in member size as the span increases while keeping basic unit loads constant.

Trusses are efficient structural members for a roof framing system. By comparison, a space with a cathedral ceiling open for the 50'-0" span would require rafters supported by the sidewalls and by a ridge beam at the center. The rafters at 16 in on center could be either 3 × 14s custom-ordered lumber for a 25'-0" span or a Trus Joist 2-5/16" wide by 16" deep. Either of these choices requires more material for the framing system compared to the light-frame truss.

Example 3. Light-frame truss

A roof framing system has wood trusses built from stock lumber and spaced at 16 inches on center. The spans are varied to illustrate the range of efficient applications using a minimum quantity of material. The top chord has a plywood deck which is nailed and continuously supports the chord laterally. The bottom chord supports a plastered ceiling and 10 inches of batt insulation. The chart shows the results of member sizes for respective spans. All members have been designed for combined axial and bending stress along with applicable adjustment factors for the lumber selected.

Roof live load = 35 psf (horizontal projection)
Roof dead load = 10 psf (horizontal projection)
Ceiling dead load = 17 psf
Truss spacing = 16 " c/c
w_1 = 45 psf x 1.33 ft. = 60 plf
w_2 = 17 psf x 1.33 ft. = 23 plf

Material: Southern Pine No. 1
F_b = 1,850 psi
F_t = 1,050 psi
F_{cII} = 1,850 psi
$F_{c\perp}$ = 565 psi
F_v = 100 psi
E = 1,700,000 psi

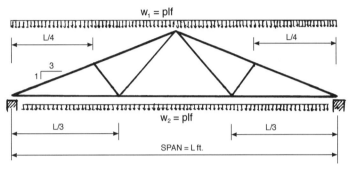

Truss Geometry and Loads

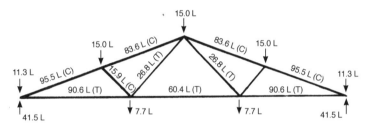

External and Internal Forces (lbs.)
in Terms of Truss Span L (ft.)

| Truss | Member sizes for spans | | |
| Span L | Top | Bottom | All diagonal |
ft.	chords	chords	webs
20'-0"	2 x 4	2 x 4	2 x 4
30'-0"	2 x 6	2 x 6	2 x 4
40'-0"	2 x 8	2 x 6	2 x 4
50'-0"	2 x 8	2 x 8	2 x 4

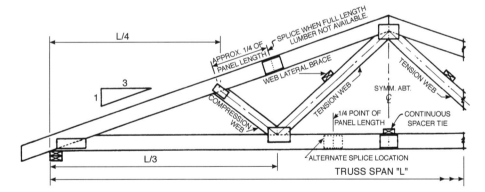

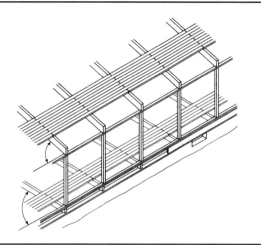

Fig. 20. Plank and beam framing.

Timber construction

Historic industrial buildings frequently used large solid wood beams supported by masonry walls and square interior wood columns. The floor deck consisted of tongue and grooved wood plank. As tools and machinery developed so did the fabricating processes for preparing wood products for construction. The larger wood sections previously identified as heavy timber construction converted to the manufacture of laminated timber sections. Connections of heavy timber construction express some very basic principles for detailing larger wood members where the transfer of heavy loads is concentrated.

Fig. 20 illustrates a schematic structural system of plank and beam. Depending on the spacing between beams, the tongue and grooved plank extended as a continuous wood deck over multiple spans. Often the plank ends are tongue and grooved in order to allow end joints to occur in a selective, random, but staggered, pattern. The intent is to develop continuity of the wood deck and therein have the opportunity to control deflections, reduce maximum bending stresses, or increase the deck span. The diagram highlights the basic system without showing the additional requirement of stability of the whole building.

Fig. 21 illustrates alternate ways to detail a connection of wood beams into a supporting masonry wall. The angular end cut on the beam represents a *fire cut*. The idea is that if a beam fails because of fire, it will collapse without damaging the masonry wall and pocket of support. Classic heavy timber beam-to-column joints, detailed in **Fig. 23,** are shown for historical reference.

Figs. 24 to **28** depict a variety of connections where secondary beams are supported by primary beams in floor framing systems. Metal hangers provide strong connections that are easy to install. However, if wood-to-wood connections are desired the designer must carefully size each member based on net sections at notches and cuts into the wood members. Such notches and cuts often require increased section size due to the reduced section at the cut. Crafted wood-to-wood connections may be developed through the study of traditional crafts, including the pinned mortise and tendon joint.

Beam-to-column connections as shown in **Figs. 29** and **30,** illustrate metal connectors commonly used in today's construction, especially for glue-laminated members.

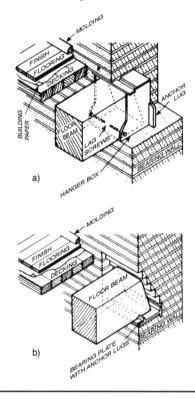

Fig. 21. Floor framing at exterior wall.

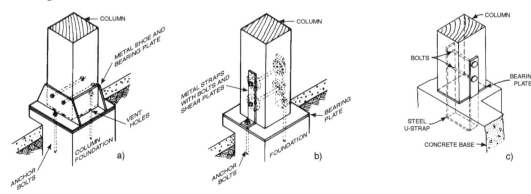

Fig. 22. Column anchorage.

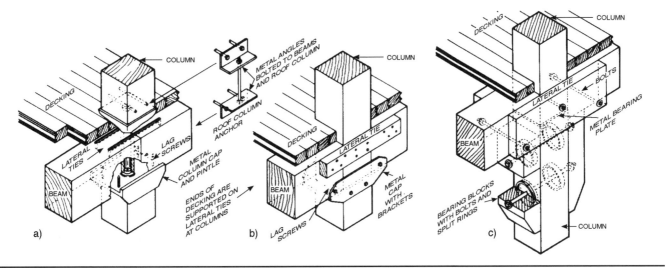

Fig. 23. Floor, beam, and column timber framing.

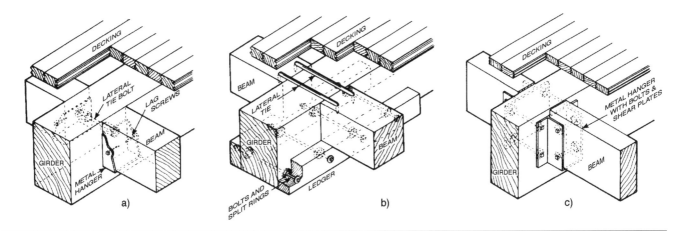

Fig. 24. Beam and girder heavy timber framing.

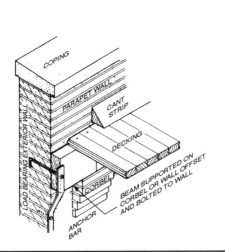

Fig. 25. Roof framing at exterior wall.

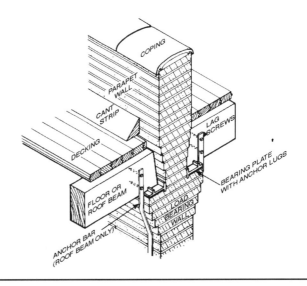

Fig. 26. Roof framing at fire or party wall.

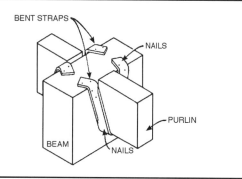

Fig. 27. Bent strap purlin hanger.

Glue-laminated timber sections can have greater depth and greater length than are attainable in natural solid timber. Sections may be laminated with varied widths, depths, curvatures, and tapers to create numerous choices of beams and arches. In a section where bending stresses dominate, outer plies can be selected for high strength or appearance, with lower grade wood relegated for the inner plies. Each piece of wood can be inspected before fabrication to avoid hidden defects that may occur in solid timber. All pieces to be laminated can be seasoned uniformly before fabrication, reducing chances of shakes and checks found in solid timbers. Inspection and seasoning before fabrication permit the use of higher design stresses as compared to solid timber. The *Timber Construction Manual* (AITC 1994) contains extensive data on laminated beams, arches, columns, decks, diaphragms, and fasteners.

For preliminary design purposes, **Table 3** shows common structural wood members and the range of applicability within common structural system types.

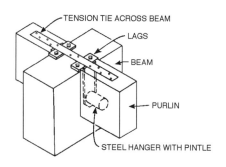

Fig. 28. Concealed purlin hanger.

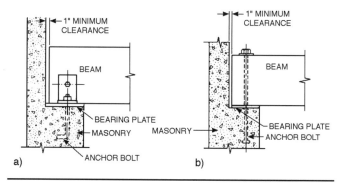

Fig. 29. Beam anchorage.

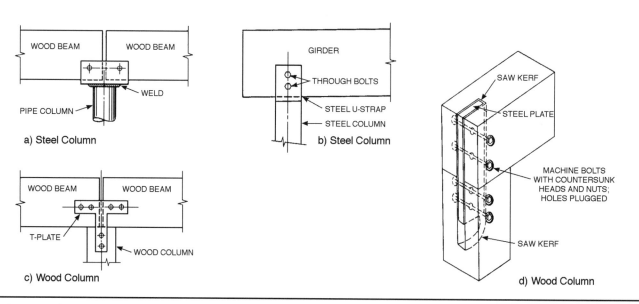

Fig. 30. Beam-to-column connections.

Table 3. Common Structural Wood Member Sizes and Range of Applicability

Type of Structural Unit	Section Size Range		Spacing center to center	Span Range, ft.
	b, inches	*d, inches*		
Plank deck	continuous	2", 3" & 4"	n/a	4 ft. to 16 ft.
Laminated deck	continuous	3" & 4"	n/a	4 ft. to 20 ft.
Lumber rafters	2"[1]	4" to 12"	12", 16" or 24"	6 ft. to 20 ft.
Trus-joist rafters	1-1/2" to 3-1/2"	9-1/2" to 16"	12", 16" or 24"	6 ft. to 30 ft.
Lumber joists	2"[1]	4" to 12"	12" or 16"	6 ft. to 20 ft.
Trus-joist joists	1-1/2" to 3-1/2"	9-1/2" to 16"	12" or 16"	6 ft. to 24 ft.
Solid timber beams	3" to 12"[1]	8" to 24"	4 ft. to 16 ft.	8 ft. to 26 ft.
Laminated beams	2-1/2" to 10-3/4"	6" to 60"[3]	4 ft. to 20 ft.	8 ft. to 60 ft.
Microlam beams	1-3/4" & 3-1/2"	5-1/2" to 18"	[2]	6 ft. to 30 ft.
Paralam beams	1-3/4" to 7"	9-1/4" to 18"	[2]	6 ft. to 30 ft.
Light frame wood trusses	2"[1]	varies	16" or 24"	20 ft. to 50 ft.
Wood trusses	varies	varies	8 ft. to 16 ft.	30 ft. to 60 ft.
Arch rafter (laminated)	varies	varies	16" or 24"	20 ft. to 50 ft.
Three hinged arch	varies	varies	8 ft. to 16 ft.	40 ft. to 100 ft.
Lamella arch (rise/span = 1/8 to 1/4)	continuous	8" to 16"	n/a	40 ft. to 120 ft.

[1] Nominal lumber dimension
[2] Member best used as a single beam in light frame construction
[3] Deeper sections up to 81" are possible

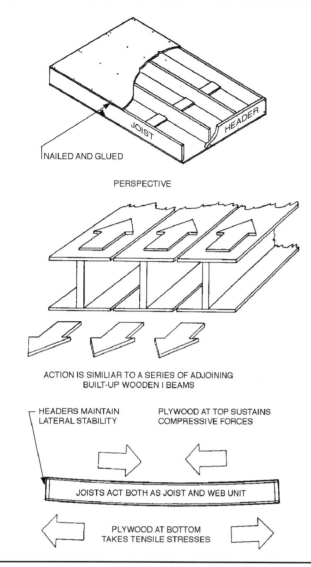

PERSPECTIVE

ACTION IS SIMILIAR TO A SERIES OF ADJOINING
BUILT-UP WOODEN I BEAMS

NAILED AND GLUED

HEADERS MAINTAIN
LATERAL STABILITY

PLYWOOD AT TOP SUSTAINS
COMPRESSIVE FORCES

JOISTS ACT BOTH AS JOIST AND WEB UNIT

PLYWOOD AT BOTTOM
TAKES TENSILE STRESSES

Fig. 31. Stressed-skin panel concept.

Stressed-skin panels

Stressed-skin panel construction provides a means to extend the strength of separate wood materials by their composite action. In stressed-skin panels, plywood is firmly fastened to one or both edges of ribs (joists, rafters, or studs) to make the skins, which act integrally with the ribs and provide enhanced resistance to bending or buckling. **Fig. 31** illustrates these principles and presents cross sections of stressed-skin plywood panels for floors and roofs of houses. All panels use standard 4 ft wide plywood with the face grain parallel to the joists. The lengths of the panels vary, the maximum safe length in each case being a function of loading, joist grade, size, spacing, and plywood thickness and grade. References include *Design of Plywood Stressed-Skin Panels* and *Fabrication of Plywood Stressed-Skin Panels* (American Plywood Association).

The structural action of a stressed-skin panel is similar to a wide-flange steel beam. The top skin carries compressive stress and the bottom carries tension. Because the skins tend to slip horizontally in relation to one another, important shearing stresses exist between the plywood and the ribs and also within the ribs. The only practical way to transmit this shear is by a rigidly glued joint between the plywood and the ribs.

The top face of the panel has additional stresses since it must carry loads between joists. When the top face serves as a floor with only an asphalt tile, linoleum, or carpet covering, it must be ⅜ in minimum if joists are 16 in on center. For roof construction not intended for use as a deck, a ½ in thick top cover is usually satisfactory.

To obtain satisfactory glued joints, pressure must be applied along the glue line. The best technique, obtainable only in a shop, is to use presses to apply a pressure of at least 150 lb/in² of contact area uniformly along the entire glue line. In place of mechanical pressure methods, nail-gluing may be used.

Nails shall be at least 4d for plywood up to ⅜ in thick, 6d for ½ to ⅞ in plywood, and 8d for 1 to 1-⅛ in plywood. They shall be spaced not to exceed 3 in along the framing members for plywood through ⅜ in, or 4 in for plywood ½ in and thicker, using one line for lumber 2 in thick or less, and two lines for lumber more than 2 in and up to 4 in thick.

The glue employed is extremely important. For panels that are not exposed to weather or high relative humidity, casein and urea resin glues will provide satisfactory bonds. For panels exposed to moisture, a highly moisture-resistant adhesive such as resorcinol formaldehyde or, with heated presses, phenol formaldehyde resins and melamine formaldehyde resins may be used.

Typical connections are shown in **Fig. 32.** For panels longer than 8 ft, the plywood faces must be spliced, since plywood is usually not readily obtainable in longer sheets. These splices can be located anywhere within the span, but it is best to locate the splices as near the ends as possible. The splice may be made with a strip of plywood of the same thickness as the plywood joined, and glued under pressure.

Engineered wood framing compared to conventional wood framing

Architects are familiar with traditional wood platform framing as previously described, which is fast and efficient (**Fig. 33**). Critics claim that wood-framed structures perform poorly in hurricanes and earthquakes, although designers and builders compensate by "overbuild-

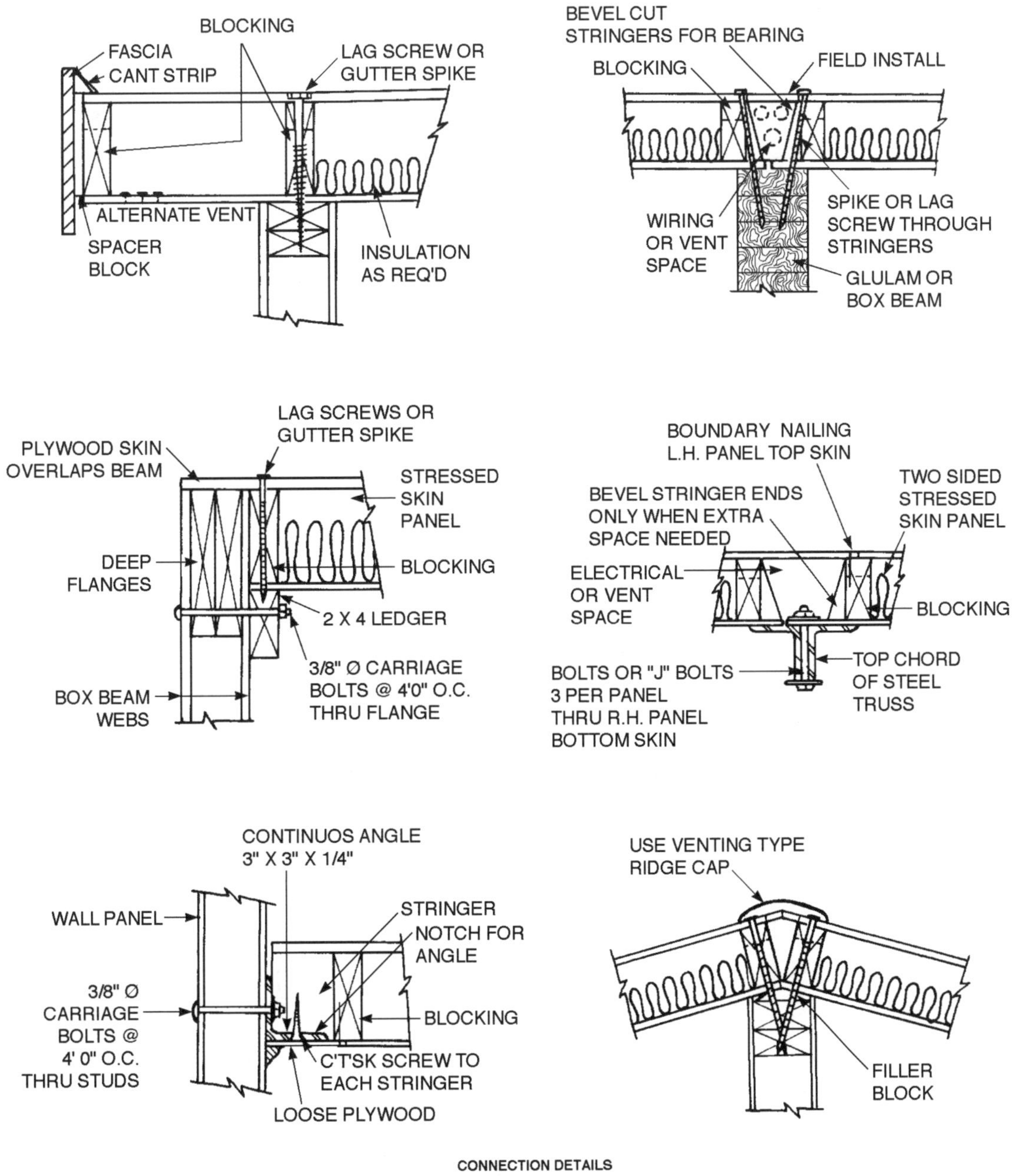

CONNECTION DETAILS

Fig. 32. Stressed-skin panel details.

ing" with structure redundancies for added stability. Wood can be manufactured from a renewable, biodegradable resource and according to practices established for sustainable forest yield. Forest restrictions have limited the overall amount of timber available for lumber production. Limits on harvesting old-growth trees in particular have reduced the amount and availability of large-dimension framing, which are now typically milled from younger, second-growth trees, resulting in finished lumber with greater amounts of imperfections, such as knots and rounded edges. Lumber manufacturers are reevaluating their present forest management and harvesting techniques to better meet market demands and ensure sustainable resources. At the same time, pressure on supply of lumber for construction has led to popularity in engineered wood products (Barreneche 1994).

The term "engineered wood" is used to describe wood composites fabricated by assembling, gluing, and pressing small wood fibers from recycled wood, crushed logs with bark removed, or lower grade hardwoods or weaker woods such as birch or aspen. The terms can apply to laminated veneer lumber, wood I-joints, glue-laminated beams, and oriented-strand board (OSB). It is manufactured from tree fibers and then treated with resins and formed into beams, studs, and I-joints. Lengths of lumber can also be glued together to create laminated beams. These engineered members eliminate natural defects, such as knots, and do not warp or bow like traditional lumber because moisture from the wood is removed during manufacture. Deeper laminated beams and I-joints are able to carry greater loads with fewer members than traditional wood beams (**Fig. 34**).

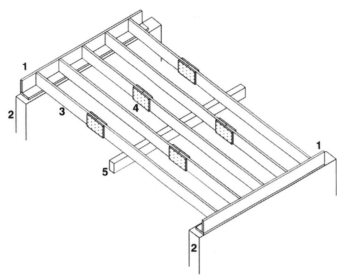

1 HEADER JOIST
2 CONCRETE FOUNDATION
3 FLOOR JOIST
4 PLYWOOD OR METAL
  JOIST SPLICE
5 CENTER BEAM
6 TOP PLATE
7 WINDOW HEADER
8 CORNER BRACING
9 STUD
10 SOLE PLATE
11 STRINGER JOIST
12 ANCHORED SILL PLATE

WOOD FLOOR FRAMING

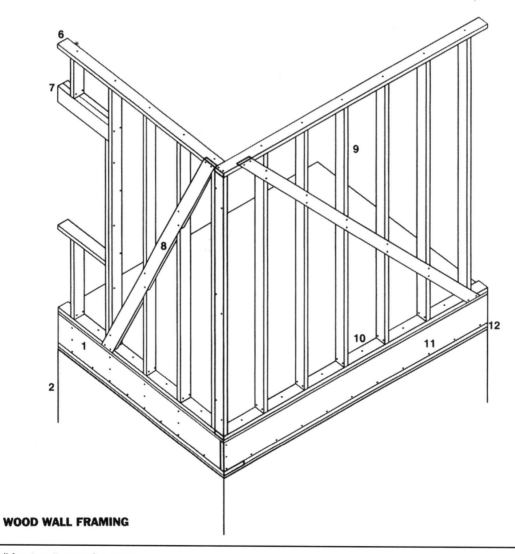

WOOD WALL FRAMING

Fig. 33. Wood-wall framing. (Barreneche, 1994)

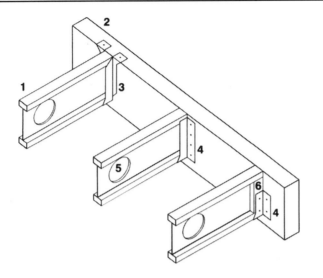

1 FLOOR I-JOIST
2 PARALLEL-STRAND-
   LUMBER BEAM
3 TOP-MOUNTED HANGER
4 FACE-MOUNTED HANGER
5 DUCT OPENING
6 WEB STIFFENER
7 WOOD CANTILEVER
8 METAL CROSS-BRACING
9 PLYWOOD WEB STIFFENER
10 ROOF I-JOIST
11 BLOCKING PANEL

ENGINEERED-WOOD FLOOR FRAMING

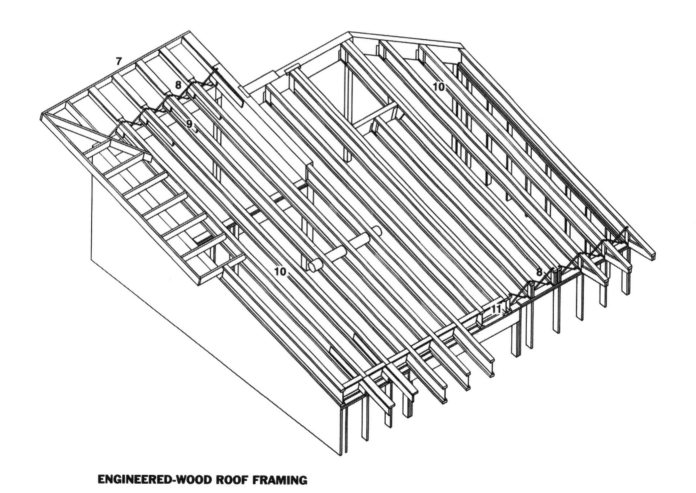

ENGINEERED-WOOD ROOF FRAMING

Fig. 34. Engineered wood roof framing. (Barreneche, 1994)

Manufacturers claim that engineered wood products convert almost 50 percent more of a typical log into structural framing than does traditional milling. While currently more expensive than dimensional light framing lumber, engineered lumber sections offer increased strength compared to regular framing of similar depth, enabling longer spans. This in turn offers ease of construction and compensating cost advantages by eliminating intermittent framing. Webs of engineering joists can be drilled for crossing pipe and electric conduits. A built-in curvature can be provided in longer glue-laminated beams to counter deflections under gravity loads and to prevent sagging.

See comparable comments on light-gauge steel framing at the end of the following article. ■

REFERENCES

AFPA, *ANSI/NFoPA NDS-1991 National Design Specification for Wood Construction,* revised 1991 ed., American Forest & Paper Association, Washington, 1992.

AFPA, *ANSI/NFoPA NDS-1991 National Design Specification Supplement, Design Values for Wood Construction,* revised ed., American Forest & Paper Association, Washington, 1992.

American Institute of Timber Construction (AITC), *Timber Construction Manual,* 4th ed., John Wiley & Sons, New York, 1994.

American Plywood Association (APA)—The Engineered Wood Association, *Grades and Specifications,* American Plywood Association, Tacoma.

Barreneche, Raul A., "Framing Alternatives," *Architecture,* October 1994.

Canadian Wood Council (CWC), *Wood Reference Handbook,* Canadian Wood Council, Ottawa, 1991.

Western Wood Products Association (WWPA), *Western Woods Use Book, Structural Data and Design Tables,* 4th ed., Western Wood Products Association, Portland, 1996.

Jonathan Ochshorn

Summary

This article describes the material properties of structural steel; related steel products and systems with structural applications; preliminary structural design methods for steel columns, beams, and tension elements; connections for structural steel elements; and steel systems for floor framing, trusses, and building frames.

Key words

beam, bolt, column, fireproofing, frame, girder, light-gauge framing, steel, structure, tension, truss, weld

Deere Company Headquarters. Moline, Illinois. Eero Saarinen, Architect. 1967.

Structural design—steel

1 OVERVIEW OF STEEL MATERIAL PROPERTIES

Only certain material properties of steel are discussed here—specifically, those that have bearing on the structural behavior of steel members. The most obvious, and important, structural properties are those relating force to deformation, or stress to strain. Knowing how a material sample contracts or elongates as it is stressed up to failure provides a crucial model for its performance in an actual structure. Not only is its ultimate stress (or strength) indicated, but also a measure of its resistance to strain (modulus of elasticity), its linear (and presumably elastic) and/or nonlinear (plastic) behavior, and its ability to absorb energy without fracturing (ductility).

Ductility is important in a structural member because it allows concentrations of high stress to be absorbed and redistributed without causing sudden, catastrophic failure. Ductile failures are preferred to brittle failures, since the large strains possible with ductile materials give warning of collapse in advance of the actual failure.

A linear relationship between stress and strain is an indicator of elastic behavior—the return of a material to its original shape after being stressed and then unstressed. Structures are expected to behave elastically under normal "service" loads; but plastic behavior, characterized by permanent deformations, needs to be considered when ultimate, or failure, loads are being computed.

Typical stress-strain curves for steel are shown in **Figs. 1** and **2**. The most striking aspects of these stress-strain curves are the incredibly high strength (both yield and ultimate strength), modulus of elasticity (indicated by the slope of the curve), and ductility (related to the area under the stress-strain curve) of steel relative to other commonly used structural materials such as concrete and wood.

As shown in Figs. 1 and 2, steel has a distinct elastic region in which stresses are proportional to strains (up to point "A"), and a plastic region that begins with the yielding of the material and continues until a so-called "strain-hardening" region is reached (from point "A" to point "C"). The yield stress defines the limit of elastic behavior, and can be taken as 36 ksi [kips per square inch. One kip = 1000 pounds] for the most commonly used structural steel (designated ASTM A36).

Within the plastic range, yielded material strains considerably under constant stress (the yield stress), but does not rupture. In fact, rupture only occurs at the end of the strain-hardening region, at an ultimate or failure stress (strength) much higher than the yield stress (point "D"). Bending cold-formed steel (see below) to create structural shapes out of flat sheets or plates of steel stretches the material at the outer edges of these bends beyond both the elastic and plastic regions, and into the strain-hardening region. This actually increases the strength of these structural elements, even though the direction of stretching is perpendicular to the longitudinal axis of the element.

High-strength steels (with yield stresses up to 65 ksi or higher) are available, but their utility is limited in the following two ways:

- First, the modulus of elasticity of steel does not increase as strength increases, but is virtually the same for all steel (29,000 to 30,000 ksi). Reducing the size of structural elements because they are stronger makes it more likely that problems with serviceability (that is, deflections and vibrations) will surface since these effects are related, not to strength, but to the modulus of elasticity.

- Second, increased strength is correlated with decreased ductility, and a greater susceptibility to fatigue failure. Where dynamic and cyclic loading is expected, high-strength steel is not recommended; where dead load dominates, and the load history of the structural element is expected to be relatively stable, high-strength steel may be appropriate, as long as the first criteria relating to stiffness (modulus of elasticity) is met. Commonly used steels, along with minimum yield and ultimate stresses, are listed in **Tables 1** and **2**, as well as in the *Manual of Steel Construction* (AISC 1989).

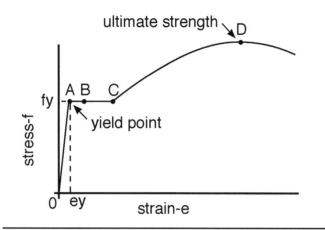

Fig. 1. Stress-strain curve for steel.

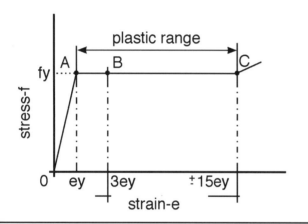

Fig. 2. Detail of plastic range of stress-strain curve.

Table 1. Types of structural steel for use in building construction

ASTM designation	Primary use in construction
	Carbon steel
A36	All-purpose carbon-grade steel used for construction of buildings and bridges
	High-strength low alloy steel
A242	For exceptionally high corrsion resistance: more expensive; suitable for use in uncoated conditions.
A441	Welded structures where weight saving is important; excellent impact resistance; corrosion resistance twice that of carbon steel.
A572	Excellent formability and weldability; economical where strength and light weight are vital design objectives; the range of yield strengths offers designers a selection of steel to closely match their varied requirements.
A588	The atmospheric corrosion resistance of this steel is 4-6 times that of carbon steel; if unpainted, a tightly adhering oxide coating forms on surface to prevent progressive oxidation; for use where weight reduction, weldability, and maintenance costs are considerations.

Table 2. Minimum yield and ultimate stresses for structural steel

ASTM designation	Thickness, in	F_y Minimum yield stress, ksi	F_u Minimum tensile stress, ksi
A36	To 8" incl.	36.0	58.0
A242	To 3/4" incl.	50.0	70.0
	3/4" to 1-1/2" incl.	46.0	67.0
	1-1/2" to 4" incl.	42.0	63.0
A441	To 3/4" incl.	50.0	70.0
	3/4" to 1-1/2" incl.	46.0	67.0
	1-1/2" to 4" incl.	42.0	63.0
	4" to 8" incl.	40.0	60.0
A572 grade 42	To 4" incl.	42.0	60.0
A572 grade 50	To 1-1/2" incl.	50.0	65.0
A572 grade 60	To 1" incl.	60.0	75.0
A572 grade 65	To 1/2" incl.	65.0	80.0
A588	To 4" incl.	50.0	70.0
	4" to 5" incl.	46.0	67.0
	5" to 8" incl.	42.0	63.0

In addition to stress-strain data, environmental conditions, manufacturing processes, or the way in which loads are applied can also influence material properties. Steel is subject to corrosion if not protected, and loss of strength and stiffness at high temperatures if not fireproofed. While these are extremely important material properties, the structural design of steel elements presupposes that these issues have been addressed within the architectural design process. Specifically, steel is typically fireproofed by being encased in a fire-resistive material such as gypsum board, plaster, or concrete; or by the application of a sprayed-on thin film intumescent paint (expanding when heated); or, most commonly, by the application of a sprayed-on or troweled cementitious coating (**Fig. 3**). Steel can be protected from corrosion by being encased within various fireproofing materials, or by being painted.

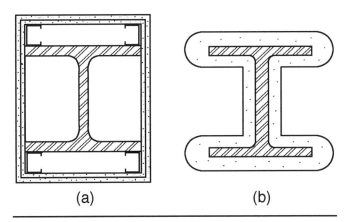

Fig. 3. Fireproofing of steel members with (a) gypsum board and (b) sprayed-on cementitious fireproofing.

Hot-rolled steel shapes contain residual stresses even before they are loaded. These are caused by the uneven cooling of the shapes after they are rolled at temperatures of approximately 2000 F. The exposed flanges and webs cool and contract sooner than the web-flange intersections; the contraction of these junction points is then inhibited by the adjacent areas that have already cooled, so they are forced into tension as they simultaneously compress the areas that cooled first. Residual stresses have an impact on the inelastic buckling of steel columns, since partial yielding of the cross section occurs at a lower compressive stress than would be the case if the residual compressive stresses "locked" into the column were not present.

The behavior of structural elements is conditioned by the particular shapes into which these materials are formed, and the particular material qualities selected. Steel structures can be fabricated from elements having an enormous range of strengths, sizes, and geometric configurations, subject only to the constraints imposed by manufacturing technologies, transport and handling, and requirements of safety and serviceability. In practice, the usual range is smaller, limited to standard shapes and sizes endorsed by industry associations.

Wide-flange shapes are commonly used for both beams and columns within steel-framed structures. They are designated by a capital W, followed by the cross section's nominal depth and weight per linear foot. For example, a W14 × 38 has a nominal depth of 14 in and weighs 38 pounds per linear foot. While any wide-flange shape may be used as either a column or beam, in practice beam sections tend to be more elongated (with much greater resistance to bending about their strong axes), while column sections tend to have more square proportions (in order to lessen the disparity between radii of gyration about the two potential axes of buckling). Unlike "I-beam" sections, whose flange surfaces are not parallel (the inner surface slopes about 16 percent relative to the outer surface), wide-flange sections have parallel flange surfaces, making it easier to make connections to other structural elements. Wide-flange sections are manufactured in groups with a common set of inner rollers. Within each of these groups, the dimensions and properties are varied by increasing the overall depth of the section (thereby increasing the flange thickness) and letting web thickness increase as well. For this reason, actual depths may differ considerably from nominal depths given to each group of shapes.

Dimensions and section properties of commonly available W shapes are tabulated in the "Dimensions and Properties" section of the *Manual of Steel Construction* (AISC 1989). Other shapes, such as channels (C or MC), angles (L), standard "I-beams" (S), and various hollow structural shapes (HSS) such as pipes and tubing also have many structural applications. Standard dimensions and properties for these shapes are also tabulated (AISC 1989). The designation for channels

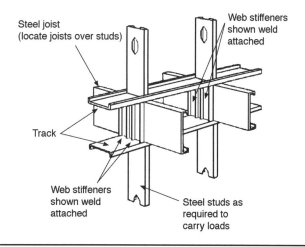

Fig. 4. Cold-formed steel studs and joists.

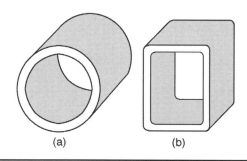

Fig. 5. Hollow structural shapes: (a) pipes; and (b) square and rectangular tubes.

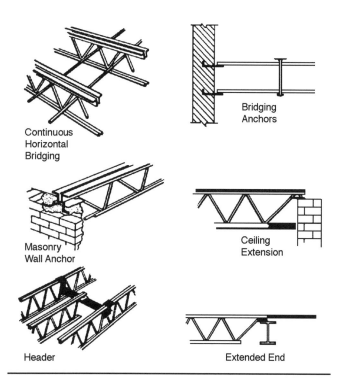

Fig. 6. Open-web steel joists.

(C and MC) follows that for wide-flange sections, with the nominal depth in inches followed by the weight in pounds per linear foot. For angles, three numbers are given after the symbol, L: the first two are the overall lengths of the two legs; the third is the leg thickness (always the same for both legs).

Related products

Aside from standard rolled structural shapes, several other structural applications of steel should be noted:

- Cold-formed steel is made by bending steel sheet (typically with 90-degree bends) into various cross-sectional shapes, used primarily as studs (closely spaced vertical compression elements), joists (closely spaced beams), corrugated decks, or elements comprising lightweight trusses (**Fig. 4**). Corrugated steel decks constitute the floor and roof system for almost all steel-framed buildings. For floor systems, they are often designed compositely with concrete fill, effectively creating a reinforced concrete floor system in which the reinforcement (and formwork) consists of the steel deck itself. Manufacturers of these cold-formed products provide tables containing section properties and allowable loads, or stresses.

- Hollow structural shapes can be formed from flat sheets or plates bent and then welded under pressure; these can be formed into circular-shaped pipes, or square and rectangular structural tubing (**Fig. 5**).

- Open-web steel joists are lightweight prefabricated trusses made from steel angles and rods (**Fig. 6**). Spans of up to 144 ft are possible with "deep longspan" or DLH-series joists; regular "longspan" (LH-series) joists span up to 96 ft, while ordinary H-series joists span up to 60 ft. These products are relatively flexible, subject to vibration, and are most often used to support roof structures in large one-story commercial or industrial buildings.

- Space-frame (actually space-truss) systems consisting of linear elements and connecting nodes are manufactured by numerous companies.

- Cables and rods can be used as structural elements where the only expected stresses are tension, or where the element is prestressed into tension: the flexibility of these elements prevents them from sustaining any compressive or bending stresses. Applications include elements within trusses, bridges, and membrane structures.

2 STEEL DESIGN CALCULATION METHODS

Allowable stress design

Uncertainties abound in structural engineering. These include not only the nature of loads and the strength and stiffness of structural materials in resisting these loads; but also the appropriateness of mathematical models used in design and analysis, and the degree to which actual built structures conform to the plans and specifications produced by their designers. Structural design approaches can be characterized by the extent to which these uncertainties are made explicit. The simplest approach to designing steel structures uses a single factor of safety to define an allowable stress for a given type of structural behavior, that is, bending. If actual (that is, calculated) stresses do not exceed these allowable stresses, the structure is considered to be safe.

In steel Allowable Stress Design [ASD], the factor of safety is made explicit, and is most often multiplied by the yield stress to obtain the allowable stress. In practice, the factor of safety ranges from ⅔ for adequately braced and proportioned beams to ¹²⁄₂₃ or lower for slender steel columns.

In allowable stress design, dead and live loads are simply added together, in spite of the fact that dead loads can be predicted with a higher degree of certainty than live loads. Thus, if two structures carry the same total load, but one structure has a higher percentage of dead load, the structures will have different degrees of safety when designed using the allowable stress method. That is, the structure with more dead load will be statistically safer, since the actual dead load acting on the structure is more likely to correspond to the calculated dead load than is the case with live load.

Allowable stress design is sometimes called working stress design, since the loads used in the method ("service loads") represent those expected to actually occur during the life of the structure.

Load and resistance factor design

A more recent approach to the design of steel structures explicitly considers the probabilistic nature of loads and the resistance of structural materials to those loads. Instead of regulating the design of structural elements by defining an upper limit to their "working stresses," Load and Resistance Factor Design [LRFD] is based upon the highest stress that the steel can withstand before failing or otherwise becoming structurally useless—this "limit state" is most often taken as the onset of buckling for columns, or the complete yielding of a cross section for beams (that is, the creation of a so-called "plastic hinge").

Using this method, the required strength of a structural element, calculated using loads multiplied by load factors (that correspond to their respective uncertainties), must not exceed the design strength of that element, calculated by multiplying the strength, or "failure" stress, of the material by resistance factors (that account for the variability of those stresses, and the consequences of failure). In the discussion that follows for steel elements, we use allowable stress design.

Tension elements

Elements subjected to tension provide the simplest mathematical model relating internal force and stress: axial stress = force / cross-sectional area.

This equation is simple and straightforward because it corresponds to the simplest pattern of strain that can develop within the cross section of a structural element, assumed to be uniformly distributed across the entire cross section. For this reason, it can be defined as force per unit area. Classical "strength of materials" texts use the symbol, σ, for axial stress, so that we get $\sigma = P / A$, where P is the internal force at a cross section with area, A. By axial stress, we mean stress "acting" parallel to the longitudinal axis of the structural element, or stress causing the element to strain in the direction of its longitudinal axis. Tension is an axial stress causing elongation; compression is an axial stress causing shortening or contraction.

In considering particular structural materials, including steel, stresses are often represented by the letter F rather than σ, and capitalized when referring to allowable yield or ultimate stresses. For example, F_y refers to the yield stress of steel; F_u refers to the ultimate stress of steel

(the highest stress, or "strength," of steel reached within the strain-hardening region); while F_t (not to be confused with the "top-story force" F_t used in seismic calculations) symbolizes allowable tensile stress and F_a refers to allowable axial compressive stress. Lowercase f, with appropriate subscripts, is often used to refer to the actual stress being computed. An exception to this convention occurs in reinforced concrete strength design, where the yield stress of reinforcing steel (F_y in steel design) is given a lowercase designation, f_y. In any case, for axial tension in steel, allowable stress design requires that $f_t \leq F_t$.

Unlike tension elements designed in timber, two modes of "failure" are considered when designing bolted steel tension members. First, the element might become functionally useless if yielding occurs across its gross area, at the yield stress, F_y. Since internal tensile forces are generally uniform throughout the entire length of the element, yielding would result in extremely large deformations. On the other hand, if yielding commenced on the net area (where bolt holes reduce the gross area), the part of the element subjected to yield strains would be limited to the local area around the bolts, and excessive deformations would not occur. However, a second mode of failure might occur at these bolt holes: rupture of the element could occur if, after yielding, the stresses across the net area reached the ultimate stress, F_u.

Another difference in the design of wood and steel tension elements occurs because non-rectangular cross sections are often used in steel. If connections are made through only certain parts of the cross section, as illustrated in **Fig. 7**, the net area in the vicinity of the connection will be effectively reduced, depending on the geometry of the elements being joined, and the number of bolts being used. This reduced effective net area, A_e, is obtained by multiplying the net area, A_n, by a reduction coefficient, U, ranging from 0.9 to 0.75 as described in **Table 3**.

Where all parts (that is, flanges and webs) of a cross section are connected, and the so-called shear-lag effect previously described cannot occur, the coefficient U is taken as 1.0, and the effective net area equals the net area. For short connection fittings like splice plates and gusset plates, U is also taken as 1.0, but $A_e = A_n$ cannot exceed 0.85 times the gross area. Finally, the lengths of tension members, other than rods and cables, are limited to a slenderness ratio (defined as the ratio of length to least radius of gyration) of 300, to prevent excessive vibrations and protect against damage during transportation and erection.

From the previous discussion, it can be seen that two values for the allowable stress in tension need to be determined: one for yielding of the gross area; and one for failure (rupture) of the effective net area. These two values are $F_t^{gross} = 0.6 F_y$ and $F_t^{net} = 0.5 F_u$ where F_t^{gross} and F_t^{net} are the allowable tensile stresses for steel corresponding to the two modes of "failure"; F_y is the yield stress; and F_u is the ultimate stress for steel.

The following example illustrates the application of these principles to a steel tension problem. Note that different procedures are used for cables, eyebars, and threaded rods.

Example 1: steel tension element analysis

Find the maximum tension load, P, that can be applied to a W8 × 24 element connected to gusset plates within a truss with ¾" diameter bolts, as shown in **Fig. 8**. Assume A36 steel. Note that bolt hole diameter can be taken as bolt diameter plus ⅛", or ⅞".

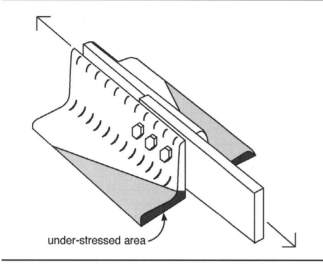

Fig. 7. Shear lag in bolted tension connection.

Table 3. Shear lag coefficient, bolted steel connections in tension

Condition	U
• W,M,S and tees • connection to flange • 3 bolts per line, minimum • flange width at least 2/3 beam depth	0.90
• 3 bolts per line, minimum • any other condition	0.85
• 2 bolts per line, minimum	0.75

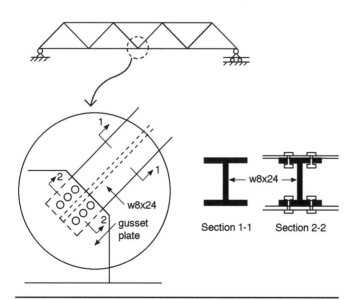

Fig. 8. Truss member stressed in tension.

– *Solution overview:* Find cross-sectional dimensions and material properties; find gross area capacity; find effective net area capacity; governing capacity is the lower of the two values.

– *Problem solution:* The cross-sectional dimensions of a W8 × 24 are found from "Dimensions and Properties" tables of the Manual (AISC 1989):

• A_g = 7.08 in²

• d = 7.93 in.

• b_f = 6.495 in.

• t_f = 0.400 in

The yield and ultimate stresses of A36 steel are F_y = 36 ksi; and F_u = 58 ksi (AISC 1989).

To find the capacity, P, based on yielding of the gross area:

• F_t^{gross} = 0.6 F_y = 0.6(36) = 22 ksi

• P = $F_t^{gross} \times A_g$ = 22(7.08) = 156 k

To find the capacity, P, based on rupturing of the effective net area:

• U = 0.90 (Table 3) since the following criteria are met: W-shape? yes; connection to flange? yes; b_f at least ⅔ d? yes; 3 bolts per line, minimum? yes

• A_n = A_g – (no. of holes) (hole diameter × t_f) = 7.08 – 4(⅞ × 0.400) = 5.68 in²

• A_e = U × A_n = 0.9(5.68) = 5.11 in²

• F_t^{net} = 0.5 F_u = 0.5(58) = 29 ksi

• P = $F_t^{net} \times A_e$ = 29(5.11) = 148 k

Conclusion: failure on effective net area governs since 148 k < 156 k. The capacity (allowable load) is 148 k.

Solution for steel threaded rods: Since the size of tension elements is not constrained by the consideration of buckling, relatively small-diameter steel rods are often used, threaded at the ends to facilitate their connection to adjacent elements. Threaded rods are designed using an allowable tensile stress, F_t = 0.33F_u, which is assumed to be resisted by the gross area of the unthreaded part of the rod. While there are no limits on slenderness, diameters are normally at least ⅟₅₀₀ of the length; and the minimum diameter rod permitted in structural applications is ⅝ in.

Columns

Columns are vertical elements subjected to compressive stress; nothing, however, prevents us from applying the same design and analysis methods to any compressive element, whether vertical, horizontal, or inclined. Compression is similar to tension, since both types of structural actions result in a uniform distribution of axial stresses over a cross section taken through the element. But allowable stress in compression is often limited by the phenomenon of buckling, in which the element suddenly deforms out of its axial alignment at a stress that may be significantly lower than the stress causing compressive crushing.

Leonhard Euler calculated in the 18th century that deflections perpendicular to the member's axis increase rapidly in the vicinity of a particular ("critical") load, at which point the column fails; and that the value of this load is independent of any initial eccentricity. In other words, even with the smallest imaginable deviation from axiality, a column will buckle at some critical load. Since no perfectly axial columns (or loads) can exist, all columns behaving elastically will buckle at the critical buckling stress derived by Euler:

$$\sigma_{cr} = p^2 E / (KL / r)^2$$

In this well-known equation,

– E is the modulus of elasticity;

– K is a coefficient that depends on the column's end constraints;

– L is the unbraced length of the column; and

– r is the radius of gyration with respect to the unbraced length, equal to the square root of the quantity I / A.

Where the unbraced length is the same for both axes of the column, r (or I) is taken as the smaller of the two possible values, that is, r_{min} (or I_{min}). The term L/ r, or KL/ r, is called the column's slenderness ratio. Values for K can be found in Table C-C2.1 in AISC (1989).

The strength of a steel column is limited in two ways: either it will crush at its compressive stress, or buckle at some critical stress that is different from, and independent of, its strength in compression. Euler's equation for critical buckling stress works well for slender columns, but gives increasingly inaccurate results as the slenderness of columns decreases and the effects of crushing begin to interact with the idealized conditions from which Euler's equation was derived.

Slender steel columns are designed using the Euler buckling equation, while "non-slender" columns, which buckle inelastically, or crush without buckling, are designed according to equations formulated to fit empirical data. Residual compressive stresses within hot-rolled steel sections precipitate this inelastic buckling, as they cause local yielding to occur sooner than might otherwise be expected. Unlike timber column design, the design equations corresponding to elastic and inelastic buckling have not been integrated into a single unified formula, so the underlying rationale remains more apparent. The slenderness ratio dividing elastic from inelastic buckling is set, somewhat arbitrarily, at the point where the Euler critical buckling stress equals one-half of the yield stress.

Additionally, the maximum slenderness ratio should not exceed 200 for steel axial compression elements.

Rather than directly applying the equations for elastic and inelastic buckling to the solution of axial compression problems in steel, allowable stress tables (for analysis, Tables C-36 and C-50) or allowable axial load tables (for design, Allowable Concentric Loads on Columns) are more often used (AISC 1989).

Example 2: steel column design

Select the lightest (most economical) wide-flange section for the first-floor column illustrated in **Fig. 9**. Assume office occupancy (with live load = 50 psf); a roof (construction/maintenance) live load = 20 psf; a typical steel floor system and an allowance for steel stud partitions resulting in a dead load of 55 psf on each floor. Assume pin-ended (simple) connections. Use A36 steel.

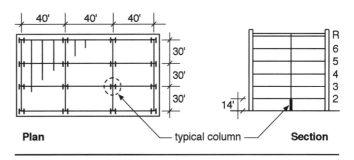

Fig. 9. Typical column in steel-framed building.

– *Solution overview:* Find total load on column; find effective length; select lightest section from table (AISC 1989).

– *Problem solution:* Find total column load:

- "Unreduced" live load (LL) = 50 psf;

- Live load reduction: The maximum live load is unlikely to occur simultaneously on all floors of the office building; according to procedures outlined in *Minimum Design Loads for Buildings and Other Structures* (ASCE 1994), the maximum live load reduction coefficient of 0.4 may be used in this case, so that the reduced live load = 50(0.4) = 20 psf. Dead load (DL) = 55 psf; roof live load (CL) = 20 psf;

- Find total column load:

LL = 5 floors × (25′ × 40′) × (20 psf) = 100,000#

DL = 6 floors × (25′ × 40′) × (55 psf) = 330,000#

CL = 1 floor × (25′ × 40′) × (20 psf) = 20,000#

Total column load = 450,000# = 450 k

Find the unbraced effective length: Kl = (1.0) (14) = 14 ft

Select the most economical section:

- Using the "Allowable axial loads in kips" column tables (AISC 1989), pick the lightest acceptable section from each "nominal depth" group (that is, one W10, one W12, one W14), to assemble a group of "likely candidates"; that is:

W10 × 100 can support 503 k

W12 × 87 can support 459 k

W14 × 90 can support 497 k

- Choose lightest section: W12 × 87 is the most economical since its weight per linear foot (87 lb) is smallest.

Beams

Like all structural elements, beams are both stressed and subject to deformations when loaded. Both of these considerations must be accounted for in the design of steel beams.

Beams are stressed when they bend because the action of bending causes an elongation on one side, resulting in tension; and a shortening on the other side, resulting in compression. From this geometry, the basic bending stress relationship can be derived:

$$f_{b\,max} = M / S, \text{ where:}$$

$f_{b\,max}$ is the maximum bending stress at a given cross section;

M is the bending moment at that section; and

S is the section modulus.

To design a beam using the allowable stress method, find the required section modulus by dividing the maximum bending moment by the allowable bending stress, that is:

$$S_{required} = M_{max} / F_{b\,allowable}$$

Then, using tabulated design aids (AISC 1989), select a cross section whose section modulus is at least as large as the required value. It should be emphasized that this selection is provisional, and must be checked for both deflection and shear.

Laterally unsupported beams

When the compression flange of a beam is not continuously braced, lateral-torsion buckling can reduce the allowable bending stress. How much this stress is reduced depends on whether the beam buckles before or after the cross section begins to yield. Three different cases are possible:

- *Case I:* If a beam can develop a "plastic hinge" without buckling, the maximum allowable bending stress of $0.66F_y$ is used. In addition to lateral-torsion buckling, various types of local flange and web buckling must also be prevented from occurring before this so-called plastic moment is reached. Local buckling is prevented by limiting the ratio of flange width to flange thickness, as well as web width to web thickness. Sections proportioned so that local buckling will not occur are called compact sections; these sections must be used to qualify for the allowable stress of $0.66F_y$. As it turns out, all the wide-flange shapes listed in the *Manual of Steel Construction* (AISC 1989) are compact sections when made from A36 steel. For 50 ksi steel, all but three (W8 × 10, W10 × 12, and W40 × 192) are compact.

- *Case II:* A smaller nominal allowable bending stress of $0.6F_y$ is given to beams that can sustain an elastic moment without buckling, but not a plastic moment.

- *Case III:* When lateral-torsion buckling occurs before the elastic moment is reached, the allowable bending stress is reduced below $0.6F_y$, based on the explicit calculation of the critical buckling stress.

For a given "compact" cross-sectional shape, it is the unbraced length between lateral supports, L_b, that determines which of the cases previously described applies. As L_b approaches zero, that is, as the compressive flange of the beam becomes more or less continuously braced, Case I governs. At the other extreme, for large unbraced lengths, Case III governs. For a given cross section, the critical lengths separating Case I from Case II, and Case II from Case III, can be computed.

These critical lengths, L_c and L_u, are shown in relationship to the cases depicted in **Fig. 10a**. For a given cross-sectional shape, L_c is the largest unbraced length that can sustain a plastic moment; while L_u is the largest unbraced length that can sustain an elastic moment. **Fig. 10b** shows schematically how the allowable bending stress, F_b, changes as the unbraced length increases. Alternatively, the unbraced length can be plotted against allowable moment by multiplying the allowable bending stress by the section modulus, as shown in **Fig. 10c**. It is this latter form that serves as a design aid for steel beams whose compression flanges are not continuously braced. For any bending moment (in foot-kips) and unbraced length (in feet), the "Allowable Moments in Beams" graphs in the *Manual of Steel Construction* (AISC 1989) can be used to locate the lightest acceptable wide-flange cross section, using 36 or 50 ksi steel.

Laterally braced beams

Where the compression flange is laterally braced against buckling, the required section modulus (in³) can be found directly from:

$$\text{required } S_x = M_{max} / F_b, \text{ where:}$$

- M_{max} = the maximum bending moment (in-k); and

- F_b = the allowable bending stress = $0.66F_y$ for compact sections (ksi).

Choosing the lightest (that is, most economical) section is facilitated by the use of the "Allowable Stress Design Selection Tables" (AISC 1989) in which steel cross sections are ranked, first in terms of section modulus, and then by least weight (indicated by bold-faced entries).

Internal forces perpendicular to the longitudinal axis of beams may also exist along with bending moments at any cross section, consistent with the requirements of equilibrium. These shear forces are distributed over the cross-sectional surface according to the general shear stress equation derived in strength of materials texts. For steel wide-flange shapes, simplified procedures can be used, based on average stress on the cross section, neglecting the overhanging flange areas; that is, the actual maximum shear stress in a beam can be taken as:

$$f_v = V / (d\, t_w), \text{ where}$$

- f_v = the maximum shear stress within the cross section;

- V = the total shear force at the cross section;

- d = the cross-sectional depth; and t_w = the web thickness. This value for the actual shear stress can then be compared with the allowable shear stress for steel—taken as $F_v = 0.4\, F_y$ (or 14.5 ksi for A36 steel)—in order to check whether a beam designed for bending stress is acceptable for shear.

While the elongation or contraction of axially loaded members along their longitudinal axes is usually of little consequence, beams may experience excessive deflection perpendicular to their longitudinal axes, making them unserviceable. Limits on deflection are based on several considerations, including minimizing vibrations, thereby improving occupant comfort; preventing cracking of ceiling materials, partitions, or cladding supported by the beams; and promoting positive drainage (for roof beams) in order to avoid ponding of water at mid-span. These limits are generally expressed as a fraction of the span, L (**Table 4**). Formulas for the calculation of mid-span deflections are given in the Manual of Steel Construction (AISC 1989).

Example 3: Steel beam design

Using A36 steel, design the typical beam and girder for the library stack area shown in **Fig. 11**. Assume a dead load of 47 psf and a live load of 150 psf. Assume that the floor deck continuously braces the beams, and that the girders are braced only by the beams framing into them.

- *Solution overview:* Find loads; compute maximum bending moment and shear force; use appropriate tables to select beams for bending; then check for shear and deflection.

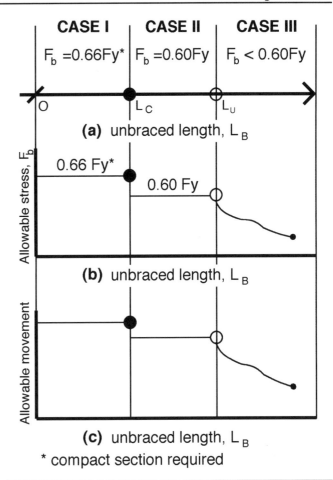

Fig. 10. Unbraced length of beams: relationship to (a) L_c and L_u; (b) allowable stress; and (c) allowable moment.

Table 4. Recommended minimum depths for deflection control

floor beams	roof beams
[1]L/800Fy)or [2]L/20	[1]L/(1000/Fy)

[1]Fy is in ksi units, *eg.*, 36 ksi for A36 steel: L is the span.
[2]Use L/20 for vibration control over large partition-free floor areas.

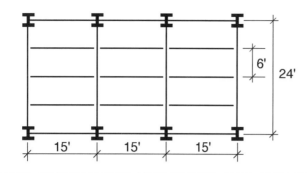

Fig. 11. Framing plan.

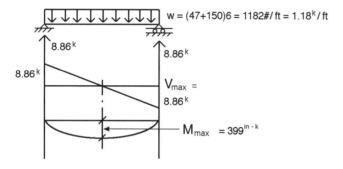

Fig. 12. Load, shear, and moment diagrams.

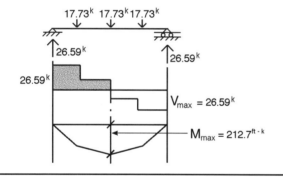

Fig. 13. Load, shear, and moment diagrams.

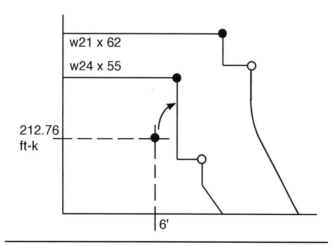

Fig. 14. Use of "Allowable Moment" design graphs.

– *Problem solution, beam design:*

• Create load, shear, and moment diagrams (**Fig. 12**) to determine critical (that is, maximum) shear force and bending moment. The total distributed load, w = (150 + 47) 6 = 1182 #/ft = 1.18 k/ft.

• Find allowable bending stress: since beam is laterally braced by floor deck and section is compact, $F_b = 0.66F_y = 0.66(36) = 24$ ksi;

• Compute required $S_x = M_{max}/F_b = 399/24 = 16.62$ in³.

• Select W12 × 16 with actual $S_x = 17.1$ in³ from "Allowable Stress Design Section Table" (AISC 1989).

• Check shear: Allowable shear stress, $F_v = 0.4F_y = 0.4(36) = 14.5$ ksi; actual shear stress, $f_v = V / (d\ t_w) = 8.86 / (11.99 \times 0.22) = 3.36$ ksi < allowable shear stress, so beam is OK for shear.

• Check deflection: The allowable live load deflection for a floor beam = span/360 = L/360 = 15(12)/360 = 0.5 in (from Table 4); the actual deflection, from "Beam Diagrams and Formulas" (AISC 1989), is equal to $5wL^4/(384EI_x) = 0.34''$.

In this equation, the modulus of elasticity of steel, E, can be taken as 29,000 ksi, the moment of inertia, I_x (in⁴) can be found in "Dimensions and Properties" tables (AISC 1989), and the distributed load, w, is calculated for live loads only. Note that where the distributed load is measured in units of kips/ft and the span, L, is measured in units of feet, the deflection equation must be multiplied by 12³ to reconcile the incompatible units. Since the actual deflection of 0.34″ < allowable deflection = 0.5 in, the beam is OK for deflection.

– *Problem solution, girder design:*

• Create load, shear, and moment diagrams (**Fig. 13**) to determine critical (that is, maximum) shear force and bending moment. Each concentrated load is twice the typical beam reaction, or 17.73 k. [Alternatively, compute using tributary areas; that is, P = (150 + 47)(15 × 6) = 17730 # = 17.73 k.]

• Since allowable bending stress cannot be determined directly (girder is not continually braced), use "Allowable Moment" design graphs (AISC 1989) to select beam directly for M = 212.76 ft-k and $L_b = 6$ ft. Select W24 × 55 (**Fig. 14**).

• Check shear: Allowable shear stress, $F_v = 0.4F_y = 0.4(36) = 14.5$ ksi; actual shear stress, $f_v = V / (d\ t_w) = 26.595 / (23.57 \times 0.395) = 2.86$ ksi < allowable shear stress, so beam is OK for shear.

• Check deflection: The allowable live load deflection for a floor beam = span/360 = L/360 = 24(12)/360 = 0.8 in; the actual deflection, from "Beam Diagrams and Formulas, Table of Concentrated Load Equivalents" (AISC 1989), is equal to:

$$ePL^3/(EI);\ \text{where:}$$

– e = 0.0495 for three equally spaced concentrated loads on a simply supported span, and

– L = span in inches = 24(12) = 288 in.

As before, the modulus of elasticity of steel, E, can be taken as 29,000 ksi; the moment of inertia, $I_x = 1350$ in⁴, can be found in "Dimensions and Properties" tables (AISC 1989); and the concentrated load, P = 13.5 kips, is calculated for live loads only. Substituting these values into the equation, we get an actual live load deflection = 0.4 in. Since this value is less than the allowable deflection of 0.5 in, the beam is OK for deflection.

3 TYPICAL CONSTRUCTION DETAILS

Steel building frames typically consist of beams, girders, and columns that are fastened together using high-strength bolts or welds. Welded connections are often used to create rigid ("Type 1") joints, while bolts are commonly used for simple shear ("Type 2") connections, although bolts or welds can be used in either case. In fact, welds and bolts can be used within the same connection, even in cases where a simple connection is desired. This occurs, for example, where clip angles, welded to one structural element in the shop, are bolted to another structural element in the field. Semi-rigid ("Type 3") connections fall somewhere between the first two types. In general, connections are detailed so that welding, where necessary, occurs as much as possible under shop conditions, whereas connections that must be made in the field are designed to be bolted. Examples of typical simple and rigid connections (beam to girder, girder to column) are illustrated in **Fig. 15.**

Aside from the intersection of beams, girders, and columns, two other connection conditions should be noted: column to column; and column to foundation. In the first case, column joints are typically placed somewhat above the floor elevation, so as not to interfere with the connection of beams and girders to the column (**Fig. 16**). Additionally, the columns are often fabricated in lengths of two stories to reduce the number of field connections. The connection of columns to the concrete foundation is most often mediated by a steel base plate, welded to the column in the shop, that can be precisely aligned using leveling nuts or shims and then grouted as shown in **Fig. 17.**

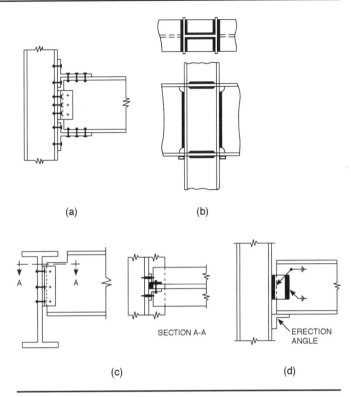

Fig. 15. Typical steel connections: (a) Type 1 bolted; (b) Type 1 welded (with stiffener plates); (c) Type 2 bolted; and (d) Type 2 welded.

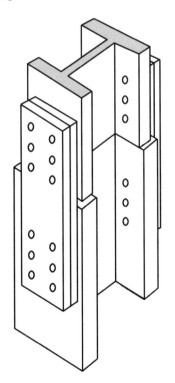

Fig. 16. Bolted column-to-column splice.

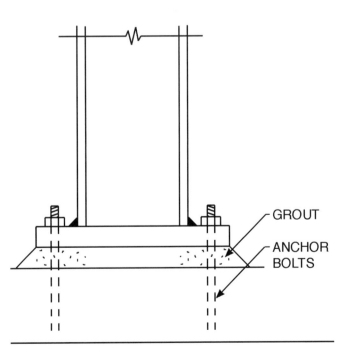

Fig. 17. Typical column base plate.

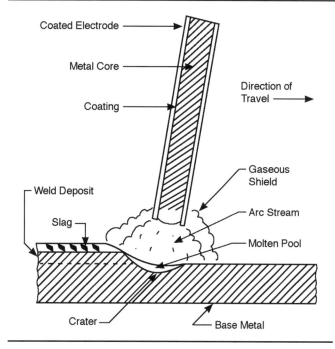

Fig. 18. Shielded metal arc welding.

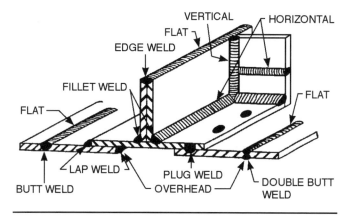

Fig. 19. Types of welds.

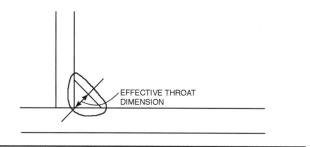

Fig. 20. Section through convex fillet weld.

Welded connections

Structural elements can be monolithically connected when the surfaces to be joined are heated sufficiently and then allowed to cool. In practice, the surfaces to be joined are not fused directly; instead, metal from a separate electrode is fused with the base metal of the two steel surfaces to be joined. In Shielded Metal Arc Welding [SMAW], a 6500F electric arc forms in the gap between the electrode and steel as the electrode is moved along the weld line (**Fig. 18**), melting the electrode into the base metal to form a continuous metal connection. A coating on the electrode containing flux forms a gaseous shield that protects the molten weld from reacting chemically with oxygen and nitrogen in the atmosphere, and facilitates the removal of oxides in the weld metal. Flux can be supplied separately from the electrode in submerged arc welding, an automated process associated more with shop welding than with field welding.

Various shapes of welds can be created, the most common being the triangular fillet weld. The position of the weld is also of interest: flat and horizontal welds are easiest to create, while vertical and overhead welds are more difficult, and therefore more expensive (**Fig. 19**).

The design of SMAW fillet welds is governed by their strength in shear, so that the capacity of a particular weld can be found by multiplying the allowable shear stress of the weld material (taken as $0.3 \times$ the ultimate strength of the electrode used; that is, 0.3×70 ksi for an E70 electrode) by the area of the anticipated failure plane in shear. The area of this failure plane is simply the length of the weld multiplied by the effective throat dimension, as shown in **Fig. 20**.

Standard welding symbols and examples of their use are illustrated in **Figs. 21** and **22**.

Bolted connections

Allowable loads for ordinary and high-strength bolts used in shear are given in Table I-D of the *Manual of Steel Construction* (AISC 1989). There are several parameters in this table that influence bolt capacity:

- Bolt strength: the two commonly used high-strength bolt types are designated A325 and A490, the latter being significantly stronger. For secondary structural members, ordinary A307 bolts (also known as machine bolts, or common bolts) can be used.

- Connection type: although all high-strength bolts are tightened to the point where some friction develops between the metal pieces being joined, bolted connections can be designed either on this basis (slip critical, SC connections) or by using the bearing strength of the bolt and "plate" material as a criteria (bearing N or X connections). "N"-type bearing connections occur where bolt threads appear in the shear plane; "X"-type bearing connections are designed so that the bolt threads are excluded from the shear plane. Note that SC connections must also be designed to resist bearing stresses.

- Hole type: various types of bolt holes can be used, including standard round holes (STD) and long-slotted holes (LSL), allowing some flexibility in detailing.

- Loading: values for both single and double shear are given (double shear refers to a condition where three plates rather than two engage the bolt in shear, so that the total shear force is divided into two shearing planes, effectively cutting the stress in half).

For both slip critical and bearing connections, the bearing capacity of the steel plate material to be joined must also be considered. Table I-E (AISC 1989) lists allowable loads for various thicknesses of steel plate, various commonly used bolt sizes (¾, ⅞, and 1 in diameter), and various steel strengths (ranging from F_u = 58 ksi to F_u = 100 ksi).

For bolts subjected to tension, Table I-A (AISC 1989) gives allowable loads for bolt sizes ranging from ⅝ to 1-½ in. Where both tension and shear act simultaneously on a bearing connection, the allowable shear and tension stresses are limited to values listed in Tables J3.2 and J3.3 (AISC 1989).

Steel floor and roof framing systems

The flat floor surfaces characteristic of steel-framed buildings are most often designed using corrugated steel deck with concrete fill spanning between evenly spaced steel beams, which are in turn supported by steel girders framing into a grid of steel columns. The framing module is thus determined by the spanning capacity of the steel deck. This, in turn, depends on the deck's gauge (the thickness of the steel plate from which it is formed), the depth of its corrugations, the total depth of the slab (including the concrete fill), and the live and dead floor loads. Typical spans ranging from 8 to 12 ft can be achieved using 2-in steel decks with a total slab depth of approximately 4 in. A schematic detail section showing the relationship between beam, girder, and deck for a steel-framed building is illustrated in **Fig. 23.**

Precast concrete slab panels can also be used in place of corrugated steel decks and steel beams, spanning directly between steel girders. Cast-in-place concrete slabs over steel beams are much less commonly encountered since they introduce the additional cost of concrete formwork without eliminating the cost of structural steel elements.

Roof framing systems are similar to floor framing systems except for two important differences. First, concrete fill is often eliminated, and the steel deck alone is designed to span between beams. The roofing membrane is then placed over a substrate that has been fastened to the steel deck. For conventional roofs, the substrate is often rigid insulation, as shown in **Fig. 24.**

The second important difference between roof and floor framing systems is that roof framing elements are often sloped towards roof drains. While this does not ordinarily have much of an effect on the

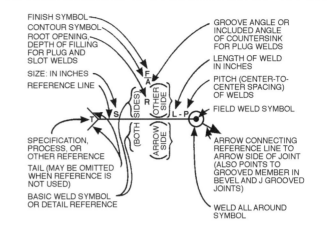

Fig. 21. Standard welding symbols.

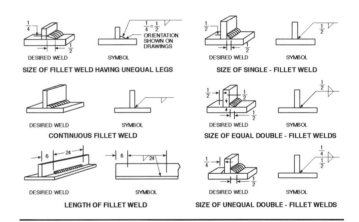

Fig. 22. Use of welding symbols.

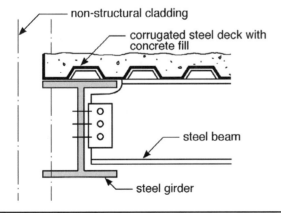

Fig. 23. Typical steel floor framing.

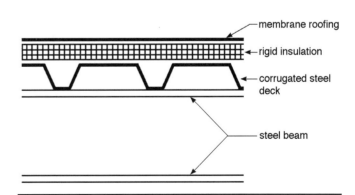

Fig. 24. Typical steel roof deck.

framing plan, the minimum slope requirements for low-sloped roofs can have a major impact on the building section. For example, where a 100 ft wide roof is designed to slope up ¼ in for each foot measured horizontally from a centrally placed roof drain, the height added to the building elevation due to the slope of the roof would be (50 ft) × (¼ in per ft) = 12-½ in. As an alternative to sloping the structural steel roof framing elements to accommodate the need for roof drainage, it is possible to design a flat roof deck and create a sloping surface with either lightweight concrete fill, or tapered roof insulation.

Steel trusses

Steel trusses range in size from the relatively lightweight standardized open-web steel joists previously described, to wind and seismic bracing systems spanning from the foundation to the roof of multistory buildings. The design of each truss element starts with the calculation of the axial force to be resisted. For trusses acting as simply supported spanning members, elements comprising the top chord are generally in compression and those in the bottom chord are generally in tension—echoing the pattern of internal forces that emerges in a conventional beam, similarly loaded. Once the axial force has been computed, the design of a particular truss bar is no different in principle than the design of either a steel column (where the axial force is compression) or a steel tension element.

In practice, the bars of the top and bottom chords are often made continuous, and the connection of these chords to the vertical and diagonal bars becomes the major detailing issue. Gusset plates are commonly used as a mediating device between the various intersecting

steel members in bolted construction; whereas in welded tubular steel trusses, the individual truss members are brought directly into contact with each other. **Fig. 25** shows typical connection details for bolted and welded steel trusses.

Steel building frames

The structural design of a steel building frame must account for both vertical loads (typically live, dead, and snow loads) as well as horizontal loads (typically wind and seismic loads). Strategies for resisting the vertical loads have already been suggested in the section on floor and roof framing, and are essentially the same for all steel buildings: loads originating at any point are transferred by the structural deck to the supporting beams and girders, at which point they are picked up by the building columns and transferred ultimately to the foundation system. What distinguishes one framing system from another is really the way in which lateral loads are resisted. Two general strategies are available for resisting these horizontal forces: either the joints between columns and girders are made rigid (creating a moment-resisting frame), or diagonal bracing elements are placed within the rectilinear frame (creating a truss).

Where trusses are used, they are most often hidden within the building core or behind opaque cladding material at the outside wall (so that the programming of building functions is not compromised by the appearance of truss diagonals); less frequently, they are expressed as part of the building's external form. Where moment-resisting frames are used, they are most commonly located at the outside faces of the building. Schematic examples of these bracing strategies are illustrated in **Fig. 26.**

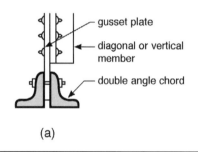

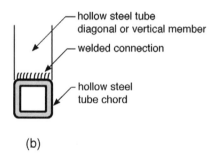

(a) (b)

Fig. 25. Typical connection details for (a) bolted, and (b) welded steel trusses.

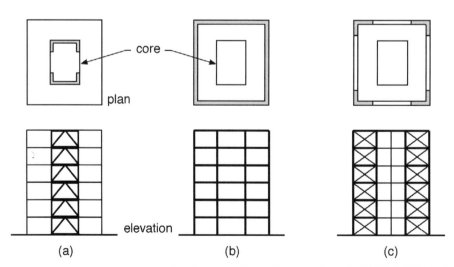

(a) (b) (c)

Fig. 26. Bracing strategies include: (a) truss bracing in core; (b) moment-resisting frame at exterior face; and (c) truss bracing at exterior face.

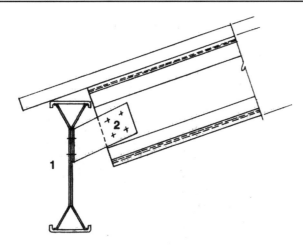

1 STEEL BEAM
2 BENT PLATE
3 STEEL DECK
4 WOOD NAILER
5 METAL PIN
6 ELECTRICAL CONDUIT

STEEL ROOF CONNECTION

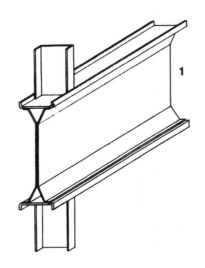

STEEL BEAM-STUD CONNECTION

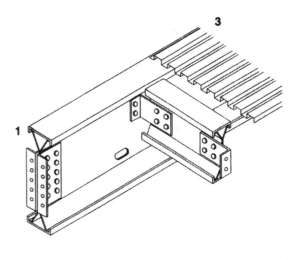

STEEL BEAM CONNECTION

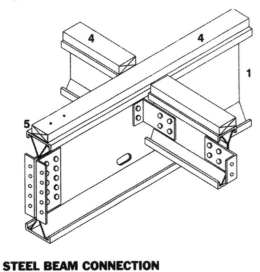

STEEL BEAM CONNECTION

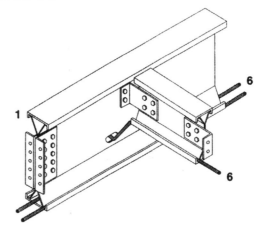

STEEL BEAM CONNECTION

Fig. 27. Light-gauge steel framing details. (Barreneche 1994)

Light-gauge steel framing

As conventional wood framing costs have risen, light-gauge steel framing systems have become available and competitive for residential and small commercial applications (**Fig. 27**). Light-gauge steel framing offers simplified framing, due to its structural strength: fewer beams and joists can span greater distances and studs can be placed up to 24 in (60 cm) o.c. There is no shrinkage as in wood structures. Hurricane strength and bracing is more easily achieved than in comparative wood structures. Structural shapes accommodate electric conduits. A drawback is thermal bridging, of concern in both the heating period (heat loss) and in cooling (condensation and its effects within the construction envelope). On-site construction time for assembly is reportedly longer, perhaps due to its relatively recent introduction. Reports of environmental benefits vary: claims of recycled steel content in a typical stud range from 24 to 66 percent (Barreneche 1994). See comparable comment on wood framing at the end of the prior article. ■

REFERENCES

AISC, *Manual of Steel Construction. Allowable Stress Design,* 9th ed., American Institute of Steel Construction, Chicago, 1989.

AISC, *Manual of Steel Construction. Load & Resistance Factor Design,* 1st ed., American Institute of Steel Construction, Chicago, 1986.

ASCE, *Minimum Design Loads for Buildings and Other Structures,* American Society of Civil Engineers, New York, 1994.

Barreneche, Paul A., "Framing Alternatives," *Architecture,* October 1994.

Sweet's General Building & Renovation Catalog File, McGraw-Hill, New York, 1996.

Robert M. Darvas

Summary

This article presents the basic design concepts of reinforced concrete structures, including beams, columns, and floor/roof deck systems. It is intended to enable the reader to understand the basic ideas underlying the design of reinforced concrete structures. It should be helpful in formulating a framing concept, and in the selection of a preliminary design.

Key words

concrete, floor systems, modulus of elasticity, prestressed concrete, reinforcement, shear, T beams, tilt-up concrete, Ultimate Strength Design

Railway station Lyon-Satolas, France. Santiago Calatrava, Architect and Engineer. 1989–94.

Photo: Alexander Tzonis

Structural design—concrete

Introduction

Reinforced concrete structures are inherently indeterminate structures, the analysis of the internal forces (moments, shears, and axial forces) cannot be performed by statically determinate models. Furthermore, in the analysis of indeterminate structures the length of the members and their relative sizes all influence the resulting shears and moments in the members.

This article can be used by the architectural designer to understand the ramifications of a selected framing system, and to arrive at some reasonable preliminary estimates of layout and member sizes. Final design of members, reinforcing quantities and details should be left to the consulting structural engineer.

1 CONCRETE MATERIALS

Concrete is a mixture composed of a filler material (aggregate) bound together by a hardened paste. The hardened paste is the result of a chemical reaction, called hydration, between cement and water. In addition admixtures—various chemicals, usually in liquid form—are often used to impart desirable qualities to the freshly mixed and/or hardened concrete. The paste fills the voids between the aggregate particles, gravel or crushed stone and sand, and binds them together. The aggregate size distribution is carefully controlled in order to minimize the resulting voids that must be filled with the paste. Minimizing the amount of paste helps to minimize the amount of cement, which is the most expensive ingredient of the mixture, for it requires a large amount of energy in its manufacture. The proportions of the

aggregate in normal weight concrete is approximately 65 to 75 percent by volume, while the paste makes up approximately 33 to 23 percent. The remaining volume is air.

The quality of the concrete depends upon the binding agent, i.e., the quality of the paste. The hydration process requires the presence of moisture. Since the cement can utilize only so much moisture, excess water will evaporate through capillaries, leaving voids behind, which reduces practically all the desirable qualities of the hardened concrete. Thus it is important to keep the amount of water in the mix to an absolute minimum that still permits the concrete to be workable and moldable. Concrete made with just enough water for the hydration process will not be sufficiently workable; furthermore, during handling and placement there will be inevitably some water loss due to evaporation and absorption by the formwork, leaving insufficient moisture behind for the hydration process.

Practically all of the physical and mechanical properties of the hardened concrete are related to the ratio of water to the cement by weight. Thus, for example, a water/cement ratio of 0.45 means that in the mix 45 lb of water is used for every 100 lb of cement.

Keeping the water/cement ratio as small as practicable helps, among other attributes: to increase the compressive and flexural strength; to reduce the permeability; to reduce shrinkage and the formation of shrinkage cracks; to increase durability and resistance to wear. **Fig. 1** illustrates the relationship between the compressive strength and the water/cement ratio in concretes made with equal amounts of cement per cubic yard.

Credits: Concluding section on tilt-up concrete systems is adapted from Barreneche (1995).

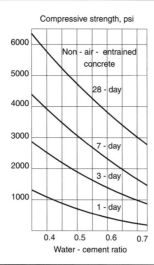

Fig. 1. Concrete compressive strength (psi). (Source: Portland Cement Association)

Admixtures are often used to enhance the properties of the freshly mixed or hardened concrete. Admixtures are most commonly used to:

- accelerate or retard the setting time and the hardening;

- reduce the amount of water in the mix, while maintaining good workability;

- increase water tightness;

- intentionally entrain air for increased freeze/thaw resistance.

Properties of hardened concrete

Compressive strength

In architectural structures the most commonly required strengths are between 3000 to 6000 psi, measured on 6″ diameter, 12″ high cylinders at 28 days of age. Stronger concretes are sometimes used in columns of high-rise buildings. The cylinder strength is symbolized as f'_c.

Tensile strength

Concrete has rather limited tensile strength. The ultimate flexural tensile strength (also known as the Modulus of Rupture) shows a great variability, but it may be assumed to be $f_r = 7.5\sqrt{f'_c}$

(f'_c must be entered in psi units)

Modulus of Elasticity

$E_c = 33w^{1.5}\sqrt{f'_c}$; where w is the weight of the concrete in pcf units.

Weight

Normal weight concrete (made with gravel or crushed stone as coarse aggregate) weighs approximately 145 pcf. Reinforced concrete is usually taken as 150 pcf to account for the higher unit weight of the steel reinforcing.

Lightweight structural concretes are also produced using rotary kiln expanded clays, shales and clays, or expanded slags. These concretes weigh significantly less, in the range of 110 to 120 pcf, thus their use

may be warranted when the benefit of the reduction in self-weight exceeds the added cost for the more expensive aggregate.

Thermal expansion coefficient

6×10^{-6} in/in/F, very close to that of steel, thus the two materials may expand or contract without significant stresses resulting.

Durability

This is usually used to refer to the freeze/thaw resistance of the concrete, although sometimes the reference is to resistance to other environmental factors. Chemicals that attack concrete are many. Chlorides (road salts) attack concrete as well, although the major problem is the corrosion of the reinforcing in the presence of chlorides.

Air entrainment

During the mixing of the fresh concrete, chemicals form tiny air bubbles (approximately 300 billion per cubic yard) uniformly distributed in the mixture. When concrete saturated with water in its capillary voids is subject to freezing, the expanding ice produces hydraulic pressures in the yet unfrozen liquid. These pressures result in tensile stresses in the concrete that can lead to rupture. The entrained air voids are thought to act as reservoirs into which the excess fluid volume can be pushed; 5 to 7 percent of entrained air volume is practical for this purpose, and its use does not lead to significant strength loss. Air entrainment also helps workability, thus the amount of water can be reduced.

Volumetric changes in concrete structures

Volumetric changes, i.e., deformations, are caused chiefly by four different effects.

Elastic deformations (or instantaneous deformations) occur in all structural elements when loaded. They may be calculated using methods established by elastic theory. However, since reinforced concrete is a composite material, the calculation becomes more complicated (and the resulting accuracy less certain) than with more homogenous materials, like steel. A further difficulty presents itself with the fact that beams and slabs in monolithic structures crack in the tensile region even if the cracks are largely invisible at normal service loads. At the location of the cracks, the Moment of Inertia of the section is drastically reduced, which in turn leads to larger deflections than calculated values obtained by using gross section properties throughout.

Control of deflections is a primary design objective. Deflections, both instantaneous and long term (see below), if excessive, may seriously compromise the structure and may jeopardize the performance of the attached "nonstructural" elements of the building. Roofs may not drain properly; partitions supported by the structure may crack; doors and windows may distort if excessive deflections take place. The most important action in this respect is the selection of appropriately deep structural elements. In the paragraph discussing typical floor systems, values of minimum overall structural depth are given. Experience shows that the use of such minimum depths lead to good serviceability, i.e., adequate control of deflections.

Shrinkage occurs when the fresh concrete sets (setting shrinkage), and then during the hardening process (drying shrinkage). The amount of shrinkage varies with many factors. Low water/cement ratio of the concrete mix, limiting the length of a concrete pour, and a careful curing process helps to minimize shrinkage. While it is difficult to predict, an average contraction of 0.0002 to 0.0003 inch per inch may be used to estimate the length change in reinforced concrete structures. If the resulting length change could freely take place without restraint, no stresses would result. However most concrete structures are restrained against free change of length by either their physical ties to an already constructed portion, or by friction forces on the formwork or the subgrade. These restraints result in tensile stresses in the concrete structure. Concrete, especially at the early stages of strength development, has very limited tensile strength, and when the shrinkage-caused stresses exceed the then available tensile strength, cracking will result.

Thermal movements occur due to the change of temperature. Expansion or contraction takes place at the rate of 0.000006 (six millionth) inch per inch per degree of Fahrenheit. While it seems to be a small number, a 50 degree change will cause ⅜″ change in every 100 ft. Just as in the case of shrinkage, unrestrained length change will not cause stresses in the structure; however, if the movement is restrained, tensile or compressive stresses will result. Even more problematic is when a structural element is subject to differential temperature changes. For example, exterior building panels may bend or warp when there is a differential temperature between their faces. In columns that are partially exposed, additional bending moments develop due to the differential temperature between their inside and outside face. In tall buildings, an exposed exterior column will change its length with respect to the interior columns, forcing the floor structure to bend in order to follow the differential length change.

Creep is a phenomenon identified with long-term deformations due to sustained stresses. Columns will shorten, and flexural members (beams, slabs, etc.) will show increased deflections with age. Creep deformations add 100 to 200 percent to the instantaneous deformations. Creep begins as soon as a concrete element starts to carry loads, and continues at a diminishing rate for as long as the concrete carries load. Most creep deformation, however, takes place in the first two years. Among many factors, the most important is the age of the concrete when it is first loaded, i.e., the further along in its strength development, the less creep deformation will result.

2 DESIGN CONCEPT

Design of concrete structures (or any other structure, for that matter) that begins with the selection of a structural system may be viewed as satisfying several concurrent goals:

- functional layout

- adequate strength

- good serviceability (usually means control of deflections)

- economy

- aesthetic requirements (architectural appearance)

Most monolithic reinforced concrete structures will require extensive mechanical and electrical services, which are usually provided within the space between the concrete floor structure and the suspended ceiling below it. Very often the availability of maximum structural depth and economy, i.e., the overall cost, governs the selection of the structural system.

Ultimate strength design (USD)

In the present context *design* means finding the appropriately sized members (together with the required reinforcing) that have adequate strength. *Adequate strength* means to design a section that has a certain amount of reserve capacity, over and beyond the strength that is called upon in the everyday service life of the structure.

Structural elements are subject to service load effects (moments, shears, axial forces) acting on a particular section of a member. The service effect comes from two parts. One comes from loads that are *permanently* present, inherent within or attached to the structure: these are referred to as *dead loads*. The other part comes from loads whose nature is *transitory*, sometimes they are present, other times they are not, such as people, furnishings, wind, seismic loads, and so on. These are referred to as *live loads*. Together the two form the expected true loads that a structure may encounter during its lifetime.

The nature of the dead and live loads are such that the former are more predictable and therefore easier to estimate magnitude. Live loads on the other hand are more difficult to predict; their nature may be such that either the magnitude cannot be defined with any reasonable certainty, or their action is far from being static in nature, and so they more closely resemble quick dynamic impulses. Since dynamic impulses create an, albeit temporary, overstress on structural elements, live loads need more careful handling to ensure that temporary excess live loads will not result in the failure of the structure or element.

Load factors

In order to have a *safe design,* or adequate strength, we need strength so that the structure is not going to fail if either we underestimated somewhat the actually occurring loads, or for whatever reason there is a certain amount of excess load placed on our structure. Hence we employ load factors, i.e., we arbitrarily magnify the actual loads (or the moments therefrom) and thus create the demand on the strength. The demand states, for example, that the structure (or more precisely: the section under investigation) must have an ultimate strength (i.e., before it may fail) not less than

$$U = 1.4 \times D + 1.7 \times L$$

$$\text{or } U = 0.75 \times (1.4 \times D + 1.7 \times L + 1.7 \times W)$$

$$\text{or } U = 0.9 \times D + 1.3 \times W$$

(when seismic loads are considered, substitute $1.1 \times E$ for W)

where

U = Required (Ultimate) Strength

D = Effect from dead loads

L = Effect from prescribed live loads

W = Effect from wind loads

E = Effect from seismic loads

The multipliers applied to the effects in the various load combinations are the *load factors*. These are intended to guard against accidental overloading of the structure; they also recognize our incomplete knowledge in establishing loads more precisely.

Design (ultimate) strength

Ultimate strength of the section comes from the sizes, materials employed, and the amount of reinforcing furnished. This is the *supply,* i.e., the strength furnished by the design. For example, in flexural design this will be designated as M_n or "nominal moment strength."

Flexure (Bending) of rectangular concrete beams

In the following we shall establish the value of the expected nominal strength as a function of the size of the beam, the amount of reinforcement, the quality of the materials used, *i.e.* the strength of the concrete and that of the steel.

Notation : (Fig. 8)

a = depth of equivalent stress block (in.)

A_s = area of tensile reinforcement (sq. in.)

b = width of compression face of member (in.)

d = distance from the extreme compression fiber to centroid of tensile reinforcement ("effective depth") (in.)

h = overall depth of member (in.)

ρ = ratio of tension reinforcement = A_s/bd

$\varnothing$ = strength reduction factor ($\varnothing$ = 0.9 for flexure)

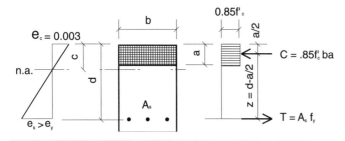

Fig. 8. Typical rectangular reinforced concrete beam.

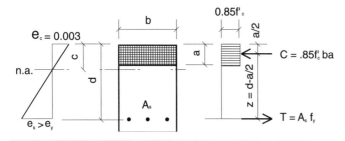

Fig. 9. Strain and stress on reinforced concrete beam.

Nominal strength is an assumed strength, provided everything goes according to plan. To allow things to go slightly wrong during construction we take this nominal strength and employ a *strength reduction factor* ($\varnothing$-factor) to define the *useful (or useable) strength*.

Hence the problem of ultimate strength design may be stated as follows:

- **Demand ≤ Supply**

- (required strength ≤ design strength)

For example, for a beam subject to gravity loads only:

$$M_u \leq \varnothing M_n \quad \text{or} \quad 1.4 \times M_D + 1.7 \times M_L \leq \varnothing M_n$$

Different $\varnothing$ factors are used for different effects.

Flexure	$\varnothing = 0.90$
Shear	$\varnothing = 0.85$
Axial compression (tied columns)	$\varnothing = 0.70$

On the left-hand side of the above *inequality* is the demand. The demand as was previously noted depends only on the span, type of beam (i.e., simply supported, cantilevered, etc.), and the loads. All information comes from static analysis.

On the right-hand side, however, we have the supplied strength of the section, which depends upon the size (shape) of the cross section, the quality of the materials employed (f'_c and f_y), and the amount of reinforcing furnished. Thus one may see that while the left-hand side is unique, the right-hand side is undefined, i.e., there are infinite different sizes, shapes, and reinforcing combinations that may satisfy a given problem. Economy, among other considerations, dictates that we should not *overdesign*.

Figs. 8 and **9** indicate a typical reinforced concrete beam and depict the strain distribution over the cross section at failure and the assumed (for calculation purposes) stress distribution. The internal couple forming the resisting moment is shown. C is the sum of the compressive stresses, while T is the tension in the reinforcement.

From equilibrium: T = C, *i.e.* $A_s f_y = 0.85 f'_c ba$

From here "a" (the depth of the equivalent stress block) may be expressed as:

$$a = \frac{A_s f_y}{0.85 f'_c b}$$

The nominal flexural strength of the section then may be calculated from the value of the internal couple.

$$M_n = Cz = 0.85 f'_c ba \ (d-a/2)$$

$$\text{or } M_n = Tz = A_s f_y \ (d-a/2)$$

(Note that the same concrete cross section may have different flexural strengths with different amounts of reinforcing in it.)

The usable moment capacity is then: $\varnothing M_n$

The above equations are then adequate to calculate the flexural strength of a section, when everything is known about the section.

Assumptions for ultimate strength design

(The Code Requirements and Commentary following below are extracted from ACI 318-92 Building Code Requirements for Reinforced Concrete)*

Code requirements	Commentary

Code requirements

10.2.1 - Strength design of members for flexure and axial loads shall be based on assumptions given in Sections 10.2.2 through 10.2.7 and on satisfaction of applicable conditions of equilibrium and compatibility of strains.

Commentary

The strength of the member computed by the strength design method of the Code requires that two basic conditions be satisfied: (1) static equilibrium and (2) compatibility of strain. Equilibrium between the compressive and tensile forces acting on the cross section at nominal strength must be satisfied. Compatibility between the stress and strain for the concrete and the reinforcement at nominal strength conditions must also be established within the design assumptions allowed by Section 10.2.

10.2.2.- Strain in reinforcement and concrete shall be assumed directly proportional to the distance from the neutral axis

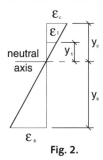

Fig. 2.

Many tests have confirmed that the distribution of strain is essentially linear across the reinforced concrete section, even near ultimate strength.

Both the strain in reinforcement and in concrete are assumed to be proportional to the distance from the neutral axis.

$$\frac{\varepsilon_1}{y_1} = \frac{\varepsilon_c}{y_c} = \frac{\varepsilon_s}{y_s}$$

10.2.3 - Maximum usable strain at extreme concrete compression fiber shall be assumed equal to 0.003

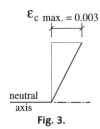

Fig. 3.

The maximum concrete compressive strain at crushing of the concrete has been observed in tests of various kinds to vary from 0.003 to higher than 0.008 under special conditions. However, the strain at which ultimate moments are developed is usually about 0.003 to 0.004 for members of normal proportions and materials.

10.2.4 - Stress in reinforcement below specified yield strength f_y for grade of reinforcement used shall be taken as E_s times steel strain. For strains greater than that corresponding to f_y stress in reinforcement shall be considered independent of strain and equal to f_y

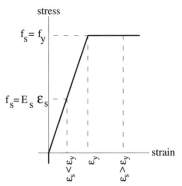

for $f_y = 40$ ksi, $\varepsilon_y = 0.00138$
for $f_y = 60$ ksi, $\varepsilon_y = 0.00207$

Fig. 4.

For the reinforcement it is reasonably accurate to assume that the stress in the reinforcement is proportional to strain below the yield strength f_y. The increase in strength due to strain hardening after yielding is neglected. The assumptions are:

when $\varepsilon_s < \varepsilon_y$ (yield strain)
then $A_s f_s = A_s E_s \varepsilon_s$

when $\varepsilon_s \geq \varepsilon_y$
then $A_s f_s = A_s f_y$

The modulus of elasticity of steel reinforcement E_s may be taken as 29,000,000 psi.

*American Concrete Institute, 1992. *Building Code Requirements of Reinforced Concrete* (ACI 318-89) and Commentary (ACI 318R-89), Detroit, MI.

Assumptions for ultimate strength design* (continued)

Code requirements

10.2.5 - Tensile strength of concrete shall be neglected in axial and flexural calculations of reinforced concrete.

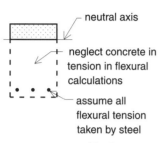

Fig. 5.

10.2.6 - Relationship between concrete compressive stress distribution and concrete strain may be assumed to be rectangular, trapezoidal, parabolic, or any other shape that results in prediction of strength in substantial agreement with results of comprehensive tests.

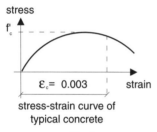

stress-strain curve of typical concrete

Fig. 6.

10.2.7 - Requirements of 10.2.6 are satisfied by an equivalent rectangular concrete stress distribution defined by the following:

10.2.7.1 - Concrete stress of 85f′$_c$ shall be assumed uniformly distributed over an equivalent compression zone bounded by edges of the cross section and a straight line parallel to the neutral axis at a distance a = β₁c from the fiber of maximum compressive strain.

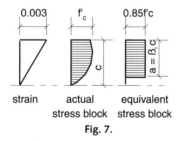

Fig. 7.

10.2.7.2 - Distance c from fiber of maximum strain to the neutral axis shall be measured in a direction perpendicular to that axis.

10.2.7.3 - Factor β shall be taken as 0.85 for concrete strengths f′$_c$ up to and including 4000 psi. For strengths above 4000 psi, β₁ shall be reduced continuously at a rate of 0.05 for each 1000 psi of strength in excess of 4000 psi, but β₁ shall not be taken less than 0.65.

Commentary

The tensile strength of concrete in flexure (modulus of rupture) is a more variable property than the compressive strength and is about 10–15 percent of the compressive strength. Tensile strength of concrete is neglected in strength design. For members with normal percentages of reinforcement, this assumption is in good agreement with tests.

The strength of concrete in tension, however, is important in cracking and deflection considerations at service loads.

This assumption recognizes the inelastic stress distribution of concrete at high stress. As maximum stress is approached, the stress strain relationship of concrete is not a straight line but some form of a curve (stress is not proportional to strain). The general shape of a stress strain curve is primarily a function of concrete strength and consists of a rising curve from zero to a maximum at a compressive strain between 0.0015 and 0.002, followed by a descending curve to an ultimate strain (crushing of the concrete) from 0.003 to higher than 0.008. As indicated under 10.2.3, the Code sets the maximum usable strain at 0.003 for design.

For practical design the Code allows the use of a rectangular compressive stress distribution (stress block) to replace the more exact concrete stress distributions. In the equivalent rectangular stress block, an average stress of 0.85f′$_c$ is used with a rectangle of depth a = β₁c. The β₁ of 0.85 for concrete with f′$_c$ ≤ 4,000 psi and 0.05 less for each 1,000 psi of f′$_c$ in excess of 4,000 psi was determined experimentally.

*American Concrete Institute, 1992. *Building Code Requirements of Reinforced Concrete* (ACI 318-89) and Commentary (ACI 318R-89), Detroit, MI.

(Problem of *investigation*, i.e., we try to verify that a section has adequate strength to satisfy the demanded ultimate strength.)

Example:

Given: $h = 20''$ $b = 12''$ $f'_c = 3$ ksi $f_y = 60$ ksi

              $A_s = 3$-#7 bars $= 1.80$ in^2

Solution: The working depth, $d = h$ – concrete cover – stirrup diameter – ½ of reinf. bar diameter

              $d = 20.0 - 1.5 - 0.375 - 0.875/2 = 17.69''$

              $a = (1.80) 60 / 0.85 (3)12 = 3.53''$

              $\varnothing M_n = 0.9 (1.80) 60 [17.69 - 3.53/2] = 1548$ k-in

The problem of *design*, that is, the search for a section with a certain amount of reinforcement to satisfy a demanded ultimate strength, is somewhat more involved. We may notice that in the expression(s) defining the nominal strength, there are five different items (f'_c, f_y, b, d, and A_s). Unfortunately there is only one equation that expresses the fact that,

$$M_u \leq \varnothing M_n$$

The normal design procedure is to select four of the unknowns and calculate the fifth from the above equation. Usually, we decide on the strength of the concrete (f'_c) and the quality of steel (f_y) for the whole project. Then we select an estimated concrete section (b and h). This leaves only the required amount of reinforcing to be calculated.

$M_u = \varnothing A_s f_y (d-a/2)$ substituting $a = \dfrac{A_s f_y}{0.85 f'_c b}$

and reorganizing we may obtain

$$\left(\frac{0.5294\ f_y^2}{f'_c b} \right) A_s^2 - (0.9\ f_y\ d)\ A_s + M_u = 0$$

let $K_1 = \left(\dfrac{0.5294\ f_y^2}{f'_c b} \right)$ and $K_2 = 0.9\ f_y\ d$ then

$$A_s = K_2 - \frac{\sqrt{K_2^2 - 4\ K_1\ M_u}}{2K_1}$$

All units must be consistent!

Example:

Given: $M_u = 210$ k-ft $= 2520$ k-in

Select: $h = 24''$ $b = 14''$ $f'_c = 4$ ksi $f_y = 60$ ksi

(because we do not yet know the size of the reinforcing, we can only estimate the value of d; a good and practical estimate is $d = h - 2.5''$) then: $d_{est} = 21.5''$ then

$$\left[0.5294\ \frac{(60^2)}{4 \times 14} \right] A_s^2 - [0.9\ (60)\ 21.5]\ A_s + 2520 = 0$$

$A_s = 2.33$ in^2 select: 3-#8 bars; $A_s = 2.37$ in^2

There are other methods and design aids that help with the solution. By introducing a parameter called "steel ratio,"

$$p = \frac{As}{bd}, \text{ and letting } R = \varnothing\ p\ f_y \left(\frac{1 - p\ f_y}{1.7\ f'_c} \right)$$

the design equation can be brought to:

$$M_u \leq R\ b\ d^2 \quad \text{or} \quad R \geq M_u / (b\ d^2)$$

There are design tables that list R as a function of p, f'_c and f_y, thus p can be selected to correspond to a required R value, after which A_s can be found.

3 CONCRETE STRUCTURAL ELEMENTS

T beams

In a monolithic floor construction we rarely have isolated rectangular beams. Instead we have beams that are continuous over several spans with slabs spanning between them. The adjacent slabs in the positive moment regions help to carry the compressive stresses. The stress block at ultimate strength becomes wider and more shallow, increasing the (d-a/2) moment arm, thus helping to reduce the amount of required reinforcing.

Fig. 10 illustrates the point. On the cantilevers (or more precisely in the zone of negative moments) tension is on the top and compression is on the bottom. There the beam is like a rectangular section, the adjacent slabs are in the tension zone, and only the web of the beam is available to carry compression.

On the other hand in the positive moment region compression is on the top and the slab, which forms part of the beam due to monolithic action, helping the beam to carry the compressions. The ACI Code provides instructions about the width of slab that may be used in the design of T beams. Width of the slab effective as a T beam flange shall not exceed one-quarter of the span length of the beam, and the effective overhanging flange width on each side of the web shall not exceed (**Fig. 11**):

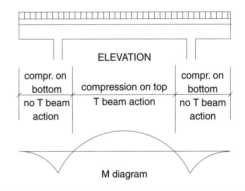

Fig. 10. T beam.

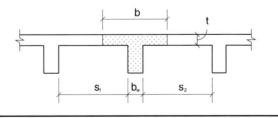

Fig. 11. T beam effective flange.

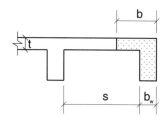

Fig. 12. Effective flange on one side only.

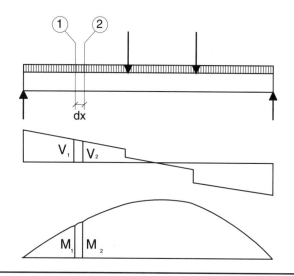

Fig. 13. Shear and moment diagram.

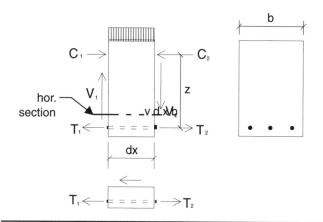

Fig. 14. Beam detail.

(a) 8 times the slab thickness, and

(b) one-half the clear distance to the next web.

In other words:

b is the least of   span/4

or $16t + b_w$

or $b_w + S_1/2 + S_2/2$

For beams that have a slab on one side only, the formulae modify as follows (**Fig. 12**):

b is the least of: $b_w + span/12$

or $b_w + 6t$

or $b_w + S/2$

Shear in reinforced concrete beams

Fig. 13 shows a reinforced concrete beam, its shear and moment diagrams due to some kind of load as indicated. We selected a small length of the beam, bounded by sections 1 and 2. The small length is designated as "dx." As we may observe there are differences in the shear and the moment at the two respective sections, i.e., $V_1 > V_2$ and $M_1 < M_2$.

As the reader may recall, the change in the moment equals the area under the shear diagram, and the rate of change in the moment equals the magnitude of the shear. Mathematically this was expressed as:

$$\frac{dM}{dx} = V \text{ or } \frac{M_2 - M_1}{dx} = V$$

If we substitute the moments with the internal couples, i.e., $M_1 = T_1 z = C_1 z$ and $M_2 = T_2 z = C_2 z$, then we may observe that $T_1 < T_2$ since $M_1 < M_2$

When we further isolate a small part of the beam that is below the "horizontal section" indicated on **Fig. 14**, then we find that for equilibrium purposes we must have a horizontal force acting on that horizontal section that helps restore equilibrium on that small part. The area of that "horizontal section" is b dx and if the stress (i.e., the force per unit area) is designated by "v" then we can derive the following relationship:

$$T_2 - T_1 = \frac{M_2}{z} - \frac{M_1}{z} = \frac{dM}{z}$$

from equilibrium: $T_2 - T_1 = v \, b \, dx$

hence: $\frac{dM}{z} = v \, b \, dx$

rearranging the terms we may write: $V = \frac{dM}{dx} = v \, b \, z$

And thus the horizontal shear stress value may be calculated as:

$$v = \frac{V}{bz}$$

Fig. 15 indicates an isolated part of the beam, shown in elevation. Within this portion of the beam (somewhere inside) a small $1'' \times 1'' \times 1''$ cube is selected. On the elevation of this cube the shear stresses are also indicated. Previously we showed what causes the horizontal shears. Notice that the horizontal shears form a couple (on the sketch it is a counterclockwise couple). Since a couple can be kept in equilibrium by another couple, we conclude that a clockwise couple is needed on this cube. This clockwise couple is furnished by equal magnitude shears on the vertical side of the cube. The appearance of shears both on the horizontal sections and on the vertical sections of a beam is known as the "duality of shears," meaning that shears are always present on both the horizontal surface and on the vertical surface of a little elementary cube inside the beam and that they are equal in magnitude.

Shears do not cause a problem for concrete, as a matter of fact concrete is quite strong in shear. However, when we isolate the unit cube and continue our "detective" work, we may examine the resultant of two of the shears on the top and the left, and also from the bottom and the right, respectively. These shears are trying to tear our cube apart perpendicular to the diagonal shown. When we separate the cube into two triangular wedges, we note that for equilibrium purposes we need stresses perpendicular to that diagonal cut. The sum total of these tensile stresses must be equal to $v \sqrt{2}$. Since the area of the diagonal cut is $1 \sqrt{2}$, we may conclude that the stresses acting on that diagonal cut are equal to "v" psi (or ksi), i.e., the magnitude of the *diagonal tensile stresses* equal that of the shear stresses (**Figs. 16 to 18**).

Concrete is weak in tension, therefore there is the potential that the diagonal tensions may tear the beam apart. There are many such potential cracks. The horizontal component of the diagonal tension can be resisted by the horizontal reinforcing. The vertical component requires a special reinforcing called stirrups, which are usually small diameter bars (#3 or #4).

Since we may have a potential crack at any place where the shears are large, stirrups are needed along a good portion of the beam at both ends where the shears are large (**Fig. 19**).

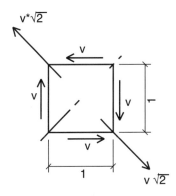

Fig. 16. Shear forces on isolated concrete cube.

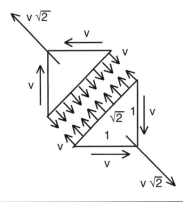

Fig. 17. Cracking potential in beam.

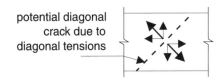

Fig. 18. Diagonal tension.

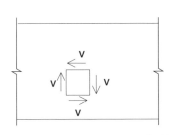

Fig. 15. Isolated beam detail.

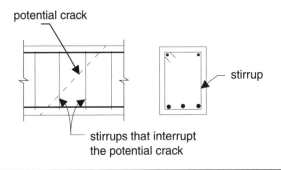

Fig. 19. Stirrup reinforcing.

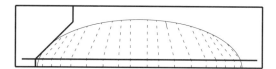

Fig. 20. Simple model of beam stresses.

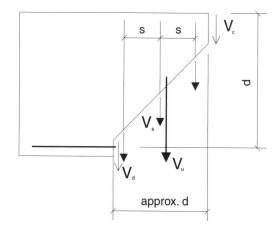

Fig. 21. Shear forces.

While the explanation above created the impression that the cracks are exactly "diagonal," i.e., 45 degrees to the axis of the beam, the truth is more complicated than that, because the longitudinal stresses (compression above the neutral axis and tension below) modify the direction of these tensions; but for design purposes a simple model can be created as shown in **Fig. 20**.

Accordingly we assume that there is a potential crack crossed by a number of stirrups (n) that are at "s" spacing apart. The action of V_u is resisted by "friction" created in the compression zone (V_c), the sum of the tensions created in the stirrups' legs (V_s), and a so-called dowel action from the vertical shear resistance of the horizontal reinforcing (V_d). V_d is neglected by the ACI Code. The remaining two, i.e., V_c plus V_s, then form the resistance, the so-called shear strength (**Fig. 21**). (Remember that the shear is used as a measure of the diagonal tension.)

The design equation is then:

$$V_u \leq \varnothing\, V_n = \varnothing\, (V_c + V_s)$$

V_c is the assumed nominal shear strength contributed by the concrete and it can be calculated in beams as:

$$V_c = 2\,\sqrt{f'_c}\; b\, d \quad (f'_c \text{ must be entered in psi units})$$

V_s is the nominal shear strength provided by the stirrups:

$$V_s = A_v\, f_y\, d/s$$

Notation:

A_v = sum of the cross section of stirrup legs

s = spacing of stirrups

b_w = width of the web of concrete beams

d = distance from extreme compression fiber to centroid of tensile reinforcement

$\varnothing$ = strength reduction factor (0.85 for shear)

Derivation of V_s: $V_s = n\,(A_v\, f_y)$, assuming that "n" stirrups cross the potential 45 deg. crack.

$$\text{since } n\, s \approx d, \text{ thus } n = d/s$$

$$\text{hence: } V_s = A_v\, f_y\, d/s$$

Design procedure for shear in concrete beams:

1. Find V_u at section under investigation

2. Calculate $Vc = 2\,\sqrt{f'_c}\; b\, d$

3. Calculate $V_s = (V_u/\varnothing) - V_c$

4. Select stirrup size (usually #3 or #4)

5. Calculate the spacing required at the section under investigation as

$$s = \frac{A_v\, f_y\, d}{V_s}$$

(Since a single stirrup has two legs, they will both work as part of V_s, thus A_v equals twice the cross-sectional area of a stirrup.)

Notes:

a. The maximum permitted spacing is *the least* of the following:

    1. the spacing calculated above, or

    2. $s_{max} = d/2$ when $V_s \leq 4 \sqrt{f'_c}\, b_w\, d$, or

        $s = \dfrac{d}{4}$ when $4 \sqrt{f'_c}\, b_w\, d < V_s < 8 \sqrt{f'_c}\, b_w\, d$, or

    3. $s_{max} = A_v\, f_y / (50\, b_w)$

b. A minimum area of shear reinforcement must be provided where

$$V_u > \varnothing\, V_c / 2 \quad \text{except in slabs and footings;}$$

$$\text{or in concrete joist construction;}$$

c. Sections located less than distance "d" from the face of the support may be designed for the same V_u as that computed at a distance "d" from the face of the support.

Reinforced concrete columns

Fig. 22 shows part of a concrete frame. The deformation shown is that of a simply supported beam. Simply supported beams are characterized by free rotations at the ends. Free rotation means lack of restraints, or in other words, lack of end moments. However, in a monolithically built reinforced concrete structure the ends of the beams cannot rotate freely, since at the joints beams and columns must rotate an identical amount. The columns are trying to resist the rotation of the beam, the beam "drags" them along to some equilibrium position as shown in **Fig. 23**.

For the equilibrium of the joint, $\Sigma M = 0$, the beam moment(s) are kept in equilibrium by the column moments, as shown in **Fig. 24**.

When one examines a system of beams and columns as shown in **Fig. 25**, it is easy to follow the transfer of shears and moments from beams to columns and vice versa. Shears at the ends of the beams become axial loads on the columns. In addition, the moments from the floor above and below the column tend to bend the column into a "double curve." This is much more pronounced at exterior columns than at interior columns, where loads on the neighboring beams try to rotate the common node in opposite directions, thus the bending on the columns is not as great, at least not from gravity loads.

As it may be seen, at any section of the column we may find an axial force (P_u) and a moment (M_u). These were calculated from factored loads and represent the demand on the section under consideration. The design equations now are much more complex, since the strength must satisfy two (or three, when in the truly general situation the column is bent around two axes!) items simultaneously.

If we examine a column section (or a short length of a column) on which a given P_u and M_u act (**Fig. 26**), the axial force creates compression throughout the section (both concrete and vertical steel are in compression), while the bending moment creates compression on the right-hand side and tension on the left-hand side. On the right-hand side the compressive effects of the axial force and the moment add up. On the left side we cannot be sure what will happen. There the tension from the moment and the compression from the axial force work

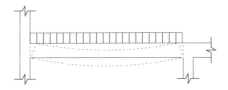

Fig. 22. Simply supported concrete frame.

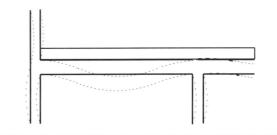

Fig. 23. Monolithic concrete frame.

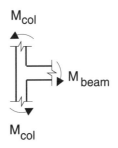

Fig. 24. Equilibrium of the joint.

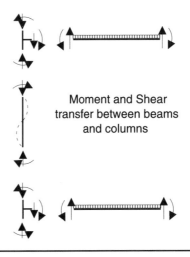

Moment and Shear transfer between beams and columns

Fig. 25. Transfer of shears and moments.

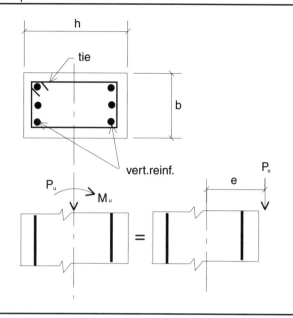

Fig. 26. The effect of axial forces.

against each other. If the tension from the moment is small, then the compression will "win" and the whole section will be in compression with the maximum occurring on the right side. On the other hand, if the moment is large, the tension on the left side will "overwhelm" the compression from the axial force and a net amount of tension will result. Since the concrete is assumed to take no tension, only the reinforcing steel on the tension side will be available to resist it.

Note: A system consisting of an axial force and a moment may also be represented by a statically equivalent system of a force at an eccentricity. For the two systems to be equivalent we must have

$$P_u e = M_u \quad \text{or} \quad e = \frac{M_u}{P_u}$$

In flexure a given section with a given amount of reinforcing has an easily calculable ultimate moment. In columns, however, a given column section with a given amount of reinforcing *may fail either due to excessive compression* under the combined effects of the axial load and the moment, or *it might fail in tension.* Either failure mode is possible depending on the relative magnitudes of P_u and M_u. There are an infinite number of axial force and moment combinations that represent failure condition for a given column (i.e., a column with known materials, cross section, and reinforcing). These ultimate axial force and moment combinations can be represented in a graph called an *interaction diagram.*

The different possibilities of failures may be shown in the following five diagrams, each of which represents a particular "failure mode." The interpretation of the P_u force is such that it is just large enough to create the conditions shown on the *strain diagrams* (**Fig. 27**).

Fig. 28 is a so-called interaction diagram. For every imaginable column section with a given amount of reinforcing one can construct an

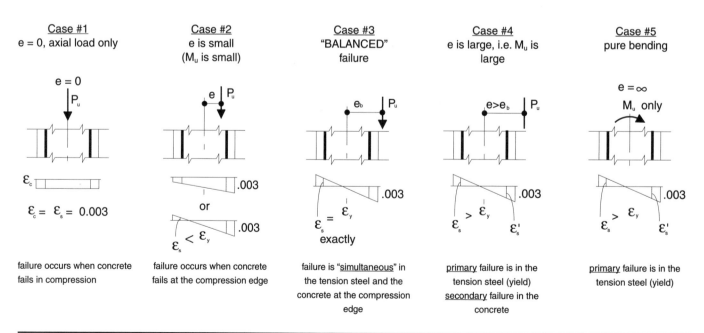

Fig. 27. Failure analysis.

interaction diagram. Any pair of force and moment can be represented in the coordinate system as a point, and the force and moment pair will not cause failure in the given column as long as the point falls within the curve. Any point on the curve or outside of the curve represents the combined action of a force and a moment that will cause failure in the column section. The "safe zone" on the diagram simply means the scaling of the failure curve by a factor $\emptyset$. The ACI Code selects this as $\emptyset = 0.7$ for tied columns.

Ties are used to enable the reinforcing bars that are long and slender compression elements to develop their full yield strength without buckling. In order to achieve that goal we select the following as the maximum allowable spacing of the ties:

spacing $\leq 16\,D$ (where D = diameter of the longitudinal bars)

≤ 48 tie diameters

$\leq b$ (where b is the *shorter* cross-sectional dimension of the column)

Ties are at least #3 up to and including #10 longitudinal bars

#4 for longitudinal bars #11 and larger

Typical floor systems

Flat plate (**Fig. 29**) structures are often used for moderate spans and loads. The forming cost is the least of all possible systems; it provides for the least structural depth and thus for the least floor to floor height. The span/depth ratios most commonly used are between 28 and 32; the lower value should be used when the exterior or corner panels are unstiffened by the incorporation of an edge beam. It is also the most economical, when the spans are approximately 26 ft or less. Beyond 26 ft, the slab becomes too thick, with the corresponding increase of its self-weight. If larger spans are desired, the architect either has to select a different structural system, or a prestressed (post-tensioned) version must be used.

Fig. 30 shows the schematic deformation diagram of a flat plate under load. While the largest deflections are in the center of the bay, the most highly stressed zones occur in the vicinity of the supports. Since all the loads must travel toward the columns, the available zone (**Fig. 31**)

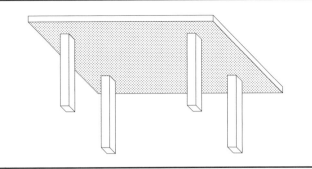

Fig. 29. Flat plate.

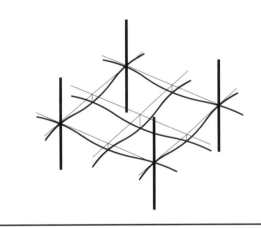

Fig. 30. Schematic deformation diagram.

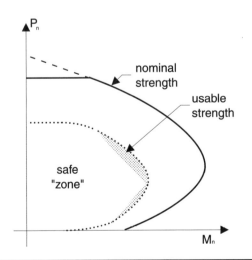

Fig. 28. "Interaction diagram."

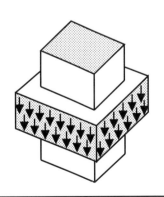

Fig. 31. Failure surface at shear zone.

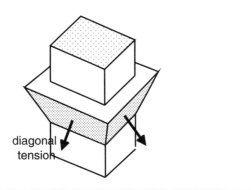

Fig. 32. Failure surface at shear zone.

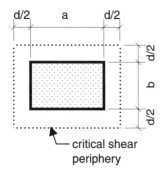

Fig. 33. Plan of column.

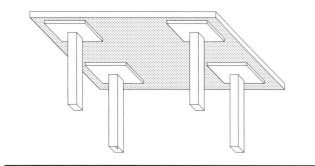

Fig. 34. Flat slab with drop panels.

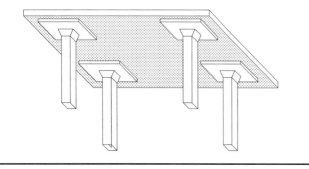

Fig. 35. Flat slab with drop panels and column capitals.

through which shears must travel becomes smaller and smaller, thus the unit shear increases and reaches a maximum at or near the interface of the column and the slab. The large shears are also indicative of sharp change in the moments that occur in the vicinity of the columns. Shears cause diagonal tensions (see later) in structures subject to flexure. Since concrete is quite weak in resisting tension, failure can result. The failure surface may be envisioned as a truncated pyramid (**Fig. 32**). This phenomenon is known as punching shear, that is, the column "punches" through the slab, or more precisely the slab fails and falls down around the column.

The ACI Code deals with this rather complex problem by offering a simple model for design, shown by tests to offer an appropriate safety measure against failure. Instead of working with the tension on a slanted surface, it assumes a *critical shear periphery* located at d/2 distance from the face of the column in every direction (**Fig. 33**, where d = the working depth of the slab), and may be assumed approximately as [h − 1.25″] for preliminary design purposes.

$$V_u \leq \phi V_n = \phi V_c \text{ where } V_c = \left(2 + \frac{4}{\beta_c}\right)\sqrt{f'_c}b_o d$$

$$\text{but } V_c \leq 4\sqrt{f'_c}b_o d$$

b_o = length of the shear periphery = (2a + 2b + 4d)

βc = the aspect ratio of the longer face to the shorter face of the column. It does not become significant unless it is larger than 2.

Note that the size of the critical shear surface, upon which the available shear strength depends, is governed by the thickness of the slab on the one hand, and the dimensions of the column section on the other. Furthermore, openings through the slab near the column create discontinuity in the shear surface and seriously weaken the available strength. Thus, in the planning of the building layout, vertical chases should not be located in the immediate vicinity of columns. Special reinforcing made up of either reinforcing bars, or of wide-flange steel sections, are sometimes used to increase the shear strength of the critical zone.

Flat plate and flat slab structures need not necessarily be laid out in a regular fashion. Columns may be offset from a regular pattern so long as the slab span/depth ratios between the columns do not increase beyond the values given above in either direction. Moderate length cantilevers are actually beneficial, for they provide increased shear surface at exterior columns and also help to reduce the deflections of the slab in exterior or corner bays.

Flat slab structures (**Figs. 34** and **35**) are actually plates that are reinforced by either drop panels, or column capitals, or both. Its use is warranted for moderate spans (up to 30 to 32 ft) and high superimposed loads. The increased forming cost may be justified, for the system provides maximum ceiling space between the drop panels, and even in the area of drop panels, the loss of depth is quite minimal. The column capitals help to enlarge the column/slab interface periphery, thus helping with the critical shear transfer from the slab to the column. The drop panels help in many ways. The increased slab thickness provides the potential of greater flexural strength, it increases the size (and therefore the strength) of the critical shear periphery. Furthermore, the greater thickness also represents greater stiffness, i.e., resistance to deformation, and thus helps reduce the deflections in the middle of the bay. Drop panels, if used, must extend to a distance at least one-sixth of the span in each direction, and its depth below the slab must be at least one-quarter of the thickness of the slab. The thickness of the slab for good serviceability should be selected between span/32 to span/36.

Waffle slab structures (**Fig. 36**) are thick flat plate structures, with the concrete removed in zones where not required by strength considerations. They are economical structures for spans up to 60 ft. square, or nearly so, bays, loaded with light and moderate loads. The voids are formed by steel (or fiberglass) "domes," which are reusable and thus very economical. These domes are available in standardized sizes (**Fig. 37**), although wider or odd-shaped domes are also used to satisfy some design objectives. The domes are tapered, usually 1 in 12, which permits easy removal after the concrete has sufficiently cured. When carefully done, and finished after the removal of the forms, the two-way joists provide a pleasing appearance as well.

While the lips on the domes, when laid out side by side, form 5″ wide joists for the 19″ voids and 6″ wide joists for the 30″ wide voids, it is not a requirement that forces the designer to work with 24″ or 36″ planning modules. Since the domes are always laid out on a flat plywood deck, the spacing between the domes can be adjusted, so by making the joists wider than standard at the base, virtually any column spacing can be accommodated, while maintaining a uniform appearance. By leaving out the domes around the columns, a shear head is automatically formed to provide increased shear strength. The slab over the domes is typically 3″ thick, unless large concentrated loads or increased fire rating requirements warrant the use of a thicker slab. The slab is reinforced with a light welded wire fabric that helps control potential shrinkage and temperature cracks.

Another popular form of structure is shown in **Fig. 38**. Wide beams form a two-way grid of beams between columns, and the depth is equal to the depth of the two-way joist system. This arrangement provides a somewhat easier layout of reinforcing in the negative moment regions around the columns.

One-way joists spanning between beams are essentially closely spaced beam elements (**Fig. 39**). In order to qualify for the joist designation by the ACI Code, the space between them must not exceed 30″. The forms used are made of various materials. Steel, fiberglass, fiberboard, and corrugated cardboard forms are readily available, made with or without the edge lip (**Fig. 40**). However, forms without

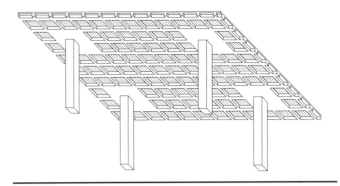

Fig. 36. Waffle slab.

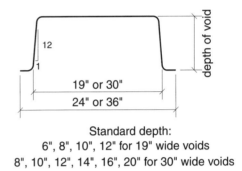

Standard depth:
6″, 8″, 10″, 12″ for 19″ wide voids
8″, 10″, 12″, 14″, 16″, 20″ for 30″ wide voids

Fig. 37. Standard void dimensions of waffle systems.

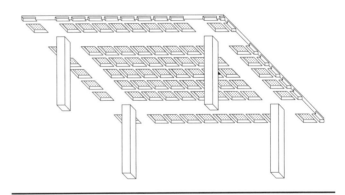

Fig. 38. Waffle slab with two-way beams.

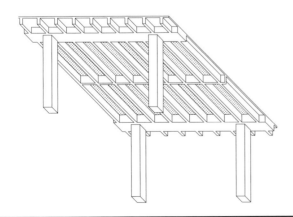

Fig. 39. One-way joists and beams.

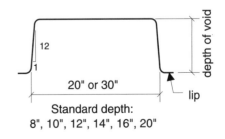

Standard depth:
8″, 10″, 12″, 14″, 16″, 20″

Fig. 40. Standard steel form dimensions of one-way systems.

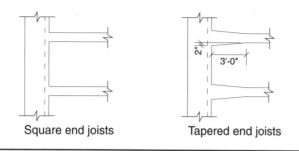

Fig. 41. Ends of concrete joists.

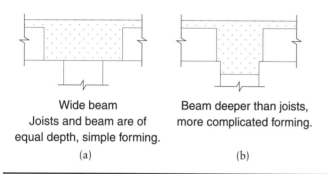

Fig. 42. Beams for one-way systems.

Table 1. Minimum thickness of non-prestressed beams or one-way slabs, unless deflections are computed.*

Member	Simply supported	One end continuous	Both ends continuous	Cantilever
Solid one-way slabs	span/20	span/24	span/28	span/10
Beams or joists	span/16	span/18.5	span/21	span/8

Values given shall be used directly for members with normal weight concrete and Grade 60 reinforcement. For other conditions the values shall be modified as follows:

a) For structural lightweight concrete having unit weight in the range of 90-120 pcf, the values shall be multiplied by $(1.65 - 0.005w_c)$ but not less than 1.09, where w_c is the unit weight in pcf.

b) For f_y other than 60,000 psi, the values shall be multiplied by $(0.4 + f_y/100,000)$.

*ACI 318-89, Building Code Requirements for Reinforced Concrete, American Concrete Institute, Detroit, MI.

From note b) it is clear that if the depth must be minimized beyond the values listed in the table, the designer has the choice of using Grade 40 ($f_y = 40,000$ psi) reinforcing. This will result in approximately 50 percent more reinforcing in the member, which in turn reduces the strain in the reinforcing steel at service load condition. Reduced strain in the reinforcing provides reduced deflection in a member. Since it is not a wise thing to use a different grade reinforcing for a few selected members on a project, it is permissible to use Grade 60 steel equal in cross-sectional area as the calculated amount of steel that would be necessary with the use of Grade 40 steel.

the edge lip tend to bulge sideways during construction under the lateral pressure of the freshly poured concrete, and the resulting joist widths are going to be uneven. Forms are also available with square or tapered ends. The tapered ends provide increased shear capacity as well as increased moment capacity at the negative moment regions (**Fig. 41**). The one-way joist system is often used when the bays are elongated, i.e., in one direction the column spacing exceeds the spacing in the other direction by approximately 40 percent or more. At such span ratios, the advantage of two-way behavior is greatly reduced, and it is more economical to use one-way systems, i.e., beams spanning between columns, and joists spanning between the beams. It is most economical to span the beams in the shorter spans and the joists in the longer span. For ease of forming, the depths of beams are often selected to be equal to the depth of the joists. In order to provide the necessary shear and moment capacity, the beams are made considerably wider than the column faces into which they frame. Beams deeper than the joists occupy additional ceiling space, and require additional forming cost (**Figs. 42a** and **b**).

The slab over the voids is typically 3 in thick, unless large concentrated loads or increased fire rating requirements warrant the use of a thicker slab. The slab is reinforced with a light welded wire fabric that helps with control of potential shrinkage and temperature cracks. The overall depth of the joist (including the slab's thickness) should be selected in accordance with **Table 1** from the ACI Code. The ratios listed therein give satisfactory performance for most structural elements. However, the designer should be aware that these are minimum depth values, and as the fine print in the Code warns the user, should be used for "Members not supporting or attached to partitions or other construction likely to be damaged by large deflections."

Thus special attention should be given to the attachment of walls to the underside of concrete structural elements, so that due to creep-caused long-term deflections, such elements do not start to use such walls as supports. Furthermore, for crack-free performance masonry walls require that the deflection of the supporting beams should not exceed span/600.

The *slabs and beams* system (**Fig. 43**) is an economical choice when the bays are elongated and the superimposed loads are large, especially when the structure is subject to large line loads. Large through-the-slab openings can be easily accommodated virtually anywhere in the floor. It results in larger structural depth than the other systems described previously, but the forming cost is also usually higher. These apparent disadvantages are balanced by the economical concrete and reinforcing usage in the system. The system also provides a clear and un-ambiguous transfer of moments between beams and columns, which is a real advantage in high wind and/or seismic zones, when the structural frame is called upon in the resisting of large lateral loads on the building.

Prestressed concrete

The concept of prestressing means the introduction of stresses into the concrete structural element, that when combined with other stresses created by self-weight and superimposed loads, results in a desirable state of stresses in the element. Since, as was mentioned before, the tensile strength of concrete is rather limited (and not very reliable), it is discounted in design.

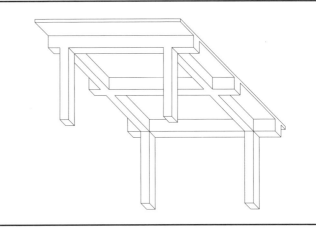

Fig. 43. Slab and beam system.

Fig. 44 illustrates the principle involved. An F prestressing force creates a stress distribution shown in **Fig. 44a**. Depending on the eccentricity (e), the stress at the top may be compression as shown, or tension. The uniformly distributed loads create tension at the bottom and compression at the top (**Fig. 44b**). When the two are combined, the stress distribution (shown in **Fig. 44c**) is obtained. Again, depending on the magnitude and the eccentricity of the F force, the section will have compression throughout as shown, or a small amount of tension may result in the bottom.

Prestressing has two different approaches: pre-tensioning and post-tensioning. In the former, the prestressing wires or strands are tensioned by stretching and fixing against a bulkhead, and then the concrete is poured around them in the desirable shape and form. After the concrete has gained sufficient strength, the strands are released and the force in them is transferred into the concrete element by the bond established between the strands and the cured concrete. This method is applicable for precast and prestressed elements produced in manufacturing plants. The production techniques often involve casting of elements in long casting beds, up to 600 ft (180 m), permitting simultaneous fabrication of many elements with a single tensioning of the strands. Accelerated curing techniques permit the release of the strands in only 8 to 12 hours after the placement of the concrete, thus a 24-hour manufacturing cycle can be maintained. The production is highly mechanized and great quality control can be obtained.

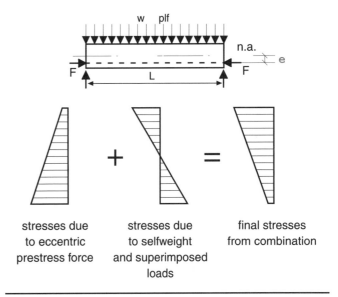

stresses due to eccentric prestress force + stresses due to selfweight and superimposed loads = final stresses from combination

Fig. 44. Prestressed concrete principles.

In post-tensioning, as the name aptly indicates, the concrete structure is poured in situ with conduits containing the prestressing strands pre-placed into the formwork. After the concrete has gained sufficient strength with one end of the strand fixed into position, a hydraulic prestressing jack is applied to the other end. Using the cured concrete as the bulkhead, the strand is tensioned by stretching. After the stressing, the end is anchored, thus preventing its snapping back to its original length. The space around the strand within the conduit may be grouted (grouted tendons), or left free (ungrouted tendons), in which case only the end anchorages provide for the maintenance of the prestressing force. There are many proprietary prestressing (post-tensioning) systems on the market, using different anchorage designs.

Tilt-up concrete

In the typical process of tilt-up concrete construction, concrete wall panels are poured on-site and horizontally onto a floor slab or a casting bed, then moved upright into place (**Figs. 45 and 46**). While not widely used until recently, the process was pioneered in the early 20th century by architects in California including Irving Gill and R. M. Schindler, whose own 1922 house in Los Angeles is constructed of tilt-up panels separated by glass strips.

Most tilt-up buildings are load bearing to increase structural efficiency. After being poured on the ground, panels are lifted with cranes that grab hold of steel anchors cast into the slabs. Once in place, telescoping steel braces support the panels until the walls are secured to footings and roof decking is installed. The size of the build-

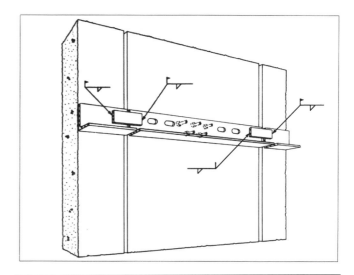

Fig. 45. Tilt-up concrete wall with prepositioned connectors. Steel angles fastened to wall panels support metal roof. (Barreneche 1995)

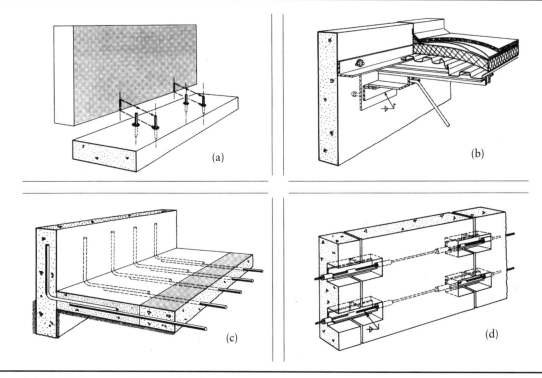

Fig. 46. Tilt-up wall details: (a) Concrete walls are anchored to footings with steel rods inserted into predrilled holes; (b) Tilt-up structures are typically fitted with metal deck roof system; (c) Steel rods anchor tilt-up wall panel and floor slab; (d) Chord bars cast into concrete wall panels. (Barreneche 1995)

ing's floor plate dictates the size of tilt-up panels. Once erected, tilt-up walls can be repositioned and even disassembled and moved to another site.

Tilt-up concrete construction has the advantages of simplicity of forming and elimination of element transport. But there are important differences between tilt-up and other concrete construction methods:

– Load bearing tilt-up walls require both vertical and horizontal reinforcement.

– Vertical rebars are typically inserted into the wall panel at 12 to 16 in (30 to 40 cm) intervals. The amount of horizontal reinforcement depends on size and thickness of the panel. Precast Concrete Institute recommends that horizontal rebars cover a minimum of 0.1 percent of the panel's cross-sectional area. Shear walls require additional reinforcement.

– Temporary braces support the panels against surface winds until the roof structure is installed. The placement of these braces must be planned, since the anchors that hold them are cast into the panel while it is poured. Consult Tilt-up Concrete Association bracing guidelines.

Once the panels are erected, a 2 to 4 ft (60 to 120 cm) gap is typically left between the wall panel and the concrete floor slab. After wall panels are fastened to their foundations with steel rods, concrete is poured in to fill the gap, covering net reinforcement rods cast into the wall. The width of the gap depends on factors such as soil conditions and slope. ■

REFERENCES

American Concrete Institute, *ACI Manual of Concrete Practice, Parts 1–5,* American Concrete Institute, Detroit, 1996. A collection of the Institute's Standards offers state-of-the-art reports on any aspect of concrete materials, manufacturing, design, and construction standards and methods.

Barreneche, Raul A., "Tilt-Up Concrete on the Rise," *Architecture,* September 1995.

Concrete Reinforcing Steel Institute, *CRSI Handbook,* Concrete Reinforcing Steel Institute, Schaumburg, 1996. A large collection of design tables for sizing concrete structural elements, including columns, beams, joists, slabs, one- and two-way systems, including size and reinforcing required for given loading.

Precast / Prestressed Concrete Institute, *PCI Design Handbook,* Prestressed Concrete Institute, Chicago, 1992. Product information and design selection tables of standard precast and prestressed products (hollow-core slabs, single and double T sections, beams, etc.). Problems of Architectural Precast Concrete, connections between precast elements are also discussed in great detail.

Tilt-Up Concrete Association (TCA), product information and publications, Mount Vernon, IA, (319) 895-6911, <www.tilt-up.org>

Martin D. Gehner, P.E.

Summary

A review of structural masonry construction is provided with guidelines for structural design of masonry, including details for brick and concrete masonry units and construction considerations.

Key words

brick, concrete masonry, masonry, engineered masonry, retaining walls

Roman arch construction enduring in situ after two millennia. Le Kef, Tunisia, North Africa.

Structural design—masonry

1 INTRODUCTION

Masonry is construction that uses brick, block, stone, or glass manufactured or cut in easily handled units and bonded together through mortar, grout, reinforcing, and metal ties. Throughout history masonry has been a construction material where its strength in compression is paramount. Recent research of this material and method of construction has developed for reinforced masonry significant advantages in performance, especially when subjected to earthquake loads.

Masonry codes historically were product driven. A brick code, a concrete masonry code, and a clay tile code all had similar standards but each was different according to industry standards combined with the industry's empirical methods. The 1995 *Building Code Requirements for Masonry Structures and Specifications for Masonry Structures* (ACI 530.1-95/ASCE 6-95/TMS 602-95) results from years of research and coordinated efforts to establish one comprehensive masonry code that includes the many different masonry materials. Nearly all forms of masonry are covered including clay and shale brick, concrete block, stone, unreinforced, reinforced, empirical, glass unit masonry, and anchored veneer masonry along with mortar, grout, and metal accessories.

The analysis and design for masonry structures is based on the allowable stress design (ASD) methodology. Allowable stresses have been used in masonry design for many years and reflect the extensive research and experience documented over the last century. The allowable stress design provisions are based on the following assumptions:

1. Masonry materials are linearly elastic under service loads;

2. Stress is directly proportional to strain under service loads;

3. Masonry materials behave homogeneously; and

4. Sections plane before bending remain plane after bending. Service loads are used as the basis of design, and the masonry unit of brick or block, together with the mortar and grout, essentially act as one unit rather than separately.

Allowable stresses are based on failure stresses with a factor of safety in the range of 2 to 5. The 1995 code also has a provision, not included in previous masonry standards, that requires the effects of restraint of movement due to prestressing, vibrations, impact, shrinkage, expansion, temperature changes, creep, unequal settlement of supports, and differential movements to be considered in the design. The code states design coefficients for thermal expansion, moisture expansion, shrinkage, and creep for masonry.

For strength, the specified compressive strength of masonry, f'_m, must be determined by the designer and verified by the contractor. The modulus of elasticity, E_m, may be determined by the secant method from prism tests. Deflection limits are imposed for masonry beams and lintels that support unreinforced masonry. The deflection should not exceed L/600 or 0.3 in where L is the span of the member.

In unreinforced masonry, the small tensile stresses are taken into consideration in the design of members. Allowable flexural stresses reflect a factor of safety of 2.5 to 3.5. Any reinforcement placed in unreinforced masonry, by definition, is for shrinkage or for other reasons. Allowable shear stresses are based upon a parabolic shear stress distribution rather than on an average shear stress as in previous codes. For axial compressive stresses, the slenderness ratio for unreinforced masonry is a function of the radius of gyration of the member's cross section. The factor of safety is 4 for unreinforced masonry.

Previous codes imposed limits on slenderness as they were defined relative to thickness of wall. In the 1995 code the slenderness reduction factor becomes very small as the structural element gets more slender.

In reinforced masonry, steel reinforcement carries all tensile forces in a bending member. Reinforcement may also provide resistance to shear forces. Minimum amounts of reinforcement are determined by design except for seismic provisions. The allowable flexural compressive stress is the same as for unreinforced masonry.

2 MASONRY MATERIALS

Stone

As a natural inorganic substance stone is identified by its geologic origin. *Igneous rock* is formed by the solidifying and cooling of molten material lying deep within the earth and thrust to its surface by volcanic action. Granite is the only building stone of this origin. *Sedimentary rock* is formed by waterborne deposits of minerals produced by the weathering and destruction of igneous rock. Sandstone, shale, and limestone are building stone from this source. *Metamorphic rock* is either igneous or sedimentary material whose structure has been changed by extreme heat and pressure. Marble, slate, and quartzite are building stone in this category. Good building stone contains silica and calcareous materials.

Stone masonry is a structural material very good in compression but also is a durable finish material. All stone used in stone masonry must satisfy requirements of strength, hardness, workability, durability, and appearance. **Table 1** shows properties of common building stones.

Brick

Clay and shale as raw materials contain ceramic characteristics. When a ground mixture is shaped and subjected to a controlled firing temperature in a kiln, the silicates melt to fuse the particles to a specified level of vitrification (crystallization from heat fusion). The resulting strength and weathering characteristics of the brick unit make it one of the most durable building materials.

Bricks are manufactured in many different types, shapes, and sizes. Building brick is used as a structural material where strength, durability, and appearance must be specified according to the building application and location. Durability and weather resistance is governed by the American Society of Testing Materials (ASTM) *Standard Specification for Building Brick, C62*. Grades are SW (severe weathering), MW (moderate weathering) and NW (negligible weathering). Most reference sources include a map of the United States, which shows the zones where SW, MW, and NW grades are permitted. Brick of grade SW are used where there is a high resistance to frost action and exposure conditions and where the masonry is exposed to water and freezing temperatures. In addition grade SW brick is used for below grade structures and for all horizontal surfaces under all weathering conditions. Brick of grade MW is used in regions subject to freezing when the brick is not exposed to water permeation. It is used for vertical walls and piers above grade in regions with moderate weathering conditions. NW brick is used in interior installations and in vertical application in regions where there will be little weathering exposure. Most manufacturers make brick to meet the SW weathering grades so that their product may be shipped to all regions of the country. Some brick manufacturers may select to produce only MW grades. The manufacturers can furnish certification of the grade of brick furnished. Further standards for appearance, dimensional tolerances, and moisture absorption are elaborated in the published information of the referenced documents.

Brick sizes and shapes are varied and custom orders are always possible. **Fig. 1** shows common brick sizes with nominal dimensions. Actual dimensions vary according to the thickness of the mortar joint. In general, higher quality brick construction will have mortar joints ⅜ in thick. For best coordination with other construction dimensions, actual dimensions of bricks and mortar joints in courses and stretchers must be detailed and specified. Normally brick is listed by the dimensions of thickness × height × length.

Bricks are classified as solid or hollow. A solid brick is one whose net cross-sectional area in every plane to the bearing surface is 75 percent or more of its gross section measured in the same plane. Simplified, a solid brick has a maximum coring of 25 percent of the gross area. A hollow brick is one whose net cross-sectional area in every plane parallel to the bearing surface is less than 75 percent of its gross section

Table 1. Properties of common building stones
Source: National Bureau of Standards Reports

Rock type	Origin	Principle ingredient	Weight lb./cu. ft.	Specific gravity	Compressive strength, psi
Granite	Igneous	Silica	170	2.61-2.70	7,000-60,000
Marble	Metamorphic	Calcium carbonate	165	2.64-2.72	8,000-50,000
Slate	Metamorphic	Calcium carbonate	170	2.74-2.82	10,000-15,000
Limestone	Sedimentary	Calcium carbonate	165	2.10-2.75	2,600-28,000
Sandstone	Sedimentary	Calcium carbonate	155	2.14-2.66	5,000-20,000

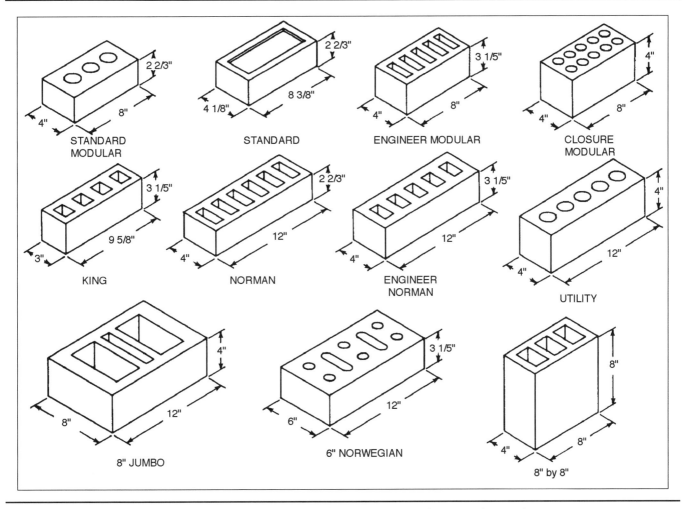

Fig. 1. Brick sizes (nominal dimensions). (Source: Technical Notes on Brick Construction 9B, Brick Institute of America)

area measured in the same plane. Holes in brick permit more even drying and firing of the units, reduce the amount of fuel to fire the units, and reduce the weight for shipping costs. Frogs in bricks are depressions located on the bed surface of the unit and are useful for the same purposes as core voids. Cores and frogs increase the mechanical bonding of individual brick units and improve the structural performance of walls. They also improve the ease of handling each unit for masons when constructing a wall.

The brick pattern on the wall surface reflects the method for constructing the wall as well as the bonding of wythes together. **Figs. 2** through **6** depict five very common patterns. The running bond consists entirely of stretchers. Since there is no header brick connecting two wythes, metal ties must be used for structural connection. Common bond has header brick every sixth course. Flemish bond consists of alternate stretcher and header brick in every course, and English bond has alternate courses of stretchers and headers. For a more elaborate illustration of variations of bonds, refer to the referenced documents.

Type of joint

The mortar joints that bond the masonry units together are of great importance for durability of masonry, and are vital to the aesthetic

appearance. Four types are shown in **Fig. 7**, and other variations are possible. These four are:

1 Weathered

2 Flush

3 Vee

4 Concave

A mason has a separate tool to create each type. Although all four are considered weather resistant, types 3 and 4 have the best resistance to weather. The tool used to create the finish also presses and spreads the mortar tightly in the joint after it has been partially set. For appearance decisions, sample walls are readily built on the job site so as to compare the color, the joint, the joint color, and the quality of craft to review and establish the standard for masons to achieve for a specific project.

Concrete masonry units

Concrete masonry units (CMUs) are made from cement and aggregate materials, which are hardened by chemical reactions rather than

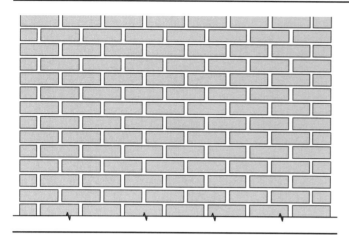

Fig. 2. Running bond.

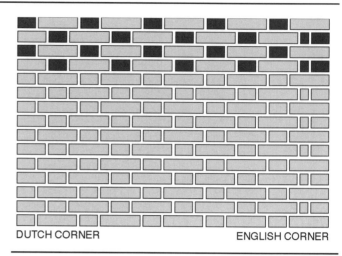

DUTCH CORNER   ENGLISH CORNER

Fig. 5. Flemish bond.

Fig. 3. Common bond with headers every sixth course.

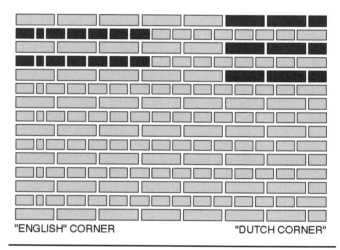

"ENGLISH" CORNER   "DUTCH CORNER"

Fig. 6. English bond.

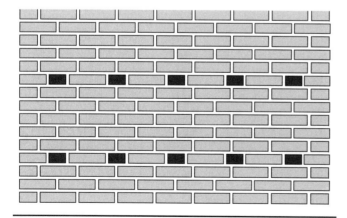

Fig. 4. Common bond with Flemish headers every sixth course.

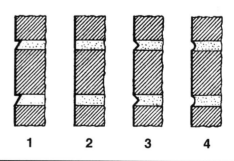

1   **2**   **3**   **4**

Fig. 7. Joint treatments.

by ceramic fusion as in the manufacture of clay brick. Concrete masonry units include concrete brick, concrete block, cast stone, and cellular concrete block. Concrete masonry units are produced from a mixture of Portland cement and aggregates in sizes and colors. Aggregates may be gravel, crushed stone, cinders, burned clay, blast furnace slag, and sand. Combinations permit normal concrete weight units or lightweight units. Raw materials are proportioned with water, and the controlled mixed is pressed into preformed casting dyes. The pressure-formed units are removed from the dyes, stacked, and cured in high-pressure autoclaves.

Unit sizes and shapes, including core size, vary according to the type of unit manufactured. **Fig. 8** shows typical shapes of concrete masonry units. The dimensions are modular based on a nominal 8 in high by 16 in long. The widths are commonly 4, 6, 8, 10, 12, and 16 in. With mortar joints of ⅜ in, the actual sizes are the nominal dimensions less ⅜ in in all directions. The number and size of cores vary according to manufacturer and application. Solid units and hollow units are defined the same as for brick. A solid unit has void cores up to 25 percent of the gross area in cross section. Hollow units will have up to 75 percent void cores. Standard specifications are controlled by criteria established by The American Society for Testing and Materials (ASTM). *The Concrete Masonry Handbook for Architects, Engineers and Builders* (1991) provides an excellent reference for design, detailing, and specification data on masonry construction.

Cast stone is widely used in masonry construction in products such as lintels, sills, copings, and veneer units. Selected aggregates of granite or marble may be used for color. The faces may be ground and polished as desired for the application.

Mortar

Mortar is the bonding medium for masonry. It must function to bond the masonry units together as well as to seal the construction against air and moisture penetration. Also, it must bond with steel reinforcing, which strengthens the masonry, and with metal ties and anchor bolts, which join the building components together. For structural components, mortar strength, performance, and durability are as equally important as the masonry unit. The quality of craft and installation not only controls the mortar but also the integrity of the whole of masonry elements being constructed.

The ingredients of mortar and grout are cement, lime, sand, and water. Cement gives the mortar strength and durability. Lime adds workability and elasticity. Sand acts as a filler and gives the mix strength and economy. Water gives the mix plasticity. Together these ingredients must be proportioned to achieve the highest quality for this cement-based bonding agent. Five types of mortar are available, of which only four are appropriate for structural masonry. **Table 2** lists the types along with their respective prism test requirements of strength.

Selection of mortar type is a function of the requirements for the finished structural element. Where high lateral strength is required on walls or piers, a mortar with high tensile bond strength is desired. For load bearing walls, high compressive strength or shear strength may govern the design. Consideration of durability or color may be a primary determinant for the mortar. Not all mortar types have the same qualities, so recommended uses are illustrated in **Table 3**.

Type M mortar has high compressive strength and greater durability than other mortar types. It is recommended for reinforced and unre-

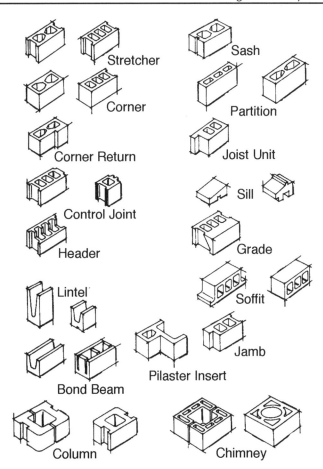

Fig. 8. Typical shapes of concrete masonry units.

Table 2. Mortar types (ASTM C270-73)

Mortar type	Minimum average compressive strength of three 2 in. cubes at 28 days, psi	Parts by volume			Aggregate measured in damp, loose condition
		Portland cement	Msonry cement	Hydrated lime or lime putty	
M	2,500	1 1	1 (Type II)	1/4	Not less than 2 1/2 and not more than 3 times the sum of the volumes of the cements and lime used.
S	1,800	1/2 1	1 Type II)	Over 1/4 to 1/2	
N	750	1	1 (Type II)	Over 1/2 to 1 1/4	
O	350	1	1 (Type I or II)	Over 1 1/4 to 2 1/2	

Table 3. Types of mortar required for various kinds of masonry

Foundations:	
Footings	M or S
Walls of solid units	M, S, or N
Walls of hollow units	M or S
Hollow walls	M or S
Masonry other than foundation masonry:	
Piers of solid masonry	M, S, or N
Piers of hollow units	M or S
Walls of solid masonry	M, S, N, or O
Walls of solid masonry, other than parapet walls or rubble stone walls, not less than 12 in. thick nor more than 35 ft. in height, supported laterally at intervals not exceeding 12 times the wall thickness	M, S, N, or O
Walls of hollow units; loadbearing or exterior, and hollow walls 12 in. or more in thickness	M, S, or N
Hollow walls, less than 12 in. in thickness where assumed design wind pressure:*	
(a) exceeds 20 psf	M, or S
(b) does not exceed 20 psf	M, S, or N
Glass-block masonry	M,S, or N
Nonbearing partitions or fireproofing composed of structural clay tile or concrete masonry units	M, S, N, O, or gypsum
Gypsum partition tile or block	Gypsum
Fire brick	Refractory air setting mortar
Linings of existing masonry, either above or below gradde	M or S
Masonry other than above	M, S, or N

* For design wind pressures, see section on Design Loads

inforced masonry that is subject to high compressive loads, severe frost action, or high lateral forces. Because of its durability, it is specifically recommended for unreinforced masonry below grade and for masonry in contact with the earth such as foundation walls, retaining walls, walks, sewers, and manholes.

Type S mortar has reasonably high compressive strength. Tests indicate that the tensile bond strength with brick approaches the maximum attainable with cement-lime mortars. It is recommended for use in reinforced masonry, for unreinforced masonry where maximum flexural strength is required, and for use where mortar adhesion is the sole bonding agent between facing and backing as with ceramic veneers.

Type N mortar is a medium strength mortar suitable for general use in exposed masonry above grade. It is highly recommended for parapet walls, chimneys, and exterior walls subjected to severe exposure.

Type O mortar is a low strength mortar suitable for general interior use in non-load bearing masonry. It is never recommended in masonry potentially subject to freezing. Because of its high lime content it has excellent workability and therefore is the favorite among masons.

Masonry accessories

Accessory items are an integral part of masonry construction. Horizontal joint reinforcement, metal anchors, metal ties, anchor bolts, flashing materials, and control or expansion joint materials all are part of good masonry construction. Steel is most frequently used, and it must be galvanized or coated in order to protect it from corrosion. Caused by oxidation corrosion, requires careful consideration for all accessories used in masonry construction.

Horizontal joint reinforcement is used primarily to control shrinkage cracks in the masonry. It is also used to tie multiple wythes of masonry together and to anchor masonry veneer. Horizontal joint reinforcement consists of two or more longitudinal wires, 9 gauge or slightly larger, with 12-gauge cross wires welded to the longitudinal wires. Two basic types are produced: a ladder type and a trussed type. The ladder type has the cross wires welded at 90 degrees to the longitudinal wires and spaced at about 16 in. The trussed type has cross wires bent like webs of a truss with the bend welded to the longitudinal wires. Both types have several variations. The longitudinal wires are laid in the mortar joint along the faces of the masonry. The cross wires should also be embedded in mortar over the webs of the masonry. **Fig. 9** shows a plan view of typical joint reinforcement, and **Fig. 10** shows a plan view of adjustable joint reinforcement. Joint reinforcement needs to turn corners (Fig. 30 shows one illustration of that condition).

Masonry anchors secure the masonry wall to its structural support such as beams, columns, or another wall. Examples are shown in the construction details in **Figs. 11** through **14**. Masonry ties connect masonry wythes together or connect a veneer to a backup wall of some other material, such as a stud wall. Several unit tie details are illustrated in

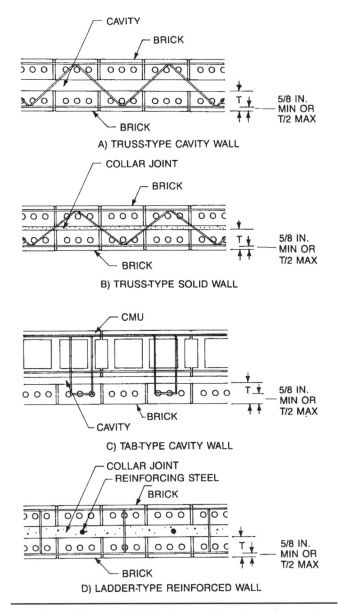

Fig. 9. Joint reinforcement details. (Source: Brick Institute of America)

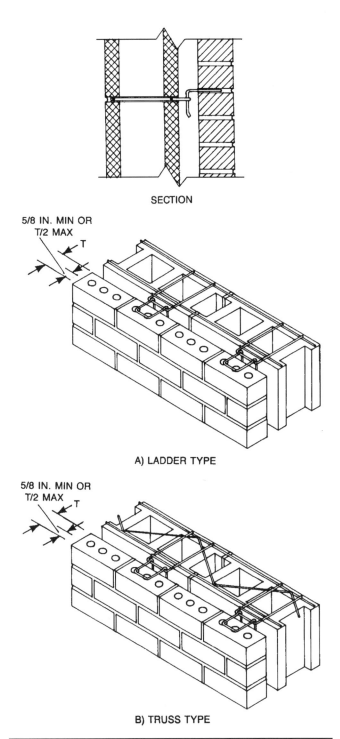

Fig. 10. Adjustable assembly details. (Source: Brick Institute of America)

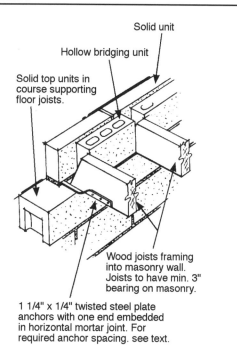

Solid unit

Hollow bridging unit

Solid top units in course supporting floor joists.

Wood joists framing into masonry wall. Joists to have min. 3" bearing on masonry.

1 1/4" x 1/4" twisted steel plate anchors with one end embedded in horizontal mortar joint. For required anchor spacing. see text.

Fig. 11. Anchoring wood joists to masonry wall.

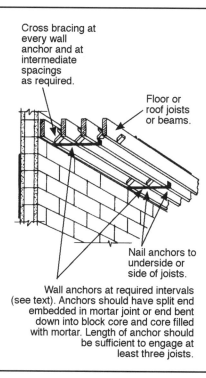

Cross bracing at every wall anchor and at intermediate spacings as required.

Floor or roof joists or beams.

Nail anchors to underside or side of joists.

Wall anchors at required intervals (see text). Anchors should have split end embedded in mortar joint or end bent down into block core and core filled with mortar. Length of anchor should be sufficient to engage at least three joists.

Fig. 13. Anchoring parallel joists to masonry wall.

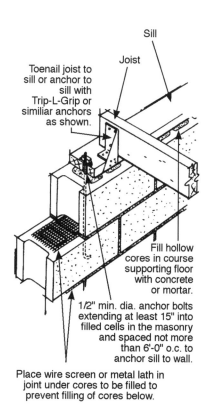

Sill

Joist

Toenail joist to sill or anchor to sill with Trip-L-Grip or similiar anchors as shown.

Fill hollow cores in course supporting floor with concrete or mortar.

1/2" min. dia. anchor bolts extending at least 15" into filled cells in the masonry and spaced not more than 6'-0" o.c. to anchor sill to wall.

Place wire screen or metal lath in joint under cores to be filled to prevent filling of cores below.

Fig. 12. Anchoring wood sill to foundation.

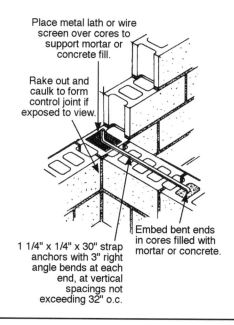

Place metal lath or wire screen over cores to support mortar or concrete fill.

Rake out and caulk to form control joint if exposed to view.

Embed bent ends in cores filled with mortar or concrete.

1 1/4" x 1/4" x 30" strap anchors with 3" right angle bends at each end, at vertical spacings not exceeding 32" o.c.

Fig. 14. Anchorage of intersecting bearing walls.

Fig. 15. Adjustable unit tie details are referenced in **Fig. 16.** Masonry fasteners are used to attach other building elements to the masonry such as the case where wood furring strips are secured to a masonry wall.

All metal accessories must be galvanized and spaced at intervals that are recommended by industry standards. In masonry veneers attached to a reinforced concrete frame building, steel shelf angles will support the masonry vertically at one floor level and at the next level the masonry connection should be one that supports lateral loads only. Above the lateral connection, a soft masonry joint is necessary to accommodate any differential movements within the veneer and the supporting structure. A variety of construction details are included in **Figs. 17** through **29** to depict different applications of masonry being used as panel walls connected to other structural frames or as bearing walls in relation to foundations, floors, and roofs.

Figs. 30 through **32** suggest versions of control joints in masonry walls. A control joint is used in masonry to create a plane of weakness that controls the location of cracks due to shrinkage and creep. Control joints are located so that the structural integrity of the masonry is not impaired.

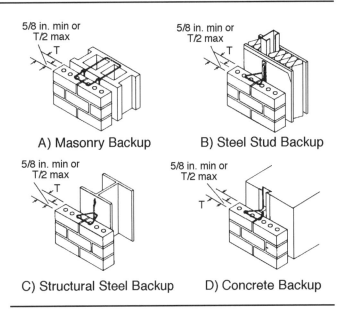

Fig. 16. Adjustable unit tie details. (Source: Brick Institute of America)

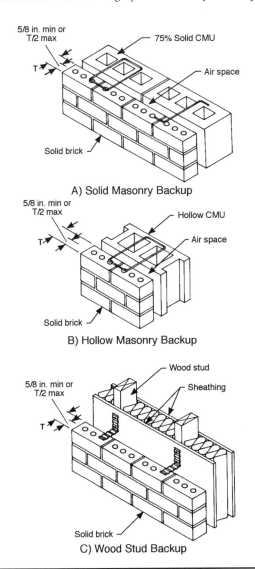

Fig. 15. Unit tie details. (Source: Brick Institute of America)

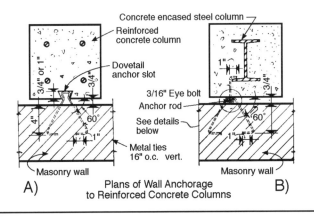

Fig. 17. Plans of wall anchorage to reinforced concrete columns.

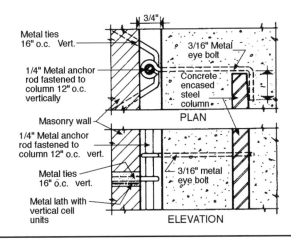

Fig. 18. Wall anchorage details.

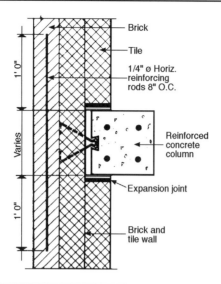

Fig. 19. Column partially enclosed in masonry.

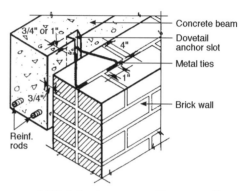

a) Wall Anchorage to Concrete Beam

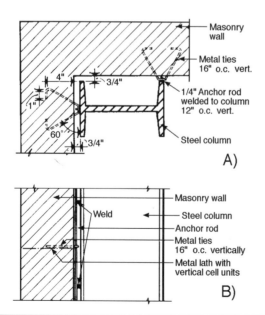

Fig. 20. Wall anchorage to steel column: (a) plan; (b) elevation.

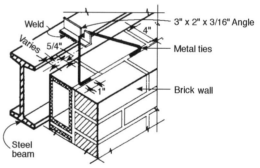

b) Wall Anchorage to Steel Beam

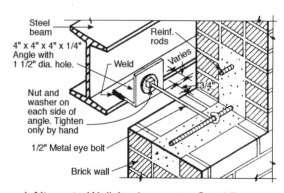

c) Alternate Wall Anchorage to Steel Beam

Fig. 21. Typical beam-wall anchorage: (a) wall anchorage to concrete beam; (b) wall anchorage to steel beam; (c) alternate wall anchorage to steel beam.

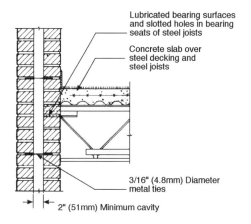

Fig. 22. Anchorage of steel floor joists.

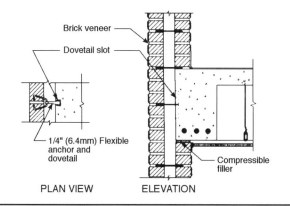

PLAN VIEW   ELEVATION

Fig. 23. Flexible anchorage to concrete frame.

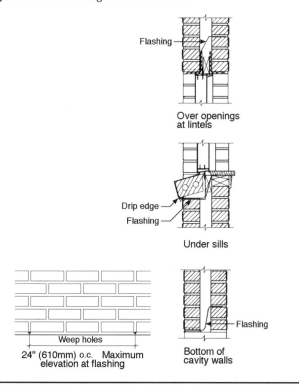

Over openings
at lintels

Under sills

Bottom of
cavity walls

24" (610mm) o.c. Maximum
elevation at flashing

Fig. 24. Flashing and weep holes.

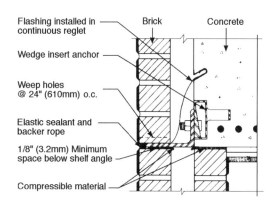

Fig. 25. Steel shelf angles.

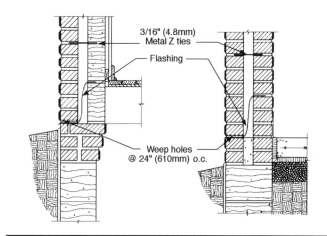

Fig. 26. Foundation details.

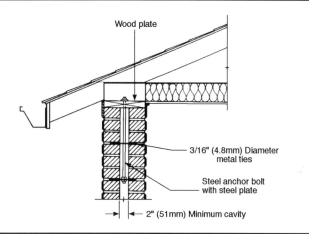

Fig. 27. Anchorage of wood roof framing.

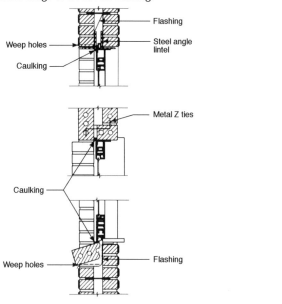

Fig. 28. Commercial metal window.

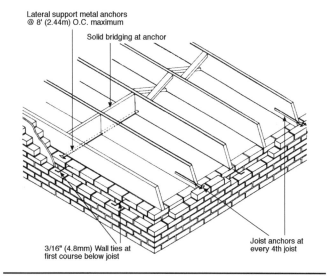

Fig. 29. Anchorage of wood floor framing.

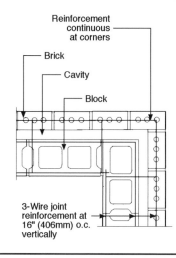

Fig. 30. Horizontal wall reinforcement at corner.

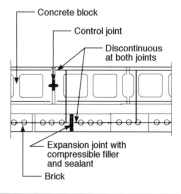

Fig. 31. Masonry control joint detail.

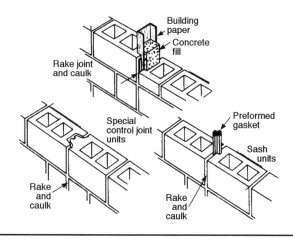

Fig. 32. Typical control joint details.

3 STRUCTURAL DESIGN OF MASONRY

Masonry is construction that provides excellent compressive strength. Its usual mass and weight creates an opportunity for its compressive strength to be emphasized in forms and structures dependent on that property. Even though it is a brittle construction element, masonry does have a small tensile strength but not enough to rely on as a principal stress. Whether brick, concrete block, stone or glass, the basic unit is stronger in compression than the composite structural element as units are bonded together with mortar joints. The skill required to construct a well-crafted masonry wall is very important to the structural integrity of a building.

Codes distinguish methods of structural analysis as engineered masonry design and empirical design. The latter format allows traditional approaches based on historical experience. Although experience is an asset in the design of any structure, empirical design of masonry structures uses conservative allowable stresses that underestimate the real strength of quality material and construction methods.

Engineered masonry is further distinguished for unreinforced and reinforced masonry. Obviously the major distinction is whether tensile reinforcement is required to maintain the integrity of the structural elements. By current codes, the design and analysis of structural elements and systems rely on the *allowable stress design* (ASD) method. Accordingly, structures and their component members are designed by elastic analysis using service loads and allowable stresses.

Together with the allowable stress design method the actual working section of masonry that is carrying load must be distinguished from the gross section that has voids as the products are manufactured. Furthermore not all webs have mortar between units. Details and specifications must be clear about gross section and the net section that is actually providing the strength and transmitting load. **Figs. 33** and **34** convey the idea about determining the net section for various types of walls, some grouted, some solid, and some hollow.

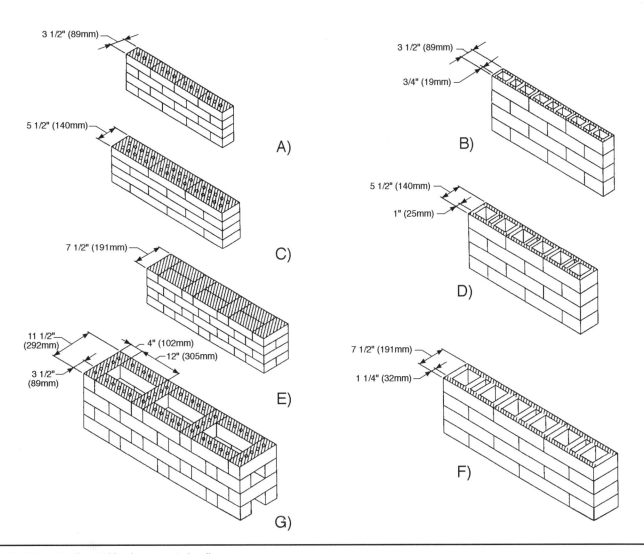

Fig. 33. Net section for axial load—ungrouted walls.

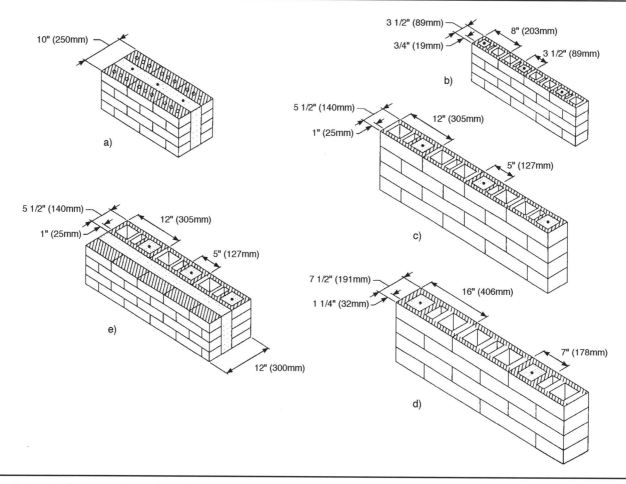

Fig. 34. Net section for axial load—grouted walls.

General Criteria

General criteria for clay masonry and concrete masonry includes considerations regarding loads and materials. Load combinations that must be considered to determine the governing conditions of design are as follows:

1. D   where: D = dead load or related internal moments and forces

2. D + L   L = live load or related internal moments and forces

3. D + L + (W or E)[1]   W = wind load or related internal moments and forces

4. D + W[1]   E = load effects of earthquake or related internal moments and forces

5. 0.9D + E[1]   H = lateral pressure of soil or related internal moments and forces

6. D + L + (H or F)   F = lateral pressure of liquids or related internal moments and forces

7. D + (H or F)

8. D + L + T   where T = load due to movements from thermal changes

9. D + T

NOTE 1: Allowable stresses may be increased by $\frac{1}{3}$ when considering this load combination.

Material Properties: General material properties that must be considered to determine the applicable specified materials are indicated in **Tables 4** and **5**.

Engineered design of unreinforced masonry— Allowable stress criteria

Axial compression and flexure:

$$f_a \leq F_a$$

$$f_b \leq F_b$$

$$P \leq 0.25 \, P_e$$

$$F_a = 0.25 \, f'_m \, [1 - (h/140r)^2] \text{ for } h/r \leq 99$$

$$F_a = 0.25 \, f'_m \, (70 \, r/h)^2 \text{ for } h/r \geq 99$$

$$F_b = 0.33 \, f'_m$$

$$P_e = (\pi^2 \, E_m \, I/h^2) \, (1 - 0.577 \, e/r)^3$$

$$(f_a/F_a) + (f_b/F_b) \leq 1$$

where:
- e = eccentricity of axial load, in
- f_a = calculated axial compressive stress, psi
- F_a = allowable axial compressive stress, psi
- f_b = calculated flexure compressive stress, psi
- F_b = allowable flexure compressive stress, psi
- f'_m = specified compressive stress of masonry, psi
- h = effective height of a column or wall, in
- I = moment of inertia, masonry net section, in^4
- P = design axial load, lbs
- P_e = Euler buckling load, lbs
- r = radius of gyration, in

Shear: in-plane shear shall not exceed any of:

$$F_v \leq v + 0.45 \, N_v/A_n$$

$$F_v \leq 1.5 \, \sqrt{f'_m}$$

$$F_v \leq 120 \text{ psi}$$

where:
- A_n = net cross section area of masonry, in^2
- F_v = allowable shear stress in masonry, psi
- N_v = force acting normal to shear stress, lbs
- v = shear stress of masonry in running bond, psi
  - 37 psi for partially grouted masonry
  - 60 psi for solid grouted masonry

Allowable flexural tension **(Table 6)**

Engineered design of reinforced masonry— allowable stress criteria

Reinforced masonry construction requires special consideration of the placement of the unit masonry, the placement of the steel reinforcing rods both vertically and horizontally, and the grout which fills and bonds all the pieces together to create an effective structural wall. Vertical reinforcement is placed in aligned cores, which must have potential for grout to surround the steel rod and yet bond with the masonry units. The running mortar joints are limited in size, thereby creating the need to detail the horizontal reinforcing in appropriately fashioned longitudinal joints that must be filled with grout. **Figs. 35** to **40** identify a few examples of reinforced masonry construction. More complete information is available in the references noted.

Axial compression and flexure:

$$P_a = (0.25 \, f'_m \, A_n + 0.65 \, A_{st} \, F_s) \, [1 - (h/140r)^2] \text{ for } h/r \leq 99$$

Table 4. Clay Masonry

Net area compressive strength of units, psi	Moduli of Elasticity, E_m, psi x 10^6		
	Type N mortar	Type S mortar	Type M mortar
12,000 and up	2.8	3.0	3.0
10,000	2.4	2.9	3.0
8,000	2.0	2.4	2.8
6,000	1.6	1.9	2.2
4,000	1.2	1.4	1.6
2,000	0.8	0.9	1.0

Table 5. Concrete Masonry

Net area compressive strength of units, psi	Moduli of Elasticity, E_m, psi x 10^6	
	Type N mortar	Type M mortar
6,000 and up	-	3.5
5,000	2.8	3.2
4,000	2.6	2.9
3,000	2.3	2.5
2,500	2.2	2.4
2,000	1.8	2.2
1,500	1.5	1.6

Modulus of elasticity, steel $E_s = 29,000,000$ psi
Modulus of elasticity, grout $E_g = 500 \, f_g$
Thermal expansion coefficients:
    Clay masonry, $k_t = 4 \times 10^{-6}$ in/in/degree F
    Concrete masonry, $k_c = 4.5 \times 10^{-6}$ in/in/degree F
Shrinkage coefficients:
    Concrete masonry, $k_m = 0.15 \, s_l$, where s_l is not more than 6.5×10^{-4} in/in
Moisture expansion coefficients:
    Clay masonry, $k_e = 3 \times 10^{-4}$ in/in
Creep coefficients:
    Clay masonry, $k_c = 0.7 \times 10^{-7}$ per psi
    Concrete masonry, $k_c = 2.5 \times 10^{-7}$ per psi

Table 6. Allowable flexural tension, F_b, psi

Masonry type	Portland cement/lime mortar		Masonry cement mortar	
	M or S	N	M or S	N
Normal to bed joints				
Solid units	40	30	24	15
Hollow units[1]				
Ungrouted	25	19	15	9
Fully grouted	68	58	41	26
Parallel to bed joints in running bond				
Solid units	80	60	48	30
Hollow units				
Ungrouted	50	38	30	19
Partially grouted	50	38	30	19
Fully grouted	80	60	48	30

[1]. For partially grouted masonry, allowable stresses shall be determined on the basis of linear interpolation between hollow units that are fully grouted or ungrouted and hollow units based on amount of grouting.

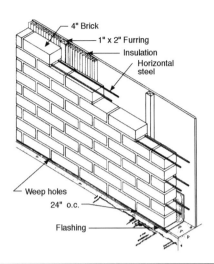

Fig. 35. Isometric of 4-in reinforced brick curtain wall with furring, insulation, and interior finish.

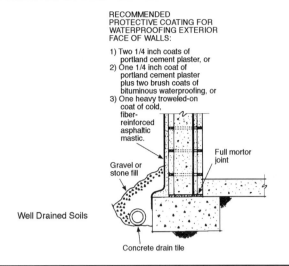

Well Drained Soils

Fig. 38. Typical footing detail.

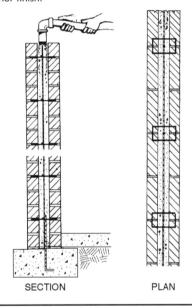

SECTION   PLAN

Fig. 36. "High-lift" grouted reinforced masonry wall.

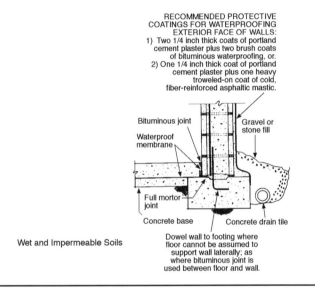

Wet and Impermeable Soils

Fig. 39. Footing detail for very wet soil.

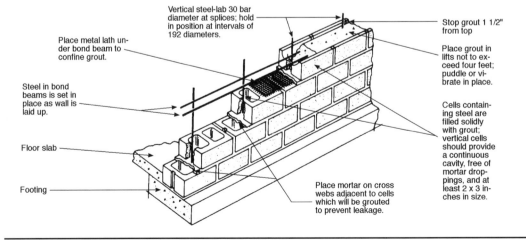

Fig. 37. Typical reinforced concrete masonry construction.

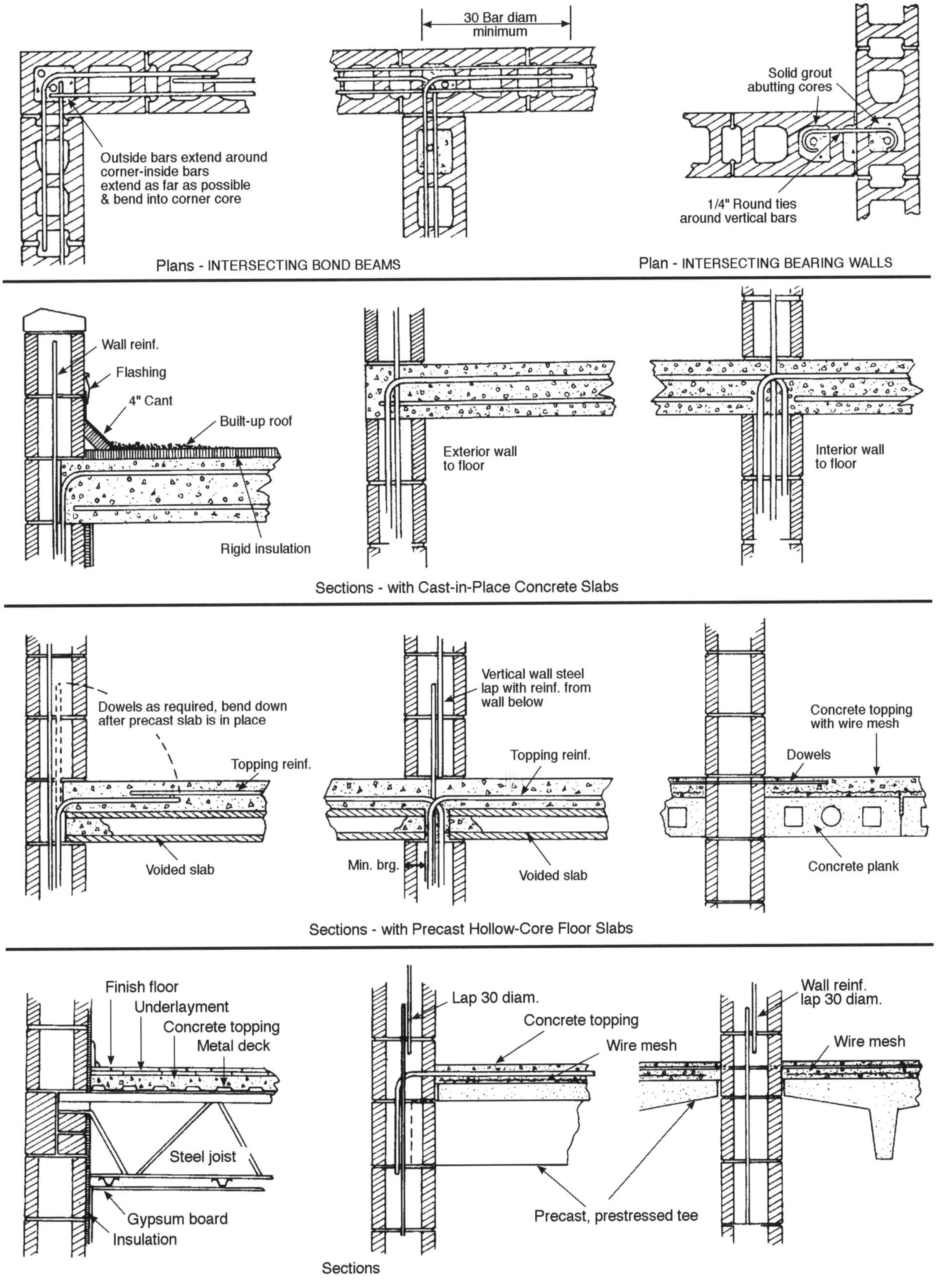

Outside bars extend around corner-inside bars extend as far as possible & bend into corner core

30 Bar diam minimum

Solid grout abutting cores

1/4" Round ties around vertical bars

Plans - INTERSECTING BOND BEAMS

Plan - INTERSECTING BEARING WALLS

Wall reinf.
Flashing
4" Cant
Built-up roof
Rigid insulation

Exterior wall to floor

Interior wall to floor

Sections - with Cast-in-Place Concrete Slabs

Dowels as required, bend down after precast slab is in place
Topping reinf.
Voided slab

Vertical wall steel lap with reinf. from wall below
Topping reinf.
Min. brg.
Voided slab

Concrete topping with wire mesh
Dowels
Concrete plank

Sections - with Precast Hollow-Core Floor Slabs

Finish floor
Underlayment
Concrete topping
Metal deck
Steel joist
Gypsum board
Insulation

Lap 30 diam.
Concrete topping
Wire mesh
Precast, prestressed tee

Wall reinf. lap 30 diam.
Wire mesh

Sections

Fig. 40. Construction details, reinforced concrete masonry.

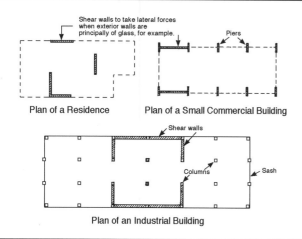

Fig. 41. Reinforced masonry shear walls.

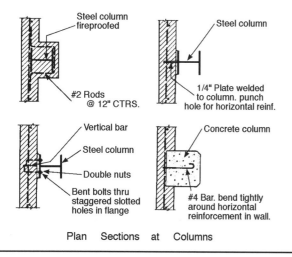

Fig. 42. Attachment of reinforced masonry shear walls to structural column.

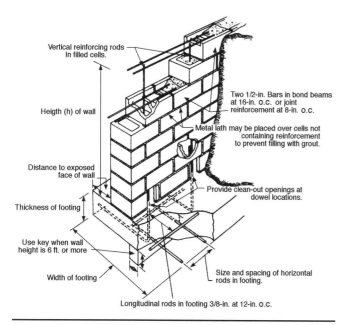

Fig. 43. Reinforced concrete masonry retaining wall.

$$P_a = (0.25 \, f\,'_m \, A_n + 0.65 \, A_{st} \, F_s)(70 \, r/h)^2 \text{ for } h/r \le 99$$

$$F_b = 0.33 \, f\,'_m$$

where: A_{st} = total area of longitudinal reinforcing steel, in^2

d = distance from extreme compression fiber to centroid of tensile reinforcement, in

F_s = allowable tensile or compressive stress in reinforcing steel, psi

M = maximum moment at point of shear design, in lbs

P_a = maximum allowable compressive force in reinforced masonry due to axial force, lbs

V = design shear force, lbs

Shear:

Flexural member $F_v \le \sqrt{f\,'_m}$, with 50 psi max.

Shear wall (M/Vd v 1) $F_v \le 0.33 \, [4 - (M/Vd)\sqrt{f\,'_m}$, with $80 - 45 \, (V/Md)$ max.

Shear wall (M/Vd y 1) $F_v \le \sqrt{f\,'_m}$, with 35 psi max.

Tension in reinforcement:

Grade 40 or 50 $F_s = 20,000$ psi

Grade 60 $F_s = 24,000$ psi

Joint reinforcement $F_s = 30,000$ psi

All of these criteria must be translated into actual structural members that have strength, proportion, and stability. The basic requirements of axial stress, bending stress, shear and deflection are fundamental to the design of structural components. The building's structural system must function as a whole structure that has strength and stability yet compatibility with the architectural requirements. The references contain charts and guides that help to gain insight regarding size and proportion of members. This information is useful for preliminary evaluations about the relationship of structural strength and form to architectural design development.

When reinforced masonry walls have the potential to resist lateral forces on a building, these walls are referred to as shear walls. Schematic plans are suggested in **Fig. 41.** Such walls must be tied to the structural frame so that forces may be transmitted through the frame and applied to the shear walls. **Fig. 42** depicts typical connections to columns. Similar connections to beams in the system may be required.

Retaining walls

Reinforced masonry may be used for retaining walls. The masonry unit may be concrete block with filled cores, as shown in **Fig. 43,** or brick with a grouted cavity, as shown in **Fig. 44.** The brick with grouted cavity type is recommended for low retaining walls. A 10 in thick reinforced brick wall with grouted cavity has the capacity to retain earth up to a height of 6 ft. By comparison, a 12 in thick reinforced concrete masonry retaining wall, with reinforcement in grouted cores, may be designed for a height of about 8 ft. Beyond these heights for retaining earth, reinforced concrete is more efficient structurally and it may be built with a masonry veneer. All walls must be properly capped to prevent the entry of water into any voids of the masonry.

Provision should be made to prevent accumulation of water behind a retaining wall. Recommended are 4 in diameter weep holes located at 5 to 10 ft spacing. The backfill behind the retaining wall should be gravel and granular material so that water may drain away from the wall.

Waterproofing the back face of the retaining wall is recommended in locations of severe frost and heavy rainfall. During construction of a reinforced masonry retaining wall, backfill should be accomplished until at least seven days after grouting. Heavy surcharges of force should be avoided.

Lintels

A lintel is a horizontal beam placed over a wall opening to carry the load in the wall above it. Lintels may be structural steel, reinforced masonry, or reinforced concrete. Historically, arches, including flat arches, were alternative options. Structural steel lintels are common lintels for masonry walls. Steel angles are the simplest shapes to accommodate the masonry and still provide strength to carry moderate loads. For heavier loads, I-beams or channels together with steel plates may be selected options (refer to **Fig. 46**). The outstanding leg of the angle or plate should be 3-½ in to support a nominal 4 in masonry wythe.

The determination of the load to be carried by the lintel is illustrated in **Fig. 45**. The weight of the masonry above the lintel is assumed as the weight of a triangular section whose height is one-half the clear span of the opening. To the dead load of the wall must be added the uniform dead and live loads of floors and roofs that frame into the wall above the opening and below the apex of a 45-degree triangle. Assessment of this load may be completed by comparing the dimensions D and L/2 in Fig. 45. Concentrated loads from beams framing into the wall above may be distributed over the wall from the edge of the beam's bearing on the wall projected at a 60-degree angle.

The lintel's bearing area must be determined in accordance with the allowable masonry stresses permitted for compressive axial load. Deflection of the lintel must be limited to L/600 where L is the span of the lintel in inches. Refer to **Figs. 46** and **47** for one sample detail of a reinforced masonry lintel. In order to reduce the potential for cracks occurring at the corners of openings, reinforcement is often installed as shown in the elevation of **Fig. 48**. This reinforcement is best accomplished with the installation of reinforced masonry structural lintels and in conjunction with reinforced masonry walls. Further data for common lintel sizes and capacities is available in the industry's resources.

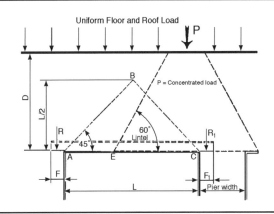

Fig. 45. Computing loads on a lintel.

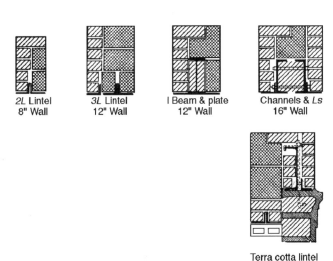

Fig. 46. Reinforced brick lintel in cavity wall.

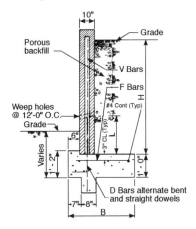

Fig. 44. Section through typical low, reinforced brick masonry retaining wall.

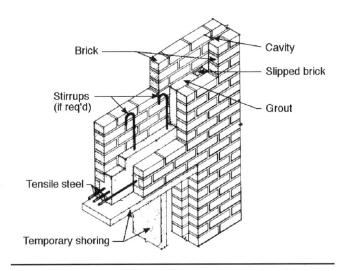

Fig. 47. Reinforced brick lintel in cavity wall.

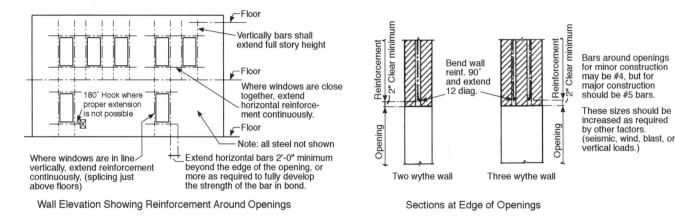

Wall Elevation Showing Reinforcement Around Openings

Sections at Edge of Openings

Fig. 48. Typical reinforcement around wall openings.

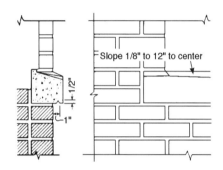

Fig. 49. Sill detail to prevent wash.

4 BRICK MASONRY TREATMENTS

The formation of efflorescence is from water-soluble salts migrating to the surface of the masonry. As water evaporates the salts show up as white deposits. The way to eliminate efflorescence is to reduce all contributing factors to a minimum. The following procedures are recommended as a means to that end.

1. Reduce the amount of soluble salts in the masonry materials by:

– Specifying that all wall facing and trim materials pass a "wick test" for efflorescence.

– Testing mortar for efflorescence.

2. Prevent contact between facing and backup by use of cavity-wall construction or flashing.

3. Keep moisture out of wall by use of:

– Hard-burned brick or tile facing.

– Cavity-wall or solid metal-tied wall construction.

– Good workmanship (all joints thoroughly filled).

– Protection of the tops of walls during construction.

– Projecting sills and copings, with drip slots underneath (**Fig. 49**).

– Flashing, especially at all intersections of wall and roof, under all horizontal elements such as copings and sills, and just above finished grade, to prevent rise of moisture by capillarity from the foundation.

– Caulking, carefully applied, around all door and window frames.

– Vapor barrier and ventilation to prevent condensation within walls.

Cleaning

Improper cleaning irreparably damages many new buildings. The most common causes of such damage are:

1. Failure to saturate masonry before application of cleaning agent;

2. Use of too strong acid solution;

3. Failure to protect windows and trim.

It is recommended that any cleaning agent be tried first on a sample wall, using a minimum area of 20 sq ft, and left for at least a week.

To clean unglazed masonry surfaces, remove large particles with a wood paddle and saturate the surface with water. Apply a 10% solution of muriatic acid, not more than 1 part acid to 9 parts water, to an area of not more than 15 to 20 sq ft. Then wash the surface with clear water.

To cut labor costs, high-pressure water is sometimes used; nozzle pressures range between 400 and 700 psi at a flow rate of 3 to 8 gal/min. Two hoses may be used: one with cleaning solution, the other with plain water. Dry sandblasting is also sometimes used.

To clean glazed surfaces, scrub with soap and water only. Use no acid and no metal scrapers on glazed surfaces.

Efflorescence can usually be removed with soap and water and a stiff scrubbing brush. If necessary, use dilute muriatic acid, as described above. A type of efflorescence known as "green stain" may be caused by the action of muriatic acid on some types of masonry. Since this type cannot be foreseen it is important to make a preliminary test on a sample wall. Green stain is difficult to remove: try oxalic acid, 2 lb per 5 gal of water, brushed or sprayed on and washed off after several hours. If necessary follow with sodium hydroxide, such as one 12-oz can of "Drano" per qt of water, applied liberally with paintbrush and hosed off after three days.

Methods for cleaning old buildings are listed in order of frequency of use as follows:

1. High-pressure steam—best for relatively impervious facing materials.

2. Sandblasting—used mostly on porous materials such as limestone, sandstone, and unglazed brick; cannot be used on glazed or polished surfaces.

3. Hand washing—expensive; used only on small buildings.

4. High-pressure cold water—good if there is ample water supply and suitable method of disposing of waste.

5. Chemical and steam—used for removing coatings such as paint.

Before deciding to clean an old building, consider carefully whether it is advisable. The "dirt" may be simply weathered masonry, not accumulated deposits, and the cleaning process may remove the actual surface of the masonry.

Stain removal

The removal of stains, such as those caused by rust, smoke, copper, oil, and the like, requires special treatment appropriate to the type of stain and the type of masonry. See *Technical Notes on Brick Construction No. 20 Revised*, published by the Brick Institute of America.

Painting

Paints are applied to masonry walls for decorative effect and as a barrier to rain penetration. They must not, however, prevent the wall from "breathing," that is, prevent moisture within the wall from escaping by evaporation from the surface. Cement-based paints and water-thinned emulsion paints are highly permeable to water vapor and are recommended for exterior use. New masonry walls to be painted should not be cleaned with acid.

Cement-based paint should be applied to a wall only after it has cured for at least a month and has been dampened thoroughly by spraying. Apply heavy coats with a stiff brush, allowing at least 24 hours between coats. During this time and for several days after the final coat, keep the wall damp by periodic spraying. Water-thinned emulsion paints, commonly called latex paints, can be applied to damp, uncured walls; since they are quick-drying, additional coats can be applied without waiting. Polyvinyl acetate and acrylic emulsions are generally the most satisfactory of the water-thinned paints.

Solvent-thinned paints should be applied only to completely dry, clean surfaces. Oil-based and alkyd paints are nonpermeable and are not recommended for exterior masonry. Oil-based paints are highly susceptible to alkalides, and new masonry must be thoroughly neutralized before being painted; zinc chloride or zinc sulfate solution, 2 to 3-½ lb/gal of water, is often used for this purpose. Several days of drying are usually required between coats. Synthetic rubber and chlorinated rubber paints can be applied to damp, alkaline surfaces, and can be used on exterior masonry.

Waterproofing

Silicones are widely used for waterproofing, or more correctly damp-proofing, masonry walls. Without actually sealing openings, silicones retard water absorption by creating a negative capillarity that repels water. Silicones may be water-based or solvent-based and may be applied by brush or spray. Normally, silicones cause no perceptible color change, but they sometimes bleach artificially colored mortar. They penetrate the masonry to a depth of ⅛ to ¼ in, and their effective life is from 5 to 10 years. Foundation walls below grade should be waterproofed with one or preferably two coats of Portland cement mortar (1 : 1-½); after curing, apply hot bituminous coating or a cold asphalt emulsion coating.

Coatings for concrete masonry

Fill coats. Fill coats or primer-sealers are used to fill the voids in porous concrete masonry and on coarse-textured masonry before the application of finish coats. Fill coats contain regular Portland cement as a binder and finely graded siliceous sand filler. An alternate product is acrylic latex or polyvinyl acetate latex combined with the Portland cement binder. Fill coats are applied by brushing the material into the voids of the surface. Skilled workmanship is necessary for successful results. Those fill coats that do not contain latex require application to a moist surface and moist curing for hydration of the Portland cement constituent. The fillers containing latex do not require moist curing because the latex retards evaporation of moisture, thereby making it available for hydration of the cement binder.

Portland cement paints. These paints are sold in powdered form in a variety of colors and are mixed with water just before use. They are produced in standard and heavy-duty types. The standard type contains a minimum of 65 percent Portland cement by weight and is suitable for general use. The heavy-duty type contains 80 percent Portland cement and is used where there is excessive and continuous contact with moisture, such as in swimming pools. Each type is available with a siliceous sand additive for use as a filler on porous surfaces. Portland cement paints set by hydration of the cement, which bonds to the masonry surface. The paints are applied to moist surfaces by stiff brush. The surface is dampened by fine water spray for 48 to 72 hours until the cement cures. Portland cement paints contain little organic material and are not subject to attack from alkali found in new concrete. They have a history of success in waterproofing masonry when properly applied and cured.

Latex paints. Latex paints, inherently resistant to alkali, are made of water emulsions of resinous materials. They dry throughout as soon as the water of emulsion has evaporated, usually within 1 to 2 hours. Styrene-butadiene is one of the original synthetic chemical coatings and is still in use. Other latex coatings such as polyvinyl acetate and acrylic resin are presently in greater demand and are also available as clear coatings for colorless applications. All latex paints are available as opaque coatings. Latex paints may be applied to damp or dry surfaces and require no curing. Although acrylic latex is somewhat higher in cost than the other latex waterproofing materials, it has demonstrated superior resistance to penetration by rain and shown greater overall durability.

Oil-base paints. Oil-base paints are manufactured from natural oil resins or synthetic alkyd resins. Similar to conventional house paints, the oil-base paints designed for use on masonry are usually reinforced by certain resins to improve their resistance to alkali. They may be applied by brush, roller, or spray. A dry masonry surface is required at the time of application, and the effective alkalinity of the surface must be reduced through aging the masonry or application of surface pretreatment. Oil-base paints that are subjected to dampness from within the masonry may fail from blistering and peeling.

Epoxy coatings. These coatings are based on epoxy or urethane resins to which a catalyst is added just before application. The epoxies are highly resistant to alkali and form an impervious film. Outdoor exposure of epoxy paints results in chalking, which must be removed by washing with soap and water to restore the original appearance. The high cost of the material and difficulty experienced in application has limited the use of epoxies to specialized requirements. They are not recommended for general use on concrete masonry.

Silicone-based coatings. Silicone is a colorless resinous material produced by a synthetic process from silicon dioxide. When applied to masonry surfaces, silicone-based coatings do not cause a change in color or texture. Without actually sealing openings, silicones retard water absorption by changing the contact angle between water and the walls of capillary pores in the masonry. Silicones do not bridge large openings; therefore, fill coats are desirable on coarse-textured masonry. Application of silicone-based coatings is commonly accomplished by flooding the surface with a low-pressure spray head.

Bituminous coatings. These coatings are produced from coal tar or asphalt and are furnished in solid form to be melted for hot application. They are also available in liquid form, either diluted in solvent or emulsified with water, for application at normal temperature. Hot application of bituminous coatings may be made alone or in combination with felt or other reinforcing fabric to form a built-up membrane. Where considerable hydrostatic pressure is exerted upon the coating, the built-up membrane has the distinct advantage of main-taining continuity of waterproofing over possible imperfections in the wall. The low cost and excellent resistance to penetration of water favor the use of bituminous coatings where appearance is not important, such as below-grade portions of basement walls.

Cold weather construction

With special provisions, masonry construction in cold weather is a wide-adopted practice throughout the northern United States and Canada. The advantages of early occupancy, and the reduction of construction time, more than compensate for the additional cost of special provisions including heating of the construction area. The recommendations outlined below call for supplementary heat when the daily mean temperature is 20F (–7°C) or lower.

A clear distinction should be made between cold weather concreting and masonry construction. Generally, concrete is placed in forms that absorb little water from the concrete and prevent evaporation into the atmosphere. By contrast, in masonry construction, thin layers of mortar are placed between thicker absorbent units that absorb water from the mortar and stiffen it. The degree of saturation of the mortar is therefore lowered and the water-cement ratio is reduced. Hence little water is actually left to freeze in the mortar and cause damage by expansion.

The International Masonry Industry All-Weather Council has issued Guide Specifications for Cold Weather Masonry Construction, the principal provisions of which are summarized as follows:

– All materials must be delivered dry and kept fully covered at all times.

– Brick units should be more absorbent than those used in normal construction.

– Before placement, absorbent brick should be sprinkled with heated water above 70F if the units (that is, ambient conditions) are above 32F (0°C) and rising, and with water heated above 130F (55°C) when ambient conditions are below 32F and lowering.

– Type S or Type M mortar is recommended, or the use of mortar made with Type III Portland cement, high early strength.

– Sand, if frozen, must be heated before mixing. Ideal mortar temperature is 80F (27°C). The mixing temperature selected should be maintained within 10 percent.

– Admixtures in general, and antifreezes in particular, are not recommended.

– Accelerators, such as calcium chloride, may be used up to a maximum of 2 percent of the Portland cement by weight provided that the masonry does not contain metal, which is severely corroded by the salt.

– Coloring pigments should be limited to 10 percent (carbon black to 2 percent) of the cement content by weight; they may retard the setting of the mortar, an undesirable effect in cold weather construction.

– Masonry must not be laid on a frozen or snow- or ice-covered bed. Such a bed must be heated until it is dry to the touch.

– Masonry damaged by freezing must be removed before continuing construction.

Construction enclosures may be of many types. Small buildings are often completely enclosed in a tent or inflated structure. A simple type of scaffold enclosure is shown in **Fig. 50.** A digest of recommendations for cold-weather construction is listed in **Table 7.** ■

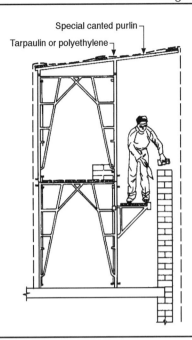

Special canted purlin ⌐
Tarpaulin or polyethylene ⌐

Fig. 50. Scafford-type enclosure.

Table 7. Summary of recommendations for cold weather construction

Temperature* F	Construction	Protection
40-32	Heat sand or mixing water to produce mortar temperatures between 40°and 120 F.	Protect top of masonry from rain or snow by waterproof membrane extending down sides a minimum of 2 ft for 24 hr.
32-24	Heat sand and water to produce mortar temperatures between 40° and 120 F. Maintain temperatures of	Cover masonry completely with waterproof membrane for 24 hr.
25-20	Heat sand and water to pruduce mortar temperatures between 40° and 120 F. Maintain mortar temperatures on boards above freezing. Provide supplementary heat on both sides of walls. Provide windbreaks when wind is over 15 mph (Table 76).	Cover masonry completely with insulating blankets for 24 hr.
20 and below	Heat sand and water to provide mortar temperatures between 40° and 120 F. Provide enclosure and supplementary heat to maintain air temperature above 32 F. Temperature of units when laid shall be not less than 20 F.	Maintain masonry temperatures above 32 F for 24 hr. by enclosure and supplementary heat supplied by electric blankets, infrared lamps, or other methods.

*Air temperature at time of construction, and mean daily air temperature during period of protection.

REFERENCES

American Concrete Institute (ACI), American Society of Civil Engineers (ASCE), and The Masonry Society (TMS), *Building Code Requirements for Masonry Structures* (ACI 530-95/ASCE 5-95/TMS 602-95); and *Specifications for Masonry Structures* (ACI 530.1-95/ASCE 6-95/TMS 602–95), American Concrete Institute, Detroit, MI, 1995.

Beall, Christine, *Masonry Design and Detailing for Architects, Engineers and Builders,* Prentice-Hall, Englewood Cliffs, NJ, 1994.

Brick Institute of America (BIA), *Technical Notes on Brick Construction,* Brick Institute of America, Reston, VA, 1996.

International Masonry Institute, *Masonry Bibliography: 1830–1982; Masonry Bibliography, Volume II: 1983–1987; Masonry Bibliography, Volume III: 1987–1990,* International Masonry Institute, Washington, DC, 1991.

National Concrete Masonry Association (NCMA), *TEK Manual for Concrete Masonry Design and Construction,* National Concrete Masonry Institute, Herndon, VA, 1996.

Orton, Andrew, *Structural Design of Masonry,* John Wiley & Sons, New York, NY, 1992.

Portland Cement Association (PCA), *The Concrete Masonry Handbook for Architects, Engineers and Builders,* Portland Cement Association, Skokie, IL, 1991.

Summary

An overview is provided of exterior wall assemblies, including performance and preliminary design selection criteria, system types, and schematic details.

Key words

bearing walls, curtain walls, framed walls, panel systems, pressure equalization, wall facings, wind pressure

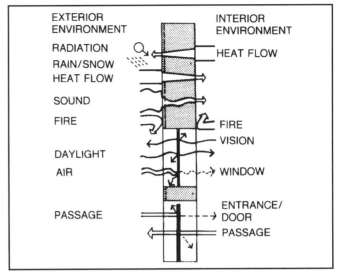

Fig. 1. Exterior wall performance factors.

Overview of exterior wall systems

1 EXTERIOR WALLS: AN OVERVIEW

Exterior walls and assemblies separate the external environment and function as a barrier and/or selective filter (**Fig. 1**). Their multiple functions may be included into one assembly, or separated into distinct components. Their combined performance criteria include:

- *Aesthetic*

- provide views, controlled visibility, and awareness of the external environment.

- present the architectural design intentions within a cultural and environmental context.

- provide for life-long maintenance, repair, replacement, and disassembly.

- *Structural and safety*

- carry vertical loads or protect the building structure that does so.

- resist lateral wind forces and may also be subject to seismic loads.

- minimize the effects of external or internal fire hazard.

- provide basic security.

- *Environmental control*

- control of heat flow between the two environments, utilizing bioclimatic advantages of sun, light, breeze and fresh air.

- controlling water vapor migration from one environment to another, including minimizing damaging condensation on or within the wall construction.

- admit daylight to the interior environment, or control its transmittance.

- allow controlled movement of air from one environment to another, while minimizing uncontrolled air infiltration/exfiltration through the envelope.

- minimize the transmission of sound.

- screen and protect the structure and interior from penetration of rain, snow, and ice.

Structural loads and forces

The structural role of walls includes providing stability under all environmental conditions, while allowing for movement (**Figs. 2 and 3**).

Walls that do not carry superimposed loads of the structural frame must only resist wind loads between horizontal and/or vertical supports, and transmit such loads to the supporting frame. On medium- to high-rise buildings, and buildings within the wind flow around adjacent buildings, wind pressures are complex and varied within the aerodynamic microclimate. Provisions for resistance to extreme wind are somewhat similar to, but are nonetheless distinct from, earthquake resistance design. Provisions for one set of conditions may or may not address the other. Each requires separate analysis.

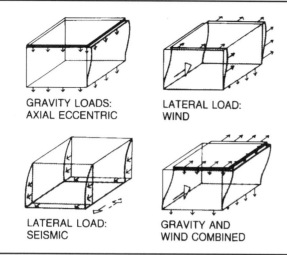

Fig. 2. Structural forces and exterior wall stability.

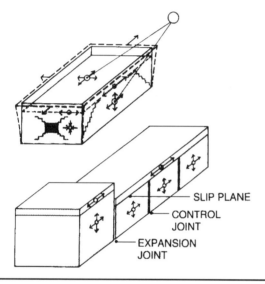

SLIP PLANE

CONTROL JOINT

EXPANSION JOINT

Fig. 3. Structural forces and exterior wall movement.

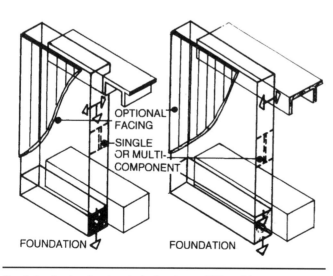

OPTIONAL FACING

SINGLE OR MULTI-COMPONENT

FOUNDATION   FOUNDATION

Fig. 4. Bearing/nonbearing stacked and monolithic wall types.

Wind pressure may be:

- positive, pushing the wall against the supporting horizontal frame and causing it to deform or deflect inward.

- negative, pulling the wall away from supporting frame and causing outward deflection.

- parallel to wall, which may result in shearing stresses in the wall due to interaction between it and the supporting horizontal frame.

Walls that carry superimposed loads of the structural frame may also be subject to eccentric loading, which will result in further deflection in them, either adding to that induced by lateral loads or counteracting it.

Walls will be affected by thermal expansion/contraction within them as well as in the structural frame to which they are connected:

- Solar radiation striking a wall or parts thereof will cause expansion, and such expansion may be differential. The juncture of walls with different exposures to solar radiation should provide for differential movement between the walls joined.

- Long walls may require control joints to limit extent of cumulative movement thus magnitude of resultant stresses; expansion joints, when the structural frame itself is divided into sections to limit expansion/contraction.

- Differential movement may occur between walls and horizontal assemblies: flat roof assembly may be expanding while walls which are continuously connected to it or are supporting it may be expanding at different rates, or may be contracting depending on their exposure.

- Monolithic walls of concrete and walls of masonry units may also be subject to shrinkage-induced stresses in addition to thermal stresses, and may require control joints to minimize the possibility of cracking.

2 EXTERIOR WALL TYPES

Bearing/nonbearing: stacked and monolithic walls

Stacked or monolithic assemblies normally use compatible structural frame: steel, concrete, light-gauge metal or wood framed. Careful consideration must be given to location and spacing of joints to control temperature/moisture-induced expansion and contraction. Bearing and nonbearing wall assemblies are constructed of both stacked units, generally at the job site often manually, and monolithic units, assembled with lift equipment.

Stacked types, typically assembled as shown in **Fig. 4,** include:

- Single or double wythe of concrete block, generally with reinforcing in horizontal joints to control shrinkage-induced cracking; bearing or nonbearing. Outer wythe may be left exposed, may receive applied coating, or may be faced.

- Single wythe of reinforced brick masonry, generally nonbearing; or outer wythe of brick bonded to an inner wythe of concrete block or structural tile, bearing or nonbearing.

– Cavity: two wythes separated by an airspace. Outer wythe usually of brick, inner wythe either brick or concrete block, bonded with metal ties.

Monolithic units, also indicated in Fig. 4, include:

– Concrete, poured-in-place, reinforced as a minimum to control shrinkage stresses when nonbearing.

– Concrete, site precast large panels, reinforced to control erection and shrinkage and/or superimposed load-induced stresses.

Bearing/nonbearing framed walls

Typically constructed of closely spaced light-gauge metal or wood studs, with exterior faces secured against lateral displacement in the plane of the wall by structural sheathing connected to them, or by diagonal braces when the sheathing that is used is nonstructural (**Fig. 5**). These wall types are generally used with framed floor/roof assemblies only and are generally capable of supporting superimposed loads, whether thus used or not:

– posts of support-concentrated loads of the structural frame may be incorporated into the framing.

– studs may be faced both sides with structural sheathing, generally plywood glued or glued and nailed to studs, to function as stressed-skin panels.

– exterior generally faced over sheathing; some facings may act as combined facing and/or structural sheathing.

– interior generally faced, with the facing often also functioning as secondary bracing to the framing.

– insulation generally placed between studs, wiring and small diameter piping may be run through studs.

– moisture control through site-built assemblies must be carefully designed and installed.

Curtain walls: grid type

Curtain wall grid-type assemblies and systems (**Fig. 6**) include:

– mullions spanning between floor, or floor and roof framing, supported and laterally braced by such framing.

– rails connected to, supported by, and laterally braced by mullions.

– in-fill panels, also referred to as glazing panels, generally with edges of the same thickness whether transparent or opaque, held in place by mullions and rails. Windows and/or doors may be used in lieu of panels.

In-fill panels may be:

– monolithic of single thickness; glazing of tinted, patterned, opaque glass; panels of cement-bound mineral fiber, patterned, pigmented, coated.

– monolithic, spaced: glazing of two or more lights of glass or of

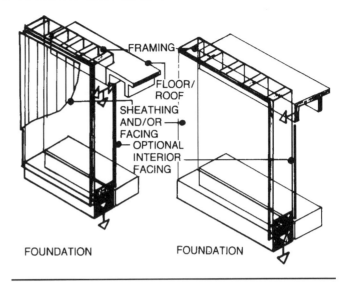

Fig. 5. Bearing/nonbearing framed wall types.

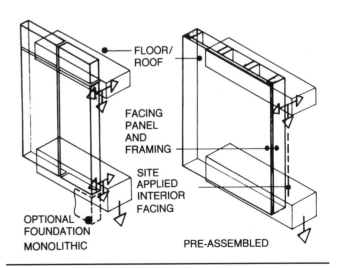

Fig. 6. Curtain walls: grid type.

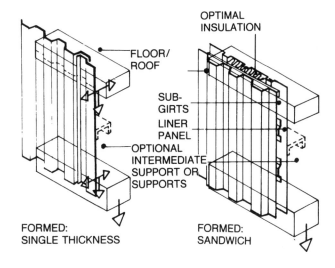

FORMED: SINGLE THICKNESS

FORMED: SANDWICH

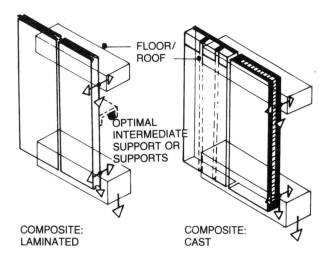

COMPOSITE: LAMINATED

COMPOSITE: CAST

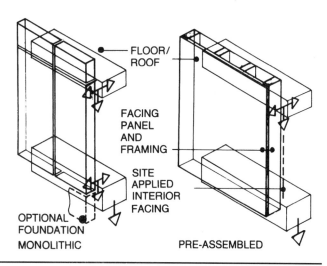

MONOLITHIC

PRE-ASSEMBLED

Fig. 7. Curtain wall panel types.

plastic, or combinations thereof, assembled into units with air spaces between them to reduce flow of heat through them.

- composite, laminated: glazing of glass and plastic, panels of pre-finished metal faces with cores of rigid insulation or rigid boards.

- formed: panels of metal faces with formed edges, generally with insulation between them.

3 CURTAIN WALL PANELS

Curtain wall panels are generally intended to function as the entire wall assembly spanning between floor/roof assemblies; supported and laterally braced by such assemblies (**Fig. 7**):

- intermediate supports between the floor/roof assemblies may be used to reduce the span of thin panels for more economical installation.

- length of panels may be limited by manufacturing processes and/or shipping constraints.

• *Formed panels*

- Single thickness panels: of metal, either nonferrous or anticorrosion-treated ferrous, formed in various configurations to impart rigidity to the section; of plastic in various configurations; of cement-bound mineral fiber, generally corrugated.

- Sandwich panels: single thickness metal panel outer face, connected to and supported through subgirts by a formed metal inner face, generally with insulation between the two faces. The inner face is attached to and supported by continuous structural steel framing. The outer face is connected to subgirts using exposed fasteners or concealed clips.

- Sandwich panels are available as fire-resistant rated assemblies.

- Metal panels may be unfinished when nonferrous, surface treated or coated.

- Compatible structural frame: steel. May be installed on concrete frame if structural steel supports are added.

• *Composite panels*

The two generic types of composite panels are: laminated and cast.

Composite, laminated: Outer face of: metal either flat, formed, or stamped, generally with applied coating; flat cement-bound mineral fiber, either textured or coated.

- panel interior cores of rigid boards, rigid insulation, fiber or metal honeycomb.

- interior face may be exposed core or similar to outer face.

- panels secured to steel supports with concealed fasteners or formed metal clips.

- compatible structural frame: steel. May be used with concrete frame if steel supports are added.

Composite, cast: of polymer or regular concrete with insulation between the outer and inner faces.

– outer face may be lightly to heavily textured or of exposed aggregate inner face generally smooth

• secured to framing with structural steel clips

• intermediate supports not commonly used.

– compatible structural frame: steel, concrete.

• *Monolithic panels*

Solid or monolithic masonry panels are generally of regular concrete, with either normal or lightweight aggregate:

– outer face either flat, textured, or molded/sculptured

– inner face generally smooth

– secured to framing with structural steel clips

– intermediate support are seldom used when one or two stories in height may be supported directly on foundation and laterally braced by the structural frame.

– compatible structural frame: steel, concrete.

• *Preassembled panel systems*

Total envelope and structural systems are available with prefinished facing panels, attached to preassembled framing and shipped to the site as ready-to-be-installed units. Compatible structural frame includes steel or concrete.

4 WALL FACING TYPES

All walls, whether exterior or interior, consist of at least two elements: the outer faces, and the core or body between them. The wall may be single component, such as the fabric of a tent, or it may be an assembly of multiple layers of different components, but the two basic elements will still be present.

The outer surfaces of a solid stone or brick wall may be finished for appearance or durability, but that will not constitute a facing. But when stone is combined with a concrete wall to protect and enhance it, it becomes a facing, whether dependent on the concrete for stability or not. A sheet of metal such as aluminum will always constitute a facing, whether single thickness or laminated to a backing, formed or flat, when used as the outer surface of a solid core wall assembly or attached to open framing. Generic exterior wall facing types indicated in **Fig. 8** include:

• *Facing panels*

Facing panels are applied over a back-up wall and secured to the wall and/or structural frame:

– backup may be of stacked units, generally concrete block, or framed.

PANELS

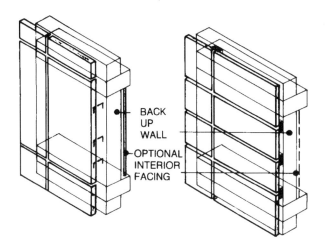

UNITS/STRIPS: ATTACHED

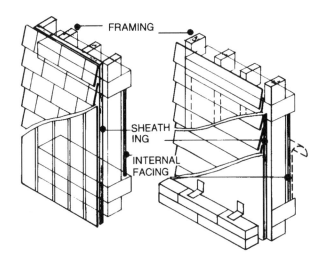

UNITS/SURFACING: BONDED

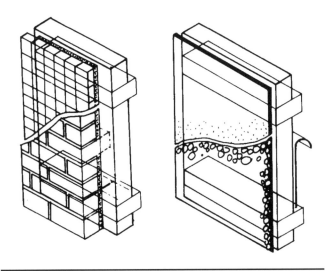

Fig. 8. Wall facing types.

- facing panels may require subframing to be installed over the back-up wall for proper attachment and/or alignment.

- light, thin panels may be attached to solid plumb surfaces using adhesives, such as high modulus silicone, but such methods of attachment are not common.

- *Unit assemblies*

Assemblies of units, such as shingles, stone, tile, or brick masonry; and strips such as vertical or horizontal siding; applied over a back-up wall:

- backup generally framed with nailable sheathing, may also be stacked units, such as concrete block, but nailable furring strips have to be then installed over the wall.

- horizontal siding, when sufficiently rigid, may be attached directly to the studs of a framed wall, and sheathing omitted when the structural frame provides the required rigidity.

- *Surfacing*

Surfacing includes factory-applied or site applications such as stucco, select aggregate, bonded to a back-up wall:

- backup may be: stacked units, generally concrete block, monolithic concrete, either cast-in-place or precast, sheathed framing, or rigid insulation secured to back-up wall.

- stucco applied over framed back-up wall may be over sheathing, or the sheathing may be omitted.

5 EXTERIOR WALLS: SELECTION CRITERIA

Principal design considerations during selection of an exterior wall assembly include:

- Function of the building and requirements it imposes. Extensive areas of glazing required and their distribution over the plane of the walls may narrow the choice of wall type, or preclude the efficient use of bearing walls.

- Form of the building, whether low- or high-rise, may influence the choice of a particular type. Bearing walls are generally only economical up to about 10 stories in height.

- Structural frame, whether short- or long-span, and the spacing of horizontal framing members may affect the choice. Short spans and closely spaced horizontal framing members would allow for efficient use of bearing walls, as would uniform compartmentalization of interior space.

- Ground conditions may impose limitations on the entire building. Soils with poor bearing capacity may require that all components be as light as practicable. Differential settlement to be expected may preclude the use of rigid wall assemblies.

- Structural stability and integrity under all loads. Walls may interact with the structural frame to contribute to its strength or rigidity, or the structural frame may impose loads on walls they

were not intended to resist through dimensional changes in the frame.

- Durability under all environmental factors, or service life as a measure of the time until some loss of function occurs. It is critical that all wall components be selected to endure and/or to be replaced in an accessible and nondisruptive maintenance and repair process. The environment at any plane of the wall assembly is determined by the arrangement and properties of its components, and durability is reflected in the ultimate cost of maintaining all the required functions of the wall assembly over its intended service life.

- Economy in initial and maintenance costs. Initial cost may be reduced by selecting lower quality components, but generally only at the expense of increased maintenance cost or reduced service life.

- Aesthetic quality. Form, overall pattern of components, color, and texture may be varied over a wide range without affecting other considerations, but inadequacies in design that allow problems such as cracks or runoff staining to develop may severely affect the aesthetic quality of a building.

6 CURTAIN WALLS

Typical curtain wall system types are indicated in **Fig. 9**. Mullion types are indicated in **Fig. 10**.

- *Grid curtain walls*

Grid systems are pressure-equalized arrangements of vertical and horizontal framing members attached to the structural frame and supporting transparent, translucent, or opaque in-fill panels. The grid curtain wall can be generally characterized, depending on method of delivery and assembly:

- Stick system: with the vertical members, or mullions, and horizontal members, or rails, assembled at the site using sleeves to connect mullions and splines to connect the rails. Movements in the wall assembly and/or the structural frame are generally accommodated at splices of framing members and in the glazing pockets of rails.

- Unitized stick system: with prefabricated vertical mullions and two-piece interlocking rails, which are connected to mullions with splines. Movements in wall and/or the structural frame are taken at joints in mullions and in the interlocking rails. This system is generally more expensive than the stick system, but is able to better accommodate thermal expansion and contraction.

- Unit system: with shop prefabricated interlocking mullions and rails, often pre-glazed and shipped to the site as units. Movements in the wall assembly and/or structural frame are accommodated in the interlocking mullions and rails. This system has the advantage of closer tolerances and greater capacity for accommodating movement. The disadvantages are increased material and fabrication costs, and necessity of maintaining closer tolerances in the structural frame.

Additional considerations applicable to all grid systems are:

- amount of adjustment available within the system to accommodate field conditions, such as misalignments in the structural frame.

STICK

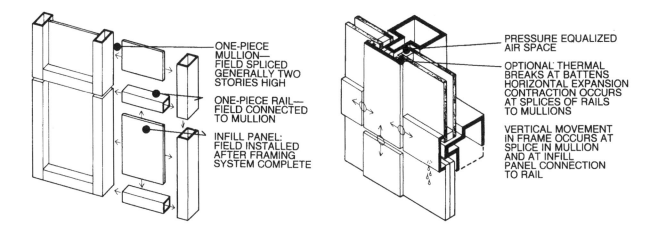

ONE-PIECE MULLION—FIELD SPLICED GENERALLY TWO STORIES HIGH

ONE-PIECE RAIL—FIELD CONNECTED TO MULLION

INFILL PANEL: FIELD INSTALLED AFTER FRAMING SYSTEM COMPLETE

PRESSURE EQUALIZED AIR SPACE

OPTIONAL THERMAL BREAKS AT BATTENS HORIZONTAL EXPANSION CONTRACTION OCCURS AT SPLICES OF RAILS TO MULLIONS

VERTICAL MOVEMENT IN FRAME OCCURS AT SPLICE IN MULLION AND AT INFILL PANEL CONNECTION TO RAIL

UNITIZED STICK

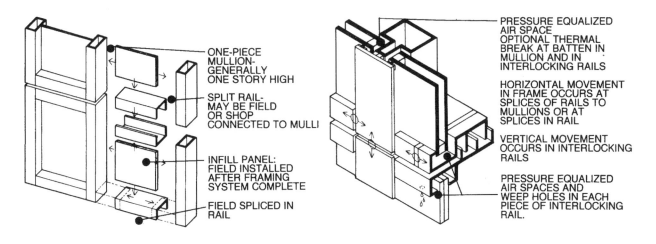

ONE-PIECE MULLION-GENERALLY ONE STORY HIGH

SPLIT RAIL-MAY BE FIELD OR SHOP CONNECTED TO MULLI

INFILL PANEL: FIELD INSTALLED AFTER FRAMING SYSTEM COMPLETE

FIELD SPLICED IN RAIL

PRESSURE EQUALIZED AIR SPACE OPTIONAL THERMAL BREAK AT BATTEN IN MULLION AND IN INTERLOCKING RAILS

HORIZONTAL MOVEMENT IN FRAME OCCURS AT SPLICES OF RAILS TO MULLIONS OR AT SPLICES IN RAIL

VERTICAL MOVEMENT OCCURS IN INTERLOCKING RAILS

PRESSURE EQUALIZED AIR SPACES AND WEEP HOLES IN EACH PIECE OF INTERLOCKING RAIL.

UNITIZED

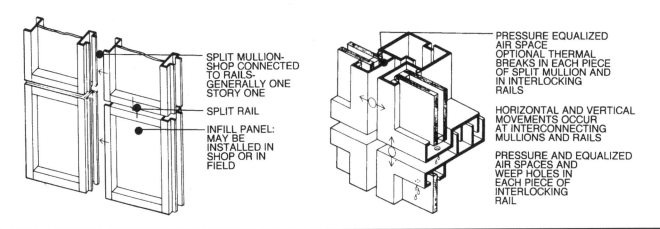

SPLIT MULLION-SHOP CONNECTED TO RAILS-GENERALLY ONE STORY ONE

SPLIT RAIL

INFILL PANEL: MAY BE INSTALLED IN SHOP OR IN FIELD

PRESSURE EQUALIZED AIR SPACE OPTIONAL THERMAL BREAKS IN EACH PIECE OF SPLIT MULLION AND IN INTERLOCKING RAILS

HORIZONTAL AND VERTICAL MOVEMENTS OCCUR AT INTERCONNECTING MULLIONS AND RAILS

PRESSURE AND EQUALIZED AIR SPACES AND WEEP HOLES IN EACH PIECE OF INTERLOCKING RAIL

Fig. 9. Grid type curtain walls.

BATTEN GLAZING

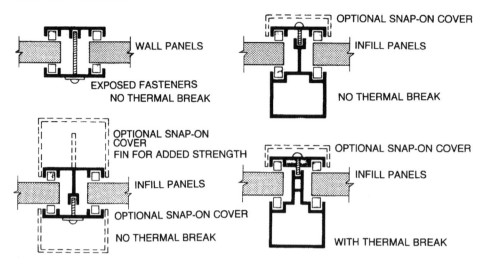

STOP GLAZING

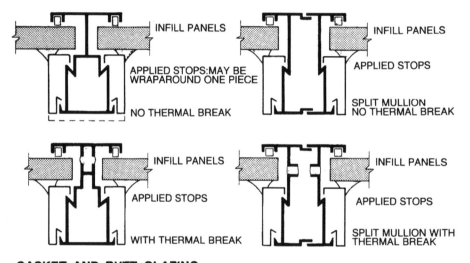

GASKET AND BUTT GLAZING

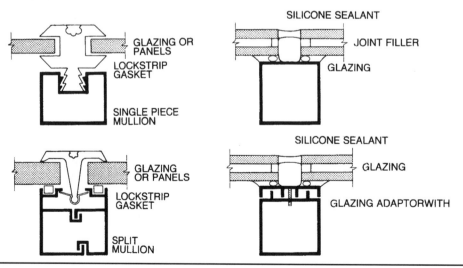

Fig. 10. Curtain wall mullion types.

– maintaining the structural integrity of the system under in-service conditions, such as horizontal displacement, or sway, in the structural frame under lateral loads.

– window washing equipment is required for high-rise buildings with fixed glazing, and the additional load imposed thereby on mullions becomes a factor.

• *Wall panel systems*

Wall panel systems include an array of panel assemblies capable of functioning as a complete wall assembly. Preliminary considerations of the wall panel system may be influenced by:

– Functional considerations: when occupancy activities require either a virtually opaque wall, or when a limited amount only of openings, such as windows and/or doors is required.

– Openings in most wall panels require secondary framing to support the frame of the opening and the free edges of adjacent panels.

– Erection considerations: wall panels are always erected from the outside, and connections to the structural frame are generally also made from the outside, except for some types that may be back fastened.

– Weight: ranges from very light, such as single thickness of formed metal, to very heavy, such as sculptured of precast concrete.

• *Deformation in curtain walls*

Negative air pressure on a given wall of a tall building, especially at corners, may significantly exceed positive air pressures that the same wall could be subjected to if direction of wind reverses. Negative air pressure may also be augmented when buildings are maintained under positive pressure:

– Air pressure, either negative or positive, acting on a grid curtain wall, will cause bending in the framing members and in-fill panels held by them, with each component then deflecting proportionately to its relative rigidity.

– Mullions as the principal framing members are relatively rigid and can easily be reinforced, thus bending stresses and resulting deflections can be kept within safe limits.

– Rails are generally short members and relatively rigid.

– In-fill panels, especially transparent ones, may deform when subjected to the same air pressures, and as a result may fail in tension, or be pulled out of the framing members.

– In grid curtain walls, excessive deformation or deflection of the framing members under lateral loads may affect the in-fill panels or their connections to framing member, or may be visually unacceptable.

– Generally deflections should not exceed $\frac{1}{180}$ of the span or a ¾ in (19 mm) maximum deviation from a straight line between supports.

– Deflections in panels of curtain wall panel systems may generally be as high as $\frac{1}{120}$ of span if not visually objectionable; alternatively, allowable stresses in bending will determine maximum spans.

Pressure equalization in curtain walls

Pressure equalization in curtain wall assemblies provides one means of, or line of defense against, undesired water penetration. In such approaches, confined air spaces, or air pressure equalization chambers, are incorporated into mullions and rails, with openings to the outside generally located in soffit areas of rails to protect them from heavy wetting. Air pressure equalization chambers are compartmentalized to prevent differential air pressures developing within each chamber. Double seals are provided at connections of in-fill panels to mullions and rails: the outer seal acts as a deferent seal to water penetration but is not relied upon to completely prevent it; the inner seal acts as an air seal to substantially reduce air from the interior to the air chamber. Pressures in air chambers will not be effectively equalized unless the aggregate area of all openings to the outside is considerably larger than the total area of all openings to the inside. The ratio of 10 to 1 is considered minimal by the Architectural Aluminum Manufacturers Association.

7 BEARING WALLS

Bearing walls act simultaneously as structure and enclosure to support superimposed loads from floor, roof, and other wall assemblies and transfer the resultant forces downward to the foundations. Bearing walls withstand the flexural moment and shears caused by lateral and vertical loads and serve as bracing to other parts of the structure. Bearing walls below grade withstand lateral soil and sometimes also hydrostatic pressure and resist seismic tremors in some areas.

Bearing walls may be identical to a curtain wall in construction and a nonbearing wall, or a partition when one story or less in height; or may become a curtain wall without any change if its bearing capacity is not utilized; or may be bearing for a certain portion of it and nonbearing, or curtain wall, for remaining portions.

When numerous large openings have to be provided, even with uniformly applied floor/roof framing loads, the wall will become a series of piers or posts; the loading on the footing will be uneven and the wall assembly will no longer function as a true bearing wall. Under such conditions, a portion or the entire wall may have to be replaced with a structural frame.

Bearing walls can be generally classified as:

• *Stacked unit walls*

Made up of relatively small units stacked upon each other:

– in various patterns or bonds in one or more wythes, contiguous or separate.

– in various forms: brick, block, ashlar, rubble.

– of various materials: stone, burned clay, concrete.

– bonded by mortar of various types or laid dry.

– reinforced or unreinforced.

• *Monolithic reinforced concrete*

There are three major types: cast-in-place, tilt-up, and precast:

– Cast-in-place thin concrete walls are usually integrally connected to the floor and roof slabs and to each other, thus forming a crate-like form with excellent lateral stiffness. Buildings of 16 stories and more have been erected by this method.

– An often more convenient method is the so-called "tilt-up," where walls are cast flat on the ground or on a platform next to their final position, then picked up by a crane and tilted into place. Connecting pours to surrounding structure are then generally made.

– Precast concrete bearing walls are generally ribbed panels, single or double tee's. Connections are usually made by preformed fasteners with/without additional concrete placed.

• *Framed construction*

Made of small, closely spaced vertical members, connected to plates top and bottom and covered by a skin.

– wood framed walls of which balloon and platform frames are best known.

– metal framed walls, where metal studs replace wood.

• *Deformations in bearing and nonbearing walls*

Lateral stability of walls is always a consideration:

– for bearing and nonbearing walls, the allowable stresses in bending under lateral load, or under combined lateral and gravity loads will determine maximum unsupported height or length.

– empirically established ratios of unbraced height/length to thickness of wall, or slenderness ratio, may be used for some types in lieu of calculating actual stresses.

Concentrically loaded, single component wall assembly will be in compression throughout its thickness:

– horizontal loads will cause bending in the assembly and change the magnitude of compressive stresses; in slender wall assemblies tension may occur under heavy wind loads.

– effect on facings is seldom if ever significant.

Eccentrically loaded wall assemblies may develop tensile stresses due to bending depending on the magnitude and/or eccentricity of the load. Facings may be affected when eccentric loading, horizontal forces and thermal expansion combine to increase bending stresses in the wall assembly.

Multicomponent bearing wall assemblies, such as a bearing cavity wall, may not develop bending stresses even when carrying an eccentric load, provided the load is distributed between the two wythes:

– bending may develop in slender exterior facing wythes under extreme horizontal load and the influence of thermal expansion/contraction.

– thermal and moisture induced movements rather than horizontal loads will generally be the more important considerations.

– vertical loads will affect wall assembly only when safe working stresses in component materials are exceeded.

When walls are faced to enhance their resistance to detrimental effects of external environment, or because of aesthetic considerations, the physical properties of such facings may dictate the structural requirements of the wall:

– deflection in walls faced with stucco, plaster, or other inelastic materials may be limited to minimize the possibility of cracks developing in such facings.

Walls when supported by or connected to the structural frame will generally be affected by deformations in the frame. The entire envelope must therefore be considered during the selection of its constituent parts.

Figs. 11 to **15** (on following pages) give schematic and representative details of bearing wall assemblies. Critical considerations of insulation, moisture control, weathertightness, and related design details are discussed in subsequent articles. ■

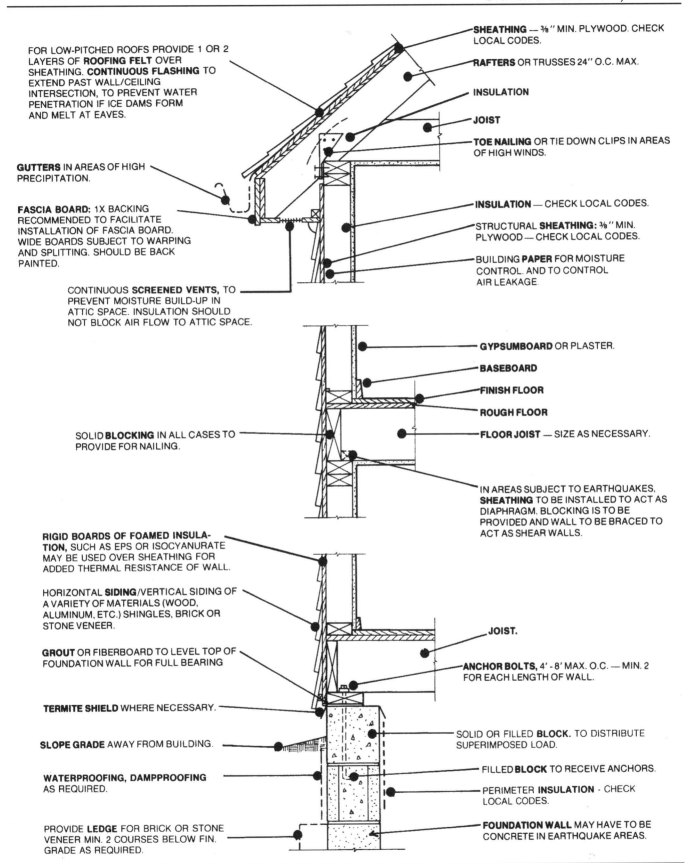

FOR LOW-PITCHED ROOFS PROVIDE 1 OR 2 LAYERS OF **ROOFING FELT** OVER SHEATHING. **CONTINUOUS FLASHING** TO EXTEND PAST WALL/CEILING INTERSECTION, TO PREVENT WATER PENETRATION IF ICE DAMS FORM AND MELT AT EAVES.

GUTTERS IN AREAS OF HIGH PRECIPITATION.

FASCIA BOARD: 1X BACKING RECOMMENDED TO FACILITATE INSTALLATION OF FASCIA BOARD. WIDE BOARDS SUBJECT TO WARPING AND SPLITTING. SHOULD BE BACK PAINTED.

CONTINUOUS **SCREENED VENTS**, TO PREVENT MOISTURE BUILD-UP IN ATTIC SPACE. INSULATION SHOULD NOT BLOCK AIR FLOW TO ATTIC SPACE.

SOLID **BLOCKING** IN ALL CASES TO PROVIDE FOR NAILING.

RIGID BOARDS OF FOAMED INSULATION, SUCH AS EPS OR ISOCYANURATE MAY BE USED OVER SHEATHING FOR ADDED THERMAL RESISTANCE OF WALL.

HORIZONTAL **SIDING**/VERTICAL SIDING OF A VARIETY OF MATERIALS (WOOD, ALUMINUM, ETC.) SHINGLES, BRICK OR STONE VENEER.

GROUT OR FIBERBOARD TO LEVEL TOP OF FOUNDATION WALL FOR FULL BEARING

TERMITE SHIELD WHERE NECESSARY.

SLOPE GRADE AWAY FROM BUILDING.

WATERPROOFING, DAMPPROOFING AS REQUIRED.

PROVIDE **LEDGE** FOR BRICK OR STONE VENEER MIN. 2 COURSES BELOW FIN. GRADE AS REQUIRED.

SHEATHING — ⅜" MIN. PLYWOOD. CHECK LOCAL CODES.

RAFTERS OR TRUSSES 24" O.C. MAX.

INSULATION

JOIST

TOE NAILING OR TIE DOWN CLIPS IN AREAS OF HIGH WINDS.

INSULATION — CHECK LOCAL CODES.

STRUCTURAL **SHEATHING**: ⅜" MIN. PLYWOOD — CHECK LOCAL CODES.

BUILDING **PAPER** FOR MOISTURE CONTROL. AND TO CONTROL AIR LEAKAGE.

GYPSUMBOARD OR PLASTER.

BASEBOARD

FINISH FLOOR

ROUGH FLOOR

FLOOR JOIST — SIZE AS NECESSARY.

IN AREAS SUBJECT TO EARTHQUAKES, **SHEATHING** TO BE INSTALLED TO ACT AS DIAPHRAGM. BLOCKING IS TO BE PROVIDED AND WALL TO BE BRACED TO ACT AS SHEAR WALLS.

JOIST.

ANCHOR BOLTS, 4' - 8' MAX. O.C. — MIN. 2 FOR EACH LENGTH OF WALL.

SOLID OR FILLED **BLOCK.** TO DISTRIBUTE SUPERIMPOSED LOAD.

FILLED **BLOCK** TO RECEIVE ANCHORS.

PERIMETER **INSULATION** - CHECK LOCAL CODES.

FOUNDATION WALL MAY HAVE TO BE CONCRETE IN EARTHQUAKE AREAS.

Fig. 11. Bearing walls: wood framed anchorage and connections.

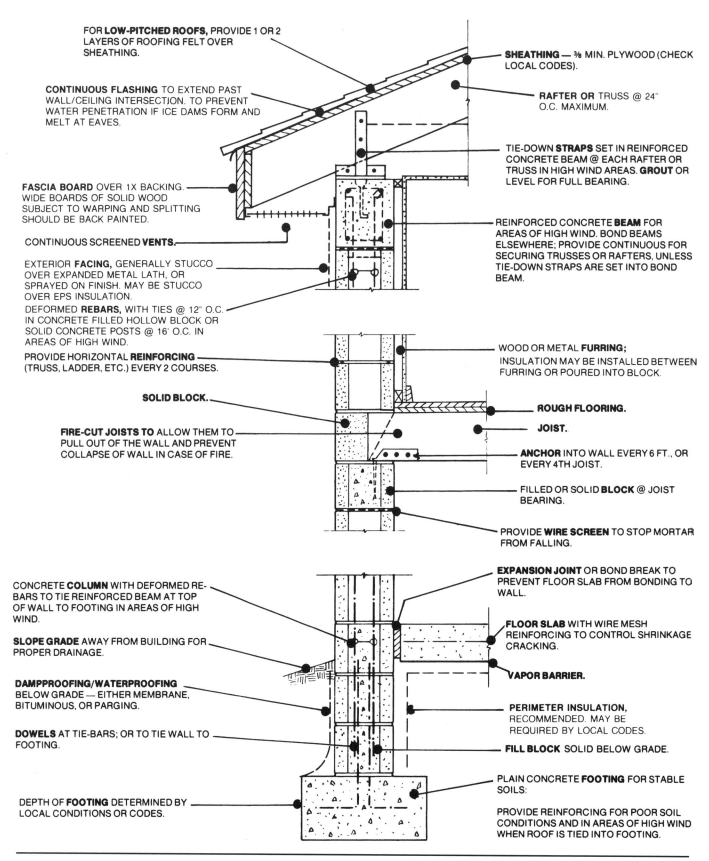

FOR **LOW-PITCHED ROOFS,** PROVIDE 1 OR 2 LAYERS OF ROOFING FELT OVER SHEATHING.

CONTINUOUS FLASHING TO EXTEND PAST WALL/CEILING INTERSECTION. TO PREVENT WATER PENETRATION IF ICE DAMS FORM AND MELT AT EAVES.

FASCIA BOARD OVER 1X BACKING. WIDE BOARDS OF SOLID WOOD SUBJECT TO WARPING AND SPLITTING SHOULD BE BACK PAINTED.

CONTINUOUS SCREENED **VENTS.**

EXTERIOR **FACING,** GENERALLY STUCCO OVER EXPANDED METAL LATH, OR SPRAYED ON FINISH. MAY BE STUCCO OVER EPS INSULATION.

DEFORMED **REBARS,** WITH TIES @ 12" O.C. IN CONCRETE FILLED HOLLOW BLOCK OR SOLID CONCRETE POSTS @ 16' O.C. IN AREAS OF HIGH WIND.

PROVIDE HORIZONTAL **REINFORCING** (TRUSS, LADDER, ETC.) EVERY 2 COURSES.

SOLID BLOCK.

FIRE-CUT JOISTS TO ALLOW THEM TO PULL OUT OF THE WALL AND PREVENT COLLAPSE OF WALL IN CASE OF FIRE.

SHEATHING — ⅜ MIN. PLYWOOD (CHECK LOCAL CODES).

RAFTER OR TRUSS @ 24" O.C. MAXIMUM.

TIE-DOWN **STRAPS** SET IN REINFORCED CONCRETE BEAM @ EACH RAFTER OR TRUSS IN HIGH WIND AREAS. **GROUT** OR LEVEL FOR FULL BEARING.

REINFORCED CONCRETE **BEAM** FOR AREAS OF HIGH WIND. BOND BEAMS ELSEWHERE; PROVIDE CONTINUOUS FOR SECURING TRUSSES OR RAFTERS, UNLESS TIE-DOWN STRAPS ARE SET INTO BOND BEAM.

WOOD OR METAL **FURRING;** INSULATION MAY BE INSTALLED BETWEEN FURRING OR POURED INTO BLOCK.

ROUGH FLOORING.

JOIST.

ANCHOR INTO WALL EVERY 6 FT., OR EVERY 4TH JOIST.

FILLED OR SOLID **BLOCK** @ JOIST BEARING.

PROVIDE **WIRE SCREEN** TO STOP MORTAR FROM FALLING.

CONCRETE **COLUMN** WITH DEFORMED RE-BARS TO TIE REINFORCED BEAM AT TOP OF WALL TO FOOTING IN AREAS OF HIGH WIND.

SLOPE GRADE AWAY FROM BUILDING FOR PROPER DRAINAGE.

DAMPPROOFING/WATERPROOFING BELOW GRADE — EITHER MEMBRANE, BITUMINOUS, OR PARGING.

DOWELS AT TIE-BARS; OR TO TIE WALL TO FOOTING.

DEPTH OF **FOOTING** DETERMINED BY LOCAL CONDITIONS OR CODES.

EXPANSION JOINT OR BOND BREAK TO PREVENT FLOOR SLAB FROM BONDING TO WALL.

FLOOR SLAB WITH WIRE MESH REINFORCING TO CONTROL SHRINKAGE CRACKING.

VAPOR BARRIER.

PERIMETER INSULATION, RECOMMENDED. MAY BE REQUIRED BY LOCAL CODES.

FILL BLOCK SOLID BELOW GRADE.

PLAIN CONCRETE **FOOTING** FOR STABLE SOILS:

PROVIDE REINFORCING FOR POOR SOIL CONDITIONS AND IN AREAS OF HIGH WIND WHEN ROOF IS TIED INTO FOOTING.

Fig. 12. Bearing walls: masonry single wythe.

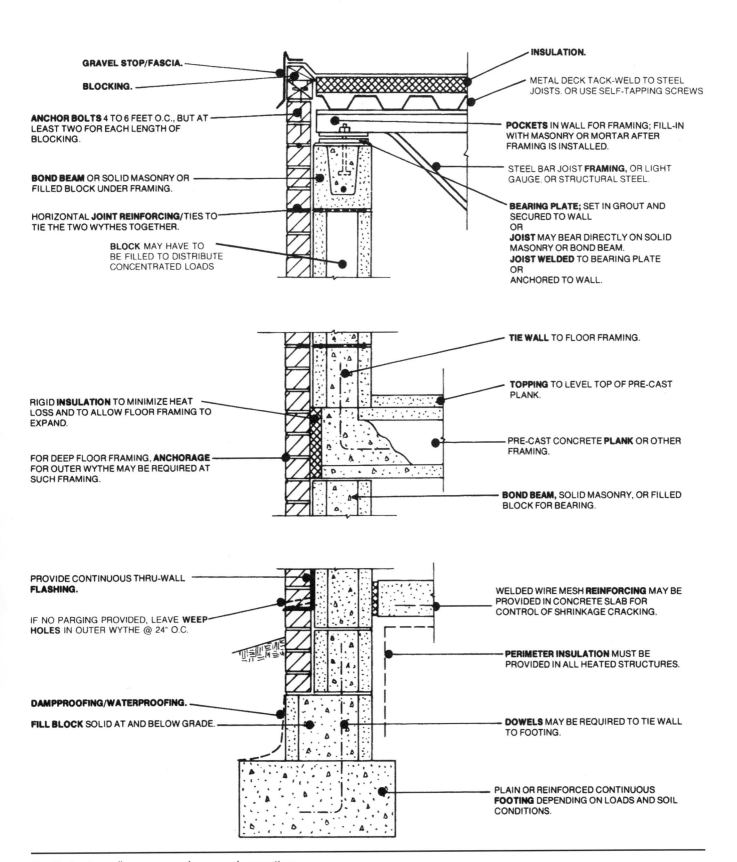

GRAVEL STOP/FASCIA.

BLOCKING.

ANCHOR BOLTS 4 TO 6 FEET O.C., BUT AT LEAST TWO FOR EACH LENGTH OF BLOCKING.

BOND BEAM OR SOLID MASONRY OR FILLED BLOCK UNDER FRAMING.

HORIZONTAL JOINT REINFORCING/TIES TO TIE THE TWO WYTHES TOGETHER.

BLOCK MAY HAVE TO BE FILLED TO DISTRIBUTE CONCENTRATED LOADS

INSULATION.

METAL DECK TACK-WELD TO STEEL JOISTS. OR USE SELF-TAPPING SCREWS

POCKETS IN WALL FOR FRAMING; FILL-IN WITH MASONRY OR MORTAR AFTER FRAMING IS INSTALLED.

STEEL BAR JOIST FRAMING, OR LIGHT GAUGE. OR STRUCTURAL STEEL.

BEARING PLATE; SET IN GROUT AND SECURED TO WALL
OR
JOIST MAY BEAR DIRECTLY ON SOLID MASONRY OR BOND BEAM.
JOIST WELDED TO BEARING PLATE
OR
ANCHORED TO WALL.

RIGID INSULATION TO MINIMIZE HEAT LOSS AND TO ALLOW FLOOR FRAMING TO EXPAND.

FOR DEEP FLOOR FRAMING, ANCHORAGE FOR OUTER WYTHE MAY BE REQUIRED AT SUCH FRAMING.

TIE WALL TO FLOOR FRAMING.

TOPPING TO LEVEL TOP OF PRE-CAST PLANK.

PRE-CAST CONCRETE PLANK OR OTHER FRAMING.

BOND BEAM, SOLID MASONRY, OR FILLED BLOCK FOR BEARING.

PROVIDE CONTINUOUS THRU-WALL FLASHING.

IF NO PARGING PROVIDED, LEAVE WEEP HOLES IN OUTER WYTHE @ 24" O.C.

DAMPPROOFING/WATERPROOFING.

FILL BLOCK SOLID AT AND BELOW GRADE.

WELDED WIRE MESH REINFORCING MAY BE PROVIDED IN CONCRETE SLAB FOR CONTROL OF SHRINKAGE CRACKING.

PERIMETER INSULATION MUST BE PROVIDED IN ALL HEATED STRUCTURES.

DOWELS MAY BE REQUIRED TO TIE WALL TO FOOTING.

PLAIN OR REINFORCED CONTINUOUS FOOTING DEPENDING ON LOADS AND SOIL CONDITIONS.

Fig. 13. Bearing walls: masonry anchorage and connections.

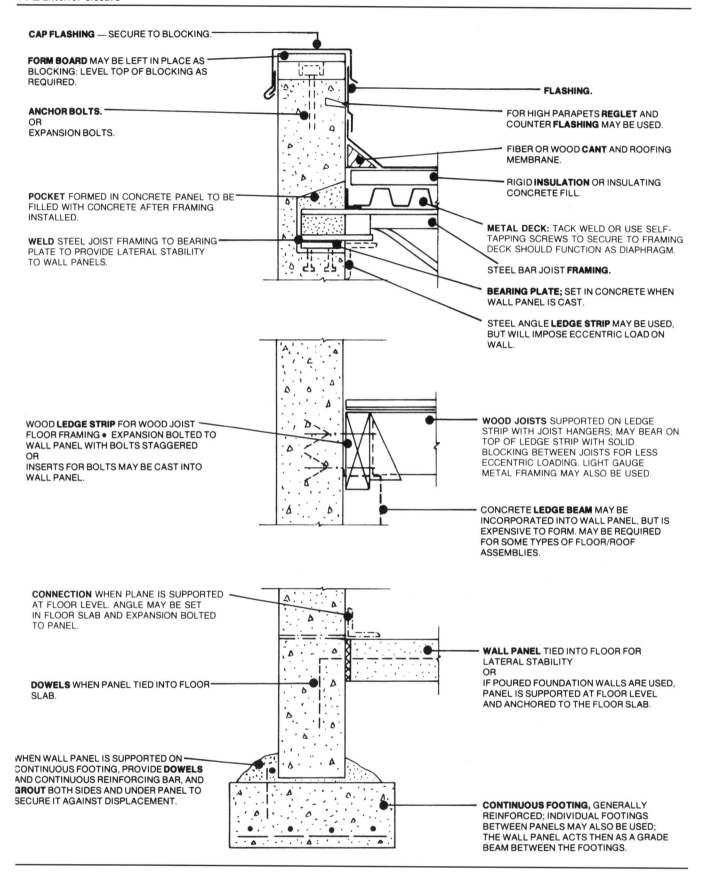

CAP FLASHING — SECURE TO BLOCKING.

FORM BOARD MAY BE LEFT IN PLACE AS BLOCKING: LEVEL TOP OF BLOCKING AS REQUIRED.

ANCHOR BOLTS.
OR
EXPANSION BOLTS.

POCKET FORMED IN CONCRETE PANEL TO BE FILLED WITH CONCRETE AFTER FRAMING INSTALLED.

WELD STEEL JOIST FRAMING TO BEARING PLATE TO PROVIDE LATERAL STABILITY TO WALL PANELS.

FLASHING.

FOR HIGH PARAPETS **REGLET** AND COUNTER **FLASHING** MAY BE USED.

FIBER OR WOOD **CANT** AND ROOFING MEMBRANE.

RIGID **INSULATION** OR INSULATING CONCRETE FILL.

METAL DECK: TACK WELD OR USE SELF-TAPPING SCREWS TO SECURE TO FRAMING DECK SHOULD FUNCTION AS DIAPHRAGM.

STEEL BAR JOIST **FRAMING.**

BEARING PLATE; SET IN CONCRETE WHEN WALL PANEL IS CAST.

STEEL ANGLE **LEDGE STRIP** MAY BE USED, BUT WILL IMPOSE ECCENTRIC LOAD ON WALL.

WOOD **LEDGE STRIP** FOR WOOD JOIST FLOOR FRAMING ● EXPANSION BOLTED TO WALL PANEL WITH BOLTS STAGGERED OR INSERTS FOR BOLTS MAY BE CAST INTO WALL PANEL.

WOOD JOISTS SUPPORTED ON LEDGE STRIP WITH JOIST HANGERS; MAY BEAR ON TOP OF LEDGE STRIP WITH SOLID BLOCKING BETWEEN JOISTS FOR LESS ECCENTRIC LOADING. LIGHT GAUGE METAL FRAMING MAY ALSO BE USED.

CONCRETE **LEDGE BEAM** MAY BE INCORPORATED INTO WALL PANEL, BUT IS EXPENSIVE TO FORM. MAY BE REQUIRED FOR SOME TYPES OF FLOOR/ROOF ASSEMBLIES.

CONNECTION WHEN PLANE IS SUPPORTED AT FLOOR LEVEL. ANGLE MAY BE SET IN FLOOR SLAB AND EXPANSION BOLTED TO PANEL.

DOWELS WHEN PANEL TIED INTO FLOOR SLAB.

WHEN WALL PANEL IS SUPPORTED ON CONTINUOUS FOOTING, PROVIDE **DOWELS** AND CONTINUOUS REINFORCING BAR, AND **GROUT** BOTH SIDES AND UNDER PANEL TO SECURE IT AGAINST DISPLACEMENT.

WALL PANEL TIED INTO FLOOR FOR LATERAL STABILITY OR IF POURED FOUNDATION WALLS ARE USED, PANEL IS SUPPORTED AT FLOOR LEVEL AND ANCHORED TO THE FLOOR SLAB.

CONTINUOUS FOOTING, GENERALLY REINFORCED; INDIVIDUAL FOOTINGS BETWEEN PANELS MAY ALSO BE USED; THE WALL PANEL ACTS THEN AS A GRADE BEAM BETWEEN THE FOOTINGS.

Fig. 14. Bearing walls: concrete precast and tilt-up.

FRAMED:

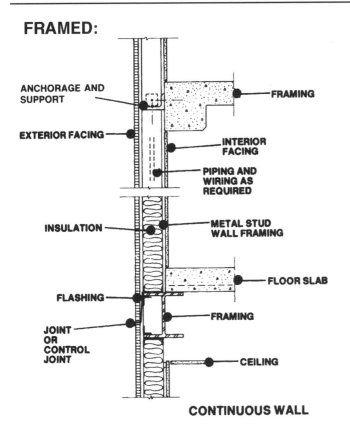

ANCHORAGE AND SUPPORT
EXTERIOR FACING
FRAMING
INTERIOR FACING
PIPING AND WIRING AS REQUIRED
INSULATION
METAL STUD WALL FRAMING
FLOOR SLAB
FLASHING
FRAMING
JOINT OR CONTROL JOINT
CEILING

CONTINUOUS WALL

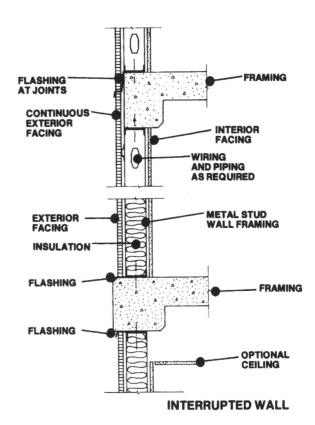

FLASHING AT JOINTS
FRAMING
CONTINUOUS EXTERIOR FACING
INTERIOR FACING
WIRING AND PIPING AS REQUIRED
EXTERIOR FACING
METAL STUD WALL FRAMING
INSULATION
FLASHING
FRAMING
FLASHING
OPTIONAL CEILING

INTERRUPTED WALL

STACKED:

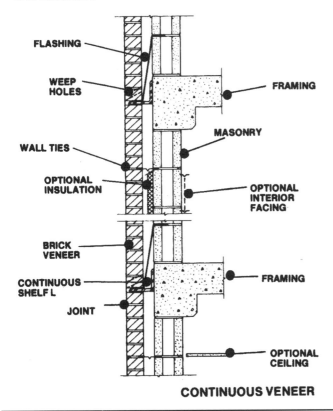

FLASHING
WEEP HOLES
FRAMING
MASONRY
WALL TIES
OPTIONAL INSULATION
OPTIONAL INTERIOR FACING
BRICK VENEER
FRAMING
CONTINUOUS SHELF L
JOINT
OPTIONAL CEILING

CONTINUOUS VENEER

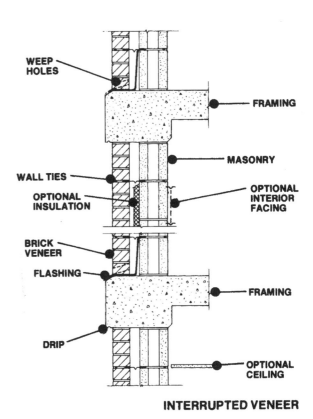

WEEP HOLES
FRAMING
MASONRY
WALL TIES
OPTIONAL INTERIOR FACING
OPTIONAL INSULATION
BRICK VENEER
FLASHING
FRAMING
DRIP
OPTIONAL CEILING

INTERRUPTED VENEER

Fig. 15. Bearing walls: used as curtain walls.

Donald Baerman, AIA

Summary

Thermal insulation helps improve comfort, conserves energy, and protects structures from thermal and freezing damage. Reviewed here are principles of heat flow through the building envelope and design guidelines for placement of insulation.

Key words

attic, comfort, condensation, conductivity, convection, emissivity, envelope, foundation, heat gain, heat loss, humidity, infiltration, roof, thermal insulation, thermal resistance, U value

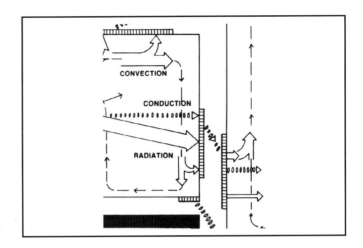

Thermal insulation

1 THEORY OF HEAT FLOW DYNAMICS

This section reviews the thermodynamic principles of heat flow with respect to the building envelope in order to provide a theoretical background to the role of thermal insulation in designing buildings.

Human thermal comfort

There are six major variables in human thermal comfort (Fanger 1970):

– Air temperature

– Ambient radiant temperature

– Humidity

– Dress (a 1940s business suit is given the thermal insulation value of 1 "clo")

– Air velocity

– Metabolic rate, or activity level.

Variables that do not appear to vary in thermal comfort studies with experimental subjects include age, gender, place of origin and residence, skin color, and body form and weight. The perceived "discomfort" and physiological ability to tolerate discomfort and thermal stress may vary according to these and other variables. In other words, the human "comfort" zone is relatively universal, independent of age, health, and sex. However, reports of "discomfort" and actual stress appear to vary as a function of many variables, such as acculturation (Fanger 1970).

Of the variables listed, architects and engineers have some control of air temperature, ambient radiant temperature, humidity, and air velocity. Thermal insulation affects mainly air temperature and ambient radiant temperature, and those variables are very important to thermal comfort inside most buildings.

Body comfort in an enclosed space largely depends on the balance between heat produced internally in the body and the temperature and humidity of the surrounding air and the surface (radiant) temperatures of the surrounding envelope. Any changes in the ambient or surrounding surface temperature, when humidity is disregarded, will change the comfort level. The dynamics of heat flow within and through a building envelope at low exterior temperatures is depicted in **Fig. 1.**

Forms of heat transfer

The classical principles of heat dynamics describe how heat passes through materials, restated here as an introduction to understanding the design principles and applications of insulation.

• *Conduction,* the transfer of heat by direct contact between two parts of a stationary system, caused by a temperature difference

---

Credits: The author is indebted for contributions to this article by Larry Berglund, Ph.D., John B. Pierce Foundation, Yale University.

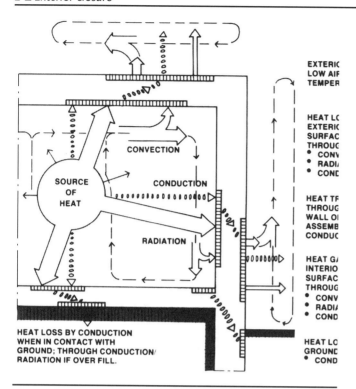

Fig. 1. Heat flow in and around the building envelope.

between those two parts. An example of conductive heat loss is warming your feet in bed by pressing them to your partner's back; an example of insulation from conductive heat loss is wearing socks while doing so.

• *Convection,* the transfer of heat from one material to another by the circulation or movement of an intermediary fluid, such as a liquid or gas. Diffusion can be considered a form of convection for the purposes of this definition. An example of convection is warming your hands by blowing on them; an example of convective insulation is stepping behind a wind shelter.

• *Radiation,* the transfer of heat by electromagnetic waves, irrespective of the temperature of the intervening medium such as air. An example of radiation is warming yourself by standing in sunlight; an example of radiant insulation (radiant barrier) is walking in the shade on a hot summer day.

• *Evaporation* is also a form of heat transfer by phase change, not directly relevant to insulating properties of materials but part of thermal heat loss, such as water cooling a roof surface when it evaporates, absorbing "latent heat" in order to drive the evaporation process. Similarly, when ice melts on a roof surface, it "gives back" the latent heat originally required to freeze water into ice. In well-insulated roofs, neither of these effects is major.

• *Thermal time lag,* or heat storage effect of heat in materials with high thermal mass or capacitance, is a related process, important in thermal performance of materials such as adobe or masonry. Heat moves into and out of such materials very slowly, and for this reason, we say it is "stored" in the material's mass. Time-lag effects explain some effects related to insulating buildings.

Infiltration (or exfiltration of warm air to outside cooler air) is not considered in the classic definition of heat transfer but is an unintended source of temperature and humidity flow through the building envelope. The importance of infiltration losses in design of insulated envelope is represented in **Box A.** Also see the article elsewhere in this volume, "Moisture Control."

To illustrate the issues raised in design of insulation details, an example of a complex heat and mass transfer that occurs in buildings is offered in **Box B.**

Radiation and reflectivity

Radiation is the phenomenon of heat transfer by radiant energy through space (without the need of a medium of transfer) from a body or material at a higher temperature to bodies or materials at lower temperatures that are in its line of sight (**Fig. 2**).

Heat transfer by radiation increases significantly as the temperature of the emitting surface rises. Solar energy striking a surface will be partially reflected and partially absorbed, with the fractions primarily dependent on the selectivity or reflectance of the surface: a dark (selective) surface may absorb about 90 percent, while a white (reflective) surface will absorb from 20 to 40 percent, reflecting the balance. The difference between temperatures of different surfaces exposed to solar irradiation may be as much as 60F (15°C) as a result of their surface reflectance.

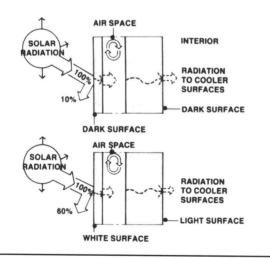

Fig. 2. Radiation: reflectivity.

Box A

Sources of infiltration

Location	% Contribution*	Responsibility
Envelope, wall: sill plate-foundation joint, electrical outlets, plumbing penetrations, top plate-attic joint, gaps in sheathing	18-50 (35 typ)	architect's detailing, builder's workmanship
Envelope, ceiling: leaks into attic via light fixtures, plumbing and electrical penetrations, attic access	3-30 (18 typ)	architect's detailing, builder's workmanship
Doors and windows: generic type rather than manufacturer, most important	6-22 (15 typ)	architect's design, specifier's selection
Exhausts and vents: fireplaces (indoor air supply, faulty dampers)	0-30 (12 typ)	architect's design; hardware, accessories
Exhausts and vents: vents in conditioned spaces (usu. lacking dampers)	2-12 (5 typ)	architect's design, specifier's selection
Heating system: location of and leaks in ductwork, absence of outdoor combustion intake	3-28 (15 typ)	engineer's design, installer's workmanship
Door openings and closings	significant* (varies)	occupants' habits; architect's plan and space relationships

*Values from ASHRAE *Fundamentals* does not account for door operations.

Box B

Illustrative example of a complex heat and mass transfer that occurs in buildings
(an actual case, occurring in cold weather)

– Water enters an insulated steep roof system through a leak.

– The interior finish is warmed by a combination of convective and radiant heat from the room below.

– The heat passes by conduction from the interior through the finish and vapor retarder.

– The water is warmed by conduction, and it undergoes a phase change, becoming water vapor.

– The water vapor diffuses through the insulation in all directions and passes by diffusion and convection to the underside of the roof sheathing.

– At the roof sheathing, which is cold, the water vapor condenses, transferring phase change heat to the sheathing.

– The heat passes through the roof sheathing and covering by conduction, and it leaves the system by a combination of radiation to the sky, convection to the air, and convection to the rainwater running down the roof.

– After building up droplets on the underside of the roof sheathing, the water drips down through the insulation to the vapor retarder, and the process continues.

– After a while the entire system is sopping wet, and it is difficult to find the source of the moisture. The architect is called to explain why the whole building is wet and filled with mold spores.

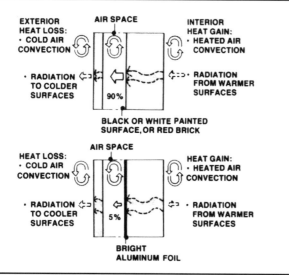

Fig. 3. Radiation: emissivity.

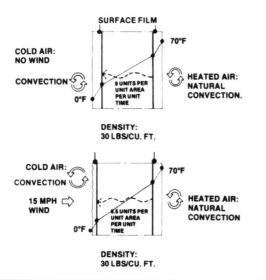

Fig. 4. Convection: surface conductance.

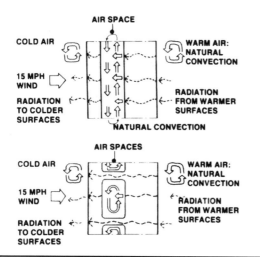

Fig. 5. Convection and radiation: vertical air space.

Radiation and emissivity

Temperature and emissivity of the surface will determine how heat gained is radiated (**Fig. 3**).

The visible color of most painted surfaces has limited effect on emissivity: black and white lacquers at 100F (37°C) to 200F (93°C) both have an emissivity range of 0.80 to 0.95. Metallic surfaces, especially when polished, have much lower coefficients of emissivity. Unpainted metallic surfaces therefore will reradiate more slowly than painted surfaces and remain hotter.

The term "infrared" includes a range of wave frequencies. Sunlight includes this whole range. However, the infrared radiation given off by building surfaces has longer wave lengths and lower wave frequencies. The emissivity of surfaces differs depending on the wave length. Thus dark roofing materials will absorb more radiant heat than light surfaces, but both dark and light surfaces emit about the same amount of low frequency radiation.

Glass and some transparent plastics make use of the differing emissivity to long and short wave infrared radiation. Clear and tinted glass transmits most of the sunlight but absorbs much of the heat radiated by objects in a building. This is called the "greenhouse effect." "Low-e" glass and plastic transmit most of the sunlight but reflect much of the heat radiated by objects in a building, thus lowering heat loss.

Convection and surface conductance

Heat will flow through a solid body when there is a temperature differential on opposite sides (**Fig. 4**).

Heat gain and heat loss by and from the body will be by convection: air in contact with the surfaces will either give up heat to the body, or pick up heat from it. Natural convection will take place when the motion of air is due entirely to differences in density. Forced convection occurs when external forces augment the air motion.

The heat flow through a surface film, the convective surface conductance, in general use is the design value for interior surfaces: still air generally assumed at 0.65 Btu/hr sq ft per degree F. Because this varies somewhat depending on surface material, relative position of surface, direction of heat flow and temperature, and other design values are sometimes used. The design value for exterior surface, whether vertical or horizontal, with 15 mph wind is 6 Btu/hr sq ft per degree F. These design values are incorporated into the temperature gradient calculations offered below.

Convection and radiation: vertical air space

Heat transfer through an air space incorporated into a vertical assembly will be by natural convection within the air space: temperature differences between the surfaces of components facing the air space will set up convective currents within the air space (**Fig. 5**).

The amount of heat transferred will increase with increase in temperature differences of the two surfaces and will not be significantly affected by the temperature level. Radiation will occur through the air space from the warm surface to the cold one. At low temperature levels, convection will be the controlling factor: at very high temperatures, the controlling factor is radiation.

Convection and radiation: horizontal air space

Heat transfer through horizontal air spaces will differ depending on the direction of heat flow (**Fig. 6**).

Upward heat flow through an air space will be by convection and radiation, similar to that for vertical air space. The transfer by radiation is the same through vertical and horizontal air spaces. Assuming that at normal temperatures, the emitting surface has a coefficient of 0.9—such as for painted surfaces or red brick—the heat transfer by radiation might be about 50 percent of the total heat transferred. If a bright metallic surface is substituted, heat transfer by radiation may be reduced to about 5 percent of the total.

Conduction

Conduction is the transfer of heat from one part of the body to another, or from one body to another which is in physical contact with it, without any appreciable displacement of the particles of the body or bodies (**Fig. 7**). Heat continues to flow as long as a temperature difference exists within the body, or between bodies in contact with one another.

The rate of heat flow depends upon the conductivity of the body. Conductivity of materials varies with differences in their densities: low density materials have voids in them, which contain air or other gaseous substances and which impede the transfer of heat by increasing the cross-sectional area or length of travel.

Temperature variations and units of measure

Equivalent temperature

Heat gain and heat loss in assemblies is normally calculated at the time of greatest heat flow, which implies that such conditions remain the same at all times. This approach is referred to as the steady state of heat flow.

Actual conditions do change almost constantly, especially when an assembly is exposed to variable solar radiation, resulting in an unsteady state of heat flow. An assembly may be exposed to instantaneous heat gain through solar radiation, which will first be absorbed by the surface layer. The temperature of this layer will rise above the temperature of the remainder of the assembly, and also above the temperature of outdoor air.

The unsteady flow of heat or dynamic response generally is accounted for by using the equivalent temperature difference (**Fig. 8**):

− The temperature difference that reflects the total heat flow through an assembly caused by variable solar radiation and outdoor temperature.

− The solar irradiation required to establish its amount at a given location can be found in ASHRAE *HVAC Applications* (ASHRAE 1991 or latest edition).

− Design temperature differentials for a given location are available from NCDC (see References).

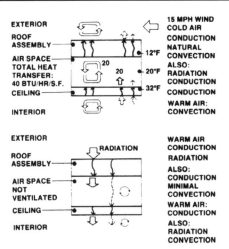

Fig. 6. Convection and radiation: horizontal air space.

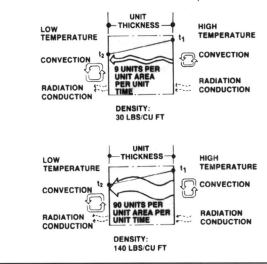

Fig. 7. Conduction.

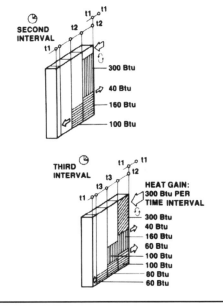

Fig. 8. Equivalent temperature.

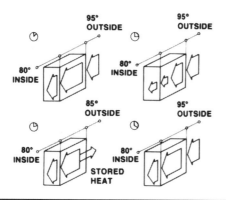

Fig. 9. Varying outdoor temperatures.

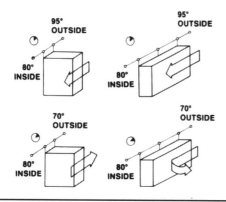

Fig. 10. Time lag.

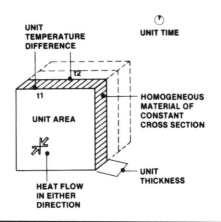

Fig. 11. Conductivity.

Varying outdoor temperatures

The equivalent temperature difference must take into account the duration of the exposure during various times of the day (**Fig. 9**). Outside temperatures vary with a resultant immediate effect on the flow of heat.

For example, if outdoor temperature suddenly drops from 95 to 85F (35 to 29.5°C):

– heat continues to flow from the interior surface of the assembly into an interior space at 80F (26.6°C).

– there is also heat flow from the outer surface of the assembly to now cooler outside air.

– therefore the amount of heat stored within the assembly is reduced.

If the outside temperature rises again to 95F (35°C) after several hours and the outer surface of the assembly begins to gain heat, the flow of heat from the inner surface of the assembly into the interior space does not immediately rise to its previous level:

– the inner surface remains slightly above the temperature of the interior air due to negligible heat flow when outdoor temperature was at 85F (29.5°C).

– heat flow into the interior increases gradually, returning to the previous level only after the temperature of the entire assembly has risen to a point where the steady state condition is re-established.

Time lag

The interval between the change in outdoor temperature and the temperature of the inner surface is known as the time lag (**Fig. 10**). It is due mostly to the heat required to raise the temperature of the assembly itself. Time lag is the time required to establish steady state condition through an assembly: for heat to travel through an assembly from the warm surface to the colder one. Thin lightweight assemblies have little mass and do not require large amounts of heat to raise their temperature. Dense, thick assemblies have a large heat storage capacity.

Conductivity

Thermal conductivity designated k, is a property of homogeneous material (**Fig. 11**). Thermal conductivity is measured by the quantity of units of heat passing through a unit thickness, per unit area, in unit time, when a unit temperature difference is maintained between the outer surfaces of the material. Coefficients of conductivity cannot be added to yield the U value.

Generally used units are:

– units of heat given by British thermal unit, or Btu, which is the amount of heat required to raise the temperature of 1 lb of water from 63 to 64F.

– unit thickness: 1 in

– unit area: 1 sq ft

– unit time: 1 hr

– unit temperature difference: 1F

Conductance

Thermal conductance designated C measures the rate of heat flow through the actual thickness of homogeneous, nonhomogeneous, or composite materials (**Fig. 12**):

- Conductance is defined as the heat flow in Btu per hour through one square foot area of given thickness for one degree F difference in temperature between the outer surfaces.

- Coefficients of conductance should not be added.

Thermal resistance, designated R or 1/C, is the reciprocal of conductance:

- It is a unit for the resistance to heat flow through a given thickness of a homogeneous, nonhomogeneous, or composite material.

- It is measured by the temperature difference in degrees F between the outer surfaces required to cause one Btu to flow through one square foot per hour: R = temperature difference in degrees F divided by Btu per one square foot per hour.

- Resistance (R) values may be added.

U value

Thermal transmittance, designated as U value, is the measure of heat flow through a component of the building, whether vertical or horizontal, when a difference between air temperatures on either side of such component exists (**Fig. 13**):

- The effect of air spaces ¾ in and wider, incorporated into the assemblies, and that of surface air films is included in the coefficient of thermal transmittance.

- Thermal transmittance is measured by Btu per hour through one square foot, when the temperature difference of the air is one degree F between the two surfaces of the assembly.

- The U value is the reciprocal of the sum of all thermal resistances of the components, or the total resistance to heat flow through a complete assembly: Sum. R = R of surface film + R of outer component or components + R of air space or spaces + R of inner component or components + R of surface film.

  - U values cannot be added to determine the total U value; when modifications of an assembly are investigated, thermal resistances (R values) should be used.

In *ASHRAE Fundamentals,* Chapter 20 "Thermal Insulation and Vapor Retarders" gives the standard procedure for calculating heat flow. Box B offers a short-form method, intended as a very brief summary, illustrating the above definitions.

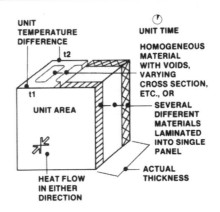

Fig. 12. Conductance.

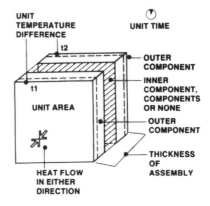

Fig. 13. Transmittance.

Box C

Calculating heat flow: a short-form method

- Heat passes from the warm side of materials and systems to the cold side. If the temperature at the two sides is the same, heat does not pass. Coldness is not considered a quality; it is simply less heat.

- Heat transfers through different materials at different rates. Gold, aluminum, and other metals conduct heat at very high rates, while plastic foams and other insulating materials, conduct heat poorly. The time rate of heat conduction through gold is approximately a thousand times as great as the rate through polyisocyanurate foam. Also, foam is less expensive.

- The time rate of thermal conductivity of materials is represented by the symbols "C" and "k," and the time rate of the total heat flow from the fluid on the warm side of the construction to the fluid on the cool side is represented by "U" or "U factor."

- "C" (conductance) is the time rate of heat flow through the unit area of a body per unit of temperature difference.

- "k" (conductivity) is the time rate of heat flow through the unit area of a homogeneous material per unit of thickness.

- "Btu" (British thermal units) is a measure of heat energy required to raise the temperature of one pound of water one degree Fahrenheit (F).

- The resistance to heat flow is the reciprocal of thermal conductance, and is represented by "R." The reciprocal of conductivity is resistivity, represented by "r." (Although it is convenient to assume that these factors and rates are constant for any material, this is not the case. Many materials vary in their insulating value according to such factors as temperature and dampness.)

Heat flow can be calculated by knowing the temperatures on both sides of construction and the thermal resistance, or insulating value, of the construction. Thermal resistance values can be added to give the total thermal resistance of the construction system.

Consider the wall of a wood frame house. The composition of the wall, from outside to inside, is as follows. The values in this example are given in inch-pound units as degrees Fahrenheit (F), Btu, and inches. Comparable units can be transposed for the SI (metric) system.

- *Given that:*

- The air film on the outside of the wall. At 15 mph the thermal resistance of that air film is assumed to be 0.17.

- ½ in (1.27 cm) wood siding. The thermal resistance is approximately 0.81.

- Underlayment or air infiltration retarder. The thermal resistance is so low as to be negligible.

- ½ in (1.27 cm) plywood sheathing. The thermal resistance is approximately 0.63.

- Nominal 2 × 6 studs 24 in o.c. The thermal resistance is approximately 5.5. The portion of the wall with studs is 1.5 / 24 = 0.06.

- Between the studs: nominal 6 in (15 cm) fiberglass batt insulation. The thermal resistance is approximately 19. The portion of the wall between the studs is 0.94.

- Vapor retarder. The thermal resistance is so low as to be negligible.

- ½ in (1.27 cm) gypsum wallboard. The thermal resistance is 0.45.

- Inside air film. The thermal resistance is approximately 0.61. Note: one of the reasons why blowing air against the inside of a

window clears condensation is that it lowers the thermal resistance of the inside air film and thus warms the glass.

- *Solution:*

- The total thermal resistance between the studs is the sum of the appropriate figures above, 21.67.

- The total thermal resistance at the studs is the sum of the appropriate figures above, 8.17.

- Multiplying the thermal resistance between the studs × 0.94, and multiplying the thermal resistance at the studs × 0.06: the average thermal resistance for the wall, combining studs and insulated spaces between the studs, is 20.86.

- The heat loss through this wall will be the reciprocal of the total thermal resistance. 1 / 20.86 = 0.048. This is the U factor, meaning that 0.048 Btu of heat will pass through the wall per hour per square foot of wall per degree F temperature difference.

- The U factor and resistance are the reciprocal of one another, and a graph showing their relationship is hyperbolic. The curve is asymptotic (approaching but never reaching zero). No matter how much insulation is used, the heat loss will always be above zero, and no matter how little insulation is used, the heat loss will be finite. The heat loss advantage of using a little insulation is great, but adding the same amount again has less advantage.

There is a point of little return, where adding more insulation has virtually no advantage. For example:

- Adding 1 in of extruded, expanded polystyrene to a thin sheet of aluminum increases the R value and resistance to heat flow from 0.79 to 5.79, or more than seven-fold. It decreases the U factor from 1.26 to 0.17, which is a difference of 1.09.

- Adding an additional inch of extruded, expanded polystyrene to the previous system changes the R value from 5.79 to 10.79. It decreases the U factor from 0.17 to 0.09, which is a difference of 0.08, much lower than the previous figure.

- Adding an additional inch of extruded, expanded polystyrene to the previous system changes the R value from 10.79 to 15.79. It decreases the U factor from 0.09 to 0.06, a difference of 0.03.

- Adding an additional inch of extruded, expanded polystyrene to the previous system changes the R value from 15.79 to 20.79, or less than 1⅓ times the previous value. It decreases the U factor from 0.06 to 0.05, a difference of 0.01.

The U value is (approximately) proportional to the money spent on fuel. If the money value per Btu per year is $2.00, the savings per square foot in going from no insulation to 1 in of insulation, as calculated above, is 1.09 × $2.00 = $2.18 (example in southern New England). Under the same conditions, adding 3 in of additional insulation will save $0.24.

As the calculation shows, it makes more sense to add insulation to parts of a building that have little or no insulation, while adding more insulation to a well-insulated building may not pay for itself. Even more important, however, are the quality of the workmanship in installing the insulation and the proper operation of the building. Improperly installed or missing insulation does no good. The architect should be on the job to verify proper installation of the insulation, air infiltration barrier, and vapor retarder.

Table 1 indicates common thermal resistance factors, compiled from various sources, principally from *ASHRAE Fundamentals*. A complete tabulation along with the thermal properties of common building materials and assemblies can be found in additional tables at the end of this article.

There are also doors and windows in walls, for which thermal resistance figures are available from manufacturers (often given only for the center of the units, but properly calculated for the entire assembly, including perimeter losses). A typical 1-¾ in (4.5 cm) solid core wood flush door would have a thermal resistance of approximately 3.0. A typical clad double-hung wood window with insulating glass might have a thermal resistance of approximately 3.0.

For fixed glazing and other glazing not listed in manufacturers' literature, the following figures are typical. Note, however, that the thermal resistance figures for glass include the insulating values for interior and exterior air films, not the glass alone.

– One sheet of ³⁄₃₂-in (2.3 mm) monolithic glass: 0.89.

– One sheet of ¼-in (6.3 mm) float glass: 0.92. Note that the thickness of the glass has little effect on the thermal resistance; glass by itself is a very poor insulator.

– Insulating glass composed of two sheets of ¼-in (6.3 mm) float glass and ½-in (12.6 mm) dry air space: 2.08.

– Insulating glass, as above, with low-emissivity coating, which reflects radiant heat back inside: 3.0.

– Insulating glass, as above, with low-emissivity coating and also argon-filled space: 3.57.

For skylights, manufacturers' data are available. Most skylights have deep metal rafters, so that the metal area exposed to the inside air is large. The relative areas of glass and frame are important in estimating heat loss. The primary route of heat transfer from the outer rafter covers to the inner rafters is probably the metal fasteners. This suggests a good use of reinforced polymer fasteners, which have much lower thermal conductivity.

2 TYPES OF INSULATION

The practical ideal insulation is a vacuum or air when kept completely motionless in a space separating two solid components. Air, however, cannot be kept motionless even in a narrow vertical cavity (as in a wall assembly).

– Convective currents develop, which transfer heat from the warm side of the cavity to the colder one.

– Radiation from the warm side to the colder one takes place whether the air moves or is still.

– In an air space broken up horizontally into tiny compartments convective currents can be effectively minimized, and the excellent insulating properties of still air utilized.

Mass type insulation reduces the flow of heat by preventing convection in entrapped air and also by forming a barrier to radiation. Some types (such as foamed plastics, or cellular glass) trap small quantities

Table 1. Thermal resistance of common building materials.

Material *R-value*	*Thickness*	
Air film, exterior, 15 mph wind		0.17
Air film, interior		0.52
Aluminum	per inch	0.008
Asphalt shingles	normal	0.44
Brick, common		
80 lb.	cubic ft./inch	0.45-0.31
100 lb.	cubic ft./inch	0.30-0.23
120 lb.	cubic ft./inch	0.23-0.16
Built-up roofing	3/8"	0.33
Carpet and fibrous pad	normal	2.08
Cellular glass	per inch	2.86
Cellulosic insulation (milled paper or wood pulp)	per inch	3.70-3.13
Cellular polyisocyanurate (gas-impermeable facers)	per inch	7.20
Cellular polyurethane/ polyisocyanurate (unfaced)	per inch	6.25-5.56
Concrete, normal weight	per inch	0.08
Concrete masonry units, lightweight	8 inch	3.2-1.90
Same with perlite filled cores		5.3-3.9
Concrete masonry units, normal weight	8 inch	1.11-0.97
Same with perlite filled cores		2.0
Douglas Fir-Larch	per inch	1.06-0.99
Expanded perlite, organic bonded	per inch	2.78
Expanded polystyrene, extruded (smooth skin surface)	per inch	5.00
Expanded polystyrene beadboard	per inch	4.00
Cellular glass	per inch	2.7
Foil-faced polyethylene foam, heat flow down	1/4"	10.74
Glass fiber, organic bonded	per inch	4.00
Gypsum or plaster board	0.5 inches	0.45
Gypsum plaster: sand aggregate	per inch	0.18
Mineral fiber batts processed from rock, slag, or glass	nom. 6 inch	22
Oak	per inch	0.89-0.80
Particleboard		
low density	per inch	1.41
medium density	per inch	1.06
high density	per inch	0.85
Plywood (Douglas Fir)	per inch	1.25
Shingles, wood, 16 inches, 7-1/2" exposure		0.87
Siding, wood	0.5 thick	0.81
Stucco	per inch	0.20
Western redcedar	per inch	1.48-1.11
Wood, hardwood finish	0.75 inches	0.68

of air or other gaseous substances in closed cells. The heat flow through the cells is greatly reduced because convection currents are virtually eliminated in small cells.

Fibrous materials will perform best at a specified optimum density:

– if compressed to higher than optimum density, heat flow will increase since fiber will touch fiber and some of the surface air film will be lost.

– if fluffed up too much, more heat may be transmitted by convection or radiation through the large voids.

Reflective insulation—properly called *radiant barriers*—reduces the transfer of heat through air spaces by minimizing radiation of energy from the warmer, or emitting, surface of one of the components that enclose an air space to a colder, or receiving, surface of the other component:

– The emissivity of various building materials at the same surface temperature vary: radiation across an air space between two polished aluminum surfaces will be only approximately 3 percent of that between two black surfaces.

– Reflective materials act as insulation because of their low surface emissivity by reflecting incident radiant energy: in a cavity wall up to 60 percent of heat transfer is estimated to be by radiation.

Of all of these, the principal way in which thermal insulation works is the capacity of that material to resist heat flow by forming a tortuous path through the material, around voids. The more efficient insulation types are also made from materials with poor thermal conductance. Low emissivity materials and coatings reflect radiant heat.

Inorganic fibers include fiberglass, mineral wool, spun basalt, asbestos, ceramic fibers, and others. These may be in the form of loose fibers, batts, and semi-rigid boards.

Asbestos was used in the past for thermal insulation. It has been found to cause cancer, and its use is restricted today. Other fibers are being used where asbestos was once used. The following caution is the final paragraph in Skinner (1988): "After a thousand years of use, asbestos is being replaced by other, often fibrous, materials. It remains to be seen whether the substitutes will be as successful, commercially and financially, or more or less hazardous. We are certainly not going to do without fibrous inorganic materials nor expunge them from our environment."

Representative insulation materials include:

• Organic fibers, including cellulose fibers, bagasse, thatch, and wood fibers.

• Inorganic foams, including foamed glass, cellular concrete, hollow glass bead concrete, perlite, and vermiculite. Expanded polystyrene bead concrete can also be considered in this category, since the main function of the beads is to create voids in the concrete.

• Organic foams, including expanded polystyrene, polyurethane foam, and polyisocyanurate foam. Cork is a natural form of void-filled organic material.

• Metal foils and metal foil laminated on other materials. One form combines shiny aluminum foil with flexible polyethylene foam, and its manufacturer reports very favorable insulation values, especially where radiant heat is the predominant mode of heat transfer.

• Composite materials combining several of the materials listed above.

• Natural materials of low thermal resistance that, nevertheless, act as thermal insulators and also provide thermal storage include earth, masonry, and turf.

Perimeter and foundation insulation

Perimeter and other foundation insulation reduce heat loss through the foundation walls. It may be installed outside the foundations, inside the foundations, integral with the foundations, under slabs-on-grade, or in a combination of these locations. Common perimeter insulation types include expanded polystyrene board and fibrous glass board. There is some evidence that insects can attack polystyrene insulation, and cellular glass and fibrous glass insulation may be a good alternative material.

Wall insulation

Selection of the type of insulation to be used should also include consideration of the method of its installation within the wall assembly. Wall assemblies may be insulated by:

• Batt insulation, between studs, available unfaced or with reflective foil or paper face.

• Foamed-in-place insulation between studs.

• Rigid-board insulation sheathing, placed outside, within, or on the inside face. Each location has an impact on constructability and attachment details.

• Foamed-in-place insulation may be placed within masonry cavities.

• Concrete Masonry Units (CMU) available with rigid insulation inserts cast-in during fabrication.

• Rigid board insulation, laminated or clip attached, to inside face of masonry walls. Furring strips may have to be provided between the boards to facilitate attachment of interior facing materials.

• Loose insulation fill within masonry cavities.

• Monolithic in-place concrete assemblies may be insulated with rigid board insulation laminated or clip attached to interior face.

• Precast and tilt-up concrete assemblies may be insulated by rigid board insulation between interior and exterior courses of a sandwich panel.

Water vapor migration is either by diffusion, or by air leakage, and is generally controlled by providing a vapor retarder on the warm side of the wall. Vapor retarders consist of materials that resist the diffusion of vapor through them under the action of a difference in pressure, such as plastic film metallic foil, coated paper, and, to a certain extent, applied coatings.

Walls in existing buildings may be insulated with blown-in or foamed-in insulation. Consideration should be given to:

– ensuring that all voids in wall assembly are completely filled.

– possible settlement of blown-in insulation.

– water vapor migrating by diffusion or by air leakage into the wall assembly, condensing within the wall and causing rapid deterioration of exterior facing or even the wall assembly itself.

Masonry wall insulation

– Expanded polystyrene board and some other materials can be installed in the cavities of masonry cavity walls and veneer walls. It can be made with an integral drainage course to keep the cavity drainage from being clogged with mortar.

– Fibrous glass and other inorganic fiber insulation boards may also be used in wall cavities.

Workmanship is especially important for masonry wall insulation. Once the walls are built, inspection is impossible. Unless the insulation is secured tightly to one of the wythes, cold air can circulate around and behind the insulation, greatly reducing its effect. Unsecured cavity insulation acts like a warm coat unbuttoned.

– Expanded polystyrene inserts are available for concrete masonry units, installed in the factory or field.

– Foam-in-place polyurethane and polyisocyanurate can be placed in wall cavities, where they expand and fill the space.

– Various types of insulation can be installed on the inside of masonry walls, and special furring systems with little or no thermal bridging are available.

– An innovative system used for fruit storage and other uses incorporates a thick extruded, expanded polystyrene core and concrete faces, held together through the insulation with permanent reinforced polymer form ties.

– Exterior insulation and finish systems (EIFS) can be applied to the masonry exterior. The insulation may be extruded, expanded polystyrene board or expanded polystyrene bead board. This system may be applied over other types of structure.

Frame wall insulation

– The most common type of insulation is fibrous glass batts. Other types of insulation for stud spaces include foam-in-place polyurethane, polyisocyanurate, and other plastic foams, other inorganic fiber batts, blown-in fibrous glass, blown-in cellulose fibers, and reflective foil systems.

– If there are plumbing lines in exterior walls (not a good idea, but sometimes necessary), the insulation should be installed outside the pipes and, just as important, not inside the pipes. If the separation is small, use a highly efficient insulation.

– Various types of board insulation can be installed inside or outside the frame. They have the advantages of potentially high insulation value per unit thickness and not being penetrated by the framing members. The siding or interior finish is installed over them. If they are used instead of plywood sheathing, other forms of bracing are required to replace the shear value of the plywood.

– Integral wall materials and insulation.

– Wood fiber Portland cement roof panels have been used as wall panels with integral insulating qualities.

– Cellular concrete panels have been used as bearing and non–load-bearing walls with integral insulation. Expanded polystyrene bead concrete has been used in the same way.

– Log houses have thick wooden walls, with fair insulating properties.

Roof and attic insulation

Roof insulation may be installed above the roof structure. It has the advantage of being an unbroken layer. Available materials include organic foam board, organic and inorganic fiberboard, cellular concrete, and cellular glass board. Protected membrane roof systems have the insulation above the membrane, and the insulation is extruded, expanded polystyrene board. The insulation above the membrane must be protected from sunlight, and it must be ballasted to prevent its blowing off. *ASHRAE Fundamentals* recommends that roof insulation be placed above the structure of low-slope roofs. One important advantage is that the roof structure is protected from thermal changes and potential resulting damage.

• Roof insulation may be integral with the roof structure. Thick wood plank roof decks have enough insulating quality for mild climates. Another form of integral roof deck is Portland cement-wood fiber planks. Reinforced cellular concrete planks have been used as roof decking.

• Roof insulation may be installed under the roof. This is the normal method for steep roofs, and it is also used for low-slope roofs. The insulation may be between the attic floor joists, between the rafters, or in between. Common materials include fibrous glass batts, blown-in fibrous glass, and blown-in cellulose fibers. Other materials can also be used. It is difficult to avoid multiple penetrations of the insulation, and, in the author's experience, it is common for there to be voids in the insulation.

• There are several other cautions regarding the use of roof and ceiling insulation between framing members. Unless the insulation is secured at the eaves, the insulation may impede proper ventilation above it. Also, and probably more important, the insulation may lift the eaves, and cold winter air may pass under the insulation. Attic insulation is sometimes omitted over walls containing plumbing lines, thus chilling the occupants and freezing the pipes. It is prudent for the architect to inspect the attic insulation carefully before substantial completion of the construction. It is worth the expense to have thermographic studies made of buildings during their first winter, to verify proper placement of insulation.

• One of the most important functions of roof and attic insulation is to limit summer heat gain. The sun's heat is delivered as radiant heat. Light, heat-reflective roof coverings are available at little or no additional cost, and they are very effective. Radiant barrier systems, with the reflective surfaces facing air spaces, are also effective.

Soffit insulation has the same characteristics as ceiling insulation. If there are plumbing lines between the framing members, they should be above the insulation, and there should be no insulation above the pipes.

Basement insulation

Basement ceiling insulation may be used in place of perimeter insulation and interior basement wall insulation. Depending on the use of the basement and the relative areas of the basement ceiling and walls, the choice may be one or the other. The most common fault with basement ceiling insulation is that it tends to be incomplete. Even if just a few voids in the insulation exist per joist space, cold air from the basement will circulate above and below the insulation. Careful, void-free installation and application of a gypsum board ceiling or poultry netting retainer is essential. Plumbing pipes are best kept above the insulation, and all mechanical equipment and pipes in the cold basement must be insulated.

• There might be a problem with insulated water pipes in very cold areas. If the water does not flow often, the insulation will only slow the water's freezing, not stop it. A heat source is needed to stop freezing.

3 SUMMARY: INSULATED ENVELOPE DESIGN

Design, calculation, and installation details of insulation are often specified by rote reference to prevailing codes and standards. This approach, however expeditious, fails to benefit from the interactive role of thermal insulation, moisture control and protection of building materials. There are substantial economies to be realized through optimally insulated envelopes that account for the role that thermal mass, solar, and other time-lag factors might serve to reduce HVAC equipment sizing and operating costs.

Thermal storage capacity

The thermal mass of masonry and concrete walls can be used in heat loss calculations to show lowered heat loss. The method is described in Brick Institute of America and National Concrete Masonry Association publications. Heat storage capacity of walls can be used to significant advantage:

– to reduce peak heat gain and thereby reduce cooling loads on mechanical equipment (when the masonry surface is exposed to interior air).

– to reduce heat losses through time lag (when there is partial to significant heat flow through the envelope).

– to store heat absorbed through solar energy and release it when needed (as in glass-covered masonry walls or in interior masonry exposed to solar irradiation).

To analyze time lag and heat storage capacity of a design, a "dynamic analysis" of heat gain/loss is required that takes into account the hourly changes in weather conditions as well as the thermal storage capacity of the structure, and closely predicts the peak loads required to determine the size of equipment needed to control the interior environment of a structure.

Water vapor condensation

The dew point method of calculating whether or not water vapor condensation will occur is made determinate by the existence of one vapor retarder. However, recent research has shown that vapor movement in buildings is much more complex than was thought when this method was first devised. Air almost always contains a certain amount of water vapor. The maximum amount of vapor that can be contained at constant pressure increases with the temperature of the air/vapor mixture, and the curve is upwardly concave:

– When air at a given temperature, saturated with water vapor, is cooled, or comes into contact with a colder surface, water vapor will continuously condense as long as the temperature of the air/vapor mixture drops.

– Insulation incorporated into assemblies of an enclosure changes the temperature gradients through them, thereby increasing the likelihood of condensation within the assemblies.

– Condensation may occur within the insulation, if it is permeable, and increase its density, thereby lowering its thermal resistance.

Insulation and moisture control issues must be considered together in designing the building envelope and assembly. In its simplest form, water vapor condensation requires low temperatures and high partial vapor pressure. "Partial vapor pressure" is the absolute (not relative) humidity, or the part of the air pressure that is exerted by the water vapor in the air. Under normal temperatures fit for human life, water vapor makes up a relatively small part of the total air pressure:

– at 0F (–18°C), partial vapor pressure at saturation is approximately ⅒th of 1 percent of the air pressure.

– at 32F (0°C), partial vapor pressure is ⁵⁄₁₀ of 1 percent.

– at 70F (21°C), partial vapor pressure is 2-½ percent.

– at 100F (38°C), partial vapor pressure is 6 percent.

Condensation will not occur unless the partial vapor pressure is high enough and the temperature is low enough. To predict whether water vapor condensation will occur, the conditions must be quantified, and fairly complex calculations are required. Most building construction is affected by water vapor condensation, and the effect is mostly harmful. Examples are wet insulation, rotting wood structure, damp, spalling masonry, and mildew spores in the air.

Insulation, envelope, and HVAC systems

Determining how much insulation to use should involve the following minimum considerations:

– Conforming to code requirements. This step alone may come close to determining a proper level or amount of insulation, but this judgment has to be considered in terms of site and building specific factors. Higher insulation values may permit lower mechanical system installation sizing and usage.

– Making a best guess as to the likelihood of future energy costs and cost escalation compared to general inflation. Unless one has special information, assume that energy inflation will approximate general inflation.

- Drawing a graph, or making a series of calculations, of dollar savings vs. the cost of additional insulation. After a certain increase in insulation thickness, the added provision of insulation may require higher costs for the envelope. For complex buildings, utilization of computer simulation programs is required for more accurate thermal dynamic analysis.

- Adding factors having to do with the durability of the building and its possible vulnerability to condensation, as affected by insulation.

- Adding the time-value of money.

- Note that too much insulation may be wasteful of irreplaceable resources and money.

- Adding ethical factors regarding non-cash values of reducing fuel use and using resources to increase the insulation.

The role and effectiveness of thermal resistance of the building envelope is dependent on these dynamic variables:

- daily and seasonal temperatures imposed by weather, as a function of average and extreme climate norms.

- daily flux of internal heat gain, as a function of occupancy, building type, electric lighting, and equipment loads.

- amount and placement of windows and skylights, especially the respective benefit or liability of solar heat gain during underheated or overheated periods.

- HVAC system type, thermal controls, and response time of the HVAC system.

- occupancy profile of the building; for example, limited to daytime use compared to 24-hour occupancy.

For example:

- a well-insulated exterior wall (including High-R windows), may preclude the need for perimeter heating, or may permit downsized heating and cooling plant capacity, thus saving in HVAC installation and operating costs.

- thermal mass exposed to the building interior and insulated on the outside will serve as a "heat sink" for typically overheated hours and occupancy conditions, thus reducing cooling plant sizes and operating costs.

- poorly insulated masonry structures will require longer "start up" of heating time to reach comfortable indoor air and radiant surface temperatures.

- the interior temperature of a well-insulated structure that is used only during the day may "float," that is, remain relatively stable with the HVAC system turned down or off, requiring less energy and less "start up" time at the beginning of the following day.

- well-insulated structures, on the other hand, require careful provision of fresh-air ventilation supplied to all portions of the space, but especially those subject to temperature flux (such as near window areas).

- an improperly insulated building envelope (wall or roof) may create moisture control and condensation, potentially damaging to both the building envelope and to objects within (such as in art museums).

For all of these reasons, the determination of insulation values for major building components (ceilings/roofs, walls and windows) needs to be analyzed alongside thermal mass, building occupancy and equipment loads, lighting and mechanical system design and sizing.

The relative effectiveness of insulation, thermal mass for heat storage, and solar irradiation through windows requires complex calculations, now possible through computer simulation programs. Such analysis is needed to "optimize" the building envelope design and often demonstrates that reduced mechanical system sizing and reduced cycling are cost effective benefits of increasing insulation.

Various tabulated values of representative building components are given in the tables that follow. ■

REFERENCES

ASHRAE Fundamentals, Atlanta, American Society of Heating, Refrigerating and Air Conditioning Engineers, 1993 (or latest edition).

Fanger, P. O., *Thermal Comfort, Analysis and Applications in Environmental Engineering,* McGraw-Hill, New York, 1970.

NCDC Subscription Services Center, 310 State Route 956 Building 300, Rocket Center, WV 26726.

Sixth Canadian Masonry Symposium, *Proceedings of the Sixth Canadian Masonry Symposium,* Civil Engineering Department, University of Saskatchewan, Saskatoon, 1992.

Skinner, H. Catherine, et al., *Asbestos and Other Fibrous Materials,* Oxford University Press, New York, 1988.

Trechsel, Heinz R., ed., *Moisture Control in Buildings,* American Society for Testing and Materials (ASTM), Philadelphia, 1994.

Thermal resistances of plane air spaces[a,e]

(Reproduced by permission from *ASHRAE Handbook of Fundamentals*, 1977.)

All resistance values expressed in (hour)(square foot)(degree Fahrenheit temperature difference) per Btu

Values apply only to air spaces of uniform thickness bounded by plane, smooth, parallel surfaces with no leakage of air to or from the space.

Thermal resistance values for multiple air spaces must be based on careful estimates of mean temperature differences for each air space.

Position of Air Space	Direction of Heat Flow	Mean Temp,[b] (F)	Temp Diff,[b,d] (deg F)	0.5-in. Air Space[a] Value of E[b,c] 0.03	0.05	0.2	0.5	0.82	0.75-in. Air Space[a] Value of E[b,c] 0.03	0.05	0.2	0.5	0.82
Horiz.	Up	90	10	2.13	2.03	1.51	0.99	0.73	2.34	2.22	1.61	1.04	0.75
		50	30	1.62	1.57	1.29	0.96	0.75	1.71	1.66	1.35	0.99	0.77
		50	10	2.13	2.05	1.60	1.11	0.84	2.30	2.21	1.70	1.16	0.87
		0	20	1.73	1.70	1.45	1.12	0.91	1.83	1.79	1.52	1.16	0.93
		0	10	2.10	2.04	1.70	1.27	1.00	2.23	2.16	1.78	1.31	1.02
		−50	20	1.69	1.66	1.49	1.23	1.04	1.77	1.74	1.55	1.27	1.07
		−50	10	2.04	2.00	1.75	1.40	1.16	2.16	2.11	1.84	1.46	1.20
45° Slope	Up	90	10	2.44	2.31	1.65	1.06	0.76	2.96	2.78	1.88	1.15	0.81
		50	30	2.06	1.98	1.56	1.10	0.83	1.99	1.92	1.52	1.08	0.82
		50	10	2.55	2.44	1.83	1.22	0.90	2.90	2.75	2.00	1.29	0.94
		0	20	2.20	2.14	1.76	1.30	1.02	2.13	2.07	1.72	1.28	1.00
		0	10	2.63	2.54	2.03	1.44	1.10	2.72	2.62	2.08	1.47	1.12
		−50	20	2.08	2.04	1.78	1.42	1.17	2.05	2.01	1.76	1.41	1.16
		−50	10	2.62	2.56	2.17	1.66	1.33	2.53	2.47	2.10	1.62	1.30
Vertical	Horiz.	90	10	2.47	2.34	1.67	1.06	0.77	3.50	3.24	2.08	1.22	0.84
		50	30	2.57	2.46	1.84	1.23	0.90	2.91	2.77	2.01	1.30	0.94
		50	10	2.66	2.54	1.88	1.24	0.91	3.70	3.46	2.35	1.43	1.01
		0	20	2.82	2.72	2.14	1.50	1.13	3.14	3.02	2.32	1.58	1.18
		0	10	2.93	2.82	2.20	1.53	1.15	3.77	3.59	2.64	1.73	1.26
		−50	20	2.90	2.82	2.35	1.76	1.39	2.90	2.83	2.36	1.77	1.39
		−50	10	3.20	3.10	2.54	1.87	1.46	3.72	3.60	2.87	2.04	1.56
45° Slope	Down[d]	90	10	2.48	2.34	1.67	1.06	0.77	3.53	3.27	2.10	1.22	0.84
		50	30	2.64	2.52	1.87	1.24	0.91	3.43	3.23	2.24	1.39	0.99
		50	10	2.67	2.55	1.89	1.25	0.92	3.81	3.57	2.40	1.45	1.02
		0	20	2.91	2.80	2.19	1.52	1.15	3.75	3.57	2.63	1.72	1.26
		0	10	2.94	2.83	2.21	1.53	1.15	4.12	3.91	2.81	1.80	1.30
		−50	20	3.16	3.07	2.52	1.86	1.45	3.78	3.65	2.90	2.05	1.57
		−50	10	3.26	3.16	2.58	1.89	1.47	4.35	4.18	3.22	2.21	1.66
Horiz.	Down[d]	90	10	2.48	2.34	1.67	1.06	0.77	3.55	3.29	2.10	1.22	0.85
		50	30	2.66	2.54	1.88	1.24	0.91	3.77	3.52	2.38	1.44	1.02
		50	10	2.67	2.55	1.89	1.25	0.92	3.84	3.59	2.41	1.45	1.02
		0	20	2.94	2.83	2.20	1.53	1.15	4.18	3.96	2.83	1.81	1.30
		0	10	2.96	2.85	2.22	1.53	1.16	4.25	4.02	2.87	1.82	1.31
		−50	20	3.25	3.15	2.58	1.89	1.47	4.60	4.41	3.36	2.28	1.69
		−50	10	3.28	3.18	2.60	1.90	1.47	4.71	4.51	3.42	2.30	1.71

Position of Air Space	Direction of Heat Flow	Mean Temp (F)	Temp Diff (deg F)	1.5-in. Air Space[a] 0.03	0.05	0.2	0.5	0.82	3.5-in. Air Space[a] 0.03	0.05	0.2	0.5	0.82
Horiz	Up	90	10	2.55	2.41	1.71	1.08	0.77	2.84	2.66	1.83	1.13	0.80
		50	30	1.87	1.81	1.45	1.04	0.80	2.09	2.01	1.58	1.10	0.84
		50	10	2.50	2.40	1.81	1.21	0.89	2.80	2.66	1.95	1.28	0.93
		0	20	2.01	1.95	1.63	1.23	0.97	2.25	2.18	1.79	1.32	1.03
		0	10	2.43	2.35	1.90	1.38	1.06	2.71	2.62	2.07	1.47	1.12
		−50	20	1.94	1.91	1.68	1.36	1.13	2.19	2.14	1.86	1.47	1.20
		−50	10	2.37	2.31	1.99	1.55	1.26	2.65	2.58	2.18	1.67	1.33
45° Slope	Up	90	10	2.92	2.73	1.86	1.14	0.80	3.18	2.96	1.97	1.18	0.82
		50	30	2.14	2.06	1.61	1.12	0.84	2.26	2.17	1.67	1.15	0.86
		50	10	2.88	2.74	1.99	1.29	0.94	3.12	2.95	2.10	1.34	0.96
		0	20	2.30	2.23	1.82	1.34	1.04	2.42	2.35	1.90	1.38	1.06
		0	10	2.79	2.69	2.12	1.49	1.13	2.98	2.87	2.23	1.54	1.16
		−50	20	2.22	2.17	1.88	1.49	1.21	2.34	2.29	1.97	1.54	1.25
		−50	10	2.71	2.64	2.23	1.69	1.35	2.87	2.79	2.33	1.75	1.39
Vertical	Horiz.	90	10	3.99	3.66	2.25	1.27	0.87	3.69	3.40	2.15	1.24	0.85
		50	30	2.58	2.46	1.84	1.23	0.90	2.67	2.55	1.89	1.25	0.91
		50	10	3.79	3.55	2.39	1.45	1.02	3.63	3.40	2.32	1.42	1.01
		0	20	2.76	2.66	2.10	1.48	1.12	2.88	2.78	2.17	1.51	1.14
		0	10	3.51	3.35	2.51	1.67	1.23	3.49	3.33	2.50	1.67	1.23
		−50	20	2.64	2.58	2.18	1.66	1.33	2.82	2.75	2.30	1.73	1.37
		−50	10	3.31	3.21	2.62	1.91	1.48	3.40	3.30	2.67	1.94	1.50
45° Slope	Down[d]	90	10	5.07	4.55	2.56	1.36	0.91	4.81	4.33	2.49	1.34	0.90
		50	30	3.58	3.36	2.31	1.42	1.00	3.51	3.30	2.28	1.40	1.00
		50	10	5.10	4.66	2.85	1.60	1.09	4.74	4.36	2.73	1.57	1.08
		0	20	3.85	3.66	2.68	1.74	1.27	3.81	3.63	2.66	1.74	1.27
		0	10	4.92	4.62	3.16	1.94	1.37	4.59	4.32	3.02	1.88	1.34
		−50	20	3.62	3.50	2.80	2.01	1.54	3.77	3.64	2.90	2.05	1.57
		−50	10	4.67	4.47	3.40	2.29	1.70	4.50	4.32	3.31	2.25	1.68
Horiz.	Down[d]	90	10	6.09	5.35	2.79	1.43	0.94	10.07	8.19	3.41	1.57	1.00
		50	30	6.27	5.63	3.18	1.70	1.14	9.60	8.17	3.86	1.88	1.22
		50	10	6.61	5.90	3.27	1.73	1.15	11.15	9.27	4.09	1.93	1.24
		0	20	7.03	6.43	3.91	2.19	1.49	10.90	9.52	4.87	2.47	1.62
		0	10	7.31	6.66	4.00	2.22	1.51	11.97	10.32	5.08	2.52	1.64
		−50	20	7.73	7.20	4.77	2.85	1.99	11.64	10.49	6.02	3.25	2.18
		−50	10	8.09	7.52	4.91	2.89	2.01	12.98	11.56	6.36	3.34	2.22

[a] Credit for an air space resistance value cannot be taken more than once and only for the boundary conditions established.

[b] Interpolation is permissible for other values of mean temperature, temperature differences, and effective emittance E. Interpolation and moderate extrapolation for air spaces greater than 3.5 in. are also permissible.

[c] Effective emittance of the space E is given by $1/E = 1/e_1 + 1/e_2 - 1$, where e_1 and e_2 are the emittances of the surfaces of the air space (See section B of Table 3.)

[d] Resistances of horizontal spaces with heat flow downward are substantially independent of temperature difference.

[e] Thermal resistance values were determined from the relation $R = 1/C$, where $C = h_c + Eh_r$, h_c is the conduction-convection coefficient, Eh_r is the radiation coefficient $\cong 0.00686E [(460 + t_m)/100]^3$, and t_m is the mean temperature of the air space. For interpretation from Table 4 to air space thicknesses less than 0.5 in. (as in insulating window glass), assume $h_c = 0.795 (1 + 0.0016)$ and compute R-values from the above relations for an air space thickness of 0.2 in.

Thermal properties of typical building and insulating materials—(design values)[a]

These coefficients are expressed in Btuh-ft² (deg F difference in temperature between the air on the two sides), and are based on an outside wind velocity of 15 mph

These constants are expressed in Btu per (hour) (square foot) (degree Fahrenheit temperature difference). Conductivities (*k*) are per inch thickness, and conductances (*C*) are for thickness or construction stated, not per inch thickness. All values are for a mean temperature of 75°F, except as noted by an asterisk (*) which have been reported at 45°F.

Description	Density (lb/ft³)	Conductivity (k)	Conductance (C)	Resistance[b] (R) Per inch thickness (1/k)	Resistance[b] (R) For thickness listed (1/C)	Specific Heat, Btu/(lb) (deg F)	SI Unit Resistance[b] (R) (m·K)/W	SI Unit Resistance[b] (R) (m²·K)/W
BUILDING BOARD								
Boards, Panels, Subflooring, Sheathing								
Woodboard Panel Products								
Asbestos-cement board	120	4.0	—	*0.25*	—	0.24	1.73	
Asbestos-cement board. . . . . 0.125 in.	120	—	33.00	—	*0.03*			*0.005*
Asbestos-cement board. . . . . 0.25 in.	120	—	16.50	—	*0.06*			*0.01*
Gypsum or plaster board . . . . 0.375 in.	50	—	3.10	—	*0.32*	0.26		*0.06*
Gypsum or plaster board . . . . 0.5 in.	50	—	2.22	—	*0.45*			*0.08*
Gypsum or plaster board . . . . 0.625 in.	50	—	1.78	—	*0.56*			*0.10*
Plywood (Douglas Fir).	34	0.80	—	*1.25*	—	0.29	8.66	
Plywood (Douglas Fir). . . . . 0.25 in.	34	—	3.20	—	*0.31*			*0.05*
Plywood (Douglas Fir). . . . . 0.375 in.	34	—	2.13	—	*0.47*			*0.08*
Plywood (Douglas Fir). . . . . 0.5 in.	34	—	1.60	—	*0.62*			*0.11*
Plywood (Douglas Fir). . . . . 0.625 in.	34	—	1.29	—	*0.77*			*0.19*
Plywood or wood panels. . . . . 0.75 in.	34	—	1.07	—	*0.93*	0.29		*0.16*
Vegetable Fiber Board								
Sheathing, regular density. . . . . 0.5 in.	18	—	0.76	—	*1.32*	0.31		*0.23*
. . . . 0.78125 in.	18	—	0.49	—	*2.06*			*0.36*
Sheathing intermediate density . . . . 0.5 in.	22	—	0.82	—	*1.22*	0.31		*0.21*
Nail-base sheathing. . . . . 0.5 in.	25	—	0.88	—	*1.14*	0.31		*0.20*
Shingle backer. 0.375 in.	18	—	1.06	—	*0.94*	0.31		*0.17*
Shingle backer. . . . . 0.3125 in.	18	—	1.28	—	*0.78*			*0.14*
Sound deadening board . . . . 0.5 in.	15	—	0.74	—	*1.35*	0.30		*0.24*
Tile and lay-in panels, plain or ·								
acoustic	18	0.40	—	*2.50*	—	0.14	17.33	
. . . . 0.5 in.	18	—	0.80	—	*1.25*			*0.22*
. . . . 0.75 in.	18	—	0.53	—	*1.89*			*0.33*
Laminated paperboard.	30	0.50	—	*2.00*	—	0.33	13.86	
Homogeneous board from								
repulped paper	30	0.50	—	*2.00*	—	0.28	13.86	
Hardboard								
Medium density	50	0.73	—	*1.37*	—	0.31	9.49	
High density, service temp. service								
underlay	55	0.82	—	*1.22*	—	0.32	8.46	
High density, std. tempered	63	1.00	—	*1.00*	—	0.32	6.93	
Particleboard								
Low density	37	0.54	—	*1.85*	—	0.31	12.82	
Medium density	50	0.94	—	*1.06*	—	0.31	7.35	
High density.	62.5	1.18	—	*0.85*	—	0.31	5.89	
Underlayment. . . . . 0.625 in.	40	—·	1.22	—	*0.82*	0.29		*0.14*
Wood subfloor. 0.75 in.		—	1.06	—	*0.94*	0.33		*0.17*
BUILDING MEMBRANE								
Vapor-permeable felt	—	—	16.70	—	*0.06*			*0.01*
Vapor-seal, 2 layers of mopped								
15-lb felt	—	—	8.35	—	*0.12*			*0.02*
Vapor-seal, plastic film	—	—	—	—	Negl.			
FINISH FLOORING MATERIALS								
Carpet and fibrous pad	—	—	0.48	—	*2.08*	0.34		*0.37*
Carpet and rubber pad	—	—	0.81	—	*1.23*	0.33		*0.22*
Cork tile . . . . 0.125 in.	—	—	3.60	—	*0.28*	0.48		*0.05*
Terrazzo . . . . 1 in.	—	—	12.50	—	*0.08*	0.19		*0.01*
Tile—asphalt, linoleum, vinyl, rubber	—	—	20.00	—	*0.05*	0.30		*0.01*
vinyl asbestos						0.24		
ceramic.						0.19		
Wood, hardwood finish . . . . 0.75 in.			1.47		*0.68*			*0.12*
INSULATING MATERIALS								
BLANKET AND BATT								
Mineral Fiber, fibrous form processed								
from rock, slag, or glass								
approx.[e] 2–2.75 in.	0.3–2.0	—	0.143	—	*7*[d]	0.17–0.23		*1.23*
approx.[e] 3–3.5 in.	0.3–2.0	—	0.091	—	*11*[d]			*1.94*
approx.[e] 5.50–6.5 in.	0.3–2.0	—	0.053	—	*19*[d]			*3.35*
approx.[e] 6–7 in.	0.3–2.0		0.045	—	*22*[d]			*3.87*
approx.[d] 8.5 in.	0.3–2.0		0.033	—	*30*[d]			*5.28*

Notes are located at the end of the table.

(cont.). Thermal properties of typical building and insulating materials—(design values)[a]

Description	Density (lb/ft³)	Conductivity (k)	Conductance (C)	Resistance[b] (R) Per inch thickness (1/k)	Resistance[b] (R) For thickness listed (1/C)	Specific Heat, Btu/(lb) (deg F)	SI Unit Resistance[b] (R) (m·K)/W	SI Unit Resistance[b] (R) (m²·K)/W
BOARD AND SLABS								
Cellular glass	8.5	0.38	—	2.63	—	0.24	18.23	
Glass fiber, organic bonded	4–9	0.25	—	4.00	—	0.23	27.72	
Expanded rubber (rigid)	4.5	0.22	—	4.55	—	0.40	31.53	
Expanded polystyrene extruded Cut cell surface	1.8	0.25	—	4.00	—	0.29	27.72	
Expanded polystyrene extruded Smooth skin surface	2.2	0.20	—	5.00	—	0.29	34.65	
Expanded polystyrene extruded Smooth skin surface	3.5	0.19	—	5.26	—		36.45	
Expanded polystyrene, molded beads	1.0	0.28	—	3.57	—	0.29	24.74	
Expanded polyurethane[f] (R-11 exp.)	1.5	0.16	—	6.25	—	0.38	43.82	
(Thickness 1 in. or greater)	2.5							
Mineral fiber with resin binder	15	0.29	—	3.45	—	0.17	23.91	
Mineral fiberboard, wet felted Core or roof insulation	16–17	0.34	—	2.94	—		20.38	
Acoustical tile	18	0.35	—	2.86	—	0.19	19.82	
Acoustical tile	21	0.37	—	2.70	—		18.71	
Mineral fiberboard, wet molded Acoustical tile[g]	23	0.42	—	2.38	—	0.14	16.49	
Wood or cane fiberboard Acoustical tile[g] ... 0.5 in.	—	—	0.80	—	1.25	0.31		0.22
Acoustical tile[g] ... 0.75 in.	—	—	0.53	—	1.89			0.33
Interior finish (plank, tile)	15	0.35	—	2.86	—	0.32	19.82	
Wood shredded (cemented in preformed slabs)	22	0.60	—	1.67	—	0.31	11.57	
LOOSE FILL								
Cellulosic insulation (milled paper or wood pulp)	2.3–3.2	0.27–0.32	—	3.13–3.70	—	0.33	21.69–25.64	
Sawdust or shavings	8.0–15.0	0.45	—	2.22	—	0.33	15.39	
Wood fiber, softwoods	2.0–3.5	0.30	—	3.33	—	0.33	23.08	
Perlite, expanded	5.0–8.0	0.37	—	2.70	—	0.26	18.71	
Mineral fiber (rock, slag or glass) approx.[e] 3.75–5 in.	0.6–2.0	—	—		11	0.17		1.94
approx.[e] 6.5–8.75 in.	0.6–2.0	—	—		19			3.35
approx.[e] 7.5–10 in.	0.6–2.0	—	—		22			3.87
approx.[e] 10.25–13.75 in.	0.6–2.0	—	—		30			5.28
Vermiculite, exfoliated	7.0–8.2	0.47	—	2.13	—	3.20	14.76	
	4.0–6.0	0.44	—	2.27	—		15.73	
ROOF INSULATION[h]								
Preformed, for use above deck Different roof insulations are available in different thicknesses to provide the design C values listed.[h] Consult individual manufacturers for actual *thickness of their material.*			0.72 to 0.12		1.39 to 8.33		— —	0.24 to 1.47
MASONRY MATERIALS								
CONCRETES								
Cement mortar	116	5.0	—	0.20	—		1.39	
Gypsum-fiber concrete 87.5% gypsum, 12.5% wood chips	51	1.66	—	0.60	—	0.21	4.16	
Lightweight aggregates including expanded shale, clay or slate; expanded slags; cinders; pumice; vermiculite; also cellular concretes	120	5.2	—	0.19	—		1.32	
	100	3.6	—	0.28	—		1.94	
	80	2.5	—	0.40	—		2.77	
	60	1.7	—	0.59	—		4.09	
	40	1.15	—	0.86	—		5.96	
	30	0.90	—	1.11	—		7.69	
	20	0.70		1.43			9.91	
Perlite, expanded	40	0.93		1.08			7.48	
	30	0.71		1.41			9.77	
	20	0.50		2.00		0.32	13.86	
Sand and gravel or stone aggregate (oven dried)	140	9.0	—	0.11		0.22	0.76	
Sand and gravel or stone aggregate (not dried)	140	12.0	—	0.08			0.55	
Stucco	116	5.0	—	0.20			1.39	
MASONRY UNITS								
Brick, common[i]	120	5.0	—	0.20	—	0.19	1.39	
Brick, face[i]	130	9.0	—	0.11	—		0.76	

(cont.). Thermal properties of typical building and insulating materials—(design values)ᵃ

Description	Density (lb/ft³)	Conduc-tivity (k)	Conduc-tance (C)	Resistanceᵇ(R) Per inch thickness (1/k)	Resistanceᵇ(R) For thick-ness listed (1/C)	Specific Heat, Btu/(lb) (deg F)	Resistanceᵇ (R) (m·K) W	Resistanceᵇ (R) (m²·K) W
Clay tile, hollow:								
1 cell deep . . . . 3 in.	—	—	1.25	—	0.80	0.21		0.14
1 cell deep . . . . 4 in.	—	—	0.90	—	1.11			0.20
2 cells deep. . . . . 6 in.	—	—	0.66	—	1.52			0.27
2 cells deep. . . . . 8 in.	—	—	0.54	—	1.85			0.33
2 cells deep. . . . . 10 in.	—	—	0.45	—	2.22			0.39
3 cells deep . . . . 12 in.	—	—	0.40	—	2.50			0.44
Concrete blocks, three oval core:								
Sand and gravel aggregate . . . . 4 in.	—	—	1.40	—	0.71	0.22		0.13
. . . . 8 in.	—	—	0.90	—	1.11			0.20
. . . . 12 in.	—	—	0.78	—	1.28			0.23
Cinder aggregate . . . . 3 in.	—	—	1.16	—	0.86	0.21		0.15
. . . . 4 in.	—	—	0.90	—	1.11			0.20
. . . . 8 in.	—	—	0.58	—	1.72			0.30
. . . . 12 in.	—	—	0.53	—	1.89			0.33
Lightweight aggregate . . . . 3 in.	—	—	0.79	—	1.27	0.21		0.22
(expanded shale, clay, slate . . . . 4 in.	—	—	0.67	—	1.50			0.26
or slag; pumice) . . . . 8 in.	—	—	0.50	—	2.00			0.35
. . . . 12 in.	—	—	0.44	—	2.27			0.40
Concrete blocks, rectangular core.*ʲ								
Sand and gravel aggregate								
2 core, 8 in. 36 lb.ᵏ* . :	—	—	0.96	—	1.04	0.22		0.18
Same with filled coresʲ*	—	—	0.52	—	1.93	0.22		0.34
Lightweight aggregate (expanded shale,								
clay, slate or slag, pumice):								
3 core, 6 in. 19 lb.ᵏ*	—	—	0.61	—	1.65	0.21		0.29
Same with filled coresˡ*	—	—	0.33	—	2.99			0.53
2 core, 8 in. 24 lb.ᵏ*	—	—	0.46	—	2.18			0.38
Same with filled coresˡ*	—	—	0.20	—	5.03			0.89
3 core, 12 in. 38 lb.ᵏ*	—	—	0.40	—	2.48			0.44
Same with filled coresˡ*	—	—	0.17	—	5.82			1.02
Stone, lime or sand.	—	12.50	—	0.08	—	0.19	0.55	
Gypsum partition tile:								
3 × 12 × 30 in. solid	—	—	0.79	—	1.26	0.19		0.22
3 × 12 × 30 in. 4-cell	—	—	0.74	—	1.35			0.24
4 × 12 × 30 in. 3-cell	—	—	0.60	—	1.67			0.29
PLASTERING MATERIALS								
Cement plaster, sand aggregate	116	5.0	—	0.20	—	0.20	1.39	
Sand aggregate . . . . 0.375 in.	—	—	13.3	—	0.08	0.20		0.01
Sand aggregate . . . . 0.75 in.	—	—	6.66	—	0.15	0.20		0.03
Gypsum plaster:								
Lightweight aggregate. . . . . 0.5 in.	45	—	3.12	—	0.32			0.06
Lightweight aggregate . . . . 0.625 in.	45	—	2.67	—	0.39			0.07
Lightweight agg. on metal lath . . . . 0.75 in.	—	—	2.13	—	0.47			0.08
Perlite aggregate.	45	1.5	—	0.67	—	0.32	4.64	
Sand aggregate	105	5.6	—	0.18	—	0.20	1.25	
Sand aggregate . . . . 0.5 in.	105	—	11.10	—	0.09			0.02
Sand aggregate . . . . 0.625 in.	105	—	9.10	—	0.11			0.02
Sand aggregate on metal lath. . . . . 0.75 in.	—	—	7.70	—	0.13			0.02
Vermiculite aggregate.	45	1.7	—	0.59	—		4.09	
ROOFING								
Asbestos-cement shingles	120	—	4.76	—	0.21	0.24		0.04
Asphalt roll roofing	70	—	6.50	—	0.15	0.36		0.03
Asphalt shingles.	70	—	2.27	—	0.44	0.30		0.08
Built-up roofing . . . . 0.375 in.	70	—	3.00	—	0.33	0.35		0.06
Slate. . . . . 0.5 in.	—	—	20.00	—	0.05	0.30		0.01
Wood shingles, plain and plastic film faced	—	—	1.06	—	0.94	0.31		0.17
SIDING MATERIALS (ON FLAT SURFACE)								
Shingles								
Asbestos-cement.	120	—	4.75	—	0.21			0.04
Wood, 16 in., 7.5 exposure	—	—	1.15	—	0.87	0.31		0.15
Wood, double, 16-in., 12-in. exposure	—	—	0.84	—	1.19	0.28		0.21
Wood, plus insul. backer board, 0.3125 in.	—	—	0.71	—	1.40	0.31		0.25
Siding								
Asbestos-cement, 0.25 in., lapped.	—	—	4.76	—	0.21	0.24		0.04
Asphalt roll siding	—	—	6.50	—	0.15	0.35		0.03
Asphalt insulating siding (0.5 in. bed.)	—	—	0.69	—	1.46	0.35		0.26
Hardboard siding, 0.4375 in.	40	1.49	—	0.67	—	0.28	4.65	
Wood, drop, 1 × 8 in.	—	—	1.27	—	0.79	0.28		0.14

(cont.). Thermal properties of typical building and insulating materials—(design values)[a]

Description	Density (lb/ft³)	Conductivity (k)	Conductance (C)	Resistance[b] (R) Per inch thickness (1/k)	Resistance[b] (R) For thickness listed (1/C)	Specific Heat, Btu/(lb) (deg F)	SI Unit Resistance[b] (R) (m·K)/W	SI Unit Resistance[b] (R) (m²·K)/W
Wood, bevel, 0.5 × 8 in., lapped............	—	—	1.23	—	0.81	0.28		0.14
Wood, bevel, 0.75 × 10 in., lapped........	—	—	0.95	—	1.05	0.28		0.18
Wood, plywood, 0.375 in., lapped........	—	—	1.59	—	0.59	0.29		0.10
Aluminum or Steel[m], over sheathing								
Hollow-backed........................	—	—	1.61	—	0.61	0.29		0.11
Insulating-board backed nominal								
0.375 in.........................	—	—	0.55	—	1.82	0.32		0.32
Insulating-board backed nominal								
0.375 in., foil backed.............			0.34		2.96	0.32		0.52
Architectural glass......................	—	—	10.00	—	0.10	0.20		0.02
WOODS								
Maple, oak, and similar hardwoods..........	45	1.10	—	0.91	—	0.30	6.31	
Fir, pine, and similar softwoods............	32	0.80	—	1.25	—	0.33	8.66	
Fir, pine, and similar softwoods...........0.75 in.	32	—	1.06	—	0.94	0.33		0.17
...........................1.5 in.		—	0.53	—	1.89			0.33
...........................2.5 in.		—	0.32	—	3.12			0.60
...........................3.5 in.		—	0.23	—	4.35			0.75

Notes for Table 5

[a] Representative values for dry materials were selected by ASHRAE Technical Committee on Insulation and Moisture Barriers. They are intended as design (not specification) values for materials in normal use. For properties of a particular product, use the value supplied by the manufacturer or by unbiased tests.

[b] Resistance values are the reciprocals of C before rounding off C to two decimal places.

[c] Also see Insulating Materials, Board.

[d] Does not include paper backing and facing, if any. Where insulation forms a boundary (reflective or otherwise) of an air space, see Tables 3 and 4 for the insulating value of air space for the appropriate effective emittance and temperature conditions of the space.

[e] Conductivity varies with fiber diameter. Insulation is produced in different densities; therefore, there is a wide variation in thickness for the same R-value among manufacturers. No effort should be made to relate any specific R-value to any specific thickness. Commercial thicknesses generally available range from 2 to 8.5.

[f] Values are for aged board stock. Conductivity increases slowly with time as air permeates the cells.

[g] Insulating values of acoustical tile vary, depending on density of the board and on type, size, and depth of perforations.

[h] The U. S. Department of Commerce, *Simplified Practice Recommendation for Thermal Conductance Factors for Preformed Above-Deck Roof Insulation*, No. R 257-55, recognizes the specification of roof insulation on the basis of the C-values shown. Roof insulation is made in thicknesses to meet these values.

[i] Face brick and common brick do not always have these specific densities. When density is different from that shown, there will be a change in thermal conductivity.

[j] Data on rectangular core concrete blocks differ from the above data on oval core blocks, due to core configuration, different mean temperatures, and possibly differences in unit weights. Weight data on the oval core blocks tested are not available.

[k] Weights of units approximately 7.625 in. high and 15.75 in. long. These weights are given as a means of describing the blocks tested, but conductance values are all for 1 ft² of area.

[l] Vermiculite, perlite, or mineral wool insulation. Where insulation is used, vapor barriers or other precautions must be considered to keep insulation dry.

[m] Values for metal siding applied over flat surfaces vary widely, depending on amount of ventilation of air space beneath the siding; whether air space is reflective or nonreflective; and on thickness, type, and application of insulating backing-board used. Values given are averages for use as design guides, and were obtained from several guarded hotbox tests (ASTM C236) or calibrated hotbox (BSS 77) on hollow-backed types and types made using backing-boards of wood fiber, foamed plastic, and glass fiber. Departures of ±50% or more from the average may occur.

Coefficients of transmission (U) of frame walls*

(Reproduced by permission from *ASHRAE Handbook of Fundamentals*, 1977)

These coefficients are expressed in Btuh-ft² (deg F difference in temperature between the air on the two sides), and are based on an outside wind velocity of 15 mph

Replace Air Space with 3.5-in. R-11 Blanket Insulation (New Item 4)

Construction	1 Between Framing	1 At Framing	2 Between Framing	2 At Framing
1. Outside surface (15 mph wind)	0.17	0.17	0.17	0.17
2. Siding, wood, 0.5 in.× 8 in. lapped (average)	0.81	0.81	0.81	0.81
3. Sheathing, 0.5-in. asphalt impregnated	1.32	1.32	1.32	1.32
4. Nonreflective air space, 3.5 in. (50 F mean; 10 deg F temperature difference)	1.01	—	11.00	—
5. Nominal 2-in. × 4-in. wood stud	—	4.38	—	4.38
6. Gypsum wallboard, 0.5 in.	0.45	0.45	0.45	0.45
7. Inside surface (still air)	0.68	0.68	0.68	0.68
Total Thermal Resistance (R)	R_i=4.44	R_s=7.81	R_i=14.43	R_s=7.81

Construction No. 1: U_i = 1/4.44=0.225; U_s=1/7.81 =0.128. With 20% framing (typical of 2-in. × 4-in. studs @ 16-in. o.c.), U_{av} = 0.8 (0.225) + 0.2 (0.128) = 0.206 (See Eq 9)

Construction No. 2: U_i = 1/14.43 = 0.069; U_s = 0.128. With framing unchanged, U_{av} = 0.8(0.069) + 0.2(0.128) = 0.081

* See text section on overall coefficients for basis of calculations.

Determination of *U*-value resulting from addition of insulation to the total area[e] of any given building section

(Reproduced by permission from ASHRAE Handbook of Fundamentals, 1977.)

Given Building Section Property[a,b]		Added R[c,d,e]						
		R = 4	R = 6	R = 8	R = 12	R = 16	R = 20	R = 24
U	R	U	U	U	U	U	U	U
1.00	1.00	0.20	0.14	0.11	0.08	0.06	0.05	0.04
0.90	1.11	0.20	0.14	0.11	0.08	0.06	0.05	0.04
0.80	1.25	0.19	0.14	0.11	0.08	0.06	0.05	0.04
0.70	1.43	0.19	0.13	0.11	0.07	0.06	0.05	0.04
0.60	1.67	0.19	0.13	0.10	0.07	0.06	0.05	0.04
0.50	2.00	0.18	0.13	0.10	0.07	0.06	0.05	0.04
0.40	2.50	0.16	0.12	0.10	0.07	0.05	0.05	0.04
0.30	3.33	0.14	0.11	0.09	0.07	0.05	0.04	0.04
0.20	5.00	0.11	0.09	0.08	0.06	0.05	0.04	0.03
0.10	10.00	0.06	0.06	0.06	0.05	0.04	0.04	0.03
0.08	12.50	0.06	0.06	0.05	0.04	0.04	0.03	0.03

[a] *For U- or R-values not shown in the table, interpolate as necessary.*
[b] *Enter column 1 with U or R of the design building section.*
[c] *Under appropriate column heading for Added R, find U-value of resulting design section.*
[d] *If the insulation occupies a previously considered air space, an adjustment must be made in the given building section R-value.*
[e] *If insulation is applied between framing members use equation given on sheet 4 to determine average U-value.*

Determination of *U*-value resulting from addition of insulation to uninsulated building sections

(Reproduced by permission from ASHRAE Handbook of Fundamentals, 1977.)

U Value of Roof without Roof-Deck Insulation[a]	Conductance C of Roof-Deck Insulation					
	0.12	0.15	0.19	0.24	0.36	0.72
	U	U	U	U	U	U
0.10	0.05	0.06	0.07	0.07	0.08	0.09
0.15	0.07	0.08	0.08	0.09	0.11	0.12
0.20	0.08	0.09	0.10	0.11	0.13	0.16
0.25	0.08	0.09	0.11	0.12	0.15	0.19
0.30	0.09	0.10	0.12	0.13	0.16	0.21
0.35	0.09	0.10	0.12	0.14	0.18	0.24
0.40	0.09	0.11	0.13	0.15	0.19	0.26
0.50	0.10	0.12	0.14	0.16	0.21	0.29
0.60	0.10	0.12	0.14	0.17	0.22	0.33
0.70	0.10	0.12	0.15	0.18	0.24	0.35

[a] *Interpolation or mild extrapolation may be used.*

Note: for U-values for solid wood doors and for glass windows, doors; also see Tables 3 and 4 in section on Heating, Ventilating, and Air Conditioning.

Effective resistance of ventilated attics[a] (summer condition)

(Reproduced by permission from ASHRAE Handbook of Fundamentals, 1977.)

PART A. NONREFLECTIVE SURFACES

Ventilation Air temp., F	Sol-air[d] temp., F	No Ventilation		Natural Ventilation		Power Ventilation[e]					
		___		___		Ventilation rate, cfm/sq ft					
		0		0.1[b]		0.5		1.0		1.5	
		1/U Ceiling resistance, R[c]									
		10	20	10	20	10	20	10	20	10	20
80	120	1.9	1.9	2.8	3.4	6.3	9.3	9.6	16	11	20
	140	1.9	1.9	2.8	3.5	6.5	10	9.8	17	12	21
	160	1.9	1.9	2.8	3.6	6.7	11	10	18	13	22
90	120	1.9	1.9	2.5	2.8	4.6	6.7	6.1	10	6.9	13
	140	1.9	1.9	2.6	3.1	5.2	7.9	7.6	12	8.6	15
	160	1.9	1.9	2.7	3.4	5.8	9.0	8.5	14	10	17
100	120	1.9	1.9	2.2	2.3	3.3	4.4	4.0	6.0	4.1	6.9
	140	1.9	1.9	2.4	2.7	4.2	6.1	5.8	8.7	6.5	10
	160	1.9	1.9	2.6	3.2	5.0	7.6	7.2	11	8.3	13

PART B. REFLECTIVE SURFACES[f]

Ventilation Air temp., F	Sol-air temp., F	0		0.1		0.5		1.0		1.5	
80	120	6.5	6.5	8.1	8.8	13	17	17	25	19	30
	140	6.5	6.5	8.2	9.0	14	18	18	26	20	31
	160	6.5	6.5	8.3	9.2	15	18	19	27	21	32
90	120	6.5	6.5	7.5	8.0	10	13	12	17	13	19
	140	6.5	6.5	7.7	8.3	12	15	14	20	16	22
	160	6.5	6.5	7.9	8.6	13	16	16	22	18	25
100	120	6.5	6.5	7.0	7.4	8.0	10	8.5	12	8.8	13
	140	6.5	6.5	7.3	7.8	10	12	11	15	12	16
	160	6.5	6.5	7.6	8.2	11	14	13	18	15	20

[a] *The term effective resistance is used when there is attic ventilation. A value for no ventilation is also included. The effective resistance of the attic may be added to the resistance (1/U) of the ceiling (Table 6G) to obtain the effective resistance of the combination based on sol-air (see section on HVAC) and room temperature. These values apply to wood frame construction with a roof deck and roofing having a conductance of 1.0 Btu/(hr·ft²·°F).*
[b] *When attic ventilation meets the requirements of Table 2 in section on Condensation Control, 0.1 cfm/ft² may be assumed as the natural summer ventilation rate for design purposes.*
[c] *Resistance is one (hr·ft²·°F)/Btu. Determine ceiling resistance from Tables 6G and 7A and adjust for framing. Do not add the effect of a reflective surface facing the attic to the ceiling resistance from Table 6G, as it is accounted for in Table 8, Part B.*
[d] *Roof surface temperature rather than sol-air temperature may be used if 0.25 is subtracted from the attic resistance shown.*
[e] *Based on air discharging outward from attic.*
[f] *Surfaces with effective emissivity E of 0.05 between ceiling joists facing the attic space.*

Donald Baerman

Summary

Causes for building movement include changes in thermal, moisture, and humidity conditions, and structural failure and imposed stresses, including expansive clay movement under foundations. This article discusses how to design details to accommodate such dimensional movement.

Key words

expansion coefficient, frost expansion, joint sealants, movement joints, thermal expansion

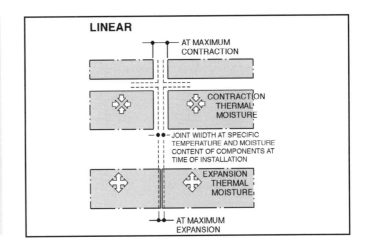

Building movement

All materials expand or contract when heated or cooled and/or when taking on moisture or drying. For design analysis, three types of movement in buildings can be characterized as linear, differential, and transverse.

• *Linear movement* (**Fig. 1**), or dimensional change within building components, is a continual process due to variations:

– in internal temperature of the components regardless of material used.

– in exterior temperatures.

• *Differential movement* (**Fig. 2**), differential dimensional changes between components:

– different coefficients of expansion and contraction of the components. For example, a 10 ft sq (3 m sq) panel of aluminum will contract 0.155 in (3.9 mm) for a temperature drop of 100F (35°C); an adjacent masonry panel of the same size will only contract 0.037 in (0.94 mm), or only 20 percent as much, under the same conditions.

– different rates of shrinkage and swelling due to changes in internal moisture content between components, or within the component. Dimensional changes in wood during loss or gain of moisture vary depending on whether expansion is tangential in the direction of growth rings, or radial across growth rings. A piece of green Dou-

glas fir will shrink about 1.5 percent tangentially and about 2.5 percent radially when dried to 20 percent moisture content, the volumetric change being about 3.7 percent.

– differential movement may also result from movements in the supporting frame acting simultaneously with thermal and/or moisture movements.

• *Transverse movement* (**Fig. 3**), or movement perpendicular to the plane of components, may result from differences in the magnitude of lateral loads action on adjacent components or from bending stresses:

– differences in pressures on vertical components, such as wall panels.

– moving loads over horizontal components, when the edge of one is free to deflect.

– deflection due to thermal or moisture movement in a component with two edges restrained and adjacent to an unrestrained component.

– deflection due to horizontal loads on a free edge of a component next to an attached edge of another component.

– differences in deflection between a relatively stiff component next to a flexible one.

Credits: Figs. 1 to 3 are from *Sweets Catalog File.* Other drawings created by Wynne Mun. Photos are by the author.

LINEAR

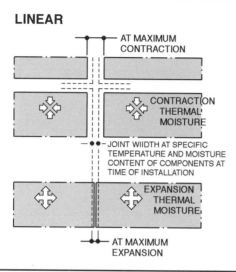

Fig. 1. Linear movement.

DIFFERENTIAL

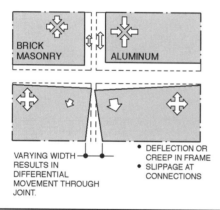

Fig. 2. Differential movement.

TRANSVERSE

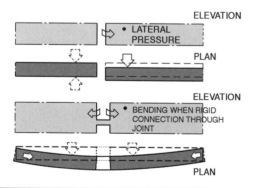

Fig. 3. Transverse movement.

– deflection in two components with rigid, spaced connections between them, when they are restrained at their edges or when under lateral load.

– deformation in components due to differentials in temperature between opposite faces of one component, or differences in moisture gain/loss, such as warping in wood.

The thermal movement behavior of common building materials is indicated in **Table 1.** Coefficients of expansion are listed in unit-per-degree temperature difference. Coefficients of expansion are without linear dimension, being feet/feet, meter/meter, and cubit/cubit. The values differ according to which temperature scale one uses. Coefficients of expansion for other materials are listed in the "Miscellaneous" section of the *A.I.S.C. Steel Construction Manual,* where the coefficients listed are per 100F (37°C), while those listed below are per degree, as in Brick Institute of America (1991) and other references.

Caution: values for coefficients of thermal expansion vary, sometimes greatly, according to source and exact material. For example, while single values for concrete are listed in various references, other references indicate a 100 percent difference in coefficient of expansion depending on the aggregate used. Also, the coefficient of expansion is not truly uniform throughout the full range of temperatures. Prudent practice is to assume a little more movement than tabulated values and resulting calculations indicate.

For coal-tar bitumen, the coefficient listed in Table 1 is higher than that shown for built-up roofing, organic felt, and asphalt. At higher temperatures, the coefficient is less. This is why some roofs split in very cold weather. Fiberglass felts, with greater strength than organic felts, are more resistant to splitting. Organic felts are weaker in the transverse direction; fiberglass felts are approximately equal in strength in all directions. Membrane roofing materials generally become flexible when warm, so thermal expansion of the roof membrane is not a problem. These materials become more rigid when cold, so shrinkage may cause damage if the membrane is not adequately anchored.

Possible causes of thermal movement

• Daily or seasonal air-temperature changes.

• Diurnal movement of the sun and its heating effects, including reflection from adjacent surfaces, cooling winds, snow, ice, and rain.

• Thin materials exposed to the environment and coupled to massive materials, even if the coefficients of expansion of the two materials are similar, will change temperature more rapidly.

• Loss of initial heat from hydration of massive concrete.

• Cooling by operation of building environmental control equipment, such as air conditioning and cold storage systems.

• Heating by operation of fuel-burning equipment and chimneys.

• Fire is normally the most severe thermal change that can affect buildings. Even components that are not destroyed by fire can be severely damaged by thermal movement, and the damage may not be immediately evident.

- Low temperatures before occupancy of building and during abandonment. Some of the greatest "normal" stresses may be imposed during construction.

- Differential movement occurs when different parts of a system are exposed to different temperatures. For example, a highly insulated building with closely controlled interior temperatures experiences little temperature change and therefore little thermally induced movement on the inside of the walls. The outer portion of the walls may vary greatly in temperature, from below 0F (–17.8°C) up to 140F (60°C) or more for dark surfaces in the sun. Roofs, oriented nearly perpendicular to the noonday sun in summer, may get even hotter. The exterior of well-insulated buildings will experience greater thermal movement than those of poorly insulated buildings.

- Building components intended not to change temperature may be exposed to temperature changes as a result of insulation failure. If, for example, the roof insulation becomes saturated with water, then the structural roof deck may get hotter in summer and cooler in winter than was anticipated by the design.

Examples of thermal movement problems

- Masonry walls expand in summer due to seasonal warming. In winter, due to seasonal cooling and having little tensile strength, they may crack rather than returning to their initial size (**Fig. 4**). Brick arches and lintels, especially soldier and rowlock-coursed lintels, having more mortar joints than the adjoining masonry, are highly resistant to thermal cracking. Heavy, solid masonry buildings with heated interiors do not generally suffer damage from thermal movement as much as insulated buildings, but elements exposed on both sides to the exterior, such as parapets, do suffer damage.

- Damage from thermal expansion and shrinkage does not necessarily occur within the first year. Such damage can take many years to become visible.

- Tinted glass that is partly exposed to the sun and partly in shade might shatter.

- Massive concrete structures might become hot during hydration of the cement, and shrink and crack when this internal heat has passed out of them.

- In winter the outside of chimneys becomes cold while the flue becomes hot. If the two are rigidly connected, the outside is exposed to tensile stresses and possibly to cracking.

- Concrete lintels in brick walls often show cracks at the end mortar joints. There are several causes:

– Concrete shrinks with age (**Fig. 5**), while brick expands with age.

– There are multiple mortar joints in the brick, while the lintel has joints at the ends only. Mortar joints are, or should be, more flexible than the masonry units.

– Concrete has a higher coefficient of thermal expansion than brick.

- Rigid building elements may expand to the extreme during fires, thus destroying or lessening the structural integrity of the building.

Table 1. Coefficients of expansion of common building materials.

Material	Coefficient of expansion per Degree F.	Coefficient of expansion per Degree C.	Movement per 100F per 100'
Aluminum	.0000128	.0000230	1.54"
Milled Steel:	.0000065	.0000117	0.78"
Granite; limestone similar:	.0000047	.0000085	0.56"
Brick masonry:	.0000036	.0000065	0.43"
Fire clay brick masonry:	.0000025	.0000045	0.30"
CMU, normal aggregate:	.0000052	.0000094	0.62"
CMU, lightweight aggregate:	.0000031 to .0000046	.0000056 to .0000083	0.37" to 0.55"
Concrete, limestone aggregate:	.0000033	.0000060	0.40"
Concrete, traprock aggregate.	.0000039	.0000070	0.47"
Concrete, granite aggregate:	.0000044	.0000080	0.53"
Concrete, certain l.w. agg.:	.0000050	.0000090	0.60"
Concrete, quartzite aggregate:	.0000067	.0000120	0.80"
Fir, parallel to the grain:	.0000021	.0000038	0.25" [1]
Fir perpendicular to the grain:	.000032.	.000058	6.91"
Glass:	.000008.	.000014	0.96"
"Pyrex" glass:	.0000018	.0000032	0.22" [2]
Polycarbonate glazing sheet:	.000037	.000067	4.44" [3]
Built-up roofing, felt and asphalt, range 0F—30F:	.000037	.000067	4.4"
Reinforced plastics:	.000035	.000063	4.2"
Aramid fibers:	.000001	.0000018	0.12" [4]
Polyethylene:	.000195	.000351	23.4"

Notes:
[1] This is a very low value (but not zero).
[2] Source: Corning Glass Works.
[3] This value is almost 5 times as great as that of glass; glazing details may have to be modified to accommodate this movement.
[4] Note that this is an extremely low value. Source: Akzo Fibers Division.

Fig. 4. Movement along brick wall.

Fig. 5. Movement of concrete, leading to cracking.

Fig. 6. Expansion joint in masonry wall.

- A building interior designed to undergo slight change of temperature during its service life might be exposed to very low or high temperatures during construction.

Calculating movement

It is possible to calculate the probable maximum movement of building components, using the coefficients listed in Table 1. The length of the element multiplied by the thermal difference multiplied by the coefficient of expansion gives the movement length.

- *Example 1:* A dark masonry wall 100 ft (30.5 m) long in New England. Assume that it was built at 50F (10°C) average temperature.

- In summer assume that the wall is heated by sunlight to 130F. The temperature difference from built condition to service condition is 80F (26°C). Therefore, 80F × 100′ × 0.0000034 = 0.0271 ft = 0.33 in (8.4 mm).

- In winter assume that the wall occasionally chills to 0F. The temperature difference is 50F (10°C). Therefore, 50F × 100′ × 0.0000034 = 0.2 in (5 mm).

Since the summer condition causes the greater movement, design for that figure. If the wall were built in hotter or colder weather, the expansion or contraction from the "as built" size would be greater. In this case the extremes are unlikely, since it would be improper to build the wall below 40F (6°C) or above 90F (32°C).

It is not always evident why a wall develops one large crack rather than several smaller cracks. To some extent this can be predicted empirically by observing similar construction. For example, it appears that a long, narrow panel is more likely to crack than a similar panel that is broader, and cracks usually occur where walls are weakened by doors and windows. "Fracture mechanics" relates to such phenomena; see Gordon (1988) for an elementary discussion of fracture mechanics.

There are numerous examples of uninsulated solid masonry buildings that do not undergo cracking from thermal movement. The probable reason is that the interior is always at a stable temperature and the exterior is structurally bonded to it. The stress is accommodated by elastic behavior in the masonry. It is common, however, for parapets of such buildings to crack.

Design of flexible movement joints

Flexible movement joints may extend through the building, dividing the building into parts, which may expand and contract independently of one another. It is important that the flexible movement joints in the various components be located in line or close together. Traditionally such joints are called "expansion joints" (**Fig. 6**).

Flexible movement joints may simply extend through walls and other parts of the exterior closure. They allow differential movement of the components in which they occur. Such joints are sometimes called "control joints," but that term is not in accord with current usage. For brick masonry, see Brick Institute of America (1991). For concrete masonry, see NCMA (1973). **Fig. 7** shows one type of movement joint.

Rules of thumb for placement of flexible movement joints for different types of construction in temperate climates include:

- Solid brick wall, heated and not insulated: joints placement every 250 ft (76 m) is the industry recommendation; a better recommendation is 80 ft (24 m).

- Insulated brick cavity or veneer wall with window and door openings, outer wythe: placement every 100 ft (30.5 m) is industry recommendation; a better recommendation is 40 ft (12 m). This guideline is also recommended for parapets and unheated buildings. The brick recommendations do not mention the ratio of height to length. If the height is small, the author recommends spacing the joints closer to one another.

- For concrete masonry ("block") walls, insulated and heated and with masonry joint reinforcement placed 16 in (40.6 cm) o.c., the industry recommendation is that the "panel length" ("panel" being defined as the section isolated by movement joint) should be no more than 3 times as long as it is high and no more than 50 ft (15 m) in length between joints. A better recommendation is 30 ft (9 m) between joints. If the wall is longer than 3 times as long as it is high, or if it is unheated, consider 20 ft (6 m).

The above guidelines assume a temperate climate similar to that of the middle part of the United States, which experiences an average temperature range of from −10 to +90F (−23 to +32°C). In climates with a smaller temperature range, the spacing for movement joints may be increased. In climates with larger temperature range, they should be decreased. For example, Saskatoon, Canada has a temperature range from −40 to 104F (−40 to +40°C), and thus the temperature range differential is 144F (80°C)!

Also recommended is the use of grouted, reinforced bond beams and grouted, reinforced intermittent cores in masonry. This practice permits longer panels between joints. Post-tensioned bond beams permit yet longer panels between joints.

Openings and abrupt changes in shape create stress concentrations and may require strategically located movement joints even if the spacing is not great. Movement joints should not intersect lintels over openings (**Fig. 8**).

To design the movement joints

- Calculate the temperature differential. The extent of movement will vary with the temperature during construction and in service. Since the designer may not be able to predict this, assume the worst. For example, if a wall will vary in temperature from −10 to 130F (23 to 55°C), and if the specifications permit work to take place between 40 to 90F (4 to 32°C), the possible extremes are:

– Wall built at 40F. In service it may get 50F (10°C) colder and 90F (32°C) warmer. Use 90F (32°C) as the temperature differential.

– Wall built at 90F (32°C). In services it may get 100F colder and 40F warmer. Use 100F as the temperature differential.

– The larger temperature differential is 100F.

- *Example 2a:* Assume, for example, insulated brick masonry with movement joints 40 ft (12.2 m) apart. The 40 ft panel length × 100F temperature differential × coefficient of thermal expansion of 0.0000034 = 0.014 ft = 0.16 in (4 mm). If the sealant to be used in the joint permits 25 percent movement, the joint must be at least 4 times the movement, or 0.67 in (17 mm). With more ex-

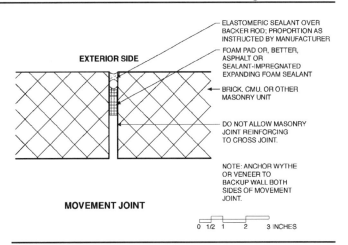

Fig. 7. Flexible movement joint.

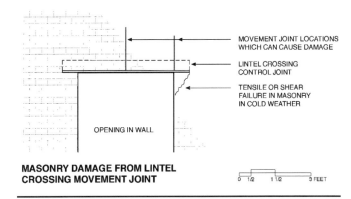

Fig. 8. Masonry damage from lintel crossing movement joint.

tensible and compressible sealants, the joint width can be less wide. The author recommends never designing movement joints less than approximately ⅜ in (10 mm) wide.

- *Example 2b:* As a second example, you wish to follow industry recommendations instead of the author's more conservative ones. Suppose that the panels are 100 ft (30.5 m) long and that the other parameters do not change. The movement will then be 0.034 ft = 0.41 in (10 mm). If the sealant permits 25 percent movement (such as acrylic polymeric sealant), the joint should be 1.63 in (41 mm) wide! If the sealant permits 50 percent extension or compression, the joint could theoretically be 0.81 in (21 mm) wide. However, buildings do not always perform as intended. We cannot reasonably assume that the center of each panel will remain fixed and that the ends will move equally. Sometimes the fixed portion of the panel is at one end or near it. Suppose the two adjacent panels, as described in this example, "stick fast" near their far ends. The common joint will then move more than ¾ in (19 mm), and a ¾ in wide joint may extend to 1-½ in (38 mm). Recommendation: be conservative; few architects can reasonably regret having called for too many and too wide movement joints. Careful design can make movement joints nearly invisible.

One should consider the penetrations that may resist the intended movement. A solidly grouted pipe passing through a wall may be subjected to stress when the wall moves. A metal roof may impose stresses on flashed vents and skylights that penetrate it. Windows anchored both to the inside and the outside of a wall may be stressed by movement of the outer wythe.

Components with differing thermal expansion characteristics, such as a steel frame and a masonry wall, should be isolated from one another enough to allow differential movement. Anchorage should be flexible. Although steel and masonry have similar coefficients of expansion, they are often exposed to different temperatures.

A masonry wall composed of brick, with a lower coefficient of expansion on the outside, and Concrete Masonry Units (CMU), with a higher coefficient of expansion on the inside, is somewhat self-compensating. The outer wythe is exposed to greater temperature changes and has a lower coefficient of thermal expansion. Thus the joints on the inside may be reasonably placed far apart.

Moisture expansion and shrinkage
Wood

Wood, as cut, contains several kinds of moisture. Free moisture filling the cells does not affect shrinkage. Chemically combined water (the "hydrate" of carbohydrate) is not lost unless the wood burns, rots, and is digested by insects. The water, and the loss of water, which causes shrinkage, is absorbed and adsorbed on the cell walls.

When wood is dried below 25 to 30 percent moisture content, the water on the cell walls is lost, and the wood experiences shrinkage. The point at which shrinkage starts is called the "fiber saturation point." Throughout the normal range of service conditions, the wood expands during periods of high humidity and shrinks during periods of low humidity. The expansion of wood varies approximately (but only approximately) with the relative humidity. A table giving moisture content at various temperatures and relative humidity is found in Forest Products Laboratory (1999). By combining the results of this table with tables giving the expansion by moisture content in the same reference, one can calculate the relationship of humidity and moisture expansion as a function of grain or cut (**Fig. 9**).

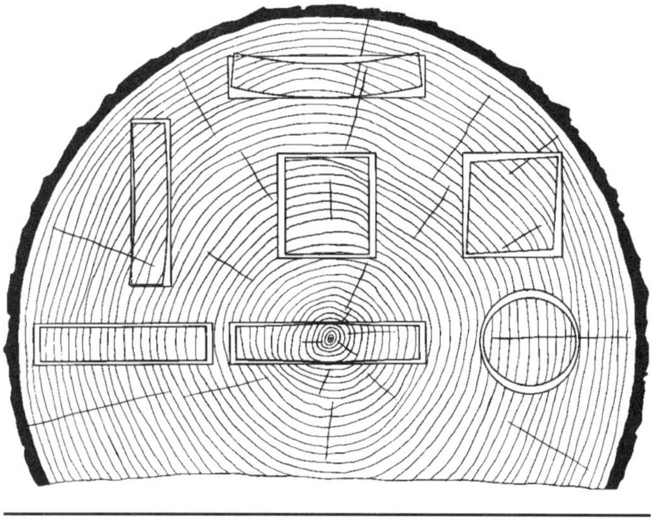

Fig. 9. Variations in woodcuts and grains. (Source: Forest Products Laboratory 1987.)

- Expansion and shrinkage is least in the direction of the grain, almost (but not quite) nil.

- Expansion and shrinkage is moderately high perpendicular to the growth rings. For Douglas fir the difference, from fiber-saturated to oven dry, is approximately 4.1 percent.

- Expansion and shrinkage is highest tangential to the growth rings. For Douglas fir the difference from fiber-saturated to oven dry is approximately 7.6 percent.

- The in-service range of moisture content of wood is not always as great as is shown above. However, the shrinkage from "S-GRN" to the dryness experienced in an unhumidified building in winter in cold climates may approximate that range.

- Shrinkage is approximately proportional; for a given change in moisture from fiber-saturation point to oven dry, the same proportional change occurs in shrinkage.

Normally, for rough framing of buildings, the moisture content should be below 19 percent by weight, and for critical applications, it is available dried to 15 percent moisture content. If the lumber is first dried, then surfaced (planed to a standard size), the grade stamp will show "S-DRY" or "MC-15" (15 percent moisture content). Since all lumber is not identical, the lumber is more uniform in size if it is surfaced after drying. If uniformity is not important, lumber that is labeled "S-GRN" (surfaced "green" before drying) may be used if it is tested for moisture content before use. Or if shrinkage does not matter at all, the wood may be used at whatever moisture content it happens to have upon delivery.

Relatively inexpensive moisture meters are available for testing wood on the job. A number of such instruments are sold by PRG and by Delmhorst (see Additional References). To measure the inner parts of framing lumber, order hammer-driven electrodes.

Finish woodwork is normally milled at approximately 12 percent moisture content and allowed to reach equilibrium moisture content in its place of installation.

There is an incorrect belief that it makes no difference whether the wood is dry or not, since, after the first rain, it becomes saturated with water anyway. That is not usually true.

To avoid problems with movement of wood:

- Avoid wood framing with a lot of horizontal-grain wood framing in conjunction with a material that does not have the same expansion characteristics. For example, if you intend to apply conventional stucco or brick veneer to a wood frame building, use balloon framing instead of platform framing. If you must apply stucco or brick veneer to a building with platform framing, consider continuous vertical furring or horizontal expansion joints at the floor framing.

- The depth of horizontal wood framing should be the same throughout the structure. If you design the framing above foundations with 12 in of horizontal framing lumber, there should be 12 in (30.5 cm) of horizontal framing lumber at the girders also. This can be accomplished by using steel girders or by framing the joists nearly flush with wood girders, using multi-nailed joist hangers, not straps (**Fig. 10**).

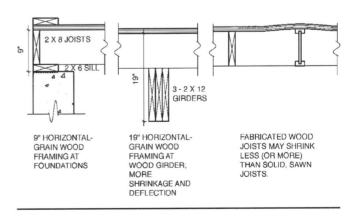

Fig. 10. Differential wood framing shrinkage.

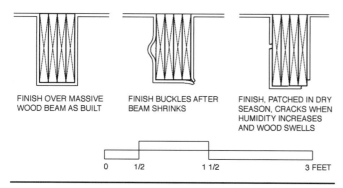

FINISH OVER MASSIVE
WOOD BEAM AS BUILT

FINISH BUCKLES AFTER
BEAM SHRINKS

FINISH, PATCHED IN DRY
SEASON, CRACKS WHEN
HUMIDITY INCREASES
AND WOOD SWELLS

0   1/2   1 1/2   3 FEET

Fig. 11. Rigid finish over massive wooden members.

- Be careful about using sawn lumber and fabricated structural wood products together; if one shrinks more than the other the floors and ceilings may be uneven (**Fig. 10**).

- Avoid massive wooden members over which gypsum wallboard or plaster is to be applied. Such a detail will almost certainly crack. If you must have massive wooden members covered with wallboard, detail resilient furring between the two, or separate the support for the finish from the structural members (**Fig. 11**).

- When applying wood siding, do not nail each course with multiple nails too far apart. For board-and-batten siding, nail boards midway between battens, and nail battens through the joint between the boards. Nail wide clapboards just above the top of the course below. Do not allow T&G or board siding to be installed too tight; allow for expansion. Leave gaps between wooden shingles.

- Leave gaps of at least ⅛ in (3.2 mm) between the sides and ends of plywood panels. If the plywood is for ceramic tile installation, follow Tile Council of America recommendations (⅛ in gaps).

- Detail woodwork not to show shrinkage cracks.

- Real stile and rail paneling must have expansion space around the panels, and the panels should not be rigidly mounted.

- Do not install wood shingles tight to one another.

- If possible, allow woodwork and wood floors to reach equilibrium moisture before installing them. Use a moisture meter to verify this. If at all possible, the humidity in the space while the woodwork is being installed should be close to that which would prevail during occupancy.

- Wooden flooring is prone to moisture expansion problems, and "floating" wooden flooring is especially prone to such problems.

- For "floating" wooden flooring, the subfloor should be in two layers, and the layers should be thoroughly adhered and fastened to one another to act as a continuous diaphragm. As the floor shrinks in times of low humidity, it must have the strength to retain its integrity.

- There should be an expansion space around the entire perimeter. This can be hidden by the wall base (**Fig. 12**).

- If the humidity conditions are expected to vary greatly between installation and service, or during service, make allowances during installation. If the floor is installed during very dry conditions (cold weather, heated interior, and no humidification), the flooring should not be installed tight; leave a little space between the strips. If the floor is installed during very humid conditions, drive the strips tight to one another.

- For extreme variation in humidity, as in a vacation house left unoccupied in winter, treat the wood with a preservative water-repellent solution before installation. Sanding will remove the treated top wood, but the finish will serve the same purpose. And do not expect a smooth-as-glass finish and total absence of gaps in such buildings.

For demanding applications, wood should be aged long enough not only for drying but to relax its internal stresses and become stable

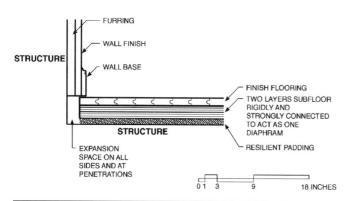

FURRING

WALL FINISH

STRUCTURE

WALL BASE

FINISH FLOORING

TWO LAYERS SUBFLOOR
RIGIDLY AND
STRONGLY CONNECTED
TO ACT AS ONE
DIAPHRAM

STRUCTURE

RESILIENT PADDING

EXPANSION
SPACE ON ALL
SIDES AND AT
PENETRATIONS

0 1 3   9   18 INCHES

Fig. 12. Floating wood floor.

with prevailing site conditions. In the author's opinion, the frequent splitting and disintegrating of exterior wood columns is mainly due to the wood's not being aged and selected as it once was. To offer an extreme but illustrative case of the level of care taken in woodcraft, one major concert piano manufacturer selects its wood, ages it outdoors under cover for a year, then discards 90 percent, kiln-dries the remainder, and further rejects half of that, retaining only 5 percent of the original for use in manufacture of the final instrument.

Concrete and concrete masonry

Concrete shrinks as the water adsorbed on the surfaces of the calcium silicate hydrate crystals in the hydrated cement paste dries, and it shrinks as the water in the small capillaries dries. In general the shrinkage of concrete is minimized if the water/cement ratio is kept as low as practicable.

- Concrete masonry is subject to expansion and shrinkage as is concrete. Lightweight masonry units are more likely to exhibit this characteristic than normal weight units.

- Moisture-controlled masonry units are more stable than uncontrolled ones.

- The partially completed and completed masonry should be protected against rain and snow by covering the work.

Tile and other thin finishes

The backer board should have low expansion and shrinkage from moisture and temperature, similar to those of the tile. Glass-reinforced mortarboard and glass-reinforced and faced gypsum sheathing are appropriate; products containing wood fiber are not.

- The backer board edges should be spaced apart as recommended by its manufacturer. Joints in the tile should correspond to joints in the backer board.

- Ceramic tile will expand as it ages. Sealant in the joints, or an elastic latex mortar, or both will help absorb the movement harmlessly (**Fig. 13**).

Expansive clays

Certain clays, such as Bentonite, absorb many times their volume in water and expand accordingly. This expansion in and around building foundation soils reportedly represents one of the largest natural building destroyers in the United States, contending in numbers with building losses from earthquakes, floods, and windstorms. The usual mechanism is that the placement of the building on the expansive clay soil interrupts normal evaporation and causes the clays to become wetter and to expand. Other types of moisture change, such as discharge of roof and paving drainage near a building, have similar effects. The expansive force is probably most destructive on large, lightly loaded members such as slabs-on-grade. These members are displaced upward.

If the proposed site has expansive clay soils, or if there is any substantial probability of its having them, the safe course is to retain a geotechnical engineer familiar with the local conditions and to design accordingly. The local building department should be consulted as to the prevalence of expansive clays in the area.

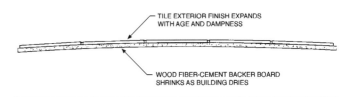

TILE EXTERIOR FINISH EXPANDS WITH AGE AND DAMPNESS

WOOD FIBER-CEMENT BACKER BOARD SHRINKS AS BUILDING DRIES

Fig. 13. Bowing from coupled materials with different expansion characteristics and exposures.

One effective method of avoiding damage from expansive clay soil is called "void forming." A compressible material such as thick corrugated cardboard is used to form slabs-on-grade, which slabs must be reinforced as supported slabs. The void forms serve only as the base on which the concrete is placed. When the clay expands, it crushes the cardboard. Another method is to form the slabs above the soil. Void forming and other construction methods to avoid damage from expansive clay soils should be designed by geotechnical engineers familiar with the problem.

Freezing, frost heaving, and salt crystallization

Freezing of water in absorbent building materials may cause the materials to burst. For example, water-saturated masonry and concrete can disintegrate after freezing.

Frost heaving can move and damage buildings. Water-laden soil can expand upon freezing and cause enough upward pressure to damage the building or component.

Keep water away from the footings by providing porous fill and drainage. Prevent freezing of the soil under the footings by using adequate soil cover or, under special conditions, by using insulation below grade. Use of insulation to allow the footings to be closer to grade is described in ASCE/SEI Standard 32 (2001), which is listed as an approved method of foundation protection in the *International Building Code*. The insulation method of frost protection is especially useful in building alterations. Remember that frost heaving could damage slabs-on-grade before the building is enclosed and heated.

In some cold climates, with lightly loaded foundations, freezing soil to the sides of the foundation can lift the foundations up above the footings. An inch of polystyrene insulation on the cold side(s) will help avoid this problem (**Fig. 14**).

Movement of salt-laden moisture within porous building materials can cause salts to crystallize near the surfaces where the water evaporates. The salts exert great expansive forces (9000 psi; 1305 MPa for halite) that can cause surface spalling. If the moisture movement is upward in the walls, it is called "rising damp." For a discussion of "rising damp" and methods to remedy it, see Massari, Giovanni, and Ippolito (1985). Other *Association for Preservation Technology* publications describe ways of desalinating salt-saturated masonry.

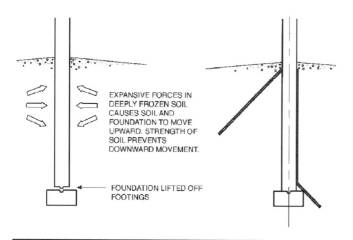

EXPANSIVE FORCES IN DEEPLY FROZEN SOIL CAUSES SOIL AND FOUNDATION TO MOVE UPWARD. STRENGTH OF SOIL PREVENTS DOWNWARD MOVEMENT.

FOUNDATION LIFTED OFF FOOTINGS

Fig. 14. Thermal protection of foundation in cold climates.

Building movement from failure, degradation, or change of its components

Some examples of such materials failure-induced movement include:

- Expansion of concrete from alkali-silica and sulfate reactions.

- Expansion of corroding steel lintels and reinforcing; expansion and spalling of concrete reinforcing; corrosion of other iron and steel products. See the following article on corrosion of metals.

- Decay and insect damage in wooden structures.

- Excessive and differential foundation settlement.

- Shrinkage (and embrittlement) of some organic materials, such as plasticized polymers. ■

REFERENCES

ASCE/SEI Standard 32, *Design Guide for Frost-Protected Shallow Footings,* American Society of Civil Engineers, Structural Engineering Institute, Reston, 2001.

Brick Institute of America, "*Movement; Design and Detailing of Movement Joints,*" Technical Notes, No. 18A, Reston, Brick Institute of America, 1991.

Forest Products Laboratory, *Wood Handbook: Wood as an Engineering Material,* Forest Service, U.S. Department of Agriculture, Madison, 1999.

Gordon, J. E., *Structures, or Why Things Don't Fall Down,* Da Capo Press, New York, 1978.

Gordon, J. E., *The Science of Structures and Materials,* Scientific American Library, New York, 1988.

Hoadley, R. Bruce, *Understanding Wood,* The Taunton Press, Newtown, 1980.

Massari, Giovanni and Ippolito, "Damp Buildings Old and New," *Association for Preservation Technology Bulletin,* XVII-1-85, Association for Preservation Technology, Williamsburg, 1985.

NCMA, "Design of Concrete Masonry for Crack Control," NCMA-TEK 53, National Concrete Masonry Association, Herndon, 1973.

U.S. HUD, Office of Policy Development and Research, *Design Guide for Frost-Protected Shallow Footings,* U.S. Department of Housing and Urban Development, Washington, 1994.

Sources of moisture meters for testing wood:

Delmhorst Instrument Company, 51 Indian Lane East, Towaco, NJ 07082. (800) 222-0638

PRG, Inc., P.O. Box 1768, Rockville, MD 20849. (301) 309-2222

Donald Baerman

Summary

Corrosion of metals affects nearly all parts of buildings and their environment, evidenced in still extant but corroding iron masonry dowels used by the ancient Greeks in the Parthenon to vastly more critical corrosion of contemporary parking garages and highway structures. Design guidelines are offered to mitigate and control corrosion conditions in buildings.

Key words

anodic protection, cathodic protection, coatings, corrosion, metals, paint, rust-resistant treatments

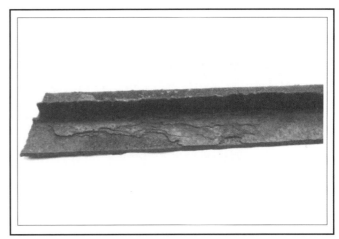

Steel beam, with web totally destroyed by corrosion in a masonry-bearing wall.

Corrosion of metals

1 CORROSION IN GENERAL

Current opinion is that all metal corrosion reactions are electrochemical, and that these reactions are best understood by application of thermodynamic principles. The following summary, however, is in terms of "classic" corrosion theory. For a discussion of modern thermodynamic corrosion theory, see Fontana and Greene (1986). For more information on corrosion of different iron and steel structures, see Steel Structures Painting Council (1993).

Even if only one metal is involved, small differences in electric potential cause electrons to flow in the metal. If adjoining metals are different, and especially if they are far apart on the galvanic series, the reaction will be more rapid. In a fresh-water environment, the following galvanic series, from "more noble" to "less noble" applies (in a wet environment, metals toward the bottom of the series will corrode in contact with those toward the top).

Monel
Copper
Stainless steel
Lead
Tin on steel
Galvanized iron or steel
Zinc
Aluminum
Magnesium

One of the most common examples of galvanic corrosion with dissimilar metals is the corrosion of steel domestic water pipe coupled to copper pipe. The galvanic series is different in seawater and other aqueous solutions (Fontana and Greene 1986); the series above is approximate for fresh water only.

In "biological corrosion" living organisms affect the corrosion. Examples are destruction of protective coatings and changing the pH of the environment. One actual example is the rusting of a microwave tower, in which shrouding of the tower was required by a local architectural review board. The shrouding protected the tower from rain and high winds. The shelter allowed pigeons to nest within and also prevented the droppings from being washed away by the rain. The droppings produced ammonia-rich conditions against the protective paint on the steel, which then saponified and peeled off. After the ammonia passed off, the droppings fermented, producing acidic conditions at the steel, retaining water from dew and other sources. The steel then corroded. After cleaning, the diagnostic remedy was relatively simple: close the small openings through which pigeons gained access and to maintain the tight closure.

Iron and steel corrosion

The corrosion of iron and steel is among the most harmful natural environmental forces acting on buildings. Iron can corrode under a number of different conditions in damp environments. The following are some of the more common modes:

- *Iron in oxygen-free acid environment.*

$$Fe + 2 (HCl) \rightarrow FeCl_2 + H_2$$

Cathodic reaction: $2H^+ + 2e \rightarrow H_2$

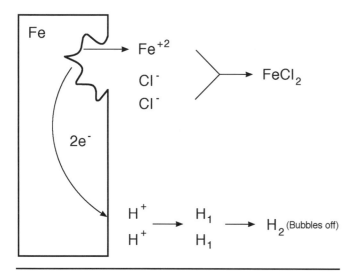

Fig. 1. Iron in oxygen-free acid environment (solution).

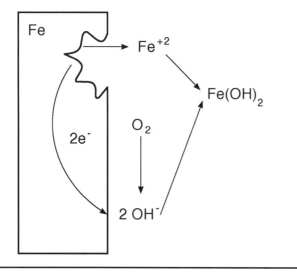

Fig. 2. Iron in aerated environmental, neutral or basic.

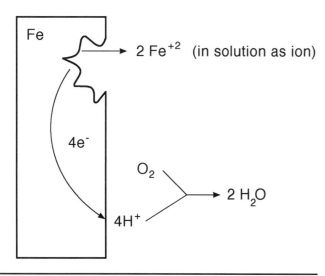

Fig. 3. Iron in aerated acid-water.

(Hydrogen ions in solution combine with electrons at the cathode to form hydrogen.)

Anodic reaction: $Fe \rightarrow Fe^{+2} + 2e$

(Iron gives off electrons that pass through the metal to the cathode; ferric ions go into solution; **Fig. 1.**)

- *Iron in aerated environment, neutral or basic.*

$$O_2 + 2H_2O + 2Fe \rightarrow 4OH^- + 2Fe^{+2} \rightarrow 2\ FeOH_2$$

Cathodic reaction: $O_2 + 2H_2O + 4e \rightarrow 4OH^-$

(Oxygen in solution and water combine with electrons at the cathode and form hydroxyl ions in solution.)

Anodic reaction: $Fe \rightarrow Fe^{+2} + 2e$

(Iron gives off electrons, which pass through the metal to the cathode; ferric ions go into solution.)

Then: $Fe^{+2} + 2\ (OH)^- \rightarrow Fe(OH)_2$

(Ferric ions and hydroxyl ions combine to form ferric hydroxide.)

Then: $2Fe\ (OH)_2 + O_2 \rightarrow Fe_2O_3 + H_2O$

(Ferric hydroxide and oxygen combine to form hematite (brown rust) and water.)

And this product can be further oxidized to FeO (ferric oxide• Iron in aerated acid water; **Fig. 2**).

- *Iron in aerated acid water.*

$$2Fe + O_2 + 4H^+ \rightarrow 2H_2O + 2Fe^2$$

Cathodic reaction: $O_2 + 4H^+ + 4e \rightarrow 2H_2O$

(Oxygen and hydrogen ions in solution combine with electrons at the cathode to form water.)

Anodic reaction: $Fe \rightarrow Fe^{+2} + 2e$

(Iron gives off electrons that pass through the metal to the cathode; ferric ions go into solution; **Fig. 3.**)

- *Iron and copper, or other "noble" metal, coupled.*

The reactions are similar to those described above, but the coupled metals might create a greater differential in potentials between the anode and cathode, and the reaction is more rapid (**Fig. 4**).

In aerated water, it is as follows:

The primary harm from steel corrosion is the weakening of the structural steel itself.

Some of the products of corrosion reactions, in addition to destruction of the steel itself, can be harmful to the building.

- *Hydroxyl ions can attack the paint.* Atomic hydrogen, produced in some corrosion reactions, can embrittle certain steels, especially high-strength steels, and it can form "blisters" where there are voids within the metal. Note the unfortunate coincidence: parking garages are often built with prestressed concrete, which contains reinforcing strands of high-strength steel under stress. Parking garages in cold regions have salt tracked into them. The cover of precast, prestressed concrete over reinforcing is generally less than 1-½ in (3.8 cm), because the flanges are thin.

- *Rust expansion is a major destroyer of the built environment.* The iron oxides and hydroxide are hydrates; they contain bonded water. They are roughly about 10 times as voluminous as the iron. Their expansive force is mighty; they can burst concrete and masonry, and they can break fasteners (**Fig. 5**).

Other types of corrosion of concern

In building locations subject to acid deposition (acid rain), a residue of acid may remain on roofs after the rain dries and acid aerosols may settle there. When the acid rain dries on chemically inert surfaces, and when additional acid aerosols settle, the acids become concentrated. Rain will dilute the acid and wash it off, but mist and dew on the roof may dissolve the acid residue without diluting it much, and the resulting acid may attack copper, lead-coated copper, and some other roofing metals, removing the protective patina. Without a coating of protective patina, copper's durability is reduced. If the copper is designed not to accept runoff from other surfaces, or if it is protected by zinc sacrificial anodes, it is very durable (**Fig. 6**).

- Intergranular corrosion (corrosion of one alloy component) may occur in alloys. One type is dezincification of brass, commonly called "crystallization."

- Lead may leach out of domestic water lines, solder, and fixtures, and make the domestic water toxic.

- Stainless steel in an environment with halide ions suffers "autocatalytic corrosion"; the corrosion occurs in small pits and may cause premature failure. Thus, stainless steel ceiling hangers over chlorinated swimming pools are not a wise design choice.

- Aluminum will corrode in the presence of hydroxyl ions. Hydroxyl ions are found in concrete and masonry mortar. This is a rapid reaction. If aluminum is embedded in fresh concrete, an area of hydrogen bubbles can sometimes be seen at the surface above it. Since concrete is rich in hydroxyl ions, wetting of the concrete-aluminum boundary may continue to cause corrosion in the completed building.

2 SOME METHODS OF CORROSION PREVENTION

In general, subvert any part of the corrosion reaction. The following are some of the strategies for doing so:

- *Prevent metals from getting wet.* Since the reactions listed above are aqueous reactions, prevention is to keep metals from moisture. This protection must be highly reliable. The author has seen unpainted, uncorroded steel in the attics of buildings nearly a century old and an un-rusted 20-year-old tobacco can in the Nevada desert. However, if a leak occurs and the steel gets wet, corrosion will proceed.

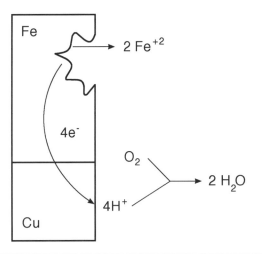

Fig. 4. Galvanic couple (similar to example in Fig. 3).

Fig. 5. Brick masonry cracked by expansion due to corrosion.

Fig. 6. Pitting and corrosion of copper clashing as a result of runoff from membrane roof.

- *Select proper materials.* For severe service, consider high-silica cast iron, certain types of wrought iron (if available), stainless steel, bronze, or other noncorroding metals. Where materials vulnerable to corrosion are used in a damp environment, protect them by one of the methods listed below.

- *Provide anodic protection.* This is based on a property of iron and some other metals to "passivate" at an intermediate level of oxidizing power. Paint coatings such as zinc chromate and red lead protect by this mechanism.

- *Provide cathodic protection.* This is similar to the galvanic corrosion noted above, but the protective metal is less noble than the material being protected. The protected base metal becomes the cathode, and the less noble metal, such as zinc or aluminum, becomes the sacrificial anode. This is the basis for protection by the zinc coating on galvanized steel. However, since the protective anodic metal is sacrificed, there is a time limit to this protection. In some cases the sacrificial anode may be replaced, but galvanized steel inside construction cannot easily be replaced.

Cathodic protection can be provided by blocks of sacrificial anodic metal. Cathodic and anodic protection can also be provided by applying a direct current to the metal and its environment. Protection using these methods should be designed by a corrosion engineer. A commonly seen use of cathodic protection is the zinc blocks coupled to underground steel fuel tanks.

Maintaining a high pH (hydroxyl-rich) environment will protect steel unless there are halide ions present. ("pH" is a measure of the acidity and alkalinity of a solution. A rating of 7 is neutral, below 7 is acid, and above 7 is alkaline. The numbers are on a logarithmic scale; each unit above 7 is 10 times the previous unit, and every unit below 7 is $\frac{1}{10}$ the previous unit.) Thus steel framing and reinforcing steel encased in concrete and masonry are generally not subject to corrosion. However:

- The embedment must be great enough to avoid neutralizing the alkaline environment by acid deposition. Special quality control is needed to maintain the proper separation of embedded steel from exterior surfaces. Using "chairs" between the reinforcing and the side and bottom forms is one method of maintaining proper separation. Vigilant inspection with a mirror or flashlight is another.

- The concrete or masonry must be sound and relatively uncracked.

- There must be no penetration by chloride and other halide ions. Chlorides and other halides "depassivate" the surface of the metal. The chemical mechanism by which they do this is apparently not known with certainty, but appears to concern complex reactions with the passivation layer. Therefore some methods, which protect steel in a salt-free environment, do not work in an environment rich in chlorides and other halides.

- Corrosion-inhibiting admixtures for concrete are available. Also, highly impermeable concrete and concrete with durable coatings will resist the penetration of halide ions.

- *Apply coatings.* This is the predominant method of corrosion protection, but it has its problems. Most paints of most types are somewhat porous, and many paints do not contain corrosion-inhibitive pigments. Corrosion-protective coatings for each spe-

cific environment should be selected through consultation with a technical representative of the selected paint manufacturer or, for critical applications, a corrosion engineer. The *Steel Structures Painting Manual* (1993) contains recommendations for preparing, priming, and painting steel structures under numerous service conditions. Preparation, priming, and painting may be specified by reference to SSPC standard specifications.

- A few coatings, including coal-tar enamel, are totally nonporous, but it is prudent to assume that paint coatings are somewhat porous.

- Most organic corrosion-resistant coatings (paints), such as red lead and zinc chromate, protect by creating an oxidizing polarized layer at the metal surface. See "anodic protection" above. They are not recommended for total or frequent immersion, however.

- A few organic corrosion-resistant coatings (paints), such as zinc dust primer, protect by becoming sacrificial anodes and thus making the steel the cathode. The zinc must be tightly packed and within a few angstrom units of the surface of the metal (the zinc-rich primer must be applied almost immediately after abrasive blasting). These paints are called "zinc-rich primers and paints."

- Epoxy coatings are commonly applied to concrete reinforcing bars in critical environments. Epoxy coatings are not harmed by an alkaline environment, while most alkyd and oleoresinous paints are saponified and loosened in that environment.

- Applying most finish paints directly to metal does not give good protection; they need a proper primer. The preparation must also be proper.

- There is a synergistic effect with the use of coatings and catalytic protection. There is an advantage to using zinc dust polymer coatings over abrasive-blasted steel, in that both cathodic protection and an impermeable layer are employed. Applying a proper protective coating over galvanized steel protects the zinc coating and thus prolongs the life of the coating and its protection.

Good design practice

While specialized corrosion protection may require the services of a corrosion engineer, the following good design practices can be implemented by the architect, and can be highly effective.

- Protect corrosion-vulnerable components from water. Design all details to be free-draining.

- Maintain a proper environment near corrodible metals. For example, do not locate lead-acid batteries near structural steel. Do not locate steel structures in a place formerly or presently used to store salt. Low temperatures retard corrosion. Hot, steamy environments hasten corrosion.

- Protecting steel from corrosion in a halide-rich environment is difficult and often unreliable. Parking garage decks in areas where melting salts are used in winter, especially the floors that are not exposed to rain washing, are highly vulnerable to corrosion. Cathodic and anodic protection is currently being used for bridge structures, and such protection can be used for parking structures as well. The design of such protection is performed by corrosion engineers, but it is the architect's role to request consultation with the corrosion engineer when appropriate. One beneficial maintenance operation is to wash the lower floors of parking garages with clear water in the spring, but the designer cannot be sure that this maintenance will be performed.

- Increase wall thickness to allow some corrosion without affecting required strength. Example: cast-iron roof drains corrode, but their thickness, together with the slow corrosion rate of cast iron, allows them to function for the life of the roof.

- Avoid open joints. Welded joints and rolled sections resist internal corrosion, while riveted and bolted connections are more prone to such corrosion. Where it is appropriate to use riveted or bolted connections exposed to a corrosive environment, provide special protection (**Fig. 7**).

- Design to facilitate cleaning, maintenance, and replacement. Design inspection panels at critical joints.

- Avoid corrosive conditions at stress concentrations (or, avoid stress concentrations in corrosive environments). Stress concentrations cause differences in potential and thus galvanic corrosion.

- Avoid electrical circuits in metal in corrosive environments. Electrical circuits cause differences in potential and thus galvanic corrosion.

- Avoid heterogeneity of metals, especially metals far apart in the galvanic series.

- Observe and learn from experience in the locale where you practice. What works in Houston will not necessarily work in Boston. When practicing outside of your familiar area, confer with architects and engineers familiar with the environmental factors specific to the locale of the building project.

- Insulate galvanic couples. For example, isolate steel from copper pipe in water supply lines.

- Keep the exposed area of the cathode small, and keep the exposed area of the anode large. A copper nail in a steel sheet is not very harmful, but a steel nail in a copper sheet is harmed. If you can only protect half the system, protect the cathodic part.

- Note that "weathering steel" (Corten and Miari-R) resists corrosion except in salt atmospheres and where exposed to standing water. Follow the manufacturer's precautions.

- In metals imbedded in concrete:

- Maintain adequate cover, following the recommendations of the American Concrete Institute and increasing the cover where practicable. Exercise tight quality control regarding this. Inspect the formwork, using a good flashlight on dark days and a mirror on bright days. Do not permit the concrete to be placed until certain that there is no metal near the outside forms. This applies to tie wires as well as reinforcing. Specify "chairs" between the reinforcing and the outside forms.

- Maintain a high pH. Note that acid deposition can neutralize the concrete, especially if the concrete cover is thin. To some extent,

Fig. 7. Corrosion between bolted steel plates.

coating old concrete with lime wash (calcium hydroxide plus binders and other admixtures) may stop the neutralizing that occurs from environmental acid deposition.

– Concrete should be of high quality and nonporous. Avoid excess water in the mix. Use water-reducing admixture or other means to lower the water content. Consider silica fume precipitate. Remember that nonstructural concrete must be treated with the same care as structural concrete.

– Avoid chlorides. Do not add them, and do not allow use of aggregates and water containing chlorides (salt sand; salt used to melt ice in the mixer, etc.). Note that some proprietary products may contain chlorides without saying so. Consider having plastic concrete tested for chlorides. The chloride content allowed under codes may not be safe; consider using a lower limit. A desirable limit, but one hard to attain, is 0.1 percent by weight of cement. ACI permits 2 percent, with less for prestressed work.

– If the concrete will be exposed to chlorides (near ocean, in parking garage, in swimming pool, etc.), the integral or applied protection to exclude chlorides must be in place before exposure. Such methods do not work after the chlorides have already penetrated the concrete. Methods of sealing the concrete include coatings, penetrating water repellents, and very nonporous concrete. Some success has been reported regarding removal of chlorides by setting up an electrical current. A positive charge is imposed on the top of the concrete, drawing the chloride anions to the top where they can be washed off.

– Avoid cracking. Discuss methods with the structural engineer. Remember that nonstructural concrete must be protected from cracking as well as structural concrete. Cracking is especially likely at areas of tension and thermal movement concentration.

– Galvanize reinforcing, or use epoxy-coated reinforcing, or use stainless steel, or use nonmetallic reinforcing such as alkali-resistant fiberglass and aramid fiber. These methods should be used in conjunction with good design; they may not be adequate by themselves.

– Patches in concrete at reinforcing can create a galvanic cell that makes other parts of the reinforcing anodic. For this reason the steel should be coated with an electrically insulating coating before the concrete is patched.

– Salt splash zones in concrete and masonry are vulnerable to corrosion. Salt splash zones that are covered and not washed by rain are especially vulnerable.

– Do not trust older concrete; the problem of chloride was not adequately recognized until the mid-1960s. Older buildings may be in the process of corroding. Many of the buildings on Alcatraz Island were allegedly built of concrete mixed with seawater, and they are in ruin.

– Apply phosphate or other pretreatment of steel surfaces. This offers corrosion protection, and it aids in paint adhesion.

• On every project consider possible corrosion problems, and seek professional advice when in doubt. For example:

– Parking garages in climates where melting salt is used.

– Swimming pools.

– Structures near highways where melting salt is used.

– Structures near salt water.

– Structures with strong underground electrical currents.

– Structures in contaminated soil.

– Structures with critical metal components that cannot be inspected and repaired in the future. ■

REFERENCES

Brantley, L. Reed, and Ruth T. Brantley, *Building Materials Technology: Structural Performance and Environmental Impact,* McGraw-Hill, New York, 1995.

Fontana, Mars G, and Norbert D. Greene, *Corrosion Engineering,* McGraw-Hill, New York, 1986.

Steel Structures Painting Council, *Steel Structures Painting Manual,* Steel Structures Painting Council, Pittsburgh, 1993.

Other sources of information

MIT Corrosion Laboratory, Cambridge, MA and other university-affiliated corrosion laboratories.

National Association of Corrosion Engineers (NACE), 1440 South Creek Drive, Houston, TX 77084

Joseph Lstiburek, P.E.

Summary

This article presents the fundamentals and applications of controlling moisture migration through the exterior envelope, including provision for rain, water drainage, condensation, and moisture transport. Design and detailing strategies are discussed appropriate to specific climate, rainfall, and temperature characteristics.

Key words

airflow retarder, condensation, moisture vapor control, perm, rain control, vapor diffusion, wall section

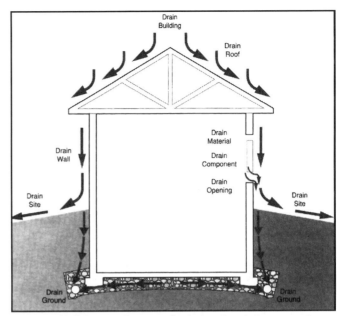

Surfaces of building envelope must be designed to drain away water.

Moisture control and the building envelope

1 RAIN CONTROL

Rain control strategies are varied based on the frequency and severity of rain.

– The amount of annual rainfall determines the type of approach necessary to control rain.

– Rainwater flow over the building surface will be determined by gravity, wind flow across the surface, and wall-surface features such as overhangs, flashings, sills, copings, and mullions.

Rain penetration into and through building surfaces is governed by capillary, momentum, surface tension, gravity, and wind (air pressure) forces. Capillary forces draw rainwater into pores and tiny cracks, while the remaining forces direct rainwater into larger openings.

– Capillarity can be controlled by capillary breaks, capillary-resistant materials, or by providing a receptor for capillary moisture (**Fig. 1**).

– Momentum can be controlled by eliminating openings that go straight through the wall assembly (**Fig. 2**).

– Rain entry by surface tension can be controlled by the use of drip edges and kerfs (**Fig. 3**).

– Using flashings, and layering the wall assembly elements to drain water to the exterior (providing a "drainage plane") can be used to control rainwater from entering by gravity flow (**Fig. 4**), along

with simultaneously satisfying the requirements for control of momentum and surface tension forces.

– Sufficiently overlapping the wall assembly elements or layers comprising the drainage plane can also control entry of rainwater by air pressure differences.

– Finally, locating a pressure-equalized air space immediately behind the exterior cladding can be used to control entry of rainwater by air pressure differences by reducing those air pressure differences (**Fig. 5**).

Combining a pressure-equalized air space with a capillary-resistant drainage plane—which typify state-of-the-art for Norwegian and Canadian rain control practices—addresses all of the driving forces responsible for rain penetration into and through building surfaces under the most severe exposures.

• The first level approach to rain control involves overall architectural design decisions including:

– locating buildings so that they are sheltered from prevailing winds,

– providing roof overhangs and massing features to shelter exterior walls and reduce wind flow over building surfaces,

– providing architectural detailing to shed rainwater from building faces.

• The second level approach to rain control involves details that deal with capillary, momentum, surface tension, gravity, and air pressure forces acting on rainwater deposited on building surfaces.

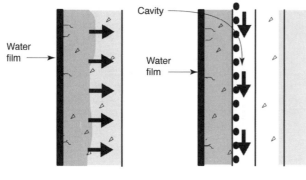

Capillary suction draws water into porous material and tiny cracks

Cavity acts as capillary break and receptor for capillary water interrupting flow

Fig. 1. Capillarity as a driving force for rain entry
- Capillary suction draws water into porous material and tiny cracks.
- Cavity acts as capillary break and receptor for capillary water interrupting flow.

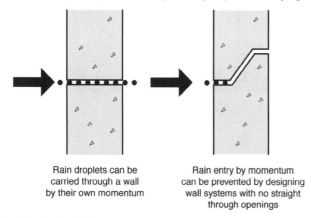

Rain droplets can be carried through a wall by their own momentum

Rain entry by momentum can be prevented by designing wall systems with no straight through openings

Fig. 2. Momentum as a driving force for rain entry
- Rain droplets can be carried through a wall by their own momentum.
- Rain entry by momentum can be prevented by designing wall systems with no straight through openings.

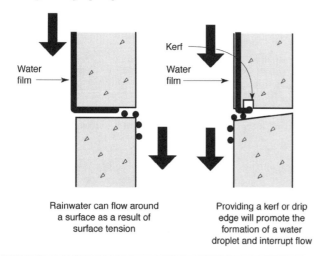

Rainwater can flow around a surface as a result of surface tension

Providing a kerf or drip edge will promote the formation of a water droplet and interrupt flow

Fig. 3. Surface tension as a driving force for rain entry
- Rainwater can flow around a surface as a result of surface tension.
- Providing a kerf or drip edge will promote the formation of a water droplet and interrupt flow.

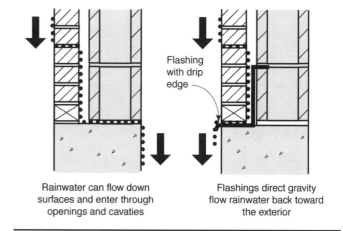

Rainwater can flow down surfaces and enter through openings and cavaties

Flashings direct gravity flow rainwater back toward the exterior

Fig. 4. Gravity as a driving force for rain entry
- Rainwater can flow down surfaces and enter through openings and cavities.
- Flashings direct gravity flow rainwater back toward the exterior.

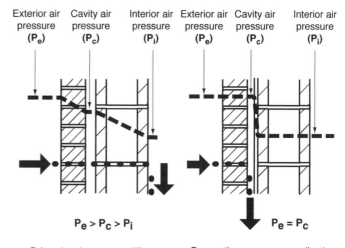

$P_e > P_c > P_i$

$P_e = P_c$

Driven by air pressure differences, rain droplets are drawn through wall openings from the exterior to the interior

By creating pressure equalization between the exterior and cavity air, air pressure is diminished as a driving force for rain entry.

Fig. 5. Air pressure difference as a driving force for rain entry
- Driven by air pressure differences, rain droplets are drawn through wall openings from the exterior to the interior.
- By creating pressure equalization between the exterior and cavity air, air pressure is diminished as a driving force for rain entry.

This second level detailing approach employs two general design principles:

- *Face-sealed/barrier approaches*

– **Storage/reservoir systems (Fig. 6)**, appropriate for all rain exposures.

– **Non-storage/non-reservoir systems (Fig. 7)**, appropriate for locations with less than 30 in average annual precipitation.

- *Water-managed approaches*

– **Drain-screen systems (Fig. 8)**, appropriate for locations with less than 50 in (127 cm) average annual precipitation.

– **Rain-screen systems (Fig. 9)**, appropriate for locations with less than 60 in (152 cm) average annual precipitation.

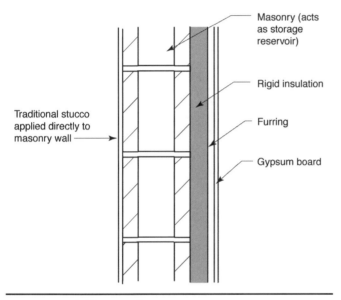

Fig. 6. Face-sealed barrier wall storage reservoir system
- Some rain entry past exterior face permitted.
- Penetrating rain stored in mass of wall until drying occurs to interior or exterior.

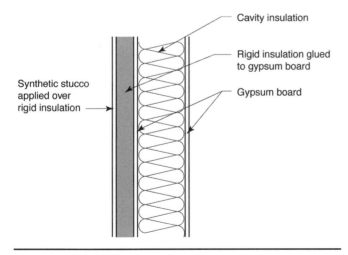

Fig. 7. Face-seated barrier wall non-storage non-reservoir system
- No rain entry past exterior face permitted.

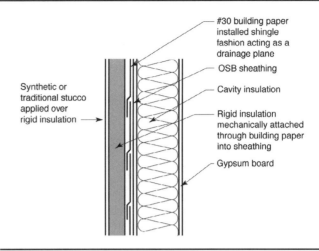

Fig. 8. Water managed wall drain-screen system (drainage plane)
- Should not be used in regions where the average annual precipitation exceeds 50 inches.
- Should not be used in regions where the average annual precipitation exceeds 30 inches.

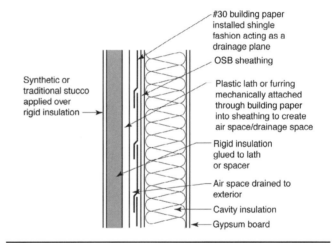

Fig. 9. Water managed wall rain-screen system (drainage plane with drainage space)
- Should not be used in regions where the average annual precipitation exceeds 60 inches.

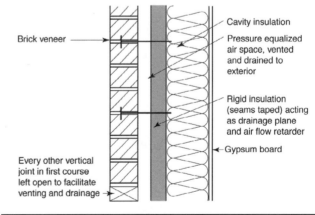

Fig. 10. Water managed wall pressure equalized rain-screen system (drainage plane with pressure equalized drainage space)
- Should be used in regions where the average annual precipitation exceeds 60 inches.

– **Pressure-equalized rain-screen (PER) systems (Fig. 10)**, appropriate for all rain exposures.

Rain is permitted to enter through the cladding skin in the three systems listed above as the water-managed approach: drain-screen, rain-screen, or pressure-equalized rain-screen (PER) systems. "Drain the rain" is the cornerstone of water-managed systems. In the three water-managed systems, drainage of water is provided by a capillary-resistant drainage plane or a capillary-resistant drainage plane coupled with an air space behind the cladding. If the air space has sufficient venting to the exterior to equalize the pressure difference between the exterior and the cavity, the system is classified as a PER design.

In the face-sealed barrier approach, the exterior face is the only means to control rain entry. In storage/reservoir systems, some rain is permitted to enter and is stored in the mass of the wall assembly until drying occurs to either the exterior or interior. In non-storage/non-reservoir systems, no rain can be permitted to enter.

Frequency of rain, severity of rain, system designs, selection of materials, workmanship, and maintenance determine the performance of a specific system.

– In general, water-managed systems outperform face-sealed/barrier systems due to their more forgiving nature.

– However, face-sealed/barrier systems constructed from water-resistant materials that employ significant storage have a long historical track record of exemplary performance even in the most severe rain exposures.

The least forgiving and least water-resistant assembly is a face-sealed/barrier wall constructed from water-sensitive materials that does not have storage capacity. Most external insulation finish systems (EIFS) are of this type and, from the point of view of moisture control, should be considered as best limited to climate zones that see little rain, less than 30 in (76 cm) average annual precipitation.

The most forgiving and most water-resistant assembly is a pressure-equalized rain-screen wall constructed from water-resistant materials. These types of assemblies perform well in the most severe rain exposures, e.g., more than 60 in (152 cm) average annual precipitation.

Water-managed strategies should be used in climate regions where average annual rainfall exceeds 30 in (76 cm) (**Fig. 11**).

Face-sealed/barrier strategies should be carefully considered. Non-storage/non-reservoir systems constructed out of water-sensitive materials should be limited to regions where average annual rainfall is less than 30 in (76 cm). Storage/reservoir systems constructed with water-resistant materials can be built anywhere. However, their performance is design, workmanship, and materials dependent. In general, these systems should be limited to regions or to designs with high drying potentials to the exterior, interior or, better still, to both.

Drainage plane continuity. The most common approach to rain control is the use of a drainage plane. This drainage plane is typically a "tar paper" or building paper. More recently, the term "house wrap" has been introduced to describe building papers that are not asphalt-impregnated felts ("tar papers"). Drainage planes can also be created by sealing or layering water-resistant sheathings such as a rigid insulation or a foil-covered structural sheathing.

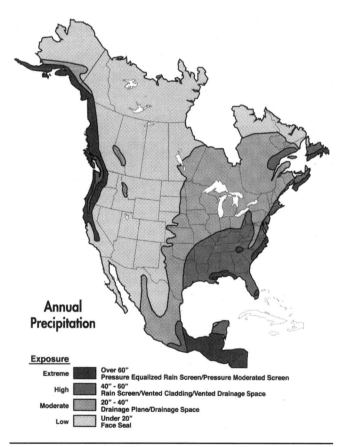

Annual Precipitation

Exposure

Extreme		Over 60" Pressure Equalized Rain Screen/Pressure Moderated Screen
High		40" - 60" Rain Screen/Vented Cladding/Vented Drainage Space
Moderate		20" - 40" Drainage Plane/Drainage Space
Low		Under 20" Face Seal

Fig. 11. Annual precipitation. (Source: Building Science Corporation)

In order to effectively "drain the rain," the drainage plane must provide drainage plane continuity especially at "punched openings" such as windows and doors. Other critical areas for drainage plane continuity are where roofs and decks intersect walls.

2 MOISTURE VAPOR CONTROL

Two seemingly innocuous requirements for building envelope assemblies challenge designers and builders almost endlessly:

• Keep moisture vapor out.

• Let the moisture vapor out, if it gets in.

It gets complicated because sometimes the best strategies to keep moisture vapor out also trap moisture vapor in. This can be a problem if the assemblies start out wet because of rain and the use of wet materials (wet framing, concrete, masonry or damp spray cellulose, fiberglass or rock wool cavity insulation).

It gets more complicated because of climate. In general, moisture vapor moves from the warm side of building assemblies to the cold side of building assemblies. This means that different strategies are needed for different climates. The designer also has to take into account differences between summer and winter.

Water vapor moves in two ways: *vapor diffusion* and *air transport*. If the designer understands the two ways, and knows the climate zone, the problem can be addressed and solved. However, techniques that are effective at controlling vapor diffusion can be ineffective at controlling air-transported moisture, and vice versa.

Building assemblies, regardless of climate zone, need to control the migration of moisture that results from both vapor diffusion and air transport. Techniques that are effective in controlling vapor diffusion can be very different from those that control air-transported moisture.

Vapor diffusion and air transport of vapor

Vapor diffusion is the movement of moisture in the vapor state through a material as a result of a vapor pressure difference (concentration gradient) or a temperature difference (thermal gradient).

– **Vapor diffusion** moves moisture from an area of higher vapor pressure to an area of lower vapor pressure, as well as from the warm side of an assembly to the cold side.

– **Air transport of moisture** will move moisture from an area of higher air pressure to an area of lower air pressure if moisture is contained in the moving air (**Fig. 12**).

Vapor pressure is a term used to describe the concentration of moisture at a specific location. It refers to the density of water molecules in air. For example, a cubic foot of air containing 2 trillion molecules of water in the vapor state has a higher vapor pressure (or higher water vapor density) than a cubic foot of air containing 1 trillion molecules of water in the vapor state. Moisture will migrate by diffusion from where there is more moisture to where there is less. Hence, moisture in the vapor state migrates by diffusion from areas of higher vapor pressure to areas of lower vapor pressure.

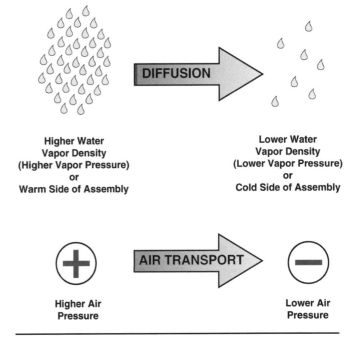

Higher Water Vapor Density (Higher Vapor Pressure) or Warm Side of Assembly

Lower Water Vapor Density (Lower Vapor Pressure) or Cold Side of Assembly

Higher Air Pressure

Lower Air Pressure

Fig. 12. Water vapor movement

In most cold climates, 1/3 of a quart of water can be collected by diffusion through gypsum board without a vapor diffusion retarder; 30 quarts of water can be collected through air leakage.

Moisture in the vapor state also moves from the warm side of an assembly to the cold side of an assembly. This type of moisture transport is called *thermally driven diffusion*. Transported moisture vapor condenses on cold surfaces. These cold surfaces act as "dehumidifiers" pulling more moisture towards them.

Vapor diffusion and air transport of water vapor act independently of one another

– Vapor diffusion will transport moisture through materials and assemblies in the absence of an air pressure difference if a vapor pressure or temperature difference exists.

– Furthermore, vapor diffusion will transport moisture in the opposite direction of small air-pressure differences, if an opposing vapor pressure or temperature difference exists. For example, in a hot, humid climate, the exterior is typically at a high vapor pressure and high temperature during the summer.

– In addition, the interior air-conditioned space is maintained at a cold temperature and at a low vapor pressure through the dehumidification characteristics of the air conditioning system. This causes vapor diffusion to move water vapor from the exterior towards the interior. This will occur even if the interior conditioned space is maintained at a higher air pressure (a pressurized enclosure) relative to the exterior (**Fig. 13**).

Vapor diffusion retarders

The function of a *vapor diffusion retarder* is to control the entry of water vapor into building assemblies that would occur by the mechanism of vapor diffusion. The vapor diffusion retarder may be required to control the diffusion entry of water vapor into building assemblies from the interior of a building, from the exterior of a building, or from both the interior and exterior.

Vapor diffusion retarders should not be confused with *airflow retarders* whose function is to control the movement of air through building assemblies. In some instances, airflow retarder systems may also have specific material properties, which also allow them to perform as vapor diffusion retarders. For example, a rubber membrane on the exterior of a masonry wall installed in a continuous manner is a very effective airflow retarder. The physical properties of rubber also give it the characteristics of a vapor diffusion retarder. Similarly, a continuous, sealed polyethylene ground cover installed in an unvented, conditioned crawl space acts as both an airflow retarder and a vapor diffusion retarder. The opposite situation is also common. For example, a building paper or a house wrap installed in a continuous manner can be a very effective airflow retarder. However, the physical properties of most building papers and house wraps (they are vapor permeable, that is, they "breathe") do not allow them to act as effective vapor diffusion retarders.

Water vapor permeability

The key physical property that distinguishes vapor diffusion retarders from other materials is permeability to water vapor. Materials, which retard water vapor flow, are said to be impermeable. Materials, which allow water vapor to pass through them, are said to be permeable.

The unit of measurement typically used in characterizing permeability is a *perm*. Many building codes define a vapor diffusion retarder as a material, which has a permeability of 1 perm or less.

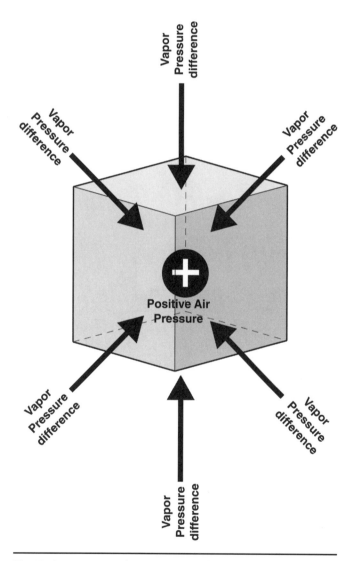

Fig. 13. Opposing air and vapor pressure differences

• Cube is under higher air pressure but lower vapor pressure relative to surroundings.
• Vapor pressure acts inward in this example.
• Air pressure acts outward in this example.

Materials that are generally classed as impermeable to water vapor are: rubber membranes, polyethylene film, glass, aluminum foil, sheet metal, oil-based paints, bitumen-impregnated Kraft paper, almost all wall coverings and their adhesives, foil-faced insulating and non-insulating sheathings.

Materials that are generally classed as semi-permeable to water vapor are: plywood, OSB, expanded polystyrene (EPS), extruded polystyrene (XPS), fiber-faced isocyanurate, heavy asphalt impregnated building papers (30# building paper) and most latex-based paints. Depending on the specific assembly design, construction, and climate, all of these materials may or may not be considered to act as vapor diffusion retarders. Typically, these materials are considered to be more vapor permeable than vapor impermeable.

Materials that are generally classed as permeable to water vapor are: un-painted gypsum board and plaster, fiberglass insulation, cellulose insulation, dimensional lumber and board lumber, unpainted stucco, some latex-based paints, masonry, brick, lightweight asphalt-impregnated building papers (15# building paper), asphalt-impregnated fiberboard sheathings, and "house wraps."

3 AIRFLOW RETARDERS

The key physical properties that distinguish airflow retarders from other materials are *continuity* and *the ability to resist air pressure differences*. Continuity refers to absence of holes, openings, and penetrations. Large quantities of moisture can be transported through relatively small openings by air transport if the moving air contains moisture and if an air pressure differential also exists. For this reason, airflow retarders must be installed in such a manner that even small holes, openings, and penetrations are eliminated.

Airflow retarders must also resist the air pressure differences, which can act across them. These air pressure differences occur as a combination of wind, stack, and mechanical system effects. Rigid materials such as interior gypsum board, exterior sheathing and rigid draft stopping materials are effective air retarders due to their ability to resist air pressure differences.

Magnitude of vapor diffusion and air transport of vapor

The differences in the significance and magnitude of vapor diffusion and air-transported moisture are typically misunderstood. Air movement as a moisture transport mechanism is typically far more important than vapor diffusion in many (not all) conditions. The movement of water vapor through a ¾ in (19 mm) square hole as a result of a 10 Pascal air pressure differential is 100 times greater than the movement of water vapor as a result of vapor diffusion through 32 sq ft, (2.9 sq m) sheet of gypsum board under normal heating or cooling conditions (see **Fig. 14**).

– In most climates, if the movement of moisture-laden air into a wall or building assembly is eliminated, movement of moisture by vapor diffusion is not likely to be significant. The notable exceptions are hot, humid climates or rain-wetted walls experiencing solar heating.

– Furthermore, the amount of vapor that diffuses through a building component is a direct function of area. That is, if 90 percent of

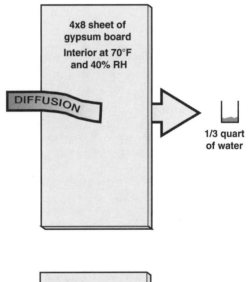

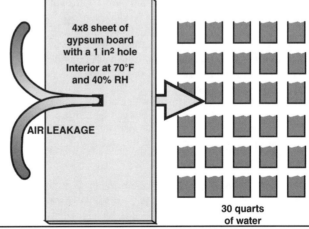

Fig. 14. Diffusion vs. air leakage

In most cold climates, ½ of a quart of water can be collected by diffusion through gypsum board without a vapor diffusion retarder; 30 quarts of water can be collected through air leakage.

the building envelope area is covered with a vapor diffusion retarder, then that vapor diffusion retarder is 90 percent effective. In other words, continuity of the vapor diffusion retarder is not as significant as the continuity of the airflow retarder.

– It is possible and often practical to use one material as the airflow retarder and a different material as the vapor diffusion retarder. However, the airflow retarder must be continuous and free from holes, whereas the vapor diffusion retarder need not be.

In practice, it is not possible to eliminate all holes and install a "perfect" airflow retarder. Most strategies to control air-transported moisture depend on the combination of an airflow retarder, air pressure differential control, and interior/exterior moisture condition control in order to be effective. Airflow retarders are often utilized to eliminate the major openings in building envelopes in order to allow the practical control of air pressure differentials. It is easier to pressurize or depressurize a building envelope made tight through the installation of an airflow retarder than a leaky building envelope. The interior moisture levels in a tight building envelope are also much easier to control by ventilation and dehumidification than those in a leaky building envelope.

4 COMBINING SEVERAL APPROACHES

In most building assemblies, various combinations of materials and approaches are often incorporated to provide for both vapor diffusion control and air-transported moisture control.

– For example, controlling air-transported moisture can be accomplished by controlling the air pressure acting across a building assembly. The air pressure control is facilitated by installing an airflow retarder such as glued (or gasketed) interior gypsum board in conjunction with draft stopping.

– For example, in cold climates during heating periods, maintaining a slight negative air pressure within the conditioned space will control the exfiltration of interior moisture-laden air.

– However, this control of air-transported moisture will not control the migration of water vapor as a result of vapor diffusion.

– Accordingly, installing a vapor diffusion retarder towards the interior of the building assembly, such as the Kraft paper backing on fiberglass batts is also typically necessary.

– Alternatives to the Kraft paper backing are low permeability paint on the interior gypsum board surfaces, the foil backing on foil-backed gypsum board, sheet polyethylene installed between the interior gypsum board and the wall framing, or almost any interior wall covering.

In the above example, control of both vapor diffusion and air-transported moisture in cold climates during heating periods can be enhanced by maintaining the interior conditioned space at relatively low moisture levels through the use of controlled ventilation and source control. Also, in the above example, control of air-transported moisture during air-conditioning periods (when moisture flow is typically from the exterior towards the interior) can be facilitated by maintaining a slight positive air pressure across the building envelope, thereby preventing the infiltration of exterior, hot, humid air.

Overall strategy

Building assemblies need to be protected from wetting that may result from air transport and vapor diffusion. The typical strategies used involve vapor diffusion retarders, airflow retarders, air pressure control, and control of interior moisture levels through ventilation and dehumidification via air conditioning. The location of airflow retarders and vapor diffusion retarders, pressurization versus depressurization, and ventilation *versus* dehumidification depend on climate location and season.

The overall strategy is to keep building assemblies from getting wet from the interior, from getting wet from the exterior, and allowing them to dry to either the interior or exterior should they get wet or start out wet as a result of the construction process or through the use of wet materials.

In general, moisture moves from warm to cold. In cold climates, moisture from the interior conditioned spaces attempts to get to the exterior by passing through the building envelope. In hot climates, moisture from the exterior attempts to get to the cooled interior by passing through the building envelope.

Cold climates

In cold climates and during heating periods, building assemblies need to be protected from getting wet from the interior. As such, vapor diffusion retarders and airflow retarders are installed towards the interior warm surfaces. Furthermore, conditioned spaces should be maintained at relatively low moisture levels through the use of controlled ventilation (dilution) and source control.

In cold climates, the goal is to make it as difficult as possible for the building assemblies to get wet from the interior. The first line of defense is the control of moisture entry from the interior by installing interior vapor diffusion retarders, interior airflow retarders along with ventilation (dilution with exterior air), and source control to limit interior moisture levels. Since it is likely that building assemblies will get wet, a degree of forgiveness should also be designed into building assemblies, allowing them to dry should they get wet. In cold climates and during heating periods, building assemblies dry towards the exterior. Therefore, permeable ("breathable") materials are often specified as exterior sheathings.

Therefore, in general, in cold climates, airflow retarders and vapor diffusion retarders are installed on the interior of building assemblies, and building assemblies are allowed to dry to the exterior by installing permeable sheathings towards the exterior. A "classic" cold climate wall assembly is presented in **Fig. 15**.

Hot climates

In hot climates and during cooling periods the opposite is true. Building assemblies need to be protected from getting wet from the exterior, and allowed to dry towards the interior. Accordingly, airflow retarders and vapor diffusion retarders are installed on the exterior of building assemblies, and building assemblies are allowed to dry towards the interior by using permeable interior wall finishes, installing cavity insulations without vapor diffusion retarders (unbacked fiberglass batts), and avoiding interior wall coverings such as vinyl wallpaper. Furthermore, conditioned spaces are maintained at a slight positive air pressure with conditioned (dehumidified) air in order to limit the infiltration of exterior, warm, humid air. A "classic" hot climate wall assembly is presented in **Fig. 16**.

Mixed climates

In mixed climates, the situation becomes more complicated. Building assemblies need to be protected from getting wet from both the interior and exterior, and be allowed to dry to either the exterior or interior. Three general strategies are typically employed:

- Selecting either a classic heating climate assembly or classic cooling climate assembly, using air pressure control (typically only pressurization during cooling), using interior moisture control (ventilation/air change during heating, dehumidification/air conditioning during cooling), and relying on the forgiveness of the classic approaches to dry the accumulated moisture (from opposite season exposure) to either the interior or exterior. In other words, the moisture accumulated in a cold climate wall assembly exposed to hot climate conditions is anticipated to dry towards the exterior when the cold climate assembly finally sees heating conditions, and vice versa for hot climate building assemblies;

- Adopting a "flow-through" approach by using permeable building materials on both the interior and exterior surfaces of building assemblies to allow water vapor by diffusion to "flow-through" the building assembly without accumulating. Flow would be from the interior to exterior during heating periods, and from the exterior towards the interior during cooling periods. In this approach, air pressure control and using interior moisture control would also occur. The location of the airflow retarder can be towards the interior (sealed interior gypsum board), or towards the exterior (sealed exterior sheathing). A "classic" flow-through wall assembly is presented in **Fig. 17**; or

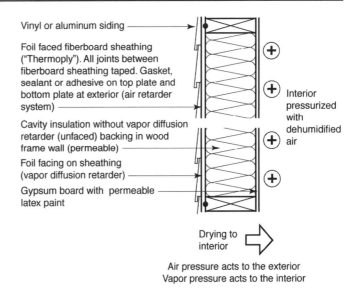

Fig. 16. Classic hot climate wall assembly
- Vapor diffusion retarder to the exterior
- Air flow retarder to the exterior
- Pressurization of conditioned space
- Impermeable exterior sheathing
- Permeable interior wall finish
- Interior conditioned space is maintained at a slight positive air pressure with respect to the exterior to limit the infiltration of exterior, hot, humid air.

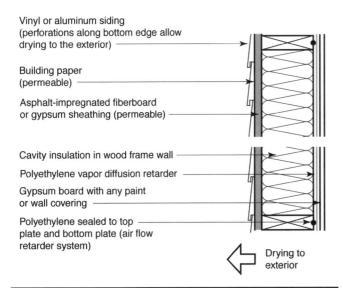

Fig. 15. Classic cold climate wall assembly
- Vapor diffusion retarder to the interior
- Air flow retarder to the interior
- Permeable exterior sheathing
- Ventilation provides air change (dilution) and also limits the interior moisture levels.

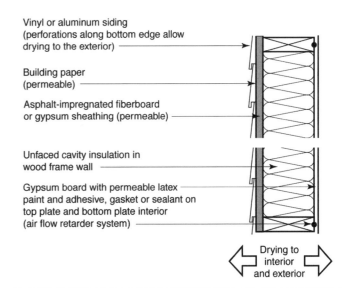

Fig. 17. Classic flow-through wall assembly
- Permeable interior surface and finish and permeable exterior sheathing
- Interior conditioned space is maintained at a slight positive air pressure with respect to the exterior to limit the infiltration of exterior moisture-laden air during cooling.
- Ventilation provides air change (dilution) and also limits the interior moisture levels during heating.
- Air conditioning/dehumidification limits the interior moisture levels during cooling.
- Air conditioning also provides dehumidification (moisture removal) from interior.

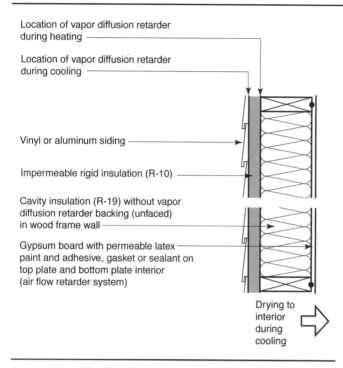

Location of vapor diffusion retarder during heating

Location of vapor diffusion retarder during cooling

Vinyl or aluminum siding

Impermeable rigid insulation (R-10)

Cavity insulation (R-19) without vapor diffusion retarder backing (unfaced) in wood frame wall

Gypsum board with permeable latex paint and adhesive, gasket or sealant on top plate and bottom plate interior (air flow retarder system)

Drying to interior during cooling

Fig. 18. Vapor diffusion retarder in the middle of the wall
- Air flow retarder to the interior
- Permeable interior wall finish
- Interior conditioned space is maintained at a slight positive air pressure with respect to the exterior to limit the infiltration of exterior moisture-laden air during cooling.
- Ventilation provides air change (dilution) and also limits the interior moisture levels during heating.
- Air conditioning/dehumidification limits the interior moisture levels during cooling.

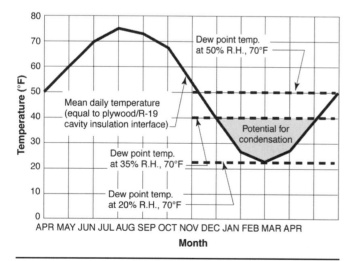

Fig. 19. Potential for condensation in a wood frame wall cavity in Chicago, IL
- By reducing interior moisture levels, the potential condensation is reduced or eliminated.

- Installing the vapor diffusion retarder roughly in the middle of the assembly from a thermal perspective. This is typically accomplished by installing impermeable or semi-permeable insulating sheathing on the exterior of a frame cavity wall. For example, installing 1.5 in (3.8 cm) of foil-faced insulating sheathing (approximately R 10) on the exterior of a 2 × 6 in (5 × 15 cm) frame cavity wall insulated with unfaced fiberglass batt insulation (approximately R 19). The vapor diffusion retarder is the interior face of the exterior impermeable insulating sheathing (Fig. 18). If the wall assembly total thermal resistance is R 29 (R 19 + R 10), the location of the vapor diffusion retarder is 65 percent of the way (thermally) towards the exterior (19/29 = 0.65). In this approach air pressure control and utilizing interior moisture control would also occur. The location of the airflow retarder can be towards the interior or exterior.

The advantage of the wall assembly described in **Fig. 18** is that an interior vapor diffusion retarder is not necessary. In fact, locating an interior vapor diffusion retarder at this location would be detrimental, as it would not allow the wall assembly to dry towards the interior during cooling periods. The wall assembly is more forgiving without the interior vapor diffusion retarder than if one were installed. If an interior vapor diffusion retarder were installed, this would result in a vapor diffusion retarder on both sides of the assembly, significantly impairing durability.

Note that this discussion relates to a wall located in a mixed climate with an exterior impermeable or semi-permeable insulating sheathing. Could a similar argument be made for a heating climate wall assembly? Could one construct a wall in a heating climate without an interior vapor diffusion retarder? How about a wall in a heating climate with an exterior vapor diffusion retarder and no interior vapor diffusion retarder? The answer is "yes" to both questions, but with caveats.

5 CONTROL OF CONDENSING SURFACE

The performance of a wall assembly in a cold climate without an interior vapor diffusion retarder (such as the wall described in Fig. 18) can be more easily understood in terms of condensation potentials and the control of condensing surface temperatures.

Fig. 19 illustrates the performance of a 2 × 6 in (5 × 15 cm) wall with semi-permeable plywood sheathing (perm rating of about 0.5 perms, dry cup; 3.0 perms, wet cup) covered with building paper and painted wood siding located in Chicago. The wood siding is installed directly over the building paper without an air space or provision for drainage. The interior conditioned space is maintained at a relative humidity of 35 percent at 70F (21°C). For purposes of this example, it is assumed that no interior vapor diffusion retarder is installed (unpainted drywall as an interior finish over unfaced fiberglass!). This illustrates a case we would never want to construct in a cold climate: a wall with a vapor diffusion retarder on the exterior (semi-permeable plywood sheathing and painted wood siding without an air space) and no vapor diffusion retarder on the interior.

The mean daily ambient temperature over a one-year period is plotted. The temperature of the insulation/plywood sheathing interface (back side of the plywood sheathing) is approximately equivalent to the mean daily ambient temperature, since the thermal resistance values of the siding, building paper, and the plywood sheathing are small compared to the thermal resistance of the insulation in the wall cavity. The dew point temperature of the interior air/water vapor mix is approximately 40F (4.4°C). This can be found from examining a psychrometric chart. In other words, whenever the back side of the plywood sheathing drops below 40F (4.4°C), the potential for condensation exists at that interface should moisture migrate from the interior conditioned space via vapor diffusion or air movement.

From the plot it is clear that the mean daily temperature of the back side of the plywood sheathing drops below the dew point temperature of the interior air at the beginning of November and does not go above the dew point temperature until early March. The shaded area under the dew point line is the potential for condensation, or wetting potential for this assembly should moisture from the interior reach the back side of the plywood sheathing.

Fig. 20 illustrates the performance of the wall assembly described in Fig. 18, a 2 × 6 in (5 × 15 cm) wall insulated on the exterior with 1.5 in (3.8 cm) of rigid foil-faced impermeable insulating sheathing (approximately R 10, perm rating of about 0.5 perms, wet cup and dry cup), located in Chicago. The wall cavity is insulated with unfaced fiberglass batt insulation (approximately R 19). Unpainted drywall is again the interior finish (no interior vapor diffusion retarder). Now this wall assembly also has a vapor diffusion retarder on the exterior, but with a huge difference. This exterior vapor diffusion retarder has a significant insulating value since it is a rigid insulation. The temperature of the first condensing surface within the wall assembly, namely the cavity insulation/rigid insulation interface (the back side of the rigid insulation), is raised above the interior dew point temperature because of the insulating value of the rigid insulation. This illustrates a case we could construct in a cold climate, a wall with a "warm" vapor diffusion retarder on the exterior and no vapor diffusion retarder on the interior.

The temperature of the condensing surface (back side of the rigid insulation) is calculated in the following manner. Divide the thermal resistance to the exterior of the condensing surface by the total thermal resistance of the wall. Then multiply this ratio by the temperature dif-

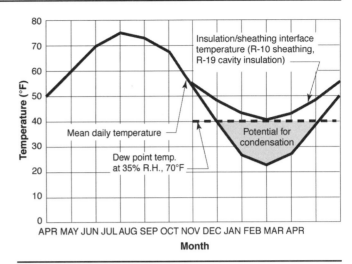

Fig. 20. Potential for condensation in a wood frame wall cavity without an interior vapor diffusion retarder in Chicago, IL

- The R-10 insulating sheathing raises the dew point temperature at the first condensing surface so that no condensation will occur when interior

Table 1. Cold climate wall assembly characteristics (All wall assemblies compatible with dry applied cavity insulations)

Permeable	Non-insulating Fiberboard	Asphalt Impregnated	Building Paper Required	Damp Spray Cellulose
	Gypsum Board	Building Paper Required	Damp Spray Cellulose	
	Insulating	Rigid Fiberglass	Can Come with Building	Damp Spray Cellulose
Semi-Permeable	Non-Insulating	Plywood	Building Paper Required	Damp Spray Cellulose only with Airspace Between Cladding and Building Paper
		O.S.B.	Building Paper Required	Damp Spray Cellulose only with Airspace Between Cladding and Building Paper
	Insulating	Expanded Polysyrene	Building Paper Not Required	Damp Spray Cellulose Not Recommended
		Extruding Polystyrene	Building Paper Not Required	Damp Spray Cellulose Not Recommended
		Fiberfaced	Building Paper Not Required	Damp Spray Cellulose Not Recommended
Impermeable	Non-Insulating	Thermoply	Building Paper Not Required	Damp Spray Cellulose Not Recommended
	Insulating	Foil Faced Isocyanurate	Building Paper Not Required	Damp Spray Cellulose Not Recommended

ference between the interior and exterior. Finally, add this to the outside base temperature.

- T(interface) = R(exterior)/R(total) × (Tin − Tout) + Tout, where:

- T (interface) = the temperature at the sheathing/insulation interface or the temperature of the first condensing surface

- R(exterior) = the R value of the exterior sheathing

- R(total) = the total R value of the entire wall assembly

- Tin = the interior temperature

- Tout = the exterior temperature

The R 10 insulating sheathing raises the dew point temperature at the first condensing surface so that no condensation will occur with interior conditions of 35 percent relative humidity at 70F (21°C). In other words, no interior vapor diffusion retarder of any kind is necessary with this wall assembly if the interior relative humidity is kept below 35 percent. This is a "caveat" for this wall assembly. Now remember, this wall is located in Chicago. This is another "caveat" for this wall assembly.

What happens if we move this wall to Minneapolis? Big change. Minneapolis is a miserable place in the winter. The interior relative humidity would have to be kept below 25 percent to prevent condensation at the first condensing surface. What happens if we move the wall back to Chicago, and install a modest interior vapor diffusion retarder, such as one coat of a standard interior latex paint (perm rating of about 2 perms) over the previously unpainted drywall (perm rating of 20)? If we control air leakage, interior relative humidity can be raised above 50 percent before condensation occurs.

What happens if we move this wall to Raleigh, North Carolina and reduce the thickness of the rigid insulation? Another big change. Raleigh, North Carolina has a moderate winter. Compare with the prior example.

In Raleigh, North Carolina, with no interior vapor diffusion retarder of any kind, condensation will not occur in this wall assembly until interior moisture levels are raised above 45 percent, 70F (21°C) during the coldest part of the heating season. Since these interior conditions are not likely (or desirable), the potential for condensation in this wall assembly is small.

6 SHEATHINGS AND CAVITY INSULATION

Exterior sheathings can be permeable, semi-permeable, impermeable, insulating, and non-insulating. Mixing and matching sheathings, building papers, and cavity insulation can be challenging. The following guidelines are offered:

- Impermeable non-insulating sheathings are not recommended in cold climates (drying not possible to interior due to requirement for interior vapor diffusion retarder, condensing surface temperature not controlled due to non-insulating sheathing).

- Impermeable and semi-permeable sheathings (except plywood or OSB due to their higher permeability) are not recommended for use with damp spray cellulose cavity insulation in cold climates (drying not possible to interior due to interior vapor diffusion retarder).

- Impermeable insulating sheathings should be of sufficient thermal resistance to control condensation at cavity insulation/sheathing interfaces.

- Permeable sheathings are not recommended for use with brick veneers and stuccos due to moisture flow reversal from solar radiation (sun heats wet brick, driving moisture into wall assembly through permeable sheathing), unless a polyethylene interior vapor diffusion retarder is installed to protect the interior gypsum board from the exterior moisture. ■

REFERENCES

Lstiburek, Joseph, *Builder's Guide: Cold Climates,* Building Science Corporation, Westford, 1997.

Lstiburek, Joseph, and John Carmody, *Moisture Control Handbook,* Van Nostrand Reinhold, New York, 1994.

Stephen S. Ruggiero, P.E. and James C. Myers

Summary

This article reviews principles of design for two categories of wall waterproofing systems, barrier walls and cavity walls, and examines applications to various types of wall systems, including single-wythe masonry veneers, precast concrete wall panels, glass/metal curtain walls, and exterior insulation and finish systems (EIFS). Features for reliable and durable waterproofing are reviewed, in view of problems found in field investigations and remedial options for leaking walls.

Key words

barrier walls, cavity walls, curtain walls, EIFS, flashings, masonry veneers, precast panels, sealants

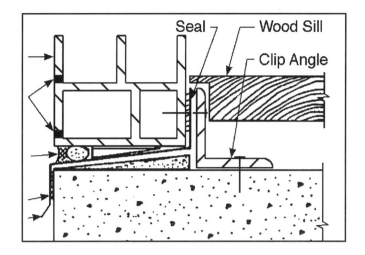

Watertight exterior walls

Exterior building walls generally consist of an exterior veneer or cladding that provides the weathering surface of the building, a backup that provides structural support for the veneer, and an interior finish applied to the backup. Buildings from the early 1900s have relatively massive exterior walls with multiple layers of thick absorptive materials separating the exterior surface from the interior finishes. The articulation of the exterior facade promoted drainage away from wall openings; these designs typically incorporated secondary waterproofing barriers or built-in flashings for long-term performance.

Current trends in exterior wall design have led to increasingly thin, lightweight veneers with little separation between exterior surfaces and interior finishes. In many cases, secondary barriers and throughwall flashings are absent from the design, and surface water flows freely over exposed joints and wall openings. As a result, the occurrence of exterior wall leakage problems has increased, including consequential degradation from such leakage, such as deterioration or corrosion of hidden wall components and damage to interior finishes, within the first few years of service.

In this article, two fundamental approaches to waterproofing exterior walls are considered:

- *barrier wall* construction: uses the exterior surfacing as the sole waterproofing barrier.

- *cavity wall* construction: provides a waterproof barrier behind the exterior surfacing to collect and drain water that penetrates the veneer back to the exterior.

1 RAINWATER ON EXTERIOR WALLS

A sound approach to aid in the waterproofing of exterior walls is to shield them from rain, such as by using cornices, overhangs, belt courses, or similar features. Unfortunately, the effectiveness of this approach is limited to low-rise construction. As building height increases, rain accompanied by even slight wind tends to wet the wall surfaces despite such shielding features. The following article examines two categories of exposure to the elements: rainwater flow over the wall surface with and without the driving pressure of wind.

Gravity-induced water flow

Water that flows down exterior walls soaks into absorbent surfacing materials and flows into cracks or other openings in or between the various wall components. Gravity, surface tension, and capillary action allow water to penetrate the openings even when wind and its driving pressure are absent. Experience in evaluating and testing various wall systems indicates that much of the leakage can be replicated by allowing water to flow over the wall system without application of a differential pressure across the wall, i.e., wind pressure. While wind is a key element in the waterproofing design of wall systems, the designer should reduce the exposure of the wall components and joinery from water flow due to gravity.

Providing slight outward slopes to horizontal surfaces avoids ponding of water and directs water away from the wall and joinery. Shingling or overlapping materials at joints in the direction of water flow reduces the severity of joint exposure to water.

Credits: This article is an updated version by the authors of an earlier paper (Ruggiero and Myers 1991), reprinted by permission of the American Society for Testing and Materials (ASTM).

Critical areas of the wall should be shielded from the flow of water down the wall. Setting windows back from the face of the wall is an example of this approach. Providing an exposed drip edge on metal extrusions or flashings above horizontal joints reduces the exposure of the joints to rainwater. Projecting subsills that extend beyond window jambs and continuous ledges or belt courses shed water away from vulnerable joints, and break up concentrated water flows and spread them more evenly over the wall surface.

These approaches use physical building features to provide permanent protection of the vulnerable areas with little maintenance requirements. However, such features do not ensure watertight wall construction; the design must account for the effects of wind-driven rain.

Wind-driven rain

Wind creates two types of driving forces on rainwater: the momentum of the raindrops (splashing) and differential pressure across the exterior wall. The momentum of wind-driven raindrops allows them to penetrate openings approximately ¼ in (6 mm) or wider. Narrower openings cause the raindrop to shatter with less penetration into the opening. Wind pressures can counteract the effects of gravity and cause water to "flow uphill." But most important, wind creates a pressure differential across the wall that forces water through cracks and openings in the wall cladding. Water held within the cladding due to capillary forces will flow readily toward the interior under small differential pressures. Designers need to consider these forces that act on wall systems, particularly on taller buildings and those in windy locations, such as shorelines of lakes and oceans. AAMA (1985) contains details on calculations of wind pressures on buildings.

Conceptually, wall waterproofing systems fall into two categories, depending upon the means by which they control rainwater and the driving forces discussed above.

– *Barrier walls* rely on the exterior cladding and surface seals at joints to prevent water penetration to the interior.

– *Cavity walls* rely, in part, on the cladding to shed rainwater, but include a backup waterproofing system to collect water that penetrates the cladding surface and drain it back outside.

These categories provide a convenient basis for examining the waterproofing fundamentals discussed below. Of course, many wall systems consist of combinations or variations of these two types. Below, we discuss the application of these fundamentals to commonly used wall systems.

Barrier walls

Barrier wall designs require that the exterior wall materials and joinery block passage of all water at the exterior face of the wall. These systems typically have no waterproofing redundancy and little tolerance for construction variations and defects. Key factors in the performance of barrier walls are discussed below.

The basic cladding element must be relatively impermeable and cannot develop through cracks in the course of weathering and reacting to thermal or moisture cycles. Some materials contain more redundancy than others and reduce the chances of leakage. For example, multi-wythe brick masonry can tolerate some deficiencies in construction of one of the wythes without creating through-cracks. Some

materials absorb and contain limited moisture without significant material deterioration or leakage to the interior. Design considerations include:

– Joints in the wall system at openings or between cladding elements must be sealed with materials that do not split or debond from the cladding.

– The cladding must be continuous and uncracked along the sealant bond line. Typically, cladding joints are sealed during construction (in the field) with liquid-applied sealants. It is unreasonable to expect the application of these materials to be perfect.

– Substrate surfaces must be sound and uncracked and then cleaned and prepared for sealing. Joint backup materials need to be positioned properly, and sealant materials must be mixed in some cases and then applied.

– The sealant materials must withstand joint movement and weathering without deterioration.

Given all of these variables, some deficiencies in the joint seals are likely to occur both upon initial installation and as the sealant ages. Under the best circumstances, the deficiencies are rare and leakage is not widespread, but maintenance of the seals is necessary to avoid increased leakage. In field surveys and testing, significant leakage problems have been found in buildings with single joint seals that contain defects along as little as 1 percent of their length. This does not provide much allowance for variability in construction of such joints. A common method to improve the watertightness of sealant joints is to provide two seals in one joint. This is discussed further below.

Incorporating shielding elements within the cladding to protect the joints can improve barrier wall performance significantly. Overlapping the wall elements at joints, recessing the seals and windows from the face of the wall, and providing overhangs and drip edges are examples of such features. Unfortunately, recent trends in wall design eliminate such features and, instead, set the glazing and joint seals flush with the exterior surface, providing little or no shielding from rainwater and from the deteriorating effects of ultraviolet (UV) radiation on organic sealants.

Elements within wall openings, such as windows, must be watertight and cannot leak from frame corners or face joints. Windows typically contain joints between the horizontal and vertical framing members that are sealed with gaskets or liquid-applied sealants. For reasons discussed above, corner seals that are constructed with liquid-applied sealants are not likely to be watertight. In addition, handling and installation of the window frame can disturb or break these seals. For these and other reasons, it is prudent to install a flashing, such as a sheet metal or sheet membrane sill pan, along the bottom of the window to collect leakage through the window glazing or frame joints and direct it back to the outside (Fig. 1). Myers (1990) provides more detailed information on window sill flashings.

Many barrier walls do not incorporate such a flashing in keeping with the concept that the surface seal is the only defense needed against water penetration. In many cases, this results in water leakage into the building.

Wall openings interrupt the cladding. Some barrier walls, such as multi-wythe brick masonry, may absorb and contain some water within the cladding. As this water seeps down within these materials, it can leak to the inside at the top of the wall openings, unless a flashing is installed in this location to collect water and drain it to the exterior.

Field experience is that barrier walls generally are problematic because the combination of imperfect average workmanship and degradation of materials by weathering result in deficiencies in the barrier that allow some water leakage. The extent and nature of leakage problems that develop depend on the types of materials used, the quality of workmanship, and the frequency of maintenance.

Cavity walls

The cavity wall concept differs fundamentally from the barrier wall concept, in that the exterior surfacing screens the rain from the waterproofing layer that is placed behind it, rather than acting as the sole barrier to water entry. This concept acknowledges, and accounts for, the inevitable penetration of some water through the exterior veneer and joinery. As such, it avoids some of the primary drawbacks of the barrier wall approach and can possess a high degree of reliability and durability. The details of cavity wall construction can take different forms depending upon the veneer type and backup construction. Its fundamental design elements include the following:

- The exterior veneer provides the initial barrier to water penetration. While the veneer is not expected to prohibit all water entry, it should not contain significant cracks, openings, or unsealed joints. Differential air pressure acts across this veneer and drives water through it.

- An air space isolates the inner, or backup wall, from the exterior veneer. Water that penetrates the veneer flows downward in this cavity, minimizing any contact with the backup wall construction. The width of the air space varies depending upon the veneer materials and the likelihood of creating obstructions during construction of the veneer, but generally ranges from 1 to 2 in (2.5 to 5 cm).

- A continuous waterproofing layer should cover the backup wall to shed any small amounts of water that inevitably cross the air space by splashing or by direct flow at cavity obstructions or at veneer anchor ties that span the cavity. Asphalt-saturated felts and a variety of sheet or fluid-applied membranes, shingled with the flow of water, are commonly placed on the exterior face of the backup wall. Because the veneer and cavity control much of the water and the veneer shields the cavity from wind-driven rain, the requirements for this waterproofing layer are much less severe than if it were exposed on the face of a building. The combination of a protective screen and a waterproofing layer provide significant redundancy in these systems with resultant long-term reliability.

- Horizontal runs of through-wall flashings must be located at regular vertical intervals to collect the water that flows downward within the veneer and cavity space. The inboard end of the flashing should turn upward at the backup wall, and the wall waterproofing layer should shingle over it. The flashing should extend from the backup wall, across the cavity, through the veneer, and terminate with an exposed drip edge at the front of the veneer to prevent water from running back underneath the flashing (**Fig. 2**). Providing slight outward slope to the horizontal part of the flashing to promote drainage and avoid ponding on the flashing enhances reliability and durability. Sloped quick-set mortar beds or closely spaced tapered shims beneath the flashing can provide such slope.

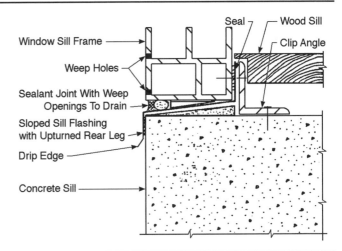

Fig. 1. Schematic cross section of windowsill flashing. The flashing collects water that penetrates the window, such as at corners, drawing it back to the exterior through weep holes. Window frame also has weep drainage detail.

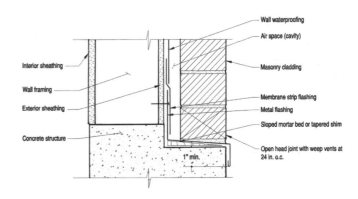

Fig. 2. Through-wall flashing of brick veneer/steel stud wall.

- Along the length of the wall, the flashing needs to be continuous and seamed watertight at joints and corners. Expansion joints should be incorporated in continuous flashings that are made with rigid materials, such as sheet metal, to accommodate thermally induced movement of the flashing and cladding. At terminations, the flashing should turn up and the corner should be sealed watertight to prevent water from draining off the end of the flashing and into the building. Weep openings are needed in the veneer at the flashing level to permit drainage of water from the flashing to the exterior. Size and spacing of these weep holes vary with the veneer materials.

Pressure-equalized design concept

An approach that is related to the cavity wall concept is pressure-equalized design, which provides an air barrier inboard of the veneer, instead of, or in addition to, a waterproofing layer. By preventing air penetration through the backup wall and by sufficiently venting the cavity (air chamber) to the outside air, the pressure differential across the exterior veneer is reduced, or eliminated, during wind-driven rains, thus removing a primary driving force for water penetration. Essential elements for pressure-equalized systems include the following:

- The air barrier must be continuous and properly sealed to all wall openings such as windows and doors. The air chamber is not simply a ventilated space. Because wind pressures vary considerably over the face of the wall, the air chamber should be compartmentalized to avoid airflow, and accompanying water flow, from high pressure to low pressure regions.

- The air barrier and its supporting wall, typically the backup wall, must have adequate strength to resist wind loads on the building.

- The exterior veneer serves as the primary rain screen or barrier to water penetration. However, the joints between veneer elements are left open to some degree to allow efficient pressurization of the air chamber behind the veneer. Wind-driven rain inevitably penetrates the open joint areas due to momentum of the raindrops.

- Backup waterproofing layers are needed at the joints or the joints should be configured to control this form of penetration, e.g., ship-lap geometry.

- Internal drainage devices, such as through-wall flashings, are required at regular vertical intervals to collect water that penetrates the cladding and direct it back to the exterior.

The balance of this article describes the composition of some common exterior wall systems, the application of the design principles discussed above, and key features to incorporate in the design and construction of these systems, with the emphasis of the discussion on control of water penetration, along with common problems with these systems, and remedial options for leaking systems.

2 CAVITY WALL MASONRY VENEERS

A typical masonry veneer wall consists of nominal 4 in (10 cm) thick brick veneer with a 2 in (5 cm) wide air space (cavity) that separates it from the backup wall. Wire ties embedded in the veneer bridge the cavity and are attached to a backup wall to stabilize the veneer against wind loads. A layer of waterproofing covers the backup wall, i.e., concrete masonry units or gypsum sheathing board/steel stud wall.

A variety of materials can be used as the waterproofing layer that covers the backup wall. A heavier layer of unperforated asphalt saturated felt (30 lb felt) is more able to withstand construction handling and exposure before installation of veneer than a 15 lb felt. "Peel and stick" membranes provide more reliable protection and can serve as secure exposed waterproofing until the veneer is installed. "Peel and stick" membranes also provide some self-sealing around anchor penetrations. Always check vapor drive when using low permeability membranes to avoid problems of condensation within the wall. For concrete block backup walls with drill-in brick anchors, a bituminous modified elastomeric coating or "peel and stick" membranes are good waterproofing options. For cast-in anchors in block backup walls mastics are generally used to avoid cutting and patching of sheet materials, but these mastics can crack as the backup moves in response to changes in thermal, moisture, and loading conditions.

Single-wythe masonry veneers must be designed as a cavity wall to properly control water penetration through the veneer. These walls contain many mortar joints and some inevitable brick-to-mortar separations due to normal material and construction variations that allow water penetration. In addition, some moisture may soak through these somewhat absorptive materials. Proper selection of masonry materials and complete filling of mortar joints can minimize, but not eliminate, water penetration through the veneer. The cavity wall approach is necessary to accommodate this inevitable water penetration.

An important aspect in the construction of these systems is maintaining a clear cavity and avoiding accumulations of mortar droppings on the through-wall flashings. Care in placing the mortar and setting the brick units can reduce the amount of mortar oozing out from the cavity-side of the mortar joint and falling into the cavity. See Brick Institute of America (1985) for further details. A cavity width of 2 in (5 cm) makes it easier to control the mortar and reduce droppings into the cavity than with narrower cavities. However, there is documentation of successful construction with narrower cavities.

Through-wall flashing is the most essential element to successful waterproofing of single-wythe veneers. Steel relieving angles that support the veneer are typically located at each floor level, and the flashings should be located on each angle to limit the accumulation of water within the wall cavity, as well as to limit the distance it travels, before being weeped to the exterior. In some cases, exposed concrete spandrel beams support the brick veneer. Through-wall flashing is necessary at these areas, particularly since the spandrel beam tends to funnel any water leakage directly to the interior floor.

Through-wall flashings are also required to protect the heads and sills of wall openings against water penetration, such as at windows. Flashings at the head of the window are absolutely essential for cavity wall construction to collect the water draining down the wall cavity above the window head. Many windows are placed directly below the veneer relieving angles, and the flashing that covers the angle serves to protect the window head as well. Avoid penetrating the flashing with fasteners used to anchor the window head.

If the windows are placed into separate, "punched" openings in the wall, a loose steel lintel typically supports the brick veneer above the opening. A head flashing should cover the angle and integrate with the backup wall waterproofing. The flashing should extend beyond the sides of the opening, and the ends of the flashing must turn up with watertight corners, i.e., bulkhead or end-dam, to prevent water from flowing off the ends of the flashing and into the wall assembly. Aligning bulkheads with a head joint in the veneer allows the bulkhead to extend outward to the face of the veneer.

Sill flashings are generally necessary to waterproofing window openings. When the interior face of the window frame aligns with the interior face of the veneer, then any leakage through the sill-to-jamb frame corner or around the window frame may flow into and be weeped out of the cavity reducing the importance of a sill flashing. Recommended practice is to use sill flashings regardless of frame position, to protect against inadvertent transmission of water to the backup at wood blocking or other "rough opening" materials and sill anchors.

Sill flashings can be created that direct the water into the cavity, rather than extending the flashing through the veneer, to avoid the aesthetic impact of an exposed flashing and drip edge. Such an approach requires careful consideration of the path of water flow within the cavity, the impact of additional water in the cavity, and the construction details. Avoid penetrating the horizontal portions of sill flashing with window anchors, and use fasteners with seals through the vertical legs of the flashing to reduce the severity of exposure of these penetrations to water. Also, provide slope to drain at horizontal portions of flashings with continuous shims (as in Fig. 1).

The sides or jambs of the opening also require some protection as the waterproofing layer terminates at this location and, therefore, provides an avenue for penetration of water to flow in the cavity. This area is particularly vulnerable when the brick veneer forms a 90-degree corner at the jambs, since the return edge of the brick may reduce the width of the cavity. Mortar tends to accumulate in such areas and directs water against the window jambs. Many jamb flashing details are available, depending upon the type of window framing. Consider the use of sheet metals or "peel and stick" membrane flashing. These flashings need to integrate with head and sill flashings and shingle properly over the sill flashing.

Flashings must be constructed from durable materials that can withstand abuse during construction of the brick veneer. Lead-coated copper and stainless steel have superior strength, corrosion and staining resistance, and can be bent and soldered to form durable watertight geometries. The seams between sections of flashing can be soldered or strip flashed with uncured rubber sheet to provide continuity of waterproofing. Also, these metals can protrude beyond the face of the veneer to form drip edges that protect vulnerable sealant joints at "soft joints" below relieving angles and at the heads of windows. Sheet membranes may also be suitable for use as flashing materials, however, the common problems discussed below must be considered before these materials are used.

To facilitate the installation of through-wall flashing—particularly its integration with the gypsum sheathing or concrete block at the backup wall—a two-piece flashing assembly consisting of waterproofing membrane and lead-coated copper or stainless steel is convenient. The waterproofing membrane can be shingled into the gypsum sheathing or concrete block slightly above the flashing level and protrude from the sheathing. When the through-wall flashing is placed at a later time, the waterproofing membrane is then lapped over the rear upturned leg of the flashing (as in Fig. 2).

The design of the through-wall flashing should provide adjustment capability to move the flashing in or out to maintain a uniform exposure of the drip edge over the masonry. Turning up the rear leg of the flashing at an angle less than 90 degrees allows such flexibility.

Common problems

Some flashing materials, such as thin unreinforced polyvinyl chloride (PVC) roll flashing (less than 1 mm, 10 to 30 mils) and thin waterproofing membranes (less than 40 mils) are readily punctured and torn during construction of the brick veneer, including after they are mounted on the backup wall when the wind slaps them against the building. These materials are not stiff enough to maintain formed shapes and must be bonded to a substrate to create the desired shape. They are also damaged by UV exposure, and therefore cannot be formed to provide an exposed drip edge. The final positioning and seaming is commonly done by the mason, not a waterproofing contractor. Forensic examination of flashing failures frequently finds that joints are lapped and unsealed, or not lapped at all, particularly at corners. Lack of coordination of the various trades and failure to integrate the wall components is a common problem with this system.

Documented investigations of a number of walls with leakage problems include cases in which PVC roll flashings have become brittle and developed cracks and splits. PVC is a rigid plastic, made flexible during manufacturing by the addition of oils and "plasticizers." Embrittlement due to plasticizer migration is common to all PVC materials and is a significant problem with the relatively thin PVC roll flashings. Such PVC can be embrittled within two years of service, particularly where the flashing is under mechanical stress (e.g., where the flashing spans over an offset or where mortar has accumulated on the flashing).

"Peel and stick" membranes should be 40 mils thick as a minimum and must be bonded to a substrate to create the desired flashing shape. Use of sheet metal angles or wood blocking around window openings is often required to provide a substrate with the proper flashing geometry (similar to **Fig. 3**). Care during installation is required to ensure that the membrane is continuously bonded to the substrate without air pockets or canting at corners, otherwise the membrane can be easily damaged by impact loads.

Aggravating any flashing deficiencies is the common problem of mortar accumulation in the wall cavity and on the flashing, and use of small, widely spaced weep holes. Keeping the cavity clear requires close attention by the mason. For weep holes, provide open head joints filled with open cell foam to maximize drainage from the flashing and prevent insect entry.

A common weakness in some flashing designs is to terminate the flashing behind the face of the veneer, concealing it from view. This practice can allow the water to run back underneath the flashing as it tries to drain from the cavity. This water then can either be conducted inside directly, such as with exposed concrete spandrel beams, or it can collect on steel support angles. The water on the steel angles can corrode the angles, and it tends to run along the angle and leak into the backup wall at joints in the angle or at the ends of the angle.

Extending the flashing through the wall and providing an exposed drip edge avoids this problem. An alternative is to fully adhere the flashing to prevent water from running underneath it. This alternative is not as reliable as the drip-edge approach, since it relies on the

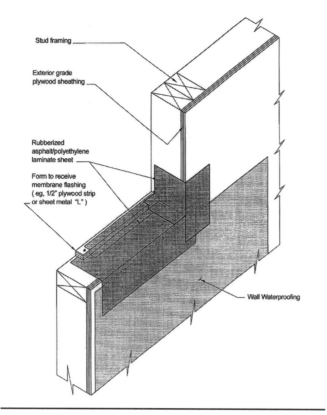

Stud framing

Exterior grade
plywood sheathing

Rubberized
asphalt/polyethylene
laminate sheet

Form to receive
membrane flashing
(eg, 1/2" plywood strip
or sheet metal "L")

Wall Waterproofing

Fig. 3. Schematic isometric elevation of window sill flashing using a "peel and stick" waterproofing membrane.

quality and durability of the adhesive installation and it requires a joint-free substrate for continuous adhesion.

Other forensic examinations include building projects where head or sill flashings are not included and leakage results. Also, a number of leakage problems result from poor flashing design, e.g., missing end-pans, unsealed joints and corners, penetrations by fasteners that anchor the window head or sill, and so on. Flexible flashings should be folded to form a watertight corner, and should not be cut at the corner.

Remedial options

Remediation for leaking masonry veneers fall into three general categories:

– surface coatings,

– flashing replacement, or

– replacement of the wall.

Attempts to eliminate leakage through use of surface sealers and water repellents, such as siloxanes, are not generally successful. They are tried frequently because they are low-cost and low-disruption options compared to flashing or wall replacement. However, this approach does not treat the root cause of the leakage problem, which is usually traceable to defects in the flashing. Instead, the sealer attempts to reduce the volume of water penetrating the veneer and reaching the flashing, in a sense, reverting to barrier wall construction.

Sealers can reduce the surface absorption and capillary draw of masonry walls and, thereby, reduce the amount of water penetrating the veneer via these paths and reaching the flashings. Generally, however, the sealers do not seal the separations or cracks between the mortar and the masonry units and water will continue to penetrate the veneer through these paths. In many masonry veneers, these separations are the predominant source of water entry, and leakage will continue despite sealer application. Frequent reapplication is necessary over the life of the building to maintain the effectiveness, if any, of the sealer.

A common repair is to replace defective flashings. This requires removing several courses of masonry at the flashing level in a "leg and leg" fashion. Sections of masonry 3 to 6 ft (1 to 2 m) are removed, while adjacent sections are left in place between these areas or shoring is installed to temporarily support the veneer above. The flashing is repaired or replaced in the areas of removed masonry. The masonry is replaced and the process is repeated until all flashing is repaired or replaced. At the same time, the base of the cavity can be cleared of any mortar obstructions, and proper weep holes incorporated.

Generally, the decision to replace the entire wall is due to other deficiencies beyond leakage problems, such as inadequate veneer ties, defects in the masonry materials, or deterioration of the backup wall components from the ongoing leakage.

3 PRECAST CONCRETE

These wall systems typically contain large prefabricated wall panels that are attached to the structure at a few discrete points to resist gravity and wind loads. There are horizontal and vertical joints between the panels. Strip windows, i.e., a continuous horizontal band of windows, are common with this system. Typically, a steel stud wall behind the panel supports the interior finishes. Alteratively, metal furring is attached to the interior face of the panel to receive interior finishes.

Precast concrete panel systems can be barrier walls or cavity walls, including pressure-equalized designs. Barrier wall construction results from sequencing the wall erection such that the panels enclose the structural frame quickly and in advance of interior wall construction. Consequently, access to the exterior face of the interior walls cannot be achieved for installation of a waterproofing layer or air barrier.

To properly implement cavity wall construction, the backup wall must be installed before the panels, and, therefore, must be capable of resisting wind loads during construction. Installation of the waterproofing layer, particularly the seal around panel attachment anchors, and the continuous through-wall flashings with associated seams and transitions typically requires access from the exterior and coordination with panel erection so that these operations can be completed as each panel is erected. Prefabrication and mounting of the flashing before erection can help reduce coordination problems. All of these factors increase the cost of the project and can reduce overall floor space. Consequently, the majority of precast panel wall systems are designed as barrier walls.

Architectural precast concrete wall panels can develop full-depth cracks, commonly at the reentrant corners in the panels. Cracking is more common in sandwich panels—i.e., those with insulation placed within the panel during casting—than in solid concrete panels, due to greater thermal gradients across the panel depth. Proper quality control in manufacturing and handling during erection can reduce full-depth cracks in the field of these panels. Using panels with simple geometries, i.e., rectangular without "punched" openings, and simple anchorage arrangements that avoid restraint of thermally induced bowing further reduces the likelihood of cracking.

Accordingly, solid precast concrete panels can provide a fairly effective, but not always perfect, barrier against water penetration. Unlike some other wall systems that rely on light-gauge steel framing and gypsum sheathing for attachment, precast concrete panel systems rely on relatively thick steel angles and similar substantial materials for structural support and the system can tolerate some water entry without rapid structural deterioration.

The joints between panels can be significant sources of water penetration. Several options for waterproofing the joints are available. The simplest form of protection at the joinery consists of a single line of sealant material, typically a liquid-applied sealant, placed in a butt joint at the face of the panels. This approach is not as reliable as other methods because some water inevitably penetrates these single sealant joints and the butt joint configuration allows direct transmission to the interior. Half-lapped or ship-lapped joints can improve single joint seal performance, particularly when the sealant is recessed within the joint (**Fig. 4**). Further, some panel-edge geometries can protect the recessed sealant by including preformed drip edges at horizontal joints and raised shoulders along vertical joints to reduce sideways flow of wind-driven water over the sealant (**Fig. 5**).

Diagnostic examinations indicate that polyurethane or polysulfide sealants shielded from prolonged UV exposure are in much better condition, i.e., less surface crazing, splitting, debonding, and hardening, than sealants placed on the face of the building under direct UV exposure.

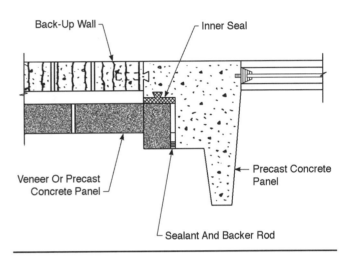

Fig. 4. Plan section showing vertical joinery in precast concrete panels. Note that panel geometry shields vertical joint from weather. Water that penetrates outer seal does not have a direct path to the interior.

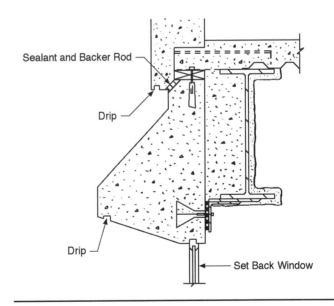

Fig. 5. Vertical section showing horizontal joinery in precast concrete panels. Note shiplap geometry and recessed sealant to shield the joint from the weather.

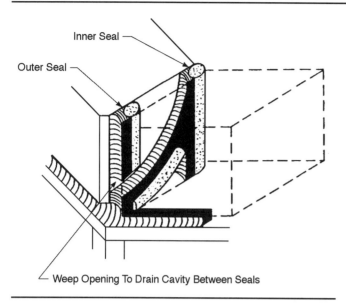

Inner Seal

Outer Seal

Weep Opening To Drain Cavity Between Seals

Fig. 6. A two-stage remedial vertical seal with weep openings at the base of the joint.

Joint reliability can be improved further by installing two seals in each joint, one near the face of the panel and the other set some distance behind the outer joint. This two-stage approach provides redundancy in the system and protects the inner seal from the elements. This approach requires the installation of weep openings in the exterior seal to allow water contained by the inner seal to exit the cavity between joint seals. At vertical joints, the inner seal must turn out to the plane of the exterior seal at regular intervals to force water out of the joint (**Fig. 6**).

This termination requires care in detailing and construction. Some outward slope or offset joinery should be incorporated in the horizontal panel joints to promote drainage. Failure to provide these weep openings results in water trapped within the wall and ponding against both seals. This accelerates deterioration of the sealant material and its bond to the substrate.

A more reliable approach is to incorporate a horizontal flashing at the base of the vertical joints. This avoids the problem-prone weep hole detail in the two-stage approach and reduces reliance on the horizontal sealants. Flashings can be incorporated easily with strip window systems, because continuous window sill and head flashings can be installed after the panels are erected. Metal flashings to drain water from the system are thus recommended.

Panel openings, such as at "punched" windows, require sill flashings. The panel edges can be configured to shield the perimeter joints, direct the flow of water away from the opening, and restrict the transmission of water to the interior, such as with steps or jogs in the panel edge inboard of the sealant joint. Head flashings generally cannot be installed, because the ends of the flashing cannot turn up into the solid concrete panel.

A common approach, instead of using a head flashing, is to install a two-stage sealant joint along the head and jambs of the windows and direct the water between the seals into the sill flashing for drainage. A proper seal of the top edge of the upturned end of the sill flashing to the concrete jamb is critical to prevent the water that flows down between the jamb seals from bypassing the sill flashing. A practical detail here is the use of sheet rubber sill flashings adhered to the concrete and separate pieces of sheet metal, i.e., counterflashing, set into a sealant-filled reglet to cover the top edge of the upturned end of the flashing.

Common problems

Exposed aggregate finishes on the panels present an irregular surface for sealant adhesion. It is nearly impossible to tool the sealant into the surface irregularities, resulting in pinholes and leakage. A better approach is to use panels where the sides and perimeter of the face of the panel is finished smooth, thus confining the exposed aggregate to the central portion of the panel.

Panels commonly develop hairline shrinkage cracks, particularly at the perimeter edges and at corners of punched openings, despite controlled curing procedures. These cracks create avenues for water to bypass shallow joint sealants, even when they have good adhesion to the panels.

Remedial options

Cracks through the panel can be epoxy-injected to prevent water penetration, provided the crack arose from overstress during improper handling and overstresses will not reoccur, such as with thermal bowing conditions. Access to both faces of the panel is required to construct a dam to retain the epoxy on one face and to inject the epoxy on the opposite face. The repair may blend well with the concrete when dry, but can stand out when the panel is wetted, due to the differences in porosity between the epoxy and the surrounding concrete.

Cracks in areas of ongoing movement require less rigid repair materials to maintain a seal and allow movement. The crack can be routed to form a shallow, narrow groove on the face of the panel, at least $\frac{3}{8} \times \frac{3}{8}$ in (9×9 cm) release tape applied to the base of the groove, and liquid-applied sealant installed. The release tape is needed to distribute the crack movement over an unbonded area of the sealant and avoid strain concentrations in the sealant. This type of repair may not match the appearance of the surrounding concrete.

Generally, joint repairs involve upgrading single-stage sealant joints to two-stage seals that are drained with weep holes through the exterior seal. This can be difficult when existing joints are narrow, since access is needed through the joint near the back of the panel to construct the inner seal. Cutting the joint wider for some partial depth of the panel can resolve this problem, but may be costly.

Depending upon the configuration of the panels and their layout, it may be possible to install flashings along the base of the panels. With certain panel layouts, one may be able to slide a flashing into a horizontal joint between panels, although this is tedious and many obstructions such as anchors and shims arise. This type of repair is not commonly used.

Where flashings have been omitted from window sills, it is possible to install such flashings. In some cases, flashings can be installed without removing the existing windows, but often window removal is necessary and less costly. If windows are not removed, any existing sill anchors need to be cut and shims have to be removed. This approach also requires substantial clearance between the frame and the supporting structure, and is not feasible when narrow sill perimeter sealant joints exist. In some cases, it is possible to remove wood blocking below the window to increase the clearance. Flexible flashing materials, such as sheet rubber, are useful, since they can be slid through narrow openings and turned up on the inside of the frame.

4 GLASS/METAL CURTAIN WALLS

Curtain walls are metal-framed walls with various in-fill materials, glass being the most common. Most frames are assembled from individual horizontal and vertical members, i.e., stick systems. Metal-to-metal framing intersections and glazing-to-framing joints are sealed commonly with foam or dense rubber gaskets, or liquid-applied sealants. At some corners, rubber plugs or pieces of metal are incorporated with the sealant to fill gaps in the framing.

These systems use a variety of cavity wall and pressure-equalized design principles for waterproofing. Manufacturers of these systems generally recognize that some water will penetrate the joints in the system, including the glazing and framing joint seals. Therefore, curtain walls generally are designed to drain the water that penetrates these joints down to each sill (horizontal framing member) where it is weeped back to the outside (**Fig. 7**).

The sill member generally acts as a trough or gutter and, as such, it must have corners and intersections sealed permanently watertight.

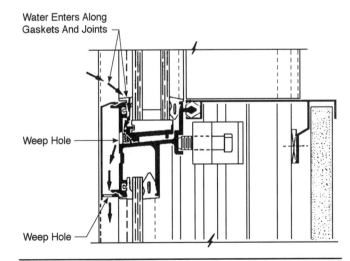

Fig. 7. Cross section of a curtain wall. Note secondary drainage capability of the pocket below the glass. The base of the pocket is sloped outward to promote drainage through weep holes.

Weep holes in the sill should be protected by covers or shielded to avoid direct inward flow of water. In many systems, the inboard side of the sill gutter is sealed airtight, resembling to some degree a pressure-equalized design.

Traditionally, curtain walls do not incorporate through-wall flashings, except at the base of the wall, relying instead on the sill gutters and their corner seals at vertical members to collect and contain penetrating water at frequent vertical intervals until it weeps out of the sill gutter. This approach lacks the reliability that a separate flashing provides, in that the corner seals are formed from liquid-applied sealants, which are not as reliable or durable as the soldered corners in sheet metal flashings.

Unfortunately, the service life of these sealants is much shorter than that expected for the wall system. While the system may perform well for many years, there typically is not a reliable means for replacing the seals in the future when they deteriorate. While this is a weakness, the systems generally perform better than barrier wall systems because they provide some secondary drainage capability and do not rely solely on a single exterior seal for waterproofing.

The critical requirement for these systems is providing a durable seal for the corner joinery where the horizontal member abuts the continuous vertical member. The most common means for creating this seal is to install preformed gaskets and/or liquid-applied sealant over the joined metal extrusions. The better designs incorporate the following features:

- A slight outward slope along the bottom of the horizontal member directs water outward and reduces the magnitude and duration of water contact with these critical joint seals. Prompt drainage limits leakage volume at any seal defects and improves the durability of the sealant, which degrades when immersed in water.

- Frame extrusions without complex geometries and differing materials, such as screw bosses, offsets and thermal breaks, increase the chances of creating a continuous seal at corner intersections.

- Systems that permit construction of the corner seals in the factory, as opposed to on-site, generally have a greater chance of success due to better control on surface preparation and cleaning and better supervision of the sealing process.

Expansion joints in vertical members are a particularly difficult area in the framing to maintain a watertight seal. Generally, the joint incorporates a backup plate behind gapped ends of the members, and the plate is bedded in a non-curing butyl-based sealant. One of the edges in such a joint faces against the flow of water, inviting water entry. Incorporating a backup plate that fits behind the upper member and laps over the lower member is one approach to avoid this weakness, but it is not commonly used. With either approach, the movement of the vertical members concentrates at one point along the glazing seal and inevitably creates an unsealed opening at this point.

Another alternative is to create a butt sealant joint at the expansion joint to avoid impeding the water flow and distribute the movement of the ends of the vertical members. This requires providing solid watertight end caps on the members, and is not commonly done. Typically, the systems accept these weaknesses and attempt to collect water that penetrates the expansion joints in the drained sills.

Common problems

The most prevalent problems are defects in the corner joinery seals, including omission of the seals altogether due to fabrication and erection oversights in some cases. Other defects include:

- Pinholes or discontinuities in the internal corner seals due to the complexity of the intersecting members and difficulty in accessing certain spots along the joint.

- Poor adhesion of sealants due to improper cleaning and surface preparation, incompatibility with various materials, particularly at plastic and rubber components such as thermal breaks, and deterioration of the sealant material with age and exposure to ponding water.

Frequently, other defects are found in the external seals that allow significant water entry into the system, which tends to exacerbate leakage at any corner seal defects. Glazing seals are the most common source of water entry to the framing system. Gasket shrinkage or improper installation causes gaskets to pull away from the frame at the glazing corners. Gaskets require proper installation methods to avoid stretching and the resulting "shrinkage" over time as the gasket relieves this built-in stretch. Some gaskets also shrink due to material behavior, i.e., weathering and loss of plasticizers. Nonuniform compression on the gaskets, due to accumulated fabrication tolerances or variable tightening of pressure bar glazing bead fasteners, can allow water penetration.

Recommended practice suggests constructing external glazing seals with liquid-applied sealants, i.e., wet seals, as opposed to preformed dry gaskets. The wet seals avoid gasket joinery and compression pressure problems, since they are continuous and adhered to the substrate. Wet seals are subject to some defects due to installation tolerances, but experience indicates they prevent more water penetration than dry-gasketed systems. They require outside access for glass installation and replacement, and sometimes are not used for this reason.

In some cases, such as at the base of a curtain wall or at windows, the sill frames are anchored to the structure with fasteners that penetrate the sill gutter and any underlying flashing. Fastener holes provide an avenue for water penetration. Sealant materials, if any, used to cover the fastener heads only provide short-term protection as they often lose bond when subject to "ponding" water. Fig. 1 shows a detail for fastening the sill frame with a clip angle and fastener into the rear of the frame to avoid penetrating the horizontal portion of the sill flashing. Penetrations through the upturned rear leg have a very minor exposure to water, compared to those in the horizontal part of the flashing.

Remedial options

Remedies for leaking glass/metal curtain walls include two approaches using sealant materials; flashing installation generally is not feasible with these systems.

- One option is to wet seal all external joints in the system, i.e., seal them with liquid-applied sealants. This option typically is tried because it imposes relatively low cost and low disruption. This approach, however, does not treat the common fundamental defects that exist in the waterproofing system, i.e., leaking internal seals, but instead attempts to make a barrier system out of the curtain wall and prevent water from reaching the corner seals. As such, it contains the drawbacks of any barrier system, and some degree of ongoing leakage is likely with the extent depending on the quality, durability, and maintenance of the wet seals. This approach can be improved by using extruded sheet "band-aids" fabricated from the sealant material and applied over the larger joints within the curtain wall system (**Fig. 8**). The sheet can resist the movement at these joints more reliably than the sealant and can be easily integrated with (bonded to) the sealant.

- Another option is to reconstruct the corner seals. This approach has included various schemes ranging from drilling portholes and blindly pumping sealant into the hidden corner areas, to partial disassembly of the curtain wall, including removal of glass lites, pressure bars, or frame members to repair the corner seals. The former approach is never found to be effective due to the inability to clean, prepare, and inspect the joint, while the latter approach can be successful, provided reasonable access to the joint for cleaning and remedial sealant application and tooling can be obtained. Wet sealing the system after corner seal repairs is prudent to reduce reliance upon the internal remedial seals.

5 EXTERIOR INSULATION AND FINISH SYSTEMS (EIFS)

Barrier EIFS

Exterior insulation and finish systems (EIFS) typically consist of polystyrene insulation boards, which are covered by a polymer-modified cementitious coating (synthetic stucco) that is reinforced with glass fiber mesh. Generally, the coating consists of two layers: a base coat and a finish coat, which is called the lamina. The insulation boards are usually adhered to exterior gypsum sheathing on a steel stud backup wall. In some systems, the insulation boards are fastened mechanically to the steel studs. Most EIFS installations have been field constructed, as opposed to panelized, and have been adhered, rather than mechanically attached, to the backup wall.

Typical EIF systems use barrier wall principles and lack any cavity or waterproofed backup. Traditional cement plaster stucco wall systems can incorporate a drainage layer through the use of asphalt-impregnated felt behind the metal lath. While this is not a clear

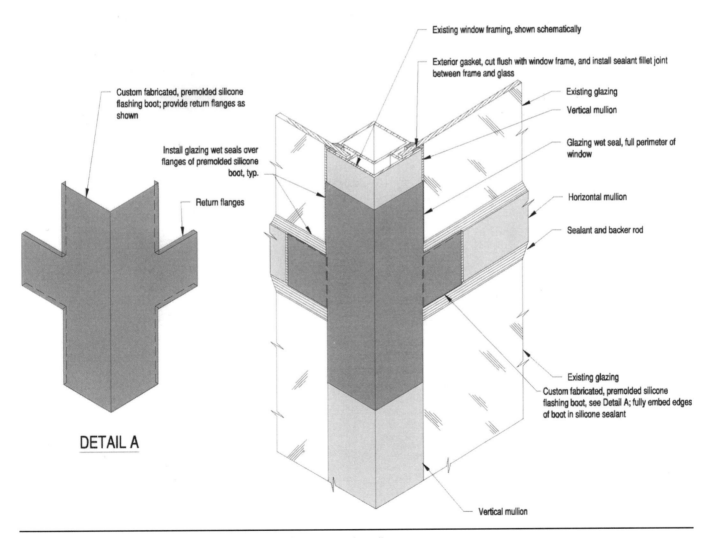

DETAIL A

Fig. 8. Schematic isometric elevation of an extruded flashing boot at a window sill.

drainage cavity, the field experience is that the felt can control water that may penetrate at cracks or joints in the stucco wall, if it directs this water onto a through-wall flashing. However, this places the metal lath and fasteners in a moist environment and invites corrosion problems.

With the barrier EIFS composite of materials, such a waterproofing layer cannot be incorporated, because it would interrupt the adhesive attachment of the insulation or plaster coats. It may be possible to incorporate a waterproofing layer if the system is mechanically attached, but such an approach has not been documented in practice. Like traditional stucco, the fasteners with mechanically attached EIF systems are in a corrosive environment and subject to premature failure.

Barrier EIF systems rely solely on the polymer-modified stucco coating and joint sealants to resist water leakage. Rain penetration through EIFS clad walls typically occurs at cracks in the lamina, at defects in the joint seals, and through unflashed window frame corners and joinery. Gypsum sheathing, if used, may degrade readily when exposed to water. Structural deterioration of the gypsum sheathing, fasteners and steel studs, and loss of attachment, become a greater concern than just discomfort of the building occupants and damage to interior finishes due to water leakage.

Control of cracking is important in these systems, particularly the control of cracks that occur over the joints between insulation boards. Hairline cracks that do not penetrate through the lamina have no leakage-related consequence. However, if cracks occur through the lamina especially over joints in the insulation boards, water has a ready path to the water-sensitive exterior gypsum sheathing board, particularly under differential air pressures across the wall. Causes of cracking are discussed further in the following section.

Methods of waterproofing the joints between panels and the need for sill flashings at windows and other wall penetrations are similar to that discussed previously for precast concrete panels.

Drainage-plane EIFS

Many EIFS manufacturers have developed systems in recent years that incorporate back-up waterproofing and/or a drainage plane to capture and evacuate intruding rainwater. Drainage plane systems that are most similar to traditional, proven cavity wall systems have components as follows, from interior to exterior (**Fig. 9**):

- Light-gauge metal or wood framing

- Gypsum or wood sheathing

- Back-up waterproofing barrier such as building paper or a rubberized asphalt/polyethylene laminate sheet

- Self-furring metal or plastic lath to create a cavity

- Expanded polystyrene insulation (EPS) (i.e., "bead board") adhered to metal lath or mechanically fastened to sheathing backup

- Acrylic-modified cement or all-acrylic base coat with coated glass fiber mesh reinforcement

- Acrylic finish coat with sand particles to provide simulated stucco texture.

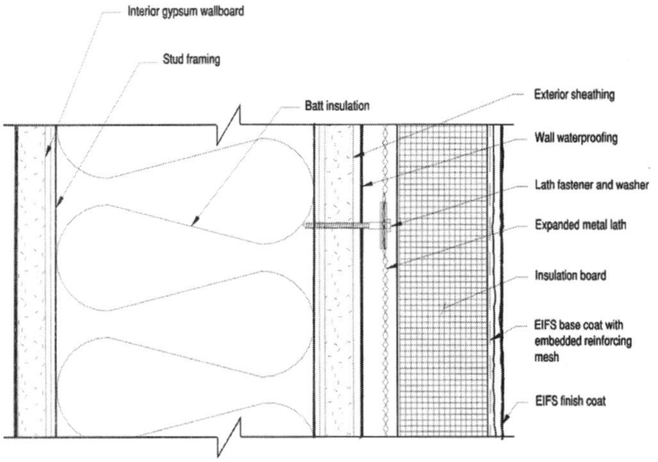

Fig. 9. Cross section of drainage-plane EIFS with back-up waterproofing membrane and drainage lath.

Additionally, some of these drainage systems prescribe detailing to address issues that surface-sealed EIF systems do not, including flashing around window penetrations and flashing at wall terminations (as in Fig. 3). Some of the more comprehensive drainage plane systems include:

- Flashing at window sill openings that integrate with the back-up waterproofing barrier.

- Back-up waterproofing barrier that wraps window jamb openings and integrates with flashing at sill.

- Plastic, weeped "starter tracks" at wall terminations that capture the EPS board edge, integrate to the back-up waterproofing barrier, and allow water to weep to the exterior.

Common problems

Problems with barrier EIF systems can result from cracking of the lamina, which must remain unbroken for watertightness. The authors have seen buildings where vertical or horizontal control joints are omitted and this has produced significant cracking, particularly on elevations with strong solar exposures. Some manufacturers of adhered systems have asserted that the system is "soft" and can "float" in response to thermal cycles. Consequently, these systems sometimes are designed without vertical control joints to subdivide building elevations into discrete panels. The polystyrene insulation has a relatively high coefficient of thermal movement. The lamina and the composite EIFS system have a lower coefficient, based on our testing of laboratory samples and measurement of movements on actual building walls, but the coefficient is sizable and requires due consideration in design.

Wall elevations that are subject to strong solar heat gain should be subdivided by control joints. These control joints are in addition to those normally required by the manufacturer, such as at intersections of dissimilar materials or where structural movement may occur, i.e., vertical joints at intersecting walls and horizontal joints at floor levels with flexible edge beams or slabs.

Cracks typically develop at the reentrant corners formed by window openings. In many cases, the insulation board joints align with the window corner, creating a plane of weakness in the EIFS substrate aligned with a point of high stress caused by the window opening penetrating through the face of the panel. These cracks can allow direct water entry or water can bypass the window perimeter sealant where the crack and sealant intersect. Corner cracking can be reduced by cutting a single insulation board to fit each window corner such that board joints do not align with the window corners and by following manufacturers' recommendations to install extra layers of diagonally oriented reinforcing at all opening corners.

Prolonged exposure to moisture softens some EIFS finish coats. At sealed panel joints, the softening can permit cohesive failure within the lamina when the joints move and the sealant pulls on the finish coat. Using low modulus urethane or silicone sealants helps reduce the stresses on the finish coat, but there is not yet an extensive track record of use in these systems.

During field investigations and water tests, the authors have found that leakage from sill-to-jamb window frame corners penetrates behind the lamina and insulation when sill flashings are omitted from the window opening. As a result, the exterior gypsum sheathing often has significant hidden deterioration in the vicinity of such window sill corners; horizontal sliding windows, which are commonly used in residential complexes, are particularly prone to frame corner leakage.

The weather-stripping seals on the sliding joints tend to allow more water entry into the window system, especially as the weather-stripping deteriorates from use, than do seals on other styles of windows. In addition, the sill acts like a gutter as it does in a curtain wall, increasing the exposure of the corner joinery seals to water compared to other styles of windows where water does not collect in the sill.

In many leakage investigations, it has been established that these system problems are exacerbated by the flush-glazed, flat surface profile of the facade that does not shield the vulnerable surface seals.

During field investigations and water tests, the authors have found typical workmanship problems relating to the installation of both barrier and drainage plane EIFS. At bases of walls and at all EIFS terminations, manufacturers typically require installers to "back wrap" all insulation boards with reinforcing mesh and embed the mesh in base coat. The authors typically observe unembedded reinforcing mesh at board edges, which precludes the installation of a properly bonded and durable sealant joint.

Remedial options

Barrier EIFS

Since typical EIFS is a barrier system with components readily damaged by water, the system requires frequent inspection and maintenance to limit water entry and consequential damage. Further, if significant leakage is occurring, a critical evaluation of the concealed conditions is needed to determine the scope of repairs.

Repair of cracks in the lamina vary with the cause of the crack. If cracks result from movements within the system that apply concentrated stresses to the lamina, remedial control joints should be installed to accommodate the movements. This requires removing the EIFS to form a joint and grinding the adjacent finish coat back to the existing base coat, wrapping the joint edges with reinforcing mesh and base coat that extends onto the back of the insulation (backwrapping), and sealing the joint. Remediation steps are to patch nonmoving cracks and grind the finish coat back to the base coat and rout the crack; fill the routed area with new insulation and rasp flush; and install new mesh reinforcing in new base coat, and a new finish coat.

With these systems, even simply cutting out the old sealant to repair defects can be a significant undertaking. Grinding to remove all traces of the old sealant, which is generally good practice when resealing, may damage the lamina. Bonding the new sealant to the remnants of the old failed sealant is not generally good practice, depending upon the materials involved. Upgrading single-stage sealant joints to two-stage joints is more difficult than with other wall systems, since the insulation and properly applied coating may not extend deep enough to permit proper installation of dual seals. Significant cutting and patching would be needed to install a remedial flashing to drain the joints in this system.

Drainage Plane EIFS

The inclusion of a drainage plane within the wall system has several advantages over the barrier EIF system. Drainage plane systems eliminate difficult and vulnerable terminations of localized flashings and drainage elements on or through the surface of a surface-sealed barrier system. Further, it can be implemented to control moisture intrusion anywhere on the wall.

The relatively short performance history of EIFS drainage plane systems makes them somewhat experimental and their long-term performance characteristics are, as yet, unknown. Nevertheless, those systems that utilize similar technology as traditional stucco systems, i.e., a back-up waterproofing layer, drainage medium (a material such as expanded lath), and application of a standard EIF system over these components, should perform well. Details for the back-up waterproofing barrier should include rubberized asphalt/polyethylene laminate sheet at building corners, window perimeters, and integrated sill flashings.

In climates where the predominant vapor drive is from outside to inside (e.g., much of the deep South), a rubberized asphalt/polyethylene laminate sheet provides a vapor retarder on the appropriate side of the wall and also provides a reliable, self-sealing waterproofing layer. In this application, a vapor retarder should not be installed at the interior side of the wall assembly. In climates where the predominant vapor drive is from the inside to the outside (e.g., many northern states), a high grade, asphalt-saturated felt paper provides a serviceable waterproofing layer in the field of the EIFS. The rubberized asphalt/polyethylene laminate sheet can be then used at critical details, such as window and door openings.

Summary

Exterior wall systems that incorporate cavity-wall waterproofing principles are the most reliable in preventing water leakage to the building interior. The key component for these systems is the through-wall flashing that should be durable and have an expected service life equivalent to that of the entire wall system. Proper attention to the detailing and installation of these flashings is crucial to the success of a cavity wall system. Lower durability flashings with limited track records should be avoided due to the high cost of future replacement of failed flashings.

Barrier wall systems with modifications to incorporate some degree of secondary drainage capability, particularly at vulnerable joints, can provide levels of watertightness acceptable to some building owners, if sound, durable materials are used to form the barrier. Barrier walls that rely solely on surface seals and use components that deteriorate readily from water that penetrates flaws in those seals do not provide a level of waterproofing reliability acceptable to most building owners.

All wall systems, and in particular barrier walls, can benefit from shielding provided by proper articulation of the wall surface to promote water drainage away from vulnerable joints.

Ultimately, the building owner and architects should make an informed decision when selecting the wall system, based on analysis of waterproofing reliability and the contractor's estimate of costs, i.e., affordability. An established maintenance protocol is necessary for all buildings. Given the expected level of maintenance, design and construction detailing should provide for reliability over the life of the building. Critical to the owner's evaluation is a clear understanding of the likelihood of leakage, the consequential damages from leakage, and life cycle costs and disruption associated with repairs, maintenance, and replacement of the various cladding systems. ■

REFERENCES

AAMA, *Design Windloads For Buildings and Boundary Layer Wind Tunnel Testing,* AAMA Aluminum Curtain Wall Series No. 11, American Architectural Manufacturers Association, Des Plaines, 1985.

Brick Institute of America, "Water Resistance of Brick Masonry, Construction and Workmanship," *Technical Notes on Brick Construction Revised,* Brick Institute of America, Reston, 1985.

Myers, J. C., "Window Sill Flashings: The Why and How," *Progressive Architecture,* June 1990.

Ruggiero, S. S., and J. C. Myers, "Design and Construction of Watertight Exterior Building Walls," *Water in Exterior Building Walls: Problems and Solutions,* ASTM STP 1107, Thomas A. Schwartz, ed. American Society for Testing and Materials, Philadelphia, 1991.

Timothy T. Taylor

Summary

This article provides an overview of exterior doors and entrances, both for pedestrian and vehicular traffic, with criteria for their selection and specification. Included are swinging doors, sliding doors, revolving doors, fire doors and other special constructions and hardware.

Key words

aluminum, closers, energy efficiency, entrances, environmental influences, hardware, fire doors, fire rating, frame, overhead doors, revolving doors, safety, sliding doors, steel, swinging doors, veneers, wood

Exterior doors and hardware

1 OVERVIEW

Design and selection criteria

Exterior door assemblies separate exterior from interior environments while controlling passage, isolating and resisting the effects of external/internal factors such as differential wind pressures, sound, light, air infiltration/exfiltration, water penetration, fire, explosion, forced entry, building frame deformations, and pests. Entrance doors are movable segments of the envelope of a space made to open and close quickly and easily whenever passage to and from an enclosed space through its envelope is required (**Fig. 1**).

Occupancy and use

Building type and occupancy will be the most important design determinant. Total capacity, or the number of exit units needed, will be determined by the applicable building codes. The configuration will be determined by:

- the circulation pattern of the building occupants coming and leaving.

- maximum number of people entering/leaving the building at peak load time.

- number of people entering/leaving at other times of the day.

- number of hours when building remains open.

- minimum distance or separation between sets of doors in vestibules, based on the need to create an airlock separation between outdoor and indoor climate. Many people wait for rides inside entry vestibules, which might be best accommodated by seating.

- capacity as a means of egress to satisfy code requirement.

- when considered as an emergency egress or exitway, the direction of swing must be in direction of flow of traffic to a place of refuge.

For both average and peak load conditions, consider:

- number, distribution, and type by operation of the entrance doors, including consideration of universal design goals to assist persons with limited physical capacities, those carrying packages, and so forth.

- number and distribution of the fixed dividing components—sidelights and transoms, principally as a function of the need for visibility and security.

- design and location of sheltering components: awnings, canopies, vestibules, air curtains.

- design and structure of the assembly encompassing frame. The frame system can also develop into a curtain-wall system.

- all possible and conceivable uses as might be presented by people with open umbrellas, baby carriages, service deliveries, or bicycles

Credits: This article is based upon data in *Time-Saver Standards for Building Materials and Systems* (2001), with updates provided by Timothy T. Taylor. Tables courtesy of American Architectural Manufacturers Association, National Association of Architectural Metal Manufacturers, and Wood & Door Manufacturers Association.

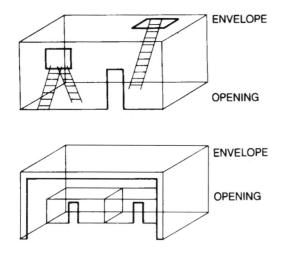

ENVELOPE

OPENING

ENVELOPE

OPENING

DOOR

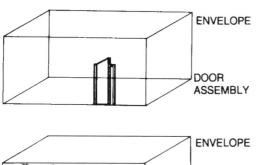

ENVELOPE

DOOR ASSEMBLY

ENVELOPE

DOOR ASSEMBLIES

ENTRANCE

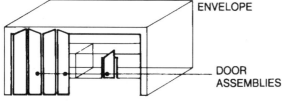

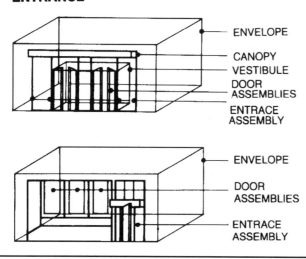

ENVELOPE
CANOPY
VESTIBULE
DOOR ASSEMBLIES
ENTRACE ASSEMBLY

ENVELOPE
DOOR ASSEMBLIES
ENTRACE ASSEMBLY

Fig. 1. Exterior door system concepts.

must be considered to avoid conflicting and possibly unsafe patterns of use.

– vision panels for safety and security; size and location, to be coordinated with the location and type of lighting.

Security

Security requirements of the building envelope at the entrance should be considered:

– What security requirements are created by the design program?

– Is vandalism a concern?

– Is visual surveillance and recognition through the entrance required?

– How can security be improved by lighting to allow recognition and identification?

Universal design and accessibility

Entrance selection for universal design must be concerned from the point of view of access, movement, and dimensional limitations of all individuals of varying stature, strength, mobility, and encumbrances, such as packages or baby carriages. Power-activated doors, even if not required, should be considered for universal design accommodation, for safety and convenience. For doors whose operation is impaired by air pressure, consider balanced pivots or power actuators. Related items for the design consideration are:

– including space for common courtesy, that is, to hold doors for others and for inside waiting.

– minimum door width/clear opening.

– maximum force to open door.

– level changes at entrance.

– hardware requirements and location.

Safety considerations

– Codes generally require safety glazing to reduce accidents due to broken glass.

– Door swings, location of stops, and other applied hardware must be considered to avoid interference with traffic flow through door.

– The arc of a door swing should exceed 90 degrees to allow the full width of the door opening to be unobstructed.

– Hinge jambs should be at least 6 in (15 cm) from a wall perpendicular to a building face to prevent the user's hands from being pinched between the door and the wall. If hinged jambs for two doors have to be adjacent, there should be enough distance between them to permit the doors to swing through an arc of 110 degrees.

– If doors hung on center pivots are hung in pairs, they should be hinged at the side jamb and not at the center mullion. Doors hinged off a common mullion may create problems: hardware to prevent one door from swinging into the path of the other could subject the door to excessive forces with resulting severe damage.

– All-glass doors and sidelights should be clearly identified to prevent the possibility of people walking into them accidentally. Insufficient lighting, or excessive lighting, veiling reflections and glare can create complicating vision and visibility problems.

– Swinging doors should be located to clear passing pedestrian traffic without interference.

Environmental influences

Aspects of entrance design most influenced by the climatic considerations above should include:

– incorporation of sun and rain protecting devices and windscreens. Visibility of stairs, railings, and the entry doors themselves should not be impaired by sun angle and glare.

– use of vestibules and of revolving doors may minimize drafts and provide better separation of outside and inside environments.

– concern for sufficient structural strength of entrance frame. In this case, long-term durability is important, along with ease of use, which is related to door weight.

– selection of types of door operation and of hardware for efficient opening in all weather conditions and for adequate durability.

– selection of component construction, glazing, and weather-stripping to minimize air and water infiltration and heat loss.

Weathertightness

Exterior doors are subjected to all the effects of natural forces: solar heat, rain, and wind. For ordinary installations, closed doors cannot be expected to exclude water or stop air movement completely under all conditions. One explanation for this is that space clearances must be provided around each door to permit ease of operation, thermal expansion, and construction tolerances.

In mechanically ventilated buildings, there is likely to be a difference in air pressure between the inside and outside at entrances. In the case of entryways located near heavily trafficked areas or loading zones, noxious fumes can enter the building from outside. Where it is a critical concern and where doorways or service areas cannot otherwise be relocated, this air leakage can be controlled in several ways:

– entrance vestibules.

– revolving door entrances.

– weather-stripping.

Entrances may need to isolate the interior from the exterior acoustically: weather-stripping is effective in sound isolation.

Exterior door types

Plate 1 summarizes exterior door types and operations, discussed in detail below.

• *Pedestrian doors.* The closure panel, or door, is generally classified by the method used to allow its opening and closing. There are three major types of pedestrian entrance doors:

– swinging, where the door panel is anchored to a supporting frame by hinges or is pivoted top and bottom.

– sliding, where the door panel slides to one side either top hung from a supporting frame or bottom supported; with either bottom or top guides.

– revolving, where door panels are attached to a center rotating post; operating within a self-supporting enclosure.

In general, exterior door type is selected on the basis of desired operation:

• *Swinging doors,* either single-action or double-action:

– provide versatility in permitting large or small passage capacity.

– permit manual or power actuation, but:

– may require considerable strength to open in certain weather conditions.

– do not provide the best protection against drafts and heat loss.

• *Sliding doors* are:

– safest, especially where people are carrying large objects, packages, baggage, as in air terminals, shopping centers, and active delivery ways.

– present least obstruction inside and outside and will act in any weather.

– must be power-actuated when serving as entrances of any size.

– permit outside air exchange to or from the building interior unless a vestibule design is used.

• *Revolving doors* are most effective for:

– sealing the outside environment from the interior without use of a vestibule.

– handling an orderly trickle of pedestrians in and out of buildings.

– have limited capacity and cannot handle peak loads.

– are difficult for people with large objects and do not meet universal access requirements.

• *Vehicular doors.* Vehicular doors should be so located that exhaust fumes from vehicles do not enter the building. The major functional types of vehicular/service entrance doors are:

– swinging

– sliding—to one or both sides—in large or small segments

– vertical rise—in large or small segments

Plate 1. Door assemblies: types and operation.

TYPE	DESCRIPTION

SLIDING

- Single door installed to overlap opening. May also be within opening with a sidelight. Generally hung from overhead track with bottom guides. May also ride in a bottom track with top guided only.
- When fire-resistance rated, inclined top track may be used for automatic closing or door may be counterweighted; fusible link then used to hold door in open position.
- Opening width generally up to 16 feet. Side clearance required for stacking door when open; additional space required when counterweight is used.
- Opening speed when motor-operated: 4 to 8 inches per second.

- Pair of doors installed to either overlap the opening or within the opening with side panels. Generally glazed when within the opening. Hung from top track with bottom guides; or ride in bottom track. When used as entrance, operation is automatic, and doors are designed to swing out when pressure is applied from inside the building during panic exit.
- Inclined tracks available for automatic closing during fire, or doors may be counterweighted; generally for industrial application only.
- Opening speed when motor-operated: 4 to 8 inches per second.

- Multiple doors installed within opening. Generally ride in bottom tracks with top guides when large; small doors may be hung from top tracks with bottom guides only. Opening width and height not limited; often used as aircraft hangar doors. May slide to one side, or be bi-parting. Clearance required for stacking doors alongside the opening. When large, constructed of rolled structural shapes with various wall panels available for facing. Generally motor-operated: large doors may have individual motors. Opening speed for large doors: about 60 feet per minute.

REVOLVING

- Revolving entrance doors are only available as a complete package from manufacturer. Diameter varies from 6.5 to 7.5 feet, with 7 feet being the standard height. Doors are available up to 8 feet in diameter and to 9 feet in height on special order. Use of wider doors generally recommended for easier traffic flow, especially in buildings where hand-carried luggage is a factor. Revolving doors should be equipped with emergency-release mechanism to book-fold wings and should have manual or power assisted speed controller. Effective speed range is 8 to 12 revolutions per minute.

- Special type to prevent light penetration into a space when door is operated. Generally used as door to a darkroom.
- Available only as a complete package from manufacturer. Sizes are limited, and once installed will not allow any large equipment to be taken into or out of the space.
- Manual operation only.

VERTICAL RISE, SLIDING

- Single panel installed to overlap opening. Side guides and counterweight required. Clearance required over opening for stacking panel, and at sides of opening for guides and counterweight. Generally used to protect openings in fire-rated walls; automatic closing with fusible link releasing counterweight.
- Cannot be used as required exit unless a swinging door incorporated into door panel but such use not common.
- May be motor-operated. Opening speed when motorized: 45 to 60 feet per minute.

- Multiple panels installed within opening.
- Overhead clearance for stacking panels required. Guides within opening; counterweight required but may be remotely located if space near door is not available. Opening width generally up to 24 feet; wider doors also available.
- Generally used for high openings when headroom for stacking panels limited, or when speed in opening and closing is important.
- Generally motor-operated, with opening speeds from 45 to 60 feet per minute.

VERTICAL RISE, TELESCOPING

- Horizontal panels nesting one into the other.
- Installed to overlap opening. Headroom required over opening for header box and nesting of door panels; clearance at sides for guides.
- Opening size 20 by 20 maximum; door limited to 400 square feet.
- Availability limited. Motorized operation only with opening speed of 40 feet per minute.

Plate 1. Door assemblies: types and operation (continued)

VERTICAL RISE, SECTIONAL

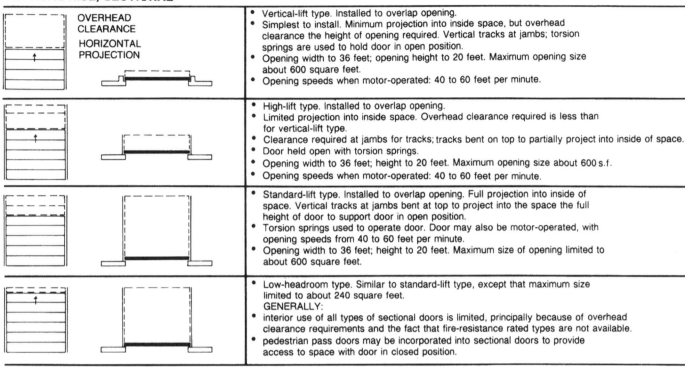

OVERHEAD
CLEARANCE

HORIZONTAL
PROJECTION

- Vertical-lift type. Installed to overlap opening.
- Simplest to install. Minimum projection into inside space, but overhead clearance the height of opening required. Vertical tracks at jambs; torsion springs are used to hold door in open position.
- Opening width to 36 feet; opening height to 20 feet. Maximum opening size about 600 square feet.
- Opening speeds when motor-operated: 40 to 60 feet per minute.

- High-lift type. Installed to overlap opening.
- Limited projection into inside space. Overhead clearance required is less than for vertical-lift type.
- Clearance required at jambs for tracks; tracks bent on top to partially project into inside of space.
- Door held open with torsion springs.
- Opening width to 36 feet; height to 20 feet. Maximum opening size about 600 s.f.
- Opening speeds when motor-operated: 40 to 60 feet per minute.

- Standard-lift type. Installed to overlap opening. Full projection into inside of space. Vertical tracks at jambs bent at top to project into the space the full height of door to support door in open position.
- Torsion springs used to operate door. Door may also be motor-operated, with opening speeds from 40 to 60 feet per minute.
- Opening width to 36 feet; height to 20 feet. Maximum size of opening limited to about 600 square feet.

- Low-headroom type. Similar to standard-lift type, except that maximum size limited to about 240 square feet.
  GENERALLY:
- interior use of all types of sectional doors is limited, principally because of overhead clearance requirements and the fact that fire-resistance rated types are not available.
- pedestrian pass doors may be incorporated into sectional doors to provide access to space with door in closed position.

VERTICAL RISE, ROLL UP

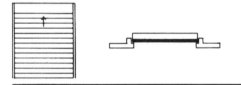

- Interlocking metal slats. May be insulated with rigid foamed insulation and also weatherstripped. May be fire-resistance rated but only up to 120 square feet in size. May be installed within opening; generally mounted to overlap opening. Guides required at jambs and torsion springs for opening.
- Opening size up to 30 feet wide by 30 feet high. Larger sizes available on special order, but width may be limited.
- May be motor-operated, with speeds from 30 to 60 feet per minute.

VERTICAL RISE, CANOPY

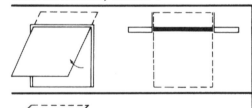

- Single panel installed within opening only. Top tracks and counterweight are required.
- Opening width generally to 60 feet; up to 130 feet wide available on special order. Height generally up to 30 feet.
- Clearance required: approximately 2/3 of door height in front of opening; 1/3 in back plus space for overhead tracks and counterweight.
- Smaller doors may be crank and gear operated; larger sizes generally motorized with opening speed of about 30 feet per minute.

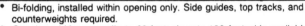

- Bi-folding, installed within opening only. Side guides, top tracks, and counterweights required.
- Opening widths generally to 60 feet; sizes to 130 feet wide available on special order. Height to 50 feet.
- Clearance required in front of opening less than for single panel: clearance in back for top tracks and counterweight similar to that required for single panel.
- Generally motor-operated only, with opening speed of about 30 feet per minute.

PLUG

 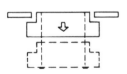

- For specific applications only, such as isolating high-level radiation. Will continue to shield outside space against radiation even when opened. Also used where resistance against explosion required.
- Generally of reinforced and/or lead-shielded concrete.
- track mounted and motorized for operation
- Always custom designed.

COMPONENTS OF ASSEMBLY

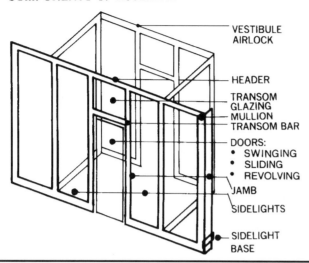

DESIGN COMPONENTS

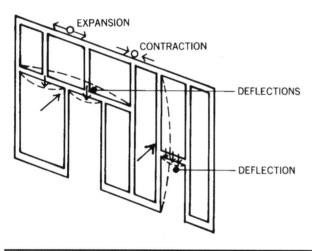

FRAMING MEMBERS

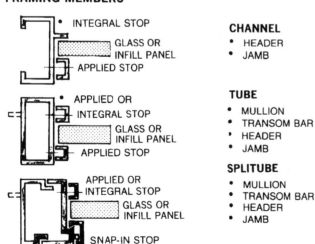

Fig. 2. Entrance assemblies.

Components of entrance door assembly (Fig. 2)

- *Jamb/header.* Vertical and horizontal frame members form the sides of an entrance or door assembly. In a door assembly, the hinge jamb is the frame member at which the hinges or pivots are mounted.

- *Mullion.* Vertical framing member holds and supports fixed glazing or opaque in-fill panels. May be single piece or split; with or without thermal breaks.

- *Transom bar.* Horizontal framing member that separates the door opening from the transom above. Transom bars may contain operating hardware for doors, such as closers or automatic operators.

- *Transom bracket.* A bracket to support all-glass transom over an all-glass door when no transom bar is used.

- *Sidelight.* Fixed light or lights of glass located adjacent to a door opening. Wet or dry glazed, with dry glazing more commonly used. Sidelight base: may be a single piece, built up of several framing members, or a masonry or concrete curb may be used for support of the bottom frame. In either case, provisions to seal the gap between the bottom of the entrance assembly and supporting construction should be incorporated in the design of the assembly.

Design components

- *Expansion/contraction.* In the assembly, must not be restricted within the opening and proper clearances in the opening and at connections must be incorporated in the design. Movement within the assembly may be accommodated by providing for slippage at joints or in split mullions.

- *Independent door frames.* Especially in large assemblies, door frames should be independent of other framing to minimize effects of thermal movement.

- *Deflection in horizontal members.* May impose loads on glass and may cause breakage and/or prevent proper operation of doors. When staggered concentrated loads have to be carried by a horizontal framing member, such member may have to be reinforced to limit deflection, or the assembly should be redesigned. Lateral loads may result in excessive deflection in long horizontal members and reinforcing may be required.

- *Deflection in vertical members.* May affect operation of doors, and may have to be less than the acceptable maximum of approximately $1/180$ of span for other framing members.

- *Split mullions.* Supporting doors hung from them may require reinforcement since they generally are not stiff enough to hold doors securely and in proper alignment.

Framing members

Door framing members are commonly available as stock items; however, custom frames are also available. They must be selected to complement the function of the door opening. Building use and environmental factors are prime considerations. Door frame types include:

– built-up frames

– brake or roll formed

– extruded, formed, or tubular

- *Built-up frames*

– assembled frames with prehung door are available.

– two-piece adjustable frames are available.

– when wood frames are used in masonry walls a subframe is recommended.

– structural shape or bent plate frames are generally limited to industrial type construction; hinges are generally surface mounted, recess for latch is drilled in the field.

– drip cap at head recommended.

– closers cannot be concealed in frame; they may be surface mounted on frame or on door.

– wood and structural shape frames are generally prepared to receive hardware in the field.

– wood frames and trim for sliding doors are available clad in aluminum or PVC.

- *Brake or roll-formed frame*

– usually available bonderized and prime painted; galvanized metal is available when specified.

– various sizes and shapes are available; wraparound shapes are generally used for drywall construction.

– when installed in masonry walls, jambs and head are typically filled solid with mortar.

– prefabricated shapes are available in standard lengths.

– drip cap is recommended when the face of the frame is flush with the outside face of the wall.

– frames should be factory prepped to receive hardware.

- *Extruded frames, formed, or tubular*

– aluminum extrusions are available in clear and color anodized as well as painted.

– various shapes and sizes are available.

– extruded sections with curved glass or metal fixed panels are used for revolving door enclosures.

– drip caps, either attached to frame or installed in the wall at the head of the frame, are recommended when the face of frame is flush with the outside face of the wall.

– frames should be factory prepared to receive hardware.

2 DESIGN CRITERIA AND SELECTION CHECKLISTS

Checklist for pedestrian traffic doors

- General considerations include:

– Provide vision panels for all swinging doors unless locked at all times to prevent the leaf from swinging in the face of a person approaching the entrance from the opposite side.

– All-glass doors should be marked for easy identification within standard vision to prevent injury to persons from walking into the glass.

- *Resistance to corrosion* may be an important factor in the selection of entrances. When corrosion resistance is reviewed, it should concern both the base materials and finishes of the components.

- *Sound transmission* (applies to exterior and interior doors) through the door and along its perimeter should fit the STC (sound transmission class) of the entire assembly; accordingly, doors selected may be:

– hollow doors with sound deadening insulation.

– solid-core doors.

– solid-core doors faced with sound absorbing material.

– doors in partitions with high STC requirements have to be completely sealed around the entire perimeter:

– even a small gap will result in sound leakage enough to drastically lower the STC of the entire assembly.

- When *pressure differentials* exist between the two sides of the door, air/gas leakage under pressure should be prevented:

– compressible or mechanically inflatable seals along the entire perimeter are required.

– seals will also effectively prevent light passage; simple weatherstripping may be adequate when resistance to light leakage only is required.

Box A—Conductivity coefficients for various door types, winter conditions

Door Type	With Wood storm door		With metal storm door		With no storm door	
	U	R	U	R	U	R
• 1″ solid wood	.30	3.3	.39	2.6	.64	1.6
• 1¼″ solid wood	.28	3.6	.34	2.9	.55	1.8
• 1½″ solid wood	.27	3.7	.33	3.0	.49	2.0
• 2″ solid wood	.24	4.2	.29	3.4	.43	2.3
•• 1¾″ steel, mineral fiber core b					.14-.24	4-7
•• 1¾″ steel, solid urethane foam core					.09-.075	11-13
•• 1¾″ steel, solid polystyrene					.13-.24	4-7.5
•• 1¾″ steel, honeycomb core					.41-.45	2.2-2.4
•• 1¾″ steel, fiberboard core					.28	3.6

* from ASHRAE Fundamentals
** from various manufacturers

- *Thermal insulation,* as a function of the door construction (**Box A**), and of the entire door assembly.

- *Heavy traffic doors.* Doors located where they are subject to the impact of constant traffic:

  - solid-core metal-clad wood doors are good in resisting frequent impact, but are high in cost.

  - hollow-core wood doors are easily broken, and hollow metal doors are easily dented.

  - doors may be reinforced to minimize damage when accidentally hit.

- *Freezer doors.* In doors used for cooler or freezer assemblies, resistance to heat flow around the entire assembly is critical:

  - freezer doors are generally provided with perimeter heating cables to prevent freeze-ups due to water vapor condensation and freezing.

- *Radiation-resistant doors.* Doors may be located in radiation-resistant assemblies. The range of requirements is:

  - from a low level such as of an X-ray machine in a physician's office to that of an atomic reactor.

  - for low-level radiation protection, lead-lined doors and frames are available.

  - most other applications require special design.

- *Resistance to impact*

  - solid-core doors have high impact resistance. Under severe conditions, metal-clad or solid-core wood doors are recommended. Flush glass doors and hollow-core wood or hollow-core metal doors are least resistant.

  - flush doors are generally stronger than stile and rail doors.

  - face width, and thickness of the stile-and-rail frame members will affect overall strength.

  - hollow-core wood doors are not recommended for exterior exposure.

- Oversized doors and lead-lined doors, because of their weight:

  - require more rugged hinges, frames, and closers.

  - power actuators may be needed if operating effort becomes excessive.

  - due to the stresses incurred by oversized doors, the choice of hardware might be limited.

- *Vision panels.* Louvers are required; and any special configurations, such as Dutch doors.

- *Fire-resistance rating requirements.* Not all door panels can be fire rated.

- *Industry standards* used in the construction of door panels are in general as follows:

  - for wood panels—WDMA and AWI.

  - for metal and glass doors—NAAMM and AAMA.

  - for all-glass doors—GANA, but safety standard ANSI as enforced by the Consumer Product Safety Commission must be followed.

Checklist for service and vehicular entrances and doors

Anticipated traffic

General considerations include anticipated traffic, which may suggest:

- For power-operated materials-handling equipment, such as fork-lift trucks: consider bi-parting sliding, multipanel vertical sliding, sectional, roll-up, and telescoping types.

- For vehicular traffic, such as automobiles and trucks:

  - Consider multipanel vertical sliding, sectional, roll-up, and telescoping types.

- For low frequency use, where available clearances between entrances must be kept to a minimum, consider swinging bi-folding, or four-folding types.

- For large equipment, such as aircraft:

  - openings up to 30 ft (9 m) high × 130 ft (40 m) wide: single-panel canopy type.

  - openings up to 50 ft (15 m) high × 130 ft (40 m) wide: bi-folding canopy type.

  - higher and wider openings: multipanel sliding. Multipanel types require room for stacking panels beyond the clear opening provided.

Frequency of use

High frequency use may preclude selection of certain types of entrances and require power operators, special controls, or other options.

- In all instances the need for power operators should be investigated; power operators add to cost of the installation and maintenance requirements.

- Ease of operation under adverse conditions, such as high winds, especially for large doors, may limit selection to horizontal sliding, vertical sliding, sectional, and roll-up types.

- Time required to open and close the door panels may also be a factor, especially for high frequency use entrances.

- Insulation within the door panel and possibility of efficient weather-stripping may be a consideration for low frequency use entrances.

- Isolation or separation of service traffic, especially standing vehicles, in ways that allow the exhaust fumes to inadvertently enter the building, such as through stairwells and/or fresh air intakes.

Environmental factors

- wind loads, especially for large entrances, affect the choice of entrance type to avoid damage to entrance, and to allow operation under high wind conditions.

- type of core material or frame construction: to resist horizontal wind forces without excessive deflection.

- canopy-type doors will, in addition, be subject to vertical wind force or uplift when in open position.

- thermal movement should be considered for very high or very wide door panels.

- impact resistance may be a consideration for high frequency use vehicular entrances.

- in general, sectional and roll-up types are easily damaged, but they also are simpler to repair.

Clearances for service and vehicular entrances and doors

Clearance required for proper operation should be considered.

- *Swinging type entrances*

- width of panels generally limited by allowable loads on hinges and frames.

- width and height limited for panels requiring fire-resistance ratings.

- select surface-mounted hinges when appearance is not a consideration.

- use mortise or unit locks/latches for durability and/or security.

- power operation should be considered for high frequency use entrances or oversized door panels and when opening speed is important.

- *Sliding entrances*

- width and height of panels generally not limited except for panels requiring fire-resistance ratings.

- top track limited to smaller sizes of single panel and bi-parting types.

- inclined top track with fusible link catch available for normally open entrances required to be self-closing in case of fire.

- counterweights may be added:

- for ease in opening and closing.

- to make door with horizontal track self-closing in case of fire.

- clear space should be provided near door for counterweights.

- multipanel types are generally power operated using endless chain, or motor-driven bottom rollers.

- for multipanel type in wide openings, excessive deflection of framing, which supports the top guides, will prevent opening or closing of door.

- side-coiling type may also be used with curving tracks. Only top track with bottom guides can be used for this type.

- *Vertical rise entrances*

- width and height of panels generally not limited except for panels requiring fire-resistance ratings.

- multipanel vertical slide and canopy types generally used for special conditions, and are individually designed for each application.

- sectional and roll-up types most widely used; standard sizes are available.

- roll-up types are limited in width by structural properties of slats, which have to transmit wind forces to jamb guides.

- multipanel vertical sliding type may also be used with curving tracks.

3 SPECIFICATION OF EXTERIOR DOOR SYSTEMS

Specification of glazed doors

This section includes selection data relevant to interior swinging stile and rail glazed doors. Types of glazed doors are discussed, along with selection criteria and glass light sizes.

- *Selection criteria include:*

- grade

- model

- door thickness

- outer face material and thickness

- veneer matching

- internal construction

- light openings

- *Grade (model)*

- steel doors: extra heavy duty

- wood doors: custom or premium (stile and rail)

- aluminum doors: custom (stile and rail)

- *Door thickness*

- steel doors: 1-¾ in (4.5 cm)

- wood doors: 2-¼ in, 1-¾ in (5.7 cm, 4.5 cm)

– aluminum doors: 1-¾ in (4.5 cm)

• *Outer face material and thickness*

– steel doors: hot or cold rolled steel sheet, galvanized steel sheet, stainless steel, bronze, or brass; 16-gauge thickness.

– wood doors: dimensional lumber stock for transparent (plain, rift, or quarter sawn) finishing or opaque finishing, or standard thickness hardwood face veneers overlaid with medium density overlay veneer, natural hardwood veneer, or plastic laminate directly applied to core construction; composed of one ply.

• *Veneer matching*

– matching between individual pieces of veneer: book, slip, or random match

– assembly of spliced veneer on a face: sequence matching from opening to opening must be specified; examples include balanced, center balanced, and running matching

• *Internal construction*

– steel doors: tubular steel

– wood doors: dimensional lumber stock for transparent or opaque finishing or veneering

– aluminum doors: tubular aluminum

• *Light openings*

– steel doors: fully tempered or laminated safety glass; minimum bottom rail, stiles, top and intermediate rail heights of 3-½ in (8.9 cm).

– wood doors: fully tempered or laminated safety glass; minimum recommended bottom rail height of 10 in (25 cm), minimum stiles, top and intermediate rail heights of 4-½ in (11 cm).

– aluminum doors: fully tempered or laminated safety glass; typical bottom rail, stiles, top and intermediate rail heights of 2-³⁄₁₆ in (5.5 cm), 4 in (10 cm), and 5 in (12.7 cm).

Specification of sliding doors

Horizontal sliding doors are advantageous for:

– unusually wide openings.

– where clearances do not permit use of swinging doors.

– operation of sliding doors is not hindered by windy conditions or differences in air pressure between indoors and outdoors.

For certain usage, horizontal sliding doors:

– may have to be motorized to increase traffic flow through the entrance.

– panic exit features may need to be incorporated to let people move through the door panels without injury during emergency egress.

Sliding entrances are manufactured as assemblies. Since a single manufacturer provides all components, the selections to be made will deal more with the style, materials, finishes, and accessories available than with the range of components and combinations available. Sliding entrances are normally selected for view and illumination as well as ingress/egress. Unless the doors are power-operated, sliding entrances are normally used for infrequent or low traffic entrances.

Sliding doors consist of one or more panels of framed, or unframed, glass, metal, or wood that, in turn, are contained in an overall frame designed so that one or more panels are moveable in a horizontal direction. Each panel may be moveable, or some panels may be moveable with others fixed in a single opening. Panels may lock, or interlock with each other, or may contact a jamb member where the panel is capable of being securely locked. Sliding doors can be fabricated principally with either aluminum or wood materials.

Aluminum sliding doors

• *Performance*

– Aluminum sliding doors are available in five performance grade designations as indicated in **Table 1**. The performance grade standards represented here are from American Architectural Manufacturers Association (AAMA/NWWDA) 101–97 *Voluntary Specifications for Aluminum, Vinyl (PVC) and Wood Windows and Glass Doors.*

– Performance is indicated by a number that follows the type and grade designation. For instance, a residential sliding glass door may be designated SGD-R15. The number establishes the design pressure, in this example 15 lb per sq ft (psf). The structural test pressure for all doors is 50 percent higher than the design pressure that, in the example, would be 22.5 psf.

– The standard maximum limit to deflection of 0.4 percent of span applies to the first four designations. A maximum limit to deflection of 0.2 percent under the structural load test applies only to the Architectural door designation. However, it is good practice to research and specify sliding glass doors that are designed to meet

Table 1. Sliding glass aluminum door designations

Designation	Type	Structural Design	Water Resistance	Air Infiltration	Force to Open
SGD-R15	Residential	15	2.86 psf	0.37 cfm @ 1.57 psf	30 lbf
SDG-C20	Commercial	20	3.00 psf	0.37 cfm @ 1.57 psf	30 lbf
SDG-HC40	Heavy Comm.	40	6.00 psf	0.37 cfm @ 6.24 psf	40 lbf
SDG-AW40	Architectural	40	8.00 psf	0.30 cfm @ 6,24 psf	40 lbf

this criteria to avoid the problems arising from excessive flexing of a sliding door and frame assembly.

– Air and water performance values shown are the minimum required to meet the designation grades indicated.

– Use of products exceeding the performance levels in Table 1 may be necessary where severe wind conditions, wind loading, special condensation and heat transmission criteria, or type of building project are encountered.

• *Materials*

– Aluminum is lightweight, non-rusting, nearly maintenance free, decorative, and non-rotting material. It can be formed by extrusion, bent from sheet, cast, and joined by heliarc welding into many shapes, sizes, and forms.

– Aluminum has a high coefficient of thermal expansion (0.000013 per in per degree F) and its thermal resistance factor is almost zero. Lower thermal resistance factors increase the tendency of interior water vapor to condense on, or in, window framing members in cold weather.

– Aluminum sliding glass doors that incorporate higher-priced thermal break construction increase thermal resistance factors. Use of insulating glass units, dual lines of high performance gaskets and weather-stripping, and careful, proper, and competent installation procedures offset the low thermal resistance factors inherent in aluminum by reducing air infiltration.

• *Finishes*

– Clear lacquer or naturally developed aluminum oxide coatings are the minimal forms of coating protection to aluminum during construction where subsequent field-applied coatings are intended.

– Aluminum components of aluminum sliding glass doors normally are factory finished with some form of a protective, decorative anodized or organic coating.

– Anodic coatings are composed of aluminum oxide and are a part of the aluminum substrate. By carefully controlling the thickness, density, and hardness of the anodized coating, a substantial performance and durability improvement over lacquered and naturally developed oxide coatings can be achieved. Anodized coatings have limited color availability.

– Organic coatings are either baked on or air-dried and are available in a great array of performance and durability levels as well as color selection. Factory applied and baked on, organic coatings typically outperform air-dried types. Some baked on, fluropolymer-based, organic coatings outperform anodized coatings for color retention, chalk, and humidity resistance.

– Most organic coatings that are used for aluminum components of sliding doors should meet or exceed the requirements of AAMA 2603 Pigmented Organic Coatings on Aluminum Extrusions and Panels or AAMA 2605 Superior Performing Organic Coatings on Aluminum Extrusions and Panels. AAMA 2605 is more stringent than AAMA 2603. The two standard classification levels of architectural anodized coatings promulgated by the Aluminum Association (AA) and the National Association of Architectural Metal Manufacturers (NAAMM) are indicated in **Table 2.**

Table 2. Architectural coating designations

Architectural Classification	Thickness (mils)	Weight (Mg/sq.in.)	Application
Architectural Class I	0.7 min.	27 min.	Interior architectural items subject to normal wear, and for exterior items that receive a minimal amount of cleaning and maitenance. Higher performing "hardcoat" Class I coatings may be achieved by increasing coating thickness to between 1 and 3 mils.
Architectural Class II	0.4 to 0.7	17 to 27	Interior items not subject to excessive wear or abrasion.

Table 3. Sliding glass wood door designations

Designation	Structural Design	Water Resistance	Air Infiltration	Force to Open
Grade 20	20	2.86 psf 1.57 psf	0.34 cfm @	25 lbf
Grade 40	40	4.43 psf 1.57 psf	0.25 cfm @	30 lbf
Grade 60	60	6.24 psf 1.57 psf	0.10 cfm @	35 lbf

Wood sliding doors

- *Performance*

– Wood sliding doors are available in five performance grade designations as indicated in **Table 3**. The performance grade standards represented in this text are from Window & Door Manufacturers Association (WDMA) Standard AAMA/NWWDA 101–97 Voluntary Specifications for Aluminum, Vinyl (PVC) and Wood Windows and Glass Doors.

– Performance is designated by a number that follows the type and grade designation. For instance a residential sliding glass door may be designated SGD-R15. The number establishes the design pressure, in this example 15 lb per sq ft (psf). The structural test pressure for all doors is 50 percent higher than the design pressure that, in our example would be 22.5 psf.

– The standard maximum limit to deflection of 0.4 percent applies to the first four designations. A maximum limit to deflection of 0.2 percent applies only to the architectural door designation.

– Air and water performance values shown are the minimum required to meet the designation grades indicated.

– Use of products exceeding the performance levels in Table 3 may be necessary where severe wind conditions, wind loadings, special condensation and heat transmission criteria, more stringent deflection criteria, or type of building project are encountered.

- *Materials*

– Wood is lightweight, non-rusting, and decorative material. It can be formed by machining into many shapes, sizes, and forms.

– Wood has a lower coefficient of thermal expansion than aluminum. However, if the moisture content of the wood is affected by ambient humidity fluctuations then shrinking and swelling may occur and result in door component dimensional change.

– The thermal resistance factor of wood is higher than aluminum. Higher thermal resistance factors reduce the tendency of interior water vapor to condense on or within window framing members in cold weather.

– Use of insulating glass units, dual lines of high performance gaskets and weather-stripping, and careful, proper, and competent installation procedures aid in increasing the high thermal resistance factors inherent in wood by reducing air infiltration.

Specification of swinging entrances

Since all components that comprise swinging entrances can be manufactured independently, the selection of the proper components for a specific application is as important as the selection of the basic entrance type.

In selecting a swinging door, consider:

– single-action doors can swing 90 degrees or more in one direction only.

– double-action doors can swing 90 degrees or more in each direction.

– far more styles, types, materials, and accessories are available for swinging entrances than for any other type.

As indicated in **Fig. 3**, doors may be mounted either on butt hinges or on pivots. Hinges provide maximum free opening width, but impose

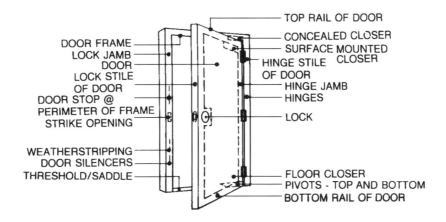

FLUSH DOORS

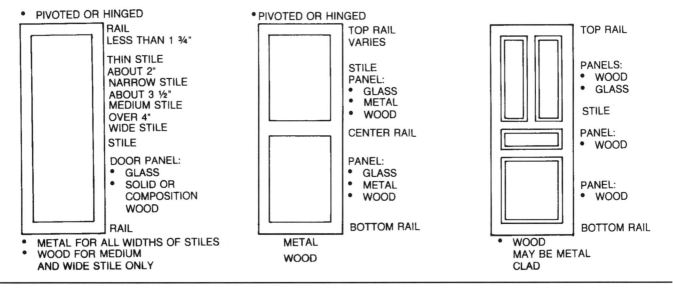

STILE AND RAIL DOORS

Fig. 3. Door assemblies (swinging door types).

strain on jamb. Commonly there are three hinges for standard height doors. Pivots may be center, offset, or swinging. Center pivots are required for double-acting doors, and generally for automatically operated doors. Pivots are preferred to hinges for heavy doors or for unusually severe service. Closers may be mounted concealed in the top rail of the frame, exposed on the top rail, or surface mounted on the door. Floor closers are recessed in the floor construction.

The following points should be considered for each swinging door assembly:

- *Size and configuration*

- Swinging doors are generally available in sizes up to 4 ft (1.2 m) wide and 10 ft (3 m) high.

- Width: The wider a door leaf the greater its weight, the higher the stresses on the hinging hardware and frames, and the more difficult it will be to open.

- Height: The taller a door leaf the greater its weight, and the higher the occurrence of door leaf deformations and excessive flexibility. Selecting wider door stiles, greater door thickness, and additional hinging hardware components can offset the effects of greater door height.

- *Building type and anticipated building use*

- building egress: when considered as an exit, direction of swing must be in direction of flow of traffic to area of refuge.

- balanced and center-pivoted doors reduce clear openings of swinging doors.

- the dynamics of building population use: a single pair of swinging doors can handle a small building population effectively.

- security requirements: swinging doors can be custom fabricated to incorporate card readers or coded number access devices coupled with magnetic locks and metal detectors.

- accessibility for the disabled: large swinging doors may be difficult to operate for disabled people, especially when excessive wind and stack pressures are encountered. In order to address this concern swinging doors can be provided with automatic door operators with opening and closing speed controls.

- weathertightness: swinging doors can be fabricated, or provided with, a positive continuous seal around each door leaf. Double-acting doors cannot be made as weathertight as single-acting doors.

- *Environmental influences and climatic conditions*

- temperature range: project-specific ambient and surface temperatures should be considered in the selection of materials for swinging doors.

- prevailing winds: swinging door assemblies should be designed to resist positive and negative wind loads as determined from local code requirements, by analytical methods, or from data obtained through wind tunnel analyses.

- precipitation: the presence of de-icing salts may cause corrosion of unprotected swinging door components.

- atmospheric conditions: project-specific humidity, salt spray, and air pollution should be considered in the selection of materials for swinging doors.

- UV exposure: project-specific sun exposure should be considered in the selection of organic and inorganic coatings on exposed components of swinging doors.

- *Other factors* influencing swinging door entrance design

- stack pressure: the greater the stack pressure, the greater the potential for energy loss. The entrance area suction, or pressure, increases as both the difference between the inside and outside air temperatures widens and as the building gets taller.

- suitable structural support for the swinging door opening frame should always be provided.

- door hardware: tall buildings, and buildings in areas with tall buildings, can create large downdrafts affecting swinging door performance. Hydraulic, electric, or pneumatic door operators and balanced door pivots are sometimes incorporated into swinging door assemblies to offset downdrafts as well as the effects of excessive stack pressures and door weight. Operators are normally set for an adjustable time to open, between one to five seconds.

- glazing and weather-stripping selected to minimize air infiltration/exfiltration and water penetration.

- codes normally require safety glazing to reduce accidents due to broken glass.

Specification of revolving doors

Revolving doors are a form of exterior door assembly that is typically selected for entries that carry a continuous flow of traffic without very high peaks and where air infiltration/exfiltration must be kept to an absolute minimum. Revolving door entrances are manufactured as assemblies. The manufacturer will provide all components required for installation. When selecting revolving doors, consider that they are generally selected for:

- entries that carry a continuous flow of traffic without very high peaks.

- they keep interchange of inside and outside air to a relatively small amount compared to other types of doors.

- they are usually used in combination with swinging doors because of revolving doors' inability to handle large volumes of people in short periods of time.

- building codes prohibit the use of revolving doors for some types of occupancy because of the limited traffic flow in emergencies.

- where permitted as exits, they have limitations imposed by local building codes.

– may not, in some instances, provide more than 50 percent of the required exit capacity at any location. The remaining capacity must be supplied by swinging doors within close proximity.

Revolving doors may be power assisted to facilitate traffic through them (**Fig. 4**). Revolving-door entrances normally provide a panic-releasing device that automatically releases a door panel in case of:

– entrapment of the user.

– accidental jamming or impact on the door leaves.

– revolving doors are provided with speed governors to limit the maximum speed at which the door leaves will travel.

The following points should be considered for each revolving door assembly:

• *Size and configuration*

– Revolving doors are only available as a complete package. Diameters vary from 6 to 8 ft (1.8 to 2.4 m) as standard, with 7 ft (2.1 m) as the standard height. Wider doors are generally recommended for easier traffic flow, especially in buildings where hand-carried luggage is a factor.

– Three-wing and four-wing doors are available as standard from many manufacturers. Four-wing types are generally more energy efficient while three-wing types provide more space for people in wheelchairs.

• *Building type and anticipated building use*

– building egress: some building codes restrict the use of revolving doors to provide full exit capacity for certain building occupancies because of their limitations to traffic flow in emergencies. In such situations, exit capacity is made up by the provision of adjacent swinging entrance doors. Revolving doors should be equipped with an emergency release mechanism to book-fold wings, and a manual or power-assisted speed controller.

– dynamics of building population use: a single revolving door can handle a small building population effectively. The larger the building the greater the quantity of revolving doors required to accommodate peak building population entrance/exit times.

– security requirements: revolving doors can be custom fabricated to incorporate card readers or coded number access devices coupled with magnetic locks and metal detectors.

– accessibility: standard-size revolving doors are difficult to operate by those with limited physical capacities and by those transporting large objects. To address these concerns, custom revolving doors can be manufactured that incorporate wider wings and door speed controls.

– weathertightness: revolving doors are fabricated to incorporate a positive, continuous seal around the door assembly perimeter and completely around each door wing. In addition, with power-assisted operators revolving doors stop automatically with their wings in quarter-point position, providing an air lock within the enclosure that reduces air infiltration/exfiltration.

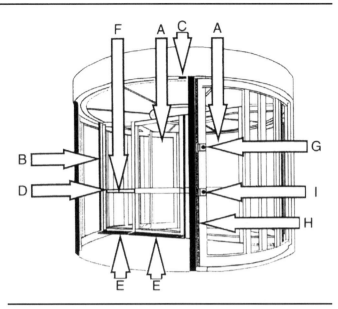

Fig. 4. Safety systems for automatically revolving doors: (A) emergency escape doors; (B) vertical compressible safety switches; (C) vertical sensors at throat openings; (D) vertical sensors on leading edges of wings; (E) horizontal compressible safety switches located on bottom leading edges of the wings; (F) horizontal safety sensors on muntin bars of rotating wings; (G) emergency stop switch (location optional); (H) vertical compressible safety switches placed on the lead edges of the wing; (I) handicap door speed reduction switch (location optional). (courtesy Besam Automated Entrance Systems)

• *Environmental influences and climatic conditions*

– temperature range: project-specific ambient and surface temperatures should be considered in the selection of materials for revolving doors.

– prevailing winds: revolving door assemblies should be designed to resist positive and negative wind loads as determined from local code requirements, by analytical methods, or from data obtained through wind tunnel analyses.

– precipitation: in geographic locations that receive heavy snowfall, foot grilles are sometimes incorporated into revolving door installations to prevent the accumulation of snow within the enclosure. The presence of de-icing salts may cause corrosion of unprotected revolving door components.

– atmospheric conditions: project-specific humidity, salt spray, and air pollution should be considered in the selection of materials for revolving doors.

– UV exposure: project-specific sun exposure should be considered in the selection of organic and inorganic coatings on exposed components of revolving doors.

• *Other factors* influencing revolving door entrance design

– energy efficiency: revolving doors are much more energy efficient than swinging doors. A single bank of revolving doors is more energy efficient than a double bank of swinging doors.

– stack pressure: the greater the stack pressure, the greater the potential for energy loss. The entrance area suction, or pressure, increases as both the difference between the inside and outside air temperatures widens and as the building gets taller.

– suitable structural support for the revolving door opening frame should be provided.

– door hardware: tall buildings, and buildings in areas with tall buildings, can create large downdrafts affecting revolving door performance. Manual or power-assisted speed controllers, often sized to comply with code-mandated speeds, are used to prevent rapid acceleration and spinning of revolving doors caused by downdrafts.

– glazing and weather-stripping should be selected to minimize air infiltration/exfiltration and water penetration.

– codes normally require safety glazing to reduce accidents due to broken glass.

Specification of fire doors

This section includes selection data relevant to interior fire rated, standard steel, and wood doors. Types of fire doors are discussed, along with selection criteria and limitations on glass light sizes.

• *Types of doors* include:

– swinging steel doors

– swinging wood doors

– sliding steel doors

• *Selection criteria* include:

– grade

– model

– door thickness

– fire-resistance ratings and sizes

– outer-face material and thickness

– veneer matching

– internal construction

– louver types

– light openings

– fabrication tolerances

• *Grade (model)*

– steel doors: standard, heavy, and extra heavy duty (full flush or seamless design)

– wood doors: economy, custom, and premium (seam-free only)

– sliding steel doors: custom (full flush or seamless design)

• *Door thickness*

– steel doors: 1-¾ in (4.5 cm)

– wood doors: 1-¾ in, 1-⅜ in (4.5 cm, 3.5 cm)

– sliding steel doors: 1-¾ to 4-⅛ in (4.5 to 10.5 cm)

• *Fire-resistance ratings and sizes*

– swinging steel doors: 20 through 120 minutes

– wood doors: 1-¾ in (4.5 cm), 1-⅜ in (3.5 cm) thick: 20 minutes; 1-¾ in (4.5 cm) thick: 45, 60, and 90 minutes

– sliding steel doors: 45 to 240 minutes

– temperature rise ratings: available in both steel and wood to 650F maximum temperature rise after 30 minutes.

• *Face sizes*

– steel doors: 4 × 10 ft (1.2 × 3 m) singles; 8 × 10 ft (2.4 × 3 m) pairs.

– wood doors: 4 × 9 ft (1.2 × 2.7 m) singles; 8 × 9 ft (2.4 × 2.7 m) parallel pairs; 8 × 8 ft (2.4 × 2.4 m) double egress 45 and 60 minutes; 4 × 10 ft (1.2 × 3 m) singles; 8 × 8 ft (2.4 × 2.4 m) parallel pairs; 8 × 8 ft (2.4 × 2.4 m) double egress 90 minutes; 4 × 10 ft (1.2 × 3 m) singles; 8 × 8 ft (2.4 × 2.4 m) parallel pairs.

– sliding steel doors; refer to **Table 4**

• *Outer-face material and thicknesses*

– *steel doors:* hot or cold rolled steel sheet, galvanized steel sheet, electro-zinc coated steel sheet, stainless steel, bronze, or brass; 20, 18, 16, 14 gauge thicknesses; embossed patterns available.

– *wood doors:* standard thickness hardwood face veneers overlaid with medium density overlay veneer, natural hardwood veneer, plastic laminate, or hardboard directly applied to core construction; composed of two, three, or four plies having an overall approximate thickness of 1/16 in (1.5 mm); one ply of 1/8 in (3 mm) for hardboard faces.

– *sliding steel doors:* hot or cold rolled steel sheet, galvanized steel sheet, stainless steel.

• *Veneer matching*

– matching between individual pieces of veneer: book, slip, or random match.

– assembly of spliced veneer on a face: sequence matching from opening to opening must be specified; examples include balanced, center balanced, and running matching.

• *Internal construction*

– steel doors: unitized steel grid, vertical steel stiffeners, mineral fiberboard.

– wood doors: 20-minute doors: particleboard and glued block core, asbestos-free incombustible mineral.

– wood doors: 45-, 60-, 90-minute doors: asbestos-free incombustible mineral.

– sliding steel doors: rectangular steel framing with intermediate steel tube members, fiberglass filler.

• *Louver types*

– may not be used on a door opening in a means of egress. Some manufacturers are permitted to use on doors fire rated up to 90 minutes; most are limited in area to 576 sq in (3700 sq cm) with maximum 24 in (60 cm) length or width.

– steel doors: some manufacturers are not permitted to mix fusible link louvers on doors having light openings, panic devices, or doors exceeding 12 ft (3.7 m) high.

– wood doors: some manufacturers are not permitted to mix fusible link louvers on doors having light openings, panic devices, hardboard faces, or doors exceeding 9 ft (2.7 m) high.

Table 4. Sliding fire door sizes (single, centerparting and 2 panel tele types)

Core	Skin Gage	Labeled Size (Max)	Oversize Label	Temperature Rise
Composite (fiberglas)	14 to 18	12'-0" x 12'-0"	40'-0" x 40'-0"	450 F
Hollow metal	14 to 20	12'-0" x 12'-0"	34'-0"x 20'-0"	not available
Composite (mineral fiberboard)	14 to 20	12'-0" x 12'-0"	34'-0" 20"-0'	not available

- *Light openings in steel fire doors*

  - 20, 30, and 45 minutes: maximum single light 1296 sq in (8360 sq cm) with no dimension exceeding 54 in (1.4 m).

  - 60 and 90 minutes: maximum single light 100 sq in (645 sq cm).

  - 120 minutes: no light permitted.

  - sliding steel doors: lights available in doors rated to 240 minutes.

- *Light openings in wood fire doors:* Same criteria is permitted for steel doors; however, the following is known to be available:

  - 20 and 30 minutes: maximum single light 1296 sq in (8360 sq cm) with no dimension exceeding 54 in (1.4 m).

  - 45 minutes: maximum 1296 sq in (8360 sq cm) singles; maximum 100 sq in (645 sq cm) parallel pairs and double egress.

  - 60 and 90 minutes: maximum 100 sq in (645 sq cm) singles and parallel pairs.

Specification of overhead doors

Overhead doors are a form of exterior door assembly that is usually selected to control door openings such as can be found at loading docks, garage entrances, and airplane hangers. Selection criteria and issues regarding door function, size, and operation are discussed. The following points should be considered for each overhead door assembly:

- *Size and configuration*

  - Width and height of panels making up overhead doors are generally available in the sizes indicated in **Table 5.** Larger, custom sizes are available. Fire-rated models have limited size availability.

  - Overhead doors are limited in width by structural properties of slats, which must transmit wind forces to jamb guides.

- *Building type and anticipated building use*

  - building egress: overhead doors are not intended as a means of egress.

  - the dynamics of building population use: estimated cycles per day varies with building type and use. Standard and high cycle spring sets are selected where lifetime door cycling is not anticipated to exceed less than 50,000 or 100,000 cycles, respectively. High cycle springs are also selected where high use or corrosive environments are anticipated.

  - operation options: manual, crank, and gear; motorized operations are typically available for all overhead doors.

  - security requirements: overhead doors can be custom fabricated to incorporate card readers or coded number access devices coupled with door controllers and operators.

  - accessibility for the universal design criteria: manually operated overhead doors are difficult to operate. To address this concern, overhead doors with motorized operators can be manufactured.

Table 5. Average available maximum sizes of overhead doors

Type	Width x Height (Feet)
Sectional	36 x 20
Roll up	30 x 30
Rolling grille	Varies
Telescoping	20 x 20
Canopy	60 x 30

– weathertightness: overhead doors are fabricated to incorporate positive seals around the door assembly perimeter that resist air infiltration/exfiltration. These seals cannot exclude water or stop air movement completely. Door curtains of perforated slat, slotted slats, or bar grille design would not be weathertight.

- *Environmental influences and climatic conditions*

– temperature range: project-specific ambient and surface temperatures should be considered in the selection of materials for overhead doors.

– prevailing winds: overhead door assemblies should be designed to resist positive and negative wind loads as determined from local code requirements, by analytical methods, or from data obtained through wind tunnel analyses.

– precipitation: the presence of de-icing salts may cause corrosion of unprotected overhead door components.

– atmospheric conditions: project-specific humidity, salt spray, and air pollution should be considered in the selection of materials for overhead doors.

– UV exposure: project-specific sun exposure should be considered in the selection of organic and inorganic coatings on exposed components of overhead doors.

Other factors influencing overhead door design

- *Energy efficiency* of overhead doors is normally made by the incorporation of neoprene, silicone, EPDM, or PVC and nylon brush-type seals at the head, jamb, and bottom bar components of the door assembly to control air infiltration/exfiltration. Curtain slats can be fabricated with foamed in place, or rigid block, type insulation to increase thermal performance. Curtain slats can be fabricated from PVC.

- *Suitable structural support* for the overhead door opening frame and hangers should be provided.

- *Door hardware* with a capacity and durability should be selected to provide adequate performance of the door assembly. Torsion springs are generally used and counterweights are usually required when door is in a fire-rated opening. Counterweights hold the door in the open position and are released by fusible link, smoke detectors, or loss of power from initiation of a fire alarm system.

- *Sheltering components* may be provided to aid in the convenient and sheltered loading and unloading of goods; includes canopies, opening seals, bumpers, guards, and loading dock shelters and air curtains.

4 DOOR FRAMES AND HARDWARE CHECKLISTS

Elements and nomenclature of entrance door frames and hardware are shown in **Figs. 5** and **6**. Steel door frame nomenclature is indicated in **Fig. 7**. Code-determined dimensions for door handles, pulls, latches and locks of publicly accessible entrances are illustrated in **Fig. 8**. The following section describes general selection criteria, in terms of:

AUTOMATIC DOOR OPERATORS

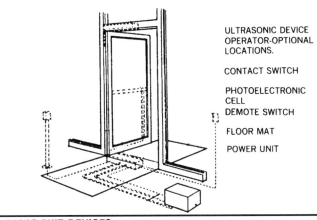

ULTRASONIC DEVICE OPERATOR-OPTIONAL LOCATIONS.

CONTACT SWITCH

PHOTOELECTRONIC CELL

DEMOTE SWITCH

FLOOR MAT

POWER UNIT

PANIC EXIT DEVICES

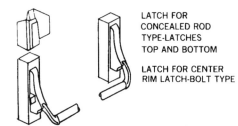

LATCH FOR CONCEALED ROD TYPE-LATCHES TOP AND BOTTOM

LATCH FOR CENTER RIM LATCH-BOLT TYPE

OVERHEAD HOLDER

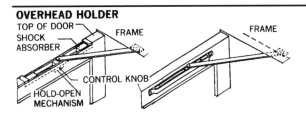

TOP OF DOOR
SHOCK ABSORBER
FRAME
FRAME
CONTROL KNOB
HOLD-OPEN MECHANISM

DEADLATHES

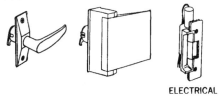

ELECTRICAL

FLUSHBOLTS

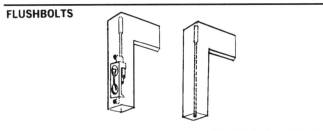

Fig. 5. Door-frame hardware.

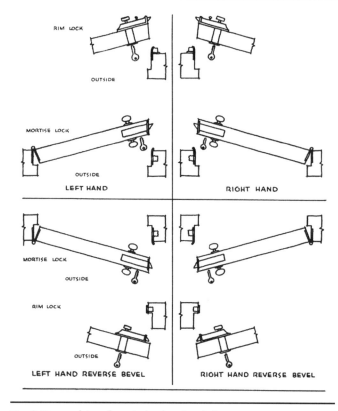

Fig. 6. Nomenclature for exterior door handedness.

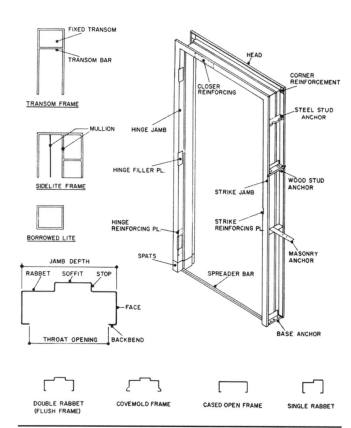

Fig. 7. Nomenclature for steel doors.

- frames

- closers

- hinges and pivots

- locks and latches

Frames

The entrance frame can be a simple frame surrounding a door panel, or a series of members holding fixed panels as well as the door panels.

- *The frame and the trim* may be integral or made of separate pieces. Entrance frame must be strong enough to resist wind load without excessive deflection, to avoid the possibility of deformation of the frame with resultant:

  - cracking of fixed glass panels.

  - binding of door panels.

  - opening of joints in frame.

- *Door frames in wood construction*

  - require rough-in bucks secured to the structural frame for secure attachment and operation.

  - can receive complete "pre-hung" door assemblies or be site fabricated.

  - joints between frame and wall are covered by trim.

  - finished wood frames are generally field fitted to exact conditions.

- *Door frames in metal construction*

  - are often set in before the wall is filled in and serve as framing members.

  - frames and doors may be pre-hung and preassembled and come as a package. Protection of metal frames and pre-hung doors during installation and remainder of construction often requires considerable care.

- *Metal entrance frames* may be of:

  - built-up rolled sections.

  - brake-formed metal sections.

  - roll-formed metal sections.

  - extrusions.

Closers

The next major entrance component to be considered is closers, manual and powered.

- Closers for doors are overhead or floor-type, and are either fully concealed, semi-concealed, or surface mounted. All manually operated closers require a certain amount of force to open the door panel. Therefore, depending on the type of entrance desired, power-actuation may be required:

- Oversize doors may become too heavy to be opened manually.

- All entrance types are generally available with power-actuation.

- When selecting power-actuation, consider safety. People must be protected from inadvertent operation of power-actuated door leaves. Review the type of sensors to be used.

- Swinging doors normally require guardrails or other architectural barriers to protect people from their swing.

- Sliding doors need a pocket or other barrier to prevent contact with people during operation.

- Revolving doors must have a speed control to limit number of revolutions.

- Some definitions of door hardware:

– Automatic closing device: causes the door to close when activated by detector through rate of temperature rise, smoke, or other products of combustion.

– Automatic closing door is normally in open position, and is closed by an automatic closing device in case of fire.

– Center latch: is used to hold two leaves of bi-parting doors together.

– Self-closing door: will return to the closed position after having been opened and released.

Hinges and pivots

The other entrance components to be considered simultaneously with the selection of closers are hinges, or devices on which doors turn or swing, to open and close:

- Hinges may be concealed or exposed.

- Butts are the most common type of hinge used today. They are usually mortised into the edge of the door.

– are generally mounted on a door 5 in (13 cm) from the head and 10 in (25 cm) from the floor.

– when a third butt is required to minimize door warping, it is mounted equidistant between top and bottom hinges.

- Pivots are stronger and more durable than hinges and are better able to withstand the racking stresses to which doors are subjected. Their use is generally recommended for

– oversize doors, heavy doors.

– entrance doors of high frequency use.

Locks and latches

Locks and latches are used to hold doors in the closed position. As indicated above, locks and latches are positioned within the height

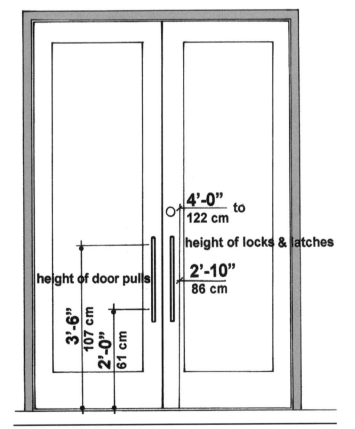

Fig. 8. Public access entry door depicting typical code-determined dimensions.

range indicated in Fig. 8 except those not routinely used and for security purposes only, which may be mounted at any height.

- A deadbolt is often used in conjunction with a latch, in which case the unit is known as a lock.

- for doors that need not be latched or locked during the normal workday, push-pull plates are normally used in lieu of latch sets or locks.

- doors with push-pull plates may be provided with a deadbolt if there is a need to secure them at certain times.

- hardware is a factor in determining the ultimate security of the entrance:

- Mortise locks are the most secure type of lock. Deadbolts provide superior protection to latch bolts.

- The proper location of door silencers on swinging entrances can prevent latch lock tampering.

- Special armor plates are available for protecting lock cylinders.

- Electronic latches, hinges, card readers, and other devices are available for specific security requirements.

- Panic devices for mass exit in emergencies are installed on exterior doors that serve as legal exits from a building.

- Entrance, exit and door hardware is a diverse and highly intricate subject. Architects rarely specify such hardware without the benefit of the expertise of a hardware consultant. Installation of some entrance types and component types create special requirements:

- one-piece hollow-metal frames are normally installed before the wall construction is complete.

- recessed floor closures need openings in floor slabs and adequate slab depth.

- revolving door entrances require special care in the installation of the floor within the enclosure for smoothness and flatness.

- hardware should be reviewed to determine its operating life. ■

REFERENCES AND RESOURCES

American Architectural Manufacturers Association, 1827 Walden Office Square, Suite 550, Schaumburg, IL 60173

Door and Hardware Institute, 14170 New Brook Drive, Suite 200, Chantilly, VA 20151

National Association of Architectural Metal Manufacturers, 8 S. Michigan Ave., Suite 1000, Chicago, IL 60603

National Fire Protection Association, One Batterymarch Park, Quincy, MA 02169

Patterson, Terry L., *Illustrated 2000 Building Code Handbook*, McGraw-Hill, New York, 2001.

Steel Door Institute, 30200 Detroit Road, Cleveland, OH 44145

Window and Door Manufacturers Association (Formally NWWDA), 1400 E. Touhy Avenue, Suite 470, Des Plaines, IL 60018

John Carmody and Stephen Selkowitz

Summary

This article provides an introduction to the energy-related aspects of windows for both residential and commercial buildings. Windows are one of the most important components affecting energy performance and comfort. New window technologies provide improved performance and an array of design options.

Key words

energy efficiency, commercial building, glazing, residence, solar heat, gain, transmittance, windows

High-performance windows in a residential building.

Windows

In residential and small commercial buildings, almost all windows are manufactured units that include glazing, operating sashes, and frame. In recent years, residential windows have undergone a technological revolution. In the winter, high performance windows reduce heat loss considerably, provide greater thermal comfort, and reduce the risk of condensation. In summer, it is possible to have expansive views and daylight while significantly reducing solar heat gain. These changes create many new options for architects, builders, and homeowners, making window selection a more complex process. Choosing a window involves many considerations related to aesthetics, function, energy performance, and cost.

1 ENERGY-RELATED PROPERTIES OF WINDOWS

Heat flows through a window assembly in three ways: conduction, convection, and radiation. When these basic mechanisms of heat transfer are applied to the performance of windows, they interact in complex ways. The key energy performance characteristics of windows are heat flow indicated by U factor, solar heat gain coefficient (SHGC), and air leakage (AL). Other important attributes are visible transmittance (VT) and condensation potential (**Fig. 1**).

- *Heat flow*

When there is a temperature difference between inside and outside, heat is transferred through the window frame and glazing by the combined effects of conduction, convection, and radiation. This is indicated in terms of the U factor of a window assembly. It is expressed in units of Btu/hr-sq ft-F (W/sq m-°C). The U factor may be expressed for the glass alone or the entire window, which includes the effect of the frame and the spacer materials. The lower the U factor, the greater

a window's resistance to heat flow. A window's insulating value is indicated in terms of its R value, which is the reciprocal of U value. **Tables 1** to **3** summarize properties of typical window types, along with insulating and shading devices.

- *Heat gain from solar radiation*

Regardless of outside temperature, heat can be gained through windows by direct or indirect solar radiation. The ability to control this heat gain through windows is indicated in terms of the solar heat gain coefficient (SHGC). The SHGC is the fraction of incident solar radiation admitted through a window, both directly transmitted, and absorbed and subsequently released inward. The solar heat gain coefficient has replaced the shading coefficient as the standard indicator of a window's shading ability. It is expressed as a number between 0 and 1. The lower a window's solar heat gain coefficient, the less solar heat it transmits, and the greater its shading ability. **Fig. 1a** indicates the effects of orientation on solar gain.

- *Air leakage*

Heat loss and gain also occur by infiltration through cracks in the window assembly. This effect is measured in terms of the amount of air (cubic feet or meters per minute) that passes through a unit area of window (square foot or meter) or window perimeter length (foot or meter) under given pressure conditions. It is indicated by an air leakage rating (AL). For energy efficiency, select a window with an AL of 0.30 or below (units are cfm/sf). In reality, infiltration varies with wind-driven and temperature-driven pressure changes. Infiltration also contributes to summer cooling loads in some climates by raising the interior humidity level. **Fig. 1b** indicates comparative air leakage of representative glazings.

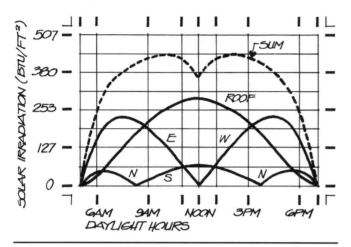

(a) Effect of window orientation upon effectiveness for passive solar gain (Watson and Labs 1993)

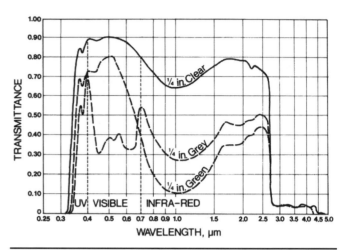

(c) Spectral transmittance for ¼ in architectural glass comparing clear, gray heat-absorbing, and green heat-absorbing types (Yellott 1979)

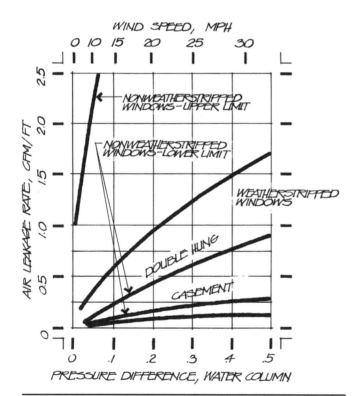

(b) Window air leakage (*Canadian Building Digest* No. 35)

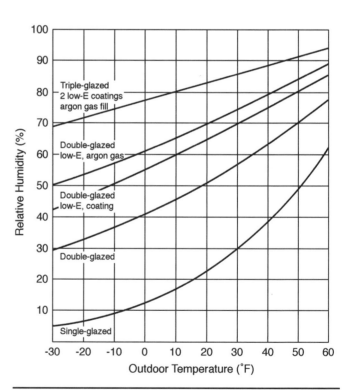

(d) Condensation potential in windows. Note: All air spaces are ½ in (1.27 cm); all coatings are e = 0.10.

Fig. 1. Defining window properties.

Table 1. Properties of some typical windows (Source: Carmody, Selkowitz and Hershong, 1996)

Window description	Total window unit U-value SHGC VT			Center of glass only U-value SHGC VT		
Single-glazed Clear glass Aluminum frame*	1.30	0.79	0.69	1.11	0,86	0.90
Double-glazed Clear glass Aluminum frame**	0.64	0.65	0.62	0.49	0.76	0.81
Double-glazed Bronze tinted glass Aluminum frame**	0.64	0.55	0.47	0.49	0.62	0.61
Double glased Clear glass Wood or vinyl frame	0.49	0.58	0.57	0.49	0.76	0.81
Double-glazed Low-E (high solar gain) Argon gas fill Wood or vinyl frame	0.33	0.55	0.52	0.32	0.74	0.74
Double-glaze Low-E (medium solar gain) Argon gas fill Wood or vinyl frame	0.30	0.44	0.56	0.26	0.58	0.78
Double-glazed Specrally selective low-E (low solar gain) Argon gas fill Wood or vinyl frame	0.29	0.31	0.51	0.24	0.41	0.72
Triple-glazed Clear glass Wood or vinyl frame	0.34	0.52	0.53	0.31	0.69	0.75
Triple-glazed Two low-E coatings Krypton gas fill Wood or vinyl frame	0.15	0.37	0.48	0.11	0.49	0.68

* No thermal break in frame.
** Thermal break in frame.
  All values for total windows are based on a 2-foot by 4-foot casement window.
  Units for all U-values are Btu/hr-sq ft-°F.
  SHGC = solar heat gain coefficient.
  VT = visible transmittance.

Table 2. Comparative thermal transmission through glazing and insulating devices (Watson and Labs 1993)

Comparative thermal transmission of glazing materials, vertical*

Glazing type	Winter U**	Overall R**
Single sheet glass, 1/4″ (e = .84)	1.14	.88
Insulating glass, double glazed (e = .84)		
1/8″ with 3/16″ air space	.62	1.6
1/8″ with 1/4″ air space	.58	1.7
1/4″ with 1/2″ air space	.49	2.0
1/2″ air space with low emittance coating†		
e = .60	.43	2.3
e = .40	.38	2.6
e = .20	.32	3.1
Insulating glass, triple glazed (e = .84)		
1/4″ air spaces	.39	2.6
1/2″ air spaces	.31	3.2
Storm window (conventional), 1″ to 4″ air space	.50	2.0
Single sheet plastic, 1/8″	1.06	.94
1/4″	.96	1.0
1/2″	.81	1.2
Insulating plastic, double glazed		
1/8″ with 1/4″ air space	.55	1.8
1/4″ with 1/2″ air space	.43	2.3
Glass block		
6 x 6 x 4″ thick	.60	1.7
8 x8 x 4″	.56	1.8
8 x 8 x 4″, double cavity	.48	2.1
12 x 12 x 4″	.52	1.9
12 x 12 x 4″, double cavity	.44	2.3
Double skinned acrylic sheet	.6	1.7
Corrulux (8 oz. corrugated fiberglass) ‡	1.09	.92
Sunwall I‡	.45	2.2
Sunwall II‡	.38	2.6
Sunwall III‡	.30	3.3
Sunwall IV‡	.25	3.9
Sunwall V‡	.22	4.5

*Values from ASHRAE Fundamentals [1981] except as noted

**U values from air-to-air, Btu/hr(ft^2)F; R=1/U

†Reflective coating on one sheet facing air space; other faces uncoated

‡From manufacturer's literature

Comparable thermal transmission through operable insulation devices, interior

Insulating device	Unit R	Winter U*	Overall R*
Drapery			
tight fitting, tight weave closed†			
loose fitting, closed†			
Window Blanket	2.0	.34	2.9
Panel type			
cellular glass†	2.5/in.		
rigid fiberglas board†	4.5/in.		
expanded polyurethane†	6.25/in.		
expanded polystyrene, extruded†	5.3/in.		
expanded polystyrene, beadboard†	3.6/in.		
Nightwall		.27	3.7
Insul Shutter	6.25	.14	7.14
Skylid		.26	3.8
Roll down shades			
ordinary roller shade, drawn†		.88	1.1
ordinary shade, with metallized film		.52	1.9
ordinary shade, with edge tracks			
or seals		.50	2.0
Insealshaid	4.0		
Curtain Wall	9.1	0.1	10.0
Window Quilt	3.2	.24	4.2
Thermo Shade		.40	2.5
High R Shade	.08	.07	14.3
Integral			
Slimshade, interior louvers, closed‡		.41	2.4
Beadwall	3.3/in.		
Interior storm window		.5	2.0

*for device in combination with single glazing

† from ASHRAE Fundamentals [1981]

‡from manufacturer's literature

Comparative thermal transmission through exterior insulating devices

Insulating device	Unit R	Winter U*	Overall R*
Roll down shutters			
Rolladen	1.1	.45-.50	
Roll-Awn	1.6	.40	
Rolsekur	1.1	.45-.50	
Everstrait	1.1	.45-.50	
Storm window, conventional		.56	1.78
Shading devices			
Koolshade solarscreen (reduces solar gain)†		.96	1.04

*for device in combination with single glazing

†from manufacturer's literature

- *Visible transmittance*

Visible transmittance (VT) is an optical property that indicates the amount of visible light transmitted through the glass. Although VT does not directly affect heating and cooling energy use, it is used in the evaluation of energy-efficient windows. For example, two windows may have similar solar heat gain control properties, however one may transmit more daylight as indicated by the visible transmittance. The visible transmittance may then be the basis for choosing one window over another. Specifically, VT is the percentage or fraction of the visible spectrum (380 to 720 nanometers) weighted by the sensitivity of the eye, that is transmitted through the glazing. The higher the VT, the more daylight is transmitted. **Fig. 1c** compares spectral transmittance of three glazing types.

- *Condensation potential*

Reducing the risk of condensation on windows is an important aspect of selecting a window. **Fig. 1d** indicates the condensation potential on glazing (center of glass) at various outdoor temperature and indoor relative humidity conditions. Condensation can occur at any points that fall on or above the curves.

- *Example 1*: At 20F (−7°C) outside temperature, condensation will form on the inner surface of double glazing any time the indoor relative humidity is 52 percent or higher. It will form at an indoor relative humidity of 70 percent or higher if a double-pane window with low-E and argon is used.

- *Example 2*: In a cold climate where winter night temperatures drop to −10F (−23°C), we want to maintain 65 percent humidity without condensation. A double-glazed window with low-E and argon will show condensation at 57 percent relative humidity, so the triple glazing with two low-E coatings and argon is needed to prevent condensation.

Technological improvements

A progression of innovations has integrated more elements of control into the window assembly or the glass itself. Some technological innovations appearing in fenestration products are described briefly below.

- *Glazing unit structure*

Multiple layers of glass or plastic films improve thermal resistance and reduce the heat loss attributed to convection between window layers. Additional layers also provide more surfaces for low-E or solar control coatings.

- *Low-emittance coatings*

Low-emittance or low-E coatings are highly transparent and virtually invisible, but have a high reflectance (low emittance) to long-wavelength infrared radiation. This reduces long-wavelength radiative heat transfer between glazing layers by a factor of 5 to 10, thereby reducing total heat transfer between two glazing layers. Low-emittance coatings may be applied directly to glass surfaces, or to thin sheets of plastic (films) suspended in the air cavity between the interior and exterior glazing layers.

Table 3. Properties of glazing and insulating devices (Watson and Labs 1993)

Properties of shading devices.

	% Transmitted	% Reflected	% Absorbed	S.C. a
Venetian blinds				
light-colored horizontal	5	55	40	.55
med.-colored horizontal	5	35	60	.64
white (closed) vertical	0	77	23	.29
Roller shades				
white color, translucent	25	60	15	.39
white, opaque	0	80	20	.25
dark, opaque	0	12	88	.59

a shading coefficient given for device in combination with ⅛″ clear float glass (87% transmittance): except for vertical blind, with 71-80% transmittance.

Solar and visible transmission of different glazing materials.

Material		%Daylight	%Solar	S.C.
Clear float glass, 1 sheet, ⅛″		90	86	1.00
2 sheets, ⅛″		82	71	.88
1 sheet, ¼″		88	77	.93
2 sheets, ¼″		78	60	.80
Sunadex "water white" 1 sheet, ⅛″			91.6	
Lo-iron	1 sheet, ⅛″		89.1	
heat absorbing	⅛″	84	65	.82
	¼″	76	48	.68
Plexiglas 1 sheet, 3/16″		92	90	
Lexan polycarbonate sheet, ⅛″		86	89	–
	¼″	82	86	–
Lascolite corrugated fiberglass				
crystal clear, 4 oz.		93	82	
clear,	5 oz.	87	81	
frost,	8 oz.	66	60	
solar white,	5 oz.	32	21	
Kalwall sunlite, 1 sheet			85-90	
sunwall 1 sheet		77		
acrylic double skinned sheet				
clear		83	83	.97
white		70	67	.81
white		20	19	.31
polycarbonate double skinned sheet		80	77	
polycarbonate double skinned sheet		73	74	.88
gray float glass, 1 sheet, ⅛″ (LOF)		62	63	.82
¼″		42	44	.67
gray reflective, 1 sheet, (LOF)		8-34	11-37	.36-.62
Crystaflex 40-A, translucent, ⅛″		83	18	
Glasshade II		Varies	Varies	

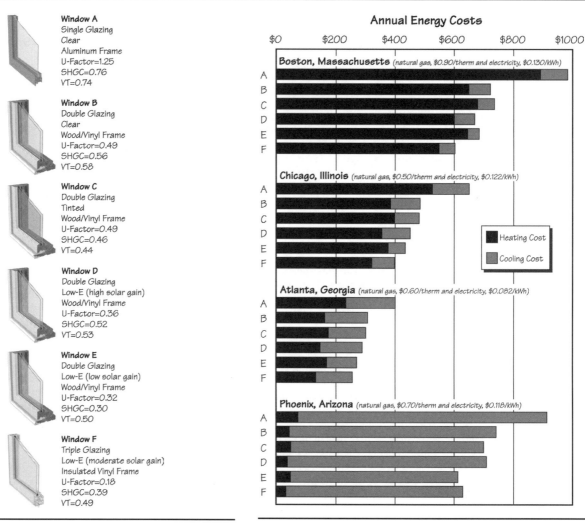

Window A
Single Glazing
Clear
Aluminum Frame
U-Factor=1.25
SHGC=0.76
VT=0.74

Window B
Double Glazing
Clear
Wood/Vinyl Frame
U-Factor=0.49
SHGC=0.56
VT=0.58

Window C
Double Glazing
Tinted
Wood/Vinyl Frame
U-Factor=0.49
SHGC=0.46
VT=0.44

Window D
Double Glazing
Low-E (high solar gain)
Wood/Vinyl Frame
U-Factor=0.36
SHGC=0.52
VT=0.53

Window E
Double Glazing
Low-E (low solar gain)
Wood/Vinyl Frame
U-Factor=0.32
SHGC=0.30
VT=0.50

Window F
Triple Glazing
Low-E (moderate solar gain)
Insulated Vinyl Frame
U-Factor=0.18
SHGC=0.39
VT=0.49

Fig. 2. Window options and properties (labeled for reference to **Fig. 3**).

Fig. 3. Annual energy performance for a 2000 sq ft house with different windows in four U.S. climates. (Source: Carmody et al. 2000)
Note: The annual energy performance figures shown here were generated using RESFEN for a typical 2000 sq ft house with 300 sq ft of window area (15 percent of floor area). The windows are equally distributed on all four sides of the house and include typical shading (interior shades, overhangs, trees, and neighboring buildings). The heating system is a gas furnace with air-conditioning for cooling. The figures are based on typical energy costs for each location. U factor, SHGC, and VT are for the total window including frame.

- *Solar control glazings and coatings*

To reduce cooling loads, new types of tinted glass and new coatings can be specified that reduce the impact of the sun's heat without sacrificing view. Spectrally selective glazings and coatings absorb and reflect the infrared portion of sunlight while transmitting visible daylight, thus reducing solar heat gain coefficients and the resulting cooling loads. These solar control coatings can also have low-emittance characteristics.

- *Low-conductance gas fills*

With the use of a low-emittance coating, heat transfer across a gap is dominated by conduction and natural convection. While air is a relatively good insulator, there are other gases (such as argon, carbon dioxide, krypton, and xenon) with lower thermal conductivities. Using one of these nontoxic gases in an insulating glass unit can reduce heat transfer between the glazing layers.

- *Warm edge spacers*

Heat transfer through the metal spacers that are used to separate glazing layers can increase heat loss and cause condensation to form at the edge of the window. "Warm edge" spacers use new materials and better designs to reduce this effect.

- *Thermally improved sash and frame*

Traditional sash and frame designs often contribute to heat loss and can represent a large fraction of the total loss when high-performance glass is used. New materials and improved designs can reduce this loss.

- *Improved weather-stripping*

Better weather-strips are now available to reduce air leakage, and most are of more durable materials that will provide improved performance over a longer time period.

2 RESIDENTIAL WINDOWS

Overall impact of improving window efficiency

The impact of changing to energy-efficient windows can be significant even though windows usually comprise a small percentage of the total building envelope by area. **Figs. 2** to **4** show the heating and cooling season energy use in a typical house in four U.S. climates. In each climate, the annual energy use with six types of windows is illustrated. The major difference between cities compared in Fig. 4 is due to climate; however, different fuel costs also play an important role. For example, Boston and Chicago have similar heating loads, but since fuel prices are greater in the Northeast, the savings from improved windows are greater in Boston.

Such energy-efficiency improvements can have a large impact on overall national energy consumption. There are approximately 20 billion sq ft of windows in the United States. These windows create additional energy bills for our nation's homeowners of $9.3 billion per year. Each time a window is specified for a new or existing house, the

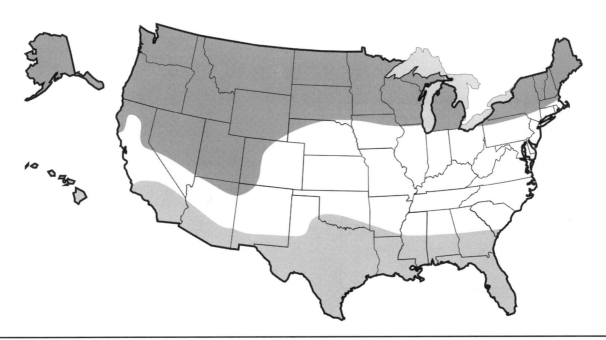

Fig. 4. ENERGY STAR zones and requirements.

Northern Zone	Central Zone	Southern Zone
Mostly heating	*Heating and cooling*	*Mostly cooling*
U factor = 0.35 or less	U factor = 0.40 or less	U factor = 0.75 or less
(0.45 or less for skylights)	(0.45 or less for skylights)	SHGC = 0.40 or less
	SHGC = 0.55 or less	

decisionmaker has the opportunity not only to save some money on the monthly energy bills but to shrink this national energy cost as well. Studies at Lawrence Berkeley National Laboratory suggest that if all windows purchased over the next 15 years incorporated low-E coatings, gas fills, and a few other readily available efficiency improvements, the collective U.S. annual energy bill could be reduced by 25 percent or over $2.5 billion per year by 2010 (Geller and Thorne 1999).

Window selection criteria

In most cases designers and specifiers base part of the decision on appearance factors such as frame style and materials. Then, basic functional issues must be considered. These include providing daylight, glare control, thermal comfort, and ventilation. Certain practical considerations, such as resistance to condensation, sound control, maintenance requirements, durability, compliance with structural codes, and watertightness are also part of the decision-making process.

Window energy performance is an important concern. Some of the basic thermal and optical properties (U factor, solar heat gain coefficient, and visible transmittance) can be identified if the window is properly labeled and compliance with energy codes determined. Basic properties of the window influence annual heating and cooling energy use. This can be determined by looking at the impact of window choice on a typical house. Finally, window selection involves cost. This includes not only initial costs but a number of costs and benefits that occur through the life of the window.

Guide to selecting energy-efficient windows for residential buildings

Beginning with the simplest and least time-consuming and moving to the more complex, here are four basic steps in efficient window selection:

1. *Look for the ENERGY STAR Label*
   The U.S. Department of Energy (DOE) and the Environmental Protection Agency (EPA) have developed an ENERGY STAR designation for products meeting certain energy performance criteria. Since energy-efficient performance of windows, doors, and skylights varies by climate, product recommendations are given for three U.S. climate zones. ENERGY STAR labels are found on windows, doors, and skylights. For making comparisons among ENERGY STAR products, use the NFRC label or directory. See **Fig. 4** for ENERGY STAR zones and requirements.

2. *Look for the NFRC Label*
   The National Fenestration Rating Council (NFRC) is a nonprofit, public/private organization created by the window, door, and skylight industry. It is composed of manufacturers, suppliers, builders, architects and designers, specifiers, code officials, utilities, and government agencies. The NFRC has developed a window energy rating system based on whole product performance (**Fig. 5**). The NFRC label provides the only reliable way to determine the window energy properties and to compare products. The NFRC label appears on all products certified to the NFRC standards and on all window, door, and skylight products that are part of the ENERGY STAR program. At this time, NFRC labels on window units give ratings for U factor, solar heat gain coefficient (SHGC), and visible transmittance (VT).

Fig. 5. NFRC label.

3. *Compare Annual Energy Costs for a Typical House in Your Region*
The annual energy use from computer simulations for a typical house in your region can be compared for different window options. **Fig. 6** illustrates this kind of comparison for six windows in four climate zones. The Efficient Windows Collaborative web site (www.efficientwindows.org) provides annual energy performance comparisons including fact sheets for typical houses using over 30 windows in more than 80 U.S. cities.

4. *Estimate and Compare Annual Energy Costs for the House Design*
Using a computer program such as RESFEN to compare window options is the only method of obtaining reasonable estimates of the heating and cooling costs for your climate, house design, and utility rates. Users define a specific "scenario" by specifying house type (single-story or two-story), geographic location, orientation, electricity and gas cost, and building configuration details (such as wall, floor, and HVAC system type). Users also specify size, shading, and thermal properties of the windows they wish to investigate. The thermal properties that RESFEN requires are: U factor, solar heat gain coefficient, and air leakage rate. The relative energy and cost impacts of two different windows can be compared. See the references for more information on RESFEN.

3 WINDOWS FOR COMMERCIAL BUILDINGS

The term *commercial building* is often used to refer to any nonresidential structure. This includes offices, hotels, restaurants, retail and entertainment facilities, as well as institutional uses such as museums, libraries, schools, and hospitals. Also included are laboratory, manufacturing, and warehouse facilities. Much of the general information about window systems and their performance applies to all building types, however there are obvious differences between these so-called *commercial* functions in terms of their specific energy performance patterns, occupancy requirements, and the desired number and appearance of windows (**Figs. 7** and **8**).

Three major types of window systems are typically used in commercial buildings:

- *Manufactured window units* placed into rough openings in a building facade. These are built in a factory and include typical aluminum and steel frame commercial units as well as wood, vinyl, fiberglass, and other composite frame materials associated with small commercial and residential construction.

- *Curtain walls* that form the entire building skin and are typically hung from the structural floors. These are commonly constructed on site and are made up of vision glass panels serving normal window functions and opaque spandrel panels set into a structural frame. Increasingly, preassembled curtain wall units are delivered to the job site.

- *Storefront windows* found on the lower levels of buildings. Also assembled on site, these are intended to provide maximum view into and out of the building and often include glazed entrance doors. Unlike curtain walls, which bypass floor levels, storefront windows are typically inset between floors.

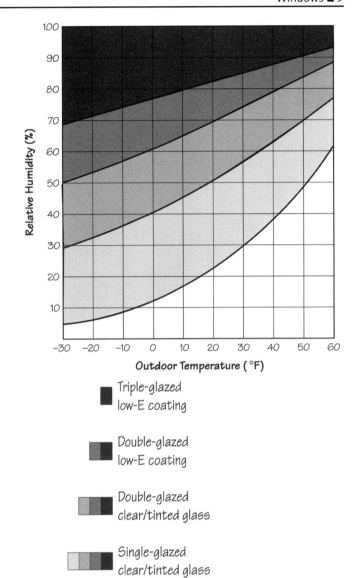

Triple-glazed
low-E coating

Double-glazed
low-E coating

Double-glazed
clear/tinted glass

Single-glazed
clear/tinted glass

Fig. 6. Window comparison in climate zones.

Fig. 7. Shade sails on the north façade of the Phoenix Central Library reduce glare and direct summer sun in the morning and evening.

Photo: Bill Timmerman

Impact of windows on energy performance in office buildings in a cold climate

In a predominantly cold climate, window design and selection must address solar heat gain control, daylight, and heat loss during cold periods. In **Fig. 9**, six representative window types are compared for a typical office building in Chicago, Illinois. A double-pane clear window is used as a base case for this climate. Annual energy use and peak demand per square foot of perimeter floor area are shown for each set of conditions being compared. Fig. 9 pertains only to a south-facing perimeter zone (the area of a building within 15 ft of the exterior facade). The degree to which the perimeter zone contributes to overall building energy use and peak demand depends on the size, shape, and use of the whole building.

The windows in Fig. 9 are compared under two conditions: with and without daylighting controls. The results show that annual electricity use always declines by installing controls that dim or turn off electric lighting when there is sufficient daylight. With such daylighting controls, for all window types except Window D, there is an average reduction of 2.0 to 2.4 kWh/sf yr (15 to 20 percent) compared to a zone without them. Lighting energy use associated with low-VT Window D does not decline significantly; little light enters Window D, giving little opportunity to dim lights and save energy. With the other window cases, however, the higher the VT, the greater the lighting load reduction.

Daylighting controls also translate into reduced cooling loads because of the diminished heat gain from the lights. Therefore, annual heating energy use increases by 0.2 to 0.6 kWh/sf-yr in zones with daylighting controls, as opposed to zones without them. Heating loads rise in proportion to reduced heat gains. For Chicago's cold climate, heating energy represents about 20 percent of the total annual energy use for moderately sized windows and 30 percent for large-area windows (assuming an electricity-to-gas fuel ratio of 3 to 1) so this increase can produce a significant effect on the total perimeter zone performance.

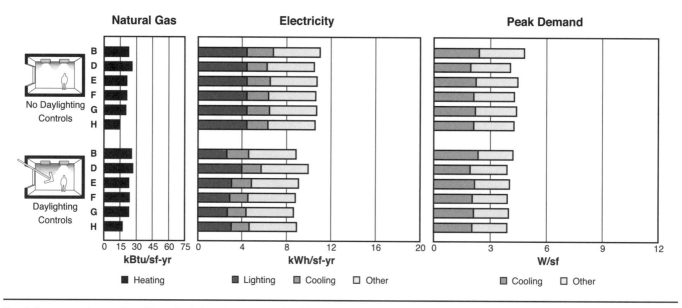

Fig. 8. Summary of properties of typical windows in commercial buildings. (Source: Carmody et al. 2004)

Window types with a very low SHGC and U factor and a moderate VT perform best. For example, a spectrally selective, low-E triple-pane window (Window H) is one of the lowest in total annual energy use. A spectrally selective, tinted double-pane window (Window F) outperforms conventional reflective glass (Window D) for all window sizes.

Fig. 9 also shows that daylight controls significantly reduce peak electricity demand in south-facing perimeter zones. With daylighting controls and a moderate window area, peak demand falls by 0.6 to 1.1 W/sf (13 to 20 percent) for all window types except Window D.

Impact of windows on energy performance in office buildings in a hot climate

In a predominantly hot climate, window design and selection must address solar heat gain control and control of plentiful intense daylight. In **Fig. 10,** six representative window types are compared for a typical office building in Houston, Texas. A single-pane clear window

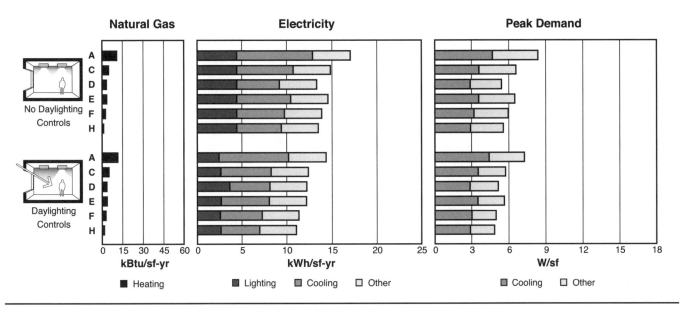

Fig. 9. Annual energy use and peak demand comparison in Chicago, Illinois.
Note: All cases are south-facing with a 0.30 window-to-wall ratio and no shading. Numbers are expressed per square foot within a 15 ft deep perimeter zone. Results were computed using DOE-2.1E for a typical office building in Chicago, Illinois. See Fig. 8 for window descriptions. (Source: Carmody et al. 2004)

Window	Number of Glazings	Frame	U-factor		SHGC		VT		LSG	
			Overall	COG	Overall	COG	Overall	COG	Overall	COG
A Clear	1	Aluminum	1.25	1.09	0.72	0.82	0.71	0.88	0.99	1.08
B Clear	2	Alum-TB	0.60	0.48	0.60	0.70	0.63	0.78	1.05	1.12
C Bronze tint	2	Alum-TB	0.60	0.48	0.42	0.49	0.38	0.48	0.90	0.98
D Reflective	2	Alum-TB	0.54	0.40	0.17	0.17	0.10	0.13	0.59	0.76
E Low-E bronze tint	2	Alum-TB	0.49	0.33	0.39	0.44	0.36	0.45	0.92	1.01
F Selective low-E tint	2	Alum-TB	0.46	0.29	0.27	0.29	0.43	0.53	1.59	1.83
G Clear with selective low-E	2	Alum-TB	0.46	0.29	0.34	0.38	0.57	0.71	1.68	1.87
H Clear with 1 low-E layer	3	Insulated	0.20	0.15	0.22	0.26	0.37	0.46	1.68	1.78
I Clear with 2 low-E layers	4	Insulated	0.14	0.13	0.20	0.24	0.34	0.42	1.70	1.73

Fig. 10. Annual energy use and peak demand comparison in Houston, Texas. (Source: Carmody et al. 2004)
Note: All cases are south-facing with a 0.30 window-to-wall ratio and no shading. Numbers are expressed per square foot within a 15 ft deep perimeter zone. Results were computed using DOE-2.1E for a typical office building in Houston, Texas. See Fig. 8 for window descriptions.

Box A—Definitions

ABSORPTANCE. The ratio of radiant energy absorbed to total incident radiant energy in a glazing system.

EMITTANCE. The ratio of the radiant flux emitted by a specimen to that emitted by a blackbody at the same temperature and under the same conditions.

AIR LEAKAGE RATING. A measure of the rate of infiltration around a window or skylight in the presence of a specific pressure difference. It is expressed in units of cubic feet per minute per square foot of window area (cfm/sq ft) or cubic feet per minute per foot of window perimeter length (cfm/ft). The lower a window's air leakage rating, the better its airtightness.

INSULATING GLAZING UNIT. In general, two or more panes of glass separated by air spaces within an opening to improve insulation against heat transfer and/or sound transmission. In factory-made insulating glazing units, the air between the glass sheets is thoroughly dried and the space is sealed airtight, eliminating possible condensation and providing superior insulating properties.

GAS FILL. A gas other than air, usually argon or krypton, placed between window or skylight glazing panes to reduce the U factor by suppressing conduction and convection.

LIGHT-TO-SOLAR-GAIN RATIO. A measure of the ability of a glazing to provide light without excessive solar heat gain. It is the ratio between the visible transmittance of a glazing and its solar heat gain coefficient. Abbreviated LSG.

LOW CONDUCTANCE SPACERS. An assembly of materials designed to reduce heat transfer at the edge of an insulating window. Spacers are placed between the panes of glass in a double- or triple-glazed window.

LOW-EMITTANCE (LOW-E) COATING. Microscopically thin, virtually invisible, metal or metallic oxide layers deposited on a window or skylight glazing surface primarily to reduce the U factor by suppressing radiative heat flow. A typical type of low-E coating is transparent to the solar spectrum (visible light and short-wave infrared radiation) and reflective of long-wave infrared radiation.

R VALUE. A measure of the resistance of a glazing material or fenestration assembly to heat flow. It is the inverse of the U factor (R = 1/U) and is expressed in units of hr-sq ft-F/Btu. A high-R-value window has a greater resistance to heat flow and a higher insulating value than one with a low R value.

REFLECTANCE. The ratio of reflected radiant energy to incident radiant energy.

SHADING COEFFICIENT (SC). A measure of the ability of a window or skylight to transmit solar heat, relative to that ability for ⅛ in (6.35 mm) clear, double-strength, single glass. It is being phased out in favor of the solar heat gain coefficient, and is approximately equal to the SHGC multiplied by 1.15. It is expressed as a number without units between 0 and 1. The lower a window's solar heat gain coefficient or shading coefficient, the less solar heat it transmits, and the greater is its shading ability.

SOLAR HEAT GAIN COEFFICIENT (SHGC). The fraction of incident solar radiation admitted through a window or skylight, both directly transmitted, and absorbed and subsequently released inward. The solar heat gain coefficient has replaced the shading coefficient as the standard indicator of a window's shading ability. It is expressed as a number between 0 and 1. The lower a window's solar heat gain coefficient, the less solar heat it transmits, and the greater its shading ability. SHGC can be expressed in terms of the glass alone or can refer to the entire window assembly.

SPECTRALLY SELECTIVE GLAZING. A coated or tinted glazing with optical properties that are transparent to some wavelengths of energy and reflective to others. Typical spectrally selective coatings are transparent to visible light and reflect short-wave and long-wave infrared radiation. Usually the term *spectrally selective* is applied to glazing that reduces heat gain while providing substantial daylight.

SUPERWINDOW. A window with a very low U factor, typically less than 0.15, achieved through the use of multiple glazing, low-E coatings, and gas fills.

TRANSMITTANCE. The percentage of radiation that can pass through glazing. Transmittance can be defined for different types of light or energy, that is, visible light transmittance, UV transmittance, or total solar energy transmittance.

U FACTOR (U VALUE). A measure of the rate of non-solar heat loss or gain through a material or assembly. It is expressed in units of Btu/hr-sq ft-F (W/sq m-°C). Values are normally given for NFRC/ASHRAE winter conditions of 0F (18°C) outdoor temperature, 70F (21°C) indoor temperature, 15 mph wind, and no solar load. The U factor may be expressed for the glass alone or the entire window, which includes the effect of the frame and the spacer materials. The lower the U factor, the greater a window's resistance to heat flow and the better its insulating value.

VISIBLE TRANSMITTANCE (VT). The percentage or fraction of the visible spectrum (380 to 720 nanometers) weighted by the sensitivity of the *eye,* that is transmitted through glazing.

is used as a base case for this climate. Annual energy use and peak demand per square foot of perimeter floor area are shown for each set of conditions being compared. Fig. 10 pertains only to a south-facing perimeter zone (the area of a building within 15 ft of the exterior facade). The degree to which the perimeter zone contributes to overall building energy use and peak demand depends on the size, shape, and use of the whole building.

The windows in Fig. 10 are compared under two conditions: with and without daylighting controls. The results show that annual electricity use always declines by installing controls that dim or turn off electric lighting when there is sufficient daylight. With daylighting controls, across all sizes of unshaded Windows C-H there is an average reduction of 2.2 kWh/sf-yr (15 percent) compared to a zone without them. Lighting energy use falls to a greater degree as VT increases, while cooling energy use diminishes slightly because of reduced heat gain from the lights. For instance, lighting energy use associated with low-VT Window D does not decline significantly with controls; little light enters Window D, giving little opportunity to dim lights and save energy. With the other window cases, on the other hand, the higher the VT, the greater the lighting load reduction.

Heating energy use rises with daylighting controls, on average 0.47 kBtu/sf-yr (12 percent) compared to a non-daylit zone, but heating represents only about 3 percent of the total annual energy use (assuming an electricity-to-gas fuel ratio of 3 to 1), so this increase has an insignificant impact on the total perimeter zone performance in Houston. Window types with a very low SHGC and U factor, and a moderate VT, generally perform better (Windows F and H). With Window H, total annual energy use can be lower than an opaque insulated wall even for large windows.

Daylight controls also reduce peak electricity demand in south-facing perimeter zones. With daylighting controls and a large window area (WWR=0.60), there is an average reduction of 0.77 W/sf (12 percent) compared to a zone without them for Windows C–H. While all the energy use comparisons in this section suggest that daylight controls offer significant savings, there is a range of possible performance. ■

RESOURCES

Center for Sustainable Building Research
College of Architecture and Landscape Architecture
University of Minnesota
1425 University Avenue SE
Minneapolis, MN 55455

Efficient Windows Collaborative
Alliance to Save Energy
1200 18th Street, N.W., Suite 900
Washington, D.C. 20036
<www.efficientwindows.org>

ENERGY STAR Program
<www.energystar.gov>

Lawrence Berkeley National Laboratory (LBNL)
Building Technologies Department
Environmental Energy Technologies Division
Berkeley, CA 94720

National Fenestration Rating Council (NFRC)
1300 Spring Street, Suite 120
Silver Spring, MD 20910

RESFEN is a computer program for calculating the annual heating and cooling energy use and costs due to fenestration systems. RESFEN also calculates their contribution to peak heating and cooling loads. It is available from the NFRC at the address above.

RESFEN can be downloaded at:
<http://eande.lbl.gov/BTP/tools/index.html>

REFERENCES

Canadian Building Digest publication series, Division of Building Research, National Research Council of Canada, Ottawa, K1A OR6.

Carmody, John, Stephen Selkowitz, Dariush Arasteh, and Lisa Hershong, *Residential Windows: New Technologies and Energy Performance,* 2nd ed., W.W. Norton, New York, 2000.

Carmody, John, Stephen Selkowitz, Eleanor S. Lee, Dariush Arasteh, and Todd Willmert, *Window Systems for High-Performance Buildings,* W.W. Norton, New York, 2004.

Geller, H., and J. Thorne, *U.S. Department of Energy's Office of Building Technologies: Successful Initiatives of the 1990s,* American Council for an Energy-Efficient Economy, Washington, 1999.

Watson, Donald, and Kenneth Labs, *Climatic Building Design,* McGraw-Hill, New York, 1983, revised 1993.

Yellott, John I., "Fenestration and Heat Flow Through Windows" in *Energy Conservation through Building Design,* Donald Watson, ed., Architectural Record Books/McGraw-Hill, New York, 1979.

Donald Watson, editor

Summary

Solar control refers to the architectural design for sun shading and reflection, dimensioned to provide beneficial sunshine for passive heating,
for daylighting, and to minimize overheating. The earth-sun geometrical relationship is described. Solar angles, graphic methods, and applications of sun path charts are reviewed, with emphasis on practical aids
for design of shading devices. Resources for web-based design tools
and various sun study aids are listed.

Key words

altitude, azimuth, ecliptic, Equation of Time, gnomon, heliodon, shading
devices, shadow angles, solar angles, sun path diagrams, sun penetration

Photo: Alexander Purves

Solar and astronomical observatory. Jaipur, India *circa* 1710.

Solar control

1 FUNDAMENTALS

The two most important climatic factors that influence the thermal behavior of a building are air temperature and solar radiation. While winds and humidity also have an effect, solar
radiation can cause severe overheating in summer (in some cases, even
in winter), or can increase the air-conditioning load. Solar gain can be
beneficial in winter, reducing the heating requirement or perhaps eliminating the need for heating by using conventional forms of energy.
Daylighting design similarly requires understanding of solar geometry
and design for directed and reflected sunlighting. One of the first tasks
of a designer is to determine when passive solar heat input is desirable
for occupant comfort and when solar radiation is to be excluded. The
next step will then be to provide the appropriate solar control.

The best approach to solar control is some form of external shading
device, which blocks direct solar radiation before it reaches window
glass when solar gain is not desirable. It is easy to design a device that
would block out all sun penetration. Such a device would unduly restrict daylighting and perhaps view. With climate data available for
most locations, and calculation of external and internal heat loads, it
is possible to design sun shading that "exquisitely" admits sun when
it is beneficial for heating and to shade it when it is not, while also utilizing reflected sunlight for illumination.

A prerequisite of designing for solar control is to know the sun's position at any time of the year and then to relate it to the building.

The following overview provides the basis for understanding solar
geometry.

Heliocentric view: earth-sun relationship viewed from space

The earth is almost spherical in shape, some 7900 mi (12,700 km) in
diameter. It revolves around the sun in a slightly elliptical (almost circular) orbit (**Fig. 1**). The earth-sun distance is approximately 93 million mi (150 million km), varying between:

- 95 million mi (152 million km) at its farthest point, *aphelion*, on
  July 1, and

- 92 million mi (147 million km) at its nearest point, *perihelion*, on
  January 1.

The plane defined by the earth's revolution around the sun is referred
to as the *ecliptic*. The earth's axis of rotation is tilted 23.45° from
ecliptic plane. The angle between the earth's equator and the ecliptic
(or the earth-sun line) is the *declination* (DEC) and varies between
+23.45° on June 22 (northern solstice) and −23.45° on December 22
(southern solstice), shown in **Fig. 1a**. For practical purposes, ±23.5°
gives an acceptable precision. On equinox days (approximately
March 22 and September 22) the earth-sun line is coincident within
the plane of the equator, thus DEC = 0°. The annual variation of this
declination is shown by a sinusoidal curve in **Fig. 2**.

Credits: This article includes excerpts from Steven V. Szokolay "Solar Control" included in the CD-ROM accompanying this volume. Figs. 12, 14, 16, and
17, by Murray Milne and John S. Fisher, are from Givoni (1969) by permission of the publisher.

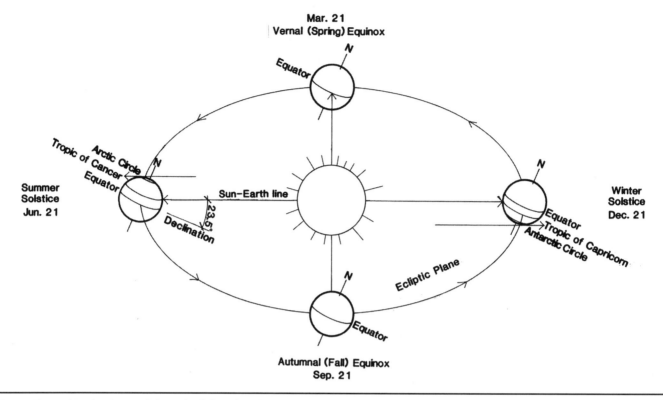

Fig. 1a. The earth's orbit. Sun-earth line orbit defines the solar ecliptic plane. (after Knowles 1967)

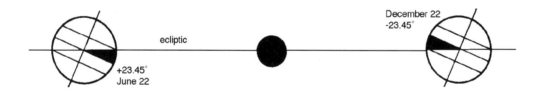

Fig. 1b. Section through ecliptic plane, the reference baseline for solar declination.

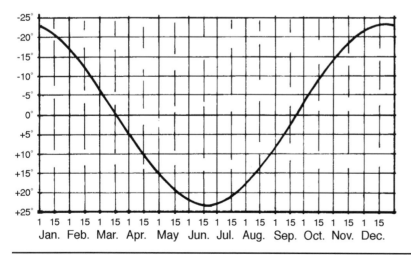

Fig. 2. Annual variation of declination (mean of the leap-year cycle).

The line we define as geographical latitude of any point on the earth's surface is the angle (from 0° at the equator to 90° at the poles) measured at the center of the earth between the plane of the equator and the line connecting with the surface point considered, as **Fig. 3a** indicates.

– Points having the same latitude form a latitude circle.

– The North Pole is +90°, the South Pole –90°, and the equator is 0° latitude.

– The extreme latitudes where the sun reaches directly overhead (the zenith) at midsummer are the tropics (**Fig. 3b**), such that:

  • LAT = +23.45° is the tropic of Cancer, and

  • LAT = –23.45° is the tropic of Capricorn.

– The arctic circles (at LAT = ±66.55°) mark the extreme positions where at midsummer the sun appears to be skirting just above the horizon all day and at midwinter the sun does not rise at all.

Lococentric view: sun viewed from earth

Figs. 4a to c depict a "solar cone" generated by the trace of the sun-earth line during one day, which takes on a different geometry on any given date (Knowles 1967). Given that from the earth's minuscule perspective, the sun rays are in effect parallel, the cones depicted in Figs. 4a and b are identical at any one time regardless of one's earth position. On two days of the year, spring or fall equinox, the "cone" is in fact a flat plane. Viewing the sun from the earth, the intersection of two geometries, the "solar cone" and an imagined sky dome hemisphere, crease the basis of sun path diagrams, depicted in **Figs. 5 and 6.**

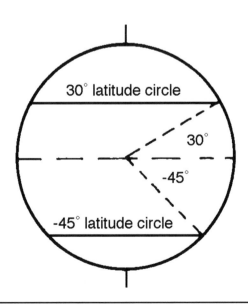

Fig. 3a. Geographical latitude.

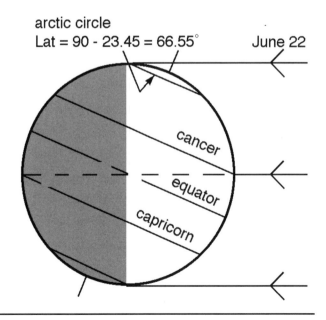

Fig. 3b. Definition of the tropics.

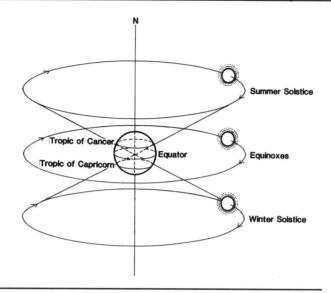

Fig. 4a. Theoretical "solar cones" derived by sun-earth line from center of earth. (after Knowles 1967)

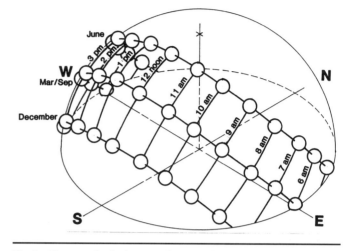

Fig. 5a. Theoretical "skydome" indicating solar position with reference to point on earth plane, varying with each latitude. (Watson 1983)

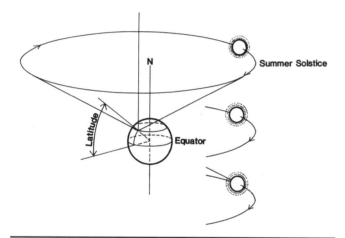

Fig. 4b. Theoretical "solar cone" derived by sun earth-line from single point (any position on earth). (after Knowles 1967)

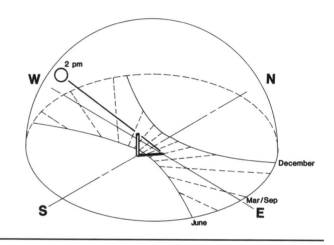

Fig. 5b. Gnomonic projection (also referred to as "flagpole" shadow) the tip of which traces the horizontal sun chart, varying with each latitude. (Watson 1983)

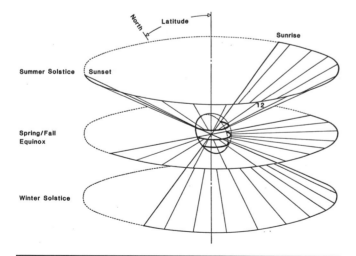

Fig. 4c. Intersection of "solar cones" with "skydome," a theoretical hemisphere of the sky as seen from any single point. (Watson 1983)

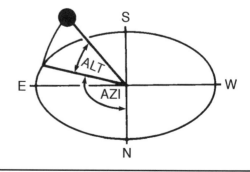

Fig. 6. Definition of solar position angles.

In solar control design, the earth (ground) is assumed to be flat and limited by the horizon circle. The sun's apparent position on this celestial dome is defined by the two angles, *altitude* and *azimuth*. These give the reference for terms useful for solar control and shading design, as follows:

- **Altitude** (*ALT*) is measured vertically, as the angle between the sun's direction and the horizon plane; in some texts this is referred to as "elevation."

- **Azimuth** (*AZI*) is the angle of position of the sun measured in the horizontal plane from north in a clockwise direction (thus east = 90°, south = 180°, west = 270°, while north can be 0° or 360°) also referred to as "bearing." Most references for solar angles (in the northern hemisphere) use 0° for south and have −90° for east and +90° for west, north being ±180°. Some in the southern hemisphere use the converse: north = 0°, going through east (+90°) to +180° for south and through west (−90°) to −180°. The 0–360° convention is the only one valid for any location.

- **Zenith angle** (*ZEN*) is measured between the sun's direction and the vertical and is the supplementary angle of the altitude: ZEN = 90° − ALT

- **Hour angle** (*HRA*) expresses the time of day with respect to the solar noon: it is the angular distance, measured within the plane of the sun's apparent path (**Fig. 7**) between the sun's position and its position at noon, i.e., the *solar meridian* (the plane of the local longitude, which contains the zenith and the sun's noon position).

As the hourly rotation of the earth is 360°/24h = 15°/h, HRA is 15° for each hour from solar noon: HRA = 15 × (h − 12)

where h = the hour considered (24-hour clock) so HRA is negative for the morning and positive for the afternoon hours

e.g., for 9 AM: HRA = 15 × (9 − 12) = −45°

but for 2 PM: HRA = 15 × (14 − 12) = +30°

- **Horizontal shading angle** (HSA) determines the performance of vertical shading devices (**Fig. 8**). HSA is defined as the difference between the *azimuth angle* of the sun and the *orientation azimuth* (ORI) of the building face (sometimes referred to as the *azimuth difference*): HSA = AZI − ORI. This will be positive if the sun is clockwise from the orientation, but negative when the sun is counterclockwise. **Fig. 9** indicates that different shading devices may have the same HSA, that is, they perform relatively equivalently.

- **Profile angle** is the angle of the sun's ray when viewed "in profile" to a wall, when the horizontal leg of the angle is perpendicular to the vertical building surface. The performance of horizontal shading devices is measured by the "*profile angle*" also called the *vertical shadow angle* (VSA) (**Fig. 10**).

- **Angle of incidence** (INC) is a common term describing the sun (beam) with respect to the specified surface, i.e., window, wall, or solar collector (**Fig. 11**). Both HSA and VSA can be used either to quantify the performance of a given shading device or to specify the required shading performance for a device yet to be designed, to be effective at given times. INC is the angle of the sun's ray striking a plane measured by reference to a line perpendicular to that plane. The incident angle is not needed for shadow construction but is the term of reference used in representing the amount of insolation received by building surface.

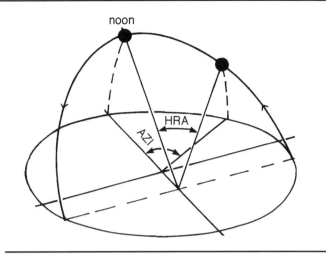

Fig. 7. Definition of hour angle (HRA).

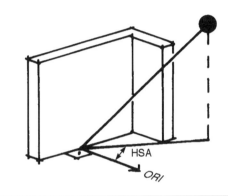

Fig. 8. Horizontal shadow angle (HSA).

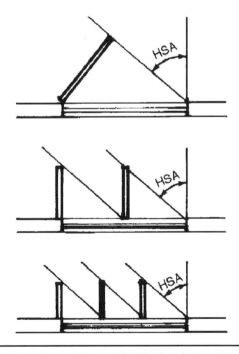

Fig. 9. Plan view of several "vertical fin" shading devices giving the same HSA.

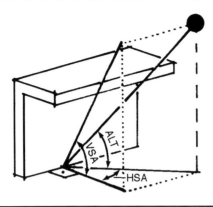

Fig. 10. Vertical shadow angle (VSA).

2 GRAPHIC METHODS OF SOLAR CONTROL DESIGN

The designer may use information from sun charts and tables to determine solar altitude and azimuth for most major latitudes, times of day and year, interpolating from tabulated values as appropriate for more site-specific analysis. Solar angle data are presented in a variety of formats, e.g., **Plate 1** indicates altitude and azimuth values for representative latitudes and times in graphic and in tabular form, whereas more complete monthly data are tabulated in **Plate 2**. The advantage of graphic representation is that it can be directly visualized on a site or building plan, such that a similar graphic could be usefully constructed by the designer for any assigned latitude of a specific design project. Longhand calculation methods for solar time and sun angles are given in Szokolay (1996), reprinted in full on the CD-ROM accompanying this volume. Applications and graphic methods using these data are described below.

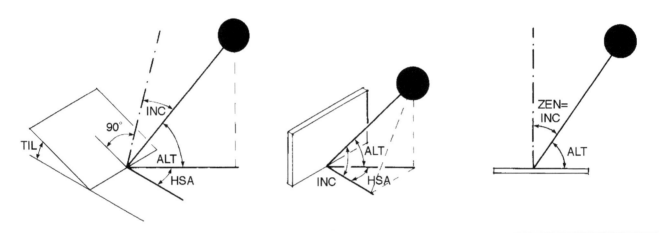

Fig. 11. Angle of incidence.

Box A—Field method of determining true north-south line

The method requires recording the sun's passage over a period of time on a sunlit day, at the very least for several hours from late morning to early afternoon. It is thus for the very patient and observant, perhaps ideally undertaken at both ends of a long lunch.

1 Drive a stake (gnomon) vertically in the ground in an open, flat area.
2 In the morning, scratch a mark and place a peg at the end of the staff's shadow.
3 Tie one end of a string loosely to the staff and at the other end of the string, with a marking tool affixed to the string.
4 Mark an arc on the ground from Point 2 well to the other side of the staff, facing north clockwise.
5 After a sufficient passage of time in the afternoon, return to observe and record the "touch point" (6) where the shadow of the gnomon transects the arc, placing another small marker stake at this intersection.
6 Draw a straight line between the two Points 2 and 6.
7 Find the halfway point along this line (Point 8) and draw a Line 9 from this point to the staff. (To be consistent with the geometric construction, Point 8 can be found as the intersection of any two

equal radius arcs centered on Points 2 and 6. The point of intersection when connected to the gnomon base will bisect Line 2–6 at its midpoint.)
8 Line 9 is the meridian line and indicates true north-south.

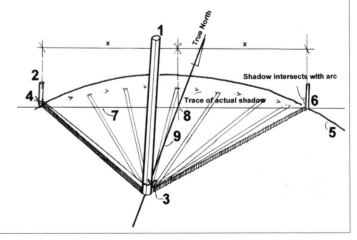

Horizontal sun path diagrams and "flagpole" method

Sun-clocks or sundials have been used for millennia. Vitruvius in *The Ten Books on Architecture* describes sundial construction applying "doctrines of Pythagoras" that is, classic geometry, based on the latitude of Rome (Morgan 1914). Solar geometry was understood by the ancients throughout the globe who devised means of determining cardinal dimensions (**Box A**) well before the compass, which needs to be corrected to correct for magnetic deviation for each locale (**Box B**).

There are two basic types of sun path diagrams: horizontal and vertical (there are also numerous tilted varieties). With a horizontal sundial, the direction of the shadow cast by the *gnomon* (a rod or pin) indicates time of day.

Conversely, if the direction of this shadow for a particular hour is known, then the direction of the sun (its AZI angle) can be predicted.

If the length of the gnomon is known, then the length of the shadow cast will indicate the solar altitude (ALT) angle. During the day the tip of the shadow will describe a curved line, which can be adopted as the sun path line for that day. (On the two equinox dates, that "curve" describes a straight line running due east-west at each and every point on the globe, the sun rising due east and setting due west and, on those two dates, is directly overhead at the equator.)

Figs. 12a and **b** represent the geometric derivation of horizontal sun path traces (the line traced by the end of the gnomon or "flagpole"). In Fig. 12, the term "asymptote" is adopted from analytic geometry to describe a line that continuously approaches a curve though infinitely extended would never reach it (Milne 1967). **Fig. 13** illustrates the characteristic patterns of sun path diagrams as a function of latitude.

Fig. 14 describes a simple method for casting shadows of any complex three-dimensional object for any orientation, altitude, and time of day. Each point in the plan can be cast graphically with protractor angle, using values interpolated as appropriate either from tabulated values, or read from a sun path diagram. The "flagpole method" (after Givoni 1969) can be useful in constructing the shadow cast by a complex object for any specified date and time. As an example, **Fig. 15** shows the plan and elevation of a small office block, located at LAT = 30°.

To construct the shadow cast on November 3, at 08:00 h.

1   The solar position angles have been read from the sun path diagram: AZI = 140° and ALT = 40°.

2   Imagine a flagpole located at each of the points 1 and 2. Draw the direction of shadow cast at both points by the sun at 140° (towards 140 + 180 = 320°).

3   Draw a line perpendicular to this direction at both flagpole points, to a length corresponding to the "flagpole" heights (6 m and 18 m respectively).

4   From the tip of these, draw a line to the ALT angle, and where this intersects the direction-line, it will mark the length of shadow.

5   Given the two corners of the shadow cast, its outline can be completed by drawing parallel lines.

Box B—Magnetic deviation from True North

Compass direction may deviate significantly from the True North-South meridian.

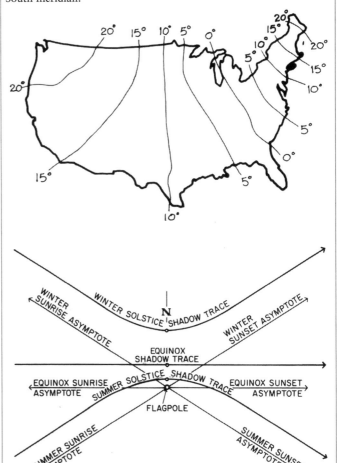

Fig. 12a. Shadows cast by a point in space (i.e., top of gnomon or "flagpole").

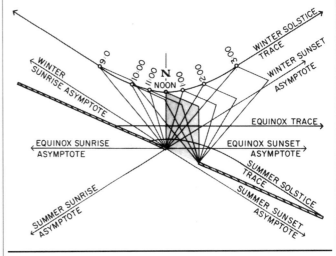

Fig. 12b. Corner of sunlight pattern follows the "flagpole" shadow trace. (Givoni 1976)

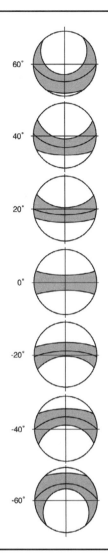

A sun path diagram for the latitude of the site can be used as an underlay, for a direct graphic reading of the azimuth angle. Horizontal sun paths for representative U.S. latitudes are given in **Plate 3** and are available in various formats on the web such as **Plate 4** (see References for web-based sources). Sun path diagrams for most latitudes (2 degree increments) are included in Burt (1969). A "Universal Sun Dial" is illustrated in **Plate 5.**

By using tabulated azimuth and attitude values or by graphic reference to the sun path diagrams, one can plot shadows cast on building interior or exteriors (**Figs. 16** and **17**). The principles of a vertical sun-

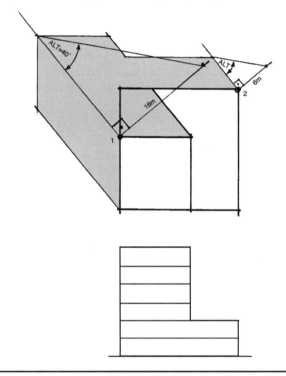

Fig. 13. The pattern of changing sun paths from the equator towards the poles.

Fig. 15. The flagpole method used for shadow casting.

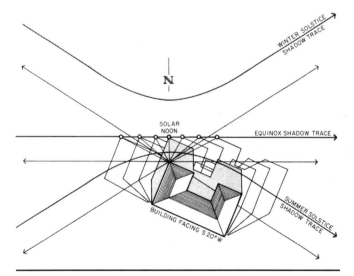

Fig. 14. Shadows cast by any complex three-dimensional object following the "flagpole" shadow trace. (Givoni 1976)

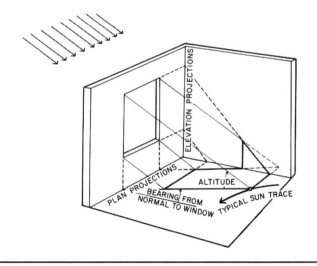

Fig. 16. Shadows cast on vertical surfaces found by projection from the horizontal. (Givoni 1976)

dial are similar, except that the gnomon is protruding horizontally from a vertical plane onto which the shadow is cast. Note in Fig. 17 that the "straight line" shadow cast on the equinox dates remains in only one angle.

Vertical sun path diagrams

The geometric basis of vertical sun path diagrams is illustrated in **Fig. 18.** The lines of latitude of the "sky dome" hemisphere are projected onto a cylinder (**Fig. 18a**) similar to the Mercator map projection. The altitude circles are compressed towards the zenith and the horizontal dimensions, correct at the horizon, are stretched increasingly with the altitude: the zenith point becomes a line of the same length as the horizon circle. This compression would normally place too much data at the top of the projected graph. This is corrected as depicted in **Fig. 18b,** creating an equidistant vertical chart, not a projection per se but a calculated construct. The advantage of vertical sun path diagrams is to more closely visualize solar position viewed from a window or wall plane, a convenience appropriate for conceptualizing sun availability or sun shading, adopted among others by Mazria (**Fig. 18c**).

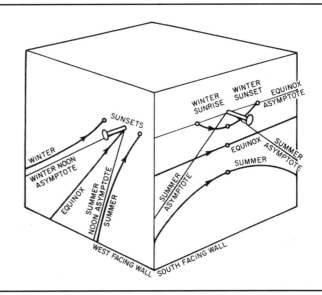

Fig. 17. Shadows cast by the head of a nail show the sun's motion relative to a vertical surface. (Givoni 1976)

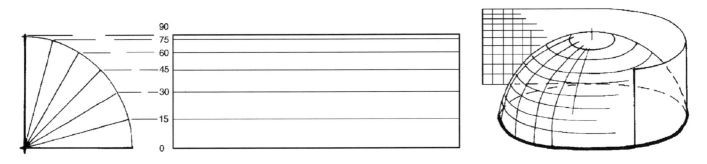

Fig. 18a. Cylindrical projection.

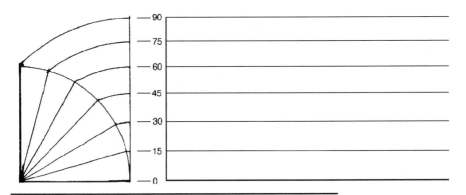

Fig. 18b. Improved construction to graph altitudes equally.

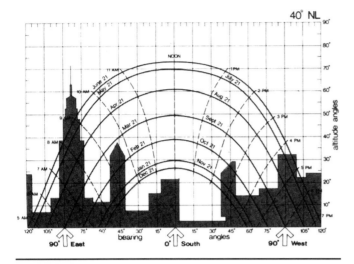

Fig. 18c. Equidistant vertical sun path diagram, overlaid on window view to show time and date of sunlight not blocked by structures on the horizon. (Mazria 1979)

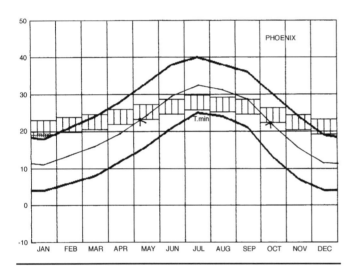

Fig. 19. Temperature plot and comfort band for Phoenix, Arizona.

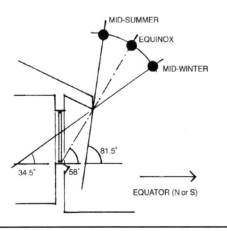

Fig. 20. Automatic seasonal adjustment: equator-facing window.

Initial sketch and preliminary design

Solar radiation falling on a window consists of three components: *beam* (direct) radiation, *diffuse* (sky) radiation, and *reflected* radiation (from ground, adjacent walls, other buildings). External shading devices can eliminate the direct beam component, normally the largest, while also serving to reduce the diffuse and reflected components. The solar orientation of the building is very important, especially so if at some part of the year solar heat input is desirable. This period of desirable passive solar heating should be determined by reference to bioclimatic data for a given location, but also accounting for internal gains of occupancy. Then the overheated period should also be determined, i.e., the dates when solar radiation should be excluded.

At the sketch design stage and for low internal gain buildings such as houses, this can be taken as the time when the mean temperature is higher than the lower comfort limit, as indicated for Phoenix in **Fig. 19**. The more exact daily temperature profile of the building can be considered at a later stage to ascertain the hours when shading is necessary. An equatorial orientation (facing the equator) is the only one where a fixed horizontal shading device can give an automatic seasonal adjustment: exclude the summer (high angle) sun, but allow sun penetration in winter, when the sun is at a low angle (**Fig. 20**).

A general principle of sun shading design proposed by Olgyay and Olgyay (1957) is that for an equator-facing (or near equator facing) window, a horizontal device gives a better performance, but for a window of east or west (or near east or west) orientation a vertical device may be more effective.

A useful starting point is to determine the solar altitude at the two equinox dates, that is, 90°-LAT (the latitude of the location) (**Fig. 21**). From this line, the sun "moves" 23.5° up at midsummer and 23.5° down at midwinter. As noted above, on the equinoxes, the Vertical Solar Angle (VSA) for an equator-facing window will be constant for the entire day. If this line were adopted initially as the VSA for a sun control device, then the sun would be fully excluded for the summer half-year and it would penetrate to an increasing extent after the autumn equinox, reaching its maximum at the winter solstice. This very preliminary assumption may be sufficient for "first pass" dimensioning of overhangs and can be adjusted later when the design is being refined.

Box C offers additional approximate "rule of thumbs" for "first pass" sketch assumptions of window shade dimensions for other orientations.

Shading masks

Developed by Olgyay and Olgyay (1957), a useful basis for design and evaluation of shading devices is indicated by shading masks. A shading mask is a graphic "calendar" of when shading is desired for a given project and site, depicted as an overlay at the same scale and size as the applicable sun path diagram.

A shading mask for any given project and site can be constructed with the aid of the shadow angle protractor (**Fig. 22**). The protractor is a semicircular transparent sheet, of the same diameter as the sun path diagram. It has a set of radial lines, marked from 0 at the center to −90° anticlockwise and +90° clockwise. This protractor is the HSA scale. It also has a set of arc lines, converging to the left and right corners and spaced at the centerline the same as the corresponding altitude circles of the sun path diagram. These indicate the VSA. Both scales in Fig. 22 are at 15° spacing.

Box C—Approximating shade design dimensions

Roughly appropriate overhang dimension W can be calculated by selecting the shade line factor (slf) from *TABLE* a and inserting in the formula:

Desirable overhang $W = \dfrac{H}{SLF}$

TABLE a

Shade Line Factors

Window faces	Latitude in degrees						
	25	30	35	40	45	50	55
East	.8	.8	.8	.8	.8	.8	.8
Southeast	1.9	1.6	1.4	1.3	1.1	1.0	0.9
South	10.1	5.4	3.6	2.6	2.0	1.7	1.4
Southwest	1.9	1.6	1.4	1.3	1.1	1.0	0.8
West	0.8	0.8	0.8	0.8	0.8	0.8	0.8

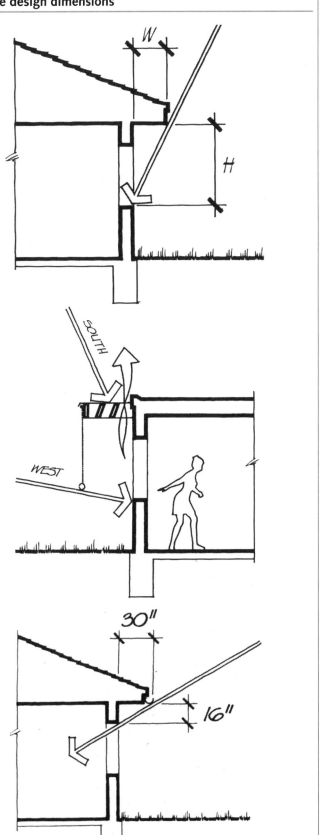

Louvered overhang is desirable because it allows hot air to escape, rather than trapping it under a hot soffit. Louvers can be field-built, prefabricated or purchased as "bolt on" items.

Support structure can be cantilevered ends of joists. Rafters or outriggers framework can also be supported on struts from below, or suspended on cable ties anchored above.

Louvers themselves may be wood or metal; fabrics are also a possibility.

The Small Homes Council of the University of Illinois suggests that a 30/16 overhang is a good solution for south elevations from 30° to 50° latitude—for conventional window sill and ceiling heights or similar proportions.

A standard overhang may be justified on the basis that as latitude increases, the duration of the overheated season decreases. So, although solar altitude decreases, the overhang need not increase.

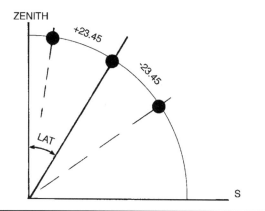

Fig. 21. Equinox sun position.

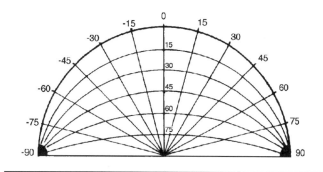

Fig. 22. The shadow angle protractor.

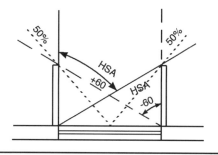

Fig. 23. Plan view of Hour Solar Angle (HSA) of a pair of vertical fins.

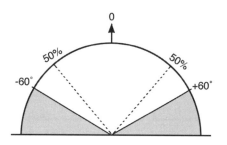

Fig. 24. Shading mask of the fins shown in Fig. 23.

A vertical shading device will give a sectoral-shaped shading mask. The pair of vertical fins shown in plan in **Fig. 23** will produce the shading mask shown in profile in **Fig. 24**. Dotted lines drawn to the center point of the window indicate 50 percent shading, represented by the dotted lines drawn parallel with these on the shading mask. This shading mask can then be superimposed on the sun path diagram, with its centerline corresponding to the orientation of the window, which will be shaded at the times covered by the shading mask (**Fig. 25**). The baseline of the protractor represents the line of building elevation examined. At any times below that, the sun would be behind the building, the elevation would be in shade. Note that the sun path lines (calendar dates) and the hour lines form a date and hour coordinate system, representing the year. The only unusual feature is that the lines are not straight, but curved.

The canopy above a window (one kind of horizontal shading device) shown in **Fig. 26** gives a vertical shadow angle (VSA) of 60°. The shading mask of this will be segmental in shape, bounded by the 60° arc, as indicated by **Fig. 27**. The dotted line drawn to the mid-height point of the window and the corresponding dotted arc of the shading mask indicate 50 percent shading. **Fig. 28** shows this shading mask superimposed on the sun path diagram.

Use of the protractor with the sun path diagram allows viewing the overall pattern of shading effects and thus the making of informed decisions. For example, once a HSA is determined for a given location and orientation, several options, equally effective in shading but of different dimension, may be quickly considered (**Fig. 29**). When a design has been adopted, it is helpful to do physical or computer modeling, and fairly easy to do a few calculations (Szokolay 1997) to verify the graphic results and determine final dimensions.

The above analyses can be executed with the *Solar Angle Calculator,* copyright of Libbey-Owens-Ford, now Pilkington Industries. While perhaps more detailed than what one needs for sun angle analysis per se, the *Calculator* has additional overlays for graphic analysis daylighting (see web-based resources in References).

Shading devices

There are three basic types of external shading devices: horizontal, vertical, and eggcrate.

A horizontal device will always give a segmental-shaped shading mask, as shown in **Fig. 30**. Some subtypes, the last three being adjustable, include:

- eaves overhang

- canopy at window head or higher

- light-shelf designed to act also as a shade

- horizontal louvers (sun-breaks or *brise-soleil*) with straight or tilted blades

- jalousie shutters

- awnings (canvas, plastic, etc.)

- combinations, e.g., a canopy with slats suspended at its edge

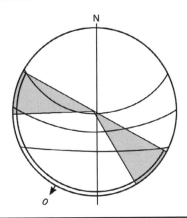

Fig. 25. Shading mask superimposed on the sun path diagram for Azimuth Orientation (ORI) = 210°.

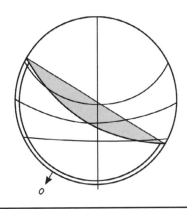

Fig. 28. Shading mask superimposed on the sun path diagram.

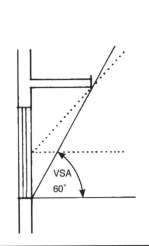

Fig. 26. Wall cross section view of Vertical Solar Angle (VSA) of a horizontal shading device: a canopy.

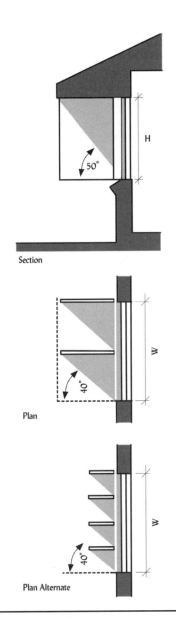

Fig. 29. Section and plan of window.

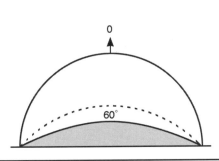

Fig. 27. Shading mask of the canopy shown in Fig. 38.

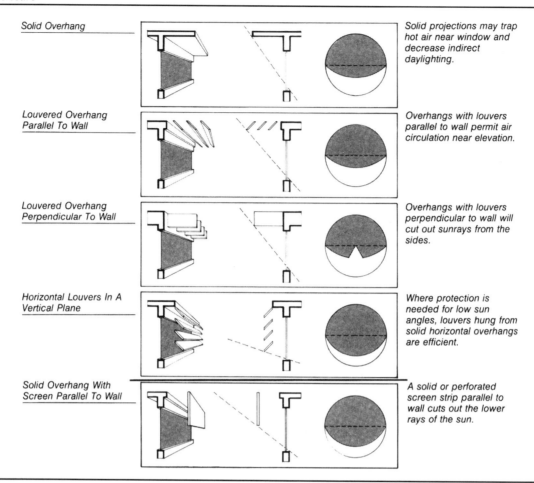

Fig. 30. Horizontal shading devices and representative shading masks.

Solid Overhang — Solid projections may trap hot air near window and decrease indirect daylighting.

Louvered Overhang Parallel To Wall — Overhangs with louvers parallel to wall permit air circulation near elevation.

Louvered Overhang Perpendicular To Wall — Overhangs with louvers perpendicular to wall will cut out sunrays from the sides.

Horizontal Louvers In A Vertical Plane — Where protection is needed for low sun angles, louvers hung from solid horizontal overhangs are efficient.

Solid Overhang With Screen Parallel To Wall — A solid or perforated screen strip parallel to wall cuts out the lower rays of the sun.

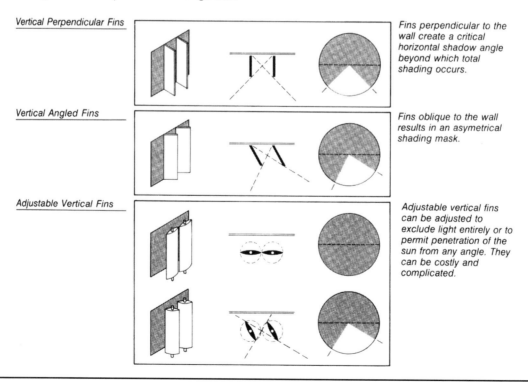

Fig. 31. Vertical shading devices and representative shading masks.

Vertical Perpendicular Fins — Fins perpendicular to the wall create a critical horizontal shadow angle beyond which total shading occurs.

Vertical Angled Fins — Fins oblique to the wall results in an asymetrical shading mask.

Adjustable Vertical Fins — Adjustable vertical fins can be adjusted to exclude light entirely or to permit penetration of the sun from any angle. They can be costly and complicated.

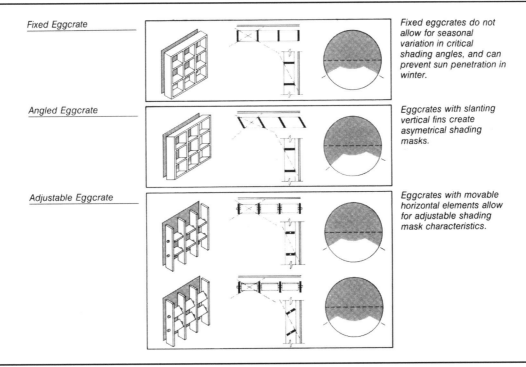

Fixed Eggcrate

Fixed eggcrates do not allow for seasonal variation in critical shading angles, and can prevent sun penetration in winter.

Angled Eggcrate

Eggcrates with slanting vertical fins create asymetrical shading masks.

Adjustable Eggcrate

Eggcrates with movable horizontal elements allow for adjustable shading mask characteristics.

Fig. 32. "Eggcrate" or combined shading devices and representative shading masks.

A vertical device will always give a sectoral-shaped shading mask, as shown in **Fig. 31,** and its performance is measured by the HSA. Some subtypes are:

- vertical fins or baffles

- vertical louvers, fixed

- vertical louvers, adjustable

Eggcrate (or combination) devices give a shading mask that is a composite of the above two, indicated in **Fig. 32.** Some subtypes are:

- grille blocks, rectangular

- grille blocks, polygonal

- fins, both horizontal and vertical (equal or unequal)

- vertical fixed fins with horizontal (adjustable) louvers

Overshadowing

The concept of shading masks can be extended to evaluate the over-shadowing effect of adjacent buildings or other obstructions. The technique is best explained by an example:

- *Question: For what period is point A of a proposed building over-shadowed by the neighboring existing building?*

Assume that the building is located at LAT = 42° and it is facing 135° (S/E). Take a tracing of the shadow angle protractor and transfer onto it the angles subtended by the obstruction at point A, both in plan and in section, as shown on **Fig. 33.** This gives the shading mask of that building for the point considered. This can be placed over the ap-

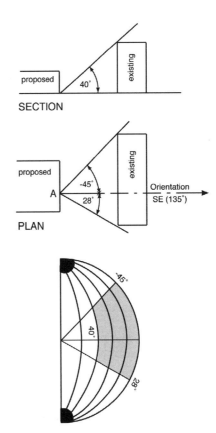

Fig. 33. Overshadowing by a building: construction of shading mask.

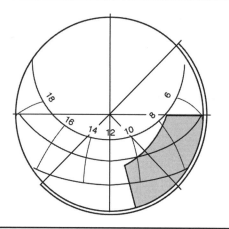

Fig. 34. Shading mask superimposed over sun path diagram.

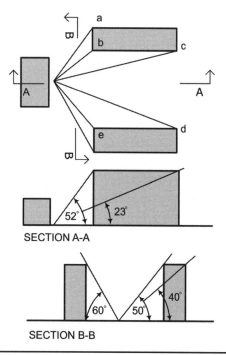

SECTION A-A

SECTION B-B

Fig. 35. Overshadowing by two buildings.

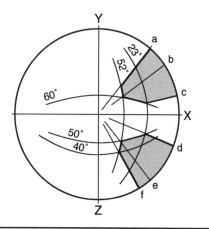

Fig. 36. Construction of shading mask.

propriate sun path diagram with the correct orientation (**Fig. 34**) and the period of overshadowing can be read. In this instance, look at the three cardinal dates:

June 22: no overshadowing

Equinoxes: shade from sunrise to 10:00 AM

December 22: shade from sunrise to about 10:45 AM

Fig. 35 shows a more complex situation, wherein two existing buildings can cast a shadow over the point considered. To construct a shading mask: for horizontal angles draw radial lines parallel to those drawn on plan to the edges of the building. The altitudes measured from section are taken as the VSAs: use the shadow angle protractor so that its centerline is in the plane of the section. For example, direction X for section A-A (mark the 52° and 23° VSA arcs), for section BB; direction Y for the upper block and direction Z for the lower one. **Fig. 36** depicts the construction of the shading mask.

The technique can also be used for a site survey: to plot all obstructing objects that may overshadow a selected point of the site. **Fig. 37** shows plan and section of the site with existing buildings, and **Fig. 38** explains the construction of the shading mask. This mask can then be laid over the appropriate sun path diagram and the period of overshadowing can be read, as indicated by **Fig. 39**. If a full-field camera with a 180° lens were to be placed at point A, pointing vertically upwards, the photo produced would be similar to this shading mask. A set of sun path diagrams may be adapted for use as overlays to such photos.

3 SUN-SIMULATORS FOR MODEL STUDIES

While computer-based tools for sun simulation are available, physical modeling has the advantages of easy use as part of the quick design and "mock-up" style of many designers.

Many ingenious heliodon devices have been developed to simulate the solar geometry and allow the study of shading with the use of physical models. These devices are useful as teaching tools in schools and in professional practice for conceptualizing design. They are also very helpful to demonstrate the shading performance on a model, possibly by photographs of the model with shadows cast on different dates and times. Such photos can be useful in some controversial building permit applications, and for presentation to clients or court cases.

Heliodon devices for indoor use employ a lamp to simulate the sun in order to provide laboratory conditions for very careful and controlled study. A small light source gives a divergent beam at the model, resulting in shadows of parallel edges becoming divergent. This effect can be reduced by increasing the lamp-to-model distance and/or by using a large diameter light source. The device must allow three sets of adjustments:

1. geographical latitude

2. calendar date

3. time of day.

First developed at Building Research Station UK in 1932, the heliodon consists of a tile table for the study model, which tilts to simulate the

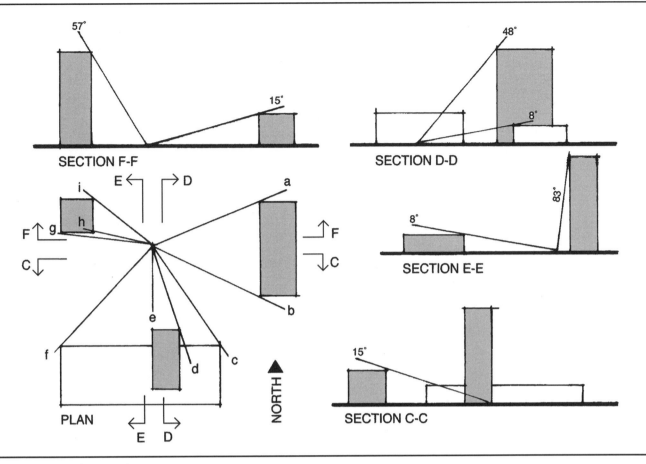

Fig. 37. Site survey: relevant angles.

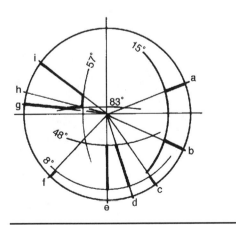

Fig. 38. Construction of shading mask.

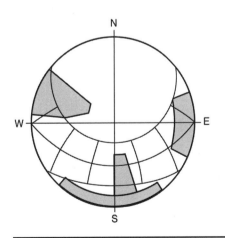

Fig. 39. Shading mask over sun paths.

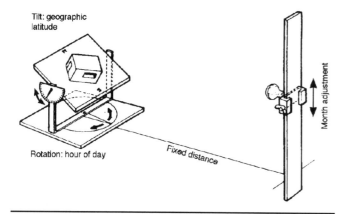

Fig. 40. A simple modeling set-up. (Building Research Station UK)

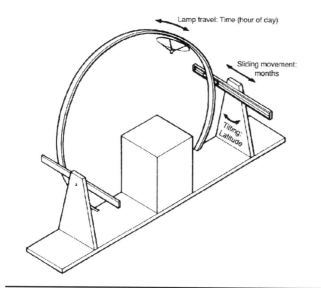

Fig. 41. Solar scope. (Polytechnic of Central London)

latitude and rotates to give the time of day (**Fig. 40**). The sun lamp is attached to a slider on a vertical rail at a known distance: the topmost position for summer solstice and the lowest position for midwinter. Positioning the lamp level with the model simulates the equinoxes. This approach has the advantage of simplicity and can be stored and easily set up for indoor model studies. A disadvantage is that as a "fixed sun/moving earth" heliodon, the model has to be moved for each solar position and does not offer the designer the intuitive clarity or dynamic of a "fixed earth—moving sun" heliodon, a limitation that has lead to development of the heliodons illustrated below.

Research applications require more accuracy and convenience of change of light position. The Solarscope developed in 1968 at the (then) Polytechnic of Central London is an effective educational tool: the arc (¼ circle) rail describes the sun's path for the given day (**Fig. 41**). A motorized carriage travels on this rail from sunrise to sunset, on which a 26 in (650 mm) diameter mirror is mounted, with a small high intensity lamp at its focal point. A similar device was constructed about the same time by Professor Ralph Knowles at the University of Southern California.

Several models have been developed for prospective commercial distribution to schools and practitioners, offering a moving sun-fixed earth heliodon (**Figs. 42 and 43**).

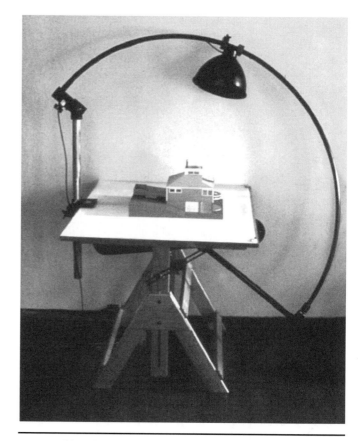

Fig. 42. Table Heliodon. Designed in 1984 by Van Altena/Olenik/Watson, Yale University. The Sunlight heliodon is a small table model that is demountable while being astronomically correct. Manually operated, one lamp powered by slide projector bulb, adjustable to all latitudes and times of the year. Sweep of arc simulates one day.

To overcome the challenge of providing bright light with parallel rays with electric light indoors is to undertake the modeling exercise out of doors on a sunlit day, positioning a tilt table and model base with a gnomon (**Fig. 44**). This has the advantage of exactly parallel light, bright enough for photographic documentation. The model is sequentially adjusted for each solar position selected for study, using the gnomon's shadow point to establish the date and hour. ■

Fig. 43. "Sun Emulater" Heliodon. Designed in 1998 by Norbert Lechner, Auburn University. Seven parallel hoops each supporting one lamp. Lamps are moved manually to simulate 21st day of each month at all latitudes. Stores in space 6 ft × 6 ft × 2ft. (High Precision Devices, Boulder, Colorado.)

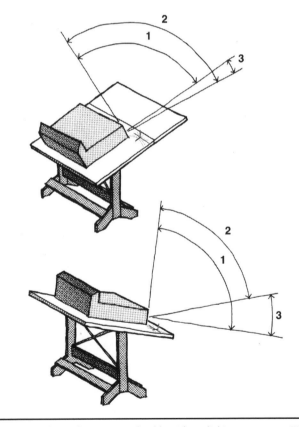

Fig. 44. Simple outdoor set-up: tilt table with sunlight as source, positioning the table and model with gnomon/sun path for date and time verisimilitude. The set-up is identical to daylight model testing. "**1**" indicates segment of sky normally "seen" by a window; "**2**" indicates sky segment actually "seen" by the model, as a subject of tilt; "**3**" indicates area where errors in daylight measurement may occur due to ground or other conditions at model test site.

Plate 1a. Representative solar angles

WINTER Dec. 22 **FALL** Sept. 23 / March 21 **SPRING** June 22 **SUMMER**

40° North Latitude

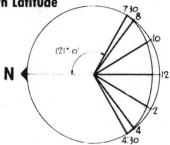 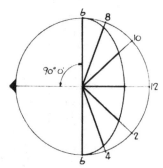 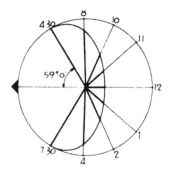

A.M.	P.M.	AZIMUTH	ALTITUDE
NOON		180°- 0'	26°-30'
10:00	2:00	150°-30'	20°-30'
8:00	4:00	127°- 0'	5°-30'
7:30	4:30	121°- 0'	0°- 0'

A.M.	P.M.	AZIMUTH	ALTITUDE
NOON		180°- 0'	50°- 0'
10:00	2:00	138°- 0'	41°-30'
8:00	4:00	110°-30'	22°-30'
6:00	6:00	90°- 0'	0°- 0'

A.M.	P.M.	AZIMUTH	ALTITUDE
NOON		180°- 0'	73°-30'
11:00	1:00	138°- 0'	69°- 0'
10:00	2:00	114°- 0'	60°- 0'
8:00	4:00	89°- 0'	37°-30'
4:30	7:30	59°- 0'	0°- 0'

45° North Latitude

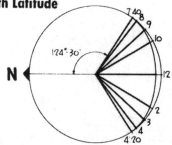 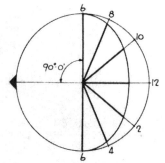 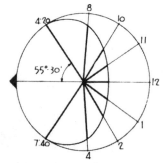

A.M.	P.M.	AZIMUTH	ALTITUDE
NOON		180°- 0'	21°-30'
10:00	2:00	151°-30'	16°- 0'
9:00	3:00	139°- 0'	10°- 0'
8:00	4:00	127°-30'	2°-30'
7:40	4:20	124°-30'	0°- 0'

A.M.	P.M.	AZIMUTH	ALTITUDE
NOON		180°- 0'	45°- 0'
10:00	2:00	141°- 0'	38°- 0'
8:00	4:00	112°- 0'	20°-30'
6:00	6:00	90°- 0'	0°- 0'

A.M.	P.M.	AZIMUTH	ALTITUDE
NOON		180°- 0'	68°-30'
11:00	1:00	145°-30'	65°-30'
10:00	2:00	121°-30'	57°-30'
8:00	4:00	93°- 0'	37°-30'
4:20	7:40	55°-30'	0°- 0'

50° North Latitude

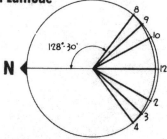 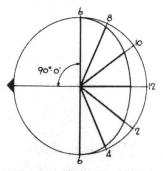 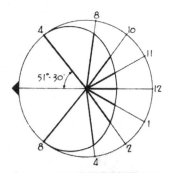

A.M.	P.M.	AZIMUTH	ALTITUDE
NOON		180°- 0'	16°-30'
10:00	2:00	152°- 0'	12°- 0'
9:00	3:00	139°-30'	6°-30'
8:00	4:00	128°-30'	0°- 0'

A.M.	P.M.	AZIMUTH	ALTITUDE
NOON		180°- 0'	40°- 0'
10:00	2:00	143°- 0'	34°- 0'
8:00	4:00	114°- 0'	18°-30'
6:00	6:00	90°- 0'	0°- 0'

A.M.	P.M.	AZIMUTH	ALTITUDE
NOON		180°- 0'	63°-30'
11:00	1:00	150°-30'	61°- 0'
10:00	2:00	127°-30'	54°-30'
8:00	4:00	97°- 0'	37°- 0'
4:00	8:00	51°-30'	0°- 0'

Plate 1b. Representative solar angles

WINTER Dec. 22 **FALL** Sept. 23 March 21 **SPRING** June 22 **SUMMER**

25° North Latitude

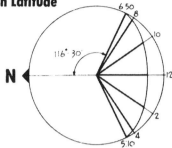

A M	PM	AZIMUTH	ALTITUDE
NOON		180°- 0'	41°- 30'
10:00	2:00	146°- 30'	33°- 30'
8:00	4:00	125°- 0'	14°- 30'
6:50	5:10	116°- 30'	0°- 0'

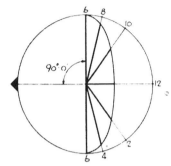

A M	PM	AZIMUTH	ALTITUDE
NOON		180°- 0'	65°- 0'
10:00	2:00	126°- 0'	51°- 30'
8:00	4:00	103°- 30'	27°- 0'
6:00	6:00	90°- 0'	0°- 0'

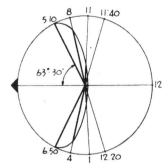

A M	PM	AZIMUTH	ALTITUDE
NOON		180°- 0'	88°- 30'
11:40	12:20	107°- 0'	85°- 0'
11:00	1:00	93°- 0'	76°- 0'
8:00	4:00	78°- 0'	35°- 30'
5:10	6:50	63°- 30'	0°- 0'

30° North Latitude

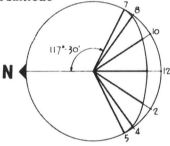

A M	PM	AZIMUTH	ALTITUDE
NOON		180°- 0'	36°- 30'
10:00	2:00	148°- 30'	29°- 0'
8:00	4:00	126°- 0'	11°- 30'
7:00	5:00	117°- 30'	0°- 0'

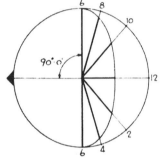

A M	PM	AZIMUTH	ALTITUDE
NOON		180°- 0'	60°- 0'
10:00	2:00	131°- 0'	48°- 30'
8:00	4:00	106°- 0'	25°- 30'
6:00	6:00	90°- 0'	0°- 0'

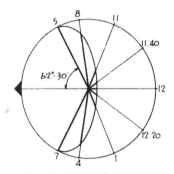

A M	PM	AZIMUTH	ALTITUDE
NOON		180°- 0'	83°- 30'
11:40	12:20	144°- 30'	82°- 0'
11:00	1:00	112°- 30'	75°- 0'
8:00	4:00	81°- 30'	36°- 30'
5:00	7:00	62°- 30'	0°- 0'

35° North Latitude

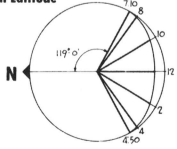

A M	PM	AZIMUTH	ALTITUDE
NOON		180°- 0'	31°- 30'
10:00	2:00	149°- 30'	25°- 0'
8:00	4:00	126°- 30'	8°- 30'
7:10	4:50	119°- 0'	0°- 0'

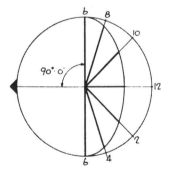

A M	PM	AZIMUTH	ALTITUDE
NOON		180°- 0'	55°- 0'
10:00	2:00	135°- 0'	45°- 0'
8:00	4:00	108°- 30'	24°- 0'
6:00	6:00	90°- 0'	0°- 0'

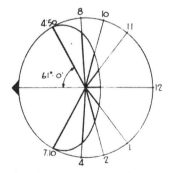

A M	PM	AZIMUTH	ALTITUDE
NOON		180°- 0'	78°- 30'
11:00	1:00	127°- 30'	72°- 30'
10:00	2:00	105°- 30'	61°- 0'
8:00	4:00	85°- 30'	37°- 0'
4:50	7:10	61°- 0'	0°- 0'

Plate 2. Tabulated values

Date	Solar Time AM	Solar Time PM	24 DEGREES N (Solar Position) ALT	24 AZM	32 DEGREES N ALT	32 AZM	40 DEGREES N ALT	40 AZM	48 DEGREES N ALT	48 AZM	56 DEGREES N ALT	56 AZM	64 DEGREES N ALT	64 AZM
Jan 21	7	5	4.8	65.6	1.4	65.2	–	–	–	–	–	–	–	–
	8	4	16.9	58.3	12.5	56.5	8.1	55.3	3.5	54.6	–	–	–	–
	9	3	27.9	48.8	22.5	46.0	16.8	44.0	11.0	42.6	5.0	41.8	–	–
	10	2	37.2	36.1	30.6	33.1	23.8	30.9	16.9	29.4	9.9	28.5	2.8	28.1
	11	1	43.6	19.6	36.1	17.5	28.4	16.0	20.7	15.1	12.9	14.5	5.2	14.1
	12		46.0	0.0	38.0	0.0	30.0	0.0	22.0	0.0	14.0	0.0	6.0	0.0
Feb 21	7	5	9.3	74.6	7.1	73.5	4.8	72.7	2.4	72.2	–	–	–	–
	8	4	22.3	67.2	19.0	64.4	15.4	62.2	11.6	60.5	7.6	59.4	3.4	58.7
	9	3	34.4	57.6	29.9	53.4	25.0	50.2	19.7	47.7	14.2	45.9	8.6	44.8
	10	2	45.1	44.2	39.1	39.4	32.8	35.9	26.2	33.3	19.4	31.5	12.6	30.3
	11	1	53.0	25.0	45.6	21.4	38.1	18.9	30.5	17.2	22.8	16.1	15.1	15.3
	12		56.0	0.0	48.0	0.0	40.0	0.0	32.0	0.0	24.0	0.0	16.0	0.0
Mar 21	7	5	13.7	83.8	12.7	81.9	11.4	80.2	10.0	78.7	8.3	77.5	6.5	76.5
	8	4	27.2	76.8	25.1	73.0	22.5	69.6	19.5	66.8	16.2	64.4	12.7	62.6
	9	3	40.2	67.9	36.8	62.1	32.8	57.3	28.2	53.4	23.3	50.3	18.1	48.1
	10	2	52.3	54.8	47.3	47.5	41.6	41.9	35.4	37.8	29.0	34.9	22.3	32.7
	11	1	61.9	33.4	55.0	26.8	47.7	22.6	40.3	19.8	32.7	17.9	25.1	16.6
	12		66.0	0.0	58.0	0.0	50.0	0.0	42.0	0.0	34.0	0.0	26.0	0.0
Apr 21	5	7	–	–	–	–	–	–	–	–	1.4	108.8	4.0	108.5
	6	6	4.7	100.6	6.1	99.9	7.4	98.9	8.6	97.8	9.6	96.5	10.4	95.1
	7	5	18.3	94.9	18.8	92.2	18.9	89.5	18.6	86.7	18.0	84.1	17.0	81.6
	8	4	32.0	89.0	31.5	84.0	30.3	79.3	28.5	74.9	26.1	70.9	23.3	67.5
	9	3	45.6	81.9	43.9	74.2	41.3	67.2	37.8	61.2	33.6	56.3	29.0	52.3
	10	2	59.0	71.8	55.7	60.3	51.2	51.4	45.8	44.6	39.9	39.7	33.5	36.0
	11	1	71.1	51.6	65.4	37.5	58.7	29.2	51.5	24.0	44.1	20.7	36.5	18.4
	12		77.6	0.0	69.6	0.0	61.6	0.0	53.6	0.0	45.6	0.0	37.6	0.0
May 21	4	8	–	–	–	–	–	–	–	–	1.2	125.5	5.8	125.1
	5	7	–	–	–	–	1.9	114.7	5.2	114.3	8.5	113.4	11.6	112.1
	6	6	8.0	108.4	10.4	107.2	12.7	105.6	14.7	103.7	16.5	101.5	17.9	99.1
	7	5	21.2	103.2	22.8	100.1	24.0	96.6	24.6	93.0	24.8	89.3	24.5	85.7
	8	4	34.6	98.5	35.4	92.9	35.4	87.2	34.7	81.6	33.1	76.3	30.9	71.5
	9	3	48.3	93.6	48.1	84.7	46.8	76.0	44.3	68.3	40.9	61.6	36.8	56.1
	10	2	62.0	87.7	60.6	73.3	57.5	60.9	53.0	51.3	47.6	44.2	41.6	38.9
	11	1	75.5	76.9	72.0	51.9	66.2	37.1	59.5	28.6	52.3	23.4	44.9	20.1
	12		86.0	0.0	78.0	0.0	70.0	0.0	62.0	0.0	54.0	0.0	46.0	0.0
Jun 21	4	8	–	–	–	–	–	–	–	–	4.2	127.2	9.0	126.4
	5	7	–	–	–	–	4.2	117.3	7.9	116.5	11.4	115.3	14.7	113.6
	6	6	9.3	111.6	12.2	110.2	14.8	108.4	17.2	106.2	19.3	103.6	21.0	100.8
	7	5	22.3	106.8	24.3	103.4	26.0	99.7	27.0	95.8	27.6	91.7	27.5	87.5
	8	4	35.5	102.6	36.9	96.8	37.4	90.7	37.1	84.6	35.9	78.8	34.0	73.3
	9	3	49.0	98.7	49.6	89.4	48.8	80.2	46.9	71.6	43.8	64.1	39.9	57.8
	10	2	62.6	95.0	62.2	79.7	59.8	65.8	55.8	54.8	50.7	46.4	44.9	40.4
	11	1	76.3	90.8	74.2	60.9	69.2	41.9	62.7	31.2	55.6	24.9	48.3	20.9
	12		89.4	0.0	81.5	0.0	73.5	0.0	65.5	0.0	57.5	0.0	49.5	0.0
Jul 21	4	8	–	–	–	–	–	–	–	–	1.7	125.8	6.4	125.3
	5	7	–	–	–	–	2.3	115.2	5.7	114.7	9.0	113.7	12.1	112.4

Date	Solar Time AM	Solar Time PM	24°N ALT	24°N AZM	32°N ALT	32°N AZM	40°N ALT	40°N AZM	48°N ALT	48°N AZM	56°N ALT	56°N AZM	64°N ALT	64°N AZM
	6	6	8.2	109.0	10.7	107.7	13.1	106.1	15.2	104.1	17.0	101.9	18.4	99.4
	7	5	21.4	103.8	23.1	100.6	24.3	97.2	25.1	93.5	25.3	89.7	25.0	86.0
	8	4	34.8	99.2	35.7	93.6	35.8	87.8	35.1	82.1	33.6	76.7	31.4	71.8
	9	3	48.4	94.5	48.4	85.5	47.2	76.7	44.8	68.8	41.4	62.0	37.3	56.3
	10	2	62.1	89.0	60.9	74.3	57.9	61.7	53.5	51.9	48.2	44.6	42.2	39.2
	11	1	75.7	79.2	72.4	53.3	66.7	37.9	60.1	29.0	52.9	23.7	45.4	20.2
	12		86.6	0.0	78.6	0.0	70.6	0.0	62.6	0.0	54.6	0.0	46.6	0.0
Aug 21	5	7	–	–	–	–	–	–	–	–	2.0	109.2	4.6	108.8
	6	6	5.0	101.3	6.5	100.5	7.9	99.5	9.1	98.3	10.2	97.0	11.0	95.5
	7	5	18.5	95.6	19.1	92.8	19.3	90.0	19.1	87.2	18.5	84.5	17.6	81.9
	8	4	32.2	89.7	31.8	84.7	30.7	79.9	29.0	75.4	26.7	71.3	23.9	67.8
	9	3	45.9	82.9	44.3	75.0	41.8	67.9	38.4	61.8	34.3	56.7	29.6	52.6
	10	2	59.3	73.0	56.1	61.3	51.7	52.1	46.4	45.1	40.5	40.0	34.2	36.2
	11	1	71.6	53.2	66.0	38.4	59.3	29.7	52.2	24.3	44.8	20.9	37.2	18.5
	12		78.3	0.0	70.3	0.0	62.3	0.0	54.3	0.0	46.3	0.0	38.3	0.0
Sep 21	7	5	13.7	83.8	12.7	81.9	11.4	80.2	10.0	78.7	8.3	77.5	6.5	76.5
	8	4	27.2	76.8	25.1	73.0	22.5	69.6	19.5	66.8	16.2	64.4	12.7	62.6
	9	3	40.2	67.9	36.8	62.1	32.8	57.3	28.2	53.4	23.3	50.3	18.1	48.1
	10	2	52.3	54.8	47.3	47.5	41.6	41.9	35.4	37.8	29.0	34.9	22.3	32.7
	11	1	61.9	33.4	55.0	26.8	47.7	22.6	40.3	19.8	32.7	17.9	25.1	16.6
	12		66.0	0.0	58.0	0.0	50.0	0.0	42.0	0.0	34.0	0.0	26.0	0.0
Oct 21	7	5	9.1	74.1	6.8	73.1	4.5	72.3	2.0	71.9	–	–	–	–
	8	4	22.0	66.7	18.7	64.0	15.0	61.9	11.2	60.2	7.1	59.1	3.0	58.5
	9	3	34.1	57.1	29.5	53.0	24.5	49.8	19.3	47.4	13.8	45.7	8.1	44.6
	10	2	44.7	43.8	38.7	39.1	32.4	35.6	25.7	33.1	19.0	31.3	12.1	30.2
	11	1	52.5	24.7	45.1	21.1	37.6	18.7	30.0	17.1	22.3	16.0	14.6	15.2
	12		55.5	0.0	47.5	0.0	39.5	0.0	31.5	0.0	23.5	0.0	15.5	0.0
Nov 21	7	5	4.9	65.8	1.5	65.4	–	–	–	–	–	–	–	–
	8	4	17.0	58.4	12.7	56.6	8.2	55.4	3.6	54.7	–	–	–	–
	9	3	28.0	48.9	22.6	46.1	17.0	44.1	11.2	42.7	5.2	41.9	–	–
	10	2	37.3	36.3	30.8	33.2	24.0	31.0	17.1	29.5	10.0	28.5	3.0	28.1
	11	1	43.8	19.7	36.2	17.6	28.6	16.1	20.9	15.1	13.1	14.5	5.4	14.2
	12		46.2	0.0	38.2	0.0	30.2	0.0	22.2	0.0	14.2	0.0	6.2	0.0
Dec 21	7	5	3.2	62.6	–	–	–	–	–	–	–	–	–	–
	8	4	14.9	55.3	10.3	53.8	5.5	53.0	–	–	–	–	–	–
	9	3	25.5	46.0	19.8	43.6	14.0	41.9	8.0	40.9	1.9	40.5	–	–
	10	2	34.3	33.7	27.6	31.2	20.7	29.4	13.6	28.2	6.6	27.5	–	–
	11	1	40.4	18.2	32.7	16.4	25.0	15.2	17.3	14.4	9.5	13.9	1.8	13.7
	12		42.6	0.0	34.6	0.0	26.6	0.0	18.6	0.0	10.6	0.0	2.6	0.0

Plate 3. Sun path diagrams

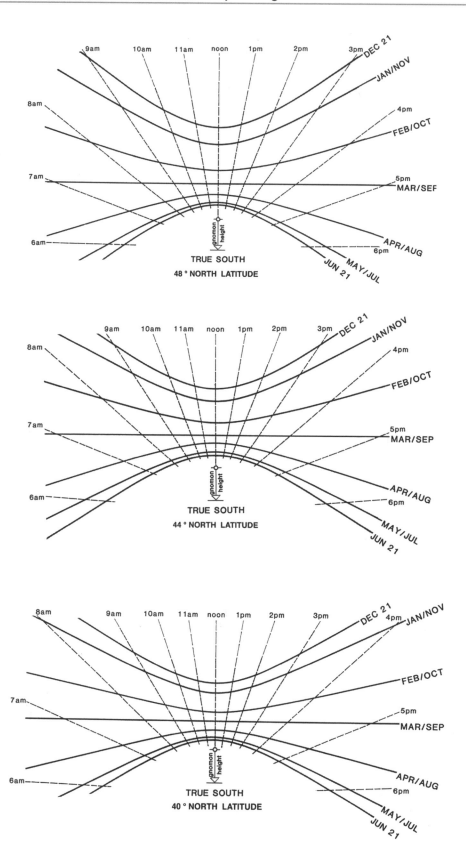

Plate 3. Sun path diagrams (continued)

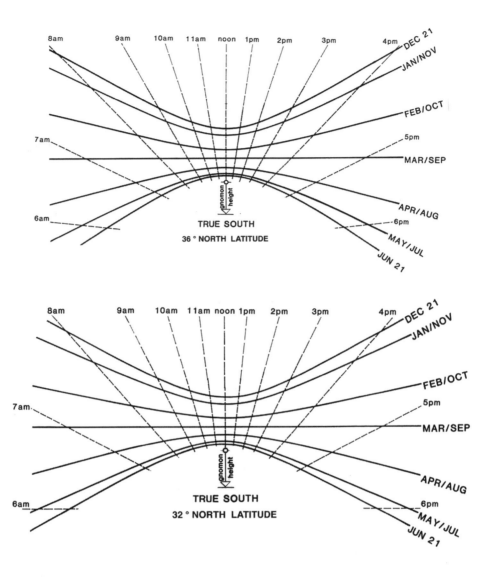

Plate 4. Sun path plot for Phoenix, Arizona, with bioclimatic data indicating time of day and year when shading is recommended or required (similar sun charts are plotted in this fashion for over 500 sites worldwide, available from Professor Murray Milne, Climate Consultant <http://www.aud.ucla.edu/energy-design-tools>)

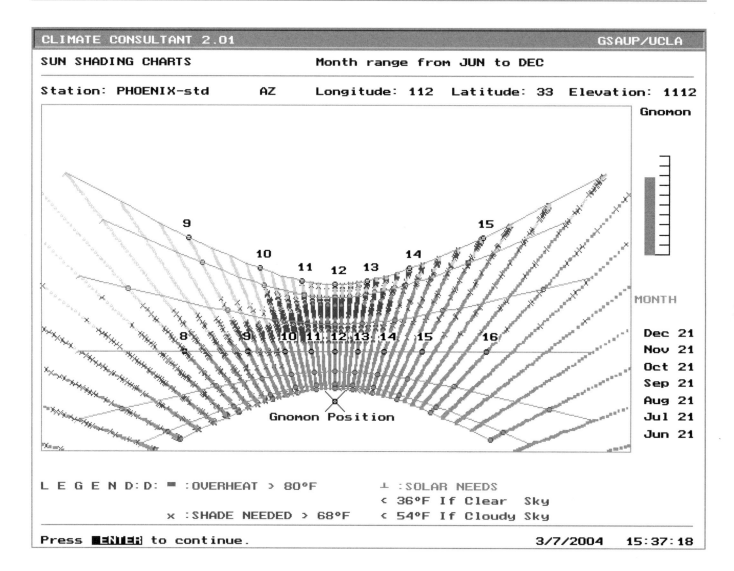

Plate 5. Universal sundial. (courtesy Pilkington Industries)

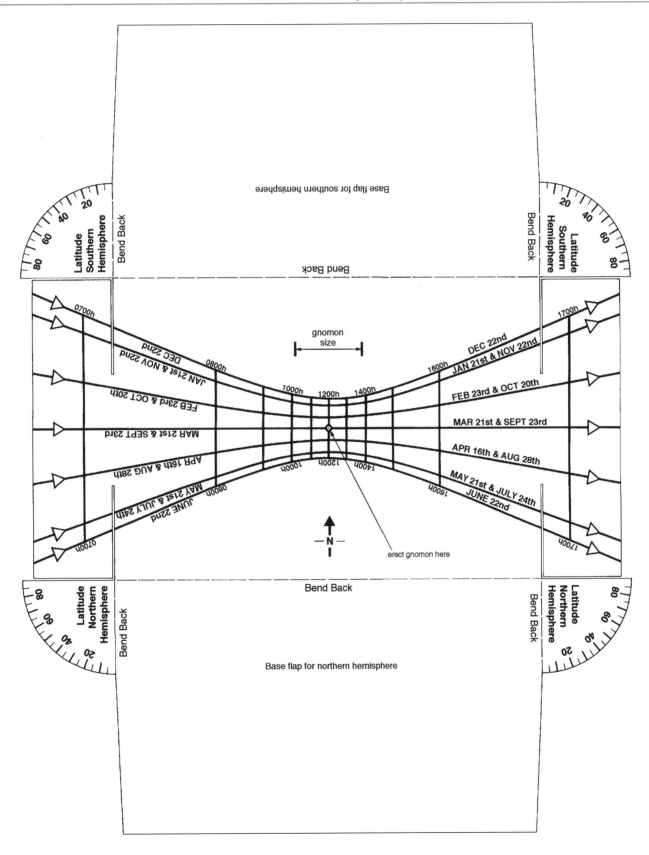

REFERENCES

Burt, W. et al., *Windows and Environment* (+ supplement), Pilkington Environmental Advisory Service / McCorquodale & Co., Newton-le-Willows, 1969.

Givoni, B., *Man, Climate and Architecture,* Applied Science Publishers, London, 1969.

Knowles, Ralph, "The Sun," Report for National Endowment for the Arts, University of Southern California, Los Angeles, 1967.

Libby-Owens-Ford (LOF) Glass Company, *Sun Angle Calculator,* Toledo, OH 43695. In 1986, the Libbey-Owens-Ford Company was acquired by Pilkington Industries, the largest global glass manufacturer, and is now referred to as Pilkington North America. In 2004, arrangements for distribution of the *Sun Angle Calculator* in North America were made with the Society of Building Science Educators, c/o Bruce Haglund, Department of Architecture, University of Idaho, PO Box 442451, Moscow, ID 83844. Prices on request.

Mazria, E., *The Passive Solar Energy Book,* Rodale Press, Emmaus, 1979.

Milne, Murray, "Sun Motion and Control of Incident Solar Radiation," in Givoni, 1969, *op. cit.*

Morgan, Morris Hicky, *Vitruvius: The Ten Books on Architecture,* Harvard University Press, Cambridge, 1914.

Olgyay, A., and V. Olgyay, *Solar Control and Shading Devices,* Princeton University Press, Princeton, 1957.

Smithsonian Institute, *Smithsonian Meteorological Tables: Sun-Path Diagrams,* Smithsonian Institute, Washington, (undated).

Szokolay, S. V., *Environmental Science Handbook for Architects,* Longman (Construction Press) and Wiley/Halsted Press, London and New York, 1980.

Szokolay, S. V., *Solar Geometry,* PLEA Note 1, PLEA/University of Queensland, Brisbane, 1996.

Watson, Donald, "Where the Sun Is: A Brief Review of Solar Geometry for Architectural Designers," in *Proceedings International Passive and Low Energy Architecture (PLEA) Conference,* Crete 1983, Pergamon Press, London, 1983.

Web-based resources for sun angle and solar control design

Climate Consultant (author: Professor Murray Milne, University of California, Los Angeles). Bioclimatic data and sun path diagrams. <www.aud.ucla.edu/energy-design-tools>

Designing with the Pilkington Sun Angle Calculator. Pilkington North America <http://pilkington.com/sunmanagement>. Also available along with other educational media from Society of Building Science Educators. <www.polaris.net/-snse/web/pnasac.html>

Suntool (author: Andrew Marsh, Western Australia University). Sun path and shading effectiveness. http://www.squl.com

Donald Baerman

Summary

Roofing must withstand the extremes of climate but also the subtle action of moisture, materials, and movement of a building over time. This chapter provides an overview to roofing, references and summary guidelines for responsible roofing design practices, along with references and resources necessary for design detailing and specification of selected roofing systems.

Key words

built-up roofing, cricket, eave, expansion joint, ice dam, flashing, green roof, membrane roofing, metal roofing, roof drain, shake, shingle, single-ply roofing, slate

Roofs of Bermuda.

Roofing systems

1 INTRODUCTION TO ROOFING DESIGN

A continuous challenge of architects and builders, the design of roofs is a significant part of the architectural vocabulary, in plain terms, "to keep the rain out." Dramatic new technological developments in materials and systems have made possible a revolution in the past few decades in the way roofs are designed and built. Technological developments and improvements continue, as does the experience from the field, represented by professional and industry-based research and publications. At the same time, architects and builders are increasingly involved in remodeling older roofing systems, in which case repair or replacement must conform to existing conditions and be informed and improved by recent developments.

This article presents an overview of technical references developed by the roofing industry, which provide recommendations of good practices for roofing systems, many of which are proprietary. Where not otherwise cited, the recommendations are those based upon more than 35 years of the author's roofing specification and forensic experience. This has led to the recommendation of some practices that may exceed industry recommendations: the adage that "if something can go wrong, it will go wrong" applies as much or more so to roofing details as to any other building component, warranted all the more because roof inspection and maintenance is often made difficult by circumstances of weather and/or inaccessibility.

Reference and use is made of definitions and guidelines of roofing industry publications, especially NRCA (1996) Chapter One, "Handbook of Accepted Roofing Knowledge" (currently out of print, but a condensed version is included in the 2001 5th edition of NRCA under "General Roofing Project Considerations"). This is for several purposes: first to use the technical terms and definitions adopted through consensus agreement in the roofing industry; and second, to introduce and make easier access to more complete technical data thus referenced.

Performance requirements for roofs

All roofing systems perform essentially the same weather-protective functions, irrespective of building type and climate. In many instances, the roofing is a strong visual element; its aesthetic character is critical.

Of all elements of a building, the roof is exposed to the greatest climatic stress. In equatorial climates, the roofing assembly is the most critical building element for protection against sun, which may include reflective surfaces and/or radiant barriers. In such climates, roofing is also exposed to extremes of torrential downpours and winds. In cold to temperate climates, the roof endures daily and seasonal cycles of freeze-thaw action and provides protection for thermal insulation. Being out of sight, many roofs suffer from neglect until they fail.

Credits: This article summarizes recommended roofing practices and details shown in publications of The National Roofing Contractors Association, whose assistance is gratefully acknowledged.

The performance requirements for roofing can thus be enumerated as:

- To protect the building interior from water and snow entry during all weather conditions that prevail at the site.

- To maintain waterproofing for a period of several decades, at least, with normal maintenance.

- To protect occupants and contents from thermal discomfort and to conserve energy (accomplished by insulation and by roof reflection and/or radiant barriers, sometimes as part of the roofing assembly, and in most cases, protected by the roofing).

- To control vapor transmission and condensation, both to protect building materials and components and to provide environmental control of interior conditions, sometimes as part of the roofing assembly, and in most cases, protected by the roofing.

- To be safely and easily accessible for inspection and maintenance, and removable with a minimum of problems when replacement is required.

- To protect occupants and the public from harm caused by falling and blowing materials from the roof surfaces, including accumulated snow and ice slides.

- In some uses, to withstand pedestrian, equipment maintenance, and other traffic without harm to occupants or to roofing materials.

- To be safe, that is, physiologically benign, during construction and use. The fumes of some roofing materials are harmful to workers and the public and they are often unpleasant.

Types of roofing systems

The major types of available roof systems are generically defined as steep-slope or low-slope systems, based upon their slope, which in turn determines or explains the principles and physical mechanics behind their design, fabrication, and assembly.

- Steep-slope systems are generally designed to shed water quickly by gravity, and are not necessarily watertight.

- Low-slope systems, while also designed to shed water, are designed as essentially water-impermeable systems.

Steep-roof systems

The primary mechanism in most steep-roof systems for keeping water out is gravity and water flow: the shingle units lap in such a way that water would have to run uphill to penetrate the system. Counteracting forces acting to allow water into the building through the roofing assembly include capillary action, air pressure differential, and the (lateral) kinetic force of driven rain. Steep roofs keep the rain out if the force of gravity is greater than the other forces acting on the roof.

The principal steep-roof systems are:

- shingle roofing

- sheet-metal roofs

- roll roofing and membrane roofing

- other systems not in widespread use, such as thatch roofs.

Low-slope roof systems

The primary mechanism in low-sloped systems for keeping water out is to form an impenetrable membrane without significant openings through which water could pass. There are currently six generic types of low-slope systems. In addition, "protected membrane" systems are characterized by positioning of elements, not its generic materials.

- Built-up roof membrane

- Modified bitumen roofing

- Thermoplastic and thermoset single-ply roof systems

- Liquid-applied roof coating systems

- Protected membrane roof systems

- Sprayed polyurethane roofs

- Soldered flat-lock seam metal roofs

Recommended slopes

A determining initial decision in roofing system selection is the desired roof slope, from which many other decisions derive. **Table 1** provides a general guide to proper slopes, assuming proper fastening of the system. For specific information on manufacturers' systems approved for certain slopes, consult the manufacturers' manuals.

Roof systems that drain fully and quickly are least likely to leak, or to leak badly. Roofs that are very steep are difficult to repair and maintain. Therefore, all other factors being equal, the "ideal" low-slope roof system would slope about 8 percent (1 in per ft, or 8 cm per m), and the "ideal" steep roof system would slope about 30 to 33 percent (4 in per ft, or 30 cm per m). In practice, many other criteria determine the slope.

Other factors for selection of roof systems

- *Appearance.* A great variety of colors and textures are available, and a roof can be a major opportunity for aesthetic expression. Determination of roof slope and roof type also leads to other important aesthetic criteria. Low-slope configurations will require a positive drainage system for quick removal of roof rainwater, which determines design decisions for scuppers, drainpipes, length of slope to outfall, and roof curb heights. These are too often underestimated out of an aesthetic intention to minimize roof appearance or curb height. Steep-slope configurations may also require gutters and downspouts, affecting the projected distance of the roof eave. If gutters are not used (to create free-falling rain, ice, and snow run-off), the eave projection and spaces and building elements below become critical. The resulting lines and shadows at the top edge of building elevations have great bearing upon the building appearance. If a building is seen from above, its "roofscape" becomes, in a sense, the "fifth facade" of the aesthetic of the building design.

Table 1. Recommended roof slopes

Roof type	Minimum slope	Maximum slope
Built-up membrane roofs		
- asphalt roof systems:	2%	
- asphalt-fiberglass membrane roofs:		50%
- aggregate-surface asphalt-fiberglass membrane		33%
- coal tar membrane roofs	2% [1]	
Modified bitumen and composite membrane	2%	
- aggregate-surface modified bitumen		33%
- mineral-surface and smooth-surface modified bitumen		50%
Single-ply thermoplastic and thermoset membrane	2%	
- ballasted systems		17%
- mechanically-attached smooth-surface systems		no limitation
Protected membrane roof systems	2%	8%
Sprayed polyurethane foam systems	2%	no limitation [2]
Asphalt shingle roofs		
- with normal underlayment	33%	no limitation
- with special underlayment installation.	25%	no limitation
Asphalt roll roofing	17%[3]	no limitation
Slate roofs	33%[4]	no limitation
Tile roofs	33%	no limitation
Wood shakes and shingles	33%	no limitation
Metal roofing	note [5]	
- flat-locked and soldered seam systems	2%	
- for limited areas	dead level.	
- metal steep roof systems	25%	no limitation

NOTES
[1] This limit is to retard the tendency of coal tar bitumen to flow.
[2] No general industry slope recommendations published for these systems; good practice guideline is shown.
[3] This material has been used on "dead level" roofs and roofs with a slope less than 2 in 12 or 17%, but such use is not recommended; use low-slope systems for such low slopes.
[4] Slates can be set essentially level as a paving over low-slope membrane roof systems and waterproofing systems.
[5] Since metal roofing varies greatly, no general slope recommendations can be given. Some metal roof systems are recommended by their manufacturers for slopes similar to that of low-slope membrane roof systems (2%).

- *Economy.* Under most conditions, the lowest first cost and life-cycle cost for steep roofs is an unlaminated asphalt shingle roof system, properly applied. The cost of the various types of low-slope roof systems varies, with no system being plainly the most economical in the short run or for the life of the installation.

- *Energy conservation.* Roofs and their assemblies are a significant element in the overall building energy system. The roofing surface is the largest outside surface for single-storied or low-rise buildings. They are, of all the building components, generally the easiest to insulate well. Probably the greatest detrimental heat exchange occurs by absorption of solar heat in summer. To conserve energy, the roof should:

- Reflect a large part of summer solar heat gain. Light-colored roofs reflect more heat than darker ones.

- Certain proprietary and generic "green" roof systems absorb heat and also cool the roof by evaporation.

- Resist conductive heat gain and loss.

- Resist air infiltration and exfiltration to and from the spaces inside the insulation barrier.

- Ventilation of the attic, rafter space, or joist space, above the insulation, has beneficial effects on moisture removal, but it has only limited effect in removing summer solar heat; the greater part of the solar heat transfer is by radiation. Thus a heat-reflective or "green" roof surface, one or more reflective heat barriers in the insulation system, or a combination of these methods is more effective than excessive venting.

- *Method of attachment (fasteners).* While virtually any system can be installed over wooden sheathing, adhered or ballasted systems are better for use over concrete slabs, to eliminate the need for any penetration of the slab. While some systems permit a variety of fasteners, others require special fasteners. For example, it is expensive to use mechanical fasteners to adhere a roof system to structural concrete; adhesion with hot asphalt or other adhesives is the normal method of attachment. Cement-wood fiber panels and gypsum panels require special fasteners made for this purpose. The usual way to fasten a roof to steel deck is self-tapping screws, but they penetrate the steel deck and look unsightly where the deck is exposed below. Alternative fastening systems include low-rise polymer foam adhesives, especially appropriate where the soffit of the steel deck is exposed to view.

- *Resistance to damage from use and abuse.* Protected membrane roof systems have the vulnerable membrane protected under ballast and insulation. Built-up roof systems have considerable resistance to damage, except that they may crack when cold. Sprayed polyurethane roof systems are highly vulnerable to damage from use and abuse. Some sprayed polyurethane roofs are also vulnerable to damage from birds.

- *Slip resistance.* Thermoplastic and thermoset systems, smooth-surface modified bitumen systems, and most metal roof systems are slippery when wet. Therefore, especially if the edges are not guarded, a person could slip and fall over the edges. It would be prudent to call for warning signs and safety anchors.

- *Long-term maintenance.* Durability under longer or life-cycle conditions can be extended with regular inspection and preventative maintenance protocols. Like all assemblies, the weakest link in the attachment and/or substrate components may account for premature failure of the entire assembly.

- *Weight of the roofing system.* Compared to required live loads that may be expected from snow, ice, and water, the weight of different roofing choices may not be a determining factor. But systems do vary in their "dead load" weight:

Roofing	Weight (lb/100 sq ft)
Clay tile	800–2000
Slate	600–1600
Felt and gravel	550–650
Asphalt shingles	130–325
Wood shingles	200–300
Corrugated metal	100–175
Copper (16 oz)	116–145

2 LOW-SLOPE ROOFING SYSTEMS

The following discussion of roofing system elements follows the definitions and recommendations as offered by National Roofing Contractors Association "Handbook of Accepted Roofing Knowledge," the first chapter of the 4th edition of NRCA Roofing and Waterproofing Manual (NRCA 1996), with minor changes.

Low-slope roofing systems and assemblies consist of the following elements:

1 structural deck or substrate

2 slope and drainage system

3 moisture control and vapor retarders

4 insulation

5 expansion joints and area dividers

6 roof coverings and membranes

7 cants, curbs, nailers, and flashing

8 aggregates and/or other surfacing

9 mechanical curbs and penetrations

Structural deck

Good roof systems depend upon the structural integrity of the substrate or roof deck. To ensure the construction of a quality roof deck, provisions for the following items should be included in the design of the roof deck:

- live loads, including moving installation equipment, workers, material stored on the roof, wind, snow, ice, and rain.

- dead loads, such as mechanical equipment, ducting, piping, or conduit, the deck itself, any element overlying the sheathing, roof membrane, insulation and ballast, and any future re-covering of the roof system. Rolling rooftop construction loads can exceed 600 lb (272 kg) in quite small areas (such as dollies used to transport roofing materials).

- deck strength.

- deflection.

- drainage.

- placement of expansion joints and area dividers.

- curb and penetration members and detailing.

- durability for the life of the building under prevailing conditions.

Common structural deck ("substrate") types include:

- cement-wood fiber deck panels

- lightweight insulating concrete decks

- poured gypsum concrete deck

- precast gypsum panel roof decks

- steel decks

- structural concrete roof decks

- wood plank and wood panel (plywood or approved OSB) roof decks

The structural deck supports the roofing and all dead and live loads on it. It resists snowdrift loading, impounded rain loading, equipment loading, wind loading, and wind uplift. Under the greatest loading, the roof should not deflect beyond the point at which full drainage occurs.

– If there are parapets or other structures containing water, include the weight of all water which can be impounded as part of the live load, or (more reasonably) provide overflow scuppers or other redundant drainage.

– Give special attention to deflection under concentrated roof loads, such as rooftop mechanical equipment. One way to limit such deflection is to provide separate structural support, independent of the main roof structural system, under heavy equipment. Another way is to make the whole roof very stiff. Do not allow local deflection to create a pond around mechanical equipment.

Slope and drainage system

NRCA recommends, as does accepted good practice, that all roofs be designed and built to ensure positive drainage, essentially considering the entire path of water removal from the roof and away from the building. Impounded ("ponding") water can be detrimental to roof systems and can result in:

– deterioration of the roof surface and membrane.

– debris accumulation, vegetation, and fungal growth, resulting in membrane damage.

– deck deflections sometimes resulting in structural and other complications.

– ice formation and resulting membrane degradation of damage.

– tensile splitting of water-weakened organic or asbestos felts.

– difficulties in repair should leaks occur.

– water entry into the building if the roof membrane is punctured or fails in an area of impounded water.

– voiding of manufacturers' warrantees.

Because every roof has its own specific set of drainage conditions, the architect must design for proper drainage for the entire roof and all related areas. The designer should not simply specify a standard slope without analysis and provision of how it is accomplished. NRCA recommends as an industry standard the design and installation criterion that there be no impounded water 48 hours after rainfall, under ambient drying conditions. No impounded water after 5 minutes is better. Tapered insulation systems can be used to achieve thorough drainage. Tapered saddles should be designed between drains, and crickets should be designed on the upslope side of mechanical, skylight, and other curbs to promote drainage of these areas.

All low-slope roof systems must be designed to drain easily, without impounded water and/or complicating connections to areas susceptible to water, ice, and freeze/thaw damage. Provision of adequate crickets and saddles may be included in the slope of the substrate or added by built-up sections (**Fig. 1**).

Moisture control and vapor retarders

The term "vapor retarders" refers to a broad range of materials that are used to control the flow of moisture vapor from the interior of the building into the roof system.

Vapor retarders for use in low-slope roof assemblies generally fall into two classes:

• *bituminous vapor retarders* utilize a continuous film of bitumen to serve as the vapor resistant element. A typical two-ply reinforced installation can provide a vapor retarder that is rated less than 0.005 perms, which for most roof construction purposes is considered so near zero permeance that it can be a very effective vapor retarder.

• *non-bituminous vapor retarders* are typically composed of a sheet material that serves as the vapor retarder and an adhesive tape or heat- or solvent-welding process is used to seal the laps. These include PVC films, Kraft paper, and aluminum-foil laminates, which may provide vapor retarders having permeability ratings ranging from 0.1 to 0.5 perms. The roof membrane is the vapor retarder in protected membrane roof systems.

Special consideration is required for design and application of vapor retarders and the entire roof assembly for specialty facilities, including buildings with high interior relative humidity (such as swimming pools) and facilities with very low relative humidity (such as cold storage and freezer facilities).

A rule-of-thumb method is offered in NRCA (1996) that the designer may consider as a preliminary guide to use of vapor retarders in low-sloped roof assemblies: the need for a vapor retarder should be considered when the two following conditions are anticipated:

1 The outside average January temperature is below 40F (4°C).

2 The expected interior winter humidity is 45 percent or greater.

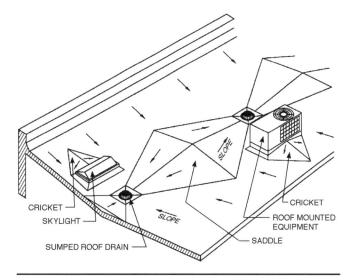

Fig. 1. Cricket and saddles are part of low-slope roof design, ensuring that water is never flowing against roof flashings. (Source: *Roofing Specifier*, January 1997)

For information on moisture control in roof assemblies, guidelines on dew point calculations and additional information on vapor diffusion and retarders, see *NRCA Energy Manual* and *NRCA Roofing and Waterproofing Manual* (2001).

Insulation

In most climates, insulation is included in the roof system to improve comfort and to minimize energy use. In addition, roof insulation may decrease the range of thermal expansion of the structure. For low-slope roof systems, the best location is usually above the structural deck. For conventional membrane roof systems, the insulation is under the membrane. For protected membrane roof systems, the insulation is above the membrane.

Except in protected membrane roof systems, rigid roof insulation usually provides in low-slope systems both the insulation for the building and a substrate to which the roofing membrane is applied. Therefore roof insulation must be compatible with, and provide adequate support for, the membrane and other rooftop materials and permit limited rooftop traffic, such as for roof inspection and maintenance.

For protected membrane roof systems, the only approved insulation is extruded, expanded polystyrene. It is resistant to water penetration, but it is vulnerable to attack from high heat and ultraviolet radiation. For roofing areas without adequate strength to support ballast, a proprietary system is available, composed of tongue and groove expanded, extruded polystyrene panels with a thin latex mortar cap, to protect against sunlight.

For conventional membrane roof systems, the following types of rigid insulation can be used:

- cellular glass

- glass fiber

- mineral fiber

- perlite

- polyisocyanurate board

- polystyrene foam (expanded or extruded)

- polyurethane foam

- wood fiberboard

- vegetable fiberboard

- composite board

Of these, polyisocyanurate has the highest insulating value per unit of thickness. It is also resistant to the temperatures that occur during roof system installation. Most manufacturers of heat-applied systems require that a thin layer of vegetable fiber, perlite board, or other vapor-porous insulation be used between polyisocyanurate insulation and the roof membrane. The reason is to allow water vapor, which may form in great volume when heat is applied during roof construction, to dissipate harmlessly.

Expansion joints and area dividers

Roof expansion joints are used to minimize the effects of stresses and movements of a building's components and to prevent these stresses from splitting, buckling/bridging, or damaging the roof system. Expansion joints in the roof assembly (here considered as combined roof membrane, insulation and roof deck) should be placed in the same location as the building's structural expansion joints (although they may also be required in other locations). Each building component has its own coefficient of expansion, and each is subject to varying temperature changes, and resultant thermal movement.

NRCA recommends that roof expansion joints should be provided wherever:

- expansion or contraction joints are provided in the structural assembly.

- steel framing, structural steel, or decking change direction.

- separate wings of L, U, and T or similar configurations exist in the building roof plan.

- the type of decking changes, for example, where a precast concrete deck and a steel deck abut.

- additions are connected to existing buildings.

- interior heating conditions change.

- differential movement might occur between vertical walls and the roof deck.

- *Area dividers.* Where expansion joints are not provided, or where the distance between expansion joints is excessive, area dividers may help control thermal stresses in a roof system (here defined as independent of the movement of the structural deck). Area dividers minimize the transmission of stress from one area of the roof to another by dividing the roof into smaller sections. NRCA recommendations indicate that these sections be of rectangular shape and uniformly spaced where possible.

Roof coverings and membranes

Low-slope systems generally use roof membranes intended to serve as water-impermeable coverings designed to protect the structure from water entry. The roof covering resists infiltration of water. It also resists attack by UV radiation, atmospheric pollution, roof traffic, thermal movement, hot and cold temperatures, and animals. Low-slope system types include the following:

- built-up roof membrane

- modified bitumen roofing

- thermoplastic and thermoset single-ply roof systems

- liquid-applied roof coating systems

- protected membrane roof systems

- sprayed polyurethane roofs

- soldered flat-lock seam metal roofs

- *Built-up roof membrane.* The built-up roof (BUR) membrane is composed of moppings or layers of bitumen (asphalt or cold tar) that are the waterproof components of the membrane. Plies of reinforcement fabric are installed between each layer of bitumen. Traditionally, bituminous membranes have been installed in multiple-ply configurations, with three to six layers of bitumen applied between layers (plies) of reinforcing fabric to compose the "built-up" membrane. Built-up roofs are highly dependent on the skill and integrity of the workers who construct them.

- *Modified bitumen roofing.* Modified bitumen roofing (MBR) is composed of a fiber mat that may contain glass fibers, polyester fibers, or both, and a mixture of asphalt and plastic that impregnates and coats the mat. The surface may be plain, coated with mineral granules, or laminated with aluminum, copper, or stainless steel foil. The back is surfaced with thin polyethylene film, which melts during application. The rolls are approximately 36 in (92 cm) in width. One common type of modified bitumen roof consists of a fiberglass-modified bitumen base sheet and a mineral granule-coated modified bitumen cap sheet. The sheets are unrolled and lapped at the joints. Some systems are installed with hot asphalt, some are installed by torch fusion, and some are a combination. Other systems make use of cold adhesives.

– Modified bitumen hybrid systems consist of a built-up base covered with modified bitumen membranes.

– Modified bitumen systems can have a surface of hot asphalt and aggregate (**Fig. 2**). This system appears to have greater resistance to mechanical damage than other modified bitumen systems.

- *Thermoplastic and thermoset single-ply systems.* "Thermoplastic" materials form because of heat of fusion without a change in chemical composition and are thus distinguished from thermosets (see below) in that there is no chemical cross-linking. Because of their nature, some thermoplastic membranes may be seamed by either heat (hot air) or solvent welding. Thermoplastic membranes are single-ply flexible sheet materials that are divided into the following categories:

– Polyvinyl Chloride (PVC)

– PVC Alloys or compounded thermoplastics (CPA, EIP, NBP)

– Thermoplastic olefin (TPO)

"Thermoset" membranes are those whose principal polymers are chemically cross-linked. This chemical cross-linkage is commonly referred to as "vulcanization" (increase of strength and elasticity of rubber due to combination of sulfur compounds with high heat) or "curing." They are strong and flexible, making them ideal for certain types of roofing applications (**Fig. 3**). The common classes of thermoset roof membranes are:

– Chlorosulfonated polyethylene—Hypalon (CSPE)

– Polyisobutylene (PIB)

– Ethylene Propylene Diene Monomer or Terpolymer (EPDM)

Fig. 2. Pouring asphalt over built-up roof felts, and embedding gravel aggregate.

Fig. 3. Thermoset membrane roof, Ingalls Ice Skating Rink, Yale University, New Haven, Connecticut. 1957. Eero Saarinen, Architect; F. J. Dahill Co., Roofing Contractor. The membrane roof protects surfaces that vary from very steep to low slope and accommodates flexing of the structure.

Thermoplastic single-ply roof systems are joined at the seams with solvent or heat. Thermoset single-ply roof systems are joined with special cement, double-sided tape, or, for some systems, with heat. Heat-joined thermoset materials are shipped to the job uncured, in which state they can be softened and joined by heat. They cure in place, after which they do not soften when heated. Some are available in white, advantageous where sunlight reflectivity is desired, such as to reduce cooling loads or to reflect light to clerestories. They can be installed in the following ways:

– loose-laid with ballast.

– fully adhered to the insulation below, the insulation being mechanically attached to the structural deck.

– mechanical attachments, either covered by the adjacent sheets or sealed watertight.

• *Liquid-applied roof coating systems.* Liquid-applied roof coating systems are relatively new. They are seamless, and so flashings are simplified. These systems are not described in the NRCA Manual.

• *Protected membrane roof systems.* "Protected membrane roofing" describes an approach to low-slope roofing in which the waterproofing membrane is protected from extreme weather conditions and mechanical damage by covering with insulating panels and ballast. The materials for protected membrane roof systems vary. The special characteristic of protected membrane roof systems is that the insulation is installed above the membrane.

Protected membrane roof systems (membranes protected by polystyrene board, also functioning as thermal insulation placed on the outside of the membrane) can incorporate any of the membrane systems listed above. Extruded, expanded polystyrene board insulation is placed over the membrane, and a sheet of water-permeable polymer fabric is laid over the insulation. Stone ballast, pavers, or a combination of them is then used to hold the insulation in place and to protect the insulation from sunlight. Since the membrane serves as a vapor retarder, and since it is under and inside the insulation, this system excels in avoiding condensation. It is the system of choice in art museums, swimming pools, and other occupancies with high humidity, roof traffic, or both.

Since the membrane is protected from harm coming from above, it is also the system of choice for rooftop terraces and similar uses. If the membrane is adhered watertight to the substrate, migration of water from leaks, under the membrane, is limited. One problem with this type of roof is that it is difficult to locate leaks from above.

– *Ballasts or pavers:* Some roof systems contain ballasts or pavers to hold the remainder of the roof system down. The roof edges must be raised a minimum 4 in (10 cm) or more to prevent the ballast from blowing off.

– *Earth-covered roof terraces:* Earth-covered roofs—also called "green roofs" and utilizing both insulation layers and earth and plant covering for combined insulation and thermal protection— follow similar principles, since the roofing is essentially characterized as a protected membrane roofing system (**Fig. 4**). Because of the difficulty of post-construction inspection and repair, earth-covered systems require double, if not triple, redundancy in design of site water coursing, drainage, and waterproofing of the entire structure as a complete system. The NRCA manual does not include earth-

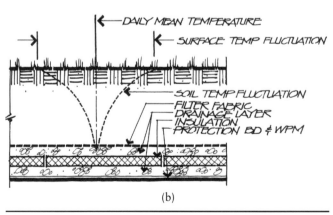

(a)

(b)

Fig. 4. Earth-covered roofing: (a) components of "green roof" (National Research Council of Canada); (b) temperature dampening effect of earth-cover on roofing. (Watson and Labs 1993)

covered construction, but the National Council of Research of Canada has sponsored recent conferences and publications on the topic (see References).

- *Sprayed polyurethane roofs.* Sprayed polyurethane roofs are formed in place by spraying liquid polymer onto the substrate. The liquid then foams and expands, after which it becomes rigid. Flashings, slopes, and other forms can be made integral with the rest of the system. The foam has limited resistance to moisture penetration and poor resistance to ultraviolet radiation, so it is coated with various types of liquid-applied protective coating. Some types of coating require aggregate to be bonded into the coating to discourage eating of the foam by birds. Traffic walkways are necessary for sprayed polyurethane roofs.

- *Soldered flat-lock seam metal roofs.* Soldered flat-lock seam metal roofs are assembled in place. With proper workmanship, they can be reliable and durable. The design must take account of thermal expansion, since the metal is rigid and has only limited ability to deform when heated and cooled. This roof type can only be applied by highly skilled sheet metal workers who know how to solder the seams (**Fig. 5**). The seams are first coated with solder ("pretinned"), unless the metal is already coated. The metal is then heated, and the solder is touched to the outside of the seam. If the procedure is proper, the solder will draw into the seam, filling it. It is suggested to observe a demonstration of soldering before the work is performed. Cut open the sample seam to make sure that the solder has penetrated fully.

Proprietary low-slope metal roof systems require complete and careful attention to the manufacturer's recommendations. The initial work should be performed in the presence, and under the supervision, of the manufacturer's trained and authorized representative. Joints are often fastened with sealant and pop rivets, and they are especially vulnerable to leaking.

Cants, curbs, nailers, and flashing

Quite often, the part of any roof system most vulnerable to water entry is the point at which the horizontal roof deck intersects with a vertical surface or penetration. Designers should carefully consider the design of all flashing details.

- *Cants.* The bending radius of bituminous roofing materials is generally limited to 45 degrees. To allow for this limited bending radius, cant strips must be provided at any 90-degree angle change such as created by roof-to-wall, roof-to-curb, or other roof-to-vertical surface intersection.

- *Unit curbs.* Mechanical units using curbs that have built-in metal base flashing flanges can be difficult to seal for the long term and, therefore, are not recommended for use with bituminous roof membranes. Some single-ply roof membranes may utilize prefabricated curbs with metal "self-flashing" flanges to be embedded in the roof membrane.

- *Nailers.* It is recommended that well-secured, decay-resistant (that is, preservative treated) wood blocking be carefully designed and provided at all roof perimeters and penetrations for fastening membrane flashing and sheet metal components. Wood nailers should be provided on all prefabricated curbs and hatches for attachment of membrane base flashing.

Fig. 5. Improperly soldered flat-lock sheet metal joint. Solder does not penetrate joint. Note corrosion from acid deposition and from western red cedar shingle runoff.

• *Flashing.* There are two types of flashing: membrane flashing and sheet metal flashing. Membrane base flashing is generally composed of strips of compatible membrane materials used to close-in or flash roof-to-vertical surface intersections or transitions. On metal units and other raised-curb equipment, metal flashing (counterflashing and cap flashing) should be installed to cover the top edge and overlap the upper portion of membrane base flashing. Plumbing vent stacks and all other pipe projections through the membrane require metal flashing collars or membrane pipe flashing "boots." Metal flanges should be stripped in with membrane flashing plies or strips.

Aggregates and/or other surfacing

Some roof membranes may require certain types of surfacing to provide fire resistance, weathering protection, reflectivity, and/or a wearing surface for traffic. Rounded river-washed or water-worn gravel, crushed stone, slag, or marble-chips are used for aggregate-surfaced and some ballasted roofs. Gravel or aggregate surfacing for built-up roof membranes is usually set in hot bitumen, which is applied either by a bitumen spreader or by hand. Gravel is placed by machine or by hand with a scoop shovel.

Mechanical curbs and penetrations

To avoid deck deflections from damaging the roof, the structural design of the roof deck should always allow for the concentrated loading of mechanical equipment. Vibrations from roof-mounted or joint-mounted mechanical equipment should be isolated from the roof membrane and flashing. Some poorly designed or poorly installed equipment may allow moisture to enter the building either from the exterior or from condensation within.

NRCA recommends clearance criteria between mechanical equipment and adjacent perimeters, curbs and walls to facilitate proper installation of roofing materials. A minimum of 12 in (25 cm) is recommended and 24 in (50 cm) for larger units. Projections through the roof should not be located in valleys or drainage areas. Condensate from roof-mounted mechanical equipment should be directed to a positive drainage or outflow.

Roofing details for low-slope systems

NRCA (2001) contains recommended details for most roof systems. It is available in printed or CD ROM format. **Plates 1 to 6** at the end of this article illustrate several details from that reference.

3 STEEP-SLOPE SYSTEMS

While similar principles may apply, the components of steep-slope roofing systems are somewhat more simplified compared to low-slope systems; many of the various roofing system functions are provided by fewer elements:

1 structural deck or substrate

2 roofing (roof coverings)

3 flashing

Slope and drainage, and expansion joints and/or area dividers are accommodated by the nature of the steep-slope systems, although flash-ing is as critical in the water drainage design. Mechanical attachments and penetrations deserve similar vigilance as low-slope systems. Moisture control and insulation functions are often separated from the roofing assembly and accommodated in the ceiling, well below the roofing assembly. Nonetheless, ventilation of, and inspection access to, roof-ceiling interstitial spaces and/or attic spaces are critical.

Structural deck or substrate

• *Substrate.* The substrate or structural deck supports the roof and all dead and live loads on it. It resists snowdrift loading, equipment loading, wind loading, and wind uplift. Positive and negative wind loadings may be major forces acting on a steep roof system.

• *Underlayment.* In virtually all climates, there should be underlayment over the whole roof, and it should be made waterproof at penetrations (this is common sense, but perhaps one in a thousand roofs has properly installed underlayment). It should extend fully to the rakes and eaves. General industry recommendations favor use of fiberglass-reinforced asphalt-saturated and, sometimes, asphalt-saturated and coated underlayment. For expensive and long-lived steep roof systems, the author recommends modified bitumen-saturated and coated fiberglass base sheet as an underlayment.

Roofing

Steep-slope roofing types include:

– Shingle roofing

– Sheet metal roofs

– Roll roofing and membrane roofing

– Other systems

• *Shingle roofing.* Shingle roofing systems of wood, metal, asphalt, clay tile, slate, synthetic tile and slate, concrete, and various others.

• *Sheet metal roofs.* Sheet metal roofs, both factory-fabricated systems and custom systems fabricated in the shop or field and assembled in the field. Sometimes designated "architectural metal panel roofing systems," these are typically designed to be used on steep enough slopes that will shed water rapidly from the metal panel surface, so typically the seams are not watertight. Solid roof sheathing is required for architectural metal panel roof systems, and underlayment is recommended.

• *Roll roofing and membrane roofing.* Mineral-surface roll roofing and some membrane roof materials, such as single-ply and modified bitumen, may be used for steep roofs. Other than slope considerations, their application in construction follows low-slope roofing practices.

• *Other systems.* Thatch roofing, while relatively esoteric in modern construction application, is also properly defined as a steep roofed system. It is used in indigenous applications throughout the world and has been restored as a building craft tradition.

Steep-slope roofs use water-shedding roof coverings, intended to shed water from upslope courses down over neighboring courses and off the roof or to a water drainage and gutter system. The shingles, slates, tiles, or other steep roof components are then applied, following the manufacturer's instructions and industry recommendations. The architect should take, read, and keep on file the manufacturer's instructions printed on the shingle wrappers (usually found in the "dumpster").

Shingle roofing

Shingle roofing systems of wood, metal, asphalt, clay tile, slate, synthetic tile and slate, concrete, and various others.

Asphalt shingles

Asphalt shingles are well understood in the industry, and their installation does not require great skill. (Steep slope asphalt materials are referred to as "prepared asphalt roofing products" in American Society of Testing Material Standards.)

Common problems are the use of smooth nails (as against annular-groove nails and other deformed shank nails), failure to leave ⅛ in (3.2 mm) gaps between plywood panels, improper anchorage of the

first courses at the eaves, improper edge conditions, and failure to install both eave flashing and underlayment. Normal warranties do not apply when wind velocity exceeds 54 mph, but there are manufacturers' and industry recommendations for greater wind resistance.

The asphalt shingles are installed with at least four deformed-shank galvanized steel nails per strip. The author recommends six nails where high wind occurs, and some codes require six nails. The first course of shingles is trimmed, removing the tabs, and then firmly nailed. The self-seal strips in the trimmed, concealed bottom course will adhere to the bottom-exposed course and make the eave shingles tight and wind-resistant. In addition, shingles at the rakes may require cementing in high wind areas.

The felt of which the shingles are manufactured may be fiberglass or organic felt. Different sizes and shapes are available. Virtually all asphalt shingles are manufactured with self-seal tabs. It is prudent to make sure that the self-seal tabs soften and adhere properly; if they do not, require sealing with roof cement, a hot air gun, or other means (**Table 2**).

Table 2. Typical asphalt shingles

PRODUCT	1 ASTM DESIGNATION	2 CONFIGURATION	3 PER SQUARE		4 APPROX. SIZE		5 TYPICAL EXPOSURE	6 UNDERWRITERS LISTING
			SHINGLES	BUNDLES	WIDTH	LENGTH		
STRIP SHINGLE MORE THAN ONE THICKNESS PER STRIP LAMINATED	FIBERGLASS D 3462 ORGANIC D 225	VARIOUS EDGE, SURFACE TEXTURE AND APPLICATION TREATMENTS	64 TO 90	3 TO 5	11-1/2" (292mm) TO 1'-3" (381mm)	3' (914mm) TO 3'-4" (1016mm)	4" (102mm) TO 8" (203mm)	A OR C
STRIP SHINGLE SINGLE THICKNESS PER STRIP	FIBERGLASS D 3462 ORGANIC D 225	VARIOUS EDGE, SURFACE TEXTURE AND APPLICATION TREATMENTS	65 TO 80	3 OR 4	1' (305mm) TO 1'-5" (432mm)	3' (914MM) OR 3'-4" (1016MM)	4" (102mm) TO 7 1/2" (191mm)	A OR C
SELF-SEALING STRIP SHINGLE "3 -TAB"	FIBERGLASS D 3462	CONVENTIONAL 3 TAB	65 TO 80	3 TYP.	1' (305mm) TO 1'-1 1/4" (337mm)	3' (914mm) TO 3'-4" (1016mm)	5 5/8" (143mm) OR 5" (127mm)	A OR C
	ORGANIC D 225	2 OR MORE TAB	65 TO 80	3 OR 4				
SELF-SEALING STRIP SHINGLE NO CUT OUT	FIBERGLASS D 3462 ORGANIC D 225	VARIOUS EDGE AND TEXTURE TREATMENTS	65 TO 81	3 OR 4	1' (305mm) OR 1'-1 1/4" (337mm)	3' (914mm) TO 3'-4" (1016mm)	5" (127mm) OR 5 5/8" (143mm)	A OR C
INDIVIDUAL LOCK DOWN BASIC "T"-LOCK DESIGN	ORGANIC	SEVERAL DESIGN VARIATIONS	72 TO 120	3 OR 4	1'-6" (457mm) TO 1'-10 1/4" (565mm)	1'-8" (508mm) TO 1'-10 1/2" (572mm)	-	A OR C

NOTE - ALL WEIGHTS AND DIMENSIONS ARE APPROXIMATE

OTHER TYPES AVAILABLE FROM SOME MANUFACTURERS IN CERTAIN AREAS OF THE COUNTRY

Fig. 6. Western red cedar shingle roof on First Presbyterian Church, New Haven, Connecticut. John Dinkeloo, Architect. 1966.

Wood shingles and shakes

Most wood shingles are made from western red cedar, but they are also made from Atlantic white cedar, eastern white pine, and other species. They can be installed over spaced nailers or solid roof sheathing (**Fig. 6**). The minimum shingle length for normal application is 3 times the exposure plus 1 in (2.5 cm) or more. Wood shakes are similar to shingles, but they are thicker and more irregular. They are installed with #30 felt or equivalent material between all courses.

The industry associations require that the joints in adjoining courses be offset substantially and that the joints in every three courses not line up exactly, as a precaution against future splitting and water entry locations (**Fig. 7**). It is recommended that joints in every three courses be offset at least 2 in (5 cm). As with all roof systems, the manufacturer and industry recommendations should be followed carefully. Eave flashings are recommended. **Figs. 8** and **9** indicate maximum permitted exposures of wood shingles and shakes.

Fig. 7. Split shingles: the first and third course joints lined up in many places. When the intermediate shingles split, there was a clear path through the shingles for rainwater.)

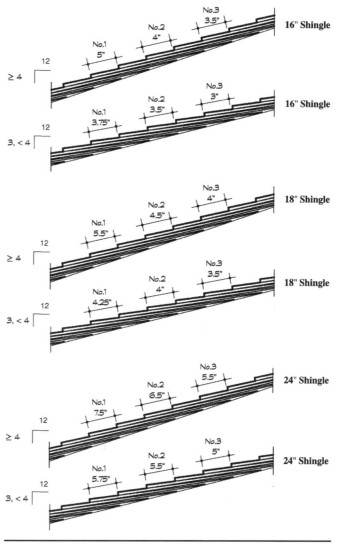

Fig. 8. Maximum permitted exposure of wood shingles. (Patterson 2001)

Slates and tiles

Slates, tiles, and synthetic slates and tiles are selected for architectural style and appearance, and may also be a system of choice in areas prone to airborne fire hazard, such as forest fires. These systems are installed over eave flashing and underlayment, best considered as a continuous and complete moisture protection system itself. Slate roofing is a durable, dense, and sound rock. It is a time-tested, weather and fire-resistant material, available in thickness from $3/16$ to 2 in (0.5 to 5 cm). Zinc-coated or copper nails are used for fastening through machine-punched holes in the slate. Nail penetrations should be protected with sealant as well as by overlapping of slate. Installation of slate and tile systems requires more skill than that of asphalt shingles. Manufacturers and industry groups publish installation instructions. **Fig. 10** indicates minimum permitted headlap of slate shingles.

Clay tile is available either molded into several shapes or flat. Vitrified clay tile has water absorption of 3 percent or less, which facilitated rapid water runoff and can withstand freeze-thaw cycling. Metal flashing is used for valleys, fastened with cleats and not soldered. Care must be taken during installation to ensure proper blending of colors and matching width and length dimensions. Corrosion of copper gutters and other valley materials should be considered where conditions of acid rain deposition prevail (most of the East Coast).

Concrete tile is available either as roll or flat shapes, similar to clay tile. Exposed surfaces are generally finished with synthetic oxide pigmented cementitious material. Moisture absorption should be investigated; if tiles absorb moisture, roofing problems may ensue.

Sheet-metal roofing

Sheet-metal roofs include both factory-fabricated systems and custom systems fabricated in the shop or field and assembled in the field. Sometimes designated "architectural metal panel roofing systems," these are typically used on steep enough slopes that will shed water rapidly from the metal panel surface, so the seams are not watertight. Solid roof sheathing is required for architectural metal panel roof systems and underlayment is recommended. Recommended thicknesses for typical roof components are listed in the SNACNA Handbook. Available metals include:

- *Copper and lead-coated copper.* These materials have a long history of successful use on roofs. They are easy to form and solder. They are highly ductile, and so they tend to yield harmlessly when stressed. In building locations subject to airborne acid deposition (acid rain residue and directly deposited acid aerosol), dew and mist might dissolve acid deposits on roofs and wash the concentrated acid onto sheet metal. Roofs made entirely from copper are usually not harmed, but copper and lead-coated copper roofs that receive drainage from most other materials are corroded (**Fig. 11**). Some protective methods:

- Detail the roof so that no water flows from other materials onto copper and lead-coated or zinc-coated copper. A roof made entirely from copper is one way to accomplish this. If the copper roof is above other roofing materials, no corrosion occurs.

- Use sheet metal not subject to acid corrosion, such as aluminum, stainless steel, and terne-coated stainless steel, where a flow of acid from above will occur.

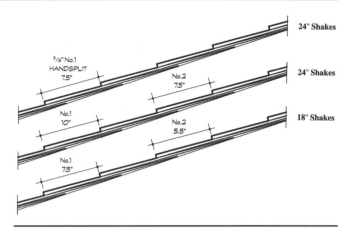

Fig. 9. Maximum permitted exposure of wood shakes. (Patterson 2001)

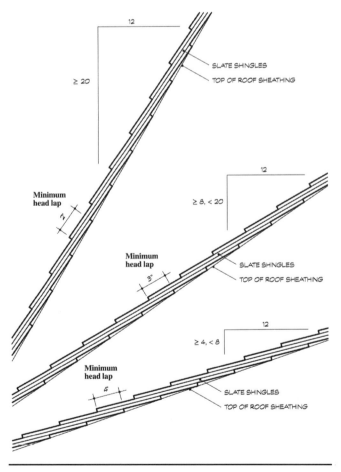

Fig. 10. Minimum permitted headlap for slate shingles. (Patterson 2001)

Fig. 11. Copper roof with well-developed light green patina. Below the glass and aluminum skylight, the patina has been removed by acid runoff.

– Install sacrificial zinc anodes at the point where the acid runs onto the copper.

- *Aluminum.* Aluminum is vulnerable to attack by hydroxyl ions, but most roofs are not exposed to alkali conditions. Aluminum is not vulnerable to attack from the concentrations of acid that occur on roofs. Although very thin aluminum is used on residences, follow the SMACNA Manual recommendations for proper minimum gauge. Aluminum is available with highly durable finishes, including fluorocarbon polymer coatings. Contrary to conventional wisdom, proper aluminum alloys with proper finish are not subject to corrosion from salt spray.

- *Steel.* Plain galvanized steel roofs are not satisfactory for roofing sheet metal exposed to acid runoff in those parts of the country with heavy rainfall and acid deposition. The protective coating erodes rapidly. They have been used successfully in many parts of the country, however. They have the advantages of economy, strength, and low coefficient of thermal expansion. Other coatings appear to be more durable, and highly durable finishes are available.

- *Terne.* Terne (trade name of Follansbee Steel Corp.), a steel that is coated with an alloy of tin and lead, has a long history of use as a roof covering. It must be painted and kept painted for durability.

- *Stainless steel.* Stainless steel and terne-coated stainless steel are highly durable metals. Terne-coated stainless steel is glossy upon first exposure, but it turns matte gray with continued exposure. Stainless steel is subject to stress hardening, and thus it is harder to work than copper, and it may rip rather than yield when exposed to great stress. Terne-coated stainless steel can be soldered well. In parts of the country exposed to acid deposition, where the metal must be soldered and where the metal will receive acid residue, Terne-coated stainless steel is the sheet metal of choice.

- *Lead.* Lead has a long history of successful use. There is a lead roofing pan on Salisbury Cathedral dated 1814, and Sir Bernard M. Feilden states that the lead roof on the Pantheon in Rome was installed in 1601. It is widely used on monumental buildings in Britain. Lead can be formed to nearly any shape, including curved, nonplanar shapes. It is highly durable. Runoff from lead and lead-coated copper roofs is toxic, and the destination of the water that washes from lead should be considered. Since lead fuel additives and lead paint pigment are no longer used, lead leached from roofing may be one of the major contemporary sources of lead pollution. Unfortunately, there are no satisfactory substitute products in all cases.

- *Zinc.* Zinc and zinc alloys have many of the same characteristics as copper. They are durable and easy to form and to solder. Acid damage due to zinc alloys might occur. One use of zinc and zinc alloy is for metal roof shingles.

- *Monel™.* Monel is a very highly durable metal occasionally used for roofing, a trademark material named after Alfred Monel, its developer and manufacturer. It is a composite alloy of nickel, copper, iron, manganese, silicon, and carbon that is very resistant to corrosion.

- *Porcelain-enameled steel.* Porcelain-enameled steel roof tiles, long associated with "your host of the highways," are very durable. Their most fragile or susceptible points are nicks that may occur in handling, installation, or maintenance.

Flashing

- *Eave flashing.* In climates that may be subject to freezing temperatures, there should be eave flashing to prevent water from ice dams from entering the building (**Fig. 12**). Detailing at the eave insulation will help reduce such freeze-thaw conditions (**Fig. 13**). Code requirements vary. In areas governed by the BOCA National Building Code, the eave flashing must extend 2 ft (61 cm) up from the intersecting plane of the interior wall surface, and 4 ft (1.2 m) or more is recommended. "Butterfly" roofs and closely spaced dormers may create deep ice dams, and eave flashings or membrane roofing for such configurations in cold climates is recommended.

- There should be metal or other valley liners, eave drips, and rake drips. Certain metals, in certain regions of the country, are subject to acid deposit corrosion. If metal valleys are used, employ a rubber or modified bitumen redundant valley under the metal. Modified bitumen and rubber may also be used as a valley liner without metal.

- Where people pass below the eaves, consider requiring snow guards. In fact, snow guards should be considered throughout the roof, up to the ridge, to avoid damage to the snow guards from an avalanche of snow. Also, where people might pass under the eaves, consider the danger of icicles. One way to avoid icicle danger is to plant shrubs under the eaves; another is to include ice-melting cable in the gutters and downspouts. Do not locate sidewalks under eaves.

Some aphorisms for use of sheet metal flashing

- Sheet metals, being rigid, will not accommodate excessive expansion and contraction. Sheet metal roofing components must be detailed to accommodate movement (**Fig. 14**). Where moving components join stable components, strict adherence to SMACNA details is especially important. In addition, joints that are not detailed to move must be fastened firmly. Solder alone may not be adequate; rivets may be necessary.

- Some sheet metals and their fasteners are subject to galvanic corrosion. If dissimilar metals cannot be kept apart, the cathode should be small and the anode should be large. Steel nails used to fasten copper, lead-coated copper, stainless steel, and Monel will corrode to destruction very rapidly. Although the practice is not recommended, fasteners of more "noble" metals are not very harmful to less noble sheet metal.

- In most cases a redundant underlayment is desirable, especially at eaves and valleys. In climates subject to ice damming, valleys and underlayment should be wider than normal. Underlayment should be lapped over eave flashing throughout and sealed to penetrations.

- Where the steep roofs adjoin walls above, turn the underlayment up. Install metal or modified bitumen step flashing lapped between the shingles. Install metal stepped counterflashings above. The metal step counterflashings should be joined to through-wall flashing at masonry walls and should be extended up behind the underlayment and siding for wood-sided walls.

- Joints made by simply lapping adjacent sheets are not waterproof. Applying sealant over the open end of a lap is not waterproof for long.

Fig. 12. Ice dam at eaves of steep roof. Thick deposit of ice causes melt water to back up and run through laps and joints in shingle roof. Eave flashing is intended to tolerate ice damming and prevent melting water from entering building.

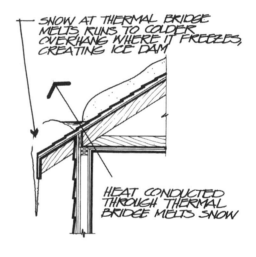

Fig. 13. Roof construction detail to reduce conditions favorable to ice dam formation. (Watson and Labs 1993)

Fig. 14. Expansion joint not properly constructed. Where moving elements were joined to fixed elements rigidly, the joint has twisted and broken.

- One way to make joints in metal flashing waterproof is to bed the lap in non-curing butyl sealant (a product offered by only a few producers). It must be in the joint, not on the outside of the joint. Avoid applying in excess, as it may work its way out of the joints.

- Another way to make metal flashing joints waterproof is to form flat-lock seams. This is an excellent method, but it requires much skill and is not often used today.

- To make sheet metal flashings waterproof with the greatest assurance of success, apply a continuous flexible flashing under the sheet metal.

4 SUMMARY

Guidelines for designing a roof system

- Be a knowledgeable designer: first, become familiar with the NRCA *Roofing and Waterproofing Manual*. If you have not read it, do not design roofs.

- Seek out local expertise and experience. Select one or more general systems appropriate to the project and the prevailing and extreme conditions of the locale. If you are not experienced in roofing design, discuss your selections with another architect, a respected roofing contractor, or both. If several systems are appropriate and equivalent, consider allowing the contractor to use whichever one he/she wishes, assigning clear lines of responsibility for contract and subcontract administration and for corrections of subsequent problems.

- Incorporate manufacturer recommendations, including the appropriate National Roofing Contractors Association and Sheet Metal and Air Conditioning Contractors Association specifications and details relevant to your design.

- Design proper vapor retarders: first determine whether a vapor retarder is to be used. Do not have more than one vapor retarder, since such practice may entrap moisture. Where there is a likelihood of vapor condensation, the protected membrane roof system is usually the system of choice for low-slope roofs. In making the decision on whether to include a vapor retarder, consult the ASHRAE *Handbook of Fundamentals* as well as the NRCA *Roofing and Waterproofing Manual*. In climates where condensation only occurs under unusual conditions, and where the roof system has the ability to absorb the moisture that may condense under those conditions, a vapor retarder is neither necessary nor desirable.

- Apply or exceed existing codes: find out what codes and regulations, such as insurance requirements for wind uplift and code requirements for fire resistance, apply, and select systems that conform to those codes and regulations. Do not assume that any product on the market conforms to code requirements.

- Create positive drainage: determine the drainage requirements from the SMACNA Handbook, the BOCA National Plumbing Code, or other codes that apply. Provide redundant drainage in case the primary drainage becomes clogged. The roof must drain freely and completely under all conditions of live load and dead load deflection. Roofing distributors may be willing to help you lay out the roof slopes; they have computers programmed to perform such layouts. If practicable, keep drains in areas of maximum deflection, and keep them away from walls and parapets that may cause leaves to pile up and/or snow and ice damage.

- Anticipate and design for extreme conditions: perform calculations to determine the required wind load, wind uplift load, and snow load, or have your structural engineering consultant do so. Design the structure and roof system accordingly.

- Be the devil in the details: after the design is mostly finished, play the devil's advocate. Try to find the ways that water can enter your system, and then correct the design to exclude water. Better yet, have this critical review conducted by a knowledgeable person, in your office or from another office, who is not part of the design team for the project.

- Design penetrations carefully: when designing roof penetrations, keep them well apart from one another and from parapets and walls. When designing supports for rooftop equipment, such as mechanical equipment, leave enough room under them for the roofers to work.

- For repair and replacement of roofing, inspect and remove unsatisfactory conditions: if there is an existing roof, determine whether it must be removed before application of the new roof. This author recommends removing the old roof in almost all cases, one reason being that you can then inspect the structure for possible decay and damage. If the existing roof is to be removed, partially or fully, have it tested for possible asbestos content, and require conformity with environmental protection, public health, and OSHA regulations.

- Help define a roof maintenance program: determine how the roof will be maintained, repaired, and removed at the end of its useful life. When replacement occurs, two-piece counterflashings make the work easier and better. For a very steep roof, consider anchors built into the system for attachment of equipment and safety lines. Access hatches and ladder guards high on the steep roof and at all levels of low-slope roofs will make it possible to perform maintenance and repairs properly. They will also allow the architect to observe and inspect the work safely.

- Use manufacturer's technical resources: require that the roof system manufacturer's representative be on the job as the work starts and at its completion. Discuss all details, and learn from the representative.

- Follow-up: go back a year later, and document what changes have occurred. Issue appropriate maintenance and/or follow-up recommendations to building owners and maintenance staff. Incorporate lessons learned from documented experience into office practices.

Accessing available information

The materials technology of modern roofing materials is constantly evolving, at times dramatically based on new materials and also upon field testing and experience. At the same time, technical information is also being constantly updated. The prudent designer and specifier of roof systems must therefore constantly refer to most recent technical literature, much of it developed by the roofing industry. There are differences in recommendations among the industry groups. For example, SMACNA recommends metal base flashings for low-slope roofs, while NRCA does not. Most roof system manufacturers have catalogs and manuals showing the proper use of their products. The following commentary provides a guide to these sources.

- For a person not familiar with roofing technology, the best single source is the National Roofing Contractors Association *NRCA Roofing and Waterproofing Manual.*

- The NRCA publishes yearly guides to major roof types, listing manufacturers, data, and available warranties under the titles "Commercial Low-slope Roofing Materials Guide" and "Residential Steep-slope Roofing Materials Guide." The Association also publishes a monthly magazine, *Professional Roofing,* with articles on low-slope and steep roofing. This is an especially current reference on problems in roofing technology applications and what is being done to solve them.

- The U.S. National Institute of Standards and Technology (NIST), together with NRCA and other professional and industry associations, sponsors international symposia on roofing every few years. The proceedings of these symposia are published and report on the very latest research information on roofs, and probable future trends.

- The sheet metal industry has published a thorough manual for the use of its products: Sheet Metal and Air Conditioning Contractors' Association (SMACNA) *Architectural Sheet Metal Manual.* Details are available for CAD use.

- The Asphalt Roofing Manufacturers Association publishes the *Residential Asphalt Roofing Manual.*

- The Cedar Shake and Shingle Bureau *Design and Application Manual* applies to this association's products.

- The Vermont Structural Slate Co., Fair Haven, Vermont, distributes *Slate Roofs,* which is a reprinting of a 1926 manual on slate roof construction.

- *The Roofing Specifier* (TRS) is a monthly trade journal with technical features and briefings available without charge to qualified professionals. 131 West 1st Street, Duluth, MN 55802 ■

Plate 1. Built-up roofing: Embedded edge metal flashing (gravel stop). (NRCA BUR-3S): This is a typical low roof edge for a built-up roof. Note that the first ply of roofing felt is folded back to form an envelope, which contains the bitumen. If the envelope is omitted, or if it breaks, coal tar will drip down the wall.

BUILT-UP ROOFING

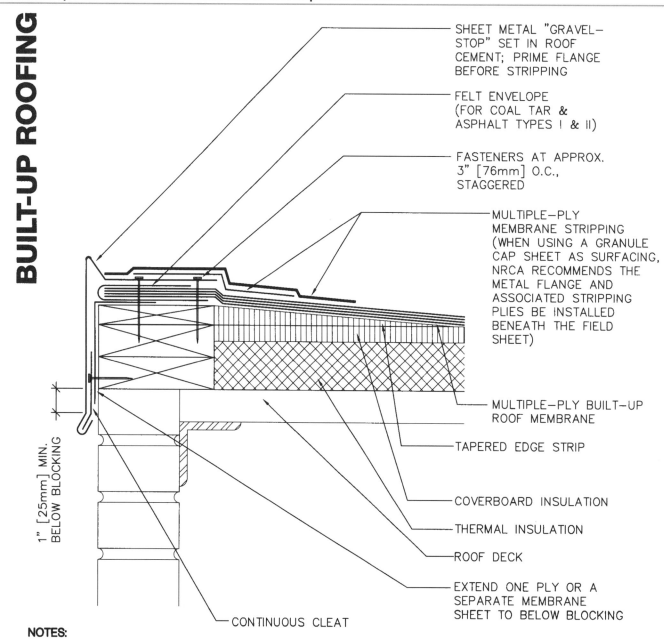

SHEET METAL "GRAVEL-STOP" SET IN ROOF CEMENT; PRIME FLANGE BEFORE STRIPPING

FELT ENVELOPE (FOR COAL TAR & ASPHALT TYPES I & II)

FASTENERS AT APPROX. 3" [76mm] O.C., STAGGERED

MULTIPLE-PLY MEMBRANE STRIPPING (WHEN USING A GRANULE CAP SHEET AS SURFACING, NRCA RECOMMENDS THE METAL FLANGE AND ASSOCIATED STRIPPING PLIES BE INSTALLED BENEATH THE FIELD SHEET)

MULTIPLE-PLY BUILT-UP ROOF MEMBRANE

TAPERED EDGE STRIP

COVERBOARD INSULATION

THERMAL INSULATION

ROOF DECK

EXTEND ONE PLY OR A SEPARATE MEMBRANE SHEET TO BELOW BLOCKING

1" [25mm] MIN. BELOW BLOCKING

CONTINUOUS CLEAT

NOTES:

1. NRCA SUGGESTS AVOIDING (WHERE POSSIBLE) FLASHING DETAILS THAT REQUIRE RIGID METAL FLANGES TO BE EMBEDDED OR SANDWICHED INTO THE ROOF MEMBRANE. (SEE BUR-1 FOR THE PREFERRED PERIMETER CONSTRUCTION.)
2. THIS DETAIL SHOULD BE USED ONLY WHERE THE DECK IS SUPPORTED BY THE OUTSIDE WALL.
3. ATTACH NAILER TO WALL WITH SUITABLE FASTENERS.
4. WOOD BLOCKING MAY BE SLOTTED FOR VENTING OF WET-FILL DECKS OR OTHER CONSTRUCTIONS WHERE APPLICABLE.
5. FREQUENT NAILING OF SHEET METAL FLANGE IS NECESSARY TO MINIMIZE THERMAL MOVEMENT.
6. REFER TO BUR/MB TABLE 1 FOR METAL THICKNESS AND CLEAT REQUIREMENT.
7. NRCA SUGGESTS THAT THE TOP STRIPPING PLY BE A HEAVY-WEIGHT REINFORCED POLYMER MODIFIED BITUMEN SHEET TO HELP STRIPPING PLIES ACCOMMODATE THERMAL MOVEMENT OF METAL.

Plate 2. Modified bitumen roofing: Embedded edge metal flashing (gravel stop). (NRCA detail MB-3S): This detail is similar to Fig. 5, but there is one major difference and advantage: the base sheet extends over the edge, behind the metal fascia. This detail will tolerate some leaking at the edge joint, since water that penetrates through the junctions of different materials will be above the base sheet and thus kept out of the building. Some manufacturers permit modified bitumen edge details with built-up roofs, and this author recommends that practice.

MODIFIED BITUMEN ROOFING

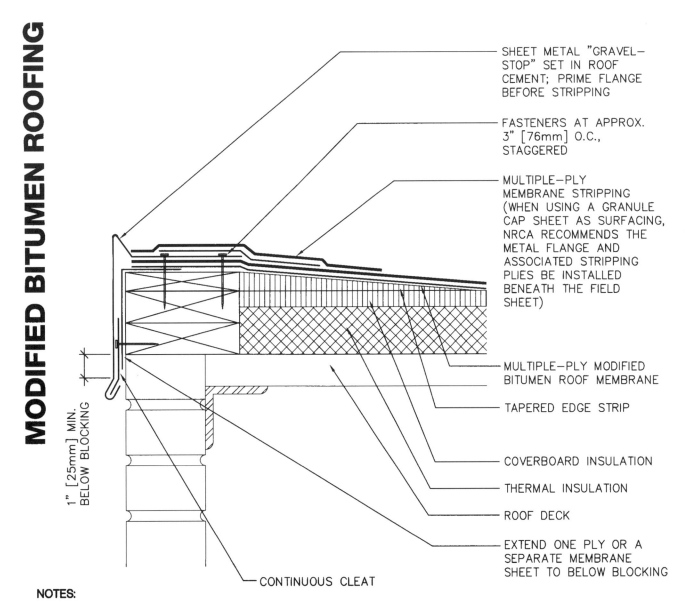

SHEET METAL "GRAVEL-STOP" SET IN ROOF CEMENT; PRIME FLANGE BEFORE STRIPPING

FASTENERS AT APPROX. 3" [76mm] O.C., STAGGERED

MULTIPLE-PLY MEMBRANE STRIPPING (WHEN USING A GRANULE CAP SHEET AS SURFACING, NRCA RECOMMENDS THE METAL FLANGE AND ASSOCIATED STRIPPING PLIES BE INSTALLED BENEATH THE FIELD SHEET)

MULTIPLE-PLY MODIFIED BITUMEN ROOF MEMBRANE

TAPERED EDGE STRIP

COVERBOARD INSULATION

THERMAL INSULATION

ROOF DECK

EXTEND ONE PLY OR A SEPARATE MEMBRANE SHEET TO BELOW BLOCKING

1" [25mm] MIN. BELOW BLOCKING

CONTINUOUS CLEAT

NOTES:

1. NRCA SUGGESTS AVOIDING (WHERE POSSIBLE) FLASHING DETAILS THAT REQUIRE RIGID METAL FLANGES TO BE EMBEDDED OR SANDWICHED INTO THE ROOF MEMBRANE. (SEE MB-1 FOR THE PREFERRED PERIMETER CONSTRUCTION.)
2. THIS DETAIL SHOULD BE USED ONLY WHERE THE DECK IS SUPPORTED BY THE OUTSIDE WALL.
3. ATTACH NAILER TO WALL WITH SUITABLE FASTENERS.
4. WOOD BLOCKING MAY BE SLOTTED FOR VENTING OF WET-FILL DECKS OR OTHER CONSTRUCTIONS WHERE APPLICABLE.
5. FREQUENT NAILING OF SHEET METAL FLANGE IS NECESSARY TO MINIMIZE THERMAL MOVEMENT.
6. REFER TO BUR/MB TABLE 1 FOR METAL THICKNESS AND CLEAT REQUIREMENT.
7. NRCA SUGGESTS THAT THE TOP STRIPPING PLY BE A HEAVY-WEIGHT REINFORCED POLYMER MODIFIED BITUMEN SHEET TO HELP STRIPPING PLIES ACCOMMODATE THERMAL MOVEMENT OF METAL.

Plate 3. Built-up roofing: Base flashing for wall-supported deck. (NRCA detail BUR-5S): This is a detail for the intersection of a roof and a masonry wall, the roof being supported by the wall. Note that the metal counterflashing is made in two pieces, so that it can be taken off for installation of the base flashing. Note also that the counterflashing is joined to through-wall flashing in the masonry wall. This writer also recommends weep tubes where the counterflashing meets the masonry wall, to let out water that may find its way into the cavity. If the wall and roof move differentially, a different detail, for expansion joints, should be used.

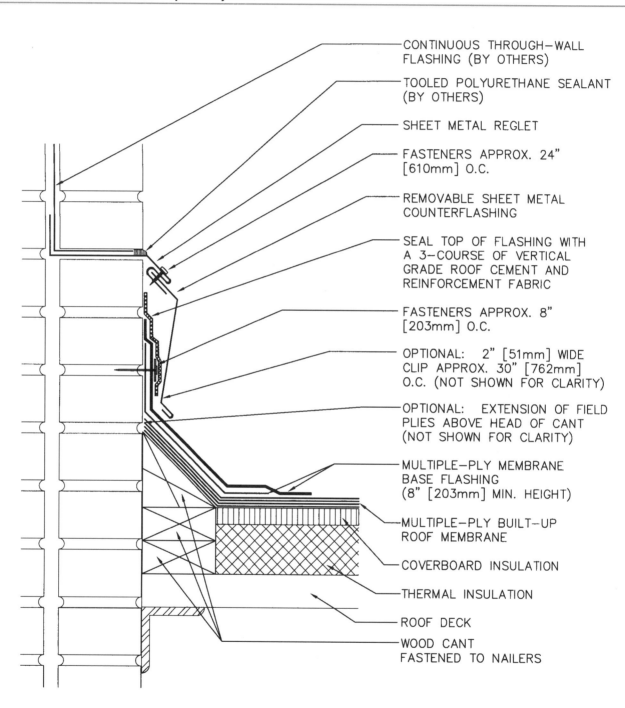

BUILT-UP ROOFING

CONTINUOUS THROUGH—WALL FLASHING (BY OTHERS)

TOOLED POLYURETHANE SEALANT (BY OTHERS)

SHEET METAL REGLET

FASTENERS APPROX. 24" [610mm] O.C.

REMOVABLE SHEET METAL COUNTERFLASHING

SEAL TOP OF FLASHING WITH A 3—COURSE OF VERTICAL GRADE ROOF CEMENT AND REINFORCEMENT FABRIC

FASTENERS APPROX. 8" [203mm] O.C.

OPTIONAL: 2" [51mm] WIDE CLIP APPROX. 30" [762mm] O.C. (NOT SHOWN FOR CLARITY)

OPTIONAL: EXTENSION OF FIELD PLIES ABOVE HEAD OF CANT (NOT SHOWN FOR CLARITY)

MULTIPLE—PLY MEMBRANE BASE FLASHING (8" [203mm] MIN. HEIGHT)

MULTIPLE—PLY BUILT—UP ROOF MEMBRANE

COVERBOARD INSULATION

THERMAL INSULATION

ROOF DECK

WOOD CANT FASTENED TO NAILERS

NOTES:

1. THIS DETAIL SHOULD BE USED ONLY WHERE THE DECK IS SUPPORTED BY THE WALL.
2. THE JOINTS IN THE SHEET METAL COUNTERFLASHING SHOULD NOT BE SOLDERED.
3. OPTION: IF WOOD NAILERS ARE NOT USED, A FIBER CANT STRIP SET IN BITUMEN OR ADHESIVE MAY BE USED.
4. SEE TABLE 2 FOR ALTERNATE SHEET METAL COUNTERFLASHING TERMINATIONS.

Plate 4. Thermoplastic roofing. (NRCA detail TP-6): This is a detail for the intersection of a concrete wall and a roof, the roof being supported on the wall. Note that the counterflashing is applied to the face of the concrete and sealed. In the author's experience, surface-applied counterflashings are more reliable than flashing inserted into cast or sawn reglets in the wall.

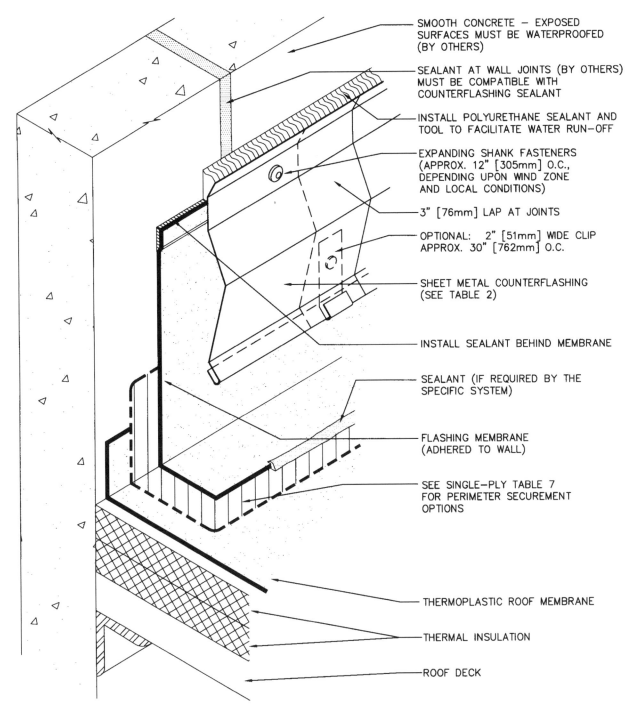

SMOOTH CONCRETE – EXPOSED SURFACES MUST BE WATERPROOFED (BY OTHERS)

SEALANT AT WALL JOINTS (BY OTHERS) MUST BE COMPATIBLE WITH COUNTERFLASHING SEALANT

INSTALL POLYURETHANE SEALANT AND TOOL TO FACILITATE WATER RUN–OFF

EXPANDING SHANK FASTENERS (APPROX. 12" [305mm] O.C., DEPENDING UPON WIND ZONE AND LOCAL CONDITIONS)

3" [76mm] LAP AT JOINTS

OPTIONAL: 2" [51mm] WIDE CLIP APPROX. 30" [762mm] O.C.

SHEET METAL COUNTERFLASHING (SEE TABLE 2)

INSTALL SEALANT BEHIND MEMBRANE

SEALANT (IF REQUIRED BY THE SPECIFIC SYSTEM)

FLASHING MEMBRANE (ADHERED TO WALL)

SEE SINGLE–PLY TABLE 7 FOR PERIMETER SECUREMENT OPTIONS

THERMOPLASTIC ROOF MEMBRANE

THERMAL INSULATION

ROOF DECK

THERMOPLASTIC ROOFING

NOTES:

1. THIS DETAIL SHOULD BE USED ONLY WHERE THE DECK IS SUPPORTED BY THE WALL.
2. TOP LAYER OF INSULATION CAN BE EITHER THERMAL INSULATION OR COVERBOARD INSULATION.
3. SLIP SHEET MAY BE REQUIRED BELOW MEMBRANE WHEN OVERLAYING SOME INSULATIONS OR SUBSTRATES.

Plate 5. Roof drain. Thermoset Roofing. (NRCA detail TS-22): The drain is shown recessed in a wide sump, to ensure that water is not impounded. The roof membrane is installed over the drain bowl flange, and then a clamping ring is installed on top of the membrane. When the bolts are tightened, the clamping ring "pinches" the membrane, creating a watertight joint. The drain strainer keeps objects out of the drain.

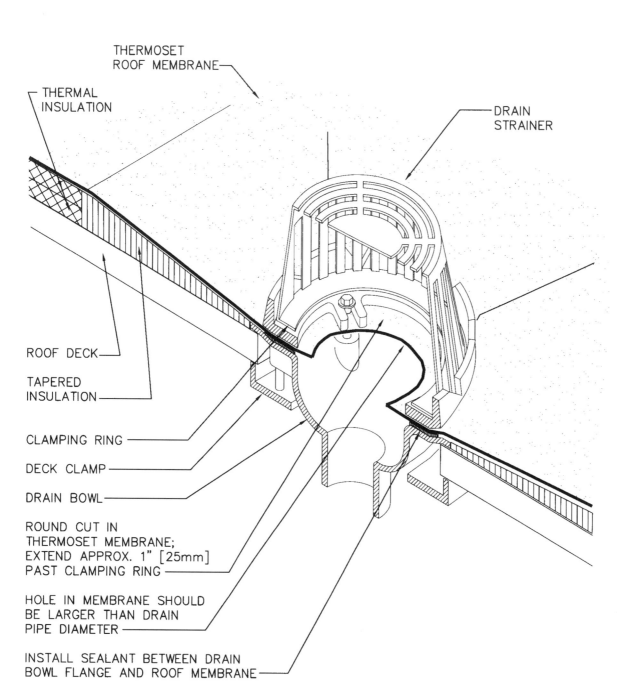

THERMOSET
ROOF MEMBRANE

THERMAL
INSULATION

DRAIN
STRAINER

ROOF DECK

TAPERED
INSULATION

CLAMPING RING

DECK CLAMP

DRAIN BOWL

ROUND CUT IN
THERMOSET MEMBRANE;
EXTEND APPROX. 1" [25mm]
PAST CLAMPING RING

HOLE IN MEMBRANE SHOULD
BE LARGER THAN DRAIN
PIPE DIAMETER

INSTALL SEALANT BETWEEN DRAIN
BOWL FLANGE AND ROOF MEMBRANE

THERMOSET ROOFING

NOTE:

1. THE USE OF A METAL DECK SUMP PAN IS NOT RECOMMENDED.   HOWEVER, DRAIN RECEIVER/BEARING PLATES ARE APPLICABLE WITH SOME PROJECTS.

Plate 6. Roof drain. Built-up roofing. (NRCA detail BUR-23): Roof drains for built-up roofs require more plies of roofing and flashing than drains for other systems. Unless the drain is placed in a wide and deep sump, the buildup of plies will create a dam around the drain, impounding water. Another advantage of the sump is that the insulation is thin there, and internal warmth from the building will tend to melt ice and snow from the drains and their immediate perimeter.

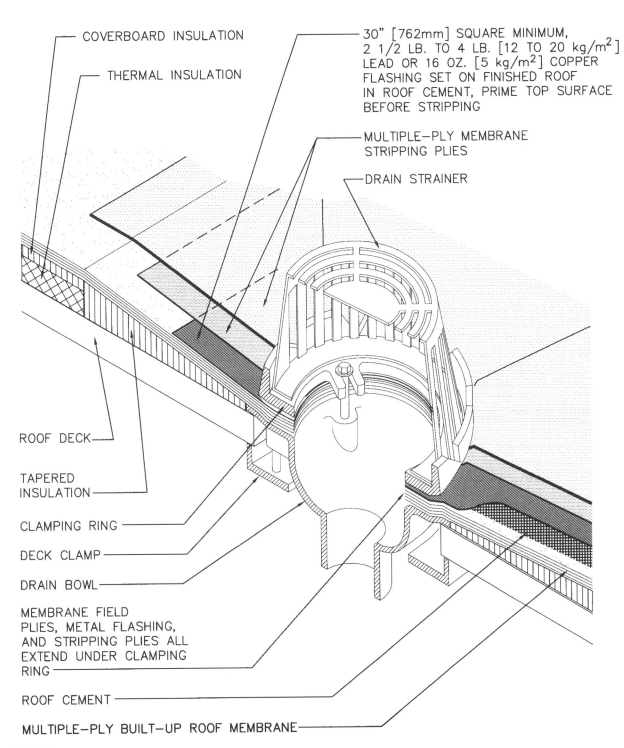

COVERBOARD INSULATION

THERMAL INSULATION

30" [762mm] SQUARE MINIMUM, 2 1/2 LB. TO 4 LB. [12 TO 20 kg/m^2] LEAD OR 16 OZ. [5 kg/m^2] COPPER FLASHING SET ON FINISHED ROOF IN ROOF CEMENT, PRIME TOP SURFACE BEFORE STRIPPING

MULTIPLE–PLY MEMBRANE STRIPPING PLIES

DRAIN STRAINER

BUILT-UP ROOFING

ROOF DECK

TAPERED INSULATION

CLAMPING RING

DECK CLAMP

DRAIN BOWL

MEMBRANE FIELD PLIES, METAL FLASHING, AND STRIPPING PLIES ALL EXTEND UNDER CLAMPING RING

ROOF CEMENT

MULTIPLE–PLY BUILT–UP ROOF MEMBRANE

NOTES:

1. THE USE OF A METAL DECK SUMP PAN IS NOT RECOMMENDED. HOWEVER, DRAIN RECEIVER/BEARING PLATES ARE APPLICABLE WITH SOME PROJECTS.
2. DO NOT APPLY COAL TAR OR DEAD LEVEL ASPHALT INTO DRAIN SUMP.

REFERENCES

Asphalt Roofing Manufacturers Association, *Residential Asphalt Roofing Manual,* Asphalt Roofing Manufacturers Association, Rockville, 1996.

National Research Council of Canada, "Design Guidelines for Green Roofs" and other information resources on earth-covered roof technology, 2004 <http://www.greenroofs.org>

NRCA, *NRCA Roofing and Waterproofing Manual,* 5th ed., National Roofing Contractors Association, Rosemont, 2001.

Patterson, Terry L., *Illustrated 2000 Building Code Handbook,* McGraw-Hill, New York, 2001.

SMACNA, *Architectural Sheet Metal Manual,* 5th ed., Sheet Metal and Air Conditioning Contractors' Association, Chantilly, 1993.

Watson, Donald, and Kenneth Labs, *Climatic Building Design,* McGraw-Hill, New York, 1983, 1993.

Donald Baerman

Summary

The most common method of rainwater removal from steep roofs is by gutters and downspouts. Other methods include direct discharge from the eaves (particularly common in cold regions), water diverters, and gutters discharging into internal leaders. Some low-slope roofs discharge through scuppers into leader heads and downspouts.

Key words

downspout, drainage, gargoyles, gutter capacity, leader capacity, rain chain, roof drainage, waterspouts

Newly cast lead leader head. Calke Abbey, Derbyshire, UK.

Gutters and downspouts

1 OVERVIEW OF ROOF DRAINAGE OPTIONS

In many locales, it is common to allow water to drain directly off the edges of steep roofs. Except in very dry areas, direct drainage should be used in conjunction with wide overhangs and, where there is a basement, a drip bed at the ground and subsurface drainage. Direct drainage is especially common in regions subject to severe cold weather, where ice and snow may remain on roofs for long periods and where gutters and downspouts do not function in winter. Water diverters may be used to avoid discharge of water over doorways and other pedestrian walkways.

The most common type of roof drainage for steep roofs is a combination of gutters and downspouts (the words "leader" and "downspout" both refer to pipes conducting water down from a roof). The gutters should be designed to accept all normal roof runoff, and the downspouts should be able to discharge all water that flows to them quickly.

Water diverters are sometimes used in place of gutters. Instead of being mounted under the eaves, water diverters are mounted above the roof plane. While diverters do not extend to the edge of the eaves, and thus they do allow some dripping, they are not as prone to clogging as gutters.

Waterspouts or gargoyles may lead the water out from the wall and allow it to drip into a pool or drip bed below. Chains, in a detail familiar in traditional Japanese architecture, are sometimes used to lead the water to the ground.

Although the predominant method of draining low-slope roofs is by internal drains, gutters and downspouts are sometimes used instead.

Some low-slope roofs are drained through scuppers at the perimeter into leader heads and then into downspouts. Some other low-slope roofs are drained from low edges into gutters, which in turn drain into downspouts, or directly to the ground from the roof edges. Still other low-slope roofs discharge from projected water spouts directly to the ground.

All roof drain systems in cold regions may form icicles, except internal leaders in heated buildings. Therefore one should not design sidewalks under the eaves. It may be prudent to design landscaping beds or rock drip beds to keep people from passing under the eaves. Alternatively, a good quality electric snow melting system in the gutters and downspouts will, when it functions, prevent problems due to icicles.

2 MATERIALS FOR GUTTERS AND DOWNSPOUTS

- *Copper, lead-coated copper, and zinc-tin coated copper.* The first two of these materials have a long history of successful use on roofs. They are easy to form and solder. They are highly ductile, and so they tend to yield harmlessly when stressed. (See "Corrosion of Metals" in this volume regarding corrosion of copper and lead-coated copper from acid deposition.) In those parts of the country subject to acid deposition (acid rain residue and directly deposited acid aerosol), dew and mist may dissolve acid deposits on roofs and wash the concentrated acid onto sheet metal. Roofs made entirely from copper might not be harmed, but copper and lead-coated copper roofs that receive drainage from other, non-neutralizing or acid-producing materials are corroded. Gutters, downspouts, and valleys, being at the bottom of the system, are especially vulnerable to acid corrosion. Some protective methods include:

- Detail the roof so that no water flows from other, non-neutralizing materials onto copper and lead-coated copper. A roof made entirely from copper is one way to accomplish this.

- Use thicker copper, such as 20-oz, and plan for replacement within 15 to 20 years.

- Use sheet metal not subject to acid corrosion, such as aluminum, stainless steel, and Terne-coated stainless steel for gutters and downspouts ("Terne" is a trade name for a product of Follansbee Steel Corp.).

- Install sacrificial zinc anodes at the eaves, where the acid runs into the gutters.

• *Aluminum*. Aluminum is vulnerable to attack by hydroxyl ions, but concentrated hydroxyl ions are rare on roofs. Aluminum is not vulnerable to attack from the concentrations of acid that occur on roofs. Although very thin aluminum is used on residences, the SMACNA Manual recommends the proper minimum gauge for architectural use. Aluminum is available with highly durable finishes, including fluorocarbon polymer coatings. Contrary to conventional wisdom, proper aluminum alloys with proper finish are not subject to corrosion from salt spray. Aluminum is the material of choice for gutters and downspouts that do not require soldering.

• *Galvanized steel*. Plain galvanized steel may not be satisfactory for gutters, downspouts, valleys, and other roofing sheet metal exposed to concentrated runoff in those parts of the country with frequent rainfall and acid deposition. The protective coating may be eroded rapidly. It has been used successfully in other parts of the country, however, and if properly maintained and periodically painted, it gives good service. Aluminized steel and aluminum-zinc alloy coated steel appear to perform better. They have the advantages of economy, strength, and low coefficient of thermal expansion. Durable finishes are available.

Fig. 1. Built-in gutter. Yale University Hall of Graduate Studies. 1932. James Gamble Rogers, Architect.

• *Stainless steel and Terne*. Stainless steel and Terne-coated stainless steel are highly durable metals. Terne-coated stainless steel is glossy upon first exposure, but it turns matte gray with continued exposure. Stainless steel is subject to stress hardening, and thus it is harder to work than copper, and it may rip rather than yield when exposed to great stress. Terne-coated stainless steel can be soldered well. In parts of the country exposed to acid deposition, where the metal must be soldered, Terne-coated stainless steel is the sheet metal of choice in the author's opinion.

• *Zinc and zinc alloys*. Zinc and zinc alloys have many of the same characteristics as copper. They are durable and easy to form and solder. Although the author has not seen acid damage to zinc alloys, it probably occurs.

• *Monel*™ is a very highly durable metal alloy occasionally used for gutters and downspouts. Metal thicknesses for gutters and downspouts are recommended in the SMACNA Handbook.

• *Wood*. Gutters may be made from decay-resistant woods, and they have given decades of satisfactory use. They are of course best detailed as easily removable to provide for replacement. They are used for historic preservation and replication details. Modern single-ply roofing materials, both thermoplastic and thermoset, are not subject to the problems of thermal expansion and corrosion that affect metal gutters. Wooden or other gutters, lined with single-ply roof membrane material, give durable and beneficial service.

3 TYPES OF GUTTERS AND WATER DIVERTERS

The simplest type of gutter, and generally the least troublesome, is a sheet metal hanging gutter installed under the eaves. These gutters may be half-round, rectangular, ogee, or other shapes. A great diversity of products to support such gutters are available, some of which are shown in the SMACNA *Architectural Sheet Metal Manual*, one of which is shown below.

Built-in gutters have been common, especially on monumental buildings with steep roofs (**Fig. 1**). Built-in gutters allow little room for error; such gutters must be fabricated and installed by highly skilled workers following the recommendations of the SMACNA *Architectural Sheet Metal Manual*. The architect should require proof of skill and experience on the part of the workers who will fabricate and install such systems; many built-in gutters look superficially like proper designs but are not properly made.

The architect should understand how seams should be soldered: the seams are first coated with solder ("pretinned"), unless the metal is already coated. The metal is then heated, and the solder is touched to the outside of the seam. If the procedure is proper, the solder will draw into the seam, filling it. One should require a demonstration of soldering before the work is performed. Cut open the sample seam to make sure that the solder has penetrated fully.

Because of the location of built-in gutters, where a leak could often result in considerable damage to the building, it is recommended that a redundant flexible gutter liner be installed under and behind the metal gutter (**Fig. 2**). The flexible liner should have its own drains, preferably in such a location that drainage from it will be seen and reported.

Metal built-in gutters, being stiff, require provisions for thermal expansion and shrinkage. Expansion joints should be designed between the drains, and the seams should be very firmly fastened, as with rivets as well as solder (details are provided in SMACNA 1993).

Gutter expansion joints are quite complex, and they should be fabricated and installed only by highly skilled sheet metal workers. While SMACNA details do not show a redundant, flexible liner under the gutter, such protection is recommended. The flexible liner should be covered with a sheet of lubricating building paper to allow movement.

Many of the problems of sheet metal built-in gutters can be avoided by using flexible materials, which do not require expansion joints, and are not subject to corrosion. They are relatively easy to repair and replace.

Wide, shallow gutters do not usually become clogged with leaves and other debris; the wind helps clear them. Most gutters, however, do become clogged, and cleaning gutters may be expensive and difficult. Light-duty gutters on multistory buildings with steep roofs are particularly difficult to clean, especially without damaging the gutters with the ladders (ladders equipped with stand-offs should be used).

One way to avoid the need for frequent cleaning is to mount a screen over the gutter. A simple screen installation is shown in **Fig. 3.** The screened gutter detail allows leaves and other debris to wash off, while the water flows through the screen. The screen should be in the

Fig. 2. Rubber-lined gutter.

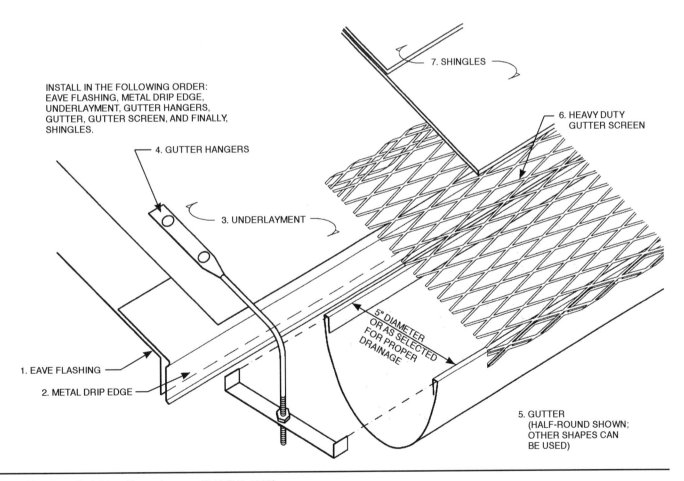

INSTALL IN THE FOLLOWING ORDER:
EAVE FLASHING, METAL DRIP EDGE,
UNDERLAYMENT, GUTTER HANGERS,
GUTTER, GUTTER SCREEN, AND FINALLY,
SHINGLES.

4. GUTTER HANGERS

3. UNDERLAYMENT

1. EAVE FLASHING

2. METAL DRIP EDGE

7. SHINGLES

6. HEAVY DUTY
GUTTER SCREEN

5" DIAMETER
OR AS SELECTED
FOR PROPER
DRAINAGE

5. GUTTER
(HALF-ROUND SHOWN;
OTHER SHAPES CAN
BE USED)

Fig. 3. Hanging adjustable gutter and screen. (SMACNA 1993)

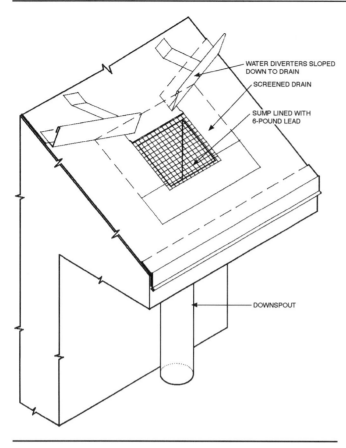

WATER DIVERTERS SLOPED DOWN TO DRAIN

SCREENED DRAIN

SUMP LINED WITH 6-POUND LEAD

DOWNSPOUT

Fig. 4. Isometric of simple basic leader head with screen.

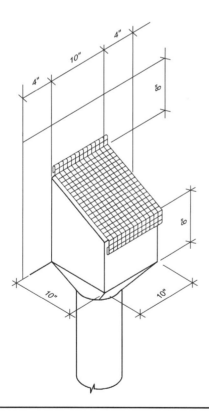

Fig. 5. Water diverter and drain.

plane of the roof, and it should pass over the gutter; it should not be mounted flat on top of the gutter. If gutter hangers are fastened to the roof sheathing, they should be installed before the shingles, to be concealed. Adjustable gutter hangers allow adjustment after installation, so that the gutters will drain thoroughly.

Gutters can make ice dams more troublesome. Eave flashing should extend behind hung gutters and, for built-in gutters, under the gutters.

Another type of drainage includes a scupper, leader head or "conductor head," and downspout. To avoid stopping up of the gutters and upper downspouts, design an air gap between the scupper and the top of the leader head. Provide a sloped screen on top of the leader head (**Fig. 4**).

In place of gutters, water diverters may be used. They are less likely than gutters to become clogged with leaves, and they are easier to keep clear. The eave flashing should extend at least 2 ft (61 cm) above the diverters. There will necessarily be some dripping from the eaves below the diverter, but most of the water will be directed to the downspout (**Fig. 5**).

Corrugated round and rectangular downspouts may expand a little from ice without being damaged. Electrical resistance heaters in the downspouts, as well as the gutters, will melt ice and help clear the downspouts. Such equipment uses energy, and power should be turned on only when required by freezing conditions.

Leader heads are an opportunity for innovative design; they may be very simple or decorative (**Figs. 6 to 9**). For cold climates, open-front downspouts are recommended by SMACNA. Except during deluge conditions, the water flow will remain in contact with the three sides of the downspout. At the transition from gutter to downspout, the back of the open-front downspout should gently curve forward and then backward to receive the flow of water from all sides of the gutter outlet. The flow has been timed at approximately 3 mph. At very high water volume, the water stream may "break away" from the downspout, but under those conditions some free-falling water will probably be tolerable.

Other approaches to rain gutters as expressive elements are indicated in **Figs. 10 and 11**.

Fig. 6. Scupper and leader head. City of York, UK.

Fig. 7. Scupper and leader head. First Church of Christ, Scientist, Berkeley, California. Bernard Maybeck, Architect.

Fig. 9. Stylized lily head on open-front leader. Donald Baerman, AIA Architect.

Fig. 8. Stylized acanthus leaf on open-front leader. Donald Baerman, AIA Architect.

Fig. 10. Rain chain. Japanese Garden Pavilion, Portland, Oregon.

Fig. 11. Water scoop or "drip gutter" of corrugated steel 60 in (152 cm) diameter. Water collects in the scoop and drips through holes drilled in the bottom of the scoop to landscape below. Cinema 12, Atlanta, Georgia. Richard Rauh & Assoc., Architects.

Photo: Peter Maus/Esto.

The drainage recommended by SMACNA (**Tables 1** and **2**) will work for open-front downspouts as well as for closed downspouts. Thus, if a 4 in (10.8 cm) wide × 3 in (7.6 cm) deep closed downspout is adequate, then a 4 in (10.8 cm) wide open downspout will also be adequate. Open-front downspouts will develop icicles in cold weather. The icicles will, however, melt faster than the ice inside closed downspouts.

Downspouts should not discharge directly on the ground near foundations of buildings with basements or crawl spaces. Proper methods of discharge include:

- Boots connected to subsurface drain lines. Do not discharge rainwater into perforated footing drains; the two should be separate. Drain boots serving open-front leaders should have sloped screens above the boots to prevent leaves from clogging the underground drain lines.

- Drained drip beds, trenches, surface gutters, swales, French drains, and other surface and shallow drains.

Downspout straps and their fasteners should be heavy-duty and resistant to corrosion; in cold climates they may have to support a column of ice. The author recommends a minimum of 0.04 in (1 mm) for light-duty residential downspouts and twice that for architectural downspouts. There should be downspout straps at the top and bottom of the downspout, above and below offsets, and (in the author's opinion) no further than 12 ft (360 cm) apart elsewhere.

Where valleys discharge into gutters, consider adding water diverters to prevent the full flow from the valleys from overshooting the gutters.

Sometimes gutters discharge into internal leaders, or into leader heads that discharge into internal leaders. As long as the internal leaders do not leak, and as long as the building is heated, this is an excellent method of drainage. The internal leaders will not become clogged with ice. As with all plumbing systems, the internal leaders should be accessible for inspection, maintenance, and replacement, and they should have cleanouts.

Waterspouts, or gargoyles, are a way of carrying water away from the building walls and foundations. The water may then fall onto a gravel or sculptural drip bed or into a pool.

Estimating rainfall and drainage capacity

The International Plumbing Code and other codes stipulate the required drainage capacity. The Sheet Metal and Air Conditioning Contractors Association's *Architectural Sheet Metal Manual* has recommended sizes for leaders and downspouts (Tables 1 and 2). This latter reference is not mandatory, but it is prudent to follow its recommendations. Recommended drainage capacity figures are given for 5-year, 10-year, and maximum storms. The accompanying plates offer a nomograph method of calculating gutter capacity as an additional reference check.

One of the factors in determining drainage capacity is the effect of delayed drainage. If the effect of delayed drainage would be catastrophic, the values for "100 Year Storms," plus a safety margin, should be used. If there is no detrimental effect from delayed drainage, a lower value, but not less than that which is code-mandated, may be used. ■

Table 1. Rainfall data and drainage factors for major U.S. locations

Intensities are based on records and statistical projections. They may occasionally be exceeded either in the general location or within microclimatic local areas. (SMACNA 1993)

	A STORMS WHICH SHOULD BE EXCEEDED ONLY ONCE IN 10 YEARS				B STORMS WHICH SHOULD BE EXCEEDED ONLY ONCE IN 100 YEARS			
	Intensity lasting 5 minutes		Calculated roof area drained per downspout area		Intensity lasting 5 minutes		Calculated roof area drained per downspout area	
	in/hr	mm/hr	sq ft/ sq in	sq mn/ 100 sq mm	in/hr	mm/hr	sq ft/ sq in	sq m/ 100 sq mm
ALABAMA: Birmingham	7.5	191	160	2.30	10.1	256	120	1.7
Mobile	8.2	208	150	2.10	10.8	274	110	1.6
ALASKA: Fairbanks	2.1	53	570	8.30	3.8	97	310	4.5
Juneau	1.7	43	700	10.10	2.3	57	530	7.60
ARIZONA: Phoenix	5.6	141	220	3.10	8.8	224	140	2.00
Tucson	6.1	155	200	2.80	9.1	232	130	1.90
ARKANSAS: Bentonville	7.4	187	160	2.30	10.2	259	120	1.70
Little Rock	7.4	187	160	2.30	10.0	253	120	1.70
CALIFORNIA: Los Angeles	4.9	124	250	3.50	6.7	170	180	2.60
Sacramento	2.5	64	480	6.90	3.9	100	310	4.40
San Francisco	2.7	68	450	6.4	3.7	93	330	4.70
San Diego	2.2	57	540	7.80	3.1	78	390	5.60
COLORADO: Denver	5.7	146	210	3.00	9.1	232	130	1.90
Boulder	6.4	164	190	2.70	9.4	238	130	1.80
CONNECTICUT: Hartford	6.2	158	190	2.8	8.7	221	140	2.00
DISTRICT OF COLUMBIA	7.1	180	170	2.4	9.7	247	120	1.80
FLORIDA: Jacksonville	7.9	200	150	2.20	10.1	256	120	1.70
Miami	7.7	195	160	2.20	9.8	250	120	1.80
Tampa	8.3	212	140	2.10	10.8	274	110	1.60
GEORGIA: Atlanta	7.3	186	160	2.4	9.9	251	120	1.70
HAWAII: Honolulu	8.7	221	140	2.00	12.0	305	100	1.40
Kahului	7.0	177	170	2.50	12.0	305	100	1.40
Hilo	17.4	442	70	1.00	19.2	488	60	0.90
Lihue	10.4	265	110	1.70	14.4	366	80	1.20
IDAHO: Boise	1.8	46	660	9.50	3.3	84	360	5.20
ILLINOIS: Chicago	6.8	172	180	2.60	9.3	236	130	1.90
INDIANA: Indianapolis	6.8	173	180	2.50	9.4	239	130	1.80
IOWA: Des Moines	7.3	186	160	2.40	10.3	262	120	1.70
KANSAS: Wichita	7.5	191	160	2.30	10.5	267	110	1.60
KENTUCKY: Louisville	6.9	175	170	2.50	9.4	238	130	1.80
LOUISIANA: New Orleans	8.3	211	140	2.10	10.9	277	110	1.60
MAINE: Portland	5.4	136	220	3.20	7.6	192	160	2.30
MARYLAND: Baltimore	7.1	181	170	2.40	9.7	247	120	1.80
MASSACHUSETTS: Boston	5.3	134	230	3.3	7.2	183	170	2.40
MICHIGAN: Detroit	6.4	162	190	2.70	8.9	226	140	1.90
MINNESOTA: Minneapolis	7.0	178	170	2.50	10.0	253	120	1.70

Table 1. Rainfall data and drainage factors for major U.S. locations (continued)

Intensities are based on records and statistical projections. They may occasionally be exceeded either in the general location or within microclimatic local areas. (SMACNA 1993)

	A STORMS WHICH SHOULD BE EXCEEDED ONLY ONCE IN 10 YEARS				B STORMS WHICH SHOULD BE EXCEEDED ONLY ONCE IN 100 YEARS			
	Intensity lasting 5 minutes		Calculated roof area drained per downspout area		Intensity lasting 5 minutes		Calculated roof area drained per downspout area	
	in/hr	mm/hr	sq ft/ sq in	sq mn/ 100 sq mm	in/hr	mm/hr	sq ft/ sq in	sq m/ 100 sq mm
MISSOURI: Kansas City	7.4	187	160	2.30	10.4	265	110	1.70
Saint Louis	7.1	181	170	2.40	9.9	251	120	1.70
MONTANA: Helena	1.8	46	660	9.50	3.1	77	390	5.70
Missoula	1.8	46	660	9.50	2.4	61	500	7.20
NEBRASKA: Omaha	7.4	188	160	2.30	10.5	267	110	1.60
NEVADA: Reno	2.3	57	530	7.60	4.5	114	270	3.90
Las Vegas	2.1	53	570	8.3	5.2	133	230	3.30
NEW JERSEY: Trenton	6.7	170	180	2.60	9.3	236	130	1.90
NEW MEXICO: Albuquerque	4.0	102	300	4.30	6.7	171	180	2.60
Santa Fe	4.5	115	270	3.80	6.4	169	180	2.60
NEW YORK: Albany	6.5	165	190	2.70	9.1	232	130	1.90
Buffalo	6.0	152	200	2.90	8.4	213	140	2.10
New York City	6.7	169	180	2.60	9.2	235	130	1.90
NORTH CAROLINA: Raleigh	7.3	185	160	2.40	9.8	250	120	1.80
NORTH DAKOTA: Bismark	6.6	167	180	2.60	9.8	250	120	1.80
OHIO: Cincinnati	6.8	172	180	2.50	9.3	236	130	1.90
Cleveland	6.3	160	190	2.70	8.8	223	140	2.00
OKLAHOMA: Oklahoma City	7.6	193	160	2.30	10.5	267	110	1.60
OREGON: Baker	2.2	56	550	7.90	3.8	97	310	4.50
Portland	2.1	53	570	8.30	3.0	76	400	5.80
PENNSYLVANIA: Philadelphia	6.8	172	180	2.60	9.4	238	130	1.80
Pittsburgh	6.4	163	190	2.70	8.8	224	140	2.00
RHODE ISLAND: Providence	5.6	143	210	3.10	7.8	198	150	2.20
SOUTH CAROLINA: Charleston	7.2	184	170	2.40	9.4	238	130	1.80
TENNESSEE: Memphis	7.4	187	160	2.30	10.0	253	120	1.70
Knoxville	6.7	169	180	2.60	9.0	229	130	1.90
TEXAS: Fort Worth	7.6	193	193	160	10.5	267	110	1.60
Dallas	7.6	194	160	2.30	10.5	267	110	1.60
Houston	8.2	208	150	2.10	10.8	274	110	1.60
San Antonio	7.6	193	160	2.30	10.5	267	110	1.60
UTAH: Provo	3.0	75	410	5.80	5.2	131	230	3.30
Salt Lake City	2.8	71	430	6.20	4.3	108	280	4.10
VIRGINIA: Norfolk	7.1	181	170	2.40	9.5	242	130	1.80
WASHINGTON: Seattle	2.1	53	570	8.30	3.3	84	360	5.20
Spokane	2.1	53	570	8.30	3.5	90	340	4.90
WEST VIRGINIA: Parkersburg	6.6	168	180	2.60	9.1	230	130	1.90
WISCONSIN: Madison	6.8	172	180	2.50	9.5	241	130	1.80
Milwaukee	6.6	168	180	2.60	9.1	232	130	1.90
WYOMING: Cheyenne	5.7	146	210	3.00	9.9	252	120	1.70

Table 2. Dimensions of standard downspouts
A = area of ¼ in. (6.4 mm) undersized inlet. (SMACNA 1993)

TYPE	AREA		"A" Size		Nominal Size		Actual	
Plain Round	sq.in.	sq.mm.	sq.in	sq.mm.	in.	mm.	in.	mm.
	7.07	4560	5.94	3831	3	76	3	76
	12.57	810	11.04	7120	4	102	4	102
	19.63	12661	17.71	11422	5	127	5	127
	28.27	18234	25.95	16737	6	152	6	152
	50.24	32404	47.15	30411	8	203	8	203
Corrugated Round	5.94	3831			3	76	3	76
	11.04	7120			4	102	4	102
	17.72	11429			5	127	5	127
	25.97	16750			6	152	6	152
Plain Rectangular	3.94	2541	3.00	1935	2	51	1.75x2.25	44x57
	6.00	3870	4.80	3096	3	76	2x3	51x76
	12.00	7740	10.31	6649	4	102	3x4	76x102
	20.00	12900	15.75	10158	5	127	3.75x4.75	95x121
	24.00	15480	21.56	13906	6	152	4x6	102x152
Rectangular Corrugated	3.80	2451	3.00	1935	2	51	1.75x2.25	44x57
	7.73	4985	6.38	4155	3	76	2.37x3.25	60x83
	11.70	7621	10.00	6513	4	102	2.75x4.25	70x108
	18.75	12213	16.63	10832	5	127	3.75x5	95x127

Plate 1. Nomographs for calculating gutter size and capacity (Sidney Shelov, AIA)

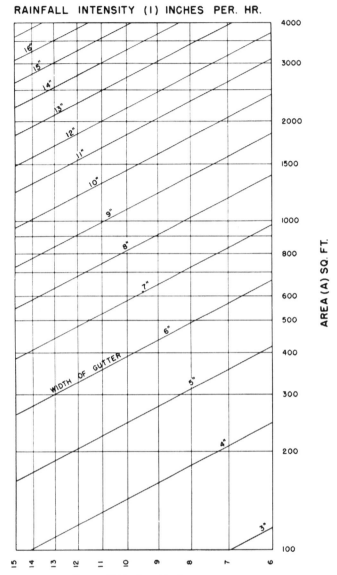

RAINFALL INTENSITY (I) INCHES PER. HR.

Fig. 4. Width of semicircular gutters

GUTTERS

In sizing gutters, the following considerations apply:

1. Spacing and size of outlet openings. (The gutter can never be any more effective than the downspout selected to drain it.)

2. Slope of the roof. (The gutter must be of such a design that water from a steep roof will not by its own velocity tend to spill over the front edge.)

3. Style of gutters to be used. (All gutters are not effective for their full depth and width.)

4. Expansion joint location. (Water cannot flow past an expansion joint.)

The size of rectangular gutters depends upon these factors:

1. Area to be drained. (A, Fig. 6.)
2. Rainfall intensity per hour. (I, Fig. 6.)
3. Length of gutter in ft. (L, Fig. 6.)
4. Ratio of depth to width of gutter. (M, Fig. 6.)

The size of half-round gutters is directly related to the downspout size. If the downspout spacing is 20 ft or less, the gutter size can be the same as the downspout size (but not less than 4 in.). If the downspout spacing is between 20 and 50 ft, add 1 in. to the downspout size for the gutter. Although it is not recommended, wherever it is necessary to drain more than 50 ft of gutter into one downspout, the gutter should be 2 in. larger than the downspout.

The required sizes of gutters other than rectangular or round can be determined by finding the semicircular or rectangular area that most closely fits the irregular cross section. The depth of a gutter should be not less than half nor more than three-fourths of its width; gutter sizes are therefore usually expressed in width only. Half-round gutters are economical and highly efficient; they are commonly used as eaves, troughs, and less often as built-in gutters.

For built-in gutters in large buildings the following formulas, and Figs. 4 and 6 which were derived from them, are recommended. These formulas were developed empirically from tests conducted by the National Bureau of Standards in Washington, D.C.

For semicircular gutters:
$$W = 1.3 \, Q^{2/5}$$

For rectangular gutters:
$$W = 0.481 \, m^{-4/7} \, I^{3/28} \, Q^{5/14}$$

Maximum distances between leaders of built-in copper gutters (with expansion joints midway between)

Width of Gutter Bottom in Inches	Side Angles of 45° and 60°				Side Angles of 60° and 90°			
	Weight of Sheet				Weight of Sheet			
	16 oz.	20 oz.	24 oz.	32 oz.	16 oz.	20 oz.	24 oz.	32 oz.
	Distance Between Downspouts in Feet							
8	30	35	45	—	35	45	55	—
12	20	30	40	65	25	35	45	80
16	—	25	30	55	—	30	40	70
20	—	20	25	50	—	25	35	60
24	—	—	25	45	—	—	30	55

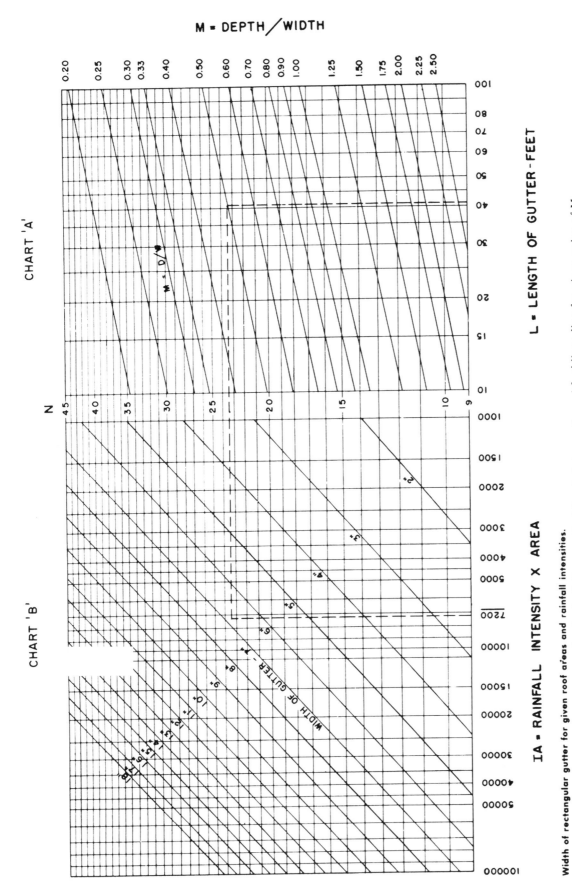

M = DEPTH/WIDTH

CHART 'A'

L = LENGTH OF GUTTER - FEET

CHART 'B'

IA - RAINFALL INTENSITY X AREA

Width of rectangular gutter for given roof areas and rainfall intensities.

Enter at the bottom of Chart A at given value for L. Follow vertical line to intersection with oblique line for given value of M. Proceed horizontally into chart B to intersection with vertical line for given value of IA. The nearest oblique line above the intersection gives width of the gutter. Dashed line illustrates an example where L = 40 ft, M = 0.59, and IA = 7,200: width of gutter is 7 in.

REFERENCES

SMACNA, *Architectural Sheet Metal Manual,* 5th ed., Sheet Metal and Air Conditioning Contractors' Association, Chantilly, 1993.

Donald Baerman

Summary

Roof openings and accessories are integral parts of a roofing assembly and include skylights, hatches, and smoke/heat vents, facilitating safety and maintenance. Also discussed briefly in this article are ridge and relief vents, roof walkways, and snow guards.

Key words

condensate gutter, heat/smoke venting, hatch, relief vent, ridge vent, scuttle, skylight, snow guard

Restaurant *Rautatalo Jurhuset*. Alvar Aalto, Architect. Helsinki, 1951.

Roof openings and accessories

1 INTRODUCTION

Roof openings include skylights, hatches, and heat/smoke venting. The design and installation of roof openings share common features. Roof openings and accessories are discussed in this article in terms of their place in a complete roofing system, accommodating design for daylighting and natural ventilation and the technical concerns of water/moisture and fire/smoke protection discussed elsewhere in this volume.

Generics forms and functions of roofing openings, depicted in **Fig. 1**, include:

- *Skylights* for daylighting and (if operable) for ventilation. Skylights provide a simple means of admitting daylighting for spaces directly below. Hinge-type skylights (for sloped roof installations) are also referred to as roof windows. Multiple glazing (double- and triple-glazed) units are available for improved resistance to heat flow. Some skylight units have integral vents, to relieve built-up overheated air temperatures within the skylight assembly, and also integral shading devices that can be used to preclude solar heat gain and glare.

- *Hatches* provide access to the roof for maintenance personnel, combined with access ladders or stairs. These may also provide for emergency escape (not classified as an exit way), access for firefighters, and access for large equipment. Operable skylights may serve the same functions.

- *Smoke/heat vents* function to reduce interior heat build-up during a fire by opening automatically in case of fire.

Skylights, hatches, and heat/smoke vents are available as preassembled units or framed assemblies of stock components. All skylight, hatchway, and vent units must be securely attached to the roof assembly: structural or miscellaneous steel frames may be required at openings in deck. Provisions for attaching a light-gauge metal flashing flange of the unit to the roof substrate/decking may be required, such as wood blocking.

2 SKYLIGHTS

Traditional skylights were and are fabricated from metal or wood frames and sheets of glass. A wood-framed glass skylight assembly supported by a cast-iron structure formed the roof of the Crystal Palace, built in 1851. Most skylights are now fabricated from aluminum, plastic, or a combination of aluminum, plastic, and wood, and are available as preassembled units shipped to the site ready to be installed, or as assemblies of units, or framed assemblies of stock components, prefabricated off-site and then site assembled (**Fig. 2**).

Skylights and assemblies of skylights must be designed for safety and protection against environmental forces to:

– prevent accidental breakage from falling or wind-blown objects and accidental falls from the roof deck.

Credits: Bruce W. Hisley, retired Chair of the Fire Protection Technical Program, National Fire Academy and by Robert Solomon, NFPA, reviewed the section on heat/smoke venting. Their contributions are gratefully acknowledged.

DAYLIGHTING, VENTILATION

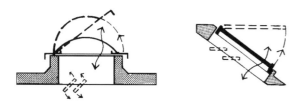

ACCESS TO ROOF

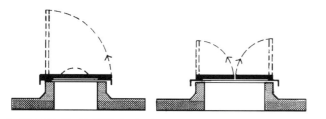

FIRE/EXPLOSION VENTING

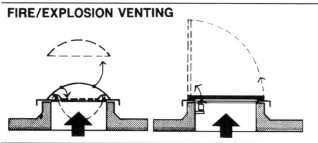

SAFETY

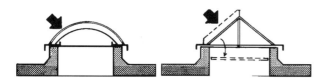

EXTERNAL FACTORS

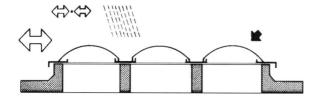

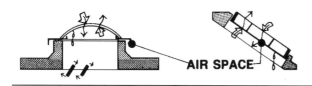

AIR SPACE

Fig. 1. Functions of roof openings.

– withstand wind pressures, both positive and negative, rain penetration, live loads of snow and ice.

– provide for drainage of condensate water and/or water that penetrates under severe conditions.

– provide for cleaning of both interior and exterior surfaces.

Basic skylight units are available as:

• *Self-flashing, without curb:*

– for installation directly into roofing.

– with flashing flange integral with glazing or with added flat flashing flange.

– generally used on pitched roofs only without a curb since flashing to prevent water penetration is difficult if not impossible to achieve on flat roofs.

• *Self-flashing, with curb:*

– shipped to site preassembled with a prefabricated curb.

– curbs generally 4 to 12 in (10 to 30 cm) high.

– curbs commonly insulated; with flashing and counterflashing flanges.

– when counterflashing flanges are short, additional counterflashing may be required to prevent water penetration.

– where deck is field cut for skylight, trim pieces may be required to finish the exposed edges of decking.

• *Framed assembly, with or without curb:*

– mounted on built-up curb with frame and counterflashing for mounting on built-up curb. Recommended minimum height for curb is 8 in (20 cm) above roofing (**Fig. 3**).

– prefabricated curbs for use in lieu of site built curbs are available without or with insulation.

All framed skylights are custom designed by manufacturers to meet necessary roof and/or wind loads.

– Mullion spacing for framed skylights is generally limited to standard glass widths.

– Dimensional limitations on a skylight assembly will further be imposed by requirements for adequate drainage of rain/storm water from roof. Additionally, condensate gutters are required in the body of the skylight assembly as well as around its perimeter (see below).

Standard plastic skylights and roof windows are available from a number of manufacturers. Metal-framed and combination wood and metal-framed skylights with pre-engineered, prefabricated components are available from many manufacturers. Large custom skylights, specially engineered for their application and often combining

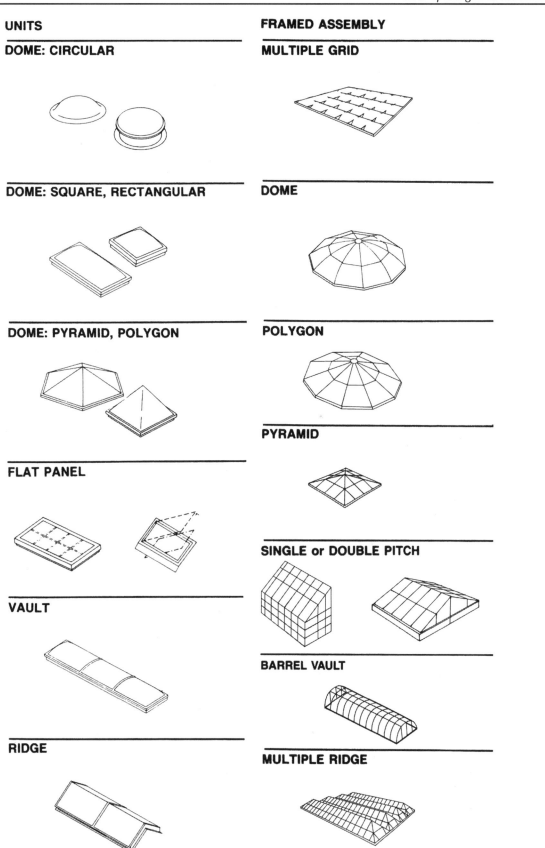

UNITS

DOME: CIRCULAR

DOME: SQUARE, RECTANGULAR

DOME: PYRAMID, POLYGON

FLAT PANEL

VAULT

RIDGE

FRAMED ASSEMBLY

MULTIPLE GRID

DOME

POLYGON

PYRAMID

SINGLE or DOUBLE PITCH

BARREL VAULT

MULTIPLE RIDGE

Fig. 2. Skylight types.

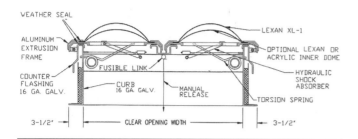

Fig. 3. Acrylic dome.

the skylights with the roof structure, are made by a few firms. Many manufacturers also make glass prism–concrete skylights.

In addition to the industry association publications listed in the references, recommendations and details are available from skylight manufacturers.

Skylight drainage and condensate control

The basic condensation control measures include:

– Condensation will occur on cool or cold surfaces exposed to the interior (moist) air. Double- or triple-glazing and thermal breaks incorporated around the framing and assembly (within it if available) will help reduce condensation.

– Usually a separation is made where the glazing member is bolted into the framing member by use of a glazing gasket.

– All good skylights should have condensation gutters, and they should drain to the exterior or to a leader.

– Mechanical (warm air system) design may properly include blanketing the skylight with warm, dry air to reduce condensation.

• Most skylights combine glazing gaskets with a system of drain channels formed integrally on the frame members. The head and purlin channels lead to rafter drains, which in turn discharge to sill flashing drained to the exterior. Moisture from interior air will condense on the coldest surface, often the skylight assembly. In very moist environments, such as pools and greenhouses, the resulting condensation and water formation can be considerable. The drains, properly designed and installed, serve to intercept both rainwater leaks and condensed water and direct it harmlessly to the outside.

• Many plastic dome, pyramid, and cylindrical skylights have perimeter drains to discharge leaks and condensation. Although building maintenance workers frequently apply sealant at the perimeter, the units are designed to function without such sealant. In restraining thermal movement, sealants so applied may also harm the skylight.

• Some framed skylights depend on a perfect seal at the glazing, without drain channels. Others have partial drain channels, eliminating the head channels. Skylight detailing and installation is thus critical in such cases to assure that channels are properly assembled and installed so as to allow the water out. In detailing the skylight assemblies and in reviewing shop drawings, the architect should check that every glass-frame joint has drain channels and that the drain channels drain continuously from top to bottom. Additional due diligence is attained by pouring water into the drain channels before glazing and verifying that it does not leak into the spaces below.

• In very cold climates, it would be prudent to heat the bottom drain troughs and weep holes to avoid freezing of the drainage system. Since the bottoms of skylights often have heaters to counteract drafts of cold air, the source of the heat may easily be available.

• Purlin framing should be designed to prevent water on the exterior from impounding above it, because such water and the dirt and algae that accumulate there are unsightly.

- Small wooden and composite sky windows do not usually incorporate drainage channels. They depend on the lapping of an upper, glazed unit over a base unit. For the most part, they give good service. If such skylights are "ganged" together, submit the joint details for review by the manufacturer, and require the manufacturer's inspection before certifying completion.

- Although some skylight manufacturers do not include drainage channels and, instead, depend on the absolute seal of wet or gasket glazing, the author's experience with them has not been good. It is likely that some of them function properly some of the time, but designer and specifier beware.

Some skylight manufacturers list the Condensation Resistance Factor, or CRF. The American Architectural Manufacturers Association Standard 1503.1-88, "Voluntary Test Method for Thermal Transmittance and Condensation Resistance of Windows, Doors and Glazed Wall Sections" sets the procedure for testing. ANAI/AAMA 101-93, "Voluntary Specifications for Aluminum and Poly (Vinyl Chloride) (PVC) Prime Windows and Glass Doors," establishes industry recommended maximum humidity levels. The Specification also lists the minimum recommended CRF (higher is better) for various outside air temperatures and inside relative humidity, up to 40 percent.

These recommendations do not include in their humidity range the conditions normally found in swimming pools and other spaces with higher humidity and higher temperatures. Therefore the architect designing and specifying skylights for high humidity applications should consult the skylight manufacturer and observe similar skylights operating under similar conditions of exterior and interior temperature and relative humidity.

Thermal control

Glass manufacturers list their thermal resistance in their catalogs. A typical insulating glass system composed of two layers of ¼ in (6.3 mm) glass with low-emissivity coating on the #3 surface and with argon gas in the sealed space, has a U factor of 0.28 at night in winter, the thermal resistance (R value) thus being 3.6 (in English units). Skylight frames usually have a larger area exposed on the inside than on the outside, and thus the relationship between heat transfer and interior temperature is not a simple calculation. The interior surfaces, exposed to the warm interior air, will be substantially warmer than would be the case if there were equivalent areas inside and outside, and that warmth will retard condensation. If the system has been tested for thermal conductivity, ask the manufacturer for the assumed or test values of interior surface temperature of the rafters and purlins.

Structural strength of skylight glazing

Structural considerations include:

- Skylight units should be adequately designed to resist forces of winds at roof level, both positive and negative. Positive pressures prevail for steep sloping surfaces; negative for flat or low pitch.

- Required resistance to live loads is generally equal to that of roof.

Forces that must be resisted by skylights include dead load, snow load, positive wind load, negative wind load, and (in some regions) seismic loads. The building code that applies to the location gives the method of calculating the combined load. The architect should stipulate and check that the skylight manufacturer submits structural calculations, performed by a structural engineer registered in the state where the project is located, showing adequate strength.

There are three ways to calculate the required glass strength. Building codes list one method, which is generally the least conservative. Most glass manufacturers provide load charts for calculating glass strength. The most conservative method, in most cases, is described in ASTM E1300-84, "Standard Practice for Determining the Minimum Thickness and Type of Glass Required to Resist a Specified Load." Thickness calculations are different from most structural calculations in that standard practice is to select glass with a probable failure of approximately eight lites per thousand. Glass is very strong, but it fails at a very small load compared to its theoretical load. It is recommended to use all three standards, meeting or exceeding the requirements of the most stringent standard select glass.

Building codes have specific requirements for skylight glazing. In some cases, protective screens below the glass are required. In all cases, a prudent design choice, even if not required by code, for spaces where people will be under the skylights is to design and specify a glazing material that will stay in place when broken, such as laminated glass.

The possibility of a person accidentally falling through a skylight should be considered, and suitable protection designed. Reported examples of such falls include a roofer falling through a plastic dome skylight when the roof ripping machine was inadvertently put into reverse gear, an adolescent falling through a cylindrical skylight while walking on it, and a campus policeman falling through a skylight while trying to chase students off. In addition, skylights may be a breach in the building's security.

Light and temperature control

Skylights can be a source of excessive solar heat gain and glare, and they can thus lead to discomfort and high air-conditioning costs. The use of shades and reflective glass are two ways to limit such conditions, but the location, orientation, and size of the skylights are the first practical means of control against solar overheating (**Fig. 4**).

Most skylights have lower thermal resistance than most wall and roof systems, and they must be integrated into a whole-building energy conservation plan. Properly configured, skylights can be part of a passive solar heating and/or lighting system design.

Many types of glazing will admit ultraviolet radiation and visible light in the violet end of the spectrum (wavelengths below 400 nanometers are most harmful). The UV radiation may fade materials. One effective way to screen UV radiation (partially) is by use of laminated safety glass with a UV-screening interlayer.

Summary: skylight selection checklist

In determining the desired form and size of the skylight unit/assembly, consider:

- *Daylight and environmental control*

- orientation and the resulting solar penetration angles, winter and summer, in the given geographic location.

- prevailing winds direction and force.

- precipitation quantity and patterns.

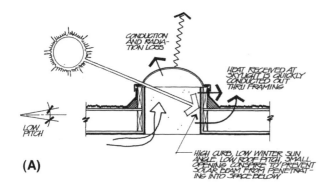

(A)

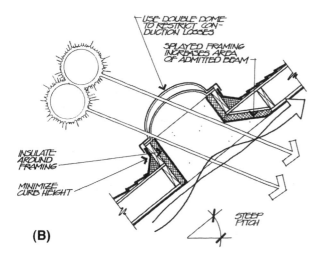

(B)

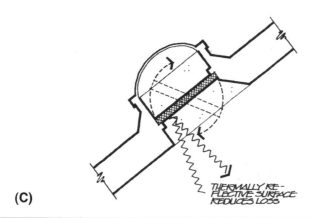

(C)

Fig. 4. Skylight considerations: (a) horizontal placement of skylights may add to heat loss and summer solar gain, with little winter sun; (b) winter heat gain is increased by orientation to the south. Lighting is improved by splaying the interior to direct and reflect light to a larger area below; (c) insulating panels may be considered to decrease heat loss. Their use requires attention to condensation forming on cold surfaces.

- *Profile of the glazing*

The more a formed plastic dome is raised, the greater its ability to refract light of the low early morning and late afternoon sun, which:

- maximizes the use of natural light; but

- increases the solar heat gain.

- *Related criteria*

- views into and out of the building through clear skylights.

- security and roof safety.

- maintainability and cleanabililty.

- susceptibility of adjoining interior materials to staining.

- inspect screening and cleaning, if skylight is operable.

Skylight glazing

The following glazing materials are listed in descending order of approximate cost:

- formed acrylic with mar-resistant finish.

- formed acrylic.

- polycarbonate.

- flat acrylic.

- laminated glass.

- tempered glass.

Proper glazing methods

- exposed gaskets of some types may be subject to material breakdown because of ultraviolet rays of the sun and ozone. EPDM gaskets do not appear to be vulnerable to such damage.

- small valleys created at the bottom of sloped glazing and horizontal glazing cap will hold water.

- sloped glazing or domed acrylic glazing is almost self-cleaning as the sloped shapes facilitate rain washing the surface.

- normal skylight glazing is not designed to support persons. Special thickness and other provisions are necessary if maintenance personnel are to walk on glazed surfaces.

Safety and security measures

Plain glass skylights should include a screen to protect occupants below in the event of breakage. Codes often permit laminated glass, tempered glass, acrylic plastic, polycarbonate plastic, and fiberglass-reinforced polymer, all subject to their individual characters for resistance to impact and breaking. Consult the provisions of local codes. Subject to security level required (which in high security areas may require security alarm devices) precautions against forced entry through a framed skylight should preclude:

– possibility of disassembly of framing.

– ease of removing snap-on cover.

– low melting point of glazing: acrylic materials are easily burned through with a torch.

3 HATCHES

Roof hatches (also referred to as "scuttles," derived from nautical terminology) are available as preassembled units, shipped to the site ready to be installed (**Fig. 5**). Non-stock sizes may be available for hatches on special order.

Roof hatches are intended to provide safe and easy access to the roof, and they have provisions for locking. Opening sizes, as well as access ways to a hatchway, should be generous, rather than minimal, to accommodate large equipment and furniture, and service and maintenance personnel and firefighters (with equipment). Manufactured units are generally safer, more convenient, and more durable than site-built hatches. It is recommended that the architect be vigilant regarding verification or specifying all-aluminum construction. Some manufactured roof hatches include safety posts that can be raised above the open hatch. For hatches on steep roofs, it is recommended that safety rings be securely fastened either inside or outside the hatches, for attaching safety ropes. The position and opening of hatches should not force a person to step near the roof edge.

Roof hatches are commonly available with integral curbs including flashing and counterflashing flanges, without or with insulation: cover is generally solid, but may incorporate glazing; usually spring assisted opening; may also be motor operated, especially for large units.

Hatchway selection considerations

Operable roof hatches and skylights must open automatically if used for smoke/fire venting (see below).

• Hatches must be able to open with a maximum snow load on them.

• In evaluating the quality of a hatchway unit, consider how often the unit will be used; this will help determine:

– type of access: ladder, ship stair, regular stair, size of opening (**Fig. 6**).

– type of operation: manual, powered, force required to open unit.

– durability of operating mechanism components, such as: compression spring operators, shock absorbers, spring latches, hold-open devices, and weather-stripping.

• Fire-resistive features required may include a "label" requirement, which certifies having passed fire resistance or operating tests performed by an acceptable laboratory, such as Underwriters Laboratories (UL) or Factory Mutual (FM) fire underwriter's approval.

• Safety features include:

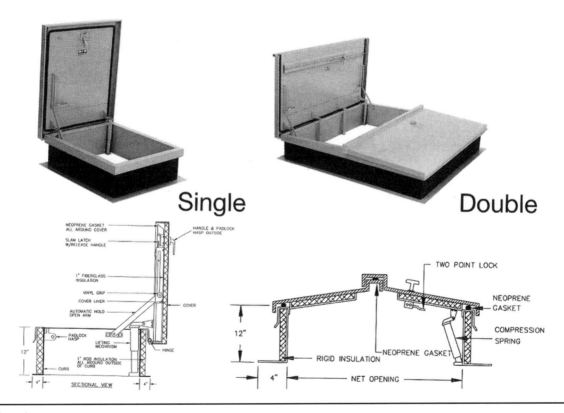

Fig. 5. Roof Hatches.

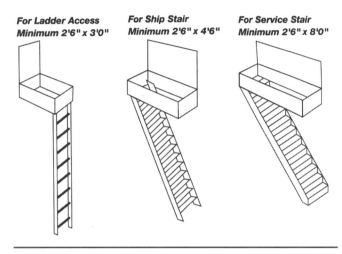

Fig. 6. Ladders.

– telescoping cylinder cover on the compression spring to prevent injuries from pinching or catching clothes in the spring coils.

– counterbalancing by spring operators to automatically lock the cover in an open position, preventing it from slamming shut on a person.

• Consider the possibility of utilizing glazed covers to provide daylighting.

4 HEAT AND SMOKE VENTS

Heat/smoke vents are roof openings designed to open upon exposure to heat. Operation usually occurs from activation of a fusible link mechanism. In some cases, operation may also be initiated by operation of a fire alarm system or by some manual mechanism. Such vents are often required for use in certain occupancies with large quantities of combustible contents such as manufacturing facilities and warehouses. Automatic venting of heat and smoke through the use of heat/smoke vents can work to reduce the loss of property and minimize damage in single-story buildings used for manufacturing. The vents should be accessible for periodic inspection, testing and maintenance, and for replacing the fusible link or other type of actuating device (**Fig. 7**).

UL Listed FM Approved heat/smoke vents are only available as preassembled units and are shipped to the site ready to be installed. Heat/smoke vents are commonly available with integral curbs provided with flashing and counterflashing flanges. There are two types

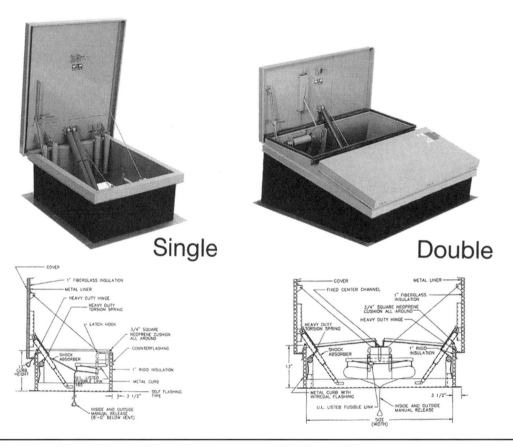

Fig. 7. Single and double vents.

of vents, both of which are designed for manual override operation from the floor of the building or from the exterior by means of a wire or cable pull release. These include:

– melt-down plastic glazing that softens and drops out of the frame when exposed to high temperature.

– automatic opening: solid or glazed cover with springs held closed by a fusible link, which melts when the temperature rises to a predetermined point and releases the springs for automatic opening of the cover.

Explosion relief vents are similar to smoke/heat vents in construction:

– plastic glazed units deform under rise in pressure and are released from frame.

– may be replaced in frame if not damaged.

– solid or glazed cover units are also rise-in-pressure activated releasing springs that automatically open the cover.

– may be reused if not damaged.

Design and selection considerations

Fires occurring in large undivided floor areas present an extremely difficult environment for firefighters, especially when the fires occur well into the interior of the building. Firefighters might be unable to enter the structure and move to the seat of the fire because of the accumulation of smoke and heat at the floor level. Heat and smoke vents open automatically when the heat generated by the fire rises to the ceiling during the fire. This in turn will:

– permit hot gases and smoke to escape.

– stop the descent of the smoke layer from the ceiling.

– lower the gas temperatures at the ceiling.

When heat from a fire reaches a predetermined temperature and melts the fusible link on the vent or vents closest to the source of the fire, the vents open. The result is:

– heated gas and smoke is removed from the building.

– spread of heated gas and smoke at the ceiling is reduced.

– firefighters are able to better identify the source of the fire, thereby enabling them to more efficiently direct their hose streams to the source of the fire.

The requirements for when heat and smoke venting should be installed can usually be found in model building codes and fire prevention codes. For example, vents are usually mandated for large area, large volume, single-story structures such as those used for storage or manufacturing. A sufficient number of vents must be distributed over the entire roof area to assure reasonable early venting of a fire regardless of its location. In warehouse occupancies, the size and spacing of the vents can be determined for each building depending upon hazard classification related to the type of storage commodity (contents), Class I to Class IV, as determined by NFPA, *Standard for General Storage*.

The following range of values represents smoke/heat vent area requirements, based upon the hazard classification of the building contents:

– ratio of roof smoke/heat vent area to floor area: 1/30 to 1/100.

– vent spacing: 75 to 120 ft (22 to 36 m) on center.

Methods and techniques are now available that permit engineered or performance-based design for these systems.

In addition to these applications, heat/smoke vents are also sometimes required in stairwells, elevator hoistways, and areas behind the proscenium in theaters.

When determining the number of vents needed to satisfy the total required vent area, it should be recognized that the venting could be accomplished more effectively through the use of several small units rather than with a few large units. The size of the vent required is based on its open area (approximately equal to its frame size). Also consider the spacing of vents in relation to interior spaces and their uses, and their possible use to also serve as skylights.

5 OTHER ROOF ACCESSORIES

Other roof accessories, as listed in the CSI MasterFormat, briefly mentioned below, include manufactured curbs, relief vents, ridge vents, roof walk boards and walkways, and snow guards. Additional roof accessories, included in *Sweet's Catalog*, are cupolas, weather vanes, and ornamental dormers.

• *Manufactured curbs.* In many cases curbs can be built of rough carpentry materials, sometimes treated for fire resistance and to resist decay. An alternative is manufactured curbs, which are produced as part of some single-ply roofing systems and also by independent manufacturers. Each manufacturer has its own design and requirements. The architect should require product information and shop drawings showing how all junctions and other conditions are to be built.

• *Relief vents (for roof and/or attic ventilation).* Relief vents and gravity vents allow movement of air in and out of the attic or other space under the roof. Generic vents are described and detailed in the SMACNA Manual. A guide to sizing relief vents is offered by the BOCA Code, which requires the ventilation aperture to be 1/150 times the horizontal attic area or, with good vapor retarders and with balanced ventilation (with inlets and outlets), 1/300 times the horizontal attic area.

• *Ridge vents (for roof and/or ventilation).* Ridge vents can be part of an attic or framing ventilation system. A number of manufactured products are available and represented in *Sweet's Catalog*. Generic vents are shown in the SMACNA Manual. Most vents are adjustable for roof slope, and many contain filter material to exclude wind-driven rain and snow. To allow ridge vents to facilitate continuous (exhaust) venting, an equal area of inlet vents should be located within the roof area, such as eave vent openings.

The most common fastening method recommended by manufacturers is simply to nail the ridge shingles through the vent material. A more reliable method is as follows:

– Make sure that there is an opening in the roof sheathing to allow air to pass through.

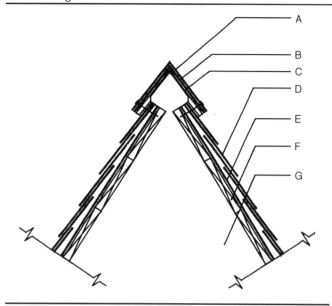

Fig. 8. Ridge with vent: (a) shingles fasted in place wwith screws through ridge vent and wood deck; (b) modified bitumen; (c) ridge vent; (d) shingles; (e) underlayment; (f) wooden decking; (g) wood framing.

Fig. 9. Installation of snow guards. (Courtesy: M. J. Mullane Co., Hudson, Massachusetts.

– Install the ridge vent.

– Install a strip of smooth-surface modified bitumen roof membrane over the ridge vent, and fasten it with corrosion-resistant screws and disks. Heat the modified bitumen until it is tacky, and embed the ridge shingles in it, using roof cement between the shingles. Alternatively, cold adhesive may be used.

– Or, install a strip of mineral-surface modified bitumen roof membrane over the ridge vent, fastening it as recommended (**Fig. 8**).

• *Roof walk boards and walkways.* One method of allowing traffic to cross roofs without injuring the membrane is to call for walk boards. They may be manufactured or made on the job from durable materials. Safe access to all parts of a roof system will encourage proper maintenance and inspection. Roof walk boards should be held in place by mechanical fastenings or by gravity. Each panel should be small enough to be lifted for maintenance, and the sleepers should be padded so as not to harm the roof.

Another method of protecting roofs from traffic is walkways, which are normally adhered to the roof membrane. Types include asphalt-saturated felts, rubber, and padded pavers. Some have been found to injure roofs; follow the roof system manufacturer's recommendations. Roof walkways should not impede drainage.

• *Snow guards.* Ice and snow can build up on steep roofs and then slide off in considerable quantities. The falling material can damage the building or injure people. Sliding ice can rip off built-in gutters and cornices. Snow guards are intended to mitigate such occurrences. They vary from simple, utilitarian designs to highly decorative ones (**Fig. 9**). Generic designs are included in the SMACNA Manual.

Except for locales in which experience has shown galvanized or painted steel to be durable (and in these areas the snow usually does not fall), snow guards should be made from highly durable materials such as copper, bronze, aluminum, and stainless steel.

Manufacturers will assist architects in determining the spacing of snow guards. To avoid damaging the snow guards from the force of sliding snow and ice, they should be installed throughout the roof, not just at the eaves. A typical installation would be 16 guards per square of roofing (1 snow guard per 6 sq ft (3.24 sq m).

If the snow guards are distributed evenly throughout the roof, the force they must resist is no greater than the force imposed on the same area by friction. The manufacturer can recommend the required fasteners, which should be of the same material as the guards. ■

REFERENCES

NFPA, *NFPA Fire Protection Handbook,* 18th ed., National Fire Protection Association, Quincy, 1996. 1-800-344-3555.

NFPA, *Guide for Smoke and Heat Venting,* National Fire Protection Association, Quincy, 1997.

NRCA, *NRCA Roofing and Waterproofing Manual,* 5th ed., National Roofing Contractors Association, Rosemont, 2001.

SMACNA, *Architectural Sheet Metal Manual,* 5th ed., Sheet Metal and Air Conditioning Contractors' Association, Chantilly, 1993.

C • INTERIORS

C1   Interior constructions

C1.1   Suspended ceiling systems   *William Hall*
C1.2   Interior partitions and panels   *William Hall*

C2   Staircases

C2.1   Stair design   *John Templer, Ph.D.*
C2.2   Stair dimensioning

C3   Dimensions

C3.1   Dimensions of the human figure
C3.2   Universal design and accessible design   *Elaine Ostroff and John P. S. Salmen*
C3.3   Design standards for pedestrian circulation   *John J. Fruin, Ph.D.*
C3.4   Parking and vehicular circulation   *Mark C. Childs*

William Hall

Summary

This article provides an overview of the most common suspended ceiling substrate and finish options, including metal ceiling and acoustical ceilings, material options, performance characteristics, specification information, and installation procedures.

Key words

acoustical tiles, linear metal ceilings, open-cell metal panels, suspension systems

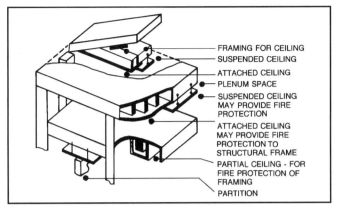

Fig. 1. Ceiling systems.

Suspended ceiling systems

Ceiling systems are nonstructural components supported by the structural frame above and provide:

– visual screen or visual/maintenance separation between the inhabited space and the underside of the structural frame.

– sound-absorbing screen.

– integral component of a fire-resistant rated roof or floor assembly, when the structural frame is not fire-resistive itself.

Ceiling membranes and substrates may be attached directly to the structural frame, or suspended from it (**Fig. 1**). This section describes the second of these approaches.

In selecting a ceiling system, the requirements of an entire system assembly should be considered (**Fig. 2**):

• *Sound control.* Sound can be controlled by minimizing sound transmission pathways through ceiling joints, penetrations, and plenums connecting adjacent spaces.

• *Fire-resistant rating.* Fire-resistive ratings are most commonly applied as part of the structural system. Ratings are established for entire roof/ceiling and/or floor assemblies, not for the ceiling components alone.

• *Heat flow.* Heat flow and moisture flow will occur through joints and penetrations in ceiling systems. Significant undesired heat gain can occur from overheated spaces below uninsulated roofs, requiring that the ceiling system provide uninterrupted and un-

breeched insulation. In practice this is not easily achieved when the ceiling plenum also contains lighting fixtures and other mechanical equipment and access.

Structural loads of the structure or HVAC system may dictate selection criteria as well:

• *Air/water vapor control* may be transported into spaces below the roofing and above ceiling systems by air movement and/or by condensation on cold surfaces, such as penetrating attachments (nails, metal hangers, and other materials that are good heat conductors). Such condensation may damage the building materials and assembly and cause staining of ceiling finishes.

• *Deflection* of the supporting floor/roof construction above will affect the ceiling membrane. The recommended deflection of a supporting member is $\frac{1}{360}$ of the span. When deflection cannot be kept well within these limits, attachment has to accommodate this movement.

• *Differential expansion/contraction* may occur because of temperature differences and/or different coefficients of expansion of materials when joined.

• *Pressurized plenums,* if not completely sealed, may force air and dust through cracks in the ceiling into the enclosed space below.

• *Lateral loads* may be imposed upon ceiling systems when long runs of partitions are connected to the system to provide them with lateral stability.

The basic design considerations in selecting a ceiling assembly are:

– type of construction and the sequence of construction.

– type and extent of mechanical and electrical service (requiring close coordination of all engineering specialties).

– performance requirements (listed above) and life-cycle maintenance.

– aesthetic and appearance criteria, along with cost, will help selection from a very broad range of textures, colors, and detailing alternatives with a range suggested by a small sampling on **Plate 1.**

The requirements of HVAC, lighting, acoustics, structure and related infrastructure services, the dimensional requirements, and sequence of construction and maintenance demand coordination during preliminary design and dimensioning. Too little space between ceiling system and the roof/floor above creates conflicts between various services. Too much space adds to building height and cost. Various choices of integration of services in open framing and closed framing are diagrammed in **Plate 2,** at the end of this article.

Along with the above criteria and system types, ceiling systems are selected based on aesthetic appearance, which may suggest concealed grid or exposed grid alternatives, as well as various shaped units (**Fig. 3**). Systems reviewed below include:

1 Metal ceiling systems, including linear, open-cell, baffle type, and metal pan systems.

2 Acoustical ceilings, including acoustical tile and panels systems.

1 METAL CEILING SYSTEMS

Metal ceilings are a specialty ceiling used where appearance is important or where a metal surface for durability or moisture resistance is desirable. They provide more difficult access to equipment than other ceilings. Within the framework of the linear design, they can handle a wide variety of shapes and colors.

Metal ceilings are composed of ceiling panel and the support system. The metal ceiling types, each discussed in turn below, are:

– Linear metal ceiling systems.

– Metallic pan ceiling systems.

Linear metal ceiling systems

• *Ceiling panels*

– Panels are formed from aluminum sheets into a variety of shapes.

– Typical metal thickness is 0.025 in (0.6 mm) and 0.032 in (0.8 mm).

– Panels can range between 4 ft (1.2 m) and 20 ft (6.1 m).

– Panels are shaped into strips that come in 2 in, 4 in, 6 in, and 8 in (51 mm, 102 mm, 152 mm, and 203 mm) in width.

– Panels are with either square or radius edges.

SOUND

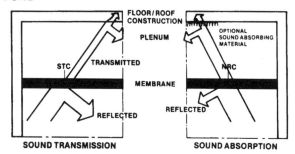

FIRE

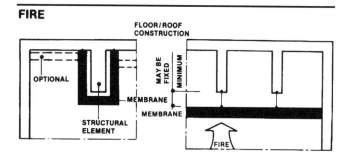

HEAT FLOW

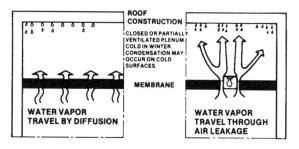

AIR/WATER VAPOR LEAKAGE

Fig. 2a. Performance criteria of ceilings in response to environment.

■ **Deflection in supporting floor/roof construction** will also affect the ceiling membrane, especially when the membrane is directly attached to it and is of inelastic material.

■ Deflection in the supporting construction **should be limited** so that the corresponding deflection in the ceiling material will not **exceed allowable bending stresses** for that material; e.g., the recommended deflection for a supporting member carrying an attached plaster ceiling membrane is 1/360 of the span.

■ **When deflection cannot be kept within safe limits,** consider resilient attachment of the membrane, or its suspension.

DEFLECTION

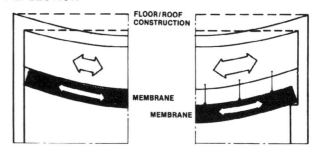

■ **Differential expansion/contraction** may occur because of differences in temperature and/or in coefficients of expansion of two materials when joined; e.g., between a roof construction exposed to solar radiation and a ceiling membrane in a cooled interior.

■ **Membranes may be:**
• restrained from free movement by adjoining vertical elements such as walls or partitions,
• separated or flexibly connected to such elements.
• differential expansion/contraction may become critical for restrained membranes, while the effects on unrestrained membranes will generally be minimal.

EXPANSION/CONTRACTION

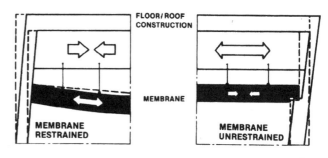

■ **Pressurized plenums,** if not completely sealed, may force air and dust through cracks in the membrane into the enclosed space.

■ **When pressure differentials such as slight negative pressure in enclosed space** exist, opening a door to the outside may result in rattling or momentary lifting of a suspended membrane.

PRESSURE DIFFERENTIALS

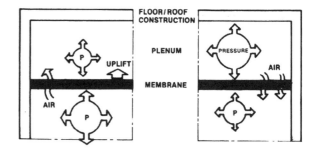

■ **Lateral loads may be imposed** upon ceiling membranes when long runs of partitions are connected to the membrane to provide them with lateral stability.

■ **The capacity of the membrane** to resist lateral loads should be investigated: some may not have the capability and the partition then should be braced to the floor/roof construction above.

■ **Vertical loads** will generally consist of light fixtures and HVAC components, e.g., air diffusers which are incorporated into, or suspended from the membrane.

LATERAL/SUSPENDED LOADS

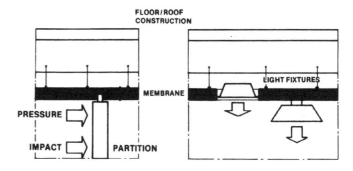

Fig. 2b. Performance criteria in response to loads.

ASSEMBLY

CONCEALED GRID, SHAPED UNITS

METAL PAN TILE

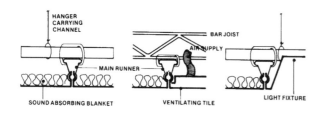

LINEAR PANELS

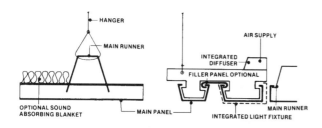

BAFFLES

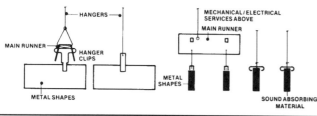

CONCEALED GRID, FLAT UNITS

KERFED EDGE

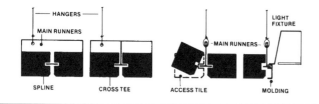

Fig. 3. Suspended ceiling types.

– Panels are designed to snap into specially designed carriers that hold them in place.

– Designed to be linear, installed with approximately ½ in (13 mm) between panels. This reveal is open to the plenum above.

– Panels also come in a design that is formed with an extension that encloses the space between the panels.

• *Panel finishes*

– Standard finish is a special, baked-on polyester paint available in a variety of colors.

– Metallic colors are available for additional cost.

– Special colors are available for additional cost.

• *Support system*

The support system is composed of the following elements, each described in turn below:

– carriers.

– support wires.

– cross channels.

– struts.

• *Carriers*

– Comprised of a cold-formed metal piece in a trapezoid shape with shaped bottom elements to which the panels are attached.

– Carriers come in 12 ft (3.7 m) lengths.

– Carriers are typically installed at 4 ft (1.2 m) on centers.

– The bottom elements are designed to allow easy, snap-on installation of the panels as well as correct alignment and spacing.

– Carriers come in straight lengths as well as radius sections for shaped installations.

• *Support wires*

– Installed in a manner and spacing typical of a standard T-bar suspension system.

– In some situations, stabilizers are installed between carriers every 4 ft (1.2 m) to increase rigidity.

• *Cross channels*

– 1-½ × ¾ in (38 × 19 mm) 20-gauge channels wired crosswise to the carriers add stability to the system.

– Where additional support is required, cross channels are installed before the support wires, and wires are attached to the channels.

- *Struts*

  – These are fastened to the channels close to the support wires and attached to the structure above, as specific conditions require.

  – Struts resist the up and down motion of a ceiling as a result of wind or seismic forces.

Open-cell metal ceiling systems

This system incorporates the ceiling support system with the ceiling design element itself, and is composed of the following elements:

  – 8 ft (2.4 m) long hanger runners.

  – 4 ft (1220 mm) long cross runners that attach perpendicular to the hanger runners at any cell location. These create a 4 × 4 ft (1.2 × 1.2 m) grid.

  – 2 ft (610 mm) long intermediate cross runners that attach to the other elements breaking down the grid to 2 × 4 ft (61 × 122 cm) or 2 × 2 ft (61 × 61 cm).

  – Ancillary grids that break down the grid into cell sizes varying from 3 to 8 in (76 to 203 mm) sq.

  – These elements are 0.20-gauge aluminum and are ⅜ in (10 mm) and 2 in (51 mm) wide by 1.2 in (30 mm), 1.6 in (41 mm), and 2 in (51 mm) high.

  – Suspension wires are used to attach to the hanger runners every 4 ft-0 in (1.2 m).

- The variety and sizes of elements available allows the creation of an open-cell ceiling system in many configurations in order to create a custom ceiling design.

- Building elements normally hidden from view are exposed through the cells of the ceiling; since the ceiling system is suspended below these elements, they are not as noticeable.

  – In many cases, everything above the grid location is painted out in a dark color to make it less noticeable.

  – Installing the light fixtures at the same height as the grid accomplishes much the same thing.

Baffle type metal ceiling systems

This type of ceiling system is similar to the open-cell systems but has a much more linear look. Baffle ceilings are composed of two parts: carriers and metal baffles.

- *Carriers*

  – Carriers support the baffles.

  – There are two different carriers for this type of ceiling: cold-formed metal shaped similar to those used with linear ceilings where baffles are attached in the same manner; and standard ¹⁵⁄₁₆ in (24 mm) T-bar suspension element similar to those used in stan-

ASSEMBLY

EXPOSED GRID: FLAT UNITS

SQUARE EDGE

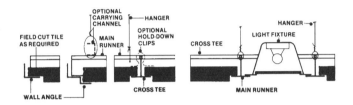

RECESSED EDGE

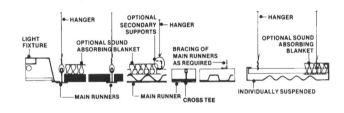

EXPOSED GRID: SHAPED UNITS

INLAY PANELS, CORRUGATED, RIBBED

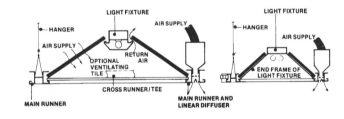

PRE-ASSEMBLED MODULES

Fig. 3. Suspended ceiling types (continued).

dard acoustic suspension systems. Baffles are attached to the bottom of the T-bar with a baffle suspension clip and are installed perpendicular to the T-bar.

– Carriers are suspended from above by support wires at 4 ft (1.2 m) o.c.

– Carriers are normally installed horizontally but can be installed at an angle.

• *Metal baffles* come in two configurations:

– A formed, 0.025 in (0.6 mm) aluminum shape with a "kinked" shape at the bottom and a flange at the top for mounting. Comes in 4 in, 6 in, and 8 in (102 mm, 152 mm, and 203 mm) deep sizes with the two deeper sizes having an additional "kink" in the middle for additional stability.

– A formed, 0.032 in (0.8 mm) aluminum shape with a mounting flange on top and a ¾ in (19 mm) radius element at the bottom. Comes in 8 in and 12 in (203 mm and 305 mm) depths but also can be special ordered in 6 in, 7 in, 9 in, 10 in, and 11 in (152 mm, 178 mm, 229 mm, 254 mm, and 280 mm) depths and in 12 ft (3.7 m) lengths.

– Metal baffles come in finishes similar to those provided for the linear systems.

Metal pan ceiling systems

Metal pan ceilings are the most common type of metal ceiling, which can be configured as a decorative element or to handle a specific utilitarian function. Composed of two parts: metal pan; and panel support system.

• *Metal pan*

– Panels are manufactured in 0.040 in (1 mm) thick aluminum as well as hot dipped, galvanized steel.

– Panels are formed up 1 in (25 mm) at the sides forming a pan. These flanges take a variety of configurations:

– Some panels have a square edge designed to fit down onto the support system in the same manner as a standard lay-in acoustic panel. These have a specially designed angled edge that is designed to snap under the bulb at the top edge of the suspension tee, creating a tight locked connection and enabling the panels to stay in place. This locking panel is ideal for installations that need frequent washing with high-pressure hoses or limited impact abuse.

– Another panel style is installed with special clips that attach to the T-bar, allowing the panel to hang below the grid so that the panel edges adjoin each other. A reveal joint between panels of this style is also available.

– Common size is 2 × 2 ft (61 × 61 cm), which is normally used in the more decorative installations. Panels are also available 2 × 4 ft (61 × 122 cm).

– Panels are designed to fit into or attach to a standard T-bar suspension.

• *Panel finishes and properties*

– Panels are available in a wide variety of standard baked-on paint colors.

– Metallic colors are available.

– Custom colors are available for an additional cost as well as a minimum square footage requirement. Check with the manufacturer for specific requirements.

– Metal pans do not have any acoustic value in their standard configuration. Panels are available in a perforated design with 0.080 in (2 mm) diameter holes staggered at 45 degrees at approximately ¼ in (6 mm) separation. This helps dissipate the sound.

– Acoustical batt insulation may be laid on top of the pans to further increase their sound dissipation. Consult with an acoustical engineer for the appropriate thickness required for a specific installation.

• *Panel support system*

– In most cases, the support system is identical with the standard T-bar suspensions system discussed elsewhere.

– The grid is available in 2 × 2 ft (61 × 61 cm) as well as 2 × 4 ft (61 × 122 cm).

– Hanger wires and seismic restraint wires are identical to the standard T-bar system.

• *Metal pan ceiling accessories*

Each type of ceiling has its own variety of specially designed accessories to handle special conditions, such as:

– Edge conditions where ceilings meet walls or where a ceiling stops and an edge cap is required.

– Trims designed to go around standard or specially designed light fixtures or HVAC grills.

– Special conditions where it is desirable to modify the spacing, angle, or location of installation.

– Radius locations.

– For any application where special conditions require a variation from the standard configuration or installation, consult with the manufacturer to determine available accessories.

2 ACOUSTICAL CEILINGS

Acoustical ceilings are composed of two parts: the acoustical tile or panel; and the support structure (**Fig. 4**). They are an inexpensive method of creating a flat ceiling surface (**Fig. 5**) with relatively easy accessibility to plenum space above the ceiling. Design issues include tile patterns, colors, textures, and edge detailing. For related installations of acoustical wall panel systems, see the following article in this chapter, "Interior Partitions and Panels."

- *Acoustical ceiling properties*

- A measure of each ceiling's sound capabilities is published by each manufacturer and indicated by the NRC rating.

- A ceiling's rating is only a part of the acoustics of the entire space. Therefore, unless consulting with an acoustic engineer, use the relative ratings between different panels to help choose the appropriate ceiling.

- Most acoustical ceilings are painted white to enhance light reflectance. A reflectance value of 0.75 is common. Light Reflectance (LR) ratings are expressed as a percentage of light reflected; 0.80 is the upper limit.

- Most manufacturers make ceiling systems with fire ratings, which are given to the entire ceiling assembly and not just a particular ceiling tile or panel.

- *Special conditions*

Most manufacturers make panel systems that address the following special conditions:

- High humidity: foil-faced and metal-faced products help the ceiling panel resist humidity.

- Chemical and corrosive fumes: The most common is chlorine such as that present in indoor swimming pools. This is commonly resisted by using stainless steel components or, better yet, nickel-copper alloy fasteners and hangers.

- Most manufacturers make abuse-resistant panels that incorporate properties such as indention resistance, friability, and sag resistance.

Acoustical panel materials

Acoustical ceilings are manufactured with two different materials:

- Cellulose- or wood-fiber–based products.

- Mineral wood-based products.

- *Cellulose-based acoustical ceilings* are:

- Manufactured from wood chips that have been washed, soaked, and densified into a thick, pulp mixture that is pressed into sheets that are cut into a variety of sizes.

- The back is sanded to a flat surface while the front is embossed into a variety of patterns or textures and painted. Some patterns are even embossed with small holes.

- Quite light in weight and more economical when compared with mineral wool.

- *Mineral wool-based acoustical ceilings* are:

- Manufactured in a manner similar to that described above.

- Made from a mixture of mineral wool and a binder made from starch, kraft paper, and clay.

Fig. 4. Suspended ceiling components. (Courtesy of USG)

Fig. 5. Suspended ceiling with relatively flat appearance. (Courtesy of USG)

– Mixture is dispensed evenly onto a moving belt or conveyor that runs under a forming wire. The stiffness of the mixture as it runs under the wire determines its texture.

– If other textures are desired, the material can be formed accordingly.

– Mineral wool ceilings are heavier and more brittle than the cellulose base product, but they yield a heavier texture and are more costly.

• *Fiberglass acoustical ceilings* are:

– Manufactured from a densified, resin-impregnated fiberglass material that is reasonably hard, stiff, will not sag in the middle of the panel, and will hold its shape after cutting into specific sizes at the factory.

– Usually used in high-performance acoustical products.

– Fiberglass panels are usually wrapped in a textured plastic membrane or with a rough textured cloth.

– Panels are made in thicknesses from ¾ to 2 in (19 to 51 mm).

– Panels may or may not be foil backed.

• *Special acoustical ceilings*

– Most manufacturers make panels that are covered or wrapped in other materials to alter their performance characteristics or appearance.

– Panels can be coated with a dense ceramic material for high moisture applications. Adds strength to the tile as well as increases its resistance to dirt and grease.

– Panels can be coated with a polymeric finish that performs similarly.

– Panels can be clad with a vinyl-faced aluminum that is extremely resistant to chlorine fumes, grease, and dirt.

– Mylar-clad panels are suitable where an extra degree of cleanliness is desired, such as computer clean rooms or hospital environments.

– To increase durability, panels can be made with an epoxy-like binder additive, or covered with metal. These are desirable in detention facilities or schools.

– Where appearance is a primary concern, panels can be wrapped in fabric, which is available in a variety of textures and colors. This type of ceiling panel is difficult to clean.

– With the variety of wood species available, wood veneer on plywood cut to the 2 × 2 ft or 2 × 4 ft (61 × 61 cm or 61 × 122 cm) can be used to upgrade ceiling appearance.

– Wood veneer panels are heavier than most; mounting structure should be given careful consideration.

Types of acoustical ceilings

There are two basic types of acoustical ceilings, each discussed in turn:

– Acoustical tile ceilings have a concealed or semi-exposed ceiling suspension system.

– Acoustical panel ceilings have an exposed ceiling suspension system.

Acoustical tile ceilings

Tile ceilings are normally made in smaller sizes, most usually in 12 in (305 mm) sq. Tiles have the following edges or joints:

– Kerfed or splined edges.

– Rabbeted edges.

– Flanged edges.

– Tongue and groove edges.

– Consult with manufacturer to determine the specific edge condition for each product.

• Tile ceilings do not allow access to elements and equipment above the ceiling as easily as with panel ceilings.

• *Access to the ceiling plenum* is provided in a number of ways:

– With an access door installed into the tile, which is visible if the door is flush with the tile; a tile installed onto the door surface can hide the door somewhat.

– Concealed systems installed with Z-clips may be accessed with a special tool or moving access clips within the grid.

Acoustical panels

Acoustical panel ceilings are most commonly made in 2 × 2 ft and 2 × 4 ft (61 × 61 cm and 61 × 122 cm) sizes. Acoustical panels are installed into a suspended T-bar grid system.

• *The most common edges*

– Square: edges of the panels are finished with a simple perpendicular edge. The panel sits flush with the bottom of the suspension grid.

– Tegular: edges are routed, enabling the tile to sit down farther into the suspension grid, for a more formal and finished look (**Fig. 6**).

– Modifications of the tegular edge, such as a radius edge or stepped edge.

• *Panels come in a variety of colors*, depending on the style.

• *Panels are available in other styles* not concerning the panel texture. In most cases, they are part of the regular edged styles. Some of these styles are as follows:

– The 2 × 4 ft (61 × 122 cm) panel has a routed groove across the tile dividing it in half, enabling it to look like a 2 × 2 ft (61 × 61 cm) panel.

– Panels can be designed with a multitude of routed grooves, dividing the tile into 12 in, 6 in, and 4 in (305 mm, 152 mm, and 102 mm) squares (**Fig. 7**). Each manufacturer has tiles that are similar to one another, and unique styles.

– Other variations add grooves in a linear manner for a distinctive appearance.

– Some of the newest designs have routed grooves in straight or radius patterns to form a distinctive appearance when all the tiles are installed. The pattern spans many tiles. The grooves have square, radius, or stepped edges.

Ceiling support system

Acoustical tile systems may use:

– direct hung systems, where the main runners of the system are hung directly from the structure.

– indirect hung systems, where the main runners are attached to channels that are hung from the structure.

– furring bar systems, where the ceiling tile is attached to wood furring strips attached to the structure above.

• *Suspended T-bar system*

The standard system for all acoustic panel ceilings (**Fig. 8**).

– A premanufactured system composed of a system of T-bars suspended at a specified height above the floor by suspension wires.

– The system is composed of the following elements:

– Main runners: T-bars that are normally supplied in 20 ft (6.1 m) pieces; installed first to form the backbone of the system.

– Intermediate runners: also T-bars, but only 4 or 2 ft (122 and 61 cm). The 4 ft (122 cm) members are installed between the main runners at 4 ft (122 cm) increments, creating a square grid. This is the system for a standard 2×4 lay-in system. The 2 ft (61 cm) runners are installed between the 4 ft (122 cm) runners, creating a 2 ft (61 cm) grid.

– T-bars are normally painted a flat, off-white color although custom colors are available.

– T-bar runners are available in a few different configurations. The most common T-bar is 15/16 in (24 mm) wide. A popular thin line or narrow line T-bar size is 9/16 in (14 mm) wide.

– T-bar designs with a small slot in the bottom of the T forming a small reveal add a minimalist style to the ceiling.

• *Suspension wires*

– Suspension wires are fastened to the T-bar at one end and to the structure above at the other.

– Wires are attached to the T-bar at 4 ft-0 in (122 cm) centers, providing overall support for the entire ceiling system.

Fig. 6. Tegular edges allow the panel to sit down into the grid. (Courtesy of USG)

Fig. 7. Panels with routed grooves and T-bars with reveals. (Courtesy of USG)

Fig. 8. Standard T-bar system. (Courtesy of USG)

• *Seismic considerations*

– Some building codes in seismic regions now require additional support for suspended ceilings.

– During a seismic event, a suspended ceiling will move vertically. Codes require a rigid strut installed between the grid and the structure above at 4 ft-0 in (122 cm) centers, resisting this upward movement.

– Codes require four angled wires installed on 12 ft (3.7 m) centers at 90 degrees to adjacent wires. This configuration resists seismic forces that tend to buckle T-bars.

– Codes also require a wire attached to each of the four corners of 2 × 4 ft (61 × 122 cm) lights installed into the grid to keep them from dropping out of the ceiling during a seismic event.

Installation

Installation of a suspended acoustic lay-in panel ceiling is relatively simple.

– A rotating laser beam device is placed in the center of the room or space at the intended height of the ceiling. The laser displays the exact height on the wall where the ceiling is to be installed.

– Hanger wires are then installed by shooting or otherwise attaching a connector into the bottom of the floor above, to which the hanger wires are attached. These wires must not be attached to the structure, but to the floor surface above.

– Edge angles are attached to the wall at the appropriate height indicated by the laser.

– T-bars are attached to the hanger wires. The bottom of the T-bars is trued up by aligning it with the laser beam.

– Lights and HVAC grills are installed into the grid. Most of the work above the grid, at this point, has been completed.

– Ceiling panels are installed last, laid into the grid at the appropriate locations.

– Installers must take care to carefully cut around any element that exists within each of the grid elements, such as recessed down lights, sprinkler heads, and ceiling-mounted speakers. ■

Plate 1. Illustrative sampling of available ceiling tile textures. (Courtesy Celotex Corporation)

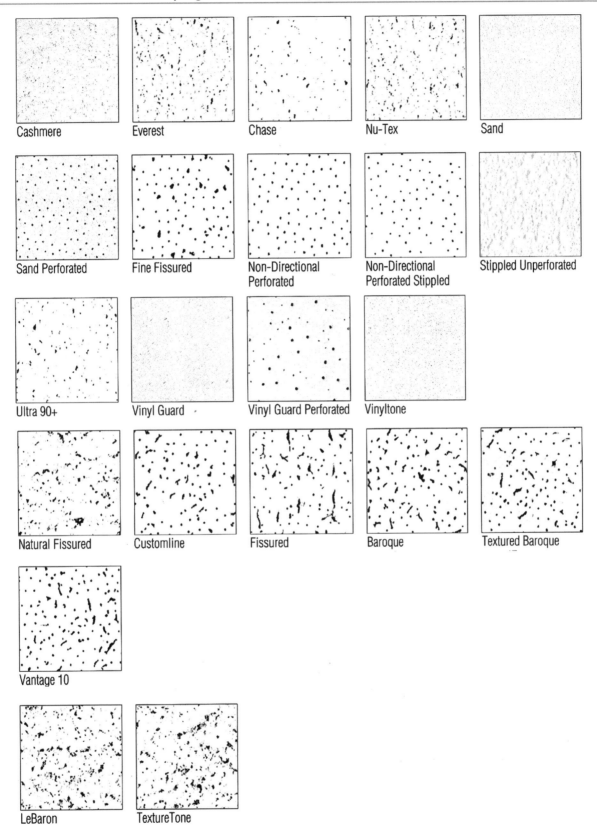

Plate 2. Integration of services above ceiling assemblies

Type and extent of mechanical/electrical services to be provided will influence the selection of the entire assembly:

■ **Space must be provided** within the plenum for feeder lines serving the enclosed space or a group of enclosed spaces; feeder lines may need to run above the ceiling membrane of one space to serve adjacent space(s).

■ **The usual arrangement** and order of installation of mechanical/electrical service lines is:
• wiring/piping first;
• ductwork, next
• lights, diffusers, return grilles, public address systems, etc., last.

■ Of all services, **only the automatic sprinkler system** must be located in a rigid prescribed pattern; all other systems allow for varying degrees of flexibility.

■ **Depth of plenum space** above a level membrane will be determined primarily:
• at points where service lines cross
• where service lines clear the deepest member of floor/roof framing.

OPEN FRAMING

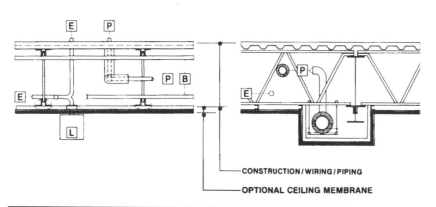

CONSTRUCTION/WIRING/PIPING

OPTIONAL CEILING MEMBRANE

■ **Framing:** open web steel bar joists and rolled steel or open web joist girders; short span wood trusses; generally 2' o.c. for floors.

■ **Wiring and piping:** may be run between or through joists and through joist girders, if provided:
• **web members** of joists should be lined up during installation.
• **clearance** between web members should be carefully checked, especially when flanged piping is used.
• **installation of piping** through joists is generally more costly since shorter lengths of pipe may have to be used and more labor is usually required.
• **running rigid ductwork** through open web joists is not practical; generally only flexible small-diameter circular ducts can be used.

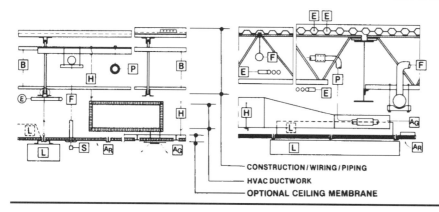

CONSTRUCTION/WIRING/PIPING

HVAC DUCTWORK

OPTIONAL CEILING MEMBRANE

■ **Framing:** open web steel bar joists and rolled steel or open web joist girders; steel or wood trusses.

■ **Wiring and ductwork:** may generally be suspended from metal deck, heavier piping should be supported from framing at panel points.
• **metal deck** with tabs for connecting hangers is available.
• **ducts** may be flattened to clear girders or where two ducts or duct and piping cross; flattening ducts will increase resistance to air flow.
• layout of **fire protection piping** should allow for draining entire system.
• **light fixtures** may be recessed, surface mounted, or suspended.

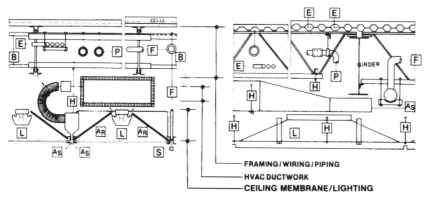

FRAMING/WIRING/PIPING

HVAC DUCTWORK

CEILING MEMBRANE/LIGHTING

■ **Framing:** open web bar joists and rolled steel or open web joist girders; or trusses.

■ **Wiring, piping and ductwork** location and supports similar to those for penetrated membranes:
• **modular components,** such as diffusers, air return grilles, and lighting fixtures to fit the suspension grid, are used;
• **pre-assembled modules** with mechanical/electrical/sound control components incorporated may be installed into a suspension grid.
• **clearances** must be provided for tilting tile, fixtures, or modules into place.
• larger diameter piping is difficult to install through joists.

Plate 2. Integration of services above ceiling assemblies (continued)

■ **The symbols used are:**
[As] Conditioned air supply ductwork and outlets.
[AR] Inlets for plenum or ducted air return to heating/cooling system.
[P] Plumbing and/or heating/cooling piping: such as domestic hot/cold water, steam, hot/chilled water for heating/cooling, roof drain leaders.

[S] Sprinkler heads.
[F] Fire protection piping: main feeders, branches.
[E] Electrical power and lighting wiring: communication systems wiring.
[L] Lighting fixtures.
[H] Hangers: either wire or strap.
[B] Bracing for framing members.

■ For information on structural frame and ceiling membranes, refer to respective sections.

SOLID FRAMING

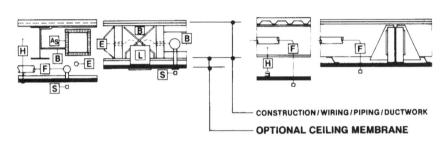

CONSTRUCTION / WIRING / PIPING / DUCTWORK
OPTIONAL CEILING MEMBRANE

■ **Framing:** rolled steel beams and girders; wood or metal joists with flush or dropped girders.

■ **Wiring and/or small diameter piping** may be run through field-drilled holes in wood joists, or through pre-punched holes in metal joists:
• installing **long straight runs** of piping through wood or metal joists is impractical; flexible tubing only can be installed.
• **steel beams/girders** can be drilled to allow wiring or small diameter piping, but drilling is costly and larger holes may require reinforcing the web.
• **ductwork** may be run parallel to rolled steel framing, but clearing lateral bracing between framing and girders may present a problem.
• **ductwork between** wood or metal joists would have to clear bracing: sizes are limited.

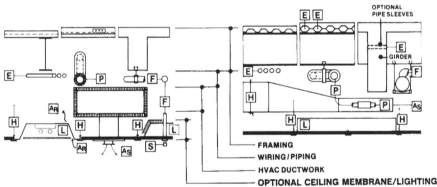

FRAMING
WIRING / PIPING
HVAC DUCTWORK
OPTIONAL CEILING MEMBRANE/LIGHTING

■ **Framing:** rolled steel beams and girders; reinforced concrete joists and beams; reinforced concrete beams and girders.

■ **Wiring and piping:** may be run between framing members, but has to clear lateral bracing members in steel framing; it is generally dropped to clear girders.
• **pipe sleeves** for wiring and small diameter piping may be cast into reinforced concrete girders.
• for fire-resistance rated assemblies, recessed **lighting fixtures are boxed-in** above the ceiling membrane to maintain its continuity.
• in **exposed grid** suspension systems, clearance for tilting tile, fixtures or panels into place must be provided.

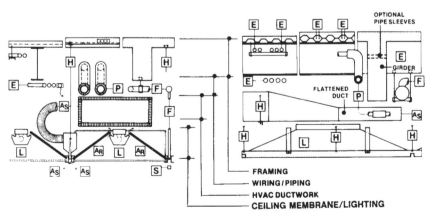

FRAMING
WIRING / PIPING
HVAC DUCTWORK
CEILING MEMBRANE/LIGHTING

■ **Framing:** rolled steel beams and girders; reinforced concrete beams and girders.

■ **Wiring, piping and ductwork:** location and supports similar to those for penetrated membranes:
• **modular components** to fit the suspension grid are generally used;
• **preassembled modules** with mechanical/electrical/sound control components may be installed into a suspended grid.
• **piping** may be run between beams, but is generally dropped to clear girders.
• **pipe sleeves** may be cast into reinforced concrete girders, but diameter is limited.
• **steel girders** may be cut to allow service lines to pass, but openings generally have to be reinforced.

REFERENCES

ASTM, ASTM E1374, *Standard Guide for Open Office Acoustics and Applicable ASTM Standards,* American Society for Testing and Materials, West Conshohocken, 1993.

CISCA, *Acoustical Ceilings: Use and Practice,* Ceiling and Interior Systems Construction Association, St. Charles, 1994.

William Hall

Summary

This article provides an overview of interior wall partitions, fixed, movable and demountable systems, bathroom partitions, and acoustical wall panel systems, including performance characteristics, sizes, and selection guidelines.

Key words

accordion partitions, acoustical wall panels, demountable partitions, toilet doors sizes, fixed partitions, panel systems, toilet partitions

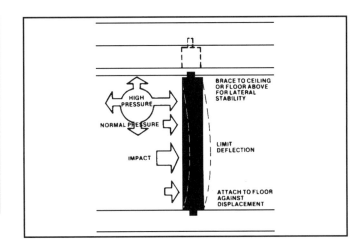

Interior partitions and panels

Interior wall and partition systems are a means for vertical division of interior spaces to provide the following performance characteristics (**Fig. 1**):

– permanent (or semi-permanent) physical, visual, or acoustical separation.

– permanent (or semi-permanent) separation of spaces for fire control and safety.

– selective and changeable partitioning to accommodate variable (in some cases unspecified) programmatic uses and/or environmental conditions.

While fixed partitions may be constructed of any standard building materials, operable partitions are available only as site-assembled manufactured components. Preliminary selection of interior partitions generally includes performance requirements of vision, control of movement or passage, sound, and desire for flexibility.

Design considerations of interior partitions include:

• Stability to resist:

– normal design air pressure experienced in pressurized interiors, generally 5 lb/sq ft (exceeded in special rooms conditions, such as testing rooms).

– suspended loads, such as equipment, shelves, and cabinets.

– concentrated horizontal loads, such as accidental impacts.

• Structural and acoustical characteristics of the adjoining floors, ceilings, and walls:

– sound may outflank the partition through the ceiling, roof, or floor construction.

– sound may also outflank adjoining spaces through closely located exterior windows or interior doors.

• Air leakage and heat flow may occur:

– around lighting fixtures recessed in the ceiling.

– between acoustical tiles and their suspension system.

– under and/or over the partition if not completely sealed.

– at electrical, plumbing, or duct penetrations through the partition or adjoining construction.

Interior partition and panel assemblies are designed and specified based on types, uses, and performance characteristics (**Figs. 2** and **3**). These factors are reviewed in this article to include:

1 Fixed partitions

2 Operable partitions, panel or accordion type

3 Demountable partitions

4 Toilet partitions

5 Acoustical wall panels

Credits: Illustrations adapted from *Time-Saver Standards for Building Materials and Systems* (Watson 2000)

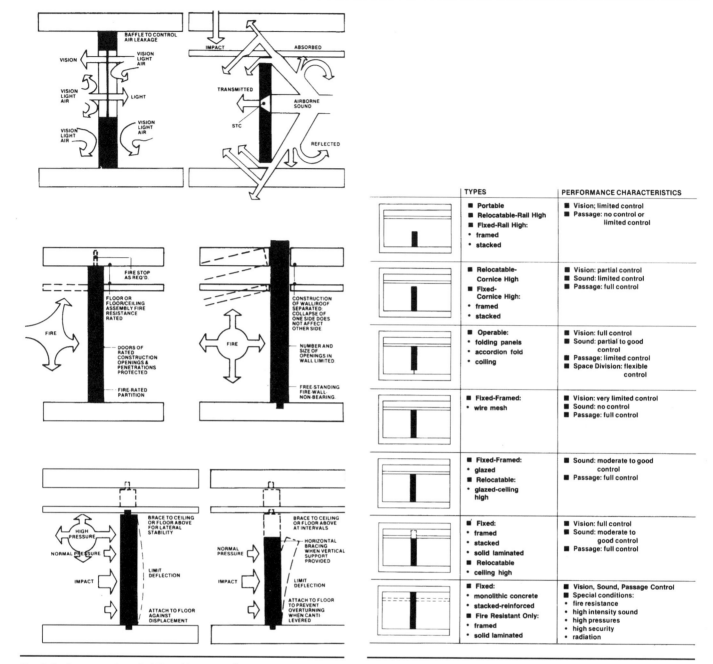

Fig. 1. Performance characteristics of interior walls.

Fig. 2. Performance characteristics of partition systems.

● denotes common usage
○ denotes possible usage

TYPE		MAXIMUM UNBRACED HEIGHT range in feet	MAXIMUM UNBRACED LENGTH, range in feet	USE/CONTROL SEPARATION				ISOLATION					
				VISION ONLY	SOUND ONLY	VISION AND SOUND	PASSAGE	FIRE	HEAT FLOW	HIGH INTENSITY SOUND	HIGH PRESSURE	RADIATION	FORCED ENTRY
FRAMED	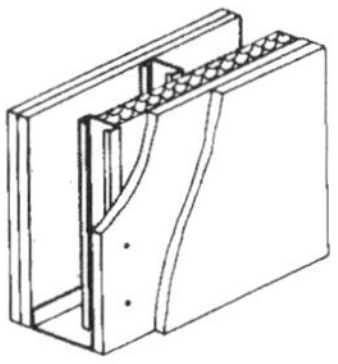	16 to 18	10 to 12	●	●	●	●	●	●	●		○	
SOLID-LAMINATED	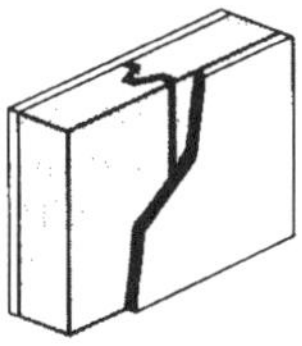	8 to 9	8 to 10	●		●	●	●					
RELOCATABLE	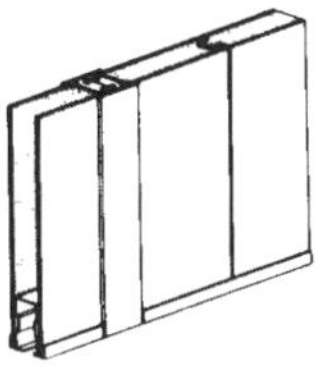	8 to 12	8 to 15	●	●	●	○	○					
OPERABLE PORTABLE	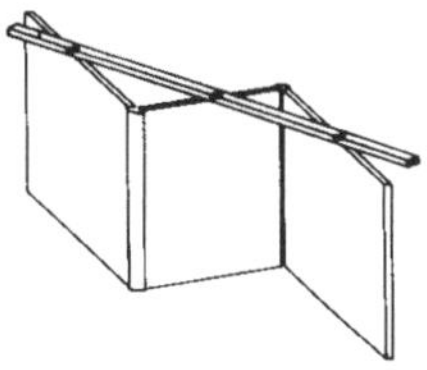	no limit for top-hung	no limit / 6 to 8	●		●	●	○					
STACKED	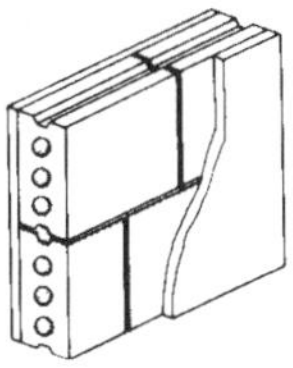	12 to 16 for 4" thick	12 to 16 for 4" thick			●	●	●		○	○	○	●
MONOLITHIC	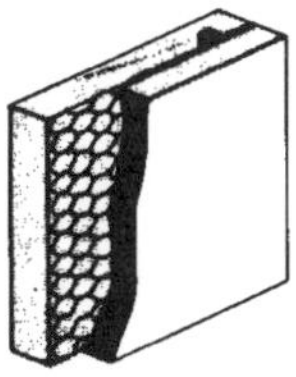	20 to 40	varies			●	●	●		●	●	●	●

Fig. 3. Partition types and uses.

Fig. 4. Fixed partitions in fire-rated corridor. (Courtesy of USG)

1 FIXED PARTITIONS

Fixed partitions offer the widest choice of materials and types of assembly. Fixed partitions are designed to be permanently installed and may provide specific fire ratings as well as sound or acoustical properties. They are generally nonload-bearing. The types of fixed partitions include:

– simple fixed partitions, used mainly to divide space.

– fire-rated fixed partitions for required fire ratings around rooms and corridors (**Fig. 4**).

– acoustically rated fixed partitions to create an acoustic isolation between spaces.

Composition of partitions

• *Gypsum board and metal studs*

– This type is by far the most common.

– Metal studs of varying dimensions are installed into a C-shaped top and bottom track.

– Tracks are installed onto the floor substrate; onto the ceiling above; suspended from diagonal support studs some specified distance above the ceiling; onto the bottom of the floor deck above.

• *Gypsum board and wood studs*

– Not common in commercial use because of obvious fire-rating limitations.

– Wood studs of varying dimensions are installed between top and bottom plates.

– Plates can be installed in a manner similar to the metal stud tracks.

• *Plaster partitions*

– Not as common as they were 25 years ago, but still an economical method of dividing space.

– Standard metal studs or specially designed plaster supports are installed with lath being applied to one or both sides.

– Plaster is then applied to the lath as directed by the manufacturer.

• *Glass blocks*

– Translucent masonry style blocks or "bricks" installed in courses in a manner to bricks.

– Available in a variety of patterns and translucency.

– Not designed to be load-bearing.

• *Masonry*

– Not commonly used as a partition material except for appearance reasons.

– When used as veneer, construction is masonry over another system.

• *Size and/or gauge*

Size and/or gauge generally depend on the height of the wall.

– 2 × 4 in wood studs are sufficient for walls up to approximately 8 to 10 ft (2438 to 3050 mm) in height.

– 22-gauge metal studs of 3⅝-in (92 mm) width is sufficient for the same height.

– For higher walls, consult the manufacturers' or suppliers' published data.

• *Spacing of framing members*

Spacing of structural elements is dependent upon the type and thickness of the surfacing material.

– ½ in (13 mm) gypsum surface material normally requires 16 in (406 mm) maximum spacing.

– ⅝ in (16 mm) gypsum board normally requires 24 in (610 mm) maximum spacing.

• *Surface material*

– gypsum board (the most prevalent).

– plaster.

– where privacy, security, acoustics, or a fire rating are not important, there are many other materials that can divide the space, and may include but are not limited to wood strips in a variety of configurations, screens or louvers, metal panels, and glass (**Fig. 5**).

– function of these materials may range from utilitarian to decorative uses.

– appearance may be an important factor.

Rated partitions

• *Fire resistance*

Fire resistance indicates the ability of a particular wall assembly to contain a fire or the heat generated from a fire. A partition's fire rating is indicated by the amount of time it will prevent the spread of fire.

– For instance, a 1-hour wall will prevent the spread of a fire across the partition for at least 1 hour.

– For a partition to obtain a specific fire rating, it must be constructed of specific materials and in a specific manner or configuration.

– Requirements for these materials and configurations are designated in *ASTM Standard E119, Fire Tests of Building Construction and Materials.*

– Fire rating requirements for partitions are set by local building code officials.

• *Fire-resistive standards*

Underwriters Laboratories (UL) publishes standards for fire-resistive construction. Most manufacturers of fire-resistive materials, such as plaster or gypsum board, publish "quick selector" lists to aid in selecting the best design for the desired fire rating. Manufacturers will normally cross reference these designs with the UL numbers and other pertinent information. Designs will indicate:

– materials (studs and gypsum board) that may be used.

– exact placement or parameters to aid in the proper placement of these materials.

– specific information regarding the type, quantity, and placement of required fasteners.

– other pertinent information needed for its proper construction.

• *Acoustical standards*

A partition's acoustical properties depend upon a wide variety of factors. Criteria for these properties are based on those aspects that can be attained by reasonably simple methods. Isolating the partition from other elements (such as one side from the other, or the partition from ceiling or floors) inhibits sound from spreading into adjacent rooms. Installing a sound absorbing material also inhibits sound transmission. Sealing all joints, penetrations, and holes with appropriate sealants or fillers will increase the function of the partitions. Most manufacturers' "quick selector" lists of fire-rated designs also included acoustical properties. They comply with the above criteria by:

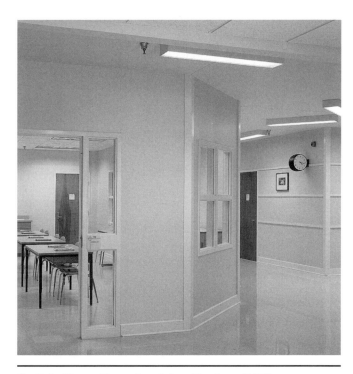

Fig. 5. Partitions with panels and glass. (Courtesy of USG)

Fig. 6. Operable wall partition allows division of space.

– filling the space between the studs with a sound absorbing material such as batt insulation.

– the two partition surfaces are isolated from one another by staggering the studs or separating them by building two one-sided walls a distance apart.

– filling all joints and holes with a special acoustical sealant.

2 OPERABLE PARTITIONS

Operable partitions are semi-permanent walls used to divide spaces. Their size and applications range from small prefabricated units similar to a multi-fold door, to entire walls which open to join several spaces into one. They are common in large conference rooms, hotel meeting rooms, schools, and other places where there is need for flexibility in the size and division of spaces (**Fig. 6**). They come in flat panel as well as folding configurations, and may be fire rated or have acoustical properties. Types of operable partitions discussed in this section are panel type and accordion type.

Panel partitions

This type of operable partition is characterized by numerous, flat panels that, when fit together, form a temporary wall.

• Panels

– Wood frame panels range from 1-¾ to 3 in (44 to 76 mm) thick.

– Steel-reinforced aluminum frame panels have face sheets of gypsum board or particleboard, in panel thicknesses between 3 to 4 in (76 to 102 mm).

– Steel frame panels range from 2-¾ to 4 in (70 to 102 mm) thick.

• *Support structure*

Depending on the type of rollers or carriers, panels are supported by a continuous, steel track mounted into the ceiling. Consult with each manufacturer regarding specific requirements for each type of track.

– Rollers or carriers, available with various types of mechanisms, move the panels within the track. The type of carrier or roller depends greatly on the weight of the panel.

– Carriers are composed of a steel rod attached to the panel with a plastic, Teflon, or other synthetic disk designed to move easily within the track, and are primarily used with panels that are relatively light.

– Rollers are composed of a steel rod attached to the panel at one end, attached to ball-bearing rollers, and are designed for heavier panels.

• *Support elements*

– The track is supported from the structure above.

– The most common method uses double-threaded steel rods at 24 in (61 cm) o.c., one on each side of the track. These rods attach to the track at the bottom side and to steel angles that are attached to the structure above.

– Since the manufacturer supplies some of these parts, and subcontractors supply others, the drawings and specifications need to be clear. Consult each manufacturer about what is supplied with their product.

• *Panel arrangement*

Depending on the length of the opening, the weight of the panels, and the manufacturer, the panels may be arranged in three ways:

– Individual panels are separate elements that are moved individually into their storage area one by one. There are two carriers per panel, and travel is restricted to a straight line.

Maximum panel height is approximately 20 ft (6.1 m), and panels are typically moved manually.

– Paired panels are hinged together so that the panels are folded together and moved as one element into their storage area. There is one carrier per panel, which can travel in straight or curved lines, with tracks intersecting. Maximum panel height is approximately 40 ft (12.2 m) and may be stored in a remote location.

– Continuously hinged panels are hinged together into a long string. Panel travel is restricted to a straight line, and large panels that are part of high and/or long partitions may need to be motorized. Maximum panel height is approximately 26 ft (7.9 m).

• *Panel weight*

– determined by size.

– determined by construction.

– influenced by STC (Sound Transmission Class) rating.

– influenced by panel accessories.

– weight of the combined panels should be considered since the structure of the building must be used to support it.

– panels exert an evenly distributed load over the entire length of the track when they are closed. Panels exert a concentrated load in the stack area when the panels are stored. The structural engineer should plan for these varying loads.

– because of the tolerances between the door bottom and the floor, excessive deflection cannot be tolerated.

– panels range from 8 to 14 lb/sq ft (300 to 525kg/sq m).

• *Fire-rated panels*

– Configuration is available only in the steel frame type.

– Most manufacturers offer a fire-rated style. Consult with manufacturer for specific characteristics.

• *Other panel characteristics*

– Panels that are electrically operated must be continuously hinged and center stacked.

– Panels are secured in place normally by a retractable element in the bottom of the door that is extended against the floor, holding it in place.

– Panels are joined edge-to-edge by a type of tongue and groove edge with resilient material within to create a sound seal.

Accordion partitions

Accordion-type partitions, used for easily moved visual screening and flexible space dividers, are composed of the track, partition components, and the following:

• *The partition track*

– made of extruded aluminum or steel.

– installed onto or into the ceiling.

– attached to a wood header or to threaded steel rods attached to the structure above in a manner similar to that described with panel type partitions.

– has one or several large slots lengthwise for the wheels attached to the folding partition to glide in.

• *Partition components*

– Top is composed of steel members to which small wheels are attached that fit into the slot(s) in the track in the ceiling.

– The steel members can be hinged or pantograph type members that enable the partition to fold up like an accordion and still provide support for the entire partition.

– Attached or anchored post or edge is a vertical member attached securely to the wall at one end.

– Partition folds away or toward this end when being opened or closed.

– Latch or moveable end is a vertical steel or aluminum element that fits into a grooved track attached to the wall. It also encompasses the latch and locking mechanism that hooks or latches to this attached element, keeping it in a closed or locked position.

– The accordion panel is composed of numerous metal, plastic, or wood pieces that are connected with a metal hinge or flexible plastic attachment strip (**Fig. 7**).

– The bottom seal is a linear plastic strip attached to the folding element and functions like a sweep to help block light and/or sound.

• *Accordion partition sizes*

– Commonly come in heights up to 20 ft (6.1 m); larger sizes are available by special order.

Fig. 7. Accordion-type partition in closed position.

– Commonly available in lengths up to 40 ft (12.2 m); special order.

• *Accordion partition configuration*

– bi-parting, in which the partition is attached at opposing walls and meets and latches in the center.

– single panel, which is one piece that attaches to the wall. It stacks where it attaches and closes and latches at the opposite wall.

• *Stack space*

– Each type and model of operable partition requires different amounts of space to stack properly.

– Whether a model stacks remotely or directly, at one side of the wall or both, stack space for the partition when it is open must be planned for.

• *Weight*

– Weight of panel is a concern because it affects the loads on the structure.

– Weight of the panel will depend on the size and height of the partition, and the construction and thickness of the partition.

3 DEMOUNTABLE PARTITIONS

Demountable partitions are wall systems designed to be placed in semi-permanent fixed positions, but are attached so that they can be moved easily and frequently, in some types without special tools or construction equipment. Such systems are usually modular on 24 in (61 cm) centers and can include windows, doors, and other elements. Demountable partitions are installed directly over the floor finish material and fasten to the bottom of the ceiling, thus allowing for re-location.

• *Advantages of demountable partitions systems*

– designed to be easily relocatable as space needs change.

– have the appearance of standard gypsum board walls.

– designed to fit together without joint treatments or painting.

– can be installed directly over carpet, making it easy to relocate walls quickly.

– approximately 40 percent less costly than standard gypsum board walls.

– 1-hour fire rating can be easily achieved.

– acoustical properties similar to standard gypsum board walls are easily attained with the addition of acoustical batt installed between the studs.

– If desired, panels are available in unfinished gypsum board that may be taped and finished to blend with permanent walls.

– may have tax code advantages in U.S. business tax interpretations, in that they may be classified as furniture or equipment, depreciated over a 7-year period, as opposed to approximately 30 years for permanent construction.

- *Disadvantages*

– Because of gypsum board component, walls are subject to damage in the same manner.

– Because some demountable partitions contain doors, sidelights, windows, and similar elements, a certain portion of the relocated wall is not reusable unless configured in the same manner.

Demountable partitions are composed of four major elements: a runner, track, studs or support frames, and panels:

- *Steel floor runner*

– made of galvanized steel.

– commonly 1-⅞ in (48 mm) wide by 1-⅛ in (29 mm) high.

– attached to the floor substrate either directly or through the floor-finish material.

- *Ceiling track*

– made of steel or aluminum.

– painted or bronze anodized (aluminum only) finish.

– commonly 3-⅝ in (92 mm) wide by 1-¼ in (32 mm) high.

– fastened to the bottom of the ceiling.

- *Studs or support frames*

– rolled, galvanized steel, or extruded aluminum.

– available in either "H" or "T" configuration.

– designed to fit between the floor and ceiling tracks at 24 in (61 cm) o.c.

- *Panels*

– most common material is gypsum board.

– tackable "Micor" panel also used.

– commonly ¾ in (19 mm) thick by 24 in (61 cm) wide.

– panels have a beveled edge to facilitate alignment of panel joints.

– panel edges are kerfed to provide a slot for the alignment clips.

– panels are wrapped in vinyl wall-covering.

– panels also available in metal surfacing as well as a tackable fabric covering.

Demountable partition trims and clips

Most partition assemblies also include trim and clip attachments, typically:

- *Base trim*

– painted or anodized aluminum.

– painted steel.

– prefinished wood.

– resilient rubber or vinyl.

- *Ceiling trim*

– aluminum.

– steel.

– wood.

- *Attachment clips*

Most typically galvanized steel, clips are attached to the studs and fit into the kerfed slot in the gypsum board during installation. Miscellaneous other clips are used in a variety of other situations depending on the manufacturer or need.

Finishes

Partition systems are commonly available with durable and decorative finishes. Standard finishes include:

– vinyl wall-covering patterns and colors.

– fabric wall-covering patterns and colors.

– baked enamel colors for metal panels.

Many manufacturers will allow wall-coverings and fabrics that are other than the standard ones they provide to be installed on the panels. Consult with the manufacturer to determine possible finishes. Many manufacturers have nonstandard finishes for their metal panels. These include:

– stainless steel.

– baked enamel colors that are nonstandard.

– powder-coated paint colors.

– porcelain enamel chalkboard finishes.

– plastic laminate colors and patterns.

4 TOILET PARTITIONS

Toilet partitions divide individual toilet stalls to provide privacy (**Fig. 8**). There are several different types of panels that may be in-

Fig. 8. Standard toilet partitions.

Fig. 9. Jamb condition on standard toilet partition.

stalled in a variety of configurations. Each panel type is available in a variety of colors. Hardware is normally provided in a variety of durable types and styles. Partition components include panels, pilasters (vertical supports), doors and/or screens, and hardware:

• *Panels*

– Typically these are the panels that form the elements between, and at the ends, of toilet stalls.

• *Pilasters*

– elements that form the jambs for the doors (**Fig. 9**).

– serve as connector elements between the panels and the doors.

– can be anywhere from a few inches to a few feet wide.

• *Doors*

Toilet stall doors are normally 2 ft (61 cm) wide and swing in. Doors to ADA accessible stalls are a minimum of 32 in (81.3 cm) wide and swing out.

• *Brackets, hinges, and latches*

– made from extruded aluminum, stainless steel, or chrome plated brass.

– used to fasten the entire partition system to the surrounding materials and to each other.

Types of toilet partition panels

• *Baked enamel steel*

– Panels are normally 1 in. (2.5 cm) thick and composed of two sheets of 20-gauge bonderized, galvanized steel laminated to a honeycomb core.

– Edges are similar steel sheets formed to a radius-edge molding.

– Different manufacturers have their proprietary methods to obtain generally the same look.

– Finish is typically a baked enamel finish with a variety of colors offered by each manufacturer.

– Powder-coated paints are also available from some manufacturers for added durability.

– This is the most common type of panel, providing the most durability for the cost.

• *Stainless steel*

– Panels are normally 1 in (2.5 cm) thick, and composed of two sheets of 20-gauge type 304 stainless steel laminated to a honeycomb core.

– Edges are similar steel sheets formed to a radius-edge molding.

- Different manufacturers have their proprietary methods to obtain generally the same appearance.

- Finish is commonly a brushed stainless steel (**Fig. 10**).

- Typically used in installations where rust is a concern.

- Stainless steel panels are more costly than baked enamel.

• *Plastic laminate*

- Panels are normally approximately ⅞ in (22 mm) thick and are composed of two 0.050 in (1.3 mm) thick pressure plastic sheets laminated over a 3-ply, resin impregnated, 45 lb density particle-board core.

- Finish colors are available from standard colors provided by the manufacturer.

• *Solid phenolic*

- Panels are normally ½ in (13 mm) thick, with doors ¾ in (19 mm) thick.

- Class B fire rating.

- Material and color is solid throughout thickness, with no core material.

- Colors are chosen from those available from the manufacturer. Many manufacturers provide phenolic colors that are the same as the plastic laminate colors.

- Phenolic partitions are suitable in areas of extremely high humidity and where frequent, direct water contact is common.

- Graffiti resistant (paint is easily removed) and extremely scratch resistant.

• *Stone*

- Panels are normally 1 in (25 mm) thick.

- Panels and pilasters are typically stone. Doors are wood, metal, or plastic laminate.

- Granite and marble are the most common stones used with color availability subject to the manufacturer.

- Stone is durable and suitable in high water and humidity situations.

• *Wood*

- Not a common choice but attractive in appearance.

- Pilasters are solid, dimensioned wood; panels and doors are commonly stile and rail construction.

Toilet stall and partition sizes

The architect determines dimensions for toilet stalls. Common sizes are as follows:

Fig. 10. Stainless steel finished toilet partition.

– Width of stalls is typically 3 ft (91.4 cm).

– ADA accessible stalls are between 42 in and 5 ft (106.7 and 152.4 cm) depending on the specific ADA and local code requirements.

– Depth of stalls is typically 5 ft (152.4 cm).

– Height of panels and doors is typically 58 in (147.3 cm); typical pilasters dimensions include: 70 in (177.8 cm) high with the floor-mounted system, and 80 in (203.2 cm) high when used with a 2-½ in (64 mm) high horizontal top railing in the overhead braced system.

Configurations

Toilet partitions are typically available from manufacturers in the following configurations:

- *Overhead braced*

– Pilasters in this style are attached to the floor at the base with expansion bolts hidden within the base.

– Panels are attached between the walls and the pilasters with brackets.

– The tops of the pilasters are fastened to each other with a horizontal top railing that attaches to each pilaster and to the adjacent wall surface.

– This type of configuration forms an extremely stable partition.

- *Floor mounted*

– Pilasters in this style are attached to a horizontal ⅜ in (10 mm) steel bar with special bolts that fasten both to the bar and a cylindrical anchor. This is attached to the floor with heavy gauge expansion bolts.

– Since this forms the major support for the partition system, this is an extremely strong connection.

– Panels and doors are fastened to the pilasters and walls with typical brackets.

– No horizontal support rail is needed.

- *Ceiling mounted*

– Similar to floor-mounted systems, except that the system is attached at the ceiling.

– Pilasters are fastened to the ceiling by a support system similar to the floor mounted system, except the expansion bolts are replaced with ⅜ in (10 mm) threaded rod and bolts that fasten to the ceiling and a support structure above the ceiling.

– Common where no connection to the floor is desired, or where ease of mopping is important.

Other design considerations

The following items should be considered when specifying and designing a toilet partition system:

– wall construction.

– floor finishes.

– ceiling structure.

– use of building (public office building, school, correctional facility).

– age of users.

– maintenance requirements.

– vandal resistance.

– moisture resistance.

5 ACOUSTICAL WALL SYSTEMS

Acoustical wall systems have specially made or installed panels, panel applications, or materials that are wrapped in fabric and attached to the wall. These panels have acoustical properties and can add refinement to the overall design of a space.

System and panel types

Acoustical wall systems come in basic configurations:

– *Rigid fiberglass,* the most common type of acoustical panel. Factory made and installed on-site.

– *Soft fiberglass batt* with separate, rigid frame is a more recent type of system.

– *Standard panels* have medium density fiberglass, with reasonable stability for panels to retain their shape after installation. They have good noise absorption and a Class A fire-resistant rating.

– *Tackable panels* have a standard panel at the core, and an additional layer of ⅛ in (3 mm) high-density fiberglass bonded to the face side of the core panel. This panel is highly tackable, has reasonable impact resistance, and the same acoustical properties as the standard panel. Fabrics are not stretchable.

– *Impact-resistant panels* have a standard panel at the core, with a woven fiberglass fabric bonded to it. This panel has high resistance to impact damage and is suitable for stretchable fabrics.

– *Specialized panels* have a standard panel at the core, with a felted fiberglass mesh bonded to it under tension and pressure. This panel is suitable for fine fabrics and/or installation on surfaces that have reasonable irregularities that might "telegraph" or show through the panel.

Special performance panels

- *High absorption panels* are two-panels-thick at the perimeter and one-panel-thick at the center, with the void filled with low-density acoustical batting, which increases its absorption.

- *Low frequency absorptive panels* are wrapped in a special non-perforated vinyl fabric. These panels are ideal where absorption of low frequency sounds is necessary, as most high and middle frequency sounds are not absorbed. Panels are useful in recording studios or concert halls.

- *Double density panels* are designed to absorb low frequency sounds. They are formed from two panels: the outside panel has a higher density than the interior one and they are separated by a 30 mil vinyl septum. This design also limits sound transmission through the panel.

- *Absorptive transmission loss panels* are formed with a standard panel attached to gypsum board. These panels are designed to absorb sound within a room while keeping out other sounds.

- Other designs are available that help to control reverberation time, double wrapped panels to help control sound within a space, and diffuser panels of varying thickness to help diffuse sound.

Typical panel edges

Panel edges are subject to a lot of wear and tear. They also contribute significantly to the overall appearance of the installation, and thus are an important design consideration.

- *Types of edge configurations*

- square edge: perpendicular to the face.

- bullnose edge: has a large radius approximately ½ to ¾ in (13 to 19 mm) depending on the thickness of the panel.

- chamfered edge: has a 45-degree chamfer starting at approximately half the panel thickness.

- radiused edge: similar to a bullnose edge but can vary from what is called a pencil radius edge to a radius equal to the thickness of the panel.

- mitered edge: at 45-degrees to the face and starts at the back edge of the panel.

- *Panel finishes*

- Panels are completely upholstered.

- Most manufacturers have a wide variety of fabrics made from polyester, wool, flannels, etc., as well as some vinyl fabrics.

- Panels may be upholstered with the client's own material to achieve the desired color or design intent.

- Almost any fabric may be used as long as it is reasonably stable. Most manufacturers will evaluate sample fabrics for appropriateness.

- When standard fabrics are used, flame spread ratings of 25 or less can be achieved. Check with manufacturer's published data on flame spread.

- *Panel mounting methods*

Panels are mounted to the wall by a variety of methods:

- *Mechanical "Z" clips:* Specially shaped clips are installed both to the wall and to the back of the panel in two or more locations.

They are designed so that the panel is pressed onto the wall and slid downward so that the clips engage each other.

- *Velcro fasteners:* Strips of Velcro are attached to both the wall and the panel in appropriate quantity and locations based on the size of the panel. The panel is then pressed into place.

- *Adhesives:* Panels may be attached with the use of adhesives. This is a more or less permanent method because the panels cannot be easily removed for cleaning or repair.

- *Magnets:* A more recent innovation for installation. Magnets are installed at specified locations on the panel, and the panel is pressed into place.

- *Specialized uses or configurations*

- Most manufacturers do custom sized or shaped panels.

- Some specialized configurations may not be possible. Consult with the manufacturer to determine capabilities and cost.

- Special edge configurations are possible. Submit design to manufacturer for approval.

- Ceiling installations are also available.

- *Rigid fiberglass panel design variations*

- Similar in construction to the standard design.

- Hardened edge is replaced with a separate plastic edge that is attached during the manufacturing process.

- Fabric is wrapped around the entire panel, including the attached edges.

- This design offers increased resistance to impact damage at the edges as well as increased torsional stability.

Site-fabricated acoustical panels

- *Composition*

- A rigid, vinyl frame that is stapled to wall surface with specially designed staples at 2 in (51 mm) o.c.

- A subsurface installed within the vinyl framework. This subsurface consists of one of the following:

- ½ in (13 mm) thick compressible, acoustical, fire-resistant polyester batt.

- ⅜ in (10 mm) thick, tackable, fire-retardant panel.

- ⅜ in (10 mm) thick, fire-retardant, plywood panel suitable for nailing or mounting heavy objects such as pictures, artwork, or signage.

- Fabric is stretched tightly over the framework and tucked into slots in the sides of the framework with a special tool.

- *Edge profiles*

Profiles of edges of panels are formed by the shape of the vinyl frame.

- Radius edge: has an approximate ⅜ in (10 mm) radius.

- Square edge: perpendicular to surface of the wall and requires a ½ in (13 mm) reveal or space between panels.

- Beveled edge: has a 60-degree angle with the edge of the panel.

- Monolithic edge: used in place of sewn seams that show stitching and press marks. Creates a clean, finished looking joint and also facilitates easier changing of fabrics.

- *Panel thickness*

- Dependent upon the thickness of the vinyl framework.

- Standard thickness is ⅜ in (10 mm).

- Alternate thickness is 1 in (25 mm) framework typical of special, high-efficiency acoustic panel design.

- *Special considerations*

- Special techniques are available to handle inside and outside edges, wrapped corners, and special reveals.

- Designs are available to cover doorframes and other elements.

- Tackable, acoustical, and nailable surfaces can be mixed under the same piece of fabric. ■

REFERENCES

ATBCB, *Americans with Disabilities Act Accessibility Guidelines for Buildings and Facilities (ADAAG)*, U.S. Architectural & Transportation Barriers Compliance Board, Washington, 1991.

NSSEA, Operable Walls Manufacturers Section, *Sound Control Performance of Operable Walls,* National School Supply and Equipment Association, Silver Spring, 1987.

OSHA, *Sanitation,* CFR 29, Section 1, Occupational Safety and Health Administration, U.S. Department of Labor, Washington, 1996.

Watson, Donald, ed., *Time-Saver Standards for Building Materials and Systems,* McGraw-Hill, New York, 2000.

John Templer, Ph.D.

Summary

A recommended design sequence and checklist of information is presented for design of stairs. A history and theoretical background of stair design and a complete discussion of design criteria are found in Templer (1994), from which this section is adapted.

Key words

balustrade, circulation, guardrail, handrail, headroom clearance, landing, Level of Service, nosing, ramp, refuge area, riser-tread dimensions

Vizcaya Museum, Miami, Florida, 1916.

Stair design

1 DESIGN OF STAIRWAYS

Design of the stair configuration depends on the floor space available, the floor-to-floor height, pedestrian movement volumes and patterns, and the groups of people who will use the stair. This article presents a discussion of stair design based upon research. A discussion of safety is in the following article.

Stair user groups

Potential users typically include able-bodied adults, specific handicapped groups, children, the elderly, or all of these groups. The potential use of the stair may be as a means of access and egress; in a public or monumental location, with a large volume of pedestrians; or in a private location. There are special design considerations for some groups, especially important in special facilities for these user groups, but applicable to all stairs where universal design is applicable:

- *Disabled:* Provide an alternative access way so those who cannot use stairs are not denied entry.

- *Elderly and disabled:* For the elderly and some handicapped people, designs that depend only on stair access and egress should be avoided.

- *People carrying food, drinks, and supplies:* Avoid placing stairs where people will routinely carry food and drink that may spill on the treads. Avoid stair designs where workers must carry bulky or heavy objects, or anything else that may limit their view of the treads or affect their balance.

- *Children:* Stairs for use by children need an additional, lower handrail. The minimum distance between balustrade members must be less than a 3-½ in (8.89 cm) sphere to prevent the passage of a small child. For control of toddlers, the stair may be closed by a gate.

Factors that affect location

- Where large crowds of people will use the stairs (theaters, stadia, fire egress for large buildings), the stair should be located so that it does not cause a hazardous bottleneck by making a sudden change of direction, such as a dogleg stair. The stair should be located to encourage continuous direct flow.

- Avoid pedestrian movement directional conflicts at the top and bottom of the stair. **Fig. 1** shows a stair leading directly to and across a passage with heavy traffic.

- Avoid direction, view, and illumination changes. **Fig. 2** illustrates several potentially hazardous layout conditions—the bottom of a stair where sunlight may blind users or a fascinating view that may distract attention.

- Avoid entry- or exit-way hazards. **Fig. 3** shows a door opening directly onto a landing.

- Avoid a configuration that violates the "keep-right" principle (the convention in the United States, which reportedly is a learned habit adapted from national driving rules of the road). Helical flights that ascend by spiraling up to the right, and dogleg and other layouts that ascend to the right, enable those ascending to

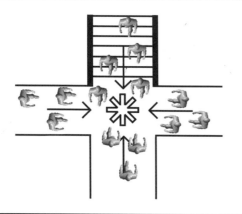

Fig. 1. Avoid conflicting pedestrian movement directions at the top or bottom of the stair.

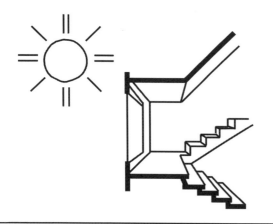

Fig. 2. Avoid direction, view, and illumination changes.

Fig. 3. Avoid entering or exit hazards.

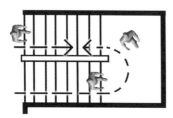

Fig. 4. Avoid keep-right conflicts.

keep to the right with little effort. This reduces the likelihood of conflicts with those descending (**Fig. 4**).

• Avoid fire-escape stairs that continue past the ground-floor egress point down into a basement. These may mislead people during an emergency, drawing them down to a dead end.

• The existing environment may limit the amount of space available for a stair. If this constraint exists, establish the size of area that is available.

Codes prescribe minimum widths and maximal protrusions of handrails and doors swings in egress stairs, with minimum width based on specified occupancies and building type. **Fig. 5** indicates these clearances for a representative case. Conforming to typical code requirements, the door swing does not intrude more than 50 percent of the specified minimum width of stair, including clearances for handrail and the door thickness and hardware in all operating positions.

Stair layout to provide areas of refuge

The Americans with Disabilities Act (ADA) along with universal design recommended practices provide for means of safe egress and refuge within smoke-protected areas and exit ways, properly considered along with stairwell design. Areas of refuge are fire-protected zones for people who are unable to use stairs to await assistance in an emergency. A wheelchair space 30 × 48 in. (76.2 × 122 cm) free and clear of the exit pathway must typically be provided for every 200 occupants or portion thereof per floor, with a minimum of two places per area of refuge. **Fig. 6** indicates provision of refuge areas for individuals in wheelchairs.

2 STAIR TYPES AND PERFORMANCE

• Direction and flow: The direction of travel that people will take to and from the top and bottom of the stair will be affected by the stair layout, and vice versa.

• Stair shape, area, and performance: The amount of floor space a staircase occupies is related to its shape. Some layouts use less space than others, and some are more effective than others for moving stretchers, furniture, crowds of people, and so on.

Determining dimensions

Stair design in buildings may be governed by several codes and standards. Refer to the applicable building code, fire code, handicapped code, occupational safety and health regulations, Department of Housing and Urban Development Standards, ANSI Specifications, and other applicable codes. While these codes establish minimum standards that must be followed, the recommendations indicated in this article are based on empirical research findings of stair use, which should be considered as a design check based on Level of Service and as appropriate to augment minimum requirements.

Width

Stair width should be a function of comfort, capacity, and reach (handrail availability). The minimum design width of stairs for single-file use should be 29 in (74 cm) for a public place. For comfort, about 38 in (97 cm) width is needed. Side-by-side walking clearance dictates a width between walls of at least 56 in (1.42 m), a module of 28 in (71.12 cm). A more comfortable module of 34.5 in (87.63 cm) dictates a minimum width of 69 in (1.75 m).

The stair must be wide enough for the expected volume of traffic. The capacity of the stair is expressed in people per minute per foot (or per meter) width. To plan for the expected flow per minute, one must consider the occupancy of the space to be served. The total occupant load per building floor can be found by dividing the floor area by the occupant density, using square feet per person (m²/person). Estimates of occupant density per building type are given in **Table 1.**

Dividing the anticipated total occupant load of the floor (for example) by the average evacuation time of the people yields the number of people per minute who will pass a point on the stair. For a walkway leading to a stair, **Table 2** indicates varying levels of service, or density of horizontal movement flows. Generally only Levels 4 to 8 are acceptable. Level 3 may be acceptable for bulk arrival (platoon) situations. Even for this use, it should be carefully considered. For the stair itself, **Table 3** indicates the recommendation that density of flow on stairs not exceed those indicated as Level E.

To avoid or minimize the likelihood of queues forming, Level E should be avoided also and Level D used in discretion. Using Level E, 13 to 17 persons per 12 in (30.1 cm) width of stair per minute, the designer might assume 15 persons per foot width of stair per minute to establish the required width of the stair. This would give the effective width. To allow for handrails, adjoining walls, and so on, another 14 in (35.6 cm) may be necessary.

For example, a stair to evacuate 200 people, who take an average of 2 minutes to reach the stair, must be able to carry 100 people per minute. At a maximum flow of 15 people per foot width per minute, an effective stair width of 6.67 ft (2.03 m) will be required. Based on a module of 28 in (71 cm), 7 ft (2.13 m) will be a better effective width. Allowing for adjoining walls and handrails, a total of about 8.17 ft (2.49 m) will be necessary.

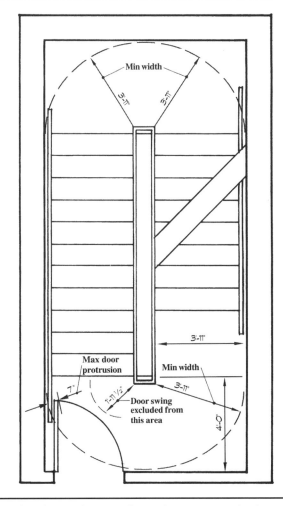

Fig. 5. Plan of stair indicating code complying provisions for door protrusion. Door swing does not protrude more than 50 percent into the stair width in all of its operating positions, including hardware and railing clearances. (Source: Ankrom Mosian Architects in Patterson, 2001).

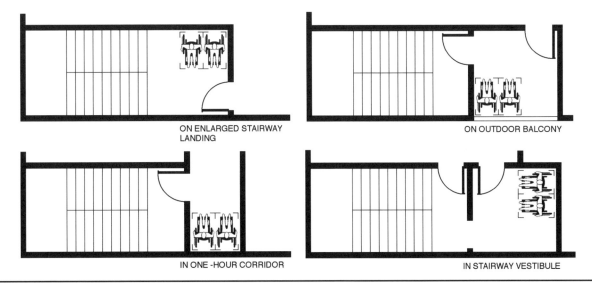

ON ENLARGED STAIRWAY LANDING

ON OUTDOOR BALCONY

IN ONE-HOUR CORRIDOR

IN STAIRWAY VESTIBULE

Fig. 6. Provision of refuge areas. (Allen and Iano 1995)

Table 1. Estimate of occupant numbers for various types of building

| | Occupant Load | | Maximum Travel Distance | |
Occupancy	Square feet per person	Square meters per person	Feet	Meters
Residential	200	18.6	100	30.5
Educational			150	45.7
classrooms	20	1.9	100	30.5
shops	50	4.7		
Institutional				
sleeping areas	120	11.2	100	30.5
treatment areas	240	22.3		
Assembly	15	1.4		
without fixed seats	6	0.6	100	30.5
standing areas	3	0.3		
Business	100	9.3	100	30.5
Mercantile			150	45.7
first floor	30	2.8		
other floors	60	5.6		
storage and shipping	100	9.3		
Industrial	100	9.3	100	30.5
Storage	300	27.9	100	30.5
Hazardous	100	9.3	75	22.9

Table 2. Levels of pedestrian density in movement on the level

Level 1:
2 to 5
(0.2—0.5)
Flow: erratic, on verge of complete stoppage
Average speed: shuffling only, 0-30 m/min.)
Choice of speed: none, movement only with the crowd
Crossing or reverse movement: impossible
Conflicts: physical contact unavoidable
Passing: impossible

Level 2:
5 to 7
(0.5-0.7)
Flow: 23-25 PPM/ft. (75-82 PPM/m), a maximum in traffic stream under pressure[a]
Average speed: mostly shuffling, 100-180 ft./min. (30±-55 m/min.)
Choice of speed: none, movement only with the crowd
Crossing or reverse movement: most difficult
Conflicts: physical contact probable, conflicts unavoidable
Passing: impossible

Level 3:
7 to 11
(0.7-1.0)
Flow: 19-23 PPM/ft. (62-75 PPM/m), attains a maximum in relaxed traffic streams
Average speed: about 70 percent of free flow, 180-200 ft./min. (55-61 m/min.)
Choice of speed: practically none
Crossing or reverse movement: severely restricted, with conflicts
Conflicts: physical contact probable, conflicts unavoidable
Passing: impossible

Level 4:
15 to 18
(1.0-1.4)
Flow: 15-19 PPM/ft. (49-62 PPM/m), 65-80 percent of maximum capacity
Average speed: about 75 percent of free flow, 200-240 ft./min. (61-73 m/min.)
Choice of speed: restricted, constant adjustments of gait needed
Crossing or reverse movement: severely restricted, with conflicts
Conflicts: unavoidable
Passing: rarely possible without touching

Level 5:
15 to 18
(1.4—1.7)
Flow: 12-15 PPM/ft. (39-49 PPM/m), 56-70 percent of maximum capacity
Average speed: about 80 percent of free flow, 240-270 ft./min. (73-82 m/min.)
Choice of speed: restricted except for slow walkers
Crossing or reverse movement: restricted, with conflicts
Conflicts: probably high
Passing: rarely possible without touching

Level 6:
18 to 25
(1.7—2.3)
Flow: 10-12 PPM/ft. (33-39 PPM/m), roughly 50 percent of maximum capacity
Average speed: more than 80 percent of free flow, 270-290 ft./min. (82-88 m/min.)
Choice of speed: unless stream similar, restricted by bunching
Crossing or reverse movement: possible, with conflicts
Conflicts: probably high
Passing: difficult without abrupt maneuvers

Level 7:
25 to 40
(2.3-3.7)
Flow: 7-10 PPM/ft. (20-33 PPM/m), roughly one-third of maximum capacity
Average speed: nearly free flow, 290-310 ft./min. (88-94 m/min.)
Choice of speed: occasionally impeded
Crossing or reverse movement: possible with occasional conflicts
Conflicts: about 50 percent probability
Passing: possible, but with interference

Level 8
Over 40
(over 3.7)
Flow: one-fifth maximum capacity or less
Average speed: virtually as chosen
Choice of speed: virtually unrestricted
Crossing or reverse movement: free
Conflicts: maneuvering needed to avoid conflicts
Passing: free, with some maneuvering

[a]PPM/ft.: pedestrians per minute per foot width of walkway; PPM/m: pedestrians per minute per meter width of walkway.

Source: Pushkarev and Zupan (1975). Flow and speed figures derived from Fruin (1987)

Table 3. Levels of pedestrian density in movement on stairs

Average Area per
Person, sq. ft. (m²)   *Characteristics*

Level F: Flow: up to 20 PPM/ft. (66 PPM/m), flow attains a maximum,
                but is Less than 4 (0.37) erratic with frequent stoppages and
                verges on complete breakdown[a]
                      Average horizontal speed: shuffling, 0—70 ft./min
                      (0—21 m/min)
                      Choice of speed: none
                      Passing: impossible
                      Queuing at stair entrance: yes

Level E: Flow: 13—17 PPM/ft. (43—56 PPM/m), intermittent stoppages
4 to 7   Average horizontal speed: 70—90 ft./min (21—27 m/min)
(0.37—0.65)   Choice of speed: none
                      Passing: impossible
                      Queuing at stair entrance: yes

Level D: Flow: 10—13 PPM/ft. (33—43 PPM/m)
7 to 10   Average horizontal speed: 90—95 ft./min (27—29 m/min)
(0.65—0.93)   Choice of speed: restricted
                      Passing: impossible
                      Queuing at stair entrance: some at higher flow level

Level C: Flow: 7—10 PPM/ft. (23—33 PPM/m)
10 to 15   Average horizontal speed: 95—100 ft./min. (29—30m/min)
(0.93—1.4)   Choice of speed: restricted
                      Passing: impossible
                      Queuing at stair entrance: none

Level B: Flow: 5—7 PPM/ft. (16—23 PPM/m)
15 to 20   Average horizontal speed: 100 ft./min. (30 m/min)
(1.4—1.9)   Choice of speed: freely selected
                      Passing: restricted
                      Queuing at stair entrance: none

Level A: Flow: 5 or less PPM/ft. (16 PPM/m or less)
More than 20   Average horizontal speed: 100 ft./min. (30 m/min)
(1.9)   Choice of speed: freely selected
                      Passing: at will
                      Queuing at stair entrance: none

[a]*PPM/ft.: pedestrians per minute per foot width of walkway; PPM/m: pedestrians per minute per meter width of walkway*

Source: Fruin (1987).

Table 4. Range of rise and going relationships for comfort and safety

Rise	Goings						
INCHES							
7.2	11						
7	11						
6.5	11	11.5	12	12.5			
6	11	11.5	12	12.5	13	13.5	14
5.5	11	11.5	12	12.5	13		
5	11	11.5	12				
4.6	11						
CENTIMETERS							
18.3	27.9						
17.8	27.9						
16.5	27.9	29.2	30.5	31.8			
15.2	27.9	29.2	30.5	31.8	33.0	34.3	35.6
14.0	27.9	29.2	30.5	31.8	33.0		
12.7	27.9	29.2	30.5				
11.7	27.9						

Riser-tread dimensions

Table 4 gives acceptable relationships for riser and *going* based on energy expenditures and potential for safer gait. (The *going* is the horizontal distance, in plan, from the nosing edge of a step to the nosing edge of the next adjoining step.)

Riser heights that are more than 7.33 in (18.6 cm) and goings less than 11 in (27.9 cm) are not recommended. Going dimensions greater than 14 in (36.6 cm) may also be acceptable, but no research is available to confirm or deny this. In the table, dimensional increments between entries are also acceptable. Applicable codes and standards may differ from these recommendations.

The *riser height* (**Fig. 7**) is the vertical height of a single step. The *tread depth* is the horizontal distance, in plan, of a tread. Some codes require a nosing overhang if the treads are small. Dimensions of adjoining risers and treads must be constructed to be constant and regular.

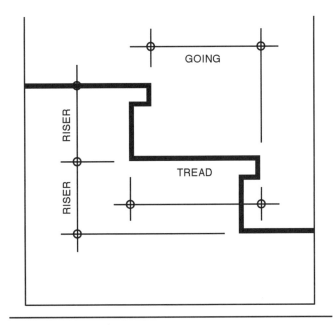

Fig. 7. Riser, tread, and going.

Landings

Landings of stairs that have no change of direction are called intermediate landings. A change in direction of 90 degrees results in a quarter-landing (wide L), and a change in direction of 180 degrees produces a half-landing (narrow U). Landings on long flights of stairs are necessary to provide a resting place for stair users, to form turning zones, and, in the event of a fall, to break the force of the fall. The minimum width of the landing must be equal to that of the widest flight of steps that reaches it. The minimum clear depth must equal the widest stair run or 48 in (1.21 m), whichever is larger.

Headroom

Headroom is measured vertically from the front edge of the nosing of a step to the finished ceiling. It should never be less than 6 ft-7 in (2 m).

Length of run

A stair flight should always consist of three or more risers. The flight should not have too many steps without a landing. In many codes the maximum number of risers permitted in a flight is 18.

Develop configuration layout

Layout techniques vary in implementation with the configuration chosen, but in all cases, an acceptable and consistent riser and tread relationship should be adhered to in order to provide a layout requiring minimum energy expenditure as well as maximum potential for safety. This section suggests techniques for laying out several types of stair. The following symbols and abbreviations are used in the discussion below:

Stair			*Ramp*	
H	=	Floor-to-floor height	=	Elevation change
L	=	Length of run between first and last riser nosing	=	Length of run from bottom to top
n	=	Number of risers		
p	=	Number of treads		
R	=	Riser height		
G	=	Going depth		

Straight flight stairs

- Determine floor-to-floor height (H). Select acceptable riser (R) and going (G) dimensions. If space is limited, choose maximum riser (R) and minimum going (G).

- Determine the number of risers (n):

$$n = \frac{H}{R}$$

Set n equal to the nearest whole number, and adjust the riser dimension accordingly.

- The number of treads is equal to the number of risers minus 1:

$$p = n - 1$$

- The length of run equals the going dimension times the number of treads:

$$L = G \times p$$

Flights with winders and splayed steps

By definition, a winder is a wedge-shaped step of varying tread width. To obtain treads of about equal widths, the steps preceding and following the turn may be splayed.

- The narrow portion of the tread should be at least 4 in (10.2 cm) at a distance of 6 in (15.2 cm) from the end of the tread or inside of the stringer. At the walking line, 10.6 in (27.0 cm) from the newel or outside handrail the going must be at least 11 in (27.9 cm).

- Do not run a step edge into a corner.

- Splayed steps and winders should rise in a clockwise direction where possible. This puts the wide portions of the treads to the right-hand side when going downstairs.

Spiral stairs

- From 12 to 20 steps can be accommodated in a full circle. The tread angle can range from 30 to 18 degrees.

- Typically, the line of the nosings does not radiate out from the geometrical center of the stair but "dances" to some extent.

- The greater the number of steps there are in the circle, the greater is the available headroom clearance but the smaller is the effective going.

- Headroom clearance should not be less than 6 ft-7 in (2 m).

- A stair that one ascends in a clockwise fashion has the advantage that, in descent, the handrail is on the right-hand side.

- The walking line is taken as 10.6 in (27.0 cm) from the outside of the newel or the inside of the outer handrail.

- At a distance of 6 in (15 cm) from the newel or inside stringer, the tread must have a depth that is greater than 4 in (10.2 cm). At the walking line, the going should not be less than 11 in (27.9 cm).

- To develop a dimensionally acceptable layout, proceed as follows:

  (1) Establish the diameter of the stair and the positions of the first and last risers.

  (2) Determine the number of risers:

  $$n = \frac{H}{R}$$

  (3) Determine the number of steps and the going dimension at the walking line by using **Table 5,** which shows the going dimension where the stair diameter and the number of treads in the plan circle are known.

  (4) Check the headroom clearance at the most unfavorable point. If the headroom is inadequate, change the number of steps.

Helical stairs with an open well

- A clockwise ascent layout is preferable.

- The actual walking line rise-going dimensions should not exceed acceptable limits. **Table 6** shows the going dimension (in the direction of the run) at 1-ft (30-cm) intervals from the center of the

Table 5. Dimensions for Spiral Stairs: Going Depth at Walking Line[a]

Inches

Exterior Diameter of Stair	54	60	66	72	78	84	90	96	102
Diameter of Walking Line	32.7	38.7	44.7	50.7	56.7	62.7	68.7		80.7

Number of treads in circle — Going depth at walking line[b]

Number of treads in circle	54	60	66	72	78	84	90	96	102
11	9.22	10.90	12.60						
12		10.01	11.57	13.13					
13		9.26	10.70	12.14	13.58				
14			9.96	11.29	12.63	13.96			
15			9.30	10.55	11.80	13.04			
16				9.90	11.07	12.24	13.41		
17				9.32	10.43	11.53	12.63	13.73	
18					9.85	10.89	11.94	12.98	
19					9.34	10.33	11.31	12.30	13.29
20						9.81	10.75	11.69	12.63

Centimeters

Exterior Diameter of Stair	140	150	160	170	180	190	200	210	220	230	240	250
Diameter of Walk Line	86	96	106	116	126	136	146	156	166	176	186	196

Number of treads in circle — Going depth at walking line[c]

Number of treads in circle	140	150	160	170	180	190	200	210	220	230	240	250
11	24.2	27.0	29.9	32.7	35.5							
12		24.8	27.4	30.0	32.6	35.2						
13			25.4	27.8	30.2	32.5						
14			23.6	25.8	28.0	30.3	32.5	34.7				
15				24.1	26.2	28.3	30.4	32.4	34.5			
16					24.6	26.5	28.5	30.4	32.4	34.1		
17					23.2	25.0	26.8	28.7	30.5	32.3	34.2	
18						23.6	25.4	27.1	28.8	30.6	32.3	34.0
19							24.0	25.7	27.3	29.0	30.6	32.3
20							22.8	24.4	26.0	27.5	29.1	30.7

[a]Exterior diameter and exterior radius are measured from the inside of the outer handrail of the stair; walking line is estimated as 10.63 inches (27 cm) from the inside of the handrail.

[b]Going at walking line is calculated from $2 \sin\alpha/2(r_{ex}-10.73)$, where r_{ex} is the exterior radius of the stair and a is the angle between the front and back lines of a tread. Values to the right of the stepped line are acceptable.

[c]Going at walking line is calculated from $\sin\alpha/2(r_{ex}-27)$, where r_{ex} is the exterior radius of the stair and a is the angle between the front and back lines of a tread. Values to the right of the stepped line are acceptable.

circle for seven different tread angles. A minimum going dimension of 11 in (28 cm) should be chosen for the walking line 10.6 in (27 cm) from the inside or outside handrail.

Ramps

By definition, a ramp is any part of a constructed pedestrian circulation way with a slope greater than 5 percent. Acceptable gradients for ramps depend on the length of ramp to be used and the location of landings.

- To determine if a ramp will be an acceptable solution for an existing site condition, the designer must determine elevation change (H) and the length of run (L). This length is the horizontal distance over which the elevation change takes place, minus the length of any landings.

- Codes in the United States generally establish a maximum gradient of $\frac{1}{12}$ for ramps qualifying as wheelchair access.

- If H/L is less than the maximum gradient given in **Table 7** for ramps of this length, then a ramp may be used. If H/L is greater than the maximum gradient, shorten the length (L) by adding an intermediate landing and check the table again.

- To establish the maximum length of the ramp between landings, consult **Table 8**.

3 DETAILS

Step shape

- Nosings: Abrupt nosing overhangs (**Fig. 8**) and any overhang that is greater than ¾ in (1.9 cm) should not be constructed. When carpets are added, they change the stair profile and thus should be carefully considered in design and installation (**Fig. 9**). Where a nosing is needed, provide backward-sloping nosing overhangs (less than ¾ in) where possible.

- Wash: A wash is needed to throw water off external steps. It should not exceed about a 1 to 60 slope.

Table 6. Going dimensions for helical stairs with an open well

Number of Treads in Circle	22.5	25.7	30	36	45	60	90	
Tread Angle (degrees)	16	14	12	10	8	6	4	
Distance from center of circle (feet)	Going dimension (inches)							
3	10.0							
4	13.4	11.7						
5	16.7	14.6	12.5	10.5				
6	20.0	17.5	15.1	12.6	10.0			
7		20.5	17.6	14.6	11.7			
8			20.1	16.7	13.4	10.0		
9				18.8	15.1	11.3		
10					16.7	12.6		
11						13.8		
12						15.1	10.1	
13						16.3	10.9	
14						17.6	11.7	
15								12.6
Distance from center of circle (meters)	Going dimension (centimeters)							
0.91	25.3							
1.22	33.9	29.7	25.5					
1.52	42.3	37.0	31.8	26.5				
1.83	50.9	44.6	38.3	31.9	25.5			
2.13			44.5	37.1	29.7			
2.44				42.5	34.0	25.5		
2.74					38.2	28.7		
3.05						31.9	21.3	
3.35						35.1	23.4	
3.66						38.3	25.5	
3.96							27.6	

Table 7. Acceptable Ramp Gradients, Maximum Rise and Length

Gradient	Maximum Rise in Single Run		Total Length, Excluding Landings		
1:8—1:10	3 inches	(7.6 cm)	24—30	inches	(61—76 cm)
1:10.1—1.11	9 feet	(2.74 m)	91—99	inches	(28—30 m)
1:11.1—1:13	14 feet	(4.27 m)	155—182	inches	(47—55 m)
1:13.1—1:15	16 feet	(4.88 m)	210—240	inches	(64—73 m)
1:15.1—1:16	20 feet	(6.10 m)	302—320	inches	(92—98 m)

Note: building, fire, and handicapped codes may require different gradients.
Source: Templer *et al.* (1980)

Table 8. Maximum length between landings on ramps

Maximum Ramp Length	Gradient 1:15.9	1:14.3	1:13.7	1:12.7	1:11.6	1:10
IN FEET						
Between bottom and landing 1	95 (5.9)	85 (6.0)	80 (5.8)	75 (5.9)	65 (5.6)	45 (4.5)
Between landing 1 and 2	75 (10.7)	70 (10.9)	65 (10.6)	55 (10.3)	55 (10.3)	45 (9.0)
Between landing 2 and 3	45 (13.5)	45 (14.0)	45 (13.9)	45 (13.8)	45 (14.2)	
Between landing 3 and 4	30 (15.4)	30 (16.1)	30 (16.1)			
Between landing 4 and 5	30 (17.3)					
Between landing 5 and 6	30 (19.2)					
IN METERS						
Between bottom and landing 1	29 (1.8)	30 (1.8)	24 (1.8)	23 (1.8)	20 (1.7)	14 (1.4)
Between landing 1 and 2	23 (3.3)	21 (3.3)	20 (3.2)	17 (3.1)	17 (3.1)	14 (2.7)
Between landing 2 and 3	14 (4.1)	14 (4.3)	14 (4.2)	14 (4.2)	14 (4.3)	
Between landing 3 and 4	9 (4.7)	9 (4.9)	9 (4.9)			
Between landing 4 and 5	9 (5.3)					
Between landing 5 and 6	9 (5.9)					

Note: figures in parentheses show total height ascended.

- Dimensional regularity: Risers, treads, and nosing projections must be constructed with a high degree of dimensional consistency, and in fact most building codes wisely insist on this. The differences in dimension between the largest and smallest in a flight and between those in adjoining steps should not exceed ³⁄₁₆ in (0.48 cm). This is by no means too exacting a standard for contemporary building practices.

Materials

The appropriate choice of material for stair treads is likely to be influenced by several factors: structural considerations, the type and volume of traffic, appearance, resistance to wear and sometimes chemicals and the climate, ease of maintenance and cleaning, cost, slip resistance, and how comfortable it is to walk on. Avoid soft woods and stone that may erode easily.

- *Floor patterns:* Avoid the use of textures or patterns or nosing strips that make it difficult to discern the edge of the nosings. Use colors to emphasize the edge.

- *Carpet fixing:* Avoid step and, particularly, nosing designs that will prevent carpeting from being fixed firmly.

- *Slip resistance:* Coefficients of Friction (COF) greater than 0.3 may be adequate to prevent slips on level, dry, step surfaces in internal stairs at normal rates of climb, but coefficients of 0.5 are considered preferable and safer. The most critical area for slips is at the nosing, but it is better to ensure that the whole tread has an adequate COF rather than to add abrasive nosing strips that may be visually confusing and may cause trips. Ramps require careful consideration to prevent slips. For a chosen COF for level surfaces, **Table 9** shows the equivalent COF that will be required to obviate slips at various ramp gradients. The left-hand column shows a range of coefficients of friction such as might be chosen for a level walkway. The remaining columns show the coefficients necessary to provide equal slip resistance for various ramp gradients (for a person who does not change pace on the ramp).

- *Tread surface:* The surface of stair treads should be smooth, free from projecting joints stable under the loads with no tendency to shift underfoot, and with nothing to catch the shoe.

- *Injurious materials:* The stair as well as the handrails and balustrading should be free from projecting elements, sharp edges and corners, and any rough surfaces, bars, rods, and other elements that have a small section. Instead, as with the interior of the

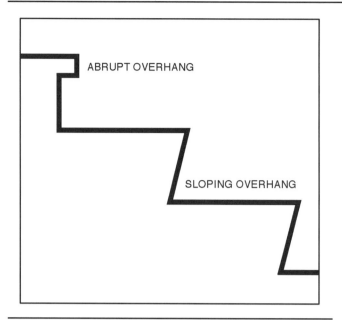

Fig. 8. Nosing overhangs.

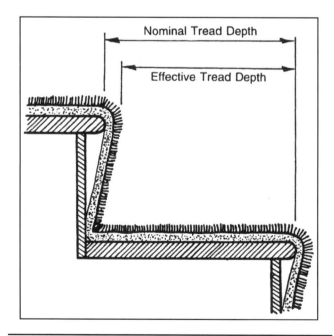

Fig. 9. Stair with carpet. Thick carpeting on stairs reduces effective tread depth. (Preiser and Ostroff 2001)

car, smooth, flat, impact-attenuating surfaces and gentle curves should be used.

Handrails

- *Location:* A stair that is 35 in (88.9 cm) wide between the walls and with a rail on one side has the maximum feasible width if the rail must fall within the reach of adult users. A 47 in (1.19 cm) wide stair with handrails on both sides is the maximum width for both rails to be always available to adult users. Current codes permit a single rail for stairs up to 44 in (0.12 m) and two rails for stairs up to 88 in (2.24 m).

- *Height:* From the forward edge of the nosing to the top of the handrail should be 36 to 40 in (0.91 to 1.02 m), but codes usually require 30 to 34 in (76.2 to 86.4 cm). For children, an intermediate rail that is 21.8 to 28.7 in (55.4 to 72.9 cm) should be provided.

- *Extent:* Handrails should extend horizontally a minimum of 12 in (30.5 cm) beyond the top of the stair and beyond the bottom riser for a distance equal to the tread width and then continue horizontally for 12 in (30.5 cm). The handrails should not project into walkways; the ends should return to the floor or adjoining walls. Handrails should continue along at least one side of a landing (**Fig. 10**).

- *Size and shape:* A circular handrail 1-½ in (3.8 cm) diameter is most effective for gripping (**Fig. 11**).

- *Spacing distance from walls:* The clearance between a handrail and an adjoining wall, assuming a circular handrail with 1-½ in (3.8 cm) diameter, should not be less than 3.65 in (9.3 cm).

- *Materials:* Handrails should not be too slippery or too rough. Rails that are lightly padded like auto steering wheels can provide the correct range of friction characteristics, may enable better grip forces to occur, and are less likely to cause trauma if they are hit in a fall. Handrail materials should not conduct or retain heat to the degree that they become untouchable. Handrails must not be permitted to deteriorate so their surfaces become splintered or pitted with rust. Finally, the color of handrails should be carefully chosen so they are always highly visible.

Guardrails

- *Height:* Guardrails should not be less than 42 in (1.07 m) high unless the width is greater than 6 in (15.2 cm). In that case, the minimum height of the guardrail should not be less than 48 in (1.22 m) minus B, where B is the minimum width of the top surface of the guardrail. Thus, if the width of the top surface of the guardrail is 20 in (25.4 cm), the height may be 38 in (0.97 m)—48 in less 10 in. The rail height should never be less than 30 in (76.2 cm). The design should discourage people from climbing onto a rail from which they may overbalance and fall.

- *Structural loading:* Most codes require the system to be able to withstand a test load without much deflection. A typical test requires the system to withstand a 200-lb (90.7 kg) vertical load at the mid-span of the rail, with a deflection that does not exceed the length of the rail divided by 96. For a horizontal load test, the system may be required to withstand 200 lb (90.7 kg), measured at the top of the rail at its mid-span, with a deflection that does not

Table 9. Static Coefficient of Friction for Level Surfaces and for Various Gradients

Level	1:20	1.18	1:16	1:14	1:12	1:10	1:8	1:6	1:4
.80	.89	.90	.91	.92	.95	.98	1.03	1.12	1.31
.75	.83	.84	.85	.87	.89	.92	.97	1.05	1.23
.70	.78	.79	.80	.81	.83	.86	.90	.98	1.15
.65	.72	.73	.74	.76	.78	.80	.84	.92	1.07
.60	.67	.68	.69	.70	.72	.74	.78	.85	1.00
.55	.62	.62	.63	.65	.66	.69	.72	.79	.93
.50	.56	.57	.58	.59	.61	.63	.67	.73	.86
.45	.51	.52	.53	.54	.55	.58	.61	.67	.79
.40	.46	.47	.47	.49	.50	.52	.53	.61	.72
.35	.41	.41	.42	.43	.45	.47	.50	.55	.66
.30	.36	.36	.37	.38	.39	.41	.44	.49	.59

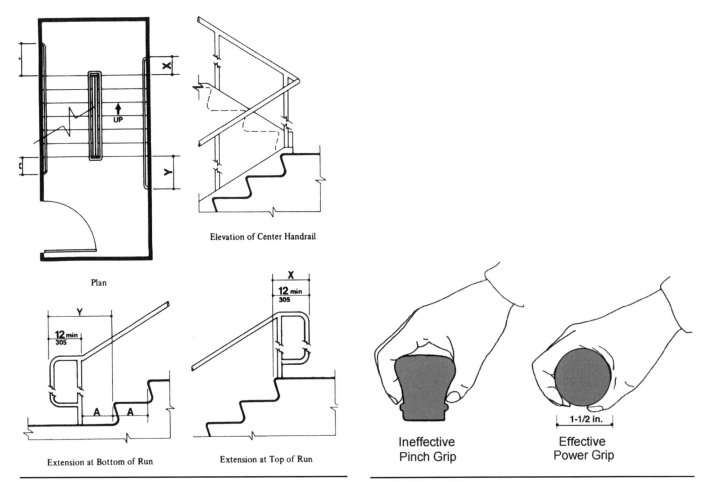

Plan

Elevation of Center Handrail

Extension at Bottom of Run

Extension at Top of Run

Ineffective Pinch Grip

Effective Power Grip

Fig. 10. Handrail extension at top and bottom of stair.

Fig. 11. Handrail. Difference in ease of grasp with common railing and functional railing. A circular shape of 1-½ in (3.8 cm) is recommended. (Preiser and Ostroff 2001)

exceed the sum of the rail height divided by 24 plus the rail length between vertical supports divided by 96. When the load is applied at a vertical support, the deflection may not exceed the rail height divided by 12. In public buildings, there is a greater danger of extreme loading, so a higher standard of structural strength is required. The test load is increased by 50 percent (or 65 percent in some circumstances, such as balconies). For one- and two-story residential buildings, the test load may be reduced by 50 percent.

- *Baluster spacing:* As a check of spacing, it should not be possible to pass a sphere of 3-½ in (8.9 cm) diameter through the balustrading.

Illumination

Proper illumination of a stairway is essential for both comfort and safety. Adequate lighting must be provided under both electric lighting and daylighting conditions, with attention to daylighting and solar glare and reflections that may occur only at specific times of the year. The following guidelines address accident prevention and safety recommendations that are restated in the following section on designing stairs to reduce and eliminate accidents.

- Adequate illumination, either natural or electric, must be provided. The IES recommendation of 5 to 20 foot-candles (54 to 215 lux) for most applications seems to be much more realistic for stair safety than minimum levels permitted by most building codes. A minimum of 8 foot-candles (86 lux) may be adequate.

- Illumination should be reasonably consistent over the entire stair.

- Window and artificial light sources should not be placed where the stair user must include them and the steps in the same direct field of vision, and shadows on the steps should be avoided.

- For reflectance, the IES recommends 21 to 31 percent for floors.

- If the stair is located where there is any risk that someone might stumble into it unexpectedly, permanent supplementary artificial illumination should be provided.

- The switches that control the stair lights should be placed sufficiently far from the stair so there is no risk of a person's falling while reaching for the switch. Three-way switches should be used at the top and bottom of the stairs. ■

REFERENCES

Allen, Edward, and Joseph Iano, *The Architect's Studio Companion: Rules of Thumb for Preliminary Design,* 2nd ed., John Wiley & Sons, New York, 1995.

Fruin, John J., *Pedestrian Planning and Design,* Elevator World, Mobile, 1987.

Patterson, Terry L., *Illustrated 2000 Building Code Handbook,* McGraw-Hill, New York, 2001.

Preiser, F. E. Wolfgang, and Elaine Ostroff, eds., *Universal Design Handbook,* McGraw-Hill, New York, 2001.

Pushkarev, Boris S., and Jeffrey M. Zupan, *Urban Space for Pedestrians,* MIT Press, Cambridge, 1975.

Templer, John, Craig Zimring, and Jean Wineman, *The Feasibility of Accommodating Physically Handicapped Individuals on Pedestrian Over- and Undercrossing Structures,* Federal Highway Administration, Washington, 1980.

Templer, John, *The Staircase: History and Theories and Studies of Hazards, Falls, and Safer Design,* MIT Press, Cambridge, 1994.

Box A: Glossary to Terms Used in Stair Design

Balustrade: the entire in-filling from handrail down to floor level at the edge of a stair.

Banister: a baluster (corruption of baluster).

Carriage (or *carriage piece, rough string, bearer, stair horse*): an inclined timber placed between the two strings against the underside of wide stairs to support them in the middle.

Circular stair: a helical stair.

Close string (or *closed string*): a string that extends above the edges of the risers and treads, covering them on the outside.

Commode step: a riser curved in plan, generally at the foot of a stair.

Dextral stair: a stair that turns to the right during ascent.

Dogleg stair (*dogleg*): a stair with two flights separated by a half-landing, and having no stairwell, so that the upper flight returns parallel to the lower flight.

Ergonomics: the interaction between work and people, particularly, the design of machines, chairs, tables, etc. to suit the body and to permit work with the least fatigue.

Flight: a series of steps between landings.

Going: the horizontal distance between two successive nosings. (In a helical stair the going varies.) The sum of the goings of a straight flight stair is the going of the flight.

Gradient of a stair: the ratio between going and riser; the angle of inclination.

Guardrail: a protective railing designed to prevent people or objects from falling into open well, stairwell, or similar space.

Handrail: a rail forming the top of a balustrade.

Handrail scroll: a spiral ending to a handrail.

Helical stair: the correct but not the usual name for a spiral stair.

Landing: a platform at the top, bottom, or between flights of a staircase.

Monkey tail: a downward scroll at the end of a handrail.

Newel (or *newel post*): the post around which wind the steps of a circular stair. Also applied to the post into which the handrail is framed.

Nosing: the front and usually rounded edge to a stair tread. It frequently projects over the riser below it.

Nosing overhand: the distance that the nosing edge of a step projects beyond the back of the tread below.

Open stair: a stair that is open on one or both sides.

Piano nobile: the principal floor of a house, raised one floor above ground level.

Ramp: an inclined plane for passage of traffic.

Riser: the upright face of a step.

Riser height (or *rise*): the vertical distance from the top of a step at the nosing to the top of an adjoining step at the nosing.

Sinistral stair: a stair that turns to the left in ascent.

Spiral stair (or *helical stair*): a circular stair in which all the treads are winders.

Stair: (1) a series of steps with or without landings, giving access from level to level; (2) one step, consisting of a tread and a riser.

Stairwell: see Well.

Step: one unit of a stair, consisting of a riser and a tread. It may be a flier or a winder.

String (or *stringer*): a sloping board at each end of the treads that carries the treads and risers of a stair.

Tread: the (usually) horizontal surface of a step; also the length (from front to back) of such a surface.

Wash (or *kilt*): a slight sloping of treads to throw off rainwater.

Well: an open space through one or more floors.

Winding stair: a spiral stair; a circular or elliptical geometrical stair.

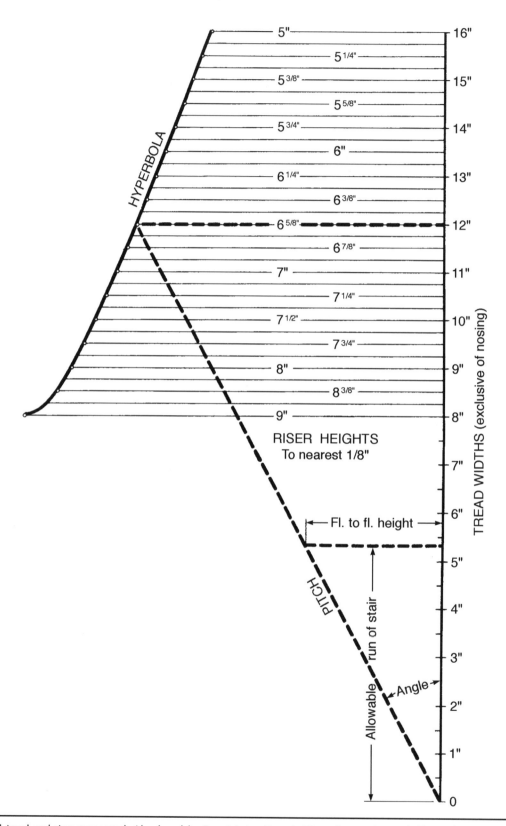

Fig. 1. Proportional tread and riser nomograph (developed by Ernest Irving Freese). Dimensions scale one-half actual size. For metric conversion: 1 in = 25.4 mm = 2.54 cm.

Summary

A graphic means for preliminary design check for stair dimensions is provided including a riser/tread nomograph and tables to standard stair designs and accessways, including exit-way refuge areas, as well as dimensioning of ramps and ladders. A nomograph and tables of common stairway design appropriate for residences is offered as a visual design guide and reference check.

Key words

handrail, gradient, ladder, ramp, refuge area, riser, stair, tread

Boston Public Library. McKim, Mead and White, Architects. 1888.

Stair dimensioning

These pages provide dimensional data of stairs for preliminary design. Due-diligence attention and understanding of the ergonomic basis of stair design offered in the prior two articles offer recommendations based on research of stair use and safety and are the basis of "best practices." Dimensions for stair design in most building types are covered in explicit terms by local building codes. References to building codes prevalent in North America are provided in Allen and Iano (1995).

Tread and riser nomograph

The nomograph (**Fig. 1**) provides a quick reference of proportional dimensions for stair layouts. Data from the nomograph indicate the relationship between tread width and riser height. The nomograph displays graphically the allowable run for stairs, the angle or pitch and floor-to-floor height and tabular material giving handrail heights, headroom, and stair gradients for stairs:

• Dimensions of stair treads and risers are proportional and can be plotted on a hyperbola. Dimensions are accurate to the nearest ⅛ in (3.2 mm).

• In all cases the width of tread is exclusive of a nosing.

• The average height of risers shown, 7 in (18 cm), is proportional to a tread of 11 in (28 cm), a combination that produces a stair that is comfortable and generally economical. At the lower extreme, a riser of 5 in (12.7 cm) produces a tread of 16 in (41 cm), which approximates the proportions of a brick step with a tread equal to two stretchers and a rise equal to two courses.

Using the nomograph

Dimensions are accurate to half-full-size. Thus, readings can be made directly and proportionally without need for calculation.

• To find proper riser for a given tread: read tread line to given width and select riser at intersection.

• To find proper tread for a given riser: select riser to nearest ⅛ in (3.2 mm) and read tread width to nearest ½ in (1.27 cm) or nearest ¼ in (0.64 cm) by interpolation at intersection with the tread line.

• To find tread and riser for given height and run of stair: scale the length of run of stair on tread line. Draw floor-to-floor height at same scale. Draw pitch of stair. Where pitch intersects hyperbola, measure riser (at half-full-size) to tread line. Read tread width directly or measure at half-full-size.

• To find run of stair for given height, tread, and riser: select riser height. Connect intersection at hyperbola with 0 on tread line, establishing pitch. Draw floor-to-floor height to scale, intersecting pitch and perpendicular to tread line. Length of stair run is found at same scale as height on tread line from 0 to intersection of floor-to-floor height.

Stairwell dimensioning

Comfortable stairways are designed in relation to dimensions of the human figure. The accompanying diagrams (**Figs. 2** to **4**) indicate the clearances required for varying ceiling clearances and the recommended handrail heights according to variations in stair gradients. These variations are included in **Table 1**, developed from the nomograph in Fig. 1. Tread and risers in curved stairs should be proportioned on an assumed "line of travel" 18 in (46 cm) from the inner (smaller radius) handrail.

For legal definition, a stair may be described as "A stepped footway having a gradient not less than 5:16 pitch (or 31-¼ percent) and not greater than 9:8 pitch (or 112-½ percent)." Below these limits, footways become "ramps." Above these limits, they are "step ladders."

All building codes have strict specifications for stairs. Many codes required that public access stairs have treads and risers within the pro-portions defined by the formula $T \times R = 70$–75, with risers not over 7-¾ in (19.6 cm) high and treads not less than 9 in (23 cm) wide, exclusive of nosings. Minimum stair width for most egress uses is 44 in (106 cm), allowing as a minimum width two 22-in lines of traffic. Winders and open risers are generally prohibited as egress. In single-family housing, stairs as steep as 8-¼ in (21 cm) riser and 9 in (23 cm) tread may be permitted, although considered steep and the maximum allowable, with a pitch or gradient preferred towards the lower end of 30 to 35 degrees. For exterior stairs risers are generally recommended not to exceed 6 in (15 cm) and treads not less than 12 in (30.5 cm). Handrails are required at all public access exterior stairs and recommended good practice at all steps or significant changes of grade.

Exact dimensions or standards for ramps or ladders have not been established, except as may be provided in applicable fire regulations, and their dimensioning is subject to specific conditions of use, as discussed below.

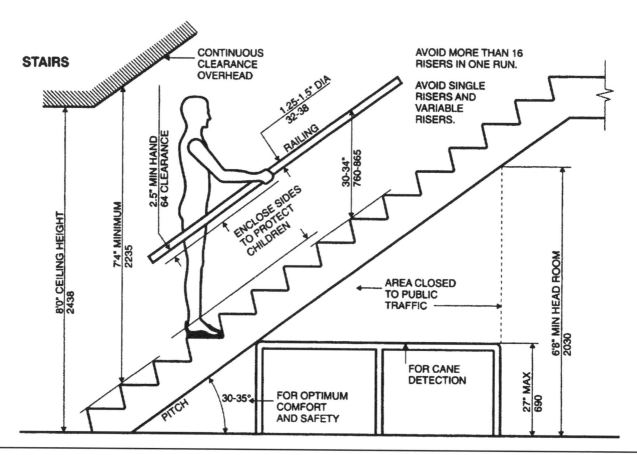

Fig. 2. Stairway dimensioning. (Source: Henry Dreyfuss Associates, 1993, by permission of the publisher)

Table 1. Dimensions for stairways

Step dimensions		Gradient designations		Headroom * Y in inches	Handrail height X in inches	NOTES
Riser **R** in inches	Tread **T** in inches	Per cent grade	Angle in degrees, minutes			
5	16	31.25	17 - 21	85		1. 7" by 11" is the proportion by which all steps are laid out
5¼	15½	33.87	18 - 43		33½	2. Risers from 5" to 6½" are suitable for exterior and "grand" interior stairs
5½	14¾	37.28	20 - 27	86		
5¾	14	41.07	22 - 20			
6	13½	44.44	23 - 58	87		3. Risers from 6⅝" to 7⅝" are most comfortable and most suitable for interior stairs
6¼	13	48.07	25 - 40			
6½	12¼	53.06	27 - 57	88	33	4. Risers for cellar and attic stairs may be up to 9" high
6¾	11¾	57.44	29 - 52			
7	11	63.63	32 - 28	89		5. Width - minimum for single-file travel, 30"
7¼	10½	69.04	34 - 37	90		6. Width - minimum for comfort, 36"
7½	10	75	36 - 52	91		
7¾	9½	81.57	39 - 12	93		7. Width - desirable (for furniture passage etc.), 42"
8	9	88.88	41 - 38	94	33½	
8¼	8½	97.05	44 - 9	96		8. Consult local building codes on all stair problems
8½	8¼	103.02	45 - 51	97		
8¾	8⅛	107.07	46 - 57	98	34	
9	8	112.5	48 - 22	99		

Minimum for head clearance only can be safely taken as 84 in. for all gradients; HUD permits 80 in.

For quick reference in preliminary layout of stairwells, dimensions are tabulated in **Table 2** and at a more detailed level in **Table 3**, each keyed to designations on the accompanying diagrams. These help to determine vertical and horizontal areas and headroom clearances for stair systems with tread and riser proportions indicated. The dimensions refer to face of treads without nosing. Tabulated data refer only to minimal conditions for straight-run stairs. All dimensions may be adjusted proportionally for more amendable or special requirements of design or stair use.

Unit planning data

The six diagrams in **Fig. 5** represent unit plans for types of non-winder stairways most frequently encountered in average residential planning. Tabular information for each is from data contained in Table 1. Plans are reproduced at ⅛ in scale. Each represents an average condition with a stair pitch well within the comfort zone. The basis is a 9 ft-6 in (2.9 m) floor-to-floor height and width of approximately 3 ft (0.9 m) from the wall. Actual width varies with requirements of design and stair use and is shown here as "W" as a guide for landings.

Ramps

Ramps as defined here are inclined pedestrian passages without vertical risers and of a lower pitch than stairs. Ramps for handicapped access require handrails and are generally limited at about 1:12 and not to exceed 6 to 8 percent gradient determined by applicable code. Ramps steeper than 10 percent normally require nonslip surfaces and handrails. Most codes limit the pitch on ramps for any purpose at about 2:12 or 16-⅔ percent. See **Table 3** for proportional dimensioning of clearances, pitch, and handrail.

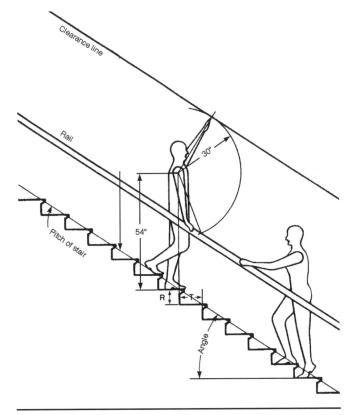

Fig. 3.

Table 2. Stair table

Floor to Floor Height	No. of Risers	Riser R	Tread T	Total Run L	Min. Headroom Y	Handrail X	Clearance C	Partition Above Z*	First Riser Below - U	First Riser Above - V*
8'-0"	† 11	8.73"	8¼"	6'-10½"	8'-2"	2'-10"	5'-8"	-1'-10"	8'-6"	-1'-7"
	† 12	8.00	9	8-3	7-10	2-9½	5-10½	-1-8½	9-7½	-1-4
	13	7.38	10¼	10-3	7-7	2-9	6-2	-1-8½	11-6	-1-1½
	14	6.86	11½	12-5½	7-4	2-9	6-4	-1-7	13-5½	-9½
	Δ 15	6.40	12½	14-7	7-3	2-9	6-7½	-1-6½	15-5½	-7½
	Δ 16	6.00	13½	16-10½	7-3	2-9	6-7½	-1-9	17-6	-8
8'-6"	† 12	8.50	8½	7-9½	8-1	2-9½	5-8½	-1-3½	8-10	-11
	† 13	7.85	9¼	9-3	7-9	2-9½	5-10½	-1-1	9-10	-7½
	14	7.29	10½	11-4½	7-6	2-9	6-2	-10½	12-9	-4
	15	6.80	11½	13-8½	7-4	2-9	6-4	-10½	13-10	-1½
	Δ 16	6.38	12½	15-7½	7-3	2-9	6-5½	-7	15-5½	+3½
	Δ 17	6.00	13½	18-0	7-3	2-9	6-7	-7	17-8	+5
9'-0"	† 12	9.00	8	7-4	8-3	2-10	5-6	-11	8-1	-8
	† 13	8.31	8½	8-6	8-0	2-9½	5-9	-9	8-11½	-5
	14	7.71	9½	10-3½	7-9	2-9½	6-0	-6	10-5	-½
	15	7.20	10½	12-3	7-6	2-9	6-2½	-3	11-10	+4½
	16	6.75	11¾	14-8¼	7-4	2-9	6-4	+2	13-11	+1-0
	Δ 17	6.35	12½	16-8	7-3	2-9	6-5½	+5	15-5½	+1-4
	Δ 18	6.00	13½	19-1½	7-3	2-9	6-7½	+6	17-8	+1-6
9'-6"	† 13	8.77	8	8-0	8-2	2-10	5-5½	-3½	8-2	-½
	† 14	8.14	9	9-9	7-10	2-9½	5-9	±0	9-5½	+5
	15	7.60	9¾	11-4½	7-7	2-9	5-11½	+4½	10-7	+10½
	16	7.13	10¾	13-5¼	7-5	2-9	6-2	+9½	12-2	+1-5½
	17	6.71	11¾	15-8	7-4	2-9	6-4	+1-1½	13-11½	+1-11
	Δ 18	6.33	12½	17-8½	7-3	2-9	6-5½	+1-5½	15-7	+2-4
	Δ 19	6.00	13½	20-3	7-3	2-9	6-8	+1-8	17-9	+2-7½
10'-0"	† 14	8.57	8½	9-2½	8-1	2-9½	5-8½	+2	8-8	+6
	† 15	8.00	9	10-6	7-10	2-9½	5-10½	+6½	9-7	+11
	16	7.50	10	12-6	7-7	2-9	6-1	+1-1	10-11½	+1-6½
	17	7.06	11	14-8	7-5	2-9	6-2½	+1-7½	12-5½	+2-2½
	18	6.67	12	17-0	7-4	2-9	6-5	+2-0	14-3½	+2-9
	Δ 19	6.32	12½	18-9	7-3	2-9	6-6	+2-5	15-8	+3-2½
	Δ 20	6.00	13½	21-4½	7-3	2-9	6-7½	+2-10	17-9	+3-8½
10'-6"	† 14	9.00	8	8-8	8-3	2-10	5-5½	+6	8-0	+9
	† 15	8.40	8½	9-11	8-1	2-9½	5-8½	+9½	8-10	+1-1
	16	7.88	9¼	11-6¾	7-9	2-9½	5-10½	+1-3½	9-10	+1-8½
	17	7.41	10	13-4	7-7	2-9	6-1	+1-9½	11-0	+2-3½
	18	7.00	11	15-7	7-5	2-9	6-2½	+2-5	12-7½	+3-0½
	19	6.63	12	18-0	7-4	2-9	6-4½	+2-11	14-4	+3-8½
	Δ 20	6.30	12½	19-9½	7-3	2-9	6-6	+3-5½	15-7	+4-3½
	Δ 21	6.00	13½	22-6	7-3	2-9	6-7½	+4-0	17-9	+5-0
11'-0"	† 15	8.80	8	9-4	8-2	2-10	5-6	+1-0½	8-1	+1-2½
	† 16	8.25	8¾	10-11¼	8-0	2-9½	5-10	+1-5	9-2½	+1-9
	17	7.76	9½	12-8	7-9	2-9½	6-0	+2-0	10-3½	+2-4½
	18	7.33	10¼	14-6¼	7-6	2-9	6-1½	+2-7½	11-4½	+3-1½
	19	6.95	11	16-6	7-5	2-9	6-3	+3-3	12-8	+3-9
	20	6.60	12	19-0	7-4	2-9	6-5	+3-10½	14-5½	+4-7½
	Δ 21	6.29	12½	20-10	7-3	2-9	6-6	+4-5	15-8	+5-3
	Δ 22	6.00	13½	23-7½	7-3	2-9	6-7½	+5-1	17-8	+6-0

Notes: Figures in bold face indicate stairs recommended for most interiors.

† Indicates stairs allowable only for attics and cellars but not recommended.

Δ Indicates stairs for exterior or monumental use.

* Dimensions given plus or minus; i.e. behind or in front of first riser (see diagram above)

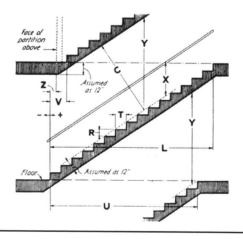

Fig. 4.

Table 3. Dimensions for ramps

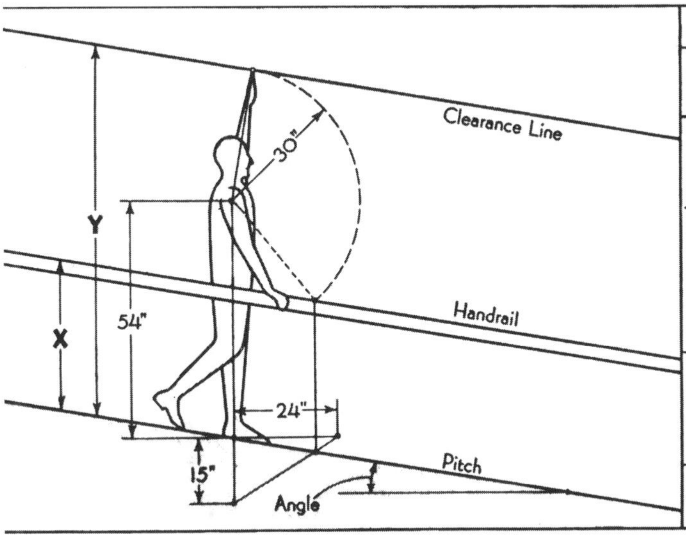

GRADIENT			HANDRAIL HEIGHT	CLEARANCE
Pitch (ratio)	Grade (%)	Angle (deg. - min.)	X (inches)	Y (inches)
½ : 12	4⅙	2 - 23	35	
½ : 10	5	2 - 52	35	
1 : 12	8⅓	4 - 46	34½	
1 : 10	10	5 - 43	34½	
1 : 8 1½ : 12	12½	7 - 7	34	84
1½ : 10	15	8 - 23	34	
2 : 12	16⅔	9 - 28	34	
2 : 10	20	11 - 19	34	
2½ : 12	20⅚	11 - 46	33½	
2½ : 10 3 : 12	25	14 - 2	33½	85
3½ : 12	29⅙	16 - 16	33½	
3 : 10	30	16 - 42	33½	

NOTES:

Overhead clearances and handrail heights may be determined graphically from the diagram

Maximum pitch:

(1) Values below the dotted line......are prohibited by the New York City Building Code for theatre aisles, except for runs not exceeding 10' - 0" which may be pitched a maximum of 1:8

(2) Values below the dash line--are prohibited by most other building codes

(3) All values above the solid line——are approved by the Workmen's Compensation Service Bureau

Ladders

Ladders have a greater pitch than stairs and may be classified as either *stepladders* or *rung ladders*. See **Table 4** for ladder dimensions and clearances for both types.

- *Stepladders* are lower in pitch than 75 degrees and require flat treads. Risers may be either "open" or "closed." Handrails may or may not be provided. In this classification belong most fire escapes and ladders for servicing boiler rooms, fly galleries, attics, decks, and so forth. Stepladders require handrails on both sides when not confined between walls or when risers are "closed." When risers are "open," treads or the ladder frame may serve as handholds. However, handrails should be provided wherever possible.

- *Rung ladders* are pitched more steeply than 75 degrees, require extremely narrow treads or round rungs to provide knee-room and do not require additional handrails. Rung ladders should have round rungs if possible both for handability and for knee clearance. Rung spacing and clearances may be determined graphically or taken from the tabulation shown in Table 4. Dimensioning of ladders for fire safety is specified in many building codes and fire regulations. ■

STRAIGHT RUN

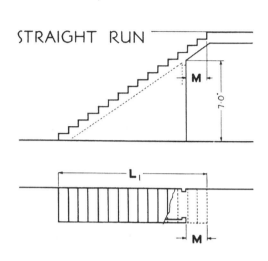

WIDE "L"

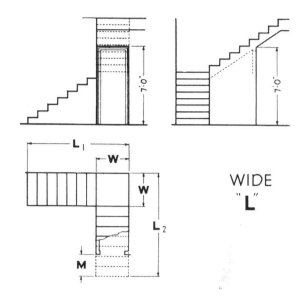

HEIGHT FLOOR TO FLOOR	NO OF RISERS	RISER	TREAD	L₁	M
8'-0"	13	7.38	10¼"	10'-3"	—
8'-6"	14	7.29	10½"	11'-4½"	4½"
9'-0"	15	7.20	10½"	12'-3"	1'-1½"
9'-6"	16	7.13	10¾"	13'-5¼"	1'-11¼"
10'-0"	17	7.06	11"	14'-8"	2'-9½"
10'-6"	18	7.00	11"	15'-7"	3'-7"
11'-0"	19	6.95	11"	16'-6"	4'-5"

HEIGHT FLOOR TO FLOOR	N° RISERS	RISER	TREAD	N° RISERS	L₁	N° RISERS	L₂	M
8'-0"	13	7.38	10¼"	7	5'-1½"+W	6	4'-3¼"+W	—
8'-6"	14	7.29	10½"	7	5'-3"+W	7	5'-3"+W	4½"
9'-0"	15	7.20	10½"	8	6'-1½"+W	7	5'-3"+W	1'-1½"
9'-6"	16	7.13	10¾"	8	6'-3¼"+W	8	6'-3¼"+W	1'-11¼"
10'-0"	17	7.06	11"	9	7'-4"+W	8	6'-5"+W	2'-9½"
10'-6"	18	7.00	11"	9	7'-4"+W	9	7'-4"+W	3'-7"
11'-0"	19	6.95	11"	10	8'-3"+W	9	7'-4"+W	4'-5"

LONG "L"

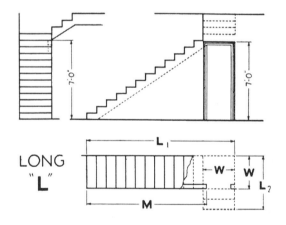

DOUBLE "L"

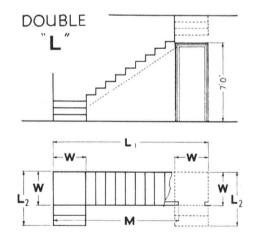

HEIGHT FLOOR TO FLOOR	N° RISERS	RISER	TREAD	N° RISERS	L₁	N° RISERS	L₂	M
8'-0"	13	7.38	10¼"	13	10'-3"+W	0	W	10'-3"
8'-6"	14	7.29	10½"	13	10'-6"+W	1	W	10'-6"
9'-0"	15	7.20	10½"	13	10'-6"+W	2	10½"+W	10'-6"
9'-6"	16	7.13	10¾"	13	10'-9"+W	3	1'-9½"+W	11'-0"
10'-0"	17	7.06	11"	13	11'-0"+W	4	2'-9"+W	11'-4"
10'-6"	18	7.00	11"	13	11'-0"+W	5	3'-8"+W	11'-5"
11'-0"	19	6.95	11"	13	11'-0"+W	6	4'-7"+W	11'-6"

HEIGHT FLOOR TO FLOOR	N° RISERS	RISER	TREAD	N° RISERS	L₁	N° RISERS	L₂	M
8'-0"	13	7.38	10¼"	13	10'-3"+2W	0	W	10'-3"+W
8'-6"	14	7.29	10½"	12	9'-7½"+2W	1	W	9'-7½"+W
9'-0"	15	7.20	10½"	11	8'-9"+2W	2	10½"+W	8'-9"+W
9'-6"	16	7.13	10¾"	10	8'-0¾"+2W	3	1'-9½"+W	8'-3¾"+W
10'-0"	17	7.06	11"	9	7'-4"+2W	4	2'-9"+W	7'-8"+W
10'-6"	18	7.00	11"	8	6'-5"+2W	5	3'-8"+W	6'-10"+W
11'-0"	19	6.95	11"	7	5'-6"+2W	6	4'-7"+W	6'-0"+W

Fig. 5. Unit planning data for residential stairs.

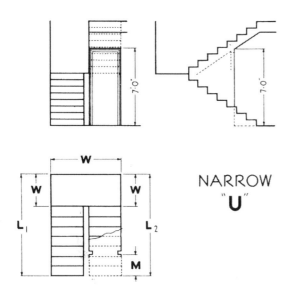

NARROW
"U"

HEIGHT FLOOR TO FLOOR	Nº RISERS	RISER	TREAD	Nº RISERS	L₁	Nº RISERS	L₂	M
8'-0"	13	7.38	10¼"	7	5'-1½"+W	6	4'-3¼"+W	–
8'-6"	14	7.29	10½"	7	5'-3"+W	7	5'-3"+W	4½"
9'-0"	15	7.20	10½"	8	6'-1½"+W	7	5'-3"+W	1'-1½"
9'-6"	16	7.13	10¾"	8	6'-3¼"+W	8	6'-3¼"+W	1'-11¼"
10'-0"	17	7.06	11"	9	7'-4"+W	8	6'-5"+W	2'-9½"
10'-6"	18	7.00	11"	9	7'-4"+W	9	7'-4"+W	3'-7"
11'-0"	19	6.95	11"	10	8'-3"+W	9	7'-4"+W	4'-5"

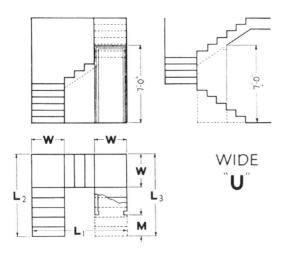

WIDE
"U"

HEIGHT FLOOR TO FLOOR	Nº RISERS	RISER	TREAD	Nº RISERS	L₁	Nº RISERS	L₂	Nº RISERS	L₃	M
8'-0"	13	7.38	10¼"	4	2'-6¾"+2W	4	2'-6¾"+W	5	3'-5"+W	–
8'-6"	14	7.29	10½"	4	2'-7½"+2W	5	3'-6"+W	5	3'-6"+W	4½"
9'-0"	15	7.20	10½"	4	2'-7½"+2W	5	3'-6"+W	6	4'-4½"+W	1'-1½"
9'-6"	16	7.13	10¾"	4	2'-8¼"+2W	6	4'-5¾"+W	6	4'-5¾"+W	1'-11¼"
10'-0"	17	7.06	11"	4	2'-9"+2W	6	4'-7"+W	7	5'-6"+W	2'-9½"
10'-6"	18	7.00	11"	4	2'-9"+2W	7	5'-6"+W	7	5'-6"+W	3'-7"
11'-0"	19	6.95	11"	4	2'-9"+2W	7	5'-6"+W	8	6'-5"+W	4'-5"

REFERENCES

Allen, Edward, and Joseph Iano, *The Architect's Studio Companion: Rules of Thumb for Preliminary Design,* 2nd ed., John Wiley & Sons, New York, 1995.

Henry Dreyfuss Associates, *The Measure of Man and Woman,* Whitney Library of Design, New York, 1993.

Ramsey/Sleeper, "Egress Planning," *Architectural Graphic Standards,* 9th ed., John Wiley & Sons, New York, 1994, pp. 23–28.

Table 4. Dimensions for ladders

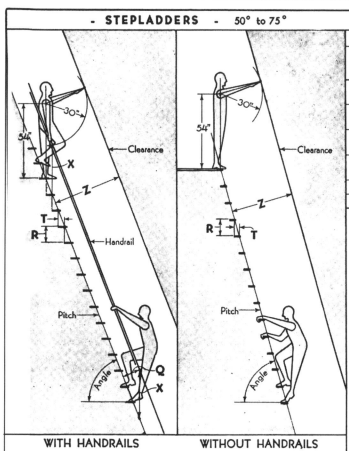

- STEPLADDERS - 50° to 75°

STEP DIMENSIONS		GRADIENT		CLEAR-ANCE	HANDRAIL HEIGHT
Riser R (inches)	Tread T (inches)	Grade (%)	Angle (deg. - min.)	Z (inches)	X (inches)
9⅜	7½	125	51 – 21	64	
9¾	7	139.28	54 – 19	62	34½
10⅛	6½	155.75	57 – 18	59	
10½	6	175	60 – 16	57	35
10⅞	5½	197.72	63 – 10	54	
11¼	5	225	66 – 2	52	35½
11⅝	4½	258.66	68 – 50	50	
12	4	300	71 – 34	47	36
12⅜	3½	353.21	74 – 12	45	36½
12¾	3	425	76 – 46	42	37

WITH HANDRAILS   **WITHOUT HANDRAILS**

NOTES:

Clearance and handrail height may be determined graphically if desired

Handrails are required on both sides of stepladders if risers are not left "open" or if not confined between side walls

Maximum and minimum widths:

With handrails: 21" to 24"
Without handrails: variable
Between sidewalls: 24" minimum

HUD requires slope between 50 and 60°; trends 6 in. min; risers 12 in. max; width, 20 in. min, 30 in. max; handrails both sides extending 30 in. above upper floor.

FORMULAE:

$$Tread = T = 20 - \frac{4}{3}R$$

$$Riser = R = 15 - \frac{3}{4}T$$

Perpendicular distance, pitch line to handrail =

$$Q = X \div \sqrt{\left(\frac{R}{T}\right)^2 + 1}$$

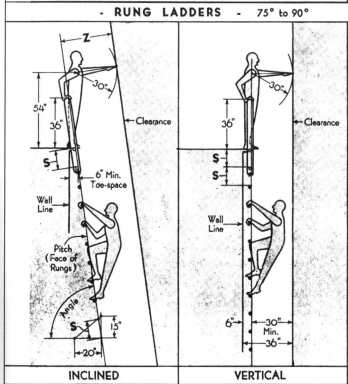

- RUNG LADDERS - 75° to 90°

	GRADIENT			RUNG SPACING S (inches)	CLEAR-ANCE Z (inches)
Pitch (ratio)	Grade (%)		Angle (deg. - min.)		
12 : 2½	480		78 – 14	13¼	41
12 : 2	600		80 – 33	13½	39
12 : 1½	800		82 – 53	13¾	37
12 : 1	1200		85 – 14	14¼	35
12 : ½	2400		87 – 37	14½	32
Vertical	90 – 0			15 maximum 12 minimum	30

INCLINED   **VERTICAL**

NOTES:

Clearances and handrail heights may be determined graphically if desired. Ladder frame should extend 3'-0" above platform

Widths:

Minimum = 15"
Desirable = 18"
Minimum between sidewalls = 24"

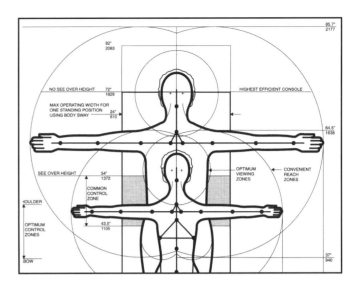

Dimensions of the human figure

The following pages include reference plates for dimensions of the human figure, the averages for which have increased with generational increments in human size (**Fig. 1**). Children do not have the same physical proportions of adults, especially during early years, and their heights vary greatly. Their proportions may be approximated from Fig. 1 (bottom).

The height of tabletops in **Fig. 2** is 29 in (740 mm); some references recommend 30 in (760 mm). A common metric standard is 750 mm. In each case, table and chair heights must coordinate. Countertops and cabinet heights are also subject to specific conditions and user preference. Most references recommend a range of heights (adjustable) for workplace settings.

Fig. 3 indicates the range of dimensions from 99th percentile to 1 percentile, including male and female. The current standard reference on the topic, Henry Dreyfuss Associates (1993) provides additional plates of dimensions by age group and motor development.

Dimensions and clearances adopted in regulations or in guidelines for planning, building layout, and furnishings may represent only minimum requirements for the average adult. Such dimensions and clearances should be used with judgment and increased to allow comfortable accommodation and improved safety for persons of larger than average stature.

Dimensions for maintenance access

Clearances for access to all spaces in a building that require servicing and maintenance are critical for worker performance and safety (**Fig. 4**).

Dimensions for accessibility

Designers of furniture and spaces where dimensioning must accommodate special conditions and/or universal design goals should investigate the range of special conditions and abilities that may characterize building users (**Figs. 5** to **7**). See also the following article "Universal Design." ■

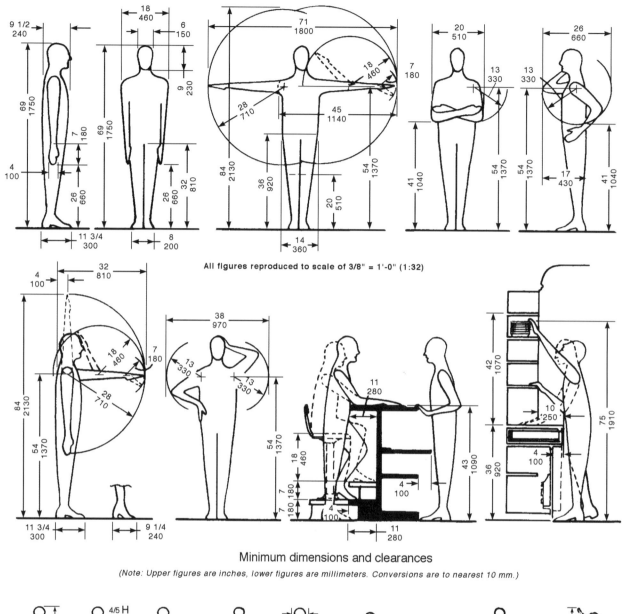

All figures reproduced to scale of 3/8" = 1'-0" (1:32)

Minimum dimensions and clearances

(Note: Upper figures are inches, lower figures are millimeters. Conversions are to nearest 10 mm.)

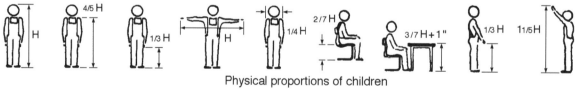

Physical proportions of children

Fig. 1. Minimum dimensions and clearances. Note: upper numbers are inches, lower are millimeters, converted to nearest 10 mm.

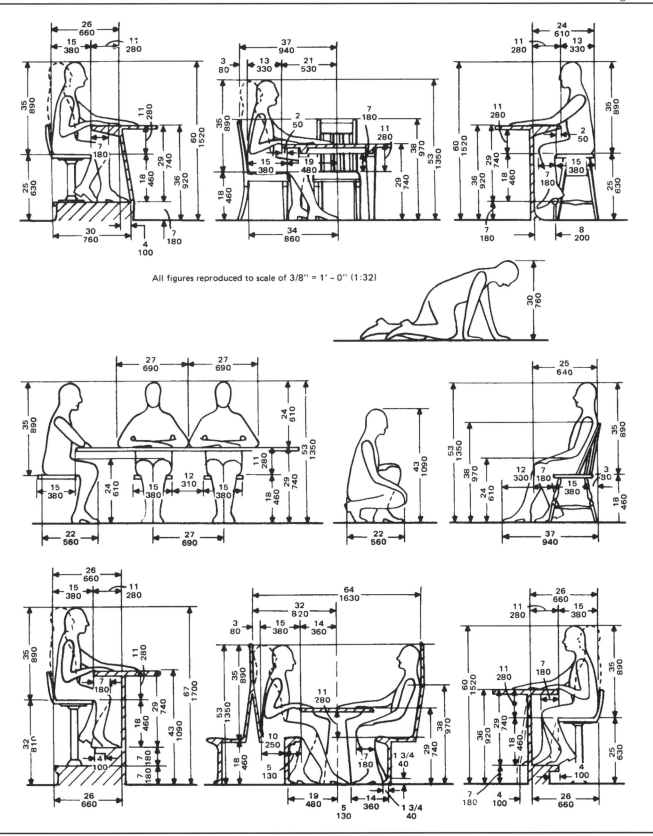

All figures reproduced to scale of 3/8" = 1' – 0" (1:32)

Fig. 2. Minimum dimensions and clearances at tables. Note: upper numbers are inches, lower are millimeters, converted to nearest 10 mm.

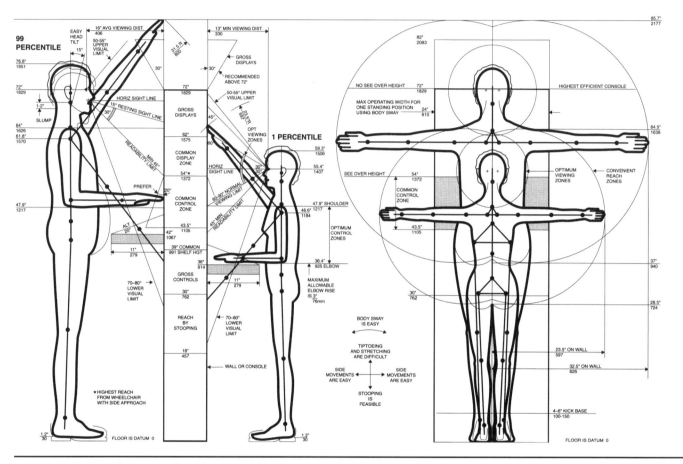

Fig. 3. Representative dimensions of standing human figure. Reprinted by permission. Henry Dreyfuss Associates, *The Measure of Man and Woman: Human Factors in Design*, Whitney Library of Design, New York, 1993.

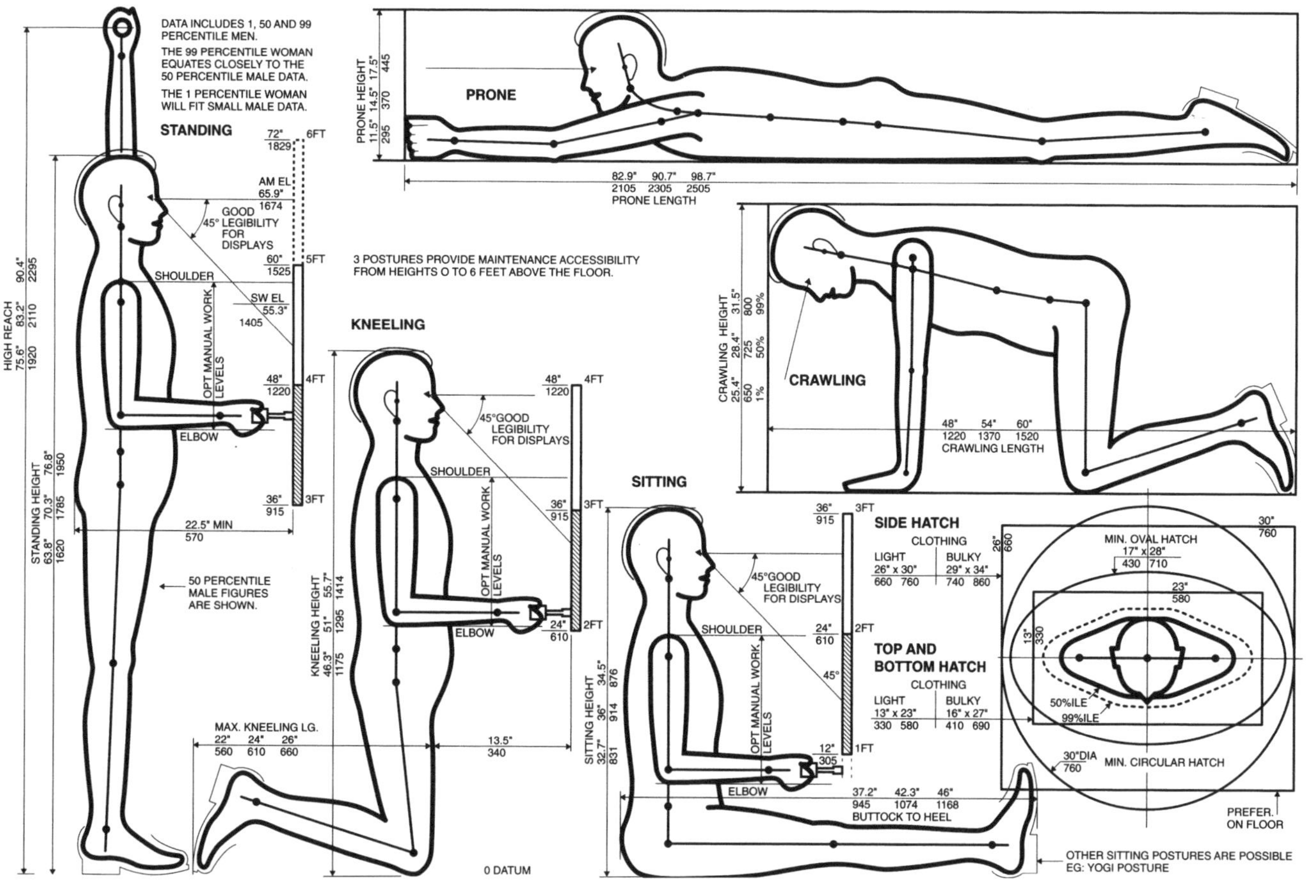

Fig. 4. Maintenance access (whole body). Reprinted by permission. Henry Dreyfuss Associates, *The Measure of Man and Woman: Human Factors in Design,* Whitney Library of Design, New York, 1993.

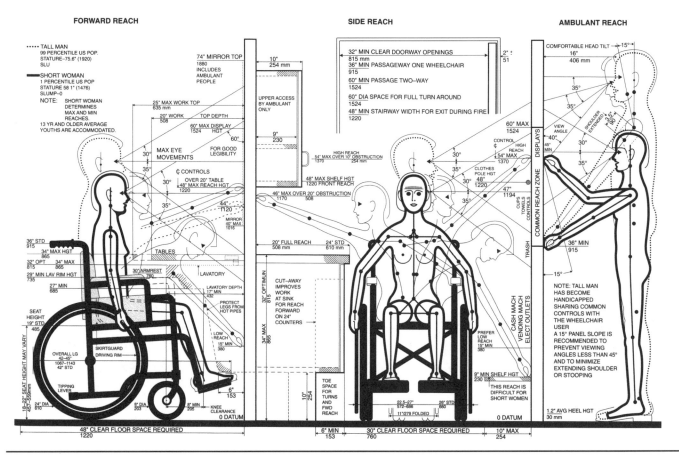

Fig. 5. Reach factors for the differently abled. Reprinted by permission. Henry Dreyfuss Associates, *The Measure of Man and Woman: Human Factors in Design,* Whitney Library of Design, New York, 1993.

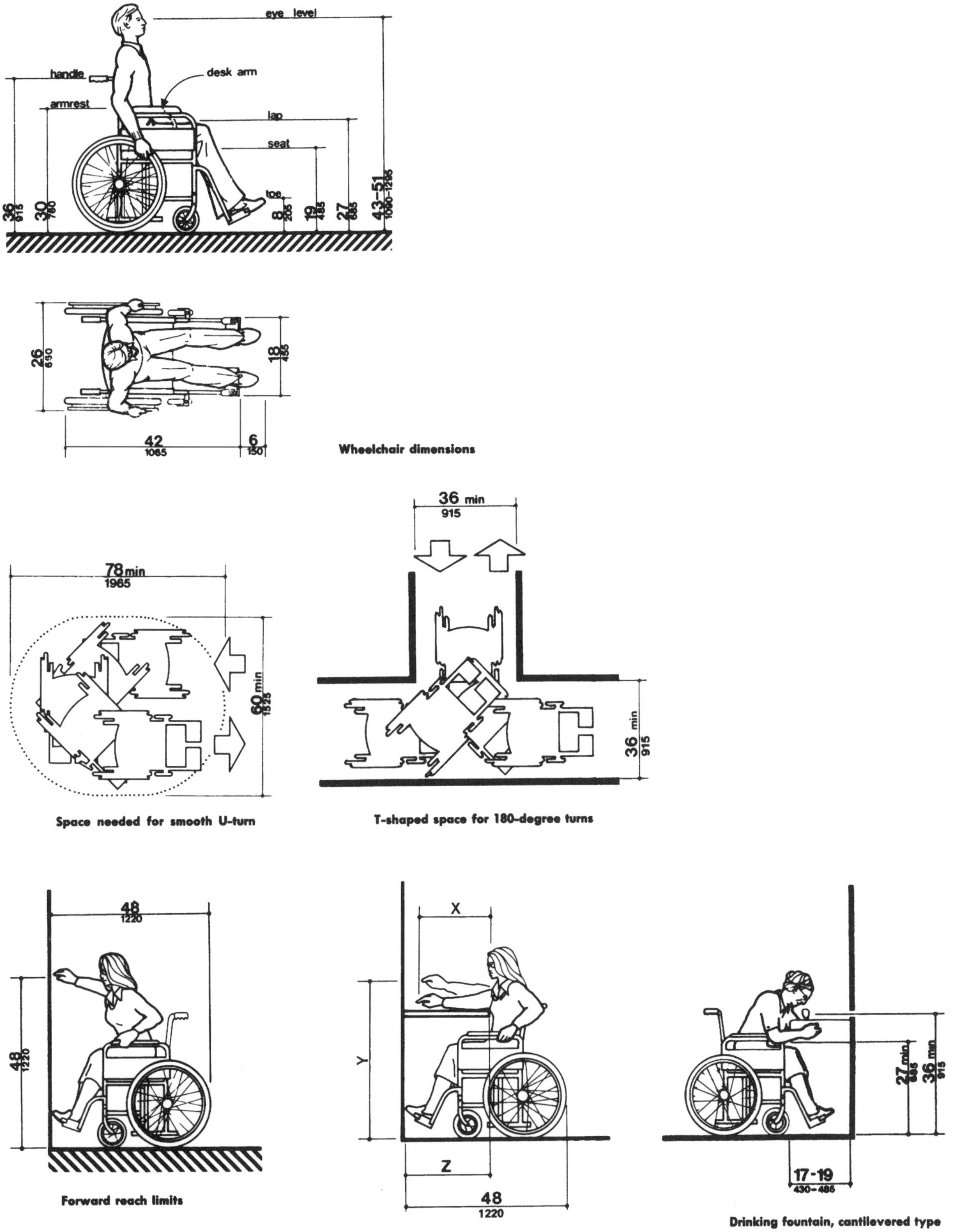
eye level
handle
desk arm
armrest
lap
seat
toe
36 915
30 760
8 205
19 485
27 685
43–51 1090–1295
26 650
18 455
42 1065
6 150
Wheelchair dimensions
78 min 1965
60 min 1525
36 min 915
Space needed for smooth U-turn
T-shaped space for 180-degree turns
48 1220
Forward reach limits
X
Y
Z
27 min 685
36 min 915
17-19 430-485
Drinking fountain, cantilevered type

NOTE: X shall be ≤ 25 in (635 mm); Z shall be ≥ X. When X < 20 in (510 mm), then Y shall be 48 in (1220 mm) maximum. When X is 20 to 25 in (510 to 635 mm), then Y shall be 44 in (1120 mm) maximum.

Fig. 6. Dimensions for accessibility.

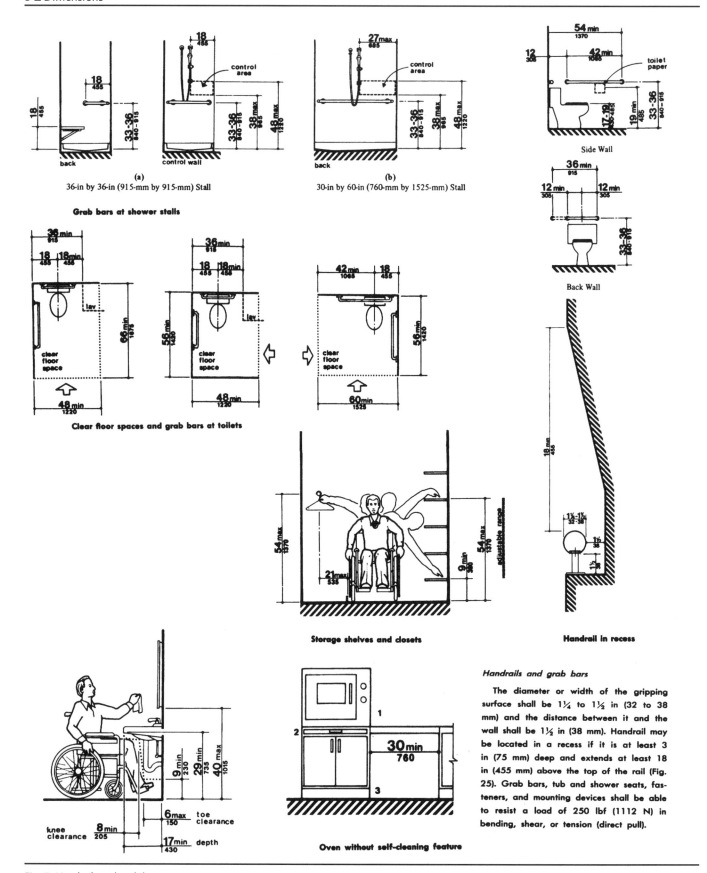

Handrails and grab bars

The diameter or width of the gripping surface shall be 1¼ to 1½ in (32 to 38 mm) and the distance between it and the wall shall be 1½ in (38 mm). Handrail may be located in a recess if it is at least 3 in (75 mm) deep and extends at least 18 in (455 mm) above the top of the rail (Fig. 25). Grab bars, tub and shower seats, fasteners, and mounting devices shall be able to resist a load of 250 lbf (1112 N) in bending, shear, or tension (direct pull).

Fig. 7. Handrails and grab bars.

Elaine Ostroff and John P. S. Salmen

Summary

Universal design is a performance-based approach to architectural design that assumes diversity of ability as a normal aspect of the human condition. It considers the wide range of people's abilities and how they use buildings and products throughout their lives. This approach establishes as the goal of design to enhance the capacities of people of all ages and abilities, going beyond minimal compliance with accessibility codes and standards.

Key words

accessibility, Americans with Disabilities Act (ADA), ergonomics, human factors, universal design

Seating with differentiated heights. Davis, California. Brian Donnelly Design.

Universal design and accessible design

1 UNIVERSAL DESIGN

The goal of universal design is to create buildings, places, and details that provide a supportive environment to the largest number of individuals throughout life's variety of changing circumstances. All people experience changes in mobility, agility, and perceptual acuity throughout their life spans. At any time in our lives, we may experience temporary or permanent physical or psychological impairments, which may be disabling or disorienting, increasing our dependence upon certain aspects of the physical environment. In addition, people are diverse in size, preferences, and abilities. Universal design responds to these normal variations in ability, situations, and conditions, and seeks to extend human capacities by accommodation of the designed environment.

Universal design involves both a design sensitivity and sensibility that seek to support the full range of human capacities. *Ergonomics* and *human factor analysis,* an approach to design pioneered in the 1930s by Dreyfuss and Tilley (Henry Dreyfuss Associates 1993), are part of the discipline and ethic of universal design. As a design approach, universal design seeks to support and enhance the changing abilities of humans throughout their life span, and the changing demographics of our society.

Universal design makes designer, user, and building owner more sensitive to what can be done to improve the long-term quality of what we build. Design and long-term building quality is improved by designing for easier access, reduced accidents, easier way finding and transit of people and goods, and design details for people of all ages, sizes, and capacities.

Demographics

The average and standard norms of human dimensions and capacities are changing. In the United States, previously determined standards for "national average" weight are increasing (**Fig. 1**). This suggests that dimensional and safety standards will also change to respond to the demographics of our society. What passed as minimal height requirements 50 years ago accommodates a decreasing portion of the population. Accommodation to an older population requires increased design sensitivity to sensory and mobility impairments.

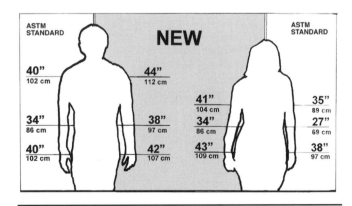

Fig. 1. Older and wider. The 2004 SizeUSA survey of over 10,000 people in the United States documents an increase in average adult measurements, indicated as "NEW," over the dimensions recognized by American Society of Testing Materials (ASTM), indicated as "OLD." (Source: ASTM and USA Project. TCA, Cary, North Carolina)

Credits: Figs. 4 to 12 are from Universal Designers and Consultants (1996) cited in the References.

The market for universally designed spaces and products is much larger than the current population of 54 million people with disabilities in the United States. Everyone over their lifetime will experience some temporary or permanent disability. The market includes children, people who must move around with luggage or other encumbrances, people with temporary disabilities, and especially older people. The aging baby-boom generation is undoubtedly the true beneficiary of universal design for three reasons.

– The United States will see continued increase in people over age 65, currently trending to 33 percent of total population.

– More than half the people over 65 have a physical disability.

– By 2025, the average life span is expected to reach 100 years of age for people in developed countries (primarily due to advances in medical technology).

Advantages of universal design

• It costs no more to universally design a space or product. It does take more thinking and attention to uses and users. Such steps are rewarded in reduced design failure and reduced costs of alterations to the environments after they are built. Buildings and places created with the needs of multiple users are economically sound, reducing costs for renovations. By thinking through all uses, the long-term durability and usefulness of a design is increased.

• The number of people who benefit from universal design is very great. It not only includes people with disabilities, but also individuals who assist them. Everyone has some vulnerability to environments at some time in one's life. Universal design attempts to address the users over their life span for the building or product over its entire life span.

• Universal design seeks to accommodate difference and variation, not minimally acceptable averages. Strategies may include adjustable or interchangeable elements, designing spaces so that they can be easily customized, and allowing flexibility of use, although sometimes a single solution may fit all.

• Universal design also addresses newly developed information related to acoustics and indoor air quality that impact the healthy functioning of all building users.

Universal design principles

The following Principles of Universal Design define guidelines developed and copyrighted by the Center for Universal Design (1997). The guidelines offer performance criteria to use in design or in evaluating designs:

1 Equitable Use

The design is useful and marketable to people with diverse abilities.

Guidelines

1a. Provide the same means of use for all users: identical whenever possible; equivalent when not.

1b. Avoid segregating or stigmatizing any users.

1c. Provisions for privacy, security, and safety should be equally available to all users.

1d. Make the design appealing to all users.

2 Flexibility in Use

The design accommodates a wide range of individual preferences and abilities.

Guidelines

2a. Provide choice in methods of use.

2b. Accommodate right- or left-handed access and use.

2c. Facilitate the user's accuracy and precision.

2d. Provide adaptability to the user's pace.

3 Simple and Intuitive Use

Use of the design is easy to understand, regardless of the user's experience, knowledge, language skills, or current concentration level.

Guidelines

3a. Eliminate unnecessary complexity.

3b. Be consistent with user expectations and intuition.

3c. Accommodate a wide range of literacy and language skills.

3d. Arrange information consistent with its importance.

3e. Provide effective prompting and feedback during and after task completion.

4 Perceptible Information

The design communicates necessary information effectively to the user, regardless of ambient conditions or the user's sensory abilities.

Guidelines

4a. Use different modes (pictorial, verbal, tactile) for redundant presentation of essential information.

4b. Provide adequate contrast between essential information and its surroundings.

4c. Maximize "legibility" of essential information.

4d. Differentiate elements in ways that can be described (i.e., make it easy to give instructions or directions).

4e. Provide compatibility with a variety of techniques or devices used by people with sensory limitations.

5 Tolerance for Error

The design minimizes hazards and the adverse consequences of accidental or unintended actions.

Guidelines

5a. Arrange elements to minimize hazards and errors: most used elements, most accessible; hazardous elements eliminated, isolated, or shielded.

5b. Provide warnings of hazards and errors.

5c. Provide fail-safe features.

5d. Discourage unconscious action in tasks that require vigilance.

6 Low Physical Effort

The design can be used efficiently and comfortably and with a minimum of fatigue.

Guidelines

6a. Allow user to maintain a neutral body position.
6b. Use reasonable operating forces.
6c. Minimize repetitive actions.
6d. Minimize sustained physical effort.

7 Size and Space for Approach and Use

Appropriate size and space is provided for approach, reach, manipulation, and use regardless of user's body size, posture, or mobility.

Guidelines

7a. Provide a clear line of sight to important elements for any seated or standing user.
7b. Make reach to all components comfortable for any seated or standing user.
7c. Accommodate variations in hand and grip size.
7d. Provide adequate space for the use of assistive devices or personal assistance.

2 ACCESSIBLE DESIGN

Accessible design is design that meets standards that allow people with disabilities to enjoy access to environments and products. The U.S. Fair Housing Act Accessibility Guidelines are more limited than the ADA Standards for Accessible Design, but apply to a wide array of privately owned multifamily dwellings not previously covered by access regulations. Since the 1988 passage of the Fair Housing Amendments Act, and the 1990 passage of the Americans with Disabilities Act (ADA), accessibility standards now cover much of what is newly constructed or renovated.

Unlike earlier federal requirements that were restricted to facilities built with federal support, these far-reaching new regulations cover privately owned as well as government-supported facilities, programs, and services. Accessibility criteria are found in building codes and in guidelines such as ADA Standards for Accessible Design, the Fair Housing Amendment Act Accessibility Guidelines or the American National Standard Accessible and Usable Buildings and Facilities CABO/ANSI A117.1. These are prescriptive technical standards, which can result in a "minimum compliance only" approach to design. By ignoring first and then adding these minimum criteria later in the design process, the final resolution often results in obvious and stigmatizing features that are not integral to the overall design.

Accessible design is a more positive term for what was previously called "barrier free" or "handicap design," both examples of unfortunate terminology that focuses on the negative process of eliminating barriers that confront people with disabilities. The standards and their minimum requirements provide a baseline that designers can build upon.

People are so diverse and adaptable that design standards to quantify how people use objects and spaces must be general. Stein-feld et al. (1979) have cataloged the major functional abilities that could be limited by disability. Their "Enabler Model" summarizes the environmental implications of limitations in the major functional areas found in people with disabilities, often in combinations (**Fig. 2**).

Accessibility standards have simplified this overwhelming diversity to three main groups of conditions shown below with the related component of the environment. By understanding the physical implications of these broad groups of disabling conditions, designers can fully respond to the criteria in the building codes and standards.

• *Sensory impairments: Design of information systems* This includes vision, hearing, and speech impairments, and total and partial loss of function. It leads to the design recommendation for redundancy of communication media to insure that everyone can receive information and express themselves over communication systems. For example, reinforcing both lighting and circulation cues, way finding can be enhanced, or, by providing both audible and visual alarms, everyone will be able to know when an emergency occurs.

• *Dexterity impairments: Design of operating controls and hardware* This includes people with limitations in the use of their hands and fingers and gives rise to the "closed fist rule," that is, testing selection of equipment controls and hardware by operating it with a closed fist. In addition, this addresses the location of equipment and controls so that they are within the range of reach of people who use wheelchairs and those who are of short stature.

• *Mobility impairments: Space and circulation systems* This includes people who use walkers, crutches, canes, and wheelchairs plus those who have difficulty climbing stairs or going long dis-

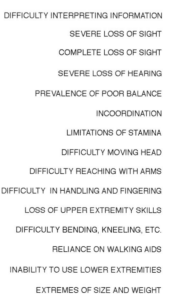
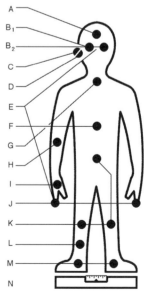

DIFFICULTY INTERPRETING INFORMATION   A
SEVERE LOSS OF SIGHT   B₁
COMPLETE LOSS OF SIGHT   B₂
SEVERE LOSS OF HEARING   C
PREVALENCE OF POOR BALANCE   D
INCOORDINATION   E
LIMITATIONS OF STAMINA   F
DIFFICULTY MOVING HEAD   G
DIFFICULTY REACHING WITH ARMS   H
DIFFICULTY IN HANDLING AND FINGERING   I
LOSS OF UPPER EXTREMITY SKILLS   J
DIFFICULTY BENDING, KNEELING, ETC.   K
RELIANCE ON WALKING AIDS   L
INABILITY TO USE LOWER EXTREMITIES   M
EXTREMES OF SIZE AND WEIGHT   N

Fig. 2. The "Enabler" model. (Steinfeld et al. 1979)

tances. The T-turn and 5 ft (1.52 m) diameter turning area provide key plan evaluation criteria here. These concepts and the accessible route of travel insure that all people have accessible and safe passage from the perimeter of a site to and through all areas of a facility.

Conflicting criteria

Accessibility has overlapping regulations and civil rights implications as established by U.S. law. Designers face the challenge of sorting out the specific accessibility regulations that apply to their work as well as of understanding the purpose and the technical requirements. In addition to overarching federal standards required by the ADA, each state has its own access regulations. There is a concerted national effort to adopt more uniform, harmonious regulations, but designers must be aware that if elements of the state regulation are more stringent, they supersede the federal standard.

In addition, the civil rights aspect of the ADA establishes requirements for existing facilities that go beyond the technical requirements previously expected in new construction or alterations. For example, the new requirement in the ADA to attempt "readily achievable barrier removal" in existing buildings (even when no renovations are planned) is not detailed in the Standards but is discussed in the full ADA regulation (U.S. Department of Justice 1994). The professional responsibilities and liability of the designer are being redefined through these regulations. Applications of these regulations as defined by ADA language, and are interpreted by evolving legal case law and in technical assistance documents published by the U.S. Department of Justice.

Housing design

Most single-family housing is not covered by the accessibility regulations noted earlier. However, there is a growing promotion of housing with "amenities" to meet the growing market of baby boomers and their parents to "age in place." The home building industry is responding to these market opportunities with more accessible features, where consumers do not want reminders of their aging. The marketing strategies of developers highlight amenities, rather than accessibility.

In 1998, the *Wall Street Journal* sought the advice of the Center for Universal Design to develop a concept for the "Next Generation Universal Home" that would define the house of the future, meeting the needs of a changing market (**Fig. 3**). The layout of the home is based on typical home designs currently being constructed in the United States and incorporates practical universal design concepts: no-step entrances, reinforced walls for grab bars, future access to second floor (item A in Fig. 4), features located at useable heights, adjustable features so that the environment adjusts to the individual, adjustable bathing fixtures (item D), improved warning and aid communication devices.

3 UNIVERSAL DESIGN PROCESS

The issues raised by accessibility regulations are best addressed and combined in a commitment to universal design. The more one knows as a designer, the better the resulting design. But universal design considerations are as complex and in a sense as unpredictable as the variety of human experience and capacities. No one "knows it all." This

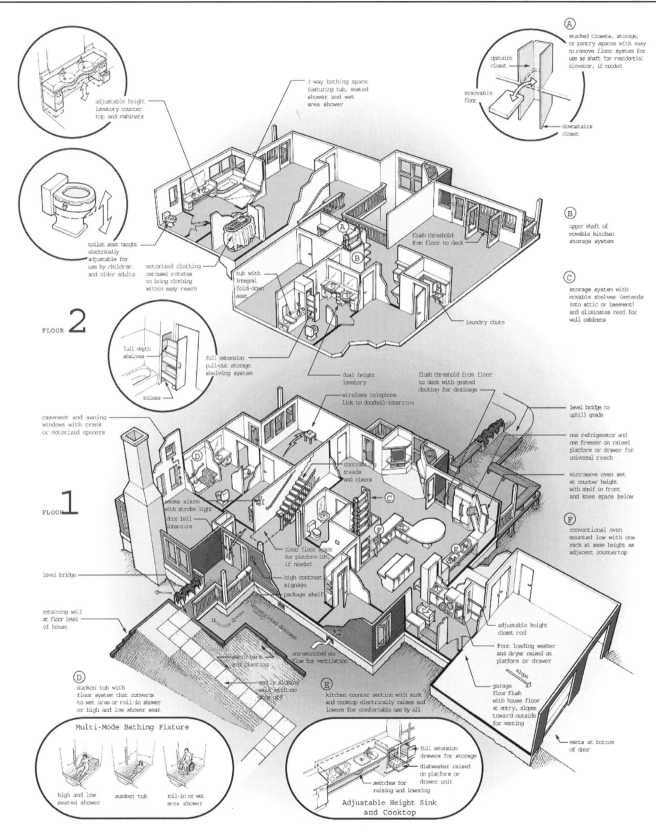

Fig. 3. Next Generation Universal Home conceived as a holistic environment to benefit multiple users in a flexible format. Ron Mace, Center for Universal Design. Drawing: Leslie C. Young and Rex J. Pace. (Preiser and Ostroff 2001)

Fig. 4. Renovated entry landscape with sloping walkway and outdoor seating platform to Visitors Center at the Arnold Arboretum. Jamaica Plain, Massachusetts. Carol R. Johnson Associates, Landscape Architects.

Fig. 5. Entry terrace modifications, including ramp and handrails, blending with historic design. Hopedale Town Hall, Hopedale, Massachusetts. Nichols Design Associates, Architects.

Fig. 6. Public toilet accommodating all users, including families. Automatic sensor controls of plumbing. Visual and tactile operating instructions in various languages. San Francisco, California. J. C. Decaux International with Ron Mace and Barry Atwood.

simple fact demands that the approach to universal design involve many people representing a range of insights from the beginning of the programming and design process. Designers cannot get such information from books, databases, or design criteria alone. Designers should involve representatives of future users, the customers of the design, through universal design reviews.

Universal design reviews undertaken at critical early and evolving phases of the design process are opportunities to improve any design, eliminate errors, improve its user friendliness, and at the same time involve and thus satisfy the special needs of owners and occupants of the resulting building. Because no one person can anticipate all possible perceptions and needs, a design should be given broad discussion and review, with input from many points of view. Designers should establish a review process that creates the opportunity to listen to and hear from perceptive spokespeople who can articulate the needs and responses of:

– People of all stages of life, from the point of view of the youngster whose eye level is half that of adults, to elders and others who have difficulty with mobility, lighting distractions, and disorientation at transition points in a building.

– Wheelchair users and people with other physical differences, which can be as common as left- and right-handedness.

– People with visual, aural, and respiratory impairments.

– Persons who maintain and service our buildings, carrying heavy loads or other potential impediments to safe travel.

– All people under conditions of emergency.

Because many persons cannot visualize actual conditions from plans or drawings, universal designing reviews may require alternative media such as three-dimensional models, virtual reality simulations, and, in some cases, full-scale mock-up prototypes, whereby all can experience, critically evaluate, and offer ways to improve a design in process.

Examples of universal design

In 1996, the National Endowment for the Arts sponsored programs to identify and promote excellence in universal design in the fields of architecture, interior design, landscape architecture, graphic design, and industrial design. These juried selections feature the work of designers worldwide to create products and environments that are useable by people with the broadest possible range of abilities throughout their lives. **Figs. 4** to **12** from Universal Designers and Consultants (1996) illustrate this range.

The more that designers learn from the diverse users of the environment, the more sensitive and sophisticated our universal designs become. Some of the best examples of special design are almost invisible because they blend in so well with their environmental context. Design inspirations such as those revealed in the photographs that accompany this article are the best way to convey both the simplicity and complexity of universal design. They exemplify the principal message of universal design: to extend our design ethic and sensibilities in order to enhance the abilities of all people who will occupy our designs. ■

Fig. 7. Dual height viewports for children of all ages in doors, part of wayfinding system at the Lighthouse, New York City, New York. Steven M. Goldberg, FAIA and Jan Keane, FAIA, Mitchell/Giurgola Architects.

Fig. 8. Full-length entry sidelight at doorways. Center for Universal Design, Raleigh, North Carolina. Ronald Mace.

Fig. 9. "G. E. Real Life Design" kitchen including adjustable height appliances and counters, natural light and high contrast trim for users with low vision. Mary Jo Peterson, Interior Design.

Fig. 10. "Home for the Next 50 Years" powder room including dual height lavatory, which provides access for standing and short-stature people or wheelchair users. Designer: Universal Designers and Consultants.

Fig. 11. Swing Clear Hinge, allowing a door to be fully opened for wider access. Gilreath and Associates, Interior Designers.

Fig. 12. Window Lock/Latch, accommodating dexterity limitations and "aging in place." Owens Residence, Chicago, Illinois. Design One, Industrial Design.

REFERENCES AND RESOURCES

ADA and Information Technology Regional Disability and Business Technical Assistance Centers, (800) 949 4 ADA.

Adaptive Environments, *Case Studies of Universal Design,* Boston, 2003. <www.AdaptiveEnvironments.org>

Barrier Free Environments, *Fair Housing Design Manual,* Publication B181, HUD, Fair Housing Clearing House, Washington, 1996.

CABO/ANSI, *American National Standard for Accessible and Usable Buildings and Facilities.* CABO/ANSI A117.1. Council of American Building Officials, Falls Church, 1997. <www.cabo.org/a117.htm>

Center for Universal Design, *Principles of Universal Design,* North Carolina State University, Raleigh, 1997. (800) 647-6777. <www.ncsu.edu/ncsu/design/cud/>

Center for Universal Design, *Universal Design Exemplars,* NC State University, The Center for Universal Design, Raleigh, 2001.

Center for Universal Design, IDEA Center, Global Universal Design Educator's Network, *Universal Design Education Online* <www.udeducation.org>

Danford, Gary S., and Beth Tauke, eds. *universal design new york,* City of New York, New York, 2002.

Henry Dreyfuss Associates, *The Measure of Man and Woman: Human Factors in Design,* Whitney Library of Design, New York, 1993.

Knecht, Barbara, "Accessibility Regulations and a Universal Design Process Inspire the Design Process," in *Architectural Record,* January 2004, New York.

Lavine, Danise, ed. *universal design new york 2,* Center for Inclusive Design and Environmental Access, University at Buffalo, Buffalo, 2003.

Mueller, James P., *Workplace Workbook 2.0: An Illustrated Guide to Workplace Accommodation and Technology,* Human Resource Development Press, Amherst, 1992.

Mueller, James P., *Case Studies on Universal Design,* Chantilly, 1997.

Preiser, Wolfgang F. E., and Elaine Ostroff, eds. *Universal Design Handbook,* McGraw-Hill, New York, 2001.

Steinfeld, Edward, et al., *Access to the Built Environment: a review of literature,* prepared for US HUD, Office of Policy Development and Research. Publication #660, Rockville, HUD Uscr, 1979, 1986.

Universal Design Newsletter, Universal Designers & Consultants, Inc., Takoma Park, <www.UniversalDesign.com>

Universal Designers and Consultants, *Images of Excellence in Universal Design,* Takoma Park, 1996 <www.UniversalDesign.com>

U.S. Access Board, *ADA Accessibility Guidelines,* (800) USA-ABLE. <www.access-board.gov>

U.S. Department of Agriculture (USDA) Forest Service, et al., *Universal Access to Outdoor Recreation: A Design Guide,* MIG Communications, Berkeley, 1993.

U.S. Department of Justice, *ADA Standards for Accessible Design,* 28 CFR Part 36, App. A., U.S. Department of Justice, Washington, 1994 revised.

John J. Fruin, Ph.D.

Summary

This article describes an empirical basis of pedestrian circulation design, developed by the author and based on extensive studies of pedestrian traffic. It presents principles used to develop the concept of "Level of Service" Design Standard. These standards enable the architect and facility planner to design for the convenience and safety of pedestrians and circulation systems.

Key words

arrival headway, capacity design, entrances, circulation, Level of Service, pedestrians, pedway, stairs, queuing, walking speeds, walkway

Lisbon Portugal Transit Terminal. Santiago Calatrava, Architect and Engineer, 1998.

Design standards for pedestrian circulation

1 PEDESTRIAN CIRCULATION

Human dimensions for pedestrian design

- *Human body dimensions: "The Body Ellipse."* Body depth and shoulder breadth are the primary human measurements used by designers of pedestrian spaces and facilities. Shoulder breadth is a factor affecting the practical capacity of doorways, passageways, stairways, and mechanical devices such as escalators and moving walks. While humans obviously vary depending on weight, clothing, etc., a compilation of body dimensions from a large number of human factors studies enables us to adopt as a practical standard for pedestrian design a "body ellipse" of 24 × 18 in (61 × 46 cm). Using this ellipse as a template provides the designer a simple visual check for accommodation of pedestrian circulation and waiting spaces (**Fig. 1**).

- *Perception of personal space: Body Buffer Zone.* Humans value person space. If freedom of choice exists, pedestrians will adopt personal spacing that avoids contact with others, except in special circumstances such as a crowded elevator, where this unwritten law may be temporarily suspended. Pedestrian contact on sidewalks and other walkways is governed by personal body buffer zone concepts and social and cultural politesse.

In the 1966 book *The Hidden Dimension*, Edward T. Hall observed that there are different cultural attitudes towards personal space throughout the world. Hall establishes four general categories: public

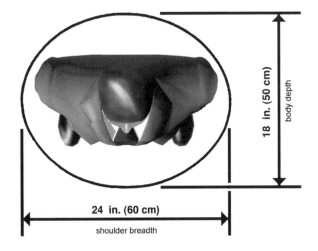

Fig. 1. Body ellipse assumed for pedestrian design. An ellipse 18 × 24 in (46 × 61 cm) is equivalent to an area of 2.3 sq ft (2 sq m).

Credits: This article is updated by the author based on research undertaken with support of The Port of New York Authority and the Howard Cullman Fellowship, and is reprinted by permission of *Elevator World*. An extended version of this article can be found in *Time-Saver Standards for Urban Design* (McGraw-Hill 2003). Illustrations by John Petrik Watson.

Box A—Definitions

The following terms are useful and necessary to design pedestrian circulation and to size building entrances, stairs, elevator halls, and passageways to accommodate anticipated circulation volumes.

- *Flow Volume* is the number of pedestrians passing a point in a unit of time. In pedestrian design, flow is expressed as pedestrians-per-foot width of the walkway or stairway per minute (PFM). Flow is the most important traffic characteristic, because it determines the width of the pedestrian way (commonly abbreviated as "pedway"). An inadequate width restricts flow. Volume has been designated as P.

- *Speed.* Pedestrian locomotion speed, expressed in distance per unit of time, generally in feet-per-minute. When related to design of a pedway, speed is the average speed of all pedestrians passing through the area during the design interval. Speed is designated as S.

- *Density.* The number of traffic units per unit of area. In pedestrian design, density is expressed in tenths of a pedestrian per-square-foot, a difficult unit to visualize. A more manageable unit, the reciprocal of density, or the sq ft of area per pedestrian, is used consistently in this article. The reciprocal of density has been designated as M, the Pedestrian Area Module.

- *Headway.* The time and distance separation between traffic units (pedestrians, in the context of this article). For example, two-second headway is the equivalent of one unit (pedestrian) passing a point each two seconds, or a flow volume of 30 traffic units per minute.

- *Queue.* In studies of traffic, a "queue" is defined as one or more traffic units—in this discussion, pedestrians—waiting in line, presumably for some service. If the pedestrian area or service function has insufficient capacity, a pedestrian queue will develop. Queue lengths and durations will vary according to traffic flow characteristics. In crowded systems, queues may be generated intermittently, due to random variations in traffic intensity.

distance, social distance, personal distance, and intimate distance, with close and far phases in each category. Hall's findings support the convention for public distance in public spaces in keeping with at least an "arm's reach" separation. As a point of reference, an opened umbrella has approximately a 43 in (109 cm) diameter with an area of about 10 sq ft (0.9 sq m).

The space required for locomotion may be divided into a *pacing zone,* the area required for foot placement, and the *sensory zone,* the area required by the pedestrian for perception, evaluation, and reaction. For personal safety, or social conventions of avoiding brushing others, or just the joy of sightseeing, the pedestrian is constantly monitoring a whole range of sensory stimuli.

The capabilities of human vision and distance judgment can have a significant effect on pedestrian activities. J. G. Gibson in *The Perception of the Visual World* (1960) uses the term "locomotor vision" to describe the specialized visual characteristics connected with judging the velocity, distance, and direction of others during walking. Pedestrians, through sight and their own internal calculation, are able to keep track of the varying speeds and angles of oncoming pedestrians and to accurately adjust their pace and speed to avoid collision (**Fig. 2**).

- *Locomotion on stairs.* Stair climbing and descent is quite different from walking. Locomotion on stairs is necessarily more restricted because of safety considerations and the restraints imposed by tread and riser configurations. Human energy consumption for climbing stairs is approximately 10 to 15 times the energy needed for walking the equivalent horizontal distance, and surprisingly, about one-third greater for descent (**Fig. 3**).

Classic flow equation

The flow equation—the classic relationship of traffic design derived from an analogy to fluid flow in channels—is expressed as follows:

$$Flow\ Volume = Average\ Ped\ Speed \times Average\ Density$$

$$or,\ P = S \times D$$

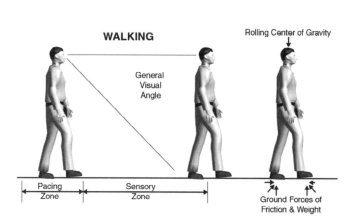

Fig. 2. Human Pacing and Walking Zones: horizontal surfaces.

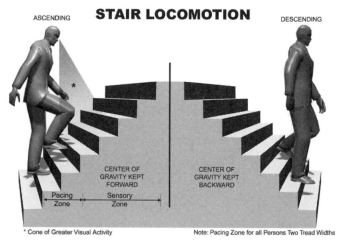

Fig. 3. Human Pacing and Walking Zones: stairs.

In analysis of "density," the reciprocal of density, sq ft area per pedestrian (M), is a common and useful way to analyze a space. The equation for pedestrian flow volume (P), in pedestrian per foot width of pedway section per minute (PFM), is expressed as follows:

$$\text{Ped Volume (P)} = \frac{\text{Average Ped Speed, ft per minute (S)}}{\text{Average Ped Area, sq ft per ped (M)}}$$

$$\text{or, } P = \frac{S}{M}$$

In this formulation, the designer has a clear concept of relative design quality, as the units are easy to manipulate. For example, a nearly normal average walking speed of 250 ft (76 m) per minute is attained with an approximate average pedestrian area of 25 sq ft (2.3 m sq) per person. The simple division of area occupancy into average speed gives an equivalent design volume of 10 pedestrians per foot width of walkway, per minute.

Time and distance headways can be determined from flow volumes by assuming a specific pedestrian lane width. For example, if a 3 ft (0.9 m) wide pedestrian lane has a flow of 10 PFM, as cited above, this is equal to a pedestrian volume per lane of 30 persons per minute, or equivalent to an average time spacing of two seconds between pedestrians. This time spacing is translated into an average distance spacing of approximately 8 ft (2.5 m) between following pedestrians, by multiplying by the 250 ft (76 m) per minute walking speed.

Walking speeds

When unimpeded by crowd density or other traffic frictions, pedestrians may vary their walking speeds over a wide range. **Fig. 4** illustrates the distribution of free-flow walking speeds obtained in surveys of approximately 1000 non-baggage-carrying pedestrians. On the basis of these surveys, average free-flow walking speed for all males, females, and the combination of all pedestrians in the surveys, were from 270, 254, and 265 ft (82, 77, and 80 m) per minute, respectively. Average speeds were found to decline with age, but slow and fast walkers were observed in all age groups. Factors as grade, and the presence of baggage or packages, have been found to have no appreciable effect on free-flow walking speed.

The remaining determinant of pedestrian walking speed is traffic density. As traffic density increases, pedestrian speed is decreased, because of the reduction in available clear area for locomotion. **Fig. 5** shows the effect of increased traffic density, or decreasing area occupancy, on pedestrian walking speeds for one directional commuter traffic flow. Similar studies of two directional commuter and multidirectional flows of shoppers resulted in only small variations from this curve, confirming its more general applicability.

Traffic flows on walkways

Pedestrian volume, or the number of persons passing a given point in a unit of time, is the most important parameter of walkway design. If traffic demand exceeds the capacity of a walkway section, crowding, uncomfortable shuffling locomotion, and delay will result.

Studies of pedestrian traffic flow on walkways have established flow volume relationships for three categories of pedestrian traffic shown in **Fig. 6**. These relationships, representing the average conditions of

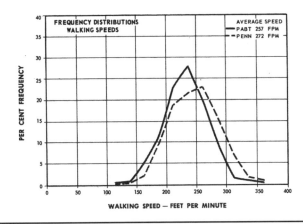

Fig. 4. Pedestrian speed (unimpeded flow). Survey data of 1000 pedestrians (without baggage). The Port of New York Authority Bus Terminal and Pennsylvania Station.

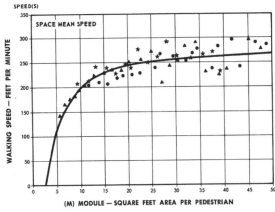

Fig. 5. Pedestrian speed (impeded one way). Data obtained from time-lapse photography.

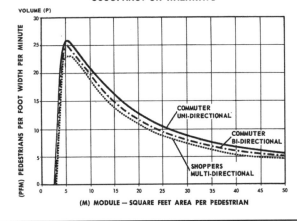

Fig. 6. Pedestrian flow volume and area occupancy. Data obtained from time-lapse photography.

three distinctive types of pedestrian traffic, show a relatively small range of variation, which suggests that reverse- and cross-flow traffic conflicts do not drastically reduce pedestrian traffic volume or speed. This characteristic makes these curves applicable to a wider range of different design conditions.

Pedestrians tend to keep a lateral clear distance between themselves and walls, typically 6 to 8 in (15 to 20 cm). This suggests that this lateral distance should be deducted from any walkway dimension (outside or inside a building) when determining effective walkway width.

Pedestrian spacing and conflicts

The discussion above established the relationships of walking speed and flow volumes to average pedestrian area occupancy. The ability to select near-normal walking speed, a qualitative measure of pedestrian flow, was found to require average areas of 25 sq ft (2.3 sq m) per person or more.

However, other measures are required to obtain a clear determination of walkway quality. Pedestrians must have additional space for maneuvering within the traffic stream to bypass slower moving pedestrians and to avoid oncoming and crossing pedestrians. This additional space is required to sense the speed and direction of others and to react without conflict or hesitation.

Pedestrian conflicts are thus a function of *walking speed* and *pedestrian spacing* in the traffic stream. Although wider pedestrian spacing provides larger crossing gaps, a corresponding increase in pedestrian speed tends to continue to make crossing the main stream difficult. The probability of conflicts due to crossing main stream traffic thus exists over a wide range of pedestrian densities.

Entrances

Entrances are, in effect, walkway sections in which pedestrians are channeled into equal, door-width traffic lanes. In addition to imposing restricted spacing in the traffic stream, entrances may require the pedestrian to perform some time-consuming function such as opening a door or turnstile. The earlier discussion of headways introduced the concept that pedestrians have different average time and distance separations in a traffic stream, dependent on the flow volume.

The headway concept is a useful one for evaluating the design of doors, turnstiles, and other entrance devices. When a pedestrian opens a door, there must be a sufficient time and headway separation between that pedestrian and the following pedestrian, to allow for the performance of this function. Because of the added time required for the door opening, entrances will be the weak links in the pedway system, and therefore they require added design attention. Observed headway distances at entrances and similar functions are summarized in **Table 1**.

Traffic flow on stairways

Pedestrian locomotion on stairs is much more restricted than walking. The dimensions of the stairs themselves determine many of the aspects of locomotion that the pedestrian may more freely choose on a level surface. A summary of results of the surveys, which involved almost 700 pedestrians, is tabulated by differences in direction, stair angle, sex, and age, in **Table 2**.

Table 1. Observed entrance headways

A summary of observed average headways for a number of entrance devices and portal-like situations. While this summary is useful for comparison purposes, the designer is encouraged to examine entrance design problems from the standpoint of traffic headways. This would provide a more qualitative insight into system adequacy and Level of Service.

TYPE OF DEVICE	OBSERVED AVERAGE HEADWAY (Seconds)	EQUIVALENT PEDESTRIAN VOLUME (Persons per minute)
DOORS		
Free-swinging	1.0 – 1.5	40 – 60
Revolving – one direction	1.7 – 2.4	25 – 35
REGISTERING TURNSTILES		
Free Admission	1.0 – 1.5	40 – 60
With Ticket Collector	1.7 – 2.4	25 – 35
COIN OPERATED (LOW)		
Single slot	1.2 – 2.4	25 – 50
Double slot	2.5 – 4.0	15 – 25
BOARDING BUSES		
Single Coin Fare	2 – 3	20 – 30
Odd Cash Fares	3 – 4	15 – 20
Multi Zone Fares	4 – 6	10 – 15

Table 2. Pedestrian stair speeds

	HORIZONTAL TIME-MEANS-SPEEDS (Feet Per Minute)			
	DOWN DIRECTION (1) (2)		UP DIRECTION (1) (2)	
Age – 29 or under				
Males	163	83	110	120
Females	117	132	106	110
Group Average	**149**	**160**	**108**	**115**
Age – 30 to 50				
Males	136	160	101	116
Females	100	128	94	107
Group Average	**127**	**153**	**99**	**114**
Age – Over 50				
Males	112	118	85	81
Females	93	111	77	89
Group Average	**108**	**117**	**83**	**83**
Average – all ages, sexes	**132**	**152**	**100**	**113**

(1) Indoor Stair: 7 in. (18 cm) riser, 11.25 in. (27 cm) tread, 32 degree angle

(2) Outdoor Stair: 6 in. (16 cm) riser, 12.0 in. (30 cm) tread, 27 degree angle

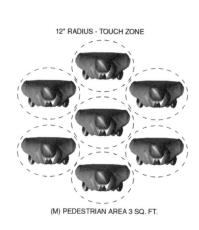

Fig. 7. Touch Zone Boundary: 3 sq ft (0.28 m sq) per person.

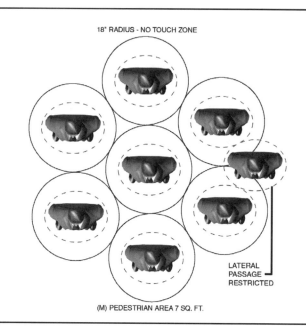

Fig. 8. No Touch Zone Boundary: 7 sq ft (0.65 m sq) per person.

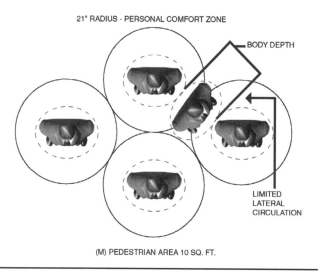

Fig. 9. Personal Comfort Zone Boundary: 10 sq ft (0.93 m sq) per person.

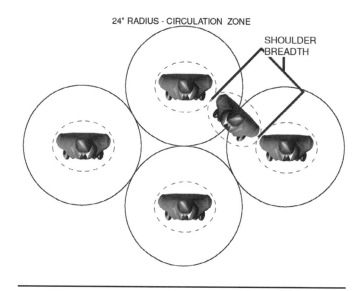

Fig. 10. Circulation Zone Boundary: 13 sq ft (1.2 m sq) per person.

Stairway volumes remain the most significant design parameter. As with walkway volumes, maximum stairway flow occurs in the region of minimum pedestrian area occupancy, about at the point of a two tread length and one shoulder breadth area, or approximately 3 sq ft (0.28 m) per person. In this confined area, movement of the pedestrian ahead determines forward progress. The maximum flow volume of 18.9 pedestrians per minute per foot of stairway width is representative of design values used by many authorities.

Pedestrian queuing

Queuing is broadly defined as any form of pedestrian waiting that requires standing in a relatively stationary position for some period of time. Queues may be of two general types: (1) a *linear* or *ordered queue,* with conventional first-come, first-served priority; or (2) a *bulk queue,* which would be unordered and without an established discipline. Bulk queuing areas may be divided into those devoted only to standing and waiting, with limited movement within the queuing area, or those devoted to waiting combined with some need for reasonably free internal circulation through the queuing area. There are no known standards for the design of queuing spaces. As a result, this aspect of pedestrian design is often overlooked.

Lines of waiting pedestrians, caused by service stoppages or capacity restrictions of any type, are an aspect of design quality that should be carefully evaluated. The pedestrian holding capacity of all public spaces should be known.

Studies by Otis Elevator Company to determine the practical capacity of elevators serve as a reference to establish the approximate upper limit of human occupancy in a confined space. The upper limit of mixed female and male occupancy on an elevator is approximately 1.8 sq ft (0.17 m sq) per person. Observations of dense bulk queues, at escalators or crosswalks, show that pedestrian area occupancies will average approximately 5 sq ft (0.46 m sq) per person in such less-confined circumstances.

Linear queues, as occur on ticket lines, are remarkably consistent with the spacing established by observational studies. Bus commuters have been found to select interpersonal spacings at approximately 19 to 20 in (48 to 51 cm), with very little variation, for both ticket purchase and bus waiting lines.

The accompanying figures illustrate human dimensions of pedestrian area occupancy by which design criteria can be established, assuming uniform interpersonal spacing and circular body buffer zones. **Fig. 7** depicts a group of pedestrians equally spaced in individual 2 ft (61 cm) diameter buffer zones. This assumption results in a queuing area of 3 sq ft (0.28 m sq) per person and is called the *boundary of the touch zone.* Below this area occupancy, frequent unavoidable contact between pedestrians is likely to occur. In **Fig. 8**, the body buffer zone has been expanded to a spacing of 3 ft (0.91 cm) and a 7 sq ft (0.65 m sq) area. This is the *boundary of the no touch zone,* because contact with others can be avoided, as long as movement within the queuing area is not necessary.

Fig. 9 illustrates the expansion of the body buffer zone to a 42 in (1.07 m) diameter and a 10 sq ft (0.93 m sq) area. This is the *boundary of the personal comfort zone,* within the range of spacial separation and area occupancy that people have selected in studies emphasizing the comfort criterion. In **Fig. 10**, the body buffer zone has been expanded to a 4 ft (1.2 m) diameter and a 13 sq ft (1.2 m sq) area. This is the *boundary of the circulation zone,* since circulation within a queuing area with an average occupancy would be possible without disturbing others.

Notes on arrival processes

Arrival processes are an important determinant of the characteristics of use of all pedestrian facilities and spaces, indoors and outdoors. The arrival sequence should be clearly visualized and accommodated by the designer before qualitative design standards are applied. There are two basic types of pedestrian arrival processes: *bulk process* and *intermittent process* arrivals. An example of a bulk process arrival pattern occurs after a sporting event, when there is an immediate mass exodus of spectators, or at a railroad terminal platform, when a fully loaded passenger train discharges in a few minutes.

Intermittent arrival and departure patterns are characteristic of a typical pedestrian facility such as a large transportation terminal, or an office building, served by multiple sources of demand. Intermittent arrival facilities have more regular overall traffic patterns, but are subject to short-term surges of traffic volume considerably higher than the average, as well as short-term gaps in which traffic volume falls far below the average.

2 LEVEL OF SERVICE DESIGN STANDARDS

Design of pedestrian spaces involves traffic engineering principles plus consideration of human convenience and the design environment. Many authorities use maximum capacity ratings for dimensioning pedestrian space. Too often, little or no consideration of human convenience is made when adopting the ratings. In such cases, the maximum capacity of a pedestrian traffic stream is attained only when there is a dense crowding of pedestrians. This is in effect a version of "planned congestion."

Since human convenience and amenity should be the primary consideration in environmental and urban design, pedestrian design standards should reflect the more generous space allocations. Level of Service standards permit a close approximation for design of pedestrian zones that are safe, convenient, and functional to a specified standard.

The Level of Service Concept was first developed in the field of traffic engineering in recognition of the fact that capacity design was, in effect, resulting in planned congestion. The Level of Service concept provides a useful standard for the design of pedestrian spaces as well. Design should offer the pedestrian the freedom to select normal locomotion speed, the ability to bypass slow-moving pedestrians, and the relative ease of cross- and reverse-flow movements at traffic concentrations.

The Level of Service standards are based on a range of pedestrian area occupancies. Design volumes for walkways and stairways are presented as a range. Walkway and stairway Levels of Service are illustrated by drawings of one directional flow at the approximate pedestrian area occupancy representing that service level. The drawings are supplemented by a written description of the qualitative aspects of each Level of Service.

Walkway standards

Breakpoints that determine the various levels of service have been determined on the basis of the walking speed, pedestrian spacing, and the probabilities of conflict at various traffic concentrations. The standards provide the means of determining the design quality of corridors, sidewalks, and entranceways. The effect width of corridors must be reduced by 18 in (46 cm) on each corridor side, to account for the human propensity to maintain this separation from stationary objects and walls, except under the most crowded conditions. Where there is a tendency for window-shopping or viewing of exhibits, net width should be reduced by an additional equal amount, to allow for standing pedestrians. When designing sidewalks, the effective walkway width must be reduced by an additional 2 ft (61 cm) or more, to account for the constricting effects of street impediments such as parking meters, light standards, fire hydrants, and receptacles.

Illustrations of *Walkway Levels of Service* are depicted in **Fig. 11**. The correspondence with pedestrian flow volume and area relationships is indicated on the curve in **Fig. 12**.

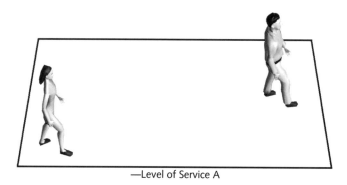

—Level of Service A

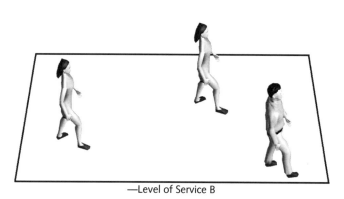

—Level of Service B

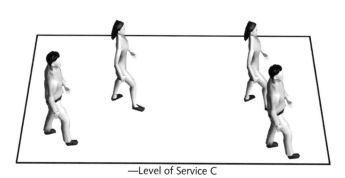

—Level of Service C

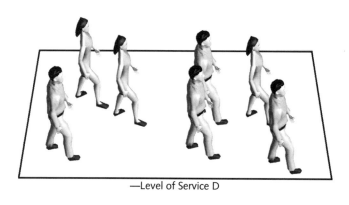

—Level of Service D

Fig. 11. Level of Service Standards of Walkways: Pedestrian flow volume and area relationships.

Walkways: Level of Service A

Average Pedestrian Area Occupancy: 35 sq ft (3.25 m sq) per person, or greater.
Average Flow Volume: 7 PFM (pedestrian foot per minute), or less.

At Walkway Level of Service A, sufficient area is provided for pedestrians to freely select their own walking speed, to bypass slower pedestrians, and to avoid crossing conflicts with others. Designs consistent with this Level of Service would include public buildings or plazas without severe peaking characteristics or space restrictions.

Walkways: Level of Service B

Average Pedestrian Area Occupancy: 25 to 35 sq ft (2.3 to 3.25 m sq) per person.
Average Flow Volume: 7 to 10 PFM.

At Walkway Level of Service B, sufficient space is available to select normal walking speed, and to bypass other pedestrians in primarily one directional flow. Where reverse directions or pedestrian crossing movements exist, minor conflicts will occur, slightly lowering mean pedestrian speeds and potential volumes. Designs consistent with this Level of Service would be of reasonably high quality, for transportation terminals and buildings in which recurrent, but not severe, peaks are likely to occur.

Walkways: Level of Service C

Average Pedestrian Area Occupancy: 15 to 25 sq ft (1.4 to 2.3 m sq) per person.
Average Flow Volume: 10 to 15 PFM.

At Walkway Level of Service C, freedom to select individual walking speed and freely pass other pedestrians is restricted. Where pedestrian cross movements and reverse flows exist, there is a high probability of conflict requiring frequent adjustment of speed and direction to avoid contact. Designs consistent with this Level of Service would represent reasonably fluid flow. However, considerable friction and interaction between pedestrians is likely to occur, particularly in multidirectional flow situations. Examples of this type of design would be heavily used transportation terminals, public buildings, or open spaces where severe peaking, combined with space restrictions, limit design flexibility.

Walkways: Level of Service D

Average Pedestrian Area Occupancy: 10 to 15 sq ft (1 to 1.4 m sq) per person.
Average Flow Volume: 15 to 20 PFM.

At Walkway Level of Service D, the majority of persons would have their normal walking speeds restricted and reduced, due to difficulties in bypassing slower-moving pedestrians and avoiding conflicts. Pedestrians involved in reverse flow and crossing movements would be severely restricted, with the occurrence of multiple conflicts with others. Designs at this Level of Service would be representative of the most crowded public areas, where it is necessary to alter walking stride and direction continually to maintain reasonable forward progress. At this Level of Service there is some probability of intermittently reaching critical density, causing momentary stoppages of flow. Designs consistent with this Level of Service would represent only the most crowded public areas.

Walkways: Level of Service E

Average Pedestrian Area Occupancy: 5 to 10 sq ft (0.46 to 1 m sq) per person.
Average Flow Volume: 20 to 25 PFM.

At Walkway Level of Service E, virtually all pedestrians would have their normal walking speeds restricted, requiring frequent adjustments of gait. At the lower end of the range, forward progress would only be made by shuffling. Insufficient areas would be available to bypass slower-moving pedestrians. Extreme difficulties would be experienced by pedestrians attempting reverse flow and cross-flow movements. The design volume approaches the maximum attainable capacity of the walkway, with resulting frequent stoppages and interruptions of flow. This design range should only be acceptable for short peaks in the most crowded areas. This design level would occur naturally with a bulk arrival traffic pattern that immediately exceeds available capacity, and this is the only design situation for which it would be recommended. Examples would include sports stadium design or rail transit facilities where there may be a large but short-term exiting of passengers from a train. When this Level of Service is assumed for these design conditions, the limited adequacy of pedestrian holding areas at critical design sections, and all supplementary pedestrian facilities, must be carefully evaluated for amenity and safety.

Walkways: Level of Service F

Average Pedestrian Area Occupancy: 5 sq ft (0.46 m sq) per person or less.
Average Flow Volume: Variable, up to 25 PFM.

At Walkway Level of Service F, all pedestrian walking speeds are extremely restricted. Forward progress can only be made by shuffling. There would be frequent, unavoidable contact with other pedestrians, and reverse or crossing movements would be virtually impossible. Traffic flow would be sporadic, with forward progress based on the movement of those in front. This Level of Service is representative of a loss of control and a complete breakdown in traffic flow. Pedestrian areas below 5 sq ft are more representative of queuing, rather than a traffic flow situation. This Level of Service is not recommended for walkway design.

Stairway standards

When designing stairs, increased attention is required to avoid and eliminate safety hazards. In addition to design judgment in evaluating the traffic patterns and peaking characteristics recommended for use of Walkway Standards, the following guidelines should be considered in stairway design:

• Stairs should be located so as to be readily visible and identifiable as a means of direct access to the levels they are designed to interconnect;

• Clear areas large enough to allow for queuing pedestrians should be provided at the approaches to all stairways;

• Stairs should be well lighted;

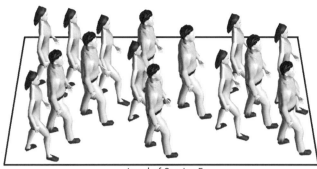

—Level of Service E

—Level of Service F

Fig. 11. cont. Level of Service Standards of Walkways: Pedestrian flow volume and area relationships.

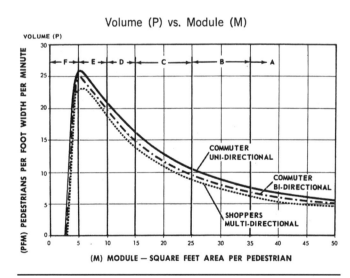

Fig. 12. Graphic summary: Level of Service Standards of Walkways—Pedestrian flow volume and area relationships.

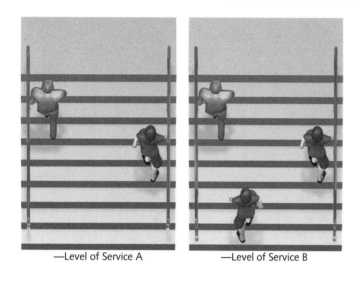

—Level of Service A —Level of Service B

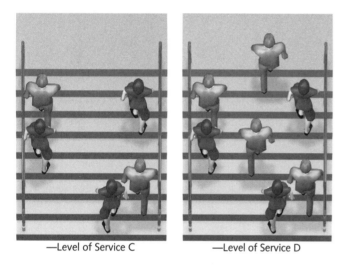

—Level of Service C —Level of Service D

—Level of Service E —Level of Service F

Fig. 13. Level of Service Standards of Stairways.

- Stair nosing, riser, tread, and railing configurations should be designed to assist human locomotion, particularly for the individuals with limited capacity;

- Riser heights should be kept below 7 in (18 cm), to reduce energy expenditure and to increase traffic efficiency;

- When a stairway is placed directly within a corridor, the lower capacity of the stairway is the controlling factor in the design of the pedway section;

- Where minor, reverse flow traffic volumes frequently occur on a stair, the effective width of the stair calculated for the major direction design flow should be reduced by a minimum of one traffic lane, or 30 in (41 cm). That is to say, actual stair width should increase to accommodate the anticipated two-way flow.

Illustrations of *Stairway Levels of Service* are depicted in **Fig. 13.** The correspondence with pedestrian flow volume and area relationships is indicated on the curve in **Fig. 14.**

Stairways: Level of Service A

Average Pedestrian Area Occupancy: 20 sq ft (1.9 m sq) per person, or greater.
Average Flow Volume: 5 PFM, or less.

At Stairway Level of Service A, sufficient area is provided to freely select locomotion speed, and to bypass other slower-moving pedestrians. No serious difficulties would be experienced with reverse traffic flows. Designs at this Level of Service would be consistent with public buildings or plazas that have no severe traffic peaks or space limitations.

Stairways: Level of Service B

Average Pedestrian Area Occupancy: 15 to 20 sq ft (1.4 to 1.9 m sq) per person.
Average Flow Volume: 5 to 7 PFM.

At Stairway Level of Service B, representing a space approximately 5 treads long and 3 to 4 ft (0.9 to 1.2 m) wide, virtually all persons may freely select locomotion speeds. However, in the lower range of area occupancy, some difficulties would be experienced in passing slower-moving pedestrians. Reverse flows would cause minor traffic conflicts. Designs at this Level of Service would be consistent with transportation terminals and public buildings that have recurrent peak demands and no serious space limitations.

Stairways: Level of Service C

Average Pedestrian Area Occupancy: 10 to 15 sq ft (0.9 to 1.4 m sq) per person.
Average Flow Volume: 7 to 10 PFM.

At Stairway Level of Service C, representing a space approximately 4 to 5 treads long and approximately 3 ft (0.9 m) wide, locomotion speeds would be restricted slightly, due to an inability to pass slower-moving pedestrians. Minor reverse traffic flows would encounter some difficulties. Design at this Level of Service would be consistent with transportation terminals and public buildings with recurrent peak demands and some space restrictions.

Stairways: Level of Service D

Average Pedestrian Area Occupancy: 7 to 10 sq ft (0.7 to 0.9 m sq) per person.
Average Flow Volume: 10 to 13 PFM.

At Stairway Level of Service D, representing a space approximately 3 to 4 treads long and 2 to 3 ft (0.6 to 0.9 m) wide, locomotion speeds are restricted for the majority of persons, due to the limited open tread space and an inability to bypass slower-moving pedestrians. Reverse flows would encounter significant difficulties and traffic conflicts. Designs at this Level of Service would be consistent with the more crowded public buildings and transportation terminals that are subjected to relatively severe peak demands.

Stairways: Level of Service E

Average Pedestrian Area Occupancy: 4 to 7 sq ft (0.4 to 0.7 m sq) per person.
Average Flow Volume: 13 to 17 PFM.

At Stairway Level of Service E, representing a space approximately 2 to 4 tread lengths long and 2 ft (61 cm) wide, the minimum possible area for locomotion on stairs, virtually all persons would have their normal locomotion speeds reduced, because of the minimum tread length space and inability to bypass others. Intermittent stoppages are likely to occur, as the critical pedestrian density is exceeded. Reverse traffic flows would experience serious conflicts. This Level of Service would only occur naturally with a bulk arrival traffic pattern that immediately exceeds available capacity. This is the only design situation for which it would be recommended. Examples would include sports stadiums or transit facilities where there is a large uncontrolled, short-term exodus of pedestrians.

Stairways: Level of Service F

Average Pedestrian Area Occupancy: 4 sq ft (0.4 m sq) per person, or less.
Average Flow Volume: Variation to 17 PFM.

At Stairway Level of Service F, representing a space approximately 1 to 2 tread lengths long and 2 ft (61 cm) wide, there is a complete breakdown in traffic flow, with many stoppages. Forward progress would depend on movement of those in front. This Level of Service is not recommended for design.

Queuing standards

Queuing Level of Service standards are based on human dimensions, personal space preferences, and pedestrian mobility. The designer should not only apply queuing standards in areas designed primarily for pedestrian waiting, such as elevator and theater lobbies, but rather in other areas in which queuing is likely to result from service stoppages of inadequate capacity of pedestrian service facilities. Pedestrian holding areas on the approaches to stairs, or other critical areas, should also be designed to hold waiting pedestrians. Areas such as railway and bus platforms have critical pedestrian holding capacities, which, if exceeded, can cause persons to be injured by being pushed onto tracks or roadways. In addition to their ability to hold standees, queuing areas have different internal circulation requirements, based on the type of use. For examples, an airport baggage claim area must be capable of

Volume (P) vs. Module (M)

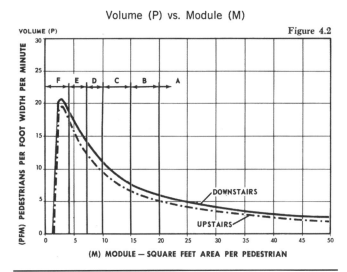

Fig. 14. Graphic summary: Level of Service Standards of Stairways—Pedestrian flow volume and area relationships.

holding persons waiting for baggage as well as those moving out of the area with baggage. Illustrations representative of several Queuing Levels of Service are shown in **Figs. 15** and **16.**

Queuing: Level of Service A—Free Circulation Zone

Average Pedestrian Area Occupancy: 13 sq ft (1.2 m sq) per person, or more.
Average Interperson Spacing: 4 ft (1.2 m) or more.

At Queuing Level of Service A, space is provided for standing and free circulation through the queuing area without disturbing others. Examples would include better-designed passenger concourse areas and baggage claim areas.

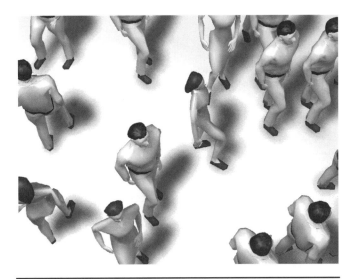

Fig. 15. Level of Service Standards (representative) of Queuing in the A to B range.

Fig. 16. Level of Service Standards (representative) of Queuing in the C to D range.

Queuing: Level of Service B—Restricted Circulation Zone

Average Pedestrian Area Occupancy: 10 to 13 sq ft (0.9 to 1.2 m sq) per person.
Average Interperson Spacing: 3-½ to 4 ft (1.1 to 1.2 m).

At Queuing Level of Service B, space is provided for standing and restricted circulation through the queue without disturbing others. Examples would include railroad platforms and passenger concourse areas.

Queuing: Level of Service C—Personal Comfort Zone

Average Pedestrian Area Occupancy: 7 to 10 sq ft (0.6 to 0.9 m sq) per person.
Average Interperson Spacing: 3 to 3-½ ft (0.9 to 1.1 m).

At Queuing Level of Service C, space is provided for standing and restricted circulation through the queuing area by disturbing others. It is within the range of the personal comfort body buffer zone established by psychological experiments. Examples would include ordered queue ticket selling areas and elevator lobbies.

Queuing: Level of Service D—No Touch Zone

Average Pedestrian Area Occupancy: 3 to 7 sq ft (0.28 to 0.6 m sq) per person.
Average Interperson Spacing: 2 to 3 ft (0.6 to 0.9 m).

At Queuing Level of Service D, space is provided for standing without personal contact with others, but circulation through the queuing area is severely restricted, and forward movement is only possible as a group. Examples would include motorstair queuing areas, pedestrian safety islands, or holding areas at crosswalks. Based on psychological experiments, this level of area occupancy is not recommended for long-term waiting periods.

Queuing: Level of Service E—Touch Zone

Average Pedestrian Area Occupancy: 2 to 3 sq ft (0.19 to 0.28 m sq) per person.
Average Interperson Spacing: 2 ft (0.6 m) or less.

At Queuing Level of Service E, space is provided for standing but personal contact with others is unavoidable. Circulation within the queuing area is not possible. This level of area occupancy can only be sustained for short periods of time without physical and psychological discomfort. The only recommended application would be for elevator occupancy.

Queuing: Level of Service F—The Body Ellipse

Average Pedestrian Area Occupancy: 2 sq ft (0.19 m sq) per person, or less.
Average Interperson Spacing: Close contact with surrounding persons.

At Queuing Level of Service F, space is approximately equivalent to the area of the human body. Standing is possible, but close unavoidable contact with surrounding standees causes physical and psychological discomfort. No movement is possible, and in large crowds there exists the potential for panic. ▪

REFERENCES

Fruin, John J., *Pedestrian Planning and Design,* Metropolitan Association of Urban Designers and Environmental Planners, New York, 1971, reprinted by *Elevator World,* Mobile, 1987.

Fruin, John J., "Planning and Design for Pedestrians," in *Time-Saver Standards for Urban Design,* McGraw-Hill, New York, 2003.

"Pedestrian Circulation" in *Time-Saver Standards for Landscape Architecture,* Charles W. Harris and Nicholas T. Dines, eds., McGraw-Hill, New York, 1998.

Mark C. Childs

Summary

This article presents the basis for dimensioning of parking spaces, including parking lots, garages, and street parking, based upon studies listed in the References. Tables and diagrams offer minimum, maximum, and recommended standards for various aspects of parking lot design, including design for universal design and accessibility.

Key words

accessibility, automobile, commercial vehicles, curb, dimensions, driveway, grades, parking, queuing, residential, stall, traffic

Santa Barbara, California, parking structure in downtown commercial/cultural district.

Parking and vehicular circulation

Comment on parking standards

Standards are not a substitute for thought. They must be used within the whole context of the design.

- *The minimum as maximum.* When a minimum dimension is given, it does not mean it is the best dimension, only that it is the least one can use in most cases without significant problems. Often a few more inches make the difference between what is minimally acceptable and a desirable amenity.

- *Escalating standards.* In 1929, recommended stall widths were 7 ft (2.13 m) and under. Today a stall width less than this is unacceptable. Parking stall dimensions are based on vehicle sizes. Traffic lanes and parking spaces have been made larger to accommodate the largest vehicles. Judgment is required for each application and special considerations of building users.

- *Note:* Dimension tables and illustrative plates are grouped at the end of the article.

1 PARKING LOTS

Bay & stall dimensions

There are a number of different approaches to the sizing and dimensioning of parking facilities. **Table 1,** "Stall and Module Dimensions," incorporates a service approach that allows a designer to vary dimensions based on the expected use of the lot. The tabulation assumes a mix of small and large cars close to the 1995 national average.

To use Table 1, three initial decisions must be made:

(1) The appropriate stall width based on the expected turnover of the lot (**Table 2**),

(2) If and how small car stalls will be provided (see below), and

(3) The angle of parking. Slightly smaller dimensions are recommended in certain conditions in a (reduced) level-of-service approach (Chrest, Smith and Bhuyan 1996) (**Figs. 1** to **3**). Parking for vehicles should be based on the vehicle's length, width, and turning radii (**Tables 3** and **4**). **Table 5** lists some special conditions for vehicle stall dimensions.

Small car stalls

It is estimated that in 1995, half the cars on the road in the United States were small cars, 5'-9" wide by 14'-11" long (1.75 by 4.55 m) or smaller (Chrest, Smith and Bhuyan 1996, p. 30). Many local regulations allow a specified percentage of stalls to be designated for small or compact cars. However, the average difference in size between small and large cars has been decreasing so that it is often confusing for motorists to decide if they are driving a small or standard car. Small car stalls are ideally designated in three different conditions:

Credits: This article is adapted by the author from Chapter 13 *Parking Spaces: A Design, Implementation and Use Manual*, McGraw-Hill, New York, 1999.

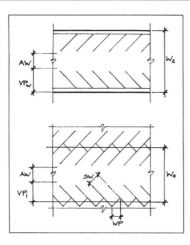

Fig. 1. Module variables.

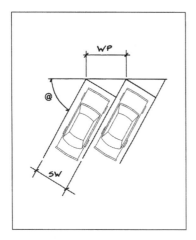

Fig. 2. Stall widths.

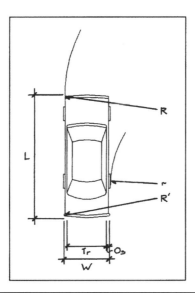

Fig. 3. Vehicle design variables.

(1) In employee parking lots, stalls for compact cars may constitute up to 40 percent of the general stalls. This standard supplies compact stalls for 80 percent of the expected number of small cars based upon the 1995 U.S. average. When a survey has been conducted and if there is reason to believe that the number of small cars varies from the average, then the supply of compact stalls should be adjusted. In order to build smaller parking lots, businesses could offer rewards to employees who drive compacts. One hundred small car stalls and aisles use approximately 5300 sq ft (~493 sq m) less land than would 100 standard stalls.

(2) At stadiums or other lots in which someone directs traffic to parking areas, cars may be sorted by size. Often stall markings are not used in these conditions to preserve flexibility. Designers should calculate the number of vehicles that may be parked under various expected conditions (*e.g.,* compacts only, mixed, large only) and provide bays that have as little waste space under each condition as possible. A 68 ft (20.7 m) long bay, for example, provides nine 7.5 ft (2.3 m) wide stalls or eight 8.5 ft (2.59 m) wide stalls.

(3) In general service lots, up to 40 percent of the stalls may be for compacts (adjusted for local conditions). Alternatively, very large cars could be given special stalls. By removing them from the mix of cars, the general stalls and aisles could be made smaller. For example, if 5 to 10 percent of stalls were designated for large cars, a stall width two sizes smaller could be used for the remainder of the lot, and aisles could be approximately 6 in (~15 cm) smaller. The large size cars, classes 10 and 11, made up 7 percent of the market in 1993 (Chrest, Smith and Bhuyan 1996, p. 33). These large car stalls should be the least convenient so that smaller cars do not occupy them. Since there is limited experience with this approach, a traffic engineer should be consulted to tailor dimensions to expected local conditions.

Lanes

Table 6 shows widths for various traffic lanes. All of these dimensions are for public streets. Local regulations and standards often specify similar dimensions for parking lot lanes. The Uniform Fire Code requires that fire lanes are a minimum of 20 ft (6.09 m) wide, have a height clearance of at least 13.5 ft (4.11 m), have a 40 ft (11.98 m) minimum radius on curves, and a maximum dead-end length of 150 ft (46.3 m).

Driveway location

The existing street and pedestrian network must be evaluated before designing a parking lot to determine the best location for entrances and exits. Local codes normally limit the size, number, and location of access points. Consideration in locating access points include:

• Avoid crossing busy pedestrian routes.

• Minimize the number and size of curb cuts to reduce conflicts with pedestrian and street traffic.

• Integrate driveways into the street system. Place entrances off of alleys when possible; otherwise integrate the driveways with intersections. If neither of these is feasible place driveways far away from intersections to avoid turning conflicts. Entrances must be "upstream" from exits.

- Avoid left turns across traffic if possible (provide turn lanes where volume is significant).

- Keep internal traffic flow simple.

- Avoid requiring cars to back up onto sidewalks in order to exit a parking stall.

- Entry control devices require at least a two-space off-street reservoir (see below to calculate queuing for large lots).

Driveway width

Driveway width should be kept to a minimum to limit sidewalk curb-cut lengths and to minimize pavement. However, sufficient width must be given to accommodate traffic flow (**Table 7**).

Number of driveway lanes

For large lots, the standard method for determining the number of lanes entering or exiting a lot is based on the highest demand for the lot during any 15 minute period. The method is given below, but some thought may be given to the use of this standard. For example, the following charts indicate that we should design stadium parking lots so that they can empty in 30 minutes.

The rate at which cars may enter a lot is affected by the angle of approach to the lot (in order of ease: straight approach, left turn to entrance, right turn to entrance), and drivers' familiarity with the lot (*e.g.*, commuters are more familiar with a lot than are tourists). Rates up to 1000 cars per lane per hour are possible. Entrance fee and control booths reduce the entrance rate by 50 to 83 percent. Attendants can park 8 to 16 cars per hour per attendant (Box 1992, p. 207).

The standard formula for the number of lanes is N = (S × R)/(P × U). N is number of lanes, S is number of stalls, R is the percent of lot capacity moving at peak hour (**Table 8**). P is the peak hour factor (**Table 9**), and U is the design capacity of the lane (**Table 10**).

Queuing

Entrance routes for lots at which people tend to arrive at the same time (*e.g.*, employee parking, special events) should have off-street queuing space to avoid having cars block the sidewalk and street. Alternatively, work hours can be staggered and special events can have incentives for arriving early. The formula to estimate the number of cars queued is: L = i²/(1 − i) where L = number of vehicles waiting, i = peak hour volume/ maximum service rate (Tables 8 and 10) (Weant and Levinson 1990, 186–187).

Grades

Table 11 shows maximum recommended grades within parking lots. Care should be taken to minimize the grades of routes used by the mobility impaired. Ramps may have a maximum slope of 1 in 12 over a maximum length of 30 ft (9.14 m) between landings (**Fig. 4**).

End islands

In lots with more than 200 cars or difficult conditions, islands should be created at the end of bays to assure sight distances, provide adequate turning radii, protect vehicles at the end of parking bays, and limit parking encroachment into cross aisles. End islands also help delineate circulation and may be used to plant trees, pile snow, or store grocery carts, and provide places for light poles, fire hydrants, low signage, and other equipment. Striped pavement in and of itself is not very effective in discouraging use of these areas for auto parking, and drivers turning into an aisle often cut the corner, putting themselves on the wrong side of the aisle. Curbs or bollards are often needed to establish the end island.

The character of these islands is a significant design feature. They line the cross street and act as gateways to each bay of parking. **Fig. 5**

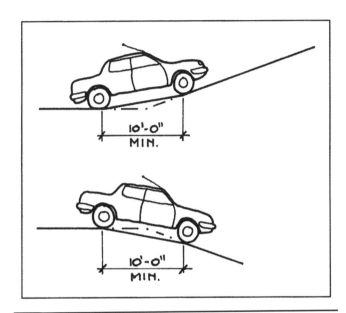

Fig. 4. Slopes at grade changes. Change grade by a maximum of 10 degree increments with 10 ft (3.05 m) minimum between changes of grade.

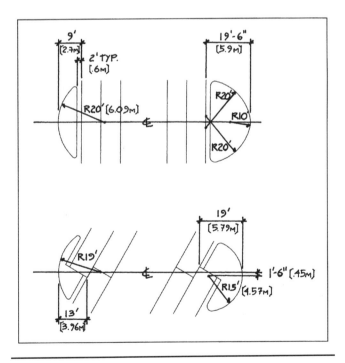

Fig. 5. Diagram of typical end islands.

shows typical end islands. The size and geometry of the islands should be adjusted for particular conditions. Design considerations include:

- A typical car has an inside turning radius of approximately 15 ft (4.57 m) and end islands with smaller radii may cause cars to "turn wide" into the opposing lane.

- Care should be taken with the placement of the radii to avoid exposing the end of an adjacent car and its disembarking passengers to "clipping" from turning cars.

- Cars parking next to the island need a walking aisle of at least 24 in (61 cm) between them and any landscaping.

- Adequate sight distance increases with the speed of cars and when the road is curved. For example, a car making a right turn onto a 20 mph (32 kph) aisle (typical small lot speeds) needs to be able to see approximately 250 ft (~76 m) ahead; turning onto a 35 mph (56 kph) aisle, the driver needs to see approximately 550 ft (168 m) ahead to judge the safety of making the turn (Stover and Koepke 1989, Table 1). Thus the depth of the island should increase next to higher speed or curved aisles/roads.

- End islands may also be increased in size to provide space for trees or other amenities.

Stall markings

Marking stalls aid in the even distribution of vehicles within a lot and is necessary for stalls for the handicapped. Painted or applied stripes are typical. Street reflectors offer higher visibility, and can be felt if a tire crosses them. Changes in pavement color and material can also help designate stalls. Painted or applied stall stripes are usually 4 in (~10 cm) wide and approximately 6 in (~15 cm) shorter than the stall to encourage drivers to pull fully into the stall. Reflective and ridged stripes are available that provide increased visibility and a tactile presence to pedestrians and drivers.

There is disagreement about the effectiveness of double stripes to encourage centering of cars. A study by Paul Box (1994) of shopping center, motel, and office building parking lots found no significant difference in parking efficiency between single and double stripes and thus recommends avoiding the expense of paired lines. However, for stalls for the mobility impaired, possibly grocery store lots, and in other conditions where the useable width of the between-doors aisle is large and critical for pedestrian access, the aisle should be marked with two stripes and crosshatching.

The design manuals of the 1950s suggest that stall marks be continued up walls to help drivers locate the stall. Careful placement of parking meters, trees, bollards, and other vertical elements can provide the same function.

Overhangs, wheel stops, and bumpers

Wheel stops, curbs, bumpers and bollards are used to protect structures, limit parking encroachment onto pedestrian pathways or planting areas, and signal to drivers when they have fully pulled into a stall. Sometimes they are used to prevent driving across rows of empty stalls because this cutting across is perceived as a hazardous activity. Backing up from parking stalls, however, generates more parking lot accidents (Box 1981), and thus cars should not be prevented from pulling through stalls when possible.

The Institute of Transportation Engineers discourages wheel stops in parking lots because they may present a tripping hazard, interfere with snow plowing, and trap trash (ITE 1990). Wheel stops should only be used to protect a wall, column, or other item at a location where pedestrians are unlikely to walk. Where wheel stops are used, an overhang of approximately 2.5 ft (76 cm) for 90-degree front-in parking and approximately 4.5 ft (1.37 m) for 90-degree back-in parking should be provided beyond the wheel stop. Concrete and recycled plastic wheel stops come in a range of sizes. Typically a 6 ft (~1.8 m) stop is used for each stall, and 6 in (~15 cm) is the maximum height for a wheel stop. Wheel stops should not be shared between adjacent stalls because it creates confusion and blocks pedestrian circulation in the aisle.

Curbs are often used in lieu of wheel stops. Curbs present a smaller tripping hazard than wheel stops because the action of stepping up or down is easier than the action of stepping over, and because they appear at an expected location. Curbs along walkways should be designed as steps with rounded, skid-resistant and contrasting-color nosings. Curbs require the same overhang setbacks as wheel stops.

Some vehicles overhang their wheels farther than the overhang setbacks recommended above and cars occasionally ride up or over curbs and wheel stops. Thus curbs and wheel stops should not be used when positive limitation is required. Bollards at least 36 in (~90 cm) tall or bumpers can be used to protect buildings, trees, fire hydrants, or other structures within harm's way.

2 BICYCLE PARKING

Some cities require that places to park and secure bicycles be provided whenever automobile parking is required. For example, Albuquerque requires that buildings provide a number of bicycle stalls equal to 10 percent of the number of required car stalls with a minimum of three bike stalls.

Bicycle stalls require either a lockable enclosure or secure stationary racks that support the frame and to which the frame and both wheels can be locked. A space with minimum dimensions of 6 ft (1.83 m) long, 2.5 ft (0.76 m) wide and with a minimum overhead clearance of 7.5 ft (2.28 m) is necessary for each stall. An access aisle 5 ft (1.52 m) wide minimum is needed beside or between each row of bike stalls.

Ideally, bike stalls should be covered to protect the bikes from rain and the heat of the sun. The parking area should be well lighted, close to the entrance of the building—*e.g.,* not more than 50 ft (15.2 m)— and visible to passersby and/or building occupants. Bikes may also be parked in secured areas within a building.

The State of Oregon Department of Transportation developed a set of questions to help evaluate bike-parking racks (ODOT 1992) including:

- Can the rack support children and adults sitting, standing, or jumping on it without bending? Is the rack safe for children to play near?

- Can rack capacity be expanded as needs increase?

- Is there adequate lighting?

- Does the rack allow a bike to be easily and securely locked to it without damage to the bike? Will the bike stand up even if bumped?

3 COMMERCIAL TRUCK PARKING

There are an estimated 185,000 commercial truck stalls near interstates at truck stops. On a typical night, 90 percent of these spaces are occupied, and a study by the Federal Highway Administration (1996) estimates that currently another 28,400 stalls are needed to make certain that exhausted truck drivers have a safe and secure place to pull off the highway.

This same report advises that public highway rest stops are not a direct substitute for private truck stops. The rest stops are used primarily during the day for short rests, while the truck stops provide longer nighttime parking. Significant factors in the preference for truck stops are the added security of the truck stop, and the services offered.

Fig. 6 shows the preferred layout of stalls for single trailer trucks. This pattern is up to 70 percent more land efficient than parallel parking (Federal Highway Administration 1996, p. *xxiii*). More than half of truck stop lots currently have no markings, providing the flexibility to accommodate double and triple trailer rigs but complicating parking maneuvers.

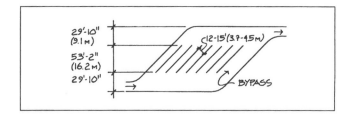

Fig. 6. Commercial truck parking layout.

4 LOTS ACCESSIBLE TO THE MOBILITY IMPAIRED

The first case brought into Federal Court that resulted in a civil penalty under Title III of the Americans with Disabilities Act (ADA) was for failure to make parking accessible. Parking is a critical element of accessibility.

The ADA is a civil rights law. The Department of Justice has the charge of enforcing the law; people who believe they have been discriminated against may sue the property owner. The guidelines issued by the government are not a building code subject to state or local approval or variances.

There are current efforts to create regulations that if followed will serve to show that the design meets the intent of the law. The information in this book was compiled from publications of the Architectural and Transportation Barriers Compliance Board (ATBCB) and other sources as noted. It should be viewed as the opinion of the author, informed by the material quoted. The law and best practices continue to evolve. The designer should review materials and conditions that apply directly to the project at hand. Lots owned by government agencies generally follow Title II rules that are usually more stringent than the Title III rules for privately owned lots discussed below.

Required number of accessible stalls

Whenever parking is supplied, no matter how the total amount of parking was determined, a portion of the stalls must be accessible to people with mobility impairment (hereafter called "accessible stalls"). Local codes may exceed the Federal requirement for required number of accessible stalls shown in **Table 12.** The more stringent rule governs. When a facility has more than one lot, the required number of stalls is determined lot by lot. In employee or contract lots, accessible stalls must be provided but "accessible spaces may be used by persons without disabilities when they are not needed by (persons) with disabilities" (ATBCB 1994). When the use of a facility, *e.g.*, a senior center, indicates that more accessible stalls are needed than are required by Table 12 criteria, a study should be conducted to determine an adequate supply of accessible stalls.

Location of stalls

The location of accessible stalls must give mobility-impaired persons preferential treatment in terms of access and must not discriminate against them in terms of amenities (*e.g.,* if the general stalls have hail protection canopies, the accessible stalls must also). The shorthand rule is that accessible stalls should be located with the shortest possible route to the entrance(s). Relevant U.S. regulations include:

Accessible parking spaces serving a particular building shall be located on the shortest route of travel from adjacent parking to an accessible entrance. In parking facilities that do not serve a particular building, accessible parking shall be located on the shortest accessible route of travel to an accessible pedestrian entrance of the parking facility. In buildings with multiple accessible entrances with adjacent parking, accessible parking shall be dispersed and located closest to the accessible entrances. (ADAAG 4.6.2)

Accessible spaces can be provided in other lots or locations, or in the case of parking garages, on one level only when equal or greater access is provided in terms of proximity to an accessible entrance, cost and convenience. . . . The minimum number of spaces must still be determined separately for each lot. (ATBCB 1994)

Van-accessible stalls

See **Table 5** for required dimensions of van-accessible stalls and Table 12 for the required number of stalls. These stalls must be marked with "van-accessible," but this does not restrict the stall to use by vans (ATBCB 1994).

Notes on the layout of stalls

Two accessible stalls may share an access aisle. However, this should only be done when the stalls are at 90 degrees and allow both front-in and back-in parking. (Title II modification to ADAAG, 14.2.6(1)(b))

Curb ramps or other obstructions may not be within the stall's access aisle, but may begin at the curb face when vehicles overhang a curb (Chrest, Smith and Bhuyan 1996, p. 212).

Car overhang may not obstruct the clear width of a sidewalk access route. Wheel stops and/or a reinforced signpost may help limit car overhang.

Signage

"Accessible parking spaces shall be designated as reserved by a sign showing the symbol of accessibility. . . . (Van) spaces . . . shall have an additional sign "van-accessible" mounted below the symbol of accessibility." (ADAAG 4.6.4)

ADAAG requires that the sign not be obscured by a car or parked van. Centering the sign on the access aisle may help its visibility.

Equipment

Equipment such as parking meters, automated teller machines, pay stations, and ticket dispensers must have accessible controls. Most such equipment is now designed with operating mechanisms that are considered accessible, and the designer's major role is to place the controls at a proper level and to provide clear access to the controls.

For example, ADAAG 14.2(2) controls the design and placement of parking meters in public rights-of-way:

Parking meter controls shall be 42 in (1065 mm) maximum above finished public sidewalk . . . Where parking meters serve accessible parking spaces, a stable, firm, and slip-resistant clear ground space a minimum of 30 by 48 in (76 cm by 122 cm), shall be provided at the controls. . . . Parking meters shall be located at or near the head or foot of the parking space so as not to interfere with the operation of a side lift or a passenger side transfer.

Existing lots

Bulletin #6 (ATBCB 1994) suggests that existing lots must be made accessible when it is possible to do so:

ADAAG established minimum requirements for new construction or alterations. However, existing facilities not being altered may be subject to requirements for access. Title III of the ADA, which covers the private sector, requires the removal of barriers in places of public accommodation where it is 'readily achievable' to do so. This requirement is addressed by regulations issued by the Department of Justice. Under these regulations, barrier removal must comply with ADAAG requirements to the extent that it is readily achievable to do so. For example, when restriping a parking lot to provide accessible spaces, if it is not readily achievable to provide the full number of accessible spaces required by ADAAG, a lesser number may be provided. The requirement to remove barriers, however, remains a continuing obligation; what is not readily achievable at one point may become achievable in the future.

When alterations are made (*e.g.,* realigning striping or resurfacing, but not routine maintenance) whatever is altered must be made accessible unless technically infeasible (ADAAG 4.1.6 (1)) *and* improvements to the path of travel to the lot must be made, up to a cost equal to 20 percent of the project budget (Title II, Rule 36.403 (f)).

Passenger loading zones

There must be at least one passenger-loading zone for the mobility impaired whenever designated loading zones are provided. There must be an access aisle at least 5 ft wide by 20 ft long (1.53 by 6.10 m) adjacent and parallel to the vehicle pull-up space. A clear height of 9.5 ft (2.90 m) is required at the loading zone and along the vehicle route, to, from, and within the zone. The vehicle space and the access aisle shall be level with surface slopes not exceeding 1 to 50 (2 percent) in all directions (ADAAG 4.6.6). Neither curb ramps nor street furniture may occupy the access aisle space (ATBCB 1994).

Curb parking and loading zones

Table 13 gives dimensions for accessible curb stalls, bus stalls, and stalls for other vehicles. Local regulations may require different dimensions.

5 CIRCULATION PATTERNS

The circulation through a parking lot is critical to its performance. Overall goals are to create a simple, legible route that allows drivers to easily circulate past all available stalls on their way in, and past as few stalls as possible on their way out. It is prudent to avoid dead-end aisles when possible, although even in high turnover lots, parking *cul-*

de-sacs for 10 to 12 cars may function well. Circulation patterns should be reviewed to remove 'choke' points—places that many cars must pass through. Additionally, stalls for the mobility impaired need to be placed as near to entrances as possible, fire lanes often are required by local codes, and conflicts between cars and between pedestrians should be minimized. Usually there are trade-offs between these goals. For the layout of vast lots, see the Urban Land Institute's *Parking Requirements for Shopping Centers* (ULI 1999). Following are some possible layouts for smaller lots. In general, any of these patterns is more efficient if the aisles run the long dimension of the lot.

The parking row

Perhaps the most common unit of parking is the two-way aisle with 90-degree stalls and exits at both ends (**Fig. 7**).

Advantages:

• Accessible stalls are easily incorporated into the design;

• The wide aisles increase separation between cars and pedestrians in the aisle;

• The two-way aisles allow drivers to exit efficiently;

• Does not require aisle directional signs and markings.

Disadvantages:

• Two-way traffic may increase the conflict between pedestrians and cars;

• This pattern cannot be fitted into all constrained sites.

One-way slot

See **Fig. 8** for an example of a one-way slot.

Advantages:

• This pattern can be fitted into narrow sites;

• One-way entrance and exit simplifies circulation and reduces required curb-cut width;

• Pedestrian/car conflict reduced;

• Angle parking is perceived as the easiest in which to park.

Disadvantages:

• Drivers cannot recirculate within the lot;

• Signage of one-way entrance and exit required;

• Stalled or slow vehicle blocks entire system;

• Requires an alley or must run block face to block face.

Herringbone

The one-way slot can be expanded into multiple one-way bays with the herringbone pattern. The advantages and disadvantages are similar to the one-way slot except that because cars cannot recirculate

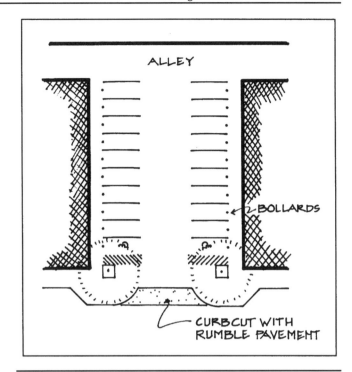

Fig. 7. Two-way bay.

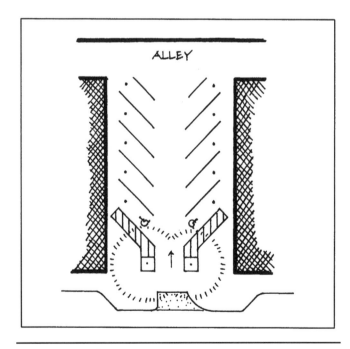

Fig. 8. One-way slot.

within the lot and cannot pass by all the stalls, there may be significant inefficiency in parking (**Fig. 9**).

One-way loop

The advantages and disadvantages of the one-way loop are similar to the one-way slot. The exit should be "downstream" of the entrance. A cross aisle can be added to allow cars to recirculate within the lot (**Fig. 10**).

Dead-end lots

Dead-end lots should be limited to 10 to 12 cars for public parking and 40 cars for low-turnover employee or contract parking and should have back-out stubs at the dead end (**Fig. 11**).

Advantages:

• All stalls are along edges allowing pedestrians to avoid crossing traffic;

• With a small lot the curb-cut width can be minimal.

Disadvantages:

• The size must be limited to reduce conflicts due to excessive turnover.

Drop-off turnabouts

See **Fig. 12** for an example.

Advantages:

• Removes the activity of dropping-off and picking-up from the street;

• Allows architectural design of the place of arrival and departure.

Disadvantages:

• Can be less time- and land-efficient than on-street drop-offs.

Accessible corners

The corners of parking lots can provide good access routes to accessible stalls. The advantages and disadvantages are dependent on the layout of the entire lot and must be evaluated on a case-by-case basis (**Fig. 13**).

Entrance aisle

Lots likely to generate significant traffic, such as grocery store lots or other high-turnover, large lots, should have entrance aisles. These aisles provide a place to slow down cars as they enter the car commons and space for cars waiting to exit the lot. They can also provide direct pedestrian paths that do not cross parking areas (**Fig. 14**).

The dimensional recommendations are indicated in the Tables below. The Plates that follow the Tables are given for visual guidance and require design judgment appropriate with each application as defined in this article.

Plates 1 to **4** following the Tables provide tabulated and visual reference for parking and vehicular circulation. ▪

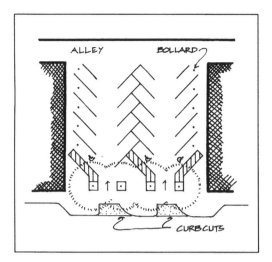

Fig. 9. Herringbone pattern.

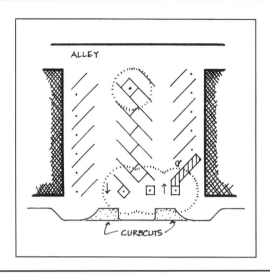

Fig. 10. One-way look.

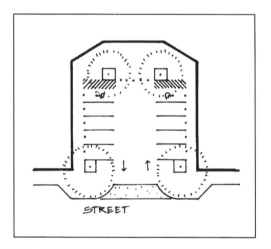

Fig. 11. Dead-end lots.

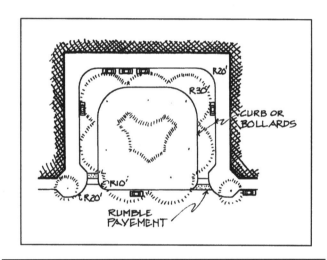

Fig. 12. Drop-off turnaround.

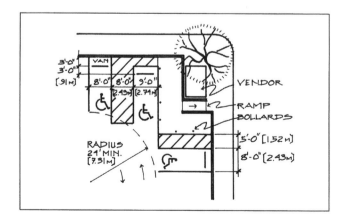

Fig. 13. Accessible corners. (after Chrest, Smith and Bhuyan 1996)

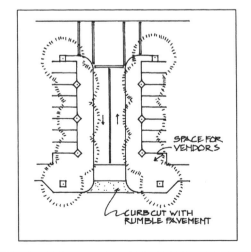

Fig. 14. Entrance aisle.

Table 1. Stall and Module Dimensions

| | | Stall Width | | Stall Depth Parallel to Aisle | | Aisle Width *Min.* | Minimum Modules | |
		Par. to Car (Sw) ft	Par. to Aisle (WP) ft	to Wall (VPw) ft	to Interlock (VPi) ft	(AW) ft	Wall to Wall (W₂) ft	Interlock (W₄) ft
Two-Way Aisle								
	90°							
Mix	G	10.00	10.0	18.4	18.4	24.0	60.8	60.8
	A	9.00	9.0	18.4	18.4	24.0	60.8	60.8
	B	8.75	8.8	18.4	18.4	24.0	60.8	60.8
	C	8.50	8.5	18.4	18.4	24.0	60.8	60.8
	D	8.25	8.3	18.4	18.4	24.0	60.8	60.8
Small	A	8.00	8.0	15.1	15.1	22.3	52.4	52.4
	B	7.75	7.8	15.1	15.1	22.3	52.4	52.4
	C	7.50	7.5	15.1	15.1	22.3	52.4	52.4
	D	7.25	7.3	15.1	15.1	22.3	52.4	52.4
Large		9.00	9.0	18.7	18.7	24.0	61.3	61.3
One-Way Aisles								
	75°						(+2 ft min. for 2-way aisle—see note)	
Mix	G	10.00	10.4	19.4	18.6	20.8	59.6	58.0
	A	9.00	9.3	19.4	18.6	21.0	59.9	58.2
	B	8.75	9.1	19.4	18.6	21.1	60.0	58.3
	C	8.50	8.8	19.4	18.6	21.2	60.0	58.4
	D	8.25	8.5	19.4	18.6	21.2	60.1	58.4
Small	A	8.00	8.3	16.2	15.4	20.0	52.5	50.8
	B	7.75	8.0	16.2	15.4	20.1	52.5	50.9
	C	7.50	7.8	16.2	15.4	20.1	52.6	50.9
	D	7.25	7.5	16.2	15.4	20.2	52.7	51.0
Large		9.00	9.3	19.7	18.9	20.9	60.4	58.7
	70°							
Mix	G	10.00	10.6	19.5	18.4	18.2	57.2	55.0
	A	9.00	9.6	19.5	18.4	18.6	57.5	55.3
	B	8.75	9.3	19.5	18.4	18.7	57.6	55.4
	C	8.50	9.0	19.5	18.4	18.7	57.7	55.5
	D	8.25	8.8	19.5	18.4	18.8	57.8	55.6
Small	A	8.00	8.5	16.4	15.3	17.9	50.6	48.4
	B	7.75	8.2	16.4	15.3	18.0	50.7	48.5
	C	7.50	8.0	16.4	15.3	18.0	50.8	48.6
	D	7.25	7.7	16.4	15.3	18.1	50.9	48.7
Large		9.00	9.6	19.8	18.7	19.1	58.7	56.4

Table 1. Stall and Module Dimensions (continued)

		Stall Width		Stall Depth Parallel to Aisle		Aisle Width *Min.*	Minimum Modules	
		Par. to Car (Sw) ft	Par. to Aisle (WP) ft	to Wall (VPw) ft	to Interlock (VPi) ft	(AW) ft	Wall to Wall (W₂) ft	Interlock (W₄) ft
One-Way Aisles (*Cont.*)								
	65°							
Mix	G	10.00	11.0	19.4	18.0	15.7	54.4	51.7
	A	9.00	9.9	19.4	18.0	16.1	54.9	52.2
	B	8.75	9.7	19.4	18.0	16.2	55.0	52.3
	C	8.50	9.4	19.4	18.0	16.3	55.1	52.4
	D	8.25	9.1	19.4	18.0	16.4	55.2	52.5
Small	A	8.00	8.8	16.4	15.0	15.7	48.5	45.8
	B	7.75	8.6	16.4	15.0	15.8	48.6	45.9
	C	7.50	8.3	16.4	15.0	15.9	48.7	46.0
	D	7.25	8.0	16.4	15.0	16.0	48.8	46.1
Large		9.00	9.9	19.7	18.3	16.6	56.0	53.2
	60°							
Mix	G	10.00	11.5	19.1	17.5	13.2	51.4	48.2
	A	9.00	10.4	19.1	17.5	13.7	51.9	48.7
	B	8.75	10.1	19.1	17.5	13.8	52.0	48.8
	C	8.50	9.8	19.1	17.5	13.9	52.2	49.0
	D	8.25	9.5	19.1	17.5	14.0	52.3	49.1
Small	A	8.00	9.2	16.3	14.7	13.6	46.1	42.9
	B	7.75	8.9	16.3	14.7	13.7	46.2	43.0
	C	7.50	8.7	16.3	14.7	13.8	46.4	43.2
	D	7.25	8.4	16.3	14.7	13.9	46.5	43.3
Large		9.00	10.4	19.5	17.8	14.1	53.1	49.8
	55°							
Mix	G	10.00	12.2	18.7	16.9	11.7	49.2	45.6
	A	9.00	11.0	18.7	16.9	11.2	48.7	45.1
	B	8.75	10.7	18.7	16.9	11.4	48.9	45.2
	C	8.50	10.4	18.7	16.9	11.5	49.0	45.4
	D	8.25	10.1	18.7	16.9	11.7	49.2	45.5
Small	A	8.00	9.8	16.0	14.2	11.5	43.5	39.8
	B	7.75	9.5	16.0	14.2	11.6	43.7	40.0
	C	7.50	9.2	16.0	14.2	11.7	43.8	40.1
	D	7.25	8.9	16.0	14.2	11.9	44.0	40.3
Large		9.00	11.0	19.1	17.2	11.7	49.9	46.1

Table 1. Stall and Module Dimensions (continued)

		Stall Width		Stall Depth Parallel to Aisle		Aisle Width *Min.* (AW) ft	Minimum Modules	
		Par. to Car (Sw) ft	Par. to Aisle (WP) ft	to Wall (VPw) ft	to Interlock (VPi) ft		Wall to Wall (W₂) ft	Interlock (W₄) ft
One-Way Aisles (*Cont.*)								
	50°							
Mix	G	10.00	13.1	18.2	16.2	11.4	47.8	43.7
	A	9.00	11.7	18.2	16.2	11.0	47.4	43.3
	B	8.75	11.4	18.2	16.2	11.0	47.4	43.3
	C	8.50	11.1	18.2	16.2	11.0	47.4	43.3
	D	8.25	10.8	18.2	16.2	11.0	47.4	43.3
Small	A	8.00	10.4	15.7	13.6	11.0	42.4	38.2
	B	7.75	10.1	15.7	13.6	11.0	42.4	38.2
	C	7.50	9.8	15.7	13.6	11.0	42.4	38.2
	D	7.25	9.5	15.7	13.6	11.0	42.4	38.2
Large		9.00	11.7	18.6	16.4	11.3	48.4	44.1
	45°							
Mix	G	10.00	14.1	17.5	15.3	11.0	46.1	41.5
	A	9.00	12.7	17.5	15.3	11.0	46.1	41.5
	B	8.75	12.4	17.5	15.3	11.0	46.1	41.5
	C	8.50	12.0	17.5	15.3	11.0	46.1	41.5
	D	8.25	11.7	17.5	15.3	11.0	46.1	41.5
Small	A	8.00	11.3	15.2	12.9	11.0	41.4	36.9
	B	7.75	11.0	15.2	12.9	11.0	41.4	36.9
	C	7.50	10.6	15.2	12.9	11.0	41.4	36.9
	D	7.25	10.3	15.2	12.9	11.0	41.4	36.9
Large		9.00	12.7	17.9	15.6	11.0	46.8	42.1

1. Figures 13.2 and 13.3 define dimensions used in Table 13.1.

2. Stalls angled between 90 and 60° confuse whether the aisle is one-way or two-way. Do not use angles between 90 and 75°. Some designers advocate using 75° stalls with two-way aisles because the right-hand-side parking maneuver is easier into an angled stall. However, making a left-hand turn to park in a 75° stall is difficult. A minimum of 22 feet is necessary for two-way aisles, and 24 to 25 feet allows ample walking space and occasional left-hand parking. Stalls at angles between 45 and 0° (parallel parking) are not generally advisable because they are often space-inefficient and confusing. The formula used to calculate Table 13.1 is given in Table 13.3; if special circumstances warrant, stall dimensions or angles other than those given may be calculated.

3. In the interest of legibility, metric dimensions are not given. The dimension in meters may be derived by dividing feet by 3.28. However, it may be better to recalculate, using Table 13.3 and appropriate metric stall dimensions.

4. Stall stripes are often painted 6 to 10 inches shorter than the stall depth to encourage drivers to fully pull into the stall.

5. The chart uses a minimum aisle width of 11 feet. This dimension is minimally sufficient to allow passage of cars and pedestrians. In high-turnover or special situations such as lots primarily serving the elderly or children, a pedestrian walkway and/or a wider aisle should be provided.

6. Sources: Adapted and recalculated from Ricker 1957; Weant and Levinson 1990; Box 1992; and Chrest, Smith, and Bhuyan 1996.

7. See Table 13.4 and Figure 13.4 for the design vehicles and clearances used to calculate this table.

Table 2. Turnover Categories and Stall Widths

Name		Stall Width Parallel to Car	Application
Mix*	G	10.00 ft (3.05 m)	Grocery stores and others that use shopping carts[†]
	A	9.00 ft (2.74 m)	Very high turnover rates—post office, convenience stores Areas with a high percentage (>20%) of passenger trucks
	B	8.75 ft (2.67 m)	High turnover rates—general retail
	C	8.50 ft (2.59 m)	Medium turnover rates—airport, hospitals, residential
	D	8.25 ft (2.52 m)	Low turnover rates—employee parking
Small	A	8.00 ft (2.44 m)	Same as categories above
	B	7.75 ft (2.36 m)	
	C	7.50 ft (2.29 m)	
	D	7.25 ft (2.21 m)	

* The mix of cars includes about 40% small cars, based on 1995 U.S. averages.

[†] There are a variety of grocery cart models ranging in width from approximately 18 to 32 inches. I recommend "hairpin" double stripes at least 2 feet wide for lots that use grocery carts. This 2-foot width is included in the 10-foot centerline-to-centerline dimensions.

Table 3. Formulas for Parking Stall and Module Dimensions

	Formula
$Sw =$	Given
$WP =$	$Sw/\sin @$
$VPw =$	$W \cos @ + (L + cb) \sin @$
$VPi =$	$.5W\cos @ + (L + cb) \sin @$
$AW =$	For lots with $@ <$ critical angle,
	$AW = R' + c - \sin @[(r - Os)^2 - (r - Os - i + c)^2]^{.5} - \cos @(r + tr + Os - Sw)$
	For lots with $@ >$ critical angle,
	$AW = R' + c + \sin @[(R^2 - (r + tr + Os + i - c)^2]^{.5} - \cos @(r + tr + Os + Sw)$
$W_2 =$	$AW + 2VPw$
$W_4 =$	$AW + 2Vpi$

Critical Angle

Mixed Stalls		Small Car Stalls		Large Car Stalls	
Stall Width	Critical Angle	Stall Width	Critical Angle	Stall Width	Critical Angle
10.00	57.6	8.00	51.6	9.0	55.0
9.00	54.8	7.75	50.7		
8.75	54.0	7.50	49.8		
8.50	53.2	7.25	48.8		
8.25	52.4				

Critical angle $= \text{arccot} \{[(R^2 - (r + tr + Os + i - c)^2]^{.5} + ((r - Os)^2 - (r - Os - i + c)^2]^{.5}]/2Sw\}$.

Critical angle chart assumes design vehicles listed in Table 13.4.

$Sw =$ stall width parallel to car; $WP =$ stall width parallel to aisle; $VPw =$ stall depth from wall parallel to aisle; $VPi =$ stall depth from interlock parallel to aisle; $AW =$ aisle width min.; $W_2 =$ module wall to wall; $W_4 =$ module interlock to interlock; $@ =$ stall angle; $W =$ design vehicle width; $L =$ design vehicle length; $cb =$ curb clearance .5 ft; R ft $=$ design vehicle wall-to-wall rear radius; $c =$ car clearance; $Os =$ design vehicle side overhang; $r =$ design vehicle curb-to-curb rear radius; $i =$ walkway between cars; $tr =$ design vehicle rear width.

For 90° lots, use 85% of the AW value given by the aisle width formula (see Weant and Levinson 1990, 160).

Aisle width formula from Edmund R. Ricker, *Traffic Design of Parking Garages,* Eno Foundation, 1957.

Table 4. Design Vehicle Dimensions

Type	Mix	Small Car	Large	Passenger truck
Length (L) inches	215 (5.46 m)	175 (4.45 m)	218 (5.54 m)	212 (5.39 m)
Width (W) inches	77 (1.96 m)	66 (1.68 m)	80 (2.03 m)	80 (2.03 m)
Wall-to-wall front radius (R) feet	20.5 (6.25 m)	18 (5.49 m)	20.75 (6.33 m)	
Wall-to-wall rear radius (R') feet	17.4 (5.31 m)	15 (4.57 m)	17.5 (5.34 m)	
Curb-to-curb rear radius (r) feet	12 (3.66 m)	9.6 (2.93 m)	12.25 (3.73 m)	
Rear width (tr) feet	5.1 (1.55 m)	4.6 (1.4 m)	5.08 (1.55 m)	
Side overhang (Os) feet	0.63 (.192 m)	0.46 (.14 m)	0.75 (.228 m)	0.66 (.201 m)
Walkway between cars (i) feet	2 (.61 m)	2 (.61 m)	2 (.61 m)	2.85 (.87 m)
Car clearance (c) feet	1.5 (.46 m)	1.5 (.46 m)	1.5 (.46 m)	

Sources: Weant and Levinson 1990, 157; passenger truck data from Dare 1985.

Table 5. Stall Dimensions for Special Conditions

	Width	Length	Clr. Height
Designated large	9 ft (2.74 m)	18.5–20 ft (5.79–6.1 m)	
Passenger truck[1]	9 ft (2.74 m)	18.5 ft (5.64 m)	
Handicap car[2]	8 ft (2.44 m) + 5 ft (1.52 m) aisle	17.5 ft (5.34 m)	
Handicap van[2]	8 ft (2.44 m) + 8 ft aisle	17.5 ft (5.34 m)	8.16 ft (2.49 m)
Universal[3]			
(handicap car or van)	11 ft (3.35 m) + 5 ft (1.52 m) aisle		8.16 ft (2.49 m)
Valet[4]	7.5 ft (2.29 m)	17 ft (5.18 m)	
Europe typical[5]	7.83–8.16 ft (2.39–2.49 m)	15.58–16.42 ft (4.75–5 m)	
Bicycle[6]	2.5 ft (.76 m)	6 ft (1.83 m)	
Motorcycle[6]	3.33 ft (1.02 m)	7 ft (2.13 m)	

SOURCES: [1] Dare 1985.
[2] ADAAG.
[3] Bulletin #6.
[4] Burrage 1957, 242.
[5] Hunnicutt 1982, 650.
[6] Weant and Levinson 1990, 167.

Table 6. Lane Widths

Type	Width	Notes
Fire lane	20 ft (6.1 m) min. typ.	
Curb parking lane	6–8 ft (2.03 m)	10 ft (3.05 m) when also a traffic lane
Parking + traffic lane	18 ft (5.49 m) min.	
No-parking one-way	10 ft (3.05 m) min.	
No-parking two-way	16 ft (4.88 m) min.	

Table 7. Driveway Widths

Type	Entry Lanes	Exit Lanes	Total Width	Corner Radii
Commercial[1]				
Typical	1	1	22–30 ft (6.71–9.15 m)	15 ft (4.57 m)
Large volume	1 @ 14–16 ft (4.29–4.88 m)	2 @ 10–11 ft (3.05–3.35 m)	34–36 ft (10.37–10.98 m)	15 ft (4.57 m)
Very high volume	2 @ 10–11 ft (3.05–3.35 m)	2 @ 10–11 ft (3.05–3.35 m)	40–44 ft (12.20–13.41 m)	20 ft (6.09 m)
Residential[2]				
Driveway for 1 car			8 ft (2.44 m) max.	
Driveway for 2 to 10 cars			12 ft (3.66 m) max.	

SOURCES: [1] Box 1992, 206.
[2] Untermann 1984, 202.

Table 8. Design Percent of Lot Capacity Moving at Peak Hour (R)

	Morning Peak		Afternoon Peak	
Land Use	In	Out	In	Out
Office	40–70%	5–15%	5–20%	40–70%
Medical office	40–60%	50–80%	60–80%	60–90%
General retail	20–50%	30–60%	30–60%	30–60%
Convenience retail	80–150%	80–150%	80–150%	80–150%
Hospital visitors	30–40%	40–50%	40–60%	50–75%
Hospital employees	60–75%	5–10%	10–15%	60–75%
Residential	5–10%	30–50%	30–50%	10–30%
Hotel/motel	30–50%	50–80%	30–60%	10–30%
	Before event		After event	
Special event	80–100%		85–200%	

SOURCE: Adapted from Chrest, Smith, and Bhuyan, 1996.

Table 9. Peak Hour Factors (PHF)

Condition	PHF
Special events	.5–.65
Single lane	.75 max.
Two lanes	.85 max.
Three lanes	.95 max.

SOURCE: Adapted from Weant and Levinson, 1990.

Table 10. Design Capacity for Lanes (U)

	Entrance Vehicles/Hour/Lane		Exit Vehicles/Hour/Lane	
Control device	Design Rate	Max. Rate	Design Rate	Max. Rate
No stop	800	1,050	375	475
Automatic ticket dispenser	525	650		
Push-button ticket dispenser	450	525		
Coin/token-operated gate	150	200	150	200
Fixed fee to cashier with gate	200	250	200	250
Fixed fee to cashier with no gate	250	350	250	350
Variable fee to cashier			150	200
Validated ticket to operator			300	350
Machine-read ticket			375	425
Coded-card reader	350	400	350	400
Proximity card reader	500	550	500	550

SOURCE: Adapted from Weant and Levinson, 1990, 186.
NOTE: This table assumes an easy or straight approach with no sharp turns.

Table 11. Grades in Parking Lots

Grade	Condition
6% max.	Continuous slope in parking lot
12% max., 30 ft long	Nonparking automobile ramps with pedestrians allowed
15% max.	Nonparking automobile ramps with signs banning pedestrians
>6% change	A vertical curve transition is required; see Figure 13.5
1% min. / 2% rec.	Slope to drain asphalt
.5% min. / 2% rec.	Slope to drain concrete
2% (1:50) max.	Slope within accessible stalls

SOURCE: Adapted from Chrest, Smith, and Bhuyan, 1996; ITE, 1982; and Untermann, 1984.

Table 12. Required Number of Accessible Stalls

Total in Parking Lot	Required Minimum Number of Accessible Spaces	Source
1–25	1	ADAAG 4.1.3 (5) (a)
26–50	2	
51–75	3	
76–100	4	
101–150	5	
151–200	6	
201–300	7	
301–400	8	
401–500	9	
501–1000	2% of total	
1001 and over	20 + 1 per 100 over 1000	

No. of Accessible Spaces	Required Minimum Number of Van-Accessible Spaces	Source
1–8	1	ADAAG 4.1.3 (5) (a)
9–16	2	
17–24	3	
25–32	4	
33 and over	1 additional van-accessible per 8 accessible spaces	

Special Cases

Place	Requirement	Source
Medical outpatient units	10% of total stalls in lots serving visitors and patients.	ADAAG 4.1.2 (5) (d) and Bulletin #6
Medical units that specialize in persons with mobility impairments	20% of total stalls in lots serving visitors and patients.	ADAAG 4.1.2 (5) (d) and Bulletin #6
Valet parking	No stalls required. However, an accessible loading zone is required, and it is strongly recommended that self-park stalls be provided.	Bulletin #6

Table 13. Curb Parking

Accessible loading	22 ft min. (6.71 m)	Platform 5 ft (1.53 m) wide, 20 ft (6.10 m) long, 9.5 ft (2.90 m) clear height	ADAAG 4.6.5 and 4.6.6
Truck loading	30–60 ft (9.15–18.29 m)	Add truck length per additional truck	Weant and Levinson
Drop-offs/taxi	50 ft (15.24 m)	Add 25 ft (7.62 m) per additional vehicle	Weant and Levinson
Paired (length per pair)	44–50 ft (13.41–15.24 m)	20 ft (6.10 m) stalls	Hunnicutt, 666 Hunnicutt, 666
Compact	19 ft (5.79 m)		Hunnicutt, 666
End stall	20 ft (6.10 m)		Hunnicutt, 666
Interior stall	22 ft–24 ft (6.71–7.32 m)		Hunnicutt, 666

Length of Curbside Bus Loading Zones

	Wheel Position from Curb		One 40-ft Bus (~12.2 m)	Additional per Bus
	6 Inches (~15 cm)	1 Foot (~30.5 cm)		
Upstream of intersection	L + 85 ft +(~25.9 m)	L + 65 ft +(~19.8 m)	105–125 ft (~32–38 m)	L + 5 ft +(~1.5 m)
Downstream of intersection				
Street width >39 ft (~11.9 m)	L + 55 ft +(~16.8 m)	L + 40 ft +(~12.2 m)	80–95 ft (~24.4–29 m)	L
Street width 32–39 ft (~9.75–11.9 m)	L + 70 ft +(~21.3 m)	L + 55 ft +(~16.8 m)	95–110 ft (~29–33.5 m)	L
Midblock				
Street width >39 ft (~11.9 m)	L + 135 ft +(~41.2 m)	L + 100 ft +(~30.5 m)	140–175 ft (~42.7–53.4 m)	L
Street width 32–39 ft (~9.75–11.9 m)	L + 150 ft +(~45.7 m)	L + 115 ft +(~35 m)	155–190 ft (~47.25–58 m)	L

Source for bus loading: Adapted from Homburger and Quinby, 1982. "Urban Transit" in *Transportation and Traffic Engineering Handbook,* 2nd edition.
L = length of bus.

Plate 1a: Parking garage space and aisle requirements at various angles

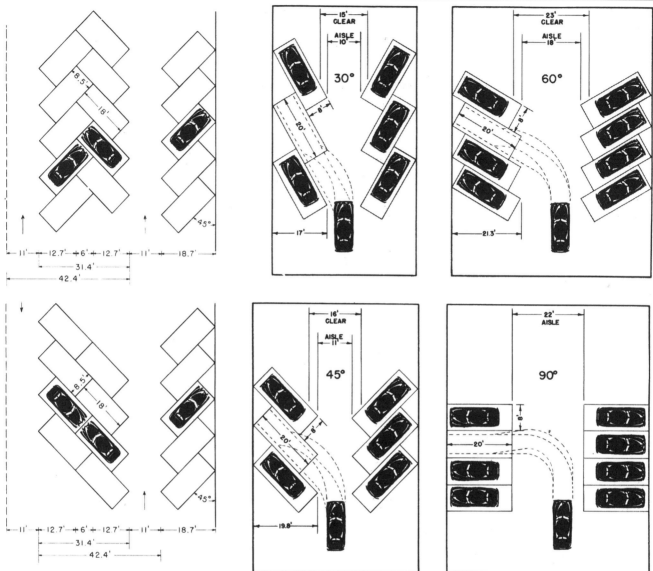

Plate 1b: Various curb parking arrangements. 22 ft (6.7 m) length is recommended for short-term parking as it allows easy exit normally with only one turning maneuver

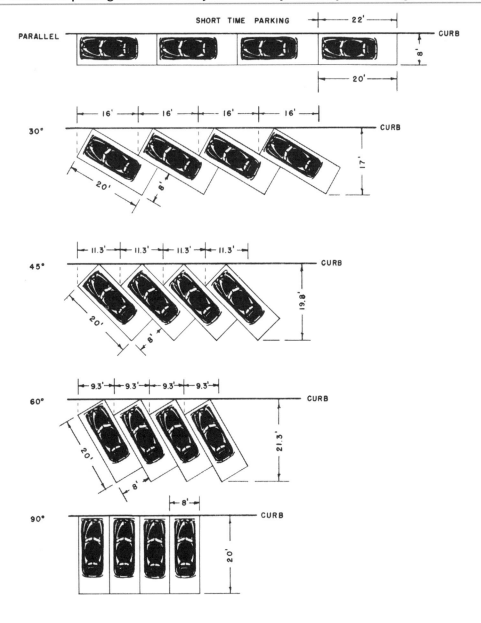

Plate 2a. Residential driveways

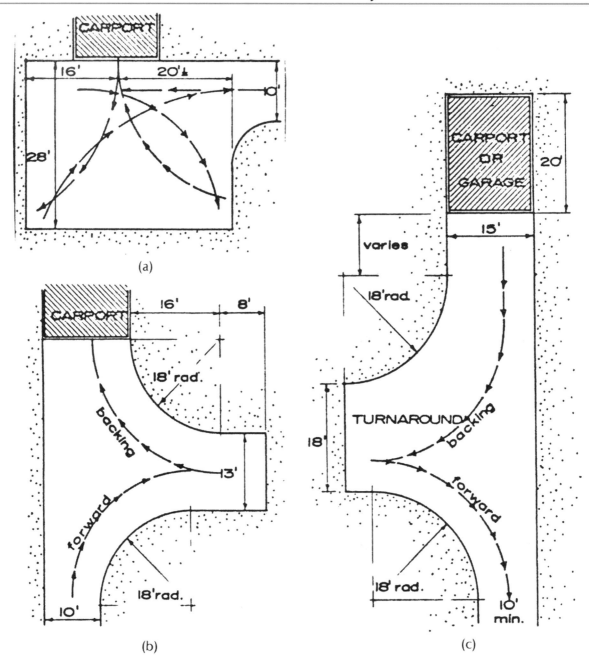

(a)

(b)

(c)

Plate 2b. Private roads

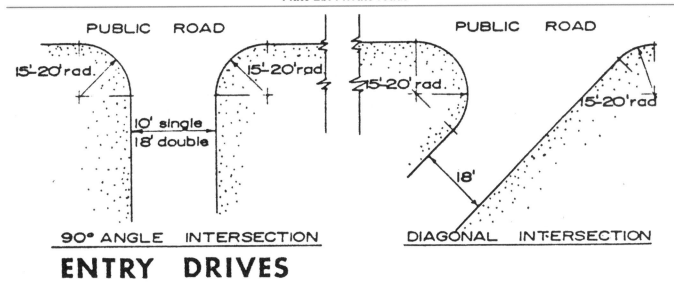

PUBLIC ROAD

15'-20' rad.   15'-20' rad.

10' single
18' double

90° ANGLE INTERSECTION

PUBLIC ROAD

15'-20' rad.

15'-20' rad.

18'

DIAGONAL INTERSECTION

ENTRY DRIVES

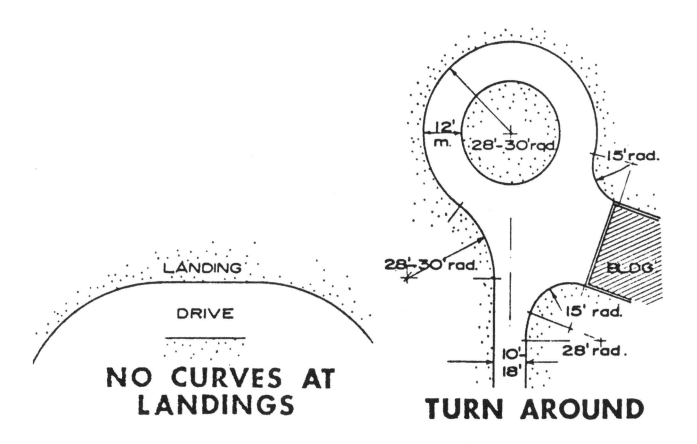

LANDING

DRIVE

NO CURVES AT LANDINGS

12' m.

28'-30' rad.

15' rad.

28'-30' rad.

BLDG

15' rad.

10'
18'

28' rad.

TURN AROUND

Plate 3a. Off-street parking option A (preferred over option B for most locations)

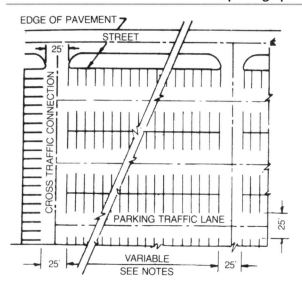

PERPENDICULAR OFF-STREET
PARKING — PLAN "A"
SEE DETAIL "A"

1. MULTIPLE LANE, OFF-STREET PARKING AREAS SHALL BE DESIGNED FOR 90 DEGREE PARKING, WITH TWO-WAY TRAFFIC LANES, IN ACCORDANCE WITH PLANS "A" AND "B".

2. NORMALLY, THE TOTAL SIZE OF THE PARKING AREA SHALL BE BASED UPON MAXIMUM ALLOWANCE OF 35 SQUARE YARDS PER VEHICLE, AND WILL INCLUDE SPACE FOR PARKING AND PARKING AREA ENTRANCES. SPACE NEEDED FOR LONG ACCESS ROADS SHALL NOT BE INCLUDED IN THE ALLOWANCE. THE AREA ALLOWANCE FOR INDIVIDUAL PARKING SPACES, WITHIN THE PARKING LANES, SHALL USUALLY BE 31.5 SQUARE YARDS.

PLAN "A"

1. NORMALLY, THE USE OF PLAN "A" IS RECOMMENDED. THE WIDE SPACING OF ENTRANCES REDUCES TRAFFIC INTERFERENCE ON THE ACCESS ROAD.

2. WHEN PARKING AREAS ARE OF EXCEPTIONAL LENGTH, CROSS TRAFFIC CONNECTIONS SHOULD BE PROVIDED ON THE BASIS OF ONE FOR ABOUT 40 VEHICLE SPACES OR 360 FEET. HOWEVER, FOR THE SMALLER ODD SHAPED LOTS THIS LIMIT MAY VARY SOMEWHAT TO PROVIDE FOR THE MOST EFFICIENT ARRANGEMENT.

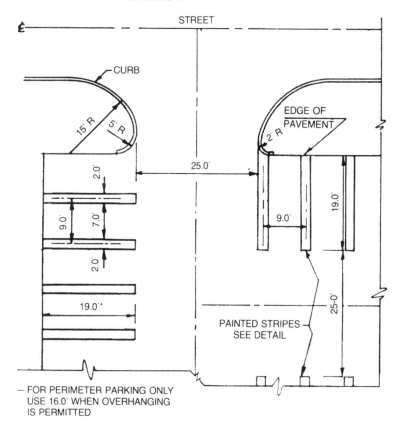

— FOR PERIMETER PARKING ONLY
USE 16.0' WHEN OVERHANGING
IS PERMITTED

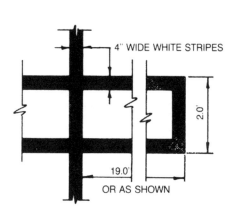

DETAIL OF PAINTED STRIPES

Plate 3b. Off-street parking option B: High density parking for secondary roadway only

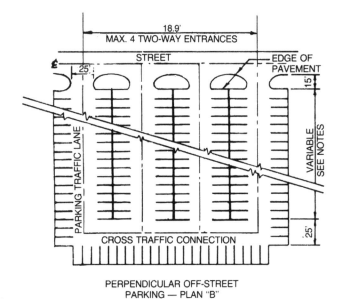

PERPENDICULAR OFF-STREET
PARKING — PLAN "B"

PLAN "B"

1. THERE SHALL BE A MAXIMUM OF FOUR TWO-WAY TRAFFIC LANES.

2. IF ACCESS IS FROM ONE ROAD ONLY, THE MAXIMUM DEPTH OF THE PARKING LOT SHALL BE APPROX. 400 FEET OR 40 VEHICLE SPACES WITH A CROSS TRAFFIC CONNECTION AT THE END OF THE TRAFFIC LANES.

3. WHEN ACCESS TO THE LOT IS FROM MORE THAN ONE ROAD, SEVERAL CROSS TRAFFIC CONNECTIONS WITH APPROX. 40 SPACES BETWEEN THEM MAY BE USED.

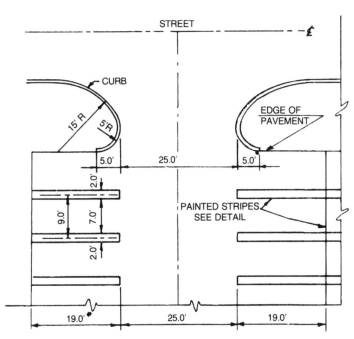

* — FOR PERIMETER PARKING ONLY
USE 16.0' WHEN OVERHANG
IS PERMITTED

Plate 4a. Alternative designs for off-street loading, single-unit truck vehicle

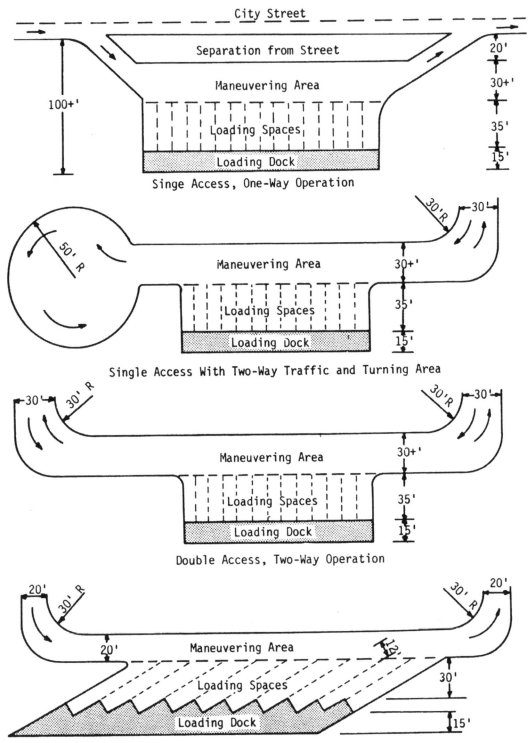

City Street

Separation from Street

Maneuvering Area

Loading Spaces

Loading Dock

100+'

20'

30+'

35'

15'

Singe Access, One-Way Operation

50' R

30'R

30'

Maneuvering Area

Loading Spaces

Loading Dock

30+'

35'

15'

Single Access With Two-Way Traffic and Turning Area

30'

30' R

30'R

30'

Maneuvering Area

Loading Spaces

Loading Dock

30+'

35'

15'

Double Access, Two-Way Operation

20'

30' R

30' R

20'

20'

Maneuvering Area

Loading Spaces

Loading Dock

12'

30'

15'

Single Entrance and Exit, One-Way Operation, Saw-Tooth Loading Bays

Plate 4b. Truck turning radius (AASHTO 1994)

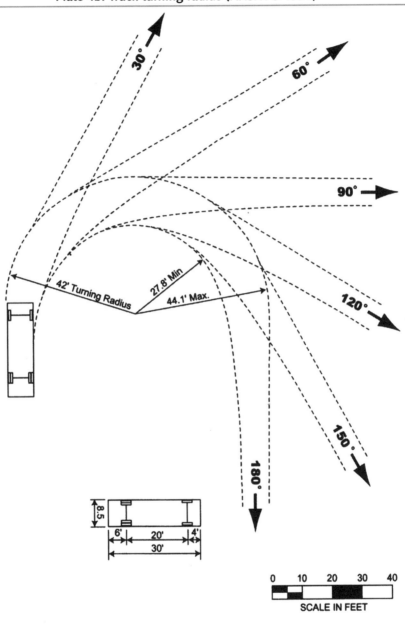

REFERENCES

AASHTO (American Association of State Highway and Transportation Officials), *Policy on Geometric Design of Highways and Streets* (AASHTO Green Book), AASHTO, Washington, 1994.

ATBCB (Architectural and Transportation Barriers Compliance Board), *Americans with Disabilities Act Accessibilities Guidelines for Buildings and Facilities; Final Guidelines,* (ADAAG) 36 CFR Part 1191, July 26, 1991.

ATBCB, *Bulletin #6: Parking,* 1994.

Box, Paul C., "Parking Lot Accident Characteristics," *ITE Journal,* December 1981.

Box, Paul C., "Parking and Terminals," *Traffic Engineering Handbook,* 4th ed., Prentice-Hall, Englewood Cliffs, 1992.

Box, Paul C., "Effect of Single vs. Double Line Parking Stall," *ITE Journal,* May 1994.

Bulletin # 6 (See ATBCB 1994).

Burrage, Robert H., and Edward G. Mogren, *Parking,* Eno Foundation for Highway Traffic Control, Saugatuck, 1957.

Childs, Mark C., *Parking Spaces: A Design, Implementation and Use Manual,* McGraw-Hill, New York, 1999.

Chrest, Anthony P., Mary S. Smith, and Sam Bhuyan, *Parking Structures: Planning, Design, Construction, Maintenance and Repair,* Chapman & Hall, New York, 1996.

Dare, Charles E., "Consideration of Special Purpose Vehicles in Parking Lot Design," *ITE Journal,* May 1985.

Federal Highway Administration, *Commercial Driver Rest and Parking Requirements,* Report no. FHWA-MC-96-0010, 1996.

ITE (Institute of Transportation Engineers), Committee 5D-8, *Guidelines for Parking Facility Location and Design,* Washington, 1990.

ODOT (Oregon's Department of Transportation), *Bicycle Parking Facilities,* 1992.

Ricker, Edmund R., *Traffic Design of Parking Garages,* Eno Foundation for Highway Traffic Control, Westport, 1957.

Stover, Vergil G., and Frank J. Koepke, "End Islands as an Element of Site Design," *ITE Journal,* November 1989.

ULI (Urban Land Institute), *Parking Requirements for Shopping Centers,* 2nd ed., Urban Land Institute, Washington, 1999.

Untermann, Richard K., *Accommodating the Pedestrian: Adapting Towns and Neighborhoods for Walking and Bicycling,* Van Nostrand Reinhold, New York, 1984.

Weant, Robert A., and Herbert S. Levinson, *Parking.* Eno Foundation for Highway Traffic Control, Westport, 1990.

D • SERVICES

D1   **Conveying systems**

D1.1   Elevators and escalators   *Peter R. Smith, Ph.D.*

D2   **Plumbing**

D2.1   Plumbing systems   *Arturo De La Vega*
D2.2   Sanitary waste systems   *Arturo De La Vega*
D2.3   Special plumbing systems   *Arturo De La Vega*

D3   **HVAC systems**

D3.1   HVAC systems for commercial buildings   *Richard Rittelmann and Paul Scanlon, P.E.*
D3.2   Special HVAC equipment   *Catheryn Bobenhausen, CIH, CSP*

D4   **Fire protection**

D4.1   Fire protection sprinkler systems   *Bruce W. Hisley*
D4.2   Special fire protection systems   *Bruce W. Hisley*
D4.3   Fire alarm systems   *Walter Cooper*

D5   **Electrical systems**

D5.1   Communication and security systems   *Walter Cooper and Robert DeGrazio*
D5.2   Electronic system specialties   *Andrew Prager*
D5.3   Lighting   *John D. Bullough*

Peter R. Smith, Ph.D.

Summary

Design principles and criteria are reviewed for planning, sizing, selection, and layout of escalators and elevators, along with mechanical and dimensional details.

Key words

elevators, escalators, Level of Service, gearless elevators, hydraulics, lobbies, moving walkways, universal design

Bradbury Building, Los Angeles, California. 1890.

Elevators and escalators

1 ESCALATORS AND MOVING WALKWAYS

An escalator or moving walk is a conveyor-belt for people. If the rate of arrival is not excessive, each passenger can step on immediately without waiting, be transported to the other end, and step off immediately. Only when the rate of arrival exceeds the transporting capacity is there any need to queue. This advantage of instant service is achieved at a considerable cost in other capabilities. In the usual types of escalators and walkways, these limitations are as follows:

- Because the equipment does not stop, the passenger must accelerate to full speed in the action of stepping on, that is in the length of one step. This effectively limits the speed of the machine to walking pace.

- Movement is linear, with passengers exiting in the order they entered. This means that each machine can only operate between two fixed points, unlike an elevator, which can have many intermediate stops.

- The angle of incline is limited. Therefore any significant vertical rise is accompanied by a far greater horizontal movement, whether this is desired or not. A moving walk (that is, with a surface that does not form steps during its travel), can be built at any angle from horizontal to 15 degrees. For escalators (which do form steps) the angle is normally 30 degrees, and deviations from this are rare.

- Riding on an escalator requires a certain degree of agility and locomotor skill. It is not suitable for a wheelchair. A baby carriage or a small baggage trolley can be carried, with some inconvenience. It presents difficulty for the visually impaired, since it is necessary to observe the arrival of the treads. These disadvantages occur to a lesser degree with a moving walkway.

Each machine operates in only one direction at a time, so that two-way traffic requires two separate escalators or walkways. However, in peak times one can be reversed, so that both operate in the major direction of travel.

Escalators are widely used to transport large numbers of people over a relatively short vertical distance. A single escalator has the same capacity as a large bank of elevators. There is little need for direction signs, since it is obvious where the escalator is going, and the passengers have the benefit of an uninterrupted view during their travel (**Fig. 1**). By contrast, an elevator disappears behind closed doors and the passengers do not see the arrival floor until the doors open.

Escalators are also useful in the planning of a building with a large pedestrian traffic flow, in directing that flow in the desired direction. This principle is used to advantage in the airport terminal building at Charles de Gaulle Airport in Paris. Incoming and outgoing passengers are transported from one side to the other of the donut-shaped building, and also from one floor to another, by a number of escalators that criss-cross the hole in the donut. This is not only quicker but also more foolproof than directing people to go "halfway around and two floors down."

Credits: This article is excerpted from a longer article by the author in Cowan (1991) and is reprinted by permission of the publisher.

Fig. 1. Escalators in multistoried atrium. (Courtesy: ThyssenKrupp Elevators)

Horizontal moving walks are less common, mainly because people are more willing to walk horizontally than they are to walk up or down stairs. If the speed of the moving walk is the same as walking pace, there is no great time advantage in using it. There is the disadvantage that, once on the walk, one is not able to stop and browse until the next exit is reached.

The use of moving walks in buildings is limited to very large horizontal buildings, such as transportation terminals. The advantages of moving walkways include the following:

- Easing long travel distances, as walking is tiring for many people.

- Many passengers are carrying baggage and may be fatigued from a long journey.

- There are definite entry and exit points (such as the terminal lounges at an airport), and little need to stop between them.

- Passengers in a hurry can walk on the moving walkway, thereby doubling their speed.

The treads of a moving walkway travel as an endless belt, returning to the original point by a path immediately under the walkway. Thus they can be installed in sidewalks or other public places with relatively little disruption to other traffic. **Fig. 2** illustrates a walkway in an airport wherein the mechanized journey between terminals is enlivened by a sunlight sculpture that changes colors as one moves past.

Mechanical details of walkways and escalators

Walkways. A moving walkway requires a firm, flat surface to stand on; close mechanical tolerances at the edges and exit point to prevent injury; and moving handrails to provide a means of maintaining balance. It is acceptable to stand on a flat surface that slopes up or down as much as 15 degrees from the horizontal (1 in 3.7), since it is not necessary to walk, and there is a handrail to hold. By way of comparison, ramps within buildings are limited by building codes to a much flatter slope, usually 1 in 10 or 1 in 12.

The surface is formed from individual panels, usually of cast aluminum, hinged together as an endless chain. Outside the United States, some moving walks are built using reinforced-rubber conveyor belting running on closely spaced rollers. The ride is slightly uncomfortable, since the rollers can be felt as one's feet passes over them. There is also some danger of the passengers' feet or clothing being caught against the edges, or at the point of exit.

Escalators. Escalators can be built steeper than moving walks because they form themselves into discrete horizontal steps. The industry standard is 30 degrees from the horizontal (1 in 1.7), although in Europe some escalators are built at 35 degrees inclination. The steps are approximately 14 in (340 mm) deep (front to back) and 8 in (200 mm) high. This is convenient for standing on, but much larger than a normal stairway. When an escalator is stopped, it forms a rather inconvenient stairway.

An escalator has the same requirements as a moving walk, and in addition the risers between the treads must be able to appear and disappear during the travel without trapping clothing or feet. The key to safety at the risers and the exits is the comb system. Both treads and risers have a grooved surface. A comb on the back of the tread engages the grooves in the riser, and a comb on the edge of the floor

Fig. 2. Moving walkway. Miami International Airport.

opening engages the grooves in the tread, so that any loose clothing or footwear is prevented from becoming caught.

In early escalators, the grooves and combs were approximately 2 in (50 mm) wide, which, along with a considerable mechanical clearance, caused some difficulty with small heels, umbrella tips, and children's toes. Modern treads are made of cast aluminum, with small and accurate grooves 4 in (100 mm) wide and minimum clearances.

Escalator treads run on wheels fore and aft, each pair of wheels following a different track. The geometry of the two tracks enables the treads to move either horizontally or along the slope, while maintaining a horizontal surface. They return underneath, thus requiring a considerable depth through the escalator enclosure. Moving walk treads are similar except they simply follow the slope of the walk, without forming risers.

Physical sizes of escalators

Since the speed of escalators is fairly standard, their carrying capacity depends on the width. In the United States and Canada the width is given between the balustrades, while in Europe the tread width is used. The balustrade width is 8 in (200 mm) greater than the tread width, since people are widest at the hips, and there is no point in making the expensive treads and mechanical components wider than necessary.

Common widths are:

– 48 in (1200 mm) between balustrades which fits two people per tread.

– 32 in (800 mm) between balustrades, which takes one person comfortably per tread, and occasionally two.

Escalator speeds and capacities

The "standard" speed for escalators is 90 feet per minute (fpm) (0.45 m/s), measured in the direction of travel. Few people have difficulty getting on at this speed. In public transport applications, the speed may be increased to 120 fpm (0.6 m/s) in peak hours. Experienced commuters who are in a hurry find this satisfactory. After peak hours the speed is reduced, because irregular users and the infirm may otherwise hesitate too long before getting on, thus negating any benefit of the higher speed. Moving walkways can run faster than escalators, mainly because it is easier to step onto a continuous flat surface

than to have to identify a tread. Walkway speeds are commonly 180 fpm (0.9 m/s) if horizontal, reducing to 140 fpm (0.7 m/s) or less for a slope of 15 degrees.

The capacity of an escalator or walkway depends on its speed and the degree of filling of the treads. It has been observed that passengers commonly fill escalators to about half their theoretical maximum capacity, although in some public transport applications the degree of filling is greater. Sometimes (for example, in the London underground) passengers are disciplined to stand on one side of the 48 in escalators so that those in a greater hurry can walk past them on the other side. In this case it is possible to achieve a carrying capacity greater than 100 percent of the theoretical maximum.

Unlike elevators, where the length of travel reduces the performance, the capacity of an escalator (**Table 1**) is independent of its length. (The longer escalator, of course, has more treads and is therefore a "bigger" escalator.)

2 ELEVATORS

Although the escalator is the logical result of mechanizing a stairway, the elevator was actually invented earlier, because it evolved from earlier machines for elevating merchandise by mechanical or animal power. In the early 19th century, elevators were used for freight movement and driven by steam power, first developed in England circa 1835 where it was called the *teagle*. In 1845 Sir William Thompson invented the first hydraulic elevator. In 1852, Elisha Graves Otis invented the safety brake for elevators, exhibited in New York City in 1854, inaugurating the era of vertical transportation in buildings, which in turn contributed to make the 20th-century skyscraper feasible. In 1878, Otis installed the first hydraulic passenger elevator in a 111-ft building in New York City. By 1903, the first gearless traction elevators were installed in the 182-ft Beaver Building in New York, operating at a speed of 500 fpm. The first "autotronic" elevators, operated without attendants, were installed in the Atlantic Refining Building in Dallas in 1950. In 1979, the first fully integrated microcomputer system was incorporated, called "Elevonic 101," designed and developed by the Otis Elevator Company to control the entire elevator operation (Dadras 1995).

The glass-walled elevator has become a popular feature of atrium designs (**Fig. 3**). Experience from such installations has resulted in the requirement of universal design that at least one elevator car be provided without windows for individuals prone to vertigo.

Table 1. Typical carrying capacities of escalators and walkways (Smith 1993)

	Width between Balustrades, in.	Tread Width, mm	Speed, fpm	Speed, m/s	Max. Capacity, Persons/ 5 min.	Nominal Capacity, Persons/ 5 min.
Escalator	32	600	90	0.45	425	170
			120	0.6	560	225
Escalator	48	1000	90	0.45	680	340
			120	0.6	900	450
Walkway	48	1000	180	0.9	1200	600
			140	0.7	900	450

fpm = feet per minute

Fig. 3. Elevators. Hyatt Regency Atrium, Atlanta, Georgia. John Portman, FAIA, Architect. 1964–1967.

The elevator is the "batch process" of transporting people in buildings. In this respect its traffic pattern has much in common with a bus, which has a fixed route but only stops when there are passengers to get on or off.

One advantage that a modern elevator installation has over most other transport systems is that all the landing and car calls are processed by a central computer, which can assess the demands and dispatch the most appropriate car to answer each call. This results in a few calls not being answered in turn, with priority being given to handling the bulk of the traffic more expeditiously.

As noted above, a single escalator does not provide a full service because it only operates in one direction. A single elevator can provide two-way service to a number of floors, but there are reasons why it is unlikely to provide a satisfactory service in most cases. The principal objections to a single elevator are the need for routine servicing, and the possibility of breakdown, either of which leaves the building with no service at all. It is possible for two elevators to be out of service simultaneously, but the probability of this is much lower than with one.

Criteria for design of an elevator installation

Elevators are called on to serve different functions according to the size and nature of the building and their location in it. The most familiar are the passenger elevators, which provide the principal passenger transport between levels in a multistory building, but may have a secondary role for carrying furniture or emergency personnel from time to time. Some elevators are used only occasionally to carry incapacitated people or goods in a low-rise building, or goods or vehicles or hospital patients or hotel guests with baggage. The criteria will therefore depend on the purpose.

An important requirement in providing an elevator service for a building is the location of the elevators (in one or more groups, depending on the size of the building) in relation to access from the entrances and also in relation to the layout of the upper floors. Since elevator shafts are normally vertical, their location on plan imposes a major constraint on every floor of the building. If the building is not of uniform height, at least one elevator group must be located in the tallest portion. The criteria for the design of an elevator group can be summarized as follows:

- *Capacity* to handle the passengers as they arrive, with minimum queuing, expressed as a percentage of the total building population that can be handled in the peak 5-minute period.

- *Frequency* to provide an available car for arriving passengers without excessive waiting, expressed as the average time interval between cars.

- *Car size* to handle the largest items required to be carried, for example, an occasional item of furniture, or a hospital bed with attendant, or a group of hotel guests with their baggage.

- *Speed of total trip,* so that passengers do not perceive the total service as excessively slow.

In addition there are many details that should be considered for the comfort and convenience of the users:

- *A means of easy way finding to the elevator lobby* that serves the user's destination floor. If there is only one zone of elevators, then a simple direction sign will suffice, but it is even better if at least one elevator door is visible from the entrance of the building. If there are multiple zones, then some signing is necessary in addition.

- *Call buttons that are easy to find, and unambiguous* for "up" and "down" calls. The location of the call buttons should encourage passengers to stand in a favorable position to watch all the cars in the group, and to move quickly to whichever comes first. The buttons should indicate that a call has been registered. People will become impatient more quickly if there is no indication that they are being served. If there are several buttons that all serve the same purpose, they must all light up to register a call, otherwise users will be uncertain whether they should press one or all the buttons.

- *Lights or indicators, and an audible indication as well,* to indicate which car is arriving and in which direction it will travel. The indicators should be above head level to be visible above a crowd. When there is a computerized control system, the indicator can be illuminated as soon as the system has decided which car will arrive next. Early indication allows waiting passengers to move in the right direction, and can save a few seconds of loading time each time a car is loaded.

- *Enough first-floor lobby space* for the crowding that is expected at peak capacity. **Fig. 4** depicts standard minimum recommendations. See John J. Fruin "Pedestrian Planning and Design" elsewhere in this volume for more careful estimation of the capacity of waiting and queuing areas based on Level of Service.

- *Universal design standards for at least one set of buttons on the landing,* and floor buttons in the car, should be at a level that can be reached by a person in a wheelchair, or a small child.

Layout of elevator groups

As mentioned, one elevator seldom provides a reliable service. In most cases, a group of three or more is needed to ensure that the waiting interval between them is not too great. To function as a group, the cars must all be close enough that an intending user can take whichever one arrives first. A moderately fast walking speed is 3 fps (0.9 m/s). If the landing doors are to remain open for 4 ss, then an unobstructed person can walk briskly a distance of 12 ft (3.6 m) before they begin to close again. Obviously, all the landing doors should be closer than this to all the waiting passengers, so that no one feels anxious that the doors will close prematurely.

Two or three cars can conveniently be located side by side. There is no need to look over one's shoulder, and they are all close by. Four in a row or two opposite two are both acceptable for a group of four. Five in a row is beginning to be too long a distance to walk. There are some installations of six in a row where the door-open time has had to be increased because of the extended walking distances mentioned above. Increasing the time spent at each landing reduces the performance of the group. Five, six, seven, or eight cars are best located opposite each other.

Grouping more than eight cars should be avoided. With larger numbers of cars, one is not filled before the next arrives, and this causes confusion. The number of people waiting in the lobby becomes excessive. Zoning of elevator groupings serving separate floor groups will provide a better service.

Fig. 5 depicts traction-type elevators, characterized by arrangements of the roping:

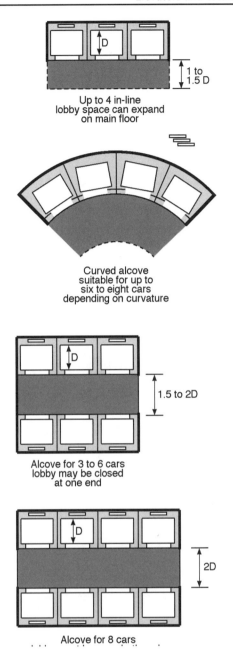

Up to 4 in-line
lobby space can expand
on main floor

Curved alcove
suitable for up to
six to eight cars
depending on curvature

Alcove for 3 to 6 cars
lobby may be closed
at one end

Alcove for 8 cars

Fig. 4. Recommended lobby dimensions for various layouts of elevator groupings. (Smith 1993)

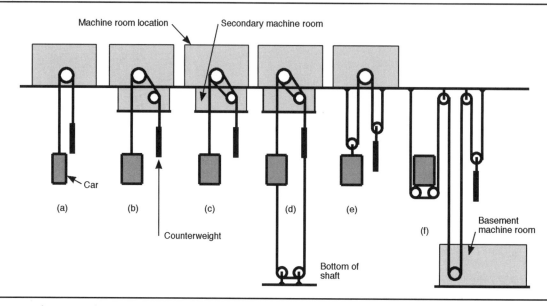

Fig. 5. Various ways of arranging the roping for traction-type elevators. (Smith 1993)

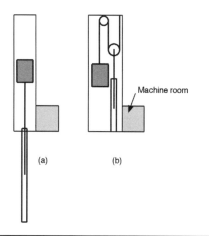

Fig. 6. Hydraulic elevator types. (Smith 1993)

Fig. 7. Gearless elevators can be installed in conventional overhead machine rooms (left) or at the top of the hoistway (top right). Some can be installed lower in the hoistway, reducing overhead space requirements (lower right). Source: Schindler Elevator Corporation.

(a) Single wrap using only the traction sheave. This is only possible for small cars because the distance between car and counterweight centers is limited.

(b) Single wrap with divertor sheave. Allows more freedom in locating the counterweight.

(c) Double-wrap. The same as (b), except that an extra wrap of the ropes gives more reliable traction.

(d) Compensator ropes are added in tall buildings. The lower ropes are merely moving ballast to compensate for the weight of the moving hoist ropes.

(e) 2:1 roping. The ropes move twice as fast as the car. This allows a gearless machine to be used on a slower car than would otherwise be feasible.

(f) Underslung car. The machine room can be located in the basement, to reduce the height needed at the top of the building.

Fig. 6 illustrates the hydraulic elevator alternatives:

(a) with a one-piece or telescopic ram beneath the car. The ram itself provides the overspeed and overtravel protection.

(b) with the ram in the shaft, using a machine chain or rope to operate the car itself. Normal safety devices are needed as with any rope-operated elevator.

Gearless Elevators

A new generation of elevators utilize a number of innovations to provide gearless permanent-magnet motors, and variable-speed, variable-frequency drives. These small motors can be mounted directly in the elevator hoistway, eliminating the need for an overhead penthouse (traction elevators) or a ground-floor machine room (hydraulic elevators) (**Fig. 7**). The smaller motors are easier to install, require less power, and promise lower operational cost and a smoother, quieter ride (Malin 2004). Selected characteristics of recently introduced models of nonhydraulic elevators are shown in Table 2.

Table 2. Selected Characteristics of Nonhydraulic Elevators. (source: Malin, 2004)

COMPANY	PRODUCT	CAPACITY lb (kg)	MAX. TRAVEL ft (m)	MAX. STOPS	SPEED fpm (m/s)	MIN. FLOORS TO COMPETE*	COMMENTS
KONE 800-956-5663 www.kone.com	MonoSpace	4,000 (1,800)	230 (70)	30	350 (1.8)	7	Larger capacities available in nonpassenger models
	EcoSpace	2,500 (1,100)	60 (18)	7	150 (0.8)	4	Fits in a smaller hoistway than most non-hydraulic elevators
OTIS 860-676-5400 www.otis.com	Gen2	4,000 (1,800)	300 (90)	30	350 (1.8)	6	Larger capacities available in nonpassenger models; uses steel-core polyurethane belts instead of steel ropes
THYSSENKRUPP 877-230-0303 www.thyssenkrupp elevator.com	ISIS	3,500 (1,600)	75 (23)	7	200 (1.0)	2	Motor mounts under elevator cab; uses aramid ropes instead of steel
	ISIS 2	5,000 (2,300)	300 (90)	30	500 (2.5)	·	Uses aramid ropes instead of steel
SCHINDLER 973-397-6500 www.us.schindler.com	400A	3,500 (1,600)	200 (60)	20	250 (1.3)	6	Models with more capacity and reach due later in 2004
FUJITEC 513-933-5560 www.fujitecamerica.com	Talon	3,500 (1,600)	190 (60)	24	350 (1.8)	7	Uses innovative belt drive with conventional steel ropes
MITSUBISHI 714-220-4700 www.mitsubishi-elevator.com	Elenessa	3,500 (1,600)	230 (70)	30	350 (1.8)	·	Not currently available in North America

*Minimum # of floors at which cost-competitive with a hydraulic elevator, according to manufacturer   Compiled from manufacturers' literature and interviews.

Table 3. Approximate sizes and ratings of elevator cars (Smith 1993)

Capacity		Passengers		Inside, W x D		Shaft, W x D	
		Max.	Average	in.	mm	in.	mm
2000	900	12	10	68 x 51	1700 x 1300	89 x 83	2200 x 2100
2500	1150	16	13	82 x 51	2100 x 1300	102 x 83	2550 x 2100
3000	1350	20	16	82 x 55	2100 x 1400	102 x 88	2550 x 2200
3500	1600	24	19	82 x 66	2100 x 1650	102 x 96	2550 x 2400
4000	1800	28	22	92 x 66	2300 x 1650	114 x 96	2850 x 2400

Tables 3 and 4 enumerate the planning criteria for elevator design and selection based upon building type and capacity. **Plates 1** to **5** illustrate various details to guide design dimensioning of elevators and escalators. ■

REFERENCES

Dadras, Aly S., *Electric Systems for Architects*, McGraw-Hill, New York, 1995.

Mailin, N., "The Elevator Revolution," *Environmental Building News*, August 2004.

Smith, Peter R., "The Movement of People and Goods," in Henry J. Cowan, ed., *Handbook of Architectural Technology*, Van Nostrand Reinhold, New York, 1991.

Table 4. Design of parameters for elevator selection

$$P = F - F\left(1 - \frac{1}{F}\right)^C$$

where P = probable number of stops
F = number of floors served above ground
C = capacity of car on average trip (taken as no more than 80 percent of the maximum number of passengers)

Plate 1

By SYSKA AND HENNESSY, INC., *Consulting Engineers*

Electric traction elevator
Passenger service
Geared machine
Capacity: 2,000 to 4,000 lbs
Speed: 200 to 350 fpm

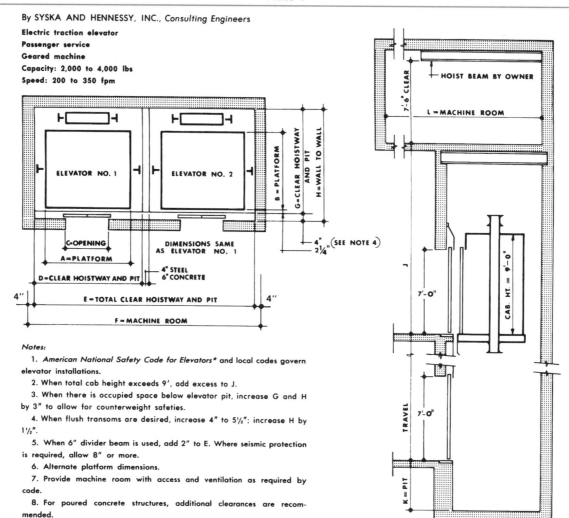

Notes:

1. *American National Safety Code for Elevators** and local codes govern elevator installations.

2. When total cab height exceeds 9', add excess to J.

3. When there is occupied space below elevator pit, increase G and H by 3" to allow for counterweight safeties.

4. When flush transoms are desired, increase 4" to 5½"; increase H by 1½".

5. When 6" divider beam is used, add 2" to E. Where seismic protection is required, allow 8" or more.

6. Alternate platform dimensions.

7. Provide machine room with access and ventilation as required by code.

8. For poured concrete structures, additional clearances are recommended.

American National Safety Code for Elevators, Dumbwaiters, Escalators, and Moving Walks, ANSI A17.1-1978

Capacity, lb	Speed, fpm	Dimensions										
		A	B	C	D	E	F	G	H	J	K	L
2,000	200	6'-4"	4'-5"	3'-0"	7'-8"	15'-8"	16'-4"	5'-9"	6'-1"	16'-0"	5'-0"	12'-6"
	300									17'-0"	5'-6"	12'-6"
	350									17'-0"	6'-0"	12'-6"
2,500	200	7'-0"	5'-0"	3'-6"	8'-4"	17'-0"	17'-8"	6'-4"	6'-8"	16'-0"	5'-0"	12'-6"
	300									17'-0"	5'-6"	12'-6"
	350									17'-6"	6'-0"	12'-6"
3,000	200	7'-0"	5'-6"	3'-6"	8'-4"	17'-0"	17'-8"	6'-10"	7'-2"	16'-0"	5'-0"	12'-6"
	300									17'-0"	6'-8"	12'-6"
	350									17'-6"	7'-6"	13'-0"
3,500 (Note 6)	200	7'-0"	6'-2"	3'-6"	8'-4"	17'-0"	17'-8"	7'-6"	7'-10"	16'-6"	5'-0"	12'-6"
	300									17'-0"	6'-9"	13'-0"
	350									17'-6"	7'-6"	14'-0"
3,500	200	8'-0"	5'-6"	4'-0"	9'-4"	19'-0"	19'-8"	6'-10"	7'-2"	16'-6"	5'-0"	13'-6"
	300									17'-0"	6'-9"	13'-0"
	350									17'-6"	7'-6"	14'-0"
4,000	200	8'-0"	6'-2"	4'-0"	9'-4"	19'-0"	19'-8"	7'-6"	7'-10"	16'-9"	5'-2"	13'-6"
	300									18'-0"	6'-9"	13'-6"
	350									18'-6"	7'-6"	14'-0"

Plate 2

Hydraulic elevator
Passenger and hospital service
Capacity: 2,000 to 4,000 lbs (passenger)
         4,000 to 5,000 lbs (hospital)
Speed: 50 to 150 fpm

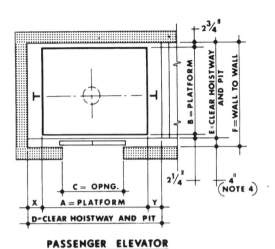

PASSENGER ELEVATOR

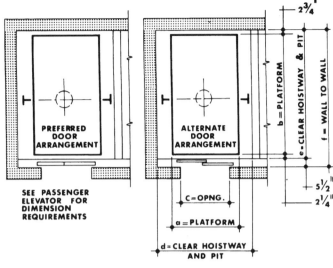

SEE PASSENGER ELEVATOR FOR DIMENSION REQUIREMENTS

HOSPITAL TYPE ELEVATOR

Notes:

1. *American National Safety Code for Elevators* and local codes govern elevator installation.

2. For vertical dimensions, see sectional view of hydraulic freight service elevator, sheet 7.

3. When total cab height exceeds 9′, add excess to H.

4. When flush transoms are desired, increase 4″ to 5½″; increase F by 1½″.

5. Alternate platform dimensions.

6. Provide machine room with access and ventilation as required by code.

7. Where seismic protection is required, allow 8″ or more for divider beam.

Passenger elevator dimensions

Capacity, lb	A	B	C	D	E	F	X	Y	G	H	J
2,000	6′-4″	4′-5″	3′-0″	7′-8″	4′-10″	5′-2″					
2,500	7′-0″	5′-0″	3′-6″	8′-4″	5′-5″	5′-9″					
3,000	7′-0″	5′-6″	3′-6″	8′-4″	5′-11″	6′-3″	8″	8″	7′-0″	13′-0″	4′-6″
3,500											
Note 5	7′-0″	6′-2″	3′-6″	8′-4″	6′-7″	6′-11″					
3,500	8′-0″	5′-6″	4′-0″	9′-4″	5′-11″	6′-3″					
4,000	8′-0″	6′-2″	4′-0″	9′-4″	6′-7″	6′-11″					

Hospital type elevator dimensions, preferred door arrangement

Capacity lb	A	B	C	D	E	F	X	Y	G	H	J
4,000	5′-8″	8′-8″	4′-0″	8′-10″	9′-1″	9′-5″	1′-7″	1′-7″			4′-6″
4,500	6′-0″	9′-0″	4′-0″	8′-10″	9′-5″	9′-9″	1′-5″	1′-5″	7′-0″	13′-0″	4′-6″
5,000	6′-0″	9′-6″	4′-0″	8′-10″	9′-5″	9′-9″	1′-2″	1′-2″			5′-0″

Hospital type elevator dimensions, alternate door arrangement

Capacity lb	a	b	c	d	e	f	x	y	g	h	j
4,000	5′-8″	8′-8″	4′-0″	7′-7″	9′-1″	9′-6½″	1′-3″				4′-6″
4,500	6′-0″	9′-0″	4′-0″	7′-4″	9′-5″	9′-10½″	8″	8″	7′-0″	13′-0″	4′-6″
5,000	6′-0″	9′-6″	4′-3″	7′-10″	9′-5″	10′-4½″	8″				5′-0″

Plate 3

Hydraulic elevator
Freight service
Capacity: 2,000 to 10,000 lbs
Speed: 50 to 150 fpm

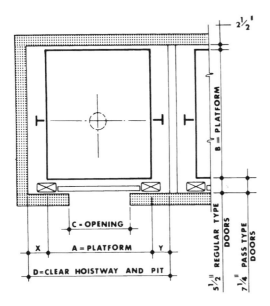

FREIGHT ELEVATOR

Notes:

1. *American National Safety Code for Elevators* and local codes govern elevator installation.

2. Dimensions provided are based on class A loading for power truck loading and/or other special loadings (Classes B, C-1, C-2, C-3) see code requirements.

3. Provide a machine room of approx. 9 x 11 x 7 ft high for a single elevator. Larger area is required when two or more power units are used or for two (2) elevators with a common machine room. Machine room can be located remote from shaft, preferably on the lowest level served. Provide machine room with access and ventilation as required by code.

4. When door height exceeds 8 ft, add excess to H.

5. See door detail sheet for vertical biparting door requirements.

6. A waterproof outer casing is recommended. It is required when water condition is known to exist.

Capacity, lb	Dimensions								
	A	B	C	D	X	Y	G	H	J
2,000	4'-4"	5'-6"	4'-0"	6'-2"					
3,000	5'-4"	6'-6"	5'-0"	7'-2"					4'-6"
4,000	6'-4"	7'-6"	6'-0"	8'-2"					
5,000	7'-4"	8'-0"	7'-0"	9'-2"	11"	11"	8'-0"	15'-0"	
6,000	8'-4"	8'-0"	8'-0"	10'-2"					5'-0"
8,000	8'-4"	10'-6"	8'-0"	10'-2"					
10,000	8'-4"	12'-6"	8'-0"	10'-2"					5'-6"

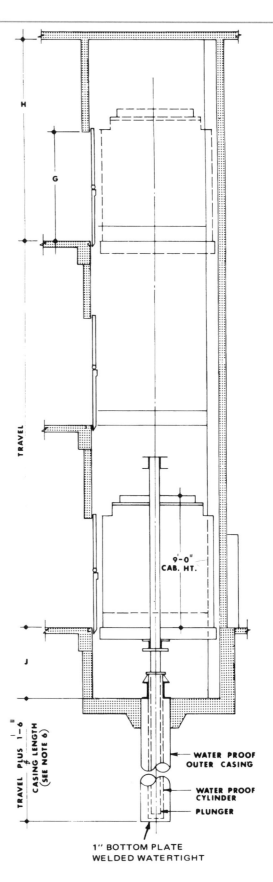

Plate 4

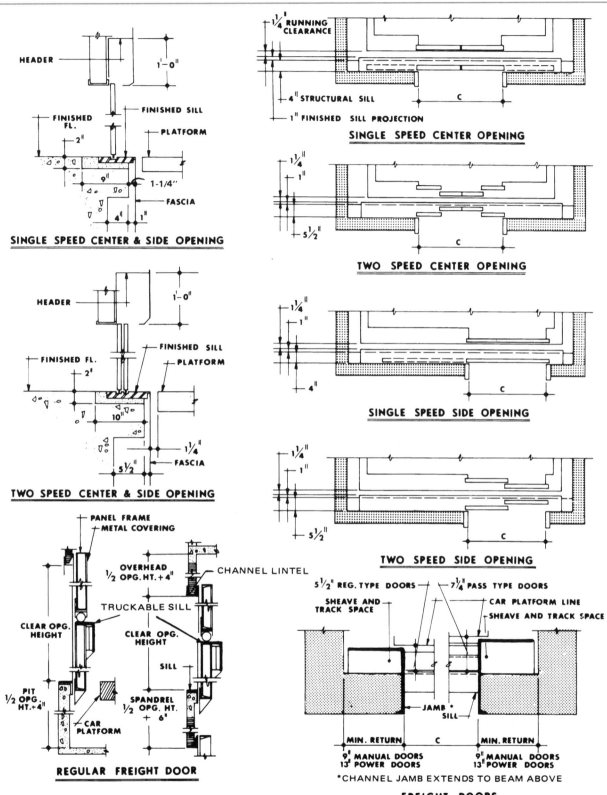

SINGLE SPEED CENTER & SIDE OPENING

TWO SPEED CENTER & SIDE OPENING

REGULAR FREIGHT DOOR

SINGLE SPEED CENTER OPENING

TWO SPEED CENTER OPENING

SINGLE SPEED SIDE OPENING

TWO SPEED SIDE OPENING

FREIGHT DOORS

NOTE:
FRONT WALLS SHOULD BE LEFT OUT UNTIL ENTRANCES ARE SET IN PLACE, OR MINIMUM ROUGH OPENING
PROVIDED 12" WIDER AND 6" HIGHER THAN DOORWAY SIZE.

Plate 5

By SYSKA AND HENNESSY, INC., *Consulting Engineers*

See American National Safety Code for Elevators, Dumbwaiters, Escalators, Moving Walks, ANSI A17.1-1978.

Electric stairway
Angle of incline: 30 deg
Speed: 90 or 120 fpm
Width: 32 or 48 in.

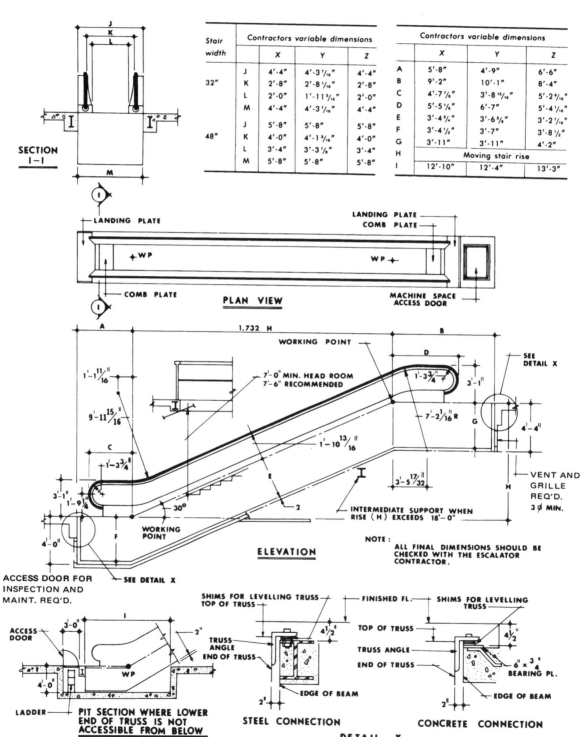

Stair width		Contractors variable dimensions		
		X	Y	Z
32"	J	4'-4"	4'-3 7/16"	4'-4"
	K	2'-8"	2'-8 1/16"	2'-8"
	L	2'-0"	1'-11 5/16"	2'-0"
	M	4'-4"	4'-3 7/16"	4'-4"
48"	J	5'-8"	5'-8"	5'-8"
	K	4'-0"	4'-1 3/16"	4'-0"
	L	3'-4"	3'-3 7/8"	3'-4"
	M	5'-8"	5'-8"	5'-8"

	Contractors variable dimensions		
	X	Y	Z
A	5'-8"	4'-9"	6'-6"
B	9'-2"	10'-1"	8'-4"
C	4'-7 7/8"	3'-8 15/16"	5'-2 9/16"
D	5'-5 1/8"	6'-7"	5'-4 1/16"
E	3'-4 3/4"	3'-6 3/4"	3'-2 1/16"
F	3'-4 1/2"	3'-7"	3'-8 1/2"
G	3'-11"	3'-11"	4'-2"
H	Moving stair rise		
I	12'-10"	12'-4"	13'-3"

SECTION I—I

LANDING PLATE
LANDING PLATE
COMB PLATE
WP
WP
COMB PLATE
MACHINE SPACE ACCESS DOOR

PLAN VIEW

1.732 H
WORKING POINT
SEE DETAIL X
1'-1 11/16"
7'-0" MIN. HEAD ROOM
7'-6" RECOMMENDED
1'-3 3/4"
3'-1"
9'-11 15/16"
7'-2 1/16" R
G
C
1'-10 13/16"
1'-3 3/4"
4'-4"
E
3'-1"
3'-5 17/32"
H
1'-9 1/4"
30°
2
VENT AND GRILLE REQ'D. 3 ⌀ MIN.
WORKING POINT
INTERMEDIATE SUPPORT WHEN RISE (H) EXCEEDS 18'-0"
4'-0"
F

ELEVATION

NOTE:
ALL FINAL DIMENSIONS SHOULD BE CHECKED WITH THE ESCALATOR CONTRACTOR.

ACCESS DOOR FOR INSPECTION AND MAINT. REQ'D.
SEE DETAIL X

ACCESS DOOR
3'-0"
2"
TRUSS ANGLE END OF TRUSS
WP
4'-0"
LADDER
PIT SECTION WHERE LOWER END OF TRUSS IS NOT ACCESSIBLE FROM BELOW

SHIMS FOR LEVELLING TRUSS TOP OF TRUSS
FINISHED FL.
SHIMS FOR LEVELLING TRUSS
TOP OF TRUSS
4 1/2"
TRUSS ANGLE
END OF TRUSS
2"
EDGE OF BEAM
STEEL CONNECTION

TOP OF TRUSS
4 1/2"
TRUSS ANGLE
END OF TRUSS
6" x 3/4" BEARING PL.
EDGE OF BEAM
2"
CONCRETE CONNECTION

DETAIL X

Arturo De La Vega

Summary

Every structure designed for human occupancy must be supplied with potable water. Potable water systems and piping distribution are sized according to codes and occupancy, related to fixture unit count or minimum water flow demand. System design includes hot and cold water lines, domestic hot water systems, pressure and flow, and tank capacities. Fixtures choices include a variety of dimensional, accessibility, finishes, and energy (water) conservation options. Water supply and storage cisterns, including rainwater harvesting, are briefly discussed and illustrated.

Key words

cistern, cold and hot water lines, pipe layouts, plumbing fixtures, pressure and flow, pump house, rainwater harvesting, tank capacity, valves, well

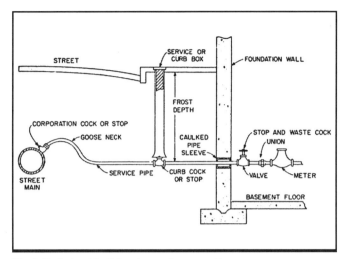

Fig. 1. Typical residential water service connection.

Plumbing systems

1 WATER SUPPLY AND DISTRIBUTION SYSTEMS

Water supply

Water supply may be provided by a public or private utility through street service (**Fig. 1**) or by an on-site well. When investigation indicates sufficient capacity, or simply as back-up supply, water may also be collected from ground or building surface sources, spring fed or rainwater collected (illustrated in the Plates at the end of this article). If used for potable water supply, ground- and building-surface–source water may be prohibited by local codes and in any case is subject to diligent sanitary provisions. As a standard minimum precaution, wells of any depth are normally not located within 50 ft (15 m) of a sewer or septic tank or within 100 ft (30 m) of a septic field.

Water distribution layouts

Pipes for hot and cold water are sized for permanently clean interior bores that are free of obstruction. It is assumed that the supply water will be relatively soft (low calcium carbonate), so that no precipitated coating will form within pipe walls, which would reduce inside pipe diameters and prevent the free flow of water. In localities where the water contains a concentration of hardness (higher levels of calcium carbonate) sufficient to cause even a slight precipitation in cold water lines, or if the water quality does not meet the health authority requirements or taste standards for human tolerance, the main line feeding the building must be filtered through a water softener. Water softeners are used to eliminate calcium and magnesium from the potable water through a process called ion exchange.

For design purposes, an architect should understand the principles of water distribution and piping system layout in order to adequately provide necessary clearances and accessible spaces for horizontal and vertical runs of piping. The piping will include insulation to prevent condensation (and resulting dripping and staining), design of proper support, hanging, and provisions for plumbing servicing and maintenance. Like any system design, the best approach is to provide chases for adequately run pipe risers and horizontal runs (typically in ceiling spaces). Water piping must run as direct as possible and free of unnecessary turns, which may unnecessarily reduce flow and create locations for blockage. Access panels must be provided in pipe chases and in inaccessible ceiling spaces for the purpose of service and maintenance where valves and other devices are located.

The values given in **Tables 1** to **3** are for water consumption evaluation and fixture unit count for water supply systems.

Cold water lines

- Taps

- Generally taps from the street water main are ¾ in (20 cm) for single-family residences containing a total amount of fixtures equivalent to those commonly found in three bathrooms, a kitchen, and laundry.

- Pipe may vary in size depending on the fixture unit count or demand, usually represented by gallons per minute (gpm) or litres/second (l/s). For pipe sizing purposes a maximum 7 fps water velocity is recommended.

- Codes

- Most regional plumbing codes in the United States require pressure-reducing valves where street main pressure exceeds 80 psi (550 kPa).

- An approved pressure-reducing valve should be installed in the water service pipe near the entrance of the water service pipe into the structure or wherever pressure exceeds the limit inside the structure, except where the water feeds a water pressure booster.

- The pressure at any fixture normally should not exceed 80 psi (550 kPa) under no-flow conditions.

- Drain valves. A drain valve should be installed in the lowest branch of the basement so that the entire system can be completely drained.

- Main shutoff valve: A main shutoff valve should be provided in each water supply pipe at each of the following locations:

- On the street side near the curb.

- At the entrance into the structure.

- On the discharge side of the water meter.

- On the base of every riser.

- At the supply of any equipment.

- At the connection to any fixture.

- Water hammer arresters

- Water hammer arresters or shock absorbers will prevent water hammering throughout the piping system. They are typically located after the first fixture of a group of fixtures.

- Arrestor devices are also recommended where quick-closing valves are utilized.

- Water softeners

- Water softeners are mechanical appliances connected to the water supply system. All water softeners use the same operating principles and are available in various sizes and types, all of which require a mineral tank and brine tank that is filled with common salt for softened water regeneration.

- Regeneration can be accomplished manually or automatically; the most popular water softeners are of automatic regeneration and generally controlled by an electric timer that controls the softening process. A floor drain for waste water is essential if water softening equipment is provided.

- Pipe insulation

- Insulation of water lines is necessary to prevent undesirable condensation from cold water lines and heat loss in the hot and recirculating water lines.

Table 1. Design criteria for daily water requirements based on building occupancy
Source: International Plumbing Code (2003)

Type of occupancy	Minimum quantity of water per person per day in gallons (or as indicated)
Small dwelling and cottages with seasonal occupancy	50
Single family dwellings	75
Multiple family dwellings (apartments)	60
Rooming houses	40
Boarding houses	50
Additional kitchen usage for nonresident boarders	10
Hotels without private baths	50
Hotels with private baths (2 persons per room)	60
Restaurants (toilet and kitchen usage per patron)	7 to 10
Restaurants (kitchen usage per meal served)	2 1/2 to 3
Additional for bars and cocktail lounges	2
Tourist camps or trailer parks with central bathhouse	35
Tourist camps or mobile home parks with individual bath units	50
Resort camps (night and day) with limited plumbing	50
Luxury camps	100 to 150
Work or construction camps (semipermanent)	50
Camp (with complete plumbing)	45 (Ind.w.s.)
Camp (with flush toilets, no showers)	25 (Ind.w.s.)
Day camp (no meals served)	15
Day schools, without cafeteria, gymnasiums, or showers	15
Day schools with cafeterias, but no gymnasiums or showers	20
Day schools with cafeterias, gymnasiums and showers	25
Boarding schools	75 to 100
Day workers at schools and offices (per shift)	15
Hospitals (per bed)	150-250
Institutions other than hospitals (per bed)	75 to 125
Factories (gallons per person per shift, exclusive of industrial wastes)	15 to 35
Picnic parks [toilet usage only (gallons per picnicker)]	5
Picnic parks with bathhouses, showers and flush toilets	10
Swimming pools and bathhouses	10
Luxury residences and estates	100 to 150
Country clubs (per resident member)	100
Country clubs (per nonresident member)	25
Motel (per bed space)	40
Motels with bath, toilet, and kitchen range	50
Drive-in theaters (per car space)	5
Movie theaters (per auditorium seat)	5
Airports (per passenger)	3 to 5
Self-service laundries (gallons per wash, i.e., per customer)	50
Stores (per toilet room)	400
Service stations (per vehicle serviced)	10

Hot water lines

A simple form of circulation can be accomplished by connecting the hot water pipe supply after the last fixture is connected to a recirculating line as a simple loop below the floor of the highest level.

Circulation serves to prevent waste of water and provides the added benefit of instantaneous hot water availability. The type of circulating hot water distribution shown is adaptable to large residences. A more elaborated system would require individual supply and return risers to serve superimposed fixtures or bathrooms.

Hot water lines should also be insulated to avoid waste of energy due to heat loss, and for this purpose typically ½ to 1 in (1.25 to 2.5 cm) fiberglass insulation is used. Shutoff valves are also required in the same fashion as indicated for cold water lines. The water heater detail diagram shown will guide the designer in where to locate check valves, recirculating pump, and relief valve.

Hot water system size

The variety of uses for domestic hot water and different lifestyles make it difficult to determine system requirements and sizing. The designer should refer to the ASHRAE Handbook, the ASPE Fundamentals of Plumbing Design, and manufacturers' catalogs.

Besides the sizing of the system, it is important to select the most efficient and economical energy source. Fuel choice will depend on local energy costs and availability. The most common sources include:

– gas fired

– oil fired

– electric (see **Fig. 2**)

– steam generated

– solar water heaters.

Other factors to be considered at the beginning of the design include:

– storage tank requirements.

– space availability.

– peak instantaneous demand.

– water temperature requirements.

– water treatment.

Table 4 provides a guide for hot water demand requirements based on the hourly hot water consumption per fixture. Special consideration should be given to the following types of facilities that have high hot-water demand, such as motels, hospitals, nursing homes, laboratories, and food service establishments.

The probable maximum demand is the result of the hourly hot water demand times the demand factor (line 19 in Table 4). The storage tank capacity is the result of probable maximum demand times the storage capacity factor (line 20 in Table 4).

Table 2. Supply fixture unit values for various plumbing fixtures
Source: International Plumbing Code (2003)

Fixture or group[a]	Type of supply control	Hot	Cold	Total[b]
		Supply fixture unit values		
Bathroom group	Flush tank	3	4.5	6
Bathroom group	Flush valve	3	6	8
Bathtub	Faucet	1.5	1.5	2
Bidet	Faucet	1.5	1.5	2
Combination fixture	Faucet	2	2	3
Kitchen sink	Faucet	1.5	1.5	2
Laundry tray	Faucet	2	2	3
Lavatory	Faucet	1.5	1.5	2
Pedestal urinal	Flush valve		10	10
Restaurant sink	Faucet	3	3	4
Service sink	Faucet	1.5	1.5	2
Shower head	Mixing valve	3	3	4
Stall or wall urinal	Flush tank		3	3
Stall or wall urinal	Flush valve		5	5
Water closet	Flush tank		5	5
Water closet	Flush valve		10	10

Note a. For fixtures not listed, factors may be assumed by comparing the fixture to a listed one using water in similar quantities and at similar rates. Note b. For fixtures with both hot and cold water supplies, the weights for maximum separate demands may be taken as three fourths of the total supply fixture unit value.

Table 3. Water distribution system design criteria required capacities at fixture supply pipe outlets
Source: International Plumbing Code (2003)

Fixture supply outlet serving	Flow rate[b] (gpm)	Flow pressure[b] (psi)
Bathtub	4	8
Bidet	2	4
Combination fixture	4	8
Dishwasher, residential	2.75	8
Drinking fountain	0.75	8
Laundry tray	4	8
Lavatory	2	8
Shower	3	8
Shower, temperature controlled	3	20
Sillcock, hose bibb	5	8
Sink, residential	2.5	8
Sink, service	3	8
Urinal, valve	15	15
Water closet, blow out, flushometer valve	35	25
Water closet, flushometer tank	1.6	8
Water closet, tank, close coupled	3	8
Water closet, tank, one piece	6	20
Water closet, siphonic, flushometer valve	25	15

Note b. 1 pound per square inch = 6.894 kPa: 1 gallon per minute = 3.785

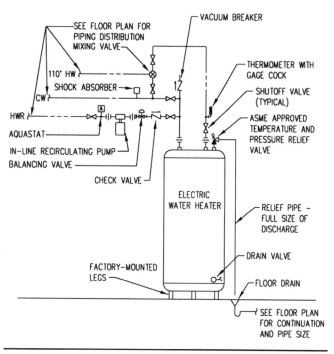

Fig. 2. Electric hot water generator detail. Note: Pipe sizes vary per flow requirements.

An efficiency factor is an important consideration. For example, gas water heaters can be expected to have an efficiency factor of 75 to 90 percent. Verification from manufacturers' data and equipment performance results reported in current literature is necessary.

Example: Hospital Facility

	Qty.		gph		Subtotal
Showers	20	×	75	=	1500
Lavatories	10	×	6	=	60
Laundry Tubs	10	×	28	=	280
Washers	18	×	28	=	504

– Possible maximum demand = 2344 gph

– Probable maximum demand = 2344 × 0.25 = 586 gph

– Heater or coil capacity 586 gph recovery

– Storage tank capacity 586 × 0.60 = 352 gal

Recovery of the unit and storage tank can be interpolated to balance or increase the capacity of the unit, based on space availability and minimum code requirements.

Table 4. Hot water demand per fixture for various types of buildings.
Gallons of water per hour per fixture, calculated at a final temperature of 140F (60°C)
Source: ASHRAE Systems and Equipment Handbook. (1995)

	Apartment House	Club	Gym- nasium	Hospital	Industrial Hotel	Office Plant	Private Building	Residence	School	YMCA
1. Basins, private lavatory	2 (7.6)	2 (7.6)	2 (7.6)	2 (7.6)	2 (7.6)	2 (7.6)	2 (7.6)	2 (7.6)	2 (7.6)	2 (7.6)
2. Basins, public lavatory	4 (15.2)	6 (22.7)	8 (30.3)	6 (22.7)	8 (30.3)	12 (45.5)	6 (22.7)	—	15 (56.8)	8 (30.3)
3. Bathtubs	20 (75.8)	20 (75.8)	30 (113.7)	20 (75.8)	20 (75.8)	—	—	20 (75.8)	—	30 (113.7)
4. Dishwashers[a]	15 (56.8)	50-150 (189.5-568.5)	—	50-150 (189.5-568.5)	50-200 (189.5-758)	20-100 (75.8-379)	—	15 (56.8)	20-100 (75.8-379)	20-100 (75.8-379)
5. Foot basins	3 (11.4)	3 (11.4)	12 (45.5)	3 (11.4)	3 (11.4)	12 (45.5)	—	3 (11.4)	3 (11.4)	12 (45.5)
6. Kitchen sink	10 (37.9)	20 (75.8)	—	30 (113.7)	20 (75.8)	20 (75.8)	10 (37.9)	20 (75.8)	20 (75.8)	
7. Laundry, stationary tubs	20 (75.8)	28 (106.1)	—	28 (106.1)	28 (106.1)	—	—	20 (75.8)	—	28 (106.1)
8. Pantry sink	5 (18.9)	10 (37.9)	—	10 (37.9)	10 (37.9)	—	10 (37.9)	5 (18.9)	10 (37.9)	10 (37.9)
9. Showers	30 (113.7)	150 (568.5)	225 (852.7)	30 (113.7)	30 (113.7)	225 (852.7)	225 (852.7)			
10. Service sink	20 (75.8)	20 (75.8)	—	20 (75.8)	30 (113.7)	20 (75.8)	20 (75.8)	15 (56.8)	20 (75.8)	20 (75.8)
11. Hydrotherapeutic showers				400 (1516.0)						
12. Hubbard baths				600 (2274.0)						
13. Leg baths				100 (379.0)						
14. Arm baths				35 (132.6)						
15. Sitz baths				30 (113.7)						
16. Continuous-flow baths				165 (625.4)						
17. Circular wash sinks				20 (75.8)	20 (75.8)	30 (113.7)	20 (75.8)		30 (113.7)	
18. Semicircular wash sinks				10 (37.9)	10 (37.9)	15 (56.8)	10 (37.9)		15 (56.8)	
19. DEMAND FACTOR	0.30	0.30	0.40	0.25	0.25	0.40	0.30	0.40	0.40	
20. STORAGE CAPACITY FACTOR[b]	1.25	0.90	1.00	0.60	0.80	1.00	2.00	0.70	1.00	1.00

[a] Dishwasher requirements should be taken from this table or from manufacturer's data for the model to be used, if this is known.

[b] Ratio of storage tank capacity to probable maximum demand/h. Storage capacity may be reduced where an unlimited supply of steam is available from a central street steam system or large boiler plant.

Pressure and flow

– Plumbing fixtures require certain pressure and flow to function properly. Street pressure is normally enough to satisfy the requirements of residences and two- to five-story buildings.

– An engineer should verify the existing pressure and flow characteristics from city authorities. For structures in excess of five stories the engineer should select any of the following means to provide adequate pressure and flow to the plumbing fixtures within the structure:

• Booster pumps can be a duplex system or multiple systems supplying different zones. A structure taller than five stories should be divided in zones of not more than 12 stories. Booster systems can be complemented with storage tanks at the highest level of each zone.

• Another alternative for pressuring the system is to provide a pneumatic booster system with the following components: booster pump, compressor, pneumatic tank, valves, and controllers.

• Tanks used in booster systems have also been used for the dual purpose of water supply and as a reserve for fire protection.

Booster pumps

When there is insufficient pressure in the water supply system, a duplex or multiple booster pump system must be provided. If minimum quantities are not satisfied the system could be supplemented by an elevated tank.

Booster pumps with hydroneumatic tanks are commonly specified to allow major operating energy savings by dividing peak flow in several capacity ranges. Use a small lead pump for low flows and one or more lag pumps for higher flows, or add a hydroneumatic tank that allows complete pump shutdown while maintaining constant system pressure under minimum or no flow conditions. Booster package systems are generally provided with pumps, tanks, valves, and control panels.

Tank capacity

The required capacity of a tank varies with the capacity and running time of the structure or fill pumps. A half-hour supply of domestic water is generally sufficient if pump capacity is equal to the hourly load. Water consumption figures typical of commercial office building usage can be used as a reference guide to determine tank and pump capacities, as follows:

Building Type	Gal. per hour/person
Commercial no air-conditioning	3.8
Commercial with air-conditioning	7.2–9

For example, assume that a commercial office building has an occupancy of 4500:

4500 times 3.8 gallons per hour per person = 17,100 gal per hour

Tank should have a half-hour supply = 8550 gal

Pump should have a one-hour supply = 17,100 gal per hour

The pump capacity will be 285 gpm (18 l/s).

Piping materials

Available water service piping materials include the following:

– Acrylonitrile butadiene (ABS plastic pipe).

– Brass pipe.

– Copper or copper-alloy pipe.

– Copper or copper-alloy tubing (Type K, WK, L, WL, M, or WM).

– Chlorinated polyvinyl chloride (CPVC plastic pipe).

– Ductile iron water pipe.

– Galvanized steel pipe.

– Polybutylene (PB plastic pipe and tubing).

– Polyethylene (PE plastic pipe or tubing).

– Polyvinyl chloride (PVC plastic pipe).

Available water distribution piping materials include the following:

– Brass pipe

– Chlorinated polyvinyl chloride (CPVC plastic pipe and tubing)

– Copper or copper-alloy pipe

– Copper or copper-alloy tubing (Type K, L, or M)

– Galvanized steel pipe

– Polybutylene (PB plastic pipe and tubing)

– Stainless steel pipe (304 and 316 in laboratories)

2 PLUMBING FIXTURES

Selection criteria

Before specifying plumbing fixtures the designer should become familiar with the plumbing fixture manufacturer's catalog information and associated components such as fitting, faucets, toilet seats, flash valves, and supports. Each plumbing fixture must include a receptor drain or strainer, trap, cold water supply or hot and cold water supply, trim, accessories, appliances, appurtenances, equipment, and supports. Selection criteria for plumbing fixtures include the following:

- *Fitting body types:* Cast brass, brass, or copper underbody with chrome-plated escutcheon, plastic underbody with chrome-plated escutcheon, plastic.

- *Finishes:* Polished chrome plated, polished brass, polished gold plated, and colored plastic finishes.

- *Handle types:* Dual handle, ornamental metal, and porcelain lever, dual three- and four-arm, dual metal or crystal knob, single lever, dual lever 4 in (10 cm) and 6 in (15 cm) wrist blade, push button, self-closing, sensor operated.

- *Fixture clearances:* Proper clearances between fixtures and between fixtures and walls must be used in the layout of washrooms and bathrooms to ensure ease of installation, ease of use, and maintenance (**Figs. 3** and **4**).

- *Accessibility for the disabled:* The layout of plumbing fixtures should be guided by considerations of universal design and accessibility, which is governed by the Americans with Disabilities Act (ADA). Accessible plumbing fixtures must be provided in public buildings and where required by code and authorities having jurisdiction providing handicapped accessibility to lavatories, sinks, water closets, and water coolers.

- *Water closets:* Two types of water closets are commonly used in new construction. Wall-hanging type fixtures, with a flush valve, are the preference in public buildings to allow toe space for wheelchair foot rest, to facilitate approach to the seat, and to allow access for cleaning below the fixture. The other type of water closet is the tank type, typically used in residential buildings. In either case, the bowl should be elongated to provide handicapped accessibility.

- *Lavatories:* The most common types of lavatories used in new construction include: wall hung, countertop, and pedestal types. Lavatories come in a variety of shapes and styles. Some common styles include backsplashes, self-rim, one-piece bowls, and under-counter mounted. Lavatories for disabled access must be provided with a clear dimension of 30 in (75 cm) under each lavatory and have insulated supply and drain lines to prevent injury and burns.

- *Showers:* Prefabricated showers and shower compartments are manufactured in several configurations. A shower compartment should have a minimum of 900 sq in (5800 sq cm) of interior cross-sectional area and have not less than 3 in (75 cm) minimum dimension measured from its finished interior dimension, exclusive of fixture valves, shower heads, soap dishes, and safety grab bars. The minimum required area and dimension is measured from the finished interior dimension at a height equal to the top of the threshold and at a point tangent to its centerline.

- *Urinals:* Urinals are typically selected for use in public men's toilet rooms. They should have a visible water trap seal without strainer to permit maintenance. For the purposes of water conservation, urinals should be selected that incorporate a maximum of 1.5 gal (5.7 l) of water per flushing cycle.

- *Sinks:* Sinks are typically selected for use in kitchens and laboratories. They can be provided with many different types of faucets and finishes. The most common sink finish is stainless steel because of its durability and resistance to foreign materials. Residential kitchen sinks often are provided with a grinder, hose spray, and faucet. Dishwashers used in residential kitchens often are designed to share the supply and drain lines used for the sink.

- *Water coolers and drinking fountains:* Because of the different applications in variety of spaces and locations, the choice of style is wide, and the designer has the freedom to select shapes and colors to improve the aesthetic appearance of the units, as long as accessibility clearances are provided.

- *Service sinks:* These fixtures are required in janitor closets or maintenance areas. The most common styles are: floor mounted, wall hung, and mop sinks. Another variety of this fixture is a laundry sink that may be used with support legs. Service sinks must be provided with hose connection and vacuum breakers.

Water conservation

The U.S. Energy Policy Act of 1992 requires that plumbing fixtures manufactured for use in the United States after January 1, 1994 have the following maximum flow rates and consumption in gallons per minute (gpm) and litre/sec (l/s), gallons (gal) and litres (l):

- Lavatory and sink faucet (public): 2.5 gpm (0.16 l/s).

- Lavatory and sink faucet (private): 2.2 gal @ 60 psi (0.16 l/s @ 413.68 kp).

- Lavatory and sink faucet (public): 0.5 gpm @ 60 psi (0.032 l/s @ 413.68 kp).

- Shower head: 2.5 gpm @ 80 psi (0.16 l/s @ 551.58 kp).

- Water closet types are as follows:

– Flush valve (public): 1.6 gal (6 l) per flushing cycle

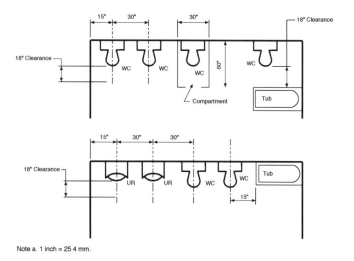

Note a. 1 inch = 25.4 mm.

Fig. 3. Plumbing fixture clearances.

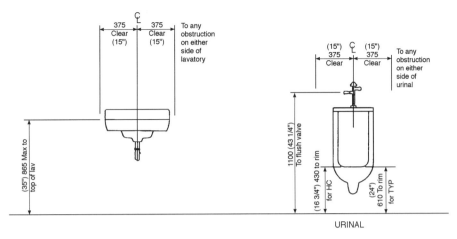

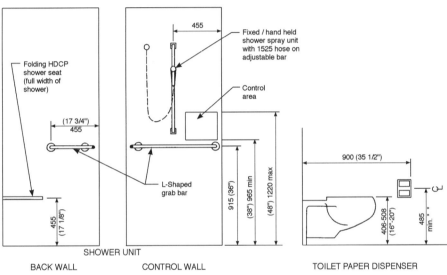

Fig. 4. Plumbing fixture typical dimensions.

- Tank type (private): 1.6 gal (6 l) per flushing cycle

- Tank type (residential): 1.6 gal (6 l) per flushing cycle

• Urinals: 1 gal (3.8 l) per flushing cycle ■

REFERENCES

American National Standards Institute, 11 West 42nd St., New York, NY 10036

American Society of Heating, Refrigeration, and Air-Conditioning Engineers, 1791 Tullie Circle, NE, Atlanta, GA 30329

American Society of Mechanical Engineers, 345 East 47th St., New York, NY 10017

American Society of Plumbing Engineers, 3617 Thousand Oaks Blvd., Suite 210, Westlake, CA 91362

American Society of Sanitary Engineering, PO Box 40362, Bay Village, OH 44140

American Society for Testing and Materials, 100 Barr Harbor Dr., West Conshohocken, PA 19428

Council of American Building Officials, 5203 Leesburg Pike, Suite 201, Falls Church, VA 22041

IPC, *International Plumbing Code,* Building Officials and Code Administration, Country Club Hills, 2003.

Plate 1. Spring water collection and protection

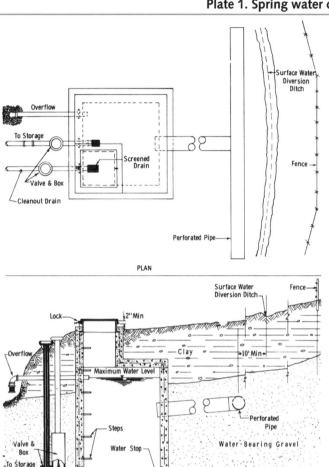

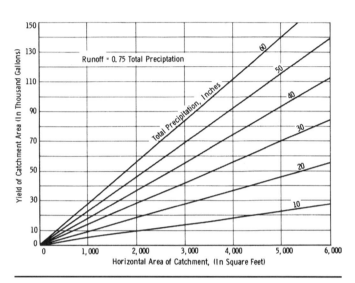

Yield of impervious catchment area.

Plate 2. Cistern

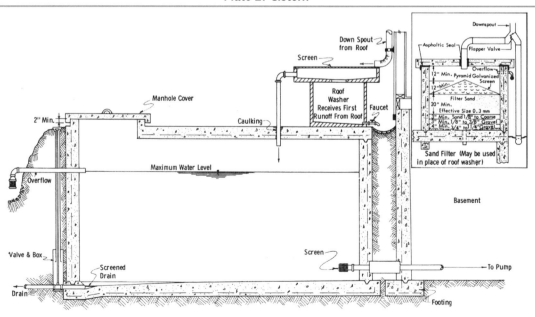

Arturo De La Vega

Summary

This section includes guidelines for sizing sanitary waste drainage piping in the forms of waste stacks and branches, building drains and sewers, drainage fixture unit values, slope of horizontal drainage, and horizontal building storm drains.

Key words

fixture unit ratings, floor drains, pipe diameter, piping, sanitary drains, septic tank, stacks, vents

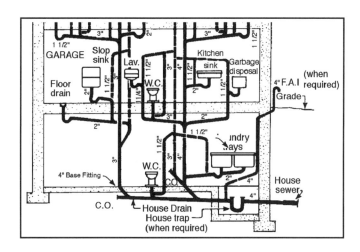

Sanitary waste systems

Waste pipe system sizing

- Sanitary drainage systems are designed to carry wastes from plumbing fixtures and floor drains to public sanitary sewers or septic tanks.

- To apply proper sizing and slope to drainage and vent pipes, the engineer should use applicable model building codes and regulations, and consult the authority having jurisdiction.

- The discharge ratings for the most commonly used plumbing fixtures are given in **Table 1**; capacities of horizontal branches and stacks are given in **Table 2**; the size and maximum lengths of vents in relation to safe carrying capacities of soil and waste pipes are found in **Table 3**; size of vent stacks and stack vents are in **Table 4**. Data on the capacities of building sewers are also shown in **Table 5**. [Tables appear at the end of this article.]

- All tables have been extracted from the IPC International Plumbing Code. Caution is advised that the values in the tables do not always agree with all current model, and local, building codes. Where differences exist, local requirements govern. However, the data indicated herewith can be used to establish limiting requirements for drainage system design.

Fixture unit ratings

- The capacities of drainage pipes are listed in fixture units, and the loads are added as they are collected in the drainage piping. To facilitate the understanding of the floor plans, and to facilitate adequate space allowance for the piping system, the designer should develop diagrams that sequentially show the system and coordi-

nate with other engineering disciplines such as civil, structural, mechanical, electrical, communication, and fire protection.

- The designer should also consider other sources of continuous or semi-continuous flow into the drainage system, such as from pumps, sump ejectors, and air-conditioning equipment. These loads are commonly computed as one fixture unit equaling 7.5 gpm (28.35 l/m). For sewer ejector detail see **Fig. 1**.

- With these parameters the designer will be able to determine the pipe sizes, slopes, and location of stacks in the safest and most economic way.

Stack capacities

- Waste stacks are the vertical pipes collecting all the horizontal drainage branches from each floor (**Figs. 2–4**). They are commonly known as "intervals." A stack can take two branches from the same level with a 45°Y fitting or sanitary T, and that also will be an interval, in other words, the collection of pipe branches in each level is an interval. For typical wet stack detail see **Fig. 5**.

Vent requirements

- The size and length of vent pipes are directly dependent upon the volume of discharge for which the soil and waste pipe are designed.

- Unless adequate venting is provided, the flow of fixture discharges through soil or waste stacks can produce pressure variations in branches that may damage the seals of fixture traps by blowing

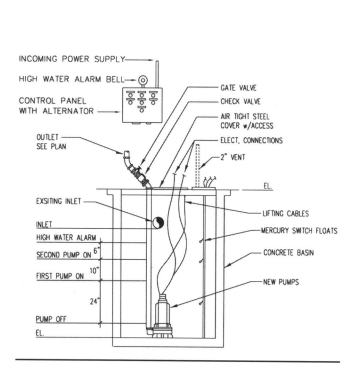

Fig. 1. Duplex ejector pump and basin. Notes: Sewage ejector and basin should have adequate capacity to prevent excessive cycling of the pumps. Each pump capacity should satisfy peak inflow. Provide duplex sewer ejectors with each pump at 100 percent of load capacity. Dimensions may vary subject to fixture load calculation.

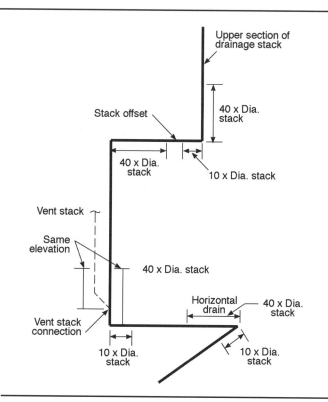

Fig. 2. Suds pressure zones.

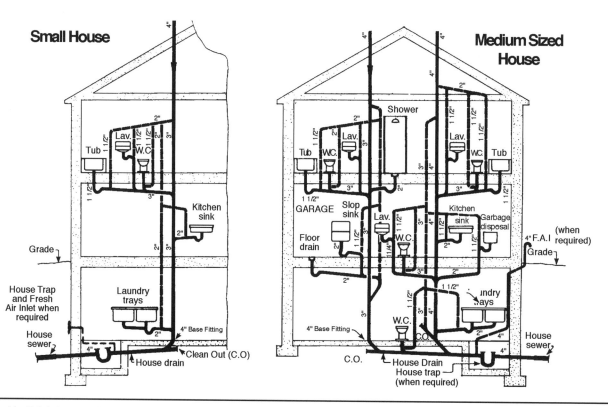

Fig. 3. Residential drainage systems.

them from positive or back pressure in lower parts of the system, or siphoning them because of negative pressure in upper sections.

• Tables list permissible sizes and lengths for the vent stack and branch vents necessary to ensure the proper functioning of a drainage system.

Sanitary building drains

• Building drains are typically placed at the lowest piping invert elevation in a drainage system. Building drains receive wastes from soil, waste, and other drainage pipes inside a structure and con-

vey them into the building sewer. The required size of the building drain for a given drainage load can be read directly from **Table 5.** Typical rules of thumb for sizing building drains are as follows:

Rule 1: Determine the total drainage requirements in fixture units from Table 1.

Rule 2: Establish pitch of drain or slope from **Tables 6** and **7,** particularly in small installations a lesser pitch would increase the possibility of fouling, generally a ¼ in/ft pitch is preferred.

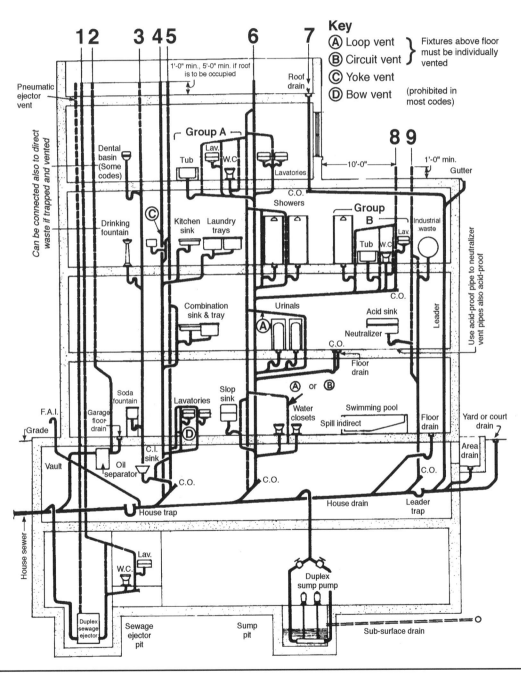

Fig. 4. Drainage system for commercial buildings.

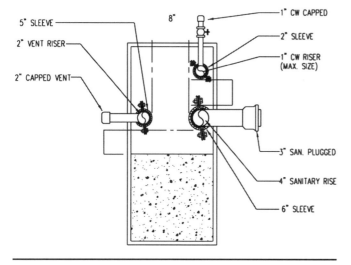

Fig. 5. Typical wet stack detail. Note: Openings through slab should be fireproofed. Dimensions vary depending on number of pipes, sizes, etc.

Rule 3: Select the required pipe diameter from Table 5. The proper sizes for branches and stacks can be taken from Table 2.

– Tables 2 and 5 are based on gravity flow of one-half full drain, and at the same time full flow capacity is reached at approximately that point because of trapped air.

– Drainage pipe going from a horizontal to a vertical line uses short turn fittings; but in going from a vertical flow to a horizontal flow, a long turn fitting is used (sweep elbow).

– The waste effluent is calculated in sequence starting from the furthest and highest fixture, or branch, and ending at the lowest fixture, or branch, to properly size the stack.

Critical limitations to consider in any drainage system

– No branch or fixture should be connected within 10 pipe diameters downstream from the base of the soil or waste stack. (See *suds pressure zones,* Fig. 2.)

– Indirect waste should be discharged through an air gap into a trapped fixture.

– Combination waste and vent should only be used for floor drains, standpipes, sinks, and lavatories, which should discharge to a vented drainage pipe.

– Chemical waste should be completely separated from the sanitary drainage system.

– The minimum size for underground drain pipe should be 2 in (50.8 mm).

– The size of the drain pipe should not be reduced in size in the direction of the flow.

– Drainage for future fixtures should be terminated with an approved cap or plug.

– Dead ends are prohibited in the installation or removal of any part of a drainage system. The application of code requirements should be accurate in this and other related matters.

Piping materials

Available aboveground drainage and vent piping materials include the following:

– Acrylonitrile butadiene styrene (ABS plastic pipe)

– Brass pipe

– Cast-iron pipe

– Copper or copper-alloy pipe

– Copper or copper-alloy tubing (Type K, L, M, or DWV)

– Galvanized steel pipe

– Polyvinyl chloride (PVC plastic pipe type DWV)

Available underground building drainage and vent piping materials include the following:

– Acrylonitrile butadiene styrene (ABS plastic pipe)

– Cast-iron pipe

– Concrete pipe

– Copper or copper-alloy tubing (Type K or L)

– Polyvinyl chloride (PVC plastic pipe type DWV)

Sizing and ratings

Figs. 3 and 5 illustrate various types of plumbing details applicable to both residential and commercial buildings. Because of the wide variance in plumbing regulations, some of these diagrammatic details may be prohibited in certain localities; other details may indicate methods far in excess of mandatory requirements in other localities. All, however, reflect solutions to typical drainage problems by methods that generally constitute good plumbing practice.

Residential drainage systems

– The pipe sizes shown in Fig. 3 will meet every requirement usually encountered in residential work. A 3 in (75 mm) main soil stack is adequate for residential use in the opinion of many authorities; a 4 in (101.6 mm) main soil stack is mandatory, however, in some localities, main house drains should never be less than 4 in (101.6 mm).

– If house sewers are connected to the septic tank of a private sewerage disposal system, no house trap or fresh air inlet is necessary. In many communities individual venting may be eliminated and a system of wet venting or combined waste and vent system can be utilized. (See representative residential drainage field and septic tanks, **Figs. 6 to 8.**)

Commercial drainage systems

Fig. 5 shows a composite of drainage problems also encountered in a wide range of commercial and industrial work; the installations are not typical for any specific kind of building. As in the house sections, soil and waste lines are shown solid; vent lines are broken.

– *Group A:* Bathroom unit is rated for five fixture units, individually vented and connected by preferred methods to main soil and vent stacks.

– *Group B:* Bathroom unit is rated at seven fixture units, individually vented and connected by the preferred method to a horizontal soil branch.

– *Loop Vent A and Circuit Vent B:* Both are types of venting in which the branch drain is a "double duty" pipe carrying both air and discharge. The use of this pipe constitutes "wet venting," prohibited by some codes. It is generally not a desirable method of venting. If used, circuit or loop vents should not be connected to a group of more than eight fixtures in series. In a loop vent, a con-

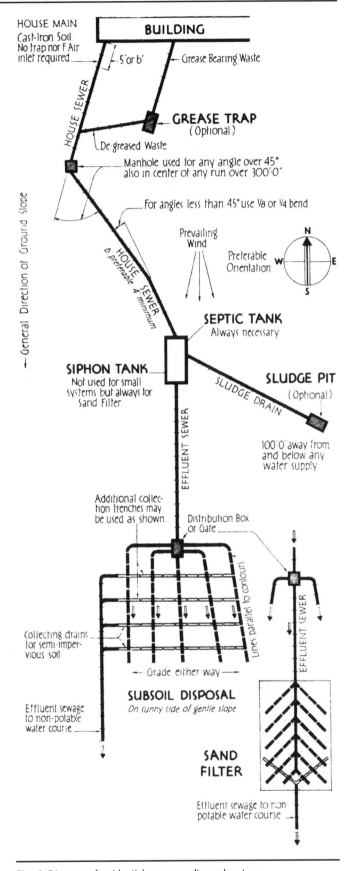

Fig. 6. Diagram of residential sewerage disposal system.

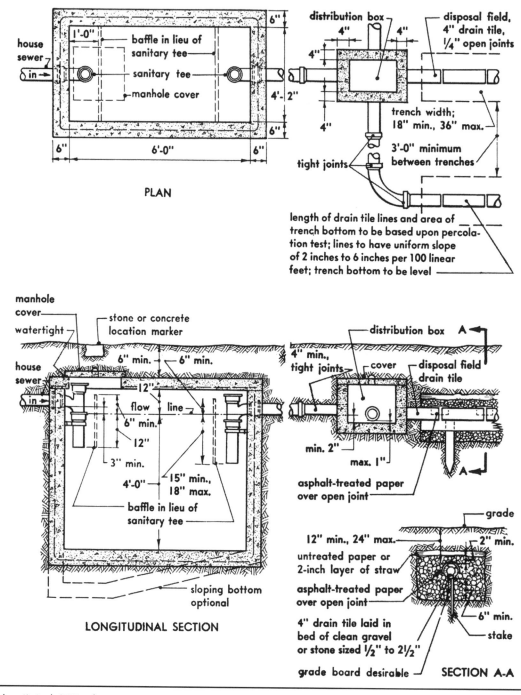

Fig. 7. Residential septic tank (750 gal).

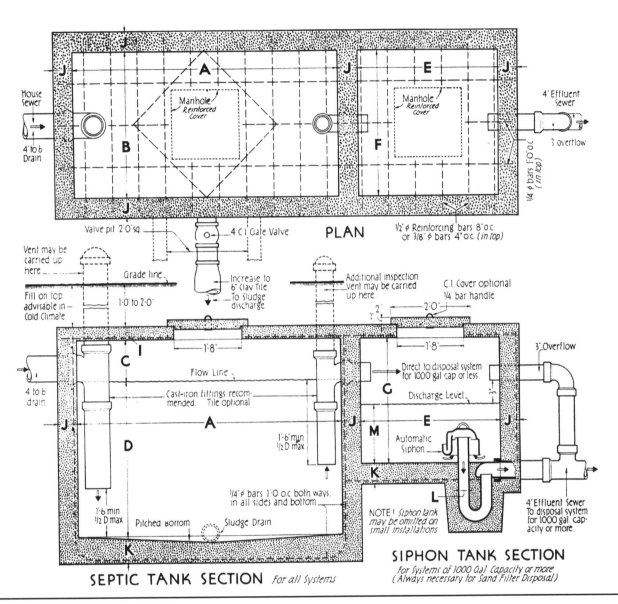

Fig. 8. Two-chamber septic tank (1000 gal).

tinuation of the branch runs up and over the fixtures to connect to the vent stack adjacent to the main soil. In a circuit vent, the connection is to a main vent stack opposite the main soil stack.

– *Yoke Vent C:* This connects the main soil and waste stacks, with the soil at the lower end of the yoke. The connection of the fixtures as at C adds greatly to the safe capacity of soil stacks. This type of connection can be made to bathroom units in residential as well as commercial buildings.

– *Bow Vent D:* This can be used for light discharge loads to avoid installation of an additional vent stack.

– *Stacks 1 and 2:* These indicate the need for separate venting of the sewage ejector and the oil separator from garage drains. The vent from a pneumatic sewage ejector should not be joined to any other pipe; sewage pumps do not require any special considerations.

– *Stack 3:* This is the vent from an indirect waste line discharging into a cast-iron sink. Its fixtures must be trapped. If an indirect waste line is over 100 ft (30 m) in developed length, it should be extended through the roof.

– *Stacks 4, 5, and 6:* The vents should be connected into these stacks at their lower ends, so that discharge will scour the connection and thus prevent fouling. Such a connection is specifically required for cast iron because of scaling.

– *Stack 9:* This applies to a special purpose type of installation. Corrosive wastes require acid-proof pipe for waste, soil, and vent lines, for fittings, and for the house drain up to the base fitting of the next main soil stack. ■

REFERENCES

American Society of Mechanical Engineers, 345 East 47th Street, New York, NY 10017

American Society of Plumbing Engineers, 3617 Thousand Oaks Blvd., Suite 210, Westlake, CA 91362

American Society for Testing and Materials, 100 Barr Harbor Drive, West Conshohocken, PA 19428

Cast Iron Soil Pipe Institute, 5959 Shallowford Road, Suite 419, Chattanooga, TN 37421

IPC, *International Plumbing Code,* Building Officials and Code Administration, Country Club Hills, 2003.

Table 1. Drainage fixture unit values for various plumbing fixtures
(Source: IPC 2003)

Type of fixture or group of fixtures	Drainage fixture unit value	Trap size (inches)
Automatic clothes washer standpipe — commercial	3	2
Automatic clothes washer standpipe — domestic	2	1 1/2
Bathroom group	6	—
Bathtub	2	1 1/2
Bidet	1	1 1/2
Combination sink and tray	2	1 1/2
Dental unit	1	1 1/4
Dishwasher	2	1 1/2
Drinking fountain	1/2	1 1/4
Emergency floor drains	0	2
Floor drains	2	2
Kitchen sink	2	1 1/2
Laundry tray	2	1 1/2
Lavoratory	1	1 1/4
Mop basin	2	2
Service sink	2	1 1/2
Shower (each head)	2	1 1/2
Sink	2	1 1/2
Urinal	4	2
Water closet, private	4	—
Water closet, public	6	—
Water closet, pneumatic assist, private or public installation	4[a]	

Note a. For the purpose of computing loads on building drains and sewers, water closets shall not be rated at a lower drainage fixture unit unless the lower values are confirmed by testing.

Table 2. Horizontal fixture branches and stacks
(Source: IPC 2003)

Diameter of pipe (inches)	Total for a horizontal branch	Maximum number of fixture units		
		Stacks[b]		
		Total discharge into one branch	Total for stack of three branch intervals or less	Total for stack greater than three branch intervals
1 1/2	3	2	4	8
2	6	6	10	24
2 1/2	12	9	20	42
3	20	20	48	72
4	160	90	240	500
5	360	200	540	1100
6	620	350	960	1900
8	1400	600	2200	3600
10	2500	1000	3800	5600
12	3900	1500	6000	8400
15	7000	Note c	Note c	Note c

Note a. Does not include branches of the building drain. Refer to Table P-603.2(1)

Note b. Stacks shall be sized and based on the total accumulated connected load at each story or branch interval. As the total accumulated connected load decreases.stacks are permitted to be reduced in size. Stack diameters shall not be reduced to less than one-half of the diameter of the largest stack size required.

Note c. Sizing load based on design criteria.

Table 3. Minimum diameters and maximum length of individual, branch, and circuit vents for horizontal drainage branches

(Source: IPC 2003)

Diameter of[a] horizontal drainage branch (inches)	Slope of horizontal drainage branch (inches per foot)	Maximum developed length of vent (feet)[b] Diameter of vent (inches)									
		1 1/4	1 1/2	2	2 1/2	3	4	5	6	8	10
1 1/4	1/4	NL[b]									
	1/2	NL									
1 1/2	1/4	NL	NL								
	1/2	NL	NL								
2	1/8	NL	NL	NL							
	1/4	290	NL	NL							
	1/2	150	380	NL							
2 1/2	1/8	180	450	NL	NL						
	1/4	96	240	NL	NL						
	1/2	49	130	NL	NL						
3	1/8		190	NL	NL	NL					
	1/4		97	420	NL	NL					
	1/2		50	220	NL	NL					
4	1/8			190	NL	NL	NL				
	1/4			98	310	NL	NL				
	1/2			48	160	410	NL				
5	1/8				190	490	NL	NL			
	1/4				97	250	NL	NL			
	1/2				46	130	NL	NL			
6	1/8					190	NL	NL	NL		
	1/4					97	250	NL	NL		
	1/2					46	130	NL	NL		
8	1/8						190	NL	NL	NL	
	1/4						91	310	NL	NL	
	1/2						38	150	410	NL	
10	1/8							190	500	NL	NL
	1/4							85	240	NL	NL
	1/2							32	110	NL	NL
12	1/8								180	NL	NL

Note a. 1 foot = 304.8 mm; 1 inch per foot= 83.3 mm/n.
Note b. NL means no limit. Actual values in excess of 500 feet.

Table 4. Size and length of vent stacks and stack vents
(Source: IPC 2003)

Diameter of soil or waste stack (in.)	Total fixture units connected to stack (dfu)	Maximum developed length of vent (feet)[b] Diameter of vent (inches)										
		1 1/4	1 1/2	2	2 1/2	3	4	5	6	8	10	12
12												
1 1/4	2	30										
1 1/2	8	50	150									
2	12	30	75	200								
2	20	26	50	150								
2 1/2	42		30	100	300							
3	10		42	150	360	1040						
3	21		32	110	270	810						
3	53		27	94	230	680						
3	102		25	86	210	620						
4	43			35	85	250	980					
4	140			27	65	200	750					
4	320			23	55	170	640					
4	540			21	50	150	580					
5	190				28	82	320	990				
5	490				21	63	250	760				
5	940				18	53	210	670				
5	1400				16	49	190	590				
6	500					33	130	400	1000			
6	1100					26	100	310	780			
6	2000					22	84	260	660			
6	2900					20	77	240	600			
8	1800						31	95	240	940		
8	3400						24	73	190	720		
8	5600						20	62	160	610		
8	7600						18	56	140	560		
10	4000							31	78	310	960	
10	7200							24	60	240	740	
10	11000							20	51	200	630	
10	15000							18	46	180	570	
12	7300								31	120	380	940
12	13000								24	94	300	720
12	20000								20	79	250	610
12	26000								18	72	230	500
15	15000									40	130	310
15	25000									31	96	240
15	38000									26	81	200
15	50000									24	74	180

Note a. 1 foot = 304.8 mm.
Note b. The developed length shall be measured from the vent connection to the open air.

Table 5. Building drains and sewers
(Source: IPC 2003)

Diameter of pipe (inches)	Maximum number of fixture units connected to a portion of the building drain or the building sewer including branches of the building drain. Slope per foot[a]			
	1/16 inch	1/8 inch	1/4 inch	1/2 inch
1 1/4			1	1
1 1/2			3	3
2			21	26
2 1/2			24	31
3		36	42	50
4		180	216	250
5		390	480	575
6		700	840	1000
8	1400	1600	1920	2300
10	2500	2900	3500	4200
12	2900	4600	5600	6700
15	7000	8300	10000	12000

Note a. 1 inch per foot = 83.3

Table 6. Drainage fixture unit values for fixture drains or traps
(Source: IPC 2003)

Size (inches)	Drainage fixture unit value
1 1/4 or less	1
1 1/2	2
2	3
2 1/2	4
3	5
4	6

Table 7. Slope of horizontal drainage pipe
(Source: IPC 2003)

Size (inches)	Minimum slope (inch per foot)[a]
2-1/2 or less	1/4
3 to 6	1/8
8 to larger	1/16

Note a. 1 inch per foot = 83.3 mm/m.

Arturo De La Vega

Summary

The trend in modern hospitals and laboratories is toward central systems to supply oxygen, vacuum, nitrous oxide, and compressed air. With the use of the tables on the following pages, central systems for these special services can be properly designed.

Key words

compressed air, low-pressure alarm, nitrous oxide, oxygen, vacuum systems

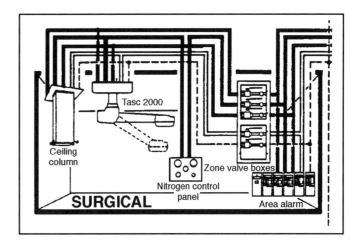

Special plumbing systems

1 MEDICAL GAS AND VACUUM SYSTEMS

Health care facilities and laboratories require more complex plumbing systems than other types of buildings. Due to the complexity of specialized equipment, close coordination is required with all the architectural, civil, structural, mechanical, and electrical work, including the commissioning process.

A medical gas system is an assembly of equipment and piping for the distribution of nonflammable medical gases as compressed air, oxygen, nitrous oxide, carbon dioxide, and nitrogen. Where medical gas and vacuum systems are required, the designer must define ahead of time what type of system will be applicable to the facility, designated by NFPA as level 1, level 2, or level 3.

Medical compressed air systems

Medical compressed air systems in health care facilities are limited for respiratory applications and are commonly supplied by medical air compressors or compressed cylinders. Air compressors are the type that must exclude oil from the air stream and compressor chamber and shall not under any condition add any toxic or flammable contaminants to the compressed air. Air compressors must be a duplex unit or multiple units as required to meet the facility load requirements. Latest technology offers package medical air compressors that include receivers, filters, medical air dryers and controllers (**Fig. 1**).

The compressors for this system may be either rotary or reciprocating. If a reciprocating pump is used, an after cooler is required to reduce the temperature of the compressed gas. The units should be lubricated by carbon rings in order to eliminate all particles in the compressed gas. A receiver is also required in a compressed air installation, and the supply header from the receiver must be provided with an air filter and regulator. See **Table 1** for pipe sizes and capacities.

Sizing example for compressed air:

Assume that there is an outlet pressure of 40 psi, 1000 ft of pipe and an allowable pressure loss of 22 psi. In Table 1 in the column for 40 psi, we read down to 22, and then across, to find that a 1-in black steel pipe of this length can supply 59 cfm; a 3-in pipe can supply 1020 cfm; and so forth. Knowing the quantity required, we can easily select the proper pipe size.

Medical vacuum system

A medical surgical vacuum system is an assembly of equipment and piping for the purpose of suction in medical patient treatment facilities. Medical surgical vacuum systems must be duplex vacuum pumps or multiple vacuum pumps capable of serving the peak calculated demand. Based on particular needs, technology offers several package options (for instance, the oil-less medical vacuum system removes any concerns with regard to potential problems with biohazard waste oil disposal).

A vacuum system consists of a central vacuum pump with control equipment, distribution piping to points where suction may be required, and alarm and signaling equipment (**Fig. 2**). A high vacuum is

---

Credits: Drawing courtesy of Chemetron.

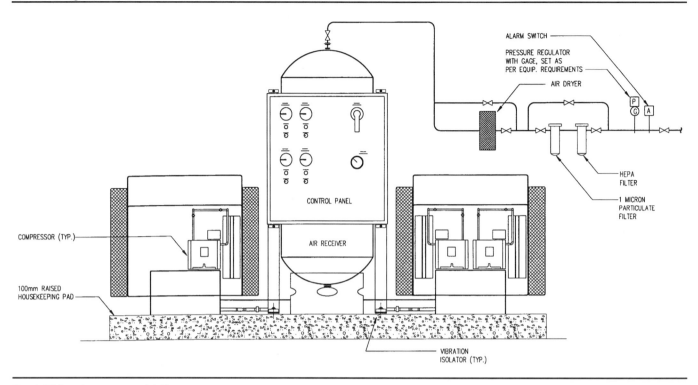

Fig. 1. Triplex air compressor detail.

Table 1. Capacity of compressed air piping

Quantities are based on IPS steel pipe.

Outlet gauge pressure, psi															Pipe size, in.											
175	150	125	100	90	80	70	60	50	40	35	30	25	20	15	3/8	1/2	3/4	1	1¼	1½	2	2½	3	4	5	6
Pressure loss, psi per 1000 ft of pipe															Factor for Type K copper tubing in per cent of IPS steel pipe											
															60	64	76	84	77	81	93	93	89	90	90	90
															Capacity, cfm											
0.4	0.5	0.6	0.7	0.7	0.8	0.9	1	1.2	1.4	1.6	1.8	2.2	2.6	3.4	1.8	3.2	8.2	15	32	48	92	150	265	540	980	1600
0.8	1.0	1.1	1.4	1.5	1.6	1.8	2	2.4	2.9	3.2	3.6	4.3	5.2	6.7	2.5	4.5	11.5	21.5	45	67	130	210	375	770	1380	2300
1.2	1.4	1.7	2.0	2.2	2.4	2.7	3	3.6	4.3	4.8	5.5	6.5	7.8	10	3.1	5.5	14.0	26.5	55	82	160	260	460	940	1700	2800
1.6	1.9	2.2	2.7	2.9	3.2	3.5	4	4.8	5.7	6.4	7.3	8.6	10.4	13.4	3.5	6.3	16.0	30.5	64	95	185	300	530	1090	1950	3200
2.0	2.3	2.7	3.3	3.6	4.0	4.4	5	5.9	7.2	8	9.1	10.8	13	16.8	3.9	8.0	18.0	34	71	108	208	330	600	1200	2160	3600
4.0	4.6	5.4	6.6	7.1	7.9	8.8	10	11.8	14.3	16	18.2	21.5	26	34	5.5	10	25.5	48	100	150	290	470	840	1700	3100	5100
6.0	6.9	8.1	10	11	12	14	15	18	22	24	28	33	41	50	6.7	12	31	59	122	185	360	570	1020	2100	3700	6200
8	9.2	11	14	15	16	18	20	24	29	32	37	43	52	67	7.7	14	36	68	142	215	410	660	1180	2450	4300	7200
10	12	14	17	18	20	22	25	26	36	40	46	54	65	84	8.6	15.8	40	76	158	240	460	720	1320	2730	4420	8000
12	14	17	20	22	24	27	30	36	43	48	55	65	78	100	9.4	17.2	44	84	172	262	500	800	1450	3000	5300	8800
14	17	19	24	25	28	31	35	42	50	56	64	76	91	118	10	18.6	48	90	186	285	545	870	1570	3250	5700	9600
16	19	22	27	29	32	35	40	48	58	64	73	86	104	134	10.8	20	51	96	200	300	580	940	1700	3400	6100	10200
20	23	27	33	36	40	44	50	59	72	80	91	108	130	168	12	22	57	108	220	340	650	1050	1880	3850	6800	11500
24	28	33	40	43	48	53	60	71	86	96	110	129	156	201	13	24	62	118	245	375	720	1150	2050	4200	7500	12600
28	33	38	47	50	56	62	70	83	100	112	128	151	182	235	14	26	67	128	260	400	770	1230	2200	4500	8000	13600
32	37	44	53	57	64	71	80	95	115	128	146	175	208	268	15	28	72	137	280	430	820	1320	2350	4900	8600	14500
36	42	49	60	64	72	80	90	107	128	144	164	194	234	302	16	30	76	145	300	460	870	1400	2500	5200	9100	15500
40	46	54	66	71	79	88	100	118	144	160	182	215	260	340	17	31	80	150	310	480	910	1480	2600	5400	9600	16200

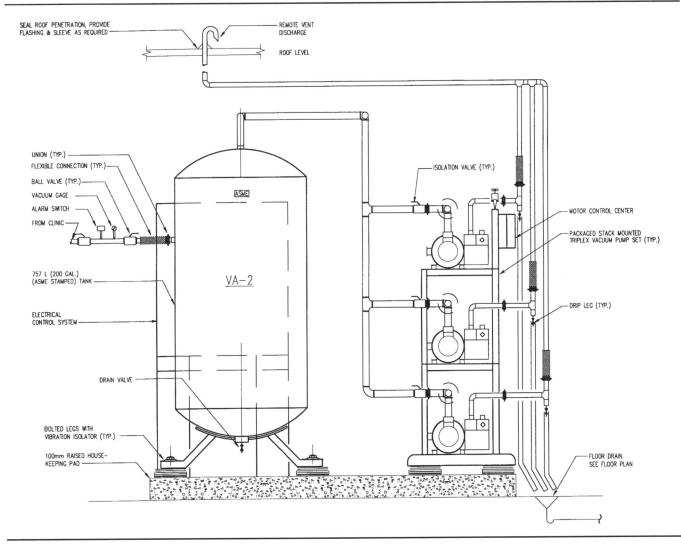

Fig. 2. Triplex vacuum pump detail.

rarely required, because even a 15 in (34 cm) (mercury column) vacuum can damage skin tissue. Quantity, not pressure, is most important.

• *System sizing*

– In this system, sizing is determined by the pressure drop required and the length of the longest run (**Table 2**). Vacuum pumps are sized for the peak draw; duplex pumps should be used to ensure a continuous source of supply.

– If the units required become too large for one pump, then two-thirds of the total capacity should be placed in each of two pumps.

– The pumps evacuate a receiving tank to which the vacuum header is connected. The exhaust from the pumps should discharge to the outside air, and should be provided with a silencer and a filter.

• *Pump types*

– Pumps may be either rotary vane or reciprocating. Care must be taken in the location and installation of reciprocating pumps,

however, because they are noisy and require a large foundation to prevent vibration and movement. The receiving tank should be hot-dipped galvanized steel, because condensation will form and collect in it.

• *Switches*

– Pressure switches for the motor starters should be mounted directly on the receiver, with only a wire running from the pressure switch to the starter, to ensure continuous vacuum supply.

2 OXYGEN

Oxygen in medical facilities is primarily used for inhalation therapy and anesthesia. Continuous supply and immediate availability throughout the facility is essential.

– Oxygen contained in a cylinder is in liquid form. When released to atmospheric pressure it becomes a gas. Although the gas is not flammable, it is dangerous to handle because it supports combus-

Table 2. Capacity of vacuum piping

gravity 1.00). Deduct 10 per cent from listed quantities for friction loss due to ... copper tubing; K = Type K or Type L copper tubing.

Pipe size, in.

Capacity, cfm

Length of pipe, ft	Pressure drop, in. Hg	3/8 P	3/8 B	3/8 K	1/2 P	1/2 B	1/2 K	3/4 P	3/4 B	3/4 K	1 P	1 B	1 K	1¼ P	1¼ B	1¼ K	1½ P	1½ B	1½ K	2 P	2 B	2 K	2½ P	2½ B	2½ K	3 P	3 B	3 K	4 P	4 B	4 K
40	20	8.6	11.2	5.3	15.8	22.0	10.3	31.6	42.3	24.6	60.8	80.0	51.6	113	153	88.3	166	216	140	308	391	283	516	641	483						
60	30	7.2	9.2	4.3	13.0	18.0	8.3	25.8	34.5	20.0	49.1	65.0	41.6	91.6	125	71.6	138	175	113	250	320	233	416	525	391						
80	40	6.2	7.8	3.7	11.3	15.3	7.2	22.5	30.0	17.5	44.1	55.8	36.3	80.0	108	61.6	118	153	98.3	216	278	200	366	450	338	600	733	533			
100	50	5.6	7.0	3.3	10.0	13.6	6.4	20.0	26.6	15.5	38.3	50.0	32.5	70.0	96.6	55.0	106	136	88.3	191	246	176	323	400	300	533	666	475			
120	60	5.0	6.6	3.0	9.2	12.6	5.8	18.3	24.1	14.1	35.0	45.8	29.1	65.0	88.3	50.8	96.6	123	80.0	176	225	161	291	366	276	491	608	433			
140	70	4.7	5.9	2.8	8.5	11.6	5.4	16.6	22.5	13.0	32.0	42.5	27.1	60.0	81.6	46.6	90.0	115	73.3	165	208	150	273	341	256	450	566	400			
160	80	4.3	5.5	2.6	7.8	10.8	5.1	15.6	21.0	12.1	30.0	39.1	25.3	55.8	76.6	43.3	83.3	108	68.3	153	191	140	255	316	236	425	525	375			
180	90	4.1	5.2	2.5	7.5	10.1	4.7	14.8	19.5	11.5	28.3	36.6	24.1	52.5	71.5	41.1	78.3	101	65.0	143	181	131	241	300	225	396	500	350			
200	100	3.8	4.9	2.3	7.0	9.6	4.5	14.0	18.6	10.8	26.6	35.0	22.8	51.6	68.3	39.1	75.0	95.0	61.6	136	173	125	228	283	213	376	475	333			
250	125	3.4	4.4	2.1	6.3	8.6	4.1	12.6	16.6	9.8	24.1	30.8	20.1	44.1	60.0	35.0	66.6	85.0	55.0	121	153	111	203	253	188	333	425	300			
300	150	3.2	4.0	1.9	5.7	7.9	3.6	11.5	15.1	8.8	21.1	28.3	18.5	40.8	55.0	31.6	60.8	78.3	50.0	111	140	103	186	233	173	308	383	271	608	716	550
350	175	2.9	3.8	1.7	5.3	7.3	3.4	10.6	14.0	8.1	20.1	26.3	17.1	37.5	50.8	29.1	55.8	71.6	46.6	103	130	95.0	171	213	160	285	355	250	558	650	508
400	200	2.7	3.5	1.6	5.0	6.8	3.2	10.0	13.1	7.6	19.0	24.6	16.0	35.0	47.5	27.5	52.5	66.6	43.3	96.6	121	88.3	161	200	150	266	333	233	525	616	475
500	250	2.4	3.2	1.5	4.4	6.1	2.9	8.8	11.8	6.8	17.0	22.0	14.3	31.6	42.5	24.5	46.6	60.0	39.1	85.0	108	78.3	143	180	133	238	300	208	466	550	430
600	300	2.2	2.8	1.3	4.0	5.6	2.6	8.1	10.8	6.2	15.3	20.0	13.0	28.3	38.6	22.0	43.3	55.0	35.1	78.3	98.3	71.6	130	163	121	216	271	191	425	500	390
700	350	2.0	2.6	1.2	3.7	5.1	2.4	7.5	9.9	5.7	14.1	18.5	12.0	26.3	35.8	20.8	40.0	50.8	32.8	73.3	91.6	66.6	120	150	113	200	250	178	391	458	363
800	400	1.9	2.4	1.1	3.5	4.8	2.2	7.0	9.3	5.4	13.3	17.3	11.3	24.6	33.3	19.5	36.5	47.5	30.6	68.3	85.0	61.6	113	140	106	188	233	165	366	433	333
1000	500	1.7	2.2	1.0	3.1	4.3	2.0	6.2	8.3	4.8	11.8	15.5	10.0	22.1	30.0	17.1	33.0	44.1	27.0	60.8	76.6	55.0	100	125	93.3	166	208	148	330	383	300
1200	600	1.6	2.0	0.9	2.8	4.1	1.8	5.7	7.5	4.4	10.8	14.1	9.1	20.0	27.3	15.6	30.0	38.8	25.0	55.0	70.0	50.8	91.6	115	86.6	151	190	135	300	350	273

tion vigorously and can cause the slightest spark to erupt into an inferno.

- For methods of installing oxygen systems consult the National Fire Protection Association (NFPA 99 and NFPA 56) Standard for Non-Flammable Medical Gas Systems.

- Great care should be exercised in handling oxygen under pressure with oils, greases, rubber, or other materials of organic nature. Regulations applicable to handling can be found in Compressed Gas Association (CGA) Pamphlet G-A Oxygen.

• *Supply systems*

- Oxygen systems may be fed from either a bulk supply or a cylinder manifold. Each should include both a normal service supply and an adequate reserve supply, which would become available automatically when the service supply is exhausted.

- Gas suppliers should be consulted on the most economical type of storage for a particular installation, considering the volume of gas to be used and the location of the installation. Bulk oxygen storage should not be located within 50 ft (15m) of any structure.

• *Alarms*

- A low-pressure alarm should be installed where oxygen supply lines from a bulk storage or cylinder manifold enters the building. This alarm, signaling a loss of pressure in the supply line due to a leak, should be both audible and visual.

- A copper tubing header Type K or L with wrought or cast copper fittings should supply all oxygen risers and outlets. Solder should have a melting point of 1000F.

• *Multiple risers*

- Each floor to be equipped for oxygen therapy should be served by more than one riser, so that if the supply to more than one riser is shut off, the entire floor will not be deprived of oxygen, and the patients can be moved to other rooms on the same floor for continuation of their oxygen therapy.

• *Piping size*

- Medical oxygen systems are typically designed to provide 50 psi at the outlet with a maximum pressure drop of 5 psi in the system. The size of the piping is usually determined by the length of the piping required from the supply to the furthest outlet. It should be noted, however, that the piping for a particular outlet closer to the supply could be sized on the basis of its own length, although generally this would not substantially reduce the overall cost of the system.

- Having determined the overall distance, and assuming a pressure drop of 2 psi, refer to **Table 3** for a direct reading of the number of liters of oxygen that a given pipe can deliver per minute.

Sizing example for oxygen:

Assume that a line is to supply 60 oxygen outlets, with a developed length of 250 ft from the source to the farthest outlet. The piping being used is Type K copper tubing, and the allowable pressure drop

is 2 psi. The required capacity can be expressed as follows: 60 outlets times 10 liters per minute per outlet times 40 percent diversity, or 240 liters per minute. Referring to Table 3, look opposite 277 ft under the column for ¾-in K and find "212 liters per minute," which is too small; under 1 in K we find 450, which is ample even after deducting the percentage for fittings. Hence the line should be 1 in in size. If screw pipe were to be used, we would select the appropriate column marked "P," and if Type TP copper tubing were to be used, we would select the column marked "B."

• *Supply valves*

Operating rooms, recovery rooms, and delivery rooms should all be supplied directly from the main, with a shutoff valve outside each room.

- The supplies for patient rooms must be zoned by valves, which should be located in boxes with break glass fronts, in order to eliminate the possibility of their being shut off by unauthorized persons. Valves can be either the ball valve type or the packless diaphragm type.

- Oxygen service riser control valves and valves 1 in (2.5 cm) or more in diameter must be specially packed in and must be free of oil. All piping in the system must be washed with a solution of trisodium phosphate to remove all grease before oxygen is admitted into the system (**Fig. 3**).

3 NITROUS OXIDE

All guidelines in reference to oxygen apply to a nitrous oxide installation with the exception of bulk storage. Because of the small quantities of gas involved, the system manifold for nitrous oxide can be located within the building in a fireproof room. **Table 4** can be used for sizing nitrous oxide piping (**Fig. 4**).

4 PIPING MATERIALS

• Compressed air piping materials include the following:

- Copper tubing seamless ACR (type K or L)

- Brass pipe standard weight (Schedule 40)

• Vacuum piping materials include the following:

- Copper tubing (Type K or L)

- Brass pipe standard weight (Schedule 40)

• Oxygen and nitrous oxide piping materials include the following:

- Copper tubing seamless ACR (type K or L)

- Brass pipe standard weight (Schedule 40)

• Acid drainage and vent piping materials include the following:

- Borosilicate glass pipe

- High silicon iron pipe

Table 3. Capacity of oxygen piping

Quantities listed are for pressure drops of 1 in. and 55.36 in. (or 2 psi) of water (at specific gravity 1.105). Assume 10 liters per minute per outlet. Deduct 10 per cent from listed quantities for friction loss due to valves and fittings. Diversity factor (percentage of simultaneous use) is 40 to 100 (see Table 11). Key: P = IPS threaded brass pipe; B = Type TP (threadless pipe) copper tubing; K = Type K threaded brass pipe; B = Type TP (threadless pipe) copper tubing or Type L copper tubing.

Capacity, liters per minute

Length of pipe, ft	Pressure drop, in. H₂O	3/8 P	3/8 B	3/8 K	1/2 P	1/2 B	1/2 K	3/4 P	3/4 B	3/4 K	1 P	1 B	1 K	1¼ P	1¼ B	1¼ K	1½ P	1½ B	1½ K	2 P	2 B	2 K	2½ P	2½ B	2½ K	3 P	3 B	3 K	4 P	4 B	4 K
55.36	1																														
50	0.9	177	230	105	310	445	205	640	840	505	1210	1580	1050	2300	3120	1750	3350	4200	2800	6400	7820	5700	10500	13000	9800						
55	1.0	165	212	100	290	420	193	610	800	480	1160	1490	980	2150	2850	1650	3200	3950	2650	6000	7400	5400	9800	12500	9100						
111	2.0	118	155	70	210	300	138	435	580	335	820	1050	700	1520	2080	1200	2250	2820	1900	4300	5400	3800	6900	8800	6500	11200	14400	10000			
166	3.0	98	125	58	170	245	112	352	470	276	670	870	580	1250	1700	980	1850	2350	1530	3500	4250	3100	5700	7200	5200	9000	11800	8300			
221	4.0	84	110	50	148	212	98	310	400	240	580	760	500	1100	1480	850	1600	2010	1320	3050	3720	2700	5000	6300	4650	7900	10000	7200			
277	5.0	75	98	45	133	192	89	275	360	212	515	680	450	980	1300	760	1440	1800	1180	2720	3350	2410	4200	5500	4125	7000	9100	6400			
332	6.0	68	89	41	122	172	80	252	330	196	490	620	405	900	1200	700	1320	1650	1100	2500	3050	2200	4050	5050	3750	6400	8100	5900			
388	7.0	63	83	38	112	160	75	235	305	182	440	580	375	840	1110	640	1220	1530	1010	2320	2820	2080	3710	4650	3500	6000	7600	5450			
443	8.0	60	78	35	103	150	70	220	285	170	415	540	350	780	1050	610	1140	1450	960	2150	2650	1920	3500	4400	3250	5500	7100	5100			
498	9.0	56	74	33	98	142	65	205	265	161	382	500	330	730	990	566	1080	1350	900	2030	2500	1850	3300	4080	3050	5200	6700	4800			
554	10	53	69	32	94	135	62	196	255	153	375	480	316	700	930	540	1020	1280	860	1910	2350	1725	3150	3900	2900	5000	6400	4600	9900	11800	9300
1107	20	38	50	28	68	96	44	138	182	108	265	340	225	500	670	380	740	920	605	1360	1650	1210	2220	2800	2100	3520	4500	3200	6950	8300	6500
1661	30	31	40	18	55	77	36	113	148	89	218	280	185	400	550	316	595	730	490	1120	1380	1000	1850	2300	1720	2900	3720	2650	5800	6800	5400

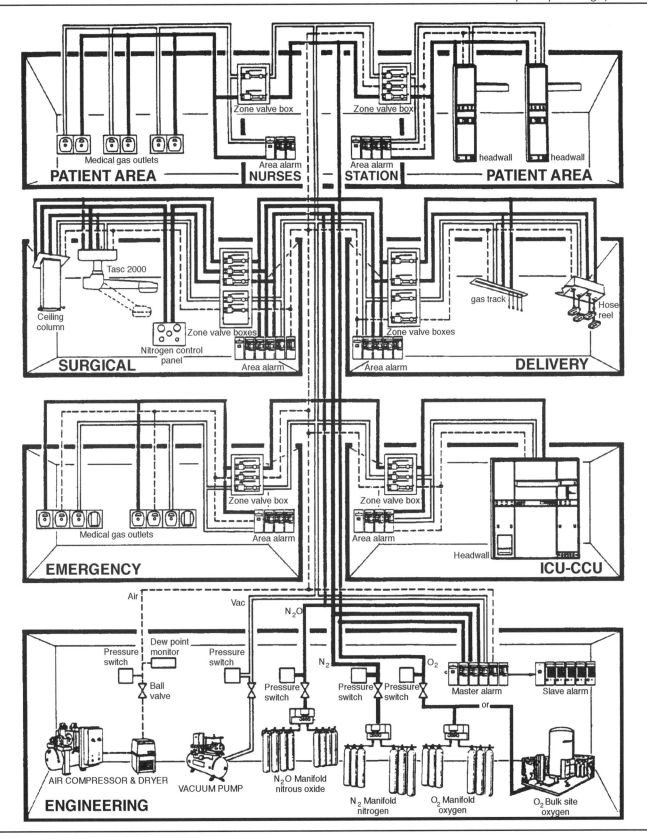

Fig. 3. Medical gas system (courtesy: Chemetron)

Table 4. Capacity of nitrous piping

Quantities listed are for pressure drops of 1 in. and 55.36 in. (or 2 psi) of water (at specific gravity 1.522). Assume 10 liters per minute per outlet. Deduct 10 per cent from listed quantities for friction loss due to valves and fittings. Diversity factor (percentage of simultaneous use) is 100. Key: P = IPS threaded brass pipe; B = Type TP copper tubing; K = Type K copper tubing.

Pipe size, in. — Capacity, liters per minute

Length of pipe, ft	Pressure drop, in. H₂O	⅜ P	⅜ B	⅜ K	½ P	½ B	½ K	¾ P	¾ B	¾ K	1 P	1 B	1 K	1¼ P	1¼ B	1¼ K	1½ P	1½ B	1½ K	2 P	2 B	2 K	2½ P	2½ B	2½ K	3 P	3 B	3 K	4 P	4 B	4 K
55.36	1																														
22	0.4	242	308	145	435	580	285	870	1150	680	1620	2180	1400	3050	4150	2420	4600	5900	3710	8200	10600	7600									
28	0.5	212	275	128	380	520	251	770	1020	600	1480	1920	1250	2720	3720	2120	4080	5300	3340	7400	9500	6700									
33	0.6	197	252	118	355	490	230	700	930	545	1320	1725	1140	2510	3400	1950	3710	4850	3050	6700	8600	6200									
39	0.7	182	230	108	327	445	210	650	860	500	1230	1600	1050	2320	3160	1820	3450	4500	2820	6210	8000	5600	10500	13000	9700						
44	0.8	170	218	100	302	417	200	608	810	470	1150	1520	970	2120	2920	1700	3260	4150	2650	5800	7400	5300	9800	12200	9100						
50	0.9	161	202	96	285	390	188	562	760	442	1090	1420	930	2050	2750	1600	3050	3900	2450	5420	7000	5000	9300	11400	8500	10100	12500	9100			
55	1.0	151	195	91	270	375	176	550	725	420	1020	1350	883	1910	2600	1510	2860	3720	2320	5100	6700	4700	8800	10800	8000	8300	10200	7300			
111	2.0	108	138	64	192	262	123	383	510	298	722	960	620	1350	1820	1060	2050	2600	1630	3620	4800	3320	6200	7800	5600	7200	8800	6350			
166	3.0	87	112	51	158	215	101	312	417	242	590	780	501	1120	1520	870	1630	2110	1350	2950	3800	2700	5000	6300	4650						
221	4.0	75	97	45	135	185	89	271	355	210	510	662	435	960	1290	745	1450	1820	1160	2550	3300	2320	4320	5500	4000						
277	5.0	68	87	40	122	165	79	243	318	188	450	600	388	860	1150	680	1280	1650	1050	2260	2950	2100	3850	4850	3520	6500	7900	5500	11300	13500	10400
332	6.0	61	79	37	110	151	77	220	290	171	418	550	355	780	1050	620	1160	1520	950	2100	2700	1900	3520	4450	3250	5900	7200	5200			
388	7.0	56	72	34	102	140	66	203	270	158	383	510	328	720	960	562	1070	1380	890	1910	2500	1760	3250	4100	3000	5420	6700	4800	10500	12500	9600

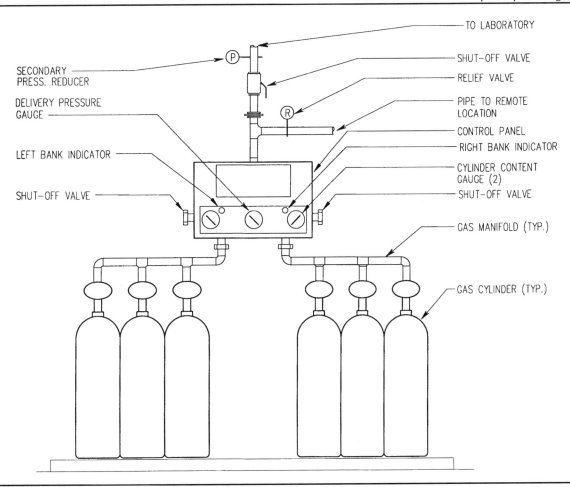

Fig. 4. Gas cylinder manifold detail.

– Polypropylene plastic pipe

– Polyethylene plastic pipe

• Ultrapure water (DI water) piping materials include the following:

– Polyvinylidene fluoride pipe (PVDF plastic pipe)

• Radioactive waste piping materials include the following:

– Stainless steel pipe (type 316)

• Natural gas piping materials include the following:

– Cast iron, wrought pipe

– Black steel pipe

– Galvanized steel pipe

– Copper pipe (Type K and L) ■

REFERENCES

American National Standards Institute, 11 West 42nd Street, New York, NY 10036

American Society of Mechanical Engineers, 345 East 47th Street, New York, NY 10017

American Society of Plumbing Engineers, 3617 Thousand Oaks Blvd., Suite 210, Westlake, CA 91362

IPC International Plumbing Code, Country Club Hills, International Code Council.

Compressed Gas Association, *Pamphlet G-A Oxygen,* CGA, Arlington.

NFPA, *56F Standard for Non-Flammable Medical Gas Systems,* National Fire Protection Association, Quincy.

NFPA 99, *Standard for Health Care Facilities,* National Fire Protection Association, Quincy.

Richard Rittelmann and Paul Scanlon, P.E.

Summary

Heating, Ventilating and Air-Conditioning (HVAC) systems provide the comfort and ventilation necessary for healthy and productive environments. This article reviews HVAC systems for commercial buildings and guidelines for preliminary system design and selection. Innovations in office buildings reviewed include underfloor supply and individual workstation modules.

Key words

air-conditioning, air-handling unit, boiler, chiller, building energy management, condenser, cooling tower, diffuser, double-skin facades, fresh air, heat pump, intelligent systems, office module systems, underfloor supply, ventilation

Ministry of France Offices, Paris, operable windows provide fresh air and save energy by shutting off perimeter heating/cooling when nearby window is open. (Loftness and Hartkopf 1997)

HVAC systems for commercial buildings

HVAC systems that are efficient, accessible for inspection, testing, and balancing, and economical to operate, are extremely important to the success of most building projects.

The HVAC system selected can significantly affect floor plan layouts. Mechanical equipment rooms and vertical distribution shafts typically occupy between 3 and 10 percent of the typical floor plan area, and an even greater percentage in high-rise buildings.

For the owner, the HVAC system can significantly affect project first costs as well as long-term operating and maintenance costs. The initial system cost (including the "hidden" cost of constructing mechanical equipment rooms and large duct shafts) can amount to a substantial percentage of total construction costs in modern fully serviced buildings. Building users are generally more affected by the long-term impacts of the system selection, annual utility bills, maintenance costs, and employee productivity. Research suggests that productivity improvements can be gained by providing occupants with more control over their personal environments than that provided by the typical HVAC system (Loftness and Hartkopf 1997).

1 BASIC COMPONENTS OF HVAC SYSTEM

HVAC systems:

- provide fresh air throughout a building

- condition air within proscribed temperature and humidity ranges

- remove and/or recondition and clean circulated air.

Piping systems for heating and cooling, and valves and dampers control and modulate the system. Recently developed microchip electronic controls bring to the HVAC system technological sophistication and capabilities, including continuous monitoring and system balancing, such as with Energy Management Systems (EMS).

In HVAC system design, the coordination of components is critical, including the designation of different space occupancy requirements, and the designation of different heating/cooling zones as influenced by building orientation. Electronic controls engineering is a significant subspecialty of HVAC design, which must be carefully reviewed to conform to the architectural program and owner and user expectations.

While HVAC systems tend to defy simple categorization, there are three basic components common to all HVAC equipment systems:

- generation equipment

- distribution system

- terminal equipment

Generation equipment

- produces the heat (steam or hot water boilers, warm air furnaces, and radiant panels) or cooling (chillers and cooling towers, and air-cooled compressors in packaged equipment).

Credits: This article was prepared with special contributions by Russ Sullivan, P.E. and Tim Beggs of Burt, Hill, Kosar, Rittelmann, Architects, PC. Section 6, "Innovations," is from Kim (1997), in the CD-ROM accompanying this volume.

- packaged equipment (equipment that is self-contained, often all-electric) requires no central mechanical equipment.

- source of heating and cooling is contained within each piece of HVAC equipment.

- type of generation equipment can limit the choices available to the designer.

- critical architectural decisions related to HVAC generation equipment are location, size, and service options of equipment rooms.

Distribution system

- method by which cooling and heating energy is "moved" throughout the building (hot/chilled water piping systems, or ductwork that distributes warm or cool air around the building).

- for packaged equipment systems, distribution is limited to a modest amount of ductwork (if any).

- limited by the capacity of the supply air fan provided as part of the packaged equipment.

- larger central system distribution is powered by large central pumps and/or air-handling units.

- critical architectural decisions in distribution system design involve coordination with all other structure and services to eliminate conflicts and to provide for effective and efficient distribution of air and water throughout the building.

- critical junctures in a distribution system must be accessible for testing and balancing.

Terminal equipment

- include devices that distribute conditioned air to the space (a diffuser is considered a terminal unit).

- either a separate or integral device is used to control the local space temperature (the "temperature control device").

- both types are usually located in close proximity to the occupant.

- in some systems, they are visible (as in the case of window air-conditioners or fan coil units, which act as both the terminal unit and temperature control device).

- in others systems, they are concealed above the ceiling (a variable air volume box acts as the temperature control device, which controls the amount of air discharged from a number of ceiling diffusers, the terminal units).

- in a single zone system, there is no separate terminal control device.

- local diffuser is the "terminal unit," and a single thermostat sends control signals straight to the distribution equipment to maintain the set-point temperature for the entire area served by the single zone system.

- multiple single-zone air handlers achieve multiple zones of temperature control within the building.

The terminal control device of the HVAC system is usually crucial in selecting the most appropriate HVAC system type.

- dictates the degree of comfort that the system will be capable of providing.

- type of terminal unit used, together with the number of thermostatic control zones desired, significantly affects both occupant satisfaction and the overall system capital cost and operating costs.

2 BASIC HVAC SYSTEM TYPES

The nomenclature used in the HVAC industry often relates to the size of the typical unit rather than the generic type of system; hence a single-zone self-contained unit might be referred to as a:

- "through-wall air-conditioner" when discussing apartment buildings.

- "unit ventilator" when discussing school buildings.

- "rooftop unit" when discussing a low-rise office building.

A variety of heating and cooling energy sources is available for each type of equipment.

To simplify understanding of the basic HVAC options, they can be classified in two categories: self-contained or central systems.

Self-contained systems

- require no central equipment to perform their function.

- all system components (air circulating fan, refrigerant compressor/condenser/cooling coil, and heating coil) are contained within one box.

- generally needs only to be plugged in to a source of electricity.

- normally appropriate for only very small load and/or small building/single room conditioning.

Fig. 1 shows five different equipment configurations used for self-contained systems. The five configurations shown are:

(1) Rooftop unit, common with small buildings with one or separate zones, especially retrofits.

(2) Split system with remote condenser and indoor fan and coil, common with residential and small commercial air-conditioning systems, and retrofits.

(3) Through-wall unit, common with single room HVAC such as hotels/motels.

(4) Window-mounted unit, commonly used for "make-do" retrofit and provisional installations.

(5) Floor-mounted indoor unit, common with larger-space single-zones, commercial/industrial, including retrofits.

Most common heating options used in self-contained systems include:

- electric resistance heating coils (sometimes called "strip heat").

- air-source heat pumps (ASHP).

Air-source heat pumps (ASHP):

- are two to three times more efficient than electric heating coils in mild weather.

- still must rely on electric resistance heating coils when the outdoor air drops to approximately 25F (–4°C).

- are only 1.5 to 2.0 times more efficient than electric resistance heating coils on an annual basis in areas characterized by cold winters.

While many self-contained systems are all-electric, larger commercial rooftop applications may also use natural gas piped to each unit.

- most frequently to provide a lower cost heating option (via direct gas-fired furnaces contained within the unit).

- a more recent product—the gas-fired desiccant air-conditioner—uses natural gas in its cooling cycle.

- these systems require a separately piped fuel.

- still categorized as self-contained systems because they require no central equipment such as boilers, pumps, and chillers.

In most applications, each unit provides a single temperature control zone, so an individual unit is often provided for each space, which has a different heating or cooling load.

- all self-contained units use air-cooled refrigeration equipment.

- a portion of the unit must be exposed to the outdoor air.

- "split system" unit is a variation of the self-contained unit.

- the condensing section (part of the air-cooled refrigeration equipment) can be separated from the rest of the unit and be located 50 ft (15 m) or more away from the indoor unit.

Self-contained systems:

- are pre-engineered units, with limited sizes available.

- almost exclusively are a commodity product designed to minimize material costs because their selection is normally price-based.

- tend to have relatively short expected service lives.

- are also limited in the type of air filtration options available.

- normally, flat panel filters capable of screening out only the largest airborne particles are provided.

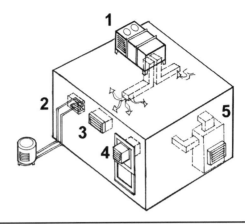

Fig. 1. Five configurations for self-contained systems: (1) rooftop unit; (2) split system with remote condenser and indoor fan and coil; (3) through-wall unit; (4) window-mounted unit; (5) floor-mounted indoor unit.

In addition to low first cost, other advantages of self-contained systems include:

- minimal maintenance

- full-system quality control/testing at the factory

- reliance on many independent units so that failure of any one unit affects only a small portion of the building.

Self-contained systems for residential applications

- quality of self-contained systems can vary substantially.

- smaller systems such as window units, through-wall units, and small split system units are considered "residential appliance" quality, with expected service lives of as low as 5 years and as high as 10 years.

- American Refrigeration Institute (ARI)–certified Package Terminal Air Conditioners (PTAC equipment) of the same size and type are manufactured to higher industry standards, and are considered commercial quality equipment with an expected service life closer to 15 years.

- because these self-contained systems have limited capacities (½ to 3 tons) and must have access to outdoor air in order to reject heat from the conditioned space, their use is limited to conditioning small individual rooms at the building perimeter.

- typical applications include single-family homes, apartments, motels, hotels, and small, residential load type offices at the perimeter of commercial buildings.

- in multistory buildings, the remote condensers of split system units are located either on grade or on the roof of the building.

Self-contained systems for commercial applications

- often referred to as "unitary equipment" or "packaged" equipment.

- common equipment configurations include rooftop units, larger split system units, and floor-mounted indoor units (located at a perimeter wall).

- in areas characterized by mild climates and reasonably low electric costs, large through-wall unit ventilators may be used in classroom applications.

- larger self-contained systems may include limited ductwork for distributing conditioned air over a relatively large area.

- multiple single-zone units are most commonly used to provide temperature control of the entire area served by each unit, but duct-mounted terminal control devices may also be used to provide additional zoning capabilities.

- self-contained rooftop multi-zone units are also available.

- a recent product introduced to the market uses multiple heating and cooling coils to provide multiple zones of temperature control (**Fig. 2**).

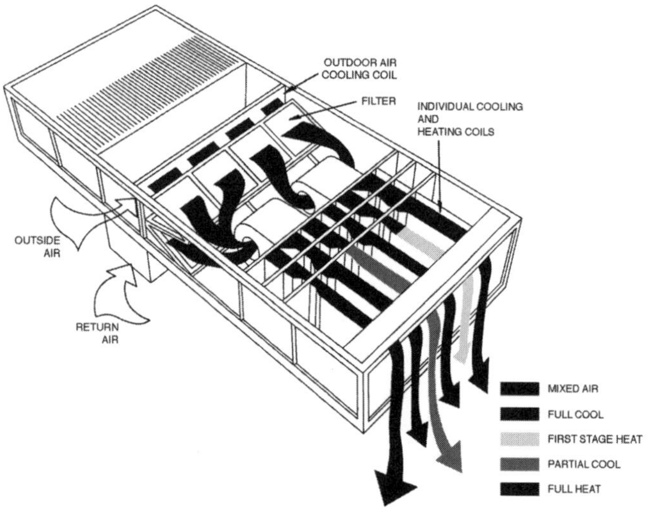

Fig. 2. Self-contained rooftop multi-zone unit. (Source: Carrier Corporation)

Heating options for each of these configurations include straight resistance electric heating coils or air source heat pumps.

- most commonly used equipment capacities range from 5 to 25 tons refrigeration capacity.

- much larger units are available for primarily industrial applications.

- equipment quality can range from "light commercial" to "commercial," with an expected service life of from 10 to 15 years.

Gas-fired desiccant air-conditioners (**Fig. 3**), a relatively new product,

- combine some of the ease-of-installation benefits of self-contained systems with the low operating costs more often associated with central systems.

- are particularly applicable to areas characterized by high humidity and in buildings with high ventilation loads, since they have the capability to remove latent heat (from humid outdoor air) very efficiently.

Air-cooled equipment of commercial self-contained systems:

- must be located at or near the outside of the building.

- use of these systems is limited to low-rise buildings.

- capacity of the supply air fans provided with this type of equipment is also limited.

- one of the most popular applications for self-contained systems is in the use of rooftop units serving a one-story structure, with multiple units, each serving up to 10,000 sq ft (929 m).

- easy to locate and require only minimum duct runs to the areas served.

Table 1 summarizes the basic choices available in self-contained systems.

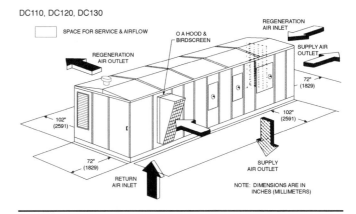

DC110, DC120, DC130

Fig. 3. Self-contained desiccant air-conditioner. (Source: Englehard/ICC)

Table 1. Basic choices for self-contained HVAC systems

Type of space	Equipment type	Typical unit cooling capacity range	Electric resistance	Air Source Heat Pump (ASHP)	Gas	Expected service life
Small [residential]	Window air-conditioner	1/2 to 3 ton	X	X		5 to 10 years
	Through-wall air-conditioner	1/2 to 5 tons	X	X		5 to 10 years
to	Unit ventilator					
	Commercial split system	3 to 5 tons	X	X		15 years
Large [commercial]	Rooftop unit	5 to 25 tons	X	X	X	15 years

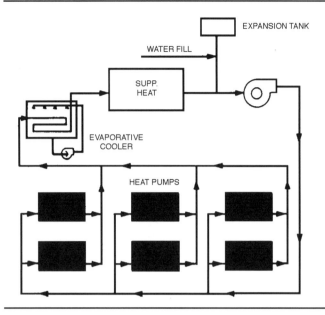

Fig. 4. Closed-loop heat pump system.

Box A—First use of central heat pump system for building heating and cooling.

Equitable Life Insurance Building, Portland, Oregon, A National Historic Mechanical Engineering landmark. Although a young French army officer proposed the theory in the early 19th century, the first major commercial installation of a central heat pump system for heating and cooling was pioneered in the Equitable Building in 1948. J. Donald Kroeker and Ray C. Chewning, system designers, Charles E. Graham, Engineer, and Pietro Bellushi, Architect.

Central systems

These systems require a central equipment space where boilers, chillers, cooling towers, pumps, and similar equipment are located and used to distribute the heating and/or cooling medium to remote terminal units.

Closed loop heat pump systems

- represent a special category of central systems.

- employ water source heat pumps (WSHP), which require only a small heating source, a circulating pump, and a small evaporative cooler (**Fig. 4**).

- each WSHP contains an air-circulating fan, a water-cooled refrigerant compressor/condenser, and a DX heating and cooling coil.

- air-source heat pumps reject heat to the ambient air (the heat sink) when operating in the cooling mode and extract heat from the air (the heat source) in the heating mode.

- water-source heat pumps use water from a closed loop piping system as both their heat source and heat sink.

- each water source heat pump can operate in either the heating or cooling mode, as required to meet varying space loads, and function in an inherent heat reclaim capability.

If one-third of the heat pumps (that is, those located at perimeter zones of a commercial office building) operate in the heating mode while the remaining heat pumps (serving interior zones) operate in the cooling mode, no external source of supplemental heating or cooling would be required. The building is internally balanced.

- temperature in the piping loop needs to be maintained between 60 to 90F (15 to 32°C) for the heat pumps to operate properly.

- if the loop temperature approaches 90F (32°C), an evaporative cooler is activated to decrease the loop temperature.

- if the water in the loop drops to 60F (15°C), supplemental heat is required.

- in conventional closed loop systems, a hot water boiler would perform this function.

- in the special case of an earth-coupled ground source heat pump (GSHP) system, a piping loop buried in the earth acts as the source for both supplemental heating and cooling.

Closed loop heat pump systems:

- strike a balance between conventional central systems (energy-efficient, but expensive and requiring large central equipment rooms) and self-contained systems (low cost but limited capabilities and service life).

- employ many small, or modular, WSHPs, which compete with residential self-contained systems in residential applications such as apartments, hotels, and dormitories.

- wall-mounted console units replace the through-wall units of self-contained systems.

- also available as pre-piped, vertically stacked closet units that offer improved aesthetics and quieter operation.

In modular WSHP systems using separately ducted ventilation air:

- horizontal concealed units can also be located above the ceiling.

- they can be used in any space (interior rooms as well as perimeter rooms) and in any height building.

- some small units require no more than a 12 in (30 cm) ceiling cavity.

- larger WSHPs also compete with commercial self-contained systems in larger commercial applications.

- available in both floor-mounted (**Fig. 5**) and rooftop units, which can be ducted to serve limited areas—approximately 10,000 sq ft (929 sq m) for the largest factory-built units commonly used.

Conventional central systems

Conventional central systems require a full complement of central equipment (boilers, chillers, cooling towers, and circulating pumps) and a distribution system (pipes and/or ducts). (Table 2.) Conventional central systems are often described as one of three types:

- all-water systems

- all-air systems

- air-water systems

All-water systems

- typically use small modular equipment, such as fan coil units or unit ventilators, to provide the local temperature control.

- hot and chilled water piping systems are the primary distribution system.

- offer more energy-efficient operation than self-contained systems, but at a higher first cost.

- use of chilled water and hot water coils offers closer control over temperature and relative humidity than do the DX refrigerant cooling coils and electric heating coils used in self-contained systems.

- also share the disadvantage of limited air filtration capabilities with self-contained terminal units.

- can be used in any size and height building; they are not limited to exterior zones or low-rise structures.

Like water-source heat pumps, terminal units for all-water systems come in the same configurations: wall-mounted console units, vertically stacked closet units, and horizontal ducted units designed to be concealed above the ceiling. **Fig. 6** indicates a stacked unit fan coil unit placement, commonly used in limited spaces.

Variations of all-water systems include two-pipe systems and four-pipe systems. While any system using chilled water coils requires a condensate drain line to carry off water that condenses on the cold

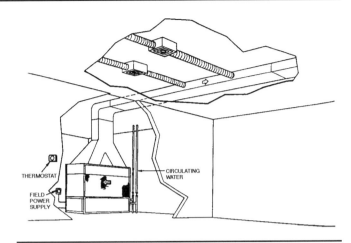

Fig. 5. Large ducted floor-mounted water-source heat pump. (Source: Carrier Corporation)

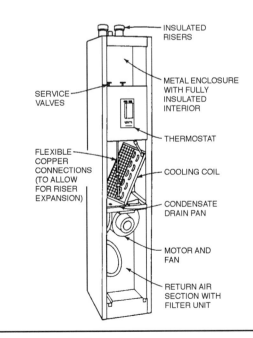

Fig. 6. Vertical "stacked" closed unit.

---

coil and collects in the condensate drain pan, the condensate piping is not counted in the nomenclature, which distinguishes two-pipe systems from four-pipe systems.

The most common type of two-pipe system is the two-pipe changeover system:

• employs a single heating/cooling coil in each terminal unit (typically called a fan coil unit) and a single set of distribution pipes.

• only one supply pipe and one return pipe, hence only hot water or chilled water can be made available to all the terminal units at any given time.

• building operator must change over the system from heating to cooling in the spring, and vice versa in the fall.

• often creates comfort problems during swing seasons (spring and fall) such as a cold but sunny, clear day when the north side of a building requires heat and the south side requires cooling.

• some two-pipe changeover systems are designed to include an electric resistance heating coil to provide partial heating capability for the changeover season.

• other systems are designed with full-size electric heating coils so either full heating or cooling is available at any time. These systems represent a compromise between the low cost of self-contained systems for residential applications such as hotels and the higher cost of four-pipe systems.

Four-pipe systems use fan coil units, which include two separate coils, a chilled water coil, and a hot water coil.

• require two sets of supply/return pipes: one for hot water, and one for chilled water.

• share the same advantages over competing systems as do two-pipe systems, but are capable of providing heating or cooling at any time at the first cost premium of an additional set of supply/return pipes and terminal coils.

• are usually the most economical all-water systems to operate.

All-air systems

• employ large, central air-handling units, from which warm or cool air is distributed throughout the building, primarily by duct distribution systems.

• central all-air systems offer the most energy-efficient equipment options, and are the most flexible of any HVAC system.

• can use a wide variety of terminal units to provide unlimited zoning capabilities, and factory-built air handlers can serve areas as large as 50,000 sq ft (4650 sq m) of conditioned space.

• quality of construction of central system equipment can range from commercial to institutional grade, with institutional grade equipment service lives exceeding 25 years.

Each component of the central station air-handling unit (AHU)—the fan, fan motor, cooling coil, heating coil, air filtration equipment, and humidification equipment—can be selected and sized *precisely* to meet the specific application needs, providing higher potential energy efficiency, comfort control, and indoor air quality. This can be accomplished with self-contained, closed loop heat pump, or all-water systems (**Fig. 7**).

Central station air-handling units are available as:

– off-the-shelf equipment that are pre-engineered and mass-produced in limited size ranges,

– modular components with the flexibility to select different sizes and configurations of each component, and

– custom units, which are designed for a specific application and built up in the field.

All-air systems are usually described by two variables: the type of air-handling unit provided, and the type of terminal control device used to control local zone comfort conditions. A system might be described as "constant volume/reheat" or "variable volume/cooling-only." Central station air-handling units are available as Constant Air Volume/Variable Air Temperature (CAV/VAT) units or Variable Air Volume/Constant Air Temperature (VAV/CAT) units.

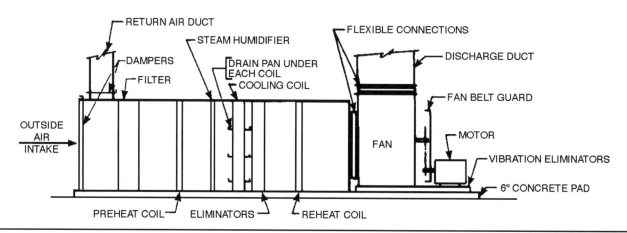

Fig. 7. Typical components of an air-handling unit.

CAV/VAT units (referred to simply as Constant Volume systems) supply a constant volume of air to the building; central heating and cooling coils vary the temperature of the air based on the building requirements (determined by local thermostats or sensors in the return air system, which indicate whether the spaces require heating or cooling). In a single zone application, this is all the control required. For some building applications with limited zoning requirements, this can be accomplished with multi-zone units, in which up to 12 sets of separate heating and cooling coils provide different temperature air to each zone.

Most central air-handling systems:

- used to serve a large number of individual temperature control zones.

- air provided by the central system must be cooled enough to meet the cooling load of the worst-case zone of conditioned space.

- to provide local control for all the other zones, some form of reheat must be used.

- an electric reheat coil or hot water reheat coil is used to reheat this central air—typically supplied around 55F (12°C)—as set by a local thermostat.

- provides the best control of temperature and relative humidity.

- very energy-inefficient to reheat the full volume of cool air supplied by the central air handler.

- systems are restricted by energy codes and limited to special uses (such as hospital operating rooms and museums) that require such a high degree of control.

To overcome the inherent energy waste of constant volume/reheat systems, Variable Volume Air (VAV) systems were developed and became very popular in the 1970s. These systems:

- include variable volume air-handling units designed to conserve fan energy by varying the amount of central air to each zone, based on local zone requirements.

- once a local control terminal (VAV box) throttles down the central air to the minimum required for ventilation and proper air circulation, reheat can be applied (at a minimum energy penalty) to the reduced volume of air to avoid overcooling the local space.

A wide range of terminal control devices, typically located above the ceiling of occupied spaces to provide local zone control, are available. To meet current energy codes, these devices must reduce the flow of central cool air to a minimum before any reheat is applied. The type of VAV box used is extremely important to the comfort conditions provided and the energy efficiency of the entire system; the types of VAV control devices available are:

- VAV cooling-only box

- VV/VT and VAV diffusers

- VAV/electric reheat coil

- VAV/hot water reheat coil

- VAV/fan-powered box, electric reheat

- VAV/fan-powered box, hot water reheat

VAV cooling-only box

- simplest type of VAV terminal control device.

- consists of dampers, which regulate the flow of cool air based on a signal from the local thermostat.

- one of the more inexpensive control devices, often used to condition large interior zones of commercial office space (which typically require no heating during occupied periods).

- can also be used to serve perimeter zones when either a separate heating system or VAV/reheat boxes are used to serve perimeter zones.

- one of the most flexible to use.

- changes to interior layouts may require only minor ducting and diffuser changes or, at the worst, changing out the VAV box with one of different capacity.

- VAV cooling-only boxes range in capacity from approximately 200 CFM (e.g., 8 × 12 × 14 in) to 3200 CFM (e.g., 18 × 65 × 54 in).

VV/VT and VAV diffusers

- rely on complex controls and mechanical volume dampers at each individual supply air diffuser to provide zoning capabilities to small commercial systems.

- both the supply air temperature delivered by the central air handler and the supply air volume at individual diffusers is varied to meet local space conditions.

- control system must continuously "poll" thermostats to determine the appropriate mode of operation (heating or cooling) of the central air handler.

- operate similarly to VAV/cooling-only boxes.

- Each diffuser has its own mechanically operated damper system to control the volume of cool air discharged from the diffuser.

- Rely heavily on sometimes-intricate control systems and many mechanical devices, which usually have a shorter service life than the equipment they operate.

- should be used to control only zones of very similar heating and cooling loads.

- system may revert to the heating mode because one or two perimeter zones require heating, even though the rest of the interior zones may be calling for cooling.

- central systems used in conjunction with these devices may or may not employ a variable speed fan; if not, all the energy efficiency benefits of "true VAV" systems are lost.

- diffusers are generally successful when applied as a low-cost alternative, in smaller commercial buildings with many small zones (many private offices in an interior area), where true VAV system costs are prohibitive.

VAV/electric reheat coil

- similar to a VAV cooling-only box, but has a small electric reheat coil attached to it.

- reheat coil is not activated until the air volume is reduced to its minimum, and the electric coil must be matched to the minimum airflow to ensure adequate flow occurs across the coil.

- flexible, low cost terminal control device, but using resistance electric heating coils involves a penalty in heating costs.

- energy efficiency of the system is enhanced if a less costly heating fuel is used at the air-handling unit, so the electric coil does not have to operate during overnight-unoccupied periods.

- during the overnight heating period, the large central air handler must operate to heat the building, incurring a cost penalty in electricity usage compared to the use of fan-powered VAV boxes (described below).

- do not provide temperature control as closely as do VAV/hot water reheat boxes because the electric coil has a limited number of stages of heating (normally from one to three).

- hot water temperature/flow through a coil can be modulated to more closely match the heating need.

VAV/hot water reheat coil

- similar in operation to the VAV/electric reheat coil, but more costly (due to additional hot water piping to each box).

- main benefit is reduced heating costs compared to the VAV/electric reheat device.

- VAV-reheat boxes range in capacity from 200 CFM (e.g., $9 \times 50 \times 22$ in) to 5000 CFM ($20 \times 60 \times 80$ in).

VAV/fan-powered box, electric reheat

- uses a small fan contained within the VAV box. Fan arrangements include:

- series fan/continuous operation arrangement

- parallel fan/intermittent operation

- series fan/continuous operation arrangement

- box fan runs continuously, and provides the motive force to distribute the central air from the box to all associated diffusers.

- as the cooling load drops and thermostat calls for heating, reduces the volume of primary air (cold air from the central air handler) to the minimum required for ventilation while drawing warm return air from the ceiling plenum through the box.

- recovers heat from the ceiling plenum, and the reheat coil is activated only when the recovered heat is insufficient to heat the zone.

- savings can be lost by the continuous use of the small (inefficient) fan, which adds heat to the primary cold air during operations in the cooling mode.

- some analyses have shown this method of operation to actually use 4 to 5 times more energy than the parallel fan/intermittent operation arrangement described below.

- provides a continuous volume of air to the occupied space.

- sometimes used in conjunction with ice storage/cold air distribution systems, which deliver colder air than the conventional 55F (12°C) supply air temperature.

- mixing cold air with warm plenum air permits the use of conventional diffusers without creating the effect of "dumping" cold air on the occupants.

- helps to prevent condensate from forming on diffusers.

- this method of handling cold air distribution now competes with recently introduced induction diffusers designed to obtain greater mixing of the supply air with room air before it enters the occupied zone.

Parallel fan/intermittent operation

- during cooling cycle, cool primary air volume is reduced as the cooling load decreases, until it reaches the minimum air volume required for ventilation.

- box is not activated until there is a call for heating.

- on the first call, it draws 100 percent warm air from the ceiling plenum, making maximum use of the recovered heat.

- if the recovered heat from the ceiling plenum is insufficient to satisfy the thermostat, there will be a second call for heating. The reheat coil will then be activated.

- parallel fan is sized only to deliver the maximum amount of air required for heating, and therefore is smaller than the fans designed for series/continuous operation.

- parallel fan only runs during the heating cycle, when the heat given off by the inefficient motor provides useful work.

- tends to be much more energy efficient than the series/continuous fan arrangement.

VAV/fan-powered box, hot water reheat

- most energy efficient of all when used in the parallel fan/intermittent operation arrangement.

- operation is similar to that described for the VAV/fan-powered box, electric reheat.

- because it is more expensive and less flexible than other VAV boxes (due to the box fan and hot water piping), this box is commonly used to condition perimeter zones, which require more heat.

- often used for relatively fixed private office layouts.

Air-water systems

- include any type of air-water system that is combined with a separately ducted ventilation air system, plus a unique system called the induction system.

- induction system uses "primary air" from a high velocity central air-handling system, which is ducted through a type of terminal unit specially designed to use the Venturi effect of the primary airstream to induce room air into the unit and across the heating/cooling coil.

- operates like a fan coil unit without requiring a local fan.

- found in high-rise buildings where a minimum amount of ductwork is desirable.

- good use is typified by building applications where modular units are desired for individual room control.

- improved air quality and humidity control is provided (since a central ventilation system air handler can be used to provide better outside air filtration, better control of relative humidity, and an opportunity to recover waste heat from building exhaust airstreams).

Due to high maintenance costs, the constant volume induction system has fallen from favor and no new induction system has been installed since about 1985, but it is still found in existing buildings. **Table 2** summarizes the basic types of central systems currently available and their general characteristics.

3 OVERVIEW OF HVAC SYSTEMS

Describing HVAC system types by category (as above) is a convenient method of explaining the nomenclature used by engineers and the engineering principles involved. However, the system selection process for any project begins with the application in mind. For this reason,

the charts in this article were developed to provide an overview of the HVAC systems to be considered in different commercial building applications. **Table 3** can be used to view all the HVAC systems commonly used in commercial building applications (densely populated buildings with high internal air-conditioning loads due to people, lights, and office equipment).

Selecting the HVAC system

The following process can be used to select, or at least to short-list, the final HVAC system options for a given building application:

1 Identify the range of HVAC system types that are appropriate for a given application from a master matrix of system types and building applications;

2 Short-list the original set of generally applicable HVAC systems using a few key screening criteria that relate to a more specific building (high-rise vs. low-rise), owner criteria, or climatic consideration;

3 Once the number of potential HVAC systems is short-listed to two or three, review the more detailed descriptions of each system's cost, equipment requirements, and performance characteristics to better understand their differences; either make the initial system selection at this point or

4 Review the final system shortlist with the Owner and engineering consultant to determine if more detailed analyses are required to select the best system, or to evaluate specific system options.

The matrices indicated in **Tables 4** and **5** illustrate the basic HVAC system types (across the top of the chart) and basic building applications (left side of the chart) for residential and commercial building systems, respectively. Using this system selection matrix allows one to quickly narrow the potential system types to be evaluated further to three or four, simplifying the decision-making process. Once a shortlist of potential system types is developed in this manner, further steps can be taken to reduce the final choices to perhaps one or two:

- Rule out any system that does not fit with the basic category appropriate to the building application (that is, a speculative builder of apartment buildings might not want to consider any central sys-

Table 2. Basic central HVAC system types

Type of space	Equipment type	Electric resistance	Air Source Heat Pump (ASHP)	Water Source Heat Pump WSHP/GSHP	Steam/hot water water	Expected service life
Small [residential]	Modular fan coil units	X	X		X	20+ years
	Modular closed loop heat pumps			X		19 years
to	Unit ventilators & induction units	X	X	X	X	20+ years
Large [commercial]	Air handling units: Off-the-shelf Modular Custom	X	X	X	X	15 + years 15-20 years 25+ years

Table 3. Overview of commercial (non-residential) HVAC system types

Legend:
- ■ = Not applicable or rarely used
- ● = Commonly Used
- ○ = Infrequently Used

NON-RESIDENTIAL HVAC SYSTEMS

Generic System Type	HVAC System Type	VAV & VAV Diffusers	Elect. Reheat Coil	H.W. Reheat Coil	VAV Box (Cooling-Only)	VAV Box, Electric Reheat Coil	VAV Box, Fan-Powered w/ Elect. Reheat Coil	VAV Box, H.W. Reheat Coil	VAV Box, Fan-Powered w/ H.W. Reheat Coil	Elect. Heating Coil	Direct Gas-Fired	Air Source Heat Pump DX and Elect. Htg. Coil	Watersource Heat Pump DX Heating Coil	Hot Water or Steam Heating Coil	Ground Source Heat Pump DX Coil	Elect. Baseboard/Wall Convectors	Elect. Radiant Panels @ Perimeter Ceiling	H.W. Baseboard/Wall Convectors	H.W. Radiant Panels @ Perimeter Ceiling
		LOW ← First Cost/Zone → HIGH								LOW ← Heating System First Cost Premium → HIGH									
SELF-CONTAINED DUCTED ALL-AIR SYSTEMS* [limited to low- and mid-rise bldgs. only]	Unitary Ducted Air Conditioners	○	○		○	○			■	●	●							○	
	Unitary Ducted Air Source Heat Pumps	○	○		○	○			■	●		●						○	
	Unitary Ducted Multizone AHU								■	●	●								
	Gas-Fired Dessicant Air-Conditioner	○	○		○	○			■	●	●								
CENTRAL DUCTED WATER LOOP HEAT PUMP SYSTEMS*	Central Water Source Heat Pump AHU								■				●						
	Central Ground Source Heat Pump AHU								■						●				
CENTRAL ALL-WATER SYSTEMS* (Small modular terminal units; may be referred to as "air-water system" if combined with central ducted ventilation air system)	2-Pipe Modular Fan Coil Unit/Unit Vent.	○	○		○	○			■	●		○		●					
	Modular Closed Loop Heat Pump	○	○		○	○			■	●		●	●	●					
	4-Pipe Modular Fan Coil Unit								■	●				●					●
	4-Pipe Modular Unit Ventilator								■	●				●					
CENTRAL ALL-AIR SYSTEMS	Central Station Multizone AHU			●	●	●	●	●	■	●				●					○
	Central Station Constant Volume AHU	●	●	●	●	●	●	●	■	●				●					
	Central Station Variable Volume AHU	●	●	●	●	●	●	●	■	●				●					
CENTRAL AIR-WATER SYSTEMS	Air-Water Induction Unit	○		●	○				■			○		●				●	●

*See Residential/Light Commercial systems chart for smaller, non-ducted system options.

EQUIPMENT OPTIONS

HVAC System Type	Mech. Equipment Locations	Central Equipment
Unitary Air Conditioner AHU	Self-Contained ROOFTOP Units,	None
Unitary Air Source Heat Pump AHU	Indoor AHU's w/ Access to Outside Air, or	
Unitary Multizone AHU	Indoor AHU's with Remote Air-Cooled Condensers	
Gas-Fired Dessicant Air-Conditioner		
Central Closed Loop Heat Pump(WSHP)	ROOFTOP Units or	Boiler, Closed Ckt. Cooler, Pumps
Central Closed Loop Heat Pump(GSHP)	Indoor Units	Ground-Coupled Piping Loop
2-Pipe Modular Fan Coil Unit	Central Mech. Eqpmt. Room,	Boiler(s)
2-Pipe Modular Unit Ventilator	Rooftop Heat Rejection Equipment, and	Air-Cooled Chiller(s) or
4-Pipe Modular Fan Coil Unit	Local Terminal Eqpmt.	Water-Cooled Chiller/Cooling Towers
4-Pipe Modular Unit Ventilator		Pumps(& AHU if separate vent. system used)
Central Station Multizone AHU	Central Mech. Eqpmt. Room &	Boiler(s) & Chiller(s)
Central Station Constant Volume AHU	Rooftop Heat Rejection Equipment	Cooling Tower(s) & Pumps
Central Station Variable Volume AHU		Central AHU's
Air-Water Induction Unit	Central M.E.R. & Rooftop Cooling Tower(s)	Boiler(s),Chiller(s),Tower(s), Pumps, AHU's

General Application Notes

Cost LOW:
- Often ALL-ELECTRIC; direct gas heat option avail.
- Multiple ROOFTOP UNITS = popular use
- Airside ECONOMIZER COOLING option avail.
- Largest units SERVE UP TO 10,000 SF AREA

First Cost:
- Most often used at bldg. perimeter
- VENTILATION thru-wall or centrally ducted
- NO airside ECONOMIZER COOLING avail.
- Largest units SERVE UP TO 1,000 SF AREA
- Most flexible systems, ECON. COOLING avail.
- Use is not limited by building size/height
- Largest units serve 40,000 SF AREA or more

HIGH:
- Limited to HIGH-RISES; 1500 SF AREA/unit

Table 4. HVAC system selection matrix for heating only applications

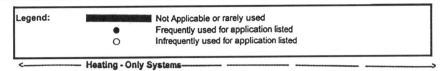

Legend:		
■■■■	Not Applicable or rarely used	
●	Frequently used for application listed	
○	Infrequently used for application listed	

←———————— Heating - Only Systems ————— ————————— ————————— —————————→

Application	Primary Building Function	Electric Baseboard	Warm Air Furnace	Infra-Red Heat	Radiant Electric	H.W. Baseboard or Convectors	Radiant H.W.
Residential	Single-Family Residence	●	●	■	○	●	●
	Low-Rise Multi-Family/Apartments	●	●	■	■	●	■
	Motels / Nursing Homes	■	○	■	○	■	○
	Dormitories	■	■	■	■	●	●
	Hotels	■	■	■	■	■	■
Light Commercial		■	■	■	■	■	■
	Country Club/Funeral Home	■	■	■	■	■	■
	Beauty/Barber Shops	■	■	■	■	■	■
	Small Retail Stores	■	■	■	■	■	■
	Department Stores	■	■	■	■	○	■
	Malls/Shopping Centers	■	■	■	■	■	■
	Restaurants	■	■	■	■	■	■
	Bowling Alleys	■	■	■	■	■	■
	Places of Worship	■	○	■	■	●	■
	Theatres	■	■	■	■	■	■
Commercial		■	■	■	■	■	■
	Auditoriums	■	■	■	■	■	■
	Class B Spec Office Building	■	■	■	■	■	■
	Class A Spec Office Building	■	■	■	■	■	■
	Corporate Office Building	■	■	■	■	■	■
	Radio/TV Studios	■	■	■	■	■	■
	Libraries (Standard)	■	■	■	■	■	■
	Libraries (Archival)/Museums	■	■	■	■	■	■
	Arenas/Exhibition Halls	■	■	■	■	■	■
	Service Garage	■	●	●	■	●	■
	Warehouse	■	●	●	■	●	■
Institutional		■	■	■	■	■	■
	Elementary Schools	■	■	■	■	●	■
	Secondary Schools	■	■	■	■	○	■
	Higher Education	■	■	■	■	■	■
	Laboratories	■	■	■	■	■	■
	Hospitals	■	■	■	■	■	■
Industrial	Light Assembly/Fabrication	■	●	●	■	●	■

tem types; a university may rule out the use of self-contained systems due to a preference for central equipment rooms or the availability of campus-wide steam, hot water, or chilled water lines from a central plant).

- Use the preliminary screening criteria noted in **Table 6.** Rule out any system type shown to be inappropriate for the given building application.

- Review the detailed system selection criteria below and the HVAC system descriptions for the remaining options to select the HVAC system most likely to meet the application's needs.

Summary of HVAC system selection criteria

- Site constraints and opportunities

– Climatic considerations: How do local weather factors affect annual utility costs, and how important are the annual energy costs to the client's business operation?

– Ambient air quality: Does the general area air quality affect the degree of air filtration and treatment required? Do local conditions affect the location of outdoor air intakes (that is, are there local pollution sources from street level traffic, or from the roofs of adjacent buildings)?

Table 5. HVAC system selection matrix for combined heating/cooling applications

Legend:

▐	Not Applicable or rarely used
●	Frequently used for application listed
○	Infrequently used for application listed

Heating & Cooling Systems — All-Air Systems — Air/Water Systems

1 Zone/Air Handling Unit — Control Terminals Above Ceiling — Multiple Zones/Air Handling Unit

Application	BASIC SYSTEM TYPE → Primary Building Function	Warm Air Furnace with Add-On A/C	Window & Thru-Wall AC with Elect. Heat	2-Pipe Changeover Fan Coil Units & Unit Ventilators	Thru-Wall or Split-System Air-Source Heat Pumps & Unit Ventilators	Modular Water-Source Heat Pumps & Unit Ventilators	4-Pipe Fan Coil Unit & Unit Ventilators	Single Zone, Constant Air Volume	Single Zone V.A.V.	Single Zone, Constant Air Volume w/ Elect. Reheat	VAV Box w/ Elect. Reheat	Multizone, Constant Air Volume	Fan-Powered VAV w/ Elect. Reheat	Single Zone, Constant Air Volume w/ H.W. Reheat Coils	Cooling-Only VAV w/ Separate Perim. Heat	VAV w/ H.W. Reheat Coils	Fan-Powered VAV w/ H.W. Reheat Coils
Residential	Single-Family Residence	●	○		●												
	Low-Rise Multi-Family/Apartments		●	○	●	●											
	Motels / Nursing Homes	○	●	●	●	●											
	Dormitories	○		●	●	●											
	Hotels				●	●	●										
Light Commercial	Country Club/Funeral Home			○	●	○		●	○		○	●	○		○		●
	Beauty/Barber Shops	●			●			●			●						
	Small Retail Stores		○		●			●									
	Department Stores	○		●		●	●	●	○		●	●	●	●	●		●
	Malls/Shopping Centers	●	○					●	○			○			○		
	Restaurants			●				●	○		●	●	●				
	Bowling Alleys							●	○			●					
	Places of Worship			○	○			●	○			●					
	Theatres							●									
Commercial	Auditoriums		○	○	○	○	○	○	○		○	●	●		●		●
	Class B Spec Office Building					●		○			●	○	○		●		●
	Class A Spec Office Building							○			●		○		●		○
	Corporate Office Building							○			○	○	○		○		○
	Radio/TV Studios							●	●	●				●			
	Libraries (Standard)							●		●		○		●			
	Libraries (Archival)/Museums													●			
	Arenas/Exhibition Halls																
	Service Garage																
	Warehouse																
Institutional	Elementary Schools		○	●	●	●	●	●			●		○		●	●	●
	Secondary Schools		○	●	●	●	●	●			●		○		●	●	●
	Higher Education																
	Laboratories																●
	Hospitals							●									
Industrial	Light Assembly/Fabrication																

Table 6. Preliminary screening criteria

IF the building application:	THEN:
is <u>not</u> a hospital operating room, laboratory, museum, or other special use space requiring exceptionally close control of temperature, relative humidity, and/or space pressurization relationships	Rule out constant volume terminal reheat systems (current energy codes prohibit the use of this system type except for special use applications, unless the source of reheat is recovered heat).
considers building aesthetics to be crucial to commercial success	Rule out self-contained through-wall and window air-conditioners (which require many visible A/C system components penetrating exterior walls).
is greater than six stories high	Rule out self-contained rooftop, split systems, and multizone units (these system types typically don't have the capability to serve tall/large buildings due to inherent equipment limitations).
requires the use of economizer cooling ("free cooling" in winter) or maximum outside air capability for "purging" the building	Rule out all-water and air/water systems (which have little or no separately-ducted outside air capability).
requires simultaneous heating and cooling for different areas of the building at any time of the year	Rule out two pipe "change-over" fan coil unit systems OR provide supplemental electric heating coils designed to provide adequate heat for "in between" seasons.
is located in a climatic area characterized by high humidity at summer design conditions (hot/humid climates)	Rule out multizone systems (due to inherent system limitations in handling high humidity/high temperature conditions).

- Available utilities and costs: Which utilities are available (electricity, gas, district or central plant steam, hot water chilled water) and at what unit cost? Are their specific rate schedules available for all-electric systems? Are equipment rebates available from local utility providers for "preferred" equipment? Should the system be designed for flexibility in fuel choices, so that the least cost fuel can be switched based on periodic utility negotiations?

- Visual sight lines: Will rooftop equipment be visible?

- Building and site boundaries: Do current buildings abut sides of this building, or could they in the future?

- *Owner/developer requirements*

- *First cost:* How important is it relative to long-term operating costs? Should systems requiring large mechanical equipment rooms, duct shafts, or increased ceiling heights be avoided?

- *Construction schedule:* Is off-the-shelf packaged equipment required to avoid long lead times for equipment procurement?

- *Annual energy and utility costs:* Are there economic criteria established for decision-making on any energy-related premiums in system first cost?

- *Capacity of building maintenance staff (number of staff and skill level):* Will custodial staff be available to change air filters and clean condensate pans on many small modular terminal units, or should most maintenance be performed in a central equipment room by more skilled staff? Will the use of high-pressure steam boilers require the presence of operating engineers around the clock?

- *Space considerations:* If rental property, how much income is lost annually for lost rental space occupied by mechanical equipment and duct and pipe shafts?

- *Equipment location considerations:* Should equipment locations at building perimeter and corner office space be avoided at all cost? Would this eliminate the use of self-contained or floor-by-floor indoor air handlers?

- *Durability:* Will exposed equipment be vulnerable to vandalism or physical abuse?

- *Reliability:* How important is redundant central equipment or multiple self-contained units?

- *Flexibility:* How often are interior space layouts expected to change, and how much will it cost to make the required changes to the HVAC system? Is the churn rate high enough, or cubicle density requirements high enough, to warrant consideration of all-air, below-floor distribution plenums rather than conventional ceiling distribution systems?

- *Adaptability:* How easily should the HVAC system be adaptable to a new space function; will the building be more marketable, now or in the future, with a more adaptable system?

- *End user and occupant requirements*

- *Degree of temperature and humidity control:* How precisely should indoor air temperature be controlled; is close control of relative humidity important?

– *Degree of air filtration required:* Are low-efficiency flat filters associated with self-contained and modular terminal units adequate, or is high-efficiency filtration available with central all-air systems required?

– *Need to avoid cross-contamination between rooms:* Should all-air systems using common return air plenums be ruled out?

– *Number of separate temperature control zones required:* What is the ratio of private spaces requiring individual thermostatic control compared to large open plan areas requiring only one temperature control zone per 1000 sq ft (TK sq m) or more of floor area? Should modular all-water terminal units be used in small perimeter spaces, with larger all-air VAV systems serving large interior cooling-only zones?

4 SPACE PLANNING

The space required to house HVAC equipment and associated pipe and duct shafts can amount to over 10 percent of the building floor area, depending upon the building application and type of HVAC system used. Heavy structural loads of central equipment will also affect the building's structural system design. Location of the mechanical equipment can influence building aesthetics and the acoustical environment in occupied areas. The spatial layout of the HVAC system needs to be programmed early in the design phase and coordinated with all other building elements.

The first step in planning the HVAC system layout is to identify the location and configuration of the central equipment. In large buildings using central systems, this often includes three types of equipment rooms:

• a central plant equipment space (usually one location in the building, housing central chillers, boilers, and related equipment),

• a rooftop location for cooling towers, and

• equipment room(s) for large central air-handling units.

Central plant equipment rooms are often located at the top of a building to:

– minimize the piping distance to connect the chillers to the rooftop cooling towers.

– minimize the length of expensive boiler flues that typically extend well above rooftop heights.

– may also be located on the lowest floor of the building.

– or the boilers and chillers may be located in two different locations.

The nomograph shown in **Fig. 8** in conjunction with **Table 7** provide a simple technique for approximating the sizes of the main air-conditioning system components, the space required to house them, and associated duct sizes.

System sizing nomograph: an example

The nomograph is used by entering with total building area on bar (A). To use an example:

• Consider a 300,000 sq ft office building. In Table 7, the data for an office building indicates a medium air-conditioning load of 400 sq ft per ton and medium air quantity of 0.9 CFM/sq ft.

– Entering the nomograph with a building area of 300,000 sq ft and proceeding vertically up to (B), and the sloped line representing 400 sq ft/ton on bar (C), the air-conditioner size can be approximated as 750 tons.

– Continuing horizontally to the right to the 45° turning line, we proceed vertically down to bar (D) and vertically up to bar (E). On bar (D) we read the mechanical equipment room volume as 45,000 cu ft.

– On bar (E), the cooling tower area would be read as 900 sq ft.

– Going back to bar (A) and proceeding vertically downward to (F) and turning to the 1 CFM/sq ft line, we read on bar (G) that the total air volume is 300,000 CFM.

• The above narrative on air-handling equipment indicates that the largest commercially available units (not custom) are about 40,000 CFM. We know that this office building will require several air handlers. For design estimating purposes, assume we are designing a 10-story office building with 30,000 sq ft per floor and that we will have one 30,000 CFM air handler on each floor.

– Enter bar (A) with 30,000 sq ft.

– Bar (G) shows 30,000 CFM.

– Bar (H) shows 12,500 cu ft. If we have a clear height of 12 ft in the fan room, it would have a floor area of 1041 sq ft.

• Typical air-handling unit data (e.g., Sweet's catalog manufacturer's literature) indicate (let us assume) an approximate unit size of 14 × 11 × 7.6 ft. This should fit comfortably within a room of 25 × 40 ft and have space for all associated ductwork and servicing. Proceeding from 3 on bar (G) horizontally to the branch duct and supply duct turning lines:

– We read on bar (I), a supply duct total area of 25 sq ft.

– We read 33 sq ft of branch duct area.

• We now know we have a supply air duct of approximately 36 × 100 in, leaving the fan room before it begins to branch to smaller sizes to serve various areas of the floor. Note that the sum of the branch duct area is larger than the total supply duct area. This is due to a lower air velocity being used in the branches.

• Remember that return air ductwork with the same area as the branch ductwork will be required for return air back to the fan room to complete the system ducting.

• Bear in mind that cooling towers can range in height from 12 to over 40 ft and should be located far away from building openings (such as windows and outside air intakes) to avoid the possibility of any carryover of moist, and possibly contaminated, air back into occupied areas.

Central equipment room planning

Central equipment rooms housing boilers, chillers, and large pumps should have between 12 to 16 ft clear height available, from the finished floor to underside of structure, to allow for adequate clearance

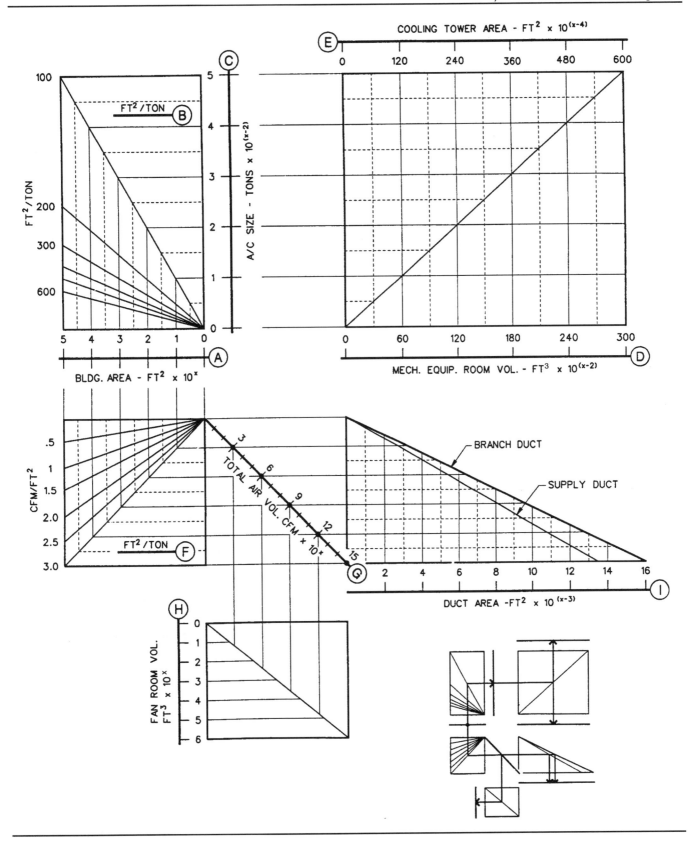

Fig. 8. Space and duct sizing nomograph.

Table 7. Air-conditioning and air quantities for various building types

	Air Conditioning Load (SF/ton)			Air Quantities (CFM/SF)		
	Low	Medium	High	Low	Medium	High
Apartments, Hi Rise	500	425	350	0.8	1.0	1.3
Auditoriums, Churches, Theaters	400	300	150	1.0	1.8	2.5
Educational Facilities	400	300	200	0.8	1.2	1.8
Factories						
Light Manufacturing	350	250	150	1.2	1.6	2.0
Heaving Manufacturing	150	100	75	2.5	3.5	4.5
Hospitals						
Patient Rooms	350	250	180	.5	.75	.9
Public Areas	300	250	150	.8	1.0	1.1
Hotels, Motels, Dormitories	500	400	300	.9	1.2	1.4
Libraries & Museums	400	350	300	.9	1.0	1.1
Office Buildings	500	400	300	.7	.9	1.2
Residential						
Large, Single Family	800	600	400	.5	.7	1.0
Medium, Single Family	800	700	600	.5	.7	1.0
Shopping Centers						
Beauty & Barber Shops	300	250	200	.9	1.3	2.0
Department Stores	500	400	300	.9	1.4	2.0
Drug Stores	250	200	150	.7	1.0	1.3
Shoe Stores	400	300	200	.8	1.0	1.2
Malls	450	350	250	1.1	1.6	2.0

above the main equipment for accessories and large piping crossovers. Long narrow rooms—with an aspect ratio (width to length) of approximately 1 to 2—usually allow for the most flexible and efficient layout of equipment. The equipment room sizes given in the nomograph above should provide adequate space for typical equipment accessories, clearances around equipment for servicing and replacement, and "tube-pull" clearances. Equipment such as chillers and shell-and-tube heat exchangers require clear space equal to the length of the equipment in order to pull the heat exchange tubes for servicing. Often a "back-to-back" arrangement of equipment minimizes the total floor area required to accommodate such needs.

Provide proper vibration isolation for large equipment, particularly rotating equipment, such as chillers and pumps. In addition to planning the location and configuration of equipment rooms, access to these rooms is an important consideration. Adequate equipment room doors and routes to freight elevators and/or the building exterior should be planned such that the largest piece of equipment can be easily installed (and possibly removed in future).

Air-handling equipment planning

The number and location of central air-handling unit equipment rooms (commonly called "fan rooms") are critical to a successful HVAC system. As noted above, the nomograph in Fig. 8 indicates an estimate of the CFM requirements for the building. Since the largest central fans typically used in commercial applications are approximately 40,000 CFM in capacity, dividing the building CFM by 40,000 yields the minimum number of air handlers required to serve the building. (If self-contained equipment, such as rooftop units, is to be used, a maximum size of 10,000 CFM per air handler is best.)

Once the number of air-handling units is determined, the next decision is how (or whether) they are to be grouped together in separate rooms. The more "centered" or centrally located within the building, the more efficient and less costly will be the distribution systems. However, other planning considerations may dictate a more beneficial arrangement. The following discussion summarizes typical air-handling unit equipment room arrangement approaches:

"Scattered" or separated units

- often used in low-rise buildings employing rooftop equipment.

- air handlers are simply located as centrally as possible to the separate zones they serve (and are thus scattered throughout the building as a function of its separate zones).

- results in the most efficient fan sizing and minimal duct sizes.

- because air handlers will be located directly above occupied areas, noise and vibration isolation are critical factors.

"Central core" placement

- all air-handling unit rooms are located together near the building core often on multiple floors in high-rise buildings.

- tends to yield the most efficient equipment room layout and duct distribution layout if one air handler can serve an entire floor.

- horizontal or vertical ducting is required to admit and reject fresh outside air and to exhaust spent air.

- air-handling unit rooms placed in the central core can take advantage of other service elements such as elevator shafts and restrooms to buffer noise.

- no equipment room wall should be located immediately adjacent to an occupied space, and equipment rooms are best stacked vertically to minimize piping and airshaft space requirements.

- at least two and preferably three sides of the equipment room are free of vertical obstructions so that supply and return ductwork can pass through them to serve the occupied areas.

- because floor-to-ceiling height is limited to the typical building floor height, the supply/return mains tend to be dimensioned "flatter" than desired for optimal airflow efficiency and noise control.

- often results in excessive fan noise and high velocity duct noise from the mains.

- place exiting ducts to pass over low occupancy service spaces, such as closets and restrooms, and also to include a duct turn above these spaces to reduce duct-transmitted noise.

"Perimeter" rooms

- minimizes the ducting required for outside air and exhaust air.

- can reduce the efficiency of the supply/return duct system, unless multiple units are required for each floor.

- potential lost use of premium perimeter floor areas.

- potential negative aesthetic impact of large air intake/exhaust louvers on the exterior.

- proximity of potentially noisy equipment close to occupied areas of the building.

"Detached" rooms

- moves the equipment room outside the main building, such as an adjacent protruding service shaft.

- sometimes allows for maximum space utilization and flexibility within the main floor plate of the building it serves.

System summaries

The descriptions that follow in tabular form (**Tables 8** to **16**) summarize the operating characteristics and key design considerations for the HVAC systems described above.

5 HVAC EQUIPMENT

Boilers

- used to provide a building with steam or hot water for space heating, processes, and services.

- steam is selected if required by the process needs.

- hot water is more common for space heating because it is more flexible and offers better space temperature control.

- boiler may be rated with a gross output in thousands of Btu per hour (MBH), boiler horsepower (33,475 Btu/hr = 1 BHP), or pounds of steam per hour (970.3 Btu per pound).

- fuels include natural gas, oil, electricity, and coal.

- outdoor air for combustion should be provided at the rate of approximately 12.5 CFM per BHP.

- net free area of direct openings in boiler rooms for combustion air should not be less than 1 sq in for every 4 MBH, or for every 2 MBH if the combustion air is ducted to the boiler.

- typically have turndown capability to reduce the boiler output in response to the load. Common turndown ratios are 4 to 1 and 10 to 1.

Boilers can be categorized by construction material:

- cast-iron boilers are built up in sections, and are expandable to add capacity.

- used in closed, low-pressure heating systems.

- steel firetube boilers include scotch marine and firebox types, which direct the flue gases through tubes surrounded by water.

- watertube boilers direct water through tubes in the combustion gas chamber.

Typical capacity ranges and other properties for a number of boiler types are shown in **Table 17**. Selection criteria are shown in **Fig. 9**.

Space requirements must allow ample room for service, which may include space to pull boiler tubes. As an example, firetube boilers, from 15 to 80 ft, have tube unit lengths of 8 to 27 ft, and widths of 4 to 10 ft. These units require an additional 5 to 23 ft of space to pull tubes as necessary. The tube-pull space provided may be within the boiler room, or may extend through a doorway. Total weight associated with these boilers varies from 300 lb per BHP (boiler horsepower) at 15 BHP, to 110 lb per BHP at 800 BHP. In general, boiler room heights should be 12 to 16 ft. For a given boiler system, multiple units should be considered. Matching total boiler capacity to a variable load requirement will provide backup capability if one boiler is out of service. Avoid gross oversizing of boiler capacity, because excessive cycling will compromise net efficiency.

Modular boilers are individual cast-iron boilers installed in banks.

- module capacities range from 9 to 57 BHP.

- supply, return, and breeching systems are common to the entire bank of boilers, but the units are step-fired, using only the number of modules necessary to meet the load.

- each module fires continuously or in long cycles, at its peak efficiency, and avoids the on-off cycling of single capacity boilers.

- can retain high efficiency through the heating season, and the entire assembly need not be shut down to repair a single unit.

- modules require less field assembly and at less than 30 in wide, are small enough to fit through standard door openings.

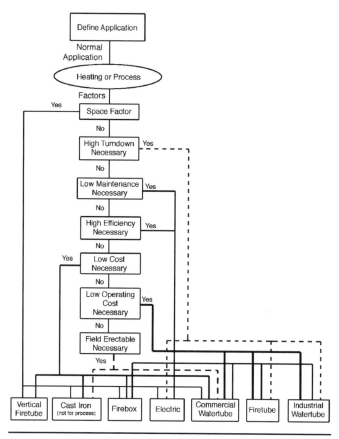

Fig. 9. General selection criteria for boilers. (Source: Cleaver Brooks)

- lengths are approximately 3 in per BHP, and heights before stacks are installed are less than 6 ft.

- condensing boilers allow cooler return water temperatures, cooler stack temperatures, and higher efficiency than noncondensing boilers.

Cooling equipment

Cooling equipment is sized by ton of cooling capacity. A ton in refrigeration terms is equal to 12,000 Btu/hr, which corresponds to the hourly heat input required to melt 1 ton of ice in 1 day at 32F (0°C). Cooling equipment capacities range from less than 1 ton for small devices such as window air-conditioners, to several thousand tons for the largest central plant equipment.

The vapor compression refrigeration cycle is the most common technology used in cooling equipment. In the basic process, a low-temperature, low-pressure refrigerant liquid is sent through an evaporator heat exchanger, where it absorbs heat (that is, from the heat load generated by the building) and evaporates into vapor form. A cooling effect is left in the building from which the heat was absorbed. The low-temperature, low-pressure refrigerant vapor is then mechanically compressed to raise its temperature and pressure. The high-temperature, high-pressure vapor is sent to a condenser heat exchanger, where it rejects the heat (to the outdoors) and condenses to a medium-temperature, high-pressure liquid. After flowing through an expansion device, the refrigerant again becomes a low-temperature, low-pressure liquid, and the cycle continues (**Fig. 10**).

The efficiency of cooling equipment is determined by the quantity of cooling generated for a given quantity of mechanical compressor energy used. There are several ways of expressing this:

- Energy Efficient Ratio (EER) rating is used for residential equipment. It represents the cooling capacity in Btu/hr divided by the electrical input in watts.

- Seasonal Energy Efficiency Ratio (SEER) is frequently used, which divides the total seasonal cooling Btu by the total watt-hours. Common SEER values range from 7 to 16.

- Coefficient of Performance (COP) is used for heat pumps and large equipment—up to a value of 7. COP is the EER divided by 3.412 Btu/watt.

- Chillers are often rated by kW/ton, with values ranging from 0.1 to 1.0.

Cooling equipment should not be oversized. Oversized cooling equipment compromises comfort (humidity) conditions, and short cycling leads to excessive equipment wear. When an oversized system short-cycles, the air is cooled but the cyclic behavior does not remove moisture adequately. The result can be a "cold and clammy" environment. If anything, a slight undersizing will allow improved comfort and operating conditions for a larger number of hours, if there are relatively few peak hours in the year.

Chillers

- primary piece of equipment in a central cooling system.

- packages together those individual components necessary to support the vapor compression cycle and create a cooling effect (the evaporator, condenser, and compressor).

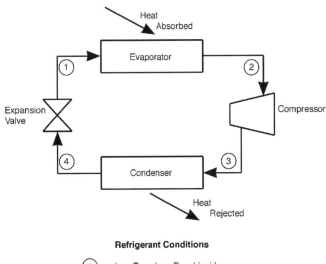

Refrigerant Conditions

①	Low T	Low P	Liquid
②	Low T	Low P	Vapor
③	High T	High P	Vapor
④	Med T	High P	Liquid

Fig. 10. Basic vapor compression cycle.

- components may be contained in one piece of equipment, or separated with the evaporator inside, and the compressor/condenser outside.

- usually classified by the type of compressor used to drive the refrigeration cycle.

- several types of compressors are available, including centrifugal, reciprocating, rotary screw, and scroll.

- centrifugal chillers compress the refrigerant with a rotating impeller.

- rated efficiencies are generally good, with values as low as 0.5 kW/ton, and COPs falling in the 4.2 to 6.0 range.

- when these units operate at less than 30 percent of full load, their efficiency drops off rapidly.

- multi-stage compressors are available to increase part load efficiencies.

- centrifugal chillers are available with capacities starting as low as 100 ton.

- used primarily in large central plants, with capacities of 1000 tons and more.

There are several types of compressors:

- Reciprocating (piston) compressors are common in the 3 to 50 ton range, where they are typically more efficient than centrifugal units. Reciprocating chillers use a proven technology, serve a wide variety of commercial applications, and generally have a lower ini-

tial cost than other chiller types. They have more individual parts than some other chiller types, and therefore require more maintenance. Reciprocating compressors produce more vibration than other machines. For this reason, care must be exercised in mounting, particularly if used on a rooftop.

- Rotating screw compressors operate with single or double interfitting rotors to compress the refrigerant. Screw compressors are rated as low as 0.57 kW/ton, and have superior part load characteristics. The COP of screw compressors is not reduced at higher condensor temperatures as much as other chillers. For this reason it is frequently selected for use as a heat recovery chiller.

- Scroll compressors generally have smaller capacities than many other types, and are becoming popular in some residential equipment. These units use two interfitting scroll members for compression. Chillers with scroll compressors are gradually taking over markets once dominated by reciprocating chillers. Scroll units have fewer parts and thus less maintenance concerns, have smoother, quieter operation, and can operate under dirtier conditions.

- Vapor compression chillers most often use electricity to drive the compressor. Gas-engine–driven chillers offer an alternative, with lower energy costs. However, space and weight requirements may increase, as well as the associated noise and vibration.

Absorption chillers use an absorption cycle rather than the vapor compression cycle to produce chilled water. The cycle, illustrated in **Fig. 11**, relies on the input of heat energy. The basic absorption cycle takes advantage of the affinity that a salt has for water. A lithium bromide salt solution acts as the absorbent, and water is the refrigerant. The cooling effect is created as the salt solution rapidly evaporates water from the low-pressure evaporator section.

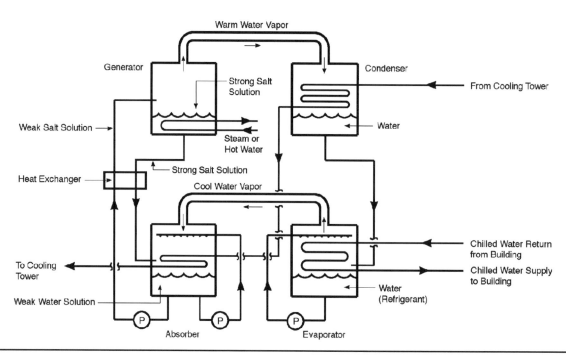

Fig. 11. Basic absorption cycle. (Source: Rowe 1994)

Absorption chillers are considered in applications where there is an existing low-cost source of heat—steam or waste heat. While their Coefficient of Performance (COP) ratings are quite low compared to vapor compression equipment (often 0.67 to 1.2 with kW/ton values as low as 0.1), the low-cost heat input makes them attractive. Absorption chillers may also be direct-fired with natural gas, as in a combination chiller/boiler unit, where utility costs or rebates offer savings over electric units. In the case of the combination unit, less space is required than for a separate chiller and boiler, and simultaneous heating and cooling is available. In addition, a heating COP up to 1.8 is possible. Maintenance requirements for absorption machines have improved, but are still higher than vapor compression equipment. The advantage is that maintenance procedures are not as complex on absorption equipment.

Table 18 outlines many of the general characteristics of common chiller systems. This is a general outline, and many of the listed characteristics vary widely with chiller size, operating conditions, application, maintenance, number of units, and manufacturer. Generally for chiller equipment, space requirements range from 0.4 sq ft/ton for large centrifugal units to 3 sq ft/ton for smaller (100 ton) absorption units, usually with a 3 or 4 to 1 length to width ratio. Height requirements range from 10 ft for 100 ton centrifugal units to 18 ft for 1000 ton two-stage steam absorption units. Operating weights range from 40 to 160 lb/ton of capacity. Absorption units typically are on the high end of the space and weight ranges, and often have more limitations in the size of opening for the individual sections that may be passed through for field erection. Heat recovery options are available with many chiller packages to use waste heat for purposes such as water heating. This option should be considered for buildings that require substantial hot water supply and space cooling simultaneously.

Heat rejection equipment

There are three common types of heat rejection equipment:

- air cooled
- water cooled
- evaporative

The purpose of heat rejection equipment in a refrigeration system is to provide a heat transfer means to reject all the heat from the air-conditioning system. This heat includes the heat absorbed by the evaporator from the space plus the heat of energy input into the compressor.

Air cooled

- typically used with refrigerant-based air-conditioning systems.

- two variations of the air-cooled heat rejection equipment are condensers and condensing units.

- a condenser has the refrigeration compressor located remotely. The condensing unit has the compressor included within the unit.

- typically contains centrifugal or propeller fans to draw air over aluminum fins with hot refrigerant running through copper tubing connected to the aluminum fins.

- air-cooled condensers and condensing units may be located indoors or outdoors and the discharge may be vertical or horizontal.

- heat transfer in an air-cooled condenser or condensing unit occurs in three phases: the superheating of the refrigerant; condensing of the refrigerant; and subcooling of the refrigerant.

- air-cooled heat rejection equipment typically has the lowest first cost installation.

Water cooled

- heat rejection equipment is commonly used in four configurations: shell and tube, shell and coil, tube and tube, and braised plate.

- type selected depends upon the capacity required, refrigerant used, temperature control required, and amount of water available.

- condenser typically takes water from an external source to be superheat, condense, and subcool refrigerant.

- compressor is located remote from the water-cooled condenser.

- condensers typically have a higher capital cost and a higher maintenance cost associated with them.

- cost is offset by the higher efficiency of the water-cooled types.

Evaporative type

- two major classifications in evaporative systems: the evaporative condenser used in refrigeration systems, and the cooling tower used in water-cooled systems.

- evaporative condenser circulates refrigerant through a coil that is continuously wetted by outside recirculating water system.

- allows evaporative condenser to be the most efficient type of condenser system.

- cooling tower is used for systems such as a water source heat pump system or chilled water system where water is used as the condenser source in lieu of refrigerant.

- where fans are used to assist in the heat rejection process, adequate space is required around the heat rejection equipment to allow proper airflow.

- if proper clearances cannot be maintained, considerable capacity reduction of the equipment will result.

- free clearance at the air inlet should equal the length of the unit.

Diffusers, registers, and grilles

There are three major types of air distribution outlets: ceiling diffuser, linear slot diffuser, and grilles and registers.

- The ceiling diffuser is the most common air outlet. Diffusers have either a radial or directional discharge, which is parallel to the mounted surface. Some diffusers have adjustable vanes that allow discharge air to be directed. Diffusers come in a variety of shapes and sizes: round, rectangular, square, perforated face, louver face, and modular type diffusers. Some typical applications for diffusers are spot heating or cooling, large capacity, mounting on exposed ductwork, horizontal distribution along a ceiling, and perimeter air distribution to handle the perimeter wall load in addition to the interior load.

• Linear slot outlets typically are a long narrow air supply device with an air distribution slot between ½ to 1 in (12.7 to 25.4 mm) in length. Linear slot outlets are available with multiple slots and may be installed in continuous lengths to give the appearance of one long device (not all need to be active). Various types of linear supply outlets are available. These types are: linear bar, T-bar slot, linear slot, and light diffuser. Some applications for linear slot outlets are high sidewall installation with flow perpendicular to the mounting surface, high sidewall installation with 15 to 30 degree upward or downward directional adjustability, perimeter ceiling installation, sill installations, and floor installations.

• A grille is a supply air outlet that consists of a frame enclosing a set of vanes, which can be mounted vertically, horizontally, or in both directions. A grille combined with a volume control damper is called a register. Some types of grilles and registers are adjustable bar grilles, fixed bar grilles, security grilles, and variable area grilles. Applications for grilles and registers are high sidewall and perimeter location in the sills, curbs, or floors. Grilles mounted in the ceiling and discharging down are unacceptable. Ceiling installation would require a special grille with curved vanes to discharge the air parallel to the mounting surface.

Fig. 12 is a sizing nomograph to approximate sizes and quantities of diffusers for various air quantities. For example, a room requiring 300 CFM (cubic feet per minute) of conditioned air could use one 12 × 12 louvered diffuser, one 10 × 10 in register or one 12 ft long one-slot linear diffuser. If multiple outlets are desired or required, read the appropriate sizes from the multiple outlet lines.

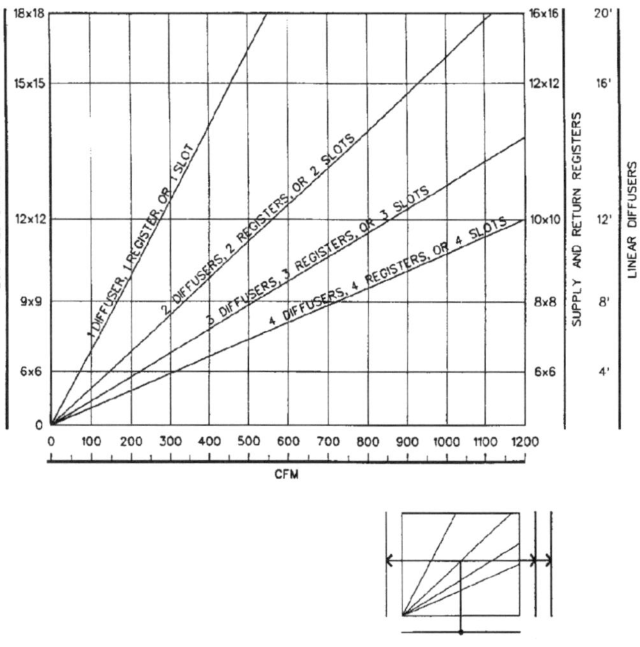

Pumps

The four most common types of centrifugal pumps are end suction, horizontal or vertical split case, in-line mounted, and vertical. The configuration of the pump shaft determines if the pump is a horizontal or vertical pump. Pumps are typically constructed of bronze or cast iron with the impeller made of steel, stainless steel, or bronze. Pumps may be arranged in a variety of configurations to provide the design flow and economical operation at partial flow or for system backup. These arrangements and control scenarios are as follows:

– multiple pumps in parallel

– one pump on, one pump on standby

– pumps with two-speed motors

– primary and secondary pumping

– variable-speed pumping

– distributed pumping

In-line pumps or circulator pumps are pipe-mounted, low pressure, low capacity pumps, typically used in residential and small commer-

Fig. 12. Diffuser, register, and grille sizing nomograph.

cial applications. End suction pumps, either close coupled or frame mounted, usually require a solid concrete pad for mounting. In addition, these pumps require a vibration isolation base to prevent vibration transmission to the floor. The coupling between the motor and the pump requires a guard. This pump takes up more room than the in-line circulator pump.

Horizontal or vertical split case pumps require mounting on a solid concrete pad with a vibration isolation base. This pump coupling requires a guard. The split case on this pump permits complete access to the impellers for maintenance. This pump is typically utilized in larger pumping systems over 1000 GPM.

Vertical turbine pumps are a multiple-stage pump that provides high pressure at normal flow rates. This unit typically has multiple impellers. Mounting requires a solid concrete pad above with a wet pit and accessibility to the pit for suction side maintenance.

Air-handling equipment

There are two common types of air-handling equipment: refrigerant type (considered air-conditioning units) and chilled water type (called air-handling units). An air-conditioning unit is typically factory assembled with refrigerant type cooling and electric, steam, or hot water heating. Typical options are economizer or free cooling cycle, increased motor size, and upgrade DDC package controls.

Advantages of air-conditioning units are fast delivery times and low installed cost. Disadvantages include higher operating costs, little or no control over indoor relative humidities, and higher maintenance costs. Units are also very inflexible relative to the type of filtration that can be provided.

Air-handling units are usually a semi-custom type of air-handling device that can be factory assembled, field assembled, or a combination of both.

- in semi-custom variety, selection is made from a standard list of components to customize the air-handling unit within set guidelines.

- custom air-handling unit will be constructed to any dimension, size, and configuration the designer chooses.

- units typically use chilled water or refrigerant as the cooling medium and electric, steam, or hot water as the heating medium.

- disadvantages are increased delivery time and a greater installed cost.

- advantages include complete flexibility with regard to size, configuration, fan size, and filtration types.

- units typically have lower operating costs.

- sufficient space is required around the air-handling system to allow for proper maintenance.

- access is required for regular maintenance: filter removal and replacement, fan and motor removal and replacement, coil pull in event of a coil failure, and access to belts and bearings.

Fans

Fans are available in a variety of impeller or wheel design and housing design. These variables affect the performance characteristics and applications for each individual type of fan. Refer to **Table 19** for impeller or wheel information, performance characteristics, and applications.

6 INNOVATIONS IN HVAC SYSTEMS FOR MODERN OFFICE BUILDINGS

Thermal comfort systems and the modern office building

Modern office buildings generally are more energy intensive than office buildings constructed in the past; the primary reason is that they are equipped with more electronic appliances, including computers, fax, television, and other building automation facilities. Electrical equipment for office automation not only consumes electric energy, but also increases the cooling load on HVAC equipment, although advancements in technology with successive models reduce heat generation. Interest in indoor air quality has led to very specific attention to ventilation, supply, and filtering of fresh air to building occupants (**Fig. 13**).

Existing buildings that are upgraded with modern telecommunications may also require increased mechanical system and cooling capacity. "Intelligent" HVAC controls, able to anticipate and rapidly respond to changes in occupancy and weather conditions, provide a means to reduce the energy requirements while increasing the electronic capacity of the modern workplace.

Innovations in thermal comfort systems in modern office buildings include:

Floor-mounted air supply units

Air supply through access floors is accomplished without ducts. In such cases, the entire access floor chamber functions as the supply duct of a conventional HVAC system. Pressurizing the entire access floor requires a good deal of fan power, and therefore significantly increases energy consumption. In order to make supply airflow efficiently without pressurizing the entire access floor chamber, floor-mounted air supply units are installed beneath the floor surfaces. A floor-mounted air supply unit is basically a variable-speed fan housed in a can. The top cover of the unit is the air diffuser grille. The direction and volume of supply air can be varied by either changing the fan speed or adjusting the grille opening size.

Floor supply and ceiling return systems

Floor air-supply systems have advantages over the ceiling air-supply systems of conventional HVAC distribution systems for both heating and cooling modes. For the winter heating mode, warm air can be directly supplied to human bodies before being exhausted to return ducts in the ceiling. This avoids the short-circuiting of warm supply air directly to return ducts that occurs in many conventional air distribution systems. It has the further advantage of supplying fresh air at the occupant zone rather than at the ceiling where likelihood of accumulated dust and pollutants is higher, and of picking up heated air from ceiling light fixtures either for removal (during overheated period) or filtering/reheating (**Fig. 14**). For the summer cooling mode, cool, heavier air stays in the lower portion of an interior space, creating a cool air zone

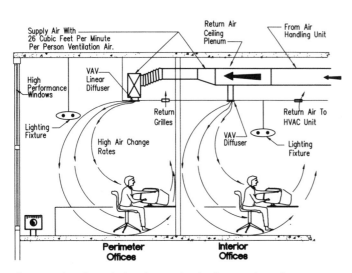

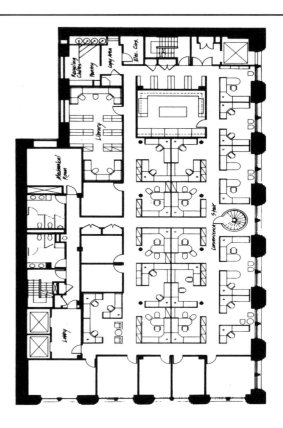

Cross section of a typical work area showing features that enhance indoor air quality. Increased frequency of variable air volume outlets in the ceiling creates improved air mixing and flow at Audubon House, helping to prevent the build-up of "stale air" pockets.

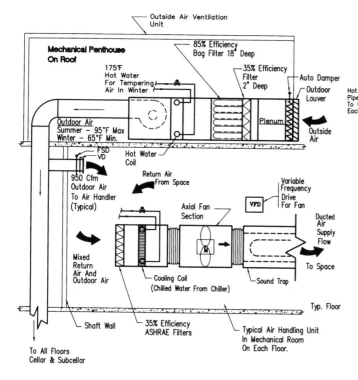

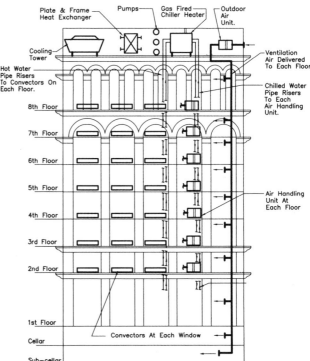

Schematic diagram showing fresh-air intake and ventilation system. Note that the fresh air is filtered twice—initially with a high-efficiency bag filter (ASHRAE 85%) and again on each exchange. (Courtesy of Flack + Kurtz.)

Audubon House—diagram of elevation with overlay of ventilation system. A high fresh air ratio and high-performance filters ensure that indoor air quality will exceed standards. (Courtesy of Flack + Kurtz.)

Fig. 13. Fresh-air ventilation system design. Audubon House, New York City. 1891 building remodeled for adaptive reuse in 1991. Croxton Collaborative, Architects. (Courtesy of Flack and Kurtz)

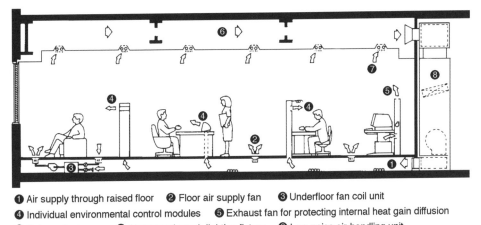

① Air supply through raised floor   **②** Floor air supply fan   **③** Underfloor fan coil unit

④ Individual environmental control modules   **⑤** Exhaust fan for protecting internal heat gain diffusion

⑥ Return air plenum   **⑦** Air return through lighting fixture   **⑧** Low-noise air-handling unit

Fig. 14. Floor supply and ceiling return supply systems. (Kim 1997)

near occupants while pushing warm air upward toward the ceiling. This again avoids the short-circuiting of supply air. A disadvantage of floor air supply systems is the increased possibility of exposing occupants to temperatures that are cooler in summer or warmer in the winter (depending on set-point temperatures of the delivery air supply). Occupants are also subject to higher speeds of air movement, creating potential draught concerns. Therefore, it is important to locate the floor-mounted air supply units at a sufficient distance away from occupants. Allowing occupants to modify the speed and the direction of supply air is beneficial in increasing individual thermal comfort.

Decentralized environmental control systems

A discernable trend is the decentralization of environmental systems, with many smaller equipment units dispersed in strategic locations throughout the building, efficiently serving separate zones. Decentralized environmental systems have many advantages over centralized systems. In case of a breakdown, decentralized systems affect only a small area of the building. Because breakdowns affect smaller areas and equipment, the replacement cost is less. By distributing mechanical equipment in many locations, the length of horizontal services (e.g., ducts and electrical wiring) can be shortened and duct sizes reduced, thus saving required clearance dimensions. Decentralized systems allow for greater flexibility of response to varying loads during the course of a day and a year. In order to fully utilize a decentralized control system, the control zone should be further individualized so that one occupant can feel free to adjust air temperature, lighting levels, and volume of ventilation without being concerned about affecting other occupants' thermal well-being.

Furniture-integrated control systems

Furniture-integrated environmental control systems allow for highly individualized environmental control. They provide occupants with full control of the ventilation, air temperature, and lighting level within their individual task areas. The supply air is typically brought up through access floors and supplied to two outlets on the partition wall, one under the desk and the other above. The volume of the air supply can be adjusted to a particular setting by an electronic controller. Thermostats can be integrated with a telephone on a user's desk. These thermostats measure air temperature within each workstation (**Figs. 15** and **16**).

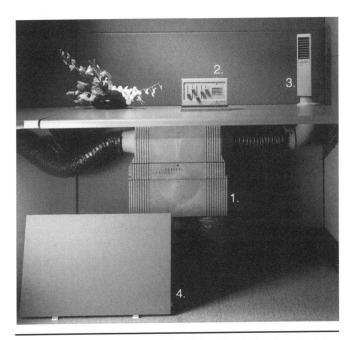

Fig. 15. Personalized Environmental Module (PEM™), developed by Johnson Controls, permits individual control of task air temperature, air speed, and air direction: (1) mixing box; (2) control panel; (3) desktop diffuser; (4) radiant panel. (Loftness and Hartkopf 1997)

Fig. 16. Personalized Harbor™ Steelcase is representative of modules that allow variable levels of closure and privacy. (Loftness and Hartkopf 1997)

Building energy management

In addition to local control systems, a centralized energy and building management system is typically installed in large modern buildings, recently promoted with the term "Intelligent Buildings" (**Fig. 17**). A computerized building management system monitors and controls security, fire safety, lighting, HVAC systems, room temperatures, vertical transportation, and other building operations. A centralized energy management system plays a major role in monitoring energy consumption patterns and provides various data useful to facility man-

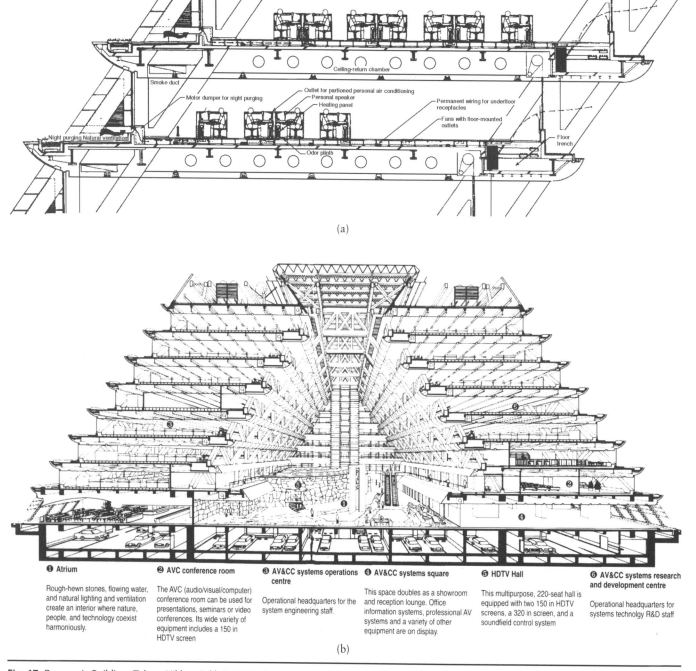

(a)

❶ Atrium

Rough-hewn stones, flowing water, and natural lighting and ventilation create an interior where nature, people, and technology coexist harmoniously.

❷ AVC conference room

The AVC (audio/visual/computer) conference room can be used for presentations, seminars or video conferences. Its wide variety of equipment includes a 150 in HDTV screen

❸ AV&CC systems operations centre

Operational headquarters for the system engineering staff.

❹ AV&CC systems square

This space doubles as a showroom and reception lounge. Office information systems, professional AV systems and a variety of other equipment are on display.

❺ HDTV Hall

This multipurpose, 220-seat hall is equipped with two 150 in HDTV screens, a 320 in screen, and a soundfield control system

❻ AV&CC systems research and development centre

Operational headquarters for systems technolgy R&D staff

(b)

Fig. 17. Panasonic Building, Tokyo. Nikken Sekkei, 1992 <http://www.nikkensekkei.com> (a) detail of access floors; (b) cross section indicating range of innovative systems.

agers in making operational decisions. Because office buildings are subject to peak load charges in determining their electricity rates, building owners must carefully control and manipulate electric energy consumption. This is required so that the peak load permissible by the contract with the utility company is not exceeded and penalty charges avoided. Typical strategies for controlling electricity consumption include switching the cooling equipment from electric chillers to gas-powered absorption ones, turning off nonessential operations (that is, lighting and air distributions), and changing thermostat set points.

Thermal storage

As a way of reducing peak loads, some commercial buildings are being equipped with thermal storage for both heating and cooling efficiency. Many new office buildings utilize ice-source thermal storage, refrigerated during off-peak and typically evening hours, and available for cooling in the following days. Ice storage systems have the advantage of being able to store more energy per unit of volume than water-source storage systems, utilizing the energy represented in the latent heat of fusion (heat represented in the change of phase of water to ice). While storage systems are most often located in belowground containers due to weight, by locating the thermal storage on the mechanical floor at the top of the building, the natural circulation of refrigerants to space air-conditioning systems can be utilized. The thermal storage tanks can also function as counterweights in the earthquake resistance system. In this case, the flexible connections supporting the storage tanks dampen the sway of the building when horizontal forces are applied during earthquakes.

Double-skin envelope design

Interest in energy-efficient operation of large buildings has led to investigation of heat recovery from an air space created by a double envelope, usually designed as an accessible air plenum. It is principally intended to capture passive thermal gain from east-, south-, and west-facing orientations, removing the heat in overheated periods and, in underheated periods, redirecting the heat for preheating the air supply. Louvers and/or other solar control and daylighting controls may also be integrated in the plenum (**Fig. 18**). ■

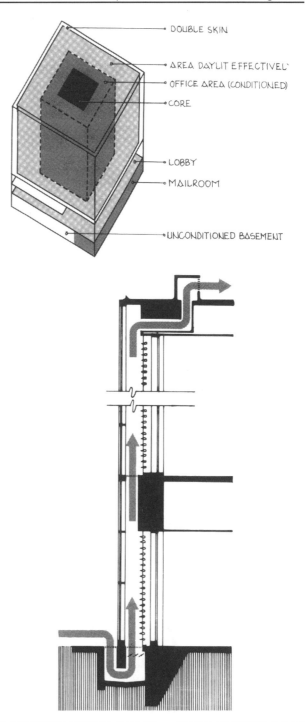

Fig. 18. Hooker Office Building, Niagara, New York. Cannon Design, Architects.

Table 8. Self-contained air-conditioners and air-source heat pumps
(window units, through-wall units, and residential split-system units)

NOTE: This system usually used for perimeter space conditioning only, with separate all-air sytem serving large interior zones.

General building applications.	Small Residential/Light Commercial Rooms @ Exterior Wall, max. 6 stories.
System classification:	Self-Contained, All-Electric Equipment (Non-Ducted)
System type:	**Self-Contained Air-Conditioners & Air Source Heat Pumps(ASHP)**
Competing systems:	Modular WSHP's and GSHP's,
	2-Pipe and 4-Pipe Fan Coil Units

Common equipment configurations:	Window Unit Through-Wall Unit	Split System Unit
General System Characteristics		
Basic operating principle:	Constant Air Volume/Variable Air Temp.	Constant Air Volume/Variable Air Temp.
Equipment quality:	Residential "appliance" unless A.R.I. rated as PTAC (commercial)	Residential "appliance" unless A.R.I. rated as PTAC(commercial)
Cooling coil type:	DX refrigerant (R-22)	DX refrigerant (R-22)
Heating coil type:	Electric	Electric
Typical capacity limitations:	150 - 450 cfm, 1/2 to 2 tons cooling	300 to 2000 CFM, 1/2 to 5 tons cooling [Larger units avail. in comm. units]
Number of zones/unit:	One	One to two
Comfort Considerations		
Degree of temperature control:	Fair	Fair
RH control:	Fair	Fair
Air circulation:	Fair	Fair
Noise Levels:	Poor (compressor & fan in occupied room)	Fair (fan in occupied room)
Indoor Air Quality Considerations		
Continuous fresh air supply for recommended vent. rate:	Good	None
Air filtration capabilities:	Fair	Fair
Room pressurization capabilities:	Poor	Poor
Humidification capabilities:	None	None
Dehumidification capabilities:	Fair	Fair
IAQ maintenance issues:	Many filters to replace, cond. pans to clean	Many filters to replace, cond. pans to clean
IAQ maintenance issues:		
Aesthetic Considerations		
In-room equipment:	Supply fan and compressor	Supply fan
Exterior wall penetrations:	Air-cooled condenser and Fresh air louvers	Refrigerant tubing penetrations
Rooftop and/or On-grade equipment:	None	Air-cooled condenser
Miscellaneous:	Coil condensate drains to exterior can stain wall surfaces	
First Cost Considerations		
System first cost:	Low	Low
Indoor equipment room space reqd.:	Minimum	Minimum
Interior pipe/duct shaft requirements:	None	None
Operating & Maintenance Cost Considerations		
Maintenance staff skill level required:	Low	Low
Maintenance hours/year required:	Low, but units easily damaged	Low
Expected service life:	10 years (15 yrs. if PTAC)	15 years
Airside economizer cooling option availability:	No	No
Energy efficiency of air-conditioning mode:	Good	Good
Energy efficiency of occupied period heating mode:	Poor	Poor
Energy efficiency during unoccupied period heating mode:	Poor	Poor
Optional energy-efficient equipment available:	ASHP heating	ASHP heating
Flexibility re: changes to space layouts:	Poor	Poor
Adaptability to changes in space function:	Poor	Poor

Table 9. Self-contained single-zone (ducted) air-conditioners
(rooftop single zone units and large split-system units)

NOTE: This system limited to LOW-RISE Buildings due to refrigerant line limitations & supply fan limitations.

General building applications:	Light Commercial Buildings	
System classification:	Unitary Ducted Single Zone Air-Conditioners & ASHP's	
System type:	**Single Zone Self-Contained (Ducted) Air-Conditioners**	
Competing systems:	Modular WSHP's and GSHP's, Central All-Air Systems	
	2-Pipe and 4-Pipe Fan Coil Units	

Common equipment configurations:	Rooftop Single Zone Units	Split System Unit
General System Characteristics		
Basic operating principle:	Constant Air Volume/Variable Air Temp.	Constant Air Volume/Variable Air Temp.
Equipment quality:	Light commercial grade	Light commercial grade
Cooling coil type:	DX refrigerant (R-22)	DX refrigerant (R-22)
Heating coil type:	Electric (or optional direct gas-fired heating)	Electric(or direct gas-fired heating)
Typical capacity range:	2,000 - 10,000 CFM, 5 to 25 tons cooling	2,000 - 10,000 CFM, 5 to 25 tons cooling
Standard Number of zones/unit:	One	One
Comfort Considerations		
Degree of temperature control:	Fair	Fair
RH control:	Fair	Fair
Air circulation:	Good	Good
Noise Levels:	Fair (good vibration control reqd.)	Fair (good vibration control reqd.)
Indoor Air Quality Considerations		
Ability to provide recommended fresh air rates on continuous basis:	Good	None
Air filtration capabilities:	Fair	Fair
Room pressurization capabilities:	Poor (air flow not continuous)	Poor (air flow not continuous)
Humidification capabilities:	None	None
Dehumidification capabilities:	Fair	Fair
IAQ maintenance issues:	Filter replacement, cond. pan cleaning	Filter replacement, cond. pan cleaning
Aesthetic Considerations		
In-room equipment:	None	None(fan above clg. or in adj. space)
Exterior wall penetrations:	None	None
	None	None
Rooftop and/or On-grade equipment:	Packaged fan/air-cooled condenser/compressor	Air-cooled condenser
Miscellaneous:		
First Cost Considerations		
System first cost:	Low	Low
Indoor equipment room space reqd.:	None	Foor-Mtd. or above-ceiling fan section
Outdoor equipment space reqd.:	Roof only	Roof or on-grade
Interior pipe/duct shaft requirements:	Min. (vert. duct shaft in multi-story buildings)	None(indoor unit typ. serves 1 floor)
Operating & Maintenance Cost Considerations		
Maintenance staff skill level required:	Low	Low
Maintenance hours/year required:	Low	Low
Expected service life:	15 years	15 years
Airside economizer cooling option availability:	Yes(optional, in units > 5 ton capacity only)	No(unless field-fabricated)
Energy efficiency of air-conditioning mode:	Good	Good
Energy efficiency of occupied period heating mode:	Poor(electric heat) to Good(direct gas-fired)	Poor(gas-fired option n/a)
Energy efficiency during unoccupied period heating mode:	Poor(electric heat) to Good(direct gas-fired)	Poor
Optional energy-efficient equipment available:	Air Source Heat Pump heating	Air Source Heat Pump heating
Flexibility re: changes to space layouts:	Good	Good
Adaptability to changes in space function:	Poor	Poor

Table 10. Self-contained ducted multi-zone air-conditioners (rooftop units)

General building applications:	Light Commercial Buildings
System classification:	Self-Contained, All-Electric Equipment (Non-Ducted)
System type:	**Self-Contained Ducted Multizone Air-Conditioners**
Competing systems:	**Central WSHP's, Central All-Air VAV Systems,**
	Multiple Self-Contained Unitary Rooftop Systems

Common equipment configurations:	**Rooftop Unit**

General System Characteristics	
Basic operating principle:	Constant Air Volume/Variable Air Temp.
Equipment quality:	Light Commercial
Cooling coil type:	DX refrigerant (R-22)
Heating coil type:	Electric, Direct Gas-Fired Option
Typical capacity limitations:	6,000 - 12,000 CFM; 15 to 37 tons cooling
Number of zones/unit:	8 to 12

Comfort Considerations	
Degree of temperature control:	Fair
RH control:	Poor
Air circulation:	Good
Noise Levels:	Fair(good vibration isolation reqd.; unit close to occupied space)

Indoor Air Quality Considerations	
Ability to provide recommended fresh air rates on continuous basis:	Good
Air filtration capabilities:	Good
Room pressurization capabilities:	Fair
Humidification capabilities:	None
Dehumidification capabilities:	Poor
IAQ maintenance issues:	Filter replacement

Aesthetic Considerations	
In-room equipment:	None
Exterior wall penetrations:	None
Rooftop and/or On-grade equipment:	Air-cooled condenser, fan

First Cost Considerations	
System first cost:	Low
Indoor equipment room space reqd.:	None
Interior pipe/duct shaft requirements:	Minimum(vert. duct shafts, multi-story bldg.)

Operating & Maintenance Cost Considerations	
Maintenance staff skill level required:	Moderate
Maintenance hours/year required:	Low
Expected service life:	15 years
Airside economizer cooling option availability:	Yes (optional)
Energy efficiency of air-conditioning mode:	Fair
Energy efficiency of occupied period heating mode:	Poor(elect.) to Good(gas option)
Energy efficiency during unoccupied period heating mode:	Poor(elect.) to Good(gas option)
Optional energy-efficient equipment available:	Economizer cooling
Flexibility re: changes to space layouts:	Fair
Adaptability to changes in space function:	Poor

Table 11. Modular water-source heat pumps
(closed-loop heat pump systems with/without central ventilation air)

General building applications:	Commercial/Institutional/Industrial Buildings	
System classification:	Central System, All-Water & Air-Water	
System type:	**Modular Water Source Heat Pumps(WSHP's)**	
Competing systems:	2-Pipe Change-Over FCU's, 4-Pipe FCU's,	
	Window/Through-Wall Air-Conditioners & ASHP's.	
	Central All-Air Systems	

Common equipment configurations:	**Wall Console Units/Unit Ventilators & Vertically-Stacked Closet Units**	**Wall Consoles, Vert. Closet Units, or Above-Ceiling Concealed Units**
Ventilation air options:	**Local Fresh Air Inlets**	**Central Ducted Ventilation System**

General System Characteristics		
Basic operating principle:	Constant Air Volume/Variable Air Temp.	Constant Air Volume/Variable Air Temp.
Equipment quality:	Commercial grade	Commercial grade
Cooling coil type:	Water-Cooled DX (R-22)	Water-Cooled DX (R-22)
Heating coil type:	Water-Cooled DX (R-22)	Water-Cooled DX (R-22)
Typical capacity range, Console & Vert. Closet Units:	200 - 800 CFM, 1/2 to 2 tons cooling	200 - 800 CFM, 1/2 to 2 tons cooling
Horiz. Cocealed Units:	n/a	200 - 1600 CFM, 1/2 to 5 tons
Unit Ventilators:	750 - 1500 CFM, 2 to 4 tons cooling	n/a
Number of zones/unit:	One	One

Comfort Considerations		
Degree of temperature control:	Good	Good
RH control:	Fair	Fair
Air circulation:	Fair	Fair
Noise Levels:	Fair (console units) to Good (closet units)	Good (unit separated from room by ceiling or closet construction)

Indoor Air Quality Considerations		
Ability to provide recommended fresh air rates on continuous basis:	Fair	Very Good
Air filtration capabilities:	Fair	Fair
Room pressurization capabilities:	Poor	Poor
Humidification capabilities:	None	None
Dehumidification capabilities:	Fair	Fair
IAQ maintenance issues:	Many filters to replace, condensate pans to clean	Many filters to replace, condensate pans to clean

Aesthetic Considerations		
In-room equipment:	Console Unit(or in-closet)	Console Unit(or concealed/ in-closet)
Exterior wall penetrations:	Fresh air louvers	None
Rooftop and/or On-grade equipment:	Cooling tower	Cooling tower

First Cost Considerations		
System first cost:	Low	Moderate
Indoor equipment room space reqd.:	Moderate	Moderate
Outdoor equipment space reqd.:	Cooling Tower	Cooling Tower
Interior pipe/duct shaft requirements:	Minimum (S/R water pipes & condensate waste lines)	Low(S/R water pipes & condensate waste lines, vert. vent. ducts)

Operating & Maintenance Cost Considerations		
Maintenance staff skill level required:	Low	Low
Maintenance hours/year required:	Moderate	Moderate; ease of access to above-ceiling units very important.
Expected service life:	19 years	19 years
Airside economizer cooling option availability:	No	No
Energy efficiency of air-conditioning mode:	Good	Good
Energy efficiency of occupied period heating mode:	Good (heat reclaim from interior zones)	Good (heat reclaim from interior zones)
Energy efficiency during unoccupied period heating mode:	Good(improved w/ thermal storage)	Good(improved w/ thermal storage)
Optional energy-efficient equipment available:	Thermal water storage for recovered heat; GSHP loop or many boiler equipment selections available; variable speed pumping.	Thermal storage for recovered heat; GSHP loop or many boiler equipment selections available; variable speed pumping, ventilation heat recovery/dessicant cooling options.
Flexibility re: changes to space layouts:	Poor	Poor
Adaptability to changes in space function:	Poor	Poor

Table 12. Central ducted water-source heat pumps
(rooftop units, floor-mounted, and horizontal indoor units)

General building applications:	Light Commercial Buildings
System classification:	Central Air-Water System
System type:	**Central Ducted Water Source Heat Pumps**
Competing systems:	Central WSHP's, Central All-Air VAV Systems, Self-Contained Unitary Single Zone Systems

Common equipment configurations:	Rooftop Unit	Floor-Mounted Indoor Unit & Horiz. Indoor Units
General System Characteristics		
Basic operating principle:	Constant Air Volume/Variable Air Temp.	Constant Air Volume/Variable Air Temp.
Equipment quality:	Commercial	Commercial
Cooling coil type:	Water-cooled DX	Water-cooled DX
Heating coil type:	Water-source DX	Water-source DX
Typical capacity limitations:	1,000 - 11,000 CFM; 3 to 25 tons cooling	300 - 4,000 CFM; 1 to 10 tons(Horiz. Unit) 340 - 9,000 CFM; 1 to 25 tons(Flr.-Mtd.)
Number of zones/unit:	One	One
Comfort Considerations		
Degree of temperature control:	Good	Good
RH control:	Good	Good
Air circulation:	Good	Good
Noise Levels:	Fair(good vibration isolation reqd.; unit close to occupied space)	Fair (vibration isolation reqd., init close to occupied space)
Indoor Air Quality Considerations		
Ability to provide recommended fresh air rates on continuous basis:	Good	Good
Air filtration capabilities:	Good	Good
Room pressurization capabilities:	Fair	Fair
Humidification capabilities:	Optional	Optional
Dehumidification capabilities:	Good	Good
IAQ maintenance issues:	Filter replacement	Filter Replacement, cond. pan cleaning
Aesthetic Considerations		
In-room equipment:	None	Fan, compressor
Exterior wall penetrations:	None	None
Rooftop and/or On-grade equipment:	Evap. cooler, air handler	Evap. cooler
First Cost Considerations		
System first cost:	Moderate	Moderate
Indoor equipment room space reqd.:	Small boiler, pump room	Small boiler, pump room
Outdoor equipment space reqd.:	None (roof only)	None (roof only)
Interior pipe/duct shaft requirements:	Minimum(vert. pipe shafts, multi-story bldg.)	Minimum(vert. pipe shafts, multi-story bldg.
Operating & Maintenance Cost Considerations		
Maintenance staff skill level required:	Low	Low
Maintenance hours/year required:	Low	Low
Expected service life:	20 years	20 years
Airside economizer cooling option availability:	Yes	Yes
Energy efficiency of air-conditioning mode:	Good	Good
Energy efficiency of occupied period heating mode:	Good (heat reclaim from interior spaces)	Good (heat reclaim from interior spaces)
Energy efficiency during unoccupied period heating mode:	Good (improved w/ thermal storage)	Good(improved w/ thermal storage)
Optional energy-efficient equipment available:	Thermal water storage	Thermal storage
Flexibility re: changes to space layouts:	Good	Good
Adaptability to changes in space function:	Poor	Poor

Table 13. Two-pipe change-over systems
(fan coil units and unit ventilators, with/without central ventilation air)

NOTE: This system is <u>sometimes</u> used for perimeter space conditioning only, with separate all-air system serving large interior zones.

General building applications:	Commercial/Institutional/Industrial Buildings	
System classification:	Central System, All-Water & Air-Water	
System type:	**2-Pipe Change-Over Systems (Fan Coil Units & Unit Ventilators)**	
Competing systems:	Modular Piped WSHP's/GSHP's, 4-Pipe FCU's	
	Window/Through-Wall Air-Conditioners & ASHP's	

Common equipment configurations:	**Wall Console Units & Vertically-Stacked Closet Units(FCU only)**	**Wall Consoles; Vert. Closet Units & Above-Ceiling Concealed Units(FCU)**
Ventilation air options:	**Local Fresh Air Inlets**	**Central Ducted Ventilation System**
General System Characteristics		
Basic operating principle:	Constant Air Volume	Constant Air Volume
Equipment quality:	Commercial grade	Commercial grade
Cooling coil type:	Chilled water	Chilled water
Heating coil type:	Shares ch. wa. coil; supplemental elect. heating optional	Share ch. wa. coil; supplem. elect. heating optional
Typical capacity range, Console & Vert. Closet Units:	200 - 1200 CFM, 1/2 to 4 tons cooling	200 - 1200 CFM, 1/2 to 4 tons cooling
Horiz. Cocealed Units:	n/a	200 - 1600 CFM, 1/2 to 5 tons
Unit Ventilators:	750 - 1500 CFM, 2 to 4 tons cooling	n/a
Number of zones/unit:	One	One
Comfort Considerations		
Degree of temperature control:	Poor	Poor
RH control:	Fair	Fair
Air circulation:	Fair	Fair
Noise Levels:	Fair(w/ fan in room) to Good(unit fan separated from room by ceiling construction)	Good (fan separated from room by room by ceiling construction)
Indoor Air Quality Considerations		
Ability to provide recommended fresh air rates on continuous basis:	Fair	Very Good
Air filtration capabilities:	Fair	Fair
Room pressurization capabilities:	Poor	Poor
Humidification capabilities:	None	None
Dehumidification capabilities:	Fair	Fair
IAQ maintenance issues:	Many filters to replace,	Many filters to replace,
IAQ maintenance issues:	condensate pans to clean	condensate pans to clean
Aesthetic Considerations		
In-room equipment:	Wall Console Unit (or above-ceiling unit)	None exposed
Exterior wall penetrations:	Fresh air louvers	None
Rooftop and/or On-grade equipment:	Cooling tower	Cooling tower
First Cost Considerations		
System first cost:	Low	Moderate
Indoor equipment room space reqd.:	Moderate	Moderate
Interior pipe/duct shaft requirements:	Minimum (S/R water pipes & condensate waste lines)	Low(S/R water pipes & condensate waste lines, vert. vent. ducts)
Operating & Maintenance Cost Considerations		
Maintenance staff skill level required:	Low	Low
Maintenance hours/year required:	Moderate	Moderate; ease of service access to above-ceiling units very important.
Expected service life:	20 years	20 years
Airside economizer cooling option availability:	No	No
Energy efficiency of air-conditioning mode:	Good	Good
Energy efficiency of occupied period heating mode:	Good	Good
Energy efficiency during unoccupied period heating mode:	Good	Good
Optional energy-efficient equipment available:	Wide range of chiller, heat rejection, ice storage, boiler equipment selections available; variable speed pumping possible;	Wide range of chiller, ice storage, boiler equipment selections available; variable speed pumping possible; central ventilation heat recovery & dessicant cooling options.
Flexibility re: changes to space layouts:	Poor	Poor
Adaptability to changes in space function:	Poor	Poor

Table 14. Four-pipe fan coil units and unit ventilators
(with/without central ventilation air)

NOTE: This system is <u>sometimes</u> used for perimeter space conditioning only, with separate all-air system serving large interior zones.

General building applications:	Commercial/Institutional Buildings
System classification:	Central System, All-Water & Air-Water
System type:	**4-Pipe Fan Coil Units & Unit Ventilators**
Competing systems:	2-Pipe Change-Over FCU's, Modular Water Source Heat Pumps,
	Window/Through-Wall Air-Conditioners & ASHP's, and Central All-Air Systems

Common equipment configurations:	Wall Console Units/Unit Ventilators & Vertically-Stacked Closet Units	Wall Consoles, Vert. Closet Units, or Above-Ceiling Concealed Units
Ventilation air options:	Local Fresh Air Inlets	Central Ducted Ventilation System
General System Characteristics		
Basic operating principle:	Constant Air Volume/Variable Air Temp.	Constant Air Volume/Variable Air Temp.
Equipment quality:	Commercial grade	Commercial grade
Cooling coil type:	Chilled Water	Chilled Water
Heating coil type:	Hot Water or Steam	Hot Water or Steam
Typical capacity range, Console & Vert. Closet Units:	200 - 1200 CFM, 1/2 to 4 tons cooling	200 - 1200 CFM, 1/2 to 4 tons cooling
Horiz. Cocealed Units:	n/a	200 - 1600 CFM, 1/2 to 5 tons
Unit Ventilators:	750 - 1500 CFM, 2 to 4 tons cooling	n/a
Number of zones/unit:	One	One
Comfort Considerations		
Degree of temperature control:	Good	Good
RH control:	Fair	Fair
Air circulation:	Fair	Fair
Noise Levels:	Fair (console units) to Good (units in closet)	Good (unit separated from room by ceiling or closet construction)
Indoor Air Quality Considerations		
Ability to provide recommended fresh air rates on continuous basis:	Good	Very Good
Air filtration capabilities:	Fair	Fair
Room pressurization capabilities:	Poor	Poor
Humidification capabilities:	None	None
Dehumidification capabilities:	Fair	Fair
IAQ maintenance issues:	Many local filters to replace, condensate pans to clean	Many local filters to replace, condensate pans to clean
Aesthetic Considerations		
In-room equipment:	Console Unit(or in-closet)	Console Unit(or concealed/in-closet)
Exterior wall penetrations:	Fresh air louvers	None
Rooftop and/or On-grade equipment:	Cooling tower	Cooling tower
First Cost Considerations		
System first cost:	High	High
Indoor equipment room space reqd.:	Moderate	Moderate
Interior pipe/duct shaft requirements:	Minimum (S/R water pipes & condensate waste lines)	Low(S/R water pipes & condensate waste lines, vert. vent. ducts)
Operating & Maintenance Cost Considerations		
Maintenance staff skill level required:	Low	Low
Maintenance hours/year required:	Moderate	Moderate
Expected service life:	20 years	20 years
Airside economizer cooling option availability:	Unit Ventilator model only	No
Energy efficiency of air-conditioning mode:	Good	Good
Energy efficiency of occupied period heating mode:	Good	Good (heat reclaim from interior zones)
Energy efficiency during unoccupied period heating mode:	Good	Good(improved w/ thermal storage)
Optional energy-efficient equipment available:	Many chiller, heat rejection, ice storage options available; many boiler/heat source options available; var. speed pumping.	Many chiller, heat rejection, ice storage options available; many boiler/heat source equipment selections available; variable speed pumping, ventilation heat recovery/dessicant cooling options.
Flexibility re: changes to space layouts:	Poor	Poor
Adaptability to changes in space function:	Fair	Fair

Table 15. Constant volume/reheat, central station air-handling systems
(with electric, hot water or steam reheat)

NOTE: These systems limited to hospital operating rooms, laboratories, museums requiring close temp./RH control unless reheat source is renewable/recovered heat.

General building applications:	Commercial/Institutional Buildings
System classification:	Central System, All Air
System type:	Constant Volume Reheat, Central Station Air Handling Units
Competing systems:	Central WSHP's, Central All-Air VAV Systems, Multiple Self-Contained Unitary Rooftop Systems

Common equipment configurations:	Electric Reheat	H.W. or Steam Reheat
General System Characteristics		
Basic operating principle:	Constant Air Volume/Variable Air Temp.	Constant Air Volume/Variable Air Temp.
Equipment quality:	Commercial to Institutional	Commercial to Institutional
Expected service life:	25 years	25 years
Cooling coil type:	Chilled Water	Chilled Water
Heating coil type:	Electric or Central Hot Water/Steam	Central Hot Water/Steam
Typical capacity limitations:	1,500 - 40,000 CFM	1,500 - 40,000 CFM
Number of zones/unit:	Unlimited	Unlimited
Comfort Considerations		
Degree of temperature control:	Very Good	Best
RH control:	Very Good	Best
Air circulation:	Very Good	Very Good
Noise Levels:	Very Good	Very Good
Indoor Air Quality Considerations		
Ability to provide recommended fresh air rates on continuous basis:	Best	Best
Air filtration capabilities:	Best	Best
Room pressurization capabilities:	Best	Best
Humidification capabilities:	Yes	Yes
Dehumidification capabilities:	Very Good	Very Good
IAQ maintenance issues:	Central M.E.R. maintenance	Central M.E.R. maintenance
Aesthetic Considerations		
In-room equipment:	None	None
Exterior wall penetrations:	Central M.E.R. only	Central M.E.R. only
Rooftop and/or On-grade equipment:	Central Cooling Tower or Air-Cooled Chiller	Central Cooling Tower or Air-Cooled Chiller
First Cost Considerations		
System first cost:	High	High
Indoor equipment room space reqd.:	High	High
Interior pipe/duct shaft requirements:	High	High
Operating & Maintenance Cost Considerations		
Maintenance staff skill level required:	High	High
Maintenance hours/year required:	Low	Low
Expected service life:	25 years+(10 years for elect. reheat coils)	25 years+
Airside economizer cooling option availability:	Yes	Yes
Energy efficiency of air-conditioning mode:	Poor(Reheat reqd.)	Poor(Reheat reqd.)
Energy efficiency of occupied period heating mode:	Poor(all-elect.)	Good(depending on central heating source)
Energy efficiency during unoccupied period heating mode:	Poor(all-elect.) to Good(central HW at AHU)	Good(depending on central heating source)
Optional energy-efficient equipment available:	Central plant equipment options	Central plant equipment options
Flexibility re: changes to space layouts:	Good	Good
Adaptability to changes in space function:	Good	Good

Table 16. VAV central station air-handling systems
(with electric and hot water reheat VAV boxes)

NOTE: Energy efficiency of central VAV systems strongly dependent on type of VAV terminal device used.

General building applications:	Commercial/Institutional Buildings
System classification:	Central System, All Air
System type:	V.A.V. Central Station Air Handling Units
Competing systems:	Central WSHP's, Central Constant Volume Reheat Systems, Multiple Self-Contained Unitary Rooftop Systems

Common equipment configurations:	Electric Reheat V.A.V Boxes	H.W. Reheat V.A.V. Boxes
General System Characteristics		
Basic operating principle:	Variable Air Volume/Constant Air Temp.	Variable Air Volume/Constant Air Temp.
Equipment quality:	Commercial to Institutional	Commercial to Institutional
Cooling coil type:	Chilled Water	Chilled Water
Central AHU Heating coil type:	Electric or Central Hot Water/Steam	Central Hot Water/Steam
Typical capacity limitations:	1,500 - 40,000 CFM	1,500 - 40,000 CFM
Number of zones/unit:	Unlimited	Unlimited
Comfort Considerations		
Degree of temperature control:	Very Good	Best
RH control:	Very Good	Best
Air circulation:	Very Good	Very Good
Noise Levels:	Very Good	Very Good
Indoor Air Quality Considerations		
Ability to provide recommended fresh air rates on continuous basis:	Good	Good
Air filtration capabilities:	Best	Best
Room pressurization capabilities:	Very Good	Very Good
Humidification capabilities:	Yes	Yes
Dehumidification capabilities:	Yes	Yes
IAQ maintenance issues:	Central M.E.R. maintenance	Central M.E.R. maintenance
Aesthetic Considerations		
In-room equipment:	None	None
Exterior wall penetrations:	Central M.E.R. only	Central M.E.R. only
Rooftop and/or On-grade equipment:	Central Cooling Tower or Air-Cooled Chiller	Central Cooling Tower or Air-Cooled Chiller
First Cost Considerations		
System first cost:	High	High
Indoor equipment room space reqd.:	High	High
Interior pipe/duct shaft requirements:	High	High
Operating & Maintenance Cost Considerations		
Maintenance staff skill level required:	High	High
Maintenance hours/year required:	Low	Low
Expected service life:	25 years+(10 years for elect. reheat coils)	25 years+
Airside economizer cooling option availability:	Yes	Yes
Energy efficiency of air-conditioning mode:	Good	Very good
Energy efficiency of occupied period heating mode:	Good(all-elect.)	Good(depending on central heating source)
Energy efficiency during unoccupied period heating mode:	Poor(all-elect.) to Good(central HW at AHU	Good(depending on central heating source)
Optional energy-efficient equipment available:	Central plant equipment options	Central plant equipment options
Flexibility re: changes to space layouts:	Good	Good
Adaptability to changes in space function:	Good	Good

Table 17. General characteristics of boilers

COMMON BOILER TYPES

	Cast Iron	Membrane Watertube	Electric	Firebox	Firetube	Vertical Firetube
Typical Applications	Heating/ Process	Heating/ Process	Heating/ Process	Heating	Heating/ Process	Heating/ Process
Typical Sizes	To 200 hp	To 250 hp	To 300 hp	To 300 hp	To 800 hp	To 100 hp
Maintenance	Medium/ high	Medium	Medium/ high	Low	Low	Low
Floor Space Required	Low	Very low	Low	Medium	Medium/ high	Very low
Initial Cost	Medium	Low/ medium	High	Low	Medium/ high	Low
Efficiency	Low	Medium	High	Medium	High	Low/ medium
No. of Options Available	Low	Medium	Medium	Low/ medium	High	Low
Pressure Range	HW/LPS	HW/LPS HPS to 600 psig	HW/LPS HPS to 900 psig	HW/LPS	HW/LPS HPS to 300 psig	HW/LPS HPS to 150 psig
Comments	Field Erectable					

HW = Hot water
LPS = Low pressure steam
HPS = High pressure steam

Table 18. General characteristics of chiller systems

GENERAL CHARACTERISTICS OF CHILLER SYSTEMS

	Centrifugal	Reciprocating	Screw	Absorption	Scroll
Capacity ranges, tons	50 - 10,000	3 - 400	20 - 1300	3 - 1700	1 - 50
Reliability/ maintenance	Good	Fair	Good - very good	Good	Good
Space requirements	Low	Low	Low	High	Low
Initial Cost	Medium	Low	Medium	High	Low
Noise/vibration	Low - medium	High	Medium	Very low	Low
Energy Costs	Good	Good	Very good	Good	Very good
Weight	Low	Low	Low	High	Low
Comments		Caution placing reciprocating equipment on the roof.	More efficient than centrifugal at less than 200 tons.	Use non ozone depleting refrigerants, i.e. water. Uses less space than electric chiller with separate boiler. Much lower kw/ton requirements.	

Table 19. Fan performance characteristics

	CENTRIFUGAL FANS			AXIAL			MISCELLANEOUS	
	Forward Curved	Backward Inclined	Air Foil	Vane Axial	Tube Axial	Propeller	Tube Centrifugal	Axial
Wheel Design	• Lowest efficiency of all centrifugals • Fan may overload if selected wrong	• Efficiency similar to air foil • Typically quieter than forward curved	• Highest efficiency of centrifugal fans • Highest speed of centrifugal fans	• Fan has good medium to high capacity and efficiency • Fan blades may be fixed or adjustable	• Less efficient than vane axial	• Low efficiency • Low pressure capabilities	• Performance similar to backward inclined • Lower efficiency than backward inclined	• Low pressure exhaust systems for factories and kitchens • Typical to a propeller fan
Housing Design	• Scroll design • Loose fit between wheel and inlet	• Scroll design • Maximum efficiency, close clearance between wheel and inlet	• Scroll design • Maximum efficiency, close clearance between wheel and inlet	• Cylindrical tube	• Cylindrical tube	• Cylindrical ring	• Cylindrical tube • Air discharges radially and turns 90° through guide vanes	• A propeller fan mounted in a structure • Air discharges from space between weatherhood
Performance	• High flow rate, low pressure • Discharge has air stream swirls	• High efficiencies with good pressure • Self-limiting toward free delivery	• High efficiencies with good pressure • Self-limiting toward free delivery	• High pressure with medium volume flow • Guide vanes correct circular motion in part by wheel	• High flow rate, medium pressure • Discharge has air stream swirls	• High flow rate, low pressure • Maximum efficiency reached near free delivery	• Performance similar to backward inclined	• Fans usually operate without ductwork • Pressure capabilities low with high volum
Applications	• Low pressure HVAC applications; residential furnaces and packaged air conditioners	• General heating, ventilating and air conditioning • Applies to larger systems with low to medium pressure • Industrial applications	• General heating, ventilating and air conditioning • Applies to larger systems with low to medium pressure • Industrial operations	• General HVAC systems, low to high pressure • Straight through air flow and compact installation • More compact than centrifugal fans	• Low and medium pressure ducted HVAC • Industrial applications	• Low pressure, high volume applications • Space ventilation through a wall without ductwork	• Low pressure, return air systems for HVAC • Straight through flow	• Low pressure exhaust systems • General factory, kitchen, warehouse exhaust • Low first cost and low operating cost

REFERENCES

ASHRAE, *ASHRAE Handbook of Fundamentals,* American Society of Heating, Refrigerating and Air-Conditioning Engineers, Atlanta, 1993.

Bobenhausen, William, *Simplified Design of HVAC Systems,* John Wiley and Sons, New York, 1994.

Kim, Jong-Kim, "Intelligent Building Systems," in *Time-Saver Standards for Architectural Design Data,* 7th ed., 1997, on CD-ROM accompanying this volume.

Loftness, Vivian, and Volker Hartkopf, "Flexible Office Infrastructure," in *Time-Saver Standards for Architectural Design Data,* 7th ed., 1997, on CD-ROM accompanying this volume.

National Audubon Society and Croxton Collaborative, *Audubon House,* John Wiley, New York, 1994.

Rowe, William H., III, *HVAC Design Criteria, Options, Selection,* R. S. Means Company, Kingston, 1994.

Catherine Bobenhausen, CIH, CSP

Summary

This article reviews items classified as "Special HVAC Equipment" in Uniformat II: D3070, including dust and fume collectors, air curtains, air purifiers, and paint spray ventilation systems. References for each topic are listed at the conclusion.

Key words

air filters, centrifugal collectors, chemical filters, curtain jet, dust collectors, industrial ventilation, pressurized air, purifiers, scrubbers, spray booths

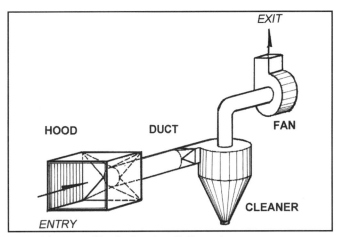

Fig. 1. Schematic of local exhaust ventilation system.

Special HVAC equipment

1 DUST AND FUME COLLECTORS

Many industrial processes (milling, grinding, abrasive blasting, welding) use dust or fume collectors to improve the quality of the air discharged to the outdoors as well as to remove dust and fumes from the work area inside the plant. The typical capacity of dust or fume collectors are loadings of 0.1 to 100 grains per cubic foot and higher. By contrast, typical air filters used in HVAC systems are designed for low concentrations, from 0.0001 to 0.1 grains per cubic foot. Fabric, wet or dry centrifugal collectors, or electrostatic precipitators may be used, depending on the application.

In industrial facilities, collectors are used in combination with a local exhaust system (**Fig. 1**) to capture dust or fumes at their point of generation. This system consists of:

– a hood (plain, flanged, slotted, or canopy) to capture the dust or fumes where they are generated,

– flexible or rigid ductwork,

– a collector, and

– an exhaust fan.

Once the collector captures dust or fumes, the relatively dust- or fume-free air is then discharged from the exhaust stack to the outdoors or is recirculated to the room or process. During system design, the maximum pressure drop through the collector must be added to overall system pressure calculations.

Collectors are chosen to:

– comply with regulatory air emission standards and regulations.

– meet occupational exposure standards.

– prevent impacts to surrounding community (property damage, public nuisance, or health hazard).

In some cases they are also chosen to:

– reclaim usable materials.

– permit recirculation of cleaned air to processes or work areas.

– eliminate highly visible (but relatively innocuous) exhaust plumes.

Generally, selection should favor the most efficient collector that can be installed at reasonable cost (capital cost plus operations and maintenance) while meeting prevailing air pollution regulations.

Factors to be considered include:

– characteristics of the airstream (emission rate, temperature, water vapor, presence of corrosive chemicals).

– type(s), particle size distribution, and concentrations of contaminants including chemical and physical properties.

– degree of removal required to meet regulatory requirements or to permit recirculation.

– fire safety and explosion control (need for explosion venting for combustible dusts).

– disposal method.

– energy requirements.

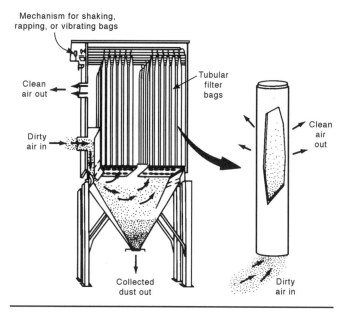

Fig. 2. Schematic of fabric collection.

Dust and fume collectors include:

- Fabric collectors.

- Wet collectors.

- Dry centrifugal collectors.

- Electrostatic precipitators.

Key features of fabric collectors (**Fig. 2**):

- High efficiencies possible (>99 percent).

- Useful for small particles (<1 micron).

- Useful for dry collection.

- Sensitive to filter velocities.

- High temperature gases must be cooled prior to entering the air cleaner.

- Affected by relative humidity.

Fabric collectors vary by:

- Type of fabric (woven or nonwoven).

- Configuration (bags or tubes; envelopes [flat bags]; pleated cartridges).

- Service (continuous or intermittent, must be shut down during dust removal).

- Reconditioning (shaker, pulse-jet, or reverse-air).

- Housing (single or multiple compartment).

Fabric collector operation. Dust particles are retained on fabric (by straining, impinging, intercepting, diffusing, or electrostatically charging) and cleaned air passes through. The collected dust improves efficiency, increases resistance to airflow, and may change flow rate unless compensation is made. Generally, the mat is cleaned (by mechanical agitation or air motion) to keep the flow rate constant before airflow reduction causes system flow to decrease.

Key features of wet collectors (scrubbers):

- Suitable for high temperatures and wet gases (will cool and clean).

- Can reduce explosion or fire hazard of combustible or explosive dust.

- Variable efficiency (<80 percent).

- May foster corrosion.

- Freeze protection will be necessary if collectors are outside in cold climates.

- Disposal may require pretreatment of wastewater.

Types of wet collectors (scrubbers):

– chamber or spray tower.

– packed tower.

– wet centrifugal collector.

– wet dynamic precipitator.

– orifice.

– Venturi.

Wet collector operation. Dust particles strike liquid droplets. Liquid droplets containing dust are then separated from the airstream by centrifugal force, impingement, or impaction.

Key features of dry centrifugal collectors (**Fig. 3**):

– simple to design and maintain.

– low to moderate pressure loss.

– temperature independent.

– low collection efficiency for small particles.

– substantial headroom required for maintenance.

– sensitive to variable loadings and flow rates.

Types of dry centrifugal collectors:

– gravity separator.

– inertial separator.

– dynamic precipitator.

– cyclone collector.

– high-efficiency centrifugal.

Dry centrifugal collector operation. Dust particles are separated from the airstream by centrifugal, inertial, or gravitational force.

Key features of electrostatic precipitators (**Fig. 4**):

– typically used for particle separation in large-volume gas streams at elevated temperature in situations with low-cost electricity.

– high efficiency (>99 percent).

– low pressure drop (usually less than 1 in wg but high electrical use).

– nominal maintenance needs; few moving parts.

– high initial cost.

– The incoming gas stream may need to be preconditioned with a cooling tower in high voltage systems or with a wet scrubber,

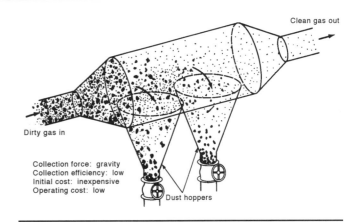

Fig. 3. Schematic of dry centrifugal collector. (gravity separator).

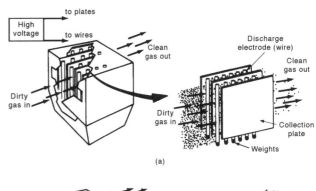

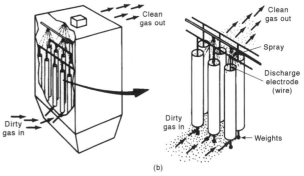

Fig. 4. Schematic of electrostatic precipitators.

evaporative cooler, or heat exchanger in low voltage systems to provide proper conditions for ionization.

– sensitive to variable loadings and flow rates.

Electrostatic precipitator operation. The airstream is ionized and then charges the dust particles, which migrate to a collecting plate of opposite polarity. The dust particles lose their charge and fall to a collecting plate where they are removed by washing, vibration, or gravity.

Types of electrostatic precipitators

- *Cottrell:* single-stage or high voltage (ionization voltage of 40,000 to 70,000 volts DC).

– heavy-duty.

– applications include utility boilers, large industrial boilers, cement kilns.

- *Penny:* two-stage or low voltage (ionization voltages of 11,000 to 14,000 volts DC).

– used in low concentration (less than 0.025 grains per cubic foot) operations.

– applications include plasticizer ovens, forge presses, die-casting machines, welding operations.

Improper selection of dust and fume collectors can result in system failure due to:

– high temperatures (searing fabric collectors).

– water vapor (plugging dry collectors).

– corrosive chemicals (damaging fabric or metal in collectors).

– presence of combustible dusts (organic or mineral dusts) creating explosion hazard.

Fig. 5. Air-curtain over bay door on interior of loading dock.

2 AIR CURTAINS

Air curtains are local ventilation devices that reduce airflow through building apertures and openings in process equipment (**Fig. 5**). They are used in place of flexible partitions such as plastic stripping, flapper doors, or canvas curtains, to create a barrier to air movement while permitting free passage of equipment and personnel through doorways and other openings. They thus reduce (although do not entirely prevent) the loss of conditioned (heated or refrigerated) air, and/or entry of humid/dry outdoor air at undesirable temperatures and/or entry of insects, dust, fumes, and odors. Typical applications are on exterior doors in warehouses, bus and air terminals, banks; and on freezer/cooler doors. Some air curtains generate an evenly distributed laminar airflow over an entryway (to create an "airlock"). Others, as in lobbies, establish a circular "curtain jet" pattern.

Air curtains are used to:

- deflect wind and reduce heat loss.

- promote the mixing of warm air to floor level and destratify room air.

- provide additional comfort in workspaces served directly by outdoor activities (such as loading docks).

- prevent loss of mechanical cooling (air-conditioning).

Types of air curtains

- *Heated* (electric, steam, and hot water heated). ASHRAE recommends that heated models be used for doors smaller than 12 × 12 ft (4 × 4 m), and for process apertures that are frequently opened (more than five times or for longer than 40 minutes during an eight-hour shift), and that are located where design outdoor winter temperatures are 5F (–15°C) or lower.

- *Unheated air at room temperature or outside temperature.* Typical applications are in spaces with a heat surplus, a vertical temperature stratification, low air temperatures—less than 46F (7.8°C)—near the building aperture, or in mild climates.

- *Laminar-flow.* These generate an evenly distributed barrier airstream over the entryway.

- *Shutter-type.* These direct air outward at an angle from 30 to 40 degrees; they may be double-sided or single-sided and projected upward or downward. Double-sided are often more effective. ASHRAE recommends upward projection when the gate width is greater than its height; additionally, upward projection provides more complete coverage of the lower part of the opening.

- *Air curtains with a lobby.* These function by directing air towards the outdoor airflow or at a small angle to it, forming a "curtain jet," which runs along the walls, slows down and makes a U-turn, reversing direction. For double-sided air curtains in this application, the length of the lobby should exceed 2.5 times its width, to prevent air from being forced outside. For shorter lobbies, air can be supplied by jet with a coerced angle of divergence.

- *Combined air curtains.* These are "double" air curtains, which can be used in very cold climates, for doors larger than 12 × 12 ft (4 × 4 m), and for spaces with several doors. Examples of combined air curtains include those that supply unheated outdoor air at the entrance (or in the lobby), and another set that supplies heated air within the building.

Special options include:

- explosion-proof motors.

- adjustable louver damper controls to regulate airflow rates.

- adjustable air directional vanes to provide draft control.

- continuously running air curtains.

- intermittent air curtains that operate whenever the door is open or an activating temperature is reached.

Selection of an air curtain depends on:

- airflow requirements (standard, high velocity, or extra power).

- application (as barrier to insects, dust, and fumes; to contain heated or cooled building air; or use in freezers or coolers).

Design calculations are provided by ASHRAE for determination of the air velocity, airflow, and temperature supplied by the air curtain.

Limitations: Air curtains may malfunction if there are indrafts caused by negative pressurization of interior space. If other outside doors, windows, or roof ventilators are open, a wind-tunnel effect may result. Some air curtains create sufficient noise to generate complaints: decibel readings are available from manufacturers. Relying on air curtains to heat nearby workspaces may result in high energy consumption for these spaces.

3 AIR PURIFIERS

"Air purifiers" include gas-phase air filters that remove low levels of airborne gas- or vapor-phase contaminants as well as filters designed to remove low levels of dust in air in HVAC building systems. Chemical filters are typically disposable (or rechargeable) cartridges containing chemically active material (adsorbent) that can be installed inside ventilation ducts to remove pollutants from the airstream. These filters may be located downstream of a respirable particulate filter (to protect them from dust) and/or upstream of air-conditioning equipment (to protect them from humidity).

- *Gas-phase air filters* include:

- activated carbon (adsorb organic solvents, ozone, sulfur dioxide, nitrogen oxide).

- activated alumina impregnated with potassium permanganate.

- acid-impregnated carbon (removes ammonia).

- base-impregnated activated carbon (removes corrosive acids, including hydrochloric and sulfuric acid).

- catalytic conversion (ozone converted to oxygen; nitrogen dioxide converted to nitrogen monoxide).

- *Granular activated carbon filters* include:

- Type I: V-bank of large-mesh carbon trays.

- Type II: cartridge of pleated dry composite media with fine-mesh carbon.

- Type III: cell of pleated, nonwoven, carbon-coated fabric.

The adsorption rate is variable and a function of:

- relative adsorptivity of multiple contaminants.

- temperature and relative humidity.

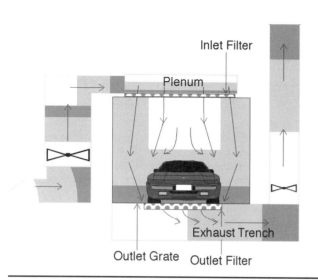

Fig. 6. Paint spray booth.

Fig. 7. Types of spray booths. Airflow indicated by arrows.

– airflow rate.

– adsorbent bed size.

– properties of the adsorbing medium.

• *Air filters* (for particulates) differ by efficiency, dust-holding capacity, and pressure drop. They operate by:

– straining.

– impingement (often use adhesive coating).

– interception.

– diffusion.

– electrostatic forces.

Efficiency ratings can be misleading if reported by mass (may not trap smaller particles). Efficiency testing for air filters includes:

– ASHRAE Arrestance (measures filter's ability to remove coarse dust particles).

– ASHRAE Efficiency (measures ability of a filter to prevent staining or discoloration determined by light reflectance readings).

– DOP (0.3 micron particles of dioctylphthalate are drawn through a high-efficiency particulate air [HEPA] filter; to be designated as a HEPA filter, filter must be at least 99.97 percent efficient).

4 PAINT SPRAY VENTILATION SYSTEMS

Commercial spray painting is usually conducted inside prefabricated enclosed and ventilated spray booths (**Fig. 6**), to ensure a good finish, to protect against fire and explosion hazards associated with flammable vapors and mists or combustible ingredients in the paints, and to prevent worker exposures (to harmful constituents of paint such as isocyanates in urethane paints). Spray booths are manufactured in a variety of forms including downdraft, semi-downdraft, crossdraft (**Fig. 7**). Downdraft systems may include a waterwash of exhaust air, using scrubbers to reduce the amount of dust entering the exhaust and allow recovery of overspray finishing material. Options may include paint recycle/reclaim systems to reclaim overspray, reduce frequency of filter replacement, increase volatile organic compounds (VOCs) and particulate removal efficiency, and reduce the amount of sludge generated.

The spray booth is typically a power-ventilated, non-combustible (steel, concrete, or masonry) structure located inside a building, which functions as an enclosure-type hood. It is constructed to:

– maintain solvent system below occupational exposure limits.

– enclose or accommodate a spray-painting operation.

– confine and limit escape of "overspray" (paint droplets dispersed in air).

– draw air towards the exhaust system to provide safe and habitable conditions during spraying.

Operation:

- A fan moves supply air through a filter bank into the spray-painting booth.

- Air is moved out of the booth by an exhaust fan through filters to the exterior of the building.

- Mechanical system is operated during and after spraying operations to exhaust vapors from dry coated articles and drying finishing material residue.

- Each spray booth has its own fan and air cleaner for fire safety.

- If more than one fan serves the booth, all fans are interconnected so that one fan cannot operate without all fans operating.

- Air exhausted during spray operations is generally not recirculated.

- Emissions are regulated by government environmental agencies.

Types of spray booths include those that differ by location of supply and exhaust:

- downdraft.

- semi-downdraft (or side-downdraft).

- crossdraft.

• *Downdraft*

- Filtered air enters from the ceiling and is exhausted through filters that cover trenches under metal grating on floor, or through water scrubbers located beneath the metal grating in a water-washing system. Downdraft ventilation spray booths are recommended as they produce lower concentrations of paint overspray and a cleaner paint job requiring less buffing. In a typical downdraft system, filtered air enters at the ceiling of the booth, flows around the car at 80 fpm, and exits through the floor.

• *Semi-downdraft* (or side-downdraft)

- Filtered air enters from ceiling and is exhausted through filters in the back of the booth.

• *Crossdraft*

- Filtered air enters in the front of the booth and is exhausted through filters in the back of the booth.

Dry type spray booths have:

- distribution or baffle plates to promote an even flow of air through the booth or reduce the overspray before it is pulled into the exhaust system;

- dry media filters, either fixed or on rolls, to remove overspray from the exhaust airstream; and/or,

- powder collection systems that capture powder overspray.

Options include:

• Paint recycle/reclaim systems can be used to:

- reclaim overspray.

- reduce the frequency of filter replacement.

- increase particulate and VOC removal efficiency.

- reduce the amount of sludge generated.

• Spray booth may include pneumatic lifts to aid operators. Booth may have a painting cycle and a curing cycle.

Ventilation requirements: NFPA recommends that vapor concentrations in the exhaust airstream be maintained below 25 percent of the lower flammable limit, requiring a sufficient flow and velocity of air through the booth.

Air velocities are to be increased to compensate for:

- high rates of spray application.

- operations where objects being coated are close to the open face or conveyor openings.

- operations where large objects are conveyed in and out of the booth at relatively high speeds.

Air velocities can be decreased for efficient application systems using heated materials, airless spray application apparatus, high-volume/low-pressure application equipment, and electrostatic application equipment. ■

REFERENCES

Dust and fume collectors

ANSI Z9.2, *Fundamentals Governing the Design and Operation of Local Exhaust Systems,* American National Standards Institute, New York.

ASHRAE, *Handbook of Fundamentals,* American Society of Heating, Refrigerating and Air Conditioning Engineers, Atlanta, 1993.

ASHRAE, *HVAC Applications,* "Chapter 24: Ventilation of the Industrial Environment" and "Chapter 26: Industrial Exhaust Systems," American Society of Heating, Refrigerating and Air Conditioning Engineers, Atlanta, 1995.

Industrial Ventilation—A Manual of Recommended Practice, American Conference of Governmental Industrial Hygienists Committee on Industrial Ventilation, Lansing, 1995.

NFPA 69, *Standard on Explosion Prevention Systems.* National Fire Protection Association, Quincy.

NFPA 91, *Standard for Exhaust Systems for Air Conveying of Materials,* National Fire Protection Association, Quincy.

NFPA 654, *Standard for the Prevention of Fire and Dust Explosions from the Manufacturing, Processing and Handling of Combustible Particulate Solids,* National Fire Protection Association, Quincy.

Air curtains

ASHRAE, *Applications Handbook,* "Chapter 24: Ventilation of the Industrial Environment," American Society of Heating, Refrigerating and Air Conditioning Engineers, Atlanta, 1995.

Air purifiers

ASHRAE, *Handbook of Fundamentals,* American Society of Heating, Refrigerating and Air Conditioning Engineers, Atlanta, 1993.

ASHRAE Standard 62: Ventilation for Acceptable Indoor Air Quality, American Society of Heating, Refrigerating and Air Conditioning Engineers, Atlanta.

ASHRAE, *HVAC Applications,* "Chapter 41: Control of Gaseous Indoor Air Contaminants," American Society of Heating, Refrigerating and Air Conditioning Engineers, Atlanta, 1995.

Committee on Industrial Ventilation, *Industrial Ventilation: A Manual of Recommended Practice,* American Conference of Governmental Industrial Hygienists, Lansing, 1995.

Paint spray ventilation systems

Committee on Industrial Ventilation, *Industrial Ventilation: A Manual of Recommended Practice,* American Conference of Governmental Industrial Hygienists, Cincinnati, 1995.

NFPA, *NFPA 33, Standard for Spray Application Using Flammable and Combustible Materials,* National Fire Protection Association, Quincy, 1995.

NFPA, *NFPA 91, Standard for Blower and Exhaust Systems for Vapor Removal,* National Fire Protection Association, Quincy, 1995.

NFPA, *NFPA 101, Life Safety Code,* National Fire Protection Association, Quincy, 1994.

U.S. Department of Labor, Occupational Safety and Health Administration, Code of Federal Regulations, Title 29, Part 1910.107. *Spray Finishing Using Flammable and Combustible Materials.*

Bruce W. Hisley

Summary

This article provides an overview of sprinkler system applications, including automatic sprinkler types, design criteria, modification in existing buildings, integrating systems with other building services, equipment, and acceptance testing requirements.

Key words

deluge systems, dry-pipe system, pre-action systems, spray pattern, sprinkler deflector, wet-pipe system

Fire protection sprinkler systems

1 SPRINKLER SYSTEMS

An automatic sprinkler system is a system of pipes with automatic sprinklers placed at various intervals. The orifice of the automatic sprinkler is normally closed by a disk or cap held in place by a temperature-sensitive releasing element. Each sprinkler is automatically activated to discharge and distribute water on a fire in quantity to either control or extinguish it. The system shall be provided with at least one automatic and reliable water supply source and provide an automatic alarm when activated (**Fig. 1**). Selection considerations include:

- Automatic sprinkler systems are one of the most reliable methods available for controlling fires. Large areas, high-rise buildings, hazardous occupancies, high content value, and concentrations of large numbers of people in one area all tend to develop risk conditions that cannot be tolerated or accepted without automatic sprinkler protection.

- Sprinkler systems are effective for life safety because they warn of fire and at the same time apply water to the burning area during the very early stages of fire.

- Automatic sprinkler systems are required to be installed by building/fire codes and fire insurance companies. These requirements are usually based on occupancy type, construction, and size of building. Many governmental jurisdictions also have adopted local automatic sprinkler requirements.

Types of automatic sprinkler systems

- *Wet-pipe system*

Automatic sprinklers are attached to a piping system that contains water under pressure at all times. When individual sprinklers are actuated, water flows through the sprinklers immediately. These systems are the most commonly installed in areas where the temperature will always be maintained above 40F (4°C).

- *Dry-pipe system*

Automatic sprinklers are attached to a piping system that normally contains air under pressure. When a sprinkler opens, air pressure is reduced to the point where water pressure on the supply side of a dry alarm valve forces open the valve. Water then flows into the system and out of any activated open sprinkler. These systems are used in areas that cannot be heated. Dry-pipe systems can be used in conjunction with wet-pipe systems to protect areas such as attics, combustible concealed spaces, or outside loading or covered storage areas. The dry-pipe alarm control valve must be kept within a heated enclosure and provided with an air compressor.

- *Pre-action system*

Automatic sprinklers are attached to a piping system in which there is air in the piping that may or may not be under pressure. When a fire occurs, a supplementary fire detection device in the protected area is actuated. A water control valve is then opened that permits water to

---

Credits: Photos courtesy of Firematic Sprinkler Devices, Inc.

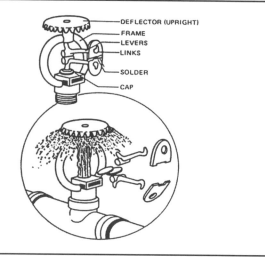

Fig. 1. Automatic sprinkler in action.

flow into the piping system before a sprinkler is activated. When an individual sprinkler is activated by heat from the fire, water flows immediately from the sprinkler. The detection devices are designed to operate before a sprinkler fuses and activates. These systems are used in locations where accidental damage to the piping or sprinklers, on a wet- or dry-pipe system, could cause damage to facilities or equipment, such as computer centers.

- *Combined dry-pipe and pre-action system*

Automatic sprinklers are attached to a piping system that includes the features of both a dry-pipe and pre-action system. The piping contains air under pressure. A supplementary heat detection device opens the water control valve and an air exhauster at the end of the feed main. The system then fills with water and operates like a wet-pipe system. If the heat detection system should fail, the system will still operate as a conventional dry-pipe system. This system has the same type of application as a standard pre-action system. In addition, these systems are used for unheated piers, and have an economic advantage by elimination of numerous dry-pipe valves that would require regular maintenance (**Fig. 2**).

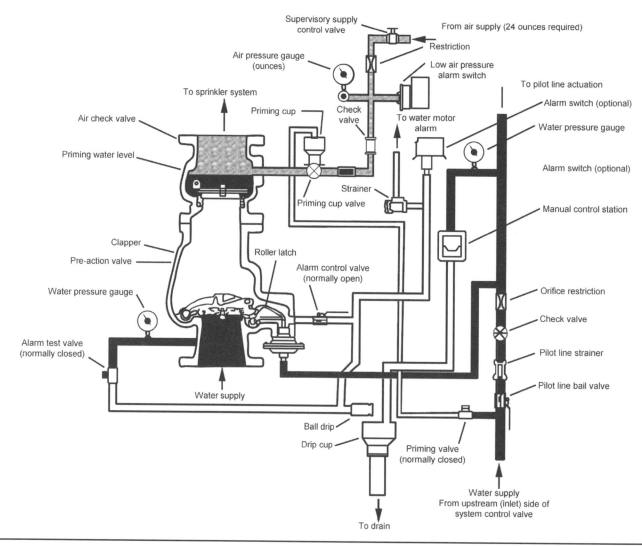

Fig. 2. Dry-pipe and pre-action system.

• *Deluge system*

In this type of system, all sprinklers are open at all times. When heat from a fire activates the fire-detecting device, the deluge valve opens and water flows and discharges from all of the sprinkler heads in the piping. The area being protected is then deluged with water. This system is used primarily in special hazard situations where it is necessary to apply water over a large area to control a fast-developing fire. It is also used to apply foam for protection of flammable liquid hazards.

• *Antifreeze system*

In this system, a wet type sprinkler system with automatic sprinklers is attached to piping that contains antifreeze solution and is connected to a water supply. Immediately upon the operation of a sprinkler, the antifreeze solution is discharged, followed by water. These types of systems are usually used in conjunction with wet type sprinkler systems to protect small, underheated areas in a building (**Fig. 3**).

• *Special types*

These depart from the normal types of systems in such areas as special water supplies and reduced pipe sizes. They are installed according to manufacturers' instructions in accordance with their listing by a testing laboratory. Examples include exterior exposure protection and circulating closed-loop systems that are part of the building's heating system. These systems require careful evaluation to determine their suitability.

Benefits of sprinkler systems

– automatic sprinklers, properly installed and maintained, provide a highly effective safeguard against the loss of life and property from fire.

– National Fire Protection Association (NFPA) has no record of a multiple death fire (a fire that kills three or more people) in a completely sprinklered building, where the system was operating properly, except in an explosion or flash fire.

– offer design flexibility, economic construction methods, and expanded choices of building materials.

– can be used to offset passive fire protection requirements such as fire resistance of building structural elements, compartmentalization, and fire-rated exitways or corridors.

– building size may be increased in areas with a lesser degree of fire-resistance rating. Some local jurisdictions have modified local subdivision development requirements for residential type development where each type of residential unit is protected with a sprinkler system.

– offset deficiencies in existing buildings related to life safety requirements.

– improve life safety related to fire in residential buildings.

– reduce problem of access to the seat of a fire or of interference due to smoke with visibility for firefighters.

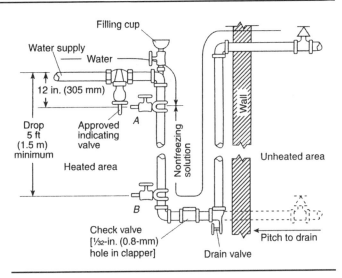

Fig. 3. Arrangement of supply piping and valves.

- generate less water damage than the water application of a hose stream by firefighters.

- sprinklers cool the smoke and make it possible for persons to remain in the area much longer than if the room were not sprinkled.

- savings from direct fire losses, business interruption caused by a fire, indirect business losses, and fire insurance costs.

2 DESIGN CRITERIA AND REQUIREMENTS

- Considering the installation of a sprinkler system before the building is designed, whether the system is required or not, is essential to take full advantage of the effectiveness and economic variables that a sprinkler system can provide. Early planning and coordination with the sprinkler designer will provide benefits in sprinkler area coverage and reduced installation costs.

- Sprinkler system design and installation is a special trade and should only be designed and installed by fully qualified, experienced, and responsible parties.

- The sprinkler system must be provided with a water source of sufficient capacity to supply the number of sprinklers that will be opened during a fire. The water must have adequate pressure to be adequately distributed to the highest and farthest sprinkler on the system.

- The sprinkler system should be designed for installation throughout the building for complete protection to life and property. In some cases local adopted requirements may only require partial sprinkler installation for hazardous areas for limited protection.

- Outdoor hydrants, indoor hose standpipes, and hand-hose connections also are frequently part of the sprinkler system.

- In older existing buildings some modifications may be needed to ensure effective sprinkler operation. These include:

- enclosing vertical openings to divide multistory structures into separate fire areas

- removing unnecessary partitions that could interfere with sprinkler discharge

- removing needless sheathing and shelving

- checking combustible concealed areas, such as attic and areas between floor/ceiling, to see if they need sprinkler protection.

- Sprinkler systems in buildings subject to flooding require special attention to the following:

- location and piping arrangement so it will not be washed out or weaken supports

- location of control valves so that they will be accessible during high water

- location of alarm devices so that they will remain operable during high water

- location and arrangement of fire pumps and their power supply and controls to provide reasonable safeguards against interference.

- Earthquake bracing, where required, is necessary to keep the pipe network in place during seismic events.

- Planning for a sprinkler system is usually based upon four general areas:

- the sprinkler system itself

- type of construction

- hazard of occupancy

- water supply

Hazard classification

- A building's use is the primary consideration in designing a sprinkler system that is adequate to protect against hazards in the occupancy. These hazard classifications affect:

- spacing of sprinklers

- sprinkler discharge densities

- water supply requirements

General classifications are:

- *Light hazard*

Quantity and/or combustibility of materials are low, and fires with relatively low rates of heat release are expected. Examples include apartments, churches, hotels, office buildings, and schools.

- *Ordinary hazard*

Quantity and combustibility of contents is moderate, stockpiles do not exceed 12 ft (3.7 m), and fires with a moderate rate of heat release are expected. Examples include laundries, textile plants, printing plants, flour mills, paper manufacturing, and storage warehouses containing paper, furniture, and paint.

- *Extra hazard*

Quantity and combustibility of contents is very high and flammable, and combustible liquids, dust, lint, or other materials are present that can produce rapidly developing fires with high rates of heat release. Examples include rubber production, upholstering operations using plastic foams, and occupancies with large amounts of flammable liquids, varnish, and paint dipping.

- *Special occupancy hazard*

Examples are storage use of flammable and combustible liquids, spray application using flammable/combustible materials, nitrate film, storage of pyroxylin plastic, laboratories using chemicals and storage (handling of liquified natural gas [LNG]).

- *Classification of commodities*

When determining the proper design considerations for a storage facility or a portion of a structure used for storage, the type, amount and arrangement of combustibles for any commodity classification is required to define the potential fire severity.

- The general hazard classifications serve as a good basic guide. It does not rule out the necessity of separately evaluating certain portions of an occupancy that may contain hazards more severe than the remainder of the building.

- In each of the broad hazard classifications, the system may be designed according to hydraulic calculation requirements (**Fig. 4**) or using a set of predetermined pipe schedule tables (**Fig. 5**). Hy-

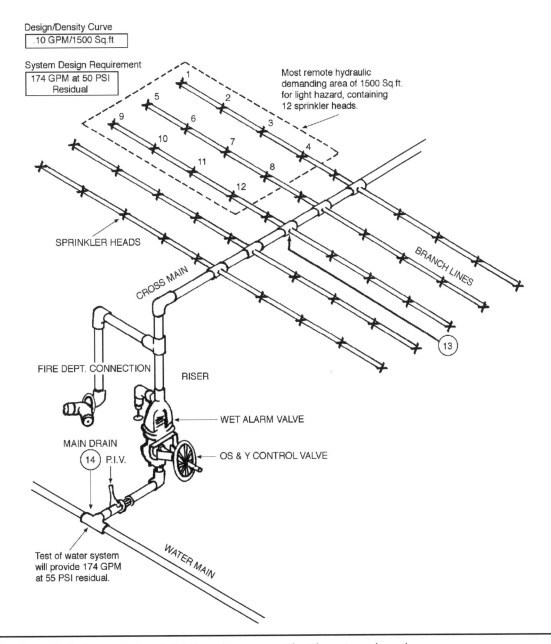

Fig. 4. Example of hydraulically designed system for light hazard occupancy without hose stream demand.

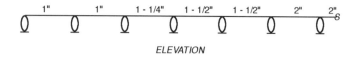

Fig. 5. Ordinary hazard pipe schedule. (Source: NSFA Fire Sprinkler Plan Review Guide)
  2 sprinklers fed by 1 in (2.5 cm) pipe
  2 + 1 = 3 sprinklers fed by 1¼ in (3 cm) pipe
  3 + 2 = 5 sprinklers fed by 1½ in (3.8 cm) pipe
  5 + 2 = 7 sprinklers fed by 2 in (5 cm) pipe (up to 10 allowable)

draulically designed systems are preferable from a fire protection standpoint and are the most prevalent type of design being used today (see **Table 1** for pipe schedule).

3 INSTALLATION SPECIFICATIONS

• All sprinkler system equipment, devices, and materials are required to be listed (approved) by a testing laboratory. Both Factory Mutual Fire Insurance Company and Underwriter's Laboratories maintain testing facilities for testing and provide a listing or approved service.

• Before a sprinkler system is installed or remodeled, a detailed working plan is prepared, identifying pertinent features of building construction and occupancy. The National Fire Protection Association (NFPA) *Standard #13: Installation of Automatic Sprinkler Systems,* is the primary standard for installation of sprinkler systems and is quite precise on the data that must be shown on the plan. This plan is required to be submitted to the local authority having jurisdiction for review and approval before installation.

• The building owner or their agent is required to provide a certificate to the sprinkler designer/installer that provides the intended use of the building, maximum height of storage, and any special knowledge of the water supply, including known environmental conditions that might be responsible for microbiologically influenced corrosion (MIC).

Integrating sprinklers with other building services and equipment

• The building designer needs to consider how the sprinkler system will be integrated into the design of the building. Examples:

– floor or roof structure elements required to support the pipe hanger.

– location of piping in ceiling spaces that will not be affected by the HVAC ductwork.

– floor plan partition layout relating to sprinkler coverage.

– location of area for sprinkler control valve and heating, if required.

Table 1. Summary of NFPA Standard 13 Pipe Schedule Systems for Steel Pipe: Number of sprinklers fed by pipe size

Pipe size	Light Hazard	Ordinary Hazard
1"	2	2
1-1/4"	3	3
1-1/2"	5	5
2"	10	10
2-1/2"	30	20
3"	60	40
3-1/2"	100	65
4"	Maximum 52,000 sq. ft. floor area	100
5"	Maximum 52,000 sq. ft. floor area	160
6"	Maximum 52,000 sq. ft. floor area	275
8"	Maximum 52,000 sq. ft. floor area	Maximum 52,000 sq. ft. floor area

– piping installation that is aesthetically pleasing.

– architectural features that may obstruct the spray pattern or cause delayed activation, such as soffits, partitions, ducts, decorative ceilings, and light fixtures.

– coordinating the operating features of the sprinkler system into the building's fire alarm system, where installed.

• Acceptance testing: NFPA Standard #13 requires that the installing contractor, in the presence of the building owner's representative and the local authority having jurisdiction, conduct system acceptance tests for major sprinkler system components. These tests are to be certified by the installing contractor in a format required by the standard. The following tests are required:

– before the underground water supply piping is connected to the inside riser, all new underground piping shall be thoroughly flushed to remove any obstructing materials that could impair the system.

– all new underground and aboveground sprinkler piping shall be hydrostatically tested for strength and leakage—at not less than 200 psi (1380 kPa) for two hours or at 50 psi (345 kPa) in excess of the maximum static pressure, when the pressure is in excess of 150 psi (1035 kPa).

– an air pressure test of 40 psi (276 kPa) for 24 hours is required for all aboveground piping for a new dry-pipe type system.

– a main drain test is required with the control valves fully open to ensure that water will be safely and properly disposed.

– an inspector's test shall be conducted to determine that the automatic water flow alarms are operational.

– an operational test to determine satisfactory performance of the control valves is required for dry-pipe, pre-action, and deluge type sprinkler systems, conducted in accordance with the valve manufacturer's specifications.

4 WATER SUPPLY

Every sprinkler system must have at least one automatic water supply of adequate pressure, capacity, and reliability. An automatic supply is one that is not dependent on any manual operation to supply water at the time of a fire. The rate of flow (capacity) and the duration (time) of that flow need to be considered as part of an automatic supply. Water supplies and environmental conditions are required to be evaluated for the existence of microbes and conditions that contribute to microbiologically influenced corrosion (MIC).

• *Types of supplies*

Sprinkler systems can be supplied from one or a combination of sources such as street mains, gravity/suction tanks, fire pumps, lakes, and wells. The most common source today is from a street main. A secondary supply may be necessary depending on the reliability of the primary supply; the value of the property, building area and height, construction type, occupancy, and outside exposures. NFPA Standard 13 requires at least one automatic, reliable water supply source (**Fig. 6**).

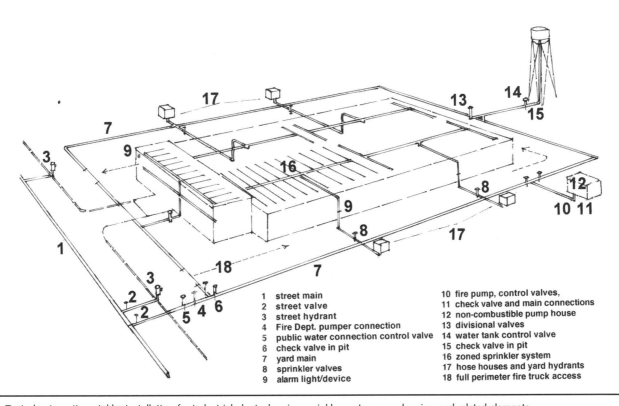

1	street main	10	fire pump, control valves,
2	street valve	11	check valve and main connections
3	street hydrant	12	non-combustible pump house
4	Fire Dept. pumper connection	13	divisional valves
5	public water connection control valve	14	water tank control valve
6	check valve in pit	15	check valve in pit
7	yard main	16	zoned sprinkler system
8	sprinkler valves	17	hose houses and yard hydrants
9	alarm light/device	18	full perimeter fire truck access

Fig. 6. Typical automatic sprinkler installation for industrial plant, showing sprinkler systems, yard mains, and related elements.

• *Connection to waterworks system*

This is the preferred single or primary method of supply if the system is reliable and of adequate capacity and pressure. In determining adequacy, a determination of probable minimum pressures and flows available at peak domestic or heavy demands must be considered.

– size and arrangement of the street mains are important.

– water mains less than 6 in (15 cm) in diameter are usually inadequate.

– feeds from long dead-end mains are also undesirable.

– water meters, if required, should be of a type approved for fire service.

– flow and pressure tests under varying conditions are required to determine the amount of water available for fire protection.

– local government or water companies may require backflow prevention devices to protect the potable water supply that also supplies the sprinkler system. These devices can affect the available water supply and pressure.

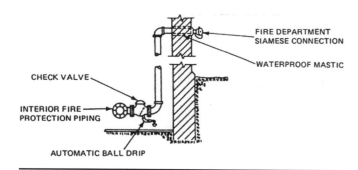

Fig. 7. Typical fire department Siamese connection at building wall.

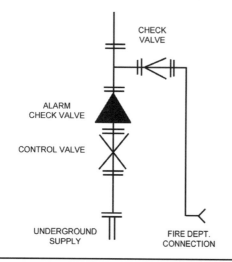

Fig. 8. Alarm check valve.

– NFPA *Standard 24: Private Fire Service Mains and Their Appurtenances* provides guidance for the installation of these devices.

• *Gravity tanks*

These types of tanks provide an acceptable supply if of adequate capacity and pressure that is provided by the available height of the water column in the tank. The sprinkler demand, hose lines, and duration of operation determine the capacity of the tank.

• *Suction tanks*

These types of tanks require a fire pump to provide the necessary pressure to the sprinkler system. Suction tanks are now being used with the advent of the hydraulically designed sprinkler system.

• *Fire pumps*

An automatic fire pump with a reliable power source and water supply is a desirable source of supply. Fire pumps:

– provide an advantage of having a water supply available at a higher pressure.

– can maintain higher pressures over a long period of time.

– can be powered by electric motors or diesel engines.

– are installed in accordance with NFPA *Standard 20: Installation of Centrifugal Fire Pumps.*

– it is important to remember that fire pumps can only provide increases in water pressure but they cannot produce water flow capacity where inadequate.

• *Pressure tanks*

Have possible uses but an important limitation is the small volume of water that can be stored. Where an adequate volume of water is available but pressure is not sufficient, a pressure tank gives a good starting point for the first sprinklers to operate. Pressure tanks can be used in tall buildings where public water pressure is too low for effective supply to the highest sprinkler, until the fire department arrives to pump into the fire department connection.

• *Fire department connections*

A connection that allows the fire department to pump water into the sprinkler system is an important secondary supply. These connections are a standard part of a sprinkler system. Fire department connections:

– shall be readily accessible at all times.

– shall be properly marked.

– shall be fitted with a check valve but not with a gate valve to prevent it from being inadvertently shut off (**Fig. 7**).

– can be designed to supply each sprinkler riser separately or connected to an outside yard system that would supply every riser (**Figs. 8** and **9**).

Factors affecting water supply requirements

Establishing the water supply requirements for a sprinkler system requires good engineering judgment based on several factors relating to fire control by sprinklers. Where conditions are favorable the fire should be controlled by the operation of only a small number of sprinklers. Factors that can affect the number of sprinklers that might open in a fire are:

- Initial water supply pressure: At higher pressures the discharge is greater. With greater discharge there is a better chance of fire control from fewer sprinklers.

- Obstructions to water patterns from sprinklers: Stockpiled high, pallets, racks, and shelving can cause obstructions to water discharge, preventing fire control and in turn a greater chance that more sprinklers needing more water supply will be required.

- Ceiling height: Ceilings of unusual heights, or 50 ft (1500 cm), can produce drafts that will carry heat away from the sprinkler directly over the fire area, resulting in the delay in the application of water and the opening of sprinklers remote from the fire.

- Unprotected vertical openings: Sprinklers are designed on the assumption that fire will be controlled on the floor of fire origin. With unprotected openings, heat and fire may spread through the openings causing additional sprinklers to operate.

- Wet type versus dry type sprinklers: With the delay in exhausting the air pressure from a dry type system, more sprinklers will open in a dry type system than a wet type system.

- Floor-mounted and ceiling-mounted obstructions and concealed spaces: Beams, girders, light fixtures, and HVAC ductwork can obstruct the water pattern, which in turn can cause additional sprinklers to operate to account for the obstruction.

- Floor obstructions such as office privacy partitions can also cause a problem.

- Concealed combustible spaces will also have an impact. When these concealed areas are not protected, the sprinkler design area is doubled to account for uncontrolled spread of fire in these areas.

Water supply requirements for sprinkler systems

The fire hazards represented by different building occupancies requires the establishment of guides to water supply for sprinkler systems. Water supply requirements will differ between a pipe schedule design and hydraulically calculated design.

- *The required total water supply* is determined by:

- occupancy hazard requirement for sprinkler.

- additional water for hose streams.

- if stored water is used, the total flow required must be multiplied by the duration of flow (time) to determine storage capacity.

Fig. 9. Check valve.

• *Pipe schedule design:* Specifies the maximum number of sprinkler heads that can be installed on a pipeline of a given size for a specific hazard type (Table 1). With the development of newer sprinkler heads this type of design is very limited because of the special pressures and water capacity requirements of the newer sprinklers. NFPA Standard 13 now limits the use of this type of design for new buildings under 5000 sq ft (450 sq m) in size without special considerations.

• *Hydraulically calculated design:* The pipe sizes are selected on a pressure-loss basis to provide a prescribed density in gallons per minute per square foot, with a reasonable degree of uniformity over a specified area. The selection of pipe sizes will depend on the water supply available. The stipulated design density and area of application (remote design area) will vary with each occupancy hazard. This is now the preferred method of sprinkler design (Fig. 4). This type of design can address the newer types of sprinklers that may require special pressures and water capacity.

Water supply for residential occupancies

With the development of the quick response residential sprinklers special water supply requirements have been developed for these types of systems (**Fig. 10**).

• One- and two-family residences: These types of systems are installed in accordance with NFPA *Standard 13D: Installation of Sprinkler Systems in One and Two Family Dwellings.* Requirements for water supply are:

– minimum flow of 18 gpm (68 l/m) to any sprinkler in the system or 13 gpm (49 l/m) for each sprinkler with a minimum of two sprinklers operating.

– system shall have an automatic water supply.

– if supply is from a stored system it shall be able to provide a minimum flow for 10 minutes or 7 minutes for one story in height and less than 2000 sq ft (180 sq m).

– system must be a wet-pipe type system using only residential type sprinklers.

– certain areas are exempt from complete coverage.

• Other residential occupancies up to four stories in height: These types of systems are installed in accordance with NFPA *Standard 13R: Installation of Sprinkler Systems in Residential Occupancies up to Four Stories in Height.* Requirements for water supply are:

– minimum flow of 18 gpm (68 l/m) for a single residential sprinkler or 13 gpm (49 l/m) for each sprinkler with a minimum of four sprinklers operating in the residential part of the occupancy.

– if supply is from a stored system it shall be able to provide a minimum flow for 30 minutes.

– system must be a wet-pipe type system using only residential type sprinklers protecting the residential areas. Dry pendent or dry-sidewall sprinklers can be used in non–living spaces not heated (**Fig. 11**).

Fig. 10. Pendent with matching flat escutcheon.

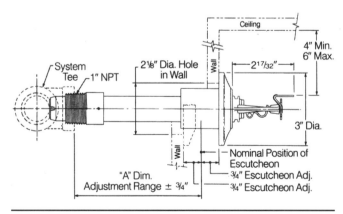

Fig. 11. Dry horizontal sidewall sprinkler.

– areas not intended for living purposes, such as attics or combustible concealed spaces are installed in accordance with NFPA Standard 13.

Piping materials, valves, and fittings shall be tested and listed by a testing laboratory as being suitable for use in a sprinkler system. The Underwriter's Laboratory publishes a fire protection equipment directory that notes the different types of piping, valves, and fittings that have been tested and listed by manufacture and model types. The NFPA Standard 13 requires that piping valves and fittings be of a type that can withstand a working pressure of not less than 175 psi (1208 kPa). Higher working pressures may be required in high-rise buildings or locations that are served by a fire pump, when the normal sprinkler system pressures exceed 175 psi (1208 kPa).

Sprinkler piping

All pipe used in sprinkler systems shall be marked continuously along its length by the manufacturer to properly identify the type of pipe. Several different types of piping materials are approved for sprinkler systems:

– ferrous piping (welded and seamless);

– copper tube (drawn and seamless);

– nonmetallic polybutylene and chlorinated polyvinyl chloride (CPVC).

• *Ferrous piping* can be either black steel, galvanized, or wrought steel pipe that are manufactured in various wall thicknesses. Most common for sprinkler systems are schedules 40, 30, and 10. NFPA Standard 13 notes minimum wall thickness for steel pipe depending on the method of joining the pipe.

• *Nonmetallic (plastic) piping* is lightweight and has favorable hydraulic characteristics for water flow. Special installation requirements are as follows:

– for use in light hazard occupancies only.

– limited to indoor wet-pipe systems.

– must have a protective membrane.

– CPVC piping can be exposed when quick response or residential sprinklers are installed.

– strict adherence to manufacturer's assembly instructions.

Sprinkler system piping components

Sprinkler piping must be carefully planned and installed in accordance with NFPA Standard 13. A system consists of the following components:

• *Branch lines:* The pipelines in which the sprinklers are placed directly.

• *Cross main:* The pipe that directly supplies the branch lines.

• *Feed main:* The piping that supplies the cross main.

• *Riser:* The main supply to the system that feeds from the underground incoming piping from the water supply source.

– must be accessible and properly identified as to what area it is protecting.

– large buildings may have several separate risers supplying different parts of the building.

– the size of the riser will be determined hydraulically by calculating the maximum number of sprinklers expected to operate on one floor during a fire, or by the pipe schedule system that is determined by the maximum number of sprinkler heads supplied by the riser on one floor (**Fig. 12**).

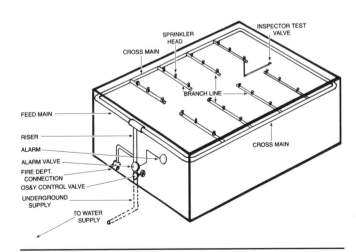

Fig. 12. Major sprinkler system components.

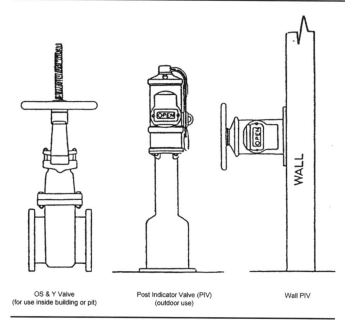

Fig. 13. OS&Y valve, post indicator valve (PIV), wall PIV.

Fig. 14. Alarm valve.

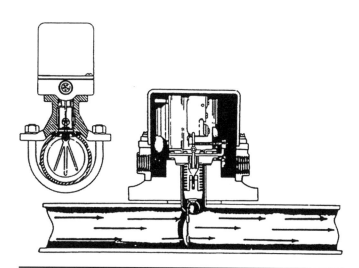

Fig. 15. Water flow detector/switch.

Valves

Valves that control the water supply to the sprinkler system are the most important. It is critical to provide supervision of the control valves that will activate a signal on the premises or at a supervising office.

- *Supply valves* controlling connections to water supplies and supplying pipes to sprinklers: These types of valves must be of the listed indicating type. When water pressures exceed 175 psi (1208 kPa) the valves shall be used in accordance with their pressure rating (**Fig. 13**).

- *Drain valves and test valves:* Shall be of an approved type and provided with permanently marked identification signs.

- all systems shall be provided with a main drain valve and inspector test valve and connection.

- valves shall be readily accessible and provided with adequate discharge that can handle the drain discharge flow.

- *Water flow alarm valves* are to be listed for the service and designed to detect water flow from one sprinkler head within 5 minutes maximum after such flow begins (**Figs. 14** and **15**). These can be either mechanical or electrical in operation or both.

- *Water flow detecting valves*, determined by the type of sprinkler provided, which are:

- wet-pipe system (**Fig. 16**).

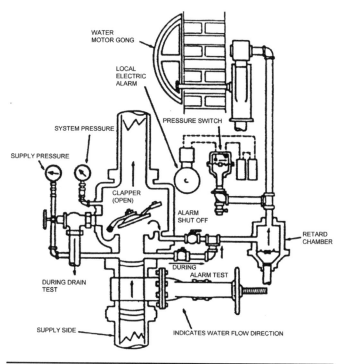

Fig. 16. Alarm check valve (wet-pipe).

– dry-pipe system (**Fig. 17**).

– pre-action and deluge system.

• *Check valves:* Can be found in various parts of a sprinkler system. They must be:

– listed for fire protection service (see Fig. 9).

– installed within the system in the correct position in accordance with the designed water flow direction.

• *Pressure-reducing valves:* Are found in systems or portions of systems where all components are not listed for pressures greater than 175 psi (1208 kPa). These valves must be listed for fire sprinkler service.

Pipe fittings and attachments

• *Pipe fittings:* Shall be designed for use in sprinkler systems. Installed by means of:

– screwed

– flanged

– mechanical joint

– brazed

– welded with specification given in the American Welding Society standard

– flexible coupling

• *Installation standards* for joining nonmetallic pipe are unique to the type of pipe used. The manufacturer's instructions are critical to ensure a correct installation.

• *Pipe hangers* are used to attach sprinkler piping to substantial structural elements of a building. The type of hangers necessary to meet various conditions of construction have been tested and listed by testing laboratories. The adequate support of sprinkler piping is an important consideration.

Corrosive conditions

Corrosive conditions call for the use of piping, fittings, valves, and hangers that are designed to resist the particular corrosive environment or for the application of a protective coating over the components.

• *Water supply:* For buildings that may contain corrosive properties, may require piping types that can resist the effects of the corrosion.

Sprinkler heads

• *Operating principles:* Under most conditions the discharge of water is restrained by a cap or valve held tightly against the orifice by a system of levers and links or other releasing devices pressing down on the cap. The operating elements can be:

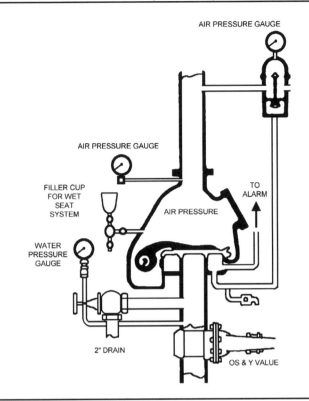

Fig. 17. Alarm check valve (dry-pipe).

Fig. 18. Fusible link sprinkler.

Fig. 19. Bulb style sprinkler.

– *fusible link style:* Operates when a metal alloy of a predetermined meeting point fuses (**Fig. 18**).

– *bulb style:* A frangible bulb, usually of glass, containing a liquid that does not completely fill the bulb. This small air bubble is then compressed by the expanding liquid and is absorbed by the liquid. Once the bulb disappears, the pressure rises and in turn shatters the glass bulb, releasing the valve cap (**Fig. 19**).

– *other thermosensitive styles:* bimetallic disc, fusible alloy pellets, and chemical pellets.

• *Deflector design:* The deflector is attached to the sprinkler frame and causes the water to be converted to a spray pattern to cover a specific area. The amount of water discharged is determined by:

– a flowing pressure of at least 7 psi (48 kPa), the minimum to develop a reasonable spray pattern and a sprinkler with a nominal ½ in (13 mm) orifice will discharge 15 gpm (57 l/m).

– to achieve the minimum flowing pressure at sprinklers that are remote from the water supply source (riser), a water supply pressure is required in the range of 30 psi (207 kPa) to 100 psi (690 kPa).

• *Pendent deflector:* Water is directed downward through the deflector, as in the bulb style sprinkler shown (Fig 19).

– used below finished ceiling, which conceals the sprinkler piping.

– heads can be recessed in the ceiling, concealed by a cover plate, or mounted flush (**Figs. 20** and **21**).

• *Upright deflector:* Water is directed upward through the deflector and then down onto the floor below (as in Fig. 18).

– are used in buildings with no finished ceiling, such as warehouses and manufacturing plants.

– must be installed within 12 in (30 cm) of the underside of the roof or floor decking.

Fig. 20. Recessed sprinkler.

Fig. 21. Concealed sprinkler.

- the design of the deflectors for pendent and upright sprinklers cause a solid stream of water from the orifice to break up to form an umbrella-shaped spray. The pattern is roughly that of a half-sphere filled with spray. Even water distribution is achieved by overlapping downward arcing coverage, by any two operating sprinklers located next to each other.

- *Sidewall horizontal deflector:* Water is directed horizontally through the deflectors to produce an arc of water that projects out from the sprinkler wall-mounted position (**Fig. 22**).

Fig. 22. Sidewall horizontal deflector.

- are limited to light hazard occupancies such as hotels, dining rooms, offices, and residential occupancies.

- supply piping is in the walls and is used where piping would be objectionable.

- directional character of the discharge from the sidewall sprinkler makes them applicable to special protection design problems.

Temperature rating

Automatic sprinklers have various temperature ratings for application in areas that will have various maximum ceiling temperatures. NFPA Standard 13 notes the various maximum ceiling temperature that may be expected and the required sprinkler rating to be installed and also notes the different sprinkler temperature classifications and the color codes used for both fusible link and glass bulb type sprinklers.

- Generally, sprinklers of ordinary 135F (57°C) to 170F (77°C) temperature ratings should not be used in areas where the temperature would exceed 100F (38°C) to prevent premature operation. Areas that require special attention are:

- areas inside buildings exposed to direct sun rays such as skylights.

- blind attics without ventilation.

- under metal or tile roofs.

- near or above heating sources.

- within confined spaces where normal temperatures can be exceeded.

- In cases where extreme speed of operation is required because of the likelihood of a rapidly developing and spreading fire, the practice is to use a deluge system with open sprinklers. The system would be activated by a special fire detection system to open a deluge control valve and quickly allow water to enter the system and discharge through all the open sprinkler heads.

Area of coverage

The fundamental idea in locating and spacing sprinklers in a building is to be sure no areas are unprotected where a fire can start or spread. No areas should be left unprotected. NFPA Standard 13 notes areas where sprinklers are sometimes questioned. These include:

- stairways

- vertical shafts

- deep blind and combustible concealed spaces

- ducts

- basements

- subfloor spaces

- attics

- electrical equipment rooms

- small closets

- walk-in coolers

- spaces under decks

- tables

- canopies

- outdoor platforms

- *Area and spacing limitations:* The location of sprinklers on a branch line and the location of the lines in relation to each other determine the size of the area to be protected by a sprinkler. A definite maximum area of coverage is defined that is dependent upon the occupancy hazard and the type of ceiling or roof construction above the sprinkler. Those types being smooth ceiling, beam and girder, bar joist, wood joist, and wood truss. In general, area coverage of sprinklers are:

- 168 to 225 sq ft (15.6 to 21 sq m) for light hazard.

- 130 sq ft (12 sq m) for ordinary hazard.

- 100 sq ft (9.3 sq m) for extra hazard.

- maximum area of coverage for any type of sprinkler not to exceed 40 sq ft (3.6 sq m).

- standard pendent and upright sprinklers maximum are not to exceed 225 sq ft (20.3 sq m).

- standard sidewall not to exceed 196 sq ft (17.6 sq m).

- extended coverage pendent and upright sprinklers not to exceed 400 sq ft (36 sq m).

- maximum spacing between any sprinklers cannot exceed 15 ft (4.6 m) for light and ordinary hazard and 12 ft (3.7 m) for extra hazard occupancies.

- the distance of a sprinkler to a wall is usually no more than half of the uniform spacing design being used.

- NFPA Standard 13 allows use of special sprinklers with greater areas of coverage when they have been tested and listed for the greater coverage. These types of sprinklers are referred to as "extended coverage" that will be addressed below.

- *Design considerations:* It is very important that the sprinkler designer be consulted as early as possible in planning for the piping installation. This planning can provide the following benefits for sprinkler placement:

- reduce the installation costs by taking advantage of the maximum spacing allowed for each sprinkler head for protection of individual rooms and areas, in turn reducing the number of heads required.

- plan individual room sizes around maximum coverage per sprinkler head.

- plan for piping runs that will not be in conflict with other mechanical systems in the ceiling.

- placement of ceiling light fixtures where they will not interfere with sprinkler placement or discharge pattern.

- improve the aesthetics of sprinkler installation that blend with the building finishes.

- reduce architectural obstructions that would affect water discharge patterns and in turn eliminate the need for additional sprinkler heads.

Obstruction to water distribution

Certain limits of clearance have been established between sprinklers and structural members such as beams, girders, and truss to keep them from obstructing water discharge from sprinklers.

- obstruction can deflect the normal sprinkler discharge pattern and in turn reduce the area of protection for the sprinkler.

- NFPA Standard 13 is explicit in the limitation it places on distances between sprinklers and both vertical and horizontal obstructions near the sprinklers.

Types of automatic sprinklers

- *Recessed sprinkler*

A type in which most of the body of the sprinkler is mounted in a recessed housing. The sprinkler is positioned in a pendent position (as in Fig. 20).

- *Flush sprinkler*

A special design for pendent mounting within the ceiling. The design allows a minimum projection of the working parts below the ceiling without affecting the heat sensitivity or water distribution pattern.

- *Concealed sprinkler*

A type whose entire body, including the operating mechanism, is above its concealed cover plate. When a fire occurs, the cover plate drops, exposing the heat-sensitive sprinkler element that in turn then operates (Fig. 21). Characteristics of these sprinklers:

- aesthetic in appearance because they do not protrude through decorated ceilings.

- cover plates are available in colors and patterns to match decorative ceiling assemblies.

- *Ornamental sprinkler*

A sprinkler that has been decorated by attachment or by plating or enameling to give the desired surface finish. These types of sprinklers are for pendent installation.

- *Dry pendent and dry upright sprinkler*

Used to provide protection in unheated areas, such as freezers, where the individual sprinklers are supplied from a wet type system outside of the unheated area. A seal is provided at the entrance of the dry sprinkler to prevent water from entering until the sprinkler fuses (**Fig. 23**).

- *Sidewall sprinkler*

Has components of standard sprinkler except for a special deflector, which discharges the water toward one side in a pattern somewhat like one-quarter of a sphere. Can only be used in light hazard occupancies. Can be mounted:

- in a vertical position along the junction between the ceiling and sidewall.

- in a horizontal position along the junction between the ceiling and sidewall (**Fig. 24**).

- *Open sprinkler*

A sprinkler that has had its valve cap and heat response element omitted and is used in deluge type systems (**Fig. 25**).

- *Residential quick response sprinkler*

Specifically listed for use in residential occupancies. These are fast-response sprinklers that have special low-mass fusible links or bulbs that make the time of temperature actuation much less than that of a sprinkler with a standard fusible link. For use in wet-pipe systems only, designed for pendent and horizontal sidewall position (**Fig. 26**).

Fig. 24. Recessed horizontal sprinkler.

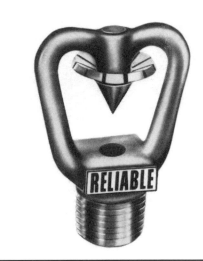

Fig. 25. Open sprinkler.

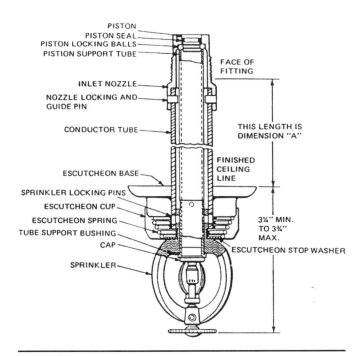

Fig. 23. Dry pendent automatic sprinkler.

Recessed Pendent

Fig. 26. Quick response sprinkler.

- *Intermediate level sprinkler*

Also referred to as in-rack sprinkler. These sprinklers are equipped with shields designed to protect the link assembly from spray of sprinklers mounted at higher levels. These heads are found in high rack storage arrangements.

- *Early suppression fast response (ESFR) sprinkler*

A fast-response sprinkler listed for its capability to provide fire suppression of specific high challenge fire hazards. The ESFR sprinklers can:

- achieve fire suppression quickly without opening more than one ring of sprinklers.

- optimize sprinkler performance by mounting a vigorous attack against a fire, regardless of its intensity or the degree of fire development when the first few sprinklers operate.

- be used in storage areas with high storage heights of highly combustible type storage.

- *Extended coverage (EC) sprinkler*

A sprinkler with special extended directional discharge patterns. The Underwriters Laboratories, Fire Protection Equipment Directory, notes that EC sidewall and pendent type sprinklers are designed to discharge water over an area having maximum dimensions indicated by the manufacturer in their individual listings. Extended coverage sprinklers:

- are designed for light hazard occupancies having smooth flat horizontal ceilings.

- deflector must be located from 4 in (10 cm) to 6 in (15 cm) below the ceiling.

- the maximum width and length dimensions are noted along with the minimum flow rate and pressure required in their individual listings. ■

REFERENCES

Byran, John C., *Automatic Sprinkler and Standpipe Systems,* latest ed., National Fire Protection Association, Quincy.

NFPA, *NFPA Fire Protection Handbook,* 19th ed., National Fire Protection Association, Quincy, 2003. 1-800-344-3555.

———. *NFPA Standard 13D: Installation of Sprinkler Systems in One and Two Family Dwellings,* National Fire Protection Association, Quincy, 2003.

———. *NFPA Standard 13R: Installation of Sprinkler Systems in Residential Occupancies up to Four Stories in Height,* National Fire Protection Association, Quincy, 2003.

———. *NFPA Standard 20: Installation of Fire Pumps,* National Fire Protection Association, Quincy, 2003.

———. *NFPA Standard 22: Water Tanks for Private Fire Protection,* National Fire Protection Association, Quincy, 2003.

Bruce W. Hisley

Summary
An overview is provided of carbon dioxide and dry chemical fire extinguishing systems, life safety considerations, applications for halon systems, foam system guidelines, design and acceptance testing, and fire protection for grease ventilation and exhaust systems.

Key words
CO_2 systems, dry chemical extinguishing properties, exhaust hood, foam expansion ratio, halogenated agent, halon

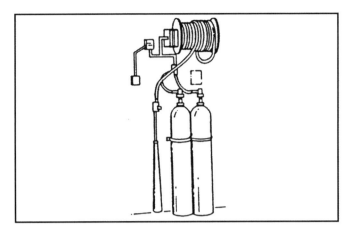

Fig. 1. Hand hose line system.

Special fire protection systems

The following special fire protection systems are described in this article:

– carbon dioxide (CO_2) systems

– dry chemical systems

– halon systems

– foam extinguishing systems

– grease exhaust hood fire protection systems

1 CARBON DIOXIDE SYSTEMS

Carbon dioxide (CO_2) has been used for many years to extinguish flammable liquid fires, gas fires, and fires involving electrical equipment. CO_2 is non-combustible, does not react with most substances, and provides its own pressure for discharge from the storage container. Because it is a gas it can penetrate and spread to all parts of a fire area, will not conduct electricity, and leaves no residue after discharge.

• *Storage*

CO_2 may be stored in high-pressure cylinders at normal temperatures or in low-pressure refrigerated containers designed to maintain a storage temperature of 0F ($-18°C$).

• *Static electricity*

The dry ice particles produced during discharge can carry charges of static electricity. Static charges can build up on ungrounded discharge nozzles. In potentially explosive atmospheres all discharge nozzles must be grounded, especially in playpipes used in hand hose line systems (**Fig. 1**).

• *Properties of CO_2*

– has a density of 1.5 times that of air.

– concentrations of 6 to 7 percent are considered the threshold level at which harmful effects become noticeable in human beings. Adequate safety precautions must be taken when designing the CO_2 system.

– is an effective extinguishing agent primarily because it reduces the oxygen content of the atmosphere by dilution, to a point where the atmosphere no longer will support combustion.

• *Life safety considerations*

Total flooding systems should not be used in normally occupied spaces unless arrangements can be made to ensure evaluation before discharge.

• *Methods of application*

– total flooding: CO_2 is discharged through nozzles to develop a uniform concentration in all parts of the enclosure. The amount of CO_2

Credits: Illustrations courtesy of Kidde-Fenwal Protection Systems.

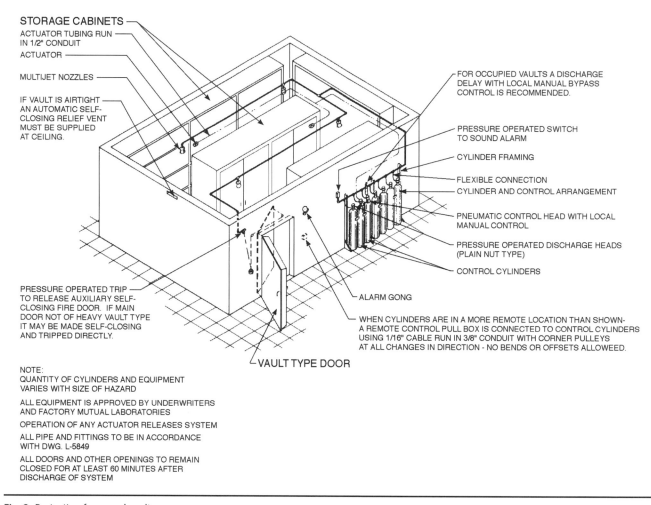

STORAGE CABINETS
ACTUATOR TUBING RUN
IN 1/2" CONDUIT
ACTUATOR

MULTIJET NOZZLES

IF VAULT IS AIRTIGHT
AN AUTOMATIC SELF-
CLOSING RELIEF VENT
MUST BE SUPPLIED
AT CEILING.

FOR OCCUPIED VAULTS A DISCHARGE
DELAY WITH LOCAL MANUAL BYPASS
CONTROL IS RECOMMENDED.

PRESSURE OPERATED SWITCH
TO SOUND ALARM

CYLINDER FRAMING

FLEXIBLE CONNECTION
CYLINDER AND CONTROL ARRANGEMENT

PNEUMATIC CONTROL HEAD WITH LOCAL
MANUAL CONTROL

PRESSURE OPERATED DISCHARGE HEADS
(PLAIN NUT TYPE)

CONTROL CYLINDERS

ALARM GONG

WHEN CYLINDERS ARE IN A MORE REMOTE LOCATION THAN SHOWN-
A REMOTE CONTROL PULL BOX IS CONNECTED TO CONTROL CYLINDERS
USING 1/16" CABLE RUN IN 3/8" CONDUIT WITH CORNER PULLEYS
AT ALL CHANGES IN DIRECTION - NO BENDS OR OFFSETS ALLOWEED.

PRESSURE OPERATED TRIP
TO RELEASE AUXILIARY SELF-
CLOSING FIRE DOOR. IF MAIN
DOOR NOT OF HEAVY VAULT TYPE
IT MAY BE MADE SELF-CLOSING
AND TRIPPED DIRECTLY.

VAULT TYPE DOOR

NOTE:
QUANTITY OF CYLINDERS AND EQUIPMENT
VARIES WITH SIZE OF HAZARD

ALL EQUIPMENT IS APPROVED BY UNDERWRITERS
AND FACTORY MUTUAL LABORATORIES

OPERATION OF ANY ACTUATOR RELEASES SYSTEM

ALL PIPE AND FITTINGS TO BE IN ACCORDANCE
WITH DWG. L-5849

ALL DOORS AND OTHER OPENINGS TO REMAIN
CLOSED FOR AT LEAST 60 MINUTES AFTER
DISCHARGE OF SYSTEM

Fig. 2. Protection for record vault.

required is based on the volume of the area and the concentration of CO_2 specified. The integrity of the enclosure is an important part of the total flooding system. All openings and ventilation systems must be closed to minimize leakage of the CO_2 after discharge (**Fig. 2**).

– local application: CO_2 is discharged directly on the burning surfaces through nozzles designed for this application. All areas that contain the combustible hazard are covered with nozzles, located so that they will extinguish all flames as quickly as possible. Local application of CO_2 can be used for fast fire knockdown (**Fig. 3**).

• *Hand hose lines*

Hand hose lines are permanently connected by means of fixed piping to a fixed supply of CO_2. These types of systems are used for manual protection of small localized hazards. They may also be used to supplement a fixed system where the hazard is accessible for manual fire-fighting.

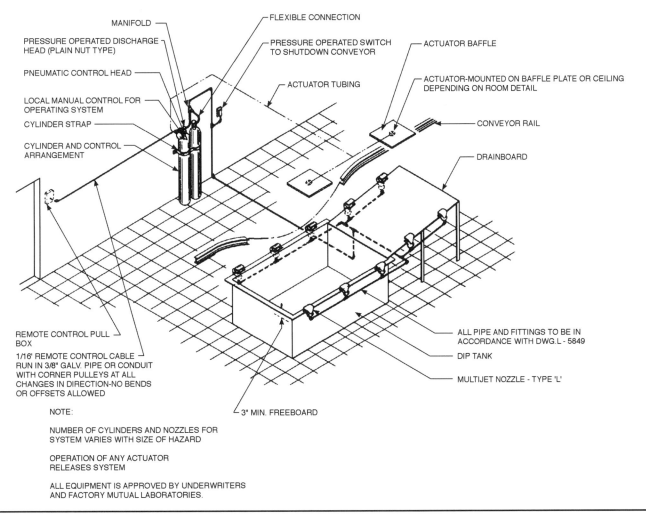

MANIFOLD
FLEXIBLE CONNECTION
PRESSURE OPERATED DISCHARGE HEAD (PLAIN NUT TYPE)
PRESSURE OPERATED SWITCH TO SHUTDOWN CONVEYOR
ACTUATOR BAFFLE
PNEUMATIC CONTROL HEAD
ACTUATOR-MOUNTED ON BAFFLE PLATE OR CEILING DEPENDING ON ROOM DETAIL
LOCAL MANUAL CONTROL FOR OPERATING SYSTEM
ACTUATOR TUBING
CYLINDER STRAP
CONVEYOR RAIL
CYLINDER AND CONTROL ARRANGEMENT
DRAINBOARD
REMOTE CONTROL PULL BOX
ALL PIPE AND FITTINGS TO BE IN ACCORDANCE WITH DWG.L - 5849
1/16' REMOTE CONTROL CABLE RUN IN 3/8" GALV. PIPE OR CONDUIT WITH CORNER PULLEYS AT ALL CHANGES IN DIRECTION-NO BENDS OR OFFSETS ALLOWED
DIP TANK
MULTIJET NOZZLE - TYPE 'L'
NOTE:
3" MIN. FREEBOARD
NUMBER OF CYLINDERS AND NOZZLES FOR SYSTEM VARIES WITH SIZE OF HAZARD
OPERATION OF ANY ACTUATOR RELEASES SYSTEM
ALL EQUIPMENT IS APPROVED BY UNDERWRITERS AND FACTORY MUTUAL LABORATORIES.

Fig. 3. Protection for dip tank and drain board.

- *Components of CO_2 systems*

The main components of a CO_2 system are:

- CO_2 supply

- discharge nozzles

- control valves

- piping

- operating devices

- fire detection equipment

- *CO_2 system design considerations*

- quantity of stored CO_2

- method of actuation

- use of predischarge alarms

- ventilation shutdown

- pressure venting

- *System control*

- CO_2 systems for total flooding and local application should be designed to operate automatically.

- the detection device may be any of the listed or approved types that are actuated by heat, smoke, flame, flammable vapors, or other abnormal process conditions that could lead to a fire or explosion.

- *Acceptance testing*

All new systems shall be inspected and tested to prove performance in accordance with design specifications.

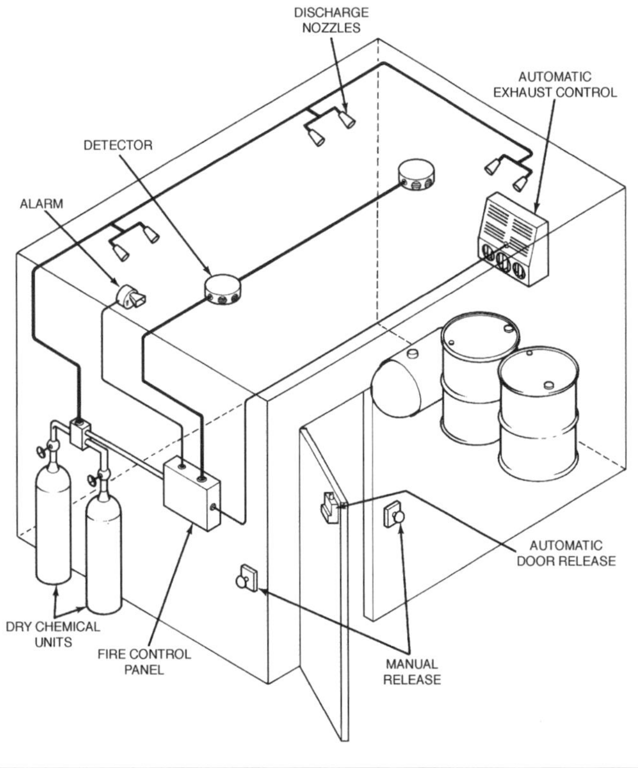

2 DRY CHEMICAL SYSTEMS

Dry chemical is a powder mixture that is used as a fire extinguishing agent for application by means of portable extinguishers, hand hose lines, or fixed systems. Regular or ordinary dry chemical are powders that are listed for use on Class B and C type fires. Multipurpose dry chemical refers to powders listed for use on Class A, B, and C type fires.

• *Application*

Dry chemical is efficient in extinguishing fires in flammable liquids and some types of electrical equipment that do not include telephone exchanges, and computer equipment rooms. Multipurpose dry chemical can be used on fires in ordinary combustible materials.

• *Extinguishing properties*

When introduced directly to the fire areas, dry chemical causes the flame to go out almost at once. Smothering, cooling, radiation shielding, and chain-breaking reaction in the flame are the causes for extinguishment.

• *Uses for dry chemical systems*

– systems are used where quick extinguishment is desired and where reignition sources are not present.

– they are used primarily for flammable liquid fire hazards, such as dip tanks, flammable liquid storage rooms, and areas where flammable liquid spills may occur.

– systems have been designed for kitchen range hoods, ducts, and range top hazards, but are now being replaced by wet chemical systems.

– systems can also be used on electrical equipment that contains flammable liquids, such as oil-filled transformers and oil-filled circuit breakers.

• *Methods of application*

– fixed systems consist of a supply of dry chemical, an expellant gas, an actuating method, fixed piping, and nozzles through which the dry chemical can be discharged. Fixed systems are of two different types:

– total flooding: A predetermined amount of dry chemical is discharged through fixed piping and nozzles into an enclosed space around a hazard. Can be used where the hazard is totally enclosed or when all openings can be automatically closed when the system is discharged (**Fig. 4**).

– local application: The nozzles are arranged to discharge directly into the fire. The principal use of local application systems is to protect open tanks of flammable liquids.

– hand hose line systems consist of a supply of dry chemical and expellant gas with one or more hand hose lines to deliver the dry chemical to the fire. They are used to provide a quick knockdown and extinguishment of relatively large fires, such as gasoline-loading racks, and aircraft hangars.

Fig. 4. Total flooding dry chemical extinguishing unit.

• *Design of dry chemical systems*

Dry chemical systems are of two different types:

– engineered systems, in which individual calculations and design are needed to determine the flow rate, nozzle pressure, pipe size, quantity of dry chemical, and number, type, and placement of nozzles for the hazard protected.

– pre-engineered systems, in which the size of the system is predetermined by fire tests for specific sizes and types of hazards. This type of design is frequently used for kitchen range and hood fire protection (**Fig. 5**).

• *System actuation*

Initiated by automatic mechanisms that incorporate sensing devices, located in the hazard area; automatic, mechanical, or electrical releases initiate the flow of dry chemical, actuate alarms, and shut down process equipment.

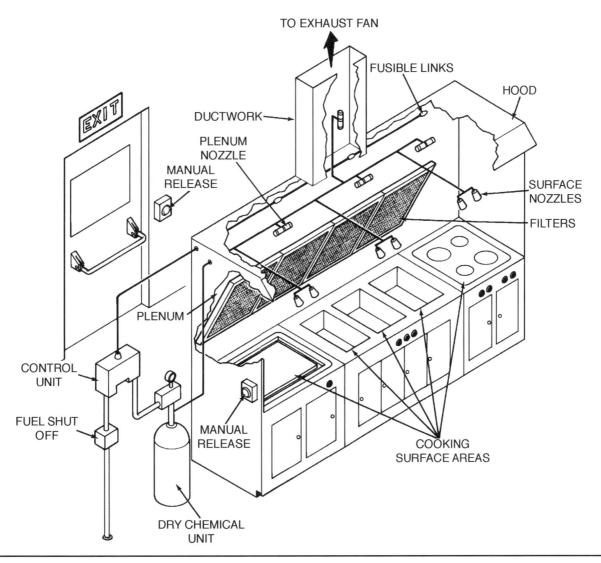

Fig. 5. Pre-engineered dry chemical system.

3 HALON SYSTEMS

Halogenated extinguishing agents are hydrocarbons in which one or more hydrogen atoms have been replaced by atoms from the halogen series: fluorine, chlorine, bromine, or iodine. Halon 1301 systems are used to protect vital electrical facilities such as computer rooms and communications equipment.

• *Halon regulation*

Halons have been identified as ozone-depletion agents. The Montreal protocol on substances that deplete the ozone layer required a complete phaseout of the production of halons by the year 2000, except to the extent necessary to satisfy essential uses for which no adequate alternatives are available.

– The U.S. Environmental Protection Agency enacted further rules regulating these products' production, use, handling, and deposition. The user of this product should consult local authorities for their current regulations.

– There are now currently over 12 commercialized total flooding clean agent alternatives to Halon 1301. The primary design guide for any installation is NFPA 2001, *Standard on Clean Agent Fire Extinguishing Systems.*

– Clean agents are defined as fire extinguishants that vaporize readily, leave no residue compounds, and invert gases and mixtures.

• *Application*

Total flooding halogenated systems are used primarily to protect hazards that are in enclosures, or equipment that in itself includes an enclosure to contain the agent. Some typical hazards are:

– electrical

– telecommunications

– flammable and combustible liquids

– gases

• *Extinguishing characteristic*

The mechanism of halogenated agents is not clearly understood. However, a chemical reaction occurs that interferes with the combustion processes. This type of extinguishing action is referred to as a chain breakdown in the flaming process. In total flooding type systems the effectiveness of flammable liquids and vapor fires are quite dramatic.

• *Halogenated components* (**Fig. 6**):

– supply of agents

– means of releasing or propelling the agent from its container

– one or more discharge nozzles

– fire detection devices

– remote or local alarms

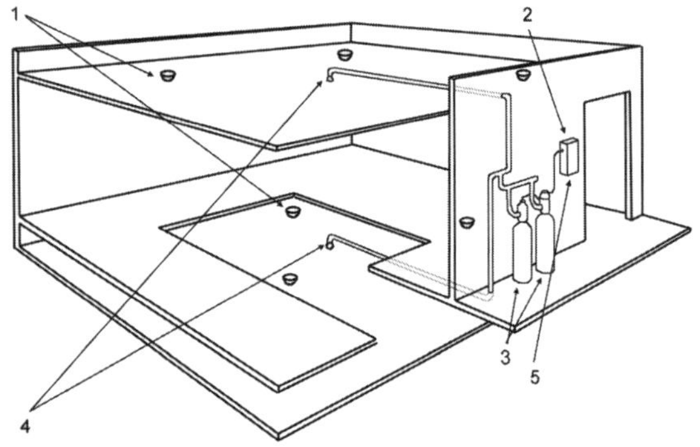

1. AUTOMATIC FIRE DETECTORS INSTALLED BOTH IN ROOM PROPER AND UNDERFLOOR AREA.
2. CONTROL PANEL CONNECTED BETWEEN FIRE DETECTORS AND CYLINDER RELEASE VALVES
3. STORAGE CONTAINERS FOR ROOM PROPER AND UNDERFLOOR AREA
4. DISCHARGE NOZZLES INSTALLED BOTH IN ROOM PROPER AND UNDERFLOOR AREA
5. CONTROL PANEL MAY ALSO SOUND ALARMS, CLOSE DOORS, AND SHUT OFF POWER TO THE AREA.

Fig. 6. Halogenated system.

– piping network

– mechanical and electrical interlocks to close doors and shut down ventilation systems to the hazard area.

• *System design and types*

The design requirements for halogenated type systems are noted in NFPA 12A, *Halon Fire Extinguishing Agent Systems.* This standard classifies systems into two types:

– total flooding: These systems protect enclosures. A sufficient quantity of agent is discharged into the enclosure to provide a uniform fire-extinguishing concentration throughout the entire enclosure.

– engineered system: Custom designed for a particular hazard. The pre-engineered type systems are determined in advance and include the description of the system's approval and listing.

– local application: This type of system discharges the agent in a manner that the burning object is surrounded locally by a high concentration of agent to extinguish the fire. Examples of application are: printing presses, dip tanks, spray booths, and oil-filled electric transformers (**Fig. 7**).

• *Acceptance testing*

– testing and inspection of the completed entire system is required to ensure proper operation and design.

– such testing would include a nondestructive test of all system functions.

– full-scale discharge tests should be avoided. Should a special need arise, a substitute test gas should be used.

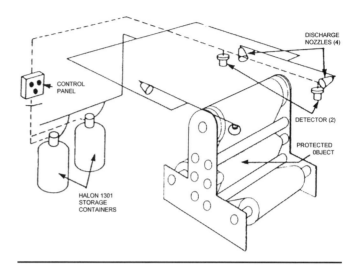

Fig. 7. Local application system.

4 FOAM-EXTINGUISHING SYSTEMS

Firefighting foam is an aggregate of gas-filled bubbles from aqueous solutions of specially formulated concentrated liquid foaming agents. The foam solution floats on the burning liquid surface to exclude the air and cool at the same time, in turn reducing and eliminating combustion. Foam is produced by mixing the concentrate solution with water in various concentrations. Foams are defined by their expansion ratio when mixed with water and air, which are low expansion, medium expansion, and high expansion.

• *Uses and limitations*

– Low-expansion foam is used to extinguish burning flammable or combustible liquid spill or tank fires.

– Medium- or high-expansion foam may be used to fill enclosures such as basement rooms or confined space hazard areas. The foam acts to halt convection and access to air for combustion.

– Some foams have very low surface tension and penetration ability. Foams of this type are useful where Class A combustible materials are present.

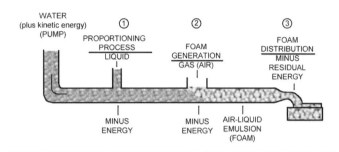

Fig. 8. Foam application.

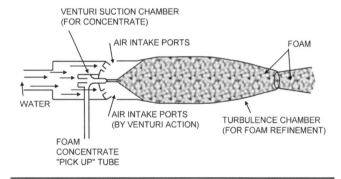

Fig. 9. Nozzle eductor.

- *Guidelines for foam systems*

- the more gently the foam is applied, the more rapid the extinguishment and lower amount of agent required.

- successful use of foam is dependent upon the rate of application, which is the amount of volume of foam solution reaching the fuel surface.

- provide the minimum application rate found by tests to be the most practical in terms of speed of control and agent required.

- air foams are more stable when generated with water at ambient temperatures from 30 to 80F (0 to 27°C).

- fixed foam makers should be located on the sides of, rather than directly over, the hazard.

- *Methods of generating foam*

The generation of foam requires three different operations: the proportioning process, the generation phase, and the distribution method (**Fig. 8**).

- nozzle eductor is the most simple in design and is widely used in portable foam-making nozzles. When foam is available in 5 gal (19 l) containers, the nozzle eductor drafts concentrate from the container through a pickup tube and mix with proper flow of water and air at the nozzle to produce foam (**Fig. 9**).

- in line eductors, the proportioner educts or drafts the concentrate from a container or tank utilizing the operating pressure of the hose water stream.

- other types of generation using different fixed-pipe systems consist of pumps, storage tanks, and proportioner eductors.

- *Types of low-expansion foam systems*

- fixed foam: piped from a central foam station, discharging through fixed delivery outlets to protect the hazard.

- semi-fixed system: the hazard is equipped with fixed discharge outlets connected to piping that terminates at a safe distance from the hazard. Foam-making materials are transported to the scene after the fire starts and connected to the piping.

- mobile system: foam-producing unit is mounted on wheels and is either self-propelled or towed by a vehicle. The unit can be connected to a water supply or can utilize a premixed foam solution. NFPA Standard 11C, *Mobile Foam Apparatus,* notes requirements for this type of system.

- portable system: foam-producing equipment and materials are transported by hand.

- *Design*

Low-expansion foam systems should be designed in accordance with NFPA Standard 11, *Low Expansion Foam.*

- *Acceptance test*

Low-expansion foam systems tests should be completed by qualified personnel and should be conducted to determine that the system has been properly installed and functions as intended.

- *Types of medium- and high-expansion foam systems*

– total flooding systems are designed to discharge into an enclosed space around the hazard. Can be used where the required amount of fire-extinguishing agent can be built up and maintained for the required period of time to ensure the control and extinguishment of fire.

– local application systems are designed to extinguish or control fires in flammable or combustible liquids, liquefied natural gas, and ordinary Class A combustibles, where the hazard is not totally enclosed. This type of system is suitable for flat surfaces such as confined spills, open tanks, drain boards, pits, and trenches.

– portable foam systems can be used to combat fires in all types of hazards where the other types of system could be used. This type of system is usually required to be transported to the designated hazard.

- *Design*

Medium- and high-expansion foam systems should be installed in accordance with NFPA 11A, *Medium and High Expansion Foam Systems.*

- *Acceptance test*

For low-expansion foam systems, tests should be completed by qualified personnel and should be conducted to determine that the system has been properly installed and functions as intended.

- *Other types of foam systems*

– deluge foam-water sprinkler and foam-water spray systems, discharge water and foam from the same discharge devices: This type of system has all of the same characteristics of a sprinkler system with the exception of the added foam discharge and special discharge nozzles. The design requirements for this type of system are found in NFPA Standard 16, *Installation of Deluge Foam-Water and Foam-Water Spray Systems.*

– closed head foam-water sprinkler systems consist of closed heads that are installed on either a wet-pipe, dry-pipe, or pre-action type sprinkler system: This type of system has all of the same characteristics of a sprinkler system with the exception of the added foam discharge and special automatic type foam/water sprinkler heads. The design requirements for this type of system are found in NFPA Standard 16A, *Installation of Closed-Head Foam-Water Sprinkler Systems.*

5 GREASE EXHAUST HOOD FIRE PROTECTION SYSTEMS

In restaurant, commercial, or institutional occupancies where cooking operations take place, grease deposits are usually present within the exhaust system. Also present are deep fat fryers that contain combustible frying oils and grills with grease deposits. Constant ignition sources can readily ignite grease, which in turn causes a rapidly spreading fire to extend throughout the exhaust system and also to the building interior. Automatic fire-extinguishing systems have been designed and approved to protect this common hazard where cooking operations are performed (**Fig. 10**).

- *Type of systems*

– wet chemical systems normally contain a solution of water and potassium, carbonate-based chemical, potassium acetate-based chemical, or a combination that forms an extinguishing agent. These systems are usually pre-engineered and must be installed in accordance with the manufacturer's listed installation instructions. This type of system is the most preferred choice today because of the minimum cleanup required after discharge (**Fig. 11**).

– grease extractors are specially designed, automatic self-cleaning water wash systems that are installed within the hood plenum and exhaust ducts. These systems, when listed, can also provide automatic fire protection for the exhaust plenum and ductwork. They may or may not be designed to also provide protection for the cooking equipment located under the exhaust hood.

- *Basic system design*

– all pre-engineered systems must be installed in accordance with the manufacturer's listed instructions.

– system must protect the exhaust ductwork, hood plenum, all surface areas of cooking appliances located below hood, and broilers if provided.

– system shall be actuated by both automatic detection and manual operation.

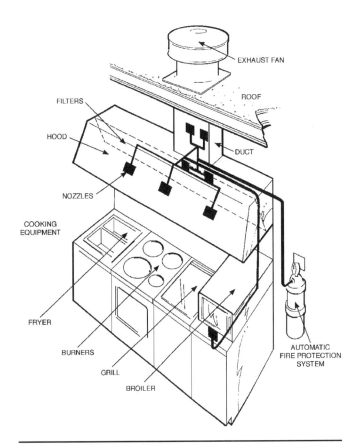

Fig. 10. Typical grease exhaust system.

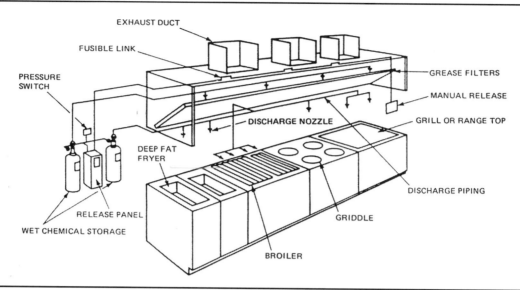

Fig. 11. Wet chemical system.

- fuel or power supply to protected cooking appliances, located under exhaust hood, shall shut off automatically when the systems actuate.

- manual actuation must be in a location away from the cooking area in a route to an exit.

- the ventilation fan control for runoff or shutoff must be in accordance with the system manufacturer's requirements.

- the entire system shall discharge to all protected areas when actuated.

• *Acceptance testing:*

Wet chemical systems should be tested by trained personnel as required by the manufacturer's listed installation requirements. The test should determine that the system has been properly installed and will function as intended. ▪

REFERENCES

NFPA, *NFPA Fire Protection Handbook*, 19th ed., *NFPA Standard 11: Low-Expansion Foam*, National Fire Protection Association, Quincy, 2003. 1-800-344-3555.

————. *NFPA Standard 11A: Medium and High Expansion Foam Systems*, NFPA, Quincy, 2003.

————. *NFPA Standard 11C: Mobile Foam Apparatus*, NFPA, Quincy, 2003.

————. *NFPA Standard 12: Carbon Dioxide Extinguishing Systems*, NFPA, Quincy, 2003.

————. *NFPA Standard 12A: Halon 1301 Fire Extinguishing Systems*, NFPA, Quincy, 2003.

————. *NFPA Standard 13: Installation of Automatic Sprinkler Systems*, NFPA, Quincy, 2003.

————. *NFPA Standard 16: Deluge Foam-Water Sprinkler and Foam-Water Spray Systems*, NFPA, Quincy, 2003.

————. *NFPA Standard 16A: Installation of Closed Head Foam Water Sprinkler Systems*, NFPA, Quincy, 2003.

————. *NFPA Standard 17: Dry Chemical Extinguishing Systems*, NFPA, Quincy, 2003.

————. *NFPA Standard 17A: Wet Chemical Extinguishing Systems*, NFPA, Quincy, 2003.

————. *NFPA Standard 96: Cooking Operations, Ventilation Controls, and Specific Listed Manufacturer's Installation Instruction*, NFPA, Quincy, 2003.

————. *NFPA Standard 2001: Standard Clean Agent Fire Extinguishing Systems*, NFPA, Quincy, 2003.

Walter Cooper

Summary

A properly designed, code-compliant fire alarm system is an essential part of the building's life safety system. It gives early warning and notification to occupants in a building, as well as notification of an off-site central station to summon the fire department.

Key words

alarm verification, command center, multiplex systems, smoke detectors, storage batteries

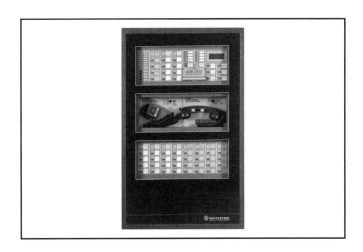

Fire alarm systems

Function

The purpose of the fire alarm system is to protect life by automatically indicating the necessity for evacuation of the building or fire area, to protect property through the automatic notification of responsible persons, and the automatic activation of fire safety functions. Fire alarm systems include one or more of the following features:

– manual alarm signal initiation

– automatic alarm signal initiation

– activation of fire suppression systems

– activation of fire safety functions

– activation of alarm notification appliances

– monitoring of abnormal conditions in fire suppression systems

– emergency voice/alarm communications

– process monitoring supervisory systems

– activation of off-premise signals

Responsibilities

Design professionals are responsible for the design of a code-compliant fire alarm system. It is very important to identify the local code requirements and their interpretation early on by reviewing local building codes and meeting with local code officials on design for code compliance. The first step is to review local building codes to establish the required system. Usually the code directs readers to the National Fire Protection Association (NFPA), an international codes and standards organization that develops and publishes fire protection codes and standards (NFPA 2003).

Design considerations

The building's height determines if the fire alarm system will have voice/alarm communication systems. Buildings over 75 ft (23 m) in height are generally considered high-rise buildings and require devices such as firefighters' telephones, warden stations, and voice notification and direction systems. For high-rise buildings, the code will direct the designer as to the type of notification required. In some jurisdictions, the alarm notification is on the floor of first alarm and on the floor above and below the floor of alarm initiation. Knowing such information allows the firefighters to direct occupants to safety.

In a building less than 75 ft (23 m) in height, the alarm notification will generally be for total evacuation of the building.

High-rise fire alarm systems are as follows:

- *A stand-alone fire alarm system,* an integrated, closed-circuit, modified two-stage, electrically supervised manual and automatic fire alarm system using addressable, multiplexed technology (**Fig. 1**) and consisting of the following:

Credits: Illustrations are reproduced by permission of Notifier / Pittway Corporation.

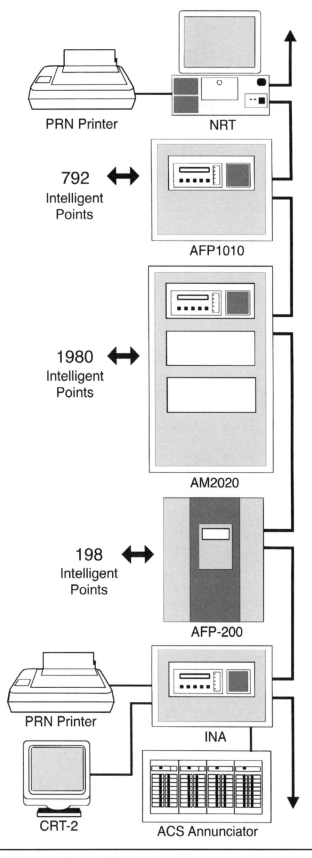

PRN Printer — NRT

792 Intelligent Points ◆➤ AFP1010

1980 Intelligent Points ◆➤ AM2020

198 Intelligent Points ◆➤ AFP-200

PRN Printer — INA

CRT-2 — ACS Annunciator

Fig. 1. Integrated network fire alarm system.

– A one-way emergency voice communication system and visual alarm system to alert building occupants.

– A two-way fire department communication system for use by the fire department.

– Fire signals automatically transmitted to the fire department via approved central station.

– Elevator recall system.

– Interface with Building Management System for ventilation, pressurization, and smoke exhaust systems.

– Interface with security system for automatic de-energization of electromagnetic locking devices.

• *Fire and smoke detection*

– Automatic sprinkler and standpipe water flow indicators.

– Area smoke detectors in all electrical and telecommunication equipment rooms and elevator machine rooms.

– Duct smoke detectors in recirculating air systems as required by code. In addition to activating alarm signals, activation of the smoke detectors will cause shutdown of related fan systems.

– Smoke detectors provided in all elevator lobbies. Activation of this detector will initiate automatic elevator recall to the designated floor.

– Manual fire alarm stations located at entry to exit doors and exit stairs.

• *Fire Command Center*

Fire command center should be located on ground level in a location approved by the fire department, and consist of:

– emergency voice communication panel.

– fire department communication panel (**Fig. 2**).

– fire detection and alarm system annunciators.

– sprinklers and standpipe supervisory display panels.

– status indicators and controls for smoke control system.

– fire and sprinkler pump control and status indicator.

– emergency and standby power indicators and controls.

– special extinguishing system monitoring.

– elevator control panels with elevator positions and status indicators.

• *Activation*

The activation of any manual or automatic alarm-initiating device:

– transmits an alarm signal to the fire department via off-site central station monitoring service.

– sounds an alert signal to all required selected locations via one-way voice communications system (**Fig. 3**).

– activates the prerecorded message and evacuation signal to those areas where the evacuation signal is required to be sounded.

– activates strobe visual alarm system in all required locations.

– activates fire door release devices.

– initiates the elevator recall operation.

– stops operation of all escalators.

– provides signals indicating alarm type and location to the smoke management/control system for fan control. ■

REFERENCES

NFPA, *NFPA Fire Protection Handbook,* 19th ed., National Fire Protection Association, Quincy, 2003. 1-800-344-3555.

Fig. 2. Voice alarm multiplex system.

Fig. 3. Voice-quality alarm speakers with and without strobe.

Walter Cooper and Robert DeGrazio

Summary

Communication and security systems have benefited from new innovations, and their design and specification involve close coordination of building design and electrical engineering specializations. This article provides the definitions and technical overview for preliminary design and integration of communication and data systems and electronic security systems.

Key words

access control, card reader, communications spaces, equipment room, intrusion detection, optical fiber, security center, telephone system, telecommunications

Communication and security systems

Electronic innovations permit greatly increased capacity for communications, both within buildings and to external sites throughout the world, including visual (video) media and computer filing systems, and telephone/teleconferencing options, along with increased security systems in buildings.

The designer should have an overview of communication and security systems and network requirements for preliminary design and layout (**Fig. 1**). This approach provides the basic integration of complex information technology systems, including the provision for long-term flexibility and access to accommodate technology upgrading over the life of the building.

The following topics are presented in this article, providing an overview of technical data for architects and engineers to integrate their work with communication and security system specialists.

1 Communication spaces and pathways

2 Communications cabling systems

3 Voice and data communication systems

4 Electronic security systems

1 COMMUNICATIONS SPACES AND PATHWAYS

Communications spaces always provide:

– physical protection and security for equipment.

– power and environmental facilities.

– provisions for cable interconnection and grounding.

– access to cables and equipment for modifications and maintenance.

In some cases, communications spaces also may provide:

– fire and smoke isolation.

– electromagnetic shielding.

– provision for electrical and lightning protection of metallic circuits.

– backbone cable pathways (riser space) between floors.

– accommodation for operating personnel.

Cable pathways always provide:

– structured wire management and organization.

– access to cables for modification and maintenance.

In some cases, cable pathways may also provide:

– physical protection and security for cables.

– fire and smoke isolation.

– electromagnetic shielding.

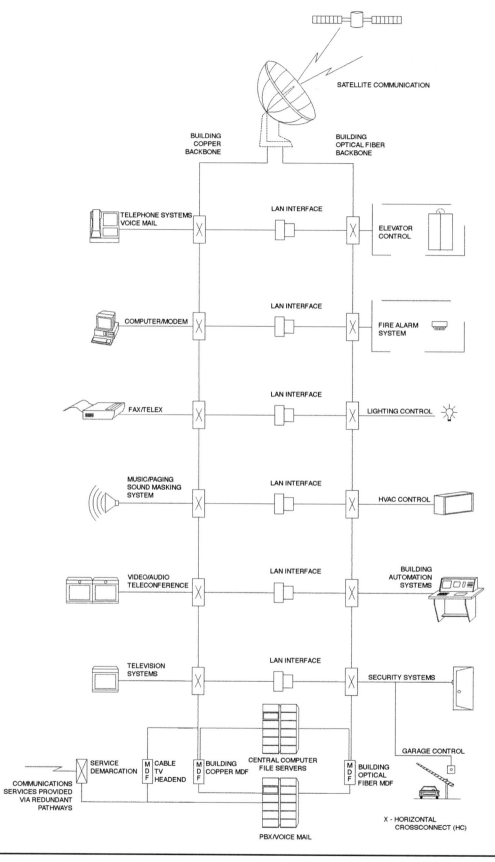

Fig. 1. Electronic communication and security system options.

Responsibilities

Base building (sometimes referred to as "backbone") communications spaces and pathways are the responsibility of the owner and are designed by the building architect and engineer team.

- In commercial buildings with rental spaces, the horizontal pathways and other communications spaces within tenant areas are typically the responsibility of the tenant or owner-occupant and are designed by the tenant architect-engineer team.

- Communications space and pathway designers and installation contractors must adhere to applicable EIA/TIA standards to ensure maximum utility, compatibility, and future flexibility of the building infrastructure system.

- In some cases (e.g., U.S. Federal Government projects), standards compliance is mandatory.

Types of communications spaces

- *Entrance room*

The entrance room is the transition point between outside cables and in-building cables. This space is usually the demarcation point between the service provider's facilities and the owner's facilities. For increased security and reliability, there may be more than one entrance room per building. An entrance room:

- Accommodates termination and interconnection points for incoming telecommunications cables, lightning protection for individual metallic conductors, and grounding for cable shields.

- Provides space, access, and a suitable environment for service provider's multiplexing and terminal equipment.

- *Telecommunications equipment room*

- Provides space and a suitable environment for telecommunications and computer equipment serving all, or part of, a building, or "campus," or group of buildings.

- May also contain the Main Distribution Facility (MDF) for building cabling and accommodation for operating and maintenance personnel.

- *Telecommunications closet*

- Typically serves a floor, or part of a floor, in a building.

- Provides space, power, and a suitable environment for electronic equipment such as Local Area Network (LAN) hubs and routers, backbone (riser) cable pathways, and Intermediate Distribution Facilities (IDF) for interconnections between backbone and horizontal cables.

- May also provide space for security, audiovisual, CATV (cable TV), building management, and other low voltage systems.

- Depending on the size of the floor plate, there may be more than one telecommunications closet per floor.

Design considerations for communications spaces

- *Entrance rooms*

- Locate on a lower building level within 50 ft (15 m) of perimeter walls where cables enter building. (Entrance rooms may also be required near the building roof to accommodate cables and equipment associated with rooftop antennas.)

- Separate by at least 10 ft (3 m) from sources of electromagnetic interference such as electric closets, switchrooms, and mechanical spaces.

- Separate from likely sources of flooding and excess humidity.

- Lighting and environmental conditions suitable for continuously operating electronic equipment (including emergency conditions).

- Maximum practical and useable wall space with plywood and other suitable blocking for wall-mounted equipment.

- Floor space for rack-mounted equipment and required service clearances.

- Without windows and finished ceiling.

- Fully accessible by service provider's maintenance personnel.

- Continuous operation and may require emergency power.

- Size in accordance with **Table 1.**

Table 1. Guidelines for sizing Communications Entrance Rooms

Building Gross Floor Area (sq. ft.)	Entrance Room Approximate Size (LxW) (ft)
70,000	12x6
100,000	12x6
200,000	12x9
400,000	13x12
500,000	16x12
600,000	18x12
800,000	22x12
1,000,000	23x12

- *Equipment rooms*

– Locate in a secure area (**Fig. 2**), centrally within building.

– In buildings with rental space, size of equipment rooms should be based on flexibility to accommodate any future tenant program.

– Somewhat similar to the communication entrance room, although smaller.

– Locate at least 10 ft (3 m) physical separation from sources of electromagnetic interference such as electric closets, switchrooms, and mechanical spaces.

– Locate with suitable separation from likely sources of flooding and excess humidity.

– Lighting and environmental conditions suitable for continuously operating, computer-grade electronic equipment.

– Without windows and possibly without finished ceilings.

– Maximize useable wall space and provided with plywood and/or other blocking for wall-mounted equipment.

– Floor space for rack-mounted equipment and required service clearances.

– May require an access floor, continuous operation and/or emergency power.

- *Telecommunications closets*

– Locate on each floor, vertically aligned within a core (vertical risers) accessway.

– sized 50 to 100 sq ft per 10,000 useable sq ft (4.6 to 9.3 sq m per 929 sq m) of serviced floor area.

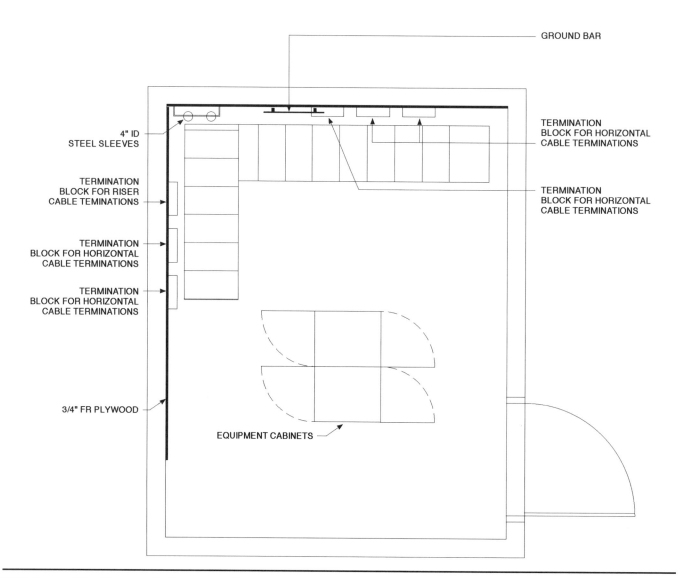

Fig. 2. Representative telecommunications equipment room plan.

– Locate so that cabling distance to work locations is 295 ft (90 m) or less.

– Floorplates greater than 10,000 sq ft (929 sq m) may require more than one closet.

– Physical separation from sources of electromagnetic interference such as electric closets, switchrooms, and mechanical spaces.

– Separate from likely sources of flooding and excess humidity.

– Provide with lighting and environmental conditions suitable for continuously operating electronic equipment.

– Without ceilings and (typically) without finished floors.

– Vertically aligned sleeves or slots for riser cables.

– Suitable fire-rating enclosure and/or fire protection.

– Maximize useable wall space with plywood and/or other blocking for wall-mounted equipment.

– Floor space for rack-mounted equipment and required service clearances.

– Outward-opening doors to maximize useable floor and wall space.

– May require an access floor and/or emergency power.

Types of communications cable pathways

Within the cabling system, the types of communication cable pathways include entrance pathways, building backbone pathways, and building horizontal cable pathways:

• *Entrance pathways*

– Ductbank or cable trenches between the property line, service provider's point(s) of access, or central campus distribution point, and individual buildings.

– Space for service provider's incoming cables and/or campus backbone cables between buildings.

– Access (via manholes, handholes, or vaults) for cable pulling, maintenance, and additions.

– May be more than one entrance pathway to a building or within a campus.

• *Building backbone pathways*

– Horizontal cable tray, conduit, j-hook supports or delineated pathways in ceiling voids or under access floor that interconnect the entrance room(s), equipment room(s), and telecommunications closets.

– Vertical backbone pathways (risers) include sleeves or slots within vertically aligned telecommunications closets, conduit, or ladder rack.

• *Building horizontal cable pathways*

– can include horizontal cable tray, conduit, j-hook supports, or delineated pathways in ceiling voids or under access floor.

– Trench headers and cells of cellular deck, and floor duct, surface-mounted raceways, and raceways within modular furniture systems may also be used as horizontal pathways.

– Conduit stub ups, poke-through fittings, preset and afterset fittings, and/or floor boxes complete the transition between horizontal pathway and the workstation.

Design considerations for communications spaces

• Entrance pathways

– Properly rated cables may be direct buried in a cable trench or placed in a utility tunnel.

– Provide with at least 4 ft (1.2 m) separation from power and other utilities in tunnels.

– Underground ductbanks are preferred for greater physical protection and cable pulling flexibility.

– Conduit or duct should be 4 in (10 cm) inside diameter and may be PVC type A, B, or C; Fiber Glass, Steel, or Multiple Plastic Duct (MPD) construction.

– All underground bends should have a radius of 40 ft (12.5 m) or greater.

– No more than two 90-degree bends are permitted between manholes/handholds.

– Provide a sufficient number of 4 in (10 cm) ducts based on type and quantity of cable and at least one empty spare per ductbank.

– Slope ductbank away from the building and provide steel sleeves at foundation wall penetrations.

– Consider providing redundant entrance pathways for increased reliability, security, and/or capacity and flexibility.

– Size the entrance pathways to accommodate multiple services (voice/data, CATV) and multiple service providers, for which **Table 2** can be used as a guide.

• Backbone cable pathways

– Provide sleeves or slots in vertically aligned telecommunications closets for vertical backbone (riser) pathways.

– Interconnect telecommunications closets on the same floor with horizontal conduit or cable tray.

– Interconnect entrance rooms and telecommunications equipment rooms to telecommunications closets on the same floor using conduit or cable tray.

– Consider providing more than one riser per floor for increased reliability, security, and/or capacity.

Table 2. Conduit provisions for entrance pathways

Building GFA (Gross Floor Area) sq. ft. (sq. m)	Minimum number of 4 in. (10 cm) conduits (including spares)*
70,000	1 + 1 spare
100,000	1 + 1 spare
200,000	2 + 1 spare
400,000	3 + 1 spare
500,000	4 + 1 spare
600,000	5 + 1 spare
800,000	5 + 1 spare
1,000,000	6 + 1 spare

* Note: conduits may be further subdivided using plastic innerduct.

Table 3. Conduit provisions for riser pathways

Total Floor Area (sq. ft.) Serviced by Riser	Minimum number of 4 in. (10 cm) sleeves (or equivalent slot area)
50,000	2 + 1 spare
100,000	3 + 1 spare
300,000	6 + 1 spare
500,000	10 + 1 spare
700,000	12 + 1 spare
800,000	13 + 1 spare
1,000,000	14 + 1 spare

– Extend backbone riser pathway to rooftop entrance room.

– Provide fire stopping to maintain fire rating of all floors and walls penetrated by backbone pathways.

– Maintain a minimum bending radius of 40 in (102 cm) in backbone pathways.

– Backbone conduit may have no more than two 90-degree bends between pull boxes or access points.

– Do not use pull boxes in lieu of conduit bends.

– Maintain at least a 1 ft (30 cm) separation between backbone pathways and electrical cables.

– Cross electrical cables only at right angles.

– Maintain at least 5 in (13 cm) separation from fluorescent light fixtures.

– Avoid horizontal offsets in riser pathways.

– Consider using metal conduit or enclosed cable tray in air plenum spaces to preclude the need for plenum-rated cable (not applicable in all jurisdictions).

• Riser pathways can be sized using **Table 3** as a guide.

• Horizontal cable pathways

– Provide pathways appropriate to the quantity of cable and necessity to provide the physical protection/radio frequency shielding.

– Maintain a bending radius at least 10 times the diameter of the largest cable to be accommodated.

– Horizontal conduit may have no more than two 90-degree bends between pull boxes or access points.

– Do not use pull boxes in lieu of conduit bends.

– Maintain at least 1 ft (30 cm) separation between backbone pathways and electrical cables.

– Cross electrical cables only at right angles.

– Maintain at least 5 in (13 cm) separation from fluorescent light fixtures.

– Avoid horizontal offsets in riser pathways.

– Consider using metal conduit or enclosed cable tray in air plenum spaces to preclude the need for plenum-rated cable (not applicable in all jurisdictions).

– Use conduit to cross inaccessible ceiling areas.

– Provide poke-through fittings, conduit stub-ups in walls, floor-mounted boxes, or cellular floor aftersets to house outlet hardware and to terminate the horizontal pathways in the vicinity of each workstation.

– Provide at least one voice and one data outlet or combined voice-data outlet fitting per 100 useable sq ft (9.29 sq m) of typical office floor area.

– Refer to and comply with Americans with Disabilities Act (ADA) requirements concerning placement of, and access to, telecommunications outlets and devices.

Grounding system

Adequate telecommunications grounding is essential for the reliable and safe operation of voice and data systems. Although telecommunications grounding and bonding systems are covered under separate standards, they are discussed together here because they are typically designed and constructed as an integral part of the spaces and pathways infrastructure and they physically interconnect major components of the spaces and pathways system. Telecommunications grounding and bonding system standard supplements, but does not replace or supersede, the requirements of NFPA 70 and other applicable electrical and safety codes.

– Provide a dedicated telecommunications bonding backbone (TBB) riser interconnecting the telecommunications closets, equipment rooms, and service entry rooms.

– Provide a telecommunications grounding busbar (TGB) in telecommunications closets and equipment rooms.

– Bond each TGB to the TBB and to building structural steel (if present) and to the local electrical panelboard.

– Provide a telecommunications main grounding busbar (TMGB) in the telecommunications entrance room.

– Bond the TMGB to the TBB, building steel (if present), the local electrical panelboard, and to the electrical service equipment grounding electrode conductor in the electrical entrance facility.

– Provide telecommunications bonding backbone interconnecting bonding conductor (TBBIBC) to interconnect multiple TBBs at a minimum of every third floor in larger buildings.

– Minimum conductor size for TBBs and TBBIBCs is No. 6 AWG. Much larger conductor sizes may be required in larger buildings. ■

References: Communication spaces and pathways

BICSI, *Telecommunications Distribution Methods Manual*, 1995. Building Industry Consulting Service International, 10500 University Center Drive, Suite 100 Tampa, FL 33612

Electronic Industries Association, *Commercial Building Standard for Telecommunications Pathways and Spaces*, ANSI/EIA/TIA-569, Electronic Industries Association, Washington, 1990.

NFPA, *National Electrical Code*, National Fire Protection Association, Quincy, 1995.

Telecommunications Industry Association, *Commercial Building Grounding and Bonding Requirements for Telecommunications*, ANSI/TIA/EIA-607, Telecommunications Industry Association, Washington, 1994.

U.S. Department of Commerce, *Federal Building Standard for Telecommunications Pathways and Spaces*, Publication FIPS PUB 175, Federal Information Processing, Springfield, 1992.

Box A—Glossary of Terms

Acronyms and Abbreviations
The following acronyms and abbreviations, useful in describing electronic communications and security systems, are referred to in this article:

ACD	Automatic Call Distribution
ATM	Asynchronous Transfer Mode
BICSI	Building Industry Consulting Service International
CATV	Cable TV
CCTV	Closed circuit TV
CPU	Computer power unit
CTI	Computer-telephone integration
EIA	Electronic Industries Association
EPN	Expansion Port Network
HC	Horizontal cross-connect
IC	Intermediate cross-connect
IDF	Intermediate Distribution Facility
ISDN	Integrated Services Digital Network
LAN	Local area network
MATV	Master antenna TV
MC	Main cross-connect
MDF	Main Distribution Facility
MPD	Multiple Plastic Duct
NFPA	National Fire Protection Association
OFN	Optical Fiber (Nonconductive)
OFC	Optical Fiber (Conductive)
PTZ	Pan-tilt-zoom (camera lenses)
PCS	Personal communications system
PBX	Private branch exchange (communication)
PPN	Processing Port Network
STP	Shielded twisted pair (wiring)
TBB	Telecommunications Bonding Backbone
TGB	Telecommunications Grounding Busbar
TIA	Telecommunications Industry Association
UL	Underwriters Laboratories
UPS	Uninterruptible power system
VDT	Video display terminals
WAN	Wide area network

2 COMMUNICATION CABLING SYSTEMS

Telecommunications service providers generally do not furnish cabling beyond the point of demarcation at the building entrance facility or project boundary. Provision of "backbone" and horizontal distribution cabling within the campus or building is the responsibility of the owner and/or tenant. Widely accepted standards for structured cabling and networks simplify the task of planning for and installing the cabling infrastructure as an integral part of the building design and construction process. In many cases (U.S. Federal Government projects, for example), compliance with structured cabling and infrastructure standards is mandatory for all renovation and new construction work.

Communications cables are used for service entry (feeder) systems, campus backbone systems, building backbone and riser systems, and building horizontal distribution systems, including distribution under access floors (**Figs. 3** and **4**). Comprehensive standards simplify the task of accommodating a wide range of services and applications using a single structured cabling infrastructure.

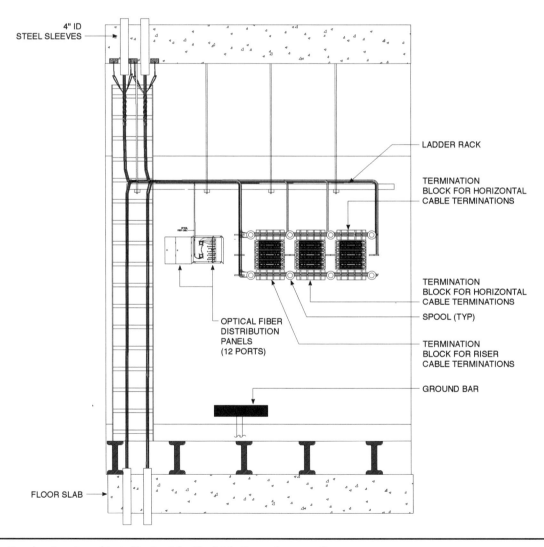

Fig. 3. Cross-section elevation view of typical horizontal cable distribution under access floor.

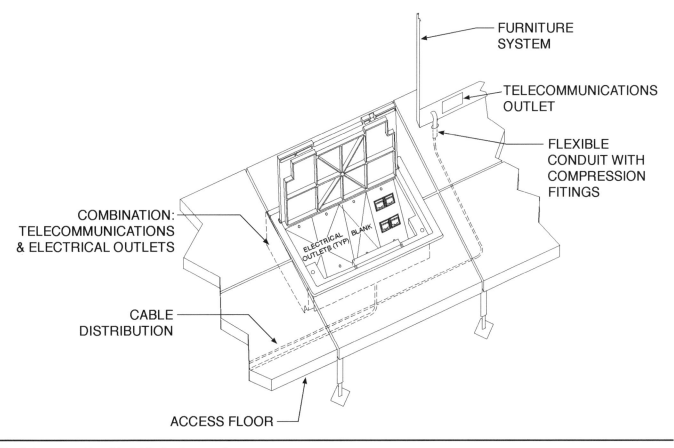

FURNITURE SYSTEM

TELECOMMUNICATIONS OUTLET

FLEXIBLE CONDUIT WITH COMPRESSION FITINGS

COMBINATION: TELECOMMUNICATIONS & ELECTRICAL OUTLETS

ELECTRICAL OUTLETS (TYP) BLANK

CABLE DISTRIBUTION

ACCESS FLOOR

Fig. 4. Access panel to cable distribution in access floor.

Communications cabling systems always provide:

– capability for voice and low- to medium-speed data transmission.

– provision for physical cable management, interconnection, and grounding.

In most cases, communications cabling systems also provide transmission of:

– high-speed data for local and wide area networks.

– video and audiovisual (including video teleconferencing) services.

– security, control, and building management services.

Responsibilities

– Service entry (feeder) cables are usually designed, installed, and owned by the telecommunications service provider(s) up to the building entrance facility or campus service demarcation point.

– Base building and campus backbone communications cabling systems are the responsibility of the owner and are designed by an engineer or telecommunications designer.

– Horizontal dedicated backbone cabling within tenant spaces is typically the responsibility of the tenant or owner-occupant.

– Cabling system designers and installation contractors must adhere to applicable EIA/TIA standards to ensure maximum utility, compatibility, and future flexibility of the cabling system. In some cases (e.g., federal government projects), standards compliance is mandatory.

Types of communications cabling

• *High pair count copper cable*

– Used as feeder cables to bring services into a campus or building and as horizontal backbone or riser cables within a building.

– Accommodates voice, low-speed data services, and some types of high-speed digital formats.

– May contain from 25 to several thousand individual twisted cable pairs, usually within an overall metallic shield.

– Being replaced by optical fiber in many backbone and riser applications, but is still widely used in buildings, especially for voice systems.

– UL classifications can include outdoor-only; riser, plenum, and general location uses.

- *Unshielded twisted pair cable (UTP)*

– almost universally used for horizontal distribution of voice and data services between horizontal cross-connect (HC) facilities in telecommunication closets and individual workstation outlets.

– available in several performance classifications (Categories 3 to 5). Category 5 will support video and high-speed local area networks.

– normally contains four unshielded twisted copper pairs per cable.

– always terminates in modular type jack at the workstation.

– UL classifications can include riser, plenum, general location, and undercarpet uses.

– undercarpet UTP seldom used if conventional alternatives exist.

- *Shielded-twisted pair cable (STP)*

– used for medium- to high-speed data transmission and for some highly specialized systems, such as point-of-sale networks.

– does not support voice networks.

– is more difficult and costly to install than UTP.

– is seldom used in new installations.

– UL classifications can include outdoor-only; riser, plenum, and general location uses.

- *Coaxial cable*

– formally widely used for data terminals and local area networks, but has been almost universally replaced by UTP in these applications.

– still used extensively for video distribution and closed-circuit TV (CCTV).

– gradually being replaced by optical fiber and/or UTP for video as digital video standards evolve.

– UL classifications can include outdoor-only; riser, plenum, general location, and undercarpet uses.

– undercarpet coaxial cable is seldom used if conventional alternatives exist.

- *Optical fiber cable*

– used mainly in outside plant, feeder, and building horizontal and backbone applications as an economical and space-saving substitute for the larger high pair count copper cables.

– may also be used to connect workstations to horizontal cross-connects (HCs) in special circumstances, providing very high transmission capacity.

– available in single mode and multi-mode versions.

– not cost-justified for low-speed/short-distance applications.

– requires costly electro-optical interfaces to operate.

– UL classifications can include outdoor-only; general location, riser, and plenum uses.

UL classifications of communications cables

Permitted uses of copper cables and optical fiber cables are summarized in **Tables 4** and **5,** respectively.

Design considerations for communications cabling

- *Entrance (feeder) cables*

– usually furnished and installed by the telecommunications service provider(s).

– terminate at the demarcation point in the building service entrance room.

Table 4. UL classification of communication cables

Marking*	Permitted use	Permitted substitutions
CMUC	Undercarpet	none
MPP	Plenums, risers & general locations	none
CMP	Plenums, risers & general locations	MPP
MPR	Risers & general locations only	MPP
CMR	Risers & general locations only	MPP, CMP, MPR
MPG, MP	General usage only	MPP, MPR
CMG, CM	General usage only	MPP, MPR, CMP, CMR
MPG, MP		

* Copper cables are marked with a two-letter designation:CM Communications Wires & Cables, MP Multipurpose Cables, "P" suffix indicates Plenum usage, "R" suffix indicates Riser usage, "UC" suffix indicates Under Carpet usage

Table 5. UL classification of optical fiber cables

UL marking*	Permitted use	Permitted substitutions
OFNP	Plenums, risers & general locations	none
OFCP	Plenums, risers & general locations	OFNP
OFNR	Risers & general locations only	OFNP
OFCR	Risers & general locations only	OFNP, OFNR, OFCP
OFNG, OFN	General usage only	OFNP, OFNR
OFCG, OFC	General usage only	OFNP, OFNR, OFCP, OFNG,
OFN		

* Optical fiber cables are marked with a three-letter designation, OFN Optical Fiber (Nonconductive), OFC Optical Fiber (Conductive),
"P" suffix indicates Plenum usage, "R" suffix indicates Riser usage, "G" suffix indicates General Purpose usage

- building owner is usually responsible for providing the service entrance pathway (ductbank) for the feeder cables and the entrance room itself.

- may consist of high pair count copper or optical fiber, or both.

- cable rated for outdoor use must be terminated and grounded within 50 ft (15+ m) of the building entry point.

- metallic cable pairs usually require high-voltage protective devices.

- all fiber and most copper feeder cables require electronic terminating equipment within the building.

- copper and fiber entrance cables have bending radius restrictions ranging from 6 to 36 in (15 to 90 cm).

- for added reliability and security, there may be more than one set of entrance cables.

- rough estimate of required entrance cable quantity is one pair per 100 useable sq ft (9.29 sq m) of floor area.

• *Backbone cabling*

- used to connect main cross-connects (MC), intermediate cross-connects (IC), and horizontal cross-connects (HC) within a campus or building.

- usually installed by the building or facility owner, not the service provider.

- may contain both horizontal and vertical (riser) elements.

- may include high pair count copper, UTP, STP, coaxial, and/or optical fiber.

- may require electronic terminating equipment at the MC, IC, and/or HC.

- generally installed in dedicated raceway, cable tray, and/or riser shaft.

- must be terminated and grounded within 50 ft (15.24 m) of building entry point.

• *Horizontal cabling*

- used to connect HCs (telecommunications closets) to individual workstation locations.

- usually furnished and installed by the tenant or system user.

- usually UTP, may also include STP, coaxial, or optical fiber.

- always installed in a "star configuration."

- usually direct home run from the HC to each workstation outlet.

- may also be distributed via "zone boxes" in open office plans.

- quantity required is at least two 4-pair UTP cables per workstation outlet.

Material and installation standards

National and international committees proscribe minimum standards for commercial building cabling systems, which must be observed for proper system performance. The most critical requirements are to:

- use standards compliant materials and hardware.

- maintain standard topology and cross-connect hierarchy.

- observe maximum cabling distances between cross-connects.

- observe minimum cable bending radii.

- maintain pair geometry and twist rates in UTP and STP.

- provide physical separation from sources of electromagnetic interference.

Cabling hierarchy

Cabling hierarchy is established by:

- one main cross-connect point (MC) per building or campus.

- one or more horizontal cross-connect points (HC) per floor of a building.

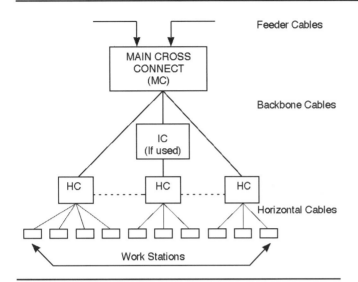

Fig. 5. Diagram of cabling hierarchy.under access floor.

Table 6. Cabling hierarchy and maximum distances indicated in ft (m)

Medium	MC to HC	MC to IC	IC to HC	HC to Outlet
Single Mode Fiber	9840 (3000)	8200 (2500)	1640 (500)	295 (90)
Multi Mode Fiber	6560 (2000)	4820 (1500)	1640 (500)	295 (90)
UTP	2624 (800)	984 (300)	1640 (500)	295 (90)
STP	2624 (800)	984 (300)	1640 (500)	295 (90)

– one or more individual outlets per work area.

– intermediate cross-connect points (IC) may be provided between the MC and HCs.

– each cross-connect element is star-connected to the subordinate elements.

– ICs and HCs may also be connected at the same level to facilitate ring-type networks.

– maximum cabling distances between hierarchical elements are shown in **Table 6** and its accompanying **Fig. 5**.

Residential and light commercial cabling less restrictive codes and EIA/TIA standards apply to these installations (see appropriate references for more information). ■

References: Communications cabling systems

BICSI, *Telecommunications Distribution Methods Manual,* 1995. Building Industry Consulting Service International, 10500 University Center Drive, Suite 100 Tampa, FL 33612

EIA, *Residential and Light Commercial Telecommunications Wiring Standard,* ANSI/EIA/TIA-570, Electronic Industries Association, Washington, 1991.

NFPA, *National Electrical Code,* National Fire Protection Association, Quincy, 1996.

TIA, *Commercial Building Telecommunications Cabling Standard,* ANSI/TIA/EIA-568-A, Arlington, Telecommunications Industry Association, 1995.

TIA, *Additional Horizontal Cabling Practices for Open Offices,* TIA-TSB 75, Telecommunications Industry Association, Arlington, 1996.

U.S. Department of Commerce, *Federal Building Telecommunications Wiring Standard,* Publication FIPS PUB 174, Federal Information Processing Standards, Springfield, 1992.

3 VOICE AND DATA COMMUNICATION SYSTEMS

All commercial and institutional buildings accommodate various voice, data, and (increasingly) video communications systems and in some cases, integrated with office automation (**Figs. 6a** to **c**). Telecommunications service providers generally do not furnish or install these systems, which are normally the responsibility of the building owner or tenant. All of these systems require spaces, pathways, cabling, and environmental support, which should be included as an integral part

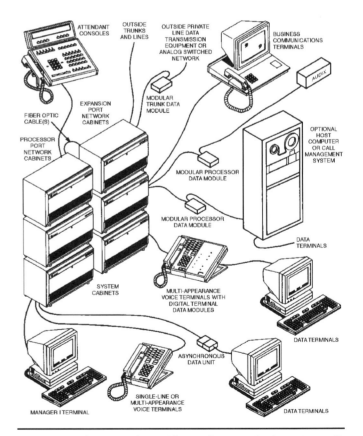

Fig. 6a. Typical integrated voice/data and communication system with processing port network (PPN) and expansion port network (EPN).

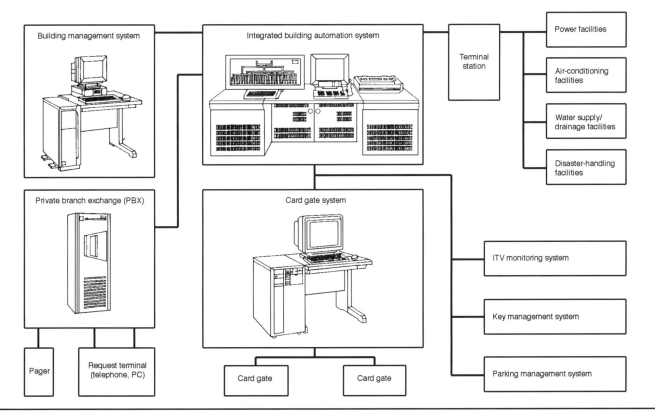

Fig. 6b. Building management network based on intelligent cards.

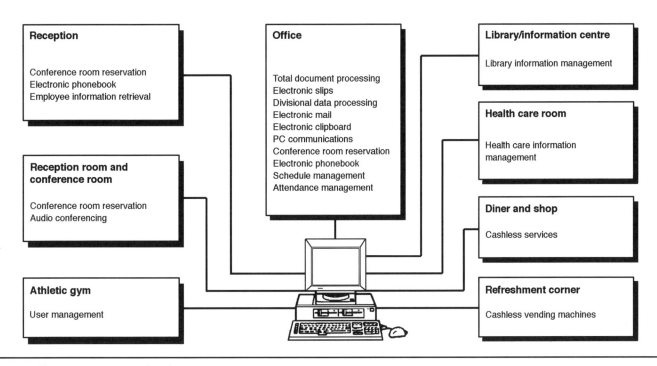

Fig. 6c. Office automation network.

of the building infrastructure design. There is increasing integration among voice, data, and video communications systems. This trend is expected to continue to the point where integrated, multifunction desktop terminals and multimedia networks will eventually support most voice, data, and video applications in the typical office environment. Voice, data, and video communications systems provide:

– the equipment, software, and terminal devices (such as telephones, computer terminals, and video displays) to transmit, process, administer, store, and retrieve sound, image, and computer data within a building, facility, or campus, or over wide areas.

– the capability to connect two or more terminals for the purpose of exchanging information electronically.

– may also provide various degrees of information routing, processing, and storage and (increasingly) interconnection/integration of systems and media.

Responsibilities

– Voice and data communications systems and equipment are usually owned and operated by the building tenant or owner-occupant.

– Telecommunications service providers typically do not provide equipment in conjunction with their voice and data network services, except under separate arrangements through equipment subsidiaries.

– Architects and engineers should design building communications spaces, pathways, and cabling systems to accommodate the tenants' communications equipment program.

– Construction schedules for new buildings and major renovations should reflect the need to have equipment spaces "room ready" well in advance of move-in to accommodate equipment installation, "burn-in," and testing.

Types of voice communications

Types of voice communications include:

• *Key telephone systems*

– small telephone switching systems supporting from two to a few dozen telephones and providing basic telephone system features, including limited data switching.

– usually a single wall-mounted cabinet.

– can be installed in a telecommunications closet or other convenient location.

– usually does not require any special environmental conditions beyond a normal office environment.

– may have a small internal or external battery back-up to retain memory and/or provide short-term operation during power outages.

– Individual telephone sets are proprietary to the system and may require electrical power for operation.

– Virtually all key systems can connect directly to EIA standard building cabling systems.

• *Private branch exchanges (PBXs)*

– support from a few to thousands of telephones within a building or campus and can provide a wide range of internal and external calling features.

– larger systems have automatic call routing and accounting software and can be partitioned electronically among multiple departments or building tenants.

– most have internal data switching capability up to at least 64 kilobits per second (kbs) and the ability to support Integrated Services Digital Network (ISDN) services from the public networks.

– common equipment can range from a single wall-mounted cabinet to multiple freestanding cabinets or equipment racks.

– small PBXs have power and environmental requirements similar to key systems.

– larger systems require a computer-like environment in a centralized equipment room.

– components of large PBXs may also be distributed within a building or campus by placing individual cabinets in telecommunications closets or additional equipment rooms.

– most large systems may be installed with or without raised access floor.

– back-up power, if provided, may require a separate rectifier-battery system of self-contain interrupt power supply (UPS).

– larger battery systems may require structural reinforcement and/or special ventilation systems.

– because larger PBXs and centralized computer equipment have similar environmental and utility needs, it is often beneficial to locate them in the same (or adjacent) spaces.

– most PBXs can support both industry standard analog telephone sets and proprietary digital/ISDN sets.

– electronic sets must be powered locally or from the telecommunications closet.

– all modern PBXs can connect directly to EIA standard building cabling systems.

Table 7 indicates approximate space and power requirements for typical PBX systems of various size ranges (actual products vary widely).

• *Central office telephone services*

– available from telecommunications service providers under trademark names such as Centrex.

– eliminate the need for major PBX equipment installations in the customer's premises.

– telecommunications switching and administration is provided at the central office using a central office switching machine that has been partitioned and programmed to function like an individual PBX.

– individual circuits extend directly from the central office to each on-premise telephone set.

– telecommunications service provider eliminates the need for most (but not all) on-premise common equipment and environmental support.

– space and environmental requirements for a typical large telecommunications service installation approximate those of a 100-line PBX.

– industry standard analog telephone sets and proprietary digital/ISDN sets are typically available.

– electronic sets may require dedicated power.

– sets can connect directly to EIA standard building cabling systems.

– central services may not be available in all localities.

• *Special-purpose voice systems*

– include high-capacity multiline phone terminals ("turrets") for securities trading desks and (in the United States) for 911 emergency consoles.

– use very specialized PBXs, characterized by very high capacity line switching equipment and station sets. Financial traders' turrets, for example, may accommodate up to several hundred direct lines on each set.

– 911 emergency consoles may integrate with computer networks and two-way radio circuits.

– station sets are proprietary, require dedicated power, and may require special millwork.

– in most cases, these systems require special cabling to the desk; some use optical fiber.

– central equipment requirements vary. On a trading floor, for example, the approximate ratio of equipment room floor space to trading floor space that is served is approximately 1 to 4.

– special voice systems almost always require back-up power and continuous environmental support.

• *Ancillary voice systems*

– provide additional features and functions to standard key, PBX, and telecommunications service providers' telephone systems.

– may require additional equipment cabinets, integrated with, or connected to, the basic system.

– include voice mail and automatic call accounting systems.

– include automatic call distribution (ACD) systems for customer service, reservation, and telemarketing call centers.

Table 7. Space and power requirements for PBX systems.

Number of Extensions	Approximate Equipment Room floor area (sq. ft.)	Approximate Connected Load (kW)	Average Demand Load (kW)
0-50	none (wall mount)	0.5 - 1.5	0.2 - 0.6
50-250	10 - 50	1.5 - 3.5	0.6 - 1.5
250-1,000	50 - 100	3.5 - 7.0	1.5 - 3.5
1,000-5,000	100 - 300	7.0 - 35.0	3.5 - 15.0
5,000-10,000	300 - 500	35.0 - 55.0	10.0 - 25.0

Fig. 7. LAN (Local Area Network) Workstation. (Courtesy: Ergotron, Inc.)

– use centralized dictation systems.

– voice-recording equipment for police, hospital, and trading floor systems.

– interfaces to computer systems and local area networks (LANs) for computer-telephone integration (CTI).

– conference bridges for high-end audio teleconferencing.

– hospitality systems for hotels may provide automated wake-up service, room environmental controls, and room status/house-keeping tracking.

• *Intercommunication systems*

– provide point-to-point or point-to-multipoint communications in conjunction with access control systems, trading floor positions, audiovisual facilities, sound and video studios, and similar applications.

– if "hands-free" operation is needed, special equipment is usually required, otherwise conventional or electronic telephone sets may be programmed as interphones.

Data communications systems

Types of data communications systems include:

• *Terminal-host systems*

– connect individual data terminals to large mini-computers or mainframes.

– becoming much less common in new installations.

– may require the use of cluster controllers to connect groups of 16 to 32 terminals to the network.

– controllers are often placed in telecommunications closets.

– may use proprietary terminals or standard PCs with emulation cards.

– are often integrated with LANs in newer installations.

– virtually all systems can connect directly to (or be adapted to) EIA standard cabling systems.

– systems required to be functional during power outages require back-up power for the terminals, controllers, and mainframe, and back-up environmental support for the controllers and mainframes.

• *Local area networks (LANs)*

– data communications systems of two or more (sometimes hundreds) of interconnected data devices, such as personal computers, printers, and file servers operating within a limited geographic area (a department, a building, or a campus).

– are becoming almost ubiquitous in the modern office and are rapidly increasing in capability and complexity (**Fig. 7**).

– most are peer-to-peer networks, meaning that all of the connected resources, such as computer programs, files, disk space, printers, and wide area communications gateways, can be shared among the users.

– vary widely in physical implementation.

– desktop terminals are typically personal computers.

– expensive resources, such as laser printers, are usually shared among several users.

– individual PCs and other devices are connected to the LAN with a hub device, typically located in the telecommunications closet.

– file servers are also PCs and are located within a using department, telecommunications closet, or centralized equipment room.

– all modern LANs can connect directly to EIA standard cabling.

– UTP cabling is almost universally used for the horizontal wiring segment and can support all current LAN speeds up to 100 megabites per second (mbs).

– LAN backbone cabling is typically EIA standard optical fiber.

– multiple LANs and LAN segments are interconnected with devices such as routers, bridges, and switchers, which may be located in telecommunications closets or equipment rooms.

– routers, bridges, and switches present heat loads in telecommunications closets and equipment rooms and require adequate environmental support.

– systems required to function during power outages require back-up power at the terminals, hubs, routers, bridges, switches, and file services, and may require back-up environmental support in telecommunications closets and equipment rooms.

– LANs frequently have back-up power only for the file servers, due to the high cost of end-to-end back-up support.

– Most offices make provisions for one LAN terminal per desk.

– It is advisable to allow additional space and environmental support for printers and LAN devices in telecommunications closets and equipment rooms.

LAN power and environmental considerations

LAN components and other data communications devices present a significant power and heat load, which may be distributed throughout a building or facility. Initiatives such as the Environmental Protection Agency's ENERGY STAR program have resulted in a new generation of products that dramatically reduce average energy consumption. In some cases (federal government projects, for example) the use of ENERGY STAR products is mandatory. **Table 8** provides approximate power requirements for typical system components comparing conventional and ENERGY STAR compliant devices.

Table 8. Power requirements of LAN equipment. Conventional and U.S. EPA Energy Star products compared.

Type of Device	Typical Connected Load - Conventional Products (W)	Average Load - Energy Star Products (W)
Personal computer	200 - 500	30 or less
Computer monitor (CRT)	200 - 300	30 or less
Small printer, copier or Fax	750 - 850	15 or less
Large printer, copier or plotter	1,000 2,000	30 or less
High end color printer	3,000 - 5,000	45 or less
Router, switch, or file server	200 - 600	30 or less

Types of LANs

Some of the most popular LANs include:

- Ethernet (currently the most widely used)

- Token Ring

- ARCnet

- Apple Talk

- FDDI

- TP-TMD

- Asynchronous Transfer Mode (ATM)

- *Wide area networks (WANs)*

- long distance voice and data networks extending beyond the limits of the individual building or campus.

- may be part of the public network provided by local and long distance telecommunications service providers, dedicated subnetworks (virtual private networks) within the public networks, or true private networks, owned and operated by the user.

- important to the architect and engineer from the standpoint of required service entry facilities (including facilities for rooftop antennas) and equipment spaces for accessing these networks and connecting them to the building cabling backbone and internal voice and data networks.

- *Typical media for WANs include:*

- copper cable

- optical fiber cable

- satellite earth stations

- microwave terminals

- mobile radio systems such as cellular

- *Integrated systems*

- telephones and computers are integrated into a single voice-data terminal in customer service facilities, reservation centers, and similar installations.

- data networks are becoming multifunctional and multimedia, with the ability to transmit, receive, and display sound, graphics, and moving images.

- newer LAN and WAN technologies such as Synchronous Optical Network (SONET) can handle voice, data, and video signals interchangeably and provide a true multimedia transport mechanism.

- the present trend toward integration is likely to continue to the point where distinctions among conventional voice, data, and video communications systems will disappear in favor of single networks of multifunction devices.

- *Wireless systems*

- increasing capability to provide similar services within buildings using wireless (radio or infrared-based systems).

- probably will not replace wired systems to any great extent due to their relatively higher cost, limited capacity, and susceptibility to interception and interference.

- necessary to "wire for wireless" to accommodate the antennas and receiver-transmitter devices needed to make these systems work.

- almost always necessary to consult specific system vendors due to the proprietary nature of the systems.

- wireless PBX: mobile telephones similar to the public cellular phones used outside buildings also known as personal communications systems (PCS).

- wireless pagers: may be radio or infrared. Some can locate and identify users automatically.

- two-way radios: "walkie-talkies" used by security and maintenance personnel.

- wireless LANS take many forms, using radio and infrared; there is little standardization.

- wireless modems: also called radio modems, are incorporated into laptop PCs for mobile computing and may also connect to a cellular phone.

- *Other data communications systems*

There are many types of special data combinations systems for:

- automatic teller machines.

- point-of-sale devices.

- specialized systems for reservation, customer service, and telemarketing centers.

- control communications used for building management systems, telemetry, and supervisory communications and data acquisition (SCADA).

- many of these systems use standard LAN components and can be accommodated on EIA standard cabling systems.

- consult manufacturers or suppliers for unique space and environmental requirements.

- *Video communications systems*

Video communications systems include closed-circuit TV (CCTV), cable TV (CATV), master antenna TV (MATV), and video teleconferencing systems (video communications systems are discussed under a separate heading within this series of articles). ■

References: Voice and data communication systems

BISCI, *Communications Distribution Methods Manual,* 1995. Building Industry Consulting Service International, 10500 University Center Drive, Tampa, FL 33612

———. *Local Area Network Design Manual,* 1995. Building Industry Consulting Service International, 10500 University Center Drive, Tampa, FL 33612

NFPA, *National Electrical Code,* National Fire Protection Association, Quincy, 1996.

TIA, *Commercial Building Telecommunications Cabling Standard,* ANSI/TIA/EIA-568-A, Telecommunications Industry Association, Arlington, 1995.

TIA, *Additional Horizontal Cabling Practices for Open Offices,* TIA-TSB 75, Telecommunications Industry Association, Arlington, 1996.

4 ELECTRONIC SECURITY SYSTEMS

Planning of electronic security systems requires understanding of electronic infrastructure as part of architectural design and electrical systems. This section discusses the range of electronic security technologies and options that effect design.

Electronic security systems provide controlled access within a facility, protection from damage and loss, and protection of information. In some cases, electronic security systems also provide alarm monitoring of critical building systems, fluid leak detection, vehicle access control, notification (also see "Fire Alarm Systems" elsewhere in this volume), and evidence for investigations.

Levels of security

* *Low level*

Simple physical barriers designed to obstruct and detect unauthorized activity, which may include electronic control of doors and locks, window bars and grates, timed or motion-detector lighting, and various intrusion detection systems.

* *Medium level*

In addition to low-level measures, institute monitored electronic perimeters beyond the boundaries of the protected area, and various advanced intrusion detection systems.

* *High level*

In addition to low and medium levels, perimeter alarm system, CCTV system, access control system, and high-security lighting.

Types of security technologies

Security systems and technologies, discussed below, include:

– access control / card entry.

– biometric Access Control technologies.

– intrusion detection.

– closed-circuit television.

• *Access control / card entry*

– able to incorporate time zone access levels, time controlled events, report generation, capability of supporting multiple workstations, video display terminals (VDT), and printers.

– most common card entry systems will support magnetic stripe readers, Wiegand effect readers, and proximity readers (choices are augmented by alphanumeric keypad and chip readers).

– once programmed, system is self-supporting, except for adding and deleting cards, acknowledging alarms, and generating reports.

Two basic card technologies are available:

– magnetic strip cards have the code located on a magnetic strip on the card back.

– Wiegand cards have a unique card code sandwiched inside the card.

• *Card readers choices*

– swipe card readers have proven their reliability and flexibility (**Fig. 8**).

– use standard credit card–size cards, which can display a company's logo and incorporate picture identification.

– insertion readers have a higher incidence of mechanical stress with insertion readers, making for a short card life span and some risk that cards may break in the reader.

– proximity card readers are more compact and have little chance of damaging the card.

Alphanumeric keypads (requiring the user to enter a code) can stand alone at security points and can augment a card reader system to raise the level of security for a given space.

Chip reader technology utilizes a programmable chip permanently affixed to the access card; the reader sensor is a flat circle or plate.

• *Biometric Access Control technologies*

– newer and constantly developing systems that directly measure physical characteristics of the individual.

– main disadvantages of current state-of-the-art technologies, compared with conventional systems, are higher cost and a less desirable trade-off between speed and accuracy.

– include fingerprint, hand geometry, eye retina scan, speech verification, signature verification, or thermogram technology.

• *Intrusion detection*

– includes the many types of sensors and alarm systems now available.

– infrared and microwave motion sensors can be ceiling- or wall-mounted (**Fig. 9**).

Fig. 8. Swipe card reader for building access. (Courtesy: Von Duprin Co.)

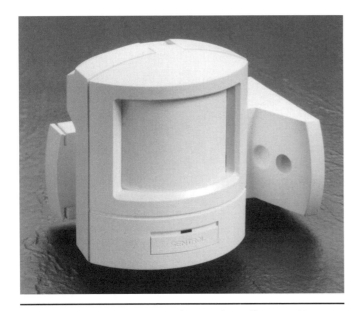

Fig. 9. Passive infrared intrusion detector for wall-mount. (Courtesy: Sentrol)

- although such detectors are mostly used to detect intrusion in interior spaces, there are motion sensors available for exterior use.

- glass break sensors are used to detect the shattering of glass.

- magnetic alarm contacts are used to detect the opening of doors and windows.

- duress alarm switches are used to notify security personnel of a crime situation or other emergency.

- fence sensors designed to detect climbing or cutting.

- buried line sensors can detect seismic activity, flooding, or presence of ferrous metals.

- *Closed-circuit television (CCTV)*

- demonstrated its effectiveness as a security tool in all sorts of facilities.

- enables multiple locations to be simultaneously monitored from a single security command center.

- CCTV console operators can direct a mobile security force to any area that requires assistance.

- CCTV recordings carry the additional value of aiding in the investigation and prosecution of crimes and disruptions that have occurred.

Design considerations for card entry systems

- *Typical locations for card entry*

- can be established wherever limited access by designated personnel or other security checkpoints logically occur.

- perimeter entrances.

- lobbies.

- vehicle entrances.

- data centers.

- telecommunications equipment rooms.

- service entry rooms.

- generator and uninterruptable power source (UPS) rooms.

- cash-handling areas.

- document control rooms.

- laboratories.

- passenger and freight elevators.

- *Electrical locking devices*

- electromagnetic locks for high-security applications.

- electromechanical strikes for medium-level security applications.

- electromechanical mortise locksets for medium to high security applications and wherever fail-safe mechanical latching is required by local code.

- electromechanical panic devices for perimeter emergency egress applications.

- coordination and compatibility with mechanical door hardware is required.

- *Card entry system power requirements*

- require low-voltage power, usually 24VDC, and are powered from security data gathering panels located in the security riser closets.

- security data gathering panels and electrical lock power supplies typically require 120VAC power.

- access control computer power unit (CPU) and workstations typically require 120VAC.

- all access control devices should be on emergency power source.

- CPU and data gathering panels must be powered by an uninterruptible power system (UPS).

- power to all systems should be dedicated and unswitched.

- good grounding system is required.

- *Card entry systems cabling requirements*

- low-voltage security cabling is typically telecommunications industry standard unshielded twisted pair copper (UTP).

- data communication cabling between the data gathering panels and the CPU is UTP copper.

- in large buildings and campuses, backbone cabling may be optical fiber or the system may be integrated with a LAN.

- *Card entry system conduit requirements*

- should include conduit stub-ups and back boxes for all devices.

- cabling must be installed in conduit where required by local code.

- high-security applications may also require all security cabling in conduit.

- cabling must be installed in conduit in all inaccessible areas.

- exposed cabling should not be permitted.

- cabling should be installed conduit where otherwise exposed exterior or other harsh environmental locations.

- *Card entry space requirements*

- security riser closets typically require 64 sq ft (6 sq m) of wall space for card entry equipment panels.

– may be contained in telecommunications closets.

– security equipment rooms typically require 64 sq ft (6 sq m) for card entry CPU and equipment.

– security riser closets and equipment rooms must be physically secure, well lighted, and ventilated.

• *Other card entry system design considerations*

– compliance with ADA requirements for accessibility.

– compliance with local building codes regarding means of egress.

– coordination of electrical locking devices with mechanical door and hardware.

– allocation of space for security equipment panels.

– number of entry exit points that will require access control devices.

– number of alarm points the access control system will process.

– number of cardholders.

– peak use throughput capacity for each door.

– flexibility and allocation for system expansion.

Design considerations for intrusion detection systems:

• *External sensors*

– should be located where they are protected from accidental or intentional damage.

– accessible for routine maintenance.

– avoid obscuring vegetation such as tall grass, movement of bushes and tree branches, and falling leaves.

– should be shielded from extreme heat and cold, lightning, wind, snow accumulation, and fog.

– ambient conditions such as electromagnetic interference from underground service, overhead power lines, and vibration from transportation vehicles might affect performance.

• *Intrusion detection*

Sensors should be placed to avoid:

– structural vibration.

– temperature fluctuations.

– direct exposure to sunlight through windows.

– reflective finishes.

– sensor positioning with respect to furniture and partitions.

– accidental damage, such as from careless maintenance.

– nearness to radiant heating.

– nearness to mechanical diffusers.

• *Intrusion detection: magnetic alarm contacts*

– flush-mount devices are more secure and less obtrusive in appearance.

– devices are typically mounted on the top of the door as far away from the hinge as possible.

– doors and windows should be well fitting and have minimal vibration in wind conditions.

• *Intrusion detection systems power requirements*

– low-voltage power, usually 12 to 24VDC.

– powered from security data gathering panels located in the security riser closets or the alarm control communicator centrally located within the protected space.

– devices must be on emergency standby power source.

– power to all systems should be dedicated and unswitched.

– good grounding system is required.

– typically, cabling for all security sensors is UTP copper.

• *Intrusion detection system conduit and cabling requirements*

– include conduit stub-ups and back boxes for all devices.

– cabling must be installed in conduit where required by local code.

– high-security applications typically require all security cabling in conduit.

– cabling must be installed in conduit in all inaccessible areas.

– install where cable would otherwise be exposed.

– install in conduit where otherwise exposed to harsh environmental locations.

– install in conduit in all exterior locations.

• *Closed-Circuit Television (CCTV) lighting*

– Codes typically require a minimum of 1 foot candle (10 lux) of illumination along exit/egress paths (note that higher levels are recommended at critical points such as stairs).

– most CCTV cameras can provide a fairly good amount of detail at 3 to 5 lux and even detect forms and motion in lighting levels as low as 1 lux.

– llumination falls off with the square of the distance. The result is that if the illumination at a door is equal to 10 lux, an area 5 ft (1.5 m) away from the door may be in near darkness at 1 lux or less, unless it is lit by a supplemental source.

- lighting along exit/egress pathways should be checked to provide sufficient illumination for all CCTV camera viewing angles and supplemented beyond the minimum standard.

- infrared illumination enables cameras to produce high-quality images in complete darkness.

• *CCTV cameras: number and location*

- monochrome (black and white) cameras provide higher resolution and better performance in low-light applications.

- color cameras require optimum lighting conditions and should be restricted to indoor applications only.

- overt camera installations provide typical surveillance and act as a deterrent.

- covert camera installations are designed to provide undercover surveillance. Their use may require legal notification (of building users) and be limited by local governance and law.

• *Camera housings*

- interior rectangle housings are designed for surface-mount wall and ceiling applications.

- interior dome housings are designed for surface or recessed ceiling-mount applications.

- interior triangle housings are designed for ceiling- and wall-mount corner applications.

- interior recessed housings are available for ceiling- and wall-mount applications.

- exterior housings are available in rectangle, dome, and recessed configurations for wall-, parapet-, and pole-mount applications.

• *CCTV monitor considerations*

- formula to calculate monitor size and viewing distance: monitor size (in) − 4 = monitor viewing distance (ft). Example 9 in − 4 = 5 ft.

- maximum vertical viewing angle is approximately 30 degrees.

- maximum horizontal viewing angle is approximately 45 degrees in either direction.

- standard security monitor sizes (measured diagonal in inches) are: 5, 9, 12, 17, 19, and 21 (in).

• *CCTV power requirements*

- cameras typically operate on either 24VAC or 120VAC provided at each camera or distributed from a central location.

- monitors, switchers, and recording equipment typically require 120VAC power.

- power to all systems should be dedicated and unswitched.

- good grounding system is required.

• *CCTV cabling requirements*

- camera signals can be transmitted over coaxial, fiber optic, or unshielded twisted pair (UTP) cable.

- most common camera signal cable in use currently is RG-59/U coaxial cable with a maximum cable distance between the camera and monitor of 1000 ft (305 m).

- fiber-optic cable can transmit camera signals over several miles.

- UTP copper cable will carry video signals up 1200 ft (365 m).

- typically each camera will require cables for power and for signal.

- PTZ (pan-tilt-zoom) camera applications will require additional multiconductor or fiber-optic cables.

• *CCTV conduit requirements*

- cabling must be installed in conduit where required by local code.

- high-security applications typically require all security cabling in conduit.

- cabling must be installed in conduit in all inaccessible areas.

- cabling should be installed in conduit where otherwise exposed to harsh environmental locations.

- cabling should be installed in conduit in all exterior locations.

• *CCTV space requirements*

- security riser closets typically require 48 sq ft (4.5 sq m) of wall space for CCTV equipment.

- security equipment rooms typically require 75 sq ft (7 sq m) of floor area for every 100 cameras.

- security riser closets and equipment rooms must be physically secure, well lighted, and ventilated.

• *Other CCTV design considerations*

- PTZ devices permit the remote control of CCTV cameras and zoom lenses.

- CCTV system may require connection to emergency power sources.

- number and location of monitoring consoles (switchers allow multiple cameras to be displayed on one or more monitors; time-lapse video cassette recorders are capable of condensing nearly 1000 hours of continuous recording onto a single 120 minute VHS tape).

- distance between camera and monitor.

- special environmental conditions for interior, exterior, and hazardous locations.

- staffing and number of console operators allocated for monitoring station. ■

References: Electronic security systems

Key references for electronic security system design are applicable codes and standards, including:

- *Underwriters Laboratories (UL)*

UL 608:	*Burglar Resistant Vault Doors and Modular Panels*
UL 609:	*Burglar Alarm Systems Local*
UL 611:	*Burglar Alarm Systems Central Stations*
UL 634:	*Standard for Connectors and Switches for Use with Burglar Alarm Systems*
UL 636:	*Holdup Alarm Units and Systems*
UL 639:	*Intrusion Detection Units*
UL 681:	*Installation and Classification of Mercantile and Bank Burglar Alarm Systems*
UL 972:	*Burglar Resistant Glazing Materials*
UL 983:	*Surveillance Cameras*
UL 1034:	*Burglary Resistant Electronic Locking Mechanism*
UL 1037:	*Antitheft Alarms and Devices*
UL 1076:	*Alarm System Units—Proprietary Burglar*
UL 294:	*Access Control Systems*

- *American Society for Testing Materials (ASTM)*

F12.10:	*Security Systems and Services*
F12.40:	*Detection and Surveillance Systems and Services*
F12.50:	*Locking Devices*
F12.60:	*Controlled Access, Security Search and Screening*

Andrew Prager

Summary

The electronic specialties described in this article include (1) audiovisual facilities; (2) video distribution and video teleconferencing, and (3) sound-masking systems. This article provides an overview of recent innovations, and the basic terminology and technology of these specialties for preliminary architectural design and coordination with electronic engineering specialists.

Key words

Articulation Index, audiovisual facilities, electrical ground, fiber optics, speech privacy, sound masking, videoconferencing

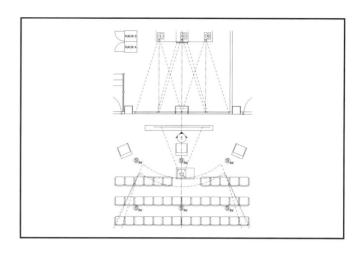

Electronic system specialties

1 AUDIOVISUAL FACILITIES

An audiovisual facility is a specialized room that demands careful attention to space requirements for projection, audio, video, control, and computer equipment as well as to positioning and seating arrangements for presenters and meeting participants. Other elements of concern are environmental issues such as lighting, acoustics, and mechanical systems. It is important that these design issues are addressed at the initial stages of the design process. Establishing the appropriate design criteria is essential not only to avoid expensive retrofitting, but to enable the AV facility to be used to its fullest potential. A successful facility may be realized only when adequate information regarding the users' needs is obtained, and by early design collaboration between the architect, engineers, and the AV designer.

An audiovisual facility provides the integration of different information technologies where presenters can interact with the systems for the purpose of presenting, training, and lecturing. Audiovisual facilities typically include:

- front and/or rear projection screens.

- projection equipment such as slide, video, and overhead transparency projectors.

- audio systems for separate speech reinforcement and program sound amplification.

- video system for playback of videotape, computer-generated images, and CATV.

- control system for remote control of AV equipment and the room environment.

- computer system(s) for presentation applications.

Audiovisual facility space requirements

- *Room size*

Proper room size is governed by the projected usage, that is, the maximum number of participants to be accommodated, ceiling height, projected image size, provisions for front or rear projection, and whether flexible seating is desired to accommodate all options (theater, classroom, U-shape, etc.). When arranging the seating plan, provide the required minimum distance between the front row of seating and the projection screen, which should be at least twice the height of the image to be projected. Also, the viewers seated closest to the screen should not need to rotate their eyes more than 30 degrees to see the top of the projected image (**Fig. 1**).

- *Ceiling height*

The minimum ceiling height is predicated on the height of the projected image. The greater the distance to the most distant viewer, the greater the finished ceiling height must be. The sill height of the projection screen should be a minimum of 4 ft (1.2 m), and if possible higher, to avoid sightline conflict with the heads of seated persons. If the image is 6 ft (1.8 m) high, the ceiling height must be at least 10 ft (3 m), plus any additional distance that may be required for framing and appearance details. If this clearance cannot be achieved, other options are:

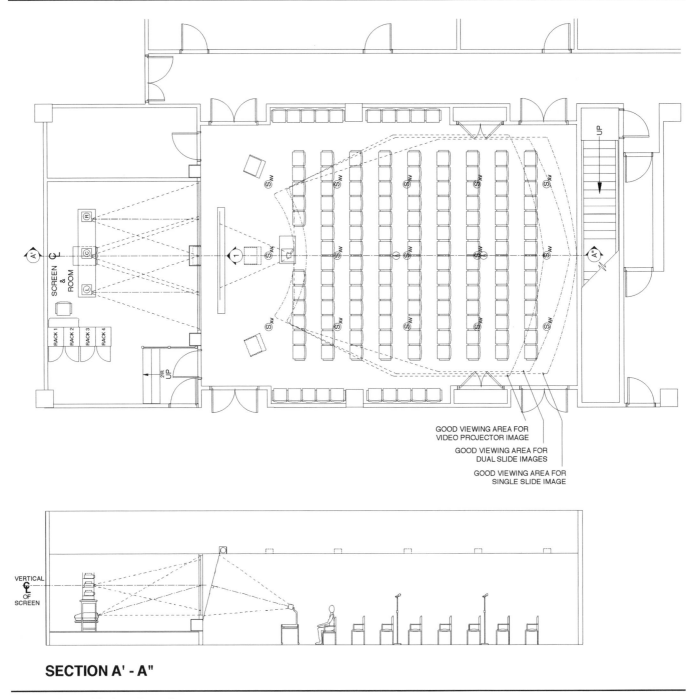

GOOD VIEWING AREA FOR
VIDEO PROJECTOR IMAGE

GOOD VIEWING AREA FOR
DUAL SLIDE IMAGES

GOOD VIEWING AREA FOR
SINGLE SLIDE IMAGE

SECTION A' - A"

Fig. 1. Audiovisual facilities plan and section.

– sloping the ceiling up towards the screen wall (dependent on structural or mechanical conditions).

– utilizing tiered levels for fixed seating in an amphitheater style (if the size of the room is adequate).

– limiting the seating arrangement to U-shape.

– rooms with staggered seating.

• *Projected image size*

The maximum distance from viewers in the last row to the projection screen should be eight times the height of the image for slides, and six times the height of the image for (current technology) computer-generated images from a video projector (**Fig. 2**). The width of the image is determined by the aspect ratio of the format projected. Typical aspect ratios are indicated in **Table 1**.

Examples:

– If the farthest viewer is 36 ft (11 m) from the projection screen, then the video image should be 6 ft (1.8 m) high. Multiplying 6 ft by the aspect ratio of 1 to 1.48 gives a projected image width of 8 ft 10-½ in. Hence, the video projected image size is 6 ft high × 8 ft 10-½ in wide (1.8 m high × 2.7 m wide).

– For slides, if the farthest viewer is 32 ft (9.75 m) from the projection screen, divide 32 by 8 and the slide image is 4 ft (1.2 m) high. Multiplying 4 ft by the aspect ratio of 1 to 1.33 equals 6 ft. Hence, the slide projected image is 4 ft high × 6 ft wide (1.2 m high × 1.8 m wide).

Table 1. Typical aspect ratios of audiovisual images

Format	Aspect ratio—H-W
Video image	1:1.48
Slide image	1:1.33
Overhead	transparency 1:1 (varies)
16mm film image	1:1.33

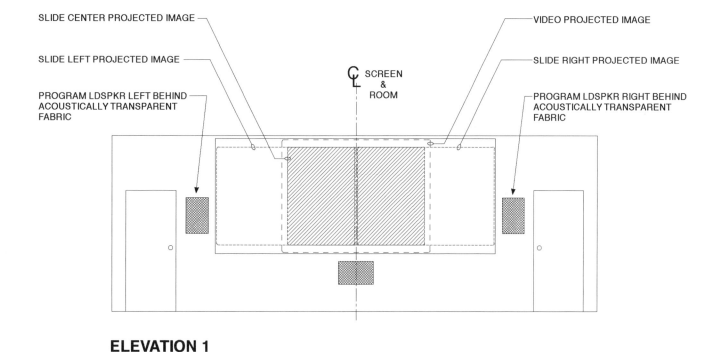

ELEVATION 1

Fig. 2. Elevation of teleconferencing facility projection wall and screen.

Keep in mind that the projection of vertical slide images requires a screen size where the horizontal image size is equal to the vertical image size; therefore, the screen must accommodate an area of 6 × 6 ft (1.8 × 1.8 m).

- *Rear projection vs. front projection*

There are advantages and disadvantages to each of these formats. Front projection is the most common. Advantages to front projection are that a separate room is not necessarily required, and it provides the highest possible color fidelity. A disadvantage to front projection is that roll-down screens are not entirely rigid and can sway during a presentation, causing in-and-out-of-focus conditions.

Advantages to rear projection include:

- allows ambient lighting levels to be higher for note-taking, maintaining meeting participant alertness, and encouraging better eye contact with the presenter.

- people or objects crossing the screen do not cast shadows on the projected image.

- associated noise from equipment and operations personnel is isolated from the presentation space.

- ambient light spilling onto the front surface of the rear projection screen will not wash out a projected image to the same extent that it will on a front projection screen.

- *Rear projection room size*

A rear projection room must contain enough depth for projection throw distance to produce an image that is the correct size. Its basic plan and section is shown in Fig. 1. Two rules of thumb are:

- The rear projection room should be ⅓ the size of the useable conference room space, or

- The rear projection room should be three times the height of the required image size.

A more accurate method to determine rear projection room size uses formulas to determine throw distance based on focal length of the slide projector lenses (i.e., throw distance = image width × lens focal length, divided by 1.34), and manufacturer's specifications for video projectors (usually around 1.5 times the video image width).

In cases where the proper room depth is not possible, an alternative is to use mirrors that fold the optics of the projected beam to increase the length of the optical path, thus utilizing a minimum of space. The mirrors are made of high-quality float glass, free from irregularities and impurities, and can be ¼ or ⅜ in (6.35 or 9.51 mm) thick depending on size. Mirrors should only be used as a last resort, due to inherent disadvantages such as vibration, cleaning maintenance, realignment requirements, and the general risk of damaging them.

Consideration should be given to providing the operator access behind the projection equipment—access of 3 ft (90 cm) is comfortable for projector loading, slide-tray changing, and maintenance. Front operation is possible but not ideal. Slide projectors are usually table mounted with an adjustable slide projector stand or height extension base on a raised platform. This enables the horizontal center of the images to be coincident with the horizontal center of the screen.

A maximum 3-degree deviation between the centers of the slide projector lens and the screen is affordable before any noticeable keystoning or distortion occurs. Alternatives to rear projection rooms are a front projection cabinet or a front projection room in the back of the conference space, where only a 6 ft (1.82 m) depth may be required.

Requirements for projection rooms

Space is required for equipment racks where the audio, video, control, and computer equipment reside.

Additionally:

- Maintain a 3 ft (90 cm) clearance behind equipment racks for installation and service.

- The footprint of a typical equipment rack is 22 in (55 cm) wide by 26 in (66 cm) deep and is 84 in (2.13 m) high.

- There may be from two to four equipment racks, depending on the system's complexity.

- An operator's position may require a shelf 30 in (76 cm) high × 12 in (30 cm) deep and attached to one or several of the equipment racks.

- A raised access floor under equipment racks and projection support table is preferred for conduit routing of power and signal to feed equipment from below without unsightly cables exposed in the room.

- Railings shall be provided adjacent to riser steps for access flooring as required by applicable code.

- Omit, cover over, or black out windows with light-tight shades.

- Paint walls and ceiling slab or finished ceiling a matte black, dark brown, or charcoal gray to avoid unwanted reflection of light within the room.

- Do not use chrome finish for items such as railings, wall plates, light fixtures, and door accessories.

- Standard building fluorescent fixtures are suitable for maintenance lighting.

- For lighting during presentations, single or dual circuit track for track light fixtures that are low profile, 75 watts, a dark finish, and have a swivel function serve well.

- Glazing for a rear projection screen should be as recommended by the screen manufacturer.

- Frames are available from the screen manufacturer where glazing is installed in the factory and only blocking for the frame rough-in work is required before installation.

– Front projection rooms require a projection port utilizing float glass that is mounted with neoprene seals to provide acoustic isolation.

– The projection port shall be tilted 5 degrees from the vertical to deflect sound back toward the ceiling of the audience area.

Requirements for the conference room space

Rooms that have as one of their principal uses the proper setting for audiovisual presentation:

– Provide for optimal technical display and control.

– Recognize that such spaces are intended for comfortable human communication and ease of accommodation.

– Design and layout should allow for different presentation styles, flexible seating, circulation within the space, and entry/exiting that does not disrupt presentation.

– Recognize that there are a wide variety of presentation formats, some involving many presenters at the front of the room, so that circulation space should permit different positions and movement of a presentation speaker or speakers.

– Lighting should be zoned in such a way that front wall wash-lighting fixtures can be dimmed to prevent light spill onto the screen during a presentation.

– Dimming control systems can be utilized to preset and activate different scenes of lighting for different projection and conference modes.

– Sophisticated lighting systems can be programmed with transitional scenes that relieve eyestrain caused by the modulation from a dark projection mode to a bright presentation mode.

– Room finishes with hard acoustical properties such as sheetrock, wood, brick, concrete block, metal or aluminum, windows, and terrazzo floors cause reflections that can decrease the intelligibility of any sound, whether amplified or natural. Acoustically treated walls, ceilings, floors, and window coverings provide absorptive qualities that minimize reverberation and improve voice communication in the space; should include carpeting with underlayment, acoustical ceiling tile (with an NRC of 0.7 to 0.9), and medium-weight drapes or curtains.

– Noise from mechanical systems should be minimized by low-velocity airflow, supply registers with the appropriate acoustical rating (such as NC25 to NC28), and ducts lined with acoustical material.

– Minimize noise from adjacent spaces with appropriate acoustical wall construction, door specifications, and glazing details for windows, front projection ports, and rear projection screens.

– Sound Transmission Class (STC) ratings for these items and an acoustical consultant should specify ratings for NC and NRC. Construction details, where appropriate, are also provided by the acoustician.

Fixtures, furnishings, and special mountings

Lecterns, built-in AV equipment, and special mounting supports are part of audiovisual facility design:

– Lecterns can either be stock items under the AV contract or custom-designed millwork.

– AV equipment such as tape machines, video document camera, and computers can be built into walls, cabinets, or credenzas for access by presenters.

– Special mounting supports will be required for ceiling-mounted video projectors and any TV monitors suspended from the ceiling.

Electrical infrastructure

Electrical power to audiovisual systems should be provided from a dedicated local circuit breaker panel, usually located in the projection room. Also note:

– Other utilities such as lighting, heavy motors, and convenience outlets (used for vacuum cleaners) should not be fed from this panel.

– Where possible, three-wire dedicated or isolated ground plus hot and neutral should feed isolated ground receptacles in order to provide clean earth as the AC power safety ground; this grounding method complies with NEC Article 250.

– A grounding system for technical earthing should also be provided to aid in preventing ground loops that are caused from differences in potential between the grounding of equipment where audio and/or video signal paths are connected.

– The frames of all equipment racks should be grounded via a grounding conductor from each rack, connected to a copper bus-bar, which is fed from the nearest cold water earth pipe, building steel with a low DC resistance to earth ground, or the isolated ground busbar within the circuit breaker panel.

– A raised access floor should be grounded from the chassis of the circuit breaker panel, also to be considered as the building ground or conduit system ground.

– The conduit system for all low-voltage cabling should be comprised of electrical metallic tubing (EMT) for physical protection and to prevent signal contamination.

– Conduits should be bonded to the building's conduit ground system to act as an additional shield to the cabling inside.

– Conduits are dedicated to specific signal levels to prevent cross-talk that can be induced from one signal level type cable to another.

– Conduits also should be separated by certain distances to deter cross-talk.

Signal characteristics and conduit separation requirements are indicated in **Tables 2** and **3**, respectively.

Table 2. Signal characteristics

Signal	Level	Voltage	Sensitivity
Audio	Mic level	100mV to 500mV	Extremely sensitive
Audio	Line level	500mV to 5V	Mildly sensitive
Video	Baseband	500mV to 2V	Moderately sensitive
Video	Broadband	500mV to 2V	Moderately sensitive
Control	Digital	5V	Moderately sensitive
Control	Analog	24V	Moderately sensitive
Power	AC mains	120V/208V	none

Table 3. Conduit separation requirements

Sensitivity	Extreme	Moderate	Mild	None
Extreme	0"	3"	6"	12"
Moderate	3"	0"	3"	6"
Mild	6"	3"	0"	3"
None	12"	6"	3"	0"

Audiovisual equipment

Projection systems such as slides, video, and overhead transparency projectors are the most common equipment that establish the formats for large screen image viewing, including:

– Single image slides or dual side by side are most common.

– Slides can be front or rear projected. The horizontal centerline of the lens is the horizontal centerline of the projected image.

– Where it is not possible for centerlines to coincide, a maximum of 3 degrees deviation from the horizontal is permissible before any keystoning or distortion is detected.

– Video projectors can also project front or rear, and can be suspended from the ceiling or mounted in a floor cradle in a portable configuration.

– The horizontal centerline of the video projector lenses is at the top of the image when ceiling mounted, and at the bottom of the image when projecting from the floor.

– The different types of video projectors (current technology) are: the three-gun (RGB) Schmidt optical system, the LCD light valve, and the LCD active matrix multimedia projector for smaller projection applications.

– Overhead transparency projectors are generally used for front projection to enable the presenters to change their own transparencies.

– Another mode for using overhead projectors is in conjunction with an LCD projection panel fed from the VGA output of a computer to enable projection of computer-generated images.

Audio systems

Audio systems required for audiovisual spaces may consist of two separate sound systems: one for speech reinforcement, and one for amplification of program sound material.

– Speech reinforcement is accomplished with microphones located at the lectern, head table, or even for the meeting participants in a larger space.

– Speech signals are mixed, processed, then amplified and delivered to flush-mounted ceiling loudspeakers.

– Loudspeakers should be placed appropriately to provide even coverage with no "hot spots" or "holes" for the audience area.

– Uniform sound level throughout the audience area is measured with a pink noise signal, where 80 dBA is the target sound pressure level (SPL); with a tolerance of + or – 1.5 dBA.

– A formula to determine the distance between ceiling loudspeaker centers for even coverage based on 90-degree loudspeaker coverage pattern for speech, is the square root of 2, which is (1.4) × (ceiling height minus listener's ear level). Example: with a ceiling height of 10 ft and with a seated ear level of 4 ft, the formula is 1.4 × (10 – 4), which equates to 1.4 × 6 = 8.4 ft spacing, center to center, on a grid pattern. (The metric equivalent would read: 1.4 × 182 cm = 255 cm space, o.c.)

– Program sound material is defined as sound tracks from videotapes, computer programs, cable TV, and laser video disc, as well as audiocassette and compact disc.

– The loudspeaker system for program sound is stereo, whereby a loudspeaker is flush mounted on each side of the projection screen.

– Another option for loudspeaker placement when the screen size is too wide for adequate center coverage is below the screen.

– The ideal placement of the loudspeakers is at the listener's ear level: 4 ft (1.21 m) seated and 5 ft-10 in (1.78 cm) standing; a compromise height of 6 ft (1.83 cm) is generally acceptable for both arrangements.

– If other room considerations dictate that the mounting requirement be higher, the loudspeakers may be tilted downwards.

– For more sophisticated applications, a surround sound program system will enable Dolby Pro-Logic or Dolby AC-3 encoded VCR tapes and laser video discs to be utilized.

– Surround sound consists of front left, center, and right loudspeakers as well as side left and right loudspeakers.

– Audio teleconferencing is available through the use of a digital telephone hybrid.

– Speech signals from the room are fed into the hybrid, sent over the telephone network to the remote caller's telephone; the remote signal is then fed in the other direction through the digital telephone hybrid and routed to the room's ceiling loudspeakers.

– Recording of these audio signals for training or archival purposes is also possible with a separately dedicated audiocassette recorder.

– If simultaneous interpretation is required, separate booths are dedicated for two interpreters for each language.

– The interpreter listens to the floor language with headphones and translates the signal simultaneously via microphone, while the signal is fed to a multichannel wireless earphone system.

Video systems

Video systems are generally intended for playback and viewing of video material, although sometimes video recording or video teleconferencing is required. While equipment can be considered to be continually changing, current technology design considerations include:

– Sources that feed video projectors and monitors are typically videotape, computer-generated images, video document camera, cable TV, internal RF distribution, laser disc, and baseband video signals via tie-lines from another facility.

– The most widely used videotape format for audiovisual presentations is ½ in (12.7 mm) VHS; others are ¾ in (19 mm) U-matic (almost obsolete) and 8mm (a popular consumer format).

– Slide-to-video units can be used to display slides via the video projector in place of a conventional slide projector. However, the currently available technology quality does not match the conventional method of showing slides.

– Video cameras can be set up in the room for the purpose of recording on videotape, or for insertion into an RF video system, or broadcast to another meeting facility.

– Permanent video cameras can be remotely controlled from pan/tilt mechanisms; all video sources are routed with their audio component via a video switcher that feeds distribution amplifiers, then the video projector, TV monitors, videocassette recorders, and external feeds.

– Video teleconferencing is achievable; however, additional special considerations for lighting, acoustics, interior finishes, seating arrangements, and camera placement are recommended (see discussion below).

Control systems

Control systems enable remote control of various AV equipment and environmental functions. It is essential in planning the types and location of controls to consider the wide variety of presenter styles, including speakers who are unfamiliar with controls and/or otherwise preoccupied with their presentation content. Ease of use and communication with the control panel function and a variety of changes of speakers and formats within a presentation and conference area suggest a control panel that is accessible to both the speaker, but possibly to one side, to permit fine-tuning adjustments of light, sound, and image by a speaker assistant without interrupting the presenter. Related design considerations include:

– Control panels can be touch screen, illuminated push-button, handheld, wired or wireless, and can be configured for flush mounting, consolette versions, or for equipment rack mounting.

– Control panels can be located at the lectern, the operator's control station at the equipment racks, in a flush-mounted wall plate, or can be portable as in the case of the wireless handheld or consolette.

– Virtually any combination or quantity of these panels can be utilized, depending on what is the best configuration for the room.

– The remote control of AV equipment typically operates the transport functions of any tape machine, such as an audio or videocassette recorder or player.

– Selection of volume control levels for speech, program, or audio teleconferencing may be remote.

– Slide projector system power is often accommodated on control panels.

– Audio teleconferencing controls are available to engage the telephone signal with the audio system.

– Audio sources to be heard and video sources to be displayed are control selectable.

– Projection screen raise/lower is a common remote control function.

– Environmental controls include the selection of different lighting scenes; drapes or curtains to open and close; movable walls or screen coverings that are motorized to open and close; controls interfaced with the mechanical system to enable remote control temperature settings for heating, air-conditioning, and ventilation.

Audiovisual facilities installation

The overall design, its circulation and seating, and its general environmental characteristics are the responsibility of the design team, including architecture, structure (if applicable), HVAC, lighting and acoustic configuration. The design of the audiovisual systems by a professional AV consultant should consist of drawings and specifications that are distributed to qualified AV contractors for a competitive bidding process. The AV contractor implements the design through fabrication, assembly, and wiring of the audiovisual systems.

Constant technological improvements are evident in audiovisual facility design, along with increasingly higher expectation of performance as users become more familiar with state-of-the-art and advanced audiovisual facilities design. Given the demanding nature of high-performance installations, the following comments describe recommended practices for specialized audiovisual facilities:

– Even if the AV contractors are not suppliers of the specified equipment, they should typically submit pricing as part of the base bid to allow bid returns to be compared as "apples-to-apples." This provides the owner and design team with designated budget estimates.

– Bidders should be given an opportunity to offer alternatives of equipment by means of demonstrating to the AV consultant, architect, and owner that there are advantages of technical performance, reliability, or cost savings. This provides for newly introduced technical developments.

- The successful bidder is required to submit shop drawings, perform pre-installation of equipment racks on their premises, then on-site installation of the equipment racks and wiring. This assures technical interface and coordination.

- After the installation is complete, the AV contractor must perform proof-of-performance testing as specified by the AV consultant. This provides documentation that the system is installed properly and performs to meet design specifications.

- The AV consultant represents the interests of the owner and the architect by witnessing and participating in all final testing. This provides a clearly defined role and responsibility for coordination and quality assurance.

- As-built documentation consisting of completed systems drawings and operations manuals must be provided by the AV contractor to the owner. This record is essential for possible future adjustments and replacements.

- Training for the use and operation of the audiovisual systems is the responsibility of the AV contractor; however, it is beneficial to the owner for the AV consultant to participate in the training process. This informs all parties in the case of future questions about system performance. ■

References: Audiovisual facilities

Ballou, Glen, 1990. *The New Audio Encyclopedia,* Howard W. Sams & Co., Indiana, 1990.

Davis, Don, and Carolyn Davis, *Sound System Engineering,* 2nd ed., Howard W. Sams & Co., Indiana, 1987.

Wadsworth, Raymond H., *Basics for Audio and Visual Systems Design,* Howard W. Sams & Co., Indiana, 1983.

2 VIDEO DISTRIBUTION AND TELECONFERENCING

As sophisticated AV installations become more common, it is important for design professionals to learn how these installations work and to be acquainted with the basic terminology used in AV design. The focus of the discussion in this section is on two widely used technologies: radio frequency (RF) video distribution and video teleconferencing. These systems can be integrated with one another, and together they carry certain design implications, both architectural and engineering, for overall facility design.

"Audiovisual" might still evoke images of slides and overhead projectors, but today's sophisticated AV installations are multimedia systems for information retrieval and display. In modern facilities with multiple meeting rooms (boardrooms, classrooms, computer training labs), a broad range of design and specification variables—cabling infrastructure, lighting, type and location of mechanical equipment, and furniture and finishes—may have a significant impact on an AV system's workability. In the past, the details of the AV design would be done in isolation from the project's architects, interior designers, and mechanical and electrical engineers. However, in an era of com-

plex and highly interactive AV installations, that approach no longer suffices. Successful audiovisual system design depends upon close coordination among AV designers and other design professionals.

Radio frequency (RF) video distribution

Radio frequency (RF) video distribution—also known as broadband signal distribution—has the following characteristics:

- Currently the most common method for distributing video and audio signals.

- May be commonly called CATV (originally Community Antenna Television, now more commonly taken to mean cable TV) or MATV (Master Antenna Television), but these may only be program sources for the system as a whole.

- CATV was originally developed for communities that were located too deep in valleys between mountains to receive a signal from a nearby transmitter. These have evolved into fully wired systems.

- MATV refers to the reception and distribution of "off-air" signals throughout an office building or apartment building.

- RF distribution within a building allows network and cable TV stations to be combined with video programming produced in-house, as well as programming from other in-house sources (VCRs, satellite feeds).

- For many applications, RF distribution is least costly and can provide the required versatility.

- Conventional RF distribution uses coaxial cable or twisted-pair cable with baluns; video may also be distributed via fiber-optic cable or through use of a LAN (Local Area Network).

- Alternate methods of video and audio distribution, which are not RF signals, but instead use electro-optics and digital processing, include using fiber optics to transport baseband or encoded multichannel MPEG streams. Transport technologies such as Asynchronous Transfer Mode (ATM) can provide a versatile protocol that allows multichannel MPEG transport over LANs.

- Each room using the system may have an outlet for use with portable monitor/receivers, or might have built-in equipment for viewing the distributed signal.

- In each of the rooms to which the system is linked, all of the system's channels can be accessed through an ordinary remote channel selector, with channel designations specific to the system: for example, channel 12 might always carry programming originating from a certain meeting room, while channel 21 might be designated for a local cable station, and channel 35 for use with a VCR.

- The available budget will play a role in determining the number of cable stations carried on an intrafacility system, because each cable station will require its own channel processor to convert the incoming signal (supplied by the local cable TV company) into a specific channel of the RF system; the greater the number of incoming channels, the greater the cost.

– A splitter/combiner takes all the separate RF sources and "squeezes" them into a single broadband signal that is distributed to the various RF outlets, or tap-offs, throughout a facility.

– The broadband signal will require greater amplification within the distribution line as the number of tap-offs increases.

– To allow for return channels, "subsplitting" can make the system bidirectional, which costs more, but provides flexibility, that is, reverse feeding a video camera to the head-end for distribution.

Baseband signals within the RF system

– Baseband refers to audio and video signals traveling separately through a system. Separate audio and video signals (from microphones and video cameras) of any programming produced on-site are combined by a device called a modulator, which converts them into a signal capable of being carried on the RF system.

– In a multipurpose, multi-meeting-room facility, flexibility can be augmented by adding baseband tie-lines between the various meeting (or other) spaces and the central location housing the RF system's modulators (called the head-end).

– Signals from cameras and microphones may be patched into the modulators via in-room audio and video connection plates, to enable the use of these locations as in-house production sites for programming.

– Baseband tie-lines can also serve as a back-up route for signals, in case of trouble with the broadband system or any of its components.

– Architects and engineers need to work closely with AV designers in mapping out areas in a facility that may be potentially used as additional production/reception sites, to ensure that the proper infrastructure is built in, and that design aspects (lighting and finishes) of these spaces are appropriate for such use.

Video teleconferencing

• *Space planning*

– Low-end, relatively inexpensive desktop video teleconferencing employs small, PC monitor-mounted cameras and can be run on ISDN voice/data lines.

– Fully equipped, dedicated video teleconferencing suites can, if desired, be interfaced with a facility's RF distribution system.

– Such suites are environments in which all design elements—lighting, mechanical systems, furniture, and finishes—are integrated, to foster conferees' comfort and to ensure high-quality transmission and reception of images.

– The layout of a video teleconferencing room usually includes two monitors at the front of the room, one small loudspeaker, and two cameras that are remotely controlled to pan, tilt, zoom, and focus (**Fig. 3**).

– The equipment is either integrated into the furniture, or housed in a "back of house" control room.

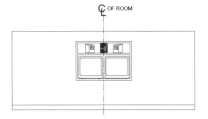

ELEVATION 1

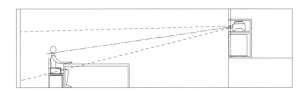

SECTION A' - A"

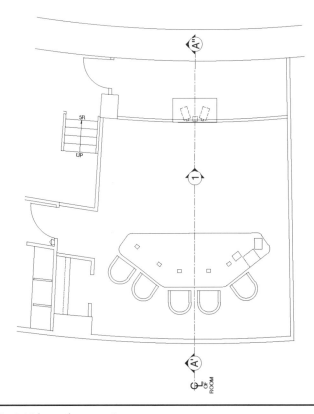

Fig. 3. Videoconference suite.

– Teleconferencing suites typically accommodate 3 to 12 people.

– At least two cameras will be needed when more than four conferees use the suite at a time, because their individual images on the TV screen might be too small for viewers to distinguish who is speaking; also, zooming and panning one camera can look awkward "on-air."

• *Lighting and HVAC*

– Color temperature of lighting must be correct for the cameras; the higher the color temperature, the more green the video camera sees.

– A good color temperature level for a video teleconferencing room is between 3200 and 3600 degrees Kelvin. For reference, daylight is 9500 Kelvin, fluorescent lighting is 2700 to 5000 Kelvin, and tungsten lights are around 2800.

– The light level for a video teleconference space is ideally 75 to 90 vertical foot candles at the desktop. For reference, typical light levels are: living room—40 foot candles, kitchen—75 foot candles, and television production studios—100 to 120 foot candles.

– The mechanical system must provide sufficient cooling to offset the heat produced by the lights and equipment.

• *Acoustics*

– The mechanical system must be designed and situated so that its noise will be minimized and will not interfere with voice transmission.

– The teleconference room should not be located near areas that create noise, such as elevator machine rooms, or electrical closets with "humming" transformers and dimmers in a video teleconferencing space, the noise criteria (NC) rating should be 25 to 28. For reference, a typical office environment NC rating is 35 to 40; a broadcast television studio is specified at NC 25.

– The amount of sound that can penetrate a wall or door into an adjacent space is specified by its STC, or Sound Transmission Class.

– An STC of 55 for a teleconferencing space can be achieved by using double sheetrock walls with 4 in insulation between them.

– The acoustic tile used in the room's ceiling should have a noise reduction coefficient rating of 0.7. These coefficients range from 0.2 to 0.9, with the highest number being the most sound absorbent.

– RT ratings describe reverberation time, or how long it takes for sound to "decay" in a space; a very reflective room has a high RT60 rating. A video teleconference room should have an RT60 of no more than 500 ms (half a second).

• *Finishes, furnishings, and controls*

– Wall finishes are important both for their acoustic and visual properties.

– The audiovisual consultant must coordinate with interior designers and lighting designers to make certain that all the suite's ele-

ments—including wall finishes, tabletop finishes, and backlighting—support the best possible transmission.

– The table for the conferees should ideally be trapezoidal or U-shaped to allow for the greatest number of participants to be seated at a consistent distance from the cameras. Tabletop finishes should not be too dark, too light, or too reflective.

– Equipment on the table typically consists of low-profile surface-type microphones, and a touch-screen control panel.

– Voice-activated switching between cameras can be used, but can be triggered by coughs and sneezes.

– A touch-screen control panel requires one of the conferees to operate it (**Fig. 4**). Additionally, a camera dedicated for the purpose of transmitting documents and transparencies, a "document-viewing camera," can be positioned pointing straight down over the table.

– A custom light box may be built into the table to provide backlighting that will allow transparencies to be transmitted via the document-viewing camera.

– Certain patterns and textures should be avoided in wall coverings and upholstery, as they can cause distracting *moiré* effects on-camera. Backlighting behind conferees—probably in the form of a wall-wash—will be needed to insure that the televised image will not appear too flat, as if the participants were painted on the wall.

– A VCR or other video player may be linked to the teleconferencing system, enabling all the conference participants at both ends of the videoconference to view videotape simultaneously.

– Video teleconferencing can be married to the RF distribution system of a multi-meeting-room facility through baseband tie-lines; people in the other rooms will be able to observe the teleconference, though they will not be able to participate.

• *Cabling and wiring*

– In designing the signal infrastructure, it is preferable to separate different signal levels. Microphone-level signals should not be mixed with loudspeaker-level signals.

– Video and audio line-level signals should be separated to avoid the possibility of signal contamination or cross-talk.

– Specifying separate conduits for RF system cables and other video/audio cables can help prevent problems during a project's installation phase, when different contractors·might be pulling cables through the same conduit.

– Conduits for power cables with high current need to be kept apart from audiovisual cable conduits to prevent the induction of a 60 Hz field caused by electromagnetic interference.

– Grounding must follow good engineering practices to minimize noise from interference and to adhere to electrical safety codes.

– If the system is grounded in too many places (creating ground loops) or the ground is not connected where it should be ("floating"

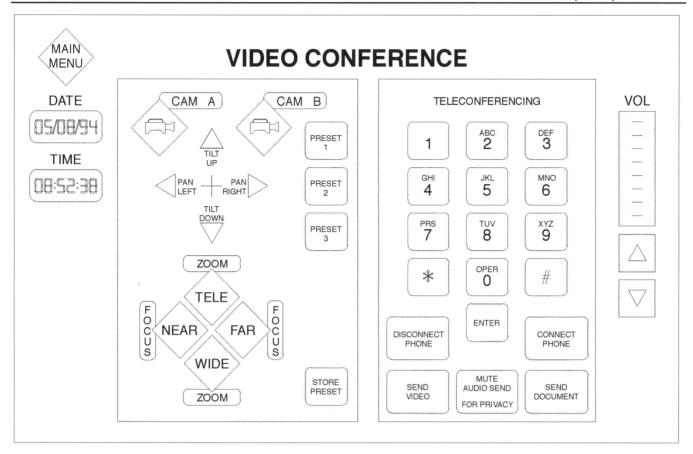

Fig. 4. Videoconference control panel.

ground), unwanted effects may be created, such as a "hum" in the audio signal and/or vertically rolling "hum-bars" in the video image.

– Careful collaboration between the AV consultant and electrical design professionals is essential to the system's performance. Refer to the discussion in the prior sections regarding quality control procedures in contracting and installation. ■

References: Video distribution and teleconferencing

Besinger, Charles, *The Video Guide,* 3rd ed., Howard W. Sams & Co., Indiana, 1983.

Cunningham, John, *Cable Television,* 2nd ed., Howard W. Sams & Co., Indiana, 1980.

Wadsworth, Raymond H., *Basics for Audio and Visual Systems Design,* Howard W. Sams & Co., Indiana, 1983.

3 SOUND-MASKING SYSTEMS

Sound masking is a relatively new technology that is able to reduce the apparent level and effective intrusiveness of ambient speech and other noise, enhancing the perception of privacy in the work environment, which in turn improves the individual's capacity for focus and efficiency. Speech privacy can be objectively assessed by reference to the *Articulation Index,* a measurement of the extent to which speech is articulate or clearly heard enough to be intelligible and is thus an inverse measure of speech privacy (**Table 4**).

A sound-masking system does not make a noisy space quiet. Rather, its function is to contribute to speech privacy by creating an acoustical background at a level that is regular and not disturbing, thus "drowning out" erratic noises. The system is designed to provide a uniform and continuous level of background sound that contains all the frequency bands where human speech occurs. The sound-masking system is functioning properly when it is not noticed, since the source of the sound is nondirectional and concealed above the finished ceiling.

Sound-masking systems are most frequently utilized in open office plan spaces, enclosed offices, hospitals, libraries, motels, and multi-tenant residences.

Characteristics of sound-masking systems

The development of these systems dates from the 1960s when it was realized that the noise from HVAC supply registers, to some degree, actually served to improve speech privacy in offices.

Table 4. Relationship between Articulation Index and degree of speech privacy

AI	Degree of Speech Privacy	% [1]
0.0		0
0.1	NORMAL	10
0.2		20
0.3		30
0.4	POOR	40
0.5		50
0.6		60
0.7		70
0.8	NONE	80
0.9		90
1.0		100

note [1] % = percent of words spoken that are intelligible

– Up to a 40 percent improvement in speech privacy can be obtained with a sound-masking system.

– Sound-absorbing materials used on open office plan partitions (without the use of sound masking) will absorb some background noise, but not the frequencies of sound that characterize speech.

– Sound masking is not appropriate for all situations. There may be open office spaces where sound masking is not desirable, as in the case of a brokerage firm with a bull pen, where vocal interaction is essential to the work process.

– Sound masking has proven to be very effective in enclosed offices where walls are constructed only to the finished ceiling level and/or are otherwise unable to be acoustically isolated.

– Intrusive speech signals are masked in enclosed offices with the same devices as are used in open office plans.

– Sound-masking systems will not be effective in areas where there is no carpet, where there are no vertical partitions, or where partitions have excessive space at their bottom edges.

– If the ceiling is essentially "hard-surfaced," such as sheetrock, plaster, metal pan, wood or even painted acoustical tile, a masking system will be ineffective.

– For the purpose of absorption, open office plan partition panels and lay-in acoustic ceiling tile should have a high NRC (Noise Reduction Coefficient) of 0.7 to 0.9.

– Air return grilles in the ceiling may cause "hot spots" in the system. The best solution to this potential problem is to carefully coordinate the locations of the mechanical system grilles with the architect, interior designer, and HVAC engineer early in the design phase, so their positions are effective for HVAC, but do not adversely affect the sound-masking system's efficiency.

Sound-masking system costs and planning

Sound masking should be planned during the initial stages of design. Although it is an element of construction that cannot be seen, one should not neglect to consider the installation of sound masking as a benefit to overall space quality. Specifically:

– The proper sound-masking "loudspeaker" devices should be installed during the construction period, when the ceiling is most accessible.

– If the sound-masking system is in place from the start of the office operation, it will go unnoticed by office personnel, and thus be more effective. Installation after the opening of the office will require that the system be adjusted in small increments (for it to be introduced so as not to disrupt what people are used to); it will take time to have the system operating at full level.

– Installation cost is reasonable if part of other construction, with access to ceiling voids during new construction or renovation. To retrofit the system once the office is in operation, installers must access the ceiling after normal working hours, which could double the cost of installation, when priced as a separate item.

– The cost of sound masking is easily offset by the avoidance of the cost of extensive acoustical treatments. For example, sound masking is also much more cost-effective than slab-to-slab wall partitions.

– Wall partitions take up more floor space than open plan furniture, so utilization of a building floor plate is poorer with partitioning that is introduced for acoustical separation, compared to an open office with sound masking.

Description of sound-masking systems

– Small sound-masking systems have devices that are stand-alone, "plug-in" units.

– Systems that combine sound masking, background music, and paging can be installed with minimal additional cost.

– In many cases, a three-in-one sound system is not advisable, due to the diminished sound quality of the background music and paging with the use of sound-masking loudspeaker devices.

– Typically, large-scale sound-masking systems are used for open office plans. This type of sound system consists of a digital noise generator that feeds the masking sound, via audio distribution amplifiers, to zones of ⅓ octave equalizers, and then to power amplifiers which feed the sound-masking loudspeaker devices, using a 70V distributed system (**Fig. 5**).

– The sound emanates upwards toward the slab from these devices and bounces or reflects off the slab to fill the plenum with sound.

– Sound-masking loudspeaker devices are suspended by chains from the upper deck slab, or from structural members using beam clamps (**Fig. 6**).

– The sound penetrates the acoustical ceiling tiles of the occupied space in a uniform manner that avoids the "hot spots" that would occur with conventional ceiling loudspeaker devices that face down from the plane of the ceiling.

– It is a misnomer to call the sound-masking signal "pink" or "white" noise; pink noise is properly defined as equal acoustic en-

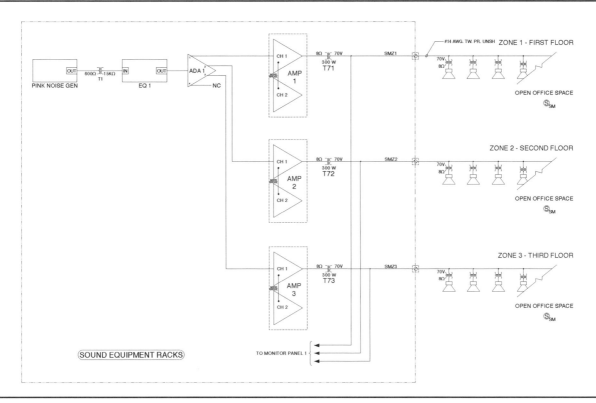

Fig. 5. Representative system layout of sound-masking equipment.

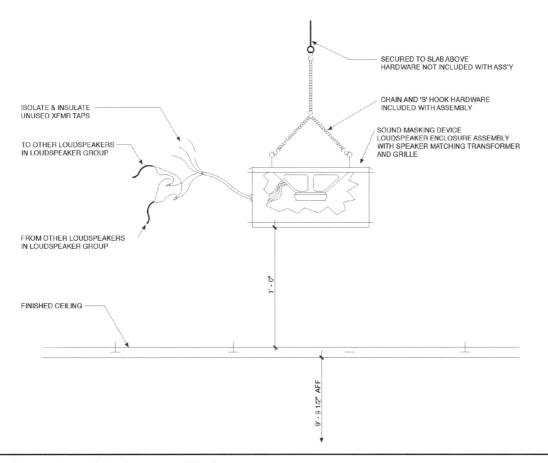

Fig. 6. Sound-masking speaker installed within a suspended ceiling.

Table 5. NC-40 Contour equalization curve

Band - hz	Relative Level in dB - SPL
200	+4
250	+3
315	+2
400	+1
500	0
630	-1
800	-2
1000	-3
1250	-4
1600	-5
2000	-6

Box A—Acronyms and Abbreviations

The following acronyms and abbreviations are useful in referring to the electronic system specialties described in this article.

AI	Articulation Index (Table 4)
ASTM	American Society for Testing and Materials
ATM	Asynchronous Transfer Mode
AV	Audiovisual
CATV	Cable TV (originally, Community Antenna Television)
CCTV	Closed Circuit Television
dB	Decibels
EMT	Electrical metallic tubing
ISDN	Integrated Services Digital Network
LAN	Local Area Network
LCD	Liquid Crystal Display
MATV	Master Antenna Television
NC	Noise Criteria
NEC	National Electric Code
NRC	Noise Reduction Coefficient
RF	Radio Frequency
RGB	Red, Green, Blue (used in video projector technology)
RT	Reverberation Time
RTA	Real Time Analyzer (used in acoustical measurement)
SPL	Sound Pressure Level
STC	Sound Transmission Class
TEF	Time-Energy-Frequency (used in acoustical measurement)
UL	Underwriters Laboratories
VDT	Video Display Terminal

---

ergy at all octaves; white noise is defined as acoustical energy with a 12dB per octave roll-off towards the lower octaves.

– In sound masking, the noise source is equalized to shape the sound to a particular curve that is best suited for sound masking and specifically intended to mask human speech, referred to as "NC-40 Contour." The NC-40 Contour consists of specific sound pressure levels at ⅓ octave frequencies between 200hz and 2Khz, below 200hz and above 2Khz, the curve provides a smooth natural roll-off (**Table 5**).

– The sound pressure level of the sound-masking signal at 500 hz (the "0" reference frequency) must be 40dB, plus or minus 2.5dB, or the system will not perform optimally.

– An installation that does not have enough loudspeaker devices per area will have uneven coverage; this will be quite noticeable and distracting.

The success of the sound-masking installation relies on the design, the installation, and the adjustment of the system with regard to equalization and level. These adjustments require a professional reading with a RTA (Real Time Analyzer) or TEF (Time-Energy-Frequency) instrument and a sound pressure level meter. Adjustments to the system are performed by the audiovisual or sound contractor initially, and then checked by the AV consultant. Sound-masking systems should be designed by a qualified AV consultant, acoustician, or electrical engineer, and installed by an experienced electrical contractor and/or audiovisual or sound systems contractor. ■

References: Sound-masking systems

Associations and Manufacturers:

American Society for Testing and Materials (ASTM) Task Group E33.04C, Conshohocken, PA (610) 832-9598

Atlas/Soundolier, Fenton, MO (314) 349-3110

Dukane Corp., St. Charles, IL (630) 584-2300

Dynasound, Norcross, GA (800) 989-6275

John D. Bullough

Summary

This article presents information on the specification of lighting for architects, engineers, and designers. General information on lighting is followed by applications, including lighting for offices, schools, institutions and public facilities, and residences.

Key words

contrast ratio, electromagnetic spectrum, lighting design, luminaire, commercial, institutional, outdoor, parking, residential, veiling reflections, visual performance

Lighting

1 LIGHTING FUNDAMENTALS

Measurement of light

Light is visually perceived radiant energy, located between about 380 and 780 nanometers (nm; 1 nm = 10^{-9} m) on the electromagnetic spectrum (**Fig. 1**). Light is only a small part of the entire electromagnetic spectrum, which also includes X-rays, ultraviolet (UV) radiation, infrared (IR) radiation, and radio and television waves.

Electromagnetic radiation is measured in terms of its radiant power in watts (W). However, not all visible wavelengths are evaluated equally by the human visual system. A given radiant power at 590 nm ("yellow" light) will not appear as bright as the same radiant power at 550 nm ("green" light). Furthermore, these relationships can change depending upon the overall ambient light level. Under typical indoor or daytime light levels, the visual system is most sensitive to a wavelength of 555 nm and sensitivity decreases for shorter or longer wavelengths. This is because photoreceptors in the retina, called *cones,* are used in daytime or *photopic* vision, and the cones are maximally sensitive to light at 555 nm (**Fig. 2**).

At very low levels, photoreceptors called *rods* are used for vision. This is called *scotopic vision.* Rods are maximally sensitive to light at 507 nm. Scotopic vision is sometimes called nighttime vision, although most nighttime levels are actually in the range of levels called mesopic vision where the transition from cones to rods occurs and the maximal sensitivity will lie somewhere between 555 nm and 507 nm,

depending upon the light level. At high mesopic light levels the maximum sensitivity will be closer to 555 nm, and at low mesopic levels it will be near 507 nm (He et al. 1997).

Light is characterized in several different ways (**Fig. 3**). A point source with a uniform luminous intensity of 1 *candela* (cd) will produce a total of 4π, or approximately 12.57 lumens (lm). Furthermore, the luminous flux density, or illuminance, on the inner surface of the sphere will be 1 lm/ft^2 or 1 foot-candle (fc) if the sphere radius is 1 ft, and will be 1 lm/m^2 or 1 lux (lx) if the sphere radius is 1 m; 1 fc is equal to 10.76 lx.

Light can also be measured in terms of luminance, which is the density of luminous intensity from a surface, in a particular direction. For many practical purposes, luminance is analogous to the perceived brightness of a surface. It is measured in cd/m^2.

The measures of light that are most commonly used by lighting specifiers and in recommendations of IESNA are *illuminance* and *luminance.* Portable meters for measuring illuminance and luminance are available.

Color properties of lighting

Color properties of light sources are characterized in several ways. Two commonly used ways are the correlated color temperature and the color rendering index.

Credits: This article is based in part on data published by the Illuminating Engineering Society of North America (IESNA and Rea, 2000) cited in the References. Reviews of the work by Mark Rea and Rita M. Harrold are gratefully acknowledged.

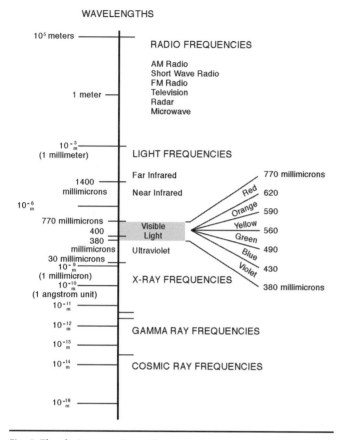

Fig. 1. The electromagnetic spectrum.

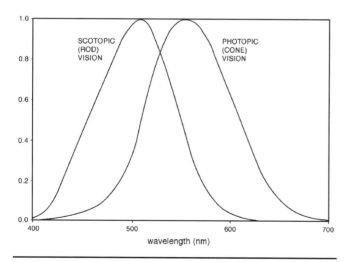

Fig. 2. The spectral sensitivity of cones (right) and rods (left).

Correlated color temperature

The Correlated Color Temperature (CCT) of a light source is a measure of its color appearance. It is based on the temperature in kelvins (K) of a blackbody radiator that produces light of a certain color. Tungsten, used in incandescent lamp filaments, behaves much like a blackbody radiator. The temperature of a tungsten filament (approximately 2800 K in incandescent lamps) is roughly equal to its CCT. CCTs of other lamp types are based on how close their color is to a blackbody radiator (or tungsten filament) of a certain temperature. At higher temperatures, a filament will become "bluer" in appearance. At lower temperatures, it will become "redder."

Color rendering index

The Color Rendering Index (CRI) of a light source is a rating that is designed to correlate with a light source's ability to render several standard test colors relative to a blackbody (incandescent-type) source. It has a maximum value of 100; a light source with a CRI approaching 100 is thought to have good color rendering properties.

Optical control

Light interacts with surfaces in several ways. It can be absorbed by materials. Dark materials have a low reflectance and absorb more light than bright materials. It can be reflected by materials, such as a mirror or a painted wall. In the case of a mirror, the reflections are called *regular* or *specular* (**Fig. 4**); in the case of a wall, most of the reflected light is diffuse (**Fig. 5**). Light can be transmitted as through glass. Light can also be refracted ("bent"). **Fig. 6** depicts how glass bends incident light rays. Luminaires can use glass or clear plastic lenses to control the distribution of light through refraction, or can redirect light (through reflection) from elements such as parabolic or ellipsoidal reflectors.

The spectral (color) properties of materials affect the way they interact with light. For example, a red surface will reflect long visible wavelengths, which are perceived as red light, and will absorb other wavelengths. A blue gel (filter) transmits short visible wavelengths that are perceived as blue light, and absorbs other wavelengths.

Lighting and vision

Visual Performance

A primary purpose of lighting in the built environment is to aid vision. Owing to the concern for energy conservation, there has been a desire to provide enough light to allow people to safely and accurately perform visual tasks, without providing excessive lighting, which could in fact waste electric energy. An understanding of visual tasks and the factors that affect visual performance can aid in providing the appropriate level of lighting for those tasks. Visual performance is affected by several factors, including:

- contrast
- size
- time

Contrast refers to the luminance difference between the critical detail of a task and its background. A reading task such as black print on white paper has a high contrast, approaching 1, while a sewing task involving white thread on white fabric will have a low contrast, approaching 0. As the contrast of a task increases, visual performance also increases (Rea 1986). However, once contrast is sufficiently high, further increases in contrast will have little effect on visual performance.

The *size* of the visual task is also important. A task with an infinitesimally small size will be invisible, with visibility increasing as size increases. As with contrast, once the size is sufficiently large, making it larger will not increase visual performance very much. For example, visual performance while reading 6-point type might be significantly better than visual performance reading 4-point type; but visual performance while reading 18-point type would only be marginally better than visual performance reading 12-point type.

The *time* a visual task is presented also affects visual performance. For visual tasks that are visible for only very brief periods of time (less than 0.1 sec), the intensity and time are traded off, such that a signal that appears for half the time of a second signal would need to be twice as intense to be as visible as the second signal. Many visual tasks for which lighting is specified, such as reading or drafting, appear for extended periods of time, so that time of presentation is not a factor.

For a visual task with a specific contrast, size, and presentation time, lighting directly affects another factor that helps determine the overall visual performance. Unless a task is self-luminous, such as a video display terminal (VDT) screen, the *task background luminance* is affected by the illuminance falling on the task surface and by the reflectance of the task. The reflectance of a surface can be determined from its Munsell value (or lightness). **Table 1** lists the approximate equivalent reflectance for Munsell values from 0 to 10. (NOTE: Tables are placed in numerical order at the end of this article.)

Task luminance affects the lowest contrast that can be detected. As the luminance is increased, the minimum contrast decreases so that contrasts that are invisible at low luminances may become visible at higher luminances. Similarly, *visual acuity* (ability to distinguish detail of the smallest objects that can be seen) improves with increasing light levels. In addition, both speed and accuracy of visual processing improve with higher light levels.

Performance of a visual task improves with higher and higher light levels, although the rate of improvement decreases when the light level is too high. This "plateau" effect is inherent to most visual tasks encountered at work or at home when objects in the field of view are well above the visual threshold (Rea 1986). For very fine, low contrast visual tasks, however, the light level will have a relatively larger impact on visual performance.

The age of the occupant should also be considered when planning the lighting in a space. The amount of light reaching the retina of a 50-year-old person is approximately 50 percent of that for a 20-year-old. As a result, lighting requirements for older persons differ from those of young people (Figueiro 2001).

Veiling Reflections and Glare

Lighting also indirectly affects visual performance in several ways. When the task contains primarily specular (shiny) surfaces, such as a VDT or glossy magazine, some light sources can cause veiling reflections that create a luminous veil over the visual task, reducing contrast and lowering visual performance. For some tasks, especially some industrial inspection tasks, reflections can actually enhance

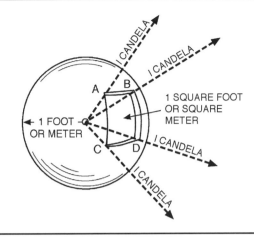

Fig. 3. Relationship between intensity, luminous flux, and illuminance.

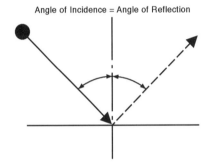

Fig. 4. Illustration of specular reflection.

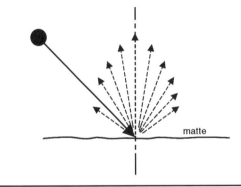

Fig. 5. Illustration of diffuse reflection.

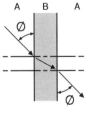

Density A:B = 1:2

Fig. 6. Refraction of a ray of light by glass.

Table 1. Equivalent reflectances and Munsell values

Munsell Value	Reflectance
0	0.00
1	0.01
2	0.03
3	0.06
4	0.12
5	0.19
6	0.29
7	0.42
8	0.58
9	0.77
10	1.00

one's ability to see, for example, scratches or chips in a metal plate (see "*Industrial Lighting*" below).

Bright sources of light, such as bare lamps or windows, can also cause disability glare by creating scattered light within the eye. This reduces the contrast of the resulting retinal image and, in essence, acts like a luminous veil, even if the scattered light does not cause discomfort. The lighting specifier should consider the task-luminaire geometry in the space and take care to avoid veiling reflections and excessively bright luminaires and lamps, by using proper positioning and shielding.

Glare becomes more of a critical issue as people age due to scattered light in the lens of the eye. When very bright sources exist within a space, they may cause discomfort glare, an annoying or painful sensation caused by the nonuniformity of lighting. Visual performance need not be impaired for discomfort glare to exist. The lighting specifier can reduce discomfort glare in spaces by the following means:

- decreasing the luminance of the offending source of light.

- reducing the area or size of the offending source.

- increasing the luminance of surfaces surrounding the offending source.

IESNA recommends that to avoid glare in spaces containing VDTs, the luminances of luminaires at specific angles from the luminaire should not exceed the following values:

- 65° above nadir: 850 cd/m^2

- 75° above nadir: 350 cd/m^2

- 85° above nadir: 175 cd/m^2

Lighting and psychology

Lighting can affect one's impressions of a space. Although visual performance will improve with increasing light levels, the light level can become excessive if people find spaces "too bright."

Spatial distributions of light are also important. Several researchers have investigated the *luminance ratios* among the visual task, immediate surround (such as a desk top), and even the room surfaces that are preferred. These results have led to the recommendation of specific luminance ratios for various applications, as described below for each application.

Lighting can reinforce the intended mood of a room. Lighting a space tends to reinforce certain subjective impressions, including the following.

- *Visual clarity:* reinforced by bright, uniform lighting combined with high brightness of the walls.

- *Spaciousness:* reinforced by uniform (not necessarily bright) wall lighting.

- *Relaxation:* reinforced by nonuniform lighting and lower ceiling brightness.

- *Privacy/intimacy:* reinforced by nonuniform lighting (low levels around the occupants, higher levels further away).

- *Pleasantness/preference:* reinforced by nonuniform lighting with high wall brightness.

Lighting and biology

Lighting also affects people's biology. Visual exposure to very intense light sources—such as discharge arcs, filaments, and the sun—can damage the retina (Bullough 2000). Shielding of these sources by luminaire housings or other means is required to prevent retinal burns. Organizations such as the American Conference of Governmental Industrial Hygienists (ACGIH) publish recommendations for exposure limits to potentially hazardous light sources.

Lighting is also an important cue for human *circadian rhythms*. Many functions, such as body temperature, hormone production, and sleep, are regulated on a near-24-hour cycle. Recent research has pointed to short-wavelength ("blue") light as the most important component of the visible spectrum for circadian regulation, which could result in changes in recommendations in the future for lighting, presently based primarily on visual needs and preferences.

2 LIGHT SOURCES

Several types of light sources (lamps) are commonly used in electric lighting systems. Common lamps for general lighting are compared according to several important characteristics in **Table 2.**

Incandescent and Tungsten-Halogen Lamps

Incandescent lamps are available in many shapes and sizes (**Fig. 7**). Lamps are designated by a letter corresponding to the bulb shape and a number corresponding to the bulb diameter (in multiples of ⅛ in). An A-19 lamp, therefore, designates a type "A" bulb (the typical household bulb shape) that is 1⅞ or 2-⅜ in (60 mm) in diameter. Incandescent lamps have a filament (usually of tungsten) inside a glass envelope (or bulb). When a current is applied across the filament, it becomes so hot (approximately 2800 K) as to radiate light. Incandescent sources also generate significant heat (radiation in the infrared or IR region of the spectrum).

Incandescent lamps are often used in applications where color rendering is very important. They have a color rendering index (CRI) ap-

Table 2. Common light source characteristics (Compiled by R. M. Harrold)

Incandescent including properties/ specifications	tungsten halogen	Fluorescent	High - intensity discharge			
			Mercury - vapor (self - ballasted)	Metal halide	High pressure sodium (improved color)	Low pressure sodium
Wattages (lamp only)	15 - 1,500	15 - 219	40 - 1,000	175 - 1,000	70 - 1,000	60 - 180
Life (hours)	750 - 12,000	7,500 - 24,000	16,000 - 24,000	1500 - 15,000	24,000 (7500)	16,000
Efficacy, lumens per watt (lamp only)	15-25	55-100	50-60 (20 - 25)	80-100	75-140 (67 - 112)	Up to 180
Lumen maintenance	Fair to excellent	Fair to excellent	Very good (good)	Good	Excellent	Excellent
Color rendition	Excellent	Good to excellent	Poor to excellent	Very good	Fair (very good)	Poor
Light direction control	Very good to excellent	Fair	Very good	Very good	Very good	Fair
Source size	Compact	Extended	Compact	Compact	Compact	Extended
Relight time	Immediate	Immediate	3 - 10 minutes	10 - 20 minutes	Less than 1 minute	Immediate
Comparative fixture cost	Low—simple fixtures	Moderate	Higher than incandescent and fluorescent	Generally higher than mercury	High	High
Comparative operating cost	High—short life and low efficacy	Lower than incandescent	Lower than incandescent	Lower than mercury	Lowest of HID types	Low
Auxiliary equipment needed	Not needed	Needed— medium cost	Needed— high cost	Needed— high cost	Needed— high cost	Needed— high cost

proaching 100. Typical incandescent lamps have luminous efficacies ranging from approximately 10 to 20 lm/W. Tungsten-halogen lamps, which use a halogen gas, are more efficient than standard incandescent lamps and have luminous efficacies ranging up to 35 lm/W.

Reducing the voltage has the following effects on an incandescent lamp:

— reducing the lumens produced by the lamp (dimming).

— increasing lamp life.

— reducing the lamp efficacy (lm/W).

— decreasing the CCT (creating a "warmer" color).

Despite the relatively low luminous efficacies of incandescent and tungsten-halogen lamps compared to other sources, they provide excellent optical control that gives them higher *application efficacy* than fluorescent lamps, for example, at creating narrow beams and directional lighting systems (Rea and Bullough 2001).

Fluorescent Lamps

Fluorescent lamps are low-pressure gas discharge sources, where light is produced mainly by fluorescent powder coatings (phosphors) that are activated by UV energy generated by a mercury arc. Fluorescent lamps usually consist of glass tubes with electrodes at either end. The tubes contain mercury vapor at low pressure with a small amount of an inert gas. The phosphors are applied to the inside of the glass tubes. When a current is applied to the electrodes, an arc forms that

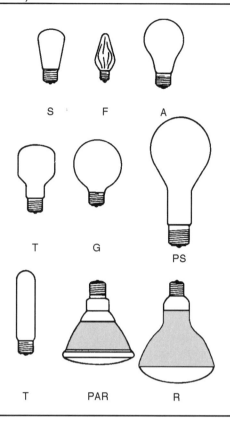

Fig. 7. Typical incandescent lamp shapes.

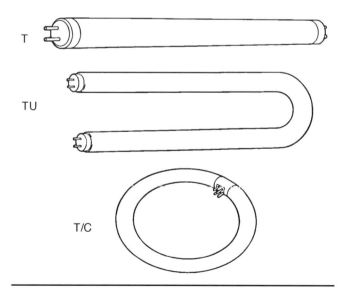

Fig. 8. Typical fluorescent lamp shapes.

radiates some light, but mostly UV energy. This UV energy excites the chemicals in the phosphors, which in turn emit light. Fluorescent lamps have a typical rated life of between 8000 and 20,000 hours.

Fluorescent lamps require a ballast to operate. The ballast provides the starting and operating voltages and currents that keep the fluorescent lamp operating properly. Several types of ballast are available: magnetic ballasts, which operate at standard ac current frequency (60 Hz in North America), and electronic ballasts, which operate lamps at frequencies between 10,000 and 50,000 Hz. Fluorescent lamp efficacy is increased by more than 10 percent when electronic ballasts are used. Ballasts that permit fluorescent lamps to be dimmed also exist.

Fluorescent lamps come in many shapes and sizes (**Fig. 8**). The notation is similar to that for incandescent lamps: for example, a T-8 lamp is one with a "T" (tubular) shape that is ⅝ or 1 in (25 mm) in diameter. They can also be tuned to produce different colors, depending upon the type and amount of phosphors they have. For most typical lighting applications, fluorescent lamps can be created with CCTs ranging from 2500 to 7500 K.

The output of fluorescent lamps is dependent upon the ambient temperature and the operating position of the lamp. The temperatures within enclosed luminaires can become quite high in some conditions and the amount of light will be affected. Ventilated luminaires can be used to alleviate this problem somewhat.

Two main types of phosphors are used in fluorescent lamps. The first are the halophosphate types. These phosphors are used to create the "warm white" and "cool white" lamps. Note that 40-W 4 ft (1220 mm) warm white and cool white T-12 lamps are being phased out of use in the United States to comply with federal energy legislation. Halophosphate coatings are still used on some energy-saving (34-W) lamps that comply with the energy legislation. CRI with halophosphate lamps tends to be between 50 and 60.

An increasingly used approach to fluorescent lamp phosphors is the triphosphor, or rare-earth phosphor system. Such lamps use three phosphors, each of which emits a narrow band of light in one of the primary color regions, mixed in various proportions to create different CCTs. Such lamps also tend to have very high CRIs (between 70 and 90).

Compact fluorescent lamps (CFLs) offer increased flexibility to lighting specifiers because their relatively small size means they can be substituted for incandescent lamps in some luminaires. Dedicated luminaires for CFLs also exist which take advantage of the better optical control that a compact source size allows. CFLs are designated by their shape and wattage: for example, a 13-W twin tube CFL will have the notation CFT13W (CFT indicates a compact fluorescent twin tube; 13W indicates the wattage). An 18-W quad (four) tube CFL will be designated CFQ18W.

Compared to incandescent lamps, fluorescent lamps are relatively diffuse, low-luminance sources. A T-8 fluorescent lamp has a surface luminance of approximately 10,000 cd/m²; a clear-bulb incandescent lamp filament can have a luminance exceeding 2,000,000 cd/m².

High-Intensity Discharge Lamps

High-intensity discharge (HID) lamps include mercury, metal halide (MH), and high-pressure sodium (HPS) lamps. Like incandescent lamps, they provide a relatively compact point of light; like fluorescent lamps, they are electric discharge lamps, tend to have long lives and require ballast. Unlike incandescent and fluorescent lamps, starting times for many HID lamps can be as long as several minutes.

Mercury lamps: Light is produced in mercury lamps by applying a current through pressurized mercury vapor. Mercury lamps are constructed with two enclosures or envelopes (**Fig. 9**): an inner arc tube that contains the mercury arc, and an outer bulb that shields the arc tube from temperature fluctuations. The outer bulb also absorbs ultraviolet (UV) radiation produced by the arc and can be coated with phosphors similarly to fluorescent lamps. Mercury lamps have very long-rated lives (16,000 to 24,000 hours).

Clear mercury lamps (with no phosphors) emit bluish-white light in several discrete wavelength bands from 405 to 579 nm. A deficiency of long wavelength energy results in poor color appearance of orange and red objects. Coated mercury lamps often use a phosphor that converts the UV radiation from the arc into long-wavelength visible light; this improves both the luminous efficacy and the CRI of the lamp. Typical mercury lamp efficacies are between 30 and 65 lm/W, and CRI ranges from 20 to 50.

Metal halide lamps: MH lamps are very similar in construction to mercury lamps, with the arc tube containing various metallic halide compounds in addition to mercury. These compounds emit light in different parts of the visible spectrum, and by using various mixtures of metallic halides, lamps with efficacies and CRIs much higher than mercury lamps are possible. Typical MH lamp efficacy ranges between 75 and 125 lm/W. CRI ranges from 60 to over 90, and CCT ranges from 3000 K (a warm white appearance) to over 6000 K (a very cool, bluish-white appearance). Rated lamp life is typically from 10,000 to 20,000 hours.

Compact MH lamps in relatively low wattages (70 to 150 W) exist that have a very high CRI (over 90) and can be used for accent display lighting. Many MH lamps are very sensitive to operating position with respect to color, efficacy, and other operating characteristics. Some MH lamps are developed to be operated in a specific orientation. MH lamps with ceramic arc tubes and improved starting gear have recently been developed that extend their life and lumen depreciation characteristics.

High-pressure sodium lamps: HPS lamps produce light by applying a current to sodium vapor. Like mercury and MH lamps, HPS lamps have two envelopes (**Fig. 10**): an inner arc tube containing sodium and mercury, and an outer glass bulb to absorb UV energy and stabilize the temperature of the arc tube. Typical HPS lamp efficacies range between 45 and 150 lm/W, with rated lamp lives of approximately 24,000 hours.

HPS lamps radiate energy across the visible spectrum, although not uniformly. Light from standard HPS lamps is a golden-white color (CCT ranging from 1900 to 2200 K) and color rendering is quite poor (CRI is 22). Improved color rendering HPS lamps can be created by increasing the sodium vapor pressure, which increases CRI to approximately 65 (while reducing efficacy and life), or by operating HPS lamps at higher frequencies (resulting in CCT between 2700 and 2800 K and CRI between 70 and 80).

Low-Pressure Sodium Lamps

In low-pressure sodium (LPS) lamps, light is generated by a current applied to sodium vapor at a lower pressure than in an HPS lamp.

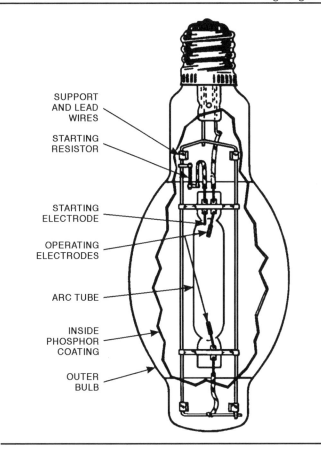

SUPPORT AND LEAD WIRES
STARTING RESISTOR
STARTING ELECTRODE
OPERATING ELECTRODES
ARC TUBE
INSIDE PHOSPHOR COATING
OUTER BULB

Fig. 9. Diagram of a mercury lamp; metal halide lamps have similar construction.

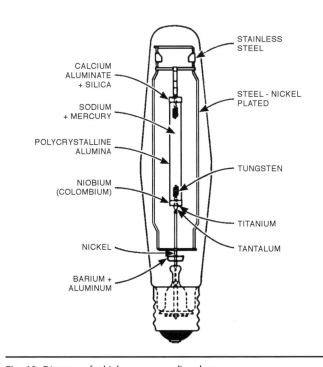

CALCIUM ALUMINATE + SILICA
SODIUM + MERCURY
POLYCRYSTALLINE ALUMINA
NIOBIUM (COLOMBIUM)
NICKEL
BARIUM + ALUMINUM
STAINLESS STEEL
STEEL - NICKEL PLATED
TUNGSTEN
TITANIUM
TANTALUM

Fig. 10. Diagram of a high-pressure sodium lamp.

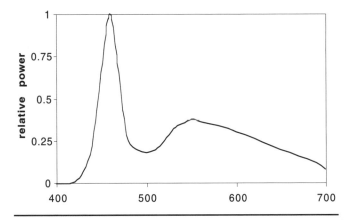

Fig. 11. Spectral power distribution of a white LED.

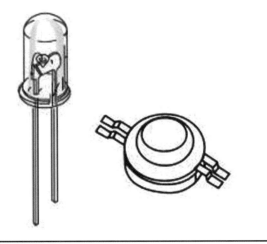

Fig. 12. LED packages (not to scale): indicator-type (left), illuminator-type (right). Adapted from National Lighting Product Information Program.

The lamp shape is also different (more linear), since the arc itself is longer. These lamps emit a very narrow wavelength band of light near 589 nm and produce light that is yellow in appearance. Ballasts are required for operation of these lamps. They have typical rated lives of approximately 16,000 hours.

LPS lamps have very high efficacy, near 180 lm/W. Because they produce monochromatic light, color rendering is essentially nonexistent with these lamps (CRI of –44). LPS lamps are sometimes used for outdoor installations in the vicinity of observatories because it is relatively simple for the astronomical observers to filter out the narrow wavelength band emitted by LPS.

Light-Emitting Diodes

First invented in the 1960s, light-emitting diodes (LEDs) have increased in efficacy, in light output, and in the range of available colors so that they are being used for a number of lighting applications. LED products presently make up the majority of the exit sign market and are rapidly transforming the traffic signal market. The development of blue LEDs that emit short-wavelength light has permitted the subsequent creation of white-light LED systems in two ways:

– combining red, green, and blue LEDs to create white light

– using phosphors together with blue LEDs that convert some of the blue light into yellow light, resulting in white light (**Fig. 11**).

Newer packages for LEDs have been developed in addition to the familiar 5-mm diameter epoxy capsule LED packages used for indicator lights (**Fig. 12**). These packages can result in wider beams than LEDs are often thought to exhibit. Some packages contain metal fins or slugs to help dissipate heat. Increased temperature inside the LED reduces its light output, and over the long term, can shorten the useful life of the source.

While LEDs have very long operating lives, typically more than 50,000 hours without failing, they do exhibit gradual reductions in light output over time. White LED indicator type packages have been shown to reach half their initial light output within 10,000 hours. Shown in **Fig. 13,** improved packages have exhibited much improved lumen depreciation characteristics (Narendran and Deng 2002).

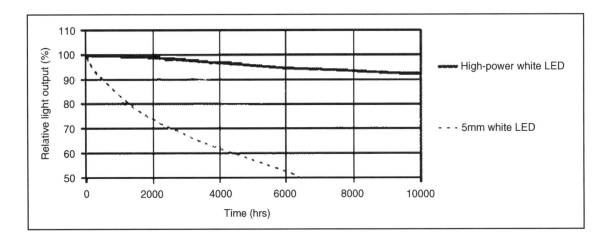

Fig. 13. Relative light output of different LED packages as a function of operating time.

Luminaires

This section briefly discusses several types of luminaires and some of their characteristics.

Interior Luminaires

The CIE has developed several categories for interior luminaires:

- direct: providing 90 to 100 percent of its luminous output downward.

- semi-direct: providing 60 to 90 percent of its output downward.

- general diffuse: providing 40 to 60 percent of its output both downward and upward.

- direct-indirect: a general diffuse luminaire with little or no output at near-horizontal angles.

- semi-indirect: providing 60 to 90 percent of its output upward.

- indirect: providing 90 to 100 percent of its luminous output upward.

Luminaires can also be classified by their physical characteristics: recessed, ceiling-mounted, track-mounted, wall-mounted, suspended, architectural, and portable luminaires such as table lamps or plug-in torchieres (**Fig. 14**). It is important to consider that luminaires in buildings contribute to the heat produced in the building and can add to the cooling load. Proper integration of the lighting and HVAC systems will result in more economical building performance.

With reference to the common interior luminaires depicted in Fig. 16, the accompanying **Box A** indicates various design-related selection criteria.

Outdoor Luminaires

For exterior luminaires, one useful classification system for characterizing a luminaire in terms of its potential for light pollution and light trespass is the *cutoff* system of the IESNA (**Fig. 15**). Many localities have begun restricting the types of luminaires that can be specified outdoors in an attempt to curb light pollution and light trespass. Applications for outdoor lighting including design to minimize "night sky light pollution" are presented in Clanton (2003).

Many outdoor luminaires use HID or LPS lamps. Outdoor fixtures include pole-mounted, surface-mounted, bollard-type, and landscape types (**Fig. 16**).

Box A—Design-Related Selection Criteria for Common Luminaire Types

	Fixture Type	Advantages	Disadvantages
a	**Recessed**	unobtrusive and out-of-the-way of space interior. many lense options. flexible wiring when used in suspended ceilings.	limited splay. can create floor area shadowing/scalloping. difficult access for maintenance if high ceilings. punctures insulated envelope if installed in top floor ceiling.
b	**Ceiling mount**	many attractive luminaires available. some luminaires will light ceiling. flexible wiring when used in suspended ceilings.	difficult access for maintenance in high ceiling application. does not use ceiling for reflector in most luminaire designs. may create veiling reflections.
c	**Track**	great flexibility for all applications.	difficult access for maintenance in high ceiling application.
d	**Wall mount**	many attractive luminaires available. recommended in lieu of puncturing insulated envelope if installed in top floor ceiling. easier access than ceiling-mount locations.	limited splay. can create "hot spot" close to wall. can create wall area shadowing/scalloping. may intrude on space (e.g., hallway/circulation). may be accessible to vandalism.
e	**Suspended**	ideal for reflected ceiling indirect lighting. many attractive luminaires available.	requires regular cleaning (dusting).
f	**Architectural molding**	ideal for architectural accents. small wattage bulbs can be used for reflective and indirect lighting. can be integrated into architectural design.	can become dust collectors. can create hot spots if not dimensioned and placed with sufficient splay and throw.

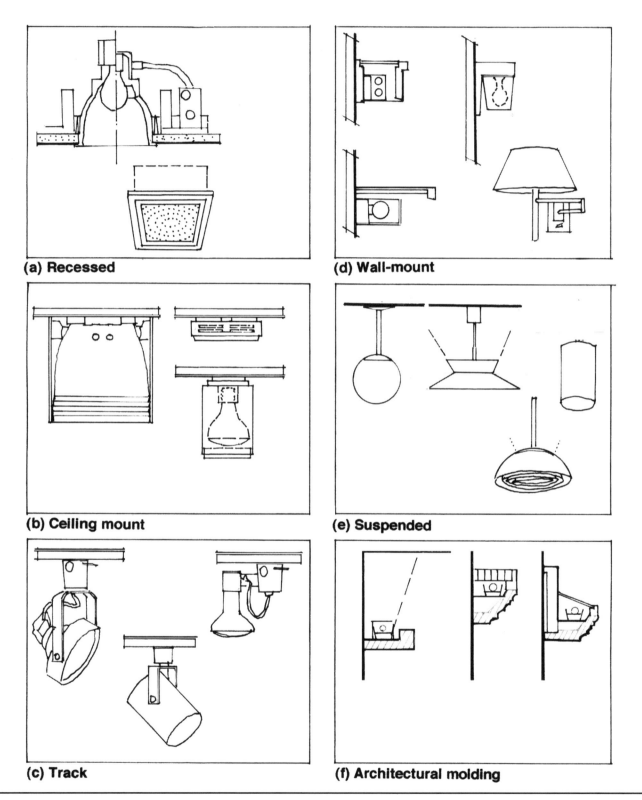

Fig. 14. Representative luminaire types: interior

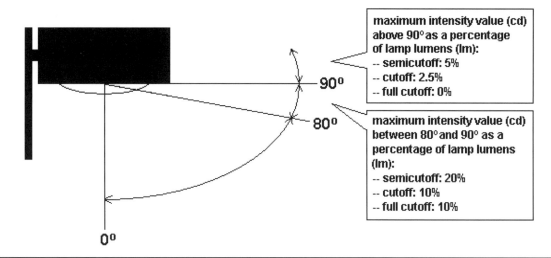

maximum intensity value (cd) above 90° as a percentage of lamp lumens (lm):
-- semicutoff: 5%
-- cutoff: 2.5%
-- full cutoff: 0%

maximum intensity value (cd) between 80° and 90° as a percentage of lamp lumens (lm):
-- semicutoff: 20%
-- cutoff: 10%
-- full cutoff: 10%

Fig. 15. Outdoor luminaire cutoff classifications. Noncutoff luminaires have no limits on luminous intensity.

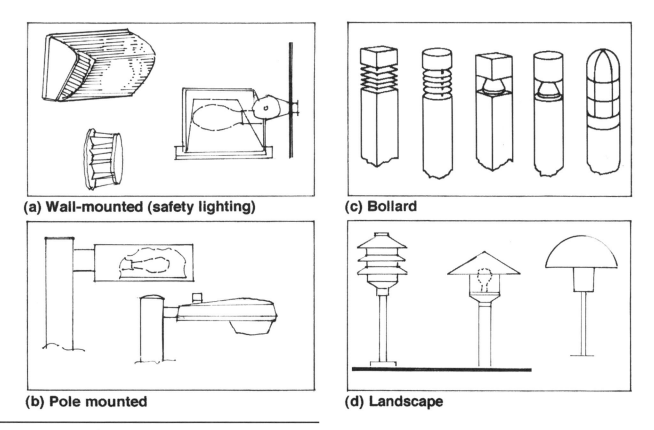

(a) Wall-mounted (safety lighting)

(b) Pole mounted

(c) Bollard

(d) Landscape

Fig. 16. Representative luminaire types: exterior

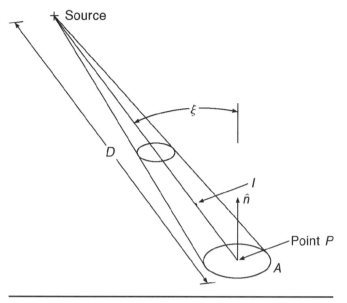

Fig. 17. Geometric arrangement for the inverse square cosine law. Adapted from IESNA *Lighting Handbook* (1993).

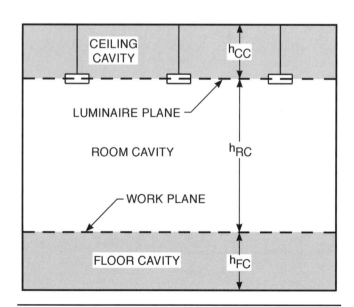

Fig. 18. Cavities used in the zonal cavity method.

3 FACTORS TO CONSIDER IN SELECTION OF LIGHTING

Lighting calculations

Ch. 9 "Lighting Calculations" of Rea (2000) describes principles and formulations that allow the specifier to predict the performance of a lighting installation. Computer programs are required to perform more complex calculations. Two methods for hand calculation useful for rough checking are detailed in the accompanying CD-ROM version of this article:

– the *inverse square cosine law* for calculating the illuminance at a point (**Fig. 17**),

– the *zonal cavity method* for estimating the average horizontal work plane illuminance in a space (**Fig. 18**).

Illuminance selection

IESNA recommends horizontal and vertical illuminances for visual tasks based on their difficulty. Generally, recommended horizontal illuminances for orientation within a location and for very simple visual tasks range between 3 and 10 fc (30 and 100 lx); for common visual tasks, recommended illuminances range between 30 and 100 fc (300 and 1000 lx). For special visual tasks where visual performance is of critical importance and where the relevant visual detail is of very small size or of very low contrast, recommended illuminances are 300 fc (3000 lx) or higher. Vertical illuminances are important because they often influence the perceptions of a space. For this reason, many recommendations include vertical as well as horizontal illuminances; these are generally one-fifth to one-third the value of the horizontal illuminance recommendation.

Table 3 lists reflectance values used for zonal cavity calculation of illuminances. **Table 4** depicts light distribution data for common luminaire types. **Table 5** lists several visual tasks and IESNA recommended illuminances.

Economic considerations

Economic concerns play a large role in the selection of a lighting system. Ch. 25 of Rea (2000), "Lighting Economics," outlines procedures for performing life-cycle cost-benefit analysis (LCCBA) recommended by IESNA.

Energy management

Approximately 20 to 25 percent of energy used in buildings is used for lighting. Since lighting contributes significantly to the cost of operating a building, energy management issues are of increasing importance.

Briefly, the elements of effective lighting energy management are:

– *Space design and utilization:* This includes the characteristics of the space that are often determined before considering the lighting system.

– *Daylighting:* The potential for effective use of daylighting should be considered early in the lighting design process (**Box B**).

Table 3. Effective ceiling cavity reflectances.

NOTE: Reflectance values are shown as two-digit numbers. For example, "64" means "0.64."

Per Cent Base* Reflectance	80								70								60								30								20								10							
Per Cent Wall Reflectance	80	70	60	50	40	30	20	10	80	70	60	50	40	30	20	10	80	70	60	50	40	30	20	10	80	70	60	50	40	30	20	10	80	70	60	50	40	30	20	10	80	70	60	50	40	30	20	10
Cavity Ratio																																																
0.2	78	78	77	77	76	76	75	74	69	68	68	67	67	66	66	65	59	59	58	57	57	56	56	55	31	30	30	29	29	29	28	28	20	20	20	20	20	20	19	19	11	11	10	10	10	10	09	09
0.4	77	76	75	74	73	72	71	70	68	67	66	65	64	63	62	61	59	59	58	57	55	54	53	52	31	30	30	29	28	28	27	26	21	20	20	19	19	19	18	18	11	11	11	10	10	10	09	09
0.6	76	75	73	71	70	68	66	65	67	65	64	63	61	59	58	57	58	57	56	55	53	51	51	50	31	30	29	28	26	26	25	25	21	21	20	19	18	18	18	17	13	12	11	11	10	10	09	08
0.8	75	73	71	69	67	65	63	61	66	64	62	60	58	56	55	53	57	56	55	54	51	48	47	46	31	30	29	28	26	25	25	23	22	21	20	19	18	17	16	16	14	13	12	10	10	09	09	08
1.0	74	72	69	67	65	62	60	57	65	62	60	58	55	53	52	50	57	55	53	51	48	45	44	43	32	30	29	27	25	24	23	22	23	22	20	19	18	16	15	15	14	13	12	11	10	09	09	08
1.2	73	70	67	64	61	58	55	53	64	61	59	57	54	50	48	46	56	54	51	49	46	44	42	40	32	30	28	25	23	22	22	21	23	22	20	19	17	16	16	14	15	14	13	12	11	10	09	07
1.4	72	68	65	62	59	55	53	50	63	60	58	55	51	47	45	44	56	53	49	47	44	41	39	38	32	30	28	24	22	21	20	19	24	22	20	18	17	15	15	13	16	14	13	12	11	09	09	07
1.6	71	67	63	60	57	53	50	47	62	59	56	53	47	45	43	41	55	52	48	45	42	39	37	35	33	29	27	23	22	20	19	18	24	22	20	18	17	15	14	13	17	15	14	12	11	09	08	07
1.8	70	66	62	58	54	50	47	44	61	58	54	51	46	42	40	38	55	51	47	44	40	37	35	33	33	29	27	23	21	19	18	17	25	23	20	18	17	15	14	12	17	15	14	13	11	09	08	06
2.0	69	64	60	56	52	48	45	41	60	56	52	49	45	40	38	36	54	50	46	43	39	35	33	31	33	29	26	22	20	18	17	16	25	23	20	18	16	13	13	11	18	16	14	13	11	09	08	06
2.2	68	63	58	54	49	45	42	38	60	55	51	48	43	38	36	34	53	49	45	42	37	34	31	29	32	29	26	24	19	17	16	15	25	23	18	16	16	14	12	10	19	16	14	13	12	10	09	06
2.4	67	61	56	52	47	43	40	36	60	54	50	46	41	37	35	32	53	48	44	41	36	32	30	27	32	29	26	23	18	16	15	14	26	23	18	16	16	14	12	10	19	17	15	13	12	10	09	06
2.6	66	60	55	50	45	41	38	34	59	54	49	45	40	35	33	30	53	48	43	39	35	31	28	26	32	29	25	23	18	16	14	14	27	23	18	16	14	11	11	09	20	17	15	13	11	09	06	06
2.8	65	59	53	48	43	39	36	32	59	53	48	43	38	33	30	28	53	47	43	38	34	29	27	24	33	29	25	23	17	15	14	13	27	23	18	15	13	11	10	09	20	18	16	13	11	09	07	05
3.0	65	58	52	47	42	37	34	30	58	52	47	42	37	32	29	27	52	46	42	37	32	28	25	23	33	29	25	22	17	15	13	12	27	23	17	15	13	11	09	09	21	18	16	14	11	09	07	05
3.2	65	57	51	45	40	35	33	28	58	51	46	40	36	31	28	25	51	45	41	36	31	27	23	22	33	29	25	22	16	14	12	12	27	23	17	15	12	11	09	09	21	18	16	13	11	09	07	05
3.4	64	56	49	44	38	34	32	27	57	50	45	39	35	29	27	24	51	45	40	35	30	26	23	20	33	29	25	22	16	14	11	11	27	23	17	15	12	10	08	09	22	18	16	13	12	10	08	05
3.6	63	54	48	43	37	32	30	25	56	49	44	38	33	28	25	22	50	44	39	34	29	25	22	19	33	29	24	21	15	13	10	10	29	23	17	15	11	10	08	09	22	19	16	14	11	09	06	04
3.8	62	53	47	41	36	31	28	24	56	49	43	37	32	27	24	21	50	43	38	33	29	24	21	19	33	28	24	21	15	13	10	10	28	23	17	15	12	10	08	06	23	19	17	14	12	10	06	04
4.0	61	53	46	40	35	30	25	22	55	48	42	36	31	26	23	20	49	42	37	32	28	23	20	18	33	28	24	21	14	12	09	09	28	23	17	14	11	09	07	06	23	20	17	14	11	09	06	04
4.2	60	52	45	39	34	29	25	21	55	47	41	35	30	25	22	19	49	42	37	32	27	22	19	17	33	28	24	20	14	12	09	09	28	23	17	14	11	09	07	06	24	20	17	14	11	09	06	04
4.4	60	51	44	38	33	28	24	20	54	46	40	34	29	24	21	18	49	42	36	31	27	22	19	16	33	28	24	20	14	11	09	09	28	24	17	14	11	08	06	05	24	20	17	14	11	08	06	04
4.6	59	50	43	37	32	27	23	19	53	45	39	33	28	24	21	17	49	41	35	30	26	21	18	16	33	28	24	20	13	10	08	08	29	24	17	14	11	08	06	04	25	20	17	14	11	08	06	04
4.8	58	49	42	36	31	26	22	18	53	45	38	32	27	23	20	16	48	41	34	29	25	21	18	15	33	28	24	20	13	10	08	08	29	24	17	13	10	08	06	04	25	20	17	14	11	08	06	04
5.0	58	48	41	35	30	25	21	18	52	44	36	31	26	22	19	16	48	40	34	28	24	20	17	14	33	28	24	19	13	11	08	08	29	24	17	13	10	08	06	04	25	20	17	14	11	08	06	04
6.0	55	44	38	31	27	22	19	15	51	41	35	28	24	19	16	13	45	37	31	25	21	17	14	11	33	27	23	18	15	11	09	06	30	24	16	13	10	08	05	04	26	21	18	14	11	08	06	03
7.0	53	41	35	28	24	19	16	12	48	38	32	26	22	17	14	11	43	35	30	24	20	15	12	09	33	26	22	17	14	10	08	05	30	24	15	12	09	07	04	03	27	21	17	13	11	08	06	03
8.0	50	38	32	25	21	17	14	11	46	35	29	23	19	15	13	08	42	33	28	22	18	13	11	08	33	26	21	16	13	09	07	04	30	23	15	12	08	06	04	03	27	21	17	13	10	07	05	03
9.0	49	36	30	23	19	15	13	10	45	33	27	21	18	14	12	09	40	31	26	20	16	12	10	07	29	25	20	15	12	09	07	04	29	23	14	11	08	06	04	03	28	21	17	13	10	07	05	02
10.0	46	33	27	21	18	14	11	08	43	31	25	19	16	12	10	08	39	29	24	18	15	11	09	07	32	24	19	14	11	08	06	03	29	22	13	10	07	05	03	02	28	21	17	12	10	07	05	02

* Ceiling, floor, or floor of cavity.

Table 4. Coefficients of utilization (CUs) and spacing-to-mounting-height ratios (S/MH) for several luminaire types

Typical Distribution and Per Cent Lamp Lumens / ρcc →		80			70			50			30			10			0
Maint. Cat.	Max S/MH Guide	RCR ↓	ρw → 50	30	10	50	30	10	50	30	10	50	30	10	50	30	10	0

Coefficients of Utilization for 20 Per Cent Effective Floor Cavity Reflectance ($\rho_{FC} = 20$)

Pendant diffusing sphere with incandescent lamp — Maint. Cat. V, Maximum S/MH Guide 1.5 (35½% ↑, 45% ↓)

RCR	80/50	80/30	80/10	70/50	70/30	70/10	50/50	50/30	50/10	30/50	30/30	30/10	10/50	10/30	10/10	0/0
0	.87	.87	.87	.81	.81	.81	.69	.69	.69	.59	.59	.59	.49	.49	.49	.44
1	.71	.67	.63	.66	.62	.59	.56	.53	.50	.47	.45	.43	.39	.37	.35	.31
2	.61	.54	.49	.56	.50	.46	.47	.43	.39	.39	.36	.33	.32	.29	.27	.23
3	.52	.45	.39	.48	.42	.37	.41	.36	.31	.34	.30	.26	.27	.24	.22	.18
4	.46	.38	.33	.42	.36	.30	.36	.30	.26	.30	.26	.22	.24	.21	.18	.15
5	.40	.33	.27	.37	.30	.25	.32	.26	.22	.26	.22	.19	.21	.18	.15	.12
6	.36	.28	.23	.33	.26	.21	.28	.23	.19	.23	.19	.16	.19	.15	.13	.10
7	.32	.25	.20	.29	.23	.18	.25	.20	.16	.21	.16	.13	.17	.13	.11	.09
8	.29	.22	.17	.27	.20	.16	.23	.17	.14	.19	.15	.12	.15	.12	.09	.07
9	.26	.19	.15	.24	.18	.14	.20	.15	.12	.17	.13	.10	.14	.11	.08	.06
10	.23	.17	.13	.22	.16	.12	.19	.14	.10	.16	.12	.09	.13	.09	.07	.05

Concentric-ring unit with incandescent silvered-bowl lamp — Maint. Cat. II, Maximum S/MH Guide 1.5 (83% ↑, 3½% ↓)

RCR	80/50	80/30	80/10	70/50	70/30	70/10	50/50	50/30	50/10	30/50	30/30	30/10	10/50	10/30	10/10	0/0
0	.83	.83	.83	.71	.71	.71	.49	.49	.49	.30	.30	.30	.12	.12	.12	.03
1	.72	.69	.66	.62	.60	.57	.43	.42	.40	.26	.25	.25	.10	.10	.10	.03
2	.63	.58	.54	.54	.50	.47	.38	.36	.33	.23	.22	.21	.09	.09	.08	.02
3	.55	.49	.45	.48	.43	.39	.33	.30	.28	.20	.19	.17	.08	.08	.07	.02
4	.48	.42	.37	.42	.37	.33	.29	.26	.24	.18	.16	.15	.07	.07	.06	.02
5	.43	.36	.32	.37	.32	.28	.26	.23	.20	.16	.14	.13	.06	.06	.05	.01
6	.38	.32	.27	.33	.28	.24	.23	.20	.17	.14	.12	.11	.06	.05	.04	.01
7	.34	.28	.23	.30	.24	.21	.21	.17	.15	.13	.11	.09	.05	.04	.04	.01
8	.31	.25	.20	.27	.21	.18	.19	.15	.13	.12	.10	.08	.05	.04	.03	.01
9	.28	.22	.18	.24	.19	.16	.17	.14	.11	.10	.09	.07	.04	.03	.03	.01
10	.25	.20	.16	.22	.17	.14	.16	.12	.10	.10	.08	.06	.04	.03	.03	.01

Porcelain-enameled ventilated standard dome with incandescent lamp — Maint. Cat. IV, Maximum S/MH Guide 1.3 (0% ↑, 83½% ↓)

RCR	80/50	80/30	80/10	70/50	70/30	70/10	50/50	50/30	50/10	30/50	30/30	30/10	10/50	10/30	10/10	0/0
0	.99	.99	.99	.97	.97	.97	.92	.92	.92	.88	.88	.88	.85	.85	.85	.83
1	.88	.85	.82	.86	.83	.81	.83	.80	.78	.79	.78	.76	.77	.75	.73	.72
2	.78	.73	.68	.76	.72	.67	.73	.69	.66	.71	.67	.64	.68	.65	.63	.61
3	.69	.62	.57	.67	.61	.57	.65	.60	.56	.63	.58	.55	.61	.57	.54	.52
4	.61	.54	.49	.60	.53	.48	.58	.52	.48	.56	.51	.47	.54	.50	.46	.45
5	.54	.47	.41	.53	.46	.41	.51	.45	.41	.50	.44	.40	.48	.43	.40	.38
6	.48	.41	.35	.47	.40	.35	.46	.39	.35	.44	.39	.34	.43	.38	.34	.32
7	.43	.35	.30	.42	.35	.30	.41	.34	.30	.39	.34	.30	.38	.33	.29	.28
8	.38	.31	.26	.38	.31	.26	.37	.30	.26	.36	.30	.26	.35	.30	.26	.24
9	.35	.28	.23	.34	.27	.23	.33	.27	.23	.32	.27	.23	.31	.26	.22	.21
10	.31	.25	.20	.31	.24	.20	.30	.24	.20	.29	.24	.20	.29	.23	.20	.18

Prismatic square surface drum — Maint. Cat. V, Maximum S/MH Guide 1.3 (18½% ↑, 60½% ↓)

RCR	80/50	80/30	80/10	70/50	70/30	70/10	50/50	50/30	50/10	30/50	30/30	30/10	10/50	10/30	10/10	0/0
0	.89	.89	.89	.85	.85	.85	.77	.77	.77	.70	.70	.70	.63	.63	.63	.60
1	.78	.75	.72	.74	.72	.69	.68	.66	.64	.62	.60	.58	.56	.55	.54	.51
2	.69	.65	.61	.66	.62	.58	.61	.57	.54	.56	.53	.50	.51	.49	.47	.44
3	.62	.57	.52	.60	.55	.50	.55	.51	.47	.50	.47	.44	.46	.44	.41	.39
4	.56	.50	.46	.54	.49	.44	.50	.45	.42	.46	.42	.39	.42	.39	.37	.35
5	.51	.45	.40	.49	.43	.39	.45	.41	.37	.42	.38	.35	.39	.36	.33	.31
6	.46	.40	.36	.45	.39	.35	.42	.37	.33	.39	.35	.31	.36	.32	.30	.28
7	.42	.36	.32	.41	.35	.31	.38	.33	.29	.35	.31	.28	.33	.29	.27	.25
8	.39	.32	.28	.37	.32	.28	.35	.30	.26	.32	.28	.25	.30	.27	.24	.22
9	.35	.29	.25	.34	.29	.25	.32	.27	.24	.30	.26	.23	.28	.24	.22	.20
10	.32	.27	.23	.31	.26	.22	.29	.25	.21	.27	.23	.20	.26	.22	.20	.18

R-40 flood without shielding — Maint. Cat. IV, Maximum S/MH Guide 0.8 (0% ↑, 100% ↓)

RCR	80/50	80/30	80/10	70/50	70/30	70/10	50/50	50/30	50/10	30/50	30/30	30/10	10/50	10/30	10/10	0/0
0	1.18	1.18	1.18	1.16	1.16	1.16	1.11	1.11	1.11	1.06	1.06	1.06	1.01	1.01	1.01	.99
1	1.09	1.07	1.04	1.07	1.05	1.02	1.03	1.01	.99	.99	.98	.96	.96	.95	.94	.92
2	1.01	.97	.93	.99	.95	.92	.96	.93	.90	.93	.90	.88	.90	.88	.86	.84
3	.93	.88	.84	.92	.87	.83	.89	.85	.81	.87	.83	.80	.84	.82	.79	.77
4	.87	.81	.76	.85	.80	.75	.83	.78	.75	.81	.77	.74	.79	.76	.73	.71
5	.80	.74	.69	.79	.73	.69	.77	.72	.68	.76	.71	.67	.74	.70	.67	.65
6	.74	.68	.63	.73	.67	.63	.72	.66	.62	.70	.66	.62	.69	.65	.61	.60
7	.69	.62	.57	.68	.62	.57	.67	.61	.57	.65	.60	.56	.64	.60	.56	.55
8	.64	.57	.53	.63	.57	.52	.62	.56	.52	.61	.56	.52	.60	.55	.52	.50
9	.59	.52	.48	.59	.52	.48	.58	.52	.48	.57	.51	.48	.56	.51	.47	.46
10	.55	.49	.44	.55	.48	.44	.54	.48	.44	.53	.48	.44	.52	.47	.44	.42

[a] ρcc = per cent effective ceiling cavity reflectance.
[b] ρw = per cent wall reflectance.
[c] RCR = Room Cavity Ratio.
[d] Maximum S/MH guide—ratio of maximum luminaire spacing to mounting or ceiling height above work-plane.

Table 4. Coefficients of utilization (CUs) and spacing-to-mounting-height ratios (S/MH) for several luminaire types (continued)

Typical Luminaire	Maint. Cat.	Maximum S/MH Guide[d]	RCR[c]	ρ_{cc}[a] → 80 (50)	80 (30)	80 (10)	70 (50)	70 (30)	70 (10)	50 (50)	50 (30)	50 (10)	30 (50)	30 (30)	30 (10)	10 (50)	10 (30)	10 (10)	0 (0)
R-40 flood with specular anodized reflector skirt; 45° cutoff (0% ↑, 85% ↓)	IV	0.7	0	1.00	1.00	1.00	.98	.98	.98	.94	.94	.94	.90	.90	.90	.86	.86	.86	.84
			1	.96	.94	.92	.94	.92	.91	.90	.89	.88	.87	.86	.85	.84	.84	.83	.82
			2	.91	.88	.86	.90	.87	.85	.87	.85	.83	.84	.83	.82	.82	.81	.80	.79
			3	.87	.84	.81	.86	.83	.81	.84	.81	.79	.82	.80	.78	.80	.78	.77	.76
			4	.83	.80	.77	.82	.79	.77	.81	.78	.76	.79	.77	.75	.78	.76	.74	.73
			5	.79	.76	.73	.79	.75	.73	.77	.74	.72	.76	.73	.71	.75	.73	.71	.70
			6	.76	.73	.70	.76	.72	.70	.75	.72	.69	.74	.71	.69	.73	.70	.68	.67
			7	.73	.69	.66	.73	.69	.66	.72	.68	.66	.71	.68	.66	.70	.67	.65	.64
			8	.70	.66	.63	.70	.66	.63	.69	.65	.63	.68	.65	.63	.67	.65	.63	.62
			9	.67	.63	.60	.67	.63	.60	.66	.62	.60	.65	.62	.60	.65	.62	.60	.59
			10	.64	.60	.58	.64	.60	.58	.63	.60	.58	.63	.60	.57	.62	.59	.57	.56
Reflector downlight with baffles and inside frosted lamp (0% ↑, 44½% ↓)	IV	0.7	0	.53	.53	.53	.52	.52	.52	.49	.49	.49	.47	.47	.47	.45	.45	.45	.44
			1	.51	.50	.49	.50	.49	.48	.48	.47	.47	.46	.46	.45	.45	.44	.44	.43
			2	.48	.47	.46	.48	.46	.45	.46	.45	.44	.45	.44	.44	.44	.43	.43	.42
			3	.47	.45	.44	.46	.45	.43	.45	.44	.43	.44	.43	.42	.43	.42	.41	.41
			4	.45	.43	.42	.44	.43	.42	.43	.42	.41	.43	.41	.41	.42	.41	.40	.40
			5	.43	.41	.40	.43	.41	.40	.42	.40	.39	.41	.40	.39	.41	.40	.39	.38
			6	.42	.40	.39	.41	.40	.38	.41	.39	.38	.40	.39	.38	.40	.39	.38	.37
			7	.40	.38	.37	.40	.38	.37	.39	.38	.37	.39	.38	.37	.38	.37	.36	.36
			8	.39	.37	.36	.38	.37	.36	.38	.37	.35	.38	.36	.35	.37	.36	.35	.35
			9	.37	.36	.34	.37	.35	.34	.37	.35	.34	.36	.35	.34	.36	.35	.34	.33
			10	.36	.34	.33	.36	.34	.33	.36	.34	.33	.35	.34	.33	.35	.34	.33	.32
Wide-distribution unit with lens plate and inside frost lamp (0% ↑, 53½% ↓)	V	1.4	0	.63	.63	.63	.62	.62	.62	.59	.59	.59	.56	.56	.56	.54	.54	.54	.53
			1	.58	.56	.54	.57	.55	.54	.54	.53	.52	.52	.51	.50	.50	.50	.49	.48
			2	.53	.50	.48	.52	.49	.47	.50	.48	.46	.48	.47	.45	.47	.45	.44	.43
			3	.48	.45	.42	.47	.44	.42	.46	.43	.41	.44	.42	.40	.43	.41	.40	.39
			4	.44	.40	.37	.43	.40	.37	.42	.39	.37	.41	.38	.36	.40	.38	.36	.35
			5	.40	.36	.33	.39	.36	.33	.38	.35	.33	.37	.35	.32	.36	.34	.32	.31
			6	.36	.32	.30	.36	.32	.29	.35	.32	.29	.34	.31	.29	.33	.31	.29	.28
			7	.33	.29	.26	.33	.29	.26	.32	.28	.26	.31	.28	.26	.30	.28	.26	.25
			8	.30	.26	.23	.30	.26	.23	.29	.26	.23	.29	.25	.23	.28	.25	.23	.22
			9	.27	.23	.21	.27	.23	.21	.26	.23	.21	.26	.23	.20	.25	.22	.20	.19
			10	.25	.21	.18	.25	.21	.18	.24	.21	.18	.24	.20	.18	.23	.20	.18	.17
Recessed unit with dropped diffusing glass (1½% ↑, 50½% ↓)	V	1.3	0	.61	.61	.61	.60	.60	.60	.57	.57	.57	.54	.54	.54	.51	.51	.51	.50
			1	.53	.51	.48	.52	.50	.47	.49	.47	.46	.47	.45	.44	.45	.44	.42	.41
			2	.46	.42	.39	.45	.42	.39	.43	.40	.38	.41	.39	.37	.39	.37	.35	.34
			3	.40	.36	.33	.40	.35	.32	.38	.34	.31	.36	.33	.31	.35	.32	.30	.29
			4	.36	.31	.28	.35	.31	.28	.34	.30	.27	.32	.29	.26	.31	.28	.26	.25
			5	.32	.27	.24	.31	.27	.24	.30	.26	.23	.29	.25	.23	.28	.25	.22	.21
			6	.29	.24	.20	.28	.24	.20	.27	.23	.20	.26	.22	.20	.25	.22	.19	.18
			7	.26	.21	.18	.25	.21	.18	.24	.20	.17	.23	.20	.17	.22	.19	.17	.16
			8	.23	.19	.16	.23	.18	.15	.22	.18	.15	.21	.18	.15	.20	.17	.15	.14
			9	.21	.17	.14	.21	.16	.14	.20	.16	.13	.19	.16	.13	.19	.15	.13	.12
			10	.19	.15	.12	.19	.15	.12	.18	.14	.12	.18	.14	.12	.17	.14	.12	.11
Intermediate-distribution ventilated reflector with clear HID lamp (1% ↑, 76% ↓)	III	1.0	0	.91	.91	.91	.89	.89	.89	.84	.84	.84	.81	.81	.81	.77	.77	.77	.75
			1	.84	.81	.79	.82	.80	.78	.79	.77	.76	.76	.74	.73	.73	.72	.71	.69
			2	.77	.73	.70	.76	.72	.70	.73	.70	.68	.70	.68	.66	.68	.66	.65	.63
			3	.71	.66	.63	.69	.65	.62	.67	.64	.61	.65	.62	.60	.63	.61	.59	.57
			4	.65	.60	.56	.64	.59	.56	.62	.58	.55	.60	.57	.54	.59	.56	.54	.52
			5	.59	.54	.50	.59	.54	.50	.57	.53	.50	.56	.52	.49	.54	.51	.48	.47
			6	.54	.49	.45	.54	.49	.45	.52	.48	.45	.51	.47	.44	.50	.47	.44	.42
			7	.50	.44	.40	.49	.44	.40	.48	.43	.40	.47	.43	.39	.46	.42	.39	.38
			8	.45	.40	.36	.45	.40	.36	.44	.39	.36	.43	.39	.35	.42	.38	.35	.34
			9	.41	.36	.32	.41	.36	.32	.40	.35	.32	.39	.35	.32	.38	.35	.32	.30
			10	.38	.33	.29	.37	.32	.29	.37	.32	.29	.36	.32	.29	.35	.31	.28	.27

Coefficients of Utilization for 20 Per Cent Effective Floor Cavity Reflectance ($\rho_{FC} = 20$)

[a] ρ_{cc} = per cent effective ceiling cavity reflectance.
[b] ρ_w = per cent wall reflectance.
[c] RCR = Room Cavity Ratio.
[d] Maximum *S/MH* guide—ratio of maximum luminaire spacing to mounting or ceiling height above work-plane.

Table 4. Coefficients of utilization (CUs) and spacing-to-mounting-height ratios (S/MH) for several luminaire types (continued)

Typical Luminaire	Typical Distribution and Per Cent Lamp Lumens	Maint. Cat.	Maximum S/MH Guide	RCR ↓	ρ_{cc} → 80			70			50			30			10			0
				ρ_w →	50	30	10	50	30	10	50	30	10	50	30	10	50	30	10	0
Intermediate-distribution ventilated reflector with phosphor-coated (HID) lamp	6½% ↑ 75½% ↓	III	1.0	0	.96	.96	.96	.93	.93	.93	.87	.87	.87	.82	.82	.82	.77	.77	.77	.75
				1	.89	.87	.84	.86	.84	.83	.82	.80	.79	.78	.76	.75	.74	.73	.72	.70
				2	.82	.79	.76	.80	.77	.74	.76	.74	.72	.73	.71	.69	.70	.68	.67	.65
				3	.76	.72	.68	.74	.70	.67	.71	.68	.65	.68	.66	.63	.66	.63	.61	.60
				4	.70	.66	.62	.69	.65	.61	.66	.63	.60	.64	.61	.58	.62	.59	.57	.55
				5	.65	.60	.56	.64	.59	.56	.62	.58	.54	.60	.56	.53	.58	.55	.52	.51
				6	.60	.55	.51	.59	.55	.51	.57	.53	.50	.56	.52	.49	.54	.51	.48	.47
				7	.56	.51	.47	.55	.50	.46	.53	.49	.46	.52	.48	.45	.50	.47	.44	.43
				8	.52	.47	.43	.51	.46	.43	.50	.45	.42	.48	.44	.41	.47	.43	.41	.40
				9	.48	.43	.39	.47	.42	.39	.46	.42	.39	.45	.41	.38	.44	.40	.38	.36
				10	.45	.40	.36	.44	.39	.36	.43	.39	.36	.42	.38	.35	.41	.37	.35	.34
Porcelain-enameled reflector with 35°CW shielding	22½% ↑ 65% ↓	II	1.3	0	.99	.99	.99	.94	.94	.94	.84	.84	.84	.76	.76	.76	.68	.68	.68	.65
				1	.88	.85	.82	.84	.81	.78	.76	.74	.72	.69	.67	.66	.62	.61	.60	.57
				2	.78	.73	.68	.74	.70	.66	.68	.64	.61	.62	.59	.56	.56	.54	.52	.49
				3	.69	.63	.58	.66	.61	.56	.61	.56	.53	.56	.52	.49	.51	.48	.46	.43
				4	.62	.55	.50	.60	.53	.49	.55	.50	.46	.50	.46	.43	.46	.43	.40	.37
				5	.55	.48	.43	.53	.47	.42	.49	.44	.39	.45	.41	.37	.41	.38	.35	.32
				6	.50	.43	.38	.48	.41	.37	.44	.39	.35	.41	.36	.33	.37	.34	.31	.29
				7	.45	.38	.33	.43	.37	.32	.40	.34	.30	.37	.32	.29	.34	.30	.27	.25
				8	.40	.34	.29	.39	.32	.28	.36	.30	.27	.33	.28	.25	.31	.27	.24	.22
				9	.36	.30	.25	.35	.29	.24	.32	.27	.23	.30	.25	.22	.28	.24	.21	.19
				10	.33	.27	.22	.32	.26	.22	.29	.24	.20	.27	.23	.19	.25	.21	.18	.17
Diffuse aluminum reflector with 35°CW x 35°LW shielding	17% ↑ 56½% ↓	II	1.5/1.1	0	.83	.83	.83	.79	.79	.79	.71	.71	.71	.65	.65	.65	.59	.59	.59	.56
				1	.75	.72	.70	.72	.69	.68	.65	.64	.62	.60	.59	.58	.55	.54	.53	.50
				2	.67	.63	.60	.65	.61	.58	.59	.57	.54	.55	.53	.51	.50	.49	.47	.45
				3	.61	.56	.52	.58	.54	.51	.54	.50	.48	.50	.47	.45	.46	.44	.42	.40
				4	.55	.49	.45	.53	.48	.44	.49	.45	.42	.45	.42	.40	.42	.39	.37	.36
				5	.49	.44	.40	.47	.42	.39	.44	.40	.37	.41	.38	.35	.38	.35	.33	.31
				6	.45	.39	.35	.43	.38	.34	.40	.36	.33	.37	.34	.31	.35	.32	.30	.28
				7	.40	.35	.31	.39	.34	.30	.36	.32	.29	.34	.30	.27	.32	.29	.26	.25
				8	.36	.31	.27	.35	.30	.26	.33	.28	.25	.31	.27	.24	.29	.25	.23	.21
				9	.33	.27	.23	.32	.26	.23	.29	.25	.22	.28	.24	.21	.26	.22	.20	.19
				10	.30	.24	.21	.29	.24	.20	.27	.22	.19	.25	.21	.19	.23	.20	.18	.16
1-ft (300 mm)-wide aluminum troffer with 40°CW x 45°LW shielding and single extra-high-output lamp	0% ↑ 42½% ↓	IV	1.1/0.8	0	.50	.50	.50	.49	.49	.49	.47	.47	.47	.45	.45	.45	.43	.43	.43	.42
				1	.46	.45	.44	.45	.44	.43	.44	.43	.42	.42	.41	.41	.41	.40	.40	.39
				2	.43	.41	.39	.42	.40	.38	.40	.39	.38	.39	.38	.37	.38	.37	.36	.35
				3	.39	.37	.35	.39	.36	.34	.37	.35	.34	.36	.35	.33	.35	.34	.33	.32
				4	.36	.33	.31	.35	.33	.31	.35	.32	.31	.34	.32	.30	.33	.31	.30	.29
				5	.33	.30	.28	.33	.30	.28	.32	.29	.28	.31	.29	.27	.30	.29	.27	.26
				6	.31	.28	.26	.30	.28	.26	.30	.27	.25	.29	.27	.25	.28	.26	.25	.24
				7	.28	.25	.23	.28	.25	.23	.27	.25	.23	.27	.25	.23	.26	.24	.23	.22
				8	.26	.23	.21	.26	.23	.21	.25	.23	.21	.25	.23	.21	.24	.22	.21	.20
				9	.24	.21	.19	.24	.21	.19	.23	.21	.19	.23	.20	.19	.22	.20	.19	.18
				10	.22	.19	.17	.22	.19	.17	.21	.19	.17	.21	.19	.17	.21	.19	.17	.16
Prismatic bottom and sides, open top, 4 lamp suspended unit—multiply by 1.05 for 2 lamps	33% ↑ 50% ↓	VI	1.4/1.2	0	.90	.90	.90	.84	.84	.84	.73	.73	.73	.63	.63	.63	.54	.54	.54	.49
				1	.80	.77	.74	.75	.73	.70	.66	.64	.62	.57	.56	.54	.49	.48	.47	.43
				2	.71	.66	.62	.67	.63	.59	.59	.56	.53	.51	.49	.47	.44	.43	.41	.38
				3	.63	.58	.53	.60	.55	.50	.53	.49	.45	.46	.43	.41	.40	.38	.36	.33
				4	.57	.50	.46	.53	.48	.43	.47	.43	.39	.41	.38	.35	.36	.34	.32	.29
				5	.50	.44	.39	.48	.42	.37	.42	.38	.34	.37	.34	.31	.33	.30	.28	.25
				6	.45	.39	.34	.43	.37	.33	.38	.33	.30	.34	.30	.27	.30	.27	.24	.22
				7	.41	.34	.30	.39	.33	.28	.34	.30	.26	.30	.27	.24	.27	.24	.21	.19
				8	.37	.30	.26	.35	.29	.25	.31	.26	.23	.27	.24	.21	.24	.21	.19	.17
				9	.33	.27	.22	.31	.26	.22	.28	.23	.20	.25	.21	.18	.22	.19	.16	.15
				10	.30	.24	.20	.28	.23	.19	.25	.21	.18	.23	.19	.16	.20	.17	.14	.13

Coefficients of Utilization for 20 Per Cent Effective Floor Cavity Reflectance ($\rho_{FC} = 20$)

[a] ρ_{cc} = per cent effective ceiling cavity reflectance.
[b] ρ_w = per cent wall reflectance.
[c] RCR = Room Cavity Ratio.
[d] Maximum S/MH guide--ratio of maximum luminaire spacing to mounting or ceiling height above work-plane.

Table 4. Coefficients of utilization (CUs) and spacing-to-mounting-height ratios (S/MH) for several luminaire types (continued)

Coefficients of Utilization for 20 Per Cent Effective Floor Cavity Reflectance ($\rho_{FC} = 20$)

Column headers: ρ_{cc} [a] → and ρ_w [b] →

	80			70			50			30			10			0
RCR [c]	50	30	10	50	30	10	50	30	10	50	30	10	50	30	10	0

2-lamp prismatic wraparound — multiply by 0.95 for 4 lamps — Maint. Cat. V — Maximum S/MH Guide [d] 1.5/1.2 — $11\frac{1}{2}\%$ ↑ / $58\frac{1}{2}\%$ ↓

RCR	50	30	10	50	30	10	50	30	10	50	30	10	50	30	10	0
0	.80	.80	.80	.77	.77	.77	.71	.71	.71	.66	.66	.66	.60	.60	.60	.58
1	.71	.69	.66	.69	.66	.64	.64	.62	.60	.59	.58	.56	.55	.54	.53	.50
2	.64	.59	.56	.61	.58	.54	.57	.54	.51	.53	.51	.49	.49	.48	.46	.44
3	.57	.52	.48	.55	.50	.47	.51	.48	.45	.48	.45	.42	.45	.42	.40	.38
4	.51	.46	.41	.49	.44	.40	.46	.42	.39	.43	.40	.37	.41	.38	.35	.34
5	.46	.40	.36	.44	.39	.35	.41	.37	.34	.39	.35	.32	.37	.33	.31	.29
6	.41	.35	.31	.40	.35	.31	.38	.33	.30	.35	.31	.28	.33	.30	.27	.26
7	.37	.31	.27	.36	.31	.27	.34	.29	.26	.32	.28	.25	.30	.27	.24	.23
8	.33	.28	.24	.32	.27	.23	.30	.26	.22	.29	.25	.22	.27	.24	.21	.19
9	.30	.24	.20	.29	.24	.20	.27	.23	.19	.26	.22	.19	.24	.21	.18	.17
10	.27	.22	.18	.26	.21	.18	.25	.20	.17	.23	.19	.16	.22	.18	.16	.15

2-lamp white diffuse wraparound — multiply by 0.90 for 4 lamps — Maint. Cat. V — Maximum S/MH Guide 1.3 — 8% ↑ / $37\frac{1}{2}\%$ ↓

RCR	50	30	10	50	30	10	50	30	10	50	30	10	50	30	10	0
0	.52	.52	.52	.50	.50	.50	.46	.46	.46	.42	.42	.42	.39	.39	.39	.37
1	.45	.43	.41	.43	.41	.39	.40	.38	.37	.36	.35	.34	.34	.33	.32	.30
2	.39	.35	.33	.37	.34	.32	.34	.32	.30	.32	.30	.28	.29	.28	.26	.25
3	.34	.30	.27	.33	.29	.26	.30	.27	.25	.28	.25	.23	.26	.24	.22	.21
4	.30	.26	.23	.29	.25	.22	.27	.24	.21	.25	.22	.20	.23	.21	.19	.18
5	.26	.22	.19	.25	.21	.19	.23	.20	.18	.22	.19	.17	.20	.18	.16	.15
6	.23	.19	.16	.23	.19	.16	.21	.18	.15	.19	.17	.14	.18	.16	.14	.13
7	.21	.17	.14	.20	.16	.14	.19	.16	.13	.17	.15	.13	.16	.14	.12	.11
8	.19	.15	.12	.18	.14	.12	.17	.14	.11	.16	.13	.11	.15	.12	.10	.09
9	.17	.13	.10	.16	.13	.10	.15	.12	.10	.14	.11	.09	.13	.11	.09	.08
10	.15	.12	.09	.15	.11	.09	.14	.11	.09	.13	.10	.08	.12	.10	.08	.07

2-lamp, 1' (300 mm)-wide troffer with 45° plastic louver — multiply by 0.90 for 3 lamps — Maint. Cat. IV — Maximum S/MH Guide 1.0 — 0% ↑ / 46% ↓

RCR	50	30	10	50	30	10	50	30	10	50	30	10	50	30	10	0
0	.54	.54	.54	.53	.53	.53	.51	.51	.51	.48	.48	.48	.46	.46	.46	.45
1	.49	.48	.46	.48	.47	.46	.46	.45	.44	.45	.44	.43	.43	.42	.42	.41
2	.44	.42	.40	.43	.41	.39	.42	.40	.38	.40	.39	.37	.39	.38	.37	.36
3	.40	.37	.34	.39	.36	.34	.38	.36	.34	.37	.35	.33	.36	.34	.33	.32
4	.36	.33	.30	.36	.32	.30	.35	.32	.30	.34	.31	.29	.33	.31	.29	.28
5	.33	.29	.26	.32	.29	.26	.31	.28	.26	.30	.28	.26	.30	.27	.26	.25
6	.30	.26	.24	.29	.26	.24	.29	.26	.23	.28	.25	.23	.27	.25	.23	.22
7	.27	.24	.21	.27	.23	.21	.26	.23	.21	.26	.23	.21	.25	.22	.21	.20
8	.25	.21	.19	.24	.21	.19	.24	.21	.19	.23	.21	.18	.23	.20	.18	.18
9	.22	.19	.17	.22	.19	.17	.22	.19	.17	.21	.18	.16	.21	.18	.16	.16
10	.21	.17	.15	.20	.17	.15	.20	.17	.15	.20	.17	.15	.19	.17	.15	.14

4-lamp, 2' (610 mm)-wide troffer with 45° plastic louver — multiply by 1.05 for 2 lamps and 0.95 for 6 lamps — Maint. Cat. IV — Maximum S/MH Guide 1.0 — 0% ↑ / 50% ↓

RCR	50	30	10	50	30	10	50	30	10	50	30	10	50	30	10	0
0	.59	.59	.59	.58	.58	.58	.55	.55	.55	.53	.53	.53	.51	.51	.51	.50
1	.54	.52	.50	.52	.51	.49	.50	.49	.48	.48	.47	.46	.47	.46	.45	.44
2	.48	.45	.43	.47	.44	.42	.45	.43	.41	.44	.42	.40	.42	.41	.39	.39
3	.43	.40	.37	.42	.39	.37	.41	.38	.36	.40	.37	.36	.39	.37	.35	.34
4	.39	.35	.32	.38	.35	.32	.37	.34	.32	.36	.33	.31	.35	.33	.31	.30
5	.35	.31	.28	.35	.31	.28	.34	.30	.28	.33	.30	.28	.32	.29	.27	.26
6	.32	.28	.25	.32	.28	.25	.31	.27	.25	.30	.27	.25	.29	.26	.24	.23
7	.29	.25	.22	.29	.25	.22	.28	.25	.22	.27	.24	.22	.27	.24	.22	.21
8	.26	.22	.20	.26	.22	.20	.25	.22	.20	.25	.22	.19	.24	.21	.19	.18
9	.24	.20	.17	.24	.20	.17	.23	.20	.17	.23	.19	.17	.22	.19	.17	.16
10	.22	.18	.16	.22	.18	.16	.21	.18	.16	.21	.18	.15	.20	.17	.15	.15

Fluorescent unit with dropped white diffuser, 4-lamp 2' (610 mm)-wide — multiply by 1.10 for 2 lamps and 0.90 for 6 lamps — Maint. Cat. V — Maximum S/MH Guide 1.2 — 1% ↑ / $60\frac{1}{2}\%$ ↓

RCR	50	30	10	50	30	10	50	30	10	50	30	10	50	30	10	0
0	.72	.72	.72	.70	.70	.70	.67	.67	.67	.64	.64	.64	.61	.61	.61	.60
1	.64	.61	.59	.62	.60	.58	.60	.58	.56	.57	.56	.54	.55	.54	.52	.51
2	.56	.52	.49	.55	.51	.48	.52	.49	.47	.50	.48	.46	.48	.46	.44	.43
3	.50	.45	.41	.49	.44	.41	.47	.43	.40	.45	.42	.39	.43	.41	.38	.37
4	.44	.39	.35	.43	.38	.35	.42	.37	.34	.40	.36	.33	.39	.36	.33	.32
5	.39	.34	.30	.38	.33	.29	.37	.32	.29	.36	.32	.29	.34	.31	.28	.27
6	.35	.30	.26	.34	.29	.25	.33	.29	.25	.32	.28	.25	.31	.27	.25	.23
7	.31	.26	.22	.31	.26	.22	.30	.25	.22	.29	.25	.22	.28	.24	.22	.20
8	.28	.23	.19	.28	.23	.19	.27	.22	.19	.26	.22	.19	.25	.22	.19	.18
9	.25	.20	.17	.25	.20	.17	.24	.20	.17	.23	.19	.16	.23	.19	.16	.15
10	.23	.18	.15	.23	.18	.15	.22	.18	.15	.21	.17	.15	.21	.17	.14	.13

[a] ρ_{cc} = per cent effective ceiling cavity reflectance.
[b] ρ_w = per cent wall reflectance.
[c] RCR = Room Cavity Ratio.
[d] Maximum *S/MH* guide — ratio of maximum luminaire spacing to mounting or ceiling height above work-plane.

Table 4. Coefficients of utilization (CUs) and spacing-to-mounting-height ratios (S/MH) for several luminaire types (continued)

Typical Luminaire	Typical Distribution and Per Cent Lamp Lumens		ρcc[a] →	80			70			50			30			10			0
			ρw[b] →	50	30	10	50	30	10	50	30	10	50	30	10	50	30	10	0
	Maint. Cat.	Maximum S/MH Guide[d]	RCR[c] ↓	Coefficients of Utilization for 20 Per Cent Effective Floor Cavity Reflectance (ρFC = 20)															
Fluorescent unit with flat prismatic lens, 4 lamp 2' (610 mm)-wide—multiply by 1.10 for 2 lamp	V	1.4/1.2	0	.73	.73	.73	.72	.72	.72	.68	.68	.68	.66	.66	.66	.63	.63	.63	.62
			1	.66	.64	.62	.65	.63	.61	.62	.60	.59	.60	.58	.57	.57	.56	.55	.54
			2	.59	.55	.52	.58	.54	.52	.56	.53	.50	.54	.51	.49	.52	.50	.48	.47
			3	.53	.48	.45	.52	.48	.44	.50	.46	.44	.48	.45	.43	.47	.44	.42	.41
			4	.47	.42	.39	.46	.42	.38	.45	.41	.38	.43	.40	.37	.42	.39	.37	.36
			5	.42	.37	.33	.41	.37	.33	.40	.36	.33	.39	.35	.32	.38	.35	.32	.31
			6	.38	.33	.29	.37	.32	.29	.36	.32	.29	.35	.31	.28	.34	.31	.28	.27
			7	.34	.29	.25	.33	.29	.25	.33	.28	.25	.32	.28	.25	.31	.27	.25	.23
			8	.30	.25	.22	.30	.25	.22	.29	.25	.22	.28	.24	.21	.28	.24	.21	.20
			9	.27	.22	.19	.27	.22	.19	.26	.22	.19	.25	.21	.19	.25	.21	.18	.17
			10	.25	.20	.17	.24	.20	.16	.24	.19	.16	.23	.19	.16	.23	.19	.16	.15
Single-row fluorescent lamp cove without reflector, mult. by 0.93 for 2 rows and by 0.85 for 3 rows.			1	.42	.40	.39	.36	.35	.33	.25	.24	.23	Coves are not recommended for lighting areas having low reflectances.						
			2	.37	.34	.32	.32	.29	.27	.22	.20	.19							
			3	.32	.29	.26	.28	.25	.23	.19	.17	.16							
			4	.29	.25	.22	.25	.22	.19	.17	.15	.13							
			5	.25	.21	.18	.22	.19	.16	.15	.13	.11							
			6	.23	.19	.16	.20	.16	.14	.14	.12	.10							
			7	.20	.17	.14	.17	.14	.12	.12	.10	.09							
			8	.18	.15	.12	.16	.13	.10	.11	.09	.08							
			9	.17	.13	.10	.15	.11	.09	.10	.08	.07							
			10	.15	.12	.09	.13	.10	.08	.09	.07	.06							
Diffusing plastic or glass. **(1) Ceiling efficiency ~60%; diffuser transmittance ~50%; diffuser reflectance ~40%.** Cavity with minimum obstructions and painted with 80% reflectance paint—use ρc = 70. **(2) For lower reflectance paint or obstructions—use ρc = 50.** (ρCC from below ~65%)			1				.60	.58	.56	.58	.56	.54							
			2				.53	.49	.45	.51	.47	.43							
			3				.47	.42	.37	.45	.41	.36							
			4				.41	.36	.32	.39	.35	.31							
			5				.37	.31	.27	.35	.30	.26							
			6				.33	.27	.23	.31	.26	.23							
			7				.29	.24	.20	.28	.23	.20							
			8				.26	.21	.18	.25	.20	.17							
			9				.23	.19	.15	.23	.18	.15							
			10				.21	.17	.13	.21	.16	.13							
Prismatic plastic or glass. 1) Ceiling efficiency ~67%; prismatic transmittance ~72%; prismatic reflectance ~18%. Cavity with minimum obstructions and painted with 80% reflectance paint—use ρc = 70. 2) For lower reflectance paint or obstructions—use ρc = 50. (ρCC from below ~60%)			1				.71	.68	.66	.67	.66	.65	.65	.64	.62				
			2				.63	.60	.57	.61	.58	.55	.59	.56	.54				
			3				.57	.53	.49	.55	.52	.48	.54	.50	.47				
			4				.52	.47	.43	.50	.45	.42	.48	.44	.42				
			5				.46	.41	.37	.44	.40	.37	.43	.40	.36				
			6				.42	.37	.33	.41	.36	.32	.40	.35	.32				
			7				.38	.32	.29	.37	.31	.28	.36	.31	.28				
			8				.34	.28	.25	.33	.28	.25	.32	.28	.25				
			9				.30	.25	.22	.30	.25	.21	.29	.25	.21				
			10				.27	.23	.19	.27	.22	.19	.26	.22	.19				
Louvered ceiling. Ceiling efficiency ~50%; 45° shielding opaque louvers of 80% reflectance. Cavity with minimum obstructions and painted with 80% reflectance paint—use ρc = 50. (ρCC from below ~45%)			1							.51	.49	.48				.47	.46	.45	
			2							.46	.44	.42				.43	.42	.40	
			3							.42	.39	.37				.39	.38	.36	
			4							.38	.35	.33				.36	.34	.32	
			5							.35	.32	.29				.33	.31	.29	
			6							.32	.29	.26				.30	.28	.26	
			7							.29	.26	.23				.28	.25	.23	
			8							.27	.23	.21				.26	.23	.21	
			9							.24	.21	.19				.24	.21	.19	
			10							.22	.19	.17				.22	.19	.17	

[a] ρcc = per cent effective ceiling cavity reflectance.
[b] ρw = per cent wall reflectance.
[c] RCR = Room Cavity Ratio.
[d] Maximum S/MH guide—ratio of maximum luminaire spacing to mounting or ceiling height above work-plane.

Table 5. Illuminance categories for several types of visual tasks.
Adapted from IESNA *Lighting Handbook* (Rea 2000)

Type of Activity	Illuminance Category	Ranges of Illuminances Lux	Footcandles
Public spaces with dark surroundings	A	20 - 30 - 50	2 - 3 - 5
Simple orientation for short Temporary visits	B	50 - 75 - 100	5 - 7.5 - 10
Working spaces where visual tasks are only occasionally performed	C	100 - 150 - 200	10 - 15 - 20
Performance of visual tasks of high contrast or large size	D	200 - 300 - 500	20 - 30 - 40
Performance of visual tasks of low medium contrast or small size	E	500 - 750 - 1000	50 - 75 - 100
Performance of visual tasks of low contrast or very small size	F	1000 - 1500 - 2000	100 - 150 - 200
Performance of visual tasks of low contrast and very small size over a prolonged period	G	2000 - 3000 - 5000	200 - 300 - 500
Performance of very prolonged and exacting	H	5000 - 7500 - 10000	500 - 750 - 1000
Performance of very special visual tasks of extremely low contrast and small size	I	10000 - 15000 - 20000	1000 - 1500 - 2000

– *Light sources:* The most efficient light sources that provide the required performance characteristics should be selected.

– *Luminaires:* As with light sources, efficient luminaires should be used; interactions with HVAC should also be considered.

– *Lighting controls:* Effective lighting control strategies should be implemented early in the design process.

– *Operation and maintenance:* A planned maintenance schedule can save energy and reduce long-term operating costs.

Lighting controls

Common lighting control technologies include switching, dimming, occupancy sensors, and photosensors. Several general guidelines for implementing lighting controls are:

– Providing each room or work area with its own control switches (possibly including occupancy sensors).

– Work areas in open-plan spaces should be grouped and controlled together.

– Adjacent luminaires (or adjacent lamps within a luminaire) should be placed on separate circuits to allow multilevel lighting.

– In addition to multilevel lighting, consideration should be given to dimming.

– Lighting for specialized work areas requiring high illuminances should be placed on separate circuits from general ambient lighting.

Box B—Daylighting Potential For Perimeter Floor Area

Typically a third or more of the operational cost of most commercial building types is electricity for lighting. Across the United States, the majority of these buildings are one-story, thus the entire building floor area has the potential of being daylit by skylights or roof monitors. For taller buildings, areas near the window wall within approximately 15 ft (4.5 m) often receive daylight that can displace a significant portion of the artificial lighting energy in the area (**B**). To accomplish this, lighting fixtures need to be circuited in zones parallel to the window wall and equipped with sensors and automatic dimming controls, so that they are turned on only when available daylight is not sufficient. Perimeter windows and interior courtyards serve to dramatically increase the percentage of floor area daylit and increase electrical lighting savings.

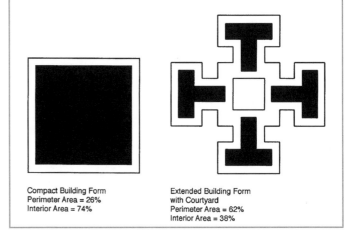

Compact Building Form
Perimeter Area = 26%
Interior Area = 74%

Extended Building Form
with Courtyard
Perimeter Area = 62%
Interior Area = 38%

– Luminaires along window walls should be controlled separately (perhaps with photosensors) so that daylight can be utilized efficiently.

Lighting codes

While this article cannot provide detailed information on lighting codes and regulations, important U.S. federal codes of which the lighting specifier should be aware are:

– The 1990 Americans with Disabilities Act (ADA), PL101-336.

– The 1992 Energy Policy Act (EPACT), PL102-486.

For example, the ADA does not permit wall-mounted objects such as luminaires to project beyond 4 in (10 cm) from the wall when they are mounted between 27 and 80 in (67 and 200 cm) from the floor in all public walkway areas such as corridors.

Emergency lighting

Emergency lighting is provided for safe egress from a building during fires or power failures. IESNA recommends that the initial minimum horizontal illuminance (on the floor) provided by emergency lighting for such conditions be at least 1 fc (10 lx) at the beginning of an emergency, and that the minimum maintained illuminance at every point along the path of egress be no less than 0.1 fc (1 lx). Higher illuminances in emergencies will likely result in faster and more confident passage through a space (Rea 2000). Additionally, high illuminances are required for such spaces as hospitals, where lighting for life-support activities is critical.

Exit signs are required in all public buildings. The National Fire Protection Association (NFPA) Life Safety Code, NFPA 101 (2003), stipulates criteria for exit sign marking and placement. One requirement is that exit signs be no more than 100 ft (30 m) apart along the path of egress.

Lighting for safety

At a minimum, the lighting in every space should be sufficient for safe working conditions, passage through a space, and identification of potential obstructions. The recommended minimum illuminances required for spaces, depending upon the degree of potential hazard and the activity level of the space, are as follows (Rea 2000):

Nonhazardous areas:

• *Low activity level:* 0.5 fc (5.4 lx)

• *High activity level:* 1 fc (11 lx)

Hazardous areas:

• *Low activity level:* 2 fc (22 lx)

• *High activity level:* 5 fc (54 lx)

Changes in elevation, such as stairways or curbs, can be considered potentially hazardous areas and must be clearly illuminated and free of obstructing shadows. Note that conditions may often require higher illuminances than the minima listed above. See Fig. 24c for an example of integrated lighting with a stair railing.

4 LIGHTING APPLICATIONS

Subsequent sections discuss lighting criteria for several common lighting applications: offices, schools, houses of worship, residences, industrial facilities, health care facilities, merchandising areas, and exterior lighting. Specific recommendations for lighting are given in Rea (2000).

Office lighting
Luminance Ratios

IESNA recommends luminance ratios that should not be exceeded in the office worker's field of view. They are specified with the goal of minimizing disability glare. The ratios are:

– Between paper task and adjacent VDT screen: 3 to 1 or 1 to 3

– Between task and adjacent surroundings: 3 to 1 or 1 to 3

– Between task and remote (nonadjacent) surfaces: 10 to 1 or 1 to 10

It is important to remember that luminance is based on the illuminance on a surface and the reflectance of that surface.

Veiling Reflections

In the office, care should be taken to avoid a situation whereby light from luminaires causes veiling reflections on specular work surfaces (glossy reading materials or a VDT screen). Luminaires should not be specified that provide high luminances within a task "offending zone" or "glare zone," shown in **Figs. 19** and **20**. Note that the location of the offending zone changes as the angle of the work plane is changed from horizontal to vertical and might be overshadowed in some positions.

Offices with VDTs

Because reflected glare on VDT screens is a potential problem in spaces containing them, IESNA recommends a maximum horizontal illuminance of 50 fc (500 lx) in office spaces with VDTs. As described above (see section entitled "Lighting and Vision"), luminaires in such spaces should not be too bright. For indirect lighting systems, the ceiling luminance does not exceed 850 cd/m^2.

School lighting
Daylighting and Glare Control in the Classroom

Care should be taken to provide sufficiently good color rendering in spaces such as art classrooms. In addition, many locations in the school use daylighting for illumination. Daylighting can:

– provide illumination for visual tasks.

– provide a relaxing distant focal point for the eyes.

– provide a psychologically pleasing view.

A glare-free and visually comfortable environment should be provided. In order to protect against glare from windows, the effective use of screens, overhangs, awnings, shades, blinds, or drapes is required to meet the luminance ratio recommendations for classrooms as depicted in **Fig. 21**.

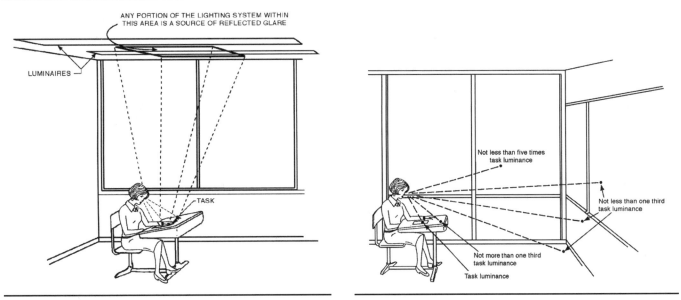

Fig. 19. Location of the "offending zone" or "glare zone" for a horizontal task such as reading at a desk.

Fig. 21. Recommended luminance ratios in the classroom.

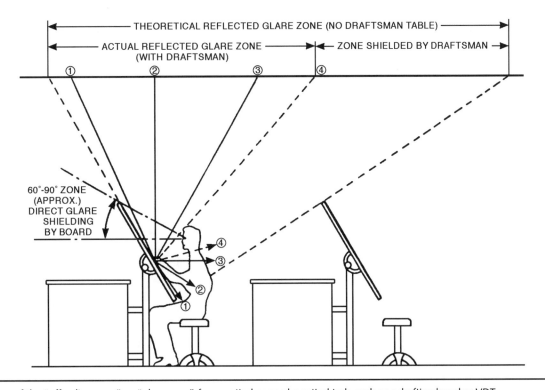

Fig. 20. Location of the "offending zone" or "glare zone" for a vertical or nearly vertical task, such as a drafting board or VDT.

Luminaire selection and arrangement in the classroom should consider the following factors:

– flexible desk arrangements and use for other activities.

– placement of the blackboard.

– location of windows.

– room geometry.

Libraries

The book stack area in the library is one of the most challenging lighting problems, because sufficient vertical illuminances must be provided between rows of shelves to read titles on the spines of books. Rows of luminaires above the aisles can be used, or when aisle placement is not known, luminaires can be oriented perpendicular to the shelves (**Fig. 22**).

Religious facilities

Proper lighting in houses of worship can enhance the religious experience of the worshippers occupying the space.

Interior Lighting

Interior lighting within the religious area serves four purposes that can be supported by up to four separate components of the lighting system. These purposes are:

– light for reading.

– accent lighting focusing on the celebrant or on religious items.

– architectural lighting to highlight building features (ceiling or walls).

– celebration lighting (candles, lanterns, and decorative elements).

For proper effect, illuminances for accent lighting (in the vertical plane) should be approximately 3 times the illuminance provided for reading; architectural lighting should be no more than 25 percent of that provided for reading. A preset control system with settings for various functions (during readings, rituals, processions) can be effective in some worship facilities.

Exterior Lighting

Lighting the facade of a house of worship can be an effective lighting technique. Consideration to the type of materials used will aid in selecting the proper light source. In addition, stained-glass windows, if available, can be illuminated from within the building to provide an attractive view to people passing by the building.

Residential lighting

Lighting in residences should reinforce the needs and desires of the occupant. The ability to easily and safely move about, the importance of considering the people within the space, flexibility, attractiveness, and economical concerns are all important factors in residential lighting. Leslie and Conway (1996) offer a guide for energy-efficient lighting techniques that can be applied to homes and residential applications.

Visual Activity Areas

Care should also be taken to provide sufficient uniformity for visual tasks by designing for the luminance ratios described in **Table 6**. Recall that for matte surfaces, if the illuminance on the surface and the reflectance are known, the luminance can be estimated. Recommended reflectances for common surfaces are given in **Table 7**.

Relaxation Areas

When relaxation is the primary consideration in the home, uniformity of illumination is not an important lighting criterion. Flexibility in the lighting, through localized lighting, dimming, or portable luminaires is important for relaxation in the home. Luminaire luminances should not exceed 1700 cd/m² in residences.

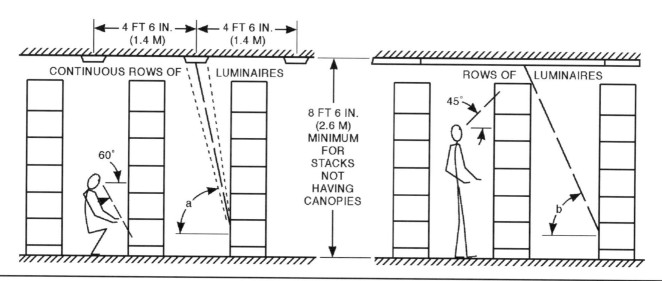

Fig. 22. Lighting for library stacks: (left) luminaires parallel with stacks; (right) luminaires at right angles to stacks provide better vertical illumination at lower shelves.

Industrial lighting

Luminance Ratios

Providing visually effective and comfortable lighting is critical in industrial facilities. Recommended illuminances for industrial lighting are described by Rea (2000). In addition, maximum luminance ratios for industrial tasks should not exceed those listed in **Table 8.**

Supplemental Task Lighting

Many industry-related visual tasks involve small details, low contrast, and are usually three-dimensional in nature (and susceptible to shadows). **Fig. 23** depicts supplemental lighting strategies for industrial tasks.

Health care facilities

Hospitals and health care facilities include populations with very different lighting requirements. Health care providers often require very high illuminances for their very critical tasks; and the psychological and emotional well-being of patients and visitors may require much lower levels and more relaxing approaches to lighting.

Visual Task Lighting

Excellent color rendering ability is often critical and should be planned in the lighting. In the event of an emergency or power failure, sufficient emergency lighting should be provided, especially in critical care and surgical areas.

Lighting for the Patient

"Patient-friendly" lighting is important, especially in longer-term health care facilities. IESNA recommends the following approaches in lighting for patients:

– Use indirect lighting whenever possible.

– Provide uniform illumination on the floors.

Table 6. Recommended maximum luminance ratios for residences

Between task and adjacent surroundings	1 to 1/10*
Between task and more remote darker surfaces	1 to 1/10
Between task and more remote lighter surfaces	1 to 10

* For special considerations (tasks of long duration and/or relatively high in luminance) no more than task and no less than 1/3 task.

Table 7. Recommended surface reflectance

Ceiling	80 - 90
Walls	40 - 60
Furniture and equipment	25 - 45
Floor	20 - 40

Table 8. Recommended maximum luminance ratios for industrial areas

	Environmental classification		
	A	B	C
1. Between tasks and adjacent darker surroundings	3 to 1	3 to 1	5 to 1
2. Between tasks and adjacent lighter surroundings	1 to 3	1 to 3	1 to 5
3. Between tasks and more remote darker surfaces	10 to 1	20 to 1	*
4. Between tasks and more remote lighter surfaces	1 to 10	1 to 20	*
5. Between luminaires (or windows, skylights, etc.) and surfaces adjacent to them	20 to 1	*	*
6. Anywhere within normal field of view	40 to 1	*	*

* Luminance ratio control not practical.

A—Interior areas where reflectances of entire space can be controlled in line with recommendations for optimum seeing conditions.

B—Areas where reflectances of immediate work area can be controlled, but control of remote surround is limited.

C—Areas (indoor and outdoor) where it is completely impractical to control reflectances and difficult to alter environmental conditions.

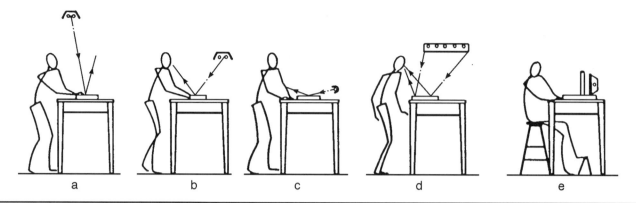

Fig. 23. Supplemental lighting for industrial tasks: (a) luminaire located to prevent veiling reflections; (b) luminaire located to cause veiling reflections; (c) low-angle lighting to emphasize surface defects; (d) large-area source is reflected toward the eye; (e) transillumination from a diffuse source. Adapted from IESNA *Lighting Handbook* (1993).

– Provide sufficient illumination for visual tasks such as reading.

– Use high-color-rendering sources.

– Reinforce the physical environment to prevent confusion.

– Use patient-controlled lighting whenever possible.

– Use adjustable task lighting.

During nighttime, luminances in health care facilities should not exceed 70 cd/m² for extended periods or 200 cd/m² for short times. Patients with specific ailments or conditions, such as premature infants (Bullough and Rea 1996), or patients with Alzheimer's disease (Figueiro et al. 2003), may also have specific visual and lighting requirements that must be met in the health care facility, as do the health workers who must provide care around the clock (Figueiro et al. 2001).

Lighting for retail areas
Objectives of Retail Lighting

Lighting in the merchandising area must support three important objectives:

– To attract and guide the customer.

– To allow the customer to evaluate the merchandise.

– To complete the sale of the merchandise.

To meet these objectives, the architectural appearance of the store, methods for maintaining lighting, and the type of store (a high-end boutique versus a wholesale discount outlet) must be considered.

Recommended Illuminances for Retail Lighting

Table 9 lists recommended illuminances for retail areas, including the merchandise, circulation, sales, and support areas. The recommendations are dependent in part upon the expected activity patterns within the store. Flexibility in lighting systems is often required, since displays of merchandise may be temporary and changed on a regular basis.

Outdoor Lighting

IESNA recommendations for outdoor lighting are described in Rea (2000). Further guidance to exterior lighting design and specification can be found in Leslie and Rodgers (1996) and Clanton (2003).

Light Pollution and Trespass

Because of the increased nighttime use of electric lighting, proper shielding and control of lighting is essential to avoid light pollution and light trespass. Light pollution is caused by stray light from luminaires that is scattered by particles in the atmosphere at night. This scattered light creates a haze that can obscure views of the nighttime sky. Using well-shielded luminaires and avoiding light spilling over in facade or sign lighting can help alleviate light pollution.

Light trespass is unwanted or excessive light, usually in an area adjacent to an outdoor lighting installation. For example, a bright street light might shine, unwanted, into a window in one's house. Like light pollution, light trespass can be minimized by carefully surveying the site before the design phase, and by specifying luminaires with appropriate cutoff characteristics and with good optical control or shielding. Refer to Fig. 15 for information on the various cutoff classifications.

Peripheral Visibility at Night

Recent research has demonstrated that light sources with higher scotopic or rod-stimulating content ("bluer" in color) result in improved detection of peripheral objects at the low light levels associated with much outdoor lighting. For example, at the same low light level, MH lamps result in shorter response times to peripheral objects than HPS lamps (He et al. 1997). This effect is not present in the central field of view (since there are no rods in the central part of the eye's retina). While these results have not been incorporated into lighting recommendations, the IESNA is actively studying these issues.

Outdoor Lighting Effects

Luminance ratios recommended to achieve specific effects in outdoor lighting design are as follows:

– 1 to 2: to blend in with surrounding areas.

– 1 to 3: to create soft accents.

Table 9. Recommended illuminances for retail lighting (IESNA 1977)

Areas or tasks	Description	Type of activity area[1]	Foot-candles	Lux[2]
Circulation	Area not used for display or appraisal of merchandise or for sales transactions	High Medium Low	30 20 10	300 200 100
Merchandise[3] (including showcases & wall displays)	That plane area, horizontal to vertical, where merchandise is displayed and readily accessible for customer examination	High Medium Low	100 70 30	1000 700 300
Feature displays[3]	Single item or items requiring special highlighting to visually attract and set apart from the surround	High Medium Low	500 300 150	5000 3000 1500
Sales transactions area	The space needed for price verification and recording of transaction	High Medium Low	70 70 70	700 700 700

[1] One store may encompass all three types within the building.

High activity area	—Where merchandise displayed has readily recognizable usage. Evaluation and viewing time is rapid, and merchandise is shown to attract and stimulate the impluse buying decision.
Medium activity	—Where merchandise is familiar in type or usage, but the customer may require time and/or help in evaluation of quality, usage, or for the decision to buy.
Low activity	—Where merchandise is displayed that is purchased less frequently by the customer, who may be unfamiliar with the inherent quality, design, value or usage. Where assistance and time is necessary to reach a buying decision.

[2] Lux is an SI unit equal to 0.0929 footcandle.

[3] Lighting levels to be measured in the plane of the merchandise.

– 1 to 5: to create accents.

– 1 to 10: to create strong accents.

Such ratios can be utilized, for example, to create a strong accent effect in the floodlighting of a building facade. Consideration should also be given to the color of the surface being illuminated. The color of red or yellow brickwork is best highlighted by a "warm" (low CCT) source such as HPS or incandescent. The color of blue flowers is best emphasized by a "cool" (high CCT) source such as mercury or MH.

Parking facilities

Care should also be taken to provide sufficiently uniform lighting in parking areas. Recommended illuminance levels for open parking lots are as follows:

Low Activity Level

– General parking and pedestrian areas: 0.2 fc (2 lx)

– Vehicle use areas: 0.5 fc (5 lx)

Box C—Glossary

Amperes (A): The unit of measure of electrical current.

Bulb: The glass enclosure of a lamp designed to contain inert gases, protect inner elements of the lamp, and occasionally to determine distribution (diffuse or reflective).

Candlepower: The intensity of light from a source in a certain direction, and measured in candelas.

Coefficient of Utilization (CU): The ratio of illuminance to the lumens radiated for the light source.

Efficacy: The ratio of the approximate initial lumens produced by a light source divided by the necessary power to produce them (lumens per watt).

Foot-candle (fc): A unit of illuminance measurement; the number of lumens that are incident on each square foot of work surface. 1 fc = 10.76 lux.

Illuminance: The light falling on a surface, measured in foot-candles or lux.

Lamp: The mechanism that converts electricity into light by means of incandescent filament or gaseous discharge. Also used as the commonplace term for luminaires.

Lens: In a luminaire, an element that is used to alter or redirect light distribution using diffusion, refraction, or filtration.

Light Loss Factor (LLF): The design factor that accounts for atmosphere dirt depreciation, normal degrading of lamp lumens over the life of the lamp, and other factors that add to the fact that less light is available over time.

Lumen (lm): A measure of total light-producing output of a source; the quantity of visible light emitted.

Luminaire: An assembly used to house one or more light sources (lamps), connect light and power sources, and distribute light (also referred to as "light fixture").

Luminance: The emitted or reflected light from a surface in a particular direction, measured in candelas per square meter (cd/m^2). Formerly called photometric brightness.

Lux (lx): A unit of measurement used to gauge the illuminance falling on a surface; the number of lumens incident on each square meter of work surface. 1 lx = 0.093 fc.

Ohms: The unit of measure of resistance.

Visual acuity: A measure of the ability to distinguish fine details.

Volts (V): The unit of measure of electrical force.

Watts (W): The unit of measure of electric power; the power required to keep a current of 1 ampere flowing under the pressure of 1 volt.

High Activity Level

– General parking and pedestrian areas: 0.9 fc (10 lx)

– Vehicle use areas: 2 fc (22 lx)

Security lighting

Security lighting should increase the security of the people or property it surrounds. It has two main goals:

– to deter potential criminals from entering the area.

– to aid in visual searching by guards.

Average illuminance of fixtures recommended for security lighting range from 0.5 to 2 fc (5 to 20 lx). The aim is to provide sufficient light to make the area's exits and entrances of entry of potential intruders and of safety escape paths highly visible. Security lighting should also be arranged to limit a potential intruder's ability to see the secure area. Areas near entrances should be lighted to higher illuminances, approximately 10 fc (100 lx).

For additional discussion of this topic, including design and specification checklists, see the longer article by Bullough in the CD-ROM accompanying this volume.

The accompanying illustrations in **Fig. 24** illustrate ways to integrate lighting into architectural design. ■

REFERENCES

Boyce, P. R., et al., "The Influence of a Daylight-simulating Skylight on the Task Performance and Mood of Night-shift Workers," *Lighting Research and Technology,* 29(3):105–134. Chartered Institution of Building Services Engineers, London, 1996.

Bullough, J. D., 2000. "The Blue-light Hazard: A Review," *Journal of the Illuminating Engineering Society,* 29(2):6–14, 141. Illuminating Engineering Society of North America, New York, 2000.

Bullough, J. D., and M. S. Rea, "Lighting for Neonatal Intensive Care Units: Some Critical Information for Design," *Lighting Research and Technology,* 28(4):189–198, Chartered Institution of Building Services Engineers, London, 1996.

Clanton, Nancy, "Urban Outdoor Lighting," in *Time-Saver Standards for Urban Design,* Donald Watson, ed., McGraw-Hill, New York, 2003.

Figueiro, M. G., *Lighting the Way: A Key to Independence,* Lighting Research Center, Rensselaer Polytechnic Institute, Troy, 2001.

Figueiro, M. G., et al., "The Effects of Bright Light on Day and Night Shift Nurses' Performance and Well being in the NICU," *Neonatal Intensive Care,* 14(1):29–32, Goldstein & Associates, Santa Monica, 2001.

Fig. 24a. Way-finding and safety lighting within stair handrail. Sackler Museum Harvard University. James Stirling, Architect.

Fig. 24c. Office lighting. Adjustable sunscreens and shielded luminaires for low-level lighting. Phoenix Mutual Offices, Hartford, Connecticut.

Fig. 24b. Retail shelf lighting combines display and ambient lighting. Body Shop, South Beach, Miami.

Fig. 24d. Office lighting. Natural lighting and electric lighting using ceiling as reflector. Shell Oil Building, Houston. CRS, Architect.

Fig. 24. Examples of lighting integration.

Fig. 24e. Skylighting and reflective surfaces for accent lighting. Ritz Hotel Tea Room, London.

Fig. 24f. Lighting programmed as interactive environment. Pedestrian walkway, Chicago O'Hare International Airport.

Fig. 24. Examples of lighting integration (continued).

Figueiro, M. G., et al., "Light Therapy and Alzheimer's Disease," *Sleep Review,* 4(1):24+, Medical World Communications, Los Angeles, 2003.

He, Y., et al., "Evaluating Light Source Efficacy Under Mesopic Conditions Using Reaction Times," *Journal of the Illuminating Engineering Society,* 26(1):125–138, Illuminating Engineering Society of North America, New York, 1997.

Illuminating Engineering Society of North America (IESNA), New York.

Leslie, R. P., and K. M. Conway, *The Lighting Pattern Book for Homes,* McGraw-Hill, New York, 1996.

Leslie, R. P., and P. A. Rodgers, *The Outdoor Lighting Pattern Book,* McGraw-Hill, New York, 1996.

Narendran, N., and L. Deng, "Performance Characteristics of Light Emitting Diodes," *Proceedings of the IESNA Annual Conference,* (pp. 157–164), Salt Lake City, Utah, August 4–7. Illuminating Engineering Society of North America, New York, 2002.

National Fire Protection Association, National Fire Protection Association, Quincy, *Life Safety Code,* NFPA 101, 2003.

National Lighting Product Information Program, *Specifier Reports* and *Lighting Answers* reports on lighting technologies, available online at <www.lrc.rpi.edu/programs/nlpip>

Rea, M. S., "Toward a Model of Visual Performance: Foundations and Data," *Journal of the Illuminating Engineering Society,* 15(2):41–57, Illuminating Engineering Society of North America, New York, 1986.

Rea, M. S., and J. D. Bullough, "Application Efficacy," *Journal of the Illuminating Engineering Society,* 30(2):73–96, Illuminating Engineering Society of North America, New York, 2001.

Rea, M. S., et al., "Circadian Photobiology: An Emerging Framework for Lighting Practice and Research," *Lighting Research and Technology,* 34(3):177–190, Chartered Institution of Building Services Engineers, London, 2002.

Rea, M. S., ed., *IESNA Lighting Handbook: Reference and Application,* 9th ed., Illuminating Engineering Society of North America, New York, 2000.

Steffy, G. R., *Architectural Lighting Design,* 2nd ed., John Wiley & Sons, New York, 2002.

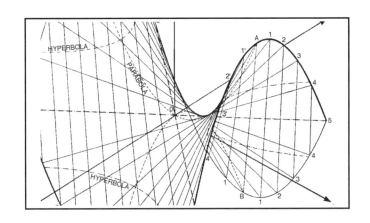

APPENDICES

Appendix 1   **Mathematics and drawing**

Appendix 2   **Units of measurement**

Appendix 3   **The SI metric system**

R. E. Shaeffer, P.E.

Appendix 1—Mathematics and drawing

NOTE: The last four pages in this section are from the classic article on analytic geometry by William Blackwell, reproduced in its entirety in *Time-Saver Standards for Architectural Design Data,* 7th edition, included in the CD-ROM accompanying this volume.

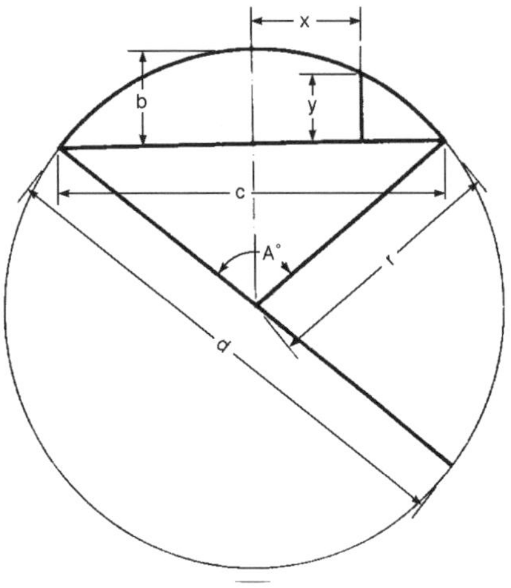

PROPERTIES OF THE CIRCLE

Circumference = C
= d π = d $\times$ 3.1416
= 2 π r = 2 $\times$ r $\times$ 3.1416

Diameter = d
= C $\div$ 3.1416
= C $\times$ 0.31831

Diameter of Circle, having circumference equal to periphery of square
= side of square $\times$ 1.27324

Side of Square, having periphery equal to circumference of circle

$$= \frac{d\pi}{4} = d \times 0.7854$$

Diameter of Circle, circumscribed about square
= side of square $\times$ 1.41421

Side of Square, inscribed in circle
= d $\times$ 0.70711

Arc, $a = \frac{\pi\, r\, A^\circ}{180} = 0.017453\, r\, A^\circ$

Angle, $A^\circ = \frac{180^\circ\, a}{\pi\, r} = 57.29578\, \frac{a}{r}$

Radius, $r = \frac{4\, b^2 + c^2}{8\, b}$

Diameter, $d = \frac{4\, b^2 + c^2}{4\, b}$

Chord, $c = 2\sqrt{2\, b\, r - b^2} = 2\, r \sin \frac{A^\circ}{2}$

Rise, Trigonometric Calculations

$$b = \frac{c}{2} \tan \frac{A^\circ}{4} = 2\, r \sin^2 \frac{A^\circ}{4}$$

Rise, Algebraic Calculations

$$b = r + y - \sqrt{r^2 - x^2}$$

$$b = r - \tfrac{1}{2}\sqrt{4\, r^2 - c^2}$$

$$x = \sqrt{r^2 - (r + y - b)^2}$$

$$y = b - r + \sqrt{r^2 - x^2}$$

Functions of π with Logarithmic Equivalents

π = 3.14159265, log = 0.4971499

$\frac{1}{\pi}$ = 0.3183099, log = $\bar{1}$.5028501

π^2 = 9.8696044, log = 0.9942997

$\frac{1}{\pi^2}$ = 0.1013212, log = $\bar{1}$.0057003

$\sqrt{\pi}$ = 1.7724539, log = 0.2485749

$\sqrt{\frac{1}{\pi}}$ = 0.5641896, log = $\bar{1}$.7514251

$\frac{\pi}{180}$ = 0.0174533, log = $\bar{2}$.2418774

$\frac{180}{\pi}$ = 57.2957795, log = 1.7581226

TABLE 1—AREAS OF CIRCLES IN SQUARE FEET—Diameter in Feet and Inches

Feet	Inches											
	0	1	2	3	4	5	6	7	8	9	10	11
0	.0000	.0055	.0218	.0491	.0873	.1364	.1963	.2673	.3491	.4418	.5454	.6600
1	.7854	.9218	1.069	1.227	1.396	1.576	1.767	1.969	2.182	2.405	2.640	2.885
2	3.142	3.409	3.687	3.976	4.276	4.587	4.909	5.241	5.585	5.940	6.305	6.681
3	7.069	7.467	7.876	8.296	8.727	9.168	9.621	10.08	10.56	11.04	11.54	12.05
4	12.57	13.10	13.64	14.19	14.75	15.32	15.90	16.50	17.10	17.72	18.35	18.99
5	19.63	20.29	20.97	21.65	22.34	23.04	23.76	24.48	25.22	25.97	26.73	27.49
6	28.27	29.07	29.87	30.68	31.50	32.34	33.18	34.04	34.91	35.78	36.67	37.57
7	38.48	39.41	40.34	41.28	42.24	43.20	44.18	45.17	46.16	47.17	48.19	49.22
8	50.27	51.32	52.38	53.46	54.54	55.64	56.75	57.86	58.99	60.13	61.28	62.44
9	63.62	64.80	66.00	67.20	68.42	69.64	70.88	72.13	73.39	74.66	75.94	77.24
10	78.54	79.85	81.18	82.52	83.86	85.22	86.59	87.97	89.36	90.76	92.18	93.60
11	95.03	96.48	97.93	99.40	100.9	102.4	103.9	105.4	106.9	108.4	110.0	111.5
12	113.1	114.7	116.3	117.9	119.5	121.1	122.7	124.4	126.0	127.7	129.4	131.0
13	132.7	134.4	136.2	137.9	139.6	141.4	143.1	144.9	146.7	148.5	150.3	152.1
14	153.9	155.8	157.6	159.5	161.4	163.2	165.1	167.0	168.9	170.9	172.8	174.8

If given diameter is not found in this table, reduce diameter to feet and decimals of a foot by aid of the following auxiliary table, and then find area from Table 4.

TABLE 2—Conversion from Inches and Fractions of an Inch to Decimals of a Foot

Inches	1	2	3	4	5	6	7	8	9	10	11
Feet........	.0833	.1667	.2500	.3333	.4167	.5000	.5833	.6667	.7500	.8333	.9167
Inches......	1/8	1/4	3/8	1/2	5/8	3/4	7/8				
Feet........	.0104	.0208	.0313	.0417	.0521	.0625	.0729				

Example. 5 ft. 7 3/8 in. = 5.0 + 0.5833 + 0.0313 = 5.6146 ft.

NOTE 1

HOW TO FIND CIRCUMFERENCES (from Table 3)

This table gives the product of π times any number *D* from 1 to 10; that is, it is a table of multiples of π. (*D* = diameter.) Moving the decimal point **one** place in column *D* is equivalent to moving it **one** place in the body of the table.

Circumference = π $\times$ diam. = 3.141593 $\times$ diam.

Conversely,

Diameter = $\frac{1}{\pi}$ $\times$ circumf. = 0.31831 $\times$ circumf.

Examples:

Diameter given; Circumference sought:
Diameter = 3.57 feet. Find 3.5 in left hand column, read right to column 7 and find 11.22 feet = circumference.

Circumference given; Diameter sought:
Circumference = 20.17 feet. Find 20.17 in body of table, read left and find 6.4, note 20.17 is in column 2, which add = 6.4 + .02 = 6.42 = diameter.

NOTE 2

HOW TO FIND AREAS (from Table 4)

Moving the decimal point **one** place in column *D* is equivalent to moving it **two** places in the body of the table. (*D* = diameter.)

Area of circle = $\frac{\pi}{4}$ $\times$ (diam.^{2}) = 0.785398 $\times$ (diam.^{2})

Conversely,

Diam. = $\sqrt{\frac{4}{\pi}} \times \sqrt{\text{area}}$ = 1.128379 $\times$ $\sqrt{\text{area}}$

Examples:

Diameter given; Area sought:
Diameter = 12.3 feet. Move decimal one point left = 1.23. Find 1.2 in left column, read right to column 3, find area of 1.23 = 1.188. Move decimal two points right = 118.8 sq. ft. = area.

Area given; Diameter sought:
Area = 4927 sq. in. Move decimal two points left = 49.27. Find 49.27. Read left and find 7.9. Note 49.27 is in column 2, which add = 7.9 + .02 = 7.92. Move decimal one point right = 79.2 inches = diameter.

TABLE 3—CIRCUMFERENCES BY HUNDREDTHS. SEE NOTE 1

D	0	1	2	3	4	5	6	7	8	9
1.0	3.142	3.173	3.204	3.236	3.267	3.299	3.330	3.362	3.393	3.424
.1	3.456	3.487	3.519	3.550	3.581	3.613	3.644	3.676	3.707	3.738
.2	3.770	3.801	3.833	3.864	3.896	3.927	3.958	3.990	4.021	4.053
.3	4.084	4.115	4.147	4.178	4.210	4.241	4.273	4.304	4.335	4.367
.4	4.398	4.430	4.461	4.492	4.524	4.555	5.587	4.618	4.650	4.681
1.5	4.712	4.744	4.775	4.807	4.838	4.869	4.901	4.932	4.964	4.995
.6	5.027	5.058	5.089	5.121	5.152	5.184	5.215	5.246	5.278	5.309
.7	5.341	5.372	5.404	5.435	5.466	5.498	5.529	5.561	5.592	5.623
.8	5.655	5.686	5.718	5.749	5.781	5.812	5.843	5.875	5.906	5.938
.9	5.969	6.000	6.032	6.063	6.095	6.126	6.158	6.189	6.220	6.252
2.0	6.283	6.315	6.346	6.377	6.409	6.440	6.472	6.503	6.535	6.566
.1	6.597	6.629	6.600	6.692	6.723	6.754	6.786	6.817	6.849	6.880
.2	6.912	6.943	6.974	7.006	7.037	7.069	7.100	7.131	7.163	7.194
.3	7.226	7.257	7.288	7.320	7.351	7.383	7.414	7.446	7.477	7.508
.4	7.540	7.571	7.603	7.634	7.665	7.697	7.728	7.760	7.791	7.823
2.5	7.854	7.885	7.917	7.948	7.980	8.011	8.042	8.074	8.105	8.137
.6	8.168	8.200	8.231	8.262	8.294	8.325	8.357	8.388	8.419	8.451
.7	8.482	8.514	8.545	8.577	8.608	8.639	8.671	8.702	8.734	8.765
.8	8.796	8.828	8.859	8.891	8.922	8.954	8.985	9.016	9.048	9.079
.9	9.111	9.142	9.173	9.205	9.236	9.268	9.299	9.331	9.362	9.393
3.0	9.425	9.456	9.488	9.519	9.550	9.582	9.613	9.645	9.676	9.708
.1	9.739	9.770	9.802	9.833	9.865	9.896	9.927	9.959	9.990	10.022
.2	10.05	10.08	10.12	10.15	10.18	10.21	10.24	10.27	10.30	10.34
.3	10.37	10.40	10.43	10.46	14.49	10.52	10.56	10.59	10.62	10.65
.4	10.68	10.71	10.74	10.78	10.81	10.84	10.87	10.90	10.93	10.96
3.5	11.00	11.03	11.06	11.09	11.12	11.15	11.18	11.22	11.25	11.28
.6	11.31	11.34	11.37	11.40	11.44	11.47	11.50	11.53	11.56	11.59
.7	11.62	11.66	11.69	11.72	11.75	11.78	11.81	11.84	11.88	11.91
.8	11.94	11.97	12.00	12.03	12.06	12.10	12.13	12.16	12.19	12.22
.9	12.25	12.28	12.32	12.35	12.38	12.41	12.44	12.47	12.50	12.53
4.0	12.57	12.60	12.63	12.66	12.69	12.72	12.75	12.79	12.82	12.85
.1	12.88	12.91	12.94	12.97	13.01	13.04	13.07	13.10	13.13	13.16
.2	13.19	13.23	13.26	13.29	13.32	13.35	13.38	13.41	13.45	13.48
.3	13.51	13.54	13.57	13.60	13.63	13.67	13.70	13.73	13.76	13.79
.4	13.82	13.85	13.89	13.92	13.95	13.98	14.01	14.04	14.07	14.11
4.5	14.14	14.17	14.20	14.23	14.26	14.29	14.33	14.36	14.39	14.42
.6	14.45	14.48	14.51	14.44	14.58	14.61	14.64	14.67	14.70	14.73
.7	14.77	14.80	14.83	14.86	14.89	14.92	14.95	14.99	15.02	15.05
.8	15.08	15.11	15.14	15.17	15.21	15.24	15.27	15.30	15.33	15.36
.9	15.39	15.43	15.46	15.49	15.52	15.52	15.58	15.61	15.65	15.68
5.0	15.71	15.74	15.77	15.80	15.83	15.87	15.90	15.93	15.96	15.99
.1	16.02	16.05	16.08	16.12	16.15	16.18	16.21	16.24	16.27	16.30
.2	16.34	16.37	16.40	16.43	16.46	16.49	16.52	16.56	16.59	16.62
.3	16.65	16.68	16.71	16.74	16.78	16.81	16.84	16.87	16.90	16.93
.4	16.96	17.00	17.03	17.06	17.09	17.12	17.15	17.18	17.22	17.25
5.5	17.28	17.31	17.34	17.37	17.40	17.44	17.47	17.50	17.53	17.56
.6	17.59	17.62	17.66	17.69	17.72	17.75	17.78	17.81	17.84	17.88
.7	17.91	17.94	17.97	18.00	18.03	18.06	18.10	18.13	18.16	18.19
.8	18.22	18.25	18.28	18.32	18.35	18.38	18.41	18.44	18.47	18.50
.9	18.54	18.57	18.60	18.63	18.66	18.69	18.72	18.76	18.79	18.82
6.0	18.85	18.88	18.91	18.94	18.98	19.01	19.04	19.07	19.10	19.13
.1	19.16	19.20	19.23	19.26	19.29	19.32	19.35	19.38	19.42	19.45
.2	19.48	19.51	19.54	19.57	19.60	19.63	19.67	19.70	19.73	19.76
.3	19.79	19.82	19.85	19.89	19.92	19.95	19.98	20.01	20.04	20.07
.4	20.11	20.14	20.17	20.20	20.23	20.26	20.29	20.33	20.36	20.39
6.5	20.42	20.45	20.48	20.51	20.55	20.58	20.61	20.64	20.67	20.70
.6	20.73	20.77	20.80	20.83	20.86	20.89	20.92	20.95	20.99	21.02
.7	21.05	21.08	21.11	21.14	21.17	21.21	21.24	21.27	21.30	21.33
.8	21.36	21.39	21.43	21.46	21.49	21.52	21.55	21.58	21.61	21.65
.9	21.68	21.71	21.74	21.77	21.80	21.83	21.87	21.90	21.93	21.96
7.0	21.99	22.02	22.05	22.09	22.12	22.15	22.18	22.21	22.24	22.27
.1	22.31	22.34	22.37	22.40	22.43	22.46	22.49	22.53	22.56	22.59
.2	22.62	22.65	22.68	22.71	22.75	22.78	22.81	22.84	22.87	22.90
.3	22.93	22.97	23.00	23.03	23.06	23.09	23.12	23.15	23.18	23.22
.4	23.25	23.28	23.31	23.34	23.37	23.40	23.44	23.47	23.50	23.53
7.5	23.56	23.59	23.62	23.66	23.69	23.72	23.75	23.78	23.81	23.84
.6	23.88	23.91	23.94	23.97	24.00	24.03	24.06	24.10	24.13	24.16
.7	24.19	24.22	24.25	24.28	24.32	24.35	24.38	24.41	24.44	24.47
.8	24.50	24.54	24.57	24.60	24.63	24.66	24.69	24.72	24.76	24.79
.9	24.82	24.85	24.88	24.91	24.94	24.98	25.01	25.04	25.07	25.10
8.0	25.13	25.16	25.20	25.23	25.26	25.29	25.32	25.35	25.38	25.42
.1	25.45	25.48	25.51	25.54	25.57	25.60	25.64	25.67	25.70	25.73
.2	25.76	25.79	25.82	25.86	25.89	25.92	25.95	25.98	26.01	26.04
.3	26.08	26.11	26.14	26.17	26.20	26.23	26.26	26.30	26.33	26.36
.4	26.39	26.42	26.45	26.48	26.52	26.55	26.58	26.61	26.64	26.67
8.5	26.70	26.73	26.77	26.80	26.83	26.86	26.89	26.92	26.95	26.99
.6	27.02	27.05	27.08	27.11	27.14	27.17	27.21	27.24	27.27	27.30
.7	27.33	27.36	27.39	27.43	27.46	27.49	27.52	27.55	27.58	27.61
.8	27.65	27.68	27.71	27.74	27.77	27.80	27.83	27.87	27.90	27.93
.9	27.96	27.99	28.02	28.05	28.09	28.12	28.15	28.18	28.21	28.24
9.0	28.27	28.31	28.34	28.37	28.40	28.43	28.46	28.49	28.53	28.56
.1	28.59	28.62	28.65	28.68	28.71	28.75	28.78	28.81	28.84	28.87
.2	28.90	28.93	28.97	29.00	29.03	29.06	29.09	29.12	29.15	29.19
.3	29.22	29.25	29.28	29.31	29.34	29.37	29.41	29.44	29.47	29.50
.4	29.53	29.56	29.59	29.63	29.66	29.69	29.72	29.75	29.78	29.81
9.5	29.85	29.88	29.91	29.94	29.97	30.00	30.03	30.07	30.10	30.13
.6	30.16	30.19	30.22	30.25	30.28	30.32	30.35	30.38	30.41	30.44
.7	30.47	30.50	30.54	30.57	30.60	30.63	30.66	30.69	30.72	30.76
.8	30.79	30.82	30.85	30.88	30.91	30.94	30.98	31.01	31.04	31.07
.9	31.10	31.13	31.16	31.20	31.23	31.26	31.29	31.32	31.35	31.38

TABLE 4—AREAS BY HUNDREDTHS. SEE NOTE 2

D	0	1	2	3	4	5	6	7	8	9
1.0	0.785	0.801	0.817	0.833	0.849	0.866	0.882	0.899	0.916	0.933
.1	0.950	0.968	0.985	1.003	1.021	1.039	1.057	1.075	1.094	1.112
.2	1.131	1.150	1.169	1.188	1.208	1.227	1.247	1.267	1.287	1.307
.3	1.327	1.348	1.368	1.389	1.410	1.431	1.453	1.474	1.496	1.517
.4	1.539	1.561	1.584	1.606	1.629	1.651	1.674	1.697	1.720	1.744
1.5	1.767	1.791	1.815	1.839	1.863	1.887	1.911	1.936	1.961	1.986
.6	2.011	2.036	2.061	2.087	2.112	2.138	2.164	2.190	2.217	2.243
.7	2.270	2.297	2.324	2.351	2.378	2.405	2.433	2.461	2.488	2.516
.8	2.545	2.573	2.602	2.630	2.659	2.688	2.717	2.746	2.776	2.806
.9	2.835	2.865	2.895	2.926	2.956	2.986	3.017	3.048	3.079	3.110
2.0	3.142	3.173	3.205	3.237	3.269	3.301	3.333	3.365	3.398	3.431
.1	3.464	3.497	3.530	3.563	3.597	3.631	3.664	3.698	3.733	3.767
.2	3.801	3.836	3.871	3.906	3.941	3.976	4.011	4.047	4.083	4.119
.3	4.155	4.191	4.227	4.264	4.301	4.337	4.374	4.412	4.449	4.486
.4	4.524	4.562	4.600	4.638	4.676	4.714	4.753	4.792	4.831	4.870
2.5	4.909	4.948	4.988	5.027	5.067	5.107	5.147	5.187	5.228	5.269
.6	5.309	5.350	5.391	5.433	5.474	5.515	5.557	5.599	5.641	5.683
.7	5.726	5.768	5.811	5.853	5.896	5.940	5.983	6.026	6.070	6.114
.8	6.158	6.202	6.246	6.290	6.335	6.379	6.424	6.469	6.514	6.560
.9	6.605	6.651	6.697	6.743	6.789	6.835	6.881	6.928	6.975	7.022
3.0	7.069	7.116	7.163	7.211	7.258	7.306	7.354	7.402	7.451	7.499
.1	7.548	7.596	7.645	7.694	7.744	7.793	7.843	7.892	7.942	7.992
.2	8.042	8.093	8.143	8.194	8.245	8.296	8.347	8.398	8.450	8.501
.3	8.553	8.605	8.657	8.709	8.762	8.814	8.867	8.920	8.973	9.026
.4	9.079	9.133	9.186	9.240	9.294	9.348	9.402	9.457	9.511	9.566
3.5	9.621	9.676	9.731	9.787	9.842	9.898	9.954	10.01	10.07	10.12
.6	10.18	10.24	10.29	10.35	10.41	10.46	10.52	10.58	10.64	10.69
.7	10.75	10.81	10.87	10.93	10.99	11.04	11.10	11.16	11.22	11.28
.8	11.34	11.40	11.46	11.52	11.58	11.64	11.70	11.76	11.82	11.88
.9	11.95	12.01	12.07	12.13	12.19	12.25	12.32	12.38	12.44	12.50
4.0	12.57	12.63	12.69	12.76	12.82	12.88	12.95	13.01	13.07	13.14
.1	13.20	13.27	13.33	13.40	13.46	13.53	13.59	13.66	13.72	13.79
.2	13.85	13.92	13.99	14.05	14.12	14.19	14.25	14.32	14.39	14.45
.3	14.52	14.59	14.66	14.73	14.79	14.86	14.93	15.00	15.07	15.14
.4	15.21	15.27	15.34	15.41	15.48	15.55	15.62	15.69	15.76	15.83
4.5	15.90	15.98	16.05	16.12	16.19	16.26	16.33	16.40	16.47	16.55
.6	16.62	16.69	16.76	16.84	16.91	16.98	17.06	17.13	17.20	17.28
.7	17.35	17.42	17.50	17.57	17.65	17.72	17.80	17.87	17.95	18.02
.8	18.10	18.17	18.25	18.32	18.40	18.47	18.55	18.63	18.70	18.78
.9	18.86	18.93	19.01	19.09	19.17	19.24	19.32	19.40	19.48	19.56
5.0	19.63	19.71	19.79	19.87	19.95	20.03	20.11	20.19	20.27	20.35
.1	20.43	20.51	20.59	20.67	20.75	20.83	20.91	20.99	21.07	21.16
.2	21.24	21.32	21.40	21.48	21.57	21.65	21.73	21.81	21.90	21.98
.3	22.06	22.15	22.23	22.31	22.40	22.48	22.56	22.65	22.73	22.82
.4	22.90	22.99	23.07	23.16	23.24	23.33	23.41	23.50	23.59	23.67
5.5	23.76	23.84	23.93	24.02	24.11	24.19	24.28	24.37	24.45	24.54
.6	24.63	24.72	24.81	24.89	24.98	25.07	25.16	25.25	25.34	25.43
.7	25.52	25.61	25.70	25.79	25.88	25.97	26.06	26.15	26.24	26.33
.8	26.42	26.51	26.60	26.69	26.79	26.88	26.97	27.06	27.15	27.25
.9	27.34	27.43	27.53	27.62	27.71	27.81	27.90	27.99	28.09	28.18
6.0	28.27	28.37	28.46	28.56	28.65	28.75	28.84	28.94	29.03	29.13
.1	29.22	29.32	29.42	29.51	29.61	29.71	29.80	29.90	30.00	30.09
.2	30.19	30.29	30.39	30.48	30.58	30.68	30.78	30.88	30.97	31.07
.3	31.17	31.27	31.37	31.47	31.57	31.67	31.77	31.87	31.97	32.07
.4	32.17	32.27	32.37	32.47	32.57	32.67	32.78	32.88	32.98	33.08
6.5	33.18	33.29	33.39	33.49	33.59	33.70	33.80	33.90	34.00	34.11
.6	34.21	34.32	34.42	34.52	34.63	34.73	34.84	34.94	35.05	35.15
.7	35.26	35.36	35.47	35.57	35.68	35.78	35.89	36.00	36.10	36.21
.8	36.32	36.42	36.53	36.64	36.75	36.85	36.96	37.07	37.18	37.28
.9	37.39	37.50	37.61	37.72	37.83	37.94	38.05	38.16	38.26	38.37
7.0	38.48	38.59	38.70	38.82	38.93	39.04	39.15	39.26	39.37	39.48
.1	39.59	39.70	39.82	39.93	40.04	40.15	40.26	40.38	40.49	40.60
.2	40.72	40.83	40.94	41.06	41.17	41.28	41.40	41.51	41.62	41.74
.3	41.85	41.97	42.08	42.20	42.31	42.43	42.54	42.66	42.78	42.89
.4	43.01	43.12	43.24	43.36	43.47	43.59	43.71	43.83	43.94	44.06
7.5	44.18	44.30	44.41	44.53	44.65	44.77	44.89	45.01	45.13	45.25
.6	45.36	45.48	45.60	45.72	45.84	45.96	46.08	46.20	46.32	46.45
.7	46.57	46.69	46.81	46.93	47.05	47.17	47.29	47.42	47.54	47.66
.8	47.78	47.91	48.03	48.15	48.27	48.40	48.52	48.65	48.77	48.89
.9	49.02	49.14	49.27	49.39	49.51	49.64	49.76	49.89	50.01	50.14
8.0	50.27	50.39	50.52	50.64	50.77	50.90	51.02	51.15	51.28	51.40
.1	51.53	51.66	51.78	51.91	52.04	52.17	52.30	52.42	52.55	52.68
.2	52.81	52.94	53.07	53.20	53.33	53.46	53.59	53.72	53.85	53.98
.3	54.11	54.24	54.37	54.50	54.63	54.76	54.89	55.02	55.15	55.29
.4	55.42	55.55	55.68	55.81	55.95	56.08	56.21	56.35	56.48	56.61
8.5	56.75	56.88	57.01	57.15	57.28	57.41	57.55	57.68	57.82	57.95
.6	58.09	58.22	58.36	58.49	58.63	58.77	58.90	59.04	59.17	59.31
.7	59.45	59.58	59.72	59.86	59.99	60.13	60.27	60.41	60.55	60.68
.8	60.82	60.96	61.10	61.24	61.38	61.51	61.65	61.79	61.93	62.07
.9	62.21	62.35	62.49	62.63	62.77	62.91	63.05	63.19	63.33	63.48
9.0	63.62	63.76	63.90	64.04	64.18	64.33	64.47	64.61	64.75	64.90
.1	65.04	65.18	65.33	65.47	65.61	65.76	65.90	66.04	66.19	66.33
.2	66.48	66.62	66.77	66.91	67.06	67.20	67.35	67.49	67.64	67.78
.3	67.93	68.08	68.22	68.37	68.51	68.66	68.81	68.96	69.10	69.25
.4	69.40	69.55	69.69	69.84	69.99	70.14	70.29	70.44	70.58	70.73
9.5	70.88	71.03	71.18	71.33	71.48	71.63	71.78	71.93	72.08	72.23
.6	72.38	72.53	72.68	72.84	72.99	73.14	73.29	73.44	73.59	73.75
.7	73.90	74.05	74.20	74.36	74.51	74.66	74.82	74.97	75.12	75.28
.8	75.43	75.58	75.74	75.89	76.05	76.20	76.36	76.51	76.67	76.82
.9	76.98	77.13	77.29	77.44	77.60	77.76	77.91	78.07	78.23	78.38

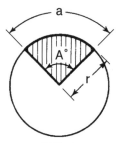

FIG. 1

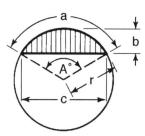

FIG. 2

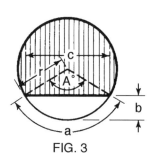

FIG. 3

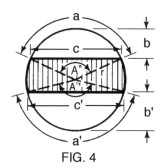

FIG. 4

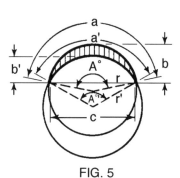

FIG. 5

Nomenclature—

$$A° = \text{Angle in degrees} = \frac{180° \, a}{\pi \, r}$$

$$a = \text{Arc} = 0.017453 \, r \, A°$$

$$b = \text{Rise} = 2 \, r \sin^2 \frac{A°}{4}$$

$$c = \text{Chord} = 2 \, r \sin \frac{A°}{2}$$

$$d = \text{Diameter} = 2 \, r = \frac{4 \, b^2 + c^2}{4 \, b}$$

$$\pi = 3.1416$$

$$r = \text{Radius} = \frac{d}{2} = \frac{4 \, b^2 + c^2}{8 \, b}$$

$$S = \text{Area} = \frac{\pi \, d^2}{4} = 0.7854 \, d^2$$

AREA OF CIRCULAR SECTOR—Figure 1

$$\text{Area} = \frac{a \, r}{2} = \frac{S \, A°}{360}$$

AREA OF CIRCULAR SEGMENT—Figure 2
(Less than half circle)

$$\text{Area} = \frac{a \, r - c \, (r - b)}{2} = \frac{S A°}{360} - \frac{c \, (r - b)}{2}$$

AREA OF CIRCULAR SEGMENT—Figure 3
(Greater than half circle)

$$\text{Area} = S - \left[\frac{a \, r - c \, (r - b)}{2} \right] = S - \left[\frac{S \, A°}{360} - \frac{c \, (r - b)}{2} \right]$$

AREA OF CIRCULAR ZONE—Figure 4

$$\text{Area} = S - \left[\frac{a \, r - c \, (r - b)}{2} + \frac{a^1 \, r - c^1 \, (r - b^1)}{2} \right]$$
$$= S - \left[\frac{S \, A°}{360} - \frac{c \, (r - b)}{2} + \frac{S A°^1}{360} - \frac{c^1 \, (r - b^1)}{2} \right]$$

AREA OF CIRCULAR LUNE—Figure 5

$$\text{Area} = \left[\frac{a \, r - c \, (r - b)}{2} \right] - \left[\frac{a^1 \, r^1 - c \, (r^1 - b^1)}{2} \right]$$
$$= \left[\frac{S A°}{360} - \frac{c(r - b)}{2} \right] - \left[\frac{S^1 A°^1}{360} - \frac{c \, (r^1 - b^1)}{2} \right]$$

AREA OF CIRCULAR SEGMENT—From Table 5
(Using Rise and Chord)
Area = c × b × coefficient.
Example: chord, c = 3.52; rise, b = 1.49

$$\frac{b}{c} = \frac{1.49}{3.52} = 0.4233$$

coefficient of 0.4233 = 0.7542
3.52 × 1.49 × 0.7542 = 3.9556 = **area of segment**

AREA OF CIRCULAR SEGMENT—From Table 6
(Using Rise and Diameter)
Area = d² × coefficient
Example: diameter, d = $5\frac{3}{32}$; rise, b = $2\frac{7}{16}$

$5\frac{3}{32} = 5.09375$; $2\frac{7}{16} = 2.4375$

$$\frac{b}{d} = \frac{2.4375}{5.09375} = 0.478528$$

Interpolation:
Coefficient for 0.479 = 0.371705
0.478 = 0.370706
.001 = 0.000999

.478528
.478000
.000528   ×   528
0.000527
Coefficient   + 0.370706
for 0.478528 = 0.371233

5.09375 × 5.09375 × 0.371233 = 9.6321 = **area of segment**

AREAS OF CIRCULAR SEGMENTS

Table 5. For ratios of rise and chord

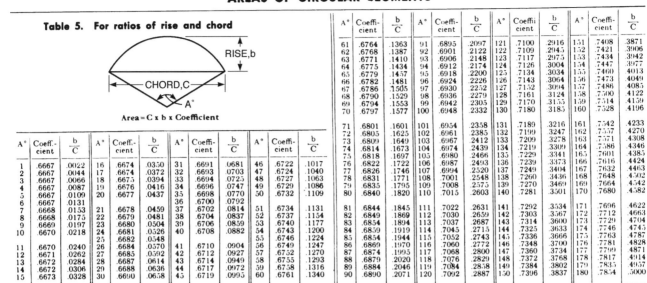

Area = C x b x Coefficient

A°	Coeff-cient	b/C	A°	Coeff-cient	b/C	A°	Coeff-cient	b/C	A°	Coeff-cient	b/C
1	.6667	.0022	16	.6674	.0350	31	.6691	.0681	46	.6722	.1017
2	.6667	.0044	17	.6674	.0372	32	.6693	.0703	47	.6724	.1040
3	.6667	.0066	18	.6675	.0394	33	.6694	.0725	48	.6727	.1063
4	.6667	.0087	19	.6676	.0416	34	.6696	.0747	49	.6729	.1086
5	.6667	.0109	20	.6677	.0437	35	.6698	.0770	50	.6732	.1109
6	.6667	.0131				36	.6700	.0792			
7	.6668	.0153	21	.6678	.0459	37	.6702	.0814	51	.6734	.1131
8	.6668	.0175	22	.6679	.0481	38	.6704	.0837	52	.6737	.1154
9	.6669	.0197	23	.6680	.0504	39	.6706	.0859	53	.6740	.1177
10	.6670	.0218	24	.6681	.0526	40	.6708	.0882	54	.6743	.1200
			25	.6682	.0548				55	.6746	.1224
11	.6670	.0240	26	.6684	.0570	41	.6710	.0904	56	.6749	.1247
12	.6671	.0262	27	.6685	.0592	42	.6712	.0927	57	.6752	.1270
13	.6672	.0284	28	.6687	.0614	43	.6714	.0949	58	.6755	.1293
14	.6672	.0306	29	.6688	.0636	44	.6717	.0972	59	.6758	.1316
15	.6673	.0328	30	.6690	.0658	45	.6719	.0995	60	.6761	.1340

A°	Coefficient	b/C	A°	Coefficient	b/C	A°	Coefficient	b/C	A°	Coefficient	b/C	A°	Coefficient	b/C
61	.6764	.1363	91	.6895	.2097	121	.7100	.2916	151	.7408	.3871			
62	.6768	.1387	92	.6901	.2122	122	.7109	.2945	152	.7421	.3906			
63	.6771	.1410	93	.6906	.2148	123	.7117	.2975	153	.7434	.3942			
64	.6775	.1434	94	.6912	.2174	124	.7126	.3004	154	.7447	.3977			
65	.6779	.1457	95	.6918	.2200	125	.7134	.3034	155	.7460	.4013			
66	.6782	.1481	96	.6924	.2226	126	.7143	.3064	156	.7473	.4049			
67	.6786	.1505	97	.6930	.2252	127	.7152	.3094	157	.7486	.4085			
68	.6790	.1529	98	.6936	.2279	128	.7161	.3124	158	.7500	.4122			
69	.6794	.1553	99	.6942	.2305	129	.7170	.3155	159	.7514	.4159			
70	.6797	.1577	100	.6948	.2332	130	.7180	.3185	160	.7528	.4196			
71	.6801	.1601	101	.6954	.2358	131	.7189	.3216	161	.7542	.4233			
72	.6805	.1625	102	.6961	.2385	132	.7199	.3247	162	.7557	.4270			
73	.6809	.1649	103	.6967	.2412	133	.7209	.3278	163	.7571	.4308			
74	.6814	.1673	104	.6974	.2439	134	.7219	.3309	164	.7586	.4346			
75	.6818	.1697	105	.6980	.2466	135	.7229	.3341	165	.7601	.4385			
76	.6822	.1722	106	.6987	.2493	136	.7239	.3373	166	.7616	.4424			
77	.6826	.1746	107	.6994	.2520	137	.7249	.3404	167	.7632	.4463			
78	.6831	.1771	108	.7001	.2548	138	.7260	.3436	168	.7648	.4502			
79	.6835	.1795	109	.7008	.2575	139	.7270	.3469	169	.7664	.4542			
80	.6840	.1820	110	.7015	.2603	140	.7281	.3501	170	.7680	.4582			
81	.6844	.1845	111	.7022	.2631	141	.7292	.3534	171	.7696	.4622			
82	.6849	.1869	112	.7030	.2659	142	.7303	.3567	172	.7712	.4663			
83	.6854	.1894	113	.7037	.2687	143	.7314	.3600	173	.7729	.4704			
84	.6859	.1919	114	.7045	.2715	144	.7325	.3633	174	.7746	.4745			
85	.6854	.1944	115	.7052	.2743	145	.7336	.3666	175	.7763	.4787			
86	.6869	.1970	116	.7060	.2772	146	.7348	.3700	176	.7781	.4828			
87	.6874	.1995	117	.7068	.2800	147	.7360	.3734	177	.7799	.4871			
88	.6879	.2020	118	.7076	.2829	148	.7372	.3768	178	.7817	.4914			
89	.6884	.2046	119	.7084	.2858	149	.7384	.3802	179	.7835	.4957			
90	.6890	.2071	120	.7092	.2887	150	.7396	.3837	180	.7854	.5000			

AREAS OF CIRCULAR SEGMENTS

Table 6. For ratios of rise and diameter

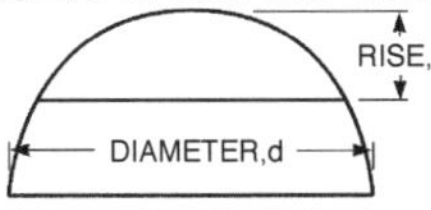

Area = d² x Coefficient

b/d	Coefficient	b/d	Coefficient	b/d	Coefficient	b/d	Coefficient	b/d	Coefficient
.001	.000042	.046	.012971	.091	.035586	.136	.064074	.181	.096904
.002	.000119	.047	.013393	.092	.036162	.137	.064761	.182	.097675
.003	.000220	.048	.013818	.093	.036742	.138	.065449	.183	.098447
.004	.000337	.049	.014248	.094	.037324	.139	.066140	.184	.099221
.005	.000471	.050	.014681	.095	.037909	.140	.066833	.185	.099597
.006	.000619			.096	.038497			.186	.100774
.007	.000779	.051	.015119	.097	.039087	.141	.067528	.187	.101553
.008	.000952	.052	.015561	.098	.039681	.142	.068225	.188	.102334
.009	.001135	.053	.016008	.099	.040277	.143	.068924	.189	.103116
.010	.001329	.054	.016458	.100	.040875	.144	.069626	.190	.103900
		.055	.016912			.145	.070329		
.011	.001533	.056	.017369	.101	.041477	.146	.071034	.191	.104686
.012	.001746	.057	.017831	.102	.042081	.147	.071741	.192	.105472
.013	.001969	.058	.018297	.103	.042687	.148	.072450	.193	.106261
.014	.002159	.059	.018766	.104	.043296	.149	.073162	.194	.107051
.015	.002438	.060	.019239	.105	.043908	.150	.073875	.195	.107843
.016	.002685			.106	.044523			.196	.108636
.017	.002940	.061	.019716	.107	.045140	.151	.074590	.197	.109431
.018	.003202	.062	.020197	.108	.045759	.152	.075307	.198	.110227
.019	.003472	.063	.020681	.109	.046149	.153	.076026	.199	.111025
.020	.003749	.064	.021168	.110	.047006	.154	.076747	.200	.111824
		.065	.021650			.155	.077470		
.021	.004032	.066	.022155	.111	.047633	.156	.078194	.201	.112625
.022	.004322	.067	.022653	.112	.048262	.157	.078921	.202	.113427
.023	.004619	.068	.023155	.113	.048894	.158	.079650	.203	.114231
.024	.004922	.069	.023660	.114	.049529	.159	.080380	.204	.115036
.025	.005231	.070	.024168	.115	.050165	.160	.081112	.205	.115842
.026	.005546			.116	.050805			.206	.116651
.027	.005867	.071	.024680	.117	.051446	.161	.081847	.207	.117460
.028	.006194	.072	.025196	.118	.052090	.162	.082582	.208	.118271
.029	.006527	.073	.025714	.119	.052737	.163	.083320	.209	.119084
.030	.006866	.074	.026236	.120	.053385	.164	.084060	.210	.119898
		.075	.026761			.165	.084801		
.031	.007209	.076	.027290	.121	.054037	.166	.085545	.211	.120713
.032	.007559	.077	.027821	.122	.054690	.167	.086290	.212	.121530
.033	.007913	.078	.028356	.123	.055346	.168	.087037	.213	.122348
.034	.008273	.079	.028894	.124	.056004	.169	.087785	.214	.123167
.035	.008638	.080	.029435	.125	.056664	.170	.088536	.215	.123988
.036	.009008			.126	.057327			.216	.124811
.037	.009383	.081	.029979	.127	.057991	.171	.089288	.217	.125634
.038	.009764	.082	.030526	.128	.058658	.172	.090042	.218	.126459
.039	.010148	.083	.031077	.129	.059328	.173	.090797	.219	.127286
.040	.010538	.084	.031630	.130	.059999	.174	.091555	.220	.128114
		.085	.032186			.175	.092314		
.041	.010932	.086	.032746	.131	.060673	.176	.093074	.221	.128943
.042	.011331	.087	.033308	.132	.061349	.177	.093837	.222	.129773
.043	.011734	.088	.033873	.133	.062027	.178	.094601	.223	.130605
.044	.012142	.089	.034441	.134	.062707	.179	.095367	.224	.131438
.045	.012555	.090	.035012	.135	.063389	.180	.096135	.225	.132273

b/d	Coefficient	b/d	Coefficient	b/d	Coefficient	b/d	Coefficient	b/d	Coefficient
.226	.133109	.281	.180918	.336	.231689	.391	.284569	.446	.338804
.227	.133946	.282	.181818	.337	.232634	.392	.285545	.447	.339799
.228	.134784	.283	.182718	.338	.233580	.393	.286521	.448	.340793
.229	.135624	.284	.183619	.339	.234526	.394	.287499	.449	.341788
.230	.136465	.285	.184522	.340	.235473	.395	.288476	.450	.342783
		.286	.185425			.396	.289454		
.231	.137307	.287	.186329	.341	.236421	.397	.290432	.451	.343778
.232	.138151	.288	.187235	.342	.237369	.398	.291411	.452	.344773
.233	.138996	.289	.188141	.343	.238319	.399	.292390	.453	.345768
.234	.139842	.290	.189048	.344	.239268	.400	.293370	.454	.346764
.235	.140689			.345	.240219			.455	.347760
.236	.141538	.291	.189956	.346	.241170	.401	.294350	.456	.348756
.237	.142388	.292	.190865	.347	.242122	.402	.295330	.457	.349752
.238	.143239	.293	.191774	.348	.243074	.403	.296311	.458	.350749
.239	.144091	.294	.192685	.349	.244027	.404	.297292	.459	.351745
.240	.144945	.295	.193597	.350	.244980	.405	.298274	.460	.352742
		.296	.194501			.406	.299256		
.241	.145800	.297	.195423	.351	.245935	.407	.300238	.461	.353739
.242	.146656	.298	.196337	.352	.246890	.408	.301221	.462	.354736
.243	.147513	.299	.197252	.353	.247433	.409	.302204	.463	.355733
.244	.148371	.300	.198168	.354	.248801	.410	.303187	.464	.356730
.245	.149231			.355	.249758			.465	.357728
.246	.150091	.301	.199085	.356	.250715	.411	.304171	.466	.358725
.247	.150953	.302	.200003	.357	.251673	.412	.305156	.467	.359723
.248	.151816	.303	.200922	.358	.252632	.413	.306140	.468	.360721
.249	.152681	.304	.201841	.359	.253591	.414	.307125	.469	.361719
.250	.153546	.305	.202762	.360	.254551	.415	.308110	.470	.362717
		.306	.203683			.416	.309096		
.251	.154413	.307	.204605	.361	.255511	.417	.310082	.471	.363715
.252	.155281	.308	.205528	.362	.256472	.418	.311068	.472	.364714
.253	.156150	.309	.206452	.363	.257433	.419	.312055	.473	.365712
.254	.157019	.310	.207376	.364	.258395	.420	.313042	.474	.366711
.255	.157891			.365	.259358			.475	.367710
.256	.158763	.311	.208302	.366	.260321	.421	.314029	.476	.368708
.257	.159636	.312	.209228	.367	.261285	.422	.315017	.477	.369707
.258	.160511	.313	.210155	.368	.262249	.423	.316005	.478	.370706
.259	.161386	.314	.211083	.369	.263214	.424	.316993	.479	.371705
.260	.162263	.315	.212011	.370	.264179	.425	.317981	.480	.372704
		.316	.212941			.426	.318970		
.261	.163141	.317	.213871	.371	.265145	.427	.319959	.481	.373704
.262	.164020	.318	.214802	.372	.266111	.428	.320949	.482	.374703
.263	.164900	.319	.215734	.373	.267078	.429	.321938	.483	.375702
.264	.165781	.320	.216666	.374	.268046	.430	.322928	.484	.376702
.265	.166663			.375	.269014			.485	.377701
.266	.167546	.321	.217600	.376	.269982	.431	.323919	.486	.378701
.267	.168430	.322	.218534	.377	.270951	.432	.324909	.487	.379701
.268	.169316	.323	.219469	.378	.271921	.433	.325900	.488	.380700
.269	.170202	.324	.220404	.379	.272891	.434	.326891	.489	.381700
.270	.171090	.325	.221341	.380	.273861	.435	.327883	.490	.382700
		.326	.222278			.436	.328874		
.271	.171978	.327	.223216	.381	.274832	.437	.329866	.491	.383700
.272	.172868	.328	.224154	.382	.275804	.438	.330858	.492	.384699
.273	.173758	.329	.225094	.383	.276776	.439	.331851	.493	.385699
.274	.174650	.330	.226034	.384	.277748	.440	.332843	.494	.386699
.275	.175542			.385	.278721			.495	.387699
.276	.176436	.331	.226974	.386	.279695	.441	.333836	.496	.388699
.277	.177330	.332	.227916	.387	.280669	.442	.334829	.497	.389699
.278	.178226	.333	.228858	.388	.281643	.443	.335823	.498	.390699
.279	.179122	.334	.229801	.389	.282618	.444	.336816	.499	.391699
.280	.180020	.335	.230745	.390	.283593	.445	.337810	.500	.392699

FORM		METHOD OF FINDING AREAS
TRIANGLE		Base × ½ perpendicular height. $\sqrt{s(s-a)(s-b)(s-c)}$, s = ½ sum of the three sides **a, b, c.**
TRAPEZIUM		Sum of area of the two triangles
TRAPEZOID		½ sum of parallel sides × perpendicular height.
PARALLELOGRAM		Base × perpendicular height.
REG. POLYGON		½ sum of sides × inside radius.
CIRCLE		$\pi r^2 = 0.78540 \times diam^2. = 0.07958 \times circumference^2$
SECTOR OF A CIRCLE		$\frac{\pi r^2 A°}{360} = 0.0087266\ r^2 A°$, = arc × ½ radius
SEGMENT OF A CIRCLE		$\frac{r^2}{2}\left(\frac{\pi A°}{180} - \sin A°\right)$
CIRCLE of same area as a square		Diameter = side × 1.12838
SQUARE of same area as a circle		Side = diameter × 0.88623
ELLIPSE		Long diameter × short diameter × 0.78540
PARABOLA		Base × ⅔ perpendicular height.
IRREGULAR PLANE SURFACE		

Divide any plane surface **A, B, C, D,** along a line **a - b** into an even number, **n,** of parallel and sufficiently small strips **d,** whose ordinates are $h_1, h_2, h_3, h_4, h_5, \dots h_{n-1}, h_n, h_{n+1},$ and considering contours between three ordinates as parabolic curves, then for section **A B C D,**

$$Area = \frac{d}{3}\left[\ h_1 + h_{n+1} + 4\ (h_2 + h_4 + h_6 \dots + h_n) + 2\ (h_3 + h_5 + h_7 \dots + h_{n-1})\right]$$

or, approximately, Area = sum of ordinates × width **d.**

METHOD OF FINDING SURFACES AND VOLUMES OF SOLIDS

SHAPE	FORMULAE	SHAPE	FORMULAE

S = lateral or convex surface   **V** = volume

Parallelopiped

S = perimeter, **P**, perp. to sides × lat. length l :   **Pl** :
V = area of base, **B**, × perpendicular height, h :   **B h**.
V = area of section, **A**, perp. to sides, × lat. length l :   **Al**.

Prism right, or oblique, regular or irregular

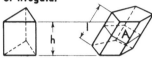

S = perimeter, **P**, perp. to sides × lat. length l :   **Pl** :
V = area of base, **B**, × perpendicular height, h :   **B h**.
V = area of section, **A**, perp. to sides, × lat. length l :   **Al**.

Cylinder, right or oblique, circular or elliptic etc.

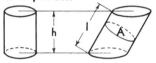

S = perimeter of base, **P**, × perp. height, h.**Ph**. **S**$_1$= perimeter, **P**$_1$, perp., × lat. length, l :   **P**$_1$ **l**.
V = area of base, **B**, × perp. height, h.**Bh**. **V**= area of section, **A**, perp. to sides × lat. length l. **Al**.

Frustum of any prism or cylinder

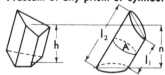

V = area of base, **B**, × perpendicular distance h, from base to centre of gravity of opposite face: **B h**.
for cylinder, ½ A (l$_1$+ l$_2$)

Pyramid or Cone, right and regular

S = perimeter of base, **P**, × ½ slant height l : ½ **Pl**.
V = area of base, **B** × ⅓ perpendicular ht., h : ⅓ **Bh**.

Pyramid or Cone, right or oblique, regular or irregular

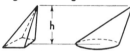

V = area of base, **B**, × ⅓ perp. height, h : ⅓ **Bh**.
V = ⅓ vol. of prism or cylinder of same base & perp. height.
V = ½ vol. of hemisphere of same base and perp. height.

Frustum of pyramid or cone, right and regular, parallel ends

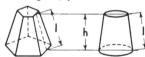

S = (sum of perimeter of base, **P**, and top, **p**) × ½ slant height l : ½ l (**P**+**p**).
V = (sum of areas of base, **B**, and top, **b**+sq. root of their products) × ⅓ perp. height, h : ⅓ h (B+b+√Bb)

Frustum of any pyramid or cone, parallel ends

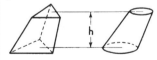

V = (sum of areas of base, **B**, and top, **b**, +sq. root of their products) × ⅓ perpendicular height, h : ⅓ h (B+b+√Bb).

Wedge, parallelogram face

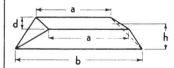

V = ⅙(sum of three edges, **a b a**, × perpendicular height, h, × perpendicular width, d) : ⅙ d h (2 a + b)

S = lateral or convex surface   **V** = volume

Sphere

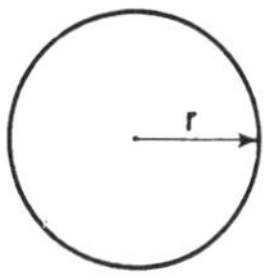

S = 4 π r² = π d² = 3.14159265 d².
V = ⁴⁄₃ π r³ = ⅙πd³ = 0.52359878 d³.

Spherical Sector

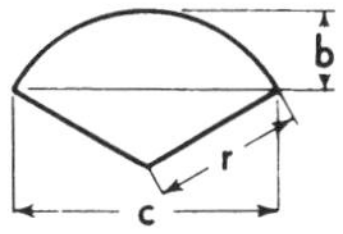

S = ½ π r (4b + c).
V = ⅔ π r² b.

Spherical Segment

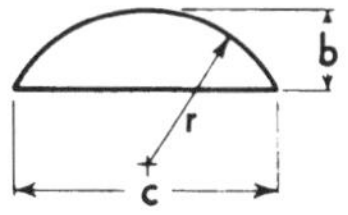

S = 2 π rb ÷ ¼ π (4 b² + c²).
V = ⅓ π b² (3r – b) = ¹⁄₂₄ π b (3c² + 4b²).

Spherical Zone

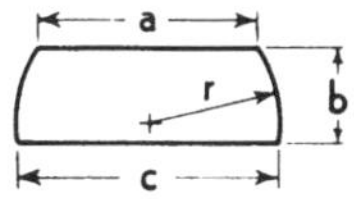

S = 2 π r b.
V = ¹⁄₂₄ π b (3a² + 3c² + 4b²).

Circular Ring

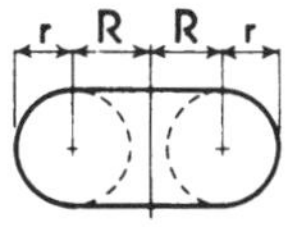

S = 4 π² R r.
V = 2 π² R r².

Ungula of right, regular cylinder
I. Base = segment, bab.   2. Base = half circle

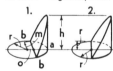

S = (2 r m – o × arc, bab) $\frac{h}{r-o}$,   **S** = 2 r h.
V = (⅔ m³ – o × area, bab) $\frac{h}{r-o}$.   **V** = ⅔ r² h.

I. Base = segment, cac.   2. Base = circle

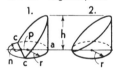

S = (2 r n + p × arc, cac) $\frac{h}{r+p}$,   **S** = π r h.
V = (⅔ n³ + p × area, cac) $\frac{h}{r+p}$.   **V** = ½ r² π h.

Ellipsoid

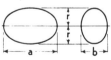

V = ⅓ π rab.

Paraboloid

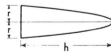

V = ½ π r² h.
Ratio of corresponding volume of a Cone, Paraboloid, Sphere & Cylinder of equal height: ⅓, ½, ⅔, 1.

RIGHT-ANGLED TRIANGLES

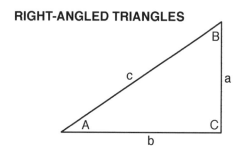

OBLIQUE-ANGLED TRIANGLES

$$S = \frac{a+b+c}{2}$$

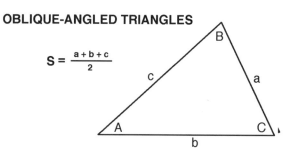

Given	Sought	Formulae
a, c	A, B, b	$\sin A = \dfrac{a}{c}$, $\quad \cos B = \dfrac{a}{c}$, $\quad b = \sqrt{c^2 - a^2}$
	Area	$\text{Area} = \dfrac{a}{2}\sqrt{c^2 - a^2}$
a, b	A, B, c	$\tan A = \dfrac{a}{b}$, $\quad \tan B = \dfrac{b}{a}$, $\quad c = \sqrt{a^2 + b^2}$
	Area	$\text{Area} = \dfrac{a\,b}{2}$
A, a	B, b, c	$B = 90° - A$, $\quad b = a \cot A$, $\quad c = \dfrac{a}{\sin A}$
	Area	$\text{Area} = \dfrac{a^2 \cot A}{2}$
A, b	B, a, c	$B = 90° - A$, $\quad a = b \tan A$, $\quad c = \dfrac{b}{\cos A}$
	Area	$\text{Area} = \dfrac{b^2 \tan A}{2}$
A, c	B, a, b	$B = 90° - A$, $\quad a = c \sin A$, $\quad b = c \cos A$
	Area	$\text{Area} = \dfrac{c^2 \sin A \cos A}{2} \text{ or } \dfrac{c^2 \sin 2A}{4}$

Given	Sought	Formulae
a, b, c	A	$\sin \tfrac12 A = \sqrt{\dfrac{(s-b)(s-c)}{bc}}$, $\cos \tfrac12 A = \sqrt{\dfrac{s(s-a)}{bc}}$, $\tan \tfrac12 A = \sqrt{\dfrac{(s-b)(s-c)}{s(s-a)}}$
	B	$\sin \tfrac12 B = \sqrt{\dfrac{(s-a)(s-c)}{ac}}$, $\cos \tfrac12 B = \sqrt{\dfrac{s(s-b)}{ac}}$, $\tan \tfrac12 B = \sqrt{\dfrac{(s-a)(s-c)}{s(s-b)}}$
	C	$\sin \tfrac12 C = \sqrt{\dfrac{(s-a)(s-b)}{ab}}$, $\cos \tfrac12 C = \sqrt{\dfrac{s(s-c)}{ab}}$, $\tan \tfrac12 C = \sqrt{\dfrac{(s-a)(s-b)}{s(s-c)}}$
	Area	$\text{Area} = \sqrt{s(s-a)(s-b)(s-c)}$
a, A, B	b, c	$b = \dfrac{a \sin B}{\sin A}$ $\quad c = \dfrac{a \sin C}{\sin A} = \dfrac{a \sin (A+B)}{\sin A}$
	Area	$\text{Area} = \tfrac12 a b \sin C = \dfrac{a^2 \sin B \sin C}{2 \sin A}$
a, b, A	B	$\sin B = \dfrac{b \sin A}{a}$
	c	$c = \dfrac{a \sin C}{\sin A} = \dfrac{b \sin C}{\sin B} = \sqrt{a^2 + b^2 - 2ab \cos C}$
	Area	$\text{Area} = \tfrac12 a b \sin C$
a, b, C	A	$\tan A = \dfrac{a \sin C}{b - a \cos C}$, $\quad \tan \tfrac12 (A-B) = \dfrac{a-b}{a+b} \cot \tfrac12 C$
	c	$c = \sqrt{a^2 + b^2 - 2ab \cos C} = \dfrac{a \sin C}{\sin A}$
	Area	$\text{Area} = \tfrac12 ab \sin C$

$a^2 = b^2 + c^2 - 2bc \cos A, \; b^2 = a^2 + c^2 - 2ac \cos B \; c^2 = a^2 + b^2 - 2ab \cos C$

SINES

Degrees	0′	10′	20′	30′	40′	50′	60′	Cosines
0	0.00000	0.00291	0.00582	0.00873	0.01164	0.01454	0.01745	89
1	0.01745	0.02036	0.02327	0.02618	0.02908	0.03199	0.03490	88
2	0.03490	0.03781	0.04071	0.04362	0.04653	0.04943	0.05234	87
3	0.05234	0.05524	0.05814	0.06105	0.06395	0.06685	0.06976	86
4	0.06976	0.07266	0.07556	0.07846	0.08136	0.08426	0.08716	85
5	0.08716	0.09005	0.09295	0.09585	0.09874	0.10164	0.10453	84
6	0.10453	0.10742	0.11031	0.11320	0.11609	0.11898	0.12187	83
7	0.12187	0.12476	0.12764	0.13053	0.13341	0.13629	0.13917	82
8	0.13917	0.14205	0.14493	0.14781	0.15069	0.15356	0.15643	81
9	0.15643	0.15931	0.16218	0.16505	0.16792	0.17078	0.17365	80
10	0.17365	0.17651	0.17937	0.18224	0.18509	0.18795	0.19081	79
11	0.19081	0.19366	0.19652	0.19937	0.20222	0.20507	0.20791	78
12	0.20791	0.21076	0.21360	0.21644	0.21928	0.22212	0.22495	77
13	0.22495	0.22778	0.23062	0.23345	0.23627	0.23910	0.24192	76
14	0.24192	0.24474	0.24756	0.25038	0.25320	0.25601	0.25882	75
15	0.25882	0.26163	0.26443	0.26724	0.27004	0.27284	0.27564	74
16	0.27564	0.27843	0.28123	0.28402	0.28680	0.28959	0.29237	73
17	0.29237	0.29515	0.29793	0.30071	0.30348	0.30625	0.30902	72
18	0.30902	0.31178	0.31454	0.31730	0.32006	0.32282	0.32557	71
19	0.32557	0.32832	0.33106	0.33381	0.33655	0.33929	0.34202	70
20	0.34202	0.34475	0.34748	0.35021	0.35293	0.35565	0.35837	69
21	0.35837	0.36108	0.36379	0.36650	0.36921	0.37191	0.37461	68
22	0.37461	0.37730	0.37999	0.38268	0.38537	0.38805	0.39073	67
23	0.39073	0.39341	0.39608	0.39875	0.40142	0.40408	0.40674	66
24	0.40674	0.40939	0.41204	0.41469	0.41734	0.41998	0.42262	65
25	0.42262	0.42525	0.42788	0.43051	0.43313	0.43575	0.43837	64
26	0.43837	0.44098	0.44359	0.44620	0.44880	0.45140	0.45399	63
27	0.45399	0.45658	0.45917	0.46175	0.46433	0.46690	0.46947	62
28	0.46947	0.47204	0.47460	0.47716	0.47971	0.48226	0.48481	61
29	0.48481	0.48735	0.48989	0.49242	0.49495	0.49748	0.50000	60
30	0.50000	0.50252	0.50503	0.50754	0.51004	0.51254	0.51504	59
31	0.51504	0.51753	0.52002	0.52250	0.52498	0.52745	0.52992	58
32	0.52992	0.53238	0.53484	0.53730	0.53975	0.54220	0.54464	57
33	0.54464	0.54708	0.54951	0.55194	0.55436	0.55678	0.55919	56
34	0.55919	0.56160	0.56401	0.56641	0.56880	0.57119	0.57358	55
35	0.57358	0.57596	0.57833	0.58070	0.58307	0.58543	0.58779	54
36	0.58779	0.59014	0.59248	0.59482	0.59716	0.59949	0.60182	53
37	0.60182	0.60414	0.60645	0.60876	0.61107	0.61337	0.61566	52
38	0.61566	0.61795	0.62024	0.62251	0.62479	0.62706	0.62932	51
39	0.62932	0.63158	0.63383	0.63608	0.63832	0.64056	0.64279	50
40	0.64279	0.64501	0.64723	0.64945	0.65166	0.65386	0.65606	49
41	0.65606	0.65825	0.66044	0.66262	0.66480	0.66697	0.66913	48
42	0.66913	0.67129	0.67344	0.67559	0.67773	0.67987	0.68200	47
43	0.68200	0.68412	0.68624	0.68835	0.69046	0.69256	0.69466	46
44	0.69466	0.69675	0.69883	0.70091	0.70298	0.70505	0.70711	45
	60′	50′	40′	30′	20′	10′	0′	

| Sines | | | | | | | | | Degrees |

COSINES

COSINES

Degrees	0′	10′	20′	30′	40′	50′	60′	Sines
0	1.00000	1.00000	0.99998	0.99996	0.99993	0.99989	0.99985	89
1	0.99985	0.99979	0.99973	0.99966	0.99958	0.99949	0.99939	88
2	0.99939	0.99929	0.99917	0.99905	0.99892	0.99878	0.99863	87
3	0.99863	0.99847	0.99831	0.99813	0.99795	0.99776	0.99756	86
4	0.99756	0.99736	0.99714	0.99692	0.99668	0.99644	0.99619	85
5	0.99619	0.99594	0.99567	0.99540	0.99511	0.99482	0.99452	84
6	0.99452	0.99421	0.99390	0.99357	0.99324	0.99290	0.99255	83
7	0.99255	0.99219	0.99182	0.99144	0.99106	0.99067	0.99027	82
8	0.99027	0.98986	0.98944	0.98902	0.98858	0.98814	0.98769	81
9	0.98769	0.98723	0.98676	0.98629	0.98580	0.98531	0.98481	80
10	0.98481	0.98430	0.98378	0.98325	0.98272	0.98218	0.98163	79
11	0.98163	0.98107	0.98050	0.97992	0.97934	0.97875	0.97815	78
12	0.97815	0.97754	0.97692	0.97630	0.97566	0.97502	0.97437	77
13	0.97437	0.97371	0.97304	0.97237	0.97169	0.97100	0.97030	76
14	0.97030	0.96959	0.96887	0.96815	0.96742	0.96667	0.96593	75
15	0.96593	0.96517	0.96440	0.96363	0.96285	0.96206	0.96126	74
16	0.96126	0.96046	0.95964	0.95882	0.95799	0.95715	0.95630	73
17	0.95630	0.95545	0.95459	0.95372	0.95284	0.95195	0.95106	72
18	0.95106	0.95015	0.94924	0.94832	0.94740	0.94646	0.94552	71
19	0.94552	0.94457	0.94361	0.94264	0.94167	0.94068	0.93969	70
20	0.93969	0.93869	0.93769	0.93667	0.93565	0.93462	0.93358	69
21	0.93358	0.93253	0.93148	0.93042	0.92935	0.92827	0.92718	68
22	0.92718	0.92609	0.92499	0.92388	0.92276	0.92164	0.92050	67
23	0.92050	0.91936	0.91822	0.91706	0.91590	0.91472	0.91355	66
24	0.91355	0.91236	0.91116	0.90996	0.90875	0.90753	0.90631	65
25	0.90631	0.90507	0.90383	0.90259	0.90133	0.90007	0.89879	64
26	0.89879	0.89752	0.89623	0.89493	0.89363	0.89232	0.89101	63
27	0.89101	0.88968	0.88835	0.88701	0.88566	0.88431	0.88295	62
28	0.88295	0.88158	0.88020	0.87882	0.87743	0.87603	0.87462	61
29	0.87462	0.87321	0.87178	0.87036	0.86892	0.86748	0.86603	60
30	0.86603	0.86457	0.86310	0.86163	0.86015	0.85866	0.85717	59
31	0.85717	0.85567	0.85416	0.85264	0.85112	0.84959	0.84805	58
32	0.84805	0.84650	0.84495	0.84339	0.84182	0.84025	0.83867	57
33	0.83867	0.83708	0.83549	0.83389	0.83228	0.83066	0.82904	56
34	0.82904	0.82741	0.82577	0.82413	0.82248	0.82082	0.81915	55
35	0.81915	0.81748	0.81580	0.81412	0.81242	0.81072	0.80902	54
36	0.80902	0.80730	0.80558	0.80386	0.80212	0.80038	0.79864	53
37	0.79864	0.79688	0.79512	0.79335	0.79158	0.78980	0.78801	52
38	0.78801	0.78622	0.78442	0.78261	0.78079	0.77897	0.77715	51
39	0.77715	0.77531	0.77347	0.77162	0.76977	0.76791	0.76604	50
40	0.76604	0.76417	0.76229	0.76041	0.75851	0.75661	0.75471	49
41	0.75471	0.75280	0.75088	0.74896	0.74703	0.74509	0.74314	48
42	0.74314	0.74120	0.73924	0.73728	0.73531	0.73333	0.73135	47
43	0.73135	0.72937	0.72737	0.72537	0.72337	0.72136	0.71934	46
44	0.71934	0.71732	0.71529	0.71325	0.71121	0.70916	0.70711	45
	60′	50′	40′	30′	20′	10′	0′	

| Cosines | | | | | | | | | Degrees |

SINES

Degrees	TANGENTS 0′	10′	20′	30′	40′	50′	60′	Cotangents
0	0.00000	0.00291	0.00582	0.00873	0.01164	0.01455	0.01746	89
1	0.01746	0.02036	0.02328	0.02619	0.02910	0.03201	0.03492	88
2	0.03492	0.03783	0.04075	0.04366	0.04658	0.04949	0.05241	87
3	0.05241	0.05533	0.05824	0.06116	0.06408	0.06700	0.06993	86
4	0.06993	0.07285	0.07578	0.07870	0.08163	0.08456	0.08749	85
5	0.08749	0.09042	0.09335	0.09629	0.09923	0.10216	0.10510	84
6	0.10510	0.10805	0.11099	0.11394	0.11688	0.11983	0.12278	83
7	0.12278	0.12574	0.12869	0.13165	0.13461	0.13758	0.14054	82
8	0.14054	0.14351	0.14648	0.14945	0.15243	0.15540	0.15838	81
9	0.15838	0.16137	0.16435	0.16734	0.17033	0.17333	0.17633	80
10	0.17633	0.17933	0.18233	0.18534	0.18835	0.19136	0.19438	79
11	0.19438	0.19740	0.20042	0.20345	0.20648	0.20952	0.21256	78
12	0.21256	0.21560	0.21864	0.22169	0.22475	0.22781	0.23087	77
13	0.23087	0.23393	0.23700	0.24008	0.24316	0.24624	0.24933	76
14	0.24933	0.25242	0.25552	0.25862	0.26172	0.26483	0.26795	75
15	0.26795	0.27107	0.27419	0.27732	0.28046	0.28360	0.28675	74
16	0.28675	0.28990	0.29305	0.29621	0.29938	0.30255	0.30573	73
17	0.30573	0.30891	0.31210	0.31530	0.31850	0.32171	0.32492	72
18	0.32492	0.32814	0.33136	0.33460	0.33783	0.34108	0.34433	71
19	0.34433	0.34758	0.35085	0.35412	0.35740	0.36068	0.36397	70
20	0.36397	0.36727	0.37057	0.37388	0.37720	0.38053	0.38386	69
21	0.38386	0.38721	0.39055	0.39391	0.39727	0.40065	0.40403	68
22	0.40403	0.40741	0.41081	0.41421	0.41763	0.42105	0.42447	67
23	0.42447	0.42791	0.43136	0.43481	0.43828	0.44175	0.44523	66
24	0.44523	0.44872	0.45222	0.45573	0.45924	0.46277	0.46631	65
25	0.46631	0.46985	0.47341	0.47698	0.48055	0.48414	0.48773	64
26	0.48773	0.49134	0.49495	0.49858	0.50222	0.50587	0.50953	63
27	0.50953	0.51320	0.51688	0.52057	0.52427	0.52798	0.53171	62
28	0.53171	0.53545	0.53920	0.54296	0.54674	0.55051	0.55431	61
29	0.55431	0.55812	0.56194	0.56577	0.56962	0.57348	0.57735	60
30	0.57735	0.58124	0.58513	0.58905	0.59297	0.59691	0.60086	59
31	0.60086	0.60483	0.60881	0.61280	0.61681	0.62083	0.62487	58
32	0.62487	0.62892	0.63299	0.63707	0.64117	0.64528	0.64941	57
33	0.64941	0.65355	0.65771	0.66189	0.66608	0.67028	0.67451	56
34	0.67451	0.67875	0.68301	0.68728	0.69157	0.69588	0.70021	55
35	0.70021	0.70455	0.70891	0.71329	0.71769	0.72211	0.72654	54
36	0.72654	0.73100	0.73547	0.73996	0.74447	0.74900	0.75355	53
37	0.75355	0.75812	0.76272	0.76733	0.77196	0.77661	0.78129	52
38	0.78129	0.78598	0.79070	0.79544	0.80020	0.80498	0.80978	51
39	0.80978	0.81461	0.81946	0.82434	0.82923	0.83415	0.83910	50
40	0.83910	0.84407	0.84906	0.85408	0.85912	0.86419	0.86929	49
41	0.86929	0.87441	0.87955	0.88473	0.88992	0.89515	0.90040	48
42	0.90040	0.90569	0.91099	0.91633	0.92170	0.92709	0.93252	47
43	0.93252	0.93797	0.94345	0.94896	0.95451	0.96008	0.96569	46
44	0.96569	0.97133	0.97700	0.98270	0.98843	0.99420	1.00000	45
Tangents	60′	50′	40′	30′	20′	10′	0′	Degrees
	COTANGENTS							

Degrees	COTANGENTS 0′	10′	20′	30′	40′	50′	60′	Tangents
0	∞	343.77371	171.88540	114.58865	85.93979	68.75009	57.28996	89
1	57.28996	49.10388	42.96408	38.18846	34.36777	31.24158	28.63625	88
2	28.63625	26.43160	24.54176	22.90377	21.47040	20.20555	19.08114	87
3	19.08114	18.07498	17.16934	16.34986	15.60478	14.92442	14.30067	86
4	14.30067	13.72674	13.19688	12.70621	12.25051	11.82617	11.43005	85
5	11.43005	11.05943	10.71191	10.38540	10.07803	9.78817	9.51436	84
6	9.51436	9.25530	9.00983	8.77689	8.55555	8.34496	8.14435	83
7	8.14435	7.95302	7.77035	7.59575	7.42871	7.26873	7.11537	82
8	7.11537	6.96823	6.82694	6.69116	6.56055	6.43484	6.31375	81
9	6.31375	6.19703	6.08444	5.97576	5.87080	5.76937	5.67128	80
10	5.67128	5.57638	5.48451	5.39552	5.30928	5.22566	5.14455	79
11	5.14455	5.06584	4.98940	4.91516	4.84300	4.77286	4.70463	78
12	4.70463	4.63825	4.57363	4.51071	4.44942	4.38969	4.33148	77
13	4.33148	4.27471	4.21933	4.16530	4.11256	4.06107	4.01078	76
14	4.01078	3.96165	3.91364	3.86671	3.82083	3.77595	3.73205	75
15	3.73205	3.68909	3.64705	3.60588	3.56557	3.52609	3.48741	74
16	3.48741	3.44951	3.41236	3.37594	3.34023	3.30521	3.27085	73
17	3.27085	3.23714	3.20406	3.17159	3.13972	3.10842	3.07768	72
18	3.07768	3.04749	3.01783	2.98869	2.96004	2.93189	2.90421	71
19	2.90421	2.87700	2.85023	2.82391	2.79802	2.77254	2.74748	70
20	2.74748	2.72281	2.69853	2.67462	2.65109	2.62791	2.60509	69
21	2.60509	2.58261	2.56046	2.53865	2.51715	2.49597	2.47509	68
22	2.47509	2.45451	2.43422	2.41421	2.39449	2.37504	2.35585	67
23	2.35585	2.33693	2.31826	2.29984	2.28167	2.26374	2.24604	66
24	2.24604	2.22857	2.21132	2.19430	2.17749	2.16090	2.14451	65
25	2.14451	2.12832	2.11233	2.09654	2.08094	2.06553	2.05030	64
26	2.05030	2.03526	2.02039	2.00569	1.99116	1.97680	1.96261	63
27	1.96261	1.94858	1.93470	1.92098	1.90741	1.89400	1.88073	62
28	1.88073	1.86760	1.85462	1.84177	1.82907	1.81649	1.80405	61
29	1.80405	1.79174	1.77955	1.76749	1.75556	1.74375	1.73205	60
30	1.73205	1.72047	1.70901	1.69766	1.68643	1.67530	1.66428	59
31	1.66428	1.65337	1.64256	1.63185	1.62125	1.61074	1.60033	58
32	1.60033	1.59002	1.57981	1.56969	1.55966	1.54972	1.53987	57
33	1.53987	1.53010	1.52043	1.51084	1.50133	1.49190	1.48256	56
34	1.48256	1.47330	1.46411	1.45501	1.44598	1.43703	1.42815	55
35	1.42815	1.41934	1.41061	1.40195	1.39336	1.38484	1.37638	54
36	1.37638	1.36800	1.35968	1.35142	1.34323	1.33511	1.32704	53
37	1.32704	1.31904	1.31110	1.30323	1.29541	1.28764	1.27994	52
38	1.27994	1.27230	1.26471	1.25717	1.24969	1.24227	1.23490	51
39	1.23490	1.22758	1.22031	1.21310	1.20593	1.19882	1.19175	50
40	1.19175	1.18474	1.17777	1.17085	1.16398	1.15715	1.15037	49
41	1.15037	1.14363	1.13694	1.13029	1.12369	1.11713	1.11061	48
42	1.11061	1.10414	1.09770	1.09131	1.08496	1.07864	1.07237	47
43	1.07237	1.06613	1.05994	1.05378	1.04766	1.04158	1.03553	46
44	1.03553	1.02952	1.02355	1.01761	1.01170	1.00583	1.00000	45
Cotangents	60′	50′	40′	30′	20′	10′	0	Degrees
	TANGENTS							

Degrees	SECANTS 0′	10′	20′	30′	40′	50′	60′	Cosecants
0	1.00000	1.00000	1.00002	1.00004	1.00007	1.00011	1.00015	89
1	1.00015	1.00021	1.00027	1.00034	1.00042	1.00051	1.00061	88
2	1.00061	1.00072	1.00083	1.00095	1.00108	1.00122	1.00137	87
3	1.00137	1.00153	1.00169	1.00187	1.00205	1.00224	1.00244	86
4	1.00244	1.00265	1.00287	1.00309	1.00333	1.00357	1.00382	85
5	1.00382	1.00408	1.00435	1.00463	1.00491	1.00521	1.00551	84
6	1.00551	1.00582	1.00614	1.00647	1.00681	1.00715	1.00751	83
7	1.00751	1.00787	1.00825	1.00863	1.00902	1.00942	1.00983	82
8	1.00983	1.01024	1.01067	1.01111	1.01155	1.01200	1.01247	81
9	1.01247	1.01294	1.01342	1.01391	1.01440	1.01491	1.01543	80
10	1.01543	1.01595	1.01649	1.01703	1.01758	1.01815	1.01872	79
11	1.01872	1.01930	1.01989	1.02049	1.02110	1.02171	1.02234	78
12	1.02234	1.02298	1.02362	1.02428	1.02494	1.02562	1.02630	77
13	1.02630	1.02700	1.02770	1.02842	1.02914	1.02987	1.03061	76
14	1.03061	1.03137	1.03213	1.03290	1.03368	0.03447	1.03528	75
15	1.03528	1.03609	1.03691	1.03774	1.03858	1.03944	1.04030	74
16	1.04030	1.04117	1.04206	1.04295	1.04385	1.04477	1.04569	73
17	1.04569	1.04663	1.04757	1.04853	1.04950	1.05047	1.05146	72
18	1.05146	1.05246	1.05347	1.05449	1.05552	1.05657	1.05762	71
19	1.05762	1.05869	1.05976	1.06085	1.06195	1.06306	1.06418	70
20	1.06418	1.06531	1.06645	1.06761	1.06878	1.06995	1.07115	69
21	1.07115	1.07235	1.07356	1.07479	1.07602	1.07727	1.07853	68
22	1.07853	1.07981	1.08109	1.08239	1.08370	1.08503	1.08636	67
23	1.08636	1.08771	1.08907	1.09044	1.09183	1.09323	1.09464	66
24	1.09464	1.09606	1.09750	1.09895	1.10041	1.10189	1.10338	65
25	1.10338	1.10488	1.10640	1.10793	1.10947	1.11103	1.11260	64
26	1.11260	1.11419	1.11579	1.11740	1.11903	1.12067	1.12233	63
27	1.12233	1.12400	1.12568	1.12738	1.12910	1.13083	1.13257	62
28	1.13257	1.13433	1.13610	1.13789	1.13970	1.14152	1.14335	61
29	1.14335	1.14521	1.14707	1.14896	1.15085	1.15277	1.15470	60
30	1.15470	1.15665	1.15861	1.16059	1.16259	1.16460	1.16663	59
31	1.16663	1.16868	1.17075	1.17283	1.17493	1.17704	1.17918	58
32	1.17918	1.18133	1.18350	1.18569	1.18790	1.19012	1.19236	57
33	1.19236	1.19463	1.19691	1.19920	1.20152	1.20386	1.20622	56
34	1.20622	1.20859	1.21099	1.21341	1.21584	1.21830	1.22077	55
35	1.22077	1.22327	1.22579	1.22833	1.23089	1.23347	1.23607	54
36	1.23607	1.23869	1.24134	1.24400	1.24669	1.24940	1.25214	53
37	1.25214	1.25489	1.25767	1.26047	1.26330	1.26615	1.26902	52
38	1.26902	1.27191	1.27483	1.27778	1.28075	1.28374	1.28676	51
39	1.28676	1.28980	1.29287	1.29597	1.29909	1.30223	1.30541	50
40	1.30541	1.30861	1.31183	1.31509	1.31837	1.32168	1.32501	49
41	1.32501	1.32838	1.33177	1.33519	1.33864	1.34212	1.34563	48
42	1.34563	1.34917	1.35274	1.35634	1.35997	1.36363	1.36733	47
43	1.36733	1.37105	1.37481	1.37860	1.38242	1.38628	1.39016	46
44	1.39016	1.39409	1.39804	1.40203	1.40606	1.41012	1.41421	45
Secants	60′	50′	40′	30′	20′	10′	0′	Degrees
	COSECANTS							

Degrees	COSECANTS 0′	10′	20′	30′	40′	50′	60′	Secants
0	∞	343.77516	171.88831	114.59301	85.94561	68.75736	57.29869	89
1	57.29869	49.11406	42.97571	38.20155	34.38232	31.25758	28.65371	88
2	28.65371	26.45051	24.56212	22.92559	21.49368	20.23028	19.10732	87
3	19.10732	18.10262	17.19843	16.38041	15.63679	14.95788	14.33559	86
4	14.33559	13.76312	13.23472	12.74550	12.29125	11.86837	11.47371	85
5	11.47371	11.10455	10.75849	10.43343	10.12752	9.83912	9.56677	84
6	9.56677	9.30917	9.06515	8.83367	8.61379	8.40466	8.20551	83
7	8.20551	8.01565	7.83443	7.66130	7.49571	7.33719	7.18530	82
8	7.18530	7.03962	6.89979	6.76547	6.63633	6.51208	6.39245	81
9	6.39245	6.27719	6.16607	6.05886	5.95536	5.85539	5.75877	80
10	5.75877	5.66533	5.57493	5.48740	5.40263	5.32049	5.24084	79
11	5.24084	5.16359	5.08863	5.01585	4.94517	4.87649	4.80973	78
12	4.80973	4.74482	4.68167	4.62023	4.56041	4.50216	4.44541	77
13	4.44541	4.39012	4.33622	4.28366	4.23239	4.18238	4.13357	76
14	4.13357	4.08591	4.03938	3.99393	3.94952	3.90613	3.86370	75
15	3.86370	3.82223	3.78166	3.74198	3.70315	3.66515	3.62796	74
16	3.62796	3.59154	3.55587	3.52094	3.48671	3.45317	3.42030	73
17	3.02030	3.38808	3.35649	3.32551	3.29512	3.26531	3.23607	72
18	3.23607	3.20737	3.17920	3.15155	3.12440	3.09774	3.07155	71
19	3.07155	3.04584	3.02057	2.99574	2.97135	2.94737	2.92380	70
20	2.92380	2.90063	2.87785	2.85545	2.83342	2.81175	2.79043	69
21	2.79043	2.76945	2.74881	2.72850	2.70851	2.68884	2.66947	68
22	2.66947	2.65040	2.63162	2.61313	2.59491	2.57698	2.55930	67
23	2.55930	2.54190	2.52474	2.50784	2.49119	2.47477	2.45859	66
24	2.45859	2.44264	2.42692	2.41142	2.39614	2.38107	2.36620	65
25	2.36620	2.35154	2.33708	2.32282	2.30875	2.29487	2.28117	64
26	2.28117	2.26766	2.25432	2.24116	2.22817	2,21535	2.20269	63
27	2.20269	2.19019	2.17786	2.16568	2.15366	2.14178	2.13005	62
28	2.13005	2.11847	2.10704	2.09574	2.08458	2.07356	2.06267	61
29	2.06267	2.05191	2.04128	2.03077	2.02039	2.01014	2.00000	60
30	2.00000	1.98998	1.98008	1.97029	1.96062	1.95106	1.94160	59
31	1.94160	1.93226	1.92302	1.91388	1.90485	1.89591	1.88709	58
32	1.88708	1.87834	1.86970	1.86116	1.85271	1.84435	1.83608	57
33	1.83608	1.82790	1.81981	1.81180	1.80388	1.79604	1.78829	56
34	1.78829	1.78062	1.77303	1.76552	1.75808	1.75073	1.74345	55
35	1.74345	1.73624	1.72911	1.72205	1.71506	1.70815	1.70130	54
36	1.70130	1.69452	1.68782	1.68117	1.67460	1.66809	1.66164	53
37	1.66164	1.65526	1.64894	1.64268	1.63648	1.63035	1.62427	52
38	1.62427	1.61825	1.61229	1.60639	1.60054	1.59475	1.58902	51
39	1.58902	1.58333	1.57771	1.57213	1.56661	1.56114	1.55572	50
40	1.55572	1.55036	1.54504	1.53977	1.53455	1.52938	1.52425	49
41	1.52425	1.51918	1.51415	1.50916	1.50422	1.49933	1.49448	48
42	1.49448	1.48967	1.48491	1.48019	1.47551	1.47087	1.46628	47
43	1.46628	1.46173	1.45721	1.45274	1.44831	1.44391	1.43956	46
44	1.43956	1.43524	1.43096	1.42672	1.42251	1.41835	1.41421	45
Cosecants	60′	50′	40′	30′	20′	10′	0′	Degrees
	SECANTS							

Drawings of the Polyhedra, shown in plan, with some of each and number of faces, vertices, and edges of each. (Cube not shown)

TETRAHEDRON

F	V	E
4	4	6

OCTAHEDRON

F	V	E
8	6	12

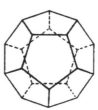

DODECAHEDRON

F	V	E
12	20	30

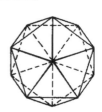

ICOSAHEDRON

F	V	E
20	12	30

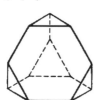

TRUNCATED TETRAHEDRON

F_3	F_4	V	E
4	4	12	18

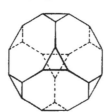

TRUNCATED CUBE

F_3	F_8	V	E
8	6	24	36

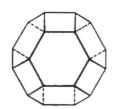

TRUNCATED OCTAHEDRON

F_4	F_6	V	E
6	8	24	36

CUBOCTAHEDRON

F_3	F_4	V	E
8	6	12	24

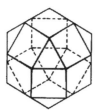

RHOMBICUBOCTAHEDRON

F_3	F_4	V	E
8	18	24	48

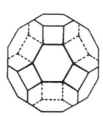

TRUNCATED CUBOCTAHEDRON

F_4	F_6	F_8	V	E
12	8	6	48	72

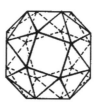

SNUB CUBE

F_3	F_4	V	E
32	6	24	60

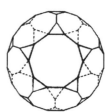

TRUNCATED DODECAHEDRON

F_3	F_{10}	V	E
20	12	60	90

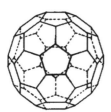

TRUNCATED ICOSAHEDRON

F_5	F_6	V	E
12	20	60	90

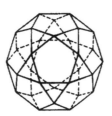

ICOSIDODECAHEDRON

F_3	F_5	V	E
20	12	30	60

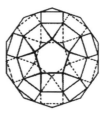

RHOMBICOSIDODECAHEDRON

F_3	F_4	F_5	V	E
20	30	12	60	120

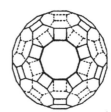

TRUNCATED ICOSIDODECAHEDRON

F_4	F_6	F_{10}	V	E
30	20	12	120	180

SNUB DODECAHEDRON

F_3	F_5	V	E
80	12	60	150

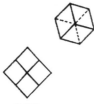

PLANS

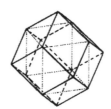

PROJECTION

RHOMBIC DODECAHEDRON

F	V	E
12	14	24

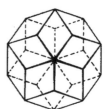

RHOMBIC TRIACONTAHEDRON

F	V	I
30	32	60

Notes:

1. Only two of the Archimedean duals are shown. The rhombic dodecahedron is drawn in an oblique or axonometric projection, as well as in two plan views. Note it is a cube (shown in fine dotted line) with a square pyramid added to each face. The others can be drawn from the corresponding Archimedean polyhedron: (a) Draw plan with vertex in center; (b) Draw on plan the perpendicular bisector of each edge which meets at vertex; (c) Extend all bisectors until they intersect; they form irregular polygonal face of the dual.

2. For making models, polygons can be drawn on a flat sheet, with some edges of each polygon in common with adjacent polygons, making a continuous strip called a net.

INDEX NO.	DUALS OF SEMI-REGULAR POLYHEDRA	E/r	DIHEDRAL ANGLE	FACE ANGLES	R/r
V.3.6²	Triakis Tetrahedron	3.127 / 1.876	129° 32'	112° 53' / 33° 33½'	1.2222
V.3.8²	Triakis Octahedron	2.083 / 1.219	147° 21'	117° 14' / 31° 23'	1.0858
V.4.6²	Tetrakis Hexahedron	1.491	143° 8'	83° 37' / 48° 11½'	1.1111
V.(3.4)²	Rhombic Dodecahedron (Octahedric Granatohedron)	1.118 / 1.225	120°	109° 28' / 70° 32'	1.3333
V.3.4³	Trapezoidal Icositetrahedron	0.887 / 0.686	138° 7'	115° 16' / 81° 34½'	1.1464
V.4.6.8	Hexakis Octahedron	1.070 / 0.878 / 0.656	155° 5'	87° 12' / 55° 1½' / 37° 46½'	1.0488
V.3⁴.4	Pentagonal Icositetrahedron (Two Enantiomorphs)	0.727 / 0.513	136° 20'	114° 48½' / 80° 46'	1.1602
V.3.10²	Triakis Icosahedron	1.254 / 0.728	160° 36'	119° 3' / 30° 28½'	1.0302
V.5.6²	Pentakis Dodecahedron	0.780 / 0.692	156° 43'	68° 36' / 55° 42'	1.0425
V.(3.5)²	Rhombic Triacontahedron (Icosahedric Granatohedron)	0.727	144	116° 34' / 63° 26'	1.1056
V.3.4.5.4	Trapezoidal Hexecontahedron	0.584 / 0.379	154° 8'	118° 16' / 86° 59' / 67° 46'	1.0530
V.4.6.10	Hexakis Icosahedron	0.689 / 0.586 / 0.373	164° 54'	89° 0' / 58° 14' / 32° 46'	1.0174
V.3⁴.5	Pentagonal Hexecontahedron (Two Enantiomorphs)	0.500 / 0.286	153° 10'	118° 8' / 67° 28'	1.0574

NOTES:

e = length of edge of regular and semi-regular polyhedra. θ = angle subtended by edge at center (for regular and semi-regular polyhedra). R = Radius of circumscribed sphere (regular + semi-regular polyhedra). r = radius of inscribed sphere (regular polyhedra and duals of semi-regular polyhedra). E = length of edges of duals of semi-regular polyhedra. R/r: This ratio, when given for the Archimedean duals, is the ratio of the radius of the circumscribed sphere of the corresponding Archimedean polyhedron to the radius of the sphere inscribed within the dual. Enantiomorph means form of opposite hand (in drawing, change broken lines to solid and solid lines to broken). There are only five possible ways of filling up three dimensional spaces with only one type of regular or Archimedean polyhedra and their duals = cubes; triangular prisms; hexagonal prisms; truncated octahedra; rhombic dodecahedra. There are three additional ways, using more than one type = tetrahedra + octahedra; tetrahedra + truncated tetrahedra; octahedra + cuboctahedra.

INDEX NO.	REGULAR POLYHEDRA	e/R	DIHEDRAL ANGLE	θ	R/r
3³	Tetrahedron	1.633	70° 32'	109° 28'	3.00
4³	Cube	1.155	90°	70° 32'	1.732
3⁴	Octahedron	1.414	109° 28'	90°	1.732
5³	Dodecahedron	0.714	116° 34'	41° 49'	1.258
3⁵	Icosahedron	1.051	138° 11'	63° 26'	1.258

INDEX NO.	SEMI-REGULAR POLYHEDRA	e/R	DIHEDRAL ANGLES Faces	Angles	θ
3.6²	Truncated Tetrahedron	0.853	6-6 / 6-3	70° 32' / 109° 28'	50° 28'
3.8²	Truncated Cube	0.562	8-8 / 8-3	90° / 125° 16'	32° 39'
4.6²	Truncated Octahedron (Tetrakaidecahedron)	0.6325	6-4 / 6-6	125° 16' / 109° 28'	36° 52'
(3.4)²	Cuboctahedron	1.00		125° 16'	60°
3.4³	Rhombicuboctahedron	0.715	4-4 / 3-4	135° / 144° 44'	41° 53'
4.6.8	Truncated Cuboctahedron	0.431	8-4 / 8-6 / 6-4	135° / 125° 16' / 144° 44'	24° 55'
3⁴.4	Snub Cube (Two Enantiomorphs)	0.744	4-3 / 3-3	142° 59' / 153° 14'	43° 40'
3.10²	Truncated Dodecahedron	0.337	10-4 / 10-6 / 6-4	116° 34' / 142° 37' / 159° 6'	19° 24'
5.6²	Truncated Icosahedron	0.4035	6-6 / 6-5	138° 11' / 142° 37'	23° 17'
(3.5)²	Icosidodecahedron (Triacontagon)	0.618		142° 37'	36°
3.4.5.4	Rhombicosidodecahedron	0.448	5-4 / 3-4	148° 17' / 159° 6'	25° 52'
4.6.10	Truncated Icosidodecahedron	0.263	10-4 / 10-6 / 6-4	148° 17' / 142° 37' / 159° 6'	15° 6'
3⁴.5	Snub Dodecahedron (Two Enantiomorphs)	0.464	5-3 / 3-3	152° 56' / 164° 10'	26° 50'

References: Cundy and Rollett, *Mathematical Models* (Oxford, 1951); Matila C. Ghyka, *Esthetique des Proportions* (Gallimard, 1927).

The hyperbolic paraboloid, a quadric surface, is shown here in isometric and orthogonal projection. It is a doubly curved surface and therefore not developable. However, since it is ruled surface, it can easily be formed or molded in a framework of straight members.

It can be generated in two ways:

1. A generating parabola (AOA in diagrams) is moved along another directrix parabola (BOB) in such a way that the successive positions of the plane of AOA are always parallel and the successive positions of the line AA are always parallel.

2. As a ruled surface: Given two straight lines (here 5'5' and 5 5) lying in a horizontal plane, two vertical planes containing these straight lines. Move one of these lines, say 5'5', called the generator, along the other (5 5), called the directrix, in such a way that its successive positions are always skew but always parallel to its initial position. Thus no plane can contain any two positions of the line 5'5'. These successive positions are the straight lines of one family, sometimes called a regulus. The other family is found by sliding the other straight line 5 5 along the line 5'5'.

The equation, with axes as shown.

$$\frac{x^2}{a} - \frac{y^2}{b^2} = \frac{z}{c}$$

(See below for the equations referred to the asymptotes as axes.)

All sections containing the z axis are parabolas. As such a section is rotated about the z axis, from one principal plane (the xz) to the other (the yz), the parabolas become wider and wider, but all with their centers of curvature above the xy plane, until at the sections containing 5 5 or 5'5', the parabola becomes a straight line; as rotation continues, the parabolas have their centers of curvature below the xy plane, and become narrower until the section plane reaches the yz plane. All sections parallel to any given plane containing the z axis are identical parabolas (or a straight line).

Every section parallel to the xy plane is a hyperbola. The lines 5'5' and 5 5 are the asymptotes of all of these hyperbolas. Every section above the xy plane will be a hyperbola with its axis parallel to the x axis; every section below the xy plane has its axis parallel to the y axis. The hyperbolas at the same distance above and below the xy plane (i.e. when z = +d or −d) are conjugate. On the xy plane the hyperbola becomes the pair of straight lines 5'5' and 5 5.

Every section which is not parallel to a plane containing the z axis is also a hyperbola (or a straight line). There are no elliptical or circular sections.

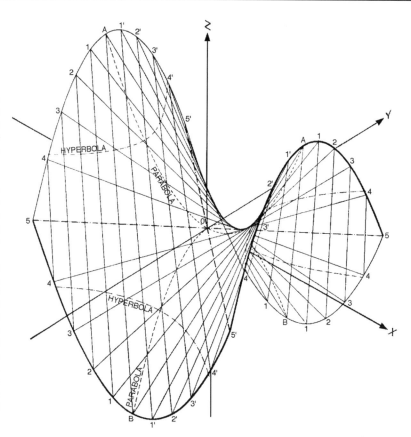

ISOMETRIC PROJECTION

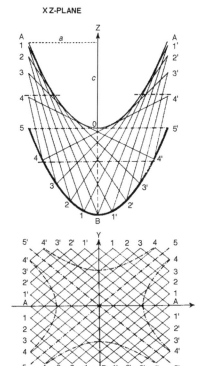

PLAN

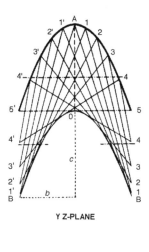

X Z-PLANE

Y Z-PLANE

Another quadric surface, the hyperboloid of one sheet (or of one nappe) is shown here in isometric and orthogonal projections. It is one of the only two possible doubly ruled curved surfaces; the other is the hyperbolic paraboloid. It is easily constructed from straight members. It can be generated in several ways:

1. As a ruled surface: A straight line (such as 3'12) is moved so that it touches at all times three given, non-intersecting straight lines (such as 3'18, 4'19 and 5'20), no two of which are in the same plane and which are not all parallel to any one plane. The three given straight lines are all members of one family or regulus; the successive position of the line 3' 12 generate the other family (such as 4' 13, 5' 14, 6' 15, etc.).

2. By the rotation of a variable hyperbola about its conjugate axis (here the z axis), with its apex always in contact with an ellipse (the throat ellipse) which is in a plane normal to this axis. When the throat ellipse is a circle, the hyperbola does not vary and the surface is a hyperboloid of revolution of one sheet.

3. By the translation of a variable (but always similar) ellipse with its plane always normal to a straight line through its center (here the z axis) and with the extremities of its axes on two fixed hyperbolas (here the sections of the xz and yz planes) whose planes are perpendicular and whose conjugate axis is this straight line.

The equation (axes as shown): $\dfrac{x^2}{a^2} + \dfrac{y^2}{b^2} - \dfrac{z^2}{c^2} = 1$

(The equation of the asymptotic cone, shown here in section as a dotted line, is $\dfrac{x^2}{a^2} + \dfrac{y^2}{b^2} - \dfrac{z^2}{c^2} = 0$)

All sections containing the z axis are hyperbolas. The xz and yz hyperbolas are principal sections. All sections parallel to any given plane containing the z axis are hyperbolas whose asymptotes are the projections on this section plane of the parallel section of the asymptotic cone containing the z axis. Such vertical sections which cut the throat ellipse will have the axes of the hyperbolas in the xy plane; sections which do not, will have their axes parallel to the z axis. The vertical section which is tangent to the throat ellipse will consist of the pair of straight lines passing through the point of tangency. (The dotted lines shown on the xz and yz planes are projections of these.) Portions of the hyperboloid as cut off by two parallel planes, both parallel to the z axis, have been used for shell roofs, such as the Hippodrome at Madrid by Torroja.

All sections parallel to the xy plane are similar ellipses.

All other sections are conics, including circles, ellipses, parabolas and hyperbolas. Circular sections are shown on Sheet 38. The contour edge of the "inside" will be an ellipse, of the "outside" a hyperbola.

The nature of such curves can be determined for each case by a simple test (see diagram). Given a curve such as ACB. Draw the chord AB and the tangents AO and BO. Find the midpoint M of AB. Draw OM, cutting the curve at C. If C lies at the midpoint of OM (such as C_2) the curve is a parabola; if C is closer to M (such as C_1) it is an elipse; if closer to O (such as C_3) a hyperbola.

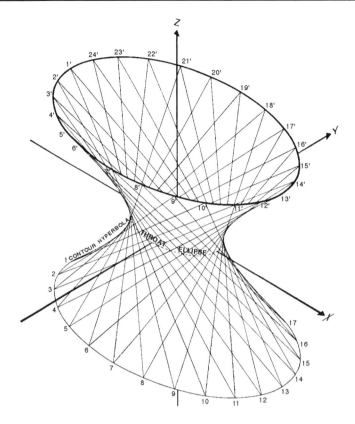

ISOMETRIC PROJECTION

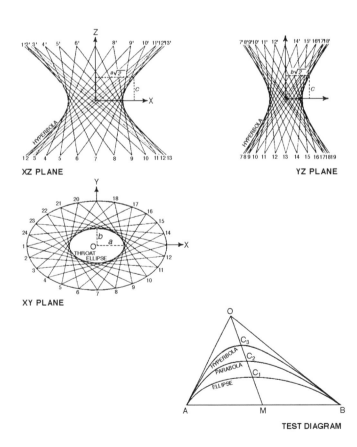

XZ PLANE

YZ PLANE

XY PLANE

TEST DIAGRAM

Appendix 2—Units of measurement

Table 1. U.S. Customary Units

Measures of weight

Weights
(The grain is the same in all systems)

Avoirdupois **weight**

16 drams	= 437.5 grains	= 1 ounce
16 ounces	= 7000 grains	= 1 pound
100 pounds		= 1 cental
2000 pounds		= 1 short ton
2240 pounds		= 1 long ton
1 std. lime bbl., small		= 180 lb. net
1 std. lime bbl., large		= 280 lb. net

Also (in Great Britain)

14 pounds		= 1 stone
2 stone	= 28 lb.	= 1 quarter
4 quarters	= 112 lb.	= 1 hundred-weight (cwt.)
20 hundred weight		= 1 long ton

Troy Weight

24 grains		= 1 pennyweight (dwt.)
20 pennyweights	= 480 grains	= 1 ounce
12 ounces	= 5760 grains	= 1 pound

1 Assay Ton = 29,167 milligrams, or as many milligrams as there are troy ounces in a ton of 2000 lb. *avoirdupois*. Consequently, the number of milligrams of precious metal yielded by an assay ton of ore gives directly the number of troy ounces that would be obtained from a ton of 2000 lb. avoirdupois.

Apothecaries' Weight

20 grains		= 1 scruple
3 scruples	= 60 grains	= 1 dram
8 drams		= 1 ounce
12 ounces	= 5760 grains	= 1 pound

Linear measure

Measures of length

12 inches		= 1 foot
3 feet		= 1 yard
5-1/2 yards	= 16-1/2 feet	= 1 rod, pole or perch
40 poles	= 220 yards	= 1 furlong
8 furlongs	= 1760 yards	
	= 5280 feet	= 1 mile
3 miles		= 1 league
4 inches		= 1 hand
9 inches		= 1 span

Nautical units

6080.20 feet	= 1 nautical mile
6 feet	= 1 fathom
120 fathoms	= 1 cable length
1 nautical mile per hr.	= 1 knot

Surveyor's or Gunter's Measure

7.92 inches		= 1 link
100 links	= 66 ft. = 4 rods	= 1 chain
80 chains		= 1 mile
33 1/3 inches		= 1 vara (Texas)

Measures of area

144 square inches	= 1 square foot
9 square feet	= 1 square yard
30-1/4 square yards	= 1 square rod, pole or perch

160 square rods	= 10 square chains	
	= 43,560 sq. ft.	= 1 acre
	= 5645 sq. *vara* (Texas)	
	= 4 roods	

640 acres = 1 square mile = 1 section of U. S. Govt. surveyed land

Volumetric measure

Measures of volume

1728 cubic inches	= 1 cubic foot
27 cubic feet	= 1 cubic yard
1 cord of wood	= 128 cu. ft.
1 perch of masonry	= 16-1/2 to 25 cu. ft.

Liquid or fluid measure

4 gills	= 1 pint
2 pints	= 1 quart
4 quarts	= 1 gallon
7,4805 gallons	= 1 cubic foot

There is no standard liquid barrel. By trade custom, 1 bbl. of petroleum oil, unrefined = 42 gal.

Dry measure

2 pints	= 1 quart
8 quarts	= 1 peck
4 pecks	= 1 bushel

1 std. bbl. for fruits and vegetables = 7056 cu. in. or 105 dry quarts, struck measure.

Board measure

1 board foot	= 144 cu. in	= volume of board 1 ft. sq. and 1 in. thick.

To calculate the number of board feet in a log = $[1/4\,(d - 4)]^2 L$, where d = diameter of log in inches (usually taken inside the bark at small end), and L = length of log in feet. The 4 in. deducted are an allowance for slab. This rule is variously known as the Doyle, Conn. River, St. Croix, Thurber, Moore and Beeman, and the Scribner rule.

Table 2. Length, Area and Volume/Capacity Equivalents

LENGTH EQUIVALENTS

	Inches	Feet	Yards	Chains	Miles	Millimeters	Meters	Kilometers
Inches	1	0.083 33	0.027 78	0.001 263	1.578×10^{-5}	25.4	0.0254	2.54×10^{-5}
Feet	12	1	0.3333	0.015 15	1.894×10^{-4}	304.8	0.3048	3.048×10^{-4}
Yards	36	3	1	0.045 45	5.682×10^{-4}	914.4	0.9144	9.144×10^{-4}
Chains	792	66	22	1	0.0125	20 116.8	20.1168	0.020 117
Miles	63 360	5280	1760	80	1	1 609 344	1609.344	1.609 344
Millimeters	0.039 37	0.003 281	0.001 094	4.971×10^{-5}	6.214×10^{-7}	1	0.001	0.000 001
Meters	39.3701	3.280 8	1.0936	0.049 710	6.214×10^{-4}	1000	1	0.001
Kilometers	39 370	3280.84	1093.61	49.7097	0.621 37	1 000 000	1000	1

AREA EQUIVALENTS

	Square inches	Square feet	Square yards	Square rods	Square Chains	Acres	Square miles	Square meters	Hectares*
Square inches	1	0.006 944	7.716×10^{-4}	2.834×10^{-6}	——	——	——	6.452×10^{-4}	——
Square feet	144	1	0.1111	0.003 673	2.296×10^{-4}	2.296×10^{-5}	3.587×10^{-8}	0.092 903	9.290×10^{-6}
Square yards	1296	9	1	0.033 058	0.002 066	2.066×10^{-4}	3.228×10^{-7}	0.836 127	8.361×10^{-5}
Square rods	39 204	272.25	30.25	1	0.0625	0.006 25	9.766×10^{-6}	25.2929	0.002 529
Square chains	627 264	4356	484	16	1	0.1	1.562×10^{-4}	404.6856	0.040 469
Acres	6 272 640	43 560	4840	160	10	1	0.001 562	4046.856	0.404 686
Square miles	——	27 878 400	3 097 600	102 400	6400	640	1	2 589 988	258.9988
Square meters	1550.00	10.7639	1.1960	0.039 537	0.002 471	2.471×10^{-4}	3.861×10^{-7}	1	0.0001
Hectares*	——	107 639	11 959.9	395.3686	24.7105	2.4711	0.003 861	10 000	1

* 1 hectare = 10 000 square meters (m²) = 0.01 square kilometer (km²)

VOLUME AND CAPACITY EQUIVALENTS

	Cubic inches	Cubic feet	Cubic yards	U.S. Fluid ounces	U.S. Quart (liquid)	U.S. Gallon (liquid)	U.S. Gallon (dry)	Liter	Cubic meter
Cubic inches	1	5.787×10^{-4}	2.143×10^{-5}	0.554 113	0.017 316	0.004 239	0.003 720	0.016 387	1.639×10^{-5}
Cubic feet	1728	1	0.037 037	957.506	29.922	7.4805	6.4285	28.3168	0.028 317
Cubic yards	46 656	27	1	25 852.7	807.896	201.974	173.57	764.555	0.764 555
U.S. Fl. oz.	1.8047	0.001 044	3.868×10^{-5}	1	0.031 25	0.007 812	0.006 714	0.029 574	2.957×10^{-5}
U.S. Quart (liq)	57.75	0.033 42	0.001 238	32	1	0.25	0.214 84	0.946 352	9.464×10^{-4}
U.S. Gallon (liq)	231	0.133 68	0.004 951	128	4	1	0.859 37	3.785 412	0.003 785
U.S. Gallon (dry)	268.8	0.1556	0.005 761	148.95	4.6546	1.1636	1	4.404 884	0.004 404
U.S. Bushel	2150.4	1.244 46	0.046 091	1191.57	37.237	9.3092	8	35.2391	0.035 239
Liter	61.024	0.035 31	0.001 308	33.814	1.0567	0.264 17	0.227 02	1	0.001
Cubic meter	61 024	35.3147	1.307 95	33 814	1056.67	264.172	227.021	1000	1

Table 3. Mass/Weight and Decimal/Fraction Equivalents

MASS (WEIGHT) EQUIVALENTS

	Grains	Ounces [Avoirdup.]	Ounces [Troy]	Pounds [Avoirdup.]	Pounds [Troy]	Short tons [2000 lb]	Long tons [2240 lb]	Kilograms	Metric tons
Grains	1	0.002 286	0.002 083	1.429×10^{-4}	1.736×10^{-4}	7.143×10^{-8}	6.378×10^{-8}	6.378×10^{-5}	6.480×10^{-8}
Ounces [Avoirdupois]	437.5	1	1.097 14	0.0625	0.075 95	3.125×10^{-5}	2.790×10^{-5}	0.028 35	2.835×10^{-5}
Ounces [Troy]	480	0.911 458	1	0.068 57	0.083 33	3.429×10^{-5}	3.061×10^{-5}	0.031 10	3.110×10^{-5}
Pounds (lb) [Avoirdupois]	7000	16	14.5833	1	1.215 28	0.0005	4.464×10^{-4}	0.453 59	4.546×10^{-4}
Pounds [Troy]	5760	13.1674	12	0.822 86	1	4.114×10^{-4}	3.673×10^{-4}	0.373 24	3.732×10^{-4}
Short Tons [2000 lb]	14 000 000	32 000	29 166.7	2000	2430.55	1	0.892 86	907.185	0.907 18
Long Tons [2240 lb]	15 680 000	35 840	32 666.7	2240	2722.22	1.12	1	1016.05	1.016 05
Kilograms	15 432.4	35.274	32.151	2.2046	2.6792	0.001 102	9.842×10^{-4}	1	0.001
Metric tons	15 432 358	35 273.96	32 150.8	2204.623	2679.23	1.102 311	0.984 207	1000	1

DECIMAL EQUIVALENTS OF FRACTIONS OF AN INCH

$\frac{1}{64}'' = 0.015\ 625$	$\frac{17}{64}'' = 0.265\ 625$	$\frac{33}{64}'' = 0.515\ 625$	$\frac{49}{64}'' = 0.765\ 625$
$\frac{1}{32}'' = 0.031\ 25$	$\frac{9}{32}'' = 0.281\ 25$	$\frac{17}{32}'' = 0.531\ 25$	$\frac{25}{32}'' = 0.781\ 25$
$\frac{3}{64}'' = 0.046\ 875$	$\frac{19}{64}'' = 0.396\ 875$	$\frac{35}{64}'' = 0.546\ 875$	$\frac{51}{64}'' = 0.796\ 875$
$\frac{1}{16}'' = 0.062\ 5$	$\frac{5}{16}'' = 0.312\ 5$	$\frac{9}{16}'' = 0.562\ 5$	$\frac{13}{16}'' = 0.812\ 5$
$\frac{5}{64}'' = 0.078\ 125$	$\frac{21}{64}'' = 0.328\ 125$	$\frac{37}{64}'' = 0.578\ 125$	$\frac{53}{64}'' = 0.828\ 125$
$\frac{3}{32}'' = 0.093\ 75$	$\frac{11}{32}'' = 0.343\ 75$	$\frac{19}{32}'' = 0.593\ 75$	$\frac{27}{32}'' = 0.843\ 75$
$\frac{7}{64}'' = 0.109\ 375$	$\frac{23}{64}'' = 0.359\ 375$	$\frac{39}{64}'' = 0.609\ 375$	$\frac{55}{64}'' = 0.859\ 375$
$\frac{1}{8}'' = 0.125$	$\frac{3}{8}'' = 0.375$	$\frac{5}{8}'' = 0.625$	$\frac{7}{8}'' = 0.875$
$\frac{9}{64}'' = 0.140\ 625$	$\frac{25}{64}'' = 0.390\ 625$	$\frac{41}{64}'' = 0.640\ 625$	$\frac{57}{64}'' = 0.890\ 625$
$\frac{5}{32}'' = 0.156\ 25$	$\frac{13}{32}'' = 0.406\ 25$	$\frac{21}{32}'' = 0.656\ 25$	$\frac{29}{32}'' = 0.906\ 25$
$\frac{11}{64}'' = 0.171\ 875$	$\frac{27}{64}'' = 0.421\ 875$	$\frac{43}{64}'' = 0.671\ 875$	$\frac{59}{64}'' = 0.921\ 875$
$\frac{3}{16}'' = 0.187\ 5$	$\frac{7}{16}'' = 0.437\ 5$	$\frac{11}{16}'' = 0.687\ 5$	$\frac{15}{16}'' = 0.937\ 5$
$\frac{13}{64}'' = 0.203\ 125$	$\frac{29}{64}'' = 0.453\ 125$	$\frac{45}{64}'' = 0.703\ 125$	$\frac{61}{64}'' = 0.953\ 125$
$\frac{7}{32}'' = 0.218\ 75$	$\frac{15}{32}'' = 0.468\ 75$	$\frac{23}{32}'' = 0.718\ 75$	$\frac{31}{32}'' = 0.968\ 75$
$\frac{15}{64}'' = 0.234\ 375$	$\frac{31}{64}'' = 0.484\ 375$	$\frac{47}{64}'' = 0.734\ 375$	$\frac{63}{64}'' = 0.984\ 375$
$\frac{1}{4}'' = 0.250$	$\frac{1}{2}'' = 0.500$	$\frac{3}{4}'' = 0.750$	$1'' = 1.000$

Table 4. Conversion of inches and fractions to decimals of a foot

Conversions have been given to six decimal places. Boldface values are exact. Factors may be rounded to the appropriate degree of precision required, for example, to three decimal places.

Common fractions	0	1"	2"	3"	4"	5"	6"	7"	8"	9"	10"	11"
0	——	0.083 333	0.166 667	**0.250**	0.333 333	0.416 667	**0.500**	0.583 333	0.666 667	**0.750**	0.833 333	0.916 667
1/16"	0.005 208	0.088 542	**0.171 875**	0.255 208	0.338 542	**0.421 875**	0.505 208	0.588 542	**0.671 875**	0.755 208	0.838 542	**0.921 875**
1/8"	0.010 417	**0.093 75**	0.177 083	0.260 417	**0.343 75**	0.427 083	0.510 417	**0.593 75**	0.677 083	0.760 412	**0.843 75**	0.927 083
3/16"	**0.015 625**	0.098 958	0.182 292	**0.265 625**	0.348 958	0.432 292	**0.515 625**	0.598 958	0.682 292	**0.765 625**	0.848 958	0.932 292
1/4"	0.020 833	0.104 167	**0.187 5**	0.270 833	0.354 167	**0.437 5**	0.520 833	0.604 167	**0.687 5**	0.770 833	0.854 167	**0.937 5**
5/16"	0.026 042	**0.109 375**	0.192 708	0.276 042	**0.359 375**	0.442 708	0.526 042	**0.609 375**	0.692 708	0.776 042	**0.859 375**	0.942 708
3/8"	**0.031 25**	0.114 583	0.197 917	**0.281 25**	0.364 583	0.447 917	**0.531 25**	0.614 583	0.697 917	**0.781 25**	0.864 583	0.947 917
7/16"	0.036 458	0.119 792	**0.203 125**	0.286 458	0.369 792	**0.453 125**	0.536 458	0.619 792	**0.703 125**	0.786 458	0.869 792	**0.953 125**
1/2"	0.041 667	**0.125**	0.208 333	0.291 667	**0.375**	0.458 333	0.541 667	**0.625**	0.708 333	0.791 667	**0.875**	0.958 333
9/16"	**0.046 875**	0.130 208	0.213 542	**0.296 875**	0.380 208	0.463 542	**0.546 875**	0.630 208	0.713 542	**0.796 875**	0.880 208	0.963 542
5/8"	0.052 083	0.135 417	**0.218 75**	0.302 083	0.385 417	**0.468 75**	0.552 083	0.635 417	**0.718 75**	0.802 083	0.885 417	**0.968 75**
11/16"	0.057 292	**0.140 625**	0.223 958	0.307 292	**0.390 625**	0.473 958	0.557 292	**0.640 625**	0.723 958	0.807 292	**0.890 625**	0.973 958
3/4"	**0.062 5**	0.145 833	0.229 167	**0.312 5**	0.395 833	0.479 167	**0.562 5**	0.645 833	0.729 167	**0.812 5**	0.895 833	0.979 167
13/16"	0.067 708	0.151 042	**0.234 375**	0.317 708	0.401 042	**0.484 375**	0.567 708	0.651 042	**0.734 375**	0.817 708	0.901 042	**0.984 375**
7/8"	0.072 917	**0.156 25**	0.239 583	0.322 917	**0.406 25**	0.489 583	0.572 917	**0.656 25**	0.739 583	0.822 917	**0.906 25**	0.989 583
15/16"	**0.078 125**	0.161 458	0.244 792	**0.328 125**	0.411 458	0.494 792	**0.578 125**	0.661 458	0.744 792	**0.828 125**	0.911 458	0.994 792

Inches

R. E. Shaeffer

Summary

The SI system—after *Le Système International d'Unites*—is the internationally adopted standard of measurement, based on the meter-kilogram-second-ampere system of fundamental units, modifying the prior European metric unit system and replacing the United States' customary measurement systems. This introduction provides a brief overview.

Key words

metrics, metrification, customary measurement units, SI units

Appendix 3—The SI metric system

What is SI metric?

SI metric is the name given to the measurement system adopted on a worldwide basis. It differs somewhat from the long-standing European metric system. SI stands for *Le Système International d'Unites*, a name given by the 36 nations meeting at the 11th General Conference on Weights and Measures (CGPM) in 1960. SI is a coherent means of measurement based on the meter-kilogram-second-ampere system of fundamental units. Conversions within the system are never necessary (e.g., as in the customary system, ounces to pounds and inches to feet, etc.).

The metric system to the United States

Developed at the time of the French Revolution, the metric system spread throughout Europe during the Napoleonic era. It was promoted in the United States first by Thomas Jefferson and subsequently by John Quincy Adams. In 1866, Congress made the metric system a legal system of units for U.S. use. In 1875 the United States and 16 other nations formed the General Conference on Weights and Measures (CGPM). The United States has been active in the periodic meetings of this group. In 1893, an Executive Order made the meter and the kilogram fundamental standards from which the pound and the yard would henceforth be derived. In 1960 the CGPM established the SI system and has subsequently modified it in several meetings.

In the United States, the Omnibus Trade and Competitiveness Act of 1988 and its amendments declared the metric system as the preferred system of measurement for the United States and mandated its use in all federal activities to the extent feasible. Federal agencies formed the Construction Metrification Council within the National Institute of Building Sciences (NIBS) in Washington, D.C. The Council is responsible for coordinating activities and distributing information and metric resources (NIBS 1991).

Some "rules of grammar"

- Double prefixes should never be used; e.g., use Gm (gigameter), not Mkm (megakilometer).

- Base units are not capitalized unless writing a symbol derived from a proper name; e.g., 12 meters or 12 m, 60 Newtons or 60N.

- Plurals are written normally except for quantities less than 1. In such cases the "s" is deleted; e.g., 2.6 meters and 0.6 meter.

- Prefix symbols are not capitalized except for M (mega), G (giga), and T (tera). This avoids confusion with m (meter), g (gram), and t (metric ton). One metric ton (t) is equal to one megagram (Mg).

- Periods are not used after symbols except at the end of a sentence. Commas should not be used to clarify groups of digits; instead, use spaced groups of three on each side of the decimal point.

832 604.789 06 not 832,604.78906
20 800 not 20,800

Credits: Adapted by the author from R.E. Shaeffer 1980, cited in the References. ASTM, 1994. Tables compiled from *ASTM E621* (a complete version of this key reference is included on the CD-ROM accompanying this volume).

Table 1—Principal SI units used in structures of concern to architect

What are the principal units used in structures which will be of concern to the architect?

Name	Symbol	Use
Meter	m	Site plan dimensions, building plans
Millimeter	mm	Building plans and details
Square millimeters	mm²	Small areas
Square meters	m³	Large areas
Hectare	ha	Very large areas (1 hectare equals 10^4 m
Cubic millimeters	mm³	Small volumes
Cubic meters	m³	Large volumes
Section modulus	mm³	Property of cross section
Moment of inertia	mm⁴	Property of cross section
Kilogram	kg	Mass of all building materials
Newton	N	Force (all structural computations)
Pascal	Pa	Stress or pressure (all structural computations; one pascal equals one newton per square meter)
Mass density	kg/ m³	Density of materials
Degree Celsius	°C	Temperature measurement

Table 2—SI units and multiplication factors

Multiplication factors	Prefix	Symbol
10^{12}	tera	T
10^9	giga (jiga)	G
10^6	mega	M
10^3	kilo	k
10^2	hecto	h
10^1	deka	da
10^{-1}	deci	d
10^{-2}	centi	c
10^{-3}	milli	m
10^{-6}	micro	m
10^{-9}	nano (nano)	n
10^{-12}	pico (peco)	p
10^{-13}	femto	f
10^{-18}	atto	a

frequently used by architects

To be consistent and avoid confusion, prefixes should change in steps of 10^3;

Exception: The space is optional in groups of four digits; e.g.,

> 1486 or 1 486
> 0.3248 or 0.324 8

- Division is indicated by a slash; e.g., a certain steel beam has a mass of 100 kg/m.

- Multiplication is indicated by a dot placed at mid-height of the letters; e.g., a certain moment or torque might be given as 100kN·m.

- Decimals (not dual units) should be used; e.g., for the length of one side of a building lot, state 118.6 m rather than 118 m, 600 mm.

- All dimensions on a given drawing should have the same units.

What is the major change from the customary system to SI for building design?

In the SI metric system of units, a clear distinction is made between mass and force. The customary system treated mass and force as if they both had force units; i.e., it would be written that a beam weighed 100 lb/foot and that the force in a truss member was 1800 lb. It was correct to use pounds for force but not for weight (mass). In the former European metric system, it was said that the beam weighed 149 kg/m and that the force in a truss member was 818 kg of force (kgf). It was correct to use kilograms for weight (mass) but not for force.

F is equal to MA   F is not equal to M

SI units do not confuse the two terms. One can "weigh" items such as cubic meters of concrete by establishing the mass in kilograms, but force is expressed in Newtons. Pressure (stress) is in Newtons per square meter (Pascals).

A commonly used illustration to explain the difference between force and mass is to look at what happens in different fields of gravity. Assume that you are holding a 1-kg mass in the palm of your hand. On earth, the kg would exert a force of 9.8 N downward on your hand. (This would vary slightly, depending upon whether you were located at sea level or on top of Mt. Everest.) At Tranquility Base on our moon, it would push with a force of 1.6 N, and on the surface of Jupiter one would feel a force of 24.1 N!

For engineering purposes on earth, we can multiply loads (if given in kg) by 9.8 to get the number of Newtons of force for which to design.

How will the new units modify design drawings?

Conceptually, the square meter is the new unit of plan area replacing the square foot. Length measurements may be in meters or millimeters, except that it is desirable to express all the measurements on a single drawing in the same units. (Among other advantages, this obviates the need for placing m or mm as a suffix to each dimension.) The millimeter is preferred for all detail, section, and plan drawings up through the scale of 1:200. On plans, this results in small numbers for wall thickness and large numbers for room dimensions, but eliminates the need for fractions. Even on details, the millimeter is small enough so that, with few exceptions, fractions can be avoided.

The basic building modules recommended are 100 mm and 300 mm. The 300-mm dimension is very close to 12 in and will be an easy concept to adopt. At the same time, it is much more flexible, in that it is evenly divisible by 2, 3, 4, 5, 6, 10, 15, 20, 25, 30, 50, 60, 100, and 150.

Tables of conversion factors are commonly available (as represented in the Tables accompanying this article). However, the more one uses conversion factors, the longer it will take to "think" in metric. In any event, one must keep the desired level of accuracy in mind when making conversions.

For example, working with a reinforced concrete beam 12 × 20 in in cross section and converting its area in square inches to millimeters squared (the dimensions imply an accuracy of plus or minus 1 square inch, or about 0.4 percent): following the table below, one could convert to metric by multiplying 240 by 6.451 600 E+02 to get an area of 154 838 mm². To use this quantity would be deceiving in terms of accuracy because it is subject to the same ±0.4 percent tolerance level, or in this case approximately 600 mm². In other words, the area could range from approximately 154 200 to 155 400. Expressing the converted area as simply 155 000 mm² would be much more consistent.

REFERENCES

ASTM, *ASTM E621-Standard Practice for the Use of Metric (SI) Units in Building Design and Construction,* American Society for Testing and Materials, Philadelphia, 1994 (complete version is included on the CD-ROM accompanying this volume).

NIBS, *Metric Guide for Federal Construction,* National Institute of Building Sciences, Washington, 1991.

Shaeffer, R. E., *Building Structures: Elementary Analysis and Design,* Prentice-Hall, Englewood Cliffs, 1980.

Table 3—Commonly used scales

Commonly Used Scales

Customary	Nearest convenient ratio	Metric equivalent
1/16" = 1'- 0"	1:200	5 mm = 1m
1/8" = 1'- 0"	1:100	10 mm = 1m
1/4" = 1'- 0"	1:50	20 mm = 1m
1/2" = 1'- 0"	1:20	50 mm = 1m
3/4" = 1'- 0"	1:10	100 mm = 1m
1-1/2" = 1'- 0"	1:10	100 mm = 1m
3" = 1'- 0"	1:5	200 mm = 1m
1" = 20'	1:200	5 mm = 1m
1" = 50'	1:500	2mm = 1m

Table 4—Selected conversion factors

A few conversion factors that may prove useful in structural analysis are presented below.

To convert from	to	Multiply by
inches	mm	2.540 000 E+01
feet	m	3.048 000 E-01
in.²	mm²	6.451 600 E+02
ft²	m²	9.290 304 E-02
in.³	mm³	1.638 706 E+04
ft³	m³	2.831 685 E-02
in.⁴	mm⁴	4.162 314 E+05
°F	°C	t°C = (t°F - 32)/1.8
lb (mass) per foot	kg/m	1.488 163 E+00
lb. (force) per foot	N/m	1.459 390 E+01
strain/°F (thermal expansion)	strain/°C	1.800 000 E+00
lb (force)	N	4.448 222 E+00
kip (force)	kN	4.448 222 E+00
lb-ft	(movement)N·m	1.355 818 E+00
kip-ft (movement)	k N·m	1.355 818 E+00
psi (stress)	kPa	6.894 757 E+00
ksi (stress)	Mpa	6.894 757 E+00
psf (uniform load)	kN/m²	4.788 026 E-02

Table 5—Conversion Tables: Basic units

For more information, consult the Construction Metrication Council, National Institute of Building Sciences,
1201 L Street NW, Suite 400, Washington, D.C. 20005, or call 202-289-7800

Base Units and Some Derived Units of SI (System International Metric)

physical quantity	name of unit	symbol for unit	physical quantity	name of unit	symbol for unit
length	meter	m	volume	cubic meter	m^3
mass (weight)	kilogram	kg	density	kilogram per cubic meter	kg/m^3
time	second	s	velocity	meter per second	m/s
electric current	ampere	A	acceleration	meter per second squared	m/s^2
thermodynamic temperature	kelvin	K	pressure	kilopascal	kPa
luminous intensity	candela	cd	force	Newton	N
area	square meter	m^2	bending moment	Newton meter	N•m

Symbols for units do not take a plural form.

Distance

Inch-Pound Units		SI System		SI System		Inch-Pound Units	
1 inch	=	25.4	millimeters	1 millimeter	=	0.03937	inch
1 foot	=	0.3048	meter	1 meter	=	3.281	feet
1 yard	=	0.9144	meter		=	1.094	yard
1 rod	=	5.029	meters	1 kilometer	=	0.6214	mile
1 mile	=	1.609	kilometer				

Mass (Weight)

1 ounce (avoir)	=	28.350	grams
1 pound (avoir)	=	453.592	grams
1 gram	=	0.035	ounce (avoir)
1 kilogram	=	2.205	pounds (avoir)

Liquid Volume (Capacity)

1 pint (U.S.)	=	0.473	liter
1 quart (U.S.)	=	0.946	liter
1 gallon (U.S.)	=	3.785	liters
1 barrel (U.S.)	=	158.98	liters

Area

1 square inch	=	645.16	square millimeters
1 square foot	=	0.093	square meter
1 square yard	=	0.836	square meter
1 acre	=	0.405	hectare*
1 square mile	=	259.0	hectares
1 square mile	=	2.590	square kilometers
1 square millimeter	=	0.00155	square inch
1 square meter	=	10.76	square feet
1 square meter	=	1.196	square yard
1 hectare*	=	2.471	acres
1 square kilometer	=	0.386	square mile

Volume

1 cubic inch	=	16387	cubic millimeters
1 cubic foot	=	0.0283	cubic meter
1 cubic yard	=	0.765	cubic meter
1 cubic meter	=	35.315	cubic feet
	=	1.308	cubic yard

*1 hectare = 1 square hectometer

FAHRENHEIT   CELSIUS

BOILING POINTS
212° F/100° C

FREEZING POINTS
32° F/0° C

Conversion °F to °C
– Subtract 32
– Divide by 1.8

Example
80° – 32   = 48
48 ÷ 1.8   = 26.66°C

Conversion °C to °F
–Multiply by 1.8
–Add 32

Example
27°C 27 x 1.8 = 48.6
48.6 + 32   = 80.6° F

Table 6—Conversion Tables: inches to millimeters

Inches/Feet to Millimeters

inches	milli-meters	inches	milli-meters	inches	milli-meters	inches	milli-meters	ft. in.	milli-meters
1/64	0.3969	1 27/32	46.8313	4 21/32	118.269	8 15/16	227.012	3 7	1092.20
1/32	0.7938	1 7/8	47.6250	4 11/16	119.062	**9**	**228.600**	3 8	1117.60
3/64	1.1906	1 29/32	48.4188	4 23/32	119.856	9 1/16	230.188	3 9	1143.20
1/16	1.5875	1 15/16	49.2125	**4 3/4**	**120.650**	9 1/8	231.775	3 10	1168.40
5/64	1.9844	1 31/32	50.0063	4 25/32	121.444	9 3/16	233.362	3 11	1193.80
3/32	2.3813	**2**	**50.8000**	4 13/16	122.238	**9 1/4**	**234.950**	**4 0**	**1219.20**
7/64	2.7781	2 1/32	51.5938	4 27/32	123.031	9 5/16	236.538	4 1	1244.60
1/8	3.1750	2 1/16	52.3875	4 7/8	123.825	9 3/8	238.125	4 2	1270.00
9/64	3.5719	2 3/32	53.1813	4 29/32	124.619	9 7/16	239.712	4 3	1295.40
5/32	3.9688	2 1/8	53.9750	4 15/16	125.412	**9 1/2**	**241.300**	4 4	1320.80
11/64	4.3656	2 5/32	54.7688	4 31/32	126.206	9 9/16	242.888	**4 5**	**1346.20**
3/16	4.7625	2 3/16	55.5625	**5**	**127.000**	9 5/8	244.475	4 6	1371.60
13/64	5.1594	2 7/32	56.3583	5 1/32	127.794	9 11/16	246.062	4 7	1397.00
7/32	5.5563	**2 1/4**	**57.1500**	5 1/16	128.588	**9 3/4**	**247.650**	4 8	1422.40
15/64	5.9531	2 9/32	57.9438	5 3/32	129.381	9 13/16	249.238	4 9	1447.80
1/4	**6.3500**	2 5/16	58.7375	5 1/8	130.175	9 7/8	250.825	4 10	1473.20
17/64	6.7469	2 11/32	59.5313	5 5/32	130.969	9 15/16	252.412	4 11	1498.60
9/32	7.1438	2 3/8	60.3250	5 3/16	131.762	**10**	**254.000**	**5 0**	**1524.00**
19/64	7.5406	2 13/32	61.1118	5 7/32	132.556	10 1/16	255.588	5 1	1549.40
5/16	7.9375	2 7/16	61.9125	**5 1/4**	**133.350**	10 1/8	257.175	5 2	1574.80
21/64	8.3344	2 15/32	62.7063	5 9/32	134.144	10 3/16	258.762	5 3	1600.20
11/32	8.7313	**2 1/2**	**63.5000**	5 5/16	134.938	**10 1/4**	**260.350**	5 4	1625.60
23/64	9.1281	2 17/32	64.2938	5 11/32	135.731	10 5/16	261.938	**5 5**	**1651.00**
3/8	9.5250	2 9/16	65.0875	5 3/8	136.525	10 3/8	263.525	5 6	1676.40
25/64	9.9219	2 19/32	65.8813	5 13/32	137.319	10 7/16	265.112	5 7	1701.80
13/32	10.3188	2 5/8	66.6750	5 7/16	138.112	**10 1/2**	**266.700**	5 8	1727.20
27/64	10.7156	2 21/32	67.4688	5 15/32	138.906	10 9/16	268.288	5 9	1752.60
7/16	11.1125	2 11/16	68.2625	**5 1/2**	**139.700**	10 5/8	269.875	5 10	1778.00
29/64	11.5094	2 23/32	69.0563	5 17/32	140.494	10 11/16	271.462	5 11	1803.40
15/32	11.9063	**2 3/4**	**69.8500**	5 9/16	141.288	**10 3/4**	**273.050**	**6 0**	**1828.80**
31/64	12.3031	2 25/32	70.6438	5 19/32	142.081	10 13/16	274.638	6 1	1854.20
1/2	**12.7000**	2 13/16	71.4375	5 5/8	142.875	10 7/8	276.225	6 2	1879.60
33/64	13.0969	2 27/32	72.2313	5 31/32	143.669	10 15/16	277.812	6 3	1905.00
17/32	13.4938	2 7/8	73.0250	5 11/16	144.462	**11**	**279.400**	6 4	1930.40
35/64	13.8906	2 29/32	73.8188	5 23/32	145.256	11 1/16	280.988	**6 5**	**1955.80**
9/16	14.2875	2 15/16	74.6125	**5 3/4**	**146.050**	11 1/8	282.575	6 6	1981.20
37/64	14.6844	2 31/32	75.4063	5 25/32	146.844	11 3/16	284.162	6 7	2006.60
19/32	15.0813	**3**	**76.2000**	5 13/16	147.638	**11 1/4**	**285.750**	6 8	**2032.00**
39/64	15.4781	3 1/32	76.9938	5 27/32	148.431	11 5/16	287.338	6 9	2057.40
5/8	15.8750	3 1/16	77.7875	5 7/8	149.225	11 3/8	288.925	6 10	2082.80
41/64	16.2719	3 3/32	78.5813	5 29/32	150.019	11 7/16	290.512	6 11	2108.20
21/32	16.6688	3 1/8	79.3750	5 15/15	150.812	**11 1/2**	**292.100**	**7 0**	**2133.60**
43/64	17.0656	3 5/32	80.1688	5 31/32	151.606	11 9/16	293.688	7 1	2159.00
11/16	17.4625	3 3/16	80.9625	**6**	**152.400**	11 5/8	295.275	7 2	2184.40
45/64	17.8594	3 7/32	81.7563	6 1/16	153.988	11 11/16	296.862	7 3	2209.80
23/32	18.2563	**3 1/4**	**82.5500**	6 1/8	155.575	**11 3/4**	**298.450**	7 4	2235.20
47/64	18.6531	3 9/32	83.3438	6 3/16	157.162	11 13/16	300.038	**7 5**	**2260.60**
3/4	**19.0500**	3 5/16	84.1375	**6 1/4**	**158.750**	11 7/8	301.625	7 6	2286.00
49/64	19.4469	3 11/32	84.9313	6 5/16	160.338	11 15/16	303.212	7 7	2311.40
25/32	19.8438	3 3/8	85.7250	6 3/8	161.925	**12**	**304.800**	7 8	2336.80
51/64	20.2406	3 13/32	86.5188	6 7/16	163.512	13	330.200	7 9	2362.20
13/16	20.6375	3 7/16	87.3125	**6 1/2**	**165.100**	14	355.600	7 10	2387.60
53/64	21.0344	3 15/32	88.1063	6 9/16	166.688	**15**	**381.000**	7 11	2413.00
27/32	21.4313	**3 1/2**	**88.9000**	6 5/8	168.275	16	406.400	**8 0**	**2438.40**
55/64	21.8281	3 17/32	89.6938	6 11/16	169.862	17	431.800	8 1	2463.80
7/8	22.2250	3 9/16	90.4875	**6 3/4**	**171.450**	18	457.200	8 2	2489.20
57/64	22.6219	3 19/32	91.2813	6 13/16	173.038	19	482.600	8 3	2514.60
29/32	23.0188	3 5/8	92.0750	6 7/8	174.625	**20**	**508.000**	8 4	2540.00
59/64	23.4156	3 21/32	92.8688	6 15/16	176.212	21	533.400	**8 5**	**2656.40**
15/16	23.8125	3 11/16	93.6625	**7**	**177.800**	22	558.800	8 6	2590.80
61/64	24.2094	3 23/32	94.4563	7 1/16	179.388	23	584.200	8 7	2616.20
31/32	24.6063	**3 3/4**	**95.2500**	7 1/8	180.975	24	609.600	8 8	2641.60
63/64	25.0031	3 25/32	96.0438	7 3/16	182.562	**25**	**635.000**	8 9	2667.00
1	**25.4000**	3 13/16	96.8375	**7 1/4**	**184.150**	26	660.400	8 10	2692.40
1 1/32	26.1938	3 27/32	97.6313	7 5/16	185.738	27	685.800	8 11	2717.80
1 1/16	26.9875	3 7/8	98.4250	7 3/8	187.325	28	711.200	**9 0**	**2743.20**
1 3/32	27.7813	3 29/32	99.2188	7 7/16	188.912	29	736.600	9 1	2768.60
1 1/8	28.5750	3 15/16	100.012	**7 1/2**	**190.150**	**30**	**762.000**	9 2	2794.00
1 5/32	29.3688	3 31/32	100.806	7 9/16	192.088	31	787.400	9 3	2819.40
1 3/16	30.1625	**4**	**101.600**	7 5/8	193.675	32	812.800	9 4	2844.80
1 7/32	30.9563	4 1/32	102.394	7 11/16	195.262	33	838.200	**9 5**	**2870.20**
1 1/4	**31.7500**	4 1/16	103.188	**7 3/4**	**196.850**	34	863.600	9 6	2895.60
1 9/32	32.5438	4 3/32	103.981	7 13/16	198.438	**35**	**889.000**	9 7	2921.00
1 5/16	33.3375	4 1/8	104.775	7 7/8	200.025	36	914.400	9 8	2946.40
1 11/32	34.1313	4 5/32	105.569	7 15/16	201.612	37	939.800	9 9	2971.80
1 3/8	34.9250	4 3/16	106.362	**8**	**203.200**	38	965.200	9 10	2997.20
1 13/32	35.7188	4 7/32	107.156	8 1/16	204.788	39	990.600	9 11	3022.60
1 7/16	36.5125	**4 1/4**	**107.950**	8 1/8	206.375	**40**	**1016.000**	**10 0**	**3048.00**
1 15/32	37.3063	4 9/32	108.744	8 3/16	207.962	41	1041.400	11 0	3352.80
1 1/2	**38.1000**	4 5/16	109.538	**8 1/4**	**209.550**	42	1066.800	12 0	3657.60
1 17/32	38.8938	4 11/32	110.331	8 5/16	211.138			13 0	3962.40
1 9/16	39.6875	4 3/8	111.125	8 3/8	212.725			14 0	4267.20
1 19/32	40.4813	4 13/32	111.919	8 7/16	214.312			**15 0**	**4572.00**
1 5/8	41.2750	4 7/16	112.712	**8 1/2**	**215.900**			16 0	4876.80
1 21/32	42.0688	4 15/32	113.506	8 9/16	217.488			17 0	5131.60
1 11/16	42.8625	**4 1/2**	**114.300**	8 5/8	219.075			18 0	5486.40
1 23/32	43.6563	4 17/32	115.094	8 11/16	220.662			19 0	5791.20
1 3/4	**44.4500**	4 9/16	115.888	**8 3/4**	**222.250**			**20 0**	**6096.00**
1 25/32	45.2438	4 19/32	116.681	8 13/16	223.838			21 0	6400.80
1 13/16	46.0375	4 5/8	117.475	8 7/8	225.425			22 0	6705.60

Millimeters to Inches/Feet

milli-meters	inches	milli-meter	inches	milli-meters	inches	milli-meters	inches	milli-meters	inches
1	0.0394	91	3.5827	181	7.1260	271	10.6693	361	14.2126
2	0.0787	92	3.6221	182	7.1654	272	10.7087	362	14.2520
3	0.1181	93	3.6614	183	7.2047	273	10.7480	363	14.2913
4	0.1575	94	2.7008	184	7.2441	274	10.7874	364	14.3307
5	0.1969	95	3.7401	185	7.2835	275	10.8268	365	14.3701
6	0.2362	96	3.7795	186	7.3228	276	10.8661	366	14.4094
7	0.2756	97	3.8189	187	7.3622	277	10.9055	367	14.4488
8	0.3150	98	3.8583	188	7.4016	278	10.9449	368	14.4882
9	0.3543	99	3.8976	189	7.4409	279	10.9843	369	14.5276
10	0.3937	100	3.9370	190	7.4803	280	11.0236	370	14.5669
11	0.4331	101	3.9764	191	7.5197	281	11.0630	371	14.6063
12	0.4724	102	4.0158	192	7.5591	282	11.1024	372	14.6457
13	0.5118	103	4.0551	193	7.6378	283	11.1417	373	14.6850
14	0.5512	104	4.0945	194	7.6378	284	11.1811	374	14.7244
15	0.5906	105	4.1339	195	7.6772	285	11.2205	375	14.7638
16	0.6299	106	4.1732	196	7.7165	286	11.2598	376	14.8031
17	0.6693	107	4.2126	197	7.7559	287	11.2992	377	14.8425
18	0.7087	108	4.4520	198	7.7953	288	11.3386	378	14.9213
19	0.7480	109	4.2913	199	7.8347	289	11.3780	379	14.9213
20	0.7875	110	4.3307	200	7.8740	290	11.4173	380	14.9606
21	0.8268	111	4.3701	201	7.9134	291	11.4567	381	15.0000
22	0.8661	112	4.4095	202	7.9528	292	11.4961	382	15.0394
23	0.9055	113	4.4488	203	7.9921	293	11.5354	383	15.0787
24	0.9449	114	4.4882	204	8.0315	294	11.5748	384	15.1181
25	0.9843	115	4.5276	205	8.0709	295	11.6142	385	15.1575
26	1.0236	116	4.5669	206	8.1102	296	11.6535	386	15.1969
27	1.0630	117	4.6063	207	8.1496	297	11.6929	387	15.2362
28	1.1024	118	4.6457	208	8.1890	298	11.7323	388	15.2756
29	1.1417	119	4.6850	209	8.2284	299	11.7717	389	15.3150
30	1.1811	120	4.7244	210	8.2677	300	11.8110	390	15.3543
31	1.2205	121	4.7638	211	8.3071	301	11.8504	391	15.3937
32	1.2598	122	4.8032	212	8.3465	302	11.8898	392	15.4331
33	1.2992	123	4.8425	213	8.3858	303	11.9291	393	15.4724
34	1.3386	124	4.8819	214	8.4252	304	11.9686	394	15.5118
35	1.3780	125	4.9213	215	8.4646	305	12.0079	395	15.5512
36	1.4173	126	4.9606	216	8.5039	306	12.0472	396	15.5906
37	1.4567	127	5.0000	217	8.5433	307	12.0866	397	15.6299
38	1.4961	128	5.0394	218	8.5827	308	12.1260	398	15.6693
39	1.5354	129	5.0787	219	8.6221	309	12.1654	399	15.7087
40	1.5748	130	5.1181	220	8.6614	310	12.2047	400	15.7480
41	1.6142	131	5.1575	221	8.7008	311	12.2441	401	15.7874
42	1.6535	132	5.1969	222	8.7402	312	12.2835	402	15.8268
43	1.6929	133	5.2362	223	8.7795	313	12.3228	403	15.8661
44	1.7323	134	5.2756	224	8.8189	314	12.3622	404	15.9055
45	1.7717	135	5.3150	225	8.8583	315	12.4016	405	15.9449
46	1.8110	136	5.3542	226	8.8976	316	12.4409	406	15.9832
47	1.8504	137	5.3937	227	8.9370	317	12.4803	407	16.0236
48	1.8896	138	5.4331	228	8.9764	318	12.5197	408	16.0630
49	1.9291	139	5.4724	229	9.0158	319	12.5591	409	16.1024
50	1.9685	140	5.5118	230	9.0051	320	12.5984	410	16.1417
51	2.0079	141	5.5512	231	9.0945	321	12.6378	411	16.1811
52	2.0473	142	5.5906	232	9.1339	322	12.6772	412	16.2205
53	2.0866	143	5.6299	233	9.1732	323	12.7165	413	16.2598
54	2.1260	144	5.6693	234	9.2126	324	12.7559	414	16.2992
55	2.1654	145	5.7087	235	9.2520	325	12.7953	415	16.3386
56	2.2047	146	5.7480	236	9.2913	326	12.8346	416	16.3780
57	2.2441	147	5.7874	237	9.3307	327	12.8740	417	16.4173
58	2.2835	148	5.8268	238	9.3801	328	12.9134	418	16.4567
59	2.3228	148	5.8661	239	9.4095	329	12.9528	419	16.4961
60	2.3622	150	5.9055	240	9.4488	330	12.9921	420	16.5354
61	2.4016	151	5.9449	241	9.4882	331	13.0315	421	16.5748
62	2.4409	152	5.9843	242	9.5276	332	13.0709	422	16.6142
63	2.4803	153	6.0236	243	9.5669	333	13.1102	423	16.6535
64	2.5197	154	6.0630	244	9.6063	334	13.1496	424	16.6929
65	2.5591	155	6.1024	245	9.6457	335	13.1890	425	16.7323
66	2.5984	156	6.1417	246	9.6850	336	13.2283	426	16.7716
67	2.6378	157	6.1811	247	9.7244	337	13.2677	427	16.8110
68	2.6772	158	6.2205	248	9.7638	338	13.3071	428	16.8504
69	2.7165	159	6.2599	249	9.8031	339	13.3465	429	16.8898
70	2.7559	160	6.2992	250	9.8425	340	13.3858	430	16.9291
71	2.7953	161	6.3386	251	9.8819	341	13.4252	431	16.9685
72	2.8347	162	6.3780	252	9.9213	342	13.4646	432	17.0079
73	2.8740	163	6.4173	253	9.9606	343	13.5039	433	17.0472
74	2.9134	164	6.4567	254	10.0000	344	13.5433	434	17.0866
75	2.9528	165	6.4961	255	10.0393	345	13.5827	435	17.1260
76	2.9921	166	6.5354	256	10.0787	346	13.6220	436	17.1654
77	3.0315	167	6.5748	257	10.1181	347	13.6614	437	17.2047
78	3.0709	168	6.6142	258	10.1575	348	13.7008	438	17.2441
79	3.1102	169	6.6535	259	10.1969	349	13.7402	439	17.2835
80	3.1496	170	6.6929	260	10.2362	350	13.7795	440	17.3228
81	3.1890	171	6.7323	261	10.2756	351	13.8189	441	17.3622
82	3.2284	172	6.7717	262	10.3150	352	13.8583	442	17.4016
83	3.2677	173	6.8110	263	10.3543	353	13.8976	443	17.4409
84	3.3071	174	6.8504	264	10.9370	354	13.9370	444	17.4803
85	3.3465	175	6.8898	265	10.4331	355	13.9764	445	17.5197
86	3.3858	176	6.9291	266	10.4724	356	14.0157	446	17.5591
87	3.4252	177	6.9685	267	10.5118	357	14.0551	447	17.5984
88	3.4646	178	7.0079	268	10.5512	358	14.0945	448	17.6378
89	3.5039	179	7.0472	269	10.5906	359	14.1339	449	17.6772
90	3.5433	180	7.0866	270	10.6299	360	14.1732	450	17.7165

Table 7—Energy, power and heat flux

Conversion Factors

Energy

Btu	X	252	=	cal	X	0.003968		
		0.252	=	kcal	X	3.968		
		0.2929	=	Wh	X	3.414	=	Btu
		1.0551	=	KJ[a]	X	0.9478		

Power, Thermal Transmission (Energy/Time)

Btuh	X	0.2929	=	W	X	3.414		
		0.252	=	kcal/hr	X	3.968		
		0.07	=	cal/sec	X	14.286	=	Btuh
		8.33×10^{-5}	=	ton[b]	X	12,000		
ton[b]	X	3.5168	=	kWh	X	0.2843	=	ton

Heat Flux [Energy/(time x area)]

Btuh/ft^2	X	3.152	=	W/m^2	X	0.3172		
Btu/ft^2 (hr)		0.2929	=	W/ft^2	X	3.414		
		2.712	=	kcal/hr(m^2)	X	0.3687	=	Btuh/ft^2
		0.00452	=	ly[c]/min	X	221.2		Btu/ft^2 (hr)
		0.2712	=	ly[c]/hr	X	3.687		
		0.0543	=	Met units	X	18.4		

Miscellaneous

ft	X	0.3048	=	m	X	3.28084	=	ft
ft^2	X	0.092903	=	m^2	X	10.7639	=	ft^2
lb	X	0.453592	=	kg	X	2.20462	=	lb
(F - 32)	X	5/9 = °C			(°C X 9/5)	+ 32	=	F

a 1 joule = 1 watt/sec

b ton of refrigeration, the cooling effect produced when 1 ton (2000 lb.) of ice at 32F melts to water at 32F in 24 hours

c ly = langley = 1 cal/cm^2; commonly used in meteorology as a measure of solar heat flux

Table 8—Lighting

Quantity (and SI Unit Symbol)	Preferred Units (Symbols)	Other Acceptable Units	Unit Name	Typical Applications	Remarks
Luminous Intensity (cd)	cd		candela		
Solid Angle (sr)	sr		steradian		
Luminous Flux (lm)	lm klm		lumen kilolumen	Luminous flux of light sources, lamps and light bulbs	1 lm = 1 cd·sr Already in general use
Quantity of Light (lm·s)	lm·s	lm·h	lumen second lumen hour		1 lm·h = 3600 lm/s
Luminance (cd/m²)	cd/m² kcd/m²	 cd/mm²	candela per square metre kilocandela per square metre candela per square millimetre	Assessment of surface brightness; luminance of light sources, lamps and light bulbs; calculation of glare in lighting layouts	Replaces stilb (1 sb = 10^4 cd/m²) and apostilb (1 apostilb = cd/πm²)
Illuminance (lx)	lx klx		lux kilolux	Luminous flux per unit area is used in determination of illumination levels and design/evaluation of interior lighting layouts. (Outdoor daylight illumination on a horizontal plane ranges up to 100 klx.)	a) Formerly referred to as illumination 1 lx = 1 lm/m² b) Replaces phot (1 ph = 10^4 lx) c) Luminous exitance is described in lm/m²
Light Exposure (lx·s)	lx·s klx·s		lux second kilolux second		
Luminous Efficacy (lm/W)	lm/W		lumen per watt	Rating of luminous efficacy of artificial light sources	

Table 9—Acoustics

Quantity (and SI Unit Symbol)	Preferred Units (Symbols)	Other Acceptable Units	Unit Name	Typical Applications	Remarks
Wavelength (m)	m mm		metre millimetre	Definition of sound wave pitch	
Area of Absorptive Surface (m²)	m²		square metre	Surface areas in the calculation of room absorption	Absorptive properties of buildings and building materials have also been expressed in the non-SI unit "metric sabin"
Period, Periodic Time (s)	s ms		second millisecond	Measurement of time, reverberation time, and duration of sound	
Frequency (Hz)	Hz kHz		hertz kilohertz	Frequency bands or ranges in acoustical calculations and measurements; frequency of vibrations	1 Hz = 1/s = s⁻¹ Replaces cycle per second (c/s or cps)
Sound Pressure (Pa)	Pa mPa		pascal millipascal	Measurement of instantaneous or peak sound pressure, normally expressed in root-mean-square (rms) values. The standard reference value for sound pressure is 20 µPa. Sound pressure levels are generally shown in the non-dimensional logarithmic unit decibel (dB) signifying the ratio of actual pressure to reference pressure.	Do NOT USE dyne (1 dyn = 10 µPa)
	µPa		micropascal	Sound pressure level $L_p = 20 \log_{10} \dfrac{\text{actual pressure (Pa)}}{20 \times 10^{-6}\ (\text{Pa})}$	
Sound Power, Sound Energy Flux (W)	W mW µW		watt milliwatt microwatt	Measurement of sound power and rate of flow of sound energy. The standard reference value for sound power is 1 pW (10^{-12} W).	
	pW		picowatt	Sound power level, $L = 10 \log_{10} \dfrac{\text{actual pressure (W)}}{20 \times 10^{-12}\ (\text{W})}$	
Sound Energy Density (J/m³)	J/m³		joule per cubic metre	Measurement of mean sound energy density	
Sound Intensity (W/m²)	W/m²		watt per square metre	Measurement of sound intensity	The standard reference value for sound intensity is 1 pW/m² (10^{-12} W/m²)
	pW/m²		picowatt per square metre	Sound intensity level $L_i: = 10 \log_{10} \dfrac{\text{actual intensity (W/m}^2)}{10^{-12}\ (\text{W/m}^2)}$	
Specific Acoustic Impedance (Pa·s/m)	Pa·s/m		pascal second per metre	Sound impedance measurement	(1 Pa·s/m = 1 N·s/m³)
Acoustic Impedance, Acoustic Resistance (Pa·s/m³)	Pa·s/m³		pascal second per cubic metre	Sound impedance measurement	

CD-ROM TABLE OF CONTENTS

Time Saver Standards for Architectural Design Data

Seventh Edition

Editors
Donald Watson, FAIA, Editor-in-Chief
Michael J. Crosbie, Ph.D., Senior Editor
John Hancock Callender (1908–1995) *in memoriam*

Associate editors
Donald Baerman, AIA
Walter Cooper
Martin Gehner, P.E.
William Hall
Bruce W. Hisley
Richard Rittelmann, FAIA
Timothy T. Taylor, AIA, ASTM

Table of Contents

- Introduction

Part I: Architectural fundamentals

1	Universal design and accessible design	John P. S. Salmen, AIA and Elaine Ostroff
2	Architecture and regulation	Francis Ventre
3	Bioclimatic design	Donald Watson, FAIA and Murray Milne
4	Solar control	Steven V. Szokolay
5	Daylighting design	Benjamin Evans, FAIA
6	Natural ventilation	Benjamin Evans, FAIA
7	Indoor air quality	Hal Levin
8	Acoustics: theory and applications	M. David Egan, P.E., Steven Haas and Christopher Jaffe, Ph.D.
9	History of building and urban technologies	John P. Eberhard, FAIA
10	Construction materials technology	L. Reed Brantley and Ruth T. Brantley
11	Intelligent building systems	Jong-Jin Kim, Ph.D.
12	Design of atriums for people and plants	Donald Watson, FAIA
13	Building economics	David S. Haviland, Hon. AIA
14	Estimating and design cost analysis	Robert P. Charette, P.E. and Brian Bowen, FRICS
15	Environmental life cycle assessment	Joel Ann Todd, Nadav Malin and Alex Wilson
16	Construction and demolition waste management	Harry T. Gordon, FAIA
17	Construction specifications	Donald Baerman, AIA
18	Design-build delivery system	Dana Cuff, Ph.D.
19	Building commissioning: a guide for architects	Carolyn Dasher, Nancy Benner, Tudi Haasl, and Karl Stum, P.E.
20	Building performance evaluation	Wolfgang F. E. Preiser, Ph.D. and Ulrich Schramm, Ph.D.
21	Monitoring building performance	William Burke, Charles C. Benton, and Allan Daly

Part II: Design data

A SUBSTRUCTURE

A1	Foundations and basement construction	
A1.1	Soils and foundation types	Philip P. Page, Jr.
A1.2	Retaining walls	Martin Gehner, P.E.
A1.3	Subsurface moisture protection	Donald Watson, FAIA and Murray Milne
A1.4	Residential foundation design	John Carmody and Joseph Lstiburek, P.Eng.
A1.5	Termite control	Donald Pearman

B SHELL

B1	**Superstructure**	
B1.1	An overview of structures	
B1.2	Design loads	Martin Gehner, P.E.
B1.3	Structural design—wood	Martin Gehner, P.E.
B1.4	Structural design—steel	Jonathan Ochshorn
B1.5	Structural design—concrete	Robert M. Darvas
B1.6	Structural design—masonry	Martin Gehner, P.E.
B1.7	Earthquake resistant design	Elmer E. Botsai, FAIA
B1.8	Tension fabric structures	R. E. Shaeffer, P.E. and Craig Huntington, S.E.

B2	**Exterior closure**	
B2.1	Exterior wall systems: an overview	
B2.2	Thermal Insulation	Donald Baerman, AIA
B2.3	Building movement	Donald Baerman, AIA
B2.4	Corrosion of metals	Donald Baerman, AIA
B2.5	Moisture control	Joseph Lstiburek, P.Eng.
B2.6	Watertight exterior walls	Stephen S. Ruggiero and James C. Myers
B2.7	Exterior doors and hardware	Timothy T. Taylor
B2.8	Residential windows	John C. Carmody and Stephen Selkowitz

B3   **Roofing**
B3.1   Roofing systems   Donald Baerman, AIA
B3.2   Gutters and downspouts   Donald Baerman, AIA
B3.3   Roof openings and accessories   Donald Baerman, AIA
B3.4   Radiant barrier systems   Philip Fairey

C INTERIORS
C1   **Interior constructions**
C1.1   Suspended ceiling systems   William Hall
C1.2   Interior partitions and panels   William Hall
C1.3   Interior doors and hardware   Timothy T. Taylor
C1.4   Flexible infrastructure   Vivian Loftness, AIA and Volker Hartkopf, Ph.D.

C2   **Staircases**
C2.1   Stair design checklist   John Templer
C2.2   Stair design to reduce injuries   John Templer
C2.3   Stair dimensioning   Ernest Irving Freese

C3   **Interior finishes**
C1.1   Wall and ceiling finishes   William Hall
C1.2   Flooring   William Hall

D SERVICES
D1   **Conveying systems**
D1.1   Escalators and elevators   Peter R. Smith

D2   **Plumbing**
D2.1   Plumbing systems   Arturo De La Vega
D2.2   Sanitary waste systems   Arturo De La Vega
D2.3   Special plumbing systems   Arturo De La Vega
D2.4   Solar domestic water heating   Everett M. Barber, Jr.

D3   **HVAC**
D3.1   Energy sources for houses   William Bobenhausen
D3.2   Heating and cooling of houses   William Bobenhausen
D3.3   Energy sources for commercial buildings   William Bobenhausen
D3.4   Thermal assessment for HVAC design   Richard Rittelmann, FAIA and John Holton, P.E., RA
D3.5   HVAC systems for commercial buildings   Richard Rittelmann, FAIA and Paul Scanlon, P.E.
D3.6   HVAC specialties   Catherine Coombs, CIH, CSP

D4   **Fire protection**
D4.1   Fire safety design   Fred Malven, Ph.D.
D4.2   Fire protection sprinkler systems   Bruce W. Hisley
D4.3   Standpipe systems   Bruce W. Hisley
D4.4   Fire extinguishers and cabinets   Bruce W. Hisley
D4.5   Special fire protection systems   Bruce W. Hisley
D4.6   Fire alarm systems   Walter Cooper

D5   **Electrical**
D5.1   Electrical systems   Benjamin Stein
D5.2   Communication and security systems   Walter Cooper and Robert DeGrazio
D5.3   Electrical system specialties   Andrew Prager
D5.4   Lighting   John Bullough
D5.5   Solar electric systems for residences   Everett M. Barber, Jr.

Appendix:

Tables and reference data
- Dimensions of the human figure
- Insulation values
- Lighting tables

Mathematics
- Properties of the circle
- Area, surfaces and volumes
- Areas-perimeter ratios   William Blackwell
- Useful curves and curved surfaces   Seymour Howard, Architect
- Drawing accurate curves   Sterling M. Palm, Architect
- Modular coordination   Hans J. Milton and Byron Bloomfield, AIA

Units of measurement and metrication
- Units of measurement
- Introduction to SI metric system   R. E. Shaeffer, P.E.
- Metrication

Index

Reader Response Form

INDEX

A

Aalto, Alvar, architect, B3.3-1
Absorbtance, *definition*, B2.8-12
Access floor, D5.1-8, D5.1-9
Accessibility (see Universal design)
Acoustics (see Sound, control)
Adaptive Environments, Inc., C3.2-8
AIA Research Corporation, xiv
Air-conditioning (see HVAC systems)
Air curtain, B2.7-1
Air distribution, D3.1-26
Air flow retarder, B2.5-1, B2.5-5
Air leakage (see Infiltration)
Air space (see Wall, cavity)
Aggregate, concrete, B1.5-1 (also see
    Concrete)
    roof, B3.1-10
Air entrainment, B1.5-2
Allen, Edward, C2.1-12, C2.2-1
Alliance to Save Energy, B2.8-13
Allowable stress design, B1.4-4 (also see
    Steel, Structure)
Aluminum, B2.4-3, B2.7-7
    door, B2.7-9, B2.7-11
    gutter, B3.2-2
    roof, B3.1-14
American Architectural Manufacturers
    Association (AAMA), B2.6-14,
    B.2.7-1, B2.7-22
American Association of State Highway and
    Transportation Officials (AASHTO),
    B1.2-10, C3.4-28
American Council of Energy Efficiency
    (ACEE), B2.8-13
American Forest and Paper Association
    (AFPA), B1.3-22
American Concrete Institute (ACI), A1.2-4,
    A1.3-2, A1.3-8, B1.5-5, B1.5-18,
    B1.6-24
American Institute of Steel Construction
    (AISC), B1.4-16, B2.3-2
American Institute of Timber Construction
    (AITC), B1.3-22
American National Safety Code for
    Elevators, D1.1-8
American National Standards Institute
    (ANSI), D3.2-7
American Plywood Association (APA),
    B1.3-18, B1.3-22
American Society of Civil Engineers (ASCE),
    B1.2-10, B1.4-16, B2.3-10
American Society of Heating, Refrigeration
    and Air Conditioning Engineers
    (ASHRAE), B2.2-3, B2.8-4, B3.1-16,
    D2.1-7, D3.1-42, D3.2-7
American Society of Mechanical
    Engineers (ASME), D2.1-7, D2.2-8,
    D2.3-10
American Society of Plumbing Engineers,
    D2.1-7, D2.2-8, D2.3-10
American Society of Sanitary Engineering,
    D2.1-7
American Society of Testing Materials
    (ASTM), B1.6-2, B1.6-4, B1.6-6,
    B2.2-13, B2.6-1, B2.6-14, C1.1-14,
    C1.2-5, C3.2-1, D2.1-7, D2.2-8,
    D5.1-24, D5.2-14, App. 3-1

Americans with Disabilities Act (ADA),
    C1.2-14, C2.1-2, C3.2-3, C3.2-4,
    C3.2-8 (also see Universal design)
Anchor, A1.1-3, B1.1-8, B1.3-14, B1.4-1,
    B1.4-4, B1.6-7–B1.6-11, B2.1-14
    bearing wall, B2.1-11
    door frame, B2.7-20
    joist anchor, B1.16-12, B2.1-12, B2.1-13
Anodic protection, B2.4-4
Arch, B1.1-15
    laminated, B1.1-16, B1.3-17
    Roman, B1.6-1
    steel, B1.1-17
Architect, B2.2-3, B2.6-14
Architectural Aluminum Manufacturer's
    Association (AAMA), B2.1-9
Architectural and Transportation Barriers
    Compliance Board (ABCB), C3.4-28
Area, units of measurement, App. 1, App. 2,
    App. 3
Asbestos, B2.2-10, B2.2-13
Asphalt Roofing Manufacturers Association,
    B3.1-24
Association for Preservation Technology
    (APT), A1.3-8, B2.3-10
Asymptote, B2.9-7 (also see Solar, angles)
Atrium, D1.1-4
Attic, B2.2-3, B2.2-11, B2.2-19, B3.1-3,
    B3.3-9
Auburn University, B2.9-19
Audiovisual facilities (see Electronic System
    Specialties)
Automobile (see Parking)
Azimuth, B2.9-4 (also see Solar, angles)

B

Backer rod, B2.6-7
Baerman, Donald, xiv, B2.2-1, B2.3-1,
    B3.1-1, B3.2-5, B3.3-1
Balustrade (see Stairs, rail)
Barreneche, Paul, B1.3-22, B1.4-15, B1.5-18
Barrier free environments, C3.2-8 (also see
    Universal design)
Barrier wall, B2.6-1, B2.6-11
Base plate (see Frame, Framing)
Basement, A1.3-1–A1.3-8, B1.3-8, B2.2-12
    (also see Wall)
Bathroom (see Plumbing, fixtures)
Beam (also see Structure)
    box, B1.1-16
    grade, A1.1-3, A1.1-4
    steel, B1.4-1
Bearing
    plate, B1.3-14, B1.3-15, B2.1-14
    wall, B2.1-2, B2.1-9
Bellushi, Pietro, architect, D3.1-6
Bentonite (see Clay, expansive)
Bermuda, roofs, B3.1-1
Bicycle (see Parking, bicycle)
Bioclimate design (see Climate)
Bobenhausen, Catherine, D3.2-1
Bobenhausen, William, D3.1-42
Body Ellipse, C3.3-1 (also see Dimensions,
    human)
Bolt, Bolted connections, B1.4-6, B1.4-11,
    B1.4-12 (also see Anchor)

Borings, A1.1-1
Bowen, Brian, xiv
Box, Paul C., C3.4-28
Boyce, P.R., D5.3-26
Bradbury Building, Los Angeles, D1.1-1
Brantley, L. Reed and Ruth T., B2.4-6
Brick (see Masonry)
Brick Institute of America, B1.6-3, B1.6-24,
    B2.2-12, B2.3-2, B2.3-4, B2.3-10,
    B2.6-14
Building Industry Consulting Service
    International (BISCI), D5.1-7, D5.1-19
Building movement (see Movement)
Building paper, Kraft paper, B2.5-4, B2.5-8,
    B3.1-5
Building Research Station, UK, B2.9-16,
    B2.9-18
Bullough, John D., D5.3-1, D5.3-26
Burnette, Charles, xiv
Bus (see Parking, bus loading)

C

Caisson, A1.1-1, A1.1-5, A1.1-6
Cable, cabling
    electric service, D5.1-8 (also see
        Communication and Security
        Systems)
    structure, B1.1-17, B1.4-4 (also see
        Structure)
    teleconferencing, D5.2-10 (also see
        Electronic System Specialties)
Calatrava, Santiago, architect and engineer,
    B1.5-1, C3.3-1
Camber (see Deflection, Movement)
Canadian Building Digest, B2.8-2, B2.8-12
Canadian Wood Council, B1.3-22
Canadian National Research Council,
    B3.1-24
Cannon Design, architect, D3.1-29
Cant, Cant strip, B2.1-14, B3.1-9
Cantilever, B1.1-18 (also see Structure)
Carmody, John, B2.5-12, B2.8-11, B2.8-12
Car (see Parking)
Carpet, carpeting, C2.1-9, C2.1-10
Cast Iron Soil Pipe Institute, D2.2-8
Cathodic protection (see Corrosion)
Cavity wall (see Wall, cavity)
Ceiling, ceiling systems, C1.1-1–C1.1-14
    integration with services, C1.1-12, C1.1-13
    lighting, D5.3-12, D5.3-13
    types, C1.1-4, C1.1-5
Ceiling and Interior Systems Construction
    Association (CISCA), C1.1-14
Cement, B1.5-1 (also see Concrete)
Center for Universal Design, C3.2-2, C3.2-7,
    C3.2-8
Ceramic tile (see Tile)
Charrette, Robert, xiv
Children, C2.1-1, C3.1-12 (also see
    Universal design)
Childs, Mark C., C3.4-1, C3.4-28
Circular stairs (see Stairs, spiral)
Cistern, D2.1-8
Crystal Palace, B3.3-1
Clanton, Nancy, D5.3-26
Clay, expansive, A1.3-4, B2.3-9

Climate, B2.5-8, B2.5-9, B2.6-14, B2.7-3, B2.7-14, B2.8-6, B2.8-7, B2.8-10, B2.8-13, B3.1-1, B2.9-26
Clo, comfort measurement, B2.2-1
Closer (see Hardware)
Coatings, B2.4-1, B2.4-4
  architectural designations, B2.7-11
  metal finishes, B2.7-11
Coefficient of Performance (COP), *definition*, D3.1-21 (also see HVAC Systems)
Color rendition (see Lighting)
Column, B1.1-1, B1.3-14, B1.4-6
  pipe, B1.3-16
Commercial building
  HVAC (see HVAC systems)
  innovation, D3.1-25
Communication and security systems, D5.1-1–D5.1-24
  cabling, D5.1-1, D5.1-8
    UL classification of, D5.1-10
  electronic security systems, D5.1-19
  equipment, servicing space requirements, D5.1-3
  glossary of acronyms and terms, D5.1-7
  LAN (Local Area Network), D5.1-16–D5.1-18
  system options, D5.1-2
  voice and data communication systems, D5.1-12
Compressed air (see Plumbing, special fixtures)
Compressed Gas Association, D2.3-10
Concrete
  beam, B1.1-12, B1.1-18, B1.5-7
  cast-in-place, B1.1-1, B1.1-2
  code requirements, B1.5-5, B1.5-6, B1.6-1
  column, A1.1-2, A1.1-3, B1.5-11
  compressive strength, B1.5-2
  cracking potential, B1.5-9
  deflection, B1.1-7, B1.1-8
  design of, B1.5-1, B1.5-3, B1.5-5
  flat-slab, B1.5-14
  folded plate, B1.1-18
  forms, B1.1-14
  foundation, A1.3-2
  masonry, A1.2-4, B1.6-21, B2.2-10, B2.3-9, B2.4-6
  materials, B1.5-1
  pile, A1.1-5
  plank, B1.1-9, B1.1-10, B1.1-14, B1.1-18, B2.1-13
  precast, prestressed, B1.5-17, B2.6-6, B2.6-7
  reinforcing steel, A1.2-4, B1.5-4
  retaining wall, A1.2-2
  shear, shear diagram, B1.5-8
  slab, B1.5-16, B2.1-12
  spans, B1.1-18
  structure, B1.1-1, B1.1-8
  thermal expansion, B1.5-2, B2.3-4, B2.3-9
  tilt-up construction, B1.5-17, B1.5-18, B2.1-14, B2.2-10
  topping, B1.1-14
  wall, B2.1-3, B2.1-12, B2.1-14
  weight, B1.5-2
Concrete Reinforcing Steel Institute (CRSI), A1.2-4, B1.5-18

Condensation, B2.2-12
  control, B2.5-10
    plumbing, D2.1-3
    skylights, B3.3-4
    windows, B2.8-2, B2.8-5
Conduction (see Heat transfer)
Conference room (see Electronic System Specialties, audiovisual facilities)
Control joint, B1.6-12, B2.1-2
Convection (see Heat transfer)
Conversion, tables of common measurement, App. 3-4
Cooling, B2.8-6
Cooper, Walter, D4.3-1, D5.1-1
Coping, B1.3-15
Copper, B2.4-3
Cork, B2.2-10
Corrosion, B1.4-3, B2.4-1–B2.4-6, B2.7-7, B3.1-9, B3.1-15, D4.1-13
Council of American Building Officials, D2.1-7
Crane, Craneway, load (see Structure, load)
Crawl space, A1.3-1, A1.3-3
Creep, *definition*, B1.5-2 (also see Movement)
Cricket, B3.1-5 (also see Flashing)
Crosbie, Michael J., xi
Croxton Collaborative, architects, D3.1-26, D3.1-42
Curtain drain, A1.3-7
Curtain wall (see Wall, curtain)

D
Dadras, Aly S., D1.1-7
Dampproofing, A1.3-1
Daylighting, B2.8-10, B2.8-12, B2.9-19, B3.3-2, B3.3-5, D5.3-19
De La Vega, Arturo, D2.1-1, D2.2-1, D2.3-1
DeGrazio, Robert, D5.1-1
Dead bolt (see Hardware)
Dead load, B1.2-6 (also see Structure, load)
Deck (see Structure)
Declination (see Solar, declination)
Deere Company Headquarters, B1.4-1
Deflection, B1.1-6, B1.1-7, B1.4-9, B1.6-1, B2.3-1, B2.7-6, C1.1-1 (also see Movement)
Deformation, B1.1-1, B1.1-6, B1.1-8, B1.5-2, B1.5-13, B2.1-9, B2.3-1
Demographics, C3.2-1
Demountable partition, C1.2-8 (also see Interior partitions and panels)
Design Load (see Structure, load)
Dimensions
  human figure, C3.1–C3.18, C3.2-1, C3.3-1
  table-top, C3.1-1
Dines, Nicholas T., C3.3-12
Dinkerloo, John, B3.1-12
Domes, B1.1-17
Door, B2.2-3, B2.7-1–B2.7-22
  clearance in stairway, C2.1-3
  conductivity coefficients, B2.7-7
  fire, B2.7-16
  handedness, B2.7-20
  overhead, B2.7-18
  sliding, B2.7-12
  swinging, B2.7-13, C3.2-8
  swipe card entry, D5.1-20
  types, B2.7-3, B2.7-4
  viewport, C3.2-7

Door and Hardware Institute, B2.7-22
Double skin envelope, D3.1-29
Downspouts (see Gutters and downspouts)
Drain, Drainage
  catchment area calculation, D2.1-8
  plane, B2.5-1, B2.5-4, B2.6-12
  roof, B3.1-2, B3.1-22, B3.1-23, B3.2-1 (also see Gutters and Downspouts)
  sanitary (see Sanitary waste system)
  screen, B2.5-3
  skylight, B3.3-4
  subsurface, A1.3-1, A1.3-2, B1.3-8
Drip edge, B1.6-11, B2.1-15
Driveway (see Parking, driveway)
Drawing, App.1-12
Duct, ductwork, B1.1-6

E
Earth, B2.9-1, B2.9-2
Earthquake, B1.1-6, B1.2-1
  load, B1.2-3, B2.1-2
Ecliptic (see Solar, ecliptic)
EIFS, External Insulation Finishing Systems (see Stucco, synthetic)
Ejector pump, D2.2-2 (also see Sanitary waste system)
Electrical services, C1.1-13
  fire alarm, D4.3-2
Electromagnetic spectrum, D5.33-2
Electronic Industries Association, D5.1-7
Electronic System Specialties, D5.2-1–D5.2-14
  acronyms and abbreviations, D5.2-14
  audiovisual facilities, D5.2-1
  sound-masking, D5.2-11
  teleconferencing facilities, D5.2-8
Elevator, B1.2-2, B1.2-9, D1.1-1–D1.1-11
  design criteria, D1.1-4
  freight, D1.1-10, D1.1-11
  gearless, D1.1-6, D1.1-7
  hospital, D1.1-9
Elevator World, C3.3-1
Emittance, Emissivity, B2.2-4
  definition, B2.8-12
Energy conservation, energy efficiency, B2.7-19, B2.8-1, B2.8-6, B2.8-9, B3.1-3, D3.1-28, D5.3-12
Energy Efficiency Ratio (EER), *definition*, D3.1-21 (also see SEER)
Energy Star rating, B2.8-7, B2.8-8, B2.8-13
Engineer, B2.2-3
Engineered wood, B1.3-18, B1.3-19, B1.3-21 (also see Wood)
  definition, B1.3-19
Entry, Entryway, B2.7-6, B2.7-21, C2.1-1, C3.2-6, C3.3-4, C3.3-5 (also see Door)
Equitable Life Insurance Company, D3.1-6
Ergonomics, C3.2-1
Escalator, D1.1-1–D1.1-12
  carrying capacity, D1.1-3
  detail, D1.1-12
Ethics, xiii
Evaporation (see Heat transfer, forms of)
Exit, Exitway, B2.7-1 (also see Door)
Expansion coefficient
  common building materials, B2.3-3
Exterior door (see Door)

Exterior wall
   exfiltration, infiltration, B2.2-3
   insulation, B2.2-12
   moisture control, B2.5-1–B2.5-12
   performance factors, B2.1-1
   pressure equalization, B2.1-1, B2-1-7
   structural loads, B2.1-1

F
Fanger, O.E., B2.2-1, B2.2-13
Fascia, B2.1-11, B2.1-12
Federal Highway Administration, C3.4-28
Figueiro, M.G., D5.3-26
Filter fabric, A1.3-7
Finishes (see Coatings)
Fire protection
   alarm system, D4.3-1–D4.3-3
   cut, B1.3-14
   door (see Door)
   protection, D4.1-1
   safety design, B3.3-2, C1.1-2, C1.2-2,
      C2.1-2, C2.1-3
   special systems, D4.2-1–D4.2-10
      carbon dioxide, D4.2-1
      dry chemical, D4.2-4
      exhaust hood, D4.2-0
      foam extinguishing, D4.2-7
      halon, D4.2-6
   sprinkler, D4.1-1–D4.1-18
      area of coverage, D4.1-15
   valves and fittings, D4.1-11
Fireproofing, B1.4-3
Flack & Kurtz, engineers, D3.1-26
Flagpole method (see Solar, graphic
      methods)
Flashing, B2.1-12, B2.1-14, B2.1-15, B2.5-1,
      B2.6-3, B2.6-5, B2.6-8, B2.6-11,
      B3.1-5, B3.1-9, B3.1-18
Flooding, A1.3-1, A1.3-2, B2.3-9
Floor, Flooring, B1.1-1, B1.3-19, B1.4-13,
      B2.3-8
Folding partition, C1.2-6–C1.2-8 (also see
      Interior partitions and panels)
Footing, A1.1-1–A1.1-4, A1.2-1, B1.3-8,
      B2.1-14
   drain, A1.3-1, A1.3-5, B1.6-16
   eccentric, A1.1-4
   pump-and-handle, A1.1-4
   spread, A1.1-3
   trapezoidal, A1.1-4
Forest Products Laboratory, B2.3-10
Foundation, A1.1-1, A1.1-2, B1.3-8,
      B1.6-11, B2.3-10
   pocket, B1.3-9
Frame, Framing, B1.1-1–B1.1-5, B1.3-7,
      B1.3-12, B1.3-17, B1.3-20, B1.4-16
   balloon frame, B1.3-4, B1.3-6
   door, B2.7-6, B2.7-7, B2.7-20
   fireplace, B1.3-10
   floor, B1.3-19
   joist, B1.3-11, B2.3-7
   plate, B1.4-11
   platform frame, B1.3-5
   plank and beam, B1.3-14
   pre-engineered, B1.1-6
   roof, B1.3-14
   sill, B1.3-6, B1.3-8, B1.3-19, B1.6-8,
      B2.5-1, B2.6-3
   space frame, B1.1-17

Frame, Framing (*Cont.*):
   stairway, B1.3-10
   timber, B1.3-15
   wall, B2.1-3, B2.2-11
   window, B2.8-1, B2.8-6
   wood, B1.3-4, B1.3-17, B1.6-12, B2.1-10,
      B2.1-11 (also see Wood)
Frampton, Kenneth, xiii
Frost, B2.3-10
   protected footings, B2.3-10
Fruin, John J., C2.1-4, C2.1-5, C2.1-12,
      C3.3-1, C3.3-12
Furniture integrated environmental control
      systems, D3.1-27

G
Galvanic series, B2.4-1
Gargoyle (see Gutters and downspouts)
Gasket, B2.6-9
Gehner, Martin D., A1.1-1, B1.2-1, B1.3-1,
      B1.6-1
Gill, Irving, architect, B1.5-17
Girder (see Structure, Wood, Steel)
Givoni, Baruch, B2.9-1, B2.9-7–B2.9-9,
      B2.9-28
Glare, D5.3-4 (also see Lighting)
Glass, Glazing, B2.1-8
   definitions, B2.8-12
   doors, B2.7-9, B2.7-16
   elevator, D1.1-3
   Low-e, B2.2-4, B2.8-3, B2.8-5, B2.8-11
   partitions, C1.2-5
   safety, B2.7-2, B2.7-8, B2.7-10
   solar transmission, B2.8-5
   spectral transmittance, visible
      transmittance, B2.8-2, B2.8-5, D5.3-3
   technological improvements, B2.8-5
   thermal transmission, B2.8-4
   thermal expansion, B2.3-3
   window, B2.8-1
Glass block, B1.2-4
Gnomon, sundial, B2.9-4, B2.9-6
Going, *definition*, C2.1-5 (also see Stairs)
Gordon, J. E., B2.3-10
Grade beam (see Beam)
Grade, Gradient
   parking (see Parking, gradient)
   ramp (see Ramp)
   walkway (see Pedestrian, design)
Granite, B1.6-2
Green roof (see Roof, vegetated)
Grid systems (see Wall, curtain)
Groundwater, A1.3-1, A1.3-2
Guardrail (see Stair, rail)
Gutters and downspouts, B2.1-11, B3.1-15,
      B3.2-1–B3.2-12
   Sizing nomograph, B3.2-10, B3.2-11
Gypsum, B1.6-6
   partitions, C1.2-4
   sheathing, B2.6-11
   wallboard, B2.5-7

H
Hall, Edward T., C3.3-1
Hall, William, C1.1-1, C1.2-1
Handicap (see Universal design)
Handedness (see Door, handedness)
Handrail (see Stair, rail)
Hardware, B2.7-1–B2.7-22, C3.2-8

Harris, Charles W., C3.3-12
Harrold, Rita M., D5.3-1, D5.3-5
Hartkopf, Volker, D3.1-1, D3.1-27, D3.1-42
Hatch (see Roof, hatch)
Heat pump, D3.1-6 (also see HVAC
      Systems)
Heat rejection equipment, D2.1-23 (also see
      HVAC Systems)
Heat transfer
   around buildings, B2.2-2
   evaporation, B2.2-2, B2.2-3
   flow, B2.8-1, B2.2-8
   forms of, B2.2-1–B2.2-7
Heliodon (see Solar, simulator)
Henry Dreyfuss Associates, C2.2-2, C3.1-1,
      C3.2-8
Hershong, Lisa, B2.8-3
High-lift masonry wall, B1.6-16
Hinge (see Hardware)
Hisley, Bruce, B3.3-1, D4.1-1, D4.2-1
Hoadley, R. Bruce, B2.3-10
Hooker Office Building, Niagara, D3.1-29
Hospital
   lighting, D5.3-23 (also see Lighting)
   plumbing (see Plumbing, special fixtures)
House wrap, B2.5-4, B2.5-7
Housing, accessibility, C3.2-4, C3.2-5 (also
      see Universal design)
Human figure, dimensions (see Dimensions)
Humidity, B2.2-1
Humpback Bridge, B1.3-1
HVAC Systems (Heating, Ventilation and
      Air-Conditioning), B2.2-12, C1.1-1,
      D3.1-1–42
   boiler types, D3.1-39
   central, D3.1-6
   equipment, B3.1-19
   fan performance, D3.1-41
   selection criteria, D3.1-13–D3.1-15
   self-contained, D3.1-2–D3.1-5
   special equipment, D3.2-1–D3.2-8
      air curtain, D3.2-4
      air purifier, D3.2-5
      dust/fume collectors, D3.2-2–D3.2-4
      local exhaust ventilation, D3.2-1
      paint spray ventilation, D3.2-6
   system types, D3.1-2, D3.1-11
   VAV system, D3.1-9, D3.1-26
   ventilation requirements, D3.1-18
Hydraulic mat, A1.1-3
Hydrostatic pressure, A1.3-3
   load, B1.2-2

I
Illuminating Society of North America
      (IESNA), D5.3-1, D5.3-12
Illumination (see Lighting)
Incidence, angle of, B2.9-5 (also see Solar,
      angles)
Industrial
   lighting, D5.3-21 (also see Lighting)
   plant fire protection, D4.1-7 (also see Fire
      protection)
Industrial ventilation, D3.2-7, D3.2-8 (also
      see HVAC Systems)
Infiltration, B2.2-2
   door, B2.7-10
   sources of, B2.2-3
   window, B2.8-2

Information, access to, xiv, B3.1-17
Institute of Transportation Engineers, C3.4-28
Insulation, A1.3-4, B1.3-19, B2.2-1
    cold climate, B2.5-11
    design values, B2.2-15–B2.2-18, B2.8-4
    doors, B2.7-7, B2.7-8
    expanded polystyrene, B2.6-12
    foundation, perimeter, B2.2-10
    frame wall, B2.2-11
    masonry wall, B2.2-11
    permeability of, B2.5-7
    pipe, D2.1-3
    polystyrene, B2.2-10
    roof, B3.1-6
    types, B2.2-9
    window, B2.8-1, B2.8-12
Interior partitions and panels, C1.2-1–C1.2-14
    acoustic, C1.2-12
    fire rating, C1.2-5
    performance characteristics, C1.2-2
    types, C1.2-3
International Building Code, B2.3-10
International Masonry Institute, B1.6-24
International Plumbing Code, D2.1-2,
    D2.1-3, D2.1-7, D2.2-8, D2.3-10

J
Japanese Garden pavilion, Portland, B3.2-5
Jefferson, Thomas, App. 3-1
Johnson, Carol R. and Associates, landscape
    architect, C3.2-6
Joist (see Framing, joist)
Joint, B1.6-6, B2.6-2 (also see Masonry,
    brick joint)
    control, B2.3-4
    expansion, B2.3-4, B2.3-5, B2.6-10,
    B3.1-16
    protection against corrosion, B2.4-5
    reinforcement, B2.1-13
    roof, B3.1-6, B3.1-16
    sealant, B2.6-8

K
Kim, Jong-Kim, D3.1-1, D3.1-27, D3.1-42
Kitchen, C3.2-7
Knowledge, ix, xiii
Knowles, Ralph, B2.9-3, B2.9-18, B2.9-28
Kraus, Richard, xiv
Kurf, B2.5-2

L
Labs, Kenneth, A1.3-3, A1.3-8, B2.8-2,
    B2.8-4, B2.8-5, B2.8-13, B3.1-8,
    B3.1-15, B3.1-24
Ladder, *definition*, C2.2-2
Lamina, *definition*, B2.6-11, C2.2-8
Landing, C2.1-2, C2.1-6 (also see Stairs)
Lawrence Berkeley Laboratory, B2.8-13
Leader (see Gutters and downspouts)
Lechner, Norbert, B2.9-19
LED (Light Emitting Diode), D5.3-8 (also
    see Lighting, lamps)
Ledger, Ledge strip, B1.3-15, B2.1-14
Leslie, R.P., D5.3-28
Lexan polycarbonate (see Glazing)
Light frame construction (see Frame, Framing)
Laminated beam (see Structure, beam)
Length, units of measurement, App. 1, App.
    2, App. 3

Level of Service, C3.3-7 (also see Pedestrian,
    design)
Library, lighting, D5.3-22 (also see Lighting)
Light shelf, B2.9-12 (also see Daylighting,
    Solar, control)
Lighting, C2.1-12, D5.3-1–D5.3-28
    building types, D5.3-20
    color rendition, D5.3-1
    codes, D5.3-20
    controls, D5.3-19
    conversion, metric units, App. 3-7
    glossary of terms, D5.3-26
    lamps, luminaries, D5.3-4,
    D5.3-14–D5.3-18
    outdoor, D5.3-9, D5.3-24, D5.3-26
    requirements per task, D5.3-19
    safety, D5.3-20
    security, D5.3-26
    selection criteria, D5.3-9
    veiling reflection, D5.3-3, D5.3-21
    vision, D5.3-2
    visual acuity, *definition*, D5.3-2
Limestone, B1.6-2
Lintel, B1.6-19, B2.3-3, B2.3-5
Lisbon, Portugal Transit Terminal, C3.3-1
Live Load (see Structure, load)
Load (see Structure, load)
Loading dock (see Parking, loading)
Locks (see Hardware)
Locomotor vision, C3.3-2 (also see
    Pedestrian, design)
Lobby, D1.1-5, D3.3-4
Loftness, Vivian, D3.1-1, D3.1-27, D3.1-42
Louver door (see Door)
Lstiburek, Joseph, B2.5-1, B2.5-12
Lumber (see Wood)
Luminaire, *definition*, D5.3-26 (also see
    Lighting, lamp)

M
Mace, Ron, C3.2-5, C3.2-6, C3.2-7
MacKinnon, D. W., xiv
Magnetic North, True North, B2.9-7
Maintenance, access dimensions, C3.1-1,
    C3.1-5
Malin, Nadav, D1.1-7
Manual of Steel Construction, B1.4-3,
    B1.4-8, B1.4-16
Marble, B1.6-2
Marsh, Andrew, B2.9-28
Masonry, A1.2-4, A1.6-19
    anchors, B1.6-8–B1.11
    brick, B1.6-2, B2.6-14
    brick joints, B1.6-3, B1.6-4
    brick sizes, B1.6-3
    brick treatments, cleaning, B1.6-20
    brick veneer, B1.3-8, B1.6-4, B1.6-16,
    B2.1-5, B2.6-3
    clay masonry, B1.6-15
    code requirements, B1.6-1
    cold weather construction, B1.6-22
    concrete masonry, B1.6-1, B1.6-3, B1.6-4,
    B1.6-15–B1.6-18, B2.1-12
    design of, B1.6-1
    foundation, A1.3-2
    thermal movement, B2.3-3
MasterFormat, xiv, xv
Mathematics, App. 1-1
Maybeck, Bernard, architect, B3.2-5

Mazria, Edward, B2.9-9, B2.9-10, B2.9-28
Measurement, App. 2-1–App. 2-5
Membrane, A1.3-4 (also see Roof, Roofing)
Metabolic rate, B2.2-1
Metal
    ceiling systems, C1.1-2
    connections, B1.3-15, B1.3-16
    corrosion, B2.4-1–B2.4-6
    gutter, B3.2-2
    roof, B3.1-3, B3.1-9, B3.1-13, B3.1-14
Metrics, metrication, App. 3-1
Miami International Airport, D1.1-2
Milne, Murray, B2.9-1, B2.9-26, B2.9-28
MIT Corrosion Laboratory, B2.4-6
Mitchell/Giurgola, architects, C3.2-7
Modulus of Elasticity, B1.3-11, B1.4-1,
    B1.4-7, B1.5-1, B1.5-2
Moisture control, moisture protection,
    A1.3-1, B1.3-8, B2.5-1–B2.5-12,
    B2.7-3, B3.1-5
Mortar, B1.6-5, B1.6-6, B2.1-9
    board, B2.3-9
Movement, B1.1-6–B1.1-9, B1.1-13, B1.1-14,
    B1.3-4, B1.5-2, B1.6-1, B2.1-2,
    B2.3-1–B2.3-10, B2.6-9, B2.7-6
    calculation of, B2.3-4
    ceiling system, C1.1-3
    masonry, B2.4-3
    wood, B2.3-7
Moving walkway, D1.1-1, D1.1-2
    carrying capacity, D1.1-3
Mueller, James P., C3.2-8
Mullion, B2.1-7, B2.1-9, B2.6-11
    definition, B2.7-6
Myers, James C., B2.6-1, B2.6-14

N
Nail, nailing, B1.3-7
Nailer, nailing strip, B1.4-15, B3.1-9
National Audubon Society Headquarters
    Building, D3.1-26, D3.1-42
National Association of Architectural Metal
    Manufacturers, B2.7-1, B2.7-22
National Association of Corrosion Engineers
    (NACE), B2.4-6
National Building Code, B1.2-10
National Concrete Masonry Institute
    (NCMI), A1.2-4, B1.6-24, B2.2-12,
    B2.3-4, B2.3-10
National Electric Code, D5.1-7
National Fenestration Rating Council
    (NFRC), B2.8-8, B2.8-12
National Fire Protection Association
    (NFPA), B2.7-22, B3.3-9, B3.3-10,
    D2.3-10, D3.2-7, D4.1-18, D4.2-10,
    D4.3-3, D5.1-7, D5.1-19
National Forest and Paper Association,
    B1.3-1
National Institute of Building Sciences
    (NIBS), App. 3-1, App. 3-3
National Institute of Standards and
    Technology (NIST), B3.1-17
National Lighting Product Information
    Program, D5.3-28
National Roofing Contractors Association
    (NRCA), A1.3-4, A1.3-8, B3.1-1,
    B3.1-16, B3.1-17, B3.1-24, B3.3-10
Nichols Design Associates, architect,
    C3.2-6

O

Observatory, Jaipur, India, B2.9-1
Occupancy, per building type, C2.1-4
Occupational Safety and Health
    Administration (OSHA), C1.2-14,
    D3.2-8
Ochshorn, Jonathan, B1.4-1
Office, lighting, D5.3-21, D5.3-27 (also see
    Lighting)
O'Hare International Airport, Chicago,
    D5.2-28
Olgyay and Olgyay, B2.9-10, B2.9-28
Optical fiber, D5.1-11 (also see
    Communication and Security Systems)
Orton, Andrew, B2.6-24
Ostroff, Elaine, C2.1-12, C3.2-1
Otis Elevator Company, studies by, C3.3-7,
    D1.1-3
Overhang
    roof, ice damage, B3.1-15 (also see
        Gutters and downspouts)
    shade design, B2.9-11 (also see Solar,
        control)
    stair, C2.1-10 (also see Stairs,
        dimensioning)
Overhead door, B2.7-18 (also see Door)

P

Paints, B2.4-4
    masonry, B1.6-22
    spray booth ventilation, B3.2-1, B3.2-8
Panasonic Building, Tokyo, D3.1-28
Panel (see Interior partitions and panels)
Parabola, App. 1-12, App.1-13
Parapet, B3.1-20
Parking, C3.4-1–C3.4-27
    accessibility, C3.4-5
    bicycle, B3.4-4
    bus loading, C3.4-19
    driveway, C3.4-2, C3.4-3, C3.4-16,
        C3.4-22, C3.4-23
    gradient, C3.4-18
    lighting, D5.3-25 (also see Lighting,
        outdoor)
    loading, C3.4-26
    peak hour factors, C3.4-17
    truck turning radius, C3.4-27
Partition (see Interior partitions and panels,
    Wall)
Patterson, Terri L., B2.7-22, B3.1-12,
    B3.1-24, C2.1-12
Pedestrian, B2.7-1, B2.7-3, B2.7-7, C2.1-1,
    C2.1-4 (also see Elevator, Escalator,
    Moving walkway)
    design, C3.3-1–C3.3-12
        Level of Service concept,
            C3.3-7–C3.3-12
        queuing, C3.3-6, C3.3-11, C3.3-12
        ramp, C2.2-3
        stairway, C3.3-9, C3.3-10 (also see Stairs)
        walking speed, C3.3-3, C3.3-9
        walkway, surface friction, C2.1-11
Perimeter, units of measurement, App. 1,
    App. 2, App. 3
Perm, *definition*, B2.5-6
Phoenix Mutual Office Building, Hartford,
    D5.3-27
Pier, Pile, A1.1-1–A1.1-5
    caps, A1.1-6

Piping (see Plumbing)
    in plenum ceilings, C1.1-12, C1.1-13
Plank (see Concrete, Wood)
Plastic
    flow (See Deformation)
    laminate, C1.2-11
Plate (see Frame, framing)
Plenum, C1.1-1, C.1.1-12, C1.1-13,
    D3.1-25
    electrical, D5.1-11 (also see
        Communication and Security
        Systems)
Plumbing, D2.1-1–D2.1-7
    clearances, D2.1-6, D2.1-7
    distribution, D2.1-1
    fire protection (see Fire protection)
    fixture, C3.2-7, D2.1-3, D2.1-7
    hot water demand, D2.1-4
    piping materials, D2.2-4
    residential, D4.1-10
    sanitary waste system (see Sanitary waste
        system)
    special fixtures
        compressed air, B2.3-1, D2.3-2
        medical vacuum system, D2.3-1,
            D2.3-3, D2.3-4
        nitrous oxide, D2.3-5, D2.3-8
        oxygen, D2.3-3, D2.3-6
        piping, D2.3-5
    stack detail, D2.2-4
    vent, D2.2-2, D2.2-10
    water supply requirements, D2.1-2
Plywood, B1.1-8, B1.3-4, B1.3-19, B2.5-7
    folded plate, B1.1-16
    joist splice, B1.3-20
    web stiffener, B1.3-21
Pilkington Industries, B2.9-27, B2.9-28
Pollution, pollutants
    indoor, C1.1-7, D3.2-1, D3.2-7
    outdoor, A1.3-2, B2.4-6
    light, D5.3-24
Portland Cement Association, B1.5-2,
    B1.6-24
Portman, John, architect, D1.1-4
Prager, Andrew, D5.2-1
Precast / Prestressed Concrete Institute,
    B1.5-18
Preiser, Wolfgang, C2.1-12, C3.2-8
Prestressed concrete (see Concrete,
    prestressed)
Pressure differential, pressure equalization,
    B2.1-7, B2.1-9, B2.5-2, B2.7-7,
    C1.1-1, C1.1-3, C1.2-1
Profile angle (see Solar, angles)
Projection booth (see Electronic System
    Specialties, audiovisual facilities)
Purlin, B1.3-16
Pushkarev, Boris, S., C2.1-12
Pythagoras, doctrines of, B2.9-7

Q

Quality control, A1.3-4
Queuing (see Pedestrian, queuing)

R

Radiant barrier, B2.2-10
Radiant temperature, B2.2-1, B2.2-2
Rafter, B2.1-11, B2.1-12
Railway Station Lyon-Satolas, France, B1.5-1

Rain chain, B3.2-5 (also see Gutters and
    downspouts)
Rainfall, A1.3-1, A1.3-3
    annual precipitation, B2.5-4, B3.2-7,
        B3.2-8
    calculation for drainage, B3.2-6
    control design for, B2.5-1,
        B2.6-1–B2.6-14
    corrosion due to, B2.4-3
    rainwater harvesting, D2.1-8
Ramps, C2.1-8, C2.1-9, *definition*, C2.2-2
    (also see Pedestrian, Stairs)
Rankine theory of earth thrust, A1.2-1
Rauh, Richard, architect, B3.2-6
Rea, Mark, D5.3-1, D5.3-28
Reflectivity, B2.2-2
Refuge (see Stairs, refuge)
Reglet, B2.1-14
Reinforced concrete (see Concrete)
Reinforcement, B1.5-13, B1.6-7 (also see
    Concrete, design of)
Remediation, A1.3-3, A1.3-8
Residential, lighting, D5.3-22, D5.3-23 (also
    see Lighting)
Retail, lighting, D5.3-23, D5.3-25, D5.3-27
    (also see Lighting)
Retaining wall (see Wall)
Revolving door, B2.7-14, B2.7-15 (also see
    Door)
Ridge vent (see Vent, ridge)
Rittelmann, Richard, D3.1-1
Ritz Hotel Tea Room, London, D5.3-28
Rogers, James Gamble, architect, B3.2-2
Roof, Roofing, B1.1-1, B1.1-11,
    B3.1-B3.1-24
    accessories, B3.3-9
    flat, B1.3-8, B2.1-13, B2.1-14
    framing, B1.3-14, B1.4-13
    hatch, hatchway, B3.3-1, B3.3-7
    load, B1.2-3, B1.2-9
    membrane, B3.1-6, B3.1-7, B3.1-21
    openings, B3.3-1 (also see Skylights)
    panel, B1.1-12
    pitch, B2.1-11
    slope, B3.1-2, B3.1-3, B3.1-10,
        B3.1-12
    smoke vent, B3.3-1, B3.3-8
    thermal movement, B2.3-1
    types, B3.1-2
    vegetated, B3.1-3, B3.1-8
    weights of, B3.1-4
Ruggiero, Stephen S., B2.6-1, B2.6-14
Rust (see Corrosion)

S

Saarinen, Eero, architect, B1.4-1, B3.1-7
Sackler Museum, Harvard University,
    D5.3-27
Safety, B2.7-2
    lighting, D5.3-20
    stair, C2.1-9
Salmen, John P. S., C3.2-1
Salt crystallization, B2.3-10
Sandstone, B1.6-2
Sanitary waste system, D2.2-1–D2.2-10
    commercial, D2.2-5
    residential, D2.2-5
    septic tank, D2.2-6, D2.2-7
Scaffold, B1.6-23

Scanlon, Paul, D3.1-1
Scupper (see Roof, Roofing, openings)
Scott, Geoffrey, xiii, xiv
Sealant, B2.3-5, B2.6-2, B2.6-6, B2.6-10,
    B2.7-7
Security, B2.7-2 (also see Communication
    and Security Systems)
    lighting, D5.3-26 (also see Lighting)
SEER (Seasonal Energy Efficiency Ratio),
    definition, D3.1-21
Seismic (see Earthquake)
Selkowitz, Stephen, B2.8-3, B2.8-12
Schindler, R.M., architect, B1.5-17
Schodek, Daniel, B1.1-16–18
Scupper, B3.2-4 (also see Gutters and
    downspouts)
Shading, Shading mask, Shadow (see Solar,
    control)
Shaeffer, R.E., App. 3-1, App. 3-3
Shakes (see Roof, Roofing, Shingles)
Sheathing, B2.5-12
Shear
    moment diagram, B1.5-8, B1.5-10, B1.5-13
    wall, B1.6-18
Sheet Metal and Air Conditioning
    Contractors Association (SMACNA),
    B3.1-16, B3.1-24, B3.2-2, B3.2-6,
    B3.2-12, B3.3-9, B3.3-10
Shell Oil Building, Houston, D5.3-27
Shielded Metal Arc Welding, B1.4-12 (also
    see Weld, Welding)
Shingles, B2.3-8, B3.1-11, B3.1-12 (also see
    Roof, Roofing)
Shrinkage (see Movement)
Sill (see Frame, Framing)
Site analysis, solar, B2.9-17 (also see Solar,
    control)
Site assembly, B1.1-4
Skinner, Catherine H., B2.2-13
Skylight, B3.3-1
    insulation, B3.3-6
    selection checklist, B3.3-5
    structural strength, B3.3-5
Slab, B1.1-1, B1.1-14 (also see Concrete)
    flat slab design, B1.5-14
    slab-on-grade, A1.3-4
    simply supported, span, B1.1-18
    structural concrete, B1.1-1, B1.1-11,
        B1.5-14–B1.5-16
    topping, B1.1-3, B1.1-14
    waffle, B1.1-18, B1.5-15
Slate
    roof, B3.1-3, B3.1-4, B3.2-2, B3.3-10
Sliding door (see Door)
Slope
    roof (see Roof, Roofing, slope)
    terrain, A1.3-1
Small Homes Council, B2.9-11
Smith, Peter R., D1.1-1, D1.1-7
Smoke vent (see Roof, Roofing, smoke vent)
Snow
    load, B1.2-2, B1.2-4 (also see Structure,
        load)
    guard, B3.3-10 (also see Roof, Roofing,
        accessories)
Soil, A1.1-1
    bearing capacity, A1.1-2, B1.2-2
    porosity, A1.3-1

Solar, Solar design
    angles, B2.9-4, B2.9-7, B2.9-9,
        B2.9-11, B2.9-12, B2.9-16,
        B2.9-20–B2.9-27
    control, B2.9-1–28
        glazing, B2.8-7
        shading coefficient, definition, B2.8-12
        shading devices, B2.8-5, B2.8-10,
            B2.9-5, B2.9-1–B2.9-15
    declination, B2.9-2
    ecliptic, definition, B2.9-1, B2.9-2
    equinox, definition, B2.9-1, B2.9-2,
        B2.9-4, B2.9-7, B2.9-12
    graphic methods, B2.9-6, B.29-7, B2.9-9
    heat gain, B2.8-12
    radiation, B2.8-1
    shading mask, B2.9-10, B2.9-13, B2.9-14,
        B2.9-16
    simulator, B2-9-16–B2.9-19
Solder, B3.1-9 (also see Weld, welding)
Soloman, Robert, B3.3-1
Sound control, sound transmission, B2.7-7,
    C1.1-1
    acoustic ceiling, C1.1-6–C1.1-11
    acoustic walls, C1.2-5, CA.2-12
    conversion, metric units, App. 3-8
    masking, D5.2-11 (also see Electronic
        System Specialties)
Space frame, space truss, B1.1-6, B1.4-4
Spalling, masonry, B1.1-8, B2.2-12
Space frame (see Frame, space)
Span (see Structure)
Specifications, xiv
Spiral stair (see Stairs, spiral)
Spread footings, A1.1-1
STC (Sound Transmission Class) (see Sound,
    transmission)
Stairs, C2.1-1–C2.1-14
    dimensioning, C2.1-5, C2.1-7,
        C2.2-1–C.2.2-8
        tables, C2.2-4, C2.2-6, C2.2-7
    ladder, C2.2-5
    pedestrian flow, C3.3-2, C3.3-4, C3.3-5,
        C3.3-10, C3.3-11
    rail, C2.1-3, C2.1-10, C2.1-11, C2.2-1,
        C3.1-8
    ramp, C2.1-8, C2.2-5
    refuge, C2.1-2, C2.1-3
    safety, C2.1-1, C2.1-12
    spiral, C2.1-6, C2.1-8
    tread and riser nomograph, C2.2-1, C2.2-2
Steel
    beam, B1.1-12, B1.1-17, B1.3-8, B1.4-11
    column, A1.1-2, A1.1-3, B1.4-6, B1.4-11
    connections, B1.4-13
    deflection, B1.1-7
    door, B2.7-9
    fireproofing, B1.4-2
    girder, B1.3-9, B1.3-10, B1.4-10
    gutter, B3.2-2
    light-gauge steel, B1.4-16
    Load and Resistance Factor Design
        (LRFD), B1.4-5
    material properties, B1.4-1
    pile, A1.1-5
    plate, B1.4-11
    spans, B1.1-17
    structure, B1.1-1, B1.1-8, B1.4-1

Steel (Cont.):
    types used in building, B1.4-2
    weathering steel, B2.4-5
Steel Door Institute, B2.7-22
Steel Structures Painting Council, B2.4-1,
    B2.4-6
Steinfeld, Edward, C3.2-3, C3.2-8
Stirling, James, architect, D5.3-27
Stirrup reinforcing, B1.5-9, B1.6-9 (also see
    Concrete, design of)
Stone, B1.6-2, B1.6-5
    ballast, B3.1-8
Stress-skin panel, B1.1-16, B1.3-1, B1.3-18,
    B1.3-19
Structure, B1.1-1
    beam, B1.1-12, B1.3-3, B1.3-12, B1.3-16,
        B1.4-8, B1.5-4
    corrosion (see Corrosion)
    deck, B1.1-1–B1.1-9, B1.1-13, B1.2-2,
        B1.3-3, B1.3-17, B1.4-13, B3.1-4
    frame, B1.1-13, B1.4-13
    load, B1.1-6, B1.1-8, B1.1-14, B1.2-1,
        B1.2-2, B1.4-5, B1.4-7, B1.5-3
        building materials, B1.2-6, B1.2-7
        live loads, B1.2-8
        load factors, B1.5-3
    masonry, design of, B1.6-13
    roof loads, B1.2-9
    roof deck, B1.1-11
    span, B1.1-14–B1.1-17, B1.3-3
Stucco, B2.1-6, B2.5-3, B2.5-7
    synthetic (EIFS), B2.5-3, B2.5-4,
        B2.6-11
Subsurface drainage, A1.3-1, A1.3-5
Suds pressure zone, D2.2-2
Sump, sump pump, A1.3-5
Sundial, B2.9-6, B2.9-27
Support (see Structure)
Surface friction (see Pedestrian, walkway)
Swail, A1.3-2
Swinging entrances (see Doors)
Swipe card entry system, D5.1-20 (also
    see Communication and Security
    Systems)
Syska & Hennessey, engineers,
    D1.1-8–D1.1-12
System International d'Unites (SI system)
    (see Metrics, Metrication)
Szokolay, Steven V., B2.9-1, B2.9-6, B2.9-12,
    B2.9-28

T
Tabletop, dimensions, C3.1-1–C3.1-3
Taylor, Timothy T., B2.7-1
Techne, Technique, xiii
Telecommunications Industry Association,
    D5.1-7, D5.1-19
Telephone (see Communication and Security
    Systems)
Temperature, B2.2-1
    Equivalent Temperature, B2.2-5
Templer, John, C2.1-1, C2.1-12
Terne, B3.1-14, B3.2-2 (also see Roof,
    Roofing)
Thermal
    break, B2.1-8
    comfort, B2.2-1
    expansion (see Movement)

Thermal (*Cont.*):
resistance, B2.2-7
of air spaces, B2.2-14
of common building materials, B2.2-9, B2.2-15
storage capacity, B2.2-12, D3.1-29
time-lag, B2.2-2, B2.2-6
Thermal insulation (see Insulation)
Tie-down strap, B2.1-12
Tile, B2.3-9
ceiling, C1.1-8
patterns, 1.1-11
roof, B3.1-3, B3.1-13
Tilt-up construction (see Concrete, tilt-up)
Tilt-Up Concrete Association (TCA), B1.5-18
Timber (see Frame, timber)
Toilet
dimensions for accessibility, C3.1-8
fixture clearances, D2.1-6
partition, C1.2-9, C1.2-10 (also see Interior partitions and panels)
public, C3.2-6
Topping (see Slab)
Transmittance, B2.8-2, *definition*, B2.8-12 (also see Heat transfer, forms of)
Transom, transom bar, *definition*, B2.7-6
Tread, *definition*, C2.1-5 (also see Stairs)
Trechsel, Heinz, R., B2.2-13
Tropic of Cancer, Tropic of Capricorn, B2.9-3
Truck (see Parking)
Truss, B1.1-1, B1.1-5, B1.1-12, B1.1-15, B1.1-16, B1.3-1, B1.3-12, B1.4-4, B1.4-13
Turn-Around (see Parking, driveway)

U
U-Value, B2.2-7, B2.2-19, B2.8-1, B2.8-6 (also see Insulation)
Ultimate Strength Design (see Concrete, design of)
Underwriters Laboratory, C1.2-5, D5.1-10, D5.1-24
Uniformat II, ix, xiv, xv
Units of measurement, App. 2-2
U.S. Department of Agriculture, C3.2-8
U.S. Department of Commerce, D5.1-7
U.S. Department of Justice, C3.2-8
U.S. Energy Policy Act, D2.1-6
Universal design, B2.7-2, C1.2-14, C2.1-12, C3.1-1, C3.1-4–C3.1-8, C3.2-1–C3.2-8
elevator, D1.1-3
hardware, C3.2-4
lighting, D5.3-2
parking, C3.4-5
principles of, C3.2-2
toilet fixtures, C3.1-8, D2.1-6, D2.1-7
signage, C3.4-6
Universal Designers and Consultants, C3.2-1, C3.2-6, C3.2-8
University of Southern California, B2.9-18
University of Minnesota, Center for Sustainable Building Research, B2.8-13

Untermann, Richard K., C3.4-28
Urban Design, ix
Urban Land Institute, C3.4-7, C3.4-28

V
Vapor
barrier, retarder, A1.3-1, B2.1-12, B2.5-6
ceiling, C1.1-1
crawl space, A1.3-3
roof, B3.1-5
diffusion, B2.5-5
Vault, B1.1-16
skylight, B3.3-3
Vehicular door, B2.7-5 (also see Door, Parking)
Veiling reflection, *definition*, D5.3-3 (also see Lighting)
Veneer
masonry, B1.3-4
wood, B2.7-17
Vent
eave, B2.1-11
exhaust hood fire protection, D4.2-0
mechanical, B2.2-3
plumbing, D2.2-2, D2.2-10
ridge, B3.3-9, B3.3-10
Ventilation (see HVAC Systems)
Ventre, Francis, xiii, xiv
Vestibule, B2.7-1
Vision, visual performance, D5.3-2 (also see Lighting)
Vitruvius, xiii, B2.9-7, B2.9-28
Vizcaya Museum, Miami, C2.1-1
Volume, units of measurement, App. 1-7, App. 2-2

W
Waffle slab (see Slab, Structure)
Walkway (see Pedestrian, design)
Wall
basement, A1.2-1–A1.2-4
bearing, A1.1-2, B2.1-9, B2.1-15
cavity, B2.2-4, B2.2-9, B2.2-14, B2.5-3, B2.5-12, B2.6-1
cold climate, B2.5-11
concrete, B2.1-3
curtain, B2.1-3, B2.1-4, B2.1-6–B2.1-9, B2.1-15, B2.6-9
exterior, B2.1-1
facing, B2.1-5
footing, A1.1-1
insulation, B2.2-10, B2.2-11
partition, B1.1-8 (also see Interior partitions and panels)
operable, C1.2-14
retaining, A1.2-1, A1.6-18
Water
conservation, D2.1-6
cooler, water fountain, D2.1-6
service, supply (see Plumbing, Fire protection)
spout (see Gutters and downspouts)
transmission, B2.2-10
vapor (see Condensation, Heat transfer, Evaporation)

Waterproofing, A1.3-1, A1.3-4, A1.3-8, B1.1-15, B1.6-21, B2.5-1, B2.6-3, B2.6-6, B3.1-6, B3.1-17
Watson, Donald, xi, B2.8-2, B2.8-4, B2.8-5, B2.8-13, B2.9-1, B2.9-18, B2.9-28, B3.1-8, B3.1-15, B3.1-24, C1.2-14
Weant, Robert A., C3.4-28
Weathertightness, B2.7-3, B2.7-15, B2.8-7 (also see Moisture, control)
Weep hole, A1.2-1, B1.3-8, B1.6-11, B2.1-13, B2.1-15, B2.6-8, B2.6-9
Weight
building materials, B1.2-6
units of measurement, App. 2-2
Weld, welding, B1.4-1, B1.4-11–B1.4-13
symbols for, B1.4-13
Western Wood Products Association (WWPA), B1.3-22
Wheelchair, C2.1-2, C3.1-6–C3.1-8 (also see Universal design)
Wind
-driven rain, B2.6-2, B2.7-3
load, B1.2-5, B2.1-2 (also see Structure, load)
Window, B2.2-3, B2.6-14, B2.8-1–13
hardware, C3.2-8
operable, D3.1-1
orientation, B2.8-2
properties of, B2.8-2, B2.8-3, B2.8-12
Window and Door Manufacturers Association, B2.7-22
Wolton, Sir Henry, xiii
Wood (also see Frame, Framing)
beam, B1.1-12, B1.1-16, B1.3-2, B1.3-8
classification of, B1.3-1
column, B1.3-14
deck, B1.1-13, B1.3-2, B1.3-3
deflection, B1.1-7
dimensions of lumber, B1.3-1, B1.3-2, B1.3-16
dimensional change, B2.3-6
door, B2.7-9, B2.7-12
girder, B1.3-8, B1.3-16, B2.3-7
grain, B2.3-6
gutter, B3.2-2
laminated, B1.3-4
moisture content, B2.3-7
nailing strip, B1.1-14
overhang, B1.3-10
pile, A1.1-5
plank, B1.1-9, B1.1-14, B1.3-2
roofing, B3.1-3, B3.1-4
shingles, B2.3-8
spans, B1.1-16
structure, B1.1-1, B1.1-8, B1.3-1, B2.1-10
testing devices, B2.3-10
veneer, B1.3-4

Y
Yale University, B2.9-18
Ingalls Rink, B3.1-7
Yellott, John I., B2.8-2, B2.8-13

CD-ROM WARRANTY

This software is protected by both United States copyright law and international copyright treaty provision. You must treat this software just like a book. By saying "just like a book," McGraw-Hill means, for example, that this software may be used by any number of people and may be freely moved from one computer location to another, so long as there is no possibility of its being used at one location or on one computer while it also is being used at another. Just as a book cannot be read by two different people in two different places at the same time, neither can the software be used by two different people in two different places at the same time (unless, of course, McGraw-Hill's copyright is being violated).

LIMITED WARRANTY

Customers who have problems installing or running a McGraw-Hill CD should consult our online technical support site at http://books.mcgraw-hill.com/techsupport. McGraw-Hill takes great care to provide you with top-quality software, thoroughly checked to prevent virus infections. McGraw-Hill warrants the physical CD-ROM contained herein to be free of defects in materials and workmanship for a period of sixty days from the purchase date. If McGraw-Hill receives written notification within the warranty period of defects in materials or workmanship, and such notification is determined by McGraw-Hill to be correct, McGraw-Hill will replace the defective CD-ROM. Send requests to:

McGraw-Hill
Customer Services
P.O. Box 545
Blacklick, OH 43004-0545

The entire and exclusive liability and remedy for breach of this Limited Warranty shall be limited to replacement of a defective CD-ROM and shall not include or extend to any claim for or right to cover any other damages, including, but not limited to, loss of profit, data, or use of the software, or special, incidental, or consequential damages or other similar claims, even if McGraw-Hill has been specifically advised of the possibility of such damages. In no event will McGraw-Hill's liability for any damages to you or any other person ever exceed the lower of suggested list price or actual price paid for the license to use the software, regardless of any form of the claim.

McGRAW-HILL SPECIFICALLY DISCLAIMS ALL OTHER WARRANTIES, EXPRESS OR IMPLIED, INCLUDING, BUT NOT LIMITED TO, ANY IMPLIED WARRANTY OF MERCHANTABILITY OR FITNESS FOR A PARTICULAR PURPOSE.

Specifically, McGraw-Hill makes no representation or warranty that the software is fit for any particular purpose and any implied warranty of merchantability is limited to the sixty-day duration of the Limited Warranty covering the physical CD-ROM only (and not the software) and is otherwise expressly and specifically disclaimed.

This limited warranty gives you specific legal rights; you may have others which may vary from state to state. Some states do not allow the exclusion of incidental or consequential damages, or the limitation on how long an implied warranty lasts, so some of the above may not apply to you.